COMPARATIVE LEGAL TRADITIONS

Text, Materials and Cases on the Civil and Common Law Traditions, with Special Reference to French, German, English and European Law

Second Edition

By

Mary Ann Glendon
Learned Hand Professor of Law
Harvard Law School

Michael Wallace Gordon
Chesterfield Smith Professor of Law
University of Florida College of Law

Christopher Osakwe
Managing Partner, Eurolaw Group
New Orleans, Louisiana

AMERICAN CASEBOOK SERIES®

WEST GROUP

Bancroft-Whitney • Banks-Baldwin • Clark Boardman Callaghan
Lawyers Cooperative Publishing • WESTLAW® • West Publishing

ST. PAUL, MINN., 1994

COPYRIGHT © 1985 WEST PUBLISHING CO.
COPYRIGHT © 1994 By WEST PUBLISHING CO.
                    610 Opperman Drive
                    P.O. Box 64526
                    St. Paul, MN 55164–0526
                    1–800–328–9352

Library of Congress Cataloging-in-Publication Data

   Glendon, Mary Ann, 1938–
   Comparative legal traditions : text, materials, and cases on the
civil and common law traditions, with special reference to French,
German, English, and European law / by Mary Ann Glendon, Michael
Wallace Gordon, and Christopher Osakwe. — 2nd ed.
   p.   cm. — (American casebook series)
   Includes index.
   ISBN 0–314–03501–X
   1. Comparative law—Cases. I. Gordon, Michael W. II. Osakwe,
Christopher, 1942–   . III. Title. IV. Series.
K583.G55 1994
340'.2—dc20
[342]   94–12240
                                          CIP

ISBN 0–314–03501–X

   (G.G. & O.) Comparative Law, 2d ACB
   2nd Reprint–2001

We Dedicate This Book to:

The Memory of Max Rheinstein

———

The Memory of Anne G. and Seery C. Gordon

———

Maria Elena Amador

*

Preface

Our purpose in this book is to provide an introduction to comparative law through discussion of several important areas in two legal traditions, that of the Romano-Germanic civil law and that of the Anglo-American common law. In our treatment of the civil law tradition, we draw mainly on the law of France and Germany. For the common law, we present the parent system, the law of England.

The materials assembled here have been used over the past several years by the authors in courses and seminars at the law schools of Boston College, the University of Florida, Harvard University, Tulane University, Whittier College of Law, and as visiting professors at Duke University Law School, the George Washington University School of Law, the University of Chicago Law School, the University of Michigan Law School, and the University of Pennsylvania Law School. Our years of comparative law teaching and our discussions with other teachers in the field have shown us that no two comparative law courses are alike and that many comparative law teachers "personalize" the course by supplementing the assigned text with their own materials. Comparative law, even more than other courses, is apt to reflect the particular background and expertise of the instructor—the substantive areas of the law in which he or she is interested, and the foreign systems with which he or she is familiar.

Thus, frequently, a comparative law coursebook will be used as background, a point of departure, or to supplement materials that have been developed by the individual teacher. Our aim is to cooperate with and facilitate these types of uses, while also furnishing a book that can stand on its own as the basis for an introductory course. We have endeavored to respond to the principal needs and desires that teachers of comparative law courses have expressed to us. Thus, this book includes: (1) an introduction to the civil law tradition and to the English variant of the common law tradition; (2) a variety of materials illustrating different legal approaches to specific common social problems; and (3) suggestions for further readings, practical exercises, student research projects and seminar reports. In this last connection, we have found that American law students who have not studied foreign languages can profitably conduct comparative research using British, Canadian, Australian and other English language materials. The fruitfulness and importance of such studies should not be underestimated, nor should the degree of intellectual challenge that they pose for Americans.

There are as many ways a course using this book might be structured as there are comparative law teachers. For example, one of the authors has used this coursebook in conjunction with Donald Kommers,

The Constitutional Jurisprudence of the Federal Republic of Germany
(1989) and John Langbein, *Comparative Criminal Procedure: Germany*
(1977). Another author has used it in conjunction with various "White
Papers," "Green Papers" and other studies and reports in England on
changes in Legal Services.

This book reproduces and translates materials from various publications. Translations, unless otherwise indicated, are our own. Footnotes
from excerpted materials have been omitted without so specifying.
Where we have retained footnotes from these materials, we have kept
their original numbering; lettered footnotes within the excerpted materials are those of the authors.

Finally, we wish to acknowledge here that in preparing this second
edition we have been greatly aided by and are deeply indebted to many
colleagues and students, here and abroad, who were generous with their
suggestions, comments and criticisms on the first edition. In particular,
we are grateful for the assistance of Paolo Wright Carozza who prepared
the new chapter on European law.

MARY ANN GLENDON
Cambridge, Massachusetts

MICHAEL WALLACE GORDON
Gainesville, Florida

CHRISTOPHER OSAKWE
New Orleans, Louisiana

Using WESTLAW
to help you understand Comparative Law

Introduction: As a law student, you want to master your courses as completely as possible. Obtaining that mastery is the key to higher levels of performance in law school and better preparedness for the bar exam. Using **WESTLAW** with **West books** is an excellent way to acquire the knowledge and information necessary to understand the legal concepts that you will encounter during law school.

The following examples will show you to use WESTLAW to quickly retrieve relevant information that will increase your understanding of the many topic areas in Glendon, Gordon and Osakwe's Comparative Legal Traditions Casebook. All you need is your WESTLAW password and WESTMATE software (if you are going to use WESTLAW from your home computer). To begin, simply type your password, enter a research session identifier and continue with one of the sections below.

I. HOW TO RETRIEVE THE FULL TEXT OF A PRINCIPAL CASE OR NOTE CASE

The principal and note cases in this text are generally not included in full. Reading the entire case, however, may help you understand the court's reasoning and holding, and give you a better grasp of the theories involved. The authors may also provide citations to note cases for additional reading to better highlight a point of law. For example, in Part 1, Introduction to the Study of Comparative Law, under note 10, the authors distinguish a case where Justice Brandeis comments on our Federal System of Justice. To see the full text of that case, *New State Ice Co. v. Liebmann*, 285 U.S. 262, 1932 (page 10 this text) type

find 285 us 1 (then press **ENTER**)

*Use the format above to retrieve cases on WESTLAW, e.g., from anywhere in WESTLAW type the word **find** (or **fi**) **followed by the volume number, reporter abbreviation**, and **page number** of the case you wish to view.*

II. HOW TO RETRIEVE LAW REVIEW AND LAW JOURNAL ARTICLES

Often a cited law review or journal article will provide valuable insight into and analysis of a particular issue or topic. Your professor may even suggest or require that you read some of these articles. For example, at the bottom of page 231, the authors cite Richard Fallon's *A Constructivist Coherence Theory of Constitutional Interpretation*, **100 Harv.L.Rev. 1189 (1987)**. To view this article, first go to the WEST-

LAW FIND PUBLICATIONS INDEX (to see if the publication is on WESTLAW and to obtain the appropriate citation format) by typing

find pubs (then press **ENTER**)

To view publication abbreviations for law reviews and Journals, locate LAW REVIEWS (it is the last entry) and type its corresponding page number (and press **ENTER**). To view publications that begin with the letter **H** (for Harvard Law Review) locate the letter H and type its corresponding page number (and press **ENTER**). Page ahead (by using the **PAGE DOWN** key or typing **p** then pressing **ENTER**) until you locate Harvard Law Review and its WESTLAW citation format. Combine the abbreviation with the appropriate volume and page then type

find 100 harv l rev 1189 (then press **ENTER**)

Use the format above to retrieve law review and journal articles, e.g., from anywhere in WESTLAW type the word **find** *(or* **fi**) **followed by the volume number, appropriate journal or review abbreviation**, *and* **page number** *of the article you wish to view.*

III. HOW TO USE WEST'S TOPIC AND KEY NUMBER SYSTEM TO OBTAIN MORE INFORMATION

Cases reported in West Publications are organized in its *topic* and *Key number system*. The cases you read on WESTLAW contain paragraphs of information called *headnotes*. The headnotes contain concise statements of law that are designated by *topic* and *key number*. The system is designed to allow you to retrieve other cases that contain the same topic and key number, meaning that the cases will have similar "on-point" law.

Page forward in any case you are viewing until you find a topic and key number discussing a point of law relevant to your research. Then enter that topic and key number in a case law database to retrieve other cases discussing the same point of law. After finding a relevant topic and key number, see how the courts in your state have decided the issue by searching for it in your state case law database, e.g., **tx-cs** (Texas), **mo-cs** (Missouri), **ny-cs** (New York), etc. (Look to the WESTLAW database list for appropriate database identifiers).

Follow up: Many, but not all of the law review and journal articles referenced in this book are contained in a WESTLAW database. If you have any questions about WESTLAW or the preceding sections, call West Customer Service at 1–800–WESTLAW (1–800–937–8529), or speak to your WESTLAW Academic or student representative.

Summary of Contents

ix

*

Table of Contents

xiii

*

COMPARATIVE LEGAL TRADITIONS

Text, Materials and Cases on the Civil and
Common Law Traditions, with Special
Reference to French, German,
English and European Law

Second Edition

*

Part I

INTRODUCTION TO THE COMPARATIVE STUDY OF LAW

SECTION 1. COMPARATIVE LAW AS AN ACADEMIC DISCIPLINE

When the first learned societies dealing with comparative law were established in France, Germany, and England in the late nineteenth century, their founders took for granted that comparative methods would advance the understanding of a broad range of legal issues. In that expectation, legal scholars were in accord with the best of their counterparts in other disciplines. Emile Durkheim had gone so far as to claim that, "Comparative sociology is not a particular branch of sociology; it is sociology itself."[1] The great legal historian F.W. Maitland had insisted that, "The English lawyer who knew nothing and cared nothing for any system but his own, hardly came in sight of the idea of legal history."[2]

The question arises, however: Why, if the benefits of comparative studies are so substantial and obvious, has comparative law remained a relative backwater in twentieth century American legal education? No doubt there are several reasons, not least of which is the increasing burden of keeping up with developments in our own legal system, the most complex the world has ever known. To achieve even minimal competence in another country's legal system requires a major expenditure of time and effort, including, in many cases, learning another language. Americans, moreover, have long tended to assume that they could get along quite well without casting their gaze beyond national borders. Like Roman lawyers of old, many American lawyers were convinced of the self-sufficiency of their legal and political arrangements.[3]

In recent years, however, that insular posture has become untenable. With unprecedented global interdependence, and with commerce

---

1. Emile Durkheim, The Rules of Sociological Method 139 (8th ed. 1964) (first published 1895).

2. F.W. Maitland, I Collected Papers 488 (1911).

3. On the inattention of Roman lawyers to comparative law, see Konrad Zweigert and Hein Kötz, Introduction to Comparative Law 48 (2d ed. 1992) (translated by Tony Weir).

1

and instant communication linking all regions of the earth, nearly every legal field has acquired an international dimension. We live in a world where national boundaries are of diminishing significance in relation to technology, ecology, information, consumerism, entertainment, the arts, commerce, and ideas of universal human rights. Legal education, accordingly, has had to adjust to demands for the skills required by lawyers in the global village. In the 1980s, international legal studies burgeoned to a degree that early comparatists could scarcely have imagined. Yet, as Basil Markesinis has written, comparative law is "still searching for an audience even where it has found a place of sorts in the university curriculum." [4]

In the years to come, it is likely that comparative law will find many different sorts of audiences as it takes its rightful place among the methods required for the effective study and practice of law. Certain fields have always had a comparative dimension: conflict of laws, international business law, public international law, and area studies where the object is to become familiar with a particular foreign legal system. In those fields, cross-national studies are now assuming greater importance than ever. According to commercial law expert John A. Spanogle Jr., business law teachers, from first-year contracts onward, ought to spend about a quarter of their time on the international aspects of their subjects if they are to keep pace with developments in the practice.[5] Increasingly, law professors in many other fields are moving in the direction counselled by Roscoe Pound in the 1930s—exploring the approaches of other legal systems to the issues that arise "in the course of teaching the law of the land." [6]

And what of the variegated courses that present themselves under the heading of "comparative law"? Is comparative law an academic subject in its own right? Consider the answer to that question given in the following essay by Professor Alan Watson.

ALAN WATSON, "LEGAL TRANSPLANTS: AN APPROACH TO COMPARATIVE LAW"

1–9 (1993).*

What is Comparative Law? The question is often put: the range of replies is startling. An extreme but not uncommon opinion is that it does not exist. More than one comparative lawyer—who, of course, will not admit the non-being of the subject—has observed that "Comparative Law" is a strange phrase. There is, it is freely conceded, no "Comparative" branch of law in the sense in which lawyers call one branch of law

4. Basil Markesinis, Comparative Law— A Subject in Search of an Audience, 53 Modern L.Rev. 1, 20 (1990).

5. John A. Spanogle Jr., American Attorneys' Use of International and Comparative Legal Analyses in Everyday Practice, 28 Wake Forest Law Review 1, 5 (1993).

6. Roscoe Pound, The Place of Comparative law in the American Law School Curriculum, 8 Tulane L.Rev. 161, 168 (1934).

* Reprinted with permission of the University Press of Virginia.

"Family Law" or another "Mercantile Law". Gutteridge tells us that the emptiness of the phrase "Comparative Law" "has been realized by German-speaking lawyers who use the term *Rechtsvergleichung* which connotes a process of comparison and is free from any implication of the existence of a body of rules forming a separate branch or department of the law". The same author also points out that the strangeness of the English term becomes manifest when attempts are made to define Comparative Law or to ascertain its relation to other forms of learning.

A variation which is frequently given on that answer is that "Comparative Law" denotes a method of study and research, or is a technique. But then it seems fair to ask, What is this method or technique? The student will find that the question tends to remain unanswered, and that the writer, having claimed that Comparative Law is a method, simply proceeds: "The method called Comparative Law can be used for a variety of practical or scholarly purposes." Presumably such a writer is of the opinion that the nature of the method or technique is obvious. But if the nature of Comparative Law is obvious, it can only be the investigation of legal rules and procedures, not of one system in isolation but in harness with the examination of the equivalent rules and procedures in at least one other system. Yet is this in itself a "method" or a "technique"? And if we answer Yes, it is a "method" or a "technique"—does the "method" or "technique" have to be specially and specifically learned? The absence of discussion on this matter can only imply that the answer is No. We are then forced to put another question: If comparative law is no more than this, a method which does not have to be learned, is it an activity worthy of academic pursuit in its own right? Is it justifiable, for instance, to have a University course in a law faculty curriculum called "Comparative Law"? The answer, it seems to me, must be No.

Other jurists, however, have held that Comparative Law is not simply a method but a science with its own distinct province. But there is no agreement as to what the province is, and the debate as to whether Comparative Law is a method or a science has turned into a debate over language. Moreover, theories that Comparative Law is a science now seem to lack support.

A more promising approach has been to hold that more than one discipline is included within the term Comparative Law. E. Lambert, for instance, was responsible for a three-fold division: Descriptive Comparative Law, Comparative History of Law and Comparative Legislation (or comparative jurisprudence proper). The first of these "is the inventory of the systems of the past and present as a whole as well as of individual rules which these systems establish for the several categories of legal relations". Comparative History of Law, Lambert tells us, "is closely allied to ethnological jurisprudence, folklore, legal sociology and philosophy of law. It endeavours to bring out through the establishment of a universal history of law the rhythms or natural laws of the succession of social phenomena, which direct the evolution of legal institutions." And he adds that "its students have been up to the present principally interested in the reconstitution of the most obscure phases of the legal history of human societies". The third branch, Comparative Legislation, "represents the effort to define the common trunk on which present national doctrines of law are destined to graft themselves as a result both of the development of the study of law as a social science, and of the awakening of an international legal consciousness". J.H. Wigmore, in his turn, also divided Comparative Law in three: Comparative Nomoscopy, which is the description of systems of law; Comparative Nomothetics, which is the analysis of the merits of the systems; and Comparative Nomogenetics, which is the study of the development of the world's legal ideas and systems.

We shall be here concerned with an approach similar to that of Lambert and Wigmore but it is not proposed to look for an all-embracing definition or an enumeration of parts. The aim is more limited; namely to determine what—if anything—Comparative Law is or should be as an academic activity worthy of pursuit in its own right and with its own proper boundaries. The answer to the question, as will be seen, has more than mere pedagogic interest.

But first of all, to clear the ground, we must say what Comparative Law (as an independent academic discipline) is not.

To begin with, Comparative Law is not the study of one foreign legal system or of part of one foreign system. A general course at a British or American university of French Private Law or a detailed study of French Contract Law may have great intellectual and practical value but it remains a course of French Law not Comparative Law. No doubt it is impossible to follow such a course without reflecting on, and making comparisons with, one's own law, and indeed, without increasing one's understanding of one's own law, but this does not change the essential nature of the course as French Law. This remains true even where an expressed aim of the course is the insight it gives into the domestic system.

Secondly, an elementary account of various legal systems or of various "families" of systems cannot be decently regarded as the proper pursuit of Comparative Law as an academic activity. The description lacks the necessary intellectual content.

Thirdly and more arguably Comparative Law cannot be primarily a matter of drawing comparisons. Those who would disagree with this proposition proceed from one of two starting points. They may start from an individual legal problem which they consider to be the same in more than one jurisdiction and examine the legal response to it. As one scholar has put it, "The fact that the problem is one and the same warrants the comparability." Or they may take a branch of law, say Contract, and investigate in detail the differences and similarities of the individual rules. But it is very doubtful if the comparisons are justifiable in academic terms as Comparative Law, whether the starting point is the legal problem or the branch of the law. Variations in the political, moral, social and economic values which exist between any two societies make it hard to believe that many legal problems are the same for both except on a technical level. For instance, the legal problem of rent restriction is not the same both in a country where rented accommodation is common and in a country where it is less common; the problem of alimony for divorced wives in a jurisdiction where it is usual for women to work differs from that in a country where women do not have jobs; that problem and the proper legal response to it may also be altered by the availability or otherwise of creches and nursery schools for young children; the legal problem of the enforceability of contracts against minors will vary with the affluence of the society, the age at which young people become accustomed to living on credit, and the extent to which residing away from their parents is prevalent. Perhaps on rare occasions one might find that the problem was identical or at least very similar, as when the matter at issue concerns international business. Yet when the starting point is the problem the weight of the investigation will always be primarily on the comparability of the problem, only secondarily on the comparability of the law; and any discipline founded on such a starting point will be sociology rather than law.

When the starting point is a branch of law, the difficulty arising from the variations of political, moral, social and economic factors for any valid comparison recedes to some extent, but is still very much present. Moreover, except where the systems are closely related as in certain states in America, a comparison of legal rules may be intellectually meaningful, but the minor nature of the differences which exist may limit the significance of the investigation. It is not surprising that Gutteridge can write in the preface to his book on Comparative Law, "No special form of technique seems to be called for if the comparison is, for instance, between Australian and Canadian law or between English law and the law of the United States."

Yet, despite the preceding paragraphs, it should be readily conceded that teaching courses of considerable educational value can be constructed on the basis of comparisons of a branch of law in various legal systems. The merit of such courses lies in alerting the student to the many approaches which are conceivable, and this merit may exist independently of any theoretical structure which would give deeper meaning to the comparisons. Likewise it should be conceded that certain legal concepts—causation is one good example—and their actual delineation in various systems can be the object of an enquiry on the highest intellectual and systematic plane. But the point of these enquiries is to explicate a concept of great importance in law by a careful examination of the way in which it operates in the detailed context of differing legal systems (as well as the way in which it is discussed by theorists). Then, I venture to suggest, the study is primarily jurisprudential and is support for the widely held view that much of jurisprudence is unthinkable without comparisons from various systems.

Comparative Law, then, if it is to be an intellectual discipline in its own right, is something other than the study of one foreign system (with glances at one's own), an overall look at the world's systems or comparison of individual rules or of branches of law as between two or more systems, and I would suggest that it is the study of the relationship of one legal system and its rules with another. The nature of any such relationship, the reasons for the similarities and the differences, is discoverable only by a study of the history of the systems or of the rules; hence in the first place, Comparative Law is Legal History concerned with the relationship between systems. But one cannot treat Comparative Law simply as a branch of Legal History. It must be something more. When one comes to treat the growth of these similarities and differences—how, for instance, has it come about that France, Germany and Switzerland, all deriving their law from Justinian's Corpus Iuris Civilis, have each different rules on the passing of risk and property in sale?—one finds oneself better able to understand the particular factors which shape legal growth and change. Indeed this may be the easiest approach to an appreciation of how law normally evolves. This seems a proper field of study of Comparative Law. So, in the second instance, I suggest that Comparative Law is about the nature of law, and especially about the nature of legal development.

These two elements coming from a study of the relationship between systems—Legal History and the step beyond into Jurisprudence—are, I submit, the essential ingredients of Comparative Law as an intellectual discipline in its own right. The importance of the history behind the legal rules has, in fact, long been recognized by comparatists, and history is prominent in the writings of the most distinguished practitioners of the art; witness, for instance, J.P. Dawson, Unjust Enrichment (Boston, 1951): F.H. Lawson, A Common Lawyer Looks at the Civil Law (Ann Arbor, 1953): J.H. Merryman, The Civil Law Tradition (Stanford, 1969): R. David, Les grands systèmes de droit contemporains, 4th edit. (Paris, 1971). O. Kahn–Freund can say of one particular instance in German and English law, "Four hundred years of legal and political history are reflected in the difference of techniques". F. Pringsheim declares roundly, "comparative law without the history of law is an impossible task".

If this approach is right and Comparative Law is best regarded as a study of the relationship between systems of law, then it follows that where there is no relationship there can be no Comparative Law, and any comparison drawn between rules will be arbitrary and without systematic worth. It thus becomes important to establish the nature of possible relationships. In the forefront, above all, stands the historical relationship: where one system or one of its rules derives from another system, probably with modifications; where more than one system or rules of such systems derived from a further system; or (where derive is too strong a term) when one system exerts influence on another. In any general or introductory work this type of relationship should have pride of place, first because the relationship itself is more obvious than any other type, secondly because the degree of borrowing and adaptation is more easily spotted, thirdly because the relevant factors in the development can be isolated more simply, and fourthly because in the Western world borrowing (with adaptation) has been the usual way of legal development. On this last point S.F.C. Milsom has spoken clearly: "Societies largely invent their constitutions, their political and administrative systems, even in these days their economies; but their private law is nearly always taken from others." Twice only have the customs of European peoples been worked up into intellectual systems. The Roman system has served two separate civilizations. The common law, governing daily relationships in very various modern societies, has developed without a break from its beginnings in a society utterly different from any of them.

A second type of relationship is what F. Pringsheim has called the "inner relationship". This rests not on any actual historical contact, but on a spiritual and psychical relationship and on an undeniable similarity between the peoples—as Pringsheim thinks—or between their development. Comparative Law can proceed from this inner relationship but one must always bear in mind that the relationship itself is an unproveable hypothesis. In terms of Western civilization, this inner relationship is to be found above all between Roman and English Law, and comparisons between the two have long been popular and fruitful. But the difficulties and dangers in this branch of study are obvious: the relationship cannot be closely defined, its nature will not always be apparent, it will not exist in all areas or at all periods of development, and above all there is no reasonably objective way of determining the importance of the similarities and differences which are observed. The great value of this branch of the study lies in the light which it can shed on major legal matters. When English law has not been influenced by Roman law it is of small significance that a detail is the same or is different in the two systems. But, in contrast, the absence of the trust in Roman law and its prominence and usefulness in English law should make us more aware of the nature of the trust and of the factors in its development. One might also come to understand Roman law better by analyzing the lack of the trust, the factors making it unnecessary or impossible for the Romans, and the institutions which took its place. Conversely the remedies against unjust enrichment in Roman law and the general lack of such until recently in the common law should make us more alive to various aspects of both systems. Likewise, much might be gained by an investigation into the role of statutes and the prominence of (what one might loosely call) case-law at Rome and in England: or into the relative degree of abstraction in juridical discussion and formulation.

A third relationship might be suggested by those scholars who believe that all legal systems in their young days pass through the same or similar stages of development. The general proposition is unsound as we shall see, though between various early systems a historical relationship exists.

Comparative Law then, as an academic discipline in its own right, is a study of the relationship, above all the historical relationship, between legal systems or between rules of more than one system.... and this is the subject of the present book. [I]n the past the boundaries of Comparative Law have been drawn too widely, ... they should define an area akin to that of comparative linguistics; that is, they should be concerned with similarities and differences in the context of a historical relationship. Yet to prevent misunderstanding it should be stressed at this stage that a knowledge of foreign systems of law—of a sort which would not be included within such a conception of Comparative Law—can be very valuable. It can have educational value as was mentioned earlier: and practical value, for instance when law reformers searching for better law for their own system look at other solutions. The investigation need have no systematic basis to produce fruitful results. And it can have academic value, for instance when a scholar who has reached particular conclusions about a development in one system can confirm the possibility of such a development by the knowledge that something similar happened elsewhere.

SECTION 2. AIMS AND USES
OF COMPARATIVE LAW

It is fair to say that comparative law, as befits a developing field, is experiencing something of an identity crisis. The existence of lively debate concerning aims and methods, however, has not hindered comparatists from happily pursuing cross-national studies in a variety of ways and for a wide range of purposes. Nor has it prevented those studies from yielding important contributions to the understanding, practice, and reform of twentieth century law. In all likelihood, the diversity of aims and methods among comparatists promotes the vitality of their work. In a world where national and cultural "difference" is often seen as posing a formidable challenge, comparatists hold up a view of diversity as an invitation, an opportunity, and a crucible of creativity. In a heterogeneous nation like the United States where empathetic understanding among groups often seems elusive, comparatists are witnesses to the joys and discoveries awaiting those who make the effort to enter imaginatively into another mental framework.

These teaching materials have been designed to lend themselves to use by instructors with many different interests and preoccupations. Like the late Professor Otto Kahn–Freund, we subscribe to the view that comparative law is "a variety of methods for looking at law." [7] Those methods may be deployed toward an even wider variety of ends. Among the aims of comparative law, we would put first the pursuit of knowledge as an end in itself: comparative law responds to that characteristic of the human species which is curious about the world and wants to understand it. That curiosity will not lead everyone in the same direction. In fact, it will take most individuals down several different paths in the course of a lifetime. Thus, we expect that emphasis will

---

7. Otto Kahn–Freund, Comparative Law as an Academic Subject, 82 Law Quar- terly Rev. 40, 41 (1966).

vary among users of this book concerning the methods to be utilized and the aims to be pursued in comparative studies. Our objective, in these introductory materials, has been to open a window to the spectrum of available techniques and to the vast range of practical and theoretical possibilities they afford.

Discussions of the goals of comparative law often draw an overly sharp distinction between its practical and its scientific aims. To be sure, comparative studies have many practical uses. Of growing interest to Americans is the way they facilitate communication on behalf of clients with one's counterparts and with officials in other countries, and enhance one's ability to be persuasive in international contexts.[8] One day, Americans, like Europeans, may also take advantage of the resources of comparative law in federal and state law-making processes. The modern systematic study of comparative law had its origins in European law reform activities, and few major legislative programs are undertaken in Europe today without extensive preliminary comparative surveys. Comparative law is indispensable as well to international endeavors such as the harmonization of laws within the European Community, and the framing, application and interpretation of supranational legal norms.

Those and other important practical applications of comparative law are typically contrasted with more theoretical aims, such as promoting an improved understanding of one's own legal system or searching for principles common to a number of legal systems. There is nothing wrong with making such a distinction between practice and theory. The only harm comes if one forgets that the practical aims just mentioned are furthered by serious pursuit of scholarly objectives, and that scholarly exercises are apt to prove sterile if they are carried on without close attention to the way law operates in the rough and tumble of daily life. The fact is that, in law as elsewhere, theory and practice are like the two blades of a scissors, complementary and indispensable to one another. The best practical work is grounded in theoretical understanding; the soundest theory emerges from constant testing against practical know-how and experience.

When we say that comparative law enables students to understand their own legal system better, we do not just mean that it will move them away from assuming their own ways are the best or the only ways of doing things. We also hope that they will acquire a better sense of what is valuable and capable of development in their own system. Above all, we are confident that those of you who are embarking for the first time on a comparative venture will have new insights that would not have occurred to you if you had remained exclusively within the framework of American law.

8. Eric Stein, Uses, Misuses, and Non-uses of Comparative Law, 72 Northwestern   Law Review 198 (1977).

What we have just said is even more true of the would-be law reformer. Investigation of the way other legal systems deal with problems confronting all societies at comparable stages of social and economic development seldom fails to help in designing research, framing hypotheses, and testing conclusions. In the law-saturated societies of developed nations, we need more than ever to know how legal norms work out in various contexts, what advantages and benefits they offer, what risks or indirect consequences they are likely to entail.

Comparative law frequently proves its worth, as we shall see, through significant contributions to specific, novel and difficult problems.[9] Indeed, the stimulus for comparative investigation is often a problem that one's home system does not handle very well. When comparatists devote their attention to a vexing or unsolved problem, it is not with the idea that they will find in some foreign land a "solution" which, like a new electrical appliance, can be fitted with an adaptor and plugged into the system back home. What they are usually looking for is, initially, a deepened understanding of the problem, and, if they are lucky, a source of inspiration. Our own way of doing things seems so natural to us that often it is only comparison with another way that establishes that there is something to be explained. Comparison often picks up issues or makes connections that remain invisible to other research strategies.

So far as increasing one's awareness of alternatives and testing one's hypotheses are concerned, one may say that comparative law gives us access to Justice Brandeis' "laboratory" concept, writ large.[10] Since controlled experimentation in law is hardly ever possible, legal scholars often use comparative law to expand their theater of observation, to see how other legal systems have dealt with problems similar to ours. The hope is that the experiences of countries at comparable stages of social and economic development will give us insight into our own situation and that they may help us to find, as John P. Dawson once put it, "our own paths through the forest."[11]

Comparative law is also an indispensable heuristic method for legal and social theory. Montesquieu, Tocqueville, Durkheim, and Max Weber all used comparative study to illuminate the history and growth of the law, its role in society, its relation to behavior and ideas. Comparative law helps us to understand the dynamics of social, as well as legal, change.

9. On this point, we are in accord with Basil Markesinis, Comparative Law in Search of an Audience, 53 Modern L.Rev. 1, 20 (1990).

10. American lawyers have long been habitual comparatists in the sense that they routinely consult the law of other states in connection with matters arising under their own state's law. Justice Louis D. Brandeis pointed out that the American federal system offers advantages to law-makers as well. In *New State Ice Co. v. Liebmann,* he remarked that it is one of the "happy incidents of the federal system that a single courageous State may, if its citizens choose, serve as a laboratory; and try novel social and economic experiments without risk to the rest of the country." (285 U.S. 262, 311 (1932) (Brandeis, J., dissenting)).

11. John P. Dawson, Unjust Enrichment: A Comparative Analysis 111 (1951).

Finally we should mention the comparatist's power and duty to make a critical evaluation of what he or she discovers through comparative analysis. If this is not done, comparative law can easily degenerate into a dizzying spiral in which everything is both cause and effect; different from, but similar to, everything else; separate but intertwined; and so on. Moreover, who is in a better position than the comparatist to follow up his or her research with a careful appraisal of its significance?

SECTION 3. METHODS OF COMPARATIVE LAW

If comparative law consists of a variety of methods for looking at law, what are those methods? Comparative analysis begins by working out a topic: Your client poses a problem. Or your government wishes to formulate and implement a policy. Or in the course of your studies, you encounter a puzzle. You investigate the facts and the opinions of others. You raise questions. You get an idea or form a hypothesis. At this stage, it may be the study of a foreign legal system that makes you aware of a problem; that suggests a hypothesis; or that helps you to form a research strategy.

When you move on to testing your hypothesis, comparative law may again be helpful. Modern thinking about how, precisely, comparative methodology enters into legal research begins with Ernst Rabel who put the systematic study of comparative law on a new basis in the 20th century. Two concepts are key to Rabel's understanding of the field: function and context. You cannot compare legal rules, institutions, or systems without knowing how they function, and you cannot know how they function without situating them in their legal, economic and cultural context. It was Rabel who insisted that it is of little use to compare paper institutions, or rules and doctrines merely as they appear in books. The comparatist's province is the operating institution and the law in action. Or, to use Kahn–Freund's analogy, comparatists are more like comparative physiologists than comparative anatomists. That functional approach, now recognized to have wide applicability, has been comparative law's principal gift to 20th century legal science.[12] Several methodological consequences follow from the emphasis on functioning systems and context:

1. The study of foreign law is an indispensable preliminary step to comparative analysis. This means that one has some grasp of the essential characteristics of the systems to be compared as functioning wholes. With regard to the particular institutions and elements under study, one needs to know how their roles fit within the whole. What values do they protect and promote? Through what technical devices do they operate?

12. For a recent elaboration of this point by one of Europe's leading comparatists, see the articles by Rodolfo Sacco, Legal Formants: A Dynamic Approach to Comparative Law (I and II), 39 Am. J.Comp.L. 1 (1991) and 39 Am.J.Comp.L. 343 (1991).

2. One has to know one's own system in the same way. That is not so simple as it sounds. In our experience, the comparative law course is often an American law student's first opportunity to reflect on our own legal system as a functioning whole. Unlike European law students, most young men or women beginning legal education in the United States receive no general overview of the legal system. That is something they are expected to pick up by themselves as they go along, putting their newly acquired legal knowledge together with what they remember from high school and college government courses. The American law school, with its curriculum divided arbitrarily into separate, overlapping subjects, affords very little opportunity to study the functions and relations of all the specialized parts of the legal order. Try to use the comparative law course, if you are a student, as an occasion for refreshing, reviewing, and supplementing the understanding you are acquiring about American law. Think about what the French historian Fernand Braudel once wrote concerning the unexpected insights that can arise from comparison:

> Live in London for a year, and you will not get to know much about the English. But through comparison, and in the light of your surprise, you will suddenly come to understand some of the more profound and individual characteristics of France, which you did not previously understand because you knew them too well.[13]

3. The need to see our own and other legal institutions in context means that comparative law by its very nature is an interdisciplinary field, one that depends heavily on empirical work. Legal norms cannot be fully understood without some knowledge of their sources; their political, social, and economic purposes; the milieu in which they operate; the role of the legal profession; the operation of the court system. The question naturally arises: How can any individual know enough languages, history, sociology, economics, and political science, or be familiar enough with practices, values, attitudes, and social conditions in another nation to be a comparatist? The answer is that comparative law is a group enterprise, characterized more than most other fields by teamwork and creative collaboration. For many of us, those cooperative endeavors are a major part of what gives the field its lasting attraction.

4. A functional approach means that legal rules and institutions at some point have to be liberated from the conceptual categories of their home systems so that they can be seen in terms of the social objectives they serve. Sometimes this will mean that an institution has to be broken down into separate parts, as, for example, when one seeks to find out how legal systems without the Anglo–American trust handle the diverse problems we treat with that single multi-purpose device. Sometimes, several seemingly unrelated legal institutions have to be studied together because it is only their joint operation that meets a particular social need. For example, in many legal systems, the problem of

13. Fernand Braudel, *Histoire et Sciences Sociales: La Longue Durée,* Annales: Economies, Sociétés, Civilisations 725, 737 (1958).

balancing freedom of testation with protection of family members against disinheritance cannot be analyzed without taking marital property law into consideration. As Zweigert and Kötz have put it, "The functional approach of comparative law concentrates on the real live problem which often lurks unseen behind the concepts of the national systems." [14]

5. The tasks comparatists set themselves may range from critical theory, to broad comparisons of entire systems, to narrower studies targeted to specific social problems. Macro- and micro-comparison tend to shade into one another, since micro-comparison furnishes examples and means of verification, while knowledge of legal systems in turn furnishes the indispensable context for the study of particular problems.

Comparative legal scholars working along the lines opened up by Rabel have produced path-breaking works. In the field of commercial law, they have discovered many essential similarities behind formal differences. Time and again, comparatists have shown, conversely, how similar legal rules produce significantly different effects in different social and procedural contexts. Sometimes our own true distinctiveness appears to us for the first time in the mirror of comparison. In the following excerpt, one of your co-authors discusses yet another way in which comparative methods can illuminate national law and even national culture.

MARY ANN GLENDON, "STORY AND LANGUAGE IN AMERICAN LAW" [15]

There is a different conception of comparative law which is both older and newer than the methods that were brought to their highest form in the 20th century by Ernst Rabel and his followers. For this, Plato's *Laws* is the foundational text. The *Laws* is the last, longest, and most political of Plato's dialogues. It probably is, or should be, of more interest to legal scholars than to philosophers, who generally consider it to be far from Plato's greatest work. But its manifest good will toward the study of foreign law warms the heart of the comparatist even as it draws us into dialogue with the text. The text, among other things, suggests a way of looking at law which comparatists often neglect.

The protagonist of the *Laws* is a traveler far from his native city, an old man who doesn't even have a name. Plato calls him the Athenian Stranger. In some ways he reminds us of the Socrates of the earlier dialogues, but he is less charming and more pious, less elegant in diction and more urgent in purpose. It may be that this is as close as we get to hearing the voice of Plato himself, but if so, it is the Plato who was approaching the end of his own journey through the world.

---

14. Konrad Zweigert and Hein Kötz, Introduction to Comparative Law 44 (1992) (translation by Tony Weir).

15. From the 1986 Rosenthal Lectures, delivered at Northwestern University in October 1986. The opening lecture, from which this excerpt is drawn, was published as the Introduction to *Abortion and Divorce in Western Law* 5–9 (1987). (Reprinted with Permission of Harvard University Press.)

The dialogue takes place between the Athenian and two other elderly pilgrims, a Cretan and a Spartan, whom he has encountered on the road from Knossos to the cave and temple of Zeus on the island of Crete. Both Crete and Sparta were renowned in the ancient world for their laws, and the shrine which is the travelers' destination commemorates the divine origin of the laws of Crete. At first it seems that the Athenian may have come to Crete to learn about these laws, for the dialogue opens with his blunt question to the others: "Is it a god or some human being, strangers, who is given the credit for laying down your laws?" When Kleinias the Cretan and Megillos the Spartan reply, somewhat equivocally, that their lawgivers were indeed gods, the Athenian Stranger proposes that it might be pleasant to beguile the time on their journey with conversation about the government and laws of Crete and Sparta. Soon we learn that Kleinias has just been appointed to a commission charged with the duty of establishing a new Cretan colony, complete with a constitution and laws. He has been told that if he and his colleagues should discover some laws from elsewhere that appear to be better than Cretan laws, they are not to worry about their being foreign. It would thus be helpful to him, Kleinias suggests, if the three travelers could spend the day founding a city in speech as they stroll and rest on the way to their common destination.

This request appears to be what the Stranger was waiting for all along. No longer the idly curious student of foreign institutions, he now dominates the ensuing discussion, which ranges over the great perennial questions of the purpose of law; the relations between law and custom, law and power, law and justice, law and what we would today call a particular culture, courts and legislatures; and the extent to which the law should attempt to regulate the private lives of citizens. Along the way no important political or moral principle is left unexamined. Family law, starting with marriage and the upbringing of children, is a central topic.

At the end of the day, the Stranger reminds his companions that their aim has been to devise laws for a real city and not some ideal republic; consequently, the law making process will have to be an ongoing one. Since the city must constantly be reexamining and revising its laws, its Guardians would do well, he advises, to send out mature citizens to study especially good laws elsewhere, and to seek assistance from wise persons wherever they may be found, even in ill-ordered cities. And, finally, he says that the city should always be willing to receive strangers of either sex who have something important to teach or who have come with a serious desire to learn. How can the comparatist not be enchanted? True, we suspect that for Plato, as for Montesquieu and Tocqueville, discourse about foreign systems is in part just a safe and convenient literary device for raising certain issues about politics and law at home. Even so, we are won over. But won over to what?

From the beginning to the end of the Laws, no matter what legal subject is raised, it is education which always comes to the fore. The ultimate concern here, as in The Republic, is not so much with the right laws for the state, but with the right education for citizenship. The Athenian Stranger continually brings the discussion around to the classical idea that the aim of law is to lead the citizens toward virtue, to make them noble and wise. The Stranger stresses, further, that the lawgiver has not only force but also persuasion at his disposal as a means to accomplish this aim. He drives the latter point home by comparing the legislator who simply issues commands to a certain kind of doctor whom he calls the slave doctor. The slave doctor, a slave himself, has learned what he knows of medicine by working as the servant of a doctor. His manner of practicing his profession is to make a hurried visit, to order whatever remedy experience suggests, and then to rush off to the next patient. By contrast, the freeman's doctor begins by getting to know the patient and his family. He inquires far back into the nature of the disorder, and when he has got as much information as possible, he then begins instructing the patient with the aim of restoring his health by persuading him into compliance. This doctor gives his prescriptions only after he has won the patient's understanding and cooperation.

As for the law maker, the Athenian Stranger asks, should he merely issue a set of commands and prohibitions, add the threat of a penalty, and then go on to another law, offering never a word of advice or encouragement to those for whom he is legislating? This kind of law may be fit for slaves, he suggests, but surely a legislator for free men should try to devise his laws so as to create good will in the persons addressed and make them ready to receive intelligently the command that follows.

I bring up these old ideas about law for two reasons. First, they are essential to understanding some of the most important differences between the approaches of Anglo–American and continental European law to specific problems.... In addition, they seem to be closely connected to some of the most interesting contemporary American thinking about law. In England and the United States the view that law is no more or less than a command backed up by organized coercion has been widely accepted. The idea that law might be educational, either in purpose or technique, is not popular among us. But on the European continent, older ideas about law somehow survived the demolition of classical political theory and have persisted, at least as undercurrents, into the modern age. The rhetorical method of law making appears not only in the great continental codifications, but also, here and there, in all sorts of contemporary European legislation....

In England and the United States, where prevailing legal theory tends to deny or downplay any pedagogical aim of law, legislation tends to be in the form of the prescriptions of the slave doctor. But recently a few American scholars have begun to talk about looking at law in a way that would not have sounded entirely strange to Plato. James Boyd White suggests, for example, that "law is most usefully seen not ... as a system of rules, but as a branch of rhetoric, ... as the central art by which community and culture are established, maintained and transformed." [17]   And from another branch of the human sciences has come a related invitation or challenge directed specifically to comparatists.   In his Storrs lectures at Yale Law School, the anthropologist Clifford Geertz advised comparative lawyers that they would learn and contribute more if they focused on the fact that law is not just an ingenious collection of devices to avoid or adjust disputes and to advance this or that interest, but also a way that a society makes sense of things.   It is "part of a distinctive manner of imagining the real." [18]   From this perspective, the interesting comparisons among legal systems should lie, first, in their manner of characterizing factual situations so that rules can be applied to them, and second, in how they conceive of the legal norms themselves. It is to be expected that legal systems compared in this manner will differ in the "stories they tell," the "symbols they deploy," and the "visions they project."   The comparatist's task thus becomes a venture into cultural hermeneutics.

Whether meant to or not, law, in addition to all the other things it does, tells stories about the culture that helped to shape it and which it in turn helps to shape: stories about who we are, where we came from, and where we are going.   The stories that are going forward at a given time in a legal system seem to have a powerful influence not only on how legal norms are invented and applied within that system, but on how facts are perceived and translated into the language and concepts of the law.   Indeed, it may be that law affects our lives at least as much by these stories as it does by the specific rules, standards, institutions, and procedures of which it is composed.   Thus it is not an unworthy task for scholars to inquire into how law interprets the world around it, what analogies and images it employs, what segments of history and what aspects of human experience it treats as relevant.

Two aspects in particular of the rhetorical activity of law deserve special attention from comparatists—the interpretive and the constitutive.   Law is interpretive when it is engaged in converting social facts into legal data and systematically summarizing them in legal language. All lawyers are aware that before legal norms can be devised or applied, those facts that are to be treated as legally relevant must be selected out from a complex manifold of words, deeds, and events.   In this process much is disregarded, and what is retained is presented in a stylized, pared-down version.   Geertz has aptly pointed out that, "Whatever law is after, it is not the whole story." [20]   This problem is, of course, not confined to law.   In every form of discourse, the choice of a word is an endowment of meaning, an act of symbolic formulation.   In the present work, some of the most interesting differences that emerge among legal systems concern the divergent ways in which social data are imaginatively reconstructed as legal facts and concepts.

17. James Boyd White, Law as Rhetoric, Rhetoric as Law, 52 U.Chi.L.Rev. 684 (1985).

18. Clifford Geertz, Local Knowledge 175 (1983).

20. Id. at 175.

The interpretive aspects of law are closely related to its constitutive qualities. Law is constitutive when legal language and legal concepts begin to affect ordinary language and to influence the manner in which we perceive reality. As White has put it, law is "an element in the perpetual remaking of the language and the culture that determines ... who we are" as individuals and as a society.[21] This way of looking at law suggests a number of questions that comparatists do well to bear in mind. What stories are being told in a given body of law at a given time? How do these stories affect what issues are raised and treated as important and which are excluded from discussion or perhaps even obscured from view? Is there a distinctively American story? What sorts of meaning are the legal norms in question creating and what sort of society are they helping to constitute?[22]

SECTION 4. THE CONCEPT
OF LEGAL TRADITION

In the minds of many people, the word "tradition" evokes a vision of the frozen and static past. As we use it here, however, it denotes a vital, dynamic, ongoing system. The civil and common law traditions are operating examples of philosopher Alasdair MacIntyre's concept of tradition: "A living tradition then is an historically extended, socially embodied argument, and an argument precisely in part about the goods which constitute that tradition. Within a tradition the pursuit of goods extends through generations, sometimes through many generations."[16]

Let us recall legal historian Alan Watson's observation that:

> Twice only have the customs of the European peoples been worked up into intellectual systems. The Roman system has served two separate civilizations. The common law, governing daily relationships in very various modern societies, has developed without a break from its beginnings in a society utterly different from any of them.[17]

Comparative law coursebooks in the United States have tended to focus exclusively on the Romano–Germanic civil law tradition. Our decision to devote equal attention to the English legal system was influenced in part by our interest in drawing attention to the shared legal and intellectual heritage that links the two great European legal traditions.[18] The elements of that heritage are discussed in the following essay by German legal historian Franz Wieacker, translated and annotated by legal philosopher Edgar Bodenheimer.

21. White, supra note at 691.

22. Id. at 699.

16. Alasdair MacIntyre, After Virtue 207 (1981).

17. Alan Watson, Legal Transplants: An Approach to Comparative Law, supra p. 7.

18. For an illuminating historical survey of many points of convergence and continuity between the civil and common law systems, see R.H. Helmholz, Continental Law and Common Law: Historical Strangers or Companions? 1990 Duke L.J. 1207.

FRANZ WIEACKER, "FOUNDATIONS OF EUROPEAN LEGAL CULTURE"

38 American Journal of Comparative Law 1, 4–29 (1990).*

European legal culture is not alone in the world. Presence and future remind Europeans daily that they have no monopoly on legal culture. There exists so far no planetary legal culture, but numerous new and old, frequently quite ancient, legal cultures have existed outside of our continent. Besides our own (which becomes intelligible as a cultural entity only in contrast to the others), there are especially the following:

On the one side, the legal and social systems of other, chiefly Asiatic high cultures, among them, as the ones reaching farthest in time and space, those of the Islamic world, India, and China. These, above all, present a challenge to Europeans to become conscious of the peculiar nature and the limitations of their own conception of law. Thus Europeans encounter in Ancient China a model that, at least originally, did not (in contrast to Europe) isolate the province of law from other societal sanction systems (that is, public morality); and they encounter in Islam a closer link between the interpersonal ("secular") law and revealed religious texts than is possible in Europe since the days when legal scholarship emerged at Bologna. (This is true also with respect to the ancient Jewish conception of law which, however, by virtue of the birth of Jesus as a Jew and, at the same time, in the Roman Empire, has been tied so closely and durably to European legal culture that we cannot regard it as the law of another continent.)

On the other hand, there are the laws of early tribal cultures and other societies called (with doubtful justification) "fragmented" or "segmented." For the legal historian they represent (as do the archaic stages of ancient and European law) valuable materials for a general and comparative legal anthropology; to us they pose difficult questions of acculturation. . . .

Thus, in this broad frame of reference, we shall discuss our own legal culture, which we call European, or more precisely, the Atlantic–European. It includes, first of all, the whole continent in the geographic sense: between the seas in the north and the Mediterranean, between the Atlantic and the Ural Mountains. It includes further the European settlements in North America, as well as large parts of Central and South America, Northern Asia (Siberia), Australia, New Zealand, and the far south of Africa. A worldwide zone of influence in the non-European world adjoins this domain. In Japan and Turkey this influence led to a full reception; beyond this it is particularly effective in the Asian countries of the Commonwealth, above all in India, but also in the

* Translated and annotated by Edgar Bodenheimer. Reprinted with permission of the American Society of Comparative Law.

Islamic countries of North Africa, in Southeast Asia and China, as well as in many new nations, especially of French-speaking black Africa.

But is it really possible to conceive of our own legal culture, so delineated, as a unitary one? The talk about "European legal culture" naturally assumes that, notwithstanding many historical, sociological, and ideological differences, that culture forms a close historical and existential unit, a distinct entity that contrasts with all other developed, or tribal, cultures. This is indeed true; but we should not accept this assertion too lightly.

Continental Europeans (such as Frenchmen, Italians, Central–Europeans both in and outside the German-language area) are tempted, in view of the old common tradition of the Roman *jus commune* and the Latin Church's *jus utrumque*,[5] and the shared experiences of humanism, enlightenment, and modern codifications, to identify their own narrower legal orbit with the totality of European legal culture. In reality, however, we have to add two areas of, at best, equal importance: first, the Anglo–American common law in Great Britain, the United States, and large parts of the British Commonwealth and, second, the contemporary socialist legal orders of Eastern and Central Europe.

1. The relationship of the Anglo–Saxon legal orders to those of the European continent poses relatively easy questions. To be sure—notwithstanding the far-reaching congruence of social structures, economic systems, and basic social values—the common law often deviates substantially from the continental legal style in matters such as organization of courts, judicial procedures, the theory of legal sources and the manner of judicial argumentation; also, these peculiarities (as a look at television shows) have had a much stronger effect on the Anglo–Saxon way of life than the more abstract and rational legal doctrine and the bureaucratic administration of justice on the continent has had on our lifestyle. Yet it is obvious that the legal systems of the common law represent the peculiarly European cultural context just as definitely as those of the continent, not only because of the similar ways of life but also because of the longstanding commonality of the crucial religious, ideological, philosophical and scientific foundations.

In particular, we should bear in mind that the common law and equity of the Anglo–Saxon orbit have shared, since the early part of the High Middle Ages, the tradition of the European *jus commune* and *jus utrumque*. Since the beginning of the Modern Age, decisive impulses shaping the continental constitutional development were received from England and the United States. As far as the theory of fundamental

---

5. From the end of the 11th century, successive generations of scholars, and especially the Glossators and Commentators at the University of Bologna, fashioned a neo-Roman law. That law, based on Justinian's *Corpus Juris Civilis,* they adapted to the needs of their time, creating a European *jus commune* which prevailed—at least as a subsidiary law supplementing the local law—throughout most of the European countries and became the foundation of European legal culture.

The term *jus utrumque* refers to the combination of secular, neo-Roman law and the canon law of the Roman Catholic Church applied by the ecclesiastical courts of Europe.

human rights and liberties and the guarantees of procedural due process are concerned, these matters require just as little discussion as the contemporary influence of the common law on conflict of laws and the progressing unification of the law of obligations.   Beyond that, the Anglo–Saxon orbit, from Hobbes and Locke over Adam Smith, John Austin, Bentham, and J. Stuart Mill up to the contemporary Anglo–American theory of law and society, has time and again provided decisive contributions to the European discussion of fundamental principles.

2.   More problematic are the questions posed by the relationship to the [former] socialist legal orders of Eastern Europe.   The central European countries of the Eastern bloc (Czechoslovakia, Hungary, and Poland) have a long tradition of affiliation with the Latin Church, the Roman law, and the occidental political system, and they belonged to the sphere of Austrian legislative power.   The crucial problem is the law of the Soviet Union (and its federated republics) and of Southeastern Europe. It cannot, however, be questioned that Russia and the Balkans belong to Europe, as it is here understood, not merely in a geographic sense.   The basis for this affiliation was already established by the religious, cultural, and political ties with the East Roman Empire, the Greek Church, and the Byzantine version of Roman law—although the peculiarities of these links engendered major differences with the legal and political conceptions established in the West by the Carolingian Empire and the Roman Church.   In the late seventeenth century, Peter the Great's enlightenment caused Russia to turn toward the constitutional and legal organization of Western Europe.   In the course of the nineteenth century, a similar turn toward the French and Central European constitutional and legal organization brought about the final liberation of the Balkan nations from Turkish rule.

It is true that the victory of Leninist Marxism in the October Revolution and, a generation later, the expansion of the Soviet sphere of domination to Central Europe as a consequence of World War II . . . fundamentally changed the face of Eastern Europe.   Nevertheless, this does not signify a turning away from the shared continental European relationships forged by history and fate.   One reason is that Marxian doctrine itself arose out of a peculiarly occidental theory of society, namely, the splitting off of dialectical materialism from the heritage of Hegel and from the reaction to the specifically West European industrial society of early capitalism.   (Less importantly, as regards the judicial organization, formal rules of procedure, and the principle of legalism, the socialist legal systems resemble those of Western Europe, especially the continental ones.)   There does remain, of course, the essential difference in the basic societal value judgments, the social and economic systems, and in the divergent conceptions of law that follow from Marxist–Leninist theory; it is not mere rhetoric to say, however, that these very differences are evidence of the precarious *concordia discors* of European experience seen as a whole.

After setting these perimeters, our actual theme, i.e., to ascertain the common elements of this enormous geographical and historical complex of relationships, remains an almost indefensible venture. If at all, it could, strictly speaking, succeed only by demonstrating common and invariable constants in each consecutive epoch of European legal history. The synchronal, so-to-speak horizontal, thrust of the intended synthesis must be preceded by a diachronous, vertical thrust corresponding to these epochs. Obviously, this initial, analytical survey can, within the limits of this paper, only be a sketch; I shall present it largely by relying on the basic ideas underlying my book *Privatrechtsgeschichte der Neuzeit (1967).*[9]

III.

By way of simplification, . . . we can distinguish four major epochs:

1. The early Middle Ages provided our legal culture with the vital impulses and, with the help of the surviving civilizing elements of late antiquity, with the basic techniques of law and administration.[10]

After the collapse of the West Roman Empire, an ethnically highly complex population faced the task of surviving and slowly rebuilding the structures of state and government beyond those of a particular region. The heirs of Rome as well as the romanized Iberians, Celts, Illyrians, and the Germans who had entered the soil of the Empire had abandoned the high classical culture of the Roman law (as well as its classicistic revival in the Byzantine East). Replacing it were, in addition to the ethnic traditions of this population, above all the remnants of legal texts, drafting practices, and law-applying techniques that had withstood the cultural regression and are now usually referred to as "vulgar law." A certain compensation for this decay of the Roman orbit and, together with it, of a legal system characterized by a highly developed intellectual discipline and conceptualist refinement was provided by a revitalization

---

9. Wieacker's book on *Private Law History of Modern Times* (2d ed. 1967) depicts the evolution of private law on the continent of Europe, with references to divergences and similarities found in the English common law. Special emphasis is given to the history of private law in Germany. Wieacker's account is not limited to what is commonly called "The Modern Age," i.e., the period extending from the beginning of the 16th century to the present. The first hundred pages contain a concise and illuminating treatment of medieval developments in secular and ecclesiastical law. The discussion proceeds on a broad-gauged philosophical level; it accentuates the jurisprudential ideas underlying the evolution of European law, such as tradition, the law-of-reason movement, humanism, positivism, welfare state reformism etc., rather than the more technical aspects of particular legal institutions.

10. Harold J. Berman's work *Law and Revolution: The Formation of the Western Legal Tradition* (1983) takes the position that distinctly Western conceptions of law

and methodological techniques came to life in the 11th and 12th centuries as a result of a "papal revolution" initiated by Pope Gregory VII. Berman also maintains that the canon law of the Catholic Church represents the first modern-type system of law. The book, which is full of interesting observations about the history of Western legal thought, appears to play down (although it does by no means ignore) the powerful influence which classical Roman law (in the form transmitted chiefly by Justinian's *Corpus Juris Civilis*) has had on European legal developments, including the canon law.

Wieacker would probably fully approve of Berman's observation that "All Western legal systems—the English, the French, the German, the Italian, the Polish, the Hungarian, and others (including, since the 19th century, the Russian)—have common historical roots, from which they derive not only a common terminology and common techniques but also common concepts, common principles, and common values." (p. 539).

of legal life itself. New personal forces stirred beneath the crust of the early Byzantine autocratic state that had crumbled in the West. The absolutist regime of coercion, which had oppressed the subjects after the destruction of the ancient municipal and civic liberties of antiquity, often yielded to the formation of new cooperative associations; impersonal offices were replaced by the personal relation of fealty. Law was no longer but the command of a distant central agency; it became part of a living tradition. The objective law, which Roman absolutism had manipulated in an almost capricious fashion, was replaced by concrete entitlements that were less susceptible to tampering. The former freedom of the urban resident or *civis Romanus* was replaced with diverse corporate freedoms; in lieu of the dead or moribund centralized judicial organization laymen adjudicated. We should not forget that these compensations for the barbarization that followed the breakdown of urban civilization in the West were rather modest; they nevertheless enriched the image of the law with new and auspicious features.

The reconstruction of civilization and of societal organization beyond the regional level would, however, have been impossible without the survival of the Roman heritage. Through painstaking "learning processes" the Roman people and the recently romanized migratory tribes were ultimately acculturated. In place of the former imperial Roman administration, the *Latin Church* became increasingly the successor organization of the imperial governmental agencies and a makeshift shelter for cultural continuity. In four ways the Church promoted these learning processes:

(1) In preserving the elementary level of the rich classical system of education, the *trivium*, the Church, by maintaining the use of writing, documentation, filing and accounting, provided the substructure required for governmental organization. It thereby forged continuous supraregional links for the Western European territories that were no longer in communication with one another and constantly threatened from outside.

(2) Primarily because of the Church, the notions of official power and jurisdiction were preserved, notions that the Byzantine absolutism, following the separation of military and civilian power, had exalted to the point of hypertrophy. This conception of office differed from the Germanic idea of a personal relation between the king and his followers, in which there was no room for fixed competences and departmental powers.

(3) The same is true for the notion of *statute*. The Germanic, and later also the Slavic nations and tribes originally did not conceive of law as a command of state power but rather as a traditional order of living. Therefore they had to resort to the conceptual framework of the late Roman Empire to explain the idea of enacted law. From Rome they learned that law is not only lived tradition but also an emanation of power and human will. At that time the foundation was laid for the

peculiar legalism of European legal culture, which has endured in the form of the statutory positivism of our days.

(4) Beyond competence and statute, a new and higher view of law entered the consciousness of early Western culture with the help of Christianity and the Church: the conviction that beyond lived tradition and the command of local rulers there exists a *universal ecumenical* law above the local traditions and enactments. This idea was nourished in its inception by the reality of an empire whose boundaries were coextensive with the *orbis terrarum.* It found, however, a spiritual basis by the identification of this universal law with the world law of the Stoics and, beyond that, by fitting it into a supernatural *ius divinum.* Christianity now related all secular law (not just Roman law) to a supernatural value, in the light of which it had to justify itself time and again. Ever since Augustine had thought of the *civitas terrena* as a reflection as well as an antithesis of the *civitas Dei,* legal metaphysics, understood as the search for an ideal law of nature, became a major theme of occidental legal culture. This perspective alone accounts for the notion of a European *ius commune* which has remained active throughout the history of European legal thought and is capable of resuscitation at any time.

2. By creating an autonomous legal science, the classical high Middle Ages fashioned a secular, juridical subsystem and mastered it intellectually. This system came to dominate life in Europe and by the end of the late medieval period had spread over the entire western and central European continent. In closest connection and coordination herewith, the church followed a similar route by transforming itself into a legal church with an articulated legal system, the canon law, and its own judicial organization.

The "learning processes" of the early Middle Ages had not as yet brought about a new, peculiar European "identity." In some respects the pre-Carolingian political establishments especially looked like provinces of the extinct empire and the surviving Christian ecumene, rather than like new creations that had appropriated an old heritage by their own free choice. Their relation to the culture of antiquity was marked by continuity and study, not by initiative and renaissance.

Only since the 11th century did the European identity begin to manifest itself in the field of the law by virtue of a genuine renaissance of Roman law. This astonishing event was based on the coincidence of rapid economic and cultural advances in Italy and Southern France with the rise of a new Rome-ideology, emanating from an intellectual elite of the clergy. In the religious realm this ideology took shape in the ecclesiastic community of the Cluny reform, in the secular area in the *renovatio* and *translatio imperii* [15] of the Salic and Staufen emperors. The counterpart in intellectual culture was the establishment of the first European philosophy to be emancipated from interpretation of the

---

15. This statement probably refers to the fact that the emperors of the medieval Holy Roman Empire regarded themselves as the legitimate successors of the Roman emperors of antiquity and the "renovators" of their political goals.

Scriptures. It took the two forms of an independent (idealistic or nominalistic) epistemology and an elaboration of an intellectual technique of argumentation, conceptualization, and logical derivation of scientific propositions.

Ideology and intellectual technique also were necessary for the well-nigh explosive renaissance of (classical) Roman law at the end of the 11th century, which found its first representative expression in the *studium civile* at Bologna. In the field of the law, the intellectual rediscovery of classical Roman jurisprudence in the form of Justinian's Pandects is the manifestation of the first genuine renaissance in Europe; from it emerged European legal science which shaped the contents of most continental European legal systems. The legitimation for the outright recognition of Roman law was furnished by the Rome-idea in its three forms: the curial one of the reformist popes, the imperial one of the Emperors' jurists, and the municipal one of the rising Italian city republics. Its social and economic precondition was the formation of a city-centered economic society with a (limited) freedom of transregional commercial and financial exchange.

What concerns us here particularly is the transference of the processes of cognition, discussion, argumentation and conceptualization offered by the new philosophy to the inexhaustible treasure trove of classical law preserved in Justinian's law books. The fathers of the new legal science at Bologna thus discovered a new intellectual world. They encountered the highest sublimation of juridical thinking that the intrinsically practical discipline of law has ever attained, and it is one of the European miracles that, with the help of the new intellectual tools, these jurists learned to respond to the old texts with an equally refined understanding. In this fashion they became the first (professional) jurists of Western civilization.[16]

In the practical world this meant that these jurists were able to claim for themselves competence to decide vital conflicts of public and social life without recourse to force or peremptory command, or within the constraints of custom and tradition, or pursuant to the dictate of unquestionable texts, or in consonance with unexamined religious or moral tenets, but rather by reasoned analysis of a specific legal problem, in terms of the prevailing scientific doctrine of their time (scholasticism). Thus, from now on there existed, apart from the vital forces and power structures, and in addition to the spiritual authority of the Scriptures, the Church fathers, and contemporary theology, a third, independent

---

16. The revival of classical Roman law (as distinguished from the vulgarized Roman law that was absorbed by the Germanic conquerors of the Western Roman Empire) in the Italian law schools, especially at Bologna, was of immense significance for the rise of European culture, including legal culture, in the 11th century. This was true especially with respect to the highly developed Roman law of obligations (including contractual obligations) and property. It was felt that these two branches of the law contained many features representing a sort of "timeless reason." There is some plausibility in this assumption when it is considered that in our time the Soviet law of obligations and property bears a great deal of similarity to the West European law notwithstanding the differences in the social and economic systems.

institution that claimed the power to decide disputes between individuals, as well as between corporate and public authorities according to a rule based on reason. To this day, the jurists' insistence on legality, i.e., on a professionalized regime of law, has, in principle, formed part of European legal culture. Compared to other civilizations, ours is characterized and distinguished precisely by this very claim. If we view the various stages of history as steps toward increasing rationality, the intellectualization of law by the glossators of the high Middle Ages and the commentators of the late Middle Ages was the first and largest step in this direction.

The actual implementation, as part of European reality, of this scheme of thought, unheard of in its novelty, was, of course, conditioned by larger cultural and socio-historical processes. The new decisional techniques did not remain the privilege of a select happy few. On the contrary, in the following centuries the Italian, French, and ultimately all continental faculties of law, from Salamanca to Cracow and Uppsala, trained entire contingents of young jurists, who later took back to their home countries the technical monopoly of knowledge for purposes of diplomacy, administration, adjudication, and drafting. By damming up the violent resolution of public conflicts, primarily by means of diplomatic, administrative, and fiscal activities in the service of Church, Empire, national states, and territories and free cities of the Empire, and by eliminating the irrational elements from adjudication, these jurists created the most important preconditions for the future growth of commerce, production, material culture and, last but not least, for new possibilities of life in the service of the spirit.

3. The early phase of the Modern Age, until the end of the *ancien régime* in 1789, perfected upon these foundations the conceptualization and systematization of law by using methodological tools of a new age dedicated to mathematics and the natural sciences; at the same time, aligned with the law-of-reason movement and the enlightenment, the demand for rationality also became victorious in the realm of political and social reality.

Because of the decline of the former universal powers of Curia and Empire, the disintegration of the *corpus christianum* due to religious schisms, the rise of national or (in Germany and Italy) territorial states, and, last but not least, because of the transatlantic colonization, the question of a new legitimation of international law, constitutional law, and ultimately even private law presented itself to this era. The response of European thought was a progressive intellectual and conceptual incorporation of the positive materials of the law into a "natural system," the law of reason. The law of reason amounts to a systematization of that ancient tradition which, as *ius naturale*, has all along provided the background for ancient Roman and medieval jurisprudence. Brought into being by the epistemology of humanistic Platonism, this new natural law had not as yet, at the time of the Spanish scholastics, Althusius and Grotius, abandoned that old traditional connection. But in its second systematic phase from Hobbes to Christian Wolff, its postulates began to shift from tradition and authority to reason (*deductio*) and empirical observation (*observatio*). The general foundation for this development had been, since Hobbes and Pufendorf, the critical method established by the *Discours* of Descartes and the notion of general laws of nature developed in Galileo's *Discorsi.*

The far-reaching consequences of this intellectual revolution persist until the present. Following the collapse of religious unity in Europe, the law of reason first provided a new supradenominational (though not necessarily secularized) foundation for law. To that extent it became the creator of a new civil religion. For the rising nations, territorial states, and city republics it supplied two models, each representing one of the two prevailing types of new European states: on the one hand, the absolute states ruled by a prince found in Western and Central Europe and extending as far as Denmark; on the other hand, the oligarchic republics (ruled either in monarchical fashion or by the estates) as in the *Generalstaaten,* in England after the Glorious Revolution,[21] but also in Sweden, Poland, at times in Hungary, as well as in the large German coastal cities. In this republican version the law of reason offered a new justification for popular sovereignty; it portrayed the historical prerogatives of the estates as individual liberties of the citizens and thereby prepared the ground for the modern constitutional state. In the absolute states ruled by the princes, on the other hand, which repressed or stifled the prerogatives of the estates, the law of reason emphasized the centralizing and rationalizing, but also the reformist features of the modern age—reformist because the law of reason as a self-contained system of natural and civic rights and duties enabled an enlightened absolutism to embark on the first planned undertakings and reforms of governments in North and Central Italy, in Prussia and Austria and, under new historical conditions, in Napoleonic France.

4. The Modern Age, from 1789 until today, moving at an ever increasing speed, is characterized by the definite collapse of Western legal metaphysics, the industrial revolution, the rise and crises of the bourgeois pioneer and entrepreneurial society, and finally the complete political and social integration of the Fourth Estate, as shown by the replacement of the "bourgeois" by the "social" law-state (*Rechtsstaat*). With all of this, our age confronts European legal culture once again, and in a more radical fashion than ever, with the question of new

---

21. The phrase "Glorious Revolution" is a somewhat misleading term referring to the deposition in 1689 of King James II in a bloodless coup and the accession to the British throne of William of Orange and his wife Mary. Their rule led to the promulgation of a Bill of Rights and the gradual establishment of a parliamentary monarchy.

The true English revolution, which resulted in a far-reaching overhauling of the social and economic system, was the Puritan Revolution beginning in 1642 under the leadership of Oliver Cromwell. Its outcome, after two civil wars, was the abolition of the monarchy and the establishment of a republican Commonwealth. (The monarchy was restored in 1660.) The Puritan Revolution eliminated or weakened many institutions of feudalism and strengthened the social position of the merchants, artisans, and middle-class gentry.

legitimations for law and the relation between the formal legal system and social justice and security in the industrial society of our time.

Contrary to first appearances, the beginning of this epoch was marked by the effectuation of the tendencies that surfaced in the late enlightenment. This is true because the French Revolution, at the zenith of *volonté générale* (i.e., the revolutionary state identified with the nation) asserted full powers over the individual rights of citizens. But once the nation, by curbing populist and egalitarian impulses, had ultimately identified itself with the *bourgeoisie,* identified by property and education, the great revolution first developed into the liberal constitutional state. This state left the economy and private law to the bourgeois entrepreneurial society as an open preserve, renouncing for the time being the attempt of guaranteeing social solidarity by a redistribution of goods. Since, however, such a society of entrepreneurs pushes for a modern and uniform private and procedural law, the European constitutional state made a full use of the legislative monopoly established at the time of enlightened absolutism. As a result, this new legislative positivism stripped the law of reason of its substance, but perpetuated it as a systematic supportive skeleton for the new codes of the bourgeois constitutional state.[23]

Only later did fundamental new approaches appear, which make up the basic theme of contemporary legal culture. I refer to the demise, in legal theory, of substantive natural law and its successors, the idealistic legal philosophies, especially in Germany; and in societal reality the question provoked by the Industrial Revolution of a just distribution of goods and of social security, more briefly: the problem of solidarity in society as a whole. At issue was how to compensate for the deficit in social equality considering the economic freedom of action which the victory of the Third Estate in the French Revolution and in the liberal constitutional state had brought about.

In order to understand these developments fully, one needs to bear in mind the increasing helplessness of jurisprudence and the judicial process in the face of modern ideological and social forces. As noted before, the law of reason as a substantive legitimation of law had become

---

23. The "law of reason" was a legal-philosophical movement of the 17th and 18th centuries that undertook to deduce general rules or principles of law from the rational part of human nature. One of the most influential representatives of the movement was Samuel Pufendorf (1632–1694), a German law professor. Pufendorf derived natural law from both the self-assertive and the social side of human nature. The former demands recognition of an individual's right to life, safety, and property; the latter requires that human beings shall not injure each other. From a combination of these principles, Pufendorf extracted a number of more specific legal concepts, all of them, in his opinion, dictated by reason and morality.

Legal positivism rejected the derivation of binding legal norms from axioms of reason and morality. It grounded the obligatory force of law chiefly on sovereign will and command. As Wieacker points out, legal positivism retained certain organizational features and system-building conceptions which had formed part of the efforts of the natural-law philosophers, especially those of Pufendorf and Christian Wolff. These systematizing and conceptualizing endeavors also influenced the structure, arrangement, choice of headings, and terminology of the codifications growing out of the law-a victim of Rousseau's *volonté générale* and Kant's epistemology; [24] yet its function as a model for systematizing and rationalizing positive law had not been discarded. In consequence what remained was a jurisprudential formalism that lacked the intrinsic support of a substantive idea of justice. To be sure, as Roman and medieval jurisprudence demonstrate, in stagnating societies positive law can remain functional for quite some time, provided it rests on a broad consensus of the dominant classes. In the 19th century, however, such consensus was confronted with the growing dynamics of the Industrial Revolution and the expectations of justice on the part of the rising working class. For this reason, juristic formalism faced for the first time the question—which had been pushed aside by positivism—of the extralegal societal values that legitimate the formal rules of law and their application.

The broad spectrum of answers to this question can only be dealt with here in a sketchy fashion. It ranges from Jeremy Bentham's utilitarianism and Jhering's purpose-in-law doctrine to the "modern school of criminal law," to the free-law movement, and to the contemporary jurisprudence of interests or value-oriented jurisprudence; from American and Scandinavian realism to the most powerful and momentous version of the answer, the socialist and, more particularly, the Marxist critique of law. Behind these critical approaches there stood the broader ideologies of economic utilitarianism, mechanistic monism, and Social Darwinism. The ultimate background was provided by the unprecedented success of the applied natural sciences which, in light of their increasing mastery and taming of natural forces also opened up the possibility of controlling social behavior, and even the psychic sphere, by social techniques and strategies.

For a long time positivism, because of its indifference toward the practical problems of justice, reacted naively and helplessly to this assault. But helpless silence could not prevent political realities from imprinting on legislation and judicial action, usually by virtue of an unconscious consensus and sometimes even involuntarily, the mark of the social state. As a result, the principle of societal solidarity, which has been legitimized and constitutionally guaranteed and implemented in the form of basic social rights, has been effectuated in relation to the weaker members of society by a "network of social guarantees." In

of-reason movement and, beyond this, of later European codes of law.

24. In Rousseau's system, the law of reason was absorbed by the *volonté générale,* understood as the genuine communitarian interest. ... The rights that the law of reason derived from the nature of human beings were put at the disposition of popular majorities, for they rather than postulates of reason bestowed legitimacy on legal rules.

According to Kant's epistemological approach, the law-of-reason philosophers committed an error in attempting to deduce the existence of rights and duties requiring rec-

ognition by the law from certain empirical traits and inclinations of human beings. Knowledge of human nature, Kant thought, cannot discover laws that can claim self-evident necessity. Only pure reason, operating in an a priori fashion, can discover such laws. According to Kant, a law must hold good for all cases and not be subject to exceptions, whereas supposed "laws" based on psychological or sociological observations are contingent and variable. The epistemology of Kant thus differs markedly from the cognitive method used by the law-of-reason philosophers.

practice, this principle has increasingly gained priority over the older ideological discussion concerning the political structure of contractual or property relationships, the disposition over the means of production or other economic assets generally.[25] The silent or self-evident manner in which this principle, or at least the hope for it, has asserted itself throughout the world, even in ancient tribal cultures, shows the compelling necessity and irreversibility of the process; it is at the same time an admonition to lawyers and ideologues not to forget for one moment the expectations of justice held by simple people of all classes, tongues, regions, and colors.

IV.

If, following this survey of historical eras, I attempt to determine the *invariables* in the historical evolution that give our legal culture its peculiar character, I can only provide a first draft of such a synopsis. With this reservation, I designate the following essential constants of European legal culture: its *personalism*, its *legalism*, and its *intellectualism*. For the time being, these are only labels that do not gain in clarity if, in colloquial language, we speak of orientation toward the individual instead of personalism, speak of thinking in terms of legal enactments instead of legalism, speak of a basic tendency to comprehend legal phenomena in the framework of scientific thought instead of intellectualism. What matters is to clarify the meaning of these broad key terms as much as possible; if it should prove impossible to fill them with content and illustrations, my undertaking to show "the foundations of European legal culture" (a risky one in any case) would have foundered. I wish to add that none of these three tendencies is altogether alien to any developed view of the law in civilized mankind, and that they determine the peculiar character of our legal culture only in their interplay and relative weight.

1. Most difficult to comprehend and to document—like most general searches for an "image of man"—is the *personalistic* trait, i.e., the primacy of the individual as subject, end, and intellectual point of reference in the idea of law. Often invoked as the hallmark of a "timeless Europeanism" from Homer over the Ionian thinkers to Descartes and Kant, that characteristic is, in the first place, a rather general and indeterminate turn of phrase. If it is at all permissible to attach such a general attribute of mankind to a particular historical culture, then the following appears to be characteristic of ours: in the realm of cognition the separation in principle of perceiving subject and perceived object, in the world in which we live the conception of human relations as a "vis-à-vis," rather than a "with one another" or "together"—both

---

25. This statement applies more obviously to continental Europe than to the common-law countries. In all or most nations of Western Europe socioeconomic rights, such as old-age pensions, national health insurance, unemployment insurance, right to paid vacations, are considered to have a rank equal with individual rights, such as rights of contract, property, and free speech. In Eastern Europe social and economic rights have enjoyed a more secure protection than individual rights.

* * *

in contrast to a stronger fusion of persons and objects, of I and We in other high civilizations and in most tribal cultures.[26]

Perhaps this personalism is as a vital heritage rooted in the free civic state of the ancient *polis* and in the associations formed by the migratory peoples of late antiquity and the early Middle Ages. The experience of a personal deity has added depth and ethical strength to this vital attitude: first in the classical religions, then, much more powerfully, in the experience of one personal God in Judaism and Christianity, inasmuch as in those religions the relationship of the human being to the absolute was experienced as the relation of an "I" to a demanding and giving "Thou," in other words, of one person to another—in contrast to the merging of an individual with a suprapersonal whole, as, for example (as we are told without claiming expert knowledge), in the Indian Nirvana and Chinese Tao. From this personal connection of an individual with a demanding and giving opposite followed, as a unique feature, the ultimate freedom of decision, and thus personal responsibility: the powerful and at the same time duty-bound *liberum arbitrium,* which manifests itself in the active response to the demands of another: as in deliberately availing oneself of a proffered salvation and also in willing and working in this world.

The best evidence of this basic relationship may well be its impact upon the conception of law. This impact is so strong that it was able to outlast the belief in a personal God—as in Deism or in the materialistic philosophies practiced in antiquity and in more recent epochs of Western history. It is only here that law becomes a network of interpersonal relationships of "ought," "can," or "may," i.e., of interaction, to fellow-citizens. Freedom and self-determination (instead of "magical" or collective constraints) in the ordering of legal relationships (whether by contract or legal norms), duty and culpability (instead of fate or doom) and thus accountability for crimes and torts: both have formed the Western idea of law developed from antiquity. They have shaped, above all, the notion of private law (which only here has become truly independent) as a bundle of subjective entitlements among responsible persons, as well as the evolution of criminal law from strict liability to culpability.

It bears brief mention that these seemingly vague statements about the religious origin of the personalistic conception of law are corroborated by concrete data of legal history: thus, for example, the major breakthrough of Greek and then early Roman law from the magic guilt based on consanguinity, the miasma by virtue of mere causation in case

---

26. Some may object to this statement on the ground that the communitarian spirit, the feeling of social "belonging" was highly developed in Europe during most of the Middle Ages. It is true, for example, that the medieval guild system was based on mutual aid and the furtherance of common vocational interests. On the other hand, the principle Wieacker calls "personalism" was clearly implicit in the rejection of collective responsibility by the medieval church and state, and in Christianity's belief in the value of the individual soul. In some early societies, an assault injuring or killing a member of a group (such as a sib or clan) obligated the group to administer retribution to the entire family or sib of the perpetrator. Such forms of group responsibility were largely unknown in European legal culture.

of even accidental homicide, to wilful, premeditated murder, as proclaimed by Apollo in the *Oresteia* of Aeschylus; and, more generally, in the genesis of liability for fault in both of the antique legal systems and, again, in the medieval canonist theory of delictual and contractual liability; and finally in converting the ancient Roman magic *fides* into the ethical principle of *bona fides,* and in characterizing subjective rights as "emanations of the individual will." The latter notion is rooted the law of reason and in the philosophical idealism of the early nineteenth century.

In the framework of such a conception, self-determination and responsibility necessarily complement each other. This has caused a persistent ambivalence between egotistic self-assertion and solidary responsibility for others. The constant tension between individualistic theories of liberty and altruistic teachings about duty, which thus furnished the basis for all legal theorizing in Europe, is expressed, in exemplary fashion, in the legend of classical natural law, which limits the primordial freedom of the original condition by a social contract that—sometimes as free consensus, sometimes as a contract of subjection or domination—establishes the social responsibility of individuals. Since then, the continuous dialogue between theories of freedom and responsibility has remained the guiding theme of all European legal and political philosophy.[a]

The ramifications of this basic pattern for the European understanding of law are immense. With respect to the relationship of the individual to the state, the theories of freedom have, in succession, helped to establish the following: the ancient freedoms of the estates; the freedom of conscience, born of religious struggles, first of the new churches and later also of the individual person; the secularized economic liberty and later also the political liberty of the rising bourgeoisie, and finally the fundamental rights of the individual enshrined in modern constitutions. The social contract or pact of domination, on the other hand, successively legitimated the following: the sovereignty of the absolute monarch (with its acknowledged responsibility for peace, security, and even the "happiness" of his subjects), the democratic people's sovereignty of the *volonté générale,* and finally the unlimited control of socialist society over the distribution of goods, opportunities to work, and the education of its subjects.

The same tension between property rights and contractual autonomy on the one hand, and the social restrictions on private rights and their exercise on the other is apparent in the private law of modern economic societies. Today, the resulting antinomy between liberal and social *Rechtsstaat* poses one of the fundamental constitutional problems in Western and Central Europe. But this tension only confirms the extent to which individual freedom and social duty (to use catchwords:

a. For discussion of the different "dialects" of the modern language of rights and responsibility, see M. Glendon, Rights Talk: The Impoverishment of Political Discourse (1991).

individualism and socialism) are two sides of the same coin: a specifically Western personalism.

2. It is easier to elucidate the second feature of our legal culture, its *legalism*. By this we mean not merely (and not even especially) the monopoly of the modern governmental legislator to create and change the law (which on the European continent did not come about until the 18th century), but more generally the need to base decisions about social relationships and conflicts on a general rule of law, whose validity and acceptance does not depend on any extrinsic (moral, social, or political) value or purpose.[28] The precondition of this exclusive power of the legal rule was the separation, characteristic for Roman as well as European professional jurisprudence, of the legal system from other social rules and sections (such as religious tenets, moral imperatives, custom, and convention). This separation can be traced back, essentially, to the growth of a specific professional administration of justice in ancient Rome (which probably derives from the expert functions performed by the ancient Roman *pontifices*) and the legacy of this jurisprudence to European legal science. In more recent times, it was reestablished and intensified by the separation of morals and law since the end of the 17th century (Thomasius and Kant) and ultimately led to the jurisprudential formalism of the 19th century and the statutory positivism of the modern constitutional state.

Thus, this separation is the root of that legalism which conceives of social duties, rights, and privileges as objectified legal relationships, removed, in principle, from arbitrariness as well as from mercy, from the *caritas* of interhuman empathy as well as the expediencies of a particular

---

28. This statement, unless it is understood in the context of subsequent qualifications, lends itself to misinterpretation. First of all, Thomist as well as classical natural law theory (Grotius, Pufendorf, Locke) did not entirely divorce the validity of a legal rule from certain moral goals lying outside of it. It was agreed that in cases of a truly outrageous violation of a moral or religious command by a legal prescription, the latter was not binding and entitled those subject to it to passive or (in some situations) even active resistance. Wieacker does not ignore this fact. He points out subsequently that during the entire European legal history "drastic correctives" have served as an antidote to formalized rule-bound justice. For example, he mentions the position taken by the canon law to the effect that legal rules are subject to equitable exceptions in appropriate cases. He also refers to the "countercurrents" against legalism during the period of the law of reason. Thus, Wieacker does not view legalism as a universally observed principle of European legal culture.

Secondly, Wieacker uses the term "legalism" in a broad sense. He does not identify legalism with literal or "plain meaning" interpretation of legal sources. His statement that legalism separates law from the moral or social purposes existing "outside" of it does not exclude construction of statutes in the light of their social objectives. Wieacker also acknowledges the existence of binding nonformal guides to judicial decisionmaking based on bona fides, the "nature of things," or accepted norms of the culture. See Wieacker, "Gesetz and Richterkunst," in 2 *Ausgewählte Schriften* 41–58 (1983).

What Wieacker appears to have in mind is that positive legal norms (which form the primary basis of judicial decisions) possess a certain degree of independence from the surrounding social and economic conditions. Their autonomy (which, as Wieacker concedes, is partial only) furnishes some guarantee that lawsuits will be decided, not on the basis of irrational sentiments or purely subjective beliefs, but on the authority of sources that impart to the judicial process some measure of objectivity, detachment, and predictability. Understood in this sense, legalism can be viewed as a pillar of European legal culture.

case. It is this legalism, if we see it correctly, which—apart from the scientific mastery of natural forces—most distinguishes European civilization from that of other high cultures, in which law emanates from an accepted social ethic as it did in classical China, or from revealed religious texts as in Judaism and Islam. Notwithstanding the evident weaknesses and dangers of such a separation of law from the living world of social values and purposes (for which professional jurists have always been criticized), legalism has bestowed upon Europe an immeasurable gain in rationality in the external world. Beyond the "legitimation by means of process" (N. Luhmann), legalism has unburdened social conflicts from force, emotions, interests, and prejudices which (contrary to accusations often heard today) has more frequently produced emancipatory rather than repressive results. As against public authorities, legalism assures the individual of greater legal certainty, and in criminal and civil procedure it has always signified freedom from the arbitrariness of irrational forms of proof and proceedings, and later, above all, greater strategic equality in litigation.

In private law, legalism led (to use the celebrated formula of Sumner Maine) "from status to contract," i.e., it accorded individuals the private autonomy to control his personal and property sphere, free from historical restrictions. More generally, legalism was the first and sole ideology to guarantee the equality of human beings before God or nature (though other highly developed cultures also derived equality from the fact that humans are children of God, or by hypothesizing the identity of everything that lives). It has thereby converted historical rights and privileges into general freedoms of citizens and ultimately into universal human rights.

Finally, legalism made possible the modern welfare state, in that it alone transformed the responsibility of society (taken for granted in the religious cultures of India, Judaism, and Islam) to help the indigent (over and above voluntary charitable activities such as alms, labors of love, and beneficent contributions) into a statutory network of social services that by now enjoys constitutional protection in the form of fundamental social rights. Regrets about the loss of spontaneity that characterizes personal generosity and about the atrophy of voluntary *caritas* because of administered assistance cannot possibly becloud the realization of the advantages that our legal culture has gained. Let us hope that they will also redound to the benefit of a future world.

These achievements of legalism did, however, come at a high price. The stringent demands it makes on rationality produce a continual tension with other fundamental postulates of justice. In legalistic systems one is painfully aware of the antinomies of generalized and individualized justice, legal certainty and material justice, equality before the law and inequality of the starting opportunities. These antinomies must, on principle, be decided in favor of the first-mentioned rational values. For this reason, throughout ancient and European legal history drastic corrections of formalized rule-bound justice became necessary: in Rome the discretionary powers of the praetor, in the Middle Ages the *aequitas canonica* (originating in the *forum internum* and then external-ized), in the age of the abstract law of reason the pragmatic and decisionist countercurrents; in modern statutory positivism the general clauses and the judicial balancing of interests.

3.   The third constant of European legal culture, *intellectualism*, relates to the peculiar way in which the phenomenon of law is understood; it is closely connected with the specific structures and traditions of European thinking. I refer to the tendency to grasp all phenomena by means of general epistemological methods. This basic tendency cannot be ade-quately understood as mere generalization or abstraction. It is more properly conceived as an idealism, provided that we strip this concept of its common linguistic meaning of an unselfish pursuit of suprapersonal goals and restrict it to epistemological idealism; or else as intellectual-ism, if we disregard the common linguistic usage that connects the term with a social attitude characterized by the priority given to the theoreti-cal activity of the mind (as in "the intellectual," "intelligentsia"). What we have in mind is that *amor intellectualis* which, again and again, drove European legal thinking in the direction of thematization, conceptualiza-tion, and contradiction-free consistency of empirical legal materials.

In the last instance, this third tendency signifies the enduring contribution of Greek philosophy to the constants of our legal culture. It dates back to the conviction of the Eleates and of Platonism about the necessary connection, even identity, of cognitive thinking and the object of cognition—and the urge it engendered to "ideate," i.e., to perceive an unchanging essence behind the bustle of empirical appearances.[29] Just as it would have been impossible for the occident to devise theologies, philosophical systems, mathematics, and the rigorous natural sciences without this impulse, it also ultimately transformed the originally quite practical and mundane acts of making and applying law into a systemat-ic science.

As a figure of formal thinking, this influence taught the Roman jurists and their legitimate heirs, the European jurists, the formation of concepts and the starting points for a general systematization of legal phenomena; beginning with the early period of the modern age it has produced the integrated systems of the law of reason and thus prepared the ground for the great modern codes. Its ultimate triumphs were these very codifications, the doctrinal systems of modern private-law

---

29. The twentieth-century philosophical movement called "phenomenology" may be regarded, to some extent at least, as a reviv-al of Platonism. It was founded by Ed-mund Husserl and has attained a sizable following, especially in Western Europe and Latin America. Phenomenology endeavors to grasp the "essence," i.e., the ideal, intel-ligible, enduring qualities of the objects of our consciousness (phenomena) with the help of intuitive vision. Phenomenology criticizes positivism on the ground that it limits the possibility of cognition to objects perceived by our senses. Nicolai Hart-mann, in his work *Das Problem des Geisti-gen Seins* (3rd ed. 1962), pointed out that in addition to sensual objects there exists a world of mental (noetic) being that includes the realm of values. This means, for exam-ple, that the concept of justice has an "es-sence" transcending the subjective reac-tions of individuals.

science and finally, the current revision of general legal theory by means of the contemporary theory of science.

The most important things, however, have not as yet been said. This third aspect is not restricted to the formal ordering of legal science. Greek intellectualism shaped the future to an even greater extent by articulating, conceptually and systematically, specific demands on justice in the form of a general idea of justice. In its general version (its mathematicalized division into "arithmetic" and "geometric" justice is not altogether accidental),[30] this idea has played a decisive role in the ideologizing of the quest for justice (a propensity characteristic for Europe): it is its blessing as well as its curse that the issue of justice has been transmuted from a matter of correct public conduct to one of intellectually cognizable judgments about truth. To be sure, in its result this ideologization has for the most part operated as a progressive, that is to say, as an equalizing and emancipatory element of European legal development. Abstract justice supplied the keynote when historical prerogatives and privileges were supplanted by civil and ultimately human rights. It did so likewise when enlightened absolutism and its progeny, the democratic *volonté générale,* encroached upon the vested rights of individuals. Today, abstract justice raises its voice, even more generally, in favor of the material equality before the law, and no longer concedes legal relevance to natural, historical, or social distinctions. In the critical legal literature of our time the ideology of general justice retains its emancipatory and egalitarian dynamism in the demand to compensate for the inequality of social starting opportunities at the expense of formal equality before the law: as, for example, by redistribution of the social product, by confiscatory progressive taxation, or by educational policies. As in the case of other antinomies found in an idea-oriented legal culture, the tension between stabilizing rationality and tendencially progressive justice remains a task that must be mastered and performed every day.

V.

We conclude with questions that lead us back from the preceding abstractions to problems of the present that, I suppose, concern everyone of us. Do the traits of our legal culture outlined here have a chance to become part of a future planetary legal culture? To answer the question

---

30. The mathematical demonstration of justice goes back to Aristotle, who distinguished between two kinds of justice: distributive and corrective. Distributive justice is concerned with the distribution of honors, wealth, and other goods among the members of the community. It is a form of "geometrical" justice in the sense that it must be thought of in terms of proportions between shares, rather than in terms of numbers. Proportional justice gives to each person that which he is entitled to in accordance with his ability and achieve-ments. Corrective justice, on the other hand, is concerned with the righting of wrongs. If a contract is breached, a tort has been committed, or an unjust enrichment has occurred, corrective justice seeks to provide compensation to the injured party, operating with the arithmetical devices of addition and subtraction. An unjustified gain, for example, is subtracted from the assets of the wrongdoer and added to the assets of the wronged person. See Aristotle, *Nicomachean Ethics,* BK. V, II.12 to IV 14 (H. Rackham transl. 1947).

one must, first of all, bear in mind the highly complex conditions of our time.

In the era of colonization, European legal systems (especially the English, French, and Dutch) were exported to non-European nations. After decolonization, some of the nations, upon attaining independence, retained that law (including its respective doctrinal apparatus and training procedures) by their own volition—similar to the way in which the peoples of the early Middle Ages retained the Roman law of late antiquity. The extent to which, in the face of this development, these nations will maintain or resuscitate their own legal tradition is a challenging problem which, however, will not be discussed here and cannot be decided by us Europeans.

Similar questions are posed for the non-European high cultures of Eastern Asia, India, and the Islamic orbit, which have either remained free of (direct) colonial domination or have retained their own, frequently religious, law in spite of it. These countries, too, after acquiring full independence or at least asserting their own identity, have often favored the reception or retention of judicial systems, modes of procedure, and codifications. That is true, first and foremost of Japan and, after its secularization, Turkey, as well as of the first Chinese Republic after 1912, Thailand, and some other countries of the Near or Far East.

In both instances, it is often noticeable that national emancipatory movements were directed not only against the European colonial masters but, at the same time, against their own former social and hierarchical structures, and that in both instances these movements operated with the legalistic and rational apparatus of European constitutional doctrines and legal techniques. In situations in which this emancipation took social-revolutionary forms, the model of socialist law from Eastern Europe was, of course, preferred. Where, however, colonial rule disappeared at an early time and without prolonged revolutionary wars of liberation, as, for example, in India and some English- or French-speaking states in Africa or the South Pacific, the inclination prevailed until now to retain Western European judicial systems and the substantive law applied by them—even if only because of the need to create a uniform political consciousness within the new boundaries (that often were determined by colonial history). Here again a prognosis as to the lasting effect would be not only pretentious but also illusory.

The crux of the problem, however, does not so much lie in these technical and regional receptions, but rather in the question which contributions, if any, European legal culture as outlined will impart to a future common world—a world whose large reserves of vitality today is challenged in equal measure by the perplexing confrontation with the Atlantic–European civilization and, at the same time, by the hope for a unique national self-realization. This situation is reflected in the paradox, just touched upon, that the identity of many young Third World nations has to articulate itself with the help of the very techniques of political rule, administration, and law borrowed from Europe. Once this is accepted as a necessity, such borrowing would, in the long run, be obviously meaningless unless these nations respect a minimum of those external modes of behavior and internalized attitudes that are at the root of European legal orders. If they do not accept this, one can no longer speak of a future planetary mission for our own legal culture, and the Europeans would have to leave the further course of events, with appropriate humility, to an uncertain future.

Yet, so far most non-European nations have in fact opted in favor of the human rights conventions and thereby for the basic inventory of individual and social rights first legally articulated in Europe; more specifically, they have embraced human dignity, personal freedom, and protection against arbitrariness, active political rights, especially freedom of voting, equality before the law, and society's responsibility for the social and economic conditions of its members. The realization of these postulates, as we have tried to show, has always been tied to the safeguarding of these rights by means of predictable legality and law-governed procedures in independent courts.

There are good reasons for hoping that the fundamental decision of these nations is more than lip service before international organizations by whatever politicians happen to be in power. For without application of these principles—and if only because of their population problems, this is true especially for many countries of the Third World—neither a bare existence nor a tolerable minimum standard of worthwhile existence is thinkable. This prognosis is not an expression of European arrogance vis-à-vis the equally valuable historical achievements of non-European high cultures and even tribal cultures. It only voices the apprehension that those venerable traditions alone cannot (as little as they did in Europe) guarantee a decent survival of the complex societies of the future, a survival all peoples of this sorely tried and damaged world are hoping for.

———

Compare with Professor Wieacker's European perspective on the commonalities between the civil and common law traditions, the following outline by an American legal historian of ten distinctive features of "Western" law. What similarities do you find in their perceptions? What differences? To what do you attribute the similarities and differences?

HAROLD J. BERMAN, "LAW AND REVOLUTION: THE FORMATION OF THE WESTERN LEGAL TRADITION *

7–10 (1983).

The principal characteristics of the Western legal tradition may be summarized, in a preliminary way, as follows:

1. A relatively sharp distinction is made between legal institutions (including legal processes such as legislation and adjudication as well as the legal rules and concepts that are generated in those processes) and other types of institutions. Although law remains strongly influenced by religion, politics, morality, and custom, it is nevertheless distinguishable from them analytically. Custom, for example, in the sense of habitual patterns of behavior, is distinguished from customary law, in the sense of customary norms of behavior that are considered to be legally binding. Similarly, politics and morals may determine law, but they are not thought to be law—as they are in some other cultures. In the West, though of course not only in the West, law is considered to have a character of its own, a certain relative autonomy.

2. Connected with the sharpness of this distinction is the fact that the administration of legal institutions, in the Western legal tradition, is entrusted to a special corps of people, who engage in legal activities on a professional basis as a more or less full-time occupation.

3. The legal professionals, whether typically called lawyers, as in England and America, or jurists, as in most other Western countries, are specially trained in a discrete body of higher learning identified as legal learning, with its own professional literature and its own professional schools or other places of training.

4. The body of legal learning in which the legal specialists are trained stands in a complex, dialectical relationship to the legal institutions, since on the one hand the learning describes those institutions but on the other hand the legal institutions, which would otherwise be disparate and unorganized, become conceptualized and systematized, and thus transformed, by what is said about them in learned treatises and articles and in the classroom. In other words, the law includes not only legal institutions, legal commands, legal decisions, and the like, but also what legal scholars (including, on occasion, lawmakers, judges, and other officials talking or writing like legal scholars) say about those legal institutions, commands, and decisions. The law contains within itself a legal science, a meta-law, by which it can be both analyzed and evaluated.

The first four characteristics of the Western legal tradition are shared by the tradition of Roman law as it developed in the Roman Republic and the Roman Empire from the second century B.C. to the eighth century A.D. and later. They are not shared, however, in many contemporary non-Western cultures, nor were they present in the legal order that prevailed among the Germanic peoples of Western Europe prior to the eleventh century. German law was embedded in political and religious life and in custom and morality—as law is today in many informal communities such as the school, the neighborhood, the factory, the village. Neither in the Frankish Empire nor in Anglo–Saxon England nor elsewhere in Europe at that time was a sharp distinction made between legal norms and procedures, on the one hand, and religious, moral, economic, political, or other standards and practices, on the other. There were, to be sure, laws, and occasionally collections of laws, issued by kings; but there were no professional lawyers or judges, no professional legal scholars, no law schools, no law books, no legal science. This was true also in the church: canon law was fused with theology, and except for some rather primitively organized collections of canons and the monastic books of penalties for sins, there was nothing that could be called a literature of ecclesiastical law.

5. In the Western legal tradition law is conceived to be a coherent whole, an integrated system, a "body," and this body is conceived to be developing in time, over generations and centuries. The concept of law as a corpus juris might be thought to be implicit in every legal tradition in which law is viewed as distinct from morality and from custom; and it is often supposed that such a concept was not only implicit but also explicit in the Roman law of Justinian. However, the phrase corpus juris Romani was not used by the Romans but by the twelfth- and thirteenth-century European canonists and Romanists who extrapolated the concept from the work of those who, one or two centuries earlier, had discovered the old Justinian texts and taught them in the European universities. It was the twelfth-century scholastic technique of reconciling contradictions and deriving general concepts from rules and cases that first made it possible to coordinate and integrate the Roman law of Justinian.

6. The concept of a body or system of law depended for its vitality on the belief in the ongoing character of law, its capacity for growth over generations and centuries—a belief which is uniquely Western. The body of law only survives because it contains a built-in mechanism for organic change.

7. The growth of law is thought to have an internal logic; changes are not only adaptations of the old to the new, but are also part of a pattern of changes. The process of development is subject to certain regularities and, at least in hindsight, reflects an inner necessity. It is presupposed in the Western legal tradition that changes do not occur at random but proceed by reinterpretation of the past to meet present and future needs. The law is not merely ongoing; it has a history. It tells a story.

8. The historicity of law is linked with the concept of its supremacy over the political authorities. The developing body of law, both at any given moment and in the long run, is conceived by some—although not by all, and not necessarily even by most—to be binding upon the state itself. Although it remained for the American Revolution to contribute the word "constitutionalism," nevertheless, since the twelfth century in all countries of the West, even under absolute monarchies, it has been widely said and often accepted that in some important respects law

transcends politics. The monarch, it is argued, may make law, but he may not make it arbitrarily, and until he has remade it—lawfully—he is bound by it.

9. Perhaps the most distinctive characteristic of the Western legal tradition is the coexistence and competition within the same community of diverse jurisdictions and diverse legal systems. It is this plurality of jurisdictions and legal systems that makes the supremacy of law both necessary and possible.

Legal pluralism originated in the differentiation of the ecclesiastical polity from secular polities. The church declared its freedom from secular control, its exclusive jurisdiction in some matters, and its concurrent jurisdiction in other matters. Laymen, though governed generally by secular law, were subject to ecclesiastical law, and to the jurisdiction of ecclesiastical courts, in matters of marriage and family relations, inheritance, spiritual crimes, contract relations where faith was pledged, and a number of other matters as well. Conversely, the clergy, though governed generally by canon law, were subject to secular law, and to the jurisdiction of secular courts, with respect to certain types of crimes, certain types of property disputes, and the like. Secular law itself was divided into various competing types, including royal law, feudal law, manorial law, urban law, and mercantile law. The same person might be subject to the ecclesiastical courts in one type of case, the king's court in another, his lord's court in a third, the manorial court in a fourth, a town court in a fifth, a merchants' court in a sixth.

The very complexity of a common legal order containing diverse legal systems contributed to legal sophistication. Which court has jurisdiction? Which law is applicable? How are legal differences to be reconciled? Behind the technical questions lay important political and economic considerations: church versus crown, crown versus town, town versus lord, lord versus merchant, and so on. Law was a way of resolving the political and economic conflicts. Yet law could also serve to exacerbate them.

The pluralism of Western law, which has both reflected and reinforced the pluralism of Western political and economic life, has been, or once was, a source of development, or growth—legal growth as well as political and economic growth. It also has been, or once was, a source of freedom. A serf might run to the town court for protection against his master. A vassal might run to the king's court for protection against his lord. A cleric might run to the ecclesiastical court for protection against the king.

10. There is a tension between the ideals and realities, between the dynamic qualities and the stability, between the transcendence and the immanence of the Western legal tradition. This tension has periodically led to the violent overthrow of legal systems by revolution. Nevertheless, the legal tradition, which is something bigger than any of the legal systems that comprise it, survived and, indeed, was renewed by such revolutions.

————

Despite their shared inheritance, the civil and common law traditions have developed in sufficiently different ways that they are now universally classified as belonging to different legal families.[19] In practical terms, this means that each system is, in important respects, inaccessible to a lawyer trained in the other system. Thus, for example, English and American lawyers unfamiliar with civil law concepts and methods can—with effort—communicate with one another, but will experience difficulty in communicating with French or German lawyers. We hasten to emphasize that, even *within* each tradition, diversity exists and communication problems arise. That is another reason we have chosen to present the English legal system here, for England and the United States are in many ways, as Robert Stevens once quipped, "two countries separated by a common law." And, as we shall see, France and Germany gave to the civil law world two very different models of codification and legal science.

Let us now turn to the older and more influential of the two great European legal traditions—that of the civil law.

19. For a comprehensive review and critical discussion of various methods of classifying the world's legal systems, see K. Zwiegert & H. Kötz, Introduction to Comparative Law 63–75 (2d ed. 1992) (translated by Tony Weir).

*

Part II

THE CIVIL LAW TRADITION

Chapter 1

HISTORY, CULTURE AND DISTRIBUTION OF THE CIVIL LAW

SECTION 1. WHAT IS THE CIVIL LAW TRADITION?

When we refer to some of the world's legal systems with a common name, such as "Romanist", "Romano–Germanic", or "civil law" systems, we are calling attention to the fact that, despite their similarities to other legal systems and despite national differences among themselves, these systems share a distinctive heritage. The tradition of the civil law is characterized by a particular interaction in its early formative period among Roman law, Germanic and local customs, canon law, the international law merchant, and, later, by a distinctive response to the break with feudalism and the rise of nation states, as well as by the peculiar role it has accorded to legal science.

SECTION 2. ROMAN LAW

To use the term Roman law to describe the entire Roman legal output of nearly a millenium stretching from the Twelve Tables (c. 450 B.C.) to the Justinian compilations (c. 534 A.D.) is about as helpful as describing the product of English legal minds from 1066 A.D. to the present as "common law." Thus, specialists in ancient Roman law subdivide their subject into various periods. It was as early as the third century B.C., during the Republic, that there appeared a class of men known as Jurisconsults, who made law their specialty. By the end of the Late Republic in the first century B.C., the Jurisconsults had acquired a monopoly of technical information and legal experience, and it can be said that they had become the first professional lawyers. In difficult cases, the lay judges began to turn to them for advice. Through this advisory role, the Jurisconsults stayed close to the practice of law and remained in constant contact with actual disputes. What we know as Roman law evolved through the accretion of the opinions they rendered case-by-case. Eventually the principles thus developed by the Jurisconsults were taught and expounded in treatises, all in a distinctive vocabulary and style.

At first rather formal and rigid, Roman law eventually supplemented fixed rules with flexible standards and moved from concrete to more abstract modes of thought. It became characterized by attention to practical details, and by terms of art which caught on and endured. The law of the Classical period (which began around 117 A.D. and came to an end with the period of anarchy, invasions, plague and civil war that commenced around 235 A.D.), represents the fullest development of ancient Roman law. Of the great Jurisconsults of this period, Ulpian, Papinian and Gaius are chiefly remembered. At its height classical Roman law constituted a body of practical wisdom of a kind the world had not seen before. It was therefore of the highest interest to Byzantine jurists after the fall of the Western empire, and, through them, of great significance to the development of the civil law systems.

Centuries later, Roman law would be called "written reason" by the medieval scholars who "rediscovered" it as Europe began to emerge from what French legal scholar Jean Carbonnier calls the "customary thicket" of the Middle Ages.[1] The Roman law that they "found" when Western society began to be ready for law to play a prominent role once again among the norms that govern human activity, was not the law of the Classical period in its original form. Most of the ancient sources had been lost. What survived was the monumental compilation of Roman law that was made at the direction of the Byzantine Emperor Justinian in the sixth century A.D. By that time, the Roman Empire in the West had been breaking up for more than a century, its fall symbolized by the sack of Rome in 410 A.D. The significance of the work of the Byzantine jurists in preserving their legal heritage would be hard to exaggerate. From Justinian's times to the present, Roman law, except to specialists, generally has meant the sixth century Corpus Juris Civilis of Justinian.

The Corpus Juris Civilis included four parts: the Institutes, the Digest, the Code and the Novels. The *Digest* was by far the most important in terms of its influence on the civil law tradition, particularly in the areas of personal status, torts, unjust enrichment, contracts and remedies. The Digest was a treatise representing the distillation of what, in the judgment of Justinian's jurists, was most valuable from the best Roman legal writings from all previous periods. Since virtually all of the books they used in composing the Digest have been lost, the Digest itself became the principal source of knowledge about what the Roman law of earlier periods had been like. The *Institutes* were simply a short introductory text for students, the *Code* was a systematic collection of Roman legislation, and the *Novels* were the imperial legislation enacted after the Code and the Digest were completed. Together, the Digest and the Code were meant to be a complete and authoritative restatement of Roman law.

1. J. Carbonnier, Essais sur les lois 250 (1979).

Byzantine Roman lawyers did not merely copy the law of earlier periods. The Corpus Juris was the product of a careful process of selection and rejection. In general outlook, as well as in matters of detail, it differed from the law of the Classical period. It continued the movement away from formalism, but this move was accompanied by a decline in technique. Equity, which in the Classical period was regarded as a principle of justice animating the whole of the law, degenerated into mere impatience with legal subtleties. Byzantine legislation was "humanitarian", in the sense of protecting "those whom it considers weak against those whom it considers strong," but Jolowicz says this tendency coincided with an "almost pathetic confidence in the power of law to do away with evils of an economic character ... and a taste for excessive regulation by statute of matters to which fixed rules can hardly, by their nature, be applied with success."[2] After the Lombard, Slav and Arab invasions that followed the reign of Justinian, the Corpus Juris Civilis fell into disuse for centuries.

SECTION 3. THE "CUSTOMARY THICKET" AND ROMAN LAW SURVIVAL

The fact that Roman law and legal science were left stranded by the collapse of the way of life that had produced them did not mean that Romanist legal influences disappeared altogether during the Middle Ages. Certainly the sophistication and technical perfection to which ancient Roman law had been brought over the centuries was not maintained during the legal and political disorder that followed the disintegration of the Roman Empire. For five centuries after the fall of Rome a series of raiders and settlers overran the areas that had once been Roman. There were no strong, centralized states. Kingdoms rose and fell. The condition of the people was one of local self-sufficiency. It would be centuries before scholars again would be capable of picking up and putting to use the technical instruments left behind by the Classical Roman and Byzantine jurists. When a reawakening of interest in Roman law did occur and when attention turned to the Corpus Juris in the 11th century, the process became known as the "revival" of Roman law.

It is quite proper to speak, nevertheless, as the legal historian Franz Wieacker does, of a "survival" of Roman law from the fifth to the tenth centuries.[3] Roman conquerors once had been all over Europe, and many of the Germanic settlers, legionnaires and migrating peoples who eventually overran the former Empire had been, to a certain extent, "Romanized." As conquerors and conquered changed places, Germanic rulers used Roman law to govern their Roman subjects, while applying their own law to their own peoples. Over time, however, the distinctions

2. H.F. Jolowicz, Historical Introduction to the Study of Roman Law 521 (1967).

3. Wieacker, The Importance of Roman Law for Western Civilization and Western Legal Thought, 4 Boston Coll.Int. & Comp. L.Rev. 257, 270 (1981).

between groups disappeared. By the end of the tenth century, the rules were the same for all persons within a given territory. Crude versions of Roman legal rules had become intermingled in varying degrees with the customary rules of the Germanic invaders to the point where historians speak of the laws during this period as either "Romanized customary laws" or "barbarized Roman laws". Thus, though Roman legal science and Classical Roman law disappeared in the welter, diversity and localism of Carbonnier's "customary thicket", a Romanist element survived and served both as a strand of continuity and a latent, potential universalizing factor in what we now think of as the civil law tradition.

The Germanic customary laws that began to be written down as early as the fifth century A.D., (as well as particular local customs), formed part of this tradition too, particularly influencing aspects of marital property and inheritance law. Many of the most ingenious and useful legal devices of the modern civil law of property and commercial law derive not from Roman, but from medieval origins, and thus remind us that the legal confusion of the Middle Ages had its fruitful and creative, as well as its fragmented and disorganized, side. The Germanic element evolved through the Middle Ages, as tribal laws became territorial laws, to the point where it produced the beginnings of a legal literature and a new legal culture that was quite different from the Roman. But its further development was arrested because of its essentially lay character, and because the crudeness of its procedures (e.g., trial by ordeal) limited its potential for adaptation to the social and economic changes that were beginning to transform feudal society.

SECTION 4. CANON LAW

With the break-up of the far-flung system of Roman administration, the Church took over some of the functions of government. Indeed, after the fall of the Roman Empire, and until the revival of Roman law in the 11th century, the single most important universalizing factor in the diverse and localized legal systems of the civil law tradition was canon law. But canon law itself was a hybrid of sorts. It had been produced by Christian notions interacting reciprocally with Roman law after the Christianization of the Empire, a process during which the reign of Constantine (d. 337 A.D.) was an important marker. The sixth-century Justinian Corpus, in particular, was affected by Christian ideas, but the Church, for its part, had borrowed freely from the structure, principles and detailed rules of ancient Roman law. Furthermore, just as there was some degree of amalgamation everywhere of Germanic customs, indigenous customs and debased Roman law, there was a certain penetration by canon law into the codes promulgated by German rulers and, later, into the legislation of the Carolingian (c. 800 A.D.) and Holy Roman Empires (c. 962 A.D.). During the Middle Ages, the Church sought and acquired jurisdiction for its own tribunals over matrimonial causes, and over certain aspects of criminal law and succession to personal property. Many of the rules and procedures it developed in these matters were accepted in secular tribunals long after the Church had lost its civil jurisdiction.

SECTION 5.   REVIVAL OF ROMAN LAW

Europe entered a period of political, economic and cultural transformation from about 1050 A.D. onward.   The gradual return of political order established conditions that facilitated speculative learning.   Economic expansion, too, with its requirements for predictability and ongoing dispute resolution, led to a renewed interest in law.   Along with scholars in other fields, jurists began to turn, with the excitement of discovery, to the accomplishments of antiquity.   The revival of Roman law that took place in northern Italy towards the end of the 11th century was a rediscovery, through the Justinian legacy, of Roman legal science.

The University of Bologna became the principal legal center to which students flocked from all over Europe to hear learned teachers (including some nuns who were the first women law professors) lecture on the Corpus Juris Civilis.   Irnerius, who is said to have given the first lectures on the Justinian Digest, proclaimed its intellectual superiority over the legal inheritance of the Middle Ages.   But the ancient text dealt with so many institutions and problems that were no longer known, that it was difficult to understand.   The first generations of scholars to study the Digest therefore made it their task to try to accurately reconstruct and explain its text.   They became known as the Glossators because of their annotations (glosses) on the Digest.   But their approach to interpretation in time gave way to the new methods of the Commentators (or Post–Glossators) of the 13th century, who saw their work as adapting the law of Roman society to the problems of their own day.   The methods of the Commentators were much influenced by the new spirit of rational inquiry and speculative dialectic that would be brought to its highest form in the work of Thomas Aquinas (d. 1274).   This way of thinking liberated them from the literalism of the Glossators and led them to search for the rationale and underlying principles of various Roman legal rules.   Bartolus (d. 1357) is remembered as the greatest of the Commentators.

The thousands of European students who had come to the Italian universities carried back to their own nations and universities, not only the law of the Corpus Juris Civilis but also the methods and ideas of their teachers.   They and their own students became the new profession of lawyers who found places not only in universities, but in the "administrations" of princes, cities and the Church.   Their work was influenced at least as much by the Bolognese method of decision making by bringing a case within the terms of an abstractly formulated authoritative text, as it was by the substantive norms of Roman law.   In Paris and Oxford, Prague and Heidelberg, Cracow and Copenhagen, a fusion took place between the medieval Romano–Germanic law and the new learning based on the revived Roman law.   In different ways and to varying degrees this amalgam formed the base on which future variations and modifications would take place in all the civil law systems. The new learning, acquired by all those trained in Northern Italy, furnished the common methodology for the further development of national laws.

It was the shared background of the influential torch bearers of the new legal science that consolidated the civil law tradition. The Roman civil law, together with the immense literature generated by the Glossators and Commentators, came to be the *jus commune,* the common law, of Europe. As Merryman has said, "There was a common body of law and of writing about law, a common legal language and a common method of teaching and scholarship." [4] Canon law continued to play a role in this shared tradition, but in a new, more refined and "Romanized" form, as Bolognese scholars systematically compiled and digested some 700 years of ecclesiastical enactments and decrees. Gratian in the 12th century is generally credited with having transformed canon law into an independent "system" which then began to be taught alongside Roman civil law in universities all over Europe.

SECTION 6. COMMERCIAL LAW [5]

In addition to Roman civil law and canon law, commercial law furnished another universalizing element as Europe emerged from the relative economic stagnation of the Middle Ages. With the rise of towns, the birth of markets, fairs and banks, the rapid expansion of maritime and overland trade, and the eventual development of large flourishing commercial centers, there appeared the need for a body of law to govern business transactions. Since Roman law did not prove readily adaptable for this purpose, guilds and merchants' associations established their own rules and their own tribunals. The merchants' courts worked out informal rules and expeditious procedures that were practical, fair, and grounded in the usages of businessmen. These rules in time came to be recognized and applied as customary law by secular and ecclesiastical authorities. Eventually the "law merchant" became international, a body of generally accepted commercial rules that transcended political boundaries. It spread even into England where the Roman law, brought back from Italy, had found favor in universities, but was stoutly resisted in the civil courts.

SECTION 7. RECEPTION OF ROMAN LAW

The Middle Ages were an era of numerous overlapping and competing jurisdictions and sources of law. In the absence of strong central states, the notion of law as command of the sovereign had no meaning. Ecclesiastical courts were apt to apply canon law; the courts of a guild would apply the law merchant; while other judges in cities and towns

---

4. J. Merryman, The Civil Law Tradition 9 (2d ed. 1985).

5. See generally, D. Tallon, Civil Law and Commercial Law, VIII Int'l Encyc.Comp.Law (Specific Contracts) (1983).

would tend to search for an appropriate rule, first, in local custom or statute, then, with the help of university scholars, filling the gaps with the *jus commune*. Aided by the expansion of economic activity, the enthusiasm of legal scholars, and by the idea of the "continued" Holy Roman Empire, the *jus commune* became the basic law of a great part of continental Europe. It proved capable of dealing with many of the new problems posed by a more complex economy; yet as part of a not entirely forgotten past, it had a certain familiarity. Through the process that civil law lawyers call *reception,* the revived Roman private law (including the writings of the Italian jurists and the canon law) moved from the universities into the courts. (It should be noted, however, that Roman *public* law, itself relatively undeveloped, was not similarly received. There was no real place for public law so long as no strong central governments existed.)

The formality and the extent of reception in a given country and the type of interaction that occurred between the *jus commune* and the medieval Romano–Germanic base varied considerably. In certain parts of Italy, the influence of Roman law had remained continuously so strong that it is perhaps not quite accurate to speak of a "reception" there. In Spain, however, the *jus commune* was always in tension with various vigorous local customary traditions. In the regions of France south of the Loire (known as the *pays de droit écrit*) where Roman law influence had been greatest, the local customary law was already heavily romanized. Thus, there was a more extensive reception there than in the northern regions of France (known as the *pays de droit coutumier*) where the various local customs had always been of greater importance than Roman law.

The *jus commune* infiltrated the law of the various regions of the Holy Roman Empire of the Germanic nation to the point where it came to be regarded as the common law of the empire. In 1495, when a central imperial court was established, its judges were obliged to decide cases according to this common law, unless a conflicting local custom or statute could be proved. The difficulty of proving a controlling German rule meant in practice that the received Roman law became the basic law of all the regions of Germany. The reception of Roman law on such a large scale in Germany is usually explained by a combination of factors. Roman law met no resistance from a strong national legal profession, court system or from the existence of a common body of "German" law. Both the weakness of the imperial power and its claim to being the successor to the Roman Empire facilitated the reception. Finally, and probably most importantly, Roman law filled the increasingly urgent need to deal with the inconvenience that the variety of local customs posed for intercourse among the many small independent territories that formed the German confederation.

The wide-scale Roman law reception in Germany was a crucial event for the later development of German legal science, producing a much more extensive systematization of law than occurred elsewhere. From the beginning, judges relied heavily on legal scholars for information and guidance concerning the local law as well as the received Roman law. Indeed, by 1600, it was a common practice for judges to send out the record of a difficult case to a university law faculty and to adopt the faculty's collective opinion on questions of law.   This practice of *Akten-versendung,* which continued until the 19th century, resulted in the accumulation of an extensive body of common doctrine that transcended the borders of the various German political entities.   Systematized in reports and essays, distillations from scholarly opinions rendered in actual controversies became, as Dawson has said, "a kind of case-law, secreted in the interstices of learned writings." [6]

In Europe generally, the *jus commune,* like the Latin language and the universal Church, was an aspect of the unity of the West at a time when there were no strong centralized political administrations and no unified legal systems, but rather a continuous struggle among the competing and overlapping jurisdictions of local, manorial, ecclesiastical, mercantile and royal authorities.   From the 15th century on, however, the relationship between the received *jus commune* and the diverse local and regional customary laws began to be affected, in varying degrees, by the rise of nationalism and the increasing consolidation of royal power.

SECTION 8.   NATION STATES AND NATIONAL LAW

Gradual political unification in Europe did not immediately bring about national legal unification, but it did arouse interest in customary law as "national" law.   The way for this development had been pre-pared, in a sense, by the 14th century Commentators who had turned scholarly attention from textual exegesis of the Digest to a consideration of the adaptability of Roman legal rules to contemporary conditions.   In the 16th and 17th centuries, as the center of legal scholarship shifted to France and Holland, the methods of the Bolognese Commentators were replaced by those of the French Legal Humanists and the Dutch Natural Law School.   The Humanists used the techniques of history and philology to study Roman law.[7]   Their view of Roman law as a historical phenomenon and of the Corpus Juris Civilis as merely an ancient text (rather than as "living law" or "written reason") marked a step toward eventual displacement of the *jus commune.*   This indirect challenge to the authority of Roman law was continued by the 17th century Dutch Natural Law School, whose members developed a systematic theory of law grounded in what they conceived to be the universal law of nature. The comprehensive legal system-building of these Dutch jurists was the prelude to modern codification.

The awakening of interest in national law was only one of several parallel developments that marked the end of the unity of the West and

---

6.   J. Dawson, The Oracles of the Law 231 (1968).

7.   See generally, D. Kelley, Foundations of Modern Historical Scholarship: Lan-guage, Law, and History in the French Renaissance (1970).

the rise of modern nation states. National literatures began to appear.
The vernacular languages began to be used in universities. Schisms
developed between national churches and Rome. In the legal area, so
long as the state had been non-existent or minimal, there was no public,
administrative or constitutional law in the modern sense. However, as
political power became sufficiently centralized, at different times in
different parts of Europe, public law, national law and the international
"law of nations" developed rapidly.

SECTION 9.   CODIFICATION

In many parts of Europe, legal nationalism early took the form of
codification. The first of these national codes appeared in the Scandinavian countries in the 17th and 18th centuries. Then, a second generation of codes not only aspired to bring about legal unity within one
kingdom, but also attempted a synthesis of the political and philosophical thought of the 18th century. These codes were the product of
"enlightened" monarchs, like Voltaire's friend Frederick II of Prussia,
and Joseph II of Austria, and their bureaucratic administrators. They
were founded on the belief that a rational, systematized, and comprehensive legal system would be an improvement on traditional law. One
consequence of the unification of national law in these early codes was
that the *jus commune* was displaced as the basic source of law. To be
sure, the draftsmen of the national codes drew heavily upon the *jus
commune* as well as on national law, but the authority of the law from
then on was derived more from the state than from tradition, or the
inherent reasonableness of the legal norms themselves. The Prussian
General Territorial Law of 1794 is chiefly remembered today as a
monument of legal hubris. In its ambition to foresee all possible
contingencies and to regulate the range of human conduct down to the
most intimate details of family life, it was hampered in operation both by
its excessive detail and its failure to acknowledge the limits of law.

Two national codes, however, have had such widespread and lasting
influence that they and their accompanying ideologies can be said to
have become part of the contemporary civil law tradition. The French
Civil Code of 1804 and the German Civil Code of 1896 have served as
models for most other modern civil codes. So different from each other,
yet growing out of a common tradition, they have both decisively affected
the shape of civil law systems of today. French revolutionary ideas and
German legal science not only gave a special stamp and flavor to their
respective national codes but affected legal thought throughout and
beyond the civil law world.

The consolidation of French royal power in the period from the end
of the 15th century to the Revolution of 1789 made France the first
modern continental nation, a politically unified society under strong
central rule. The *ancien régime,* however, never succeeded in achieving
legal unification. A traveller in France changed laws, Voltaire once said,
as often as he changed horses. It remained for Napoleon to provide

France with a unified national body of law. Under his rule, five basic codes were promulgated: the Civil Code, the Penal Code, the Commercial Code and the Codes of Civil and Criminal Procedure.

The French Civil Code of 1804, drafted in a remarkably short period of time by a commission of four eminent jurists, has a just claim to being the first modern code. Although, in form, it hewed rather closely to the framework of Justinian's Institutes, it was not, as Justinian's Code basically was, a restatement of the law. Its substantive provisions incorporated the results of a profound intellectual, political and social revolution. Though it is often referred to as the "Code Napoleon", its original name was the *Code civil des français* (the civil code of the French people). In what its title represented, as in other ways, it was unlike all earlier efforts at codification. It represented a new way of thinking about man, law and government.

The three ideological pillars of the French civil code were private property, freedom of contract and the patriarchal family. In the first of these areas, the Code consolidated the Revolution's rejection of the feudal past. Through such private law devices as prohibitions on restraints on alienation and limitations on freedom of testation, the Code's architects consciously sought to break up the estates of the powerful landed aristocracy. By the very fact of claiming the areas of property, contract and family for private, civil law, the Code was performing what may be called a constitutional function. In these three spheres, the primary role of the state was to be to protect private property, to enforce legally formed contracts, and to secure the autonomy of the patriarchal family.

At the same time that the French Civil Code was introducing new elements into the field of private law, French revolutionary ideas were contributing in important ways to the newly developing field of public law. The French Revolution and subsequent Napoleonic rule had furthered the processes of strengthening the central state and eliminating intermediate sources of power and allegiance. In this new political situation, there was little role for Roman or medieval law to play in the fashioning of the rules that henceforth would regulate the relationships of the branches and agencies of government with each other and with citizens. (We have already remarked that the Reception of Roman law had been a reception of Roman private, not public, law). In the 19th century, modern public law was emerging from a crucible where the ways of thinking about government associated with the American and French revolutions were transforming older, royal, bureaucratic traditions. To varying degrees, in different parts of the world, American, English and French ideas about equality, democracy, representative government, the separation of powers, and natural rights to life, liberty and property were helping to shape systems of public law.

In spite of all that was new in the French legal revolution, there was still much continuity with the past. First, and most obviously, continuity was provided by the sources drawn upon by Napoleon's draftsmen.

With only a few months for the drafting process, and under much pressure from the First Consul, they could not, and did not try to, create a code out of whole cloth. Naturally they turned to the *jus commune,* the royal ordinances, the learned writing, and customary law—particularly the influential Custom of Paris, which had been conveniently written down in the 16th century. Like the draftsmen of other Enlightenment codes, they thought of themselves as putting all this prior law through a "sieve of reason", retaining or rejecting it according to rational principles. But the formal tripartite structure of their end product (Persons, Property and the Different Modes of Acquiring Property) was virtually identical to that of the first three books of Justinian's Institutes. So far as the substantive rules of law were concerned, the draftsmen drew primarily, and in about equal measure, on both customary law and the *jus commune.*

A few innovations, such as divorce by mutual consent and adoption, are attributable to the influence of Napoleon. The great personal interest that Napoleon took in the Code was not so much in its substantive content, however, as in the fact of its existence. He wanted to be remembered as a great lawgiver. Because of the importance he accorded to the Code, he made its adoption a priority in France, and imposed it in his conquered territories—in Italy, Poland, the low countries and among the ruins of the Hapsburg Empire. In exile on St. Helena, Napoleon referred to the Code as a greater achievement than all his victories: "One Waterloo wipes out their memory, but my civil code will live forever."

In form and style, the French Civil Code stands in marked contrast to the German Civil Code which appeared nearly a century later. The *Code civil des français* was meant to be read and understood by the citizen. With its clear, fertile and intentionally concise provisions, its style resembles that of the United States Constitution, more than it does the German Civil Code of 1896. The founding fathers of the French Civil Code, like the framers of the United States Constitution, recognized that a legislator cannot foresee all possible applications of basic principles. The draftsmen opted for the flexibility of general rules, rather than for detailed provisions. The words of one of the draftsmen, Portalis, are still frequently referred to in this connection:

> We have equally avoided the dangerous ambition to regulate and foresee everything. . . . The function of law is to fix in broad outline the general maxims of justice, to establish principles rich in implications, and not to descend into the details of the questions that can arise in each subject.[8]

SECTION 10. GERMAN LEGAL SCIENCE

The German Civil Code (*Bürgerliches Gesetzbuch*) appeared at the end, and the French Civil Code at the beginning, of the turbulent

---

8. Quoted in A. von Mehren & J. Gordley, The Civil Law System 54 (2d ed. 1977).

century of the Industrial Revolution. The German Code emerged from an intellectual and political background that differed in many ways from the Enlightenment and revolutionary thought that informed the *Code Civil*. It is thus not surprising that Germany and France have inspired somewhat different subtraditions in the civil law world. Unlike France, where political unification had been achieved long before legal unity, Germany had remained a loose confederation of kingdoms, duchies, principalities and independent city states until it was unified under Bismarck in 1871. Indeed, as we have seen, the lack of effective central government and the need for a common law to facilitate trade had set the stage for the large scale reception of the Romanist *jus commune* in 15th century Germany. However, as German scholars worked with the *jus commune,* a certain "renationalization" of German law gradually took place, especially in the 17th and 18th centuries. Like the Bolognese Commentators, these German scholars were occupied with adapting the Romanist law to their own contemporary conditions. In the course of their work, which came to be known as the *usus modernus pandectarum* (Pandects was their name for the Justinian Digest), they increasingly introduced Germanic legal content into what remained a basically Romanist structure. This was particularly so in the areas of property and associations.

In the 19th century, as the French Civil Code began to be widely admired and imitated, the idea of codification aroused the interest of certain German jurists. By this time, Germany was already a leading center of legal scholarship on the continent, and codification became the subject of a famous scholarly dispute.[9] In 1814, a Roman law professor, Thibaut, advocated prompt adoption of a code as a means of furthering the process of political unification of Germany. Thibaut claimed that the Prussian, French and Austrian codes could serve as helpful models. The Prussian and French codes were in fact already in force in parts of Germany. Thibaut's view was disputed by members of the so-called Historical School, whose leading spokesman was Friedrich Carl von Savigny. Savigny maintained that law, like language, was part of the genius and culture of a people. It could not be derived by logic from abstract principles of natural law. Rather, he claimed, a nation's law would be revealed by the methods of historical research. It followed that a German code should not be adopted without extensive preliminary study of the development of German legal institutions.

The point of view of Savigny and the Historical School prevailed. Under the influence of their ideas, 19th century German legal scholars by and large abandoned the ahistorical natural law approach of the Enlightenment codes in favor of what they thought of as a science of law. They viewed Germanic, and classical and received Roman law as bodies of data, and regarded themselves as scientists formulating and systematizing concepts and principles from this data. Some put their principal

---

9. See generally, M. Reimann, Nineteenth Century Legal Science, 31 Boston College L.Rev. 837 (1990).

energies into the historical investigation of indigenous law. Others, including Savigny himself, turned to Roman law—looking beyond the *jus commune* to ancient Roman law. There they rediscovered that the Roman jurists had been rather pragmatic individuals. If the Romans at times reflected on the methods and underlying structure of their legal system, they did not leave records of their ideas on these matters. So it came about that in 19th century Germany, legal scholars set themselves the task of investigating classical Roman law with the aim of discovering its "latent system", which they might adapt to the needs of their own society. In the process, they brought the study of the Digest to its highest and most systematic level, and thus became known as the Pandectists. Though the Pandectist School grew out of the Historical School, in the end it came to adopt a rather ahistorical stance toward law. Believing in the superiority and lasting validity of the legal institutions of the Romans, the Pandectists tended to exclude social, ethical, economic and practical considerations from their legal work. As at the time of the Reception, there was still no organized and powerful class of practicing lawyers in Germany to leaven this tendency. The methods and concepts developed by the Pandectists came to dominate legal scholarship in Germany just at the time the preparation of the German Civil Code began in 1874.

The work on a civil code for the new German nation turned out to be a massive project. The code went through two drafts and took over 20 years to complete. It was finally promulgated in 1896, to go into effect four years later—on the first day of the new century. In the end, as Dawson has said, the Code was neither Romanist nor Germanic, but Pandectist.[10] It was constructed and worked out with a degree of technical precision that had never been seen before in any legislation. A special language was developed and employed consistently. Legal concepts were defined and then used in the same way throughout. Sentence construction indicated the location of the burden of proof. Through elaborate cross-references, all parts of the Code supposedly interlocked to form a logically closed system. The draftsmen avoided both the prolixity of the Prussian Code and the "epigrammatic brevity" of the French. Though they did not descend to regulation in detail, their system was refined to the point where, in theory, the various parts of the Code could be made to articulate tightly about nearly any given problem falling within its scope. At the beginning of the Code is the "General Part", in which definitions, concepts and principles of great breadth are set forth. These apply to all the specific subject matter areas covered by the Code. Other pervasive general principles are established within and for particular areas of law. These general provisions are in turn often qualified or restricted by specific provisions within the various sections of the Code dealing with particular subjects. The result was not a handbook for the citizen, but a system for highly trained experts. Within the civil law world, German legal science and the German style of codification developed their own sphere of influence.

10. J. Dawson, The Oracles of the Law
460 (1968).

Though the German and French civil codes differ in form, style and mood, one must not lose sight of their similarities. In the first place, they both drew heavily on a common source, the *jus commune,* as well as on their respective national law. In both codes, the influence of the Romanist *jus commune* predominated in the law of obligations and in the general structure of the system, while indigenous sources were more influential in property and succession law. Secondly, there is an ideological correspondence between the two codes. Both were grounded in 19th century liberalism. They were infused with then current notions of individual autonomy, freedom of contract and private property. But over the course of the near-century that separated the two codes, society had been changing rapidly. Thus, while the German Civil Code still resembled the French in its solicitude for private property, freedom of contract and the traditional family, it also reflected a number of changes that had taken place since 1804. Several important provisions of the German Civil Code, for example, recognize a social obligation inhering in certain private rights, as well as the idea that rights can be misused. In family law, the authority of husbands and fathers is less absolute than in the French Code. Women have somewhat more power with respect to their own property, and the definition of the family is more narrowly drawn. Certain aspects of contract and tort law show the effects of the increasing complexity of commercial transactions as well as the advance of industrialization.

In the years immediately following the promulgation of the German Civil Code, German scholars concentrated mainly on the task of making it applicable in practice by explaining its difficult text and developing its main principles. But gradually that process of interpreting the Code "out of itself" yielded diminishing returns, and the stage was set for a new phase of German legal science. A reaction against the extreme formalism of the *Pandektenrecht* had indeed already begun to set in the late 19th century when Jhering, a product of the Pandectist School himself, began to question its methods and assumptions. In a devastating satire of the movement, he placed its leading practitioners in a "heaven of legal concepts" to which no one could be admitted unless he gave up all memory of the real world.[11] But it was not until the years following World War I that German legal science generally began to turn from what had become an increasingly sterile exercise. Then, salvaging from the Pandects their genius for formulating generalizations, but joining this for the first time to an obsession with detailed facts and concrete applications, German legal science entered a new and exciting phase until interrupted by the advent of National Socialism. With its new direction, born of the ability to relate powerful abstract reasoning to irreducible and stubborn facts, German scholars began to develop the methods that came to be associated with jurisprudence of interests, legal realism and the sociological schools of legal thought. These new ways of thinking about law entered the mainstream of American legal theory,

Mehren & J. Gordley, The Civil Law System 70–72 (2d ed. 1977).

11. Excerpts from Jhering's critique of the Pandectists are translated in A. von

too. Initially, the German influence was felt through the writings of Holmes and Pound, both of whom had been much impressed by the work of Jhering. It continued to be strong in the work of the American legal scholar and codifier, Karl Llewellyn, and was given new impetus by the many eminent German jurists who fled to the United States during the National Socialist period.

SECTION 11. DISTRIBUTION
OF THE CIVIL LAW

France and Germany probably have been less influenced by each other's law, legal institutions and scholarship than have other countries within the civil law world. The distinctive French and German codifications and styles of thought each had far-reaching influence, and to some extent their influences overlapped. Thus, a case can be made that the "typical" civil law systems today are not those of France or the Federal Republic of Germany, but rather those civil law systems which in modern times have undergone the combined influence of both. Nevertheless, in the post-codification era, French law and German legal science have both become the principal tributaries to the modern civil law tradition.

Just as ancient Roman law had been introduced into the conquered territories of a vast empire, the French Civil Code was brought by Napoleon and his armies to Belgium, the Netherlands, parts of Poland, Italy and the western regions of Germany. Then, in the colonial era, France extended her legal influence far beyond continental Europe to parts of the Near East, Northern and sub-Saharan Africa, Indochina, Oceania, French Guiana and the French Caribbean islands. The influence of French law both outlived and went beyond the Napoleonic conquests and French colonialism, for the Code was widely admired for its own merits. Its clarity and elegance of style and its consolidation of the results of a Revolution which had abolished the old, unequal statuses and relations of feudalism inspired imitation in many corners of the earth. Thus, one can speak of a "reception" of the French Civil Code not only in countries which retained it after French armies and colonial governments withdrew, but also in countries that were untouched by French military or colonial power.

The Civil Code remains in effect to this day, with revisions, in Belgium and Luxembourg; and was a major influence on the Netherlands Civil Code of 1838 (replaced in 1992), the Portuguese Civil Code of 1867 (replaced in 1967), the Spanish Civil Code of 1888, some of the Swiss cantonal codes, and on the legal institutions of 19th century Italy, as well as on those of some of the Eastern European countries. French law and legal theory remained important for France's former colonies and possessions even after they gained independence in the 20th century. Furthermore, when the Spanish and Portuguese empires in Latin America dissolved in the 19th century, it was mainly to the French Civil Code that the lawmakers of the new nations of Central and South

America looked for inspiration. French culture and the French revolutionary heritage were widely admired in the Latin American countries. The language and concepts of the French codes were clear, and were already familiar because of their affinities with the legal ideas and institutions that had been introduced in Latin America by the Spanish and the Portuguese. It was natural to turn to French law as a model.

It was another story in 19th century Germany, however. Though French law and legal ideas were influential in German procedural and administrative law, they had hardly any effect on the thinking that went into the late 19th century German private law codification. The German Civil Code of 1896 put before the world an entirely different model from the French and earlier codes, but one which appeared too late to be as widely imitated as the French. By the end of the 19th century nearly all the more developed countries had already adopted codes. Apart from those that had been influenced in varying degrees by the French Civil Code, there was the Austrian General Civil Code of 1811, the product of several decades of drafting under an enlightened and authoritarian monarchy, which had in turn influenced the law of some parts of Eastern Europe. The Nordic countries, where the earliest national civil codes had appeared, historically had been and remained relatively far removed from the composite of influences from which the civil law tradition was forged.

Even if the German Civil Code had not appeared relatively late, its highly technical and reticulated structure in all likelihood would have discouraged its direct transplantation to foreign soil. Nevertheless, the German Civil Code did play a significant role in the preparation of the Italian Code of 1942, and was the major influence on the Greek Civil Code of 1940, effective in 1946. Although the German Code as a whole was not built to travel, the legal science that preceded and accompanied it has had an important influence on legal theory and doctrine in other countries, particularly in Austria, Czechoslovakia, Greece, Hungary, Italy, Switzerland and former Yugoslavia. It was one of many influences on the eclectic Brazilian Code of 1916, and on the Portuguese Code of 1967. The Japanese Civil Code drew heavily upon the first draft of the German Civil Code and, as a result, German civil law scholarship has remained important in Japan. Through Japan, the German civil law influence also spread to Korea. Since the end of World War II, however, American law, too, has had a substantial impact on the law of Japan and South Korea.

Switzerland, except for certain cantons, had remained aloof from the reception of the French Civil Code, and when Switzerland achieved legal unity through its Civil Code of 1907, and its Law of Obligations which went into effect together with the Civil Code in 1912, it did not follow either the French or the German model. A single scholarly draftsman, Eugen Huber, fashioned for the confederation a civil code that was inspired by Swiss traditions and adapted to Swiss circumstances. He drew upon German and, to a lesser extent, French sources but did not permit them to dominate. In 1926, the Swiss Civil Code (together with the Law of Obligations) was adopted, almost word for word, as the Civil Code of the newly formed Republic of Turkey.

After World War II, the civil law influence on the European continent began to diminish when the Eastern European countries adopted new civil codes. Though these codes retained many characteristic civil law features, their differences were significant enough to cause most (though not all) comparatists to classify them in the socialist family of laws.[12] With the fall of communism in 1989, most of these countries are returning to the civil law tradition. The Nordic legal systems, though touched by the Roman law revival and affected in important ways by their proximity to the modern civil law systems, are generally thought of as *sui generis,* set apart by several unique features both from the common law and the mainstream of the civil law.[13] Central and South American countries in this century have looked increasingly to North American models, particularly in the areas of public, constitutional and business law. Still, the civil law system remains the dominant one there, as it is in many former French, Belgian, Spanish and Portuguese colonies in Africa.

Civil law also survives in certain "mixed" legal systems such as the civil and common law hybrid systems of Louisiana, Quebec, the Philippines and Puerto Rico. Japan and South Korea have added so much civil, especially German, law, to their indigenous law, that some would classify them as being Romano–Germanic, rather than Far Eastern systems. However, in Japan and South Korea, as in Latin America, the law of the United States has had an important effect on public law. French-inspired civil law and legal theory remain influential in West Africa, and, in combination with Islamic law, in most North African states as well as in many Near and Middle Eastern countries. Civil law is also one of many elements in the complex legal systems of Israel and Lebanon. In Asia, civil law influence extended to, and combined with, other legal influences in Cambodia, Indonesia, Laos, Vietnam, Taiwan and Thailand. Finally, it should be noted that civil law and codification are not coextensive. A few places in the civil law world remained apart from the codification movements of the 18th and 19th centuries. Thus, for example, in Scotland and South Africa, the Roman *jus commune* survives in uncodified form, combined in the case of Scotland with common law, and in the Union of South Africa with common law and Dutch law.

As the civil law has spread and entered into combination with other legal elements, its influence has become attenuated. In the wake of codification and national law movements, each country tended to concentrate on the development of its own legal system. Legal actors turned less frequently for inspiration and ideas to the fund of sources once held in common all over Europe. As a result, it is difficult today to identify a

---

12. See, generally, R. Sacco, The Romanist Substratum in the Civil Law of the Socialist Countries, 14 Review of Socialist Law 65 (1988).

13. See J. Sundberg, Civil Law, Common Law and the Scandinavians, 1969 Scandinavian Studies in Law 181.

single "civil law rule" on any given legal problem. Indeed, there is probably as much diversity in the responses of civil law systems to various legal issues as there is between civil and common law countries. This makes it appropriate to ask what now remains that sets the civil law tradition apart from other legal traditions in the late 20th century. Law reform has become increasingly eclectic. Searching for legal approaches to new social problems common to many different countries, legislatures have been less concerned with the provenance than with the promise of new techniques and ideas. Outside the continental European cradle of the civil law, the received European law never fully penetrated the mores anyway, nor did it ever completely displace customary and religious laws.

Within the European continent, contemporary civil law systems are becoming in several important ways like the legal systems of other developed nations. Civil law, common law, and Nordic systems are associated in the European Community, a fact certain to promote legal convergence in many areas. What, then, if anything, besides history, links the civil law systems together?

The beginnings of an answer may lie in a closer examination of the various meanings of the term "civil law." Historically, the term *jus civile* (from *civis*: citizen) referred to the law applicable to Roman citizens, the law which was eventually compiled by Justinian's jurists into the Corpus Juris Civilis. Common law lawyers, and we in this book, use the phrase "civil law systems" to describe the legal systems of all those nations predominantly within the historical tradition described in the foregoing sections. But for lawyers within those systems, the term "civil law" has a narrower meaning and some such term as "Romanist" or "Romano–Germanic" is used to designate their historical connection. The meaning of "civil law" (*droit civil, Zivilrecht*) to continental European lawyers is very limited: the civil law is the law relating to those subject matter areas covered by the civil codes and their auxiliary statutes. Thus, it not only does not include the entire legal system, it does not even take in all of private law if, as is usually the case, part of the private law is contained in a commercial code and other codes and statutes.

The continental terminology leads us closer to what it is that still links the civil law systems as they move further and further from their historical roots. At the same time, it reveals the extent to which these links are becoming looser. All the major civil codes deal with a body of substantive law within the same framework staked out by, and still similar in important respects to, Justinian's Institutes: law governing personal status, including family law; property; and obligations, which may either arise from contract or result from one's conduct. One of the great links among the "civil law systems" is that the "civil law" was for centuries, in fact, the most important and fundamental part of the legal system, and is still regarded so in theory. The great legal scholars from the Bolognese Roman law revival to the German Pandectists devoted their lives to the study and refinement of the civil law. Their characteristic techniques of analysis, their ways of thinking about legal problems and formulating legal propositions were all developed within and for the civil law. This was all in marked contrast to the way the common law developed, with its obsession with facts and concrete situations, and its disdain for generalization and systematization. The contrast is particularly stark with the development of American law, where from the beginning, public law commanded the energy and attention of many of the most gifted lawyers.

Even today, though the law of the civil codes has become relatively less central in fact, the civil law remains for most continental lawyers the very heart of the legal system. In some countries it can even be said to have a quasi-constitutional character. Thus, in legal education, in practice and in the work of legal scholars, there is not only a common fund of inherited concepts, a shared passion for theory and systematization, but more importantly, there are distinctive modes of thinking and communication. Still, it is well to remember that the edges of any system of classification of human activity are bound to be indistinct. This is especially so of artificial legal constructs. The civil law systems of the late 20th century are in the midst of a process of change in which the centrality of private civil law is being constantly reduced and through which the distinctiveness of the systems is somewhat diminished.

SECTION 12. CONTEMPORARY CIVIL LAW

The evolution of 19th century civil law systems over the 20th century was closely tied to the transformation of liberal laissez-faire governments into modern social welfare states with planned or regulated economies. As noted, the classification of civil law systems proceeds as if the only law worth taking into account were the areas of law covered by the civil codes. In those areas, the 19th century codes established a large role for individual autonomy and foresaw a minimal role for governmental intervention. This scheme reflected then-prevailing views about individualism and the market economy. By the turn of the century, however, the forces that would transform the legal and social order were already at work. In the late 20th century, it has become clear that the gradual shift away from 19th century liberalism and the unfettered market economy has meant a shift in emphasis from private or civil law to public and regulatory law.

The legal order has begun increasingly to take on the characteristics of a bureaucratic, or administrative, order. The dynamics of the legal change have worked primarily through a movement away from the civil codes (via special legislation and judicial construction), and through code revision, constitutional law, harmonization of law within the European Community, and the acceptance through treaties and conventions of a variety of supranational legal norms.

Over the 20th century, legislation, in response to social and economic change, has removed large areas from the coverage of the civil codes and has created entirely new areas of law outside the codes. These areas (for example: landlord-tenant law, employment law, insurance, contracts of carriage, competition and monopoly, agricultural holdings, urban housing) are typically governed by special statutes in which the unrestricted freedom of contract of the civil codes is replaced by a network of mandatory provisions, prohibitions on certain types of agreements, and requirements of controls, permits, licenses, and the like.

While the legislatures have been creating bodies of civil law outside the civil codes, the courts have created others by interpretation or by developing new judge-made rules. Judicial adaptation of the codes to new conditions has brought into being a substantial corpus of "common law" in the form of a gloss on the legislative texts. In some systems, such as the French and those based on its model, this process has been facilitated by the structural features (gaps, ambiguities and incompleteness) of the code. Since the lawmakers of 1804 never imagined such litigation-producing aspects of modern life as industrial and traffic accidents, photographic reproduction of images, and the mass circulation of publications, it is not surprising that modern French tort law is almost entirely judge-made. In later codes, such as the German and the Swiss, judicial adaptation to changing circumstances was facilitated by the so-called "general clauses", code provisions which deliberately leave a large measure of discretion to the judge.

Although traditional civil law dogma denied that judges "make" law and that judicial decisions can be a source of law, contemporary civil law systems are more and more openly acknowledging the inescapable dependence of legislation on the judges and administrators who interpret and apply it.

To some extent, the legislatures have kept the civil codes up to date by amending their texts. The German Civil Code in particular has been amended frequently in recent years. But given the magnitude of social change since their original adoption, many civil codes have been revised less frequently and less extensively than might be expected. Indeed, many civil law countries have changed governments and constitutions more readily than they have amended their civil codes, which, to the extent this has been the case, resemble the American Constitution more than they do American statutes. Code revision has in general been more extensive in the area of family law than in other areas. Many of the family law reforms were either prompted or made necessary by post World War II constitutional provisions or international conventions promoting new ideals of equality and liberty that were at variance in several respects with the patriarchal family law of the civil codes. In other areas, where the interests of organized economic groups are more affected, the legislatures have often found it hard to make necessary reforms within the structure of the civil codes. They have resorted instead to statutes outside the codes which are more easily amended as circumstances change.

Twentieth century legislation and code revision differ in several important respects from the earlier "classical" codifications. In the first place, law reform has tended to be marked by more *eclecticism*. This takes the form of using comparative law to investigate approaches and solutions to common social problems even if the country whose law is being studied does not happen to be a member of the civil law family.

That tendency is most evident in the newest civil code, that of the Netherlands, which went into effect in 1992. The Dutch draftspersons drew not only on a variety of continental European models, but on the common law and on international conventions. With the entry of non-civil law countries into the European Community, it can be expected that the exchange of ideas among common law, civil law and Nordic systems will accelerate. This is not only because of the "harmonization of law" provisions of the 1957 Treaty of Rome, but simply as a result of increased communication, mobility and cooperation. With the reunification of Germany in 1990, and renewed communication between East and West European nations, ideas from the socialist legal family are being added to the mix. Second, law reform in the 20th century tends to take account of *diversity* in society, in contrast to the civil codes which typically upheld one model of behavior for all. Third, modern lawmakers are more *pragmatic* than the drafters of the Enlightenment codes or the highly abstract German Civil Code. This probably reflects a decline in the belief in universally valid legal postulates. Thus, private law reform in European countries today is often preceded by considerable fact and opinion research. In this way, sociology has found a place with comparative law among the tools of the lawmaker. Finally, contemporary civil law shows an awareness of the *limits of law,* and has withdrawn from the attempt to control and regulate many kinds of personal behavior.

Taken together, the shift from private to public law, the influence of new ideas about fundamental rights, the legislatures' eclecticism, pragmatism, and their senses of social diversity and the limits of law, tend in the long run to blur the distinctions between civil law systems and the legal systems of other modern states. Nevertheless, significant differences remain. Often subtle, they are more in the area of mental processes, in styles of argumentation, and in the organization and methodology of law than in positive legal norms. Thus, the distinctive characteristics of the civil law systems will become more apparent as we take up the subjects of legal education, the role of scholars, ideas concerning the divisions of the law, the working of the codes, and the judicial process, as they exist in the contemporary civil law world.

Chapter 2

LEGAL STRUCTURES IN CIVIL LAW NATIONS

SECTION 1. PARLIAMENTARY GOVERNMENT

The classification "civil law systems" has no necessary connection with public law and government. Nevertheless, if one were to categorize different countries according to the structure and relations of the organs of their governments, most of the civil law nations would be found to have governments of the type known as parliamentary. But, since many common law countries, England in particular, also have the parliamentary form of government, one cannot say this is a hallmark of civil law systems. Also, a number of civil law nations outside Europe, notably in Latin America, have adopted a presidential, rather than a parliamentary, model. France, since 1958, has gone far in this direction as well.

Parliamentary government is the form of constitutional government in which the executive authority emerges from, and is responsible to, the democratically elected legislative authority. Thus, it differs from the presidential government of countries like the United States where the members of the executive branch and the legislature are elected independently of each other. It differs, too, from socialist governments in parliamentary form to the extent that these are not based on competitive elections. Within the essential union of the legislative and executive branches that characterizes the parliamentary form of government, the legislature is supreme. The chief executive, the prime minister, usually is appointed by the head of state (a constitutional monarch or a ceremonial president chosen by the parliament). The head of state must choose as prime minister a person whom a parliamentary majority would elect. Thus, in practice, the prime minister normally is the leader of the majority party. The prime minister chooses the executive heads of government departments, the most important of whom constitute the cabinet. Together, the prime minister and the cabinet are known in parliamentary systems as "the government."

The government holds office only so long as it commands majority support in the legislature. The importance of continuing parliamentary support for the government is evidenced by the fact that the government regularly submits its program and its record for parliamentary approval. An adverse legislative vote on an important issue indicates a lack of confidence which requires the government either to resign or to try to secure a new parliamentary majority by means of a general election. Thus, the familiar American phenomenon of stalemate between an executive of one party and a legislature of another is meant to be impossible. Technically, the decision to dissolve parliament and call for new elections, like the choice of prime minister, belongs to the head of state. But in practice the head of state exercises this power only on the advice of the prime minister.

The parliamentary system has taken different forms from country to country. Thus the foregoing description of its typical features will not apply in all respects to every country whose government is organized in this general form. France, in particular, has become a special case. There, under the 1958 constitution of the Fifth French Republic, reflecting the extraordinary personal authority of President Charles de Gaulle, the powers of the head of state were increased to the point where the power of the executive is on an equal footing with that of parliament. The French president not only possesses substantial powers under the constitution (including that of dissolving parliament), but, since 1962, is chosen by direct universal suffrage. Thus, the president may have a popular mandate independent of parliament. This has led many observers within and without France to consider that France has ceased to have a parliamentary system and has instead a hybrid system with features of both presidential and parliamentary types.

The parliamentary system has become the pattern in the 20th century for governments in many of the new nations that have emerged from colonial control in Africa and Asia. Japan, too, has followed this model. The former French colonies in Africa, however, have tended to follow France in receding from the parliamentary form.

The student of comparative law should keep in mind that in some civil law countries, such as Germany, the existence of a federal system introduces important local legal structures. As in the United States, federalism creates more complexity in the legal system than is present in unitary states like England and France. The German system is, however, closer to a unitary form of government than to American-style federalism in two important respects. In the first place, the bulk of German law—criminal and civil—is federal. Secondly, federal law organizes all state and federal courts into a single nationwide system, so that the characteristic legal problems of American federalism concerning internal choice of law or forum are practically nonexistent in Germany.

Note

For further reading on the governments of Britain and several continental European countries, including France and Germany, see Government and Administration in Western Europe (F. Ridley ed. 1979). For a comparative study of the court systems in the United States, Britain and France, see H.

Abraham, The Judicial Process: An Introductory Analysis of the Courts of
the United States, England and France (6th ed. 1993).

SECTION 2. SEPARATION OF POWERS

Separation of powers means something quite different in the European context from what it has come to mean in the United States.
Historically, notions about the proper distribution of power among the
organs of government were shaped in England and in Europe generally
by the struggles of representative assemblies against the rule of monarchs. In France, the doctrine of separation of powers was further
affected by the profound revolutionary reaction there against the rear-
guard role that the judiciary had played in the *ancien régime*.[1] This
background is in marked contrast to the United States where neither the
fear of government by judges nor the dogma of legislative supremacy
played much of a role in the formative period. Many of the framers of
the American Constitution did fear, however, the unprecedented power
of relatively popular state legislatures as a threat to property and
commerce. Therefore, Chief Justice Marshall in *Marbury v. Madison*[2]
did not have to contend with deep-seated attitudes that in Europe have
been powerful obstacles to the establishment of judicial review. Separation of powers to an American evokes the familiar system of checks and
balances among the three coordinate branches of government—legislative, executive and judiciary—each with its independent constitutional
basis. To a European, it is a more rigid doctrine and inseparable from
the notion of legislative supremacy.

We have already seen the significance of the doctrine of legislative
supremacy for the role of the executive in parliamentary governments.
So far as the judiciary is concerned, the doctrine in its extreme form not
only has been thought to exclude judicial power to review the legality of
legislative, executive and administrative action, but has even been invoked to deny the courts a "lawmaking" function via interpretation of
legislative texts. However, these "logical" implications of legislative
supremacy have not prevented modern civil law systems from moving
increasingly toward some form of judicial review[3] nor have they diminished the growing de facto importance of case law.

The rigid European version of separation of powers has had long-
lasting effects on the structure of the court systems in most civil law

---

1. For over thirty years preceding the
French revolution, the French royal courts
(Parlements) used their adjudicative and
rulemaking powers to oppose moderate and
necessary reforms, always in the name of
higher law and fundamental liberties. The
resistance of this powerful group of judges
to all change, their defense of privilege
while invoking the national interest, and
their venality in office made them prime
targets for revolutionary wrath and earned
them the lasting distrust of a nation. J.
Dawson, The Oracles of the Law 263–373
(1968). See generally, on the French concept of separation of powers, M. Troper, La
séparation des pouvoirs et l'histoire consti-
tutionelle française (1980).

2. 5 U.S. (1 Cranch) 137, 2 L.Ed. 60
(1803).

3. See generally, M. Cappelletti, Judicial
Review in the Contemporary World (1971);
Rosenn, Judicial Review in Latin America,
35 Ohio State L.J. 785 (1974).

countries. The principle of legislative supremacy and, in France, mistrust of the judiciary, seemed to rule out the possibility of judicial review of the legality of administrative action or of adjudication by ordinary courts of disputes between agencies of the government. Yet some institutional mechanism for dealing with these matters was clearly needed. In France this was made one of the responsibilities of the Council of State (*Conseil d'État*), the central organ of governmental administration. A number of nations including Belgium and Italy have followed the French model. In other nations, such as Austria and Germany, such disputes are handled by the judiciary, but within a separate system of administrative courts. Thus, the typical civil law system contains at least two (and sometimes more) separate sets of courts for administrative and private law matters, each with its own supreme court, its own procedural and substantive rules, and its own jurisdiction. This is in striking contrast with the unified American system, where a single set of courts within each state and at the federal level hears both public and private law matters and even has authority to review the legality of the actions of the other branches of government.

SECTION 3. CONSTITUTIONS

A. GERMANY

S.E. FINER, "FIVE CONSTITUTIONS"
23–27 (1979).*

If one turns to the German Constitution of 1949, one is struck by its provisional character; by its emphasis on individual liberties which equals if it does not exceed that of the American Constitution; by the sheer number of the clauses that define the federal-state relationship; by the downgrading of the presidency and corresponding strengthening of the chancellorship; and by the very tight restrictions placed upon emergency powers and defence arrangements. Each of these features reflects a reaction to the special circumstances in which the Constitution was elaborated and to the régime from which the German people had just escaped.

In 1949 Germany was still occupied by the Allied forces. Step by reluctant step the three western powers (the USA, Britain and France) had united their zones of occupation for economic purposes, had licensed political parties, inaugurated municipal elections, recarved the country into provinces (*Länder*) and established *Land* governments in them. The Cold War was in full swing. The Soviet Union was bolshevizing the Eastern Zone. In March 1948, it walked out of the four-power Control Council, and in April initiated the Berlin blockade. Therefore on 1 July, the three western Allies, acting independently of the Soviet Union, asked the heads of the eleven *Land* governments (the *Landtage*) to convene a constituent assembly and draft a constitution for Germany that would be

* Reprinted by permission of Humanities Press Inc., Atlantic Highlands, New Jersey.

both democratic and federal. But the principal concern of these *Land* presidents, prior to considering any text, was to do nothing that would perpetuate, let alone legitimate, the *de facto* division of Germany. Also they found themselves forced to steer a course between the loose federalism pressed on them by the French and the Americans,—and which some of the German Christian Democrats favoured—and the tight centralization on which the German Social Democratic party insisted, even to the point of quitting the discussions at one stage.

The first of these two concerns finds expression in the Preamble, the Transitional Provisions and Article 146. The Preamble speaks of "a new order to political life for a transitional period", qualifies this by making it "on behalf of those Germans to whom participation was denied" and states further that "the entire German people are called upon to achieve in free self-determination the unity and freedom of Germany". The Transitional Provisions draw our attention to the *Land* boundaries, refugees, expellees, to occupation costs and the like. And the final Article, number 146, states: "This Basic Law shall cease to be in force on the day on which a constitution adopted by a free decision of the German people comes into force."

The second concern is reflected in the sheer complication of the Articles concerning the federation. The first draft constitution, which was completed on 23 August 1948 and submitted to the occupation authorities on 2 March 1949, was so federal that the Social Democrats walked out of the Constituent Council. They insisted that German judicial and economic unity had to be guaranteed, that the federal government must have finances adequate to its tasks and that there must be a uniform social policy. The Allies responded on 22 April, markedly softening their support for the *Länder vis-á-vis* the federal government, and it was on this basis that the draft was approved, by 53 votes to 12. Half the minority consisted of Christian Democrat delegates who thought that the document was now too centralist. The long list of powers translated as "concurrent" (a better translation would be "alternative") and the elaborate financial provisions in Chapter X, as well as the provision for the *Land* execution of federal laws, all of which make German federalism far removed from the American prototype, stand as a monument to this struggle. But so, too, does Article 79(3): there is no legal way to abandon the "division of the Federation into *Länder* " nor to terminate their "participation on principle . . . in legislation". These provisions are not amendable.

In the rest of the document the most striking idiosyncratic features represent the attempt to revert to the *Rechtsstaat* tradition after the Nazi absolutism, and to correct the faults in the Weimar Constitution which had contributed to its rise. Thus not only does the "Bill of Rights" move from its place in the middle of the Weimar Constitution to become Chapter I of the new Bonn Constitution, but there is no corresponding list of duties as there was in the Weimar text. Furthermore, whereas the Weimar Constitution sanctioned judicial review only by implication, here it is positively and explicitly affirmed and the individual himself is given license to appeal to the courts. Three features go beyond the American Constitution. First, the rights are not amendable. They stand over and above the Constitution itself. Second, they are to be interpreted so as to sustain and maintain what is described as "the free democratic order". An individual who uses (the text says "abuses") his basic rights "in order to combat the free democratic basic order" forfeits them (Article 18). Third—and unique in all written constitutions—"All Germans shall have the right to resist any person or persons seeking to abolish [the] constitutional order, should no other remedy be possible" (Article 20(4)).

Just as these provisions clearly derive from the experiences of the Third Reich, so the institutional arrangements derive from awareness of the loopholes in the Weimar Constitution which the Nazis had exploited to seize power. The presidency, abused by von Hindenburg to bring von Papen and then Hitler to office, is shorn of power and authority. Instead, the Chancellor, elected by the Bundestag, is given plenary authority over his Cabinet and can be brought down only if a majority succeeds in agreeing on his successor: thus avoiding the factitious majorities of extreme right and extreme left which had strangled parliamentary government in the Weimar Republic. Again, President Hindenburg and various Chancellors had abused the emergency-powers article (Article 48) of the Weimar Constitution to suspend the constitution and then to install Hitler as Chancellor. In the 1949 Constitution (Articles 80 and 115a) a two thirds majority is needed to authorize an emergency situation, and even when this has come into effect the legislature cannot be dissolved, the Constitutional Court must continue to sit and the basic rights contained in Articles 1–20 (except as specifically modified in the text) remain in force.

Note

On October 3, 1990, the Basic Law of 1949 ceased to be a "provisional" document and became the constitution of the entire reunited German nation. By the reunification treaty signed on August 31, 1990, the former East Germany became part of the Federal Republic of Germany and acceded to the framework of the Basic Law.[4]

B. FRANCE

S.E. FINER, "FIVE CONSTITUTIONS"

27–28 (1979).*

It is a far cry from the German text to the French Constitution of 4 October 1958. In the German text, only forty-five Articles out of 146 relate specifically to the executive, the legislature and the relationships

---

4. The treaty contained certain transitional provisions to ease the process of unification. See, for description and analysis, Peter Quint, The Constitutional Law of German Reunification, 50 Maryland L.Rev. 475 (1991).

* Reprinted by permission of Humanities Press Inc., Atlantic Highlands, New Jersey.

between them. Out of the ninety-two Articles in the French Constitution forty-six do so. We come pretty near the whole truth when we say that apart from eleven Articles concerned with the French Community (and drafted in view of the imminent dissolution of the French Empire), and three transitional Articles to bring the new instrument into effect, the Constitution is concerned with one matter alone: to redefine the powers of the executive and the legislature to the immense advantage of the former. In this document there is no detailed and specific Bill of Rights, only a Preamble which speaks of the French people's "solemn attachment" to the rights laid down in the 1789 Declaration of the Rights of Man and the Citizen, and to the Preamble to the 1946 Constitution. These rights, such as they are, are all but silent on "fair trial" procedures, and the matter relating to the structure and powers of the judiciary and of local authorities is cursory; evidently the document assumes that these will continue as before. But the President and his surrogate and/or colleague the Prime Minister (according to how one interprets the text) receive massive new powers. The President has an arbitral power under Article 5, emergency power under Article 16, and in association with the Prime Minister has the power to dissolve the legislature. Correspondingly, this legislature is now trammelled. Much of its internal procedure such as the number and the role of its commissions is now defined in the constitution and this in its turn gives the Prime Minister and his Cabinet immense procedural advantages over the Opposition (cf. for example the "block vote" provision of Article 44). Far from being omnicompetent, the legislature is confined to the passage of "laws" only and what topics constitute the subject-matter of a "law" is laid down in detail. Any matter not included in the list is reserved to the executive branch (Articles 34 and 37). This power to make regulations is conceived as the general rule; the passage of legislation as the exception.

Again, it is the different preoccupations of the constitution-makers that explain the signal difference between this constitution and the German one. The 1958 Constitution marks the triumph of an eighty-year-old effort by the French right, unsuccessful save for the puppet years of the Vichy régime (1940–44), to replace by a powerful executive supremacy the legislative prepotence—the so-called *gouvernement d'assemblée*—which, from the resignation of President MacMahon in 1879, had condemned successive Cabinets to instability and impotence during the Third Republic and, subsequently, the Fourth. In the face of the Algerian crisis, French Cabinets found themselves unable to find a broad consensus of public opinion on which to base their actions. The Algiers revolt of 1958 and the subsequent threat of a military *coup* proved the fragility of the Fourth Republic. Over its moribund body strode the Gaullists, who seized the occasion to elevate their candidate to the premiership to draft a constitution to fit his imperious nature and express his elevated conception of the presidency and his contempt for political parties and for parliamentarism.

C. POST–1989 CONSTITUTIONALISM

A new era of constitution-making opened after 1989 as the former socialist countries of Eastern Europe embarked on the transition to new forms of government. In the following excerpt, Gerhard Casper speculates about the features of constitutionalism that are likely to emerge in this process.

CASPER, "EUROPEAN CONVERGENCE"

58 University of Chicago Law Review 441, 444–46 (1991).*

... My thesis is a simple one. On the whole, Eastern Europe will follow Western European examples. The Eastern Europeans will find this path pragmatically desirable because of their aspirations to join the Council of Europe and, more importantly, the European Community. They will also find these models congenial because underlying them is a concept of the state and its role that goes back all the way to the late eighteenth century.[3]

The new constitutions will not only design what one hopes will be democratic methods for producing a social order,[4] but they themselves will identify democracy with substantive notions about the social order. The constitutions will lay down values that are to guide legislatures. Many aspects of life will be subjected to governing principles of a programmatic nature and placed under the overarching care of the state. By comparison with the socialist regimes, pluralism will be constitutionally anchored, and the private realm will receive constitutional protection, but the state will serve as the ultimate guarantor of many human aspirations.

This comprehensive ordering approach will create the immediate problem of sanctifying as constitutional law vague propositions about the appropriate scope of government. Every social issue will become a constitutional issue, and law and its oracles will be severely overtaxed. It will also create the potential for constitutional disappointments on the part of those who will come to believe that constitutional promises have been breached.

The new constitutions will have comprehensive bills of rights (even their predecessors had) that will be one of the vehicles for articulating social values. These bills of rights are likely to leave details to legislative discretion. Few rights will be truly absolute, and there will be some duties that will be viewed as concomitant to rights. Whether it will be possible under the prevailing economic and social conditions to guaran-

---

* Reprinted with permission of Gerhard Casper and the University of Chicago Law Review.

3. See Gerhard Casper, Changing Concepts of Constitutionalism: 18th to 20th Century, 1989 S.Ct. Rev 311.

4. See Hans Kelsen, Vom Wesen und Wert der Demokratie (J.C.B. Mohr, 2d ed. 1929).

tee the right to hold private property in a meaningful manner is highly dubious.

To the extent that the separation of powers may offer a measure of institutional protection where the rights approach fails, the new constitutions are likely to have a weak form of such separation. An independent executive branch along American lines is hard to imagine anywhere except as an expression of a preference for a "strong president," which is nearly the opposite of what Americans mean when they invoke separation of powers concepts. The rule will be one form or another of parliamentary democracy, though there will probably be considerable experimentation paralleling the great variety of solutions to be found in Western Europe.

Finally, Eastern Europe will follow other European countries and accept the American "higher law" concept of constitutions. The new constitutions will institutionalize judicial review, though likely on the Austrian, German, and Italian model of separate constitutional courts composed differently from ordinary courts and with their own procedures. The institutionalization of judicial review (already actively implemented in Hungary) will present one of the greatest challenges in the absence of an independent judiciary and, for all practical purposes, a high-quality legal profession. The socialist regimes prized neither independent judges nor lawyers. The legal profession found little social respect, though the situation was somewhat different in different countries. Under these conditions, it will be very difficult to create a legal profession that can avoid the pitfalls of politicization, especially in light of the legalization of many political questions that, I predict, will occur.

One of the main dangers ahead is that the organizational issues that in 1989 and afterwards were posed primarily as issues of practical politics continue to be seen mainly that way. Constitutional politics inevitably are matters of practical politics, but they also transcend practical politics. Constitutionalism does not refer simply to having a constitution, but to having a particular kind of constitution, however difficult it may be to specify its content. The task is also to assure the stability of the new order—to take the long view, rather than the short one. This is difficult under the best of circumstances. It is an awesome challenge under the conditions prevailing in Eastern Europe, where the political sorting-out after forty-five years of communist dominance must occur at the same time as the reorganization of bankrupt economies and the redefinition of national, ethnic, and other cultural identities.

SECTION 4. JUDICIAL REVIEW

Despite the difficulties that are perceived in the civil law countries as standing in the way of a system of judicial review of the constitutionality of legislation and executive action, there has been considerable movement in the years since World War II toward the establishment of some form of constitutional control over governmental power. This is

Glendon Comp. Legal Trad. -4

especially so in those countries that have adopted constitutions containing guarantees of enumerated fundamental rights, and where the constitution can be amended only by a special procedure rather than simply by the ordinary legislative process. The gradual introduction of judicial review has taken diverse forms in the civil law systems. As is the case with parliamentary government, classifications of legal systems in this area do not always coincide with civil law-common law lines of demarcation.[1] Indeed, so far as judicial review is concerned, France and England would appear to fall within one group of countries where its existence in a technical sense is denied, while Italy, Germany and the United States come within another group where judicial power to review legislation not only exists but is actively exercised by the courts. In between are several countries which in varying degrees have admitted the principle, but where the courts have been relatively cautious in implementing it.

J.A. JOLOWICZ, SUMMARY OF THE 1984 SCIENTIFIC COLLOQUIUM OF THE INTERNATIONAL ASSOCIATION OF LEGAL SCIENCE ON "JUDICIAL REVIEW AND ITS LEGITIMACY."*

Control of the constitutionality of parliamentary legislation is not necessarily exercised, if it is exercised at all, by a judicial body; instances of such control by, for example, the legislature itself or a specialised section of it can be found both in the past and in the present. Conversely, judicial control of the constitutionality of legislation does not mean only judicial control of the constitutionality of *parliamentary* legislation; it may extend to or be restricted to subordinate legislation. Nevertheless, the attention of the colloquium was directed principally, if not quite exclusively, to the *judicial* control (including the control exercised by the French *Conseil Constitutionnel*) of the acts of the legislature itself.

Control of the kind envisaged came to the United States thanks to the famous decision of Chief Justice Marshall in *Marbury v. Madison*, 5 U.S. (1 Cranch) 137, 2 L.Ed. 60 (1803); it appeared in Europe after the First World War in the Austrian Constitution of 1920 and, to a more limited extent, elsewhere. Its first great expansion came, however, after the Second World War, most notably in Austria, in the Federal Republic of Germany and in Italy. In comparatively recent times the institution in one form or another has found favour in numerous countries all over the world, usually, though not invariably, being provided for in the Constitution itself; the Federal Republic of Germany, which has had the institution since shortly after the Second World War, gave it additional scope by a constitutional amendment in 1969. In France, by contrast, it

---

4. For discussion of the various models by a leading French constitutional lawyer, see L. Favoreu, American and European Models of Constitutional Justice, in Comparative and Private International Law: Essays in Honor of John Henry Merryman 105 (1990).

* This report was prepared by Professor Jolowicz in his capacity as Director of Scientific Work for the International Association of Legal Science and is reprinted here with his permission.

was almost certainly not the intention of the Constitution of 1958 to introduce judicial review, and its existence in France today is largely due to the land-mark decision of the *Conseil Constitutionnel* of 16 July 1971; what may be seen as its confirmation in the constitutional amendment of 1974 is implicit rather than explicit. In the contemporary world, judicial review of legislation exists in many countries including even some, such as Yugoslavia, which adhere to the theory of the unity of power rather than to that of the separation of powers. Indeed, today, acceptance of judicial review in countries belonging to both the civil and the common law traditions has become so wide-spread (its acceptance in socialist countries is much less extensive) that it was generally held to be an anomaly that, notwithstanding the introduction of judicial review in the Constitutions created by Great Britain for her former colonies, the institution has not yet been accepted in that country.

In these circumstances it is not altogether surprising that, with one or two notable exceptions, little doubt should have been cast on the "legitimacy" of the institution by those attending the colloquium. As was pointed out more than once, if the Constitution is held to be a "higher" law, then logic demands that a law which conflicts with a provision in the Constitution be not applied. Nevertheless, justifications for judicial review of legislation other than that of logical necessity were put forward, in particular by way of response to the familiar argument that judicial review of legislation is "anti-majoritarian" or "anti-democratic." It was observed, for example, that democracy itself demands more than simply that the will of the majority shall prevail; it demands also that the interests of minorities and of individuals should be respected, at least to the extent that those interests are recognised in the Constitution, and to that end judicial review may be essential. Again, as was also observed, the fact that non-democratic governments which have come to power following a coup d'état or other violent means almost invariably suppress the institution of judicial review suggests that the institution protects rather than defeats the ideals of democracy.

Much of the discussion related to the "effectiveness" of judicial control, its "legitimacy" being accepted, and, though it was never so stated specifically, two distinct aspects of the matter came under consideration. First, there is the question of the effectiveness within a legal system of decisions which actually condemn a law as unconstitutional and, secondly, there is the question of the extent to which, in a given system, the institution of judicial review can operate effectively to control infringements of the Constitution by the legislative branch of government. The latter depends less than does the former on the actual form of judicial review adopted and is more dependent on political and other factors, but the chosen form of judicial review does bear upon both.

Broadly speaking judicial review conforms to one of two models, the "Austrian" and the "American." Under the former, questions of the constitutionality of legislation can be decided only by a special constitutional court on reference from an authorised person who may or may not be a judge before whom such a question is raised in the course of ordinary litigation, and the review may be *a priori or a posteriori.* Under the latter, it is the duty of any judge before whom such a question is raised in the course of litigation to deal with it there and then, although, no doubt, in important cases the question will finally be decided by the Supreme Court; review of this kind is necessarily *a posteriori.* The French system can, perhaps, be regarded as a particular version of the Austrian model, for the *Conseil Constitutionnel* alone has power to pronounce a parliamentary law unconstitutional and then only on the reference of specified persons; the challenged law is referred to the *Conseil* before promulgation, and no law or part of a law declared to be unconstitutional may be promulgated. Obviously the decisions of the *Conseil Constitutionnel* have effect *erga omnes,* for a law which is not promulgated is no law, but, generally speaking, it is typical of the Austrian model that the decisions of the constitutional court have effect *erga omnes.* Under the American model, by contrast, the decision, even if of the Supreme Court, is binding as *res judicata* only between the parties. In countries of the common law tradition this is not a serious disadvantage because the doctrine *stare decisis* has the result that the decision that a law is unconstitutional will almost invariably be applied thereafter, but elsewhere as, for example, in some countries of Latin–America where the American model has been followed, such a decision will be disregarded by other courts and the administration alike. On the whole, therefore, the American model is seen as unsuitable for countries of the civil law tradition. There was little if any disagreement with the proposition that decisions on the constitutionality or otherwise of a law should have effect *erga omnes* if the institution of judicial review is to be regarded as "effective".

So far as the second aspect of the effectiveness of judicial review is concerned, this is difficult to assess; clearly it cannot simply be measured by reference to the number of laws struck down, a statistic which varies greatly from one country to another even within continental Europe. However it was emphasised in particular that judicial review cannot be effective without judges who are genuinely independent not only in the sense that their individual decisions are not directly influenced or controlled by the political branches of government but also in the sense that their education and professional experience shall have equipped them with true intellectual independence. The institution of judicial review may be imperilled as much by its excessive exercise as by its virtual non-exercise, and the important thing is to maintain the correct balance. This intellectual independence, it was considered by some, is less likely to be produced by the kind of education and training afforded to judges in the "civil law" countries (apart from the judges specially nominated to the Constitutional Court) than in "common law" countries where the judges are generally appointed from the ranks of practitioners, and in their opinion this provided an additional reason for preferring the "Austrian" to the "American" model in countries of the "civil law."

In addition to these basic aspects of the subject, a number of other topics received attention, in particular that type of judicial control of legislation that may be exercised covertly in the guise of statutory interpretation. Most importantly, attention was directed to the emergence in more than one part of the world of inter- or supra-national control such as that provided, for example, by the European Court of Human Rights. The ultimate success of this relatively new development is, however, uncertain as is shown by experience in Latin–America (where there have been relatively few adherents to the relevant convention), and this it may be supposed is at least in part attributable to the fact that adherence to the convention or treaty which is a necessary preliminary to such control is a matter for decision by the executive branch of government.

Not unexpectedly in a gathering of lawyers, such criticism as there was of the institution of judicial review of legislation itself was relatively muted; most, though not all, apparently held the view that the period of history in which the institution itself requires justification is over and that effort should now be devoted rather to its preservation against hostile governments and to improvements in its practical operation....

A. JUDICIAL REVIEW IN FRANCE

The peculiar history of the judiciary in France—its identification with feudal oppression, its role in retarding even moderate reforms in pre-revolutionary France, the post-revolutionary reaction against and vestigial distrust of judges,[5] plus the comparatively nonprestigious role of the modern civil-servant judge,—has militated against placing the power to review the constitutionality of legislation in the judiciary. The ordinary civil courts are not even permitted to review the legality of administrative action, this task being reserved to administrative tribunals within the executive branch. So, when France in 1958 instituted a system of constitutional review of laws passed by Parliament, it created a new governmental organ, the Constitutional Council.[6] This body is authorized to review laws, but only at the request of the executive or the legislature, only *before* promulgation and only for the limited purpose of ascertaining whether the laws are in conformity with the constitutional division of powers between the executive and the legislature. As Cappelletti has written, the Constitutional Council was meant to be a "mere watchdog of the prerogatives of the executive." [7] However, in 1971 the Council claimed for itself, and has since exercised, the power to review laws, prior to their taking effect, for conformity with the constitution generally, including the unwritten "fundamental principles" of the

5. See generally, J. Dawson, The Oracles of the Law 263–373 (1968) and Beardsley, Constitutional Review in France, 1975 Sup.Ct.Rev. 189.

6. Waline, The Constitutional Council of the French Republic, 12 Am.J.Comp.L. 483 (1963).

7. Cappelletti, The "Mighty Problem" of Judicial Review and the Contribution of Comparative Analysis, 53 S.Cal.L.Rev. 409, 417 (1980).

French republican tradition.[8] This and subsequent developments indicate that even France is moving away from the older, rigid view of separation of powers.[9]

(1) The French Constitutional Council

CONSTITUTION OF THE FRENCH REPUBLIC OF OCTOBER 4, 1958

TITLE VII
THE CONSTITUTIONAL COUNCIL

ARTICLE 56

The Constitutional Council shall consist of nine members, whose terms of office shall last nine years and shall not be renewable. One third of the membership of the Constitutional Council shall be renewed every three years. Three of its members shall be appointed by the President of the Republic, three by the President of the National Assembly, three by the President of the Senate.

In addition to the nine members provided for above, former Presidents of the Republic shall be members ex officio for life of the Constitutional Council.

The President shall be appointed by the President of the Republic. He shall have the deciding vote in case of a tie.

ARTICLE 57

The office of member of the Constitutional Council shall be incompatible with that of minister or member of Parliament. Other incompatibilities shall be determined by an organic law.

ARTICLE 58

The Constitutional Council shall ensure the regularity of the election of the President of the Republic.

It shall examine complaints and shall announce the results of the vote.

ARTICLE 59

The Constitutional Council shall rule, in the case of disagreement, on the regularity of the election of deputies and senators.

---

8. Constitutional Council Decision of July 16, 1971, translated in M. Cappelletti and W. Cohen, Comparative Constitutional Law 50 (1979). See generally, Beardsley, The Constitutional Council and Constitutional Liberties in France, 20 Am.J.Comp.L. 431 (1972).

9. For a well-reasoned argument that the French experience with the Constitutional Council demonstrates that process-based judicial review aimed at assuring the separation of powers can function to protect important substantive values while remaining consistent with majoritarian democratic political theory, see Neuborne, Judicial Review and Separation of Powers in France and the United States, 57 N.Y.U.L.Rev. 363 (1982).

ARTICLE 60

The Constitutional Council shall ensure the regularity of referendum procedures and shall announce the results thereof.

ARTICLE 61

Organic laws, before their promulgation, and regulations of the parliamentary assemblies, before they come into force, must be submitted to the Constitutional Council, which shall rule on their constitutionality.

To the same end, laws may be submitted to the Constitutional Council, before their promulgation, by the President of the Republic, the Premier or the President of one or the other assembly or any sixty members of the National Assembly or the Senate.[10]

In the cases provided for by the two preceding paragraphs, the Constitutional Council must make its ruling within a time limit of one month. Nevertheless, at the request of the Government, in case of emergency, this period shall be reduced to eight days.

In these cases, referral to the Constitutional Council shall suspend the time limit for promulgation.

ARTICLE 62

A provision declared unconstitutional may not be promulgated or implemented.

The decisions of the Constitutional Council may not be appealed to any jurisdiction whatsoever. They must be recognized by the governmental authorities and by all administrative and judicial authorities.

LOUIS FAVOREU, "THE CONSTITUTIONAL COUNCIL AND PARLIAMENT IN FRANCE"

From Constitutional Review and Legislation: An International
Comparison (C. Landfried ed., 1988).
81–108 (excerpts).*

The relationship between the Constitutional Council and the legislator has evolved in France in a curious and interesting way. Although at the beginning of the Fifth Republic one could have thought, given the text of the constitution and the intention expressed by its framers, that the Constitutional Council had been created especially to oversee Parliament and to keep it from reacquiring the jurisdiction it had under the Third and Fourth Republics the opposite phenomenon took place: the

---

10. The permission for any 60 members of the National Assembly or the Senate to submit a law to the Council for constitutional review before promulgation was added by amendment in 1974. The effect was to give the parliamentary minority access to the Council. Since that time, most requests for constitutional review have come from groups of legislators. Among these requests was the challenge to the French abortion law of 1975, infra p. 85.

* Reprinted with permission of Nomos Verlagsgesellschaft.

constitutional judges contribute today to the reinforcement of the legislative powers of Parliament.

* * *

It must be noted at the very beginning that, contrary to the German, Austrian, Spanish and Italian constitutional courts, the French court does not hear cases which present ordinary public or private law questions. It is neither a super *Cour de cassation* nor a super Council of State as is often the case in other countries. Its members therefore do not need to be as technically competent as do the German, Italian or Spanish judges. It is understandable why the French judges are not required to be experienced jurists.

* * *

But what seems to us as important as strictly legal abilities is the fact that the members of the Constitutional Council generally have high level government experience, a very useful fact when they must decide, as is often the case, questions concerning the functioning of the machinery of State. First of all, we find, especially among the members named by the presidents of the legislative bodies, a great number of former legislators: 10 out of 14 of those appointed by the President of the National Assembly (including a former president of this assembly); 8 out of 12 of those appointed by the President of the Senate (including a former president and vice-president of the Senate, and the former president of the legislative committee). On the other hand, of the 14 appointed by the President of the Republic, only 5 were former legislators. All together, 23 out of 40 members had been members of the legislative bodies of the Fourth or Fifth Republics. Furthermore, many are former Ministers. It is worth noting that at one point (1977–86), the Constitutional Council counted among its members two of the five secretaries general that France has known from 1946 to 1986. This clearly influences the manner in which the Constitutional Council judges. Since the majority of its decisions concern acts of Parliament, the fact that so many of its members are specialists in the drafting and voting of legislative and parliamentary acts is of great importance: it largely explains the special relationship between the constitutional judges and Parliament.

* * *

The Manner in Which the Constitutional Council Decides on the Constitutionality of Laws

A priori control as it is exercised by the Constitutional Council contains a certain number of constraints which explain the way in which the constitutional judges hand down their decisions.

We know, in fact, that the time limit for decisions of the Constitutional Council is very short (a maximum of one month), that there are no public arguments or lawyers, and that the conditions under which the decision is made are not publicly known. Contrary to what happens in

Germany or in Spain, the number of judges voting for or against constitutionality is not made public. There are therefore no dissenting or individual opinions. Occasionally the details of the vote are known through leaks, but we can never be certain that the information is accurate. It does seem, however, that rather frequently the decisions are taken by a large majority (7 to 2, for example, for the decision of September 19, 1986 concerning the audio-visual law), or even unanimously (in the case, for example, of the decision of January 20, 1984 concerning the independence of university professors).

This apparent absence of the characteristics of a judicial proceeding should not be misconstrued, however, for, in fact, many of these characteristics reappear upon close examination of the procedure before the Constitutional Council.

First of all, we must not forget that although the time limit for decisions is very short, the Constitutional judges, unlike their European counterparts, can devote themselves entirely to the matter at hand, because they only have twenty, or at most thirty cases to resolve each year. Moreover, the legal question submitted to them has in most cases been raised and debated in the two houses well before the matter is referred to the Council. Indeed, today there is a very serious and thorough legal discussion of the important questions in the two chambers through the motions of unconstitutionality systematically introduced by the opposition. The members of the Constitutional Council are regularly informed of this debate by the legal department of the Council which prepares studies of the question using the Parliamentary documents and debates.

* * *

It appears that the Constitutional Council exercises a power of review that is becoming progressively stricter. Each successive majority has complained of the increasingly active role of the Constitutional Council using the expression, often used in France, of "government of judges".[11] This has been the case for the left-wing majority in 1981–82, and for the right-wing majority of 1986–88. The question, independently of the myth of the "government of judges", is whether the Constitutional Council has exceeded its power and invaded the domain of the legislator, usurping its place.

A further question is whether the laws which have been successfully challenged in the Constitutional Council have come from the Right or the Left, or from both in equal proportions.

* * *

In 28 years—from 1959 to 1987—the Constitutional Council has handed down 187 decisions concerning the constitutionality of laws

---

11. Concerning this mythical idea, see the incisive study by M.H. Davis, Government of Judges: An Historical Review: The   American Journal of Comparative Law, 1987, pp. 559–581.

(organic or ordinary) of which 70 were decisions of nullification (partial or total) including 103 grounds for nullification.

A comparison with other countries having a system of constitutional review shows that the number of nullifications pronounced in France is not far from the number of times the United States Supreme Court has declared a *federal* law unconstitutional (about 100) in two centuries. It is near the number of nullifications in West Germany (160 from 1951 to 1980) or in Austria (357 from 1946 to 1980), but much less than in Italy (600 decisions for the comparable period).

We may observe, however, that the proportion of nullification compared to the total number of cases decided is undoubtedly higher in France than in other countries.

In fact, there have been 70 nullifications out of a total of 187 cases or more than 36%. The proportion is even higher if we consider only the decisions concerning ordinary (i.e. non organic) laws: 64 out of 138, or almost 50%.

* * *

The Constitutional Council has always tried to respect the freedom of judgment of the legislature and has been careful not to take its place.

Thus on several occasions, beginning with the landmark decision of 15 January 1975, it has emphasized that "article 61 of the Constitution *does not give* the Constitutional Council a *general power of assessment and of decision identical to that of Parliament* but only gives it jurisdiction to judge the constitutionality of laws referred to it."

It also took pains to point out in a landmark decision of 23 August 1985 that "*the purpose of this review (of the constitutionality of laws) is not to hinder or to delay the exercise of legislative power* but to insure that it is used constitutionally."

* * *

Finally, we can observe that the Constitutional Council's power of review restricts especially the Government and that rather paradoxically this power of review can be beneficial to Parliament. We will see this later when we study the effect of the Constitutional Council's power of review.

If we attempt to determine whether the Constitutional Council has been more or less severe according to the periods or according to the political origins of the challenged laws, we can see that the constitutional judges have been consistent whatever the majority in power.

From 1974 to 1981, the referrals came mostly, but not exclusively, from the left-wing opposition challenging the validity of laws voted by the right-wing majority. The proportion of nullifications is not very high (29%), but the total number of nullifications is relatively high (5 out of 14, a proportion which we do not find later).

If we compare this to the following period (1981–86) during which the Left is in power and the Right in opposition, we are struck by the increase in the percentage of challenges sustained (50%). But we must qualify this observation by the fact that these decisions were almost all partial nullifications, often concerning mere details or with a very limited application.

Moreover, we can see that over the following period (1986–87), the success rate for challenges is even higher (56%) and the control is stricter (due to the multiplication of decisions giving qualified approval); here it is legislation of the right-wing majority which is successfully challenged by Socialist members of Parliament.

Thus, the political origins of laws do not appear to influence the severity of the examination.

On the other hand, what we do observe once more is that the review is reinforced with each change of majority. Members of Parliament are beginning to realize this. Thus, the Socialist opposition tried to limit its challenges during the period of "cohabitation" so that it would not have to submit its laws to strict examination if it recaptured the majority.

* * *

[M]ore and more, the legislature restrains itself to avoid being censured by the Constitutional Council. From the very beginning, and even before the bill is in committee, precautions are taken to avoid the nullification of certain provisions. If needs be, the questionable provisions are removed.

This of course has had an effect on Parliamentary activity, on how bills are handled in the two houses. The Government has exercised a certain degree of self-restraint and has taken care to strip its bills of everything that might risk causing a declaration of unconstitutionality. It must be said that it has been helped here by the way in which the Council of State has exercised its consultative function. We know that by virtue of article 39, par. 2 of the Constitution, the Council of State gives its opinion on bills. It appears that the High Authority has very often voiced reservations on the constitutionality of certain bills.

The tendency to "juridicize" Parliamentary debates, already noticeable before 1981, has increased considerably since then, for opposition members of Parliament rarely miss the chance to question the constitutionality of bills submitted to Parliament by the Government. In the case of the planning reform presented by the Minister of Planning in 1982, there was a rather curious coalition between the opposition and a good part of the (majority) Socialist group in the National Assembly, troubled by opposition's arguments of unconstitutionality. We have also seen members of Parliament, through a clever use of the power of referral to the Constitutional Council, oblige the Government to submit a bill where it had initially chosen to bring about the reform using its regulatory power.

More and more during Parliamentary debates we see the following scenario. The opposition Deputies or Senators file an objection of inadmissibility based on the unconstitutionality of the text submitted to them. When they do not succeed, they appeal the overruling of their objection by the majority to the Constitutional Council. The Socialists and the Communists began this new Parliamentary practice, which has since become commonplace, when they were in the opposition.

We can thus observe that in fact the influence of the Constitutional Council on the course of legislative process is especially noticeable in the self-restraint, spontaneous or contrived, of the new majority.

The drafting and voting of laws have thus become models of judicial neatness. Never before in France have laws been enacted with as much concern for their constitutionality. The members of Parliament have adapted well to this situation, even if some question the influence thus exercised by the Constitutional Council on Parliament. But is this power of review really oppressive?

Does the strengthened power of review of the Constitutional Council over the legislature weaken the role of Parliament? This is far from clear, and in fact the opposite argument could be made, i.e., that the side effect of constitutional review is to preserve the powers of Parliament as legislator.

First of all, as the Constitutional Council has become progressively stricter concerning the legislature's obligation to use its powers fully and not to leave too much of the implementation to administrative regulations, it has helped strengthen the legislative powers of Parliament. First, the Constitutional Council broadened considerably the "horizontal" power of the legislature through a very wide interpretation of articles 34 and 37 of the Constitution. Next, it extended this power in depth by requiring the legislature to leave to the regulatory power only what is strictly necessary for the implementation of laws. This happened in various ways: for ordinary laws, in extending the theory of "negative incompetence", for criminal laws, in applying strictly the principle of the legality of crimes and sentences * * *

Another phenomenon has not received much comment, although it has been occasionally remarked on, undoubtedly because it seems paradoxical. To the extent that referral to the Constitutional Council comes from members of Parliament, parliamentary rights are strengthened. These referrals must be considered not so much as criticisms of the Parliamentary majority, but as criticisms of the Government which is tempted to take advantage of the loyalty of its majority to get texts passed which are imprecise or contrary to the rights of Parliament. The referral by members of Parliament thus becomes a way to make the Government restore to Parliament its power to make laws. Even before referral, the legal debates which take place and the self-restraint exercised by the Parliamentary majority (and the Government which depends on it) are both favorable to the restoration of the legislative power of Parliament.

We should point out also that the unusual features of our system of constitutional review allow a reconciliation of constitutional review and Parliamentary rights. To the extent that this review is *a priori* it allows the legislature the possibility of legislating again, after a provision is declared unconstitutional, to correct its text itself if it so chooses. On the other hand, in a system of *a posterori* review, it is the constitutional judge who often rewrites the law through his successive interpretations. This is true to such an extent that in Italy, the Constitutional Court is considered to be a co-lawmaker.

Notes

1. In 1990, the Mitterrand Government proposed two major constitutional reforms. The first would have given private citizens access to the process of constitutional review and the second would have empowered the Constitutional Council to rule on the constitutionality of laws after they had gone into effect. Both proposals were rejected by the General Assembly. See Louis Aucoin, Judicial Review in France: Access of the Individual Under French and European Law in the Aftermath of France's Rejection of Bicentennial Reform, 15 Boston Coll. Int'l & Comp.L.Rev. 443 (1992).

2. For further reading on the French Constitutional Council from a comparative perspective, see Henry Abraham, The Judicial Process: An Introductory Analysis of the Courts of the United States, England, and France (6th ed., 1993); Alec Stone, The Birth of Judicial Politics in France: The Constitutional Council in Comparative Perspective (1992); F.L. Morton, Judicial Review in France: A Comparative Analysis, 36 Am.J.Comp.L. 89 (1988); Michael Davis, The Law/Politics Distinction, the French Conseil Constitutionnel, and the U.S. Supreme Court, 34 Am.J.Comp.L. 45 (1986).

(2) The French Abortion Decision

FRENCH CONSTITUTIONAL COUNCIL DECISION OF JANUARY 15, 1975

[1975] D.S.Jur. 529.

J.O. of January 16, 1975, 671.

[On December 20, 1974, seventy-seven legislators, acting pursuant to Article 61(2), as amended, of the French Constitution, applied to the Constitutional Council for review of the constitutionality of a law on voluntary termination of pregnancy that had been passed a few days previously by the two parliamentary assemblies. The statute at issue makes abortion available in cases of "necessity." In the first ten weeks the necessity requirement is satisfied if the pregnant woman considers herself "in distress," provided she undergoes mandatory counseling and (except in cases of emergency) observes waiting periods of one week from the date of her original request and two days from the date of counseling. After ten weeks abortion is available only when two physicians certify that the pregnancy poses a serious danger to the woman's health or that the child is likely to be born with a serious disease or defect.] [11]

THE CONSTITUTIONAL COUNCIL:

In view of the observations produced in support of the submission to this Council;

In view of the Constitution, and notably its preamble;

In view of the Ordinance of November 7, 1958, establishing the organic law of the Constitutional Council . . .;

Having heard the Reporter's report;

Whereas Article 61 of the Constitution does not confer on the Constitutional Council a general power of evaluation and decision identical to that of the Parliament, but gives it jurisdiction only to rule on the conformity to the Constitution of the laws submitted for its scrutiny;

Whereas, in the first place, according to the terms of Article 55 of the Constitution, "Treaties or accords properly ratified or approved have, from the time of their publication, an authority superior to that of the laws, with the reservation, for each accord or treaty, that it be applied by the other party";

Whereas, though these provisions, under the conditions which they define, confer on treaties a superior authority to that of the laws, they neither prescribe nor imply that respect for this superiority principle must be enforced within the framework of control of the conformity of the laws to the Constitution as provided by Article 61;

Whereas, in effect, the decisions taken on the basis of Article 61 of the Constitution assume an absolute and definitive character, as follows from Article 62, which prevents the promulgation and application of any provision declared unconstitutional; that, in contrast, the superiority of the treaties over the laws, which principle is laid down in the aforementioned Article 55, is simultaneously relative and contingent in character, stemming on the one hand from the fact that it is limited to the scope of the application of the treaty and, on the other hand, from the fact that it is subject to a condition of reciprocity, a condition whose realization may vary according to the behavior of one or more of the signatory states and according to the time when one must determine whether the condition has been respected;

Whereas a law contrary to a treaty would thus not be contrary to the Constitution;

Whereas, therefore, control over conformity to the principle of Article 55 of the Constitution could not be exercised within the framework of review provided by Article 61, by reason of the difference in nature of the two controls;

11. The statute is translated and discussed in M. Glendon, Abortion and Divorce in Western Law 155 (1987).

Whereas, under these circumstances, it is not the task of the Constitutional Council, when an application of Article 61 of the Constitution is before it, to examine the conformity of a law to the provisions of a treaty or an international accord;

Whereas, in the second place, the law relating to the voluntary termination of pregnancy respects the liberty of the persons who have resort to, or participate in, a termination of pregnancy, whether in a situation of distress or for a therapeutic reason; and that, therefore, the law does not infringe upon the principle of liberty laid down by Article II of the Declaration of the Rights of Man and of the Citizen;

Whereas the law submitted to this Constitutional Council does not authorize any violation of the principle of respect for every human being from the time of commencement of life, referred to in its Article I, except in case of necessity and according to the conditions and limitations which it defines;

Whereas none of the exceptions provided for in this law are, as it now appears, contrary to any of the fundamental principles recognized by the laws of the Republic, nor do they disregard the principle set forth in the preamble of the Constitution of October 27, 1946, according to which the nation guarantees the protection of children's health, nor any of the other provisions of constitutional value set forth in the text;

Whereas, in consequence, the law concerning the voluntary termination of pregnancy does not contradict the texts to which the Constitution of October 4, 1958, makes reference in its preamble, nor any of the articles of the Constitution itself;

[The Council] decides:

1. The provisions of the law concerning the voluntary termination of pregnancy, submitted to the Constitutional Council, are not contrary to the Constitution.

2. The present decision will be published in the Official Journal of the Republic.

JACQUES ROBERT, "THE DECISION OF THE CONSTITUTIONAL COUNCIL OF JANUARY 15, 1975, ON VOLUNTARY TERMINATION OF PREGNANCY"

27 Revue internationale de droit comparé 873–890 (1975) (excerpts).*

The real problems raised by this petition ... concerned nothing more or less than the question of how the Constitutional Council would proceed, when asked to hold that the provisions of a law, supported by the majority of public opinion and duly adopted by the legislature, but at odds with the old prohibition against abortion, were unconstitutional and contrary to an international convention.

What were the arguments in the petition for review, the elements of the controversy, and the reasons for the decision?

* Reprinted with permission of the Revue internationale de droit comparé.

I. THE ARGUMENTS IN THE PETITION FOR REVIEW

For the petitioners, the new law—which authorizes an abortion before the end of the tenth week if the pregnant woman finds herself in a situation of distress—simultaneously violates three fundamental texts.

A. In the first place, it is contrary to the preamble of the Constitution of 1958 which solemnly affirms that "on the morrow of the victory achieved by free peoples over regimes which tried to subjugate and efface the human personality, the French people proclaim once again that every human being, without distinction of race, religion or beliefs, possesses sacred and inalienable rights."

According to the opponents of the law, though one can debate the strict meaning of the term and the notion of "person", it is not permissible to dispute the quality of "human being" of an embryo less than ten weeks old and therefore to freely dispose of its life, if the mother is not physically in danger. (Everyone knows that therapeutic abortion is practiced in France; the new law, moreover, explicitly authorizes abortion when the continuation of pregnancy would put the health of the mother in grave danger or when there is a strong probability that the child would be afflicted with a particularly serious condition recognized as incurable from the moment of diagnosis).

B. The law would violate, in the second place, the tenth line of the preamble of the 1946 Constitution which reaffirms that "the nation guarantees protection of health to all, notably to children, and mothers...." This protection would commence from the time of conception, which—no one having the right to dispose of the life of another person—implies a prohibition against abortion.

C. Finally, the new provisions adopted by Parliament would be contrary to Article II of the European Convention on Human Rights which France finally, though belatedly, ratified. Under the terms of this Article II, "the right of every person to life is protected by the law...."

* * *

II. THE ELEMENTS OF THE CONTROVERSY

Two issues were immediately at the heart of the debate:

The jurisdictional issue: The Constitutional Council is certainly competent to examine the conformity of a law to the provisions of the Constitution and its preamble, but can it rule on the compatibility of this same law with the provisions of an international convention?

[Professor Robert's discussion of whether the Council is competent to determine whether the abortion law violated an international convention is omitted. Although the Council declined in the instant case to decide whether the French abortion law violated the European Convention on Human Rights, Article 55 of the French Constitution was invoked in 1975 by the highest French ordinary court, the Court of Cassation, to hold a French law invalid because it conflicted with the law of the European Economic Community.[12] Thus, paradoxically, a court which cannot review legislation for constitutionality has assumed the power to review laws for conformity to international obligations. The Court of Cassation achieved this in a manner reminiscent of Chief Justice Marshall's opinion in *Marbury v. Madison,*[13] by declaring that it was merely engaging in the time-honored process of interpretation by giving effect to a legal norm with higher authority over one of lower standing.[14]]

The fundamental question: Whether or not the Constitutional Council has such extensive jurisdiction, did the new law violate an inalienable right of the human person? Is abortion, as it is envisaged and regulated by the new law, contrary to our Constitution and to the European Convention on Human Rights?

* * *

It is true that the debate involved everyone's profound convictions. Two camps were implacably opposed to each other. On one side were the dedicated and unconditional defenders of the principle of respect for the life of all living beings whatever might be the consequences. On the other side, more realistic and less dogmatic about their assumptions, were the defenders of an equally respectable principle, the respect for human liberty, which applies to the mother as well as to the child. Irreconcilable positions! Neither of the two camps ever succeeded in convincing the other.

Primarily philosophical, the basic debate necessarily—because it was before the Constitutional Council—had to take place on the terrain of law.

The same fundamental legal texts were invoked by both sides, but obviously were interpreted in different ways.

1. Is Our Constitution Opposed to Abortion?

The opponents of the new law naturally invoked the proclamations of our charter that "every human being possess sacred and inalienable rights" and that "the nation guarantees protection of health to all, notably to children. . . ." However, for them, the fetus from the moment it comes into existence (as it does by the act of fertilization) constitutes a human being, a little person, a child. "At two months, as it has been written, the fetus is only three centimeters long and nevertheless its head, its arms, and its legs are complete. Its brain is already in place, brain activity already exists, its sex is determined, the nervous system is already developed." At all stages of growth a profound continuity exists, moreover, which makes it impossible to arbitrarily fix the moment when life begins. Man is in a perpetual state of

12. Administration des Douanes c. Société Cafés Jacques Vabre, D.S.Jur. 497 (1975), translated in M. Cappelletti & W. Cohen, Comparative Constitutional Law 156–68 (1979).

13. 5 U.S. (1 Cranch) 137, 2 L.Ed. 60 (1803).

14. See M. Cappelletti & W. Cohen, supra n. 12 at 161–63, 169.

becoming, but he is man from the beginning. Genetically, therefore, it is a human being whose rights are deliberately ended by termination of pregnancy at the tenth week.

For those who hold this thesis, the biological facts are reinforced by the law, because the law always applies the old saying that an infant *en ventre sa mere* is deemed to be born so far as its legal rights are concerned.

Thus by authorizing abortion up to the tenth week the new law would violate the sacred right to life which every human being possesses and it would therefore no longer assure the protection of health of children.... A double violation of the Constitution.

What is the response to this line of argument, not from the "partisans" of abortion ..., but from those who think that the woman must be left free to make a decision which primarily concerns her?

First, far from being outmoded and absurd, the conception which refuses to link a principle of life to the status of a human person appears singularly modern and in no way contradicted by science. Certainly, to the question: "Is the fetus a human being, a child?", metaphysics, morality and biology do not give decisive responses. Nor does law. But if biology teaches us that death is not what we take for a unique and fleeting moment, why would it be different in the case of life? When the life of the embryo, apart from the mother, begins, no one can say....

As for the [legal] adage that an infant that has been conceived is deemed to have been born, it is easy to point out that this does not concern the fetus as such; it envisages an infant which has already come into the world and as to whom it is wished to make rights retroactive to the moment of conception. The infant that has been conceived should not be considered as born except when one of his rights is in question....

It may be added that no constitutional text presently in force explicitly guarantees protection to the child from the moment of conception or before birth.

* * *

The Constitutional Council did not have an easy task. Presented with a law which everyone knew originated from the Elysée Palace, which had been adopted by a majority well-informed by the opposition, and which had received extensive support from public opinion, the Council's role was not welcomed. According to the laws which govern it, the Council had to decide, after a simple comparison of texts, whether a law, important for the evolution of the mores, was or was not in conformity with the French Constitution or an international convention. A perilous mission. For, if an affirmative answer was certainly the easiest solution, it would still be necessary to provide appropriate reasoning for the decision. As for a negative response, it would without any doubt release very strong emotions and the cry would go out yet again, but with more strength, concerning "government by judges."

The Constitutional Council was wise in two ways: by refusing to give in to the "political temptation" and by resting its decision on the notion of individual liberties. However, it perhaps lacked boldness in its categorical refusal to extend its jurisdiction to the examination of the conformity of a law to the stipulations of an international treaty.

"Article 61 of the Constitution", the Constitutional Council observes in the first part of its opinion, "does not confer on the Constitutional Council a power of evaluation and decision identical to that of Parliament, but only gives it competence to rule on the conformity to the Constitution of laws submitted for its examination."

This first consideration is fundamental, because it foreshadows all the rest. The Constitutional Council wants to warn us unequivocally at the outset that it is not ready to accept a role which does not belong to it. It is not a second Parliament, nor a court of appeal for decisions taken by the legislature. It is not up to it to take a position on the merits, but simply, at the legal level, to watch over the observance by the law of constitutional rules within the limits and under the conditions fixed by the Constitution. It is a judge, not an arbitrator. A judge who announces the law, not a judge who "governs".

But does not the very specificity of the function of the Constitutional Council inevitably, although indirectly, involve the exercise of political control? For a Parliament, to lay down general rules in a given matter is obviously to make a political choice. For a body like the Constitutional Council, to assure the conformity of this choice to the Constitution is likewise to exercise power over an act which is above all political. As has been said, "the control of constitutionality, always exercised by reference to legal norms, remains inseparable from the affirmation of a certain political ethic."

Aware that its mission as constitutional judge is not quite the same as that of another judge, judicial or administrative, but wary of the dangers that it will encounter if it agrees to decide political questions, the Constitutional Council once again makes clear that it intends to be and to remain, above all, an institution "opposing its strictly defined competence as a judge to the discretionary power of Parliament." A similar motive led it to refuse to examine the conformity of the law to the stipulations of an international treaty.

* * *

It was, in effect, essentially in the name of liberty that the Council decided that the dispositions of the law relating to abortion submitted to it were in no way contrary to the Constitution. . . .

The Constitutional Council dealt with the basic problem in three "whereas" clauses.

1. It began by affirming that the law which was submitted to it respects the liberty of persons constrained to resort to or participate in an abortion and therefore does not abrogate Article II of the Declaration

of the Rights of Man and the Citizen which proclaims that liberty is a natural and inalienable right of man.

2. It continued by noting that the law accepts that the principle of respect for life of a human being can be interfered with only in case of necessity and only according to the conditions and limitations that it defines.

3. Finally, it declares that none of the derogations from this principle that are provided for by the law are contrary to any fundamental principle recognized by the laws of the Republic nor do they contravene the Preamble of the 1946 Constitution according to which the nation guarantees protection of health to children.

In sum, for the Council, the law relating to abortion is a law of liberty which does not fundamentally abrogate either the principle of respect for life or the protection of the health of the "child".... It gives liberty to the woman to deal with her own body and with what she carries within her until the end of the tenth week; liberty also to the woman to have or not to have an abortion ... liberty to the doctor who can ... refuse ... to participate in an abortion; liberty as well to the midwife, nurse, or medical assistants....

Because it is a law of liberty, it has to provide limits to the authorizations that it gives.... The law does not in any way recognize (as has too often been said) a right to abortion on demand, but only the possibility to have recourse to it in exceptional cases. Thus, the law could and did affirm in its first Article that it effectively guaranteed respect for every human being from the time of commencement of life, derogations from this principle only existing in cases of necessity (risk to the health of the mother, situations of distress).

What in the end will be the real scope of the decision of the Constitutional Council? ... It is obvious that in the absence of particularly serious reasons, such as violation of a constitutional norm, the Constitutional Council does not in any way envisage that it can simply declare unconstitutional a law which responds to the desires of the majority. By interpreting the constitutional texts in a liberal manner, it contributes to bringing the law into conformity with social reality and thus avoids putting itself deliberately in the uncomfortable and questionable situation of the United States Supreme Court at the time of the New Deal....

B. JUDICIAL REVIEW IN GERMANY

In Austria, Italy and Germany, constitutional courts were established after World War II as part of the judicial system. These constitutional courts are special separate institutions within the judiciary with their own jurisdiction and judges. In Germany, when a party raises a constitutional objection to a statute involved in any civil, criminal or administrative case, the court hearing the case will refer the question to the Constitutional Court for decision if it thinks that the statute is unconstitutional. When the decision of the Constitutional Court is issued, the original proceeding is resumed. In contrast to France, where the courts are not competent to sanction violations of individual constitutional rights, the German Constitutional Court also hears complaints filed by individuals aggrieved by unconstitutional official actions, provided they have first exhausted their other remedies. In addition, certain governmental agencies or officials can test the validity of a statute in the Constitutional Court even though the statute is not involved in an existing dispute. The decisions of the Constitutional Court, unlike those of ordinary courts, are binding on other courts in future litigation.

(1) The German Constitutional Court

ERNEST BENDA,[15] "CONSTITUTIONAL JURISDICTION IN WEST GERMANY"

19 Columbia Journal of Transnational Law 1–13 (1981).

I. INTRODUCTION

* * *

All the vast powers and competences of the Federal Constitutional Court or FCC ... find their secure foundation in the provisions of the Basic Law *(Grundgesetz)*....

The FCC has two chambers (senates), each composed of eight judges.[a] The senates are independent of each other; each senate acts as the FCC. There is no appeal to the plenum by the litigants. But if one senate, in deciding a legal question, disagrees with the opinion of the other senate the question has to be referred to the plenum of the Court. In spite of the character of the FCC as a "twin court" the uniformity of constitutional law can be maintained.

The FCC, apart from being a judicial organ, participates in the exercise of the supreme power of the State. The status of the FCC is not inferior to that of the Federal President, the Bundestag, the Bundesrat or the Federal Government. Or, as our former Federal President, Walter Scheel, once put it:

> Each of these constitutional organs is the highest representative of the State, seen from a certain point of view: the Bundestag, in as much as the State conceives itself as a parliamentary democracy; the Bundesrat, insofar as the Federal Republic considers itself as a federal State; the Federal Government, in as much as the State is a politically active unity; the FCC, in as much as the State under-

15. Former President of the Constitutional Court of the Federal Republic of Germany. This article is reprinted with the permission of the Columbia Journal of Transnational Law.

a. Three judges in each senate are elected from other high federal courts. The Federal Parliament *(Bundestag)* and the Federal Council *(Bundesrat)* each elect one half of the remaining judges. For more details, and a description of the politics of judicial selection, see D. Kommers, Judicial Politics in West Germany: A Study of the Federal Constitutional Court 113–44 (1976).

stands itself as a State governed by the rule of law, and the Federal President because he represents the whole State in all its functions and capacities.

II. THE COURT AS "SUPREME GUARDIAN OF THE CONSTITUTION"

To be the "Supreme Guardian of the Constitution" means duty and power for the FCC at the same time.

The powers of the FCC to fill this guardianship role are extensive. One may differentiate between four kinds of competences which signify at the same time the four major facets of constitutional jurisdiction in the Federal Republic.

A. Determination of the Hierarchy of Legal Norms

The first is the determination of the hierarchy of legal norms, at the top of which stands the Constitution followed by other federal law which is superior to state law including the state constitutions.

Concrete and abstract judicial review serve this purpose. The first may arise out of an ordinary litigation before any court. If a court considers unconstitutional a statute the validity of which is relevant to its forthcoming decision, the proceedings must be stayed and a decision sought from the FCC.

* * *

Concerning *abstract judicial review,* the FCC may, at the request of the Federal Government, of a Land Government, or of one-third of the Bundestag members, be seized in case of differences of opinion or doubts of the formal and material compatibility of federal law or state law with the constitution, or of the compatibility of Land law with other federal law.

As an example of abstract judicial review I would cite the case where nearly 200 deputies of the Bundestag belonging to the Christian Democratic Party contended the incompatibility of the Abortion Reform Act of 1974 with the Basic Law. Under the Act, termination of pregnancy was no longer punishable during the first 12 weeks after conception; destruction of the fetus was permissible after that period if warranted on medical and eugenic grounds prior to the twenty-second week of pregnancy. The situation was thus adverse to that of the United States where, at the time of the Supreme Court's decisions in *Wade* and *Bolton,* the majority of state abortion laws were restrictive in the sense of legalizing abortion only on medical grounds. In 1975, the FCC—after eight months of deliberations—invalidated the relevant provision of the Abortion Reform Act. The Court invoked Art. 2, paragraph 2 of the Basic Law which says: "Everyone shall have the right to life and to the inviolability of his person," which is, in the understanding of the Senate, a fundamental or objective value decision. Human life, the Court argued, begins no later than 13 days after conception and is a continuous process which cannot be divided sharply into various stages. The majority of the Senate confirmed the obligation of the State to protect the unborn life even by penal sanctions. The Court admitted that this requirement is directed in the first instance to the legislature; yet it is the Court's duty to examine whether the legislature has fulfilled this task. . . .

B. Protection of Federalism

The second facet of constitutional jurisdiction is the protection of federalism. . . .

C. Organstreit

The separation of powers is also ensured by another procedure, the so-called Organstreit, disputes between constitutional organs of the Federal Republic necessitating an interpretation of the Basic Law.

D. Protection of Human Rights

The fourth facet is the protection of human rights. The Basic Law has provided for this purpose a special instrument, the constitutional complaint. Any person who claims that one of his basic rights has been violated by public authority may file a complaint of unconstitutionality. As a rule, the FCC may be seized of such a matter only after all legal remedies have been exhausted.

Review of constitutional complaints forms the major part of the Court's activity. In recent years there have been 2500 to 3000 constitutional complaints yearly, of which less than two per cent have been successful. The numbers reflect the public's growing consciousness of human rights violations as well as their high esteem for and confidence in our Constitutional Court. Furthermore, one must take into account that the decisions of the Court on matters of constitutional complaints have an importance far exceeding the individual cases. They give signals to the Executive, the Legislature and the Judiciary and determine their future activities.

* * *

III. The Role of Constitutional Review in a Democratic Society

[T]he fundamental aspects of constitutional review are—from the point of view of legal policy—still under discussion. Some controversial judgements of the Court, like the abortion case, were echoed by adverse criticism in the public press tending to question the justification of constitutional review against the background of a democratic society. Should eight judges really have the power to declare null and void a law which was enacted by a democratically and directly elected parliament? Different countries and people have, in the course of time, answered this question differently. Today we are witness to an extension of the idea of constitutional jurisdiction. The new Spanish constitution of 1978 has provided for a strong constitutional jurisdiction clearly based on the German model with the competences I mentioned earlier on.

The fundamental decision of our "founding fathers" in favor of a constitutional jurisdiction may well be explained by our historical experience. The Basic Law tried to avoid past faults and to learn not only

from history—if ever possible—but from our own constitutional history.... It did so secondly by creating a strong constitutional jurisdiction
to defend the constitutional order. In modern parliamentary systems
the majority of parliament generally supports the government and is no
counter-part, not an instrument of control. The controlling function is
exercised by the opposition, but this is the political minority. The
constitutional jurisdiction should not play the role of the opposition, but
in a very specific way its duty is to protect the minority. From this
point of view, the criticism that the constitutional courts are a non-
democratic power will carry no conviction as long as the majority of
today must be prepared to be the minority of tomorrow; so, in the long
run, the majority, too, is dependent upon the protection of the constitutional courts.

(2) The German Abortion Decisions

CONSTITUTIONAL COURT OF THE FEDERAL
REPUBLIC OF GERMANY, DECISION OF
FEBRUARY 25, 1975

[1975] BVerfGE 1 (Jonas and Gorby translation)
9 John Marshall Journal of Practice and Procedure 605–84 (1976) (abridged).*

[A West German statute, adopted in 1974 to liberalize abortion law,
provided that abortions performed by a physician prior to the thirteenth
week of pregnancy were not punishable by the criminal law (Fifth
Statute to Reform the Penal Law § 218a), and that abortions could be
performed legally after the twelfth week if there was certification of
grave danger to the life or health of the pregnant woman, or danger of
irreversible damage to the unborn child (§ 218b). In all cases, the
pregnant woman was required to have counselling before undergoing an
abortion (§ 218c). The governments of five West German *Länder* and
193 members of the *Bundestag* petitioned the Constitutional Court to
rule on the constitutionality of this law. Article 2 of the Basic Law of
the Federal Republic of Germany provides:

   (1) Everyone shall have the right to the free development of his
   personality insofar as he does not violate the rights of others or
   offend against the constitutional order or the moral code.

   (2) Everyone shall have the right to life and to inviolability of
   his person. The liberty of the individual shall be inviolable. These
   rights may only be encroached upon pursuant to law.]

[OPINION OF THE COURT]:

* * *

The question of the legal treatment of the interruption of pregnancy
has been discussed publicly for decades from various points of view. In

* Reprinted with the permission of the
John Marshall Journal of Practice and Procedure.

fact, this phenomenon of social life raises manifold problems of a biological, especially human-genetic, anthropological, medical, psychological, social, social-political, and not least of an ethical and moral-theological nature, which touch upon the fundamental questions of human existence. It is the task of the legislature to evaluate the many sided and often opposing arguments which develop from these various ways of viewing the question, to supplement them through considerations which are specifically legal and political as well as through the practical experiences of the life of the law, and, on this basis, to arrive at a decision as to the manner in which the legal order should respond to this social process. The statutory regulation in the Fifth Statute to Reform the Penal Law which was decided upon after extraordinarily comprehensive preparatory work can be examined by the Constitutional Court only from the viewpoint of whether it is compatible with the Basic Law, which is the highest valid law in the Federal Republic. The gravity and the seriousness of the constitutional question posed becomes clear, if it is considered that what is involved here is the protection of human life, one of the central values of every legal order. The decision regarding the standards and limits of legislative freedom of decision demands a total view of the constitutional norms and the hierarchy of values contained therein.

I.

1. Article 2, Paragraph 2, Sentence 1, of the Basic Law also protects the life developing itself in the womb of the mother as an intrinsic legal value.

a) The express incorporation into the Basic Law of the self-evident right to life—in contrast to the Weimar Constitution—may be explained principally as a reaction to the "destruction of life unworthy of life," to the "final solution" and "liquidations," which were carried out by the National Socialistic Regime as measures of state. Article 2, Paragraph 2, Sentence 1, of the Basic Law, just as it contains the abolition of the death penalty in Article 102, includes "a declaration of the fundamental worth of human life and of a concept of the state which stands in emphatic contrast to the philosophies of a political regime to which the individual life meant little and which therefore practiced limitless abuse with its presumed right over life and death of the citizen"....

b) In construing Article 2, Paragraph 2, Sentence 1, of the Basic Law, one should begin with its language: "Everyone shall have the right to life ...". Life, in the sense of historical existence of a human individual, exists according to definite biological-physiological knowledge, in any case, from the 14th day after conception (nidation, individuation).... The process of development which has begun at that point is a continuing process which exhibits no sharp demarcation and does not allow a precise division of the various steps of development of the human life. The process does not end even with birth; the phenomena of consciousness which are specific to the human personality, for example, appear for the first time a rather long time after birth. Therefore, the protection of Article 2, Paragraph 2, Sentence 1, of the Basic Law cannot be limited either to the "completed" human being after birth or to the child about to be born which is independently capable of living. The right to life is guaranteed to everyone who "lives"; no distinction can be made here between various stages of the life developing itself before birth, or between unborn and born life. "Everyone" in the sense of Article 2, Paragraph 2, Sentence 1, of the Basic Law is "everyone living"; expressed in another way: every life possessing human individuality; "everyone" also includes the yet unborn human being.

c) In opposition to the objection that "everyone" commonly denotes, both in everyday language as well as in legal language, a "completed" person and that a strict interpretation of the language speaks therefore against the inclusion of the unborn life within the effective area of Article 2, Paragraph 2, Sentence 1, of the Basic Law, it should be emphasized that, in any case, the sense and purpose of this provision of the Basic Law require that the protection of life should also be extended to the life developing itself. The security of human existence against encroachments by the state would be incomplete if it did not also embrace the prior step of "completed life," unborn life.

This extensive interpretation corresponds to the principle established in the opinions of the Federal Constitutional Court, "according to which, in doubtful cases, that interpretation is to be selected which develops to the highest degree the judicial effectiveness of the fundamental legal norm"....

d) In support of this result the legislative history of Article 2, Paragraph 2, Sentence 1, of the Basic Law may be adduced here....

The history of the origin of Article 2, Paragraph 2, Sentence 1, of the Basic Law suggests that the formulation "everyone shall have the right to life" should also include "germinating" life. In any case, even less can be concluded from the materials on behalf of the contrary point of view. On the other hand, no evidence is found in the legislative history for answering the question whether unborn life must be protected by the penal law.

* * *

II.

1. The duty of the state to protect is comprehensive. It forbids not only—self-evidently—direct state attacks on the life developing itself but also requires the state to take a position protecting and promoting this life, that is to say, it must, above all, preserve it even against illegal attacks by others. It is for the individual areas of the legal order, each according to its special function, to effectuate this requirement. The degree of seriousness with which the state must take its obligation to protect increases as the rank of the legal value in question increases in importance within the order of values of the Basic Law. Human life represents, within the order of the Basic Law, an ultimate value, the

particulars of which need not be established; it is the living foundation of human dignity and the prerequisite for all other fundamental rights.

2. The obligation of the state to take the life developing itself under protection exists, as a matter of principle, even against the mother. Without doubt, the natural connection of unborn life with that of the mother establishes an especially unique relationship, for which there is no parallel in other circumstances of life. Pregnancy belongs to the sphere of intimacy of the woman, the protection of which is constitutionally guaranteed through Article 2, Paragraph 1, in connection with Article 1, Paragraph 1, of the Basic Law. Were the embryo to be considered only as a part of the maternal organism the interruption of pregnancy would remain in the area of the private structuring of one's life, where the legislature is forbidden to encroach.... Since, however, the one about to be born is an independent human being who stands under the protection of the constitution, there is a social dimension to the interruption of pregnancy which makes it amenable to and in need of regulation by the state. The right of the woman to the free development of her personality, which has as its content the freedom of behavior in a comprehensive sense and accordingly embraces the personal responsibility of the woman to decide against parenthood and the responsibilities flowing from it, can also, it is true, likewise demand recognition and protection. This right, however, is not guaranteed without limits—the rights of others, the constitutional order, and the moral law limit it. *A priori,* this right can never include the authorization to intrude upon the protected sphere of right of another without justifying reason or much less to destroy that sphere along with the life itself; this is even less so, if, according to the nature of the case, a special responsibility exists precisely for this life.

A compromise which guarantees the protection of the life of the one about to be born and permits the pregnant woman the freedom of abortion is not possible since the interruption of pregnancy always means the destruction of the unborn life. In the required balancing, "both constitutional values are to be viewed in their relationship to human dignity, the center of the value system of the constitution".... A decision oriented to Article 1, Paragraph 1, of the Basic Law must come down in favor of the precedence of the protection of life for the child *en ventre sa mere* over the right of the pregnant woman to self-determination. Regarding many opportunities for development of personality, she can be adversely affected through pregnancy, birth and the education of her children. On the other hand, the unborn life is destroyed through the interruption of pregnancy. According to the principle of the balance which preserves most of competing constitutionally protected positions in view of the fundamental idea of Article 19, Paragraph 2, of the Basic Law; precedence must be given to the protection of the life of the child about to be born. This precedence exists as a matter of principle for the entire duration of pregnancy and may not be placed in question for any particular time. The opinion expressed in the Federal Parliament during the third deliberation on the

Statute to Reform the Penal Law, the effect of which is to propose the precedence for a particular time "of the right to self-determination of the woman which flows from human dignity vis-a-vis all others, including the child's right to life" ... is not reconcilable with the value ordering of the Basic Law.

3. From this point, the fundamental attitude of the legal order which is required by the constitution with regard to the interruption of pregnancy becomes clear: the legal order may not make the woman's right to self-determination the sole guideline of its rulemaking. The state must proceed, as a matter of principle, from a duty to carry the pregnancy to term and therefore to view, as a matter of principle, its interruption as an injustice. The condemnation of abortion must be clearly expressed in the legal order. The false impression must be avoided that the interruption of pregnancy is the same social process as, for example, approaching a physician for healing an illness or indeed a legally irrelevant alternative for the prevention of conception. The state may not abdicate its responsibility even through the recognition of a "legally free area," by which the state abstains from the value judgment and abandons this judgment to the decision of the individual to be made on the basis of his own sense of responsibility.

III.

How the state fulfills its obligation for an effective protection of developing life is, in the first instance, to be decided by the legislature. It determines which measures of protection are required and which serve the purpose of guaranteeing an effective protection of life.

1. ... It is ... the task of the state to employ, in the first instance, social, political, and welfare means for securing developing life. What can happen here and how the assistance measures are to be structured in their particulars is largely left to the legislature and is generally beyond judgment by the Constitutional Court.

2. The question of the extent to which the state is obligated under the constitution to employ, even for the protection of unborn life, the penal law, the sharpest weapon standing at its disposal, cannot be answered by the simplified posing of the question whether the state must punish certain acts. A total consideration is necessary which, on the one hand, takes into account the worth of the injured legal value and the extent of the social harm of the injurious act—in comparison with other acts which socio-ethically are perhaps similarly assessed and which are subject to punishment—and which, on the other hand, takes into account the traditional legal regulation of this area of life as well as the development of concepts of the role of the penal law in modern society; and, finally, does not leave out of consideration the practical effectiveness of penal sanctions and the possibility of their replacement through other legal sanctions.

The legislature is not obligated, as a matter of principle, to employ the same penal measures for the protection of the unborn life as it considers required and expedient for born life....

a) The task of penal law from the beginning has been to protect the elementary values of community life.... From this point of view, the employment of penal law for the requital of "acts of abortion" is to be seen as legitimate without a doubt; it is valid law in most cultural states—under prerequisites of various kinds and especially corresponds to the German legal tradition. Therefore, it follows that the law cannot dispense with clearly labeling this procedure as "unjust."

b) Punishment, however, can never be an end in itself. Its employment is in principle subject to the decision of the legislature. The legislature is not prohibited, in consideration of the points of view set out above, from expressing the legal condemnation of abortion required by the Basic Law in ways other than the threat of punishment. The decisive factor is whether the totality of the measures serving the protection of the unborn life, whether they be in civil law or in public law, especially of a social-legal or of a penal nature, guarantees an actual protection corresponding to the importance of the legal value to be secured. In the extreme case, namely, if the protection required by the constitution can be achieved in no other way, the lawgiver can be obligated to employ the means of the penal law for the protection of developing life. The penal norm represents, to a certain extent, the "ultimate reason" in the armory of the legislature. According to the principle of proportionality, a principle of the just state, which prevails for the whole of the public law, including constitutional law, the legislature may make use of this means only cautiously and with restraint. However, this final means must also be employed, if an effective protection of life cannot be achieved in other ways. The worth and the importance of the legal value to be protected demand this. It is not a question of an "absolute" duty to punish but rather one of a "relative" duty to use the penal sanctions, which grows out of the insight into the inadequacy of all other means.

* * *

3. The obligation of the state to protect the developing life exists— as shown—against the mother as well. Here, however, the employment of the penal law may give rise to special problems which result from the unique situation of the pregnant woman. The incisive effects of a pregnancy on the physical and emotional condition of the woman are immediately evident and need not be set forth in greater detail. They often mean a considerable change of the total conduct of life and a limitation of the possibilities for personal development. This burden is not always and not completely balanced by a woman finding new fulfillment in her task as mother and by the claim a pregnant woman has upon the assistance of the community (Article 6, Paragraph 4, of the Basic Law). In individual cases, difficult, even life-threatening situations of conflict may arise. The right to life of the unborn can lead to a burdening of the woman which essentially goes beyond that normally associated with pregnancy. The result is the question of exactability, or, in other words, the question of whether the state, even in such cases,

may compel the bearing of the child to term with the means of the penal law. Respect for the unborn life and the right of the woman not to be compelled to sacrifice the values in her own life in excess of an exactable measure in the interest of respecting this legal value are in conflict with each other. In such a situation of conflict which, in general, does not allow an unequivocal moral judgment and in which the decision for an interruption of pregnancy can attain the rank of a decision of conscience worthy of consideration, the legislature is obligated to exercise special restraint. If, in these cases, it views the conduct of the pregnant woman as not deserving punishment and forgoes the use of penal sanctions, the result, at any rate, is to be constitutionally accepted as a balancing incumbent upon the legislature.

In determining the content of the criterion of non-exactability, circumstances, however, must be excluded which do not seriously burden the obligated party, since they represent the normal situation with which everyone must cope. Rather, circumstances of considerable weight must be present which render the fulfillment of the duty of the one affected extraordinarily more difficult, so that fulfillment cannot be expected from him in fairness. These circumstances are especially present if the one affected by fulfilling the duty is thrown into serious inner conflicts. The solution of such conflicts by criminal penalty does not appear in general to be appropriate ... since it applies external compulsion where respect for the sphere of personality of the human being demands full inner freedom of decision.

A continuation of the pregnancy appears to be non-exactable especially when it is proven that the interruption is required "to avert" from the pregnant woman "a danger for her life or the danger of a grave impairment of her condition of health".... In this case her own "right to life and bodily inviolability" (Article 2, Paragraph 2, Sentence 1, of the Basic Law) is at stake, the sacrifice of which cannot be expected of her for the unborn life. Beyond that, the legislature has a free hand to leave the interruption of pregnancy free of punishment in the case of other extraordinary burdens for the pregnant woman, which, from the point of view of non-exactability, are as weighty as those referred to in § 218b, No. 1. In this category can be counted, especially, the cases of the eugenic (cf. Section 218b, No. 2, of the Penal Code), ethical (criminological), and of the social or emergency indication for abortion which were contained in the draft proposed by the Federal Government in the sixth election period of the Federal Parliament and were discussed both in the public debate as well as in the course of the legislative proceedings.... The decisive viewpoint is that in all of these cases another interest equally worthy of protection, from the standpoint of the constitution, asserts its validity with such urgency that the state's legal order cannot require that the pregnant woman must, under all circumstances, concede precedence to the right of the unborn.

Also, the indication arising from general emergency (social indication) can be integrated here. Finally, the general social situation of the pregnant woman and her family can produce conflicts of such difficulty that, beyond a definite measure, a sacrifice by the pregnant woman in favor of the unborn life cannot be compelled with the means of the penal law. In regulating this case, the legislature must so formulate the elements of the indication which is to remain free of punishment that the gravity of the social conflict presupposed will be clearly recognizable and, considered from the point of view of non-exactability, the congruence of this indication with the other cases of indication remains guaranteed. If the legislature removes genuine cases of conflict of this kind from the protection of the penal law, it does not violate its duty to protect life. Even in these cases the state may not be content merely to examine, and if the occasion arises, to certify that the statutory prerequisites for an abortion free of punishment are present. Rather, the state will also be expected to offer counseling and assistance with the goal of reminding pregnant women of the fundamental duty to respect the right to life of the unborn, to encourage her to continue the pregnancy and—especially in cases of social need—to support her through practical measures of assistance.

In all other cases the interruption of pregnancy remains a wrong deserving punishment since, in these cases, the destruction of a value of the law of the highest rank is subjected to the unrestricted pleasure of another and is not motivated by an emergency. If the legislature wants to dispense (even in this case) with penal law punishment, this would be compatible with the requirement to protect of Article 2, Paragraph 2, Sentence 1, of the Basic Law, only on the condition that another equally effective legal sanction stands at its command which would clearly bring out the unjust character of the act (the condemnation by the legal order) and likewise prevent the interruptions of pregnancy as effectively as a penal provision.

D.

If the challenged regulation of terms of the Fifth Statute to Reform the Penal Law is examined according to these standards, the result is that the statute does not do justice, to the extent required, to the obligation to protect developing life effectively which is derived from Article 2, Paragraph 2, Sentence 1, in conjunction with Article 1, Paragraph 1, of the Basic Law.

I.

The constitutional requirement to protect developing life is directed in the first instance to the legislature. The duty is incumbent on the Federal Constitutional Court, however, to determine, in the exercise of the function allotted to it by the Basic Law, whether the legislature has fulfilled this requirement. Indeed, the Court must carefully observe the discretion of the legislature which belongs to it in evaluating the factual conditions which lie at the basis of its formation of norms, which discretion is fitting for the required prognosis and choice of means. The court may not put itself in the place of the legislature; it is, however, its task to examine carefully whether the legislature, in the framework of the possibilities standing at its disposal, has done what is necessary to

avert dangers from the legal value to be protected. This is also fundamentally true for the question whether the legislature is obligated to
utilize its sharpest means, the penal law, in which case the examination
can extend beyond the individual modalities of punishment.

II.

It is generally recognized that the previous § 218 of the Penal Code,
precisely because it threatened punishment without distinction for nearly all cases of the interruption of pregnancy, has, as a result, only
insufficiently protected developing life. The insight that there are cases
in which the penal sanction is not appropriate has finally led to the point
that cases actually deserving of punishment are no longer prosecuted
with the necessary vigor. In addition, with respect to this offense, there
is, in the nature of the case, the frequently difficult clarification of the
factual situation. Certainly, the statistics on the incidence of illegal
abortion differ greatly and it may hardly be possible to ascertain reliable
data on this point through empirical investigations. In any case, the
number of the illegal interruptions of pregnancy in the Federal Republic
was high. The existence of a general penal norm may have contributed
to that, since the state had neglected to employ other adequate measures
for the protection of developing life.

... The statute is based upon the idea that developing life would be
better protected through individual counseling of the pregnant woman
than through a threat of punishment, which would remove the one
determined upon the abortion from every possible means of influence,
which from a criminological point of view would be mistaken and, in
addition, has proven itself without effect. On this basis the legislature
has reached the decision to abandon the criminal penalty entirely for the
first twelve weeks of pregnancy under definite prerequisites and, in its
place, to introduce the preventive counseling and instruction....

It is constitutionally permissible and to be approved if the legislature attempts to fulfill its duty to improve protection of unborn life
through preventive measures, including counseling to strengthen the
personal responsibility of the woman. The regulation in question,
however, encounters decisive constitutional problems in several respects.

1. The legal condemnation of the interruption of pregnancy required by the constitution must clearly appear in the legal order existing
under the constitution. Therefore, as shown, only those cases can be
excepted in which the continuation of the pregnancy is not exactable
from the woman in consideration of the value decision made in Article 2,
Paragraph 2, Sentence 1, of the Basic Law. This absolute condemnation
is not expressed in the provisions of the Fifth Statute to Reform the
Penal Law with regard to the interruption of pregnancy during the first
twelve weeks because the statute leaves unclear whether an interruption
of pregnancy which is not "indicated" is legal or illegal after the repeal
of the criminal penalty through § 218a of the Penal Code.... The
proposed regulation, as a whole, can therefore only be interpreted to
mean that an interruption of pregnancy performed by a physician in the

first twelve weeks of pregnancy is not illegal and therefore should be allowed (under law).

2. A formal statutory condemnation of the interruption of pregnancy would, furthermore, not suffice because the woman determined upon abortion would disregard it.... There are many women who have previously decided upon an interruption of pregnancy without having a reason which is worthy of esteem within the value order of the constitution and who are not accessible to a counseling such as § 218c, Par. 1, proposes. These women find themselves neither in material distress nor in a grave situation of emotional conflict. They decline pregnancy because they are not willing to take on the renunciation and the natural motherly duties bound up with it. They have serious reasons for their conduct with respect to the developing life; there are, however, no reasons which can endure against the command to protect human life. For these women, pregnancy is exactable in line with the principles reiterated above....

The objection against this is that women not subject to influence understand best from experience how to avoid punishment so that the penal sanction is often ineffective.... At the same time, according to this objection, the threat of punishment, by discouraging counseling of women susceptible of influence, impedes saving life in other cases because it is precisely women in whose cases the prerequisites of an indication are absent and, beyond that, also those who do not trust the result of a procedure to determine an indication who will, in the face of the penal threat, carefully keep the pregnancy secret and who to a large extent withdraw themselves from helpful influence available through counseling centers and surroundings. On the basis of such an analysis, there could not be a defense of unborn life which was free of gaps. The legislature, so this objection continues, would have no other choice than to weigh off life against life, namely the life which through a definite regulation of the abortion question could probably be saved against the life which would probably be sacrificed on account of the same regulation, since the penal sanction would not only protect but at the same time destroy unborn life....

a) To begin with, this concept does not do justice to the essence and the function of the penal law. The penal norm directs itself fundamentally to all subjects of the law and obligates them in like manner. It is true that public prosecutors practically never succeed in administering punishment to all those who have broken the penal law. The unknown incidence is variously high for the various offenses. It is uncontested that the unknown incidence of acts of abortion is especially high. On the other hand, the general preventive function of the penal law ought not be forgotten. If one views as the task of the penal law the protection of especially important legal values and elementary values of the community, a great importance accrues to its function. Just as important as the observable reaction in an individual case is the long range effect of a penal norm which in its principal normative content ("abortion is punishable") has existed for a very long time. No doubt, the mere existence of such a penal sanction has influence on the conceptions of value and the manner of behavior of the populace.... If the threat of punishment disappears in its entirety, the impression will arise of necessity in the consciousness of the citizens of the state that in all cases the interruption of pregnancy is legally allowed and, therefore, even from a socio-ethical point of view, is no longer to be condemned....

b) The weighing in bulk of life against life which leads to the allowance of the destruction of a supposedly smaller number in the interest of the preservation of an allegedly larger number is not reconcilable with the obligation of an individual protection of each single concrete life.

In the judicial opinions of the Federal Constitutional Court the principle has been developed that the unconstitutionality of a statutory provision, which in its structure and actual effect prejudices a definite circle of persons, may not be refuted with the showing that this provision or other regulations of the statute favor another circle of persons. The emphasis of the general tendency of the statute as a whole to favor legal protection is even less adequate for this purpose....

c) A dependable factual foundation is lacking for "a total accounting"—which is to be rejected on principle. A sufficient basis is lacking for the conclusion that the number of interruptions of pregnancy in the future will be significantly less than with the previous statutory regulation....

3. The counseling and instruction of the pregnant woman provided under § 218c, Par. 1, of the Penal Code cannot, considered by itself, be viewed as suitable to effectuate a continuation of the pregnancy.

The measures proposed in this provision fall short of the concepts of the Alternative Draft of the 16 criminal law scholars, upon which the conception of the Fifth Statute to Reform the Penal Law is, after all, largely based. The counseling centers provided for in [the law] should themselves have the means to afford financial, social, and family assistance. Furthermore, they should provide to the pregnant woman and her relatives emotional care through suitable co-workers and work intensively for the continuation of the pregnancy....

On the other hand, the counseling centers will give instruction about "the public and private assistance available for pregnant women, mothers, and children," "especially regarding assistance which facilitates the continuation of the pregnancy and alleviates the situation of mother and child." This could be interpreted to mean that the counseling centers should only inform, without exerting influence directed to the motivational process.... If a protective effect in favor of developing life is to accrue to the counseling, it will depend, in any case, decisively upon such an exertion of influence.... Furthermore, the prospects for success are poor since the interruption of pregnancy can immediately follow the instruction and counseling. A serious exchange with the pregnant woman and others involved in which the arguments in the counseling are contrasted with hers is not to be expected under these circumstances.... For the woman decided upon an interruption of pregnancy it is only necessary to find an obliging physician. Since he may undertake the social as well as the medical counseling and finally even carry out the operation, a serious attempt to dissuade the pregnant woman from her decision is not to be expected from him.

III.

In summary, the following observations should be made on the constitutional adjudication of the regulation of terms encountered in the Fifth Statute to Reform the Penal Law:

That interruptions of pregnancy are neither legally condemned nor subject to punishment is not compatible with the duty incumbent upon the legislature to protect life, if the interruptions are the result of reasons which are not recognized in the value order of the Basic Law. Indeed, the limiting of punishability would not be constitutionally objectionable if it were combined with other measures which would be able to compensate, at least in their effect, for the disappearance of penal protection. That is however—as shown—obviously not the case. The parliamentary discussions about the reform of the abortion law have indeed deepened the insight that it is the principal task of the state to prevent the killing of unborn life through enlightenment about the prevention of pregnancy on the one hand as well as through effective promotional measures in society and through a general alteration of social concepts on the other. Neither the assistance of the kind presently offered and guaranteed nor the counseling provided in the Fifth Statute to Reform the Penal Law are, however, able to replace the individual protection of life which a penal norm fundamentally provides even today in those cases in which no reason for the interruption of pregnancy exists which is worthy of consideration according to the value order of the Basic Law.

If the legislature regards the previously undifferentiated threat of punishment for the interruption of pregnancy as a questionable means for the protection of life, it is not thereby released from the obligation to undertake the attempt to achieve a better protection of life through a differentiated penal regulation by subjecting the same cases to punishment in which the interruption of pregnancy is to be condemned on constitutional grounds. A clear distinction of this group of cases in contrast to other cases in which the continuation of the pregnancy is not exactable from the woman will strengthen the power of the penal norm to develop a legal awareness. He who generally recognizes the precedence of the protection of life over the claim of the woman for an unrestricted structuring of her life will not be able to dispute the unjust nature of the act in those cases not covered by a particular indication. If the state not only declares that these cases are punishable but also prosecutes and punishes them in legal practice, this will be perceived in the legal consciousness of the community neither as unjust nor as anti-social.

The passionate discussion of the abortion problematic may provide occasion for the fear that in a segment of the population the value of unborn life is no longer fully recognized. This, however, does not give the legislature a right to acquiesce. It rather must make a sincere effort through a differentiation of the penal sanction to achieve a more effective protection of life and formulate a regulation which will be supported by the general legal consciousness.

IV.

The regulation encountered in the Fifth Statute to Reform the Penal Law at times is defended with the argument that in other democratic countries of the Western World in recent times the penal provisions regulating the interruption of pregnancy have been "liberalized" or "modernized" in a similar or an even more extensive fashion; this would be, as the argument goes, an indication that the new regulation corresponds, in any case, to the general development of theories in this area and is not inconsistent with fundamental socio-ethical and legal principles.

These considerations cannot influence the decision to be made here. Disregarding the fact that all of these foreign laws in their respective countries are sharply controverted, the legal standards which are applicable there for the acts of the legislature are essentially different from those of the Federal Republic of Germany.

Underlying the Basic Law are principles for the structuring of the state that may be understood only in light of the historical experience and the spiritual-moral confrontation with the previous system of National Socialism. In opposition to the omnipotence of the totalitarian state which claimed for itself limitless dominion over all areas of social life and to which, in the prosecution of its goals of state, consideration for the life of the individual fundamentally meant nothing, the Basic Law of the Federal Republic of Germany has erected an order bound together by values which places the individual human being and his dignity at the focal point of all of its ordinances. At its basis lies the concept, as the Federal Constitutional Court previously pronounced (Decisions of the Federal Constitutional Court, 2, 1 12), that human beings possess an inherent worth as individuals in order of creation which uncompromisingly demands unconditional respect for the life of every individual human being, even for the apparently socially "worthless," and which therefore excludes the destruction of such life without legally justifiable grounds. This fundamental constitutional decision determines the structure and the interpretation of the entire legal order. Even the legislature is bound by it; considerations of socio-political expediency, even necessities of state, cannot overcome this constitutional limitation (Decisions of the Federal Constitutional Court, 1, 14 36). Even a general change of the viewpoints dominant in the populace on this subject—if such a change could be established at all—would change nothing. The Federal Constitutional Court, which is charged by the constitution with overseeing the observance of its fundamental principles by all organs of the state and, if necessary, with giving them effect, can orient its decisions only on those principles to the development of which this Court has decisively contributed in its judicial utterances. Therefore, no adverse judgment is being passed about other legal orders "which have not had these experiences with a system of injustice and which, on the basis of an historical development which has taken a different course and other political conditions and fundamental views of the philosophy of state, have not made such a decision for themselves".…

E.

On the basis of these considerations, § 218a of the Penal Code in the version of the Fifth Statute to Reform the Penal Law is inconsistent with Article 2, Paragraph 2, Sentence 1, in conjunction with Article 1, Paragraph 1, of the Basic Law to the extent that it excepts interruption of pregnancy from punishability if no reasons are present which, according to the present opinion, have standing under the ordering of values of the Basic Law.…

DISSENTING OPINION

The life of each individual human being is self-evidently a central value of the legal order. It is uncontested that the constitutional duty to protect this life also includes its preliminary stages before birth. The debates in Parliament and before the Federal Constitutional Court dealt not with the *whether* but rather only the *how* of this protection. This decision is a matter of legislative responsibility. Under no circumstances can the duty of the state to prescribe punishment for abortion in every stage of pregnancy be derived from the constitution. The legislature should be able to determine the regulations for counseling and the term solution as well as for the indications solution.

A contrary construction of the constitution is not compatible with the liberal character of the fundamental legal norms and shifts the competence to decide, to a material extent, onto the Federal Constitutional Court.… Because each solution remains patchwork, it is not constitutionally objectionable that the German legislature—in consonance with the reforms in other western civilized states … has given priority to social-political measures over largely ineffective penal sanctions.… The constitution nowhere requires a legal "condemnation" of behavior not morally respectable without consideration of its actual protective effect.…

A.–I.

The authority of the Federal Constitutional Court to annul the decisions of the legislature demands sparing use, if an imbalance between the constitutional organs is to be avoided. The requirement of judicial self-restraint, which is designated as the "elixir of life" of the jurisprudence of the Federal Constitutional Court, is especially valid when involved is not a defense from overreaching by state power but rather the making, via constitutional judicial control, of provisions for the positive structuring of the social order for the legislature which is directly legitimized by the people. The Federal Constitutional Court must not succumb to the temptation to take over for itself the function of a controlling organ and shall not in the long run endanger the authority to judicially review constitutionality.

1.   The test proposed in this proceeding departs from the basis of classical judicial control. The fundamental legal norms standing in the central part of our constitution guarantee as rights of defense to the citizen in relation to the state a sphere of unrestricted structuring of one's life based on personal responsibility. The classical function of the Federal Constitutional Court lies in defending against injuries to this sphere of freedom from excessive infringement by the state power....

In the present constitutional dispute, the inverse question is presented for the first time for examination, namely whether the state *must* punish, whether the abolition of punishment for the interruption of pregnancy in the first three months of pregnancy is compatible with fundamental rights. It is obvious, however, that the disregard of punishment is the opposite of state encroachment....

2.   ... As defense rights the fundamental rights have a comparatively clear recognizable content.... On the other hand, it is regularly a most complex question, *how* a value decision is to be realized through affirmative measures of the legislature.... The decision, which frequently presupposes compromises and takes place in the course of trial and error, belongs, according to the principle of division of powers and to the democratic principle, to the responsibility of the legislature directly legitimized by the people.

Certainly, because of the growing importance of promoting social measures to effectuate fundamental rights even in this area, every judicial control of constitutionality cannot be renounced; the development of a suitable instrument which respects the freedom of the legislature to structure will probably be among the main tasks of judicial decision making in the next decades. As long as such an instrument is lacking, the danger exists that judicial control of constitutionality will not limit itself to reviewing decisions of the legislature but rather will substitute another decision which the Court determines to be better. This danger will exist in a heightened degree, when—as here—in sharply controversial questions a decision made by the parliamentary majority after long debate is challenged before the Federal Constitutional Court by the defeated minority. Without prejudice to the legitimate authority of those entitled to petition the Court to resolve constitutional doubt in this manner, the Federal Constitutional Court is unwarily falling in this case into the position of a political arbitration board to be used for the choice between competing legislative projects.

The idea of objective value decisions should however not become a vehicle to shift specifically legislative functions in the formation of social order onto the Federal Constitutional Court. Otherwise the Court will be forced into a role for which it is neither competent nor equipped....

This Court should confront the legislature only when the latter has completely disregarded a value decision or when the nature and manner of its realization is obviously faulty. On the other hand, in spite of supposed acknowledgment of legislative freedom to structure, the majority effectively charges the legislature with not realizing a recognized value decision in, according to the majority's view, the best manner possible. Should this become the general standard for judicial examination, the requirement of judicial self-restraint would accordingly be sacrificed.

II.

1. ... Quite obviously the constitution presupposes that the state can also resort to its power to punish to protect an orderly social life; the thrust of fundamental rights, however, does not go to the promotion of such a utilization but rather to the drawing of its boundaries. In this way the Supreme Court of the United States has even regarded punishment for the interruption of pregnancy, performed by a physician with the consent of the pregnant woman in the first third of pregnancy, as a violation of fundamental rights. This would, according to German constitutional law, go too far indeed. According to the liberal character of our constitution, however, the legislature needs a constitutional justification to punish, not to disregard punishment....

2. Even the *history of the origins* of the Basic Law speaks against deriving a duty to punish from norms of fundamental rights.... [T]he decisive renunciation completed with the Basic Law of the totalitarian National Socialist state demands rather the reverse conclusion, that is, restraint in employing criminal punishment, the improper use of which in the history of mankind has caused endless suffering.

B.

Even if one, contrary to our position, agrees with the majority that a constitutional duty to punish is conceivable, no constitutional violation can be charged to the legislature. Although it is not necessary to go into every detail, the majority reasoning encounters the following objections:

I.

1. ... In its adjudication of the factual basis and the effectiveness of the intended measures, the Court must accept as a basis the view of the legislature so long as it has not been refuted as obviously erroneous....

The reasoning of the judgment does not satisfy these requirements. It is repeatedly entangled with contradictions and in the end directly shifts the burden of proof: the legislature shall be allowed to forgo penal sanction, only when it is established without doubt that the milder measures favored by it to fulfill the duty of protection are "at least" equally effective or more effective....

According to the *view of the undersigned Madame Justice,* the refusal of the pregnant woman to permit the child *en ventre sa mere* to become a human being is something essentially different from the killing of independently existing life, not only according to the natural sensitivities of the woman but also legally. For this reason the equating in principle of abortion in the first stage of pregnancy with murder or intentional killing is not allowable from the outset. Firstly, it is mistaken, if not irrelevant, to relate the term solution to euthanasia or even the "killing of unworthy life" in order to distinguish it therefrom, as has occurred in the public discussion. The fact that an independently existing living being separable from the maternal organism first exists after a lengthy process of development rather suggests or at least permits with regard to legal judgment consideration of lines of demarcation based on time, which correspond to this development. . . .

The *undersigned Justice [Simon]* is inclined from a legal standpoint to attribute less significance to these further considerations about the relationship between the pregnant woman and her child *en ventre sa mere*. If however the repeal of the penal sanction during the first three months of pregnancy is not constitutionally objectionable on other grounds—those already mentioned or to be discussed later—then the legislature does not in any case act in ignorance when it takes account in its regulation of the circumstances mentioned.

2. The examination whether, despite the aforementioned special circumstances, a duty to punish in order to protect unborn life is to be required as *ultima ratio* must proceed from the *social problem,* which provided the occasion for the legislature to pass this regulation. . . .

. . . [T]he legislature cannot be indifferent to the fact that illegal interruptions of pregnancy lead even today to injuries of health; and this is true not only in the case of abortions by "quacks" and "angel-makers," but also, to a greater extent, in the case of procedures undertaken by physicians because illegality discourages the full use of modern equipment and assistance of the required personnel or hinders the necessary follow-up treatment. Further, the commercial exploitation of women inclined to an abortion in Germany and in foreign countries and the social inequality connected with it appears as a drawback; better situated women can, especially by traveling to neighboring foreign countries, much more easily obtain an abortion by a physician than poorer or less clever ones. . . .

It was especially significant for the legislature in deciding how best to reform these situations that the decision for an abortion generally grows out of a conflict situation based on varied motivations which are strongly imprinted with the circumstances of the individual case. . . .

3. In this whole situation, "the containing of the abortion epidemic" is not only a "goal desired socially and politically," but also is urgently required precisely for a better protection of life and to restore the credibility of the legal order. In striving toward the solution of this most difficult problem the legislature has exhaustively evaluated all essential points of view. . . .

In the solution chosen the legislature was within its authority to proceed on the assumption that, in view of the failure of the penal sanction, the suitable means toward a remedy are to be sought in the social and community realm and that involved is, on the one hand, facilitating the bearing of the child to term by the mother through preventive psychological, *social, and social-political promotional measures* and strengthening her willingness to this end; and, on the other hand, decreasing the number of unwanted pregnancies through better information about the possibilities for preventing conception. Even the majority does not apparently doubt that such measures seen as a whole are the most effective and are in accord with the earliest effectuation of fundamental rights in the sense of greater freedom and increased social justice....

We do not dispute that this counseling regulation—as explained in the judgment—still displays weaknesses. To the extent that these weaknesses could not have been removed by a construction of the statute which conforms to the constitution and by a corresponding implementation of regulations of federal states, a constitutional objection would have to be limited solely to these shortcomings and may not challenge the regulation of terms and counseling in their fundamental conception. Furthermore, the success of the counseling regulation depends essentially on whether help can be offered to or arranged for the pregnant woman which opens for her ways out of her difficulties. If this fails, even the penal law is nothing other than an alibi for the deficit of effective help; the responsibility and the burdens would be shifted onto the weakest members of society. The majority—in agreement with previous judicial opinions—finds itself unable to limit the freedom of formulation of the legislature and prescribes for it an expansion of the social-preventive measures. If, however, judicial self-restraint has validity, the Constitutional Court *a fortiori* should not compel the legislature to employ the power of punishment, which is the strongest means of state coercion, to compensate for the social neglect of duty with the threat of punishment. This certainly does not correspond to the function of penal law in a liberal social state.

4. Even the majority recognizes the legislative intention to preserve life through counseling as a "goal worthy of respect", but holds in agreement with the petitioners the ordering of *flanking penal sanctions* to be unalterable because comprehensive foregoing of punishment leaves a "gap in protection" in the cases in which the interruption of pregnancy is based on reasons which are in no way worthy of respect.

a) The ability of penal sanctions to protect life as intended, however, immediately appears to be doubtful.... The majority still owes the explanation incumbent upon it of how, in the era of "abortion-tourism," domestic penal provisions will directly and favorably influence those women who are decided upon abortion for imprudent reasons. Such a success is possible, if at all, only in a certain number of cases—especially with those belonging to socially weaker groups. With women subject to influence the ambivalent effect of penal threats is shown *inter alia* by the fact that, on the one hand, penal threats might offer support against the abortion demands of the father or of the family, but, on the other hand, can contribute to an increase in abortions by driving the pregnant woman into isolation, thereby exposing her more than ever to such pressures and occasioning short-circuited treatment.

b) ... The legislature found itself therefore in the dilemma that in its judgment preventive counseling and repressive penal sanction are partially [mutually] exclusive. The legislature's decision to forgo penal sanctions which could possibly prevent abortions in a probably small number of cases, conceivably to save other life in a greater number of cases, cannot be dismissed with the comment that it would be a "lump sum weighing of life against life," which would be incompatible with the constitutional duty of protection of each individual unborn life. With this argumentation the majority closes its mind in a manner difficult to understand to the fact that it is itself doing that for which it reproaches the legislature. This is so because the majority requires, for its part, for constitutional reasons an accounting from the legislature by compelling it through a requirement to retain the penal provision to leave such unborn life without protection, which could be preserved by the repeal of the penal sanction and through suitable counseling....

II.

* * *

Our most important objection is directed to the majority's failure to explain how the requirement of condemnation as an independent duty is constitutionally derived. According to our view the constitution nowhere requires that ethically objectionable behavior or conduct deserving of punishment must *per se* be condemned with the help of the statutory law without regard to the desired effect. In a pluralistic, ideologically neutral and liberal democratic community, it is a task for the forces of society to codify the postulates of opinion. The state must practice abstention in this matter; its task is the protection of the legal values guaranteed and recognized by the constitution. For the constitutional decision it matters only whether the penal provision is imperatively required to secure an effective protection of developing life, having taken into consideration the interests of the woman which are deserving of protection.

III.

That the decision of the German legislature for the regulation of terms and counseling neither arises from a fundamental attitude which is to be morally or legally condemned nor proceeds from apparently false premises in the determination of the circumstances of life is confirmed by identical or similar *provisions for reform in numerous foreign states.* In Austria, France, Denmark, and Sweden an interruption of pregnancy, performed during the first twelve weeks (in France, ten) of pregnancy by a physician with the consent of the pregnant woman, is not punishable; in Great Britain and in The Netherlands a regulation of indications is in effect which amounts to the same thing in its practical application. These states can boast that they are a part of an impressive constitutional tradition and all-in-all certainly do not lag behind the Federal Republic in unconditional respect for life of each individual human being; some of them likewise have historical experience with an inhuman system of injustice. Their decision required coming to grips with the same legal and social problems which exist in the Federal Republic. In all of these countries, the European Human Rights Convention is legally binding, Article 2, Paragraph 1, of which ("Everyone's right to life shall be protected by law.") is similar to the constitutional provision of Article 2, Paragraph 2, Sentence 1, of the Basic Law and which as a whole could easily go further than the domestic German norm. The Constitutional Court of Austria has expressly determined that the term solution of that country is compatible with the Human Rights Convention, which in Austria enjoys constitutional rank.

IV.

On the whole therefore, in our opinion, the legislature was not prevented by the constitution from dispensing with a penal sanction which, according to its unrefuted view, was largely ineffective, inadequate, and even harmful. Its attempt to remedy through socially adequate means the manifestly developing inability of state and society in the present conditions to serve the protection of life may be imperfect; it corresponds, however, more to the spirit of the Basic Law than the demand for punishment and condemnation.

Notes and Questions on the Abortion Cases

1. Do the majority and the dissenters in the 1975 German decision disagree about whether the state has an affirmative duty to protect developing human life? What are the precise areas of their disagreements? How does the majority reconcile its permission of abortion under certain circumstances with its insistence on the state's duty to protect unborn human life?

2. Read *Roe v. Wade*, 410 U.S. 113, 93 S.Ct. 705, 35 L.Ed.2d 147 (1973). What do you make of the fact that the highest courts of two nations, both committed in principle to human rights and individual liberties, decided the abortion question in different ways? Note that *both* courts, in so doing, reached results at variance with the outcomes of the legislative process. For a German constitutional law professor's analysis of the cases, see W. Brugger, A Constitutional Duty to Outlaw Abortion? A Comparative Analysis of the American and German Abortion Decisions, 36 *Jahrbuch des öffentlichen Rechts der Gegenwart* 41 (1987).

3. Compare the 1975 French and German decisions. Note especially the differences in form and style of the opinions. Can the divergent results of these two cases be attributed to differences in the language of the two constitutions? When you compare the 1975 French and German decisions with *Roe v. Wade*, do you find significant similarities or differences related to the constitutional texts being interpreted? Are there significant differences in the way the three tribunals approach the *process* of interpretation?

4. After the 1975 German decision, the legislature amended the Criminal Code to provide that abortion after implantation of the fertilized ovum was illegal except when a doctor (not the one performing the abortion)

issued a non-binding opinion concerning "whether" the pregnancy posed a serious danger to the life or physical or mental health of the pregnant woman, which could not be averted by any other means the woman could reasonably be expected to bear. In making this determination, the doctor was permitted to consider the "present and future living conditions" of the woman. In addition, abortion was permitted through the 22nd week of pregnancy if a doctor stated whether the child was likely to be born with a severe defect, and through the 12th week if a doctor stated whether the pregnancy resulted from an illegal act against the woman (i.e., rape, incest) or the pregnancy placed her in a situation of serious hardship that could not be averted in any other way. Except in emergencies, at least three days had to elapse after a mandatory counselling session in which the woman had to be advised of services available to her, especially those that would facilitate continuation with the pregnancy. German Criminal Code Sections 218 through 219c, as amended in 1976.

5. Under the Unification Treaty of 1990, a statute permitting and funding abortion on request during the first trimester of pregnancy was allowed to remain in effect in the territory of former East Germany until an all-German parliament should enact a new law. In 1992, the German legislature adopted a statute similar in many respects to the 1975 French abortion law. It would have permitted first trimester abortions on request if the pregnant woman declared she was in distress and waited three days after neutral informational counselling. The statute provided that, after twelve weeks, abortion would be permitted only if a doctor attested that the pregnancy posed a threat to the life of the woman or that the fetus had grave medical problems.

6. In 1993, the Federal Constitutional Court held the 1992 statute partially unconstitutional. Reaffirming its 1975 decision, the Court held that the state has an affirmative duty to protect developing life. As in 1975, the Court found that the state might permit abortion in situations involving severe hardships, e.g., rape, incest, serious threat to the health of the pregnant woman or likelihood of serious defect in the fetus. In all other cases, however, the Court held that abortion must remain "unlawful" (*rechtswidrig*). That did not necessarily mean, the Court went on, that first trimester abortions had to be criminalized. As in 1975, the Court acknowledged that the *means* of carrying out the state's duty to protect unborn life need not include criminal punishment, if adequate counselling and social supports (e.g., family leave, maternity benefits, day care) were provided to the pregnant woman. The counselling provisions in the new statute were held constitutionally defective, however, because they were "merely informational", rather than actively encouraging and aiding women to continue with their pregnancies.

The state's duty to protect unborn human life also includes keeping the public aware of the "unlawfulness" of abortion, according to the Court. That was the basis of the Court's ancillary ruling that non-hardship abortions cannot be covered in the ordinary national health insurance system. An exception was made for women receiving public assistance, however, with the Court reasoning that the prospect of funding might be the key factor that would bring a poor woman within reach of life-affirming counselling and assistance.

As in 1975, there were two dissents, taking issue with the majority on the means of protecting unborn life, but not on the state's duty to do so. Federal Constitutional Court Decision (Second Senate) of May 28, 1993, 20 EuGRZ 229 (1993).

7. For students who read German, it would be a worthwhile project to compare the 1993 Federal Constitutional Court decision with *Planned Parenthood of Southeastern Pennsylvania v. Casey,* ___ U.S. ___, 112 S.Ct. 2791, 120 L.Ed.2d 674 (1992). What are the uses and limits of comparative legal analysis regarding hotly contested social issues?

Notes and Questions on Judicial Review

1. What is the optimum resolution of the tension between the need to protect individuals and minorities from the majority and the commitment to government by elected representatives? How are both of these political concerns of modern republics to be accommodated, while preserving the legitimacy of the judicial power? The experience of the United Kingdom indicates that judicial review of legislation is not essential to the functioning of a democratic political system. In fact, judicial review is, in a sense, anti-democratic because it permits the courts to be used as means for continuing political battles which have been lost in the elected legislature, and possibly to reverse majoritarian outcomes. Nevertheless, most modern nations have deemed it desirable to institutionalize some form of check on the power of the majority.

Among these, the United States is distinguished by three factors: (1) the fact that the Constitution can be and is enforced by ordinary courts as part of the everyday process of adjudication of disputes; (2) the power and readiness of its courts at all levels to decide questions that require the kind of choice among policies and values, or the kind of commitment of public funds, that other countries in varying degrees prefer to leave to the "democratic" alternative: majority rule as expressed through imperfectly representative assemblies; and (3) the "constitutionalization" of a great many legal issues with the result that the legislative process for resolving these issues is often stopped cold in its tracks. Once the Supreme Court has decided, for example, that abortion rights are constitutionally protected, the underlying social controversy does not come to an end, but it can no longer proceed along the lines of bargaining, persuasion and education within the state legislatures and among citizens. The law in the area can change or evolve only through the extraordinary process of constitutional amendment or through reversal or gradual erosion of the Court's decision. Should Americans be concerned about what may happen to the legitimacy of Supreme Court decisions if the court is to have the last word concerning numerous legal issues on which the society is deeply divided? Courts in countries like France and Germany whose histories have furnished them with, in the former case, an old but deep-seated suspicion of the arbitrary power of judges, and, in the latter, with a commitment to the rule of law as the best protection against tyranny, are more reluctant to test the outer limits of their power.

It should be further recalled, however, that there is a very great legal difference between France, on the one hand, and England and Germany on the other, even though all three differ from the United States by the depth of their commitment to parliamentary rule. In France, as we have seen, parliamentary rule has been tempered significantly by executive and administrative power. Thus, the possibility of resolving highly controversial legal-political issues through the rough-and-tumble of the legislative process is often foreclosed in France by the power of the administration just as it often is in the United States by the power of the courts.

2. A court interpreting a constitution will often encounter vague language and abstract principles whose application in a particular case is uncertain. The hermeneutic process it must then engage in is not markedly different from what courts do when dealing with general concepts in other areas of law. Once case law accumulates and endows concrete content upon general constitutional norms, it serves as a guide to parties and courts in the future. How a court then deals with the body of constitutional case law may raise problems of legitimacy. How do you think the United States Supreme Court would compare with constitutional tribunals of other countries in bringing prior holdings to bear on current questions in such a way as to promote confidence in the judicial process and continuity in the development of the law? See the discussion of the judicial process in Chapter 5 infra.

3. Consider the following observation by Sheldon S. Wolin on modern governments in connection with the current discussions among lawyers about the legitimacy of judicial review: "... [G]reat changes ... have taken place in the system of national political institutions during this century. Stated briefly, there has been an evolution from a loose structure of 'government' to something like a state system. A state exists when power and authority are centralized; when their scope and application are, in principle and for the most part, unlimited except by procedural requirements; and when the basic tendency is toward the integration of the various branches of government rather than toward their separation. It is, I would emphasize, these basic tendencies, not the perfect realization of them, that warrants the description 'state system'." Wolin, Reagan Country, The New York Review of Books, December 18, 1980, p. 9.

SECTION 5.   PUBLIC LAW COURTS

In a typical civil law system, the various types of disputes that are handled by courts of general jurisdiction in the United States are entrusted to two or more separate hierarchies of specialized courts, each with its own supreme court. The jurisdiction of the ordinary courts typically is limited to criminal law and private law disputes. The tribunals which adjudicate most public law matters and most disputes in which the government is a party are separate from the ordinary courts. In some countries, as in France, the administrative courts are within the executive rather than the judicial branch, although care is taken to assure their independence from regular executive functions. In other countries, Germany for example, the administrative courts are one of two main court systems within the judiciary.

In either model, it is necessary to have some mechanism for resolving disputes about which court system has jurisdiction over a particular case. In France, a special Tribunal of Conflicts has been created to decide whether a case falls within the administrative or the ordinary jurisdiction. In the German system, where there are a number of separate hierarchies of courts, the basic rule is that the courts have power to determine their own jurisdiction and to transfer cases over which they decline jurisdiction. A final decision refusing jurisdiction is binding in the transferee court, which may, however, transfer the case to still another court system.

Although the French model was shaped by specifically French historical circumstances, it has been more widely imitated than the German system of separate judicial jurisdictions. Because administrative law was largely a creation of the 19th century, it was natural that the early French experience would be drawn on by many other countries as they searched for mechanisms to control their rapidly growing public administrations. As noted earlier, the French revolutionary doctrine of separation of powers seemed to require that the actions of administrative bodies and disputes among or involving them should not be subject to control by the judiciary. Thus the administrative dispute-settling mechanism had to be located elsewhere. In Napoleonic times this authority was vested in the Council of State *(Conseil d'État)* which began as a body of advisors to the king under the *ancien régime* and later developed into the central organ of governmental administration. The membership of the present Council of State is composed of professional public administrators, whose backgrounds and training are quite different from those of the ordinary judiciary. (In the terminology commonly used in Europe, the "administration" is the civil service, while the "government" consists of the prime minister and the cabinet).

To this day, the Council of State performs its dispute-settling function through a special "section" which is separate from its regular administrative functions. In the first instance, an administrative dispute normally is brought before one of several lower administrative courts. There is no intermediate court of appeal. The Council of State functions as the appellate court for all these lower courts, and also as the court of first and last instance for certain types of cases, such as where the constitutional status of an administrative act is challenged. It will be recalled that constitutional review by the Constitutional Council extends only to parliamentary legislation, not to other governmental actions. But under the 1958 French Constitution, the legislature has power to legislate only in enumerated areas, leaving an extensive residuary law-making power to the executive. In a landmark decision of 1959,[16] the Council of State boldly asserted, and has since regularly exercised, power to review this "executive legislation". The surprising result is that an institution which is, at least theoretically, part of the executive branch has the exclusive power to review the legality or constitutionality of the acts of the executive. The great independence

---

16. Syndicat Général des Ingenieurs–Conseils, Council of State Decision of June 26, 1959, D.Jur.1959, 541. See, generally, Brown, DeGaulle's Republic and the Rule of Law: Judicial Review and the Conseil d'État, 46 B.U.L.Rev. 462 (1966).

and prestige of the Council of State, however, support it in its assumed role as a second constitutional court in France.

Figure 1 depicts the French court system with the Council of State *(Conseil d'État)* at the head of the administrative courts, the *Cour de Cassation* at the head of the ordinary courts, and the *Tribunal des Conflits* standing ready to resolve conflicts of jurisdiction. It should be noted that the Council of State, while serving as a supreme court for administrative litigation in its *Section des Contentieux,* is a purely administrative organ in its *Sections Administratives.* Fewer than half the members of the Council of State are chiefly engaged in judicial work; the remainder carry out its administrative functions which include serving as general legal advisor to the government and to individual ministers on matters of finance, internal affairs, public works and social programs. It is this internal physical division of labor between the administrative sections and the judicial sections that has permitted the Council of State to overcome the charge of being judge in its own cause.[17] But as Brown and Bell point out, "At bottom, the *Conseil d'État statuant au contentieux* . . . remains part of the administrative machinery of the French state, although a highly specialized part." [18]

Figure 1.   Court System in France [19]

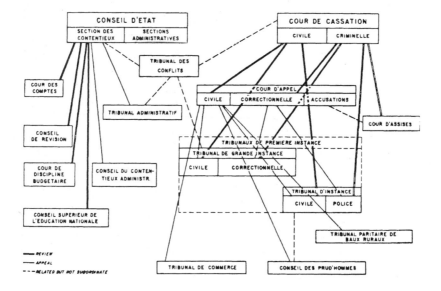

17. L.N. Brown & John S. Bell, French Administrative Law 77 (4th ed. 1993).

18. Id.

19. Kock, The Machinery of Law Administration in France, 108 U.Pa.L.Rev. 366, 368 (1960). Reprinted with the permission of the University of Pennsylvania Law Review.

Of the countries that have followed the French model, Belgium and Italy have done so rather closely, while most others have considerably varied and adapted it to suit their own circumstances over the years. Some of the developing nations which have followed French law in other respects, have adopted a unified court system for want of a sufficient number of judges to staff a dual hierarchy of courts.

Historically in Germany, unlike in France, separation of powers was not understood to require the administrative courts to be outside the judicial system. Rather they constitute one of five principal separate court systems within the judiciary (Figure 2). In contrast to the United States, where a single federal Supreme Court stands at the apex of a

Figure 2.

Court System in the Federal Republic of Germany [20]

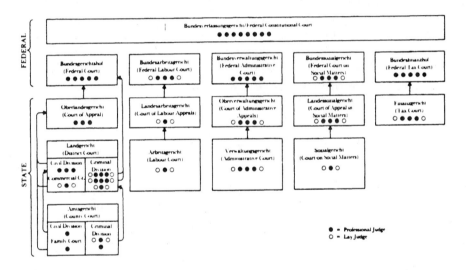

20. © Hein Kötz 1982. Reprinted from German Private and Commercial Law: An Introduction, by Norbert Horn, Hein Kötz, and Hans G. Leser, translated by Tony Weir (1982), by permission of Oxford University Press, and Professors Horn, Kötz, and Leser.

pyramid of all lower and intermediate federal courts (with considerable power over state judicial determinations), Germany has several judicial pyramids, each with its own jurisdiction and each headed by its own Supreme Court. The two main hierarchies are the ordinary (civil and criminal) courts headed by the *Bundesgerichtshof,* and the administrative courts, headed by the *Bundesverwaltungsgericht.* In addition, there are hierarchies of labor courts, tax courts and social security courts. The highest court in each system is a federal court, but the trial courts and intermediate appellate courts are state courts. The Federal Constitutional Court is yet another separate part of this system, not only exercising the power of judicial review, but also hearing complaints about violations of constitutional rights and deciding disputes of a constitutional nature among the various governmental organs and entities.

The German administrative courts have jurisdiction over public law disputes generally, except for constitutional issues, and except for those administrative matters which have been assigned to the specialized tax and social security courts. There are three levels of administrative jurisdiction: the administrative tribunals, intermediate appellate courts, and the *Bundesverwaltungsgericht* which is the supreme administrative court.

SECTION 6. ORDINARY COURTS

Just as the civil law is the heart of the substantive law in civil law countries, the so-called "ordinary courts" which hear and decide the great range of civil and criminal litigation are the core of the judicial system. These courts are the modern-day successors to the various civil and criminal courts that existed in Europe during the long period of the *jus commune,* before the modern state with its panoply of public and administrative law came into being. In the post-codification era, the main concern of the ordinary courts became the interpretation and application of the basic codes, but today they also routinely apply a great deal of law that is not found within the civil, commercial and criminal codes. The ordinary courts of first instance may, as in France, include a number of specialized courts.[21] Intermediate appellate courts, as well as the highest court, usually sit in specialized panels or chambers.

In the French system and its variants, as illustrated by Figure 1, the ordinary law courts and the administrative law courts form two separate and independent hierarchies, the public law system headed by the administrative Council of State *(Conseil d'État)* on the one side, and the

---

21.   See generally, Pugh, Cross–Observations on the Administration of Civil Justice in the United States and France, 19 Univ. of Miami L.Rev. 345 (1965); Kevorkian, The French Court System (Or Miracles will Happen), Boston Bar Journal, September 1980, p. 6.

private and criminal law system headed by the Court of Cassation *(Cour de Cassation)* on the other. Technically, only the second system composes what is known as the "judicial order." The Tribunal of Conflicts stands between the two systems as a kind of traffic officer for jurisdictional disputes. At the first level of ordinary court jurisdiction, several specialized courts co-exist with the regular civil and criminal trial courts. Matters arising under the Commercial Code, for example, are first heard in one of France's many commercial courts where the part-time judges (sitting in panels of three) are businessmen elected by their colleagues.[22] Disputes between employers and individual employees in the first instance are brought before one of the labor courts *(Conseils de Prud'hommes)* where two elected representatives each from labor and management sit together.[23] These labor courts attempt to settle disputes first by conciliation. If the matter proceeds to adjudication, and the judges become deadlocked, a professional judge sits with the panel. There are also special courts for agricultural leases and social security disputes. Except where minor civil or criminal matters are involved, courts of the first instance are collegial.

An appeal from a court of first instance is heard in the Court of Appeal *(Cour d'Appel)* within whose territorial jurisdiction the lower court is situated. At the highest level, the Court of Cassation has jurisdiction over the ordinary courts of the entire country. It is composed of about 100 judges who sit in varying combinations on panels in six specialized chambers (five civil and one criminal), and, in certain situations, in mixed chambers or plenary assembly.

In the German system, as Figure 2 shows, there are not two, but several, independent court systems, each with its own supreme court.[24] The "ordinary jurisdiction" there includes all the criminal and civil (including commercial) cases which are handled within the regular courts, and labor cases which are handled in a separate Federal Labor Court system. Traditionally, in Germany, as in most other civil law countries, the first-instance courts of general jurisdiction have sat in panels consisting of a presiding judge and two associate judges. However, legislation in the 1970s made it possible for many types of cases to be decided by a single judge. In commercial matters, the judge of first instance sits with two lay judges who are specialists in this field. Appeals from the first instance are heard in an intermediate appellate court *(Oberlandesgericht),* with final review by the Federal Supreme Court *(Bundesgerichtshof).* In the labor court system, appeals from the lower courts are taken first to the Labor Court of the state where the

---

22. For a general comparative survey of systems with specialized commercial courts, see Tallon, Civil Law and Commercial Law, Ch. 2 in VIII Int'l Encyc. Comp. Law 136–42 (K. Zweigert ed. 1983). Today, arbitration and other non-judicial modes of settling commercial disputes are increasingly utilized in the business world. Tallon concludes that separate commercial courts are presently in decline, in part because of the ancient dislike in commercial circles for official courts. Id. at 140, 142.

23. Napier, The French Labour Courts—An Institution in Transition, 42 Mod.L.Rev. 270 (1979).

24. See, generally, N. Horn, H. Kötz & H. Leser, German Private and Commercial Law: An Introduction 27–34 (1982).

lower court is located, and finally to the Federal Labor Court. At the first and second levels, the judge acts in consultation with labor and management representatives.

Notes and Questions

1. Does it make sense to have specialized courts or special divisions of courts, as civil law countries typically do, to deal with disputes arising in such areas as commercial law, labor law, and social security law? To what extent has administration of justice in the United States moved in this direction? To what extent could or should it move further? Consider, in this connection, the following excerpt from an article by a judge of the United States Court of Appeals for the Third Circuit. For a defense of the American "generalist judge", see Posner, Will the Federal Courts of Appeals Survive until 1984? An Essay on Delegalization and Specialization of the Judicial Function, 56 Southern California Law Review 711 (1983).

ALDISERT, "RAMBLING THROUGH CONTINENTAL LEGAL SYSTEMS"

43 University of Pittsburgh Law Review 935, 947–49 (1982).*

As a result of my German experience, I have now become a convert to the concept of specialized courts. I rush to add that I would not go so far as endorsing the establishment of six judicial hierarchies as found in Germany, but they have established a pattern that we should start to think about. I have previously expressed my disenchantment with the diet now imposed on United States circuit judges. I have explained how much of our work is a hum-drum review for substantial evidence in cases from the Social Security Administration, the NLRB, the Board of Immigration Appeals, the Occupational Safety and Health Review Commission, and under the Longshoremen and Harbor Workers' Compensation Act.

In Germany, social security appeals go first to the *Sozialgerichte*, a panel of one judge and two laymen, then to the *Landessozialgerichte* (three judges and two laymen) which sits at Kassel. I would adopt a version of the German system immediately for review of all "substantial evidence" appeals from the Secretary of Health and Human Services to replace the appellate hierarchy of district court to court of appeals to the United States Supreme Court in the cases. A physician and an industrial relations engineer could be the lay members of these courts that would handle all such appeals from the Secretary's adverse determinations. . . .

I also endorse the concepts of labor-management courts of West Germany. There, all questions relating to collective bargaining agreements, workmen's compensation, and the employer-employee relationship, including safety and working conditions, are processed through a specialized labor law judicial hierarchy. Like the social security courts, if these were established in the United States they could be structured to reflect the public policy of the executive and legislative branches during their terms. Because our national labor policy is determined by the Congress, and implemented by the President, I would limit the terms of the members of this court to that of the appointing president, and, of course, limit their jurisdiction to questions of substantial evidence *vel non*.

Another example of the German penchant for specialized courts is the *Bundespatentgerichts,* the patent court, located in Munich.... [T]his 100 judge court ... takes appeals directly from the patent office, a jurisdiction similar to our Court of Customs and Patent Appeals (which in 1981 had a complement of five active judges).... [This] court also has jurisdiction over all patent infringement cases, matters tried in our system in the district courts with review in the courts of appeals. When an issue of patent invalidity or infringement arises in the ordinary civil courts in Germany, the cause is immediately transferred to the *Bundespatentgerichts.* New legislation in 1982 has created a Washington-based United States Court of Appeals for the Federal Circuit that will combine the present Court of Patent and Custom Appeals with the Court of Claims and divest the other circuit courts of jurisdiction over patent validity appeals.

2. So far as the work of American appellate courts is concerned, Professor Daniel Meador argues that we may have much to learn from the way cases are allocated by subject matter *within the ordinary courts* in Germany.

MEADOR, "APPELLATE SUBJECT MATTER ORGANIZATION: THE GERMAN DESIGN FROM AN AMERICAN PERSPECTIVE"

5 Hastings International and Comparative Law Review 27–28, 55–58 (1981).*

Appellate courts can be organized in several ways. One way is on the basis of the subject matter of the cases. Under this method the court's entire docket is divided into several groupings based on the subject matter of the litigation—for example, suits involving building construction contracts, suits over interests in land, and so on. Such groupings of cases are then assigned on a continuing basis to the same designated group of judges—a division or a panel—within the court.

Although this method of judicial organization exists in some courts in the United States, there is a traditional American aversion to structuring courts and allocating judicial business on this basis. Yet its desirability is becoming increasingly evident within American appellate courts, both state and federal, especially at the intermediate appellate level. Since one of the best-functioning appellate systems embodying a subject matter design is in Germany, American lawyers and judges can gain insights into this kind of appellate structure by a clearer understanding of the German plan....

* Reprinted with permission of Daniel J. Meador and the Hastings International and   Comparative Law Review.

To appreciate the significance of this German arrangement from the American standpoint, one must first understand the problem afflicting appellate courts in the United States. The problem has grown acute, and will worsen, in the federal courts and in the larger state systems. The cause of the problem is the growth in appellate case loads over the past fifteen to twenty years, which in turn has caused a substantial increase in the number of judges sitting on appellate courts, chiefly at the intermediate level. Increases in the number of judges result in increases in the number of decisional units within a given appellate system. In the federal system there are now twelve courts of appeals established on a geographical basis. Within each of those courts, however, there are multiple and continually shifting panels of three judges. On the Ninth Circuit, for example, there are twenty-three judges; it is theoretically possible to have 1,771 different panels of three. Eight circuits have more than nine judges each, and they all sit in shifting threesomes. The state judicial systems have a variety of organizational structures at the intermediate appellate level, but they, like the federal appellate courts, are not structured or organized internally on any subject matter concept. The single court of last resort sitting at the apex of each judicial system is unable, because of the sheer quantity of decisions being turned out at the intermediate appellate level, to resolve conflicts among the decisional units, to eliminate uncertainties and unevenness in the case law, and, in general, to monitor an overall, evenhanded development of the jurisdiction's law.

As appellate litigation continues to grow, the natural tendency is to add more judges and hence more decisional units; this, of course, will heighten the threats to stability and uniformity in the law. In short, the challenge to American judicial architects is to devise a structure and procedure that will accommodate the number of appellate judges needed to handle the volume of business without destroying doctrinal uniformity and stability.

* * *

The two characteristics of the German appellate courts which most sharply differentiate them from their American counterparts are the large number of judges and the subject matter style of organization. These two characteristics are closely related. The large number of judges makes the subject matter style of organization imperative in order to maintain doctrinal coherence. This style of organization in turn permits the employment of a cadre of judges large enough to handle the docket without impairing doctrinal stability.

In Germany there are far more judges on the intermediate appellate courts and the supreme court in the ordinary civil and criminal jurisdiction than in any single American judicial system, or, indeed, in several of the largest American systems combined. With 110 judges on the *Bundesgerichtshof* and 1,382 judges on the nineteen *Oberlandesgerichte,* there are altogether 1,492 appellate judges in the ordinary jurisdiction. If one adds the judges at the intermediate appellate levels and top appellate levels in the other four German jurisdictions, the numbers become almost staggering to the American mind. This is the judiciary for a nation of sixty-two million people. By comparison, in the largest American state—California, with a population of nearly twenty-four million—there are fifty-eight judges at the intermediate appellate level and seven judges on the state Supreme Court. The German total still would not be reached if all of the intermediate appellate and supreme court judges in the states of Illinois, Michigan, Ohio, and New York were added to the number of California appellate judges. In the United States federal judiciary there are only 132 court of appeals judges and nine Supreme Court justices. Another sharp contrast with the German judiciary is found in England, where the appellate judiciary consists only of the eighteen judges on the Court of Appeal, ten Lords of Appeal (the full-time judges in the House of Lords), and a few other high-ranking judicial officers.

If one disregards system-wide figures and examines only the numbers of judges sitting on individual appellate courts, the contrast is equally startling. One of the largest American appellate courts, in terms of number of judges, is the United States Court of Appeals for the Ninth Circuit, with twenty-three judges. Appellate courts with twelve or fifteen judges are considered large in the United States. When the figure rises much above that, apprehensions increase about unmanageability and threats to coherent, uniform jurisprudence. Indeed, there is a wide-spread American belief that a single appellate court having more than nine judges is unmanageable. In Germany, by contrast, the smallest of the intermediate appellate courts has seventeen judges; the largest has 149 judges. The average number of judges on all of the nineteen intermediate appellate courts is seventy-two. If these appellate courts, or the top court with its 110 judges, were organized and operated like American appellate courts, there would be chaos in the law.

The key to the viability of appellate courts of such sizes lies in the system of internal subject matter organization. With a carefully designed plan of subject matter allocation of the docket among the judges, there is almost no limit to the total number of judges who may serve on the court without destroying the coherence of the decisional law. Subject matter organization may indeed be the ultimate answer to the problem of high volume in appellate courts. To handle the volume, numerous judges are necessary, but without an internal subject matter organization, the number of judges necessary to handle the volume of appeals would threaten the stability and uniformity of the law.

An examination of the *Bundesgerichtshof*['s] work distribution plan ... will show that subject matter organization of an appellate docket need not lead to the kind of narrow specialization about which there is much apprehension in the United States. The docket of any appellate court can be distributed among groups of judges in such a way that no one group is restricted to an overly specialized slice of the law. Each group can be given a varied mixture of legal questions drawn from different subject matters and different legal areas....

This approach holds rich possibilities for high-volume American intermediate appellate courts, either state or federal, where an increasing number of judges is necessary to decide the cases within a reasonable time. In any such court the docket can be divided into packages containing a variety of types of legal questions drawn from various subject matters and areas of the law.[71]

Whenever the idea of subject matter docket assignments is discussed among American lawyers and judges, two objections are voiced. One stems from ingrained fears of specialization. The other stems from apprehensions about boredom in the work of appellate judges. Both objections can be overcome in a carefully designed subject matter plan.

The specialization objection can be avoided by grouping cases for assignment to a particular panel so as to include a variety of subject matter. Illustrations of such varied groupings can be seen in several of the division assignments in the work distribution plan of the *Bundesgerichtshof.* The specialization point would be relevant only if an appellate panel were assigned one specific and relatively narrow category of cases.

A mixed grouping of cases going to each appellate panel would also prevent boredom among the judges. The business of each judge would be sufficiently diverse to obviate attitudes among the judges that they were dealing with the same questions day after day. Another means of avoiding boredom is to provide for a gradual, staggered rotation of judges among panels. Each judge, for example, could be assigned to a given panel for a three-year period, but each would come and go at a different time. On a division of five judges, for example, no more than one or two judges would rotate to other divisions each year. This would prevent the kind of rapid turnover that destabilizes the decisional law.

A well-designed comprehensive plan of subject matter organization has never been tried in any American appellate court. Without such experience there is no way to know with assurance how well such a plan would work. While the German plan cannot be copied precisely in an American court, it does provide a useful source of ideas for experimentation. Moreover, the German experience does provide evidence that this style of organizing appellate business is an effective way of accommodating large numbers of judges within a single court. As the volume of cases and the number of judges continue to grow in the United States, we may come increasingly to see this as the most promising method of preventing doctrinal chaos in the legal system. Certainly it is worth a try.

3. A 1978 article comparing certain features of the American court system with the judiciary in Canada, England, France, Italy, Sweden and what was then West Germany suggested that "it may be that the American judicial system ... is currently being sabotaged by an inadequate public investment." Emphasizing, in particular, the contrast between the United States and West Germany, the authors found: (1) "The U.S. judiciary seems

---

71. A proposal to incorporate subject matter docket assignments in the U.S. Courts of Appeals was made in Carrington, Crowded Dockets and the Courts of Appeals: The Threat to the Function of Review and the National Law, 82 Harv.L.Rev. 542 (1969). This idea was developed further in P. Carrington, D. Meador & M. Rosenberg, Justice on Appeal 204–07 (1976). In the latter at pages 205–06 there is a table illustrating a proposed subject matter docket assignment plan for a U.S. Court of Appeals with 16 judgeships and 1,500 dispositions on the merits annually.

to be undermanned, relative to that in several comparable jurisdictions. For example, U.S. jurisdictions employed only one-third as many judges, per capita, as West Germany...." (2) "Compared with foreign systems, the U.S. judiciary appears overwhelmed statistically by the size of the legal profession which constitutes one of its major input (case generating) factors. The number of practicing lawyers for each judge in California is more than ten times West Germany's ... ratio...." (3) "The U.S. judiciary also appears underfinanced relative to several jurisdictions. Over the period studied, the United States spent about half as much on its courts per capita as West Germany...." Johnson and Drew, This Nation has Money for Everything—Except its Courts, 17 Judges' J. (No. 3, Summer 1978) 8, 10. Before drawing conclusions from comparisons of the relative proportions of judges and lawyers in each system, you will want to consider the material on German civil procedure in Chapter 4.

Chapter 3

LEGAL ACTORS IN THE CIVIL
LAW TRADITION

A legal system, like any other system, is a group of functionally related, interacting, interdependent elements, which together give the system its special character. The formal legal structures just examined are but one set of such elements. None of these structures is a necessary feature of a civil law system. However, these institutions enter into a nation's legal culture, absorbing particular characteristics from, and imparting them to, that underlying culture. We have already traced the historical evolution of the common legal culture of civil law systems in Chapter 1 of this book. Now it is appropriate to turn to the modern-day individuals who have inherited this tradition—the practicing lawyers, the judges, the attorneys in government service, the prosecutors and professors. It is they who give life and a distinctive imprint to the legal structures of their societies. The way a society defines their legal roles and the status it accords to them is as revealing of its legal culture as are the composition and the relations of the organs of government. Of equal importance are the background and identity of the legal actors who are assigned or permitted to play these roles. Therefore, our next step into the legal culture of the civil law world takes us to law school.

SECTION 1. LEGAL EDUCATION

What might first strike an American lawyer as a major difference between legal education in the civil law countries and in our own system is that civil law training is undergraduate university education. Like most college training everywhere, it tends to be general and interdisciplinary rather than professional. But this way of organizing legal studies is also found in England. What is really distinctive about civil law legal education grows out of its methodology, which perpetuates the tradition of scholar-made law, just as our "case method" emerged from and contributes to the maintenance of the common law tradition of judge-made law. In both cases, a discrepancy is appearing between the tradition and the reality. In fact, a good argument can be made that changes now occurring will in the long run diminish the differences between the civil and common law systems of legal education.[1] At present, however, legal education in both systems still draws its basic approach from the historical circumstances in which it developed. In England, legal education from early times was in the hands of the bar. On the continent, from the time of the Roman law revival, it was the province of the universities.

Against this background, it is not surprising that one of the greatest differences between legal education in common law and civil law systems appears in the manner in which the student is initiated into the study of law. While an American law student typically spends the first days of law school reading cases and having his or her attention directed over and over again to their facts, a student of the civil law is provided at the outset with a systematic overview of the framework of the entire legal system. The diagram on the following page, for example, from a widely used German introductory text,[2] purports to be a picture of "The Law" *(Recht)*.

Notice how all "law" is represented as falling into one of two great divisions, *Privatrecht* (private law) or *Öffentliches Recht* (public law). Private law is then divided into civil law (which is further subdivided into areas we would classify under property, contracts, torts, family law, succession law, etc.) and commercial and business law (with subdivisions of corporations law, negotiable instruments, securities law, etc.) Public law has many more divisions, chief among them being administrative law, criminal law, procedure, social welfare and tax law. Administrative law *(Verwaltungsrecht)*, criminal law *(Strafrecht)* and procedure *(Prozessrecht)* are all shown with various subdivisions and interconnections of their own. With labor law *(Arbeitrecht)* and landlord-tenant law *(Mietrecht)* the categories revealingly break down. They are placed in that part of civil law dealing with assets, but the author is obliged to add in parentheses: "mit offentl. rechtl. Elementen"—(with public law elements).

1. M. Glendon, The Sources of Law in a Changing Legal Order, 17 Creighton L.Rev. 101 (1984).

2. J. Baumann, Einführung in die Rechtswissenschaft 29 (7th ed. 1980). Reproduced with permission of Verlag C.H. Beck, Munich.

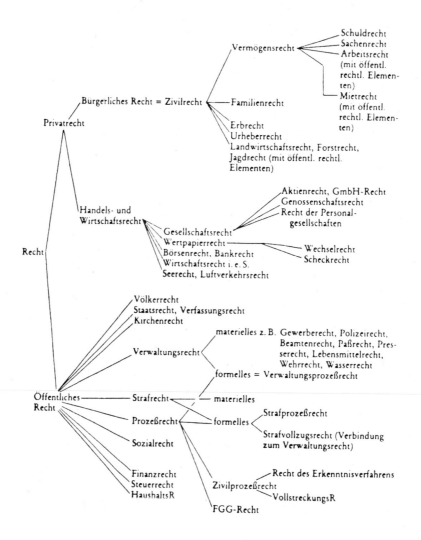

In civil law countries, each of the many subdivisions and categories of private and public law becomes, in time, the subject of study in a curriculum consisting mainly of required courses in programmed series. The first year "introduction to law" course itself, however, is apt to be taught by a professor of civil law and to deal mainly with the basic concepts of private law, the law of the civil codes.

While the common law student is taught to mistrust generalization and is expected to ferret out individually whatever patterns and structure are there to be found, the civil law beginner is kept at a certain distance from the facts and starts out with a ready-made version of the organization, methods and principles of the system. The student is introduced to a particular style of legal reasoning and learns what Mirjan Damaska has called "the grammar of law": a "network of precise interrelated concepts, broad principles and classificatory ideas." [3] All this is, of course, in keeping with the tradition of legal science so firmly ingrained in the civil law culture.

The methods of civil law legal education are a natural outgrowth of its principles. Teaching materials ordinarily consist of systematic treatises and, where appropriate, an annotated code. Typically the professor lectures rather than engaging in discussion with the class. It is not uncommon for one professor to have several hundred students in traditional lecture courses. Lectures and treatises both are relatively less concerned with practical application of legal theory and with concrete social problems than class discussion and teaching materials in a common law system would be.

Much has happened in recent years, however, to lessen these contrasts. Both common law and civil law schools are seeking a better balance between theory and practice. American law professors increasingly consider the case method only one of several useful teaching methods, while civil law faculties have come to recognize the importance of practical work, tutorials and small classes where discussion is possible. In some German universities, legal education has become less general and more professional. In Europe generally, where nearly all legal education is public and relatively easily accessible, there has been considerable pressure for change.

In the following essay, a German law graduate describes the system of legal education in her country and speculates about the probable course of reform in the light of European integration.

3. M. Damaska, A Continental Lawyer in an American Law School: Trials and Tribulations of Adjustment, 116 U.Pa. L.Rev. 1363, 1365 (1968).

JUTTA BRUNNÉE, "THE REFORM OF LEGAL EDU-CATION IN GERMANY: THE NEVER–ENDING STORY AND EUROPEAN INTEGRATION

42 Journal of Legal Education 399, 400–26 (1992).*

I. CONTEMPORARY LEGAL EDUCATION IN GERMANY

To many lawyers in other countries, German legal education is synonymous with great academic tradition; it has created jurists with solid theoretical knowledge and high capacity for hard work. By contrast, in Germany one often hears that the path to becoming a lawyer is far too long, that it covers too little of too much along the way, and that even after years of training, young (or no longer young) lawyers are not ready for the job.

As often is the case, the truth lies somewhere in the middle. To understand why, one need look no further than the fact that the present system has its roots in the ideology of legal science of the nineteenth century. While well suited to that period, it was not designed for the challenges it faces today: mass participation, ever-growing subject areas, diversification of careers, and internationalization.

The most fundamental features of German legal education are its two stages—university education and practical training—and its aim to produce "Einheitsjuristen," jurists qualified for all legal professions. The qualifications required for the profession continue to be modeled on those thought appropriate for the judge. All German lawyers have to earn the "Befähigung zum Richteramt," a status which enables them to become judges, district attorneys, or lawyers in private practice, business settings, or administrative agencies. These central aspects are set out in Section 5 of the Deutsches Richtergesetz *(DRiG):* "The qualification to the office of a judge is earned by those who complete studies of legal sciences with the First State Examination and the subsequent preparatory service with the Second State Examination."

A. *University Education*

The limpidly expressed requirement of *DRiG* Section 5 belies the very long path that leads young lawyers to the First and then Second State Examination. Unlike North American students, German law students may begin legal studies without undergraduate degrees. While some study law after earning practical experience and qualifications in other areas or as paralegals, most students move from high school directly into university. There are no tuition fees. There are also no entry examinations for the law faculties. Students generally must have successfully completed thirteen years of schooling and then passed the "Abitur," a uniform graduation examination.

While access to medical schools, for example, requires exceptional performance on that examination, the required score for entry into the law faculties is less of a barrier. This in part accounts for the high number of students (about three hundred on average) in entry semesters. But few stay the course. About fifty percent of all entering students abandon their legal studies along the way. Another twenty-five to thirty percent fail their First State Examination. Only twenty-five percent go through to the Second State Examination. . . .

---

* Reprinted with permission of the Journal of Legal Education.

According to the *DRiG* the "normal duration" of legal studies at the university level is seven semesters (3.5 years). During that time the students have to cover a number of compulsory subjects and an optional element. They must also complete a practical component of at least three months during one or more summer breaks.

The nuts and bolts of legal education are set out in the *DRiG,* but it creates only a framework, leaving detailed regulation of the curriculum to the Bundesländer (states). For example, the federal law does not set out a list of compulsory subjects; it merely mentions as "core subjects" civil law, criminal law, public law, procedural law, and historical and social foundations of law. This rather general description is fleshed out by the "compulsory subject" catalogs of the Länder.[21] For the electives the *DRiG* provides a model catalog, and the subject groups do not vary much among the Länder. They include legal theory, philosophy, sociology of law; history of law; family law and law of successions; company law and foundations of tax law; competition law; labor law; conflict of laws and comparative law; criminology and juvenile delinquency law; administrative studies; social security law; and international law and European law.

To a large extent, university education consists of formal lectures—typically, an organized, abstract, one-way presentation by the professor. Students are not required to prepare or rework the material covered or even to attend the lectures. In-term control is exercised only through the so-called "Übungen" (exercises), special classes complementing the lectures in the compulsory subjects. Here students are presented with hypothetical fact situations and instructed in methods of delivering legal opinions. The purpose is mainly the application of statutes, doctrines, and cases to these factual situations. While the case method of North American law schools encourages the development of argumentation and rhetoric, German students are always asked to render impartial opinions on "the legal situation" presented. From the very beginning of their university course, they are trained in the demeanor of the judge rather than that of the advocate or private practitioner.

---

21. For example, according to § 6 II of the Hessisches Juristenausbildungsgesetz, Hess.GVBl. 1985 I, 212, the following are compulsory subjects:

1. General Legal Science: Legal methodology, foundations of legal theory, legal philosophy, and legal and constitutional history.

2. Constitutional and Administrative Law: Constitutional law including its links to international and European law, with particular consideration of organization and competence of the European Community; general administrative law; foundations of the law of police and public order; building codes; municipal law and social security law.

3. Civil Law: The general part of the Bürgerliches Gesetzbuch (Civil Code); the law of obligations; property law; general principles of the law of successions; foundations of trade law and law of negotiable instruments.

4. Labor Law: Law of employment contracts and foundations of collective labor law.

5. Criminal Law: The general and special parts of the Criminal Code.

6. Procedural Law: Foundations of civil, criminal, and administrative procedure; noncontentious litigation; procedural aspects of labor law cases; foundations of execution and insolvency law.

During each Übung, students have to write two or more examinations and one paper on such fact patterns. After completing these assignments they receive a certificate (Schein) which is a prerequisite for admission to the First State Examination. As a minimum, admission to the First State Examination requires beginner and advanced certificates in civil, criminal, and public law as well as a certificate earned in a course on legal theory, philosophy, or history. Candidates must also have successfully completed a seminar or an exercise in their elective subject. The seminars are often the only occasion for students to carry out more in-depth research, to participate in academic discussion, and to interact more closely with their professors.

The programs of legal studies in Germany are much less structured than those at a North American law school. While each university has a formal curriculum, it is only precatory; much is left to the student's own judgment and self-discipline. Some students take a wide variety of offerings, while others take the minimalist approach and do little more than acquire the required certificates. More often than not, students fail to take advantage of their academic environment and simply focus on the requirements of the First State Examination. Not surprisingly, most find that after several semesters of leisurely student life they are not prepared for the threatening shadow cast by this postponable but ultimately unavoidable examination. Between seventy and ninety percent then resort to the services of private review classes (Repetitorium), which drill required knowledge and methodology for the examination. Students who attend university at no cost wind up spending considerable amounts of money for up to two years of Repetitorium.

The First State Examination, as its name indicates, is run not by the individual universities, but by the Ministry of Justice for each Bundesland. Practitioners and university professors comprise the examination boards and set the examination—a comprehensive final examination that tests knowledge acquired during all semesters of university study. Throughout Germany, the examination consists of a written and an oral portion, the latter generally worth thirty-three percent. The actual make-up of the written portion varies between the northern and the southern Bundesländer. In the North, candidates are required to write a number of supervised examinations and one major paper. In the South, candidates write only papers.

The First State Examination plays a dual role as the university final examination and the entry examination into the second, practical stage of legal education. In the ideal world of the *DRiG,* the student should have reached this stage after seven semesters of study. In reality students take around 11.5 semesters to reach the First State Examination. Moreover, the examination period itself may be between six and nine months, mainly because of waits for dates and results.

With a 1984 reform of the *DRiG,* the federal parliament sought to lower the average duration of studies by introducing intermediate examinations (Studienbegleitende Leistungskontrollen) to be taken by the end of a student's second year. These examinations were also supposed to weed out unsuited or unmotivated students early on, but they have yet to achieve any of the desired results.

B. Practical Training

Depending on the results of the First State Examination,[38] students (now called Referendare) may have to wait several months until they are placed for practical training. During the two and a half years of this "Vorbereitungsdienst" (preparatory service), they have the status of civil servants and receive a stipend. The preparatory service is designed to expose the Referendare to the various areas of legal practice, but the emphasis is clearly placed on public service and, in particular, the judiciary. Currently practical instruction takes place during several compulsory stages (at a civil court, a criminal court or the state attorney's office, an administrative agency, and a firm of private practitioners) and an optional stage toward the end of the practical training. In that optional stage the Referendare may choose to gain additional experience in one of the compulsory settings or to try some other field (e.g., Administrative or Tax Court, legislative bodies, notarial practices, commercial enterprises, and international or foreign businesses or law firms).

During the different stages of their training, the Referendare are assigned to supervisors—judges, state attorneys, or private practitioners, as the case may be—who are to provide individual training and to evaluate the Referendar's performance at the end of each stage. The individual instruction is supposed to expose the Referendare to daily practice in the different branches of the legal profession. But again the focus is on skills required in the judiciary—preparation of opinions and judgments—rather than on the lawyerly skills of negotiating, advocacy, and drafting. Normally, the Referendare would participate in court hearings and act on behalf of state attorneys or private lawyers. In practice the process can be quite different. Frequently, supervisors have more than one Referendar or are otherwise overworked or unmotivated. "Individual instruction" is reduced to occasional visits at the supervisor's office and homework on assigned files or problems. In addition to working with the individual instructor, the Referendar participates in work groups at each stage. Here practitioners discuss relevant theoretical and practical problems and evaluate the Referendar's performance by way of tests or papers. Like the university exercises, these evaluations have no real significance for the final examination.

---

38. The German system evaluates using seven categories: very good, good, very satisfactory, satisfactory, sufficient, insufficient (fail).... A mere pass ("sufficient") is the most common result. In 1987, 35.35 percent of all candidates (German average) achieved "sufficient," while only 12.7 percent of all candidates achieved the grades "very good" (3), "good" (103), and "very satisfactory" (706). See Steiger, *supra* note 15, at 284. In 1989, 6867 candidates submitted to the Second State Examination with the following results: 10.7 percent "fail"; 43.9 percent "sufficient"; 33.4 percent "satisfactory"; and 12.15 percent "very satisfactory" and better....

The Second State Examination is another comprehensive final examination in which the Referendare are required to show that they are capable of "practically useful" solutions to real-life cases in the different areas of law. This second examination may also take up to a year. It is cause for much anxiety, since the Referendar's career prospects depend heavily on the results. Often approaching the age of thirty, many find that their results are not good enough for them to pursue their desired career; or they may be excluded from a legal career altogether because they failed the examination. After passing the Second State Examination, the Referendar receives the title of Assessor and joins the ranks of the Einheitsjuristen, theoretically qualified for the office of judge or for any other legal career.

C. Career Choices

Not all careers, however, are open to all Einheitsjuristen. As mentioned above, much depends on the results of the examination. Only candidates achieving a certain predetermined average will be considered for the position of judge. The system intends that only the best Assessoren become judges, but this is not always the case. Though it is certainly esteemed, a judge's position is not nearly so prestigious as in common law jurisdictions. Judges do not become "legal legends"; they generally render their decisions anonymously and, with the exception of the Federal Constitutional Court, do not publish dissents. At the same time the judge's role in the proceedings is far more expansive and controlling than in common law jurisdictions. Pursuant to German procedural law, judges guide the proceedings, decide when and what witness or expert to hear, conduct the hearing, propose settlements, and render lengthy decisions based on their own research of the law. This powerful position and the demanding entry requirements assure the prestige of the German judge. Yet, while enjoying considerable independence, judges are civil servants and have much lower incomes than lawyers in the private sector. They do not join the bench after years of distinguished practice, but gain their experience on the job (where they must often battle with the bureaucracy). As a result the best Assessoren increasingly choose a career in the private sector.[61] This seems to be especially true for male candidates.[62]

Outside of the private sector the most prestigious careers open to Assessoren are those of State Attorney and careers in public service, where entry is at a relatively high level. Of course, many young lawyers decide to become private practitioners, but the percentage entering private practice is not as large as it is in North America. This may be because only recently have large firms on the North American model begun to spread over Germany and to offer interesting and highly paid careers. Because of conservative rules of ethics (Standesregeln), the

61. Out of 100–120,000 employed "full jurists," only 21,000 work within the judiciary....

62. Female candidates are more attracted to the benefits of a secure civil service position: as civil servants they are entitled to maternity leave, a secured return to their position, changes in and out of part-time positions, pension plans, and so on....

typical German law office has had between one and eight partners and worked strictly locally. For many practitioners with poor examination results, hanging out a shingle was a last resort; it was not so much the attraction of the profession, as the increasing number of graduates and stagnant numbers of public service positions, at the heart of this trend to solo private practice. Whereas private practice itself is highly regulated, entry into the profession is open to anyone with both State Examinations. The Bar Association (Anwaltskammer) may not exert its own control.

Careers in legal or management departments of commercial enterprises or banks enjoy increasing popularity. The pattern noted in the mid–1980s by Rueschemeyer, that the best law graduates in Germany enter the judiciary and civil service, is eroding. High salaries and increasingly international job profiles attract many of the best Assessoren to this sector. Often they must submit to additional training and ultimately work in nonlegal fields. German business and banking (as well as government) have traditionally preferred lawyers for their highest positions. It is no accident that a common trait of much of Germany's elite is a legal education.

What about academic careers? They are less popular among young lawyers than in Canada or the United States. There is a perception of universities as bureaucratic, rigid, and hierarchical institutions removed from day-to-day reality. Many Assessoren are also deterred by the lengthy qualification process and by salaries far lower than in the private sector. While a university career does not require the Second State Examination, most professors hold that qualification. In addition to a doctorate, young academics have to spend four to five years for their university qualification (Habilitation). During that period they are usually assistants, subordinate to a supervising professor and teaching one or more classes. They also have to prepare a substantial thesis which will be evaluated by a committee of professors. Having gained the Habilitation, the candidate will remain a simple lecturer until called by a university to a professorship. . . .

D. Historical Aspects of the German System

To understand the particularities of the German system of legal education, one needs to consider both its history and that of what is now Germany. The two-stage approach, the lengthy examination process, and the focus on the judiciary all have their roots in the eighteenth century and were shaped to an important extent by Prussian initiatives. Yet legal education in Germany was born in the late Middle Ages. Until well into the twelfth century legal training in German territories was seen as the acquisition of knowledge about the mostly local or regional customs handed down through time. But with the development of law teaching in eleventh-century Italy an academic tradition, founded in Roman law, began to appear in Germany.

German students have been documented as present at the University of Bologna since the twelfth century. In the fourteenth century the first German universities began to train students in Roman law: Prague (1348), Vienna (1365), and Heidelberg (1386). These universities paved the way for more widespread reception of Roman law in Germany, where it developed into the *jus commune*—what may be called a German "common law" in the sense that it served as a fall-back system where the local or regional law (Partikularrecht) provided no solution. In all other cases, however, local law prevailed over *jus commune*.

From this cleavage between Roman and local law emerged the division between academic and practical training. Even though academically trained jurists working in ecclesiastical or judicial administration applied Roman law in some cases, German legal practice predominantly relied on the relevant Partikularrecht. Given the multitude of rival territories then comprising the German Reich, such regional laws remained important. The different territories jealously guarded control over their judiciary, civil service, and legal education. The refusal of the universities to teach the "unintellectual" Partikularrecht and their focus on Roman law left them with only a relatively small role in the legal education of the time. As early as the sixteenth century, for example, the Reichsgericht, a state organism, introduced its own admission tests for the selection of its judges.

The greatest influence on the development of the current legal education system was exerted by one of the largest of the German territorial states: Prussia. Itself made up of several territories, Prussia sought to create a homogeneous and loyal administration, in an effort to give greater weight to the central powers. Thorough and uniform training of its governmental elites—its judiciary and civil service—was recognized early on as being of great importance. There is evidence of State Examinations since about 1713. The *Corpus Juris Fridericianum* of 1781 contained the first uniform regulation of legal education. In subsequent reforms of procedural law (1815), the *Corpus Juris* laid down the fundamental rules for the judiciary, which became a benchmark for the entire public service as well as legal education. Friedrich the Great, however, was known for his distrust of the judiciary, a distrust magnified by the judiciary's efforts to establish greater independence and protection from political interference. As a result an even tighter state regulation of the judiciary and more and more stringent control over legal education were established. Leaving only the training in the theoretical foundations of law to the universities, which were asked merely to attest to the "diligence and decent behavior" of their students, Prussia established a rigorous and long (four years) practical training program for jurists—the Referendarzeit. A final Große Staatsprüfung, held in Berlin, was developed to ensure the maintenance of a "unified profession."

The system thus established remained largely unchanged through the revolution of 1848 and the creation of the German Reich in 1871. Indeed, the German unification did not lead to the transfer of control of legal education to the Reich, but merely vested it with the power to regulate the general features of legal education. As Prussia and the southern German states could not agree on a uniform system in its detail, the Gerichtsverfassungsgesetz (Court Constitution Act) of 1877 set out only certain cornerstones: the judge as the model jurist, the two-stage process of academic and practical training, and the notion of the Einheitsjurist.

Around the turn of the twentieth century, the State Examination system assumed its current contours. The First State Examination required for entry into the preparatory service assumed its dual function of also attesting the graduation from university. By this point university education had gained greater practical value in the eyes of state functionaries. With the codification of administrative and procedural law and the entry into force of the Bürgerliches Gesetzbuch (1900), it was possible to shift emphasis from Roman law to the written law that was seen to be of practical relevance throughout Germany.

This quick review of the history of German legal education reveals the primary reasons for its current features. The importance of the judiciary to the state helps explain why the judge is the model of legal education. It also suggests why the state controls the examination process and runs the practical training of lawyers within the civil service. We can recognize a certain circular effect: the focus on the judiciary generated its reputation as the legal elite. That, in turn, made the judiciary the most sought-after career choice. Accordingly, the judiciary retained considerable influence within the legal profession as well as over legal education.

But this circularity may soon be broken. If the judiciary is no longer the career of choice, the educational focus on it may no longer be appropriate, even in theory. Certainly the State Examination process became a victim of changing conditions some time ago. Geared to the selection of a small elite, the process applied to masses of applicants created long examination periods. The unregulated character of the university portion of legal education may also become a victim of change. Rooted in traditional notions of academic freedom and meant to shield universities from government and ideological control, the liberty of both teachers and students is one of the fundamental rights entrenched in the German Grundgesetz (Constitution) of 1949. But recent reforms to legal education and accepted practice in other areas of study have shown considerable room for regulating the framework within which academic freedom is operative.

II. Prospects for Legal Education in Germany

Although everyone agrees that there are problems, the legal profession—if there is *a* profession—appears unable to agree on reforms. Various proposals have been discussed for a long time, but apart from minor changes here and there, none has as yet been adopted. Before I assess why the German Einheitsjuristen cannot agree what legal education should be like, it is worth detailing some of the problems about which agreement has been reached.

A. Everybody Knows the Troubles It Has Seen

1. Duration

One of the long-standing complaints about German legal education is its duration. Entering professional life on average at the age of thirty and even then not necessarily ready for the job, German lawyers typically have invested nine to eleven years in their legal education. They begin with years of university study before the First State Examination. Three causes postpone that examination: the timing is left almost entirely to the students; there is a gap between the university's offerings and the final examination's requirements; and the intermediate examination is now an additional hurdle. Intended to give students an earlier indication of their future and to reduce their numbers, the new examination had the reverse effect. Afraid of failing it, students now spend extra time studying and end up taking the examination long after the four semesters projected.

Another delaying factor is the administrative side of the examination process. Because examinations are written at set times during the year, there may be waiting periods between registering for and writing the examination. Most important, the process was never designed to deal with the masses now facing it. The requirement that all written examinations (especially the Second State Examination) be reviewed by two jurists—usually busy practitioners—creates long waiting periods for the results.

Finally there is the two-and-a-half-year practical training devoted to judicial and government service at the expense of private practice. Critics say that instead of becoming solid all-rounders, young lawyers are left with a little of everything—so little that they are unable to perform tasks independently once they enter the "real world." Why, the recurring question is, must all German lawyers be trained to be public prosecutors or public servants when so many of them will never use these skills?

The complaint about duration has assumed heightened significance with the increasing integration of the European Community. Many caution that German law graduates will have difficulty competing with generally younger graduates from other European countries. The domestic market will no longer be insulated from lawyers of other European countries, since pursuant to a 1988 EC Directive, university degrees from within the European Community are to be recognized in all member countries. After an adaptive course of no more than three years or upon passing a qualifying examination, lawyers from one EC country must be admitted to practice in another. This means that it will be possible for non-German graduates—and for Germans willing to train in another European country—to side-step the lengthy German process and to enter private practice without having to qualify for judicial office.

2. Subject Matter

Another line of complaints about the current system has addressed its educational content. A first concern is that the expansive subject catalogs contain much unnecessary weight. Rather than focusing on areas that are theoretically or practically essential to legal training, the catalogs require students also to cover an array of marginally important topics. The inevitable result is that students concentrate on only a few areas, guided by what the State Examination demands, gaining a scattered perspective on law that is divorced from social, philosophical, and historical foundations and filtered through formulae and schematic outlines. Students, it is argued, learn to categorize, reproduce, and score passing grades on the examinations, but do not learn what legal reasoning and equity are all about.

A second, related concern is that the needlessly comprehensive requirements leave no room for expansion of existing core areas or addition of new areas that should be part of the curriculum—for example, environmental law, European law, tax law, and immigration law. There were some attempts in the last round of reforms to cut down required subject matter and encourage specialization through electives, but the actual cuts were half-hearted and the grouping of electives resulted in continued utilitarian choices. Many students simply took the easiest electives.

A third complaint about content is that the historical, theoretical, and philosophical foundations of law and relevant neighboring sciences are marginal in the curriculum. Students must take an examination in only one of these foundational areas. And since "foundations" are not part of the final examination, the average student just goes through the motions of obtaining the necessary credit. Finally, critics of the current system have long called for a rapprochement of theory and practice. The experiment of integrating theory and practice did not lead to the replacement of the traditional model, but rather introduced, in 1984, a practical component into the university phase. This reform, most feel, has had no real effect; it is just another motion for the students and educators to go through.

3. Examination System

A third complaint is the examination system. It is time consuming, and it is unrelated to earlier university courses. Since students tend to learn what they will be examined on, the current examinations do not complement university education in a meaningful way. Critics also point to the monumental dimensions: the vast subject matter of a comprehensive final examination that aims to cover years of university work. Another concern goes to the very heart of the present approach: many say that the examinations should no longer be uniform State Examinations, but should be administered by the universities or the different professions.

4. Focus on the Judiciary

This concern about examinations is related to yet another area of dissatisfaction: the focus on the judiciary. Not only do the law faculties fail to offer training in any practical skills (such as negotiation, drafting, advocacy, and moots), but they focus exclusively—in training as well as in evaluation—on impartial opinions rather than advocacy. While this may be justifiable as an academic approach, it is inadequate for the state-run portion of training, given the profession's current profile and its likely further diversification.

B.   The Post–War Reform Debate

Although calls for reform began in the last century, educational soul searching became widespread only after World War II. The reconstruction of German law and the increasing number of law students made many of the previously discussed issues more pressing, and a series of proposals ensued between the 1950s and the mid–1980s.

1.   The Past Debate (1956–1984)

The first round of post-war discussions generated the "Hattenheimer Plan" of 1956, which demanded a reduction of subject matter and other changes in the universities' approaches to legal education. Though it was commissioned by the Conference of Law Deans, in the end the plan did not win the deans' support. Four years later the Arbeitskreis für Fragen der Juristenausbildung (Working Circle for Questions of Legal Education) put forward its proposals. Again the aim was to reduce the required subject matter. The group suggested a division of university education into "base" and "intensification" phases, each followed by university-run examinations replacing the First State Examination. No specific reforms resulted from these proposals either.

The now-famous "Loccumer Memorandum" of 1969, coming on the heels of the university events of 1968, laid the groundwork for subsequent experimentation with one-phase models of integrated theoretical and practical education. The memorandum also advocated an increased integration of social sciences and new learning theories into legal education. The forty-eighth Deutscher Juristentag (Convention of German Jurists) in 1970 concluded with a majority's endorsing a one-phase training experiment.

Even though debate was often passionate, surprisingly little legislative change resulted. For example, the *DRiG* of 1961 made seven semesters the minimum instead of the average duration of legal education at the university level. In response to complaints about the overall duration of legal education, the law was changed in 1965 to reduce practical training from an overly long three and a half years to two and a half years. Then in 1971, responding to the Loccumer Memorandum and the recommendation of the Juristentag, Section 5b was inserted into the *DRiG*. It gave the Länder the freedom to launch experimental one-phase education models. Section 5b initially permitted such models for a period of ten years (it was subsequently extended to 1984) and allowed intermediate examinations or even grades received for courses and practical elements to substitute for the First State Examination.

The one-phase models set out to reduce the duration of legal education and to achieve a harmonization not only of theory and practice, but also of education and examination. But some advocates of these goals aimed well beyond the familiar structural questions. Their concerns were far more fundamental and ideological than those of previous reformers. Rather than merely ensuring more efficient and effective education and the training of "better" jurists, the proponents of the one-phase models wanted to train different, "new" jurists. Some charged that previous changes had been too insignificant to train the kind of person that the era needed. In a well-known essay, Wassermann argued that legal education had historically been "education into the establishment," and complained that the relative unimportance of historical and theoretical subjects deprived students of the tools needed to recognize the relativity of legal norms and the extent to which they reflected the dominant interests of the time. "Realism," concealing political and social implications of law, he argued, promoted the training of jurists unable to recognize that their decisions were often political. Wassermann called for the replacement of "unenlightened, apolitical" jurists by politically conscious jurists who considered change not an evil, but a necessity. Other advocates of one-phase models went further than Wassermann, placing even greater emphasis on the need to train jurists open to change. Lawyers, they argued, had to be conscious of and active in their role as "social engineers" and policy makers.

Justified though some of these concerns were, they had the effect of stigmatizing many one-phase models as "left-wing" or even "Marxist." Ultimately, this may have caused the legislature to return to the traditional model. Officially, however, one-phase education was rejected because it allegedly had not met the objectives it had set for itself. Neither the "parallel models," seeking to alternate theory and practice, nor the "interval models," relying on a more substantial introductory phase of theoretical education, satisfied their critics. The parallel models created substantial organizational problems and exposed the students to practical experience before sufficient theoretical foundations had been laid. The interval models could not meet the demands of specialization and intensification within the constraints of the second theoretical phase.

All one-phase models managed to reduce the duration of legal education and the drop-out rates while meeting the same academic standards as the two-phase model. But they were criticized for not achieving their goal of integrating social sciences. Above all, they were labeled as "deluxe education," unsuited for the reality of mass education. There appeared to be widespread agreement that the models, which relied on small-group education and placement of the students in a variety of practical settings, could not process the existing numbers of law students. Accordingly, in the 1984 amendments to the *DRiG,* the experimental clause of Section 5b was abolished and the traditional two-phase model reinstated as the only option.

2. *The Present Debate (1986–1992)*

Given this return to the traditional model, it is hardly surprising that the debate flared up anew. Only two years after the 1984 amendments, there were calls again for substantial reform. While nothing now proposed is entirely new, two things give reason to hope that there finally will be change—and soon. First, never before has there been such diverse and weighty support for tackling the previously sacrosanct state monopoly on examinations and the notion that the Einheitsjurist must be modeled on the judiciary. Second, the prospect of increased European competition and of German education's being side-stepped via training elsewhere has given new urgency to the demands for change. The original goal of this intense new reform effort was to bring changes into effect by 1992. Although advocates of minimalist approaches remain, they are a distinct minority. Equally rare are those supporting nothing less than the complete abolition of the state examinations and the introduction of specialized rather than unified legal education.

The first item on the majority agenda is a tightening of university education to just four or five years. Though approaches may vary, it is suggested that academic training be divided into a Grundstudium (base or introductory study element) and a Vertiefungsstudium (intensive or in-depth study element), either with or without a practical component. The latter is to promote some degree of specialization even at the university level.

This goes hand in hand with the second concern of the majority agenda—the demand for a reduction of subject matter. Rather than tinkering with compulsory and elective subjects, the call is now for a narrow but solid core curriculum and subsequent specialization. In this context some demand that both "foundations" and European law should play a role for all students.

Most reformers also want to modify the current examination process. While some argue that the First State Examination should be put in the hands of the universities, others want to maintain its character as a State Examination. But all agree that education and examination must finally be better coordinated. So everyone wants some stratification of the examination process and increased control by the universities. The suggestions range from dividing the examinations into portions following the Grund-und Vertiefungsstudium, to counting performance in different courses in the final result.

The reformers also urge changes in the preparatory service which, in the differing views, would then last between one and a half and two and a half years. Interestingly, one of the more radical proposals comes from the Deutscher Richterbund (German Association of Judges), which—deviating from a previously held position—now demands only that future judges and state attorneys be trained by the state. Lawyers trained in other branches of the profession could qualify for judicial office by taking supplementary examinations. More widespread is the view that the practical part of legal education should continue to be unified and state-monitored but should allow for specialization. Again with some variation, a consensus appears to be developing that practical training should provide a general and a specialized component. During the general stage students should continue to be exposed to judicial work, but then they should be allowed to prepare for a career of their choice. The Second State Examination is to remain, although suggestions similar to those made for the First Examination are being discussed.

The current discussion, then, reveals a consensus in several areas. The education should be shortened; specialization is necessary and overall subject matter must be reduced; the Einheitsjurist will remain the focus of German legal education, but with redefinition; examinations must be more realistic in scope and consistent with what is taught; and the system will continue to have two phases but strive to integrate them more effectively.

An expert actively involved in the reform process predicted in 1991 that the redesigned version would probably look like this. University education would be divided into three years of Grundstudium devoted to core subjects and one year of Vertiefungsstudium devoted to an elective. The First State Examination would be replaced by a stratified university examination conferring the degree of Magister Legum. Possibly, early submission to the examination would be encouraged by allowing students to rewrite examinations and count the better result. Though the concept of the Einheitsjurist would be maintained, preparatory service would be reduced to two years, including six months' mandatory training in the civil branch of the judiciary but with other elements flexible. Students would have to submit to a Second State Examination.

While this may have been the consensus in 1991, a proposal agreed upon by the German Länder in 1992 did not live up to those expectations. It also failed to bring the more fundamental changes demanded by many of those involved in the reform debate. Pursuant to the proposal, the "normal duration of university studies would continue to be seven semesters." But the material covered by the final examination would be limited in such a way as to permit students to finish their studies after eight semesters at the latest. Students would also be given the opportunity to take their examinations as they go along.

Contrary to the consensus that had appeared to emerge in the previous year, the proposal does not envisage a transfer of authority over the final examinations to the universities. Instead it seeks to preserve the First State Examination. But it does follow the previous agreement by shortening the preparatory service. It calls for a two-year training period during which students would be given more opportunity to focus on international and European practice than is currently the case. A comprehensive Second State Examination would continue to be required for all legal professions. Under the Länder proposal, the Einheitsjurist would thus survive yet another round of reforms.

What reforms will eventually be enacted remains to be seen. The Länder proposal has been criticized as falling far short of what is "urgently needed." Certainly the initial schedule which envisaged the implementation of reforms by the summer of 1991 has not been met. German reunification rendered consensus on a uniform legal education system more difficult. Given the desolate state of the judicial system in Germany's new eastern Länder, more urgent issues drove legal education from its top position on the Ministries' agendas.

Another article could be written on the rebuilding of a functioning legal system in the eastern part of Germany. Suffice it to highlight only a few of the emerging problems: integrating inadequately trained law students into the (West) German education system, since no practical education system is currently available in the East; establishing a functioning judiciary from judges unfamiliar with (West) German law and those few that can be lured away from more attractive careers in the West; establishing a private practice, previously next to nonexistent; re-establishing law faculties and staffing them with qualified and politically untainted teachers.

III.   The European Dimension

The preceding review begs the question of whether German legal education lives up to its reputation or its own goals. The answer must be that for most purposes it does not meet its potential. That is true for the large number of students who are driven out of the universities and practical training placements and into mechanical learning which, ironically, makes passing grades in the final examinations easier to achieve. It is less true with respect to those who choose to go beyond such superficial learning experiences and look for deeper understanding. But even for these relatively few students the system neither provides nor facilitates access to some of the training that the market increasingly demands. The market looks for young graduates who, beyond their law degrees, have qualifications in economics, languages, and international relations. An educational system that wants to remain relevant and competitive must incorporate or at least accommodate this reality.

* * *

What, then, are the answers to the many questions arising from the German debate? A reform of the system must not only provide answers to the long-standing questions presented in this paper: a successful reform must accommodate the European dimension. This, I submit, goes far beyond the notion that Europeanization is an added incentive to shorten lawyer training. The challenge, as will be argued below, is not only structural; it is also substantive, and legal education in Germany—as elsewhere in Europe—must be prepared for it. How reform is to be effected must be decided in two steps. First, we must ask what the system should achieve. Then we must determine how to achieve these goals without losing sight of the European dimension.

The first step of inquiry requires coming to grips with the recurring themes of the reform debate. It is clear that the system will continue to be one of mass education and open access. Some of its current flexibility will have to be sacrificed to achieve the changes widely seen as necessary: a reduction in duration, a sizing-down of the material covered, the addition of certain new subjects, and the creation of a more meaningful examination system. In all this the Einheitsjurist ... is likely to survive another round of reform, albeit with some alteration.

All these aspects—and this is why a second step of inquiry is important—have European dimensions. While the Einheitsjurist model is valued because it implies mobility between careers in Germany, mobility between careers in European legal systems will soon become a far greater asset to members of the legal community. As we will see, this, in turn, has direct implications for the questions of access to, and structure, length, and subject matter of, German legal education.

The current German debate is, with some exceptions, still largely introspective, preoccupied with the first of the two steps suggested here. As yet it has not incorporated the European debate. This failure could prove to be of consequence, for the debate sheds some light on the future demands on legal education in all European countries. According to some of the visionaries of European legal education, far more comprehensive renewals than those discussed in Germany will be required. Two themes that have emerged are the notions of a "European Law School" and of a "European Common Law."

* * *

This directly translates into three demands that national law schools and legal education systems will have to meet if they want to remain competitive. First, they must pay greater attention to European content. Law faculties must offer more instruction not only in European Community law and comparative law, but also in the kinds of areas advocated by the proponents of more radical changes. Knowledge of common historical, philosophical, and theoretical foundations will provide lawyers with the basic vocabulary and grammar needed to explore other legal systems. While this type of instruction may not immediately proceed from a European perspective, it could take into account parallels to other European legal orders and thus prepare the ground for increasing Europeanization.

The second demand will be for universities to offer programs that encourage or at least accommodate exchanges, permitting their own students to earn credits elsewhere in Europe and opening their own programs to students from other countries. This is not only a question of access, but also one of creating a curriculum that allows foreign students to complement their education in a meaningful way.

Last, but not least, all this implies a greater emphasis on languages. It is already evident in many branches of the profession that knowledge of one or more foreign languages will be indispensable for the European lawyer.

German reformers would be well advised to give more consideration to these implications of European integration. While drastic changes toward European common law and law schools are neither likely nor necessarily desirable, the goal should be to create the foundations on which to build the future. The new legal education system should prepare educators and students for the challenges of the future, and it must be flexible enough to accommodate the ensuing changes.

In my view these goals could be attained by designing a four- to four-and-a-half-year university curriculum consisting of a "foundation" and a "specialization phase." During the foundation phase of two and a half to three years the students would be required to take courses in legal history and theory emphasizing European legal traditions. In addition, they would have a slimmed-down catalog of core subjects including European Community law. Evaluation would be on the basis of either stratified university examinations or examinations within each course, enabling students from foreign countries to gain qualifications pertaining to German law. At the same time, German students could satisfy some of their overall requirements by taking courses elsewhere in Europe. In the specialization phase students could choose to Europeanize their qualifications with study in other countries, or they might concentrate on a more national orientation.

The practical training period should be cut to two years and should contain a compulsory element of training in the civil judiciary. Not only does the civil judge's approach to law provide students with valuable technical and analytical skills, it also provides a good opportunity to reinforce the foundations of the students' knowledge of law. The second training element, however, should be optional and should allow a student to specialize in a chosen area. Arguably this scenario would make students less likely to side-step German legal education; many will prefer the all-round qualification in its new shape to a shortcut through another country. But since some shortcutting must be expected and since foreign practitioners will have to be accommodated, a portion of the relevant specialization training should be made suitable for such candidates. Naturally, they would not be admissible to the State Examination, which I envision at the end of the practical training period. Rather they would have to submit to a separate examination qualifying them to practice in Germany.

Notes and Questions

1. What Rudolph Schlesinger has said about German legal education is equally true of other civil law countries: the fundamental problem is the unfavorable ratio of teachers to students.[4] In recent years, a climate of economic austerity has made it unlikely that civil law faculties will be able to advance much further toward furnishing alternatives to the lecture method and toward providing students with regular examinations and feedback.

2. Professor John H. Merryman identifies three "fundamental differences" between the civil law and American systems of legal education: (1) the civil law schools with their relatively open admissions and low fees "tend to be more democratic while in American law schools meritocracy is the dominant ideal"; (2) private law schools do not exist in most civil law

---

4. R. Schlesinger, H. Baade, M. Damaska, and P. Herzog, Comparative Law 179   (5th ed. 1988).

countries, whereas in the United States they are arguably the pace-setters for legal education; there is thus less standardization and less governmental control of legal education in the United States; (3) the educational process itself is of much more interest and concern in the United States; a "higher degree of self-consciousness" about the aims and methods of legal training characterizes American legal educators. J. Merryman, Legal Education There and Here: A Comparison, 27 Stanford L.Rev. 859 (1975).

3. After reading about German legal education, as described by Brunnée, how do you think American law schools measure up? Has either system effectively bridged the gap between theory and practice? What is the potential of American clinical education as compared to European practical training programs? Are European systems as vulnerable as American ones to the criticism that legal education is neither rigorously theoretical nor practically useful?

4. Would American legal education benefit from a more ordered, systematic approach to the study of law? For Professor Mirjan Damaska, the "essence" of continental legal education consists of (1) an exposure to the "network of precise interrelated concepts, broad principles and classificatory ideas" that he calls the "grammar of law"; (2) the presentation of a comprehensive overview of the major areas of law; and (3) an initiation into the characteristic methods of legal reasoning. He finds that, in American legal education, by contrast, "very little importance is attached to the conceptual digestion of the law." His discussion of differences in mentalities between continental and American lawyers is well worth reading. M. Damaska, A Continental Lawyer in an American Law School: Trials and Tribulations of Adjustment, 116 U.Pa.L.Rev. 1363 (1968).

5. If you find Damaska's observations persuasive, consider the fact that the typical introduction-to-law course in a continental law school is basically just an introduction to civil law. Such an orientation to the fundamental concepts of private law in the civil codes, (like that of the common law student to case law), largely fails to take account of the legal materials and types of law (statutes, especially of the regulatory sort, administrative law and public law of all kinds) that are in fact predominant in modern legal systems. Because of their division of labor between "public" and "private" law specialists, European law schools find it especially difficult to construct comprehensive courses on the legal system as a whole. See generally, M. Glendon, The Sources of Law in a Changing Legal Order, 17 Creighton Law Review 663 (1984).

6. In the future, it is likely that comparative legal studies will play an increasingly important role in European legal education. According to Brunnée, the "visionaries" among European law professors are reviving the notion of a European common law and looking forward to the establishment of European law schools:

> Writers such as Helmut Coing and Hein Kötz predict that beyond the law of the European Community and the harmonization of national laws, European jurists will need to lay the foundations of a European *jus commune*. As the common market will require common laws, Coing argues, a European jurisprudence, drawing upon common traditions, will have to develop. Coing suggests that necessary steps on this way

include the transition from largely national legal thinking to an exploration of foreign legal orders, their histories, and their methodologies; an enhanced role for comparative law; and, not least, a Europeanization of legal education.

The latter aspect is taken up by those advocating the "European Law School." The most radical of these proposals envision institutions that have little in common with the contemporary national law faculties. Two Belgian jurists suggest that the European law school of the future should devote the initial stage of education to the European *jus commune*. This stage should familiarize students with basic concepts and principles of law, legal traditions, and legal methodologies common to European legal cultures, and should emphasize the study of comparative law. Only in a second phase will students be trained in the respective national laws.

Although such a law school is unlikely to emerge soon, contemporary European law teaching cannot be blind to three immediate implications of the Europeanization process. First, the laws of Europe will be increasingly harmonized or even unified, and in national legal situations the laws of other European countries will be more and more directly relevant. Second, more and more lawyers will have to be capable of working in several languages and legal systems. Finally, as a result, more students will have to study in other countries, and universities will have to accommodate more foreign students.

Jutta Brunnée, "The Reform of Legal Education in Germany: The Never–Ending Story of European Integration," 42 Journal of Legal Education 399, 424 (1992).

SECTION 2. LEGAL PROFESSIONS

It is apparent that undergraduate legal education of the kind described by Brunnée does not produce graduates who are trained to embark immediately on the practice of law. In fact, many students who take their general university education in law in civil law countries do not do so as a prelude to a career in the legal professions. By graduation, a student will have acquired facility in the "grammar of law" and a knowledge of the basic principles of the most important fields of law, but only a limited ability to do legal research and a nodding familiarity with the practical aspects of law. In contrast, the American law graduate is supposed to be prepared to do any kind of legal work (although to be sure a kind of de facto apprenticeship is needed before a beginning lawyer is capable of handling many matters alone). If the civil law graduate wants to enter a legal profession, some further practical training is required.

The type and duration of such training varies from country to country and often depends in part on the kind of legal career the graduate wishes to pursue. The civil law graduate is faced upon graduation or shortly thereafter with a choice among the various branches of the profession, a choice which is likely to be final. In a fundamental way this puts the civil law graduate in a quite different position from that of a budding American lawyer. It is uncommon for a civil law lawyer to change, as American lawyers often do, from one kind of legal career to another, or to combine careers during one's professional life. Once trained to be a practicing lawyer, a judge, a civil servant or a scholar, the civil law lawyer is more apt to remain so than a common law lawyer, even though the latter often experiences a gradual reduction in mobility over time through increased specialization.

In France, the crucial choice is made early since different kinds of practical training are required for different branches of the profession. The German *Referendar* system, discussed by Brunnée, which serves as an apprenticeship for several different legal careers, gives the law graduate more time and a better opportunity to make an informed choice of career.

A. PRIVATE PRACTITIONERS

In order to enter private practice, the civil law graduate must ordinarily prepare for and pass a special examination and serve a practical internship in a legal setting, as under the German *Referendar* system. In France, however, there is no such multi-purpose training period. A French law student who wishes to become a practicing lawyer must first obtain the *licence en droit* (the university degree awarded after three years of law study); the *maîtrise* (the degree awarded upon successful completion of a fourth year); and then pass a bar examination. Upon passing the bar, the graduate becomes a probationary lawyer for at least three years, during which time there is further course work and practical training.

In most civil law countries, the practicing legal profession is officially divided to some extent, at least between lawyers and notaries. The *notary* occupies a special position in civil law systems.[5] Unlike the common law figure with the same name, the civil law notary is an important legal personage. The notary has three major functions: drafting certain documents such as marriage contracts, wills, mortgages, and conveyances; certifying documents which then have a special evidentiary status in court proceedings; and serving as a depositary for the original copies of wills and the like. Part of the uniqueness of the notary's position comes from the fact that a notary is a public official with a state-protected monopoly over some of these functions (typically marriage contracts and mortgages) within a given region. There are a limited number of notarial offices established by law. A law graduate who wishes to be a notary must pass a special examination and then wait for a vacancy. Unlike the regular lawyer, a notary is supposed to be impartial and to instruct and advise all parties involved in the transactions he or she handles. Because of the nature of these transactions, the

---

5. See generally, L. Neville Brown, The Office of the Notary in France, 2 Int'l & Comp.L.Q. 60 (1953); N. Horn, H. Kötz & H. Leser, German Private and Commercial Law: An Introduction 44 (1982).

notary often becomes a trusted family legal advisor whose assistance is needed in connection with the property aspects of such major events as marriages, divorces and death of a family member.

Whether or not the bar is officially divided, there tends to be in most civil law countries, as in the United States, a de facto division of labor between those lawyers who advise clients and those who appear and argue before courts, as well as among the various legal sub-specialties. In recent years, especially in the more developed countries, the practice of law has been profoundly affected by the types of legal services demanded by large enterprises. It is often observed that this kind of client requires planning and drafting more than litigation services, and that a certain bureaucratization of the private bar has resulted. The increase of lawyers engaged in serving large organizations has brought about an expansion of the roles of the legal consultant and the notary, and, although small law firms have been the rule in civil law countries, a certain trend has emerged toward larger-sized firms. At the same time, with the expansion of government in modern times, large public bureaucracies have absorbed increasing numbers of lawyers.

B. GOVERNMENT LAWYERS

As in common law countries, many civil law graduates enter government service after completing their training and examinations. In some places, Germany for example, lawyers dominate the higher offices in the civil service, while in others, such as France, the various official bureaus and agencies are apt to be staffed by persons who have been trained in a special school of administration. In Italy and Spain, a central government agency serves as the "law firm of the state", providing legal advice and representation to other government departments.

The public prosecutor in civil law countries is a civil servant, too. Like a district attorney in the United States, the public prosecutor prepares and argues the government's case in criminal matters. But in this role he is much more an officer of the court than an American prosecutor normally is. In most civil law systems, the prosecutor has an additional function—that of representing the public interest in certain ordinary civil cases. On the theory that the parties to such proceedings will not always provide the judge with a full presentation of the facts and law, and will never provide an impartial view, the prosecutor is permitted, and in some cases required, to intervene in civil cases. In this role, the prosecutor is supposed to represent the interest of "society" as distinct from the interest of the state. Some civil law systems, like the German, are content to let the judge perform this function.

An interesting aspect of the position of the public prosecutor in Italy and France is that the prosecutor is a member of the judiciary. A prosecutor follows the same course of training as a judge, and they both may move from one role to the other in the course of their advancement in the civil service. In France, the judges are known as the *magistrature assise* (sitting judiciary) and the prosecutors as the *magistrature debout* (standing judiciary). In Germany, although the prosecutor is not technically a member of the judiciary, he or she is not strictly separate from it either and prosecutors and judges move easily from one position to the other.

Notes

1. The legal profession in the United States, predominantly composed of private practitioners, is often contrasted with its continental counterparts whose members are more often found in government service. For example, 70 percent of the American bar were engaged in private practice in 1980 as compared to only 33 percent of the West German bar in 1975. In the same years, 13 percent of American lawyers and 38 percent of West German lawyers occupied government positions. Law Practice, 67 A.B.A.J. 1098 (1981); Geck, The Reform of Legal Education in the Federal Republic of Germany, 25 Am.J.Comp.L. 86, 87 (1977). It should be noted, however, that bureaucratization seems to be a long-term convergence trend. In the United States, the number of solo practitioners is in decline, while the numbers employed by large private and public organizations is steadily increasing. See Clark, The Legal Profession in Comparative Perspective: Growth and Specialization, 30 Am.J.Comp.L. 163 (1981).

2. Differences from country to country in the training of lawyers and the structure of the legal profession have given rise to knotty difficulties as European integration proceeds. Nevertheless, as Roger Goebel writes, "There is unmistakable progress toward an integrated market for the practice of law throughout the [European] Community." Goebel, Lawyers in the European Community: Progress Towards Community–Wide Rights of Practice, 15 Fordham International Law Journal 556 (1991–1992). For a discussion of how the European Court of Justice and European Community legislation have handled the problem of harmonization of the legal profession, see Dominik Lasok, The Professions in the European Community: The Treaty Framework, 20 Colum.J.Trans.Law 11 (1991).

3. For further reading on legal roles and actors in various societies, see the three-volume Lawyers in Society (1988–89), edited by Richard Abel and Phillip Lewis.

C. JUDICIARY

A law student in a common law country who gives any thought to becoming a judge one day is apt to consider a judgeship as something one might look forward to as a recognition of a long and distinguished career at the bar. In civil law systems, by contrast, a judicial career is just one of many options open to a beginner. A new law graduate who aspires to be a judge can expect to be sitting on the bench as soon as he or she completes a training period and successfully passes an examination. This is because the judiciary, except at the highest levels, is just another civil service hierarchy in civil law countries. A young judge enters at the lowest level and over time works up through a regular series of promotions. Ordinarily, only positions on the highest courts are open to distinguished practitioners or professors as well as to career civil servants. Lateral entry into the judiciary at any level is uncommon.

In some countries, such as France, Spain and Japan, there are special schools for training judges. In others, such as Germany and the Nordic countries, judicial training is acquired in the post-law school practical internship period.[6] In Germany, for example, a law graduate may be appointed to a lower court after completing the *Referendarzeit* and passing the Second State Examination. After serving a three-year probationary period, he or she becomes eligible for an appointment for life. In France, the first step to becoming a judge is to pass an annual competitive examination for which students prepare by taking a special program in their last year of law studies. Successful candidates then must undergo 28 months of training consisting of a period of formal study at the National School of the Judiciary in Bordeaux, followed by a series of short practical internships in such settings as police departments, law offices, prisons and the Ministry of Justice in Paris. This training culminates in a judicial apprenticeship, during which the future judge participates on a daily basis in all the activities of a variety of courts. Upon completion of their training period, the students are ranked on the basis of their grades and the evaluations of supervisors, and then assigned to their first positions in the judicial system. Since the administrative law courts in France are not part of the judiciary, but rather of the administration, most judges for these courts are drawn, not from the lawyers trained in the National School of the Judiciary, but from the civil servants trained in the National School of Administration.[7]

DANIEL J. MEADOR, "GERMAN APPELLATE JUDGES: CAREER PATTERNS AND AMERICAN–ENGLISH COMPARISONS"

67 Judicature 16, 25–27 (1983) *

Judges on the appellate courts in the Federal Republic of Germany differ from appellate judges in the United States, as well as in England, most significantly in the stage of professional career at which they enter the judicial service. German judges, like judges in other European civil law countries, enter the service near the beginning of their professional careers—typically upon completion of the two-year period of practical training following several years of university study. Contrary to widespread American belief, however, this does not mean that a German judge has no experience outside the judiciary; ... many German appellate judges have served as prosecuting attorneys and ministry officials.

---

6. On recruitment and training of West German judges, see generally, Schram, The Recruitment of Judges for the West German Federal Courts, 21 Am.J.Comp.L. 691 (1973), and Meador, German Appellate Judges: Career Patterns and American–English Comparisons, 67 Judicature 16 (1983).

7. Recruitment to the administrative courts, including the Conseil d'État, also takes place by invitation. Although the majority of judges achieve their positions by performing well on a competitive examination, others are recruited from among civil servants who have "distinguished themselves in the practice of public administration." L.N. Brown & J.S. Bell, French Administrative Law 79 (4th ed. 1993).

* Reprinted with permission of Daniel J. Meador.

What they do lack is substantial experience as private practitioners. In the two leading common law nations, England and the United States, persons do not usually enter the judiciary until after lengthy experience at the bar or in other legal work outside the public service.

That difference is well known. What is not so well understood is that there are similarities between the German and English systems for choosing appellate judges that differentiate both from American selection procedures. The most striking similarity is the system of career management through an official agency—a well-organized and directed process through which a person is made a judge at the trial level, and, based on performance there, is eventually promoted to the appellate bench.

In Germany this career management is handled by the various *Land* ministries of justice. In England the process is managed through the Lord Chancellor's office. The latter office, like the German ministries of justice, maintains comprehensive files on every barrister beginning with the time that he "takes silk," that is, when the barrister is appointed Queen's Counsel. Those having that status form the pool from which appointments are made by the Lord Chancellor's office to the High Court of Justice—the major trial court—and it is from the judges of that court that the judges on the Court of Appeal are chosen.[13] In no American jurisdiction—state or federal—is there a permanent office that continually scrutinizes lawyers or judges with an eye toward filling judicial vacancies and promoting judges from one court to another.

The German and English concept of a permanent office with a professional career staff engaged continually in this work is an idea that can be usefully adapted in the United States. Such an office could be established in the federal government as well as in state governments; it would not in any way be inconsistent with American customs and traditions concerning the selection of judges. Whatever method of judicial selection may be employed, this type of office and staff could provide useful continuity and more fully developed information, thereby improving the quality of persons brought to the bench and the process of appraising persons for promotion to higher courts. The value of the office would be greatest where judicial selection is through nominating commissions or executive appointment; but even where judges are elected by popular vote, the office would provide valuable assistance to the executive since even in elective systems many judges are appointed to fill vacancies.

The promotion concept is another aspect of the German and English systems differentiating them from the American. It is a concept that needs to be given more attention in the United States. Although in England a person does not become a judge until well into his professional career as a practitioner, once he is brought into the judicial service he is on a promotional track under the control of the Lord Chancellor's office, much as German judges are under their *Land* ministry of justice. In the

---

13. This selection procedure is more fully described in Meador, English Appellate   Judges from an American Perspective, 66 Geo.L.J. 1349, 1371–83 (1978).

United States more serious attention to the promotion idea would enhance prospects for recruiting abler people into the first judicial levels. It is sometimes difficult to attract the best legal talent into judgeships on the lower state trial courts and into federal magistrate positions. If there were a substantial prospect of advancement to higher courts, based on performance, a larger number of able persons would likely think more seriously about a career in the judiciary.[15]

The implementation of a promotion system and the maintenance of a permanent office on the judiciary go together. The former could not be achieved without the latter. Although there is much about the German legal system and the German judiciary that would not fit comfortably with American traditions and institutions, the existence of such arrangements in England indicates that they are not inconsistent with Anglo–American legal concepts.

The advantages of the civil law systems of judicial recruitment are that they make the career more accessible to members of diverse groups in society and provide greater assurance that all judges will be able to perform in a competent manner. Thus, there are proportionately more women judges in European countries than in the United States and the likelihood of a person with no particular judicial qualifications becoming a judge is practically ruled out. On the debit side, however, it is frequently observed that civil law judges, because of their standardized training, tend to share a common outlook, and that their concerns about advancement promote a civil-service mentality which discourages initiative and independence.[8]

Though there are signs of change, the judge still has a relatively low profile in most civil law systems. As John Merryman has put it, the standard image of the civil law judge is as a civil servant who performs important but essentially uncreative functions.[9] While the common law tradition reveres the names of the great judges who created the system and accords prestige and power to their modern successors, the names of civil law judges of the past are hardly remembered and their present-day successors work largely in obscurity. The tendency toward judicial anonymity is reinforced by the fact that civil law judges, even at the

---

15. Evidence to support this theory is contained in Davidow, Law Student Attitudes Towards Judicial Careers, 50 U.Cinn. L.Rev. 247, 371 et seq. (1981). A persuasive presentation of the idea of judicial promotion in the American setting is developed in Davidow, Beyond Merit Selection: Judicial Careers Through Merit Promotion, 12 Tex.Tech.L.Rev. 851 (1981).

8. E.g., N. Luhmann, The Legal Profession: Comments on the Situation in the Federal Republic of Germany, 20 Jurid.Rev. 116, 121 (1975): "The candidates for judi-

cial careers ... show a lesser degree of professional ambition. They tend to attribute events rather to circumstances than to themselves, they are less prepared to take risks and less capable of tolerating ambiguities. Their professional values are concentrated on security and on independence of their salaries from success or failure; they are directed more towards order than towards enterprise."

9. J. Merryman, The Civil Law Tradition 38 (2d ed. 1985).

lowest levels, usually sit in panels and their decisions are presented per curiam. Except in a few courts, such as the German Constitutional Court, any disagreement among the judges will not show, either in the form of a dissenting opinion, or in a notation of the judges' votes.

Today this area of contrast between the civil and common law systems is diminishing somewhat as lower court judgeships in the United States cease to attract the best candidates, while appointments to certain civil law high courts, such as the German Constitutional Court, tend to be made from among outstanding jurists. As with the bar, bureaucratization seems to be responsible for a certain convergence.[10] Increased litigation and crowded dockets have made much of the work of American judges administrative in nature, at the same time that civil law judges and their societies are slowly becoming conscious of the real law-making power of the judiciary. Furthermore, the German experience shows that prestige and civil service are not mutually exclusive. Nevertheless, in contemporary reality as well as in folklore, the common law judge remains a more powerful, creative and respected figure than his or her civil law counterpart.

One need not search far for the historical roots of the difference. From the time the administration of English justice was centralized in the King's Courts at Westminster by the end of the 13th century, the law was developed by judges, and the practicing bar dominated legal education. Although there were moments in history when things might have gone differently, the existence of a powerful English legal profession was an important, perhaps the crucial, factor in preventing an English reception of the Roman law brought back by English scholars from Bologna, and in checking the influence and power of university legal scholars. In our historical survey of the civil law tradition, we have already seen that the central actors were not judges, but great lawgivers, like Justinian and Napoleon, and the great scholars. Next to these towering figures, the judges are almost invisible. This was so even in the classical Roman times when the lay *judex* who decided cases and the *praetor* who gave him the formulae for decisions turned to the Jurisconsult for expert advice on the law. We have also seen how medieval judges depended on University law faculties for opinions on the law. The idea of the judge as a legal actor without inherent law-making power, who applies the will of the sovereign and looks outside for advice, is thus quite deeply rooted. When French judges, in support of the social order of the *ancien régime,* began to break out of this traditional judicial role and to behave more like English judges, making new rules and dealing creatively with the sources of law, they became the targets of revolutionary fury and post-revolutionary reaction. Then, when French ideas, law and institutions spread to other countries in the 19th century,

---

10. On the bureaucratization of the administration of justice in the United States, see generally, Clark, Adjudication to Administration: A Statistical Analysis of Federal District Courts in the Twentieth Century, 55 S.Cal.L.Rev. 65 (1981); Vining, Justice, Bureaucracy and Legal Method, 80 Mich.L.Rev. 248 (1981); McCree, Bureaucratic Justice: An Early Warning, 129 U.Pa.L.Rev. 777 (1981).

this reinforced the traditional civil law conception of the judicial function as a strictly limited one.

The narrow conception of the judge's role is nowhere so evident as in France. We have seen that the doctrine of legislative supremacy took an especially rigid form there, to the point of forbidding judges to announce general rules when deciding cases, and denying that law could be made by judges. Indeed, to this day, French legal writers say that the judiciary is not really a third "branch" of government. It seemed at first to follow, logically, that a court could not decide a case on the basis of its own or even a higher court's prior decision. The judge was merely to find and apply the law made by the legislative representatives of the people. Today, France has long since retreated from the extremes of these positions, but civil law judges in most countries still are far from exercising the kind of leadership that traditionally characterizes their American and English counterparts.

SECTION 3.   LEGAL SCHOLARS

When the renowned sociologist Max Weber turned his attention to the study of the world's legal systems, he observed that each had been decisively shaped by a particular group of leaders to whom he gave the name *Rechtshonoratioren,* the honored men of the law.[11] The religious legal systems of Islamic, Jewish and Hindu secular communities were fashioned by theologians. The English common law was the creation of those judges whom Blackstone called the "living oracles" of the law.[12] And, as we have seen, European continental laws received their characteristic features through the work of learned jurists.

It is the names of scholars, not judges, that have come down to us over the centuries of the civil law tradition, as the centers of high legal learning shifted from ancient Rome, to sixth century A.D. Byzantium, to 13th century Bologna, to 16th century France and Germany, to 17th century Holland and back to Germany in the 19th century. The civil law world venerates such names as Gaius, Bartolus, Domat, Pothier, Grotius, Pufendorf, Savigny, Gény and Jhering, as the common law world does Coke, Mansfield, Marshall, Story, Holmes, Hand, and Cardozo.

In Chapter 1 of this book, we traced the ascendancy of academic jurists in the civil law world through the 19th century. The longstanding practice of judges to ask professors for their opinions in difficult cases was, in some places, institutionalized so that binding decisions in lawsuits were rendered by university faculties. The absence, at crucial formative periods, of centralized government and unified legal systems assisted the university scholars in gaining and holding their dominant position. As the "law" in civil law systems increasingly became codified or statutory, and as the doctrine of legislative supremacy took hold, one

---

11. M. Weber, Law in Economy and Society 198–223 (M. Rheinstein ed. 1954).

12. W. Blackstone, I Commentaries on the Laws of England *69.

might well wonder why the law-maker did not fully supplant the scholar as the central actor in the civil law tradition. The answer seems to be related to the fact that it was the scholars and the professors who were the architects of the doctrine of legislative supremacy and the draftsmen of the codes (or important influences on the draftsmen). After the codes appeared, reliance on pre-code authorities declined, but the need for interpretation intensified. Legal scholars became the authoritative ex-pounders and interpreters of the codes. The law of the codes thus remained, in an important way, scholar-made law.

This is still largely the case today so far as the civil codes are concerned. When the family law provisions of the French Civil Code were extensively recast in the 1970s, the government turned the task over to the highly respected French civil law scholar and legal sociologist, Jean Carbonnier. And in the American state of Louisiana, the drafting work for civil code revision is carried on under the supervision of the Louisiana State Law Institute housed at Louisiana State University. The situation is different, however, when we depart from the domain of the civil codes.

As civil law systems, like those of the common law, have become increasingly dominated by frequently amended public and regulatory statutes outside the codes, one may wonder whether this change in the law itself in time will affect the position of the civil law scholars. John P. Dawson has pointed out that it was important for the success of the 19th century German legal scholars (culminating in the adoption of the German Civil Code) that their activities were almost exclusively concen-trated within the supposedly apolitical and relatively non-controversial area of private law.[13] In the 20th century, legislation increasingly is perceived as the product of conflicts resolved by majority vote, rather than of reasoned elaboration and adaptation of fundamental principles. As law becomes more public and bureaucratic, will the university jurist remain a protagonist of the civil law tradition?

Thus far it seems that the prestige of the academic lawyer in the civil law systems is relatively secure. In the first place, all other actors in the system receive their training from the scholars who transmit to them a comprehensive and highly-ordered model of the legal system that to a great extent controls how they organize their knowledge, pose their questions and communicate with each other. This model is not only taught in the universities but constitutes the latent framework of the treatises and articles produced by the professors. Furthermore, legal periodicals, which in civil law countries are run by professors rather than students, play a much more important role there than in common law countries in bringing new legislation and court opinions to the attention of the profession. The official reports of cases do not necessar-ily report all court opinions, nor do they always set forth the opinions in full. The bar tends therefore to rely on the editors of the privately published legal journals who select and print what they consider to be

---

13. J. Dawson, The Oracles of the Law 457 (1968).

the important cases. Typically each case is followed by an annotation written by an expert (not necessarily a professor) who may amplify the facts of the case, relate the case to other decisions, and discuss its general significance. Such legal periodicals are an indispensable tool of legal research.

Though not a formal source of law, the weight of scholarly authority, known in civil law terminology as "the doctrine," is everywhere taken into account by legislators and judges when they frame, interpret or apply law. Unlike in the United States, with its complex federal structure, the expert authors of this critical literature can concentrate on the relatively manageable output of a single legislature and, basically, of two sets of courts. The interaction between these legal institutions and the scholars who closely watch them tends to result overall in a more coherent and predictable body of national law than that generated by the legislatures and courts in the 50 states and the federal system in the United States. A critical case note by a leading author, is, in effect, like an important dissenting opinion, indicating where controversy exists and the possible future direction of the law.

Given the influence and prestige of the academic branch of the profession, it is not surprising that the career of a law professor is not one that is easily accessible to law graduates in civil law countries.

In order to become a law professor in France, a law graduate must first obtain the degree of *Doctorat d'État* (a process that can take several years). That degree makes him or her eligible to take a rigorous national examination called the *Agrégation*. There are separate *Agrégations* for public and private law, a circumstance that tends to reinforce the strong separation that exists in legal pedagogy between those fields. After successfully passing that examination, the candidate becomes eligible for governmental appointment to a university position.

In the following excerpt, the author describes the background and status of German law teachers.

WILHELM KARL GECK, "THE REFORM OF LEGAL EDUCATION IN THE FEDERAL REPUBLIC OF GERMANY"

25 American Journal of Comparative Law 86, 105–108 (1977).*

Statutory law qualifies a full university professor *per se* for a position as judge or higher civil servant without the two normally required state examinations. In practice however the law professor has usually passed these two examinations with good grades, written a doctoral dissertation and worked as a professor's assistant. He then qualifies for a professorship (becoming a *Privatdozent*) in a formal procedure before a law faculty (*Habilitationsverfahren*). This requires an additional monograph (*Habilitationsschrift*) or a number of shorter

* Reprinted with permission of the American Journal of Comparative Law.

but significant publications and a test-lecture before the faculty council. High ranking judges and other jurists who have excelled in their fields through practice and publications are sometimes called to a chair without these formal procedures. All this produces, on the whole, scholars well qualified in their special fields. Capability as a teacher has not usually played the role it should have. In fact, for a long time a German professor often considered himself a scholar who also taught, rather than an individual whose scholarly research and teaching were equally balanced. Recent developments have made it very difficult to retain this self-image; in the many fields with masses of students, it is impossible.

Traditionally, German professors are not promoted at their own university, but better their working conditions, as well as salaries, only when they receive a call from another faculty. Since such calls again depend more on scholarly writing than on success in teaching, some German professors are more interested in research and publication than in teaching.

The freedom of research and university teaching is protected by the federal and state constitutions. The full and associate professor has life tenure, i.e. to a retirement age of 65 or 68 years. Depending largely on the calls he has had, he has one or more assistants and a half or full-time secretary. The full professor's salary is at least equal to that of a judge presiding over a 3–judge senate in a court of appeals. In extremely rare cases, it could reach the salary of the presidents of the highest federal courts, with the exception of the Federal Constitutional Court. The majority of the professors are somewhere in between. They are better off than most attorneys, but earn much less than the stars in that field.

As a body the full professors formerly practically ruled the university; they also elected its head, usually for a term of one or two years. Only ten years ago—according to public opinion polls—the full professor enjoyed the highest social prestige in the Federal Republic. During the last years, this picture has changed considerably.... The student explosion has ... contributed towards changing the traditional *Einheit von Forschung und Lehre* (unity of research and teaching) gradually into an *Einheit von Lehre, Prufung und Verwaltung* (unity of teaching, examining and administration). Research is on the decline almost everywhere.

There has been some inflation of professors. Under the influence of democratization postulates and political pressure, the state authorities decided on wholesale promotions of members of the junior staff, who were frequently not fully qualified and now block these positions for better qualified candidates. The state authorities also conferred the title of professor on the teaching staff of other institutions of higher learning besides universities. In consequence, new statutory regulations have been passed which will greatly curtail the chances of future professors to improve their working conditions, as well as their salaries. The fact that we have no shortage of qualified candidates now, due to the glamor of the past, contributes to this development. Before long, the professorship will likely lose its attraction. The times when a judge of the highest federal court would gladly accept a professor's chair may already be over.

As professorial publications have a considerable influence on the practice of the judiciary and the executive, I have always regretted that many German law professors had no practical experience except for their time as legal trainee. Even so there are valuable contacts between theory and practice. The law qualifies the full university professor for all the legal careers I have mentioned, even if he has not taken the two state examinations. He may act occasionally as a defense counsel, but is not permitted to engage permanently in private law practice. Still, a number of professors are actively engaged in legal work outside the university, not to mention the ones who go into politics as parliamentarians or state or federal cabinet ministers.... Professors of constitutional or economic law are called upon to write advisory opinions on difficult legal questions, or to represent a party in procedures before a constitutional court.... The law faculties have been very well represented on the Federal Constitutional Court during its first twenty years. At the moment, there are two full and two honorary professors among the sixteen judges....

Most professors have at some time or another worked as assistants. The assistants play an important role in the university. It is impossible for the professors alone to grade the numerous papers in the practical courses. The assistants do most of the teaching in smaller groups. If there is still time, they help the professors in their research. The full-time assistants have passed the second state examination, usually with well above average success. They have almost the same salary as a beginning judge of a lower court. For those assistants who later enter the judiciary or the higher administrative service, two years of university service may be counted toward obtaining life tenure. The full-time assistants are usually also working on their doctorates or on a monograph towards the *Habilitation*.

––––––

It is easy to overstate the contrast with the role of legal academics in the United States. Especially in Germany, the status and influence of civil law judges has reached the point where their relationship with legal scholars has become what John P. Dawson has termed "a close working partnership" that has greatly benefited the legal system as a whole.[14] At the same time, in the United States, Max Rheinstein traced the rise of law teachers and scholars as a "new group of co-leaders of the law," and the tendency of American law to assume some of the traits of "professorial" law, which, however, because of the active role of professors here in social reform, assumes a different character from European professorial

14. Dawson, Unconscionable Coercion: 1124 (1976). The German Version, 89 Harv.L.Rev. 1041,

law.[15]

To summarize then, even in modern administrative states where scholar-made civil law is in decline, it is still the scholars who supply the vocabulary, concepts, and methodology of the system. Though the word of the legislator is accorded the supreme position among the sources of law, the word often issues from, and its ultimate meaning is often determined by, the academy. With the rising power and prestige of civil law judges and the growing influence of legal scholars in the United States, however, the traditional distinctions between these legal roles are tending to diminish.

15. Rheinstein, Leader Groups in American Law, 38 U.Chi.L.Rev. 687 (1971).

Chapter 4

PROCEDURE IN CIVIL LAW SYSTEMS

SECTION 1. CIVIL PROCEDURE

In civil law countries, civil procedure occupies the same central position in procedural law that the civil law occupies within substantive law. The basic source of law in this area is typically a code of civil procedure. Modern procedural codes stress that judicial proceedings must be public and that, in principle, the control of the allegations and proof belongs to the parties. This latter principle, however, tends to be tempered in practice by the civil law judge's extensive power to supervise and exercise initiative in the proceedings as well as by the role that the public prosecutor can play in private actions.

In a typical civil action, after the pleadings are filed, a period of evidence taking begins. From the outset, several differences from common law civil procedure appear. These differences can be summed up by noting that on the one hand, there is no real counterpart to our pre-trial discovery and motion practice, while on the other hand there is no genuine "trial" in our sense of a single culminating event. Rather, a civil law action is a continuous process of meetings, hearings, and written communications during which evidence is introduced, testimony is taken, and motions are made and decided. During this process, the judge plays an active role in questioning witnesses, and in framing or reformulating the issues. Although the questioning is typically done by the judge, the questions are often submitted by the parties' counsel who sometimes are permitted to question a witness directly. As the action proceeds, the judge may inject new theories, and new legal and factual issues, thus reducing the disadvantage of the party with the less competent lawyer. In addition, the court may obtain certain types of evidence, such as expert opinions, on its own motion. There are no requirements that documents be formally admitted into evidence, nor are there any rules against hearsay and opinion evidence. Rather, the parties informally introduce documents after providing the other side with notice and an opportunity to inspect. The weight to be accorded the evidence is for the free evaluation of the court.

Except for minor matters which do not concern us here, the bench is usually collegial, but as a rule only one judge will preside over the evidence-taking stage of the proceedings. In some countries, it may happen that the case is decided by an entirely different judge or panel from the one or ones who heard the parties and took the evidence. The better practice, as exemplified by Germany, requires the judge who conducted the proceedings to render the decision in the case. A money judgment on the merits is generally executed out of the defeated party's property. As civil law courts traditionally had no contempt power, it is said that their decrees are *in rem* rather than *in personam*. However, today some civil law judges are authorized to hold persons in contempt of court and, in other jurisdictions, the judge may impose financial sanctions (the French *astreinte*) [1] on persons who refuse to comply with a court order. Costs of litigation are taxed in such a way as to discourage severely hopeless or frivolous causes: as a rule, the defeated party bears the cost of litigation, including attorney's fees. If each party wins and loses in part, costs are allocated proportionately.

Many of the differences between the foregoing model and the usual American trial seem attributable to the absence of the civil jury in civil law countries. The civil law countries have never felt the need to bring the parties, their witnesses, their lawyers and the judge all together on one occasion because they have not had to convene a group of ordinary citizens to hear all the evidence, to resolve factual issues, and to apply the law to the facts. The factor of the civil jury also helps to explain the relatively great number of exclusionary rules in the common law of evidence and the relatively few restrictions on admissibility in the civil law systems. However, recent developments in both systems tend once again in the direction of a certain convergence. American discovery practice and pre-trial hearings bring us close to a situation where, as in the civil law, there are few surprises at trial. Meanwhile, civil law desire for efficiency and economy has led, notably in Germany, to experiments with a single comprehensive hearing model that is said to work well for the relatively simple cases that form the great bulk of civil litigation.

Pointing out that the usual distinction between our adversarial procedure and the civil law's supposedly nonadversarial procedure is often overdrawn, Professor Langbein has noted:

> Apart from fact-gathering, ... the lawyers for the parties play major and broadly comparable roles in both the German and American systems. Both are adversary systems of civil procedure. There as here, the lawyers advance partisan positions from first pleadings to final arguments. German litigators suggest legal theories and lines of factual inquiry, they superintend and supplement judicial examination of witnesses, they urge inferences from fact, they

---

1. For a description of the development of the *astreinte,* see Beardsley, Compelling Contract Performance in France, 1 Hastings Int'l & Comp.L.Rev. 93 (1977).

discuss and distinguish precedent, they interpret statutes, and they formulate views of the law that further the interests of their clients.[2]

The main difference, Langbein suggests, between continental and American litigators is that the former are mostly "law-adversaries", while the latter are "law-and-fact adversaries." The central difference between the two systems, in his view, is that the American system leaves to partisans the work of gathering and producing the factual material upon which adjudication depends, while the civil law systems place greater responsibility for investigation of the facts upon the judge.[3]

A. CIVIL PROCEDURE IN THE FEDERAL REPUBLIC OF GERMANY

NORBERT HORN, HEIN KÖTZ AND HANS LESER, "GERMAN PRIVATE AND COMMERCIAL LAW: AN INTRODUCTION"

43, 45–50 (1982).*

The conclusion that legal institutions are essentially the same throughout the Western world is one that comparative lawyers often like to draw, but while it is true that certain common features will be found whenever and wherever judges try to resolve disputes in a rational manner, it is nevertheless undeniable that important differences of style and atmosphere emerge when one compares the civil procedure of Germany with that of a common law jurisdiction. Trial by jury may have practically disappeared from civil litigation in England, but it has still had a deep influence on the way civil matters are decided today. It is this tradition that helps to explain why trials tend to be so concentrated even when the judge sits alone, why the parties must be apprised of the precise issues and be fully prepared to meet and debate them when they appear in court, and why the trial is prepared so elaborately with the aid of discovery devices and pre-trial conferences.

In Germany there is no live tradition of trial by jury, and a civil suit is quite unlike the common law trial. In a civil case pending before the Landgericht there will be a number of isolated meetings and written communications between the parties, their attorneys and the judge; during the course of these meetings evidence will be introduced, testimony given, motions and rulings on procedure made, and areas of agreement and disagreement gradually marked out. The proceedings tend to be very unconcentrated.

This has a number of consequences. First, the pleadings are very general. Issues are defined as the case proceeds, and it is possible to

---

2. Langbein, The German Advantage in Civil Procedure, 52 U.Chi.L.Rev. 823, 824 (1985).

3. Id.

* © Hein Kötz 1982. Reprinted from German Private and Commercial Law: An Introduction, by Norbert Horn, Hein Kötz, and Hans G. Leser, translated by Tony Weir (1982), by permission of Hein Kötz and Oxford University Press.

introduce new motions, causes of action and issues with relatively few sanctions. Second, there is much less pressure on the German attorney to forearm himself with information and argument on every fact or claim that might possibly arise and prove relevant; if unsuspected facts do emerge or unforeseen allegations are made he will always be given an opportunity to search for and present additional proof. It is therefore hardly surprising that the German attorney is not equipped with the common lawyer's powers of discovery—those effective means, backed by the power of the court, for tracking down and finding out the facts that may be relevant. Nor is the German attorney especially active in pursuing information on his own. Of course, he will have full consultations with his client and will examine his papers and files before the action starts; but he will not feel at all free to talk to prospective witnesses or take statements from them. Only in special circumstances is it thought advisable to question witnesses out of court: if a witness has previously discussed the case with counsel, a German judge might be very suspicious of his testimony.

In England the many decisions that may have to be made in preliminary proceedings before the trial really begins are made by a master or registrar. In Germany they fall to the judge himself, who will hold a series of meetings with the parties and their lawyers to raise and resolve such questions as whether the court has jurisdiction, whether certain statements of fact can be agreed, whether an expert is required, which witnesses should be called, and whether a settlement is possible and, if so, on what terms. German civil procedure lays much less stress than the common law on having everything done by word of mouth. Matters that are raised in oral conference are usually put in writing forthwith; and if one of the attorneys raises a new point orally, the other often asks the court to give him a certain period of time to put his answer in writing, a request that the court usually grants.

Nor is it by any means left to the parties to drum up as many witnesses as they choose. The German judge will do his very best to minimize the number of factual issues that can only be resolved by hearing witnesses. Significantly enough, witnesses can only appear pursuant to a special order made by the judge, stating which witnesses are to be examined and on what factual issues. Such an order is not subject to appeal and will be made only on controverted issues which the judge believes crucial to the disposition of the case.

Finally, German civil procedure has no counterpart to the highly complicated rules of the common law regarding the exclusion of various kinds of evidence. Doubtless these rules were intended to prevent the jury being misled by untrustworthy testimony, but since in German civil procedure the evidence is evaluated by professional judges, any evidence, including hearsay evidence, is admissible in principle, and it is for the judge to decide how much weight to give it.

In the last few years people in Germany have realized that the practice of having a number of isolated meetings and written communications between the parties, their attorneys and the judge, with the ensuing loss of concentration, is one of the causes of the length of time that civil suits often take. Accordingly, a new method of handling civil suits has been devised and tried out in many Landgerichte. It is known as the Stuttgart procedure (Stuttgarter Verfahren), and consists of preparing the case so thoroughly, by means of written procedure and at the most one preliminary meeting, that the matter can be resolved conclusively through a single comprehensive hearing in court. The Code of Civil Procedure was amended in 1976 so as to permit the judge, if he chooses, to adopt this method of proceeding, but of course one must wait and see how widely the Stuttgart procedure is adopted in practice.

A common lawyer who attended one of the conferences in a German civil suit would think the judge rather vocal and dominant and the attorneys relatively subdued. In part this is because the court is supposed to know and apply the law without waiting for counsel to deploy it *("iura novit curia")*, but more importantly, the court is under a statutory duty to clarify the issues and help the parties to develop their respective positions fully (§ 139 ZPO). Accordingly, the court asks questions and makes suggestions with the aim of inducing the parties to improve, modify, or amplify their allegations, to submit more documents, to offer further proof, to correct misunderstandings, and to throw light upon what may be obscure.

The extent to which a court will do this depends on a number of factors. Of course, the court must not commandeer the case or manage the litigation in the place of the parties, and it goes without saying that only the parties may make allegations, offer proof, and submit motions; but if a party is appearing in person or is represented by inexperienced or incompetent counsel, and the judge feels that he may be put at a disadvantage by oversight, inadvertence, or a clear misapprehension of the applicable law, the judge may make his suggestions with some vigour in order to reach the right result, notwithstanding any faults of advocacy. Similar considerations underlie the judge's duty to avoid "surprise decisions" (Überraschungsentscheidungen), that is, decisions that in the circumstances the parties had no reason to expect. Thus the Code of Civil Procedure provides that, if the court is to found its judgment on a view of the law whose validity or relevance a party may well not have realized, it must first give him a chance to be heard on it (§ 278 par. 3 ZPO).

The way in which a witness is interrogated also indicates the somewhat inquisitorial nature of German civil procedure. The court itself asks the witness his name, age, occupation, and address, admonishes him to tell the truth, invites him to recount what he knows of the matter without undue interruption, dictates periodic summaries to the clerk, and questions the witness so as to test, clarify, and amplify what he has said. Once the court is satisfied, the attorneys are invited to ask further questions, but in general the attorney's role in examining witnesses is relatively modest, in part because the court has normally covered the ground already, in part because a lengthy examination might suggest that the court had not done its job properly.

It should be added that experts are not, technically speaking, witnesses at all. They are usually appointed by the court, act under the court's instructions, and owe the court a duty of loyalty and impartiality. Accordingly, in a German court one rarely sees head-on clashes between experts called by the parties and paid to be partial, subjected to fierce examination and cross-examination by attorneys who have just acquired a smattering of their expertise for the purpose. "The German system puts its trust in a judge of paternalistic bent acting in co-operation with counsel of somewhat muted adversary zeal." [13]

Expenses of Litigation and Legal Aid

The expenses of litigation consist of attorneys' fees and court costs. Court costs, unlike those in England, are by no means negligible. They are fixed by statute, and consist of one or more "basic units". The number of units payable depends on the number of stages the proceedings have run to, but not on how long the proceedings take or how complex they are or how much work they require of the court. In a fully contested case three units will be payable, the amount of the unit being fixed by the statute in relation to the amount involved in the litigation. According to the Code of Civil Procedure, the principle that "the loser pays" applies to attorneys' fees and court costs (§ 91 ZPO). A party must therefore bear the litigation expenses of that part of the case as to which he turns out to be the loser. He must reimburse the winner, not only for the court costs he may have had to pay, but also for his attorney's fees, including disbursements by counsel incident to the case and other expenses. This applies, however, only to expenses that a reasonable litigant would have incurred under the circumstances, and a loser who thinks he is being overcharged in the bill presented by his opponent may ask the court to review it....

A person who is too poor to sue or defend a suit may ask for legal aid (Prozess–Kostenhilfe) whatever the proceedings. If he wishes to sue, he goes to the attorney of his choice and the attorney submits a petition for legal aid along with the statement of claim. In contrast to the English system, the court itself then decides whether legal aid should be granted or not. There are two preconditions. First, there is a fairly rigorous means test; the court may require monthly contributions from a petitioner whose income exceeds the limits specified by law. Second, the court must satisfy itself at a preliminary stage of the proceedings that the petitioner's allegations disclose a prima facie case. If legal aid is refused, the petitioner may appeal. If it is granted, the court normally appoints the plaintiff's attorney as legal aid attorney and allows the plaintiff a provisional exemption from court costs.

13. Kaplan, Civil Procedure–Reflections on the Comparison of Systems, 9 Buffalo L.Rev. 409, 432 (1960) (a brilliant article). [For a discussion of important changes made in 1977, see Gottwald, Simplified Civil Procedure in West Germany, 31 Am. J.Comp.L. 687 (1983) Eds.].

If the assisted party succeeds in his suit or defence, his attorney recovers his full fees and expenses from the loser just as in a normal case. If the assisted party loses, his attorney recovers fees and expenses from the legal aid fund, though if the case involves more than DM5,600 (= £1,400) the fees will be lower than those normally payable. For example, in a case worth DM10,000, the legal aid attorney receives 83 per cent of the normal fees; in a case worth DM20,000, only 60 per cent; and in a case worth DM40,000, only 48 per cent. A successful opponent may claim reimbursement of his litigation expenses from the assisted party personally, but he has no claim against the legal aid fund even if the assisted party is a person of no substance at all. This is certainly unjust in cases where the assisted party was the plaintiff, for the state ought to be bound to indemnify the defendant for his expenses if its grant of legal aid enabled the plaintiff to molest him with an unfounded suit. The present system of legal aid has met with increasing criticism in recent years. The main complaints are, first, that a poor party cannot obtain legal aid if all he wants from an attorney is legal advice rather than assistance with litigation, and, second, that legal aid is unavailable to those whose financial position is slightly above subsistence level, although they are unable to bear the full cost of litigation. A bill has been drafted by the Federal Ministry of Justice which would improve the situation substantially . . . .

It is worth adding that in Germany it is quite lawful and fairly common to take out insurance against the financial consequences of having to sue or be sued in certain fields, such as civil and criminal cases arising from the operation of a motor vehicle.

ADDENDUM

On 18 June 1980 the Law on Legal Advice in Non–Contentious Matters (Beratungshilfegesetz) was enacted. This provides that a poor person is also entitled to legal aid if all he wants is legal advice rather than assistance with litigation. The idea that legal advice should be provided at the state's expense by public citizen's advice bureaux and similar publicly-funded institutions gave rise to heated debate in Germany, but the Bar was strongly opposed to such schemes and in the end its opposition was successful. The statute now provides that the poor person may make a direct approach to an attorney who will, before or after giving advice, file a petition for legal aid with the Amtsgericht: the petition contains information on the petitioner's financial means and the nature of the business on which the advice is sought. Legal aid is available in matters of civil, criminal, administrative and constitutional law, but not in labour law matters. Here it was believed that the services provided by the advice bureaux of the trade unions were adequate—a doubtful assumption in view of the fact that only unionized workers are entitled to such advice. Legal aid is not available in Hamburg or Bremen, for these states have for many years funded a well-established system of citizens' advice bureaux.

* * *

As to attorneys' fees, there is a statute which lists and defines in minute detail every possible act of advice or litigation, and lays down that for every act so defined the attorney is entitled to one "basic fee" or to a multiple or fraction thereof.[8] For instance, an attorney is normally entitled to three "basic fees" for conducting a lawsuit, one being payable when the action starts, another when the oral argument begins, and the third when evidence is taken. The amount of the "basic fee", under the statute, is related to the amount involved in the action or other matter handled by the attorney. In principle, therefore, the attorney's fee is the same whether the case involves a lot of work or a little, whether it is complex or simple, whether the client is rich or poor, whether the attorney is well-known and experienced or not, and whether or not he is successful in the case. Where the lawyer gives advice or acts for the client in some other way outside court, there may be some scope for flexibility in putting a value on the matter, so the schedule of statutory fees may operate less rigidly; but in litigation the value of the matter will be evident from the sum claimed, or else it will be fixed by the court, as in the case of divorces and other nonpecuniary claims. An agreement to pay a fee higher than the statute prescribes has to be in writing; to charge a lower fee is considered unethical. To work for a contingent fee is not just a breach of etiquette: the Bundesgerichtshof has held such an agreement void as contrary to public policy.

The advantage of this method of charging for legal services is that the client may make a reasonably accurate pre-estimate of the cost of his lawsuit, since the attorney's fee is based on the value of the claim rather than on the relatively unpredictable amount of time he may have to spend on it. On the other hand, it may be argued that the attorney will be underpaid if a case of small value involves a lot of work, while he may receive a windfall for handling a simple matter with a large price-tag. This danger is probably more apparent than real. In the former case, the attorney may stipulate for a fee above the statutory tariff, or he may do only as much work as the statutory fee justifies. As to the second situation, cases involving a lot of money and little work are fairly rare, but if one should arise, the attorney may agree to "split the cause of action" and limit the claim to part of the sum at stake in the hope that the opponent, having lost the case, will pay the balance without more ado.

Note on the Importance of Procedural Context in Comparative Law

Recall that the American system of administration of justice seemed to suffer in comparison with the German in the study by Johnson and Drew of resources allocated to the courts, supra pp. 128–129. In the article excerpted below, Langbein illustrates how such comparisons can be misleading if divorced from the procedural context in which judges and lawyers operate.

---

8. See Federal Statute on Attorneys' Fees (Bundesgebührenordnung für Recht-   sanwälte) of 26 July 1957, as amended.

JOHN H. LANGBEIN, "JUDGING FOREIGN JUDGES BADLY: NOSE–COUNTING ISN'T ENOUGH"

18 Judges' Journal (Fall 1979) 4, 6, 50.*

The authors' premise in making these extrapolations from German to American data is that the two legal systems are what they call "comparable jurisdictions." For Johnson and Drew, a judge is a judge—no matter where he works or what he does—which is why they think to use German judicial manpower figures to show that American courts are "undermanned."

In truth, the judicial function changes radically when we move from adversarial to nonadversarial procedural systems. In a nonadversarial system like the German, the bench has a more active (and time-consuming) role in the handling of litigation, and it is this—rather than German fiscal munificence—that explains the size of the German judicial corps.

German Civil Procedure. American civil procedure places upon the lawyers for the parties—our so-called adversaries—the tasks of gathering evidence, shaping the issues and presenting the evidence. Our lawyers conduct pretrial discovery, select and prepare witnesses, and examine and cross-examine at trial. We expect our judges to exercise important checks upon the conduct of the adversaries in pretrial and especially in trial procedure, but the responsibility for propulsion and the vast preponderance of the workload remains with the litigants' lawyers.

The German system, by contrast, allocates to the court the primary role in gathering the evidence and shaping the litigation. There is no litigant-conducted discovery procedure, indeed German law does not even recognize our division between pretrial and trial procedure. The German system does not expect its lawyers (in the phrase of a splendid English-language account of German civil procedure) to go "quarrying for the facts. It is the judges, primarily, who conduct the proof-takings...." [10] The court's investigation, guided by the motions of the parties, extends across a series of hearings—as many as the court finds necessary in order to frame the issues and to establish the facts. The court carefully records the results of these hearings in the official file that it keeps for the case. A case that goes to judgment requires the court to prepare a full written opinion of law and fact; the Germans have no counterpart to the American civil jury, hence no general verdict to spare the court the work of opinion writing.

In so brief a summary I have already said enough about German civil procedure for the reader to see why it is preposterous for Johnson and Drew to claim that American and German judicial manpower statistics are drawn from "comparable jurisdictions." The real reason

---

* Reprinted with permission of the Judges' Journal and John H. Langbein.

10. Kaplan, von Mehren & Schaefer, Phases of German Civil Procedure I, 71 Harv.L.Rev. 1193, 1201 (1958).

that the Germans need more judges is the same reason that they need fewer lawyers: their civil procedure assigns to the judiciary much of the workload that we leave to private counsel.

Collegiality and Appeal. German civil procedure shares with the other Continental nonadversarial systems two further characteristics that dictate higher levels of judicial manpower. First, in cases above a relatively low jurisdictional amount, currently 3,000 marks or about $1,600, the German first-instance bench is collegial. A panel of three professional judges sits on each case (although one of the three customarily takes a more active role in the case). In a system that does not have a civil jury trial, it is easy to understand why such a safeguard has been thought desirable, even though the cost in judicial resources is significant.

Another notable characteristic of Continental procedure is the extreme liberality of appeal. The German rule in civil matters (which is also applied to the largest portion of the criminal caseload) is that the first-instance judgment is subject to full review de novo, with the taking of new evidence allowed. Needless to say, a system that so encourages appeal is required to maintain appellate benches that are enormous by our standards.

The "Bottleneck." The Johnson and Drew article makes no mention of these traditional Continental practices of collegial first-instance staffing and liberal appellate review. The authors relegate to a footnote their admission that on account of procedural (and substantive-law) differences, "Judges may play a larger role and spend more time on each case in a country like West Germany than in the United States." Astonishingly, the authors dismiss these differences by likening them to those "among states within the United States."

This insistence on treating European data as though it arose in American contexts leads the authors to mishandle their figures on the numbers of European lawyers. Their premise is that legal systems as disparate as the American and the German should somehow be expected to have constant per capita lawyer populations. Accordingly, when the authors discover that the number of practicing lawyers per judge in California is ten times that in West Germany, they infer that the American judiciary is being "overwhelmed" by the lawyers, who are seen as " 'input' (case generating) factors." These disproportionate lawyerly "inputs" must be leading to a "bottleneck" in the courts.

What Lawyers Do. Part of the reason why this inference is fallacious has already been set forth. Americans allocate the workload in civil (and criminal) procedure differently; when lawyers rather than judges do the basic investigative and forensic work in the legal system, more lawyers and fewer judges will be required than in a nonadversarial system like the German.

Johnson and Drew also ignored another factor that bears on the question of why the American legal system needs more practicing lawyers per capita than the German: Americans make somewhat larger use of private lawyers in preventive law. For example, will drafting and estate administration, which we think of as basic lawyerly functions, are rarely handled by lawyers in Germany, because of a variety of differences in the procedural and substantive law of testation. Similarly, in American business practice lawyers play a more central role in shaping and drafting transactions than do Continental commercial lawyers. For such reasons, said a Belgian law professor to an audience of New Yorkers, "Of all countries, the United States is the lawyers' paradise." [22]

Case Duration. Another reason why Johnson and Drew fail in attempting to extrapolate an American "bottleneck" from German data is that they do not adjust for differences in the ways that the two legal systems define and dispatch their caseloads. For example, Johnson and Drew compute that "California's rate of dispositions per judge in 1975" was 20 times that of West Germany, or six times if automobile-related offenses are set aside. However, this notion of "disposition per judge" conceals a host of variables.

Thus, the authors admit, but do not correct for, the fact that the Europeans tend to handle in specialized courts or nonjudicial tribunals matters that we process as lawsuits in our ordinary courts. The footnote that contains this admission invites readers to console themselves with the thought that something called the "law of large numbers" will cause these differences to "cancel themselves out...." The authors also ignore differences in criminal procedures: American courts still process a host of petty and regulatory offenses that the Germans have long since decriminalized; and American figures, which reflect our much higher rates of serious crime, are deeply distorted by the pretrial diversion and plea bargaining process that is so strongly suppressed in West Germany.[25]

In contrast, West Germany's nonadversarial procedure in both the civil and the criminal process appears extraordinarily efficient by comparison with our own. German law neatly avoids the profligacy of our discovery procedures; it knows no real counterpart to our complex motion practice and our law of evidence; and it taxes the costs of civil litigation (including attorney fees) in a manner meant to give constant incentive to litigants to abandon hopeless causes.

Learning from Others. I hope that the message of this article will not be mistaken. I do not mean to say that Americans have nothing to learn from the study of comparative legal institutions. I have elsewhere emphasized my belief that we can find suggestive models for the reform of American procedure in the sophisticated and efficient traditions of Continental law. My point is that Johnson and Drew have not studied the Continental systems in a reasonable way.

22. van Hecke, A Civilian Looks at the Common–Law Lawyer, in International Contracts: Choice of Law and Language 5, 8 (W. Reese ed.) (Parker School Studies in Foreign and Comparative Law) (1962).

25. See Langbein, Controlling Prosecutorial Discretion in Germany, 41 U.Chi. L.Rev. 439 (1974).

Johnson and Drew have fallen victim to the cardinal error of comparative legal studies, the one that will doom any comparative inquiry. They have neglected to look at the contexts from which they have drawn their comparative data, and thus inevitably they have misunderstood and misapplied the data.

[In a response to Langbein's criticism, Johnson stated that the "principal thrust" of the Johnson and Drew article had been "that the statistical facts were, on the whole, inconsistent with a widely accepted view that our justice system is huge and overly expensive compared with other countries." He disclaimed any intent to suggest that the major problems of the American justice system could be cured merely by increased funding as opposed to restructuring the methods of dispute resolution. Johnson, Maybe Statistics have Something to Tell us After All, 18 Judges' Journal (Fall 1979) 5.]

Notes

Suggestions for Research and Further Study

1. In recent reforms of our own system of civil procedure, to what extent have we moved along lines familiar to civilians? To what extent could we or should we move further along these lines? Claiming that "The success of German civil procedure stands as an enduring reproach to those who say that we must continue to suffer adversary tricksters in the proof of fact," John Langbein made a provocative proposal in The German Advantage in Civil Procedure, 52 U.Chi.L.Rev. 108, 866 (1985). Langbein pointed to "growing manifestations of judicial control of fact-gathering" in complex litigation, and stated: "Having now made the great leap from adversary control to judicial control of fact-gathering, we would need to take one further step to achieve real convergence with the German tradition: from judicial control to judicial conduct of the fact-gathering process. In the success of managerial judging, I see telling evidence ... that judicial fact-gathering could work well in a system that preserved much of the rest of what we now have in civil procedure." Id. at 825. For an argument that Americans could not adopt the "German advantage" without radically changing other aspects of our legal culture, see John Reitz, Why We Probably Cannot Adopt the German Advantage in Civil Procedure, 75 Iowa L.Rev. 987, 988 (1990).

2. Claims are often made that the United States is uniquely litigious. In Litigation–Mania in England, Germany and the U.S.A.: Are We so Very Different? 49 Camb.L.J. 233 (1990), Basil Markesinis points to serious comparability problems in assessing relative litigiousness in the tort area. The United States' experience with litigation seems distinctive in many respects. See Per H. Lindblom and Garry D. Watson, Complex Litigation— A Comparative Perspective, in Beyond Disputing: Exploring Legal Culture in Five European Countries 33, 34 (Plett & Meschievitz eds., 1991). On the basis of their cross-national study, Lindblom and Watson concluded that "Complex litigation as a significant and sustained problem appears to be one 'Born in the U.S.A.' out of a range of factors largely peculiar to that country."

3. In England and most civil law countries, an agreement between a lawyer and a client for a contingent fee is considered unethical and treated as void. R. Schlesinger, H. Baade, M. Damaska, & P. Herzog, Comparative Law 353–58, 702–10 (5th ed. 1988). The absence of the contingent fee, together with the "loser pays all" rule, raises the financial stakes of litigation considerably in such countries. However, the use of legal insurance, which is more common in Europe than in the United States, alleviates the risks to some extent for persons of moderate means. Also, access to the courts for indigents is provided by extensive, publicly regulated, legal assistance schemes. See generally, as to these, M. Cappelletti, J. Gordley & E. Johnson, Jr., Toward Equal Justice: A Comparative Study of Legal Aid in Modern Societies (1975) and M. Cappelletti & B. Garth, I Access to Justice (1978).

4. John P. Dawson has pointed out that no adequate explanation has ever been given for the fact that the standard American rule which excludes attorneys' fees from recoverable costs is at variance with the practice in continental European countries and in England that the "loser pays all". Dawson, Lawyers and Involuntary Clients: Attorney Fees from Funds, 87 Harv.L.Rev. 1597, 1598–1601 (1974). Should our rule, which is now subject to several exceptions, be changed? Could it be changed without making other substantial changes in our civil procedure systems? See R. Schlesinger et al., Comparative Law 354, 358 (5th ed. 1988). For an extensive study of the rules concerning the allocation of attorney fees and other costs among the parties to civil litigation in 12 European countries, with an appendix containing translations of all the relevant statutory provisions, see Pfenningstorf, The European Experience with Attorney Fee Shifting, 47 Law & Cont. Problems 37 (1984). The article appeared in a symposium containing several other articles on fee shifting including Leubsdorf, Toward a History of the American Rule on Attorney Fee Recovery, 47 Law & Cont. Problems 9 (1984).

5. Should judges have more control than they do presently in the United States over the framing of issues and the structuring of civil litigation? Why or why not? What assumptions concerning the role of courts in civil litigation underlie your answer? Are courts merely to assist in the peaceful settlement of individual disputes or do they perform other, more "public", roles as well? See Jolowicz, Some Twentieth Century Developments in Anglo–American Civil Procedure, 1 Studi in Onore di Enrico Tullio Liebman 217 (1979).

6. Problems of overcrowding, expense and delay in the courts have led not only to efforts in the world's legal systems to make courts more efficient and accessible, but also to the exploration of alternatives to the courts for dispute resolution. For discussion of what, in recent years, has become a trend of worldwide importance to experiment with informal methods of resolving disputes, see the various reports of the Florence Access-to-Justice Project. They include M. Cappelletti & B. Garth eds., Access to Justice: A World Survey (1978) (Volume I, in two books); M. Cappelletti & J. Weisner eds., Access to Justice: Promising Institutions (1979) (Volume II, in two books); M. Cappelletti & B. Garth eds., Access to Justice: Emerging Issues and Perspectives (1979) (Volume III); K. Koch, Access to Justice: The Anthropological Perspective (1979) (Volume IV). See also M. Cappelletti ed.,

Access to Justice and the Welfare State (1981). For essays presenting a critical view of the alternative dispute resolution movement, see The Politics of Informal Justice, 2 vols. (R. Abel ed. 1982).

7. For further reading in English on civil procedure in Germany, see Gottwald, Simplified Civil Procedure in West Germany, 31 Am.J.Comp.L. 687 (1983); and the three classic articles: Kaplan, von Mehren and Schaefer, Phases of German Civil Procedure I, and II, 71 Harv.L.Rev. 1193 and 1443 (1958); and Kaplan, Civil Procedure—Reflections on the Comparison of Systems, 9 Buffalo L.Rev. 409 (1960). For France, see, New Code of Civil Procedure in France, Book 1 (F. Kerstrat & W. Crawford transl. 1978) and Herzog, Civil Procedure in France (1967). For Italy, see M. Cappelletti & J. Perillo, Civil Procedure in Italy (1965).

SECTION 2. CRIMINAL PROCEDURE

There are three common misconceptions in the common law world about criminal procedure in the civil law countries: that the accused is presumed guilty until proved innocent, that there is no jury trial, and that the trial is conducted in an "inquisitorial" fashion (with connotations of Inquisition-like unfairness to the accused.) The first of these notions is simply false. The second is incorrect as to some systems and, as to others, overlooks the fact that lay judges who participate on mixed courts with professional judges are a functional analog to the jury. The third misapprehension has resulted from the fact that the usual mode of proceeding in criminal cases in civil law systems is quite different from that which evolved in the common law. The epithet "inquisitorial" apparently derives from the active role played by the judge in the conduct of the trial, and, often, in investigating the facts. A better word to describe this process would be nonadversarial.

The first phase of a criminal proceeding is an extensive pre-trial investigation, conducted in some countries by a judge, in others by the public prosecutor. This official decides whether there is sufficient evidence to warrant formal charges, after interrogating the witnesses, collecting the other evidence, and questioning the suspect. Under modern codes of criminal procedure, the accused has the right to be represented by counsel during the interrogation and to remain silent.

If the examining magistrate or prosecutor determines that there is what we would call reasonable cause, the dossier compiled during the preliminary investigative phase is forwarded to the criminal court. There is considerable variation among systems as to the composition of this court. Typically, one or three professional judges sit with a number of lay judges. Both the professional and lay judges participate in the decision of all factual and legal issues relating to the determination of guilt, and also in the sentencing decision.

In contrast to the accused in an American criminal prosecution, the defendant in a civilian prosecution has an unlimited right to discovery of all the evidence assembled by the prosecution. During the trial, the presiding judge takes the lead in examining the witnesses and the defendant.   Two major differences from the common law adversary model are that the judge is less a passive arbiter between the parties, while the prosecutor is less partisan.   The system seems to elicit no such dissatisfaction and controversy in the major Western European democracies as have plagued the American criminal justice system.   "Except for political cases, which no system handles well, ... the task of detecting and punishing crime is generally perceived to be handled effectively and fairly," according to John Langbein, a leading American specialist in comparative criminal procedure.[4]

A peculiarity of criminal procedure in the civil law systems is the role accorded to the victim.[5]   In some countries, if the same wrongful act gives rise to both criminal and civil liability, the injured person is permitted to intervene directly in the criminal action rather than bring a separate civil suit.   If the victim chooses to become a party to the criminal suit, and is successful, the court may order civil damages to be paid to the victim at the termination of the proceedings.   In France, this *action civile* is not uncommon.   But in Germany, procedural and practical difficulties have discouraged its use.   However, Germany, like many other civil law countries, has another way of permitting the victim to join the prosecution.   In recognition of the victim's interest in seeing justice done, a victim who does not seek damages may sometimes be allowed to intervene on the side of the prosecution.   A guilty finding in such a case will then play an important role in any subsequent civil action by the victim.   Also, in certain types of cases, if the prosecutor declines to bring charges, an injured person may be permitted to bring a criminal proceeding individually.   However, in Germany and some other countries, the prosecutor has no discretion not to prosecute (and therefore no power to plea bargain) if there is reasonable cause to believe that the defendant has committed a serious offense.

RUDOLF B. SCHLESINGER, "COMPARATIVE LAW"

475–90 (5th ed. 1988).*

I.   OUTLINE OF THE COURSE OF A CRIMINAL PROCEEDING IN A CONTINENTAL COUNTRY

In the civilian systems, as in our own, the policeman normally is the first public official to arrive at the scene of an alleged crime, or to receive a report concerning it.   He may conduct an informal investigation; but his power to arrest the suspect without a judicial warrant, or to proceed to warrantless searches and seizures, generally is more limited than here.   Thus, at least as a rule, it becomes necessary at a very early stage of the investigation to involve the prosecutor and the court.

4. J. Langbein, Comparative Criminal Procedure: Germany 1 (1977).

5. J.A. Jolowicz, Civil Remedies in Criminal Courts, XI (Torts) Int'l Encyc. of Comp. Law, Ch. 13 (A. Tunc ed. 1972).

* Reprinted with permission of Rudolf B. Schlesinger and The Foundation Press.

There is no grand jury. The official phase of the pretrial investigation is in the hands of a judge—whom the French call *juge d'instruction*—or of the prosecutor. Both the judge and the prosecutor are essentially civil servants. The judge enjoys the usual guarantees of judicial independence. The prosecutor does not; he may be a link in a hierarchical chain of command, often leading up to the Minister of Justice. Nevertheless, except perhaps in cases having strong political overtones, the civil-servant prosecutor operating in a continental system can be expected to be reasonably impartial. He does not have to run for re-election; and his promotion within the civil service hierarchy may depend as much on his efficiency in sorting out and dropping investigations mistakenly commenced against innocent suspects as it does on his record of procuring convictions of the guilty.[4]

The magistrate or prosecutor conducting the investigation will build up an impressive dossier by interrogating all available witnesses, including those named by the suspect, and collecting other relevant evidence. The suspect himself will be interrogated, and in the most progressive continental countries such interrogation will take place in the presence of his counsel. In many civil law countries the law expressly provides that the suspect has a right to remain silent and that he must be informed of this right. Of course, there is no physical compulsion to make him talk. Experience in continental countries shows, nevertheless, that in the preliminary investigation as well as at the trial itself the defendant usually does talk. The reasons for this will be explored below.

At the conclusion of the official investigation, the prosecutor (or, in some countries, the investigating magistrate) must decide whether in his judgment the evidence is strong enough to warrant the bringing of formal charges against the suspect. If charges are brought, the accused still does not necessarily have to stand trial. Under the traditional civil law practice, the dossier now goes to a three-judge panel—on a higher level of the judicial hierarchy. Only if this panel, having studied the dossier and having given defense counsel an opportunity to submit arguments and to suggest the taking of additional evidence, determines that there exists what we would call "reasonable cause," will the accused have to stand trial. (It should be noted here how misleading it can be to call the Continental procedure "inquisitorial" and to contrast it with our allegedly "adversary" process. Under continental procedure, the accused has a two-fold opportunity to be heard—first in the course of the preliminary investigation, and again when the three-judge panel examines the dossier—*before* any decision is made whether he has to stand trial. This should be compared with the completely nonadversary grand jury proceeding by which a prosecutor under our system can obtain an indictment.)

---

4. In many of the continental systems, moreover, the discretionary powers of the prosecutor are much more narrowly circumscribed than in this country. See Herrmann, The Rule of Compulsory Prosecution and the Scope of Prosecutorial Discretion in Germany, 41 U.Chi.L.Rev. 468 (1974); Langbein, Controlling Prosecutorial Discretion in Germany, 41 U.Chi.L.Rev. 439 (1974).

In every civil law country, counsel for the accused has the absolute right to inspect the whole dossier. This will be discussed later.

At the trial, the bench normally (though not uniformly) will consist of one or three professional judges and a number of lay assessors. The jury system, which was introduced in Continental Europe in the wake of the French Revolution, more recently was replaced in most Continental countries by the system of the mixed bench.[a] Under this system, the professional judges and the lay assessors together form the court, which as a single body passes on issues of law as well as fact, and determines both guilt and sentence. Thus, the trial does not have to be bifurcated into a first hearing devoted solely to the issue of guilt, and a subsequent second hearing dealing with the sentence. The issue of guilt and the measure of punishment are determined simultaneously and by the same body of adjudicators.

The dossier, reflecting the pretrial investigation, plays a role during the trial as well. Three of the *dramatis personae* at this point are thoroughly conversant with its contents: the prosecutor, the defendant's counsel, and the Presiding Justice. The Presiding Justice has the dossier in front of him during the trial. On the other hand, the lay judges, and often the professional judges other than the Presiding Justice of the court, are unfamiliar with the dossier. Consequently, only the evidence received in open court (as distinguished from the contents of the dossier) may be considered in reaching a decision.

After a reading of the charges, the Presiding Justice normally will call upon the defendant to give his name and occupation and to make a statement concerning his general background. Then, after a warning that he has the right, at his option, to remain silent concerning the charges against him, the defendant will be asked what (if anything) he wishes to say about the charges. The defendant, who is not put under oath, at this point has the opportunity to tell his side of the story by way of a coherent statement. This will be followed by questions addressed to the defendant. In practice most of the questioning will be done by the Presiding Justice, who is well prepared for this task by previous study of the dossier in his hands. Prosecution and defense counsel may suggest, or be permitted to ask, additional questions.

After this interrogation of the defendant, the witnesses will be examined in similar fashion. Normally, the witnesses will be the same individuals whose preliminary testimony is recorded in the dossier, but additional witnesses, not discovered in the course of the pretrial investigation, may be subpoenaed by the defense or may appear voluntarily at the trial. Nontestimonial evidence, especially physical evidence, also may be produced, and the court may inspect the place of the crime.

No technical rules of evidence impede the process of proof-taking.

a. See Langbein, Mixed Court and Jury Court: Could the Continental Alternative Fill the American Need? 1981 Am.Bar Fndn.Res.J. 195; Casper & Zeisel, Lay Judges in the German Criminal Courts, 1 J.Leg.Stud. 135 (1972).

After closing arguments by prosecution and defense, and after the defendant has been accorded the last word, the court retires to deliberate. The lay judges, whose vote in most (but not all) continental countries carries the same weight as that of their professional colleagues, may outnumber the latter. In the great majority of civil law countries, the judgment does not have to be unanimous; and the fact that it is not unanimous will not be disclosed. Unless the judgment is one of acquittal, it will pronounce conviction and sentence. It will say, for example, that defendant is found guilty of armed robbery and for such crime is sentenced to four years in the reformatory.

As a rule, the judgment of the court of first instance is subject to an appeal on both the law and the facts. New evidence may be presented to the appellate court, and the proceedings before that court, which has power to review the sentence as well as the determination of guilt or innocence, may amount to a trial de novo. The decision of the appellate court normally can be attacked by a second appeal to a court of last resort, but in this last court only questions of law will be reviewed. The right to appeal is given not only to the defendant but to the prosecutor as well.

* * *

II.   Arrest and Pretrial Detention in Civil-Law Countries

With the above comments as a background, let me now turn to a discussion of some of the procedural devices and arrangements to be found in civil law countries that might provide American reformers with food for thought.

The first two items—treated together because they are so closely connected—are arrest and pretrial detention.

In this country, it is still the general rule that criminal proceedings routinely "start with the harsh, and in itself degrading, measure of physical arrest." In the federal courts, and in less than one-half of the states, this brutal and (as a rule) unnecessary routine has been modified by statutory provisions that in certain situations authorize the issuance of a summons in lieu of arrest. But these modifications are halfhearted; frequently they are limited to cases of minor violations, and most of the relevant provisions leave it to the discretion of the police or the prosecutor whether a summons should take the place of physical arrest.

The civil law countries, on the other hand, unanimously recognize that the initiation of a judicial proceeding, whether civil or criminal, never requires the defendant's physical arrest. It follows, according to civilian thinking, that the necessary notification of the defendant is to be effected by a summons, in criminal as well as civil proceedings, and that it is unthinkable to use physical arrest as a routine measure against a suspect who has not yet been tried and who, consequently, must be presumed innocent.

The question whether a suspect should be detained pending trial is, in the civilians' view, completely separate and distinct from the routine of initiating the proceeding. Such detention is regarded as the exception rather than the rule. Except in carefully defined emergency situations, a judicial order is required to detain the suspect before trial. The requirements for the issuance of such an order are strict. In West Germany, for instance, it can be issued only if the court, by definite findings of fact, determines that the following three elements exist: First, there must be strong reasons for believing that the suspect has committed the crime. Second, the evidence before the court must show a specific, rational ground for pretrial detention, such as danger of flight or danger of tampering with the evidence. Third, such detention must meet the requirement of proportionality; that is, it will not be ordered if the hardship caused by it is disproportionate to the gravity of the offense. The order, which must state the grounds on which each of these requirements is thought to be met, is subject to immediate appeal.

Compare this rational system of pretrial detention to our traditional bail procedure, still prevailing in the majority of states, under which the wealthy suspect will be released even though he is likely to flee or to intimidate witnesses, while the indigent defendant will be kept in jail despite the absence of any rational justification for detaining him....

III.   THE PROSECUTOR'S AND THE DEFENDANT'S CONTRIBUTION TO THE SEARCH FOR TRUTH

The two remaining topics I should like to discuss have one feature in common: both of them bear, directly and importantly, upon the central function of the criminal process, the ascertainment of truth.

A.   Discovery

The first of these two related topics comes under the heading of "discovery." The continental systems invariably provide that at an early stage of the proceedings, and in any event well before the trial, the defendant and his counsel acquire an absolute and unlimited right to inspect the entire dossier, that is, all of the evidence collected by the prosecution and the investigating magistrate. Thus it is simply impossible to obtain a conviction by a strategy of surprise. It must be remembered, moreover, that in most cases there can be a trial de novo on appeal, which, of course, acts as a second barrier against the successful use of surprise evidence.

To facilitate inspection of the dossier by defense counsel, German law provides that upon his request he should normally be allowed to take the dossier to his office or home for thorough and unhurried study.

Concerning this latter point, and generally concerning details of inspection procedure, other continental systems may not go quite so far as the German Code. But defense counsel's basic right to timely inspection of the entire dossier has become an article of faith throughout the civil law world—and, indeed, in the socialist orbit as well....

In its aversion to unlimited pretrial discovery in criminal proceedings, the American legal system today stands virtually alone. In England, the older common law tradition of trial by surprise has long been abandoned, and present English practice, by a combination of procedural devices and informal arrangements, permits defense counsel, well before the trial, to become fully familiar with every element of the facts known to the prosecution.

* * *

I submit that experience gained under the continental systems could be exceedingly useful in dealing with the classical anti-discovery arguments that continue to mold the attitude of our courts and legislators. Let us look, first of all, at the "abuse" argument, which is born of the fear that the defendant, once he is apprised of the State's evidence, will be enabled to prepare perjured testimony and to bribe or intimidate, or perhaps even eliminate, the witnesses for the prosecution. It must be conceded that in many situations, and especially in cases involving organized crime, this danger is real. American advocates of discovery have replied that the danger can be minimized by giving the court discretionary power to issue protective orders. *Quaere,* however, whether it is a satisfactory solution to leave everything to the court's discretion. The civil law has a better answer to the "abuse" argument. Under the continental systems—and I shall soon explain this more thoroughly—the defendant normally will have stated his own version of the facts in considerable detail at a very early stage of the proceedings. Thus, at the time when he or his counsel inspects the dossier, his position has assumed a sufficiently firm shape so that it can no longer be effectively improved by fabrications. The further danger, that prosecution witnesses might be bribed or intimidated, usually is neutralized in the civil law systems by the sensible rule that if at the trial the witness suddenly suffers a loss of memory or seeks to contradict his prior statements, his previous testimony can be used not only to assist his power of recall but even as substantive evidence. A slight modernization of our antediluvian rules of evidence (including the rule against impeaching one's own witness) would permit our courts to reach the same result.

To kill or incapacitate a prosecution witness before the trial, again will not help the defendant at all in a civil law country; the previous testimony of the witness is recorded in the dossier, and if the witness in the meantime has become unavailable, this particular portion of the dossier may be read at the trial. . . .

It follows, I submit, that the answers by which the civilians have neutralized the "abuse" argument against effective discovery are relevant in our system as well.

The only other respectable argument against unlimited discovery is that of prosecutors crying "one-way-street." Even if one is free from prosecutorial bias, one must wonder why, in an allegedly adversary system, one party should have to play with completely open cards, while the other party—the party who presumably has the most intimate knowledge of the facts—has the right to sit back and in effect to limit his utterances to two taunting words: "Prove it." . . . As a practical matter, it does not seem likely that unlimited discovery—the hallmark of civilized criminal procedure—will be widely and effectively introduced into our system unless the "one-way-street" argument can be laid to rest.[28] To do that, one must take a fresh look, aided by comparison, at the whole problem of the defendant's contribution to the ascertainment of the true facts. This brings me to the final topic of the present discussion.

B.   The Accused as a Source of Information

The role of the accused as a source of information in the truth-finding process is an important and thorny topic in any system of criminal procedure. It is also the topic concerning which—upon superficial inspection—the gap between common law and civil law appears most unbridgeable.

Closer analysis, however, shows that the rock-bottom principle that is the foundation of all specific rules in this area of the law today is shared by virtually all civilized legal systems: no physical compulsion may be used to make the suspect talk. In this sense, almost all civilized legal systems give the suspect, even before he becomes the defendant, the right to remain silent. The more enlightened legal systems, whether of the common law or the civil law variety, also are in agreement today on the principle that from the very beginning of the investigation the accused is entitled to the assistance of counsel. It follows that when the suspect, at any stage of the proceedings, is called upon to exercise his all-important option—to talk or not to talk—at least the more enlightened legal systems will make it possible for him to be guided by counsel's advice.

Up to this point, I repeat, there is a large measure of agreement among civilized and enlightened legal systems, regardless of whether they belong to the common law or the civil law orbit. Crucial differences, however, come to light when we ask the next question: Which course will counsel advise the defendant to take? Under our system, "any lawyer worth his salt will tell the suspect in no uncertain terms to make no statement to police under any circumstances." [30] Quite often, counsel will keep his client equally silent at the trial; indeed, in the many cases where the client has a criminal record, our rule permitting the prosecution to unearth such record on cross-examination makes it almost impossible for counsel to let the defendant take the stand. In its

---

28. The basis of the argument against "one-way-street" discovery is plain enough. If a criminal proceeding is regarded as essentially a sporting contest between opposing counsel, it follows that no greater burden of making pretrial disclosures should be imposed on the prosecution than is imposed on the defense. If, on the other hand, the ascertainment of truth is perceived as the major and essential objective of such a proceeding, then it is clear that defendant's silence is at least as inimical to the attainment of that objective as lack of discovery, because "[m]any offenses are of such a character that the only persons capable of giving useful testimony are those implicated in the crime." Kastigar v. United States, 406 U.S. 441, 92 S.Ct. 1653, 32 L.Ed.2d 212 (1972), quoted with approval in United States v. Mandujano, 425 U.S. 564, 573, 96 S.Ct. 1768, 1775, 48 L.Ed.2d 212 (1976).

30. Watts v. Indiana, 338 U.S. 49, 59, 69 S.Ct. 1347, 1351, 93 L.Ed. 1801 (1949) (Jackson, J., concurring and dissenting). See also Freedman, Judge Frankel's Search for Truth, 123 U.Pa.L.Rev. 1060, 1064 (1975).

perverse striving to keep the defendant silent, our law, furthermore, seeks to assure the defendant and his counsel that legal rules can repeal the laws of logic, and that by legal rules the jury can be induced not to draw the natural inferences from defendant's silence. In *Griffin v. California* [31] the Warren Court—over a powerful dissent by Mr. Justice Stewart—held that no state may permit intelligent judicial comment upon defendant's failure to testify.

In thus encouraging the accused to remain silent, our legal system stands virtually alone. In England, defendants rarely opt for silence, because English law differs from ours in two crucial respects. If the accused takes the stand, the English rule is to the effect that he cannot by reason of that alone be cross-examined as to previous convictions. And if he remains silent, the judge is authorized by English law to "suggest to the jury that it draw an adverse inference from the defendant's failure to explain away the evidence against him."

Implementing a similar policy by partly different techniques, the continental systems likewise discourage the accused from standing mute. In many (though not all) of those systems the defendant's silence may serve as corroborating evidence of guilt. Even where, as in West Germany, this traditional rule has been modified, a defendant generally is not well advised to remain silent. At the very outset of the trial, he has to stand in front of the judges, to be questioned by the Presiding Justice of the court. True, he may refuse to answer any questions relating to the charges against him; but he must announce such refusal in open court and cannot simply, as he might under a common law system, remove himself from the questioning process by deciding not to take the stand. Moreover, only in the event of a *total* refusal by the defendant to answer any questions relating to the charges does German law prohibit the drawing of inferences from his silence. If he answers any of such questions, but then refuses to answer others, the court may draw logical inferences from his refusal. Thus, selective silence is strongly discouraged. Total silence of the defendant (although in theory under the present German rule it does not support adverse inferences) will occur only rarely in a German court because it carries with it a grave disadvantage for the defendant: since there will be no separate hearing regarding the sentence, a totally silent defendant may forfeit the opportunity to present facts tending to mitigate his punishment.

The continental systems, moreover, reject our dysfunctional rule that previous convictions of the defendant can be proved if, but only if, he takes the stand. The rules developed in those systems regarding admissibility of previous convictions are neither simple nor uniform, but they exhibit unanimity on the crucial point: the admissibility of previous convictions *never* hinges on whether or not the defendant testifies.

---

31. 380 U.S. 609, 85 S.Ct. 1229, 14 L.Ed.2d 106 (1965). The arguments against this holding are cogently stated in Justice Stewart's dissent, id. at 617, and even more elaborately in Chief Justice Traynor's opinion in People v. Modesto, 62 Cal.2d 436, 42 Cal.Rptr. 417, 398 P.2d 753 (1965).

Thus he will never be dissuaded from testifying by the fear that his decision to do so will open the door to evidence of his criminal record.

Nor does a defendant who decides to testify before a continental court have to dread that a prosecution for perjury might arise out of such testimony. What he says in his defense is not under oath.

Thus the inducement to speak, and not to stand mute, is very strong in the civil law systems. Experience shows that "almost all continental defendants choose to testify" at the trial. This being so, the accused normally has little to lose and much to gain by presenting his side of the story not only at the trial, but also in the earlier phases of the proceeding. If the accused is innocent, this may lead to an early dismissal of the charges. In any event, the combination of a talking defendant and unlimited discovery will clarify the issues well before trial and make the trial both shorter and more informative—much to the benefit of an innocent defendant.

In cases where the accused is clearly guilty, the same combination of factors will prove equally potent. Through active colloquies between the accused and the investigator, combined with inspection of the dossier, such an accused and his counsel are apt to become persuaded that a denial of guilt simply will not stand up. The usual result is a confession, followed by an attempt to present evidence of mitigating circumstances.

Thus, by combining unlimited discovery for the benefit of the defense with rules making it advantageous for the accused to talk, the continental systems have fashioned a highly efficient vehicle for the ascertainment of truth. If the accused is in fact innocent, unlimited pretrial discovery will give him the best possible chance—a much better chance than he would have under a system of trial by surprise—to meet whatever evidence there may be against him. And if he is guilty, the unavailability of silence as a viable strategy will make his conviction more probable and less time consuming.

Notes

Suggestions for Further Reading and Research

1. For further reading on the subject of comparative criminal procedure see the two thought-provoking articles by Mirjan Damaska, Evidentiary Barriers to Conviction and Two Models of Criminal Procedure: A Comparative Study, 121 U.Pa.L.Rev. 506 (1973), and Structures of Authority and Comparative Criminal Procedure, 84 Yale L.J. 480 (1975). For a review of the recent American literature, from a European point of view, see Volkmann–Schluck, Continental European Criminal Procedures: True or Illusive Model? 9 Am.J.Crim.L. 1 (1981).

2. In recent years, widespread dissatisfaction with the American criminal justice system has provoked lively interest in foreign models. Especially useful as a stimulus for student reports and a basis for class discussions would be the work of John H. Langbein: Torture and Plea Bargaining, 46 U.Chi.L.Rev. 3 (1978); Land without Plea Bargaining: How the Germans Do It, 78 Mich.L.Rev. 204 (1979), and Mixed Court and Jury Court: Could

the Continental Alternative Fill the American Need? 1981 Am.Bar.Fndn. Res.J. 195. Among other authors who have found a comparative approach helpful in analyzing the defects of our own system are Lloyd L. Weinreb, Denial of Justice (1977); Richard S. Frase, Comparative Criminal Justice as a Guide to American Law Reform: How Do the French Do It, How Can We Find Out, and Why Should We Care? 78 California L.Rev. 539 (1990); Gordon Van Kessell, Adversary Excesses in the American Criminal Trial, 67 Notre Dame L.Rev. 403 (1992). William Pizzi has entered a note of caution about efforts to reform one system of criminal justice by incorporating elements drawn from another legal tradition. He examines Italy's interesting attempt to transplant features of the American adversarial system in Pizzi and Marafioti, The New Italian Code of Criminal Procedure: The Difficulties of Building an Adversarial Trial System on a Civil Law Foundation, 17 Yale J.Int.L. 1 (1992), and warns Americans about borrowing from the civil law in Understanding Prosecutorial Discretion in the United States: The Limits of Comparative Criminal Procedure as an Instrument of Reform, 54 Ohio State L.J. (forthcoming, 1994).

3. A comparative law teacher who wishes to devote a significant part of his or her course to these subjects would do well to consider adopting Langbein's supplementary coursebook, Comparative Criminal Procedure (1977). This 151–page book is not only an excellent introduction to continental criminal procedure, but provides the basis for a searching and constructive critique of the common law adversarial criminal justice system.

4. In the conclusion of his above-excerpted essay on comparative criminal procedure, Schlesinger speculates about the lessons the United States might draw from foreign experience in this area. He observes:

> In every system of criminal procedure, the ultimate policy issues are bound to center on the conflict between the value of truth and the competing "other values." A comparative approach, I submit, demonstrates that—for historical and political reasons that are complex and require further elucidation—the tendency is stronger in our system than in any other to sacrifice truth to the "other values." This in itself does not prove that the position of the majority of legal systems is superior to our minority view. But it does call for reflection and open-minded rethinking of many of our assumptions, including those which lazy traditionalism would label as "fundamental."

> Such rethinking, using comparison as one of its tools, will have to begin by classifying every rule of criminal procedure and evidence as truth-seeking or truth-defeating. Every rule (or lack thereof) recognized as truth-defeating should be seriously re-examined and should be preserved only if it meets three minimum requirements: First, the "other value" invoked as overcoming the value of truth must be clearly spelled out. Secondly, it must be shown in the light of reason and experience that the truth-defeating rule actually serves such other value. And thirdly, the other value must be found to be so strong that it justifies suppression of the truth, even though such suppression may lead to conviction of the innocent or to massive release of the guilty.

What "other values" are typically at stake in debates about reform of American criminal procedure? Why do you suppose our system tends more than any other to sacrifice truth-seeking to "other values"? Is the traditional American approach changing?

SECTION 3. APPELLATE REVIEW

Decisions of the ordinary civil and criminal courts of first instance may as a rule be appealed to an intermediate appellate court. In criminal cases, the prosecution as well as the defense has the right to appeal. Unlike a common law appeal of a trial court's decision, the proceedings in this intermediate court may involve a full review *de novo* of the facts as well as the law of the case. The panel of appellate judges initially will make its independent determination of the facts on the basis of the original record. In addition, however, the appellate court may question the witnesses again, or even take new evidence or send out for expert opinions. A party dissatisfied with the results of the appeal may seek review by the highest court which, like a common law appellate court, in theory considers only questions of law. (It may be noted in passing that civil law high courts have not been more successful than common law appellate courts in distinguishing factual from legal issues.) Some of these high courts follow the French system of "cassation", while others follow the German system of "revision." (In some civil law countries, appellate procedure in *criminal* cases does not follow the above pattern of review *de novo* of both law and facts. In Germany, for example, decisions of the courts which have first instance jurisdiction in cases of serious crime are subject to appeal only on points of law, and such appeals are heard, not by intermediate courts, but by a court of last resort. The right to appeal *de novo* does exist, however, for minor criminal offenses which are first heard before a single judge or a local court.)

The French Court of Cassation has several peculiar features which can only be explained historically.[6] The Court, as originally conceived, was to act on behalf of the legislature to supply authoritative interpretations of the law and to guarantee the obedience of the judicial system as a whole to the norms of legislatively-given law. Article 5 of the French Civil Code specifically forbids judges to decide cases submitted to them by way of pronouncing a general rule.[7] They were supposed only to find and apply the law of the Code or other legislation. The Court of Cassation was supposed to see that lower courts did not exceed this role. Its own functions were narrowly drawn. When a case is appealed to it, the Court can decide only the question of law referred to it, not the case itself. This means that it has only the option to affirm, or to quash the decision and remand the case for reconsideration by a lower court in the light of the Court's opinion on the legal questions (hence its name, Court of Cassation, from *casser:* to break or quash). It may not substitute its

---

6. See generally, Kock, The Machinery of Law Administration in France, 108 U.Pa. L.Rev. 366, 373–77 (1960).

7. French C.C. Art. 5: "Il est défendu aux juges de prononcer par voie de disposition générale et réglementaire sur les causes qui leur sont soumises."

own decision for that of the lower court. If it disagrees with the original lower court's decision, it sends the case, with its own interpretation of the law, to a different lower court. In France, the court to which the case is remanded theoretically is free to decide the case the same way as the previous lower court. If this happens, a second appeal may be made to the Court of Cassation, which will sit this time in a plenary session. If the lower court decision is again set aside, the case must still normally be remanded to a third lower court which, by an 1837 statute, is then required to give judgment as directed by the Court of Cassation. Legislation in 1967, and again in 1979, has expedited this archaic procedure somewhat, and has permitted the Court of Cassation to dispose of some cases without remand after the second appeal. The cassation system as practiced in Italy is much simpler. There, the first time the Court of Cassation remands a case, the lower court is bound to follow the high court's views.

Under the system of revision as practiced in Austria, Switzerland and Germany, the high court may, if it finds reversible error, either reverse and remand, or it may modify the decision and enter final judgment itself.

It will be recalled that the administrative courts in most civil law countries are in a separate hierarchy from the ordinary courts. The procedure in lower administrative courts, by comparison with civil procedure, from which it is to a certain extent derived, tends to be more informal, less expensive and more controlled by the administrative law judge.[8] In France, as we have seen, the decisions of these lower courts are reviewed by the Council of State. The procedure of the Council of State differs in material respects from that of the Court of Cassation. In the first place, decisions of the Council of State are final. Second, the statutory rules of administrative procedure are supplemented by a number of judge-made rules. The bulk of substantive French administrative law, which is uncodified, consists mainly of the case law which has been built up by the Council of State. A number of civil law countries, including Belgium, Italy and several developing countries formerly within the French sphere of influence, have followed the French model.

In countries, like Austria and Germany, where the administrative courts are part of the judiciary, the procedure for appellate review is essentially similar to that for civil cases in the ordinary courts. The lower court decision is reviewed *de novo* in an intermediate level administrative court, and the supreme administrative court hears appeals only on questions of law.

---

8. See generally, L.N. Brown & J.S. Bell, French Administrative Law 86–121 (4th ed. 1993).

Chapter 5

SOURCES OF LAW AND THE JUDICIAL PROCESS IN CIVIL LAW SYSTEMS

SECTION 1.   INTRODUCTION

Civil law theorists make a fundamental distinction between primary sources of law, which can give rise directly to binding legal norms, and secondary sources, sometimes called *authorities*.[1] The primary sources in all civil law systems are enacted law and custom, with the former overwhelmingly more important.[2] Sometimes "general principles of law" are also considered a primary source. Authorities may have weight when primary sources are absent, unclear or incomplete, but they are never binding, and they are neither necessary nor sufficient as the basis for a judicial decision. Case law and the writings of legal scholars are such secondary sources, and in The Netherlands, the draft of the new civil code was treated as an authority for many years prior to its enactment.

In theory, enacted law is the pre-eminent source of law, and court decisions are not binding in subsequent cases, either on the courts that issue them or on lower courts in the same hierarchy. A study of the process of *interpretation* of enacted law, however, reveals a considerable discrepancy between theory and practice. For purposes of comparison, it is essential to supplement formal sources of law theory, not only with an examination of what happens to the primary sources through interpretation, but also with a functional analysis of the mechanisms which promote the values of certainty and predictability while permitting growth and adaptation within the system. Finally, it must be cautioned

---

1. See generally, on French and German sources-of-law theory: R. David, French Law: Its Structure, Sources and Methodology (M. Kindred transl. 1972); J. Carbonnier, Droit Civil: Introduction 185–294 (1991); N. Horn, H. Kötz & H. Leser, German Private and Commercial Law 51–64 (1982).

2. In 19th century France, learned writers denied that custom was a course of law, because any other view seemed inconsistent with legislative supremacy as then understood. Though traces of this view still can be found in the literature, custom is usually mentioned as a source of law in modern treatises. See J. Carbonnier, Droit Civil: Introduction 28, 45, 236 (1991).

that the significance of the sources of law within civil law systems, and the range of judicial behavior with respect to them, varies from country to country, and, even within a country, from time to time and from subject matter to subject matter.

SECTION 2. PRIMARY SOURCES

A. ENACTED LAW

The concept of enacted law includes not only those legal rules adopted by legislatures, but those issued by executives and by administrative agencies, or adopted by popular referendum. The various types of enacted law form a hierarchy with the constitution at the pinnacle, followed by legislation (which, in France, as we shall see, may emanate from the executive as well as from the parliament), then by executive decrees pursuant to delegated legislative power, then by administrative regulations, and finally by local ordinances. In federal states, this hierarchy must be supplemented by the rules concerning the relationship of state to federal law. Account must also be taken of the increasing importance of international treaties and conventions and the effect given to them under local law. Within the European Community, for example, community law may take primacy over internal law.[3]

In general it can be said that parliamentary legislation is today the principal source of law in civil law countries. Within this category, the various codes, though still of great importance, now constitute only a small part of the total volume of existing legislation. The ever-growing body of separate statutes reinforces the traditional pre-eminence of enacted law within civil law systems, but draws attention away from the codes.

Special mention should be made here of the role played in France since 1958 by executive legislation. Recall that a cardinal tenet of the French Revolution was that all law-making power was to be vested in a representative assembly. However, it soon became apparent in France, as elsewhere, that the complexity of modern government requires the legislature to delegate substantial power to the executive to implement legislation and to issue administrative regulations. Such delegated power was not thought to derogate from the principle of separation of powers.

But the 1958 Constitution of General Charles de Gaulle's Fifth Republic went a step further, by putting the law-making power of the executive on an autonomous non-delegated basis.[4] In Article 34 of the Constitution, those matters falling within the parliamentary law-making domain are enumerated. Then, in Article 37, the Constitution states that matters other than those reserved for the legislative domain by Article 34 are of an executive character. Thus, the legislative law-making power, though it covers the most important matters, has become

---

3. Infra, Chapter 7.   4. Supra, Chapter 2, section 3.

the exception and the executive-administrative jurisdiction the rule—a direct repudiation of the traditional French doctrine of legislative supremacy. This grant of autonomous law-making power to the executive is in addition to the executive's delegated power to issue regulations in the course of executing parliamentary laws.

Two further aspects of the modern French development of the law-making power of the executive are noteworthy. The first is the treatment of the problem of the constitutionality of executive legislation. The Constitutional Council, it will be recalled, has power to review only parliamentary legislation for conformity to the Constitution.[5] The concern that executive legislation might escape review altogether was allayed by the Council of State which promptly claimed and has continuously exercised constitutional control over it.[6] The second aspect of the 1958 changes in the distribution of power between the executive and legislative branches is that these changes conferred upon the executive a privileged position in the parliamentary law-making process. As the French code reformer and civil law scholar, Jean Carbonnier, has put it: "Legislation has become to a great extent the work of the Ministry of Justice and other departments. It is something of a return, if not to the Justinian style, at least to that of the Juris-consults." [7]

B. CODES

FERDINAND FAIRFAX STONE, "A PRIMER ON CODIFICATION"

29 Tulane Law Review 303, 305–09 (1955).*

What then is this method called codification . . .? The first tenet of the method in its developed form is that law shall be written; thus it approximates more closely to legislation than to what was formerly with exactness called the common law. Man vacillates between a fear of putting things in writing lest he be bound and a desire to put things in writing so that someone else will be bound. These conflicting attitudes have manifested themselves in the debates over written versus unwritten laws as well as in the compromises adopted (witness the American Law Institute's carefully debated, much "caveated" restatements of the law which are, however, declared to be of no binding force). Although in this day and age the amount of unwritten law is infinitesimal as compared to written law and more often referred to in plays and novels than in legal treatises, yet we continue the argument in some places that to put the law into writing is unwise.

The second tenet of codification is that the laws contained in the code should be arranged according to some system. The systems

---

5. Supra, Chapter 2, section 4.

6. Supra, Chapter 2, section 5.

7. J. Carbonnier, Essais sur les lois 235 (1979).

adopted display considerable variation. That used by Trebonius in the codification of Roman Law has exerted great influence upon later codifications but the style and arrangement have been much modified. In the modern civil law countries, the French and German codes have often served as models and each has its supporters as the most perfect system, even as the newer Soviet Code will find supporters in some quarters. The faith in the ability of reason to produce order in the greatest areas of chaos, so dominant in the period of the drafting of the Code Napoleon, and the faith in the methods of science, so dominant in the period of the German Code, contributed largely to the acceptance of these codes as embodying proper methods. The cautious and greatly detailed table of contents of one of the Restatements is as typical of the concept of order of this age as were the elegant, deceptively simple generalizations of the articles of the French Code.

A third tenet is the position that a code should be drafted, considered, revised and in all ways dealt with as a single fabric. To this position some of the more ardent proponents, such as Napoleon and, in the early period, Justinian, whether from reasons of vanity or logic, would add that the fabric was complete in itself.... The notion of a single fabric, a corpus, is one dear to man's heart. Maitland's beautiful phrase of the "seamless web of history" is illustrative. The idea that all the laws could be brought together in one place, in one volume if possible, all interrelated, all neatly cross-indexed, with no tag ends, no supplements, no obscure references outside, was an ambition greatly cherished. Undoubtedly, the fact that the French and German Civil Codes could be held within the boards of a volume while the common law required a full library has, in some measure, perhaps greater than usually recognized, been responsible for the fact that these codes have been widely used as models outside the drafting countries while the common law has developed only within the original parent systems. The notion of containment in a single fabric has also been responsible in some degree for the fact that a state normally has more than one code, for example, a civil code, a penal code, a mercantile code and in California the division is even more particular. In welding the laws into a single fabric, stress has been laid upon uniformity of terminology, sometimes with sections on definitions and rules of construction. Some of the more ardent devotees of codification compare a well drafted code to a symphony with its motifs and its careful development of basic themes.

A fourth tenet of codification is that it should be done by experts. The Louisiana Civil Code was the work of three principal draftsmen. The Commission which served in drafting the French Code was more numerous, while there have been codes that represent the work of a single man. Usually the draftsmen are chosen from the ranks of the judiciary, the legislature and the bar, but perhaps the most interesting modern use of the codification method in the American scene has been in the field of industrial relations, trade practices and administrative law, beginning with the Codes of Fair Competition under the NIRA and now extensively used by the Federal Trade Commission in connection with the trade practice conferences. Here the codes are actually debated out step by step, formulated and agreed upon by the men who have the greatest interest in what they provide, an important example of a new type of law-making, and one that is coming to the fore increasingly in both business and labor relations. While some of the purists may deny to these the name of codes or to the method the name of codification, such an attitude is unfortunate since it makes of codification a creed rather than a functioning method. It is frequently in the innovations that the method is tested and made sound. Finally, it is contemplated in the method of codification that the resulting code will have binding force and effect. No particular form or device for achieving this effect is prescribed but most proponents of the method consider the result necessary.

Now having stated the problem to be that of stating the law clearly and concisely so that man may know the rules and principles which are to govern his actions, and having stated briefly the tenets of the method of codification, we can turn to an appraisal of the merits of the method. The principal advantage lies in the fact that it can be used to introduce order and system into the mass of legal concepts and ideas and so present the law as a homogeneous, related whole rather than as a series of isolated propositions. While it is true that many of the fundamental legal ideas evolved slowly and sometimes sound more in experience than in logic, yet this in itself is no valid reason why they cannot be stated in such relation as they bear to other legal ideas.

A second advantage arises from the fact that codification as a method demands that stock be taken of existing legal materials and so forces an examination not only of those ideas existing in the State that is engaged in codification but also in all other civilized States. This normally results in the type of comparative law studies that would delight the most learned professor of that subject in the universities. Unfortunately, it must be admitted as true that only when man is faced with a project of this kind or the "unprovided for case" does he engage in such inventory-taking of his own stock piles or those of his neighbor.

A third advantage comes from the bringing together of law into one place or book. The ordinary man with his book of published rules, even though he realizes that some of them are of unclear expression, feels infinitely more secure than when he exists under a law that is unpublished, that can be found only by the lawyer and judge. There is in man, even as Hamlet says, a preference to bear those ills we have than fly to others that we know not of. The sense of security that the average man feels in the Constitution or Magna Carta, even though he may not understand what is in them, is a factor which cannot be overlooked. In the common law, one wonders if the traditional faith of the average man in trial by jury does not stem in part from his lack of certainty as to what exactly the common law says.

A fourth advantage is found in that the average man, if he so desires, can find and read the law that governs him. He need not rely solely upon professional advice. This is not to say that he is guaranteed an understanding of what the words mean, nor that he will not be well advised to seek trained counsel. It is to say that insofar as words are capable of conveying meaning, the average man with a well drawn code can feel less a stranger in his own land than when he is left with little guide except the "brooding omnipresence in the sky" or the determination of what the particular judge had for breakfast on the particular day.

Finally, there is an advantage to those engaged in the exposition of law in that they are provided with an authorized framework within which to conduct their work. While such a predestined framework will not please all, there are many who would welcome its authoritative stamp.

What then are the shortcomings of the method? They are those of man himself. Man has consistently tried to build a frame for the universe and to squeeze it into that frame however much it may bulge over the sides or pinch in the corners. Always there are the bulges, the parts left over like the dismantled watch that belonged to your father. So too when man essays to imprison the law into a single, homogeneous fabric, or when he tries to encompass the whole of man's legal personality in a single set of articles, either he spells out the particulars in such detail, providing for every conceived eventuality, that man is lost in the forest, or else he retreats into generalities so vague that man shrugs them off as too indefinite to constitute notice.

The world in which the French Civil Code was created was a world of simplicity compared with our own. No industrial age or revolution had occurred. Relativism had not yet permeated all areas of thought. No factory system, railways or airplanes made the field of delict difficult. No telephone, cable or air freight made the law of contractual obligations complex. Even the world in which the German Civil Code appeared fell far short of modern complexity and even the German Code had lost some of that pristine simplicity of its French predecessor, and the critics referred to it as "more scientific."

Our age has somehow lost the knack of simplicity. Our speech, our writing, our lives attest this loss. Our age is rapidly ceasing to believe in general principles. We seem to dote on itemization. Yet, even as we lean toward particularization, our age also is ceasing to use words with disciplined precision and this everyday habit is being reflected in our more serious work. Our age is also fast becoming an age of relativism and the nineteenth century codes, as well as many of the twentieth century Latin American ones, profess to believe in absolutes. Finally, our age, particularly in the newer jurisprudential writings, has shifted attention from the word of the law to the man who interprets the word. Such an attitude is not one in which serious interest in codification as an art can flourish.

Whatever codes are produced in this century, unless produced in a controlled atmosphere such as in Russia, will bear evidences of these characteristics of our age. The particularization of the American Law Institute's Restatements, as compared to the generalization of the French Civil Code, is not alone a product of common law method; it is also a reflection of the age in which they are written.

This brings us to the principal defect of codification as a method which is that the code is, so to speak, struck off at a single time in a single age by men who are necessarily products of that age. We have listed this characteristic as an advantage and now in all fairness we must list it as a defect for in fact it possesses both aspects. The French Civil Code reflects the mores of a pre-industrial France and it is to the great credit of the legislators and judges of France that it has been kept from anachronism in these matters. Both the German and French codes reflect the high sense of individualism then dominant and so become subject to criticism by those who foster the increasing paternalism of the State.

The second defect is linked with the first but it deserves separate mention, namely, that the codifiers have not come forward with a successful method for keeping the code up-to-date. Many suggestions have been made for accomplishing this continued vitalization, ... but again the human element enters and once the main and arduous labors of codification have resulted in a code, the tendency is to consider the task done, to disband and take a well deserved rest.

H.R. HAHLO, "HERE LIES THE COMMON LAW"
30 Modern Law Review 241, 246–53 (1967).*

The belief in codification as a cure for the uncertainties, illogicalities and inconsistencies of the law harks back to eighteenth-century rationalism when philosophers and lawyers believed that it was possible to construct out of the strands of pure reason a system of legal principles from which the solution for every legal problem could be derived with near-mathematical certainty by a process of logical deduction. That this facile belief is a snare and a delusion, the experience of countries with codified systems of law abundantly attests. The propositions codes enshrine are the kind of general legal principles which are trite in any system of law, codified or not. It is when it comes to their application to concrete cases that the doubts arise, and here a clause in a code is generally of no more use to the lawyer than a statement in a textbook or digest. On the contrary, he may find the textbook statement of more use to him, for whereas a code provision expresses in stark terms the rule, and leaves it at that, a good textbook explains the rule as well as the reasons behind it, discussing decided cases and speculating on open questions.

Nor is it true that, given a codified system of law, the answers to any given problem follow logically from the stated rules. If this were so,

* Reprinted with the permission of the Modern Law Review.

systems with the same principles would always arrive at the same results, systems with different principles at different ones. In fact, as has been pointed out by, *inter alios,* Professor Rudolfo Sacco, Dean of the Faculty of Law of the University of Pavia, the opposite holds true. Starting from similar general rules French, Italian and German law have frequently arrived at different solutions. Conversely, they have not infrequently arrived at substantially the same results on different general rules.

To add an example from the law of France and the law of Quebec:

Article 1053 of the Quebec Civil Code of 1866, which prescribes that

"Toute personne capable de discerner le bien du mal, est responsable du dommage causé par sa faute à autrui, soit par son fait, soit par imprudence, négligence ou inhabileté," [a]

is substantially a contraction of articles 1382 and 1383 of the French Civil Code of 1804, providing as follows:

Article 1382:

"Tout fait quelconque de l'homme, qui cause à autrui un dommage, oblige celui par la faute duquel il est arrivé, à le réparer." [b]

Article 1383:

"Chacun est responsable du dommage qu'il a causé non seulement par son fait, mais encore par sa négligence ou par son imprudence." [c]

Yet, on the same basic principles the courts of France and Quebec have erected different structures of tort law, each one rational and consistent in itself.

The point, of course, is that code provisions are of necessity so general that they provide little more than the framework to be filled in by *jurisprudence* and *doctrine.* As Professor Sacco states:

"Seulement une étonnante illusion optique nous fait souvent penser à la définition du théoricien comme à quelque chose qui éclaire, et qui n'a point besoin d'être expliquée à son tour." [d]

He continues:

"Cependant l'interprétation de la formule ne forme point l'objet d'une théorie plus ou moins compliquée. Une telle théorie devrait exister si l'interprétation des formules nous était nécessaire. Mais ce qui nous intéresse dans la formule est sa valeur pratique plutôt

a. "Everyone who is able to distinguish right from wrong is responsible for the injury caused to another by his fault, whether through his act, or through imprudence, negligence or ineptitude."

b. "Every act of man which causes injury to another obligates the one by whose fault it occurred to give redress."

c. "Everyone is responsible for the injury he has caused not only by his act, but also by his negligence or imprudence."

d. "It is only an amazing optical illusion that often makes us think of the definition of a theoretician as something which illuminates, and which has no need whatsoever to be explained in its turn."

que son interprétation. Et la valeur pratique nous est révélée par les exemples donnés par les manuels et par les décisions des tribunaux." [e]

Whether codification renders the routine work of legal practice and adjudication easier is a question on which opinions differ. Dr. E.J. Cohn, who has practised in Germany and England, asserts in an illuminating article, entitled "The German Attorney," that

> "There can be no doubt at all . . . that codification renders the task of the practising lawyer very much easier than it is in an uncodified system,"

and that

> "A question which would require a common law practitioner to search in books of reference for one or several quarters of an hour could be solved by his continental colleague completely satisfactorily in as many minutes."

Other lawyers with experience of practice, both on the Continent and under an uncodified system, have been heard to assert, with equal assurance, that the task of a French, Dutch or German lawyer in arguing a legal point is not substantially easier than that of his English, American or Scottish colleague, and that there are as many points of controversy in modern Continental systems of law as there are in the common law.

Ex cathedra statements of this sort, even if supported by an "of course" or "no doubt," are in the nature of things capable of neither proof nor disproof. Since a code wipes out the past, it generally obviates the need for historical research going back in time beyond the date of the code and, to this extent, it makes legal work easier, but how many cases arise, after all, in any system of law, in which deep historical research is required? In an uncodified as well as a codified system, it is rarely necessary to go beyond the last thirty years of law reports.

Dr. Cohn, after having told us that codification "renders the task of the practising attorney very much easier . . .," goes on to say that the German codes "have been ably commented upon by numerous authors during the last sixty years. Commentaries vary in size from a little one-volume pocket edition to huge standard works approximating in size our *Halsbury.*" He then informs us that a library consisting of "a good selection of pocket commentaries together with a more elaborate edition of one or two codes [one of the 'huge' standard works?], plus the last fifteen years of the leading legal periodical, *Neue Juristische Wochenschrift* [which contains, apart from articles, extensive case notes], and the current official Statute Book . . . supplemented by some of the

e. "However the interpretation of the formula [in the codes] does not constitute the object of a more or less complicated theory. Such a theory ought to exist if interpretation of the formulas was necessary to us. But what interests us in the formula is its practical value rather than its interpretation. And the practical value is revealed to us by the examples given in treatises and by the decisions of the courts."

better-class students' textbooks ..." will "do for the needs of a large percentage of attorneys in all but a fairly small number of cases."

Reading this, one cannot help wondering whether practice on the Continent can really be so very much easier than in England. How much more by way of materials does an English lawyer require in all "but a fairly small number of cases?"

The immediate effect of the introduction of a code, so far from making the law more certain, is to create a lengthy period of increased legal uncertainty. True, many hitherto doubtful issues will have been settled, but the re-formulation of the old rules and the adoption of new rules, added to the systematisation of the law, are bound to open up new disputes. For each head of controversy that has been cut off, there will arise, hydra-like, one or more new ones. And it will only be decades later, after the code has become overlain with a thick encrustation of case law, that the old measure of legal certainty (or uncertainty) will be restored. When in 1853 Lord Cranworth submitted to the English judges a draft bill to codify the criminal law (a bill, incidentally, which all the judges opposed), Mr. Justice Talfourd, after stating that

> "To reduce the *statute law* into a narrow compass is an object entirely free from objection, and which, if accomplished with care, can produce nothing but good; but to reduce unwritten law to statute is to discard one of the greatest blessings we have for ages enjoyed in rules capable of flexible adaptation,"

said:

> "I do not think any greater certainty can be obtained by a Code of the unwritten law to compensate for the loss; but that on the contrary, new questions of the construction of the words of the same statutes will arise, unforseen difficulties in construction would be suggested, and new decisions more unsatisfactory than those which expound and apply principles, would become necessary."

The same point was put with American bluntness by United States Attorney–General Legarée in a paper on codification:

> "A rule is laid down in a digest; if it be inaccurately enunciated you go to the *case* which has settled it. Your remedy is in the report; you detect the error and rectify it; and the precision and uniformity of the law is maintained. But from the moment you *enact* all these rules, they are adopted and promulgated as positive law, and must be interpreted as such. You are to make a great bonfire of your libraries and take a new start. If there is the least change or obscurity in the language, verbal criticism begins, everything that has been settled is afloat once more, and the glorious uncertainty continues until as many more camel loads of reports take the place of the old ones."

It is customary to blame the shortcomings of legislation on the draftsmen who failed to foresee problems which, looked at with "hindsight," were "obviously" bound to arise. The fact, however, is that even the best draftsmanship cannot prevent future disputes on the interpretation of statutory provisions. "No finite wisdom can provide for the infinite and unknown variety and complexity of future cases." The impossibility of foreseeing the future and the imperfections of language ensure that there will always be debatable points in the application of a statutory rule to borderline cases and it is, naturally, upon these points that litigants will fasten. To quote again from Mr. Justice Talfourd's statement,

> "How little the utmost learning and care which can be bestowed in framing a statute may avail to prevent a number of questions from arising in its language, may be gathered from the example of the Statute of Frauds, which, framed by one of the greatest lawyers who ever lived, has been the subject of almost numberless decisions."

But it is not only the growing body of case law which will soon provide the nakedness of the infant code with a wardrobe rivaling in its variety and complexity that of the common law prior to codification. Almost as soon as the ink on the code is dry the need for legislative amendments will become manifest.

> "It is easier to decide one case correctly and give a true reason therefor, than it is to decide all cases that may arise correctly, and by one form of words express the general rule and its exceptions."

If, as happens in the best regulated legal systems, a court of law makes a bad ruling, courts subsequently concerned with the same point will soon put the matter right by "distinguishing" or "overruling" the unfortunate precedent. No equally easy remedy offers itself if a code makes bad law. Unless the words of the code are sufficiently elastic to permit the courts to "stretch" or "bend" their meaning, the cumbersome machinery of amending legislation has to be brought into action. Moreover, since a code is necessarily based on the *mores,* philosophy and economic and social conditions of the time in which it was drafted, amendments will become necessary as *mores,* philosophy and economic and social conditions change. There is, as Continental experience shows, much the courts can do by way of interpretation to adapt the code to changing conditions, but they cannot redraft basic rules. In addition to the growing body of case law, there will soon be an ever growing body of amending legislation, followed in due course by judgments explaining the amending legislation, and amendments upon the amendments.

How long this process can continue before the need for wholesale code revision arises, depends upon the tempo of social and economic change and the readiness of the legislature and the profession to undertake the enormous task of redrafting the code. That, sooner or later, wholesale revision will be required, is certain—and sooner rather than later in a time such as ours, when the rate of social change is far quicker than it was when the Continental codes were drafted, and is accelerating at a rate undreamt of by our forbears. There is no turning back once the law is codified, you have to go on codifying. Like the sorcerer's apprentice, the codifier is forever pursued by the spirits he evoked from the deep.

Lest it be thought that this is an unduly pessimistic assessment of the situation it is only necessary to refer to the experience with the *Code Napoléon,* the German *Bürgerliches Gesetzbuch* and The Netherlands *Burgerlijk Wetboek.* All three, to use words employed by Carter in relation to the Napoleonic code, have become "buried under a heap of subsequent enactments and of judiciary law." All three stand in need of wholesale revision. . . .

It is of the nature of law that the bulk of it should be certain, but that there will always be a fuzzy zone of uncertainty around the edges. It is also of the nature of law that it stands perpetually in need of revision if it is to remain in keeping with changing conditions. To think that law could be rendered either more certain or more stable by codification, is to blame a certain form of law for attributes which are in fact inherent in the nature of law, whatever form it may take.

Notes

1. In presenting the French Civil Code of 1804 to the General Assembly, Portalis spoke eloquently on the idea of codification and on the general spirit that had guided his drafting commission. For translations of his often-quoted reflections, see Alain Levasseur, Code Napoleon or Code Portalis? 43 Tul.L.Rev. 762 (1969) and Shael Herman, Excerpts from a Discourse on the Code Napoleon by Portalis and Case Law and Doctrine by A. Esmein, 18 Loyola L.Rev. 23 (1971–72).

2. For further reading on codification by an eminent French scholar of legal method, see the article by Jean Louis Bergel of the University of Aix–Marseille, "Principal Features and Methods of Codification," 48 La.L.Rev. 1073 (1988). Bergel's discussion, which contains much useful historical information, contrasts "substantive codification" of the type described by Stone, above, with "formal codifications" which merely compile or consolidate related statutes without altering their content.

3. In connection with the above excerpt from Hahlo, see James Gordley, European Codes and American Restatements: Some Difficulties, 81 Colum.L.Rev. 140 (1981), arguing that the goals of clarity and simplicity in codification are illusory.

C. CUSTOM

In the civil law theory of sources of law, custom is regularly listed as a primary source, but routinely dismissed as of slight practical importance, except in Spain and some of the other Spanish-speaking countries. In certain provinces of Spain, notably Catalonia, the national Civil Code does not apply to matters covered by local customary laws *(fueros).* In other civil law countries, where custom is less important but still considered to have binding force, there is an apparent difference between systems, such as the German, which permit custom in certain cases to prevail over written law, and those systems which, like the French, permit custom to supplement, but not to abrogate, the written law. The real extent of this difference may be questioned, though, in view of the rigorous insistence of the former system on the establishment of a "true custom", and the relaxed attitude of the latter concerning the nicety of the distinction between "supplementation" and "abrogation." As might be expected, custom (in the form of trade usage) plays a greater role in commercial and labor law than it does in civil law generally. Some treatise writers have characterized settled case law as custom, but it is not officially recognized as such.

D. GENERAL PRINCIPLES

It is sometimes said that "general principles," derived either from norms of positive law or from the existence of the legal order itself, are a primary source of law. They are so characterized by some French writers, especially in connection with discussions of French administrative law, but also in discussions of the judicial doctrine of abuse of rights and the expansion of the notion of unjust enrichment. Such a characterization raises the question whether the source of law is really the general principle or the judge, a problem which will be discussed below in connection with interpretation.

The following excerpt from a leading treatise on comparative law contains a forceful exposition of the view that general principles are an important source of law.

RENÉ DAVID AND JOHN E.C. BRIERLEY, "MAJOR LEGAL SYSTEMS IN THE WORLD TODAY"
115–118 (1968).*

General Formulae of Legislation

The fact that the co-operation of jurists is called for in the formulation of the law, and not only in its application, is seen in the use made of certain "super-eminent principles" *(Generalklauseln, principes généraux).* These are found sometimes in the enacted law and also, if need be, outside it. The recourse to these principles, and the use made of them, are difficult for theorists of legislative positivism to explain; they bring to light the fact that in the Romano–Germanic family there is a subordination of law to the commands of justice, such as it is conceived at a given moment in a given period, and that this legal family is a *jurists' law,* not merely a system of legislative norms.

Mention has already been made of the way in which the legislators may sometimes renounce their function and expressly appeal to the co-operation of jurists in order to find the right solution to a problem among many possible alternatives. The limitations of enacted law are obvious when the legislators confer power to judge in equity and refer to usage or even to natural law (Austrian Civil Code, art. 7), or permit the application of statutory provisions to be set aside or modified in the interests of public order or good morals. No legislative system can do without such correctives or loop-holes; in their absence there would be the impermissible risk of creating a divorce between law and justice. The adage *summum jus summa injuria* is not the ideal of the Romano–Germanic laws, nor is it acquiesced in by them. Some injustice in particular cases may be the necessary price for a just social order; the jurists of this family are not prepared to accept a juridical solution which *socially* would be unjust. It is characteristic of the flexibility of the legal ideas in the Romano–Germanic family that equity *(équité)* has at all times been part of the law, and that no necessity of correcting the series of legal solutions by means of autonomous rules or courts of equity has ever been experienced.

Legislative positivism and attacks on natural law lose most of their weight when one considers the extensive use made in periods of unsuitable legislation or crisis of such general formulae *(Generalklauseln, Blankettnormen)* found in constitutions or enacted laws. The decline of this doctrine in the contemporary world becomes apparent when the legislators themselves, expressly and by their own authority, ordain such new precepts as article 2 of the Swiss Civil Code which prohibits the abuse of rights. Article 281 of the Greek Civil Code similarly provides that the exercise of a right is prohibited if it manifestly exceeds the limits imposed by good faith or good morals or by the social or economic purpose of that right.

SUPER-EMINENT PRINCIPLES NOT PROVIDED FOR BY LEGISLATION

In cases where these super-eminent principles are provided for by law, it may be said that jurists act in virtue of a kind of delegation of powers from the legislators. But even when such powers have not been expressly conferred, jurists have nevertheless considered themselves to be so empowered *by reason of the very function* they are called upon to exercise. This power has been sparingly used, because it is thought that the best way to bring about justice in our society is to conform to the order established by the legal rules themselves. Nevertheless, there has been no hesitation about making use of it on occasion.

French law, particularly, illustrates this attitude—whether in private law, for example, in the theory of the abuse of rights, or in public law with the appeal to the *principes généraux du droit administratif.* The theory of the abuse of rights might originally have been developed from that useful tool, article 1382 of the Civil Code. It has now become clear, however, thanks to the Swiss example in particular, that this principle is not one of responsibility; it involves a general principle dominating the whole law which, if legislators intend to formulate it, must come at the beginning of the Code,—the "general section" of the whole national law. Similarly, the development of the general principles of administrative law since the Second World War has pointed out the insufficiency of the legislative order and shown, with renewed clarity, the distinction in France between law *(droit)* and enacted law *(loi)*.

Because of its history, France is probably the country where it was most natural for jurists to make their contribution to the evolution of law by reacting against the propositions of legislative positivism. Since they were the first to be attracted by these arguments, it was equally natural that they be the first to break away from them. It is interesting to note, however, that today the same tendency is being established in Germany and as a healthy reaction to the doctrine which, in the National–Socialist era, tended to sacrifice justice to politics and the racial myth. The value and sharpness of the German reaction become particularly clear when it is considered that it touches even the highest forms of legislation. The Supreme Court and even the Court of Constitutional Justice of the German Federal Republic have not hesitated to confirm this in a series of judgments: constitutional law is not limited to fundamental legislative texts but is also made up of "certain general principles which the legislators have not rendered in the form of positive rules"; there exists, moreover, a supra-positive law which binds even the constituent legislators. "The adoption of the idea according to which the constituent power could provide for everything at will would indicate a return to an outmoded positivism"; one can imagine "extreme circumstances" in which the *idea* of law itself should prevail over positive constitutional law; the Federal Court of Constitutional Justice might then ... be led to appraise such "unconstitutionality." Norwegian legal doctrine admits, for its part, the idea of "emergency constitutional law" which serves to legitimize irregular constitutional acts (the secession from Sweden, or the events of 1940–1945) which are, however, consonant with the fundamental principles and values of the Norwegian Constitution.

In other countries, too, jurists have not hesitated on occasion to apply principles of a moral nature—principles such as *fraus omnia corrumpit* and *nemo contra factum proprium venire potest*—which have not been expressed in legislation. In Spain, furthermore, recourse to such principles has a legal basis: article 6 of the Spanish Civil Code enumerates, among the possible sources of law, the general principles deduced from the Spanish codes and legislation.

Finally, the theory of the sources of law in all countries of the Romano–Germanic family seems both destined to realize and capable of fulfilling the traditional concept to which the reign of law in these countries lays claim: that law cannot be laid down *a priori*, nor can it reside exclusively in legal rules. The quest for law is a task to be accomplished by all jurists in common, each acting in a given sphere and using his own techniques, but always inspired by a common ideal—that of arriving, in each instance, at the solution which best conforms to the general sense of justice,—a justice founded on a reconciliation of all kinds of interests of private individuals and the community.

SECTION 3. AUTHORITIES

A. CASE LAW

From the preceding discussion of interpretation in civil law systems, it is evident that case law (*jurisprudence, Rechtsprechung*) plays an enormous role in the everyday operation of the legal system. Because of the necessity to interpret and apply the so-called written law, the civil law systems are in a real sense case-law systems. An important area of convergence with the common law systems emerges here when we consider the extent to which the law of England and the United States has become statutory.[9] Nevertheless, unlike the common law, the civil law tradition from ancient times has regarded the judicial function as limited to deciding particular cases.

The notion goes back to Justinian that only the sovereign can make a generally applicable rule. In modern nation states, that notion developed into the idea that only a representative legislature should be able to "make" law. We have seen in the foregoing section the extent to which modern civil law systems have retreated from that principle.

As it became generally recognized that judges frequently do in fact make law, the question arose whether and to what extent judicial decisions were a source of law. Civil law theory does not recognize the existence of a formal doctrine of *stare decisis*. Thus, judicial pronouncements are not binding on lower courts in subsequent cases, nor are they binding on the same or coordinate courts. In the extreme French situation, as we have seen in Chapter 4 above, the decision of the highest civil court is not even binding on a lower court in the *same* case until the second remand, and then only by statute.

This formal civil law theory of the role of case law is, however, subject to a number of qualifications. Initially, it is not a simple matter for a high court to decide a particular case one way and later to decide a similar case another way. If a division of the high court wishes to deviate from a prior decision, the legal question involved will usually have to be referred to a super-panel of the court. This procedure has the obvious aim of assuring consistency in the output of the court charged with the ultimate responsibility for the uniformity of the application of the law within its own hierarchy. Second, in bureaucratic judicial systems, the de facto influence of higher court decisions upon lower court judges (whose promotions may be affected by too many reversals) is considerable. Third, the decisions of the Constitutional Courts of Germany and Italy on the compatibility of statutes with the constitution do have the force of law. Fourth, a settled line of cases (*jurisprudence constante, ständige Rechtsprechung*) has great authority everywhere. In some parts of the Spanish-speaking world this settled

---

9. See infra section 5.

case law is made binding by legislation.[10] Some legal theorists consider that, in rare instances, a line of cases can create a rule of customary law which is then binding as such. Fifth, it is observable that entire bodies of law in civil law systems have been built up by judicial decisions in a manner closely resembling the growth of anglo-American common law. This is notably so, for example, in the case of French tort law, and also in French substantive administrative law which is largely uncodified.

As a practical matter it is generally recognized in civil law systems that judges do and should take heed of prior decisions, especially when the settled case law shows that a line of cases has developed. Where the case law has not become "settled", prior decisions of high courts have some weight. Even in France, where the force of precedent is weaker than in Germany, the decisions of the Council of State are considered reliable precedent, and writers say that a single decision of the Court of Cassation can be important in settling the case law. Court decisions, then, are de facto sources of legal norms whose authority varies according to the number of similar decisions, the importance of the court issuing them, and the intrinsic persuasiveness of the opinion. The extent to which a court has relied on prior decisions, however, is not always easy to determine in a given case. In this respect, judicial opinions in German-speaking countries bear a certain resemblance to American decisions with their presentation of facts, reasoning and authorities. But the cryptic opinions of the French Court of Cassation summarize the facts only briefly and do not refer to prior cases. Lower court opinions in France sometimes do cite cases and provide more ample fact statements, but they are less informative than a typical German or American opinion. When the courts are not forthcoming about their reasoning processes and the sources they have relied upon, it is only by reading a line of cases that one can make inferences about the influence of precedent.

Civil law decisions have weight for the same reasons that underlie the common law doctrine of *stare decisis*. The most important of these reasons go to the very heart of the legal system: the requirements of reasonable certainty and predictability; the elementary demand of fairness that like cases be treated alike; and the related, but distinct, consideration that justice should not only be done, but should appear to have been done. In addition to serving the values of predictability, fairness and legitimacy, continuity in the case law is itself in no small way promoted by such homely considerations as the conservation of mental energy and the fear of reversal.

In view of the de facto importance of case law as a civil law authority, one might expect the differences between the common law and civil law systems in this area to diminish over time. Certainly, the presence or absence of a formal doctrine of stare decisis is not of crucial significance. As a "rule", stare decisis applies in the United States only to require a lower court to follow the decision of a higher court in the

10. E.g., Spanish Civil Code, Art. 1.6.

same jurisdiction in cases that are "on all fours" with each other. The stricter English rule, by which courts purported to be bound by their own prior decisions, was abandoned by the House of Lords in 1966.[11] Whether bound to or not, though, judges in all legal systems acknowledge an obligation to treat like cases alike. With computerized access to prior decisions, it seems likely that civil law systems will eventually develop flexible systems of precedent that will resemble the Anglo–American systems.

Thus far, however, the traditional conception that a single case has no binding effect seems to have hindered civil law judges and scholars alike from developing a workable system of precedent. A recent comparative study by a Swiss scholar, Thomas Probst, convincingly demonstrates that civil law systems have experienced considerable difficulty in developing theories and techniques for dealing with case law.[12] Probst shows, too, that these methodological failings entail serious practical consequences in terms of unequal treatment for similarly situated parties, a relative lack of predictability, and difficulty in integrating case law into the legal system as a whole.

B. DOCTRINE

The writings of legal scholars (*la doctrine, die Rechtslehre*), like the decisions of courts, are considered authorities in civil law systems. The role of doctrine is, however, quite different from that of the case law. As we have just seen, case law authority operates to settle the law and to assure a degree of consistency within a judicial hierarchy. The learned writing, on the other hand, exerts its greatest direct influence when the law is unsettled or when there is no established law on a point. But the two types of authorities are related, in that civil law systems have left the task of organizing and analyzing the case law mainly to the learned writers. Thus, the doctrine indirectly controls, to a great extent, the judges' understanding of the case law.

The weight attached by judges to doctrinal writing varies according to a number of circumstances, including the reputation of the author and whether the view expressed is an isolated one or represents the consensus of the most respected writers. In general, it can be said that civil law judges pay close attention to scholarly opinions, as expressed in general and specialized treatises, commentaries on the codes, monographs (including the best doctoral theses), law review articles and case notes, and expert opinions rendered in connection with litigation. Persistent doctrinal criticism will often prompt re-examination of a holding,

---

11. Practice Statement [1966], 1 W.L.R. 1234. It is worth noting, however, that it was only in the period from 1859–1861 that the rule that the House of Lords would not overrule its own decisions became established, and only in the 20th century that the Court of Appeal and Divisional Courts established the same rule for themselves. See Leach, Revisionism in the House of Lords: The Bastion of Rigid Stare Decisis Falls, 80 Harv.L.Rev. 797 (1967); Langbein, Modern Jurisprudence in the House of Lords: The Passing of London Tramways, 53 Cornell L.Rev. 807 (1968).

12. Thomas Probst, Die Änderung der Rechtsprechung (1993).

and will sometimes even lead to the abandonment of an established judicial position.

As we noted earlier in our discussion of the role of legal scholars in civil law systems, the importance of the academics' function in presenting analyses of cases and statutes to judges and lawyers is hard to overestimate. There is a circular chain of reinforcement among the civil law theory on the force of case law, the mechanics of law-finding, and the influence of legal writers. Since case law (theoretically) is not binding, civil law systems traditionally lacked sophisticated and comprehensive citators for direct access to cases and for the coordination of cases with each other and with statutes. The absence of such tools in turn, made it very difficult for a reliable sense of precedent to develop. Periodicals and treatises which collect and analyze the most important cases became the main sources relied upon in research. But this means that one set of authorities is pre-selected and filtered by another. It will be extremely interesting to observe the effect on civil law practice and adjudication of the introduction of computerized law-finding devices.

Once again, however, the apparent differences between the civil and common law systems should not be exaggerated.[13] In the latter, certain kinds of legal writing and certain writers have become highly influential, as evidenced by the measurable increase in citations to law review articles in contemporary judicial opinions.[14] Judges and lawyers in common law systems also rely to some extent on treatises and articles to find, organize and analyze the case law. On the other hand, the introduction of computerized law-finding devices in civil law systems will probably liberate civil law practitioners and judges somewhat from their traditional reliance on the academics. Nevertheless, differences are likely to persist in the degree of deference accorded to scholarly opinion, and, perhaps, in the degree to which the care and responsibility exercised by the respective academic professions merit such deference.

SECTION 4. INTERPRETATION

One of the many ways in which the classic codifications represented a break with the civil law past was in their transformation of the idea of sources of law. The *jus commune,* local customs, and previous authorities of all sorts were displaced by codes that were supposed to be comprehensive within the areas they covered. In the post-codification era, scholarly attention and the judicial process has focused on the codes—their language, their structure, the interrelation of their parts, and their animating spirit. An enormous volume of literature on interpretation has been generated. Indeed, one may say that the technique

---

13. See, generally, H. Kötz, Scholarship and the Courts: A Comparative Survey, in Comparative and Private International Law: Essays in Honor of John Henry Merryman (D. Clark, ed. 1990), 183.

14. The trend is documented in Merryman, Toward a Theory of Citations: An Empirical Study of the Citation Practice of the California Supreme Court in 1950, 1960, and 1970, 50 S.Cal.L.Rev. 381 (1977).

of interpretation of enacted law has become as much of an art in civil law systems, as the manner of dealing with case law has in common law systems. Since it is in connection with the civil codes that these techniques have been refined, the discussion here will be concerned primarily with code interpretation. But it must be remembered that in modern civil law systems, a judge's everyday work is as much concerned with ordinary statutes, decrees and regulations as it is with the language of the codes, and that the theory and techniques of interpretation may be modified depending on the source of the legal norm involved.

Since the time of the codifications, there has been a considerable evolution in the way the relation of the judicial process to the written law has been perceived, an evolution which has taken somewhat different courses in different countries. We may begin our consideration by distinguishing four different types of intellectual operations that are often grouped together under the general heading of "interpretation." First, there is the kind of interpretation involved in every use of language: the ascertainment of the linguistically most plausible meaning to be ascribed to the words used. If one meaning is much more plausible than others, and it covers the case before the court, the judge applies that version. This process of ascertaining meaning may be so automatic and unconscious that the judge may think of it as "law finding". The dream of the draftsmen of the Prussian Civil Code that all law could be so "found" and "applied" has long since proved to be an illusion. But the fact remains that many everyday legal questions can be and are resolved in just this way.

A second type of interpretation occurs when there is an ambiguous or unclear provision, or an apparent inconsistency between provisions in the text. A third type occurs when there is a gap in a legislative text. In these second and third situations, the process of interpretation becomes a conscious one. Here, as we shall see, all civil law systems are characterized by the presence of a number of methods devised to elucidate unclear or ambiguous texts and to help fill the gaps in legal rules. All of these methods have in common the ultimate aim of applying the legal rule as clarified or completed.

A fourth, and entirely different set of intellectual operations is involved when the usual gap-filling or ambiguity-resolving methods fail to yield a solution; when the law is completely silent on a problem; or when an old law, because of changed circumstances, has become completely unsuitable to current conditions. Though the judge's activity in these situations is often disguised or characterized as interpretation, it is clear that whatever process he or she engages in is no longer simply a search for the meaning of a legislative text. In this fourth group of situations, judges develop the law on their own, but there is great variation in the extent to which this is openly acknowledged, in the manner in which the judges proceed, and in the degree of freedom they consider themselves to possess. In France, for reasons which are largely historical, the process of judicial development is largely hidden from view, in contrast to what the German scholar Larenz has called the "open development of the law" in Germany.[15]

In the early years after the adoption of the French and German civil codes, the codes were treated, not as complete, but as self-sufficient, in the sense that they contained a comprehensive body of rules and principles, and (the German more than the French) embodied a system for applying these norms to all cases arising within the areas they purported to cover. Interpretation was thought of as the process of "enlarging the code out of itself".[16] No matter what type of problem arose, if the text failed to supply an answer, the judge was supposed to endeavor to derive its solution from the code, from the relation of its parts, from its structure, or from its general principles. To be sure, this process resulted in the creation of new judge-made norms, but the activity of judges was almost universally disguised as the finding and application of legal rules consistent with legislative intent or purpose.

So long as interpretation was viewed as the process of discovering the express or implied will of the legislature, its principal techniques were exegetical. They involved grammatical analysis, and such logical operations as reasoning by analogy or *a contrario* from code provisions, or deriving an inclusive principle from a set of related sections. In this type of interpretation, legislative history, particularly of the type known in civil law terminology as "the preparatory work" on a statute or code, is an important aid to determining legislative purposes so as to choose between conflicting or competing views of the meaning of the text. In many cases, grammatical or logical interpretation, or the search for legislative intent on a specific problem will be fruitful and will lead to the assignment of a plausible meaning to the text. But when these procedures lead to a dead end, the pretense that the judge is doing no more than carrying out the will of the legislature was facilitated by the so-called "general clauses", provisions of such breadth that, somewhat like common law equitable principles, they can be used to modify the effect of more rigid code provisions or to set the course of a new development.[17]

General clauses may range in their application over the entire subject matter of the code. For example, Article 6 of the French Civil Code forbids individuals to derogate in their private arrangements from laws concerning public order and good morals (*bonnes moeurs*), and Article 138 of the German Civil Code provides that a transaction that

15. Larenz, The Open Legal Development: Germany, in The Role of Judicial Decisions and Doctrine in Civil Law and in Mixed Jurisdictions 133–62 (J. Dainow ed. 1974).

16. "The Civil Code must, when necessary, be enlarged out of itself, out of the system of law that it contains. It does not contain a lifeless mass of legal principles placed in conjunction with each other, but rather an organic structure of inter-related norms. The principles that are basic to the Code carry within themselves the germ of further development." I Motive zu dem Entwurfe eines Bürgerlichen Gesetzbuches für das Deutsche Reich 16 (1888).

17. See the essay by John P. Dawson on the use by German and American courts of the leeway afforded by general clauses in The General Clauses, Viewed from a Distance, 29 Rabels Zeitschrift 441 (1977). (Infra Section 6).

offends good morals (*guten Sitten*) is void. Other general clauses are confined to specific subject matters, as, for example, Article 242 of the German Civil Code [18] and Article 1134 of the French Civil Code,[19] both of which require good faith in the performance of obligations.

Gradually, it has become widely recognized and accepted in both France and Germany, as well as in other systems, that the courts, at least when they are dealing with situations of the fourth type mentioned above, are engaged in a modest law-making function. Because the response to this recognition has varied significantly in different civil law systems, we must consider separately the modern process of interpretation in France, Germany and in those civil law countries whose codes contain specific directions on what the judge is to do when the law is silent.

In France, a number of factors contributed to the firm establishment and long predominance of the exegetical school of interpretation. Not the least of these was the Civil Code itself. It may be recalled that the revolutionary reaction against the royal courts found expression in Article 5 of the French Civil Code of 1804, forbidding judges to lay down general rules in deciding cases, and that it importantly affected the organization of the court system.[20] Article 4 of the Code forbids a judge, on pain of misdemeanor, to refuse to decide a case "on the pretext that the law is silent, unclear, or incomplete." It is worth noting, however, that the draftsmen of the Civil Code of 1804 had a relatively expansive conception of the judge's role. The eloquent Portalis knew full well that the law in its generality required the cooperation of the judge to fill its gaps and adapt it to change. Portalis acknowledged that the legislature could not and should not try to foresee everything: "How can one hold back the action of time? How can the course of events be opposed, or the gradual improvement of mores?" [21] Conceding that a great many things are necessarily left to be determined by the judges, he wrote: "[T]he science of the judge is to put the principles [of the law] into action, to develop them, to extend them, by a wise and reasoned application, to private relations; to study the spirit of the law when the letter killeth, and not to expose himself to the risk of being alternately slave and rebel...."

The post-revolutionary judges, however, were eager to show their submissiveness to the new order. The Court of Cassation led the way by developing a cryptic opinion style which usually consists of a single long paragraph containing a recital of the applicable legal provisions, a brief

18. German Civil Code, Art. 242: "Obligations shall be performed in the manner required by good faith, with regard to commercial usage."

19. French Civil Code, Art. 1134: "Legally formed agreements have the force of law for those who have made them.

* * *

They must be performed in good faith."

20. French Civil Code, Art. 5: "Judges are forbidden to pronounce by way of general and regulatory disposition on the cases submitted to them."

21. Portalis, Tronchet, Bigot–Préameneu & Maleville, Discours préliminaire in J. Locré, La législation civile, commerciale et criminelle de la France 251 (1827).

description of the facts, and a series of "whereas" clauses through which the decision is made to appear to emerge as though from a mechanical process of application of the enacted law to the facts. This style, an outward sign of deference to the legislature through literal obedience to Articles 4 and 5 of the Civil Code,[22] has persisted to the present time in the Court of Cassation, while the opinions of lower courts are only somewhat more ample. Within this form however, the judges have in fact been quite creative: the lower court judges through their power to find the facts, and the Court of Cassation aided by the very conciseness and generality of the French Civil Code. In recent years, the uninformative nature of French judicial opinions has not escaped attention and criticism, as the excerpt from the article by Prott reprinted below indicates.

In legal scholarship, the school of literal interpretation held sway until nearly the end of the 19th century when François Gény, in a celebrated work on methods of interpretation and sources of law, pointed out that the judges had in fact been making law all along.[23] Gény argued that, when the text is unclear or silent, the judge *should* be freed from the limitations inherent in the traditional methods of textual exegesis. The new technique of *libre recherche scientifique* which Gény expounded was supposed to liberate judges in difficult cases to look to whatever materials were available to resolve the problem—not only to case law, custom, and learned writing, but to the entire social and economic context. Gény's views transformed French legal science, but were not welcomed—at least not visibly—into the practice of the courts. The stylized form of French judicial opinions continues to this day to mask what Jean Carbonnier has called "a tactical eclecticism in methods of interpretation." [24] It is implicit in the outcomes of the cases that French judges interpret legislative texts so as to adapt them to current social and economic conditions. But their reasoning process is nowhere exposed in their brief and uninformative decisions.

LYNDEL V. PROTT, "A CHANGE OF STYLE IN FRENCH APPELLATE JUDGMENTS"

VII Etudes de Logique Juridique 51, 58–66 (1978).*

In 1968 a discussion on the form of French judgments was initiated by an article entitled *"La Mort des Attendus?"* written by the Procureur

---

22. French Civil Code, Art. 4: "The judge who refuses to decide a case on the pretext that the law is silent, obscure or incomplete, may be prosecuted for the offense of denial of justice."

French Civil Code, Art. 5: "Judges are forbidden to pronounce by way of general and regulatory disposition on the cases submitted to them."

23. Gény's Méthode d'interprétation et sources en droit privé positif first appeared

in 1899. The revised and enlarged second edition of 1919 is available in English translation: Gény, Method of Interpretation and Sources of Private Positive Law (J. Mayda Transl. 1963).

24. J. Carbonnier, Droit Civil: Introduction 288 (1991).

* Reprinted with the permission of Établissements Emile Bruylant, Brussels.

Général at the *Cour de Cassation* and a senior member of the Court of Appeal in Paris. It reported on the reasons for a change in the style of judgments undertaken by the First Chamber of the Court of Appeal in Paris and on the reactions to it. The Court was concerned at the flight of litigants to other tribunals (especially to arbitration) and at the increasing number of bodies working to make the administration of justice less expensive, faster and more responsive to current needs. It seemed to the Chamber that one way of achieving these ends would be to remedy judicial language. In particular real concern was felt that litigants themselves seldom understood on what grounds a decision had been given for or against them. The form of the judgment, it was said, should be easily understood by the litigants, not merely meet the formulae of an esoteric juristic art. In changing its style the First Chamber of the Court of Appeal in Paris followed the lead of certain other courts, in particular those of Rennes, Montpellier and Toulouse, in rejecting the chain of "whereas" clauses (*Attendus*), and in presenting the judgment in two parts: first setting out the history of the case and the facts in direct narrative style, and then the Court's decision, preceded only by the words "On these matters the Court ..." *(Sur quoi la Cour ...).*

The authors of the article pointed out that the use of the traditional *"Attendu que ..."* form of judgment was not prescribed by law and had not been used by some French courts for many years without any disastrous effects: in particular without their decisions being reversed by the *Cour de Cassation* solely on account of their form.

The experiment in the Court of Appeal was part of a rethinking about French legal procedures and part of a movement within the legal profession to simplify judicial language which abounded in obsolete and archaic formulae. In 1971 a commission for the renewal of judicial language was set up. Its Chairman was M. Adolphe Touffait.

In 1974 a controversial article written by Touffait and Tunc appeared in which there was a plea for more explicit justification of decisions, especially in the *Cour de Cassation.* The authors argued that the most important object in a judgment was to convey to the litigants why they had won or lost. The legal principle on which the syllogism was based was frequently not a statutory provision. A bare stating of that principle as the major premise left the reader guessing as to why the Court had chosen it among other possible principles. This was particularly true where France's supreme tribunal is developing the law in new areas. Furthermore the classification of facts was often debatable—but no record of the factors which influenced the Court in this respect would be available. (This applies particularly to the lower courts: in principle the *Cour de Cassation* only reviews decisions of law, not decisions as to the facts, but where she in fact decides to apply a different legal principle, she has obviously classified the facts differently). Once a principle was enshrined in a case it would be cited over and over, even though subsequent developments might prove it more and more unfortunate. Because all discussion of its social consequences were excluded it was almost impossible to change it without the appearance of a revolution: the simple negation of a principle always thought to have been settled jurisprudence, without any argument in explanation is hardly reassuring.

The most serious criticism made against the classic style of judgment in the *Cour de cassation* is that it appears to separate the law from reality. Questions of economic or simply practical effect such as the existence of insurance practices or of social security, the economic effect of holdings relating to manufacturer's responsibility or liability for nuclear damage, cannot be accommodated in the judgment.

All this is true: but the separation of law from life goes even further, for it is not only, as the authors suggest, that non-legal but also subsidiary *legal* arguments cannot be given their full weight in the highly formalistic style of judgment. The dominating principle of the judgment, *"la rigueur cartésienne de l'esprit français"*, as well as the one-sentence form, tends to emphasize one specific reason as the determining one, and to subordinate all others to it, or indeed omit them altogether as *motifs surabondants*. Yet it is typical of practical reasoning, reasoning relating to problems of how people should behave, to be an *accumulation* of various types of arguments, no one of which is in itself decisive, but the total weight of which is.

A further flaw in the classical theory of the French judgment can be illustrated from the mouths of its own supporters. A judgment, it is said, must express *"les motifs qui ont déterminé la décision"*. At the same time it is suggested that the *Cour de Cassation* has indeed considered economic and social consequences in coming to its decisions, even though it has not expressed them in its judgments and this can of course clearly be illustrated e.g. by the reversal of the rules as to liability for injury to the non-paying passenger.... Clearly then the Court has not set out in its judgment the reasons which moved it to take that decision.

This contradiction arises because most writers on the judicial process in France do not make the distinction, fundamental in Common Law legal theory, between the psychological process of the judge which leads to the decision and the justification of that decision which must conform to certain norms of judicial behaviour. In whatever way a judge reaches a decision, he must be able to justify it by acceptable methods. An intuitive decision will still be an acceptable one if he can demonstrate that it is consistent with certain standard judicial techniques. This point has been lucidly made by the German theorist Josef Esser. Judges, he says, approach a decision with a certain orientation or predisposition (*Vorverständnis*) which is drawn from the values about justice alive in the society he serves: they guide him, often almost by instinct, to what would be an "acceptable" "feasible" or "plausible" solution. He then chooses among the various judicial techniques available (e.g. in German law the historical, grammatical, teleological or structural methods of interpretation) the one which leads to the result already foreshadowed. If the *Cour de Cassation* had indeed taken account of what the community feels to be "reasonable" in cases of transport without reward in motor accident cases, then its justification of the decision in terms of purely *legal* principle does not express, any more than do the judgments of the German judges, the reasons which decided the issue. Concentrating exclusively on traditional techniques of judicial style may leave the judge without any guidance for, and society with no control of, the most crucial stage of judicial decision.

The analysis of Touffait and Tunc, though not going so far, did suggest that the judge should mention all the factors which had entered into his consideration. Not only would this be clearer to the litigants but also to counsel, academic writers, legal advisers and, not least of all, to the lower Court from whose decision the litigant appealed (and which must sometimes have difficulty in deducing, from the elliptical expressions of the *Cour de Cassation,* what would be the right way to dispose of the case). It is true that this would open up more debate about judicial decisions, but it is through debate that developments occur.

Though the authors related the inspiration for their proposals to Portalis' description of the functions of courts, which necessarily required clarity in judgments they were under no illusions as to the opposition the proposed changes would arouse in those already critical of the changes made by the Paris Court of Appeal in 1968.

This opposition is clearly brought out in another article by a member of the *Cour de Cassation* and which apparently represents a strong faction of opinion in the French judicial world, if not within the *Cour de Cassation* itself. In the changes proposed he saw serious disadvantages. A major one would be the encouragement given to judges to ramble on in the discursive and irrelevant style of German and Common Law judges. A discussion of social and economic forces would be inappropriate to judges who are not trained in these fields. The Court's deliberations would become longer and this would slow up the course of justice. If more discussion were included in the Court's decisions, and it therefore became appropriate to allow individual judicial opinions (as also raised by Touffait and Tunc), this would be "disastrous". The destruction of judicial privacy would facilitate political pressure on the judges, it would weaken the authority of the Court, not only generally but also in respect of the lower courts, which might prefer to associate themselves with a minority view. It would plunge practitioners into a sea of perplexity.

Breton saw as probably the only fault of the classic style of judgment that it is sometimes elliptical. If the judges guard against excessive brevity, then the traditional style is *"un excellent instrument d'expression de la pensée juridique".* There also seems to be a slight sense of resentment at the Touffait/Tunc suggestion that French practice could learn anything useful from the Common Law.

* * *

These words of doom must have persuaded the Commission [for the renewal of judicial language] to approach changes in the drafting of judgments gently. The ministerial circular to court presidents of 31st January 1977 recommending the drafting of judgments in a clearer and more direct style is described as "invitation to the judges, not an order".

The Minister for Justice, in distributing the recommendations of the Commission said that its proposals, including the partial elimination of the *Attendus,* had his complete approval.

> I am convinced that litigants, most of whom have difficulty in understanding a judgment in its classical construction, will be able by means of this new presentation to better distinguish the facts of the case and the claims of the parties from the reasoning of the Court itself and because of this to grasp more easily the solution to the case".

* * *

The chief proposal is to do away with the expressions *"Attendu que ..."* and *"Considérant que ..."* Some courts apparently would have favoured their total suppression, but the Commission finally followed the solution tried out by the Paris Court of Appeal in 1968, of having the first part of the judgment, describing the course of the litigation, in a simple descriptive style and retaining the *Attendus* for the Court's actual decision.

Another recommendation is to adopt a very flexible approach and to vary the style of judgment to the type of case, giving more headings or subdivisions where appropriate, or even varying the order of presentation. Subheadings are to be used to break up the text (often in the earlier style drafted as an unappetizing slab of several pages, constructed as a single sentence).

The Commission emphasized that this change of style was not to alter the aim of conciseness. Dropping the *Attendus* should simply mean the use of a simple sentence of one or two phrases. It is noteworthy in this respect that the descriptive part of the Toulouse court's judgments considered by Mallet and Touffait in 1968 could be quite simply reconstituted in the classic style by adding *"Considérant que"* before each sentence.

Finally the Commission offered a model "head-note" which should contain the essential facts about the case (e.g. names of parties, type of litigation, etc.) and those factors required by statute to be part of a judgment. The motive behind all the Commission's proposals is clearly to free judgments of esoteric juristic mysteries and make them comprehensible, an aim which, one might add, would surely have been dear to the hearts of the drafters of the French Code, a model of the expression of legal relationships in simple clear language.

Unlike the French Civil Code, but in consonance with the views of Portalis, some of the other 19th century codes openly acknowledged and dealt with the problem of the silence or insufficiency of legislative texts. The Austrian Civil Code of 1811, which had been in preparation over the latter part of the 18th century and was strongly influenced by natural law ideas, directs the judge to look to the "principles of natural justice".[26] The Spanish Civil Code of 1888 provides that deficiencies in the law shall be supplied by reference to "general principles of the law", understood as those principles which can be derived from the rules of positive law.[27] The draftsmen of the German Civil Code considered including some such general interpretive directions, but eventually rejected the idea. Their position was that their carefully constructed Code implicitly contained its own methods of interpretation. If the ordinary methods of exegesis inherent in the structure and system of the code yielded no answer, it was anticipated that the judge would resort to general principles, not limited to those discoverable in the positive law, however, but including those principles which arise from the spirit of the legal order. This concept was later made an explicit direction in Article 12 of the Italian law on interpretation of legislative texts.[28]

The most famous of all such interpretive directions is contained in Article 1 of the Swiss Civil Code of 1907, which provides that if the judge can find no rule in the enacted law, he must decide in accordance with customary law, and failing that, according to the rule which he as a legislator would adopt, having regard to "approved legal doctrine and judicial tradition."[29] This provision, with its unprecedented grant of authority to the judge, was regarded at the time by continental legal theorists as revolutionary. In fact, however, in the years since the Swiss Civil Code has been in force, Article 1 has been rarely used, Swiss judges

---

26. Austrian General Civil Code, Sec. 7: "Where a case cannot be decided according to either the literal text or the plain meaning of a law, regard shall be had to the statutory provisions concerning similar cases and to the principles which underlie other laws regarding similar matters. If the case is still doubtful, it shall be decided according to the principles of natural justice, after careful research and consideration of all the individual circumstances."

27. Spanish Civil Code, Art. 6: "Any court which refuses to render judgment on the pretext of silence, obscurity or insufficiency of the law, shall incur liability therefor. When there is no law exactly applicable to the point in controversy, the customs of the place shall be observed, and in the absence thereof, the general principles of the law."

28. Provisions on the Law in General, Art. 12: "In interpreting the statute no other meaning can be attributed to it than that made clear by the actual significance of the words, according to the connection between them, and by the intention of the legislature.

"If a controversy cannot be decided by a precise provision, consideration is given to provisions that regulate similar cases or analogous matters; if the case still remains in doubt, it is decided according to general principles of the legal order of the State." Translated in M. Cappelletti, J. Merryman and J. Perillo, The Italian Legal System 254–55 (1967).

29. Swiss Civil Code, Art. 1: "The [enacted] law governs all questions of law which come within the letter or the spirit of any of its provisions.

"If the law does not furnish an applicable provision, the judge shall decide in accordance with the customary law, and failing that, according to the rule which he would establish as legislator.

"In this he shall be guided by approved legal doctrine and judicial tradition."

almost always preferring to couch their decisions in the language of traditional methods of interpretation.

In Germany, after an initial period of conventional exegesis, the judges began to exercise their authority to adapt and develop the law openly. They have developed an opinion style which resembles the American in its attention to the facts and its exposition of the reasoning process through which the court arrives at its decision. As anticipated by the draftsmen of the German Civil Code, the courts have not considered themselves to be tightly confined within the limits of statutory authority. They have, however, taken seriously the idea that they are bound by the legal order, the idea of law as a whole. Their care, when exercising what may be called their creative function, to incorporate new institutions into the framework of the legal order and to conform them to the basic principles of the legal order has been admired by many foreign observers. In general, the courts' authority to develop the law in this fashion is undisputed in present-day West Germany, although there is there, as elsewhere, disagreement as to the limits of such power.

In summary, it can be said that while modern theory of interpretation generally acknowledges that principles are hard to identify and that judges dealing with legislative texts are often making law, the extent to which the behavior of the courts reflects this perception varies. It varies, not so much in the results achieved (which lead one to suspect that most courts are doing the same thing most of the time), as it does in the degree to which the process is open or concealed. In France, where the process tends to be hidden, Dawson has pointed out that the absence of the reasoned opinion deprives the system of a valuable tool and an important mechanism for controlling the discretion of judges.[30] In Germany, where the process is more open, criticism tends to focus on the democratic problem: what limits should there be on the legal and political decision-making power of officials who are neither representative nor politically accountable?

The following excerpt from an essay by Professor Rieg of Strasbourg is characteristic of modern civil law approaches to interpretation of legislative texts.

ALFRED RIEG, "JUDICIAL INTERPRETATION OF WRITTEN RULES"
40 Louisiana Law Review 49, 53–65 (1979).*

THE DOMAIN OF INTERPRETATION

Judicial interpretation consisting of determining the meaning of a text is permitted only where the text is obscure, ambiguous, or simply vague. Such is, in fact, the principle formulated by jurisprudence [a] and

---

30. J. Dawson, The Oracles of the Law 415 (1968).

a. Case law.

* Reprinted with the permission of Alfred Rieg and the Louisiana Law Review.

doctrine; [b] the principle, however, admits of some derogations.

The Principle

Interpretation stops when a text is clear: *interpretatio cessat in claris*. Numerous writers consider that this maxim still continues to be valid. It leads to denying all power of interpretation to the judge when he is faced with a clear and precise text. The jurisprudence, in fact, follows this pattern and refuses, in principle, to find out whether the legislative intent might have been different from what is clearly expressed in the text. This jurisprudential tendency is evident from reading the following in a decision:

> Whereas the Court is presented with a text whose clarity and precision do not permit the Court to interpret it as the party would have the Court do, even if it is likely that its draft does not correspond to the real legislative intent; whereas, to grant to the Courts the possibility, under pretext of interpretation to modify or restrict the import of a statute which is not ambiguous and is sufficiently comprehensive would amount to authorizing the judge to substitute himself for the legislator.

When utilizing this power of interpretation for obscure and ambiguous texts, the jurisprudence particularly makes recourse to preparatory works. [c] In fact, a long line of decisions has established:

> [I]f, in principle, recourse to preparatory works is permitted when a text requires interpretation, the judge, to the contrary, must refrain from recourse to preparatory works where the meaning of the law such as it appears in the draft is neither obscure nor ambiguous, and consequently, must be looked upon as certain.

Putting the adage *interpretatio cessat in claris* into practice, however, is a delicate operation. As shown by recent works on juridical logic, it is extremely difficult to know when a text is clear. No criterion for clarity imposes itself a priori; and, as a writer has seen fit to affirm, "to say that the text is clear is to stress the fact that, under the circumstances, it is not debated." Nevertheless, that does not mean that it reasonably might not be.

Thus, one cannot speak of a clear text when the legislator uses vague terms, the content of which must be determined by the judge on a case by case basis. Article 287 of the *Code civil* provides that, following divorce, custody of the children is awarded to either one of the parents, *according to the best interest* of the children. It goes without saying that such a formulation obligates the judge to proceed with an over-all view of the situation, which can lead to granting custody to either the mother or the father. Similarly, article 1397 of the *Code civil* permits spouses to modify their matrimonial regime by agreement *"in the interest of the family."* These words cannot be defined in a singular fashion, and the *Cour de cassation* itself is not in a position to give them an all-inclusive

---

b. Learned writing.   **c.** Legislative history.

definition. Indeed, in a notable decision of January 6, 1976, the Court enunciated the following general guideline: "The existence and the legitimacy of the interest of the family must be the object of comprehensive determination, the sole fact that one of the members of the family would risk being hurt should not necessarily prohibit the modification or change contemplated." The precision supplied is incontestably important since the Court indicates to lower court judges that, in the interpretation of article 1397, *the interest of the family* may turn out to be the interest of *only one* of the family members; the fact remains that in each instance the judge must make a concrete determination as to whether the legal condition has been satisfied. One can, therefore, say that the adage *interpretatio cessat in claris* can never be invoked where the draftsman has intentionally used a general clause or formulation.

A text perfectly clear in meaning from the standpoint of ordinary language may not be so from the juridical standpoint. Thus, article 333 of the *Code civil* allows the conferring of the benefit of legitimation by authority of law upon the child whose status is that of an illegitimate child "if it appears that marriage is *impossible* between the two parents." "Impossible," in ordinary language, means "that which cannot be done." In effect, the jurisprudence has acknowledged very logically that this condition is fulfilled in those cases where the parents cannot marry by reason of an obstacle, objective and beyond their control, such as the death of one of them. Additionally, however, there exist jurisdictions which consider that, according to the *ratio legis,* the meaning of the term "impossible" could not be the usual meaning and that the impossibility in the sense of article 333 encompasses both hypotheses, where the parents cannot marry and where the parents do not want to marry. Thus, in a decision of December 7, 1976, the *Cour de Paris* did not hesitate to declare: "The law, which has not distinguished between the various causes of impossibility, leaves to the judge the task of appraising, case by case, if, under the circumstances, marriage must be considered impossible." This broad conception leads to permitting legitimation by authority of law in cases where one or both parents refuse to contract marriage. The word "impossible," then, takes on a very special connotation.

This exemplifies the difficulty of putting into practice the principle that interpretation stops when a text is clear. To the extent that the clarity of a written rule is decided by the judge himself, it suffices for him, in order to exercise the power of interpretation, to pretend that there exists an ambiguity or an obscurity. Only the *Cour de cassation,* through its regulatory function of jurisprudence, can then correct possible excesses, if it at least considers it to be necessary. Thus, not only does the principle *interpretatio cessat in claris* lack scientific rigor; but it also suffers true derogations.

The Derogations

As a premise, we assume that the judge finds himself with a clear text which, therefore, he ought to apply purely and simply; and yet, he embarks upon an interpretation. These cases are of two types; while the first type may be considered as normal, the second type is much more dangerous because it threatens to empty the principle *interpretatio cessat in claris* of its very substance.

It is commonly acknowledged by the predominant doctrine and jurisprudence that, in the presence of a clear text, the judge is granted once again his power of interpretation when it is appropriate "to give meaning to a text inapplicable in its letter or rectifying an evident material error." This is the idea expressed as follows by the *Tribunal civil de la Seine:*

> Whereas all search for legislative intent by means of interpretation is forbidden to the judge where the meaning of the statute as it reads is neither obscure nor ambiguous, and consequently must be regarded as certain ... there is an exception only *if the application of the text resulted in some absurdity.*

Absurdity can arise either from a material error in drafting or from antinomic and irreconcilable provisions within the same text. The typical example is that of article 1112 of the *Code civil.* The first paragraph of article 1112 requires that the violence capable of giving rise to annulment of a contract be "of a nature to make an impression on a reasonable person" so as to make him fearful of considerable harm, while the second paragraph provides that consideration be given "to the age, sex, and condition of the persons." In the presence of these two antinomic modes of determination, the jurisprudence has allowed the subjective criterion of the second paragraph to prevail, in accord with its general conception of the vices of consent. If the power of tribunals to eliminate the absurdities and antinomies of written rules cannot be seriously contested, one may, however, hesitate in the second type of derogation.

More and more frequently it happens that, despite the clear character of a text, the text is interpreted in order to confer upon it a different meaning from that intended by the legislator. This is a clear abandonment, pure and simple, of the principle *interpretatio cessat in claris.* An illustration of this phenomenon can be found in the recent jurisprudence concerning the petition to contest the paternity of the husband provided for by a series of articles in the *Code civil* beginning with article 318. The result from these texts is that the mother can contest the paternity only for the purpose of legitimation, which supposes the dissolution of the first marriage of the mother and her marriage to the alleged father. In order for legitimation to be effected, the child must also possess the status of being the common child of the mother and the second husband, as attested to by the express reference made by articles 318(1) to 331(1). In the presence of these texts, corroborated moreover by the opinion of the reporter of the bill before the National Assembly, the lower courts have, for several years, denied the action contesting paternity in the absence of proven possession of status. However, in spite of the texts and the preparatory works of the statute, the *Cour de cassation* has censured their application and has held in two decisions of February 16, 1977, that the articles alluded to nowhere required that the child possess the status of being the child of his mother and the second husband. These decisions caused a great commotion; and an eminent writer did not hesitate to speak of the "erroneous interpretation (*dénaturation*) of the statute by the *Cour de cassation,"* especially since the high court did not deign to indicate reasons for its position.   The effect of such jurisprudence is perplexing.   One may attempt to find an explanation in the notion of "social insufficiency" of the law, suggested by a writer not long ago: "A text of a law is there, but ... [it] leads to a solution which the judge considers bad or simply maladjusted."   As a consequence, the judge deviates from the text in order to arrive at a result which he considers more satisfactory.   This explanation undoubtedly enables one to account for the many distortions that the jurisprudence imposes on texts a priori clear.   However, the concept of "social insufficiency of the law" can be criticized as being particularly vague; one departs from the domain of the rational and the foreseeable to venture into the domain of "juridical policy" in its most subjective state.   Moreover, if one can speak of "social insufficiency" with respect to old statutes which must be adapted to the modern social order, such a value judgment appears to be excessive when it is applied to statutes which date back only a few years.

In short, concerning the "domain" of interpretation of written rules, the prevailing impression is that of a very great flexibility, if not a great uncertainty.   On the one hand, the courts regularly recall to mind that there is no place for interpretation of a clear text and, therefore, are respectful of the adage *interpretatio cessat in claris.*   On the other hand, one must not be deceived by the import of the principle.   First of all, the notion of "clarity" is itself equivocal.   Undoubtedly, if article 494 of the *Code civil* provides that "guardianship may be opened for an emancipated minor as for an adult," the need for interpretation is non-existent; similarly, if article 36 of the statute of July 24, 1966, specifies that "the number of partners *[asociés]* of a limited company *[société à responsabil- ité limitée;* S.A.R.L.] may not exceed fifty (50)," all interpretation is useless.   But how numerous are the terms and formulas which the jurisprudence considers as ambiguous or obscure, thus necessitating an interpretation?   Have we not recently seen the Plenary Assembly of the *Cour de cassation* ponder over the expression "number of voters" utilized by an article of the Labor Code *[Code du travail]* in order to find its meaning?   Here is, however, an expression devoid of all ambiguity a priori!   And then, supposing even that a text is considered to be clear by the majority opinion, nothing prevents a jurisdiction, and more especially the *Cour de cassation,* from proceeding with its interpretation in order to arrive at a result which it considers preferable.   In brief, a cloud of haziness surrounds the domain of interpretation.   That is an observation which, at first sight, does not apply to the methods of interpretation.

The Methods of Interpretation

Doctrine willingly distinguishes "methods of interpretation" from "techniques or rules of interpretation," adding sometimes that "if the principles of this method are lively debated, the practical rules are less lively debated." In reality, under the term "rules of interpretation," the writers study primarily the maxims bequeathed to modern law by jurists of the Middle Ages. In truth, these maxims concern the application of the rule of law to concrete cases—namely, the determination of its domain of application, and not its interpretation, *viz,* the determination of its meaning. The best proof of this is that these maxims come into play in a general manner even when a text is perfectly clear. Therefore, we will only examine the methods or techniques available to the judge for determining the meaning of a statute or a rule.

It is to be remembered at the outset that, in contrast to certain foreign countries, France does not have strict canons of interpretation and that the *Cour de cassation* has never defined the various techniques to be used in determining the meaning of a text; neither has the Court specific instructions for their use or a hierarchy among them. Nevertheless, if one attempts to make a synthesis, one perceives that two factors are predominant: on one side, it is the formula of the written rule itself; on the other side, it is the purpose of the rule. Interpretation is articulated around one or the other of these elements.

The Formula

As an initial premise, we assume that the judge finds himself in the presence of a written rule. It is normal that any interpretation first rely upon the expression of the text. Still a duality of means is offered. The judge may at first analyze the expression taken by itself and proceed by means of what one traditionally calls a "grammatical interpretation"; but he may also, in proceeding by way of "logical interpretation," consider the expression rationally and in its relationship to other provisions of positive law.

"Grammatical interpretation" constitutes in all cases the point of departure of the task of the judge. Its object is to determine the meaning of the text with the aid of language usage and rules of syntax. As it has been said, it involves "the search for what the terms [of the statute] signify or may signify in themselves, in an objective fashion, outside of any search for the drafter's intent and of any consideration of social utility or moral justification, foreign to the letter of the text under consideration." The terms themselves are to be taken in their juridical sense, not in that of everyday language. Very often, grammatical interpretation provides the judge with the key to the text. But it is not always so, to the extent that certain terms may have several meanings. For example, the phrase "third parties" *[tiers]* sometimes denotes persons absolutely strangers to a contract, i.e., the *penitus extranei;* sometimes they denote only certain assigns or unsecured creditors of contracting parties. Similarly, the word "act" *[acte]* denotes at times the *negotium,* at another time the *instrumentum.* It is necessary, therefore, to supplement grammatical interpretation with "logical interpretation."

"Logical interpretation" consists of applying to the obscure text the multiple resources of juridical reasoning. At times, reasoning is applied to the text taken in isolation; at other times, reasoning encompasses a second text and even several texts.

The most characteristic example of reasoning applied to the text considered as an entity is that of reasoning a contrario. This reasoning consists of turning around the statement of a text in order to draw a new inference therefrom and is, therefore, founded on the premise that if a text asserts something, it is supposed to negate the contrary. Judges often resort to argument a contrario, without explaining, moreover, the reasons for choosing this type of argument. Two well known illustrations are found in the law of filiation.

Article 336 of the *Code civil,* relative to acknowledgment of an illegitimate child, provides that "[r]ecognition by the father, without indication of avowal by the mother, is effective only with regard to the father." As it is drafted, the text, which sanctions the purely individual effect of acknowledgment, is troublesome in its result; often, the father who acknowledges the child believes that this proves the two filiations, paternal and maternal. Sharing the same belief, the mother deems it useless to proceed herself with an acknowledgment; so maternal acknowledgment is not established. Therefore, a more-than-a-century-old jurisprudence of the *Cour de cassation,* using reasoning a contrario, has adopted a different interpretation of article 336. The Court infers from the text that the father's acknowledgment, when giving the identity of the mother and stating that she recognizes the child, produces an effect toward her. The solution is all the more interesting in that the avowal of the mother need not be express but may equally be tacit; it may result, for example, from the fact that the mother brings up the child as her own. Incontestably, recourse to reasoning a contrario is implicitly justified by the result to be attained.

More recently, another provision of the *Code civil* relative to acknowledgment of an illegitimate has been the subject of analogous reasoning. Article 334(9) provides that "[a]ny recognition is void, and any petition for investigation is non-receivable, when the child has a legitimate filiation already established by possession of status." Interpretation of this text has given rise to an important controversy: the point debated was the determination of whether the child having only a legal document (birth certificate) to establish his legitimacy, without the corresponding possession of status, could have his illegitimate filiation established. One could, in effect, reason by analogy and say that, the document being one of the modes of establishment of legitimate filiation, the prohibition of article 334(9) was equally valid for the case where the child had but *one* claim to legitimacy. But one could also reason a contrario and consider that, since the text only prohibits the establishment of illegitimate filiation if the child enjoys the possession of the status of a legitimate child, this filiation may be validly established when the child has only one claim of legitimacy. Such was finally the interpretation adopted by the *Cour de cassation.* Recourse to reasoning a contrario is explained herein, even though the *Cour de cassation* did not supply any indication by *ratio legis.* In fact, the statute of January

3, 1972, was intended to favor the role of possession of status in the matter of filiation by extension of its traditional consequences.

A second form of logical interpretation consists in regarding the legislative provisions in question no longer in isolation, but rather in relation to the other rules of positive law. In placing the obscure text in context, the text's meaning becomes more readily apparent. For example, article 1321 of the *Code civil* provides that "[c]ounter-letters are effective only between the contracting parties; they are not effective as against third parties." The meaning of the phrase "third parties" *[tiers]* is derived from a comparison to article 1165, which lays down the principle of the relative effect of agreements; the third parties alluded to by this latter text are those persons absolutely strangers to the contract, i.e., the *penitus extranei*. Those third parties alluded to by article 1321 cannot be the same; otherwise, the provision would be divested of all interest. Thus, the jurisprudence decided that the third parties of article 1321 are those who have an action by particular title and the unsecured creditors of contracting parties.

The text to be interpreted is often viewed in relation to general principles of law, whose belonging to the order of positive law cannot be denied. In the civil law, these principles frequently, but not exclusively, take the form of maxims and adages borrowed from learned custom; for example, *accessorium sequitur principale, nemo auditur propriam turpitudinem allegans, contra non valentem agere non currit praescriptio.* Indeed, in the majority of these cases, these principles serve to fill in legislative gaps; it is essentially on this ground that their role has been viewed. Their function, however, is broader in that the principles constitute a means of interpretation of new statutes "which will thus be integrated into the juridical order, and reconciled with it."

Grammatical interpretation and logical interpretation applied to the wording of the text do not constitute, however, the only instruments utilized by the judge. Another element which plays a primary role is the "purpose of the rule."

The Purpose of the Rule

All written norms are necessarily decreed with a view toward a determined purpose, knowledge of which serves as a guide for the judge's interpretation. The goal of a statute or a regulation may be discovered either in the intent of the drafter or by looking at the social objectives which the statute was designed to accomplish.

Interpretation founded on the "search for legislative intent" speaks to the idea that each text reflects the particular concerns of its drafter and that it then must be interpreted such that the adopted solution corresponds to this intent. This is a characteristic method of the "school of exegesis" which enjoyed an immense success during the course of the 19th century before being denounced by writers such as Saleilles and Gény. It was contended that such a method led to sterilizing the law to the extent that the legislative will to be considered is the one which prevailed during the preparation of the statute. Applied to the Civil Code of 1804, this criticism was undoubtedly valid; today one no longer asserts that a text of the Code should be interpreted exclusively in light of the ideas that motivated the legislator 175 years ago. But that, in no way, signifies that the method need be rejected outright. It is, in effect, justified each time the judge finds himself confronted with a new text. Thus, the search for the legislative intent remains a constant of interpretation.

This intent is found essentially in the preparatory works, the importance of which for the interpretation of laws has been recently stressed. Indeed, it frequently occurs that the lower courts refer to these works. It is necessary, however, to be conscious of the inherent limits of these documents. On the one hand, only the preparatory works of the statutes *per se* are published, but not the preparatory works of the regulations. On the other hand, even for statutes, one must be careful not to rely solely on the preparatory works, especially when one considers the imprecision, indeed the contradiction, inherent in parliamentary debates which do not always allow disclosure of the deep, underlying intent.

Another type of document has recently assumed a predominant position. It is the ministerial responses to written questions of parliamentarians. To the extent that most of the statutes for reforming the civil law and the commercial law have been adopted at the initiative of the government, the proposals prepared by the ministers concerned—especially those prepared by the Ministry of Justice—and the responses given to the questions of the parliamentarians may effectively reflect the intent of the drafters. However, it is important for all concerned to proceed with caution here; for one is actually dealing here with governmental interpretation which, as shown by a brilliant study, often translates "the desire . . . of breaking away from the intent of the legislator." One would, therefore, be going too far by considering ministerial responses to reflect the thinking which motivated the legislator. Nevertheless, their influence on judicial interpretation is still certain.

The search for legislative intent is only a defensible method of interpretation if the text is recent. When, on the contrary, old statutes are involved, and in particular Napoleonic codifications, the purpose of the rule is no longer discovered in the drafters' intent, but in the social objectives of the legal provision.

Interpretation founded on the "objectives of the rule" is based on the idea that "the meaning of the statute changes with time, because it is destined to be applied to conditions existing today, and not to those existing in the more distant past." [61] The text must then be interpreted in relation to the needs of society prevailing at the time of the interpretation.

Undoubtedly, one would search in vain for a jurisprudential decision which, in its rationale, refers to such a method of interpretation. It is

61. R. David, Le droit français 143–44 (1960).

recognized that whenever judges, especially those of the *Cour de cassa-tion,* have adapted obsolete statutes to modern needs,[62] they have done so implicitly by this method. The first example deals with the notion of "public order and good morals," to which article 6 of the *Code civil* refers. The significance which the jurisprudence of today attaches to that notion is very different from that of the nineteenth century. While the concept of "public order" has been broadened, notably by the creation of an "economic public order," the concept of "good morals" has been narrowed.[64] The wording of article 6 has remained that of the *Code Napoleon* of 1804, but its content has been adapted to new needs. The second example refers to the evolution of the law of delictual liability. Although articles 1382 to 1386 of the *Code civil* have, by and large, remained unchanged, their import has been modernized. The jurisprudence has in particular created a general system of liability for the acts of things, a system which the drafters of the Code had never considered. This creation was achieved by interpretation of the insignif-icant statement of article 1384(1), which the *Cour de cassation* isolated and on which the Court built a truly new theory. Other examples could be cited which demonstrate that the meaning of the text is fixed in relation to its social objectives. It is necessary, however, to add that this method of interpretation, described as "teleological," is more often resorted to by the *Cour de cassation* than by the lower courts.

Thus, a plurality of techniques is available to the courts for deter-mining the meaning of a written rule.... At the point of departure, whatever be the text, the interpretation thereof is always grammatical; but, when a problem arises, or simply when he wishes to strengthen the solution drawn from the grammatical interpretation, the judge has recourse to logical interpretation or to the search for the original intent of the legislator. It is only when the text is outdated that the courts indulge in the application of the evolutive or teleological method. In reality, although judges often deny it, one has the impression that the choice of method(s) used is a function of the result sought. This would explain in particular why, with respect to interpretation of a text, a term is taken in a new light which in no way corresponds to its usual meaning; this would also explain why the import of a rule is fixed with the aid of reasoning a contrario, while reasoning by analogy would be just as acceptable. Indeed, no formal proof of this assertion is possible; for it is excessively rare that a decision openly scans the practical consequences of the conceivable solutions. It remains, however, that many interpretations can be explained only by the search for a result considered to be more just or more equitable.

Notes and Questions

1. John P. Dawson, in a magisterial comparative study of judicial opinion-writing, pointed out that though the French opinion style creates the

62. For a critique of this notion, see Atias et Linotte, Le mythe de l'adaptation du droit au fait, D.1977. Chron. 251.

64. For instance in the 19th century, jurisprudence would consider "matchmak-er" agreements as immoral.

appearance of great judicial restraint, it leaves judges more free to exercise discretion than an opinion style in which the judges' reasoning is more fully exposed: "The chief legacy of the Revolution was not judicial submission to the discipline of the codes but a deep-seated, widely-held conviction that judges lacked lawmaking power. The judges joined in this disclaimer and expressed it though a cryptic style of opinion writing whose main purpose was to prove their dutiful submission but which left them in fact more free.... A principle directed toward restraining judicial power thus serves to enlarge it."[31] To what extent does the requirement of reason-giving operate to limit the discretion of American judges? The classic discussion of factors that help to assure stability and predictability in American law is Karl N. Llewellyn's The Common Law Tradition (1960) (pp. 19 et seq.).

2. How does the approach to interpretation outlined by Rieg above compare with the way American courts, scholars, and lawyers deal with enacted law? For further reading, see Interpreting Statutes: A Comparative Study (D.N. MacCormick & Robert S. Summers ed. 1991).

3. Should there be different methods of interpretation for precedents, statutes, and constitutions? Upon what factors should the answer to this question depend? The classic American work on this subject is Edward H. Levi's Introduction to Legal Reasoning (1948).

4. In the essay excerpted below, Heidelberg professor Winfried Brugger discusses contemporary German approaches to interpretation in the context of constitutional law. As these excerpts show, Brugger is a sophisticated observer of American constitutional law.

WINFRIED BRUGGER, "LEGAL INTERPRETATION, SCHOOLS OF JURISPRUDENCE, AND ANTHROPOLOGY: SOME REMARKS FROM A GERMAN POINT OF VIEW"

41 American Journal of Comparative Law (forthcoming, 1994) (excerpts).*

The classic method of interpretation in Germany was established by the founder of the 'historical school of jurisprudence', Friedrich Carl von Savigny, in an 1840 treatise on Roman law. Savigny distinguished, in modern parlance, *textual, verbal or grammatical interpretation, systematic, structural* or *contextual interpretation,* and *historical interpretation.* Later on, a fourth perspective was added: *teleological interpretation, which might also be termed* purposive interpretation.[2]

---

31. J. Dawson, The Oracles of the Law 431 (1959).

* Reprinted with permission of Winfried Brugger and the American Society of Comparative Law.

2. For descriptions of these methods, *see* Karl Heinrich Friauf, *Techniques for the Interpretation of Constitutions in German Law,* in Proceedings of the Fifth International Symposium on Comparative Law 9, 11–13 (1968); Siegfried Magiera, *The Interpretation of the Basic Law,* in Main Principles of the German Basic Law 89, 91–93 (Christian Starck ed., 1983); Donald P. Kommers, The Constitutional Jurisprudence of the Federal Republic of Germany 48–49 (1989); Konrad Hesse, Grundzüge des Verfassungsrechts der Bundesrepublik Deutschland § 2 II 1 (16th ed. 1988); Winfried Brugger, Rundfunkfreiheit und Verfassungsinterpretation 4–10 (1991).

In verbal or grammatical interpretation, philological methods are used to analyze the meaning of a particular word or sentence. In systematic interpretation, one attempts to clarify the meaning of a legal provision by reading it in conjunction with other, related provisions of the same section, or title, of the legal text, or even other texts within or outside the given legal system; thus, this method relies upon the unity, or at least the consistency, of the legal world. In historical analysis, the interpreter attempts to identify what the founders of a legal document wanted to regulate when they used certain words and sentences; here, both the specific and the general declarations of intent are of crucial importance. In teleological analysis, the historical will of the framers is devalued: Instead of being accorded critical emphasis as to what was then willed, their declarations of intent are only deemed indicative, not determinative, of the contemporaneous purpose of the legal provision or document. The same holds for the weight of textual and systematic interpretation in teleological analysis: These methods suggest an outcome or a certain range of outcomes, but the decisive point of reference is the interpreter's notion of a result that, according to the "independent function" or value of the pertinent legal provision, must be the correct one.

These four methods constitute the classic catalog of statutory interpretation in Germany. They also comprise the core of constitutional interpretation, as is evidenced by many cases decided by the Federal Constitutional Court (and, in the United States, by the Supreme Court[5]). For many years, German scholars have debated whether constitutional interpretation differs qualitatively from statutory interpretation, and if so, what additional or different standards should apply to constitutional adjudication.

The prevailing view holds that the Constitution differs from statutes in that it is more political, more open-ended, and less complete. From that it follows, according to this view, that vague constitutional provisions cannot be 'construed' (*ausgelegt*) but must be 'actualized' (*aktual-*

---

5. *See* the analyses by Cass Sunstein, After the Rights Revolution. Reconceiving the Regulatory State 113–32 (1990) (discussing text, structure, purpose, history, and legal process); Richard Fallon, *A Constructivist Coherence Theory of Constitutional Interpretation,* 100 Harv.L.Rev. 1189, 1194–1209 (1987) (discussing arguments from text, framers' intent, constitutional theory, judicial precedent, and moral or policy values); Walter F. Murphy & James E. Fleming & William Harris, American Constitutional Interpretation 291–301 (1986) (discussing verbal, historical, structural, doctrinal, prudential and purposive analyses); Philip Bobbitt, Constitutional Interpretation 12–13 (1991) (describing historical, textual, structural, doctrinal, ethical, and prudential modes of analyses). The classic four German criteria cover all these elements if one assumes that 'judicial doctrine' is an upshot of the four criteria, as developed and applied to specific cases or areas of law, and if one further stipulates a broad understanding of purpose that covers all overarching goals or values a legal provision or document in fact serves or is supposed to serve. Among such goals could easily fall procedural, moral, social, political and prudential values or theories. *Respect for judicial precedent* is not a formally binding guideline for judicial interpretation in Germany, because in a code law system, judicial decisions serve only as gloss on the law which is to be found in the rules and principles of the governing legal texts. In fact, however, all courts, including the Federal Constitutional Court, strive to adhere to precedent, as do American courts.

isiert) or 'concretized' (*konkretisiert*); the difference being that a strict 'construction' reveals a solution already inherent in the text, whereas an 'actualization' or 'concretization' entails a dialectic process of creatively determining results in conformity with, but not determinable by, the Constitution. According to the most influential proponent of this view, Konrad Hesse, the goal of creating constitutional law while respecting the Constitution may be reached through adherence to five points of reference for constitutional interpretation, in addition to, and relativization of, the four classic methods of statutory interpretation: (1) Each interpretation must support the unity of the constitution. (2) In cases of tension or conflict, the principle of practical concordance (*praktische Konkordanz*) must be employed to harmonize conflicting provisions. (3) All governmental organs must respect the functional differentiation of the Constitution, that is, their respective tasks and powers in the separation of powers scheme. (4) Each interpretation must try to create an integrative effect with regard to both the various parties of a constitutional dispute as well as to social and political cohesion. These points together lead to the principle of the (5) normative force of the Constitution: Each interpretation shall attempt to optimize all the aforementioned elements.

These five additional characteristics of constitutional interpretation are widely accepted and used by both scholars and judges. There is, in my view, little doubt in legal scholarship of the usefulness of categorical differentiation in general and this analysis of constitutional interpretation in particular. However, I doubt whether the peculiarities of the German Constitution are in fact so substantial as to not only permit but compel one to devise a special theory of constitutional interpretation.

Not only constitutions, but statutes as well can be hotly disputed, and in the German setting one may plausibly argue that the Constitution elicits a greater consensus than some legislative acts. Not only do constitutions comprise open-ended principles, but so do other legal texts—in referring, for example, to various standards of public interest or reasonableness. Not only are constitutions incomplete, in the sense that they do not regulate every problem in detail, but so are statutes, and the extent to which constitutions are even less complete depends upon the specific question to answer. There are sections in the German Constitution which are more specific than some passages of legislative enactments. Finally, whether or to what extent an interpretation reveals something hidden in the language or based upon the creativity of the interpreter, is a question leading up to complex problems of literary theory and construction that transcend the distinction between statutory and constitutional law.

Even if one assumes that the dissimilarities between the German Constitution and German legislation in general are so substantial as to create a qualitative difference between these two kinds of legal texts, one can argue that the additional methods of constitutional interpretation proposed by Konrad Hesse form a part of or can be viewed as an annex to the classic canon of statutory interpretation, especially the systematic and teleological perspectives: (1) It is the goal of systematic, respectively structural or contextual interpretation to clarify the meaning of a rule by reference to other related provisions, but this reference presupposes the unity or consistency of the legal order and implies (2) that if tensions arise, they may be alleviated by a reasonable accommodation of the pertinent provisions. (4) If one of the overarching aims of the legal system is the integration of the political community, then teleological interpretation clearly permits to include this goal. Within the same approach it is also possible and perfectly reasonable to advocate the view that in order to (5) further the normative force of the legal text at hand, one must attempt to optimize all the aforementioned points. The only reference point remaining, then, is (3) adherence to the functional differentiation of the Constitution—meaning that judges should adjudicate, while legislators should adopt and administrators execute the law. This point, admittedly, plays a stronger role in constitutional adjudication than in statutory interpretation, but in the process of the former, respect for separation of powers concerns falls clearly under the auspices of a contextual analysis of the text of the Constitution.

All of this suggests that, although it is possible to create particular methods of constitutional interpretation, we are not compelled to do so. Whether or not it is desirable may depend on the specific problem at hand. At any rate, for present purposes nothing is lost by adhering to the classic canon of interpretation as a method of both statutory and constitutional interpretation. What rules, then, does the German doctrine propose with regard to the use of the four interpretive methods? Legal scholars support various methods of ranking, but the standard generally relied upon by both scholars and judges does not amount to much more than the following precept: When interpreting a provision, make use of all methods. The result may then be: All methods achieve the same result; the case is therefore easily resolved. Or, the methods may point to different results; the case is therefore difficult to settle. Which rule should one follow in a hard case? There exists no detailed rule which would be universally acknowledged and adhered to in German jurisprudence, but two precepts are widely accepted:

First, each interpretation must respect the outer bounds of grammatical analysis. For example, if the constitutionality of a legal provision is in doubt, the judge should construe it in a way compatible with the constitutional command; however, this is not a license to manipulate the ordinary meaning of the language. Yet, on a closer look, one can identify decisions in which the courts have used systematic and teleological arguments in order to disregard the wording of a rule; usually these are instances in which the result reached by textual analysis is considered by the judges to be irrational or unjust.

Second, more importance must be placed on the 'objective' textual, systematic, and teleological methods than on the 'subjective' historical method. Historical analysis, indeed, generally serves only as a secondary, supplementary way of clarifying a rule's meaning. But in some cases, courts place great emphasis on this type of argument, and it is the other methods which seem to be supplementary.

The designation of the textual, systematic, and teleological analyses as objective is meant to express the view that the text of the provision is used as an independent starting point. Once a law is adopted, according to German understanding, it becomes an independent entity, and is supposed to regulate not only the present, but the future as well. What the adopters said is paramount to what they willed. Thus the provision cannot be bound by their declarations of intent. Independence, however, is too strong a characterization. It is more accurate to say that the subjective will of the adopters influences the meaning of the provision but does not totally determine it. Other aspects: the text itself, its legal context, and, especially, teleological arguments based on contemporaneous notions of rule-specific or overarching legal values, may legitimately be considered in order to affirm, broaden, or narrow the historical understanding of the reach of the provision.

There is some irony to this: In order to employ these objective methods of interpretation, one must use subjective judgment. Without an individual assessment of how to devise, weigh, and relate textual, contextual, and teleological arguments, objective interpretation cannot be undertaken. On the other hand, it is possible, at least in some cases, to come up with a valid, objective elucidation of what the framers subjectively wanted to achieve. So, if one so desires, one might reverse traditional terminology.

LEGAL METHODS AND SCHOOLS OF JURISPRUDENCE

Apart from the terminological question, one basic fact emerges in every difficult case: The interpreter, in using the four methods of interpretation, faces problems of indeterminacy which may only be eliminated if there exists a universally accepted and detailed rule as to the use and hierarchy of the relevant methods. But such a specific rule is not available, only the aforementioned, rather weak precepts. Beyond that, scholars argue for and against particular hierarchies, and courts adhere to a fairly flexible and pragmatic course, weighing the importance of the interpretive perspectives according to whichever line of argument seems the most convincing in a particular case or group of cases, or according to which musters a majority in the court.

One way of analyzing and refining the prospect of interpretive choice is to differentiate, not between statutory and constitutional interpretation, but to demonstrate that within each of the four perspectives variations can and do arise. . . .

A textual analysis may focus upon both the ordinary meaning of a word or its legal/professional usage. Contextual analysis may refer to the legal context of a rule, or its social context, of which the interpreter forms a part. In an historical analysis of the will of the rule's adopters, one may strive to identify what their actual specific or abstract intentions were or what they might have been, had the adopters been aware of key facts and ideas known to us but not to them. Regarding teleological interpretation, one can distinguish widely disparate, over-arching purposes of legal provisions, e.g., accommodating politics, rein-forcing the democratic process, securing substantive justice, including all groups equally, supporting societal stability, reconciling individual choice and social forms, maximizing lifestyle choices, interest satisfaction, or economic wealth, respecting everything that works.

This extensive (but not exhaustive) list of variations on the four interpretive perspectives captures many reference points that both schol-ars and courts employ when they expound the meaning of legal provi-sions in hard cases. The list of variations, however, does not contain more than that—an enumeration of the most important variations on the four classic perspectives, which can serve as an analytical tool in establishing which criteria courts and legal scholars do in fact use in the interpretive process. The list does not address the problem of their relations and respective weight to be given each mode of analysis.

Before I touch on these questions, however, I want to address an expansion of not only the basic but also the enlarged list of interpretive perspectives. Every one of the topics mentioned in the enlarged list of reference points identifies at least one core element [21] of each of the most prominent legal philosophies in the United States:

Textualism concentrates on the common and legal usage of words and their legal context; it is sometimes also referred to as formalism. Interpretivism or intentionalism emphasizes the importance of the actu-al or enlightened will of the adopters of a rule. Textualism and interpretivism together are sometimes called originalism; they also comprise the core of positivism, insofar as 'law' is characterized by and confined to concrete legal provisions: that is, either specific rules or abstract principles as narrowed down by their historical meaning. Legal realism concentrates on the real-life 'input' and 'output' of legal inter-pretation, be it the personal background of judges, the contribution of an interpretation to some desirable policy, or other social factors. The critical legal studies movement endorses a more skeptical, more radical, and more utopian form of Legal Realism: Behind every interpretive statement lurk political decisions; in a fragmented and divided society these value judgments generally amount to value impositions by the ruling class on minorities, as long as these minorities are not able to amend the use of language and the current institutional/political struc-ture. If an interpreter underscores the weight of arguments of justice, one moves in the direction of classic natural law theory or modern moral theories of justice. These often emphasize the problem of the fair distribution of burdens and benefits, but in feminist jurisprudence and

---

21. In order to prove the following anal-ysis, I would have to spend much time and use much space, and it is doubtful that I could persuade everyone. But I hope that many will agree, at least on the superficial level of citing catchwords, on the character-izations, especially in the light of my reser-vation that the respective catchword cap-tures one core (and not all tenets) of these jurisprudential schools. I am fully aware that within every school I refer to, many variations exist. I also realize that every school integrates, to some extent, elements of the other approaches; indeed, one could identify some close allies. . . .

race theory additional claims are brought forward: the inclusion of oppressed minorities on a basis of equal respect for their personal and cultural contributions to social life. The emphasis is different in models of democratic decisionmaking: Here it is not the fairness or inclusiveness of the result that is considered significant, but the quality of the democratic process itself, which legitimizes the respective outcome. Interest satisfaction and wealth maximization form the core of utilitarianism and the economic theory of law. Choice maximization is the guiding light of individualism, whereas social order and stability stand at the apex of conservatism. Communitarianism can be viewed as an attempt to accommodate both individualism and conservatism, in that both free choice and the cultural embeddedness of the individual are viewed as necessary for the human personality to flourish. American pragmatism is primarily concerned with discerning and supporting institutional and substantive arrangements that 'work', and they only work if they express the funded experience of a society.[22]

If indeed these relationships exist between methods of interpretation and schools of jurisprudence, does this knowledge aid the interpreter confronted with a hard case? Or does this simply show that, apart from having a choice with regard to interpretive methods, one also has a choice in jurisprudential schools? Undeniably, choice plays a role both in the use of legal methods and in support for legal philosophies. But how great a choice exists, and what kind of discretion do we encounter in hard cases? The answers to these questions depend on the specific settings of the relevant cases and the degree of determinacy or indeterminacy of the pertaining rule(s). But general preconceptions will probably also play a role, as is evidenced by the widely diverging American views on the general degree of indeterminacy of the (which one specifically?) law.

If one wishes to address this question in general terms, it is useful to distinguish three ideal-type modes of inquiry. (1) Is this choice in fact governed by the *personal fiat* of the interpreter? Should it be? Mainstream American and German legal thinkers would answer both the factual and the normative questions in the negative, but some decon-

---

22. For Americans interested in the German schools of interpretation and legal philosophy, I mention some of the schools and their approximate American counterparts. Positivism, formalism, and textualism form the main elements of the theories of *Begriffsjurisprudenz* and Hans Kelsen's *Reine Rechtslehre*. The *Historische Rechtsschule* of Savigny and others thematizes topics which in the United States would fall under the heading of conservatism or communitarianism. The main concerns of legal realism and critical legal studies are addressed in and were preceded by the German *Freie Rechtsschule* and the *Interessenjurisprudenz*. For proponents of the view that 'law is politics' it might prove enlightening to study Carl Schmitt's 1932 treatise Der Begriff des Politischen, an advocacy and radical application of the politicization of law: The Concept of the Political (George Schwab trans., 1976). The German *Wertungsjurisprudenz* comes close to American pragmatism and moral theory. Interpretivism does not have a close German ally because historical interpretation in Germany has traditionally been seen only as a secondary source of interpretation.... As regards other teleological aspects such as utilitarianism, individualism, or other overarching purposes of law, one would have to study the pertinent classic and modern literature in social and political theory....

structivist scholars or radical adherents of critical legal studies may answer 'yes'. (2) Does there or should there exist some standard guiding interpretive choices which, although not determinative, might bestow *direction* and *order* upon this inquiry? The dominant view both in Germany and America would answer this question in the positive, and, in what follows, I shall support this stance by proposing two important sets of interpretive guidelines. (3) Could one even argue for a *strict hierarchy* of methods to guide interpretation in hard cases?

In referring to a strict or strong hierarchy of methods I include two types of theories: The former is the type in which either what is said, what historically was willed, or what now reasonably might be intended governs the outcome of the interpretation, and no accommodation of these perspectives is allowed; this one could call a privileged factor theory. The latter type opts for the binding force of conclusions drawn from the text, legal context, and history irrespective of the reasonableness of the case's substantive outcome—that is, the teleological perspective; this, of course, is a variant of the privileged factor type of theory. Some scholars argue for a strict hierarchy of methods, but until now, neither in Germany nor in the United States has any proposal been generally accepted. Some of the reasons for the failure to establish a strict canon of interpretation [27] will become clear in the following discussion.

The first recommendation for the ordering of legal methods is based on the premise that any interpretation should take both the law *and* the real world seriously. It should make at least some sense in the world of legal purposes, principles, and rules, as well as in the world of social facts and ideals. From that it follows that we must begin with the legal text and context of the relevant provision. Both can indicate either a broad or narrow range of possible solutions. Within this more or less determinate range, one may then consider what the framers wanted to achieve and what the relevant provision(s) in light of contemporaneous legal values such as justice, efficiency, or some other relevant goal require(s). As Savigny has already noted, we must employ every method available. If we work in accordance with this maxim, we are not, however, assured of the absence of conflict between these methods, and there exists no guarantee that subjective judgment will not be involved. Indeed, in every intricate case, conflict and subjectivity abound.

Nevertheless, admitting this does not imply that only personal predilections count or should count. The resolution of legal problems depends on several settings which affect the context and content of the opinion: The cultural and linguistic background will at least outline the

---

27. The term 'canon' of interpretation is often held in disregard, in Germany as well as in the United States. This dislike is probably based on the widespread linkage of the word canon with a formalistic approach to interpretation. As the text wants to make clear, there are different types of canons (flexible and inflexible ones, inclu- sionary and exclusionary ones) and also different ways of using them (in the discovery mode or the interpretive mode). For an enlightening analysis of the interpretive mode in contrast to the discovery path and the path of invention in moral philosophy, *see* Michael Walzer, Interpretation and Criticism ch. 1 (1987).

outer bounds of what might be right and wrong and what meanings can be given to the text of the relevant legal provision. The institutional setting (for example: jurisdiction, case or controversy, standing, decision by collegiate body, *stare decisis*) influences what and how the question is to be adjudicated. The personal background of the judges (their integrity and competence) can also function as an (admittedly rather abstract) check on 'bad' decisions. With regard to the methodological setting—the use of interpretive methods—some conclusions, at least in the negative, can safely be drawn: A judgment that is not based on the pertaining legal text and context is not a legal interpretation but a political decision. A judgment that makes sense only in the world of the law, but not in the real world, is an unsound judgment. And a judgment that is obviously unjust will not carry the full force of law to an unwilling population.

These principal (but not exhaustive) points of reference create an array of legitimate judicial decisionmaking in which sometimes a variety of judgments may be made. The degree to which these criteria determine the outcome of a case is always contingent upon the facts of the matter, the area of law, and the respective social consensus or dissension with regard to a reasonable dispute settlement. Many social disputes are resolved by the parties themselves; others end up in court. Many cases are settled in court or adjudicated, and are not appealed; others are appealed to higher courts, and only these cases end up in casebooks.

Of greater significance, however, than the disputed question of the degree of consensus or dissension that exists in a modern society such as that of Germany or America, is another point: Each legal decision in a hard case requires an individual judgment. This, though, does not automatically entail arbitrariness, which would only be implied upon application of the all-or-nothing approach: If something is not totally rational, certain, or determined, it must then be absolutely irrational and indeterminate. This simplistic and misleading antagonism does not make sense in a liberal and pluralistic society, in which occasionally a broad range of normative judgments may be made by rational people [32], both in adopting and in interpreting legal provisions. In such a society, the basic line is the strong possibility of some dispute over the direction and the significance of both substantive and interpretive rules, and the relevant question therefore is: If rational people partially agree and partially disagree, what adequate procedures and arguments then exist to solve these problems in the best way possible?

Viewed in this light, "critical pluralism is not the inevitable consequence in the interpretation of the 'open' text, if we understand that by

32. It is a virtue and not a failure of a liberal society that it allows and constitutionally supports differing value judgments to be proclaimed and brought to bear in the political process. Hard cases in adjudication, then, can also be characterized as cases in which the governing legal provision allows for several plausible solutions, but these compete until one is selected as the binding, according to the relevant institutional, procedural, and substantive standards. Even after a binding judicial decision is handed down, the fight is not necessarily over—there may exist other bodies to which one may appeal.

determinate meaning, we are speaking probabilistically about that interpretation that is supported by the best evidence (that can reasonably be accounted for) which would resolve competing interpretations. For, determinacy is neither certainty nor propositional adequacy to facts. It is rather a matter of degree and a function of possible communal agreement about assessment procedures."

Even if we assume that a judge does not act in good faith (but why should we assume this, if there is no concrete indication for bias? if one is a cynic, should not one then be a cynic with regard to oneself as well?), this does not necessarily lead to the mere imposition of his values on the parties. The judge is required to defend and justify his decision, using the aforementioned methods of interpretation, which, according to the circumstances of the case, should indicate what an acceptable judgment could look like. In other words: The institutional and methodological 'context of justification' delimits the range of and transforms the personal 'context of discovery'. Thus, the interpreter and his product partake of a process which is both realistic and idealistic, in that its master ideal is to achieve results which make sense both in the real world and in the legal world.

Gerhard Leibholz, an influential former Justice of the German Federal Constitutional Court, has expressed this master ideal of interpretation as follows:

> If the world as it is, i.e., political reality, is left out of account by the law, the lawyer becomes detached from life, from reality, and so from the law itself. If the value of the legal rule is overlooked because of an uncritically extended theory of the normative force of fact, the choice in favour of the ever-changing forces behind constitutional reality destroys the dignity and authority of the law. It must be the task of the constitutional lawyer to reconcile rules of law and constitutional reality in such a way that the existing dialectical conflict between rule and reality can be removed as far as possible by creative interpretation of the constitution without doing violence thereby either to reality in favour of the rule, or to the rule in favour of reality.[37] ...

What exactly is the meaning of the interpretive master concept of making sense both *in* or *of* the real world and the legal world? This ideal has complex connotations which should be addressed in greater detail than is possible here. But some core elements may be characterized as follows: The ideal of making sense in the legal world is *consistency* or *legal coherence*. The ideal of making sense in the real world possesses normative and factual dimensions which one may term, on the one hand, *legitimacy* or *ethical coherence* and, on the other hand, *instrumental rationality* or *empirical coherence*.

Consistency or legal coherence entails that all provisions of the law—its purposes, principles, and rules—should form a bond of unity: of

---

37. Gerhard Leibholz, *Constitutional Law and Constitutional Reality,* in Festschrift für Karl Loewenstein 305, 308 (Henry Steele Commager et al. eds., 1971)....

mutual coordination, accommodation, and clarification. At the very least, laws should avoid contradiction and excessive vagueness, and judges should do their best to read the law as a "rational continuum" in order to promote clarity and consonance.

This last, weaker claim is the more realistic in modern pluralistic societies, whose legal systems must integrate many different values, and where the democratic process usually is not compelled by a constitutional mandate to proceed consistently; furthermore, legislatures often evade their responsibility to take difficult (read: politically potentially damaging) decisions by intentionally using open-ended language that leaves the burden of decision-making on the judiciary. Still, if there is tension between conflicting legal provisions, it is essential to interpret them in a way that avoids inconsistency, and by arguments intelligible to the people; the same requirements hold for cases in which the courts substitute for the legislature.

One aspect of the law that supports its systemic, legal coherence is its hierarchy: Lower provisions must not contradict higher provisions, especially those within the Constitution. Another related device is the doctrine of *stare decisis* and the strategy of distinguishing whose purpose it is to demonstrate that the court is moving within the confines of binding higher cases (unity), even though it does not follow their lead in this—distinguishable—case (avoidance of inconsistency). Both doctrines—supremacy of the Constitution and *stare decisis*—also support the goal of interpreting the laws in an intelligent, understandable, and predictable way: In order to construe the laws as a rational continuum, open-ended purposes and principles on the constitutional/statutory level must be read in conjunction with the more concrete statutory or judicial rules that pertain to the respective purpose and principle and give it specificity and stability.

These last remarks indicate that consistency also possesses an institutional level: Not only must substantive rules and principles be interpreted in the best way possible as far as their commensurability is concerned; the same holds for legal provisions defining institutional powers and procedures. Judicial interpretation is one aspect of determining the law which must be seen in the light of, and contrasted with, the powers of the legislature, the executive, and the administration, to both adopt and interpret law. Each branch of government should develop and adhere to a conception of its respective powers that makes sense both in the legal world and the real world; a conception that corresponds to its functional capacities as well as to its constitutional mandate.

Legitimacy or ethical coherence refers to a convincing or at least plausible interpretation of the social and political values that are referred to in legal provisions. Using the teleological approach, we ask: What purpose does and should a legal rule serve? How does this particular purpose fit into our governing ideals of social and political life? And how should these ideals shape the overall structure of the legal system as well as our understanding of its specific rules? Here the overarching purposes and values of law and society merge.

Again, I must emphasize that while each interpreter must depend on his or her judgment in concretizing these ideals, this does not reflect sophistry or arbitrariness. When all members of a society invoke concepts such as justice, freedom, equality, or the like, then every member's interpretation is potentially one of many legitimate perspectives on these ideals; the perspectivist nature of judgment is constitutive and not detrimental to it. That is why a liberal society, which constitutionally acknowledges and protects the perspectiveness of all human judgments, strives, or at least should strive, to observe the greatest possible range of value judgments in the process of adopting and interpreting law.

The ideal of an instrumental-rational or empirically coherent interpretive process requires at least informed fact-finding and the proper consideration of the scarcity of goods and of means-ends efficiency. I say 'proper consideration' because all these aspects should also (and arguably even primarily) be taken into account by the political process. Thus, the basic goals of social science, of utilitarianism, and of the economic analysis of law figure prominently under this heading.

The two facets of this master ideal must eventually be reconciled as much as possible: A persuasive interpretation should strive for a reasonable accommodation of both external/societal and internal/jurisprudential values. Or, to put it slightly differently: Judicial interpretation should strive to integrate the ideals of systemic consistency, social congruence, and stability of doctrine over time.

It is evident that I do not consider it judicious to design a strict canon for the use of these four methods and their variations; each merits consideration because textual and contextual arguments strive to make sense of the legal world, whereas historical and teleological arguments are based on what made sense then respectively what makes sense nowadays in the real world, and both perspectives count and have to be integrated as much as possible! If that is correct, however, one conclusion in the negative can safely be drawn: One should avoid to concentrate on any single one method or on any school of jurisprudence that focuses solely on the textual, contextual, historical, or teleological perspective. This may seem a trivial criterion, but it is not without consequences. It leads to the critique of simplistic premises such as: 'law is (or should only be) politics,' 'the law is (or should only be) in the books', 'law is (or should be) restricted to what historically was willed', 'law only reflects (or should only reflect) economic rationality', etcetera. Consequently, my advice may be stated thus: Let us adhere to some form of *integration theory* when applying methods of interpretation and assessing schools of jurisprudence.

SECTION 5. CONVERGENCE
AND DIVERGENCE

MARY ANN GLENDON, "THE SOURCES OF
LAW IN A CHANGING LEGAL ORDER"

17 Creighton Law Review 663, 665–84 (1984).*

The relative predominance of the various sources of law is now quite markedly at variance with the classical common and civil law descriptions. In addition, and equally important, the very nature of two of the main sources, legislation and case law, has been profoundly altered since these descriptions were formulated in the late nineteenth and early twentieth centuries. The fundamental changes that have taken place have produced significant areas of convergence between civil and common law systems, casting doubt on the utility of many of the traditionally accepted distinctions between the common and the civil law.

* * *

The traditional ways of thinking about the materials of legal reasoning began to be unsettled by the "discovery," proclaimed by several nineteenth century writers in Europe and the United States, that the judicial function is not merely a mechanical process of finding and applying legal norms contained in earlier cases or in legislation. Von Jhering in Germany, Bentham and Austin in England, Holmes in the United States, and Gény in France all effectively demolished the illusion of the internal logic and completeness of the law. While the news that judges were often engaged in a creative law-making process held the attention of the academy, however, time-honored methods of thinking and communicating about law were being decisively and permanently affected by events in a rapidly changing society. Five aspects of the transition from market to mixed and regulated economies in particular undermined classical sources-of-law notions: the rise of legislation, the increasing variety of legislation, the decline of precedent in the common law, the emergence of administrative law, and the expansion of the functions of the state.

THE RISE OF STATUTORY LAW

Starting in the late nineteenth century, in both civil and common law systems, there was an outpouring of a kind of legislation which displaced both the judge-made common law and the continental civil codes with essentially the same kind of new law. What kind of law was this? It belonged to the age of what was then called universal suffrage and to the spirit of men like Jeremy Bentham who believed that legislation could and should be used as a "scientific" instrument of social reform and control. National legislatures, elected by increasingly broader constituencies, adopted factory legislation, workmen's compensation

* Reprinted with the permission of the Creighton Law Review.

laws, rudimentary social legislation, and laws regulating employment contracts, and began to regulate commerce and public utilities. This modern legislation removed great areas wholly or partially from the coverage of the judge-made common law in the Anglo–American systems and from the civil codes in the continental systems. Moreover, it not only took territory from these traditional sources, but it was fundamentally inconsistent with their underlying ideologies of protection of private property and enforcement of private ordering through contract.

Then, in the first part of the twentieth century, mainly in response to economic crises, a second wave of modern legislation appeared. Legislatures in industrialized countries came to the assistance, at different times and to varying degrees, of farmers, debtors, and unemployed workers. The state started to attend systematically to the elementary needs of its disadvantaged citizens. Each country laid down the main lines of its legal treatment of industrial relations. The administrative apparatus of the modern state began to take on its present contours.

What is of particular interest to us in this oft-told tale is how academic lawyers did and did not respond to the new situation. The growing importance of statutes as sources of law in the United States over the first half of the twentieth century was early remarked upon by Pound and Landis in articles which are now regarded as classics.[9] In 1947, Felix Frankfurter wrote that "as late as 1875 more than 40% of the controversies before the [Supreme] Court were common-law litigation, fifty years later only 5%, while today cases not resting on statutes are reduced almost to zero."[10] In 1982, Guido Calabresi summed up the long trend: "The last fifty to eighty years have seen a fundamental change in American law. In this time we have gone from a legal system dominated by the common law, divined by courts, to one in which statutes, enacted by legislatures, have become the primary source of law."[11] In the civil law countries, of course, legislation had been the primary source of law since the acceptance of parliamentary supremacy, with the great nineteenth century codifications of civil law enjoying pride of place.[12] What is interesting there is that the civil codes have receded steadily in importance, as more and more of the matters with which they are concerned have become the subject of what civil lawyers call "special legislation." The evergrowing body of separate statutes reinforces the traditional preeminence of enacted law within civil law systems but diminishes the influence of the codes themselves.

9. Landis, Statutes and the Sources of Law, 1934 Harvard Legal Essays 214; Pound, Common Law and Legislation, 21 Harv.L.Rev. 383 (1908).

10. Frankfurter, Some Reflections on the Reading of Statutes, 47 Colum.L.Rev. 527 (1947).

11. G. Calabresi, A Common Law for the Age of Statutes 1 (1982).

12. "The 19th century was the century of codification in Western Europe, between the Napoleonic codification of 1804–1810 and the German codification of 1900. The code was considered the natural means of presenting legal norms; that is enacted law, which was then considered to be the exclusive source of law." Tallon, La Codification en France, 27 Annuaire de Législation Française et Etrangère 12 (1978).

THE MANY VARIETIES OF STATUTORY LAW

The important position of statutes alongside case law in the common law and codes in the civil law is now well recognized. Indeed, the only place where this aspect of modern legal life seems to be insufficiently appreciated, is ... in the usual law school curriculum. It has been less widely noticed, however, that modern enacted law differs in kind both from older common law statutes and from the great continental codifications. There is not just more of it; it now comes in greater variety. Some of these varieties are new in the relatively brief history of legal regulation. Part of the reason we do not notice this is because we use the single word "statute" to describe many different types of legislation. For example, in the common law systems, there are still statutes of the sort known to Blackstone—mere restatements of or patches on the common law. There are also statutes of the kind, to which Pound and Landis devoted much attention, which potentially establish new principles or directions for the common law. But in addition, and, in the United States especially since the New Deal, the body of statutory law has been greatly augmented by what one may call bureaucratic law: the statutes which create regulatory agencies with broad delegated powers to make rules and to adjudicate and the great laws of the welfare state—revenue-raising laws, social security laws, and the various public assistance laws. To the extent that the regulatory laws which increasingly dominate modern legal systems tend to be highly detailed and specific, they create a world of their own in which the role of judge-made law is limited. Insofar as such legislation represents the temporary compromise of conflicts among organized interests, or "the pressures of narrow interest groups rather than any coherent view of the public interest," it poses special interpretive problems for judges who must attempt to apply it. The judge's search for a guiding principle or policy may be futile: such statutes often have multiple purposes, some of which may be in tension or conflict with each other.

* * *

Just as modern statutes in common law systems have little resemblance to their nineteenth century predecessors, there are significant differences between modern continental legislation and the nineteenth century codes. The civil codes, which now constitute only a small part of the total volume of existing legislation in such countries, tend to lay down general principles rather than to provide specifically for particular situations. Ordinary legislation does not maintain the same level of generality, however, nor is it characterized by as much conceptual and terminological consistency as are the codes. Regulatory legislation, such as land use control, tax law, wage and price control, labor law, rent and eviction control, etc., is more particularistic and more sensitive to political and economic currents than the codes. The fact is that legislatures have often found it hard to make necessary reforms within the structure of the hallowed civil codes, especially where the interests of organized economic groups are affected. They have resorted instead to statutes outside the codes which are more easily amended as constellations of interests and power shift and as circumstances change. Modern statutes in civil law systems require different approaches from those brought to the interpretation of the codes. In both the Anglo–American and Romano–Germanic systems, therefore, statutes are not only pervasive but increasingly regulatory, volatile, and little related in form and spirit to the former primary sources of law.

The increased volume of enacted law of all kinds in modern Western legal systems has increased the necessity for its construction, interpretation, and application by courts. Thus, in this sense, common law courts have become more like their civil law counterparts in that they are now largely engaged in dealing with enacted law. But in neither system are traditional techniques of interpretation particularly well-suited to the task of dealing with the various types of modern statutes. This brings me to my next point which concerns changes in judge-made law.

THE DECLINE OF PRECEDENT

One of the major differences between case law in a common law system and case law in the civil law is that the judicial function in the civil law systems has traditionally been regarded as limited to deciding particular cases, while common law courts are not only supposed to settle disputes between the parties before the court but also to give guidance as to how similar disputes should be handled in the future.[42] The reasoned elaboration of precedent has traditionally been the principal device for achieving the optimum balance between continuity and growth in Anglo–American law. Changes occurring over the twentieth century, however, have considerably affected this function of the common law courts. We have already noted that the proliferation of regulatory law, while affording an abundance of occasions for litigation, does not necessarily offer the court wide scope for interpretation or for reasoning from principles contained in statutes. Second, courts in the United States, especially federal courts, have increasingly been called to rule upon problems of social conflict which cannot easily be resolved by the reasoned elaboration of principle.... Third, decisions of the United States Supreme Court in important cases in recent years often show little effort on the opinion writer's part to build a bridge to preexisting authority. They often seem to simply balance the interests involved or react to the facts of the particular case. Frequently, they appear to be merely the products of majority vote.

Finally, there seems to have been a significant change in the very nature of decision-making in common law courts generally. This change

---

42. As Karl Llewellyn put it:

The court can decide the particular dispute only according to a general rule which covers a whole class of like disputes. Our legal theory does not admit of single decisions standing on their own. If judges are free, are indeed forced, to decide new cases for which there is no rule, they must at least make a new rule as they decide.

K. Llewellyn, The Bramble Bush 42–43 (1960) (first published 1930) (emphasis in original).

concerns the relative importance of the two traditional functions of common law case law: that of settling the dispute between the parties and that of providing principled guidance for the future. As P.S. Atiyah pointed out in his inaugural lecture at Oxford University in 1978, there is apt to be a tension between these two functions: a decision which does justice in all the circumstances of the case is often likely to conflict with the desire to encourage or discourage certain types of behavior in the future.[44] Atiyah makes a convincing case, which seems to be applicable at least as much to the United States as to England, that modern common law courts are less inclined than their nineteenth century predecessors to resolve disputes by adhering to principle and are giving much greater weight to the problem of individualized justice in the particular case. I do not suggest that we should uncritically accept this thesis. In particular, it seems to me that the way facts were found and the outward appearance of principled decision-making in the nineteenth century must have masked some very subjective judgments in many cases. But to the extent that Atiyah is correct, Anglo–American judicial decisions have quietly come to assume in fact a role similar to that ascribed in theory to decisions of civil law courts.

* * *

While there thus seems to have been a certain diminution in the role of precedent in the common law, court decisions have increasingly come to be treated as important sources of law in the civil law systems. As a practical matter, it is now generally accepted in civil law systems that judges do and should take heed of prior decisions, especially when a consistent line of cases has developed.... Civil and common law differ, of course, in that case law is said to be binding in the common law by the rule of stare decisis, while in civil law theory cases are said to be of no authority apart from their intrinsic merits. Given the narrowness of the doctrine of stare decisis, and the fact that decisions of certain high courts in several civil law countries have been made binding by statute, however, the sometimes asserted contrast between civil and common law systems in this area begins to appear as more of a nuance than a major difference.

Finally, as courts in the United States begin to delegate brief-reading and opinion-drafting to large and layered staffs and increasingly to dispose of cases without opinion or with short memorandum opinions, another traditional legal distinction begins to fade: that between adjudication and administration. The tension between fairness for the immediate parties and guidance for the situation-type is complicated by the presence of other factors: concern for efficiency and system maintenance. No study of the judicial process is complete, in the United States at least, that does not take account of the bureaucratization of the

44. Atiyah, From Principles to Pragmatism: Changes in the Function of the Judicial Process and the Law, reprinted in 65 Iowa L.Rev. 1249, 1250 (1980).

courts. This has been one of the more recent manifestations of those changes in government which earlier in the century produced in increasing quantities a kind of law that came to be known as administrative.

THE RISE OF ADMINISTRATIVE LAW

Starting in the late nineteenth century, as we have seen, modern statutes began to displace case law in the common law systems and codes in civil law systems as the predominant sources of law. Over the twentieth century, administrative regulations and decisions became an increasingly important part of the legal landscape in modern states, rivaling both legislation and judicial decisions as sources of law.

* * *

The phenomenon was soon reflected in the caseload of the federal courts. Mr. Justice Jackson wrote in 1952: "The rise of administrative bodies probably has been the most significant legal trend of the last century and perhaps more values today are affected by their decisions than by those of all the courts, review of administrative decisions apart." [60] Felix Frankfurter, who in 1947 had called the attention of the legal community to the great proportion of the Supreme Court's work involving statutes, took up his pen in 1957 to write about the degree to which the Supreme Court by then was occupied with administrative law: "Review of administrative action, mainly reflecting enforcement of federal regulatory statutes, constitutes the largest category of the court's work, comprising one-third of the total cases decided on the merits." [62] Administrative law ... came into its own everywhere in the industrialized West in the twentieth century.[63] New areas came under regulation; government's role in providing social services increased. Despite sporadic and modest attempts at deregulation, as more areas of public concern are identified, such as protection of the environment or health and safety in the workplace, the scope of administrative law continues to expand. Today, in any highly developed Western legal system, the laws that have the most direct impact on the lives of most people, the laws that an ordinary person encounters most often in the course of a lifetime, are the predominantly administrative bodies of tax law, social security law, public assistance law, housing law, immigration and naturalization law, and so on. Administrative law adds to modern case law and particularistic legislation yet another source of law in which reckonability is problematic. Out of the necessity to deal with a multitude of unforeseeable day-to-day contingencies, it has to repose great confidence and discretion in officials. It is often, as Charles Szladits has said, an "*ad hoc creation*," uncertain, volatile and "easily affected by social, political,

---

60. Federal Trade Commission v. Ruberoid Co., 343 U.S. 470, 487, 72 S.Ct. 800, 810, 96 L.Ed. 1081 (1952) (Jackson, J., dissenting).

62. Frankfurter, The Supreme Court in the Mirror of Justices, 105 U.Pa.L.Rev. 781, 793 (1957).

63. See generally E. Freund, Administrative Powers Over Persons and Property (1928).

economic, atmospheric, *etc.* changes." [65]

* * *

The Rise of Public Law

In classical common and civil law alike, the role of direct government intervention was supposed to be minimal, and it was assumed that two of the main functions of the state were to protect private property and to enforce legally formed contracts. From this individualistic base, in which private law had predominated and property and contract reigned supreme, the civil and the common law systems alike began moving in the late nineteenth century toward modifying ownership rights, limiting or channeling the power of private persons to make their own enforceable contractual arrangements, and, at the same time, expanding the functions of the state. . . .

In the traditional private law areas, modern legislation established a new and competing set of premises. Freedom of contract was still enshrined in the common law and the civil codes, but a variety of mandatory provisions and prohibitions was introduced by statutes in the name of the public interest. In the area of property, the common law and the codes still accorded a special place to private rights, but legislation qualified the property right by subtracting elements in the public interest or modified it by adding social obligations. The new area of labor law, unlike the common law of master and servant and the employment contract in civil codes, emphasized the group over the individual, downgraded the role of the will of the parties, and was replete with mandatory rules which could not be changed by agreement. As the twentieth century wore on, courts in the United States and Germany, in particular, began, with and without direct or indirect legislative sanction, to take upon themselves the task of conforming contracts to judicially generalized notions of fairness and reasonableness. In many places, too, the authority of the civil codes and the common law as sources of principles began to be superseded, not only by statutes, but by constitutions.

While private law was thus taking on an important public dimension, public law was being augmented by the body of rules necessary for the organization and management of public services. Just as private law had been transformed by the idea that every person has social obligations, so public law had been transformed by the social functions of government. No longer limiting themselves to providing defense, police, and dispute settlement, modern states, directly and indirectly, became involved in the provision of education, social assistance to the poor, transportation, electricity, post, telephone and telegraph services, and numerous other public works and services. Contract and the market were increasingly supplanted or supplemented as ordering mechanisms

65. Szladits, The Civil Law System, § 2 in Ch. 2 of II Int'l Encyc.Comp.Law 15, 49, 56 (R. David ed. 1974).

by new kinds of law regarding competition, the structure and activities of corporations, and employer-employee relations. Yet public authorities often used government contracts and private institutions to carry out their functions. All of these developments made it difficult to maintain another traditional distinction in legal theory: that between public and private law.

The civil law systems have long been bedevilled by their formal division of the law school curriculum into public and private law and of scholars on law faculties into "publicists" and "privatists," with the result that workers in one field are sometimes unfamiliar with important developments in the other....

Though the common law lacks such a clear-cut and formal division of functions between public and private law specialists, it nevertheless suffers from similar problems. Constitutional law scholars, who comprise many of our "publicists" and who often aspire to do jurisprudence, on occasion show little knowledge of, or sensitivity to, the role of the private order or even of that part of the work of the Supreme Court which is not concerned with constitutional questions. Some of our "privatists," on the other hand—teachers of property, torts, contracts, and family law—inhabit an essentially nineteenth century world, sustained in the illusion by teaching materials that do not take sufficient account of the extent to which the private law subjects have come under statutory and administrative regulation and to which their underlying premises have been irrevocably altered....

SUMMARY

Civil and common law systems alike were fundamentally transformed in the transition from liberal laissez-faire governments to modern social welfare states with planned or regulated economies. In the process, the source of law that had distinctively characterized each legal system, and the legal methods associated with it, lost their centrality. First, case law in the common law and codes in the civil law lost ground to modern statutes; second, judicial decisions in the common law were increasingly detached from their moorings in precedent while civil law judges were becoming more conscious of and willing to exercise their law-making powers; finally, administrative law has encroached on *all* preexisting sources of law. We have entered the age of legislation triumphant, the judge militant, and bureaucracy rampant.

Taken together, the trends described above, the increase in regulatory and administrative law, the widening room for discretion, the transition from market to mixed economies, tend, as we have seen, to blur many of the usual distinctions made between the legal systems of civil law and common law countries. Zweigert and Kötz state in their treatise on comparative law that "[t]he theory of legal families has so far proceeded as if the only law worth taking into account were what

European lawyers call private law." [74] No doubt, this has been due in part to the fact that comparatists have traditionally concentrated on private law. In the future, as comparative lawyers increasingly turn to the study of constitutional and administrative law, and to particular areas, such as labor law and property, where public and private law are mixed, it is likely that the Anglo–American and Romano–Germanic systems in developed countries will be seen as parts of a single Atlantic–European legal family. Within this family, it is probable that new and unconventional groupings of legal systems will emerge and that a country may be said to belong to a given legal group for one purpose but to others for other purposes.[77] Already, differences between adversarial and non-adversarial systems, and between systems with greater or lesser degrees of judicial review are the bases for new and important classifications.

Neither the present day Anglo–American systems nor the Romano–Germanic systems exist any longer in the forms they had at the turn of the century. Their distinctive style of reasoning, which Max Weber called logical formal rationality, and contract, which he identified as their distinctive legal institution, are both in decline.[78] Many of the differences that once seemed significant between the civil and the common law are becoming blurred or hazy, as are the great separations within legal systems between public and private law, courts and legislatures, and formal adjudication and administration.

In the new situation, the traditional mechanisms for maintaining reasonable predictability and continuity, while permitting flexibility and growth, have fallen out of equilibrium. Traditionally, in the common law, predictability and continuity were afforded by legal rules developed in cases and by the doctrine and practice of stare decisis, while flexibility and growth were furnished by the rules of equity and the techniques for limiting and distinguishing precedent. In the codified systems of the civil law tradition, predictability and stability were promoted by the "written law" of the codes, while flexibility and growth were permitted, internally, by general clauses tempering rigid rules and externally by interpretation, made more supple by the absence of a formal rule of stare decisis.

In both of these traditional systems, the present-day predominance of regulatory law has diminished the role of the traditional mechanisms—case law and the codes—for maintaining continuity and reckonability. In this new situation, it would seem at first that the civil law systems have the methodological advantage, in that techniques for statutory interpretation are now of more utility than are pure case law techniques. But in both systems, the use of traditional legal methods to

---

74. K. Zweigert & H. Kötz, I An Introduction to Comparative Law 59 (T. Weir transl. 1977).

77. David, On the Concept of "Western" Law, 52 U.Cin.L.Rev. 126 (1983); N. Horn, H. Kötz & H. Leser, German Private and Commercial Law: An Introduction 13 (T. Weir transl. 1982).

78. M. Weber, Law in Economy and Society 101, 275 (M. Rheinstein ed. 1954).

gain relative predictability is of limited utility because modern statutory law, unlike the civil codes, generally is neither stable nor particularly rational (in the sense of being principled and systematic). Its susceptibility to frequent amendment does not introduce much flexibility in the traditional sense either, since it is not in the nature of the political process to develop legal rules on a reasoned or principled basis. The courts, for their part, are increasingly called upon to rule not only on particular disputes, but also on problems of social conflict which often cannot be resolved by the reasoned elaboration of principle. Thus, both the civil and the common law, still living on their Roman inheritance of legalism and administration, share common problems of legitimation in modern administrative states.

SECTION 6.   LEGITIMATION PROBLEMS

JOHN P. DAWSON, "THE GENERAL CLAUSES, VIEWED FROM A DISTANCE"

29 Rabels Zeitschrift 441 (1977).*

Of all countries whose law resides in comprehensive codes surely Germany has had the fullest experience with law manufactured by judges under the auspices of general clauses. No outsider, especially one trained in American law, could hope to say anything that would be new to a German reader concerning the great overlay of pure case law that has thus been superimposed on the codes. But it may be that the upheavals that produced it will present some different aspects when viewed by an outsider from a distance. This is more likely when the distance is great, as great as the distance supposedly is between the American and the German legal system, whose premises, sources and working methods have seemed to differ so totally over so long a time.

During the last 20 years German lawyers have become familiar with general clauses of another kind, of a kind that for not much less than 200 years have been a pervasive presence in American law. I mean of course the basic guarantees of our constitutions:—"the freedom of the individual is inviolable," "all human beings are equal before the law," government shall not deny "life, liberty or property without due process of law." Such clauses are very general indeed though they certainly do not lack meaning. They state in condensed form and reaffirm some of the deepest aspirations of human nature, those aspirations that make us human. In their primary function, as restraints on the powers entrusted to government, they provide standards that ought to be understood and complied with by all who exercise governmental powers. But the German legal system has decided as the American did long ago that organized courts provide essential leverage both in the effective exercise of publicly organized power and for testing its legitimacy. So the two

* This article is based on a talk delivered at the Law School of the University of Frankfurt a. M., on January 11, 1977. (Reprinted with the permission of John P. Dawson and J.C.B. Mohr, Tübingen.)

societies are both committed now to a venture that other countries have rejected as too risky—placing primary reliance on the judiciary for the enforcement, the detailed application, the "concretizing" of these over-riding, open-ended mandates. It seems that this relatively recent venture should have major effects on attitudes in Germany toward the capacity of judges to serve as guardians on other frontiers.

Our concern is now with private law and especially with the general clauses of the Civil Code, the famous three—138, 242, 826.[a] The central feature of all three is that they explicitly authorize the use of moral ideas—good faith and good morals—and that as phrased these ideas are completely disembodied. Even the broadest guarantees of the present German Constitution (guarantees of liberty, equality, dignity, and so on) provide immunities for human beings and encroachment on these immunities will usually occur in specific ways. But for the three most general clauses of the Civil Code there is no such living target. To insert in prominent places in a comprehensive code ideas that float at so high a level was to authorize voyages of discovery without destinations marked on any map. The three clauses could be described as roving search lights, supplied with beams that could penetrate anywhere in private law. It must have been evident from the outset that judges would play the leading role in managing this equipment. For it would be primarily through conflict, resolved by processes of litigation, that vacancies or malformations in the landscape would be exposed, so that judges would be the first to observe them.

I should mention in passing a small flurry that we have recently had in the United States over a similar issue—a much more modest general clause that relates only to sales of goods. It is part of a more ambitious project, the Uniform Commercial Code, which is now in force in all but one (Louisiana) of the 50 states. The flurry has come over one provision (sec. 2–302) in Art. II, which as I have said covers only sales of goods. It provides that if a court shall find a contract of sale or any of its clauses to be "unconscionable," the court may "refuse to enforce" the contract or clause. Instead of offense to "good morals" or "good faith," the test becomes offense to "conscience."

Voices have been raised in the United States to protest most vigorously against this attempt, by statute, to introduce "conscience" into the law of sales. The protesters, I believe, have forgotten 600 years of history. The Anglo–American legal system is divided down the middle by what used to be a gulf. The common law in England had been organized rapidly and, as it turned out, prematurely. For all its key controls were quickly captured by a group of legal technicians whose minds became locked within the system they created. The early English common law was the classic demonstration, if one were needed, of the disaster that will come to a legal order when its own rules and internal

---

a. German Civil Code, Art. 138(1): A transaction that offends good morals *(guten Sitten)* is void; Art. 242: Obligations shall be performed in the manner required by good faith, with regard to commercial usage; Art. 826: One who intentionally injures another by conduct offending good morals must make reparation.

structure come to be viewed as complete and self-sufficient, when it destroys its own capacity to respond to new needs and developing moral values in the society it serves. The revolt against the common law that followed was successful, for the highest political authority, that of the English kings, was appealed to and the revolt was conducted by the leading royal minister, the Chancellor. But the ideas to which the Chancellors appealed to explain and justify their actions could not be stated more precisely than equity, fairness, and especially "good conscience." The appeal to such moral ideas was constant. Though in most of our states (all but four) common law and equity are now "fused" in the sense that they are administered by the same judges, these moral ideas are a living part of our tradition. I bring up these matters only to reveal a cast of mind. It is really a conviction, which I think all American-trained lawyers would share—that the frontiers of law must continuously advance, often by appeal to moral ideas, and that on many fronts judges, by virtue of their function, are placed at vantage points, enabling them to perceive the directions that the advance will take. At times this means they should lead the way.

Why, then should some American lawyers now protest at the inclusion of a general clause, with an explicit appeal to "conscience," in legislation that regulates broadly the law of sales? If our courts are free to express and be guided by moral ideas when the responsibility is theirs alone, does this mean that objection arises only when the same authority is conferred by statute? The question when phrased in this way seems silly but behind it lurks another that is not at all silly. The question is—where a legislature after full deliberation has enacted comprehensive legislation, how free should courts be to amend, extend or override duly enacted law? To such a question, in such general terms, there is of course no single answer. It may seem strange that a person trained in the United States should be concerned about this at all, for we have gone as far as any country in entrusting creative powers to judges. Most of our private law was originally judge-made. Large sectors are now governed by express legislation but other large sectors remain in which whatever law we have originally was made and is still being made by judges, and the power to make includes power to amend, extend and override, since they are free to modify or overrule their own past decisions. But the reasons given by our courts are scrutinized most critically. In examining the reasons given for innovations we find that haunting questions constantly arise. How can courts acquire the information they need? In what way is their judgment superior in balancing out and appraising the interests that are in conflict, often multisided conflict? How can they surmount the limitations that are built into the particular case when they must give reasons that project beyond—to situations that the judges know not much about and perhaps have not imagined? Questions like these, and others too, cause us anxious and constant concern, even in areas where legislatures have chosen to abstain and have left law-making to judges.

These questions are simply thrown into higher relief where the legislature has bestirred itself and has produced legislation that seems to apply. The limitations and disabilities that are inherent in the judicial function should then move, I suggest, from the back to the front of the mind. The reasons why courts should hesitate are derived only indirectly from a constitutional principle of separation of powers, by which lawmaking is assigned to legislatures. For with judicial innovations that can properly be ascribed to a general clause, there is at least a formal answer to any formal charge of judicial usurpation. By including these clauses the draftsmen of the Code and legislature acknowledge both that the Code was incomplete and that it needed to be supplemented, primarily through judicial action, from sources outside the Code. The new formulas, the variations on old formulas, and new standards of value that the courts invented were then to be used as rules that would govern their own decisions. I have called this a purely formal answer. So far as it goes it is good enough. But it does not address the central questions as to when this peculiar form of lawmaking power should be exercised and what its objectives and limits should be. Nor does it reverse or seriously modify the basic decision made in our two countries when their constitutions were adopted. This decision was that rules of law binding us all, the rules to which we owe allegiance, should be approved and validated by an agency of government that is responsive and responsible to the needs and desires of our people in ways that courts cannot be.

It is true that legislatures too have deficiencies, of a different kind. The German Civil Code itself, as Professor Wieacker pointed out, was the product of a "ministerial bureaucracy," deeply imbued with Pandectist legal science [1], and the process of screening and authentication by the legislature changed the basic text very little. Something similar could be said of our own recent experience with the Uniform Commercial Code, drafted by groups of expert legal specialists in close consultation with the commercial groups most affected. The legislatures of the 49 states that have adopted the Code have on the whole complied with the urgent entreaties that were made to them not to make changes in the standard text. But this compliance did not mean that the text was not closely scrutinized and in fact many voices were heard by the 49 state legislatures before they approved their own versions. It may well be, as Professor Kübler has said, that the demands and pressures on our legislatures have reached such a degree as to foreclose their undertaking any largescale recasting or rewriting of private law, even though given much outside help. These demands and pressures also make them all too slow to respond to much more specific and immediate needs in law revision [2]. This has been our own experience also, even with our state legislatures, on which the demands and pressures are enormously less than on a national legislature such as our federal Congress or the *Bundestag.*

1. Wieacker, Privatrechtsgeschichte der Neuzeit (1967) 459.

2. Kübler, Kodifikation und Demokratie: JZ 1969, 645, 646–648.

These issues, as to where the initiative should lie as between courts and legislatures, are extremely troublesome. They continually recur in many different ways in all developed legal systems whose societies are committed to political democracy. At what point does the "creativity" of judges become callous adventurism? When do judges undermine their own authority and respect for their own function by arrogating too much power to themselves? This can happen anywhere across the far-reaching front of issues with which courts must deal. The general clauses, then, do not create these problems, they merely focus attention upon them. But I suggest that these clauses have also offered a special temptation. For in form they were, as I see them, express licenses to judges to go out hunting anywhere and bring back their trophies, to be hung then in the living room. More important, their search was described (as I think it almost had to be) as a pursuit of moral values, raised to a very high level and completely undefined. The temptation was for judges to delude themselves, to believe that by virtue of their office they had a private entrance to a carefully guarded sanctuary located in some higher place, in cloud land. On their return to a profane world they would retain the white robes that had to be worn during their frequent visits to the sanctuary and would also retain the zeal that one expects in missionaries wearing white robes.

At this point I only raise the question whether the zeal and extreme self-confidence shown by the *Reichsgericht* judges in their most spectacular adventure—in the inflation cases of the 1920's—was not due in part to their own deeply-felt conviction that they were left as the direct and only spokesmen for the moral values of all Germans. On this I have only two comments: (1) that such delusions, no matter how firmly they may be held, almost certainly serve to disguise personal prejudices and one-sided views of social policy at a much more mundane level, too mundane to be mentioned; and (2) that such abstractions, charged up with the emotion that the sense of mission generates, remove the incentives for close and careful reasoning and tend to block off thought. Our country has the best example to offer, the United States Supreme Court, which, during the nineteenth century, discovered the entrance into the sanctuary of natural law, was allowed to view the tablets in a private showing, and continued to wear the white robes for a long time thereafter, well into the present century. As to German courts I only venture the comment that since the 1920's their missionary zeal seems to have receded somewhat.

To me it is more surprising that from the outset, under the Code of 1900, German courts found entirely congenial the role that they conceived to be assigned to them as guardians of the nation's conscience. This was possible, I suppose, because the role was at first conceived to be so very much more limited than it later proved to be. But the *Reichsgericht* moved in rapidly, seemingly without hesitation, to extend liability for intentional infliction of economic harm, finding violations of "good morals" (§ 826) in wholly new kinds of injury inflicted in wholly new ways, through the acts or threats of large and powerful economic groups engaged in competition and conflict with each other. I have recently studied the long series of German court decisions on contracts that produce a *Knebelung,* which I have translated (inadequately) as "shackling." This is a concept that the *Reichsgericht* invented in a decision not quite five months after the Code took effect. As expressed in that case its essence was that "the moral ideas and perceptions of the people ... cannot and will not permit that the superior power of capital should result in the enslavement *(Knechtung)* of the working capacities of another." Since nothing like this set of ideas appeared anywhere else in the Code they could only be brought to bear through resort to the other "good morals" clause (§ 138) [3]. And very early a style of judicial writing developed, not only in condemnations of *Knebelung* but over the whole range of issues to which general clauses were applied. I would call it a thundering style in which the transaction condemned was declared to "outrage the sense of decency of all fair- and right-thinking persons and offend the conscience of the people." With these and similar formulations the courts seemed to speak with righteous indignation from a mountain top but with complete confidence that the stern moral judgments they expressed would be shared by the people down on the plain, for whom they were entitled to speak.

The only feature that is surprising about this is that German courts should have felt so free to innovate, especially for such reasons, under a Code enacted so recently, prepared over decades with such scrupulous care, a Code to which their own allegiance seemingly was total. Their allegiance was not merely to the Code itself but to the ordered system of legal ideas that the Code expressed in short-hand, the broadly conceived and highly structured system created by Pandectist "legal science"— remarkable for its internal consistency, clarity and precision. To true believers it must have seemed that all the important questions had been thought of or at least that answers could be readily found within the system. Such convictions would not have obstructed, indeed they must have strengthened, the close ties existing between high court judges and the governmental bureaucracy that took the lead in drafting the codes. Some judges were engaged in work on the Civil Code itself and the judiciary was much more heavily used in preparing the subordinate codes and accompanying legislation. The government they served had carried forward from Prussia and other German states a tradition of strong authoritarian control. But among the advancing societies of the western world Germany had shown the greatest resistance to theories of economic individualism, whose gospel it was to minimize government functions. Whether cause or effect, this resistance corresponded with a continued, even increased responsibility assumed by government for correcting the imbalances in German society and redressing social inequalities. Bismarck himself had taken a leading part in developing the working model of the authoritarian welfare state. The question I ask relates to the period roughly two decades before and two decades after

---

3. The discussion of *Knebelung* appears in Dawson, Unconscionable Coercion—The   German Version: Harv.L.Rev. 89 (1975/76) 1041, 1071–1103.

1900, the effective date of the Code. My question (which I put most hesitantly) is whether a strong sense of identification with the governing leadership in Germany could have made the judges of that earlier time more confident and more ready to assume responsibility for discerning and promoting the general welfare, invoking for this purpose the moral authority conferred on them by the Code.

However this may be, the motives of the German high court judges in their greatest adventure of all—their plunge into the jungle created by the inflation of the 1920's—were in this respect directly the opposite. Professor *Kübler* has shown that many judges, even in the early 1900's, had become dissatisfied with the recognition and rewards they received and were also growing markedly conservative in their political views. The estrangement became complete with the advent of a republican government under the Weimar Constitution, with the successive political and economic disasters that followed, bringing disorder and tragedy to German society that seemed to threaten its survival and that the government was more and more helpless to remedy. The story has been often told of the judiciary's response, its claims to a "plenitude of power" at least equal to and perhaps overriding that of the legislature. The threats the judges made to the government were not in the end carried out, solutions were found, the whole period now seems in retrospect to have been a nightmare that daylight gradually dispelled. But the daylight proved to be only a twilight before a much deeper darkness descended. It is worth remembering that in that short interlude the German judiciary did what it could, and at that with considerable success, to undermine the power of a democratic government to protect itself against implacable enemies that were determined to destroy it and very soon succeeded.

That is not at all to say the courts were not justified in intervening as they did to clear away the monumental debris left by the great inflation. Nor do I see from my distant lookout point any better solutions for the manifold injustices that the inflation had produced. A high percentage called for highly individualized treatment, rather than the cutting blade of a strict statutory rule; so by common consent they were left for the courts to deal with. The performance of the courts in my own view deserves praise. It also seems to me that this was for modern German law the great turning point, what I have called the great shift of the main axis, by which leadership in law-making was transferred from the legislature to the courts, a shift that seems to me irreversible. The courts were confronted with an enormous variety of human situations, dislocations, aberrations that no one had imagined before. Their inventions matched in some degree the novelty of the issues that they had to resolve. But the formulas they invented could not be confined to inflation cases and have become a vast network, spread out widely and deeply over German private law. There seems to be no reason to be anything but cheerful about this, as modern German lawyers generally seem to be. For there are so many clear paths and intersections in what would otherwise be a jungle—paths and intersections that the judges unaided could not have mapped out or maintained. This is a theme to which I will return. Whether the total result has been good or bad, whether it was inevitable or not, seems hardly worth discussing. But it is worth keeping in mind that this great shift began when high court judges were in a mood that verged on rebellion, when the judiciary claimed a "plenitude of power" that cannot be tolerated in a democratic society that is determined to govern itself.

For I start from the premise that judges have highest credibility and contribute most when they perform the function that is assigned to them and that is peculiarly their own—the function of applying existing law in settling disputes. This function has strict limits but the limits bring great advantages. The highly regulated adversary procedures that prepare cases for decision compel intensive study of the elements unique to each dispute. The setting, the immediate surroundings, will be disclosed but there will be severe limits otherwise on the range of inquiry. The great advantage of this narrowing of horizons is that the particular problem becomes more manageable, so that if there are numerous interconnected problems they can be taken up one by one and not settled all at once. And it is an experience constantly renewed that open-ended, vague, overlapping or conflicting ideas fall into place, are seen in different perspectives and in more ordered relations with each other when brought to bear on the concrete facts of real-life conflict. But the importance of the function goes much beyond this. Courts are continuously engaged in re-examining the legal order in the way that is most searching of all—from below, at the innumerable points at which legal rules are to be applied. It is here that their meaning and consequences are fully and effectively tested. It is here also that a crucial opportunity is given to preserve—even to create—order and coherence among the rules themselves as they are seen converging on the individual case. The reasoned judicial opinion as it has now been developed in some countries, and to a high degree in Germany, permits rationality to be achieved by segments. It is an indispensable base and take-off point for the continuous, unremitting effort in which many others also must be engaged, to preserve—or achieve—rationality in the legal order as a whole in the midst of constant change.

I have suggested that the contribution judges can make will diminish in both credibility and usefulness as they move out and away from their primary function—which is deciding, and explaining why they decide, cases. In my own view this fade-out occurs still more rapidly when the justification for the decision must depend at least in part on moral ideas existing independently of any legal rules. By this I mean that the moral ideas are made to appear not merely as supportive (to show that the legal order has managed to promote virtue after all) but as filling a gap, large or small, in the available legal rules. For I believe that judges are not endowed by their robes of office with superior insight into moral issues. More than this, it seems to me that for most moral questions of any importance or difficulty there are *no* answers that are self-evidently right, even to judges. Since the answers are and will remain contingent and debatable, any reasons given by judges that depend on them must be even more than usually tentative and revocable.

* * *

As to the need for general clauses, who can doubt it? It is impossible to imagine what German law would have been if the draftsmen of the codes had not had the wisdom to provide, through open-ended language, many avenues for entry of new ideas, including new standards of value, and of these the most important surely have been the general clauses. Their explicit appeal to moral ideas and the influence that courts have ascribed to these ideas have added, I believe, to the moral authority of German law itself. Is this a retreat from the statement just made that in the realm of moral values judges do not have and should not claim superior insight? I think not. For one can readily concede that judges are at any rate human beings and that if they have no more, they have at least as much insight as others in the human race. But they also have a great advantage derived from the key position they hold, at the main intersection between the legal order and the human affairs that it regulates. For the close-up view of human events that the judicial function provides will include a high percentage of the instances in which one person protests that the legal order had worked or is about to work injustice. The one who files the protest will usually have an advocate on hand to define and "concretize" the claim of injustice and also to suggest some specific correctives that a court could employ. If the court is persuaded, a general clause will often give authority to apply these or other correctives.

* * *

Perhaps there ... enters here [one] of my own incurable handicaps, that I have been trained in American law. For as I have said, though we have by now in the United States a very large volume of legislation, the activities of our legislatures can still be described as selective. They have intervened for the most part in areas where there is some social interest to be protected or some social policy to be advanced, important enough to concern and activate them. It is true that when our courts are called on to interpret constitutional provisions they take great liberties and conceive their mission to be very broad. But if no constitutional issue were raised we would expect our courts to be most hesitant in modifying or overriding legislative decisions, in acting not *extra* but *contra legem*. Main attitudes, of course, must differ in a legal system that has been comprehensively codified, for then there will be few important and lasting innovations made by courts, through resort to a general clause, that will not be in some degree *contra legem: contra legem* in the sense that results called for by express language in some codes are modified or reversed for reasons that are not contained—do not even lie buried—in any code language except the "good faith" or "good morals" of the general clause itself.

Attributing such innovations to "good morals", "good faith" or "conscience," with citation to a general clause, provides, I have argued, only a partial and formal answer. For the mission of judges surely is not to lead ever onward and upward toward these receding goals, to select from the welter of impulses in human nature its highest aspirations and actively work to realize them. In a society whose main directions—whose policies, purposes and moral values—are not given to courts to determine, courts can still have a vital conserving function, ensuring that essential decencies, widely shared, are not violated. If German law in the last 50 years had run a less turbulent course the goals of German judges might have been less ambitious and they might have been somewhat less disposed to conceive of their role as that of architects and planners of a better moral order.

Whether the role was conceived grandly, as it has been, or much more restrictively, there was bound to emerge much judge-made law. Much of "the judge's art" consists of the resourceful use of moral ideas that may be ascribed to a high-level source but provide standards for judgment at an intermediate level—one should not *venire contra factum proprium* (in American law "estoppel") or profit by one's own wrong, and so on. The sense of fairness responds to such admonitions and they guide analysis but their reach is too broad for them to be called rules of "law". Also, there may be situations whose elements combine in such peculiar ways that they seldom or never recur and the solutions reached are not drawn into consequence. But many situations do regularly recur, there are very strong reasons of calculability and fairness (if only, that "like cases be treated alike") for continuities to develop. Many are solutions to practical problems of every-day life and, when they consistently recur, whatever moral ideas helped to give them warrant soon fade away; attributing them to "good morals" or "good faith" becomes not much more than a formal observance of courtesies. This process has long been routine and utterly familiar in a highly developed case-law system such as the German.

I would not attempt, of course, even to summarize the vast areas of German law that have been transformed by these means. In general terms I will only say that the case-law thus developed is a vast repository of original ideas from which American lawyers have a great deal to learn. The directions taken by German and American courts are usually parallel but on some fronts you have gone well beyond us. I would like to pause for a moment on one topic to illustrate this, partly because I have lately found the results to be instructive for us.

This is the standardized form contract containing *Allgemeine Geschäftsbedingungen.* We too use such prefabricated forms and on a massive scale comparable to yours. As I have read the German sources, the treatment now given standardized form contracts was developed by court decisions with no basis whatever in the Code and with no significant aid from legislation until the comprehensive statute on the subject that became effective on April 1st, 1977. The result is to place standardized form contracts in a separate enclave, next to but detached from the law of contract. It all began in a prosaic way, through the need for uniform rules of interpretation for A.G.B. that were used uniformly in two or more districts with different *Oberlandesgerichte,* so that the *Bundesgerichtshof* concluded it must take on the interpreter's task. Then it came to be seen that most of the text on printed forms was not read and, if so, was seldom understood by the signers, that this made nonsense of the usual tests of mutual assent, that the draftsmen of such documents were in substance and effect lawmakers. So the conclusion took firm hold that there should be cast on them the responsibility of law-makers to distribute even-handed justice. Such forms are now subjected to severe scrutiny, and wide powers are used by the courts to strike out oppressive, unexpected, and one-sided clauses. This power was recently described by one distinguished German author as a notable achievement, which has made "worthy of confidence" the regime of free contract to which Germany is committed. I mention all this because our courts also are all too keenly aware of the almost universal use of mass-produced form contracts, the absence of free, comprehending assent by most signers, and the manifold abuses through one-sided draftsmanship. The only difference is that our courts have had only sporadic success in correcting the abuses. In our contract law standardized form contracts are our greatest problem, the one we are furthest from solving. The reason for this is, I think, that almost none of our courts have as yet dared to assume the Draconian powers that German courts have exercised for the last 20 years, seemingly with the utmost assurance that "good morals" and "good faith" were a sufficient warrant.

Thus in this adventurous foray German courts are far ahead of ours but not too much should be made of this. As to standardized form contracts American courts will surely move in the same direction and some may eventually catch up. There are no doubt some patterns of decision by American courts that to Germans would seem to be advanced. What seems to me notable—I have said before elsewhere—is the increasing convergence between Germany and the United States in the methods with which we administer our case law. It would be difficult to imagine two legal systems that differed so totally in their origins and that were separated for centuries by barriers that seemed so high, almost impenetrable. There are quite a few differences still. Our judges when they disagree publish their reasons for dissent. We borrowed this practice from England, as we did so much else, and have found it to be a very good thing. It adds much to the wealth and variety of useful legal ideas and to us does not seem to undermine but rather to increase confidence in the work judges do. Another difference is that we often show more disrespect for our judges and criticize them more severely. This does not mean much, for disrespect is an American trait. But all the methods of managing and appraising case law are as well known in Germany as in the United States—the distinction between *obiter dicta* and reasons that were "necessary," testing and limiting grounds for decision by imagining the effects of adding or subtracting particular facts, lining up cases in series, comparing and contrasting them, matching results against reasons given, all of this in a spirit of skepticism—let us say, with a suspension of belief. German legal scholars, many of whom in their other work have achieved the highest distinction, actively engage in examining case law in these test tubes and, more important, go on to co-ordinate, search out and define new directions, build new structures of order out of the newly created disorder and fit them all into the grand design.

This seems to me the great achievement of modern German law. The grand design is of course based on and built around the Codes themselves but the Codes, especially the Civil Code, expressed, as I have said, in shorthand the complex and integrated system of ideas that "legal science" had earlier constructed and on which consensus had been reached to a remarkable degree. The triumph of the Pandectist system in nineteenth century Germany was due in part to its basic assumptions, which happened to be in harmony with and even helped to meet the dominant needs of the time. But the triumph was at least equally due to the precision, care and thoroughness with which the structure had been contrived. It was the culmination of centuries of work in Germany by learned and devoted men. One does not need to subscribe to theories of racial consciousness to conclude that the effects of an immense organized effort of this kind do not quickly wear away. There came many protests against "pandectology" at that time and later. The certainties concerning the prospects for human society that the nineteenth century presupposed have for the most part been destroyed. Conceptions of legal method and the relations between law and society have been almost completely recast. Despite all this, despite many changes and new directions in German law itself, despite the innumerable controversies in an abundant literature, it seems to me from my great distance that certain habits of mind persist. One of them is the habit of searching for rationality and order and pursuing the search on and up through higher levels of generalization. This means climbing hill-tops quite often and trying to map the plains below—not for the purpose of thundering down some dictate of the moral law (courts do that) but simply for the purpose of mapping, to secure an overview. There would be a good chance of being misunderstood if I were to say that the search for system continues. Any "system" of German law that one would now describe would be profoundly different from any that existed before, if only because of the great overburden of judge-made law that has since been laid upon it. It would be better to say that the struggle for coherence continues with undiminished force—coherence that is to be maintained and extended over wide sectors of the legal order. In this broader effort, almost inevitably, the academic profession continues to take the leading role.

The major shift in the last 50 years has been the initiative taken by courts in the active *making* of law—the peculiar kind of law that courts can make. This has brought a change in the ancient partnership between German legal scholars and German courts: legal scholarship has receded from the front-line position that it formerly had to what amounts, much of the time, to a follow-up role. But receding in this way has by no means brought resignation from the partnership. The multifarious creations of German courts would have wandered aimlessly about in adjacent vacant spaces, if scholars had not made constant and strenuous efforts to connect them up, realign and rearrange and put them in place within the central edifice. And it seems unlikely that they would have succeeded so well if influence had not continued to work actively both ways. The influence is evident to any reader of German law reports, not only in the frequency with which the courts cite scholarly writings but in the extensive use the courts make of organizing ideas that were first proposed by scholars. I would go much further and say that predictability and coherence could not have been maintained in German law in such high degree if a close working partnership had not been maintained between a career judiciary and legal scholars, both highly trained in and firmly committed to the same highly ordered system of legal ideas.

It was this conclusion that led me to make a suggestion recently to American readers. It was made in an effort to explain the boldness and wealth of judicial innovation in Germany in the last 50 years. It was coupled with a confession that we ourselves would have serious misgivings if American courts were to attempt so much. The suggestion is almost but not quite a paradox—that German judges have been so free because they accept so fully and have learned so well the systematics and disciplines of modern German law. The thought could be put in another way—that judges felt free to wander on the uncharted open sea because they knew their way home and intended to maintain a permanent residence there. There has been one other feature that has surely added to their confidence—they had expert guides they could trust, who watched their wanderings closely and who could tap them on the shoulder if they showed any signs of losing the way.

The misgivings we might have if American courts were to wander so far—especially in the pursuit of high moral ideals—can be best explained by mentioning some aspects of your own good fortune. German legislation, almost all of it, applies uniformly nation-wide, the German judiciary comprises a career service with promotion from within, at the summit led by a high court whose jurisdiction also is nationwide. Thus all judges can be forced—perhaps against the convictions of some—to speak with one voice and an expert critical literature can concentrate on one coherent body of legislation and decisional law. I need hardly remind that in each of our 50 states there is an independent legislature grinding out statutes, and only rarely is there a legislative model to which any will try to conform. There are 50 separate systems of courts, in no way bound by each other's decisions, and they likewise speak with discordant voices. Most judges in these systems are elected by popular vote, though this is not true in the 51st, the overarching hierarchy of federal courts. Our legal literature can be described as extensive. I have read complaints about the volume of the German literature, that it has become *unübersehbar*. Wait until you have 150 periodicals devoted exclusively to legal topics, plus perhaps 100 more that lawyers would do well to read, plus massive treatises and thousands of other books. The volume alone makes our legal literature "unoverlookable" indeed and insures that its quality will remain diffuse and uneven. I do not say these things in a spirit of complaint, for we have become accustomed to this profusion and on the whole we enjoy our lot. I wish only to explain why German judges can be safely trusted with wider powers of innovation than we would think wise for our own courts. This is because when the floodtide of case law unexpectedly came, German courts and legal scholars proceeded to train each other in developing navigational skills and direction-finding devices that are superior to those found elsewhere.

Chapter 6

FIELDS OF SUBSTANTIVE LAW
IN CIVIL LAW SYSTEMS

SECTION 1. DIVISIONS OF LAW

Comparative legal analysis can be a relatively simple matter when the jurisdictions being compared share common legal structures, procedural rules and similar ideas about how legal problems ought to be classified. An American lawyer in one state, for example, need hardly reflect on the everyday process of consulting the law of sister states for guidance on a difficult or controverted question. Legal comparisons may be dangerously misleading, however, when they take place between systems with different legal institutions, different procedural settings and different methods for classification of legal phenomena. Varying rules of procedure, for example, may produce substantially different outcomes in legal systems where identical substantive rules govern a given case. Apparent contrasts in substantive law, by the same token, often diminish when the rules are seen in their institutional and procedural contexts.

In particular, the distinctive ways in which different legal systems identify and deal with legal problems, may pose obstacles for the comparatist. Consider, for example, the difficulties that our historic distinction between "legal" and "equitable" rules and remedies must pose for comparatists from civil law countries where the division between law and equity is unknown. The categories according to which civil law lawyers are accustomed to arrange their legal norms are similar enough from country to country to greatly aid transnational communication within the civil law orbit. But they are sufficiently different from common law categories to constitute a stumbling block to civil law-common law comparisons.

A fundamental distinction is made in all civil law systems between public and private law. That classification, which is only latent or implicit in the common law, is basic to an understanding of the civil law. As we have seen, it produced the distinctive patterns of organization of the court systems of civil law countries. As public law disputes became justiciable in the 19th century, separate tribunals were created to handle

265

them. The jurisdiction of the ordinary courts today remains limited to disputes governed by private law, with the one major exception of criminal matters. Besides these jurisdictional consequences, the public-private distinction has produced a characteristic division of labor within the legal profession. The members of law faculties tend to be either "publicists" or "privatists." Courses and treatises tend to focus on one or the other area, despite the fact that today any given subject matter is apt to have public law aspects.

Though a distinction between public and private law is universally recognized within the civil law world, there is no agreement among civil law lawyers on its theoretical basis or justification, and no uniformity among countries as to its scope and effects. Generally speaking, however, public law includes at least constitutional law, administrative law and criminal law; while private law includes at least civil law and commercial law. The classification of several other areas is the subject of dispute. Civil procedure, for example, is included by some systems within the private group of subjects, and treated by others as public law. Labor law, agricultural law, social security, as well as a number of other modern regulated areas, are sometimes said to be "mixed" public and private areas, and sometimes described as sui generis.

SECTION 2. PUBLIC LAW

Although the public-private law distinction has roots in Roman law, public law remained a relatively undeveloped category until modern times. It was the preserve of the sovereign, prudently left aside by jurists. As we noted in our historical introduction to the civil law tradition, nearly all the Roman legal literature that has come down to us is concerned with private law, and legal science traditionally has concentrated on private law. We observed too, that in the localism and legal diversity of the Middle Ages, there was no place for public law. But when the centralized state and its administrative organs began to emerge on the continent (coinciding with the growing influence of legally trained professionals), conditions were favorable to the development of administrative law. In the 19th century, as administrative law began to flourish, it seemed to civil law lawyers that the ordinary private law rules that applied to disputes involving private individuals or associations could not simply be carried over to relationships in which the state was a party. In France it seemed, too, that the ordinary courts could not be entrusted with the task of resolving disputes involving the state. The French view of the separation of powers led, as we have seen, to the establishment of a separate set of public law courts within the administration. In Germany, however, concern about administrative oppression was more prevalent than mistrust of the judiciary. So, to avoid having disputes between citizen and administration adjudicated by the latter, Germany created a separate system of administrative law courts within the judiciary. Today, as the French Council of State has established its own independence from the administration proper, advanced the protection of individual rights, and extended its own control over the administrative process, the fact that it is technically not a court is of diminished importance. In modern civil law states, whether on the French or German model, the tendency has been toward increasingly effective review of the legality of administrative action.

Today, when one speaks of public law in the civil law systems, what is meant is often merely administrative law. Constitutional law, as it pertains to the form and structure of the state and its organs, is still thought of as being akin to political science. As we have seen, it is only in relatively recent times that courts or other institutions have acquired the power to review the constitutionality of the acts of government. As for criminal law, though technically classified as public law, it has traditionally been the concern of the "privatists" and everywhere falls within the jurisdiction of the ordinary courts. Thus, the bulk of public law in civil law countries in fact consists of administrative law.

It is hard to specify precisely what is included within the concept of administrative law, even within a single country. Generally speaking, it consists of the norms which regulate the organization, functions, and interrelations of public authorities other than the political and judicial authorities, and the norms which govern the relationships between the administrative authorities and citizens. Tax law has become a major specialty within this field. Administrative law does not completely coincide with the jurisdiction of the administrative courts, because, in all civil law countries, certain administrative matters are relegated by special legislation to the jurisdiction of the ordinary courts.

It is primarily in the field of administrative law that the distinctive characteristics have developed which are thought to set public law apart from private law in the civil law systems. The most striking of these is the uncodified state of administrative law. The fact that the great codifications left public law (except for penal law) untouched accentuated the division between private and public law. The separation deepened as the courts assumed a large role in establishing the general principles and rules of administrative law, a role formally denied them in the area of the civil law. At the present time, administrative law in civil law systems tends to be scattered among various statutes, with case law playing a major role. The relative importance of the case law is greater in France; that of enacted law is greater in Germany and Austria.

As might be expected, public and private law often arrive at similar solutions to similar legal problems. Nevertheless, the student of comparative law must always be aware of the possibility that the classification of a dispute as private or public will bring into play a quite different substantive rule or a different method of interpretation. For example, in France during the severe inflations after World War I, the private law courts refused to grant relief to creditors whose fixed contractual claims had become practically worthless, while the Council of State developed a doctrine of unforeseeability to come to the aid of obligees in contracts governed by public law.[1] Administrative law is said, too, to be set apart from private law by its susceptibility to frequent change; by the wider scope it allows for official discretion and the little room it leaves to the discretion of the parties; and by its more vague and fluid legal concepts.[2] However, it should be noted that the general principles of private law are often carried over to supplement or to fill gaps in administrative law.

SECTION 3.   PRIVATE LAW

Just as the term "public law" is commonly used to designate administrative law, "private law" is often used interchangeably with civil law.   In civil law systems, however, private law comprises two grand divisions of its own: civil law and commercial law.   Civil law, in principle, applies to everyone and its basic provisions are found in the civil codes, supplemented by auxiliary statutes.   Commercial law, which concerns specific groups of persons and/or specific types of activities, is in most civil law countries contained in a separate commercial code.   In Italy and Switzerland, there are no commercial codes, but commercial law nevertheless is considered and taught as a separate private law subject.   Besides commercial law, there are a number of other fields which are usually classified as separate from civil law, but within the domain of private law: literary and artistic property, maritime law, insurance and industrial property.   Labor law developed from the civil law of the individual employment contract.   However, today it is variously classified as a special category of private law; as mixed public and private law; or as being a field unto itself, neither public nor private.

A.   CIVIL LAW

Civil law *(droit civil, Bürgerliches—*or *Zivilrecht)* is traditionally arranged in treatises and for teaching purposes under the following major headings: the law of persons; family law; marital property law; property law; succession law and the law of obligations.   These categories are not exhaustive, nor do they precisely correspond with the way the subjects are distributed within the civil codes of various countries. In Switzerland, for example, there is a separate Code of Obligations, and in France, family law is included within the law of persons.

The law of persons consists of all the norms concerning the status of the individuals and legal entities which are the subjects of the law.   It includes the legal rules relating to such matters as names, domicile, civil status, capacity and protection of persons under legal incapacities of various sorts.   Most legal entities have long been subjected to special regulation by administrative, commercial and labor law, so that only a few associations are now left within the domain of the civil codes.

---

1. A. von Mehren & J. Gordley, The Civil Law System 545–51, 1049–66 (2d ed. 1977).

2. Szladits, The Civil Law System, § 2 in Ch. 2 (Structure and Divisions of the Law) 48–50, II Int'l Encyc.Comp.Law (R. David ed. 1974).

Family law covers marriage formation; the legal effects of marriage; marriage termination by divorce, separation, and annulment; filiation; and family support obligations. In the first of these areas, which has remained quite stable, the civil law systems have taken from the French the requirement of a civil ceremony for the formation of a valid marriage. In all the other parts of family law, extensive code revision has taken place under the influence of three major trends: the liberalization of divorce; the equalization of the positions of women and men in the areas of family decision-making and property rights; and the assimilation of the status of children born outside legal marriage to that of children born to parents who are married to each other.

Marital property law, with close links to family law, property law and succession law, is traditionally treated as a separate area of civil law.[3] The civil codes establish and regulate a "legal regime," the system that governs the property relations of all spouses who do not choose an alternative regime by marriage contract. The legal regime is typically a form of community property, usually with pre-marital property and property acquired through gift or inheritance kept separate if it can be identified as such. The modern trend favors forms of the so-called "deferred community" in which the spouses are treated as separate owners of whatever they respectively acquire during the marriage, but property acquired during the marriage is divided equally upon termination of the marriage by divorce or death. In addition to establishing the legal regime, the marital property provisions of the civil codes typically establish and regulate a number of alternative regimes which may be chosen by contract, as well as the procedures for entering and altering marriage contracts.

Property law in civil law systems makes a distinction between movable and immovable property, which roughly corresponds to the common law distinction between personal and real property. Historically, as in the common law, land was of greater importance than chattels, and the law of the older codes, especially, reflects this. In the liberal tradition, the right of ownership was considered virtually absolute, and the protection of private property was regarded as an important function of the state. In fact, the absoluteness of property right as described in the civil codes has long since been extensively limited by public law legislation, by new constitutions and by judicial interpretation.

Another traditional attribute of civil law ownership, not found in the common law, is its unitary character. Although the civil law recognizes certain forms of co-ownership, it is hard for a civil law lawyer to conceive of ownership as divided over time as is the case with common law present and future interests; and the distinction between legal and equitable title is unknown.[4] Property is thought of as having one owner

3. See generally, M. Rheinstein & M. Glendon, Interspousal Relations, Ch. 4 in IV Int'l Encyc.Comp.Law 31–165 (1980).

4. This feature of the civil law has made it difficult for civil law nations to develop institutions which perform all of the useful social functions of the flexible common law

(or one set of concurrent owners) and other interests affecting it are generally thought of as restrictions or encumbrances on the title of the owner.   Leases of real estate are not considered property at all, but fall within the contractual area of the law of obligations.   In modern civil law, however, the idea of unitary ownership seems to be eroding somewhat as new forms of shared ownership gain in popularity.[5]

Succession law covers the disposition of property upon death by will or by intestate inheritance.   Freedom of testation in civil law systems is typically limited in favor of the testator's children who are entitled to a "reserved share" of their parent's estate.   Unlike American law, civil law systems do not traditionally accord such a forced share to the surviving spouse, whose economic interests are thought to be sufficiently protected by the division of marital property upon death.   The modern trend everywhere, however, has been to improve gradually the successoral position of the surviving spouse, and in some countries, Germany for example, this has brought about a reserved share in his or her favor.

Two typical aspects of civil law succession have attracted considerable interest in the United States.   The first is the practice of having a will authenticated before a notary during the lifetime of the testator, a procedure which dispenses with the need for probate.[6]   The second is the fact that, in the normal situation, there is nothing corresponding to our period of administration of a decedent's estate.   An inheritance simply vests upon death in the persons designated by the will or the laws of intestate succession, subject to their right of renunciation.   Another idea from the civil law of succession has already been incorporated into American probate law reforms.   This is the inclusion of certain types of inter vivos transfers within the decedent's estate for purposes of calculating the forced share.[7]

The law of obligations is the most technical, abstract and (at first sight) stable part of the civil law.   It covers all acts or situations which can give rise to rights or claims and is customarily divided into three parts: the law of contracts, the law of tort (delict), and the law of unjust enrichment.   The contract law sections of the codes typically begin with rules which are applicable to all contracts, and then set forth special rules for particular sorts of contracts: sales, leases, agency, loans, etc.[8]

---

trust. An extensive literature in English exists on this subject.   See generally, Trusts and Trust–Like Devices (W. Wilson ed. 1981) (treating, among others, the law of England, the United States, France, West Germany, The Netherlands and Louisiana); Bolgar, Why No Trusts in the Civil Law? 2 Am.J.Comp.L. 204 (1953); Fratcher, Trust, Ch. 11 in VI Int'l Encyc.Comp.Law (1973); K. Zweigert & H. Kötz, I An Introduction to Comparative Law 274 (T. Weir transl. 1977).   Research in this area by American law students with reference to the law of Louisiana can be a fruitful exercise in con-

nection with the introductory comparative law course.

5. R. Weber, Die Stockwerkeigentümergemeinschaft (1979).

6. M. Rheinstein & M. Glendon, The Law of Decedents' Estates 198 (1971).

7. E.g., Uniform Probate Code § 2–202.

8. For comparative studies of the law of contracts, see R. Schlesinger, Formation of Contracts: A Study of the Common Core of Legal Systems (2 vols.) (1968); and the articles in VII Int'l Encyc.Comp.Law (Contracts in General) (A. von Mehren ed.) and

The civil law conception of tort liability is a unified one: in contrast to the common law which developed separate pigeonholes for different kinds of harms, it is a law of *tort* rather than torts.[9] The civil law of unjust enrichment has been built up from general principles with a heavy component of case law.[10]

The distinction between contractual and delictual (tort) responsibility has been treated as fundamental in civil law theory, even though both contract and delict are regarded as parts of the single field of obligations. As with other legal classifications, however, a great deal of literature has been devoted to the distinction without successfully clarifying its precise nature. And, as with other legal categories, there is no uniformity among systems as to which acts fall within which domain. French scholar André Tunc has stated, in a comparative survey, that there is a trend in modern practice toward the decline, but not the disappearance, of the distinction, as contractual and tort liability become increasingly intertwined and as the underlying unified principles of the law of obligations (including unjust enrichment) come more prominently into view.[11]

Chief among the unifying factors within the law of obligations are the expanded range of facts that modern courts consider legally relevant, the movement away from formalism, and trends toward protecting reasonable reliance and expectations. However, at the very time that contractual and delictual responsibility appear to be converging, the scope of the field of obligations appears to be diminishing. At the outset of this section we stated that the law of obligations is at first sight the most stable area of the civil law. If one looks only at the civil codes, the parts containing the law of obligations have been little changed, and they are recognizably related to the oldest parts of the civil law tradition. Legislation outside the codes, however, has altered both the substance and the underlying philosophy of the law of obligations.

B. COMMERCIAL LAW

Commercial law (*droit commercial, Handelsrecht*) generally includes corporations and other business associations, securities, banking, and negotiable instruments, as well as other commercial transactions. We noted in our historical introduction that commercial law had developed from mercantile customs and the practice of merchants' courts into a well-established separate branch of private law even before the codification period. The dichotomy between civil and commercial law survived both codification and the centralization of justice, thanks mainly to

VIII Int'l Encyc.Comp.Law (Specific Contracts) (K. Zweigert ed.)

9. See, generally, the magisterial essay by Tunc, Introduction, Ch. 1 in XI Int'l Encyc.Comp.Law (Torts) (A. Tunc. ed. 1974).

10. For comparative studies of aspects of this subject, see John P. Dawson: Unjust Enrichment: A Comparative Analysis (1951); Erasable Enrichment in German Law, 61 Boston U.L.Rev. 271 (1981) and Restitution without Enrichment, 61 Boston U.L.Rev. 563 (1981).

11. Tunc, supra note 9 at 27–28.

France, which adopted the *Code de Commerce* in 1807 and established separate commercial courts within the first level of jurisdiction. Most other civil law countries followed suit.[12]

The division between civil and commercial law is not, however, absolute or clear-cut. First, all systems have found the concepts of "merchant" or "commercial act" difficult to define for purposes of determining whether a transaction is governed by civil or commercial law. Second, the commercial codes lack the general principles and internal coherence of the civil codes. Thus, civil law is frequently brought in to fill the gaps in the commercial codes and their supplementary laws. This is so much the case that some writers now speak of the "civilization of commercial law", by which they mean that commercial law is becoming a special field within the civil law.[13] Third, the differences are further diminished by a countertrend toward "commercialization of the civil law."[14] The commercial law influence on the civil law has manifested itself in a reduction of unnecessary formality, increased protection of reliance by third parties, and a tendency to view transactions as parts of on-going relationships, rather than as isolated legal events. Finally, in Switzerland, Italy, and The Netherlands, the decision has been made to dispense with a separate commercial code, a development which may represent the wave of the future.

However, at the same time that civil and commercial law, through mutual enrichment, are coming to resemble parts of a unified field within private law, another legal trend is operating to remove much of commercial law from private law altogether. Originally based on custom, then codified on the liberal principle of individual freedom of contract, commercial law has increasingly been affected by a body of legislation regulating commercial and corporate activity. One aspect of this movement has been the development in civil law countries, as in common law nations, of a separate body of consumer law in which the distinction between merchant and non-merchant is significant.[15] Another aspect is the subjection of commercial activity generally to requirements for licenses, permits, etc. To the extent that state economic planning replaces the market economy, it becomes hard to distinguish some parts of commercial law from administrative law. This process has progressed to the point where French and German writers have renamed the classification. Instead of "commercial law", they refer to the field of "commercial and economic law," economic law being the regulatory law of the administrative state.

12. The definitive comparative work is Tallon, Civil Law and Commercial Law, Ch. 2 in VIII Int'l Encyc.Comp.Law (K. Zweigert ed. 1983).

13. See generally, Tallon, Id.; and Kozolchyk, The Commercialization of Civil Law and the Civilization of Commercial Law, 40 La.L.Rev. 3 (1979).

14. Id.

15. Marty, La distinction du droit civil et du droit commercial dans la législation contemporaine, Revue trim. du droit commercial et du droit économique 681, 694–702 (1981).

SECTION 4.   MERGER OR DESUETUDE
OF DIVISIONS

Legal classifications, being artificial constructs, can never completely contain the fluctuating variety of human activity upon which they are imposed.   However, it does not necessarily diminish their utility that there will always be definitional problems about where they begin and end, about what is included or excluded.   The distinctions between public and private law, civil and commercial law, contractual and delictual responsibility, need not be shown to be impermeable or to have an inherent logic in order to be functional for various purposes, not the least of which is pedagogical.   Thus, it is likely that, however much some parts of contract may merge with certain areas of delict, there will still be, as the English scholar, Weir, has put it, a distinction to be made between "transactions and collisions." [16]   Similarly, though civil and commercial law have fused in many ways, it is probable that commercial law will continue to be studied as a separate subject and that it will tend to be practiced mainly by specialists.   The civil law classification that is most eroded by time and events is the "fundamental dichotomy" between public and private law, but that too survives, in the court systems and in the minds of civil law lawyers.

As we have observed throughout this section, intervention by the state in areas once reserved to private activity increasingly blurs the public-private law distinction.   Yet the French comparatist René David wrote in the 1970s that, in contrast to public law, which he described as subject to the vicissitudes of change and political crises, the Civil Code seems to French private lawyers to be "the most lasting and the only true constitution of France." [17]   There is indeed a sense in which the Civil Code is constitutional: the law of the Civil Code is the area of the law in which the function of government is limited to the recognition and enforcement of private rights.   Especially in the field of contracts, the civil codes impose few rules in the name of public policy.   Most of the law of contracts is of the type that civilians call dispositive, suppletive or directory, as opposed to compulsory.   Dispositive rules apply only if they have not been expressly or impliedly excluded by the parties.   However, one can maintain this "constitutional" view of the civil codes only if one ignores the effect that statutory law has had upon them.   Special legislation has been an institutional bypass through which the codes have been left intact but drained of much important content.

Legislation outside the civil codes has, first and foremost, undermined the constitutional function of the codes by establishing a new and competing set of premises.   While freedom of contract still appears to be a fundamental principle of the civil codes, a variety of mandatory

---

16.   Weir, Complex Liabilities, Ch. 12 in XI Int'l Encyc.Comp.Law 38 (A. Tunc ed. 1976).

17.   R. David, French Law: Its Structure, Sources and Methodology 111 (M. Kindred transl. 1972).

provisions and prohibitions have been introduced by statutes in the name of public policy—which in some cases means protection of the weaker party; in other cases, the effectuation of economic planning; and in still others the promotion of the interests of organized groups. In the area of property, the codes still promote the notion that the role of government is to protect private property, while special legislation qualifies the property right by subtracting elements in the public interest, or modifies it by adding social obligations. With the development of public and private insurance schemes, delictual liability is no longer the main source of compensation for personal injuries; there is now a wide overlap between private tort law and public social security law. The stability which is so characteristically associated with the civil codes appears as an illusion when one takes into account that all this legislation is frequently amended. Indeed, the volatility of the special legislation is often cited as a reason why the civil law cannot be re-integrated into the codes.

The contraction of the area which is left for regulation by the civil codes is not the only manifestation of the expansion of public law. Administrative law, the child of the 19th century, came into its own in the 20th century. Not only did new areas come under regulation, but government's role in providing social services increased. The public agencies that were created to perform these services have often appropriated private law means and institutions to do so. In the process, the distinction between public and private is further blurred. Also, the state's increased role in the economy not only modified the civil law of contract, tort and property, but has led to new kinds of "economic law" regulating competition, the structure and activities of enterprises, and employer-employee relations. As more areas of public concern are identified, such as protection of the environment, or protection of health and safety in the workplace, the scope of administrative law continues to expand.

Still, the distinction between public and private law has a firm hold in the habits, attitudes, and practices of civil law lawyers. For that reason, even if it is vague or dissolving, it remains important to the understanding of the civil law tradition.

Question

The French comparatist René David once wrote: "[W]hen one says public law, a Frenchman knows that it is not and cannot be law in the strict sense. . . . Law in the strict sense can only develop in the area of relations between individuals, where the state is an impartial arbiter." David, French Law: Its Structure, Sources and Methodology 119–20 (M. Kindred transl. 1972). Lenin laid down the orthodox socialist view when he wrote, "All law is public law." What does each writer mean? What assumptions about "law" underly each statement? Is there a sense in which each of these statements is true? False?

SECTION 5. TWO PROBLEM AREAS FOR COMPARATIVE LEGAL RESEARCH AND ANALYSIS

In this section, we present materials showing how civil law systems have approached two constellations of problems that have proved vexing for all societies that have reached broadly comparable levels of complexity and development. The materials show legal and institutional arrangements under pressure to respond to new social and economic circumstances. They are meant to serve as starting points for further research by students, independently or in seminar settings.

With respect to each area, begin your own analysis by trying to delineate as accurately as possible the social problem to which the legal systems under consideration seem to be reacting. Try to see it in its cultural and economic context, and to understand how it was handled by the legal systems involved until circumstances forced its reexamination. Supplement the materials in the text with your own research into the legal treatment of similar issues in the United States. See whether you can identify the competing interests that are at stake. Obviously, these are very difficult tasks that, even under the best conditions, cannot always be completed to one's own satisfaction, especially when one is dealing with a foreign system. But the effort will be rewarding. You will develop and refine your skills in coping with some of the principal difficulties of comparative law, not the least of which are determination of the proper subjects for comparison and assessment of the utility of models from one system for another.

The first problem concerns what was until recently considered a traditional private law subject in both common and civil law systems: the reallocation of property and income when a family unit is dissolved by divorce. In all developed countries, an unprecedented increase in divorce has led to extensive revision of the way the law handles marital property and support questions. At the same time, the increasing numbers and precarious financial circumstances of female-headed families has led to the sense that no country's legal system has handled these problems in a fully satisfactory way.

The second pair of problems arises in the field of contract law. The first, regarding the legal effectiveness of standard form contracts, is a contemporary manifestation of the perennial tension between the need for security of transactions and the need to police contracts for fairness and voluntariness. The second problem deals with the difficult question of what remedies should be available when the plans of the contracting parties are disrupted by unforeseen events.

As you struggle with these traditional private law topics, this would be a good place to revisit the French and German abortion cases in Chapter 2 where two constitutional tribunals attempted to deal with a politically sensitive public law question. Those cases may profitably be reviewed here as illustrations of unresolved public law dilemmas about the proper relations between governmental institutions and the amount of leeway which judges ought to have when interpreting the fundamental law.

The similarities and differences among the ways various civil and common law systems approach common social problems enable the comparatist to increase his or her understanding of how legal systems change and adapt to new circumstances. They also afford insight into the persistent and puzzling relationships among law, behavior, ideas, politics and economics. As you work your way through the problems that follow, try to keep in mind the following questions: To what extent are the systems reaching similar results through the use of different legal techniques? To what extent are the differences among systems attributable to social or cultural differences? To different doctrinal approaches? To differences in legal institutions, roles and actors? To differences in procedure? To fundamental differences in policy?

With respect to each problem area, you should also consider whether comparison among legal systems has aided you in coming to a more refined definition and improved understanding of the underlying problem itself. Has it aided you in achieving the aim we identified at the beginning of this book as one of the principal objectives of comparative legal analysis: the better understanding of our own legal system? Has it helped you to discover ways in which existing American law could be improved? Have you been enabled to see deeper issues in each problem area that American law reform discussions typically do not reach?

Problem Area 1

ECONOMIC ASPECTS OF DIVORCE

In the 1960s and 1970s family law in the United States and Western Europe underwent rapid and profound change. This period of legal change coincided with, and in great measure was in response to, unprecedented changes that were taking place in marriage and family behavior. Divorce rates and the labor force participation rates of women and mothers climbed steeply. Non-marital cohabitation became an increasingly visible social phenomenon which claimed the attention of the law in various ways. Public assistance programs felt the strain of growing numbers of female-headed, single-parent families. In retrospect, this period of intense social change may not have been ideally suited for fundamental revision of family law. Whether or not the time was right, however, there was more activity in family law in the 1960s and 1970s than there had been in the preceding hundred years. In civil law and common law nations alike, basic underlying assumptions were turned on their heads.

M.A. GLENDON, "MODERN MARRIAGE LAW AND ITS UNDERLYING ASSUMPTIONS"

13 Family Law Quarterly 441, 442–46 (1980).

[A]t about the turn of the century, many legal systems ... shared most of the following assumptions, generally speaking: Marriage and divorce took place within (or should take place within) legal categories. The wife and children of "legitimate" marriage enjoyed a preferred legal position. Marriage was in principle to last until death of a spouse, and should be terminable during the lives of the spouses only for serious cause. The community aspect of marriage was emphasized over the individual personalities of each spouse. Within the marriage, the standard pattern of authority and role allocation was that the husband was predominant in decision making and was to provide for the material needs of the family, while the wife fulfilled her role primarily by care for the household and children (i.e., marriage was a major support institution). Procreation and child-rearing were assumed to be major purposes of marriage, and sexual relations within marriage were supposed to be exclusive. Underlying all these assumptions about particular aspects of marriage were general assumptions that marriage was "a basic social institution" and that state regulation of its formation, organization and dissolution was proper. In France or Germany, these characteristics taken together describe the "family of the Civil Code"; in England or the United States, the so-called "traditional" family.

Most of the above assumptions have undergone major change in the past 50 years. Indeed, Sweden, as early as 1915, transformed several of them at once by establishing a system of divorce where the principal ground was the factual breakdown of the marriage, and by inserting in the formula prescribed for marriage ceremonies the statement that the purpose of marriage is the welfare of the individuals who enter it. From the early Swedish reforms to the revision of the legal effects of marriage to incorporate the principle of sex equality in both Spain and Italy in 1975, and the currently impending reform of Swiss marital property law, the process of transformation of marriage law has been widespread and profound. Some recent changes, such as the increased recognition of informal marriage, have come about in part because the marriage laws are serving a broader clientele and have adapted to the needs and marriage practices of the poor, of migrant populations and of racial and ethnic minorities, groups previously neglected or ignored by the private law. But many changes are also responses to alterations in the marriage behavior of the middle class majorities, as for example, the acceptance of divorce as a "normal" mode of marriage termination; the rise of informal marriage in this group; and the erosion (to varying degrees) of marriage as a support institution, of marriage as community and of the housewife-breadwinner pattern. Still other changes reflect a different role for the state with respect to marriage, as expressed through law. Thus, state regulation of the formation and dissolution of marriage has been reduced, while regulation of the economic and child-related effects of marriage (whether of the formal-legal or informal-de facto type), has expanded. Recent changes in marriage formation law, although relatively few in number, exhibit less official concern about the traditional restrictions on entry into marriage and about marriage formalities, than about population control, the collection of data to facilitate eventual enforcement of support claims, and education about the rights and duties being undertaken by the future spouses.

So far as divorce is concerned, termination of the legal bond has become easier in principle but regulation of its economic and child-related aspects has increased. This increased attention to practical matters may well render divorces involving property and children more complicated and expensive in practice in France and West Germany than they were under the prior law where an agreed fault divorce was relatively quick and cheap. The tendency to treat economic and child-related consequences of the dissolution of informal cohabitation on a functional, marriage-neutral basis, is a sign that marriage law, like family law generally, has become more realistic about dealing with pressing practical problems that require adjustment and at the same time less ambitious in promoting any given set of values concerning marriage. . . .

In dealing with the problems of property allocation and provision for economic dependents upon dissolution of legal or de facto family units, comparative legal analysis indicates that previous assumptions about the respective roles of the family and the state in providing support are unsettled and that no clear new consensus has yet emerged. In the 1978 Law Quarterly Review, Ruth Deech has characterized the area of property division upon divorce as "currently the most controversial area of family law and one to which no satisfactory solution has yet been found." The main reason these matters are so controversial and intractable is that the question of who is to bear the cost of the deadly combination of housewife-marriage and serial polygamy practiced by persons of modest means has not yet been squarely faced. The notions of "marital partnership," and the popularity in the United States of wide-ranging discretionary "equitable" property division by judges represent efforts to keep the cost of changed family behavior, so far as possible, in the private sector. But where the former provider's resources are insufficient for two families, the effort fails—as is witnessed by the proliferation of female-headed one-parent families receiving public assistance.

––––––

Among the most controversial issues in family law today are property division and support obligations when a marriage is dissolved by divorce. The following excerpts discuss the ways in which England, France, Germany, and the United States have approached the task of framing new legal norms for regulation of the economic aspects of marriage termination. As you read this material, keep in mind that, although some legal systems treat the problems of spousal support, child custody and support, and property division as separate and distinct from one another, they are nearly always closely intertwined in practice.

MARY ANN GLENDON, "THE TRANSFORMATION OF FAMILY LAW: STATE, LAW, AND FAMILY IN THE UNITED STATES AND WESTERN EUROPE"

199–233 (1989).*

[I]t is useful to begin by briefly considering how turn-of-the-century legal systems approached the aftermath of what was then a relatively uncommon event—divorce. The spouses' property, in traditional legal systems, was divided according to ownership; that is, by restoring to each partner his or her own property in separate property systems, and by dividing the common assets equally in community systems. Marital misconduct was irrelevant to this process, but it was crucial for deter-

* Reprinted with permission of the University of Chicago Press.

mining whether a husband could be ordered to make alimony payments after divorce. The legal treatment of spousal support everywhere generally followed the lines that had been laid down for it in the immediate ancestor of secular divorce: ecclesiastical separation from bed and board. A legally innocent ex-wife was entitled in principle to continuing maintenance from her legally guilty ex-husband. Custody of minor children, which had belonged to fathers so long as children were perceived as economic assets, had already begun to be regularly given to mothers by the early twentieth century, and child support to be awarded for their basic needs.

As divorce became more frequent, dissatisfaction with this traditional pattern mounted. At the level of principle, the emphasis on technical fault in support law and on ownership in marital property law was thought to neglect issues of need and dependency. Furthermore, in practice, spousal and child support were often insufficient and precarious. All the traditional systems had in common with each other (and with modern systems) a basic reliance on private agreement as the principal mechanism for adjusting economic and child-related disputes upon divorce, and to a great extent, these agreements were unsupervised by courts. Thus, weaker parties were protected, if at all, mainly by the leverage afforded to an "innocent" spouse by the possibility of withholding consent to a fault divorce until appropriate financial arrangements were made. (An economically weaker party who could be shown to have committed marital fault, or who simply wanted to divorce a legally innocent partner, was, of course, in a poor position indeed.) Starting in the late 1960s, as fault began to be eliminated or downplayed in divorce law, the need for change began to seem acute. Once the process of reexamining the law in this area began, the new postulates of sex equality seemed to require the elimination of old, gender-based support rules where they still existed. Of the countries whose law is examined here, England was the first to try to adapt marital property and support law to a new system of divorce law.

ENGLAND

The entry into effect of the English Divorce Reform Act of 1969 was postponed for two years so that a new system for regulating the economic effects of divorce could be prepared to accompany it. This new system, as worked out in the Matrimonial Proceedings and Property Act of 1970, came into force with the Divorce Reform Act in 1971. The Matrimonial Proceedings and Property Act of 1970 sounded the death knell for the old marital property system of separation of assets, so far as divorce was concerned. Instead of trying to ascertain and restore to each spouse what was his or hers, English courts were authorized, after 1971, to order one spouse to make "financial provision" for the other by way of periodical payments, a lump sum, a transfer or settlement of property, or various combinations of these devices. In this new system, title to assets could be disregarded, as could the distinction between support and property division. Courts were directed simply to decide whether to order "financial provision" and were given great discretion as to how it should be paid and in what amounts.

Until the act was amended in 1984, the courts were supposed to exercise their discretion in such a way

> as to place the parties, so far as it is practicable and, having regard to their conduct, just to do so, in the financial position in which they would have been if the marriage had not broken down and each had properly discharged his or her financial obligations and responsibilities towards the other.

To guide the court in carrying out this direction, the statute provided that the following factors relating to the needs and resources of the spouses should be taken into consideration: the present and probable future financial situation of the spouses; their financial needs and obligations; their standard of living during the marriage; their ages; their mental and physical health; the duration of the marriage; and the loss of marriage-related benefits (such as pensions) in the future. The contributions of the spouses to the marriage were to be taken into account at this time, and the statute expressly stated that these contributions included housework as well as financial payments.

Because of the broad discretion and flexible powers this statute and its amended version have conferred on the courts, English spouses can anticipate that upon the termination of their marriage by divorce, a court ordinarily will effect some kind of redistribution of their property. But beyond this, predictability is not one of the chief features of such a system. As Lord Denning has described its operation, the decision-maker

> takes the rights and obligations of the parties all together and puts the pieces into a mixed bag. Such pieces are the right to occupy the matrimonial home or have a share in it, the obligation to maintain the wife and children, and so forth. The court then takes out the pieces and hands them to the two parties—some to one party and some to the other—so that each can provide for the future with the pieces allotted to him or to her. The court hands them out without paying any too nice a regard to their legal or equitable rights but simply according to what is the fairest provision for the future, for mother and father and the children.

Palm-tree justice along these lines is administered by the matrimonial registrars, court officials who examine the evidence in contested cases and make awards, subject to the right of appeal to a judge. As a body of decisions in appellate cases accumulated over the years, it became apparent that certain rules of thumb were being developed by the courts. These clues from the case law enabled solicitors to give their clients some idea of what to expect if a given case had to be decided by adjudication rather than through negotiation. One thing became clear early on: the original statutory direction to restore divorcing spouses to the position they would have occupied if there had been no breakdown of the marriage was wholly unrealistic in all but the rare case. Similarly, the hopes of Parliament and the Law Commission that financial provision could often be made in the form of a lump-sum payment proved impossible to realize in most situations.

Variations among registrars—and the wild-card conduct factor in section 25—render the outcome of contested divorce cases in England unpredictable to a degree that continental observers find surprising. Even though one can expect in a general way that a court will order some combination of property transfer and periodic maintenance, and will try to give possession of the marital home to a custodial parent, the precise status of the couple's property and the amount of support that will be awarded are in doubt until a decree is issued. The ideal of individualized justice (which is the main justification for a system of broad discretion) seems impossible to achieve, while the degree of uncertainty the system entails seems unnecessarily high.

In an effort to prevent the conduct factor from getting out of hand, Lord Denning recommended in a 1973 case that marital misconduct should not be held to justify reduction of financial provision, unless it was "both obvious and gross," as distinct from "what was formerly regarded as guilt or blame." But judges will differ even as to what is obvious and gross, or—as the statute now puts it—what is so "inequitable" that it should not be disregarded. A hearing on financial provision can thus come to resemble a post-mortem examination of the parties' marriage. The English system contrasts in this respect with most community property systems, where as we shall see, the common fund is equally divided, irrespective of the marital (as distinct from economic) misconduct of the parties. In such systems, conduct is treated as relevant, if at all, only in deciding questions of maintenance and fitness for custody.

By the 1980s, "serious and sustained criticism" of the 1970 act prompted the Law Commission to take another look at financial provision on divorce. Some of this criticism concerned the law's potential for arbitrariness and raised the question whether it adequately protected custodial parents and children. But most of the complaints involved what many regarded as an implicit assumption that a husband should continue to support his wife after divorce. In 1984, acting on the recommendation of the Law Commission, Parliament made one important, and several minor, changes in the act. Stephen Cretney (who was the member of the Law Commission primarily responsible for family law from 1978 to 1983) has written that the 1984 amendments were not meant to bring about a radical restructuring of financial provision law, but rather to effect a certain shift of emphasis.

The main change made in 1984 was at the level of principle. The direction to try to place the parties in the positions they would have been in had the marriage not broken down was removed. In its place, the new principle was laid down that the courts were to give "first consideration" to the welfare of any minor children in making financial arrangements:

s. 25. (1) It shall be the duty of the court in deciding whether to exercise its powers ... and, if so, in what manner, to have regard to all the circumstances of the case, first consideration being given to the welfare while a minor of any child of the family who has not attained the age of eighteen.

Parliament then took account of some of the criticisms that had been made by ex-husbands and second wives, adding several new provisions directing the court to consider making awards in such a way as to recognize and promote the potential of both spouses for independence and self-sufficiency. These provisions appear in section 25(2)(a) on earning capacity and in a new section 25A. The rest of section 25, as amended, now reads in relevant part:

s. 25 [continued]

(2) As regards the exercise of the powers of the court ... in relation to a party to the marriage, the court shall in particular have regard to the following matters—

(a) the income, earning capacity, property and other financial resources which each of the parties to the marriage has or is likely to have in the foreseeable future, including in the case of earning capacity any increase in that capacity which it would in the opinion of the court be reasonable to expect a party to the marriage to take steps to acquire;

(b) the financial needs, obligations and responsibilities which each of the parties to the marriage has or is likely to have in the foreseeable future;

(c) the standard of living enjoyed by the family before the breakdown of the marriage;

(d) the age of each party to the marriage and the duration of the marriage;

(e) any physical or mental disability of either of the parties to the marriage;

(f) the contributions which each of the parties has made or is likely in the foreseeable future to make to the welfare of the family, including any contribution by looking after the home or caring for the family;

(g) the conduct of each of the parties, if that conduct is such that it would in the opinion of the court be inequitable to disregard it;

(h) in the case of proceedings for divorce or nullity of marriage, the value to each of the parties to the marriage of any benefit (for example, a pension) which, by reason of the dissolution or annulment of the marriage, that party will lose the chance of acquiring.

(3) As regards the exercise of the powers of the court ... in relation to a child of the family, the court shall in particular have regard to the following matters—

(a) the financial needs of the child;

(b) the income, earning capacity (if any), property and other financial resources of the child;

(c) any physical or mental disability of the child;

(d) the manner in which he was being and in which the parties to the marriage expected him to be educated or trained;

(e) the considerations mentioned in relation to the parties to the marriage in paragraphs (a), (b), (c) and (e) of subsection (2) above. [Subsection (4) on support of children who are not the children of both spouses is omitted].

New section 25A specifies how the policies of promoting a "clean break" and spousal self-sufficiency may be implemented by making orders of limited duration, or even by dismissing support petitions, where this is not inconsistent with the direction in section 25(1) to consider first the interests of children:

25A. (1) Where on or after the grant of a decree of divorce or nullity of marriage the court decides to exercise its powers ... in favour of a party to the marriage, it shall be the duty of the court to consider whether it would be appropriate so to exercise those powers that the financial obligations of each party towards the other will be terminated as soon after the grant of the decree as the court considers just and reasonable.

(2) Where the court decides in such a case to make a periodical payments or secured periodical payments order in favour of a party to the marriage, the court shall in particular consider whether it would be appropriate to require those payments to be made or secured only for such term as would in the opinion of the court be sufficient to enable the party in whose favour the order is made to adjust without undue hardship to the termination of his or her financial dependence on the other party.

(3) Where on or after the grant of a decree of divorce or nullity of marriage an application is made by a party to the marriage for a periodical payments or secured periodical payments order in his or her favour, then, if the court considers that no continuing obligation should be imposed on either party to make or secure periodical payments in favour of the other, the court may dismiss the application with a direction that the applicant shall not be entitled to make any further application.

The 1984 changes, with the exception of the new requirement of first consideration for children, did not represent major departures from the prior law. It will be noted, for example, that although the idea of trying to restore the *status quo ante* has been abandoned, "the standard of living enjoyed by the family before the breakdown of the marriage" is still a factor to be weighed in determining what is appropriate financial provision under section 25(2)(c). The conduct factor was retained but recast in section 25(2)(g) to provide that conduct should be treated as relevant, but only where it is of such a nature that it would be "inequitable" to ignore it. Meanwhile, however, English courts seem to be increasingly willing to investigate the conduct of both parties in some detail in order to determine whether or not it would be inequitable to disregard their behavior. New section 25A is very cautious in the degree to which it promotes the idea of a "clean break" and is of limited practical importance in view of the relative infrequency of spousal support orders. Even after the 1984 amendments, it seems that English law still implicitly presumes a continuing obligation of support after divorce, unlike many other countries which have embraced the principle of self-sufficiency as their starting point. Still, as Law Commissioner Brenda Hoggett observed, the old direction to try to restore the parties to the position that they would have been in had the marriage not broken down did at least encourage fair sharing of marital property, and its withdrawal leaves the statute without any general standard for doing justice between the spouses.

The new statutory emphasis on the interests of children has the potential to bring about major changes in practice, but whether it will do so in fact remains to be seen. In a sense, Parliament has only recognized, belatedly, the position advanced by the Archbishop of Canterbury's Group in 1966:

> The needs of any children of a marriage to be dissolved should as a rule be made first charge on all available assets, with the object of enabling them to be brought up with as nearly as possible the same standard of opportunity as they would have enjoyed had the marriage not failed. To that end, it would in some circumstances be necessary to award a spouse, *qua* guardian of children, a level of maintenance that would not otherwise be due; for provision for children should always include suitable provision for the person given the care of them.

Increasingly, legal scholars, too, have been advocating a nuanced and differentiated approach to financial provision on divorce, with a special set of principles and rules for cases involving minor children. Such cases, in England as in most countries, constitute the majority of divorces, and in England as elsewhere, although custody, under the standard of the general welfare of the child, may be awarded to either parent, to both jointly, or to a third party, mothers are the custodial parents in the vast majority of cases.

To some extent, English courts in cases involving minor children had already been according primary importance to the needs of the children, especially where the matrimonial home was concerned. The 1984 amendments, however, were meant not only to ratify and encourage this trend but also to ensure adequate recognition of the custodial parent's role and to endeavor to make payment of financial provision more acceptable to the noncustodial parent. Whether the new attention to children's interests will make a significant difference in the financial well-being of female-headed families will depend, in large part, on whether courts will begin to make awards that reflect the actual costs of maintaining children, which, it seems, have often been underestimated.

From a comparative perspective, what is most striking about the overall English approach to financial provision on divorce is its heavy reliance on judicial (registrars') discretion. Even if one can assume that the decision makers who hold such extensive powers over the economic relations among family members are men and women of competence and integrity, a discretionary distribution scheme does very little to facilitate the negotiating process through which most divorces are in fact fought out and eventually settled.

With respect to the all-important question of how English financial provision law works out in practice, the studies so far yield a rather bleak picture of the circumstances of one-parent families headed by divorced mothers. The ongoing research of John Eekelaar and Mavis Maclean at Oxford has documented a general movement into poverty by custodial mothers and their children. Four out of five such families in their sample were below the poverty line and fewer than one in ten enjoyed an average standard of living. The average income of a divorced parent caring for children was considerably lower than that of the parent without children in his household. Eekelaar and Maclean have pointed out that until the 1984 amendments, child support was envisioned legally and in practice as merely something to be "tacked on" to other financial arrangements between the spouses, and that its amount usually bore little relation to the resources actually required by a child. If one is optimistic, one may hope that the statutory shift in emphasis in 1984 may alter both of these practices. One hopeful sign is the 1985 report of the Matrimonial Causes Procedure Committee. If the Committee's proposals are eventually adopted, the statutory policy of focusing attention on the interests of children will be reinforced. The changes proposed by the Committee would require an expedited hearing in such cases and would subject them to a more elaborate screening process. This could have the practical result that divorce decrees would not be given, even when the spouses were in agreement, until a registrar found that suitable financial arrangements for their children had been made.

As of 1988, however, there was some reason to doubt whether the courts would give full scope to the potentially transformative statutory direction to consider children's interests first. The language of the 1984 amendments could be interpreted to require that all support and property issues be arranged so as to provide the best possible outcome for any children involved, giving the interests of children priority, if necessary, over those of the parents. The Court of Appeal, however, stated in 1987 that if the statutory language *first consideration* had been intended to mean that children's interests were "paramount," or that they should have priority over "all other considerations pointing to a just result, Parliament would have said so." The court continued:

> It has not. So I construe the section [as] requiring the court to consider all the circumstances ... always bearing in mind the

important consideration of the welfare of the children, and then to try to attain a financial result which is just as between husband and wife.

* * *

FRANCE

An unusual feature of the 1975 French Divorce Reform Law, with its varied menu of divorce grounds, is that it establishes different systems of economic consequences for different categories of divorces. But the reform left marital property law basically unaffected. Except in the case of divorce on joint petition, the parties need not even wind up their matrimonial property regime before their marriage terminates. When they do liquidate the regime, of course, any assets acquired by gainful activity during the marriage will normally be divided equally between husband and wife, unless they have made some other arrangement by marital contract or divorce settlement. The role of divorce law is thus confined to determining whether and how economic transfers besides the division of marital property should be made from one ex-spouse to the other.

Under the former law, where divorce was exclusively fault-based, spousal maintenance was available only to the "innocent" spouse who obtained the divorce. This approach has now been abandoned in favor of a new set of principles. Except for the special case of divorce for disruption of the life in common, the purpose of the 1975 law, so far as the economic effects of divorce are concerned, is said to be to try to minimize "après-divorce" conflict between the ex-spouses. To this end, the starting point announced in Civil Code article 270 is that in principle, "divorce puts an end to the duty of support." The economic effects, if any, are to be regulated by a new technique called the "compensatory payment." But the basic mechanism for adjusting post-divorce financial matters, in the French as in the other systems examined here, is now (as it was in the past) the parties' own agreement. In France, however, the judge's role in approving such agreements is not perfunctory. The views of a judge expressed at the outset of a case can play a significant role in shaping the agreement, and as a rule, he or she spends a good deal of time in the final interview with the parties and their counsel. One French judge has remarked that "the spouses are very often astonished at the interference by the magistrate in the arrangements they have made between themselves." Nor will the judge be superficially informed about the case. The applicable provisions of the Code of Civil Procedure require that the spouses make available to the court in advance specified information concerning their financial circumstances, including (since 1984) their tax returns for the preceding few years.

Divorce on Joint Petition

The submission of an agreement on the effects of divorce is expressly required by the provisions of the 1975 law governing the economic consequences of the form of divorce which was meant to be preferred:

divorce by mutual consent on joint petition of the spouses. Just as the divorce itself is grounded in an agreement approved by the judge, so are its economic effects. Recall from the preceding chapter that the judge can refuse approval and thus delay the divorce if he or she finds that the agreement does not adequately protect the interests of either spouse or the children. The sections on the economic effects of divorce on joint petition repeat this idea in more precise terms:

> Art. 278. In the case of joint petition, the spouses are to fix the amount and the details of the compensatory payment in the agreement which they submit for the approval of the judge. The judge is invariably to refuse approval of the agreement if it allocates the rights and obligations of the spouses inequitably.

> Art. 279. The agreement once approved has the same executory force as a judicial decision. It can be modified only by a new agreement between the spouses which must likewise be submitted for approval. The spouses nevertheless have the option to provide in their agreement that either of them may, in the case of unforeseen change in their resources and needs, petition the judge to modify the compensatory payment.

Because divorce on joint petition is the sole form of divorce in which the spouses *must* liquidate the marital property regime at the time of divorce, and because such liquidation can be quite time-consuming, and perhaps because the judge has a good deal of power to influence the mode of division, a significant number of couples who are in agreement on divorce elect not to proceed this way. The problems with leaving the marital property to be dealt with later, however, can be severe, at least for persons with significant property. It can mean that prolonged litigation on property issues may take place after divorce, or that the regime will have to be wound up under pressure when one of the ex-spouses dies or urgently needs to sell some of the community property. The requirement that *all* the effects of divorce be settled at the time the divorce is granted on joint petition is thus simultaneously one of the virtues of the legislature's preferred route and one of its disadvantages.

In cases where the spouses are not able to come to agreement, or where they choose some other form of divorce, or where one spouse opposes the divorce and has not been guilty of "fault," the divorce will be governed by a different set of rules from those just outlined. Depending on the circumstances, the parties may be required to pay, or may be entitled to receive, "compensatory payment," or support, or sometimes civil damages. Since spousal support is exceptional in practice, and civil damages even more so, the most important of these rules are those governing compensatory payment.

The System of Compensatory Payment

The idea of the compensatory payment (*prestation compensatoire*) is to remedy "so far as possible" the disparity which the termination of marriage may create in the respective living conditions of the spouses. Thus, in theory, it is different from support or property division. Unlike alimony under the prior law, it is not in the nature of a penalty on the person against whom the divorce was pronounced. Nor does it imply continuing economic responsibility of one spouse for another. And it is independent of the liquidation of the marital property regime. It depends on the establishment of the fact of a disparity between the situations of the ex-spouses, and its aim is to enable both of them to live under approximately equivalent material conditions. The types of divorce in which the compensatory payment is called into play are the form of mutual-consent divorce in which the respondent neither cooperates with nor opposes the petitioner; divorce for shared fault; and fault divorce granted for the fault of one spouse only. In the case of fault divorce granted for the fault of one spouse only, the compensatory payment is available to the plaintiff, but not, as a rule, to the defendant, although an exception can be made if the denial of a payment in such a case would be manifestly inequitable.

Compensatory payment is never mandatory. The code section which determines whether a compensatory payment is to be made provides as follows:

Art. 270. Except where it is pronounced by reason of the disruption of the life in common, divorce puts an end to the duty of support established in Article 213 of the Civil Code; but one spouse may be required to make to the other a payment designed to compensate, so far as possible, for the disparity which the disruption of the marriage creates in the conditions of their respective lives.

The judge who decides that such a disparity exists must then determine the amount of the compensatory payment according to the following guidelines:

Art. 271. The compensatory payment is to be fixed according to the needs of the spouse to whom it is made and the resources of the other, taking account of their situations at the time of the divorce and of developments in the foreseeable future.

Art. 272. In the determination of needs and resources, the judge is to take into consideration notably:

—the age and the state of health of the spouses;

—the time already devoted or which they will have to devote to the upbringing of the children;

—their professional qualifications;

—their existing and foreseeable economic entitlements;

—the possible loss of such entitlements in connection with terminable pensions;

—their wealth, in income as well as capital, after the liquidation of the matrimonial regime.

Because these sections require the judge to make guesses about the future, and since the succeeding section provides that in principle the compensatory payment is nonmodifiable,[45] the compensatory payment sections have been criticized for requiring judges "to foresee the impossible and yet forbidding them to make any mistakes." From a comparative perspective, one can see in these sections the nascent acknowledgment in France of the ideas that the spouses (but not the children) are basically on their own after divorce, and that if, after a reasonable transition period, resources derived from an ex-spouse are insufficient, the dependent spouse must meet her needs either through her own efforts or public assistance. The compensatory payment seems to be the germ, though not the full expression, of the "severance pay" idea which has become influential in Sweden, Germany, and some of the United States, and which found a limited place in the English 1984 amendments. Pensions, it should be noted, are treated as one factor to be considered in determining the compensatory payment; they are not separately regulated as quasi-marital property, as in Germany.

In keeping with the aim to minimize postdivorce conflict, the 1975 law specified not only that the compensatory payment should in principle be nonmodifiable, but that it should be made in a lump sum. The rules which are to guide the judge are as follows:

Art. 274. When the assets of the spouse who owes the compensatory payment permit, the payment is to take the form of a lump sum.

Art. 275. The judge decides on the method according to which assets are allocated or charged for the lump sum:

1. Payment of a sum of money;

2. Transfer of property in kind; movables or immovables, but where usufruct only is concerned, the judgment operates as a forced assignment to the creditor-spouse;

3. Deposit of revenue-producing securities into the hands of a third party charged with the duty of paying income to the creditor-spouse for the period fixed;

The divorce decree can be made conditional on the effective payment of the lump sum or on the establishment of the guarantees provided for in Article 277.

Art. 275–1. If the debtor-spouse of the compensatory payment does not presently dispose of liquid assets, he may be authorized, subject to the guarantees provided for in Article 277, to make up the lump sum in three annual payments.

Art. 276. In the absence of a lump sum, or if the lump sum is insufficient, the compensatory payment can take the form of periodic payments.

45. "The compensatory payment is a fixed sum by nature. It cannot be modified even in case of unforeseen change in the resources and needs of the parties, unless the absence of modification would have consequences of exceptional gravity for one of the spouses." French Civil Code, art. 273.

Art. 276–1. The periodic payments are to be granted for a time equal to or less than the life of the creditor-spouse.

They are to be indexed; the index is to be determined as in the case of support payments.

The amount of the payments prior to being indexed can be made uniform for their entire duration or may vary in successive stages according to the probable evolution of needs and resources.

Art. 276–2. At the death of the debtor-spouse, the responsibility for the periodic payments passes to his heirs.

Art. 277. Independently of any statutory or court-ordered security interest, the judge may require the debtor-spouse to give a pledge or other security to guarantee the periodic payments.

Despite the clear preference of the legislature for a once-and-for-all financial settlement which would avoid postdivorce disputes and enforcement problems, lump-sum payments in practice have turned out, as in England, to be feasible only in the relatively few cases involving well-to-do individuals. The situation which the law contemplates as the exception—the compensatory payment made in periodic installments—thus has in fact turned out to be the rule in the majority of cases where the payment is allowed. Unlike spousal support under the old law, however, the compensatory payment is not granted for an indefinite duration. Even when it is paid out over time, with the payments indexed to the cost of living, it is of a notional fixed sum. Nevertheless, as was perhaps foreseeable, French judges have been treating the compensatory payment very much like modern maintenance, even making short-term "rehabilitative" orders in cases where the wife seems able to regain self-sufficiency.

Economic Effects of Divorce for Prolonged Disruption of the Life in Common

The general principle that divorce ends the marital duty of support does not apply in divorces based on prolonged disruption of the life in common, nor does the system of compensatory payment operate in these cases. In fact, it does not seem to be an exaggeration to say that the system of economic effects prescribed under the 1975 law for divorces permitted on prolonged disruption grounds amounts to the full continuation of the matrimonial duty of support. In the first place, the plaintiff in this kind of divorce must assume all costs. The sections regulating the other economic consequences reinforce the impression that the legislature intended to make anyone wishing to terminate a marriage to an unwilling and legally guiltless partner pay, and keep paying, for the privilege. There is no evidence here of any effort to reduce postdivorce contact between the spouses. Indeed, the system is the inverse of the compensatory payment. Support continues indefinitely; it is to take the form of periodic payments; and it is always modifiable:

Art. 281.   When the divorce is granted for disruption of the life in common, the spouse who took the initiative in the divorce remains completely bound to the duty of support.

In the case of Article 238 [impairment of a spouse's mental faculties], the duty of support includes everything that is necessary for the medical treatment of the ill spouse.

Art. 282.   The performance of the duty of support is to take the form of periodic alimony.   This may always be modified in accordance with the resources and needs of each spouse.

Art. 283.   Periodic alimony terminates as a matter of law if the spouse who is the creditor contracts a new marriage.

It is terminable if the creditor is living in open and notorious concubinage.

Accordingly, in this form of divorce, the ex-spouses are bound together economically for better or worse, in sickness and in health, unless the creditor spouse remarries or cohabits with someone.   Even when death does them part, support lives on if it is the debtor-spouse who has died, for Article 284 makes alimony a responsibility of the heirs of the deceased debtor.   It terminates only upon the death of the creditor spouse.   Exactly contrary to the scheme of the compensatory payment, Article 285 provides that in an exceptional case, the duty of support can be fulfilled by a lump-sum payment rather than through a periodic allowance.

In many ways this kind of divorce resembles a continuation of a limited form of marriage, with permission for the man, but not the woman, to add another spouse.   This impression is reinforced by an amendment to the Social Security law which provides that when an insured does not remarry after divorce granted on his or her initiative for prolonged disruption of the life in common, the ex-spouse will be deemed a surviving spouse for social security purposes.   If the insured does remarry, then the death benefits are made payable to the ex-spouse and the current spouse in proportion to the duration of each marriage.

Action for Damages

Under general principles of French tort law, a spouse in any type of divorce action may bring a civil action for damages against the other spouse for such violations of marital duties as assault and battery, defamation, and adultery.   Under the pre–1975 fault-based divorce law, the spouse who obtained the divorce could also seek damages for reparation of "the material or moral prejudice caused by the dissolution of the marriage."   The 1975 law also specifically authorizes a damage action, but limits it to the case of the plaintiff in a divorce granted for the exclusive fault of the defendant.   Under the prior law, "material and moral prejudice" was interpreted to be separate and distinct from the loss of support which may be occasioned by divorce.   The case law on this point, which is presumably still relevant, authorized compensation (sometimes very substantial) for such harms allegedly resulting from the divorce as the loss of esteem suffered by a divorced person, loneliness, or the loss of social position by one who has become accustomed to a high standard of living.

GERMANY

Like French law, German law distinguishes between property and support issues in divorce. The former are governed by the marital property law provisions of the Equality Law of 1957 and a system of pension-sharing established in 1976, while the latter are regulated by the 1976 divorce law as amended in 1986. Spousal support, in theory, plays a subordinate role in this scheme, supplementing the systems of marital property and pension-sharing in situations of special need. Whereas in most other countries, the marital home and household goods are comprehensively regulated, German law regarding these matters shows an uncharacteristic lack of system and thoroughness. Despite their great practical importance, problems in this area are still basically governed by an old 1944 ordinance, revised in 1976. This ordinance, which allows the courts a certain amount of discretion in allocating the marital dwelling and household goods upon divorce, leaves it primarily up to the judge in each individual case to harmonize the treatment of this type of property with the rules of marital property and support law.

[I]n 1957, the West German legislature implemented the constitutional principle of equality in marital property law by establishing a marital property regime (the *Zugewinngemeinschaft*) that leaves the spouses essentially free to deal with their own assets so long as the regime continues, but upon divorce requires an equal sharing of the increase in the value of the estates of each spouse occurring during the marriage. Spouses who do not wish to have their property relations regulated by the statutory regime are free, within certain limits, to adopt an alternative regime by contract.

Upon divorce, the statutory regime requires an "equalization of increase" (*Zugewinnausgleich*) in all cases where one spouse, by his or her gainful activity during the marriage, has increased the value of his or her estate more than the other spouse has. The gains of the two spouses are compared, the smaller increase is subtracted from the larger one, and half the difference is paid by the spouse who has had the larger increase to the other spouse. Unless an increase can be shown to be attributable to a premarital asset or to a gift or inheritance received during the marriage, it is presumed to be a marital increase subject to division. Unlike France, the Federal Republic does not bring about the sharing of marital acquests by partition of common assets. The equalization of increase is effected by arithmetical computation; it results in a money claim and is discharged by payment of a sum of money. Like the community of acquests, however, the system was intended to, and does, take account upon divorce of the contributions of a part-time or full-time homemaker to the family. The flat rule of fifty-fifty division can be varied only if it would result in "gross unfairness" (*grobe Unbilligkeit*) under the circumstances of the case.

A problem with the 1957 marital property system was that it did not apply to a kind of savings that was coming to represent a very significant asset of many married persons—pension rights. Housewives often had no job-related benefits, except those derived from their husbands, and such derivative rights were generally destroyed by divorce. The reform law of 1976 addressed this problem by establishing a system of equalization of benefits (*Versorgungsausgleich*) under which pension rights of all sorts accumulated by the spouses during the marriage are computed, compared, and divided equally upon divorce. The division is accomplished by transferring half of the difference in value between the respective entitlements of the spouses to the spouse with the lower value. If he or she does not yet have a pension account, one is set up, usually in the general social security system. In cases of exceptional hardship or inequity, the equalization of security benefits can be omitted or postponed by the court.

Viewed as a matter of policy, the equalization of benefits is an extension of the principle of equalization of marital property increase, but there are differences in the operation of the two processes. *Zugewinnausgleich* takes place on divorce only where the couple has been living under the basic statutory regime of matrimonial property, and not where a different marital property regime has been chosen by matrimonial contract, or where the statutory regime has been terminated by operation of law or judicial decree. *Versorgungsausgleich* applies in all divorces, irrespective of whether the parties have been living under the statutory marital property regime, unless the equalization of benefits was specifically excluded by a contract executed before a notary at the time of the marriage or at a later time. While a divorce proceeding is pending, spouses are normally given considerable latitude to make their own arrangements concerning property equalization and postdivorce support, but their freedom to modify the *Versorgungsausgleich* during the pendency of a divorce proceeding is more limited. *Versorgungsausgleich* is generally to be initiated by the court on its own motion. Any agreement suggested by the parties on the equalization of benefits in connection with the divorce must not only be executed before a notary but submitted to a family court judge for approval. Approval may be withheld if the judge finds that the agreement, viewed in conjunction with the support and property arrangements made by the spouses, will not provide appropriate security against old age or incapacity for a spouse who would otherwise be entitled to pension equalization, or that the agreement does not produce an appropriate equalization between the spouses.

As mentioned above, support law was supposed to play a supplementary role in the German system of regulating the economic effects of divorce. In this respect, the 1976 family law reform on the surface appeared to represent much more of a break with the past than did the 1975 French divorce law or the 1970–1984 English reforms. Until 1976, in West Germany (as in other traditional systems), the postdivorce support rights of the parties depended in important respects on the judicial determination of "guilt." If a husband was found to be at fault, he was obliged to maintain his wife at the economic level enjoyed during their married life—insofar as her own resources were insufficient to do so. A wife found to be at fault was required, under the prior law, to maintain her husband after divorce only if he were incapable of supporting himself, and even then only at a subsistence level. The 1976 reform law replaced these rules with a fundamentally different system. Not only is regulation of support made independent of guilt in principle, but as a general rule, spousal support is not to be available after divorce except as needed to help an economically weaker partner adjust to a new situation and to become self-sufficient. It was expected that the amount received by each spouse when the marital property regime was terminated would aid in this readjustment period. A duty of support continuing beyond the transitional period exists only in cases enumerated by the law.

The basic principle is stated in paragraph 1569: "If a spouse cannot take care of his support after divorce by himself, he has a claim for support against the other spouse according to the following provisions." Thus support, as distinct from the sharing of marital property increase and the equalization of benefits, will be granted only if a spouse meets one of several enumerated conditions. Civil Code paragraphs 1570 through 1576 specify the six classes of spouses who may claim support.

The first and most important category in practice is composed of spouses caring for a child of the marriage:

§ 1570. A divorced spouse can claim support from the other so long and insofar as employability cannot be expected of him on account of the care or upbringing of a common child.

The second and third categories concern spouses who cannot be self-supporting because of age or physical or mental incapacity. The fourth category of claims relates to a spouse's unemployability; or inability to find employment suitable for a person of his age, ability, and training; or inability to earn sufficient income.

The fifth category of cases in which postdivorce support may be claimed concerns spouses who need temporary support in order to finish an interrupted course of studies or to secure more advanced training in a professional field, particularly where their employment opportunities have been impaired by what the law refers to as "marriage-conditioned delays," such as the devotion of years to child care or the interruption of studies upon marriage.

The sixth and last category of eligibility for postdivorce spousal support is more general, leaving open the possibility of an award of maintenance where an ex-spouse cannot be expected to be employed for other "grave reasons." Recognizing the potential this general clause offers for reintroduction of the marital misconduct factor, the legislature provided that "grave reasons" that may have led to the breakdown of the marriage shall not be decisive in themselves. On the other hand, such evidence is not totally excluded from the decision to grant a support claim:

§ 1576. A divorced spouse can claim support from the other, insofar and so long as employment cannot be expected of him for other grave reasons, and the denial of support, considering the interests of both spouses, would be grossly unfair. Grave reasons should not be taken into consideration solely because they have led to the failure of the marriage.

This section is applied, for example, in situations where a spouse, at a sacrifice to his or her own professional development, has devoted years to working in the business of the other spouse.

So far as the amount of support is concerned, paragraph 1578(1) lays down, as a general principle, that support is to be determined with reference to the marital standard of living. But criticism similar to that which led to the removal of the principle of restoration to prebreakdown conditions from English law in 1984, prompted the West German lawmakers in 1986 to give the courts power to reduce support to an "adequate" standard after a period of time. At the same time and for the same reasons, they provided that the support rights of a spouse who is unable to find suitable employment or to earn a sufficient income could be terminated after a specified period.

Even though a claimant meets the threshold requirements for postdivorce support, he or she may be denied it on other grounds. A court may refuse the claim of a spouse otherwise entitled to support who has sufficient personal resources to be self-supporting, or for whom the allowance of support would be "grossly unfair" under all the circumstances of the case. The question of what constitutes unfairness sufficient for denial of support to an otherwise eligible spouse is treated in paragraph 1579. As in England, an effort was made to exclude ordinary marital misconduct from consideration. As originally enacted, paragraph 1579 provided as follows:

§ 1579(1). A support claim does not exist insofar as the claim against the liable spouse would be grossly unfair, because

1. the marriage was of short duration; the duration of the marriage includes the time during which the claimant was entitled to support under § 1570 on account of the care or upbringing of a common child,

2. the claimant has been guilty of a felony or a serious intentional misdemeanor against the obligor spouse or a near relative of the obligor spouse,

3. the claimant has maliciously brought about his own state of need, or

4. another ground exists, as grave as those set out in numbers 1 to 3.

In the first decade under the new divorce law, the general language of paragraph 1579(4) was used by the courts to deny support in a wide variety of cases. This broad judicial view of unfairness apparently met the approval of the legislature, which took the occasion of the 1986 amendments to codify this developing case law. Paragraph 1579 now includes, in addition to the first three examples of gross unfairness listed above, cases where

    4. the claimant has maliciously compromised important financial interests of the obligor spouse,

    5. the claimant has neglected his obligation to contribute to the support of the family for a long period of time before separation,

    6. the claimant is responsible for obvious and serious misconduct toward the obligor spouse, or

    7. another ground exists, as grave as those set out in numbers 1 to 6.

Thus, ten years after the switch to pure nonfault divorce, fault was firmly reinstated as a major factor in maintenance issues in Germany. However, the 1986 legislature also altered the opening section of paragraph 1579 to make it clear that the needs of any child of the couple must be met before the custodial parent's support may be curtailed under this section.

The 1986 amendments to spousal support law were made in response to widespread complaints about allegedly excessive support obligations, especially where the couple had been married but a short time, or where the wife's conduct seemed to make it unfair to require the husband to continue to support her. But questions have been raised as to whether the criticisms of the 1976 act were well founded. It does seem to be the case that spousal support, when granted, was for an unspecified duration and was geared to the marital standard of living. But spousal support appears to be awarded no more frequently in Germany than in most other countries. A study by Beatrice Caesar–Wolf and her associates at the University of Hannover revealed that in most cases virtually all the effects of divorce are settled by the parties in "court-induced" agreements. As for the contents of these agreements, the Hannover study casts doubt on whether support burdens on former providers were as heavy as had been claimed. Spousal support, for example, figured in only 11 to 14 percent of the cases in the Hannover sample. The *Zugewinnausgleich* took place in only about 10 percent of the cases, either because there was no increase to be shared or because the spouses had renounced their rights. The strict rules regarding pension benefits resulted in a settlement in favor of the wife in nearly half of the cases studied, but this benefit too was frequently renounced. Thus, as in England, much of the hue and cry about the obligations and rights of divorcing spouses towards each other seems to have been misdirected.

* * *

THE UNITED STATES

The legal approaches of the various American states to the economic aftermath of divorce resemble the English pattern in their lack of emphasis on distinctions between marital property and support law. They are more similar to the continental approaches, however, in the degree to which they have accepted the principle of spousal self-sufficiency after divorce. The Uniform Marriage and Divorce Act (UMDA) is illustrative of a number of American trends. Although adopted in its entirety by only a handful of states, it has been widely influential as a source of ideas and as a model for law revision. Its authors hoped that financial matters between the spouses could be arranged in a one-time property settlement, with periodic support being called into play only when necessary:

> The Act authorizes the division of the property belonging to either spouse, or to both spouses, as the primary means of providing for the future financial needs of the spouses, as well as doing justice between them. Where the property is insufficient for the first purpose, the Act provides that an award of maintenance may be made to either spouse under appropriate circumstances to supplement the available property. But because of its property division rules, the Act does not continue the traditional reliance upon maintenance as the primary means of support for divorced spouses.

To this end, the Uniform Act, like the law of the great majority of the American states and England, gives the courts broad discretion to redistribute *all* of the spouses' property, without regard to title, in the manner that seems fair to the judge:

> Section 307. *Disposition of Property.*
>
> (a) In a proceeding for dissolution of a marriage the court, without regard to marital misconduct, shall finally equitably apportion between the parties the property and assets belonging to either or both however and whenever acquired, and whether the title thereto is in the name of the husband or wife or both.

Section 307 goes on to list several factors which the court must take into consideration in allocating the spouses' property:

> In making apportionment the court shall consider the duration of the marriage, any prior marriage of either party, any antenuptial agreement of the parties, the age, health, station, occupation, amount and sources of income, vocational skills, employability, estate, liabilities, and needs of each of the parties, custodial provisions, whether the apportionment is in lieu of or in addition to maintenance, and the opportunity of each for future acquisition of capital assets and income. The court shall also consider the contribution or dissipation of each party in the acquisition, preservation, depreciation, or appreciation in value of the respective estates, and as the contribution of a spouse as a homemaker or to the family unit.

The UMDA authors, fearing that this free-wheeling approach might not appeal to legislatures in all states, particularly those with community property traditions, provided an alternative section in which the fund to be redistributed is limited to the marital acquests. They need not have been concerned. With the enthusiastic support of not entirely disinterested groups of divorce lawyers, discretionary distribution statutes spread like wildfire through the state legislatures. In a few places, the courts simply assumed the power to disregard title on divorce without statutory authority. By 1987, all the former separate property states and all but three of the community property states had adopted, by legislation or court decision, some form of discretionary distribution of property on divorce. There are, of course, variations from state to state. The laws differ, for example, on whether and to what extent fault may be taken into consideration; on how free the spouses are to contract out of the system; on whether all assets or only acquests made during the marriage are subject to division; and on whether the court should begin with a presumption in favor of equal division.

Once the principle of discretionary distribution of property was established, the question arose in the United States, as elsewhere, of how pensions and other job-related rights should be treated. Starting in the 1970s, American courts began routinely to consider pension rights as marital property. At present, a number of special statutes accord rights to divorced spouses in various kinds of benefits earned by the other spouse during the marriage.

For those great numbers of folk who consume what they earn and have no significant property, old or new, periodic support of one ex-spouse from the earnings of the other remains the only mechanism for making some kind of financial adjustment between husband and wife upon divorce. Among the states, the approaches to spousal support range from that of Texas, where permanent alimony cannot be given at all, to those of a few states where marital misconduct is an absolute bar to alimony, to the majority of jurisdictions, where the courts have broad powers to award spousal support as they deem equitable under the circumstances. Commonly, statutes governing spousal support provide the court with guidelines for the exercise of their discretion. In these guidelines, maintenance is commonly, but not always, made independent of marital fault. Even where legislatures have attempted to eliminate marital misconduct from consideration, however, fault often continues to play an indirect role in the economics of divorce. In cases where young children are present, putting the fitness of the mother as custodian into question has been a common way for husbands to try to force reductions in demands for support and property division. Furthermore, in recent years, damage actions between spouses for torts (such as assault and battery) committed during the marriage, long a familiar feature of the French legal landscape, have begun to be prosecuted with success in some American courts.

Support guidelines usually emphasize the needs of the support debtor and the ability to pay of the support creditor. The most recent

American statutes, like the French, Swedish, and German laws, treat spousal support as in principle what it is in fact—a temporary and exceptional consequence of divorce. The Uniform Marriage and Divorce Act contains a typical set of guidelines for spousal maintenance. They make maintenance available only in specifically enumerated situations of need and treat it as essentially temporary and rehabilitative, aimed at making the recipient self-sufficient through entry or reentry into the labor force as soon as possible after the divorce. Thus one trend makes alimony exceptional and temporary and therefore would seem to limit its availability; while another might seem to widen its potential scope by making it independent of misconduct and available on the basis of need.

The spousal support section of the Uniform Marriage and Divorce Act well illustrates the ambivalent attitudes that characterize law reform in this area. The section begins with the general proposition that there is no continuing financial responsibility of one spouse for the other after divorce, but it immediately qualifies this proposition so that most older divorced wives and most divorced mothers of young children are excepted from the application of the principle:

Section 308. *Maintenance.*

(a) In a proceeding for dissolution of marriage ... the court may grant a maintenance order for either spouse, *only* if it finds that the spouse seeking maintenance [*emphasis supplied*]:

(1) lacks sufficient property to provide for his reasonable needs; and

(2) is unable to support himself through appropriate employment or is the custodian of a child whose condition or circumstances make it appropriate that the custodian not be required to seek employment outside the home.

The authors' official comment to the section underscores the objective of promoting individual self-sufficiency:

[T]he court may award maintenance only if both findings listed in (1) and (2) are made. The dual intention of this section and Section 307 [Property Division] is to encourage the court to provide for the financial needs of the spouses by property disposition rather than by an award of maintenance. Only if the available property is insufficient for the purpose and if the spouse who seeks maintenance is unable to secure employment appropriate to his skills and interests or is occupied with child care may an award of maintenance be ordered.

The section is typical of several modern tendencies in its sex-neutrality, its express exclusion of marital misconduct, and its enumeration of specific criteria to guide the court's exercise of its discretion:

Section 308 [continued]: (b) The maintenance order shall be in amounts and for periods of time the court deems just, without regard to marital misconduct, and after considering all relevant factors including:

(1) The financial resources of the party seeking maintenance, including marital property apportioned to him, his ability to meet his needs independently, and the extent to which a provision for support of a child living with the party includes a sum for that party as custodian;

(2) the time necessary to acquire sufficient education or training to enable the party seeking maintenance to find appropriate employment;

(3) the standard of living established during the marriage;

(4) the duration of the marriage;

(5) the age and the physical and emotional condition of the spouse seeking maintenance; and

(6) the ability of the spouse from whom maintenance is sought to meet his needs while meeting those of the spouse seeking maintenance.

In practice, in the United States as elsewhere, spousal support plays a relatively minor role. In 1985, only about 15 percent of all divorced or separated women had been awarded alimony, and of these, 27 percent had never received payments.

* * *

Questions and Problems for Discussion

1. Set forth below is a leading case decided under a typical American discretionary distribution statute. How do you think the parties would have fared under French law? Under German law? What is the optimum resolution of a case of this sort?

RICE v. RICE

372 Mass. 398, 361 N.E.2d 1305 (1977).

Hennessey, Chief Justice.

Nancy Ann K. Rice (wife) filed a complaint seeking a divorce from John Rice (husband) which the Probate Court judge granted in June, 1976. The husband appealed from the Probate Court's judgment in so far as it ordered payment of alimony and a division and distribution of property. Both parties applied to this court for direct appellate review, which applications were allowed.

The parties were married for almost twenty-seven years and have two grown children. The wife, age fifty, is a homemaker, has never been employed for wages or salary and has no vocational skills. She has received an annual allowance from her husband of approximately $25,000 and fixed her income requirements at roughly $68,000. The husband, aged fifty-seven, has been involved with another woman for several years. He has been employed by the A.H. Rice Company or a successor corporation since 1948, receiving annually close to $50,000 in earned income and approximately $38,000 in unearned income. His net worth exceeds $1,000,000. His assets include agency accounts, bank accounts, a joint interest in some Canadian real estate, a joint interest in the marital home, a 40% ownership interest in Rice Investment Corporation (a personal holding company, the remaining stock of which is owned by his father), and some insurance policies. In addition, the husband has received annually from his parents gifts of $6,000. The wife has a negative net worth and derives her assets entirely from her husband. Before his marriage the husband owned the agency accounts and a 20% ownership interest in the family corporation. About the time of his marriage, he obtained another 20% interest in the family corporation as a gift from his father.

The Probate Court judge ordered that "[b]y way of alimony, past, present and future," the husband shall furnish to the wife the following support: (1) his interest in the marital home (approximate value $45,-500) including its furnishings (value unstated); (2) his interest in the Canadian real estate (his contribution $10,000); (3) $25,000 cash; (4) two agency accounts (approximate value $330,000); (5) $30,000 a year in support payments; (6) status as irrevocable beneficiary for full face value of nine insurance policies on his life (face value $80,000); and (7) $7,500 toward the wife's counsel fees. In effect, this order awards the wife $30,000 of her husband's annual income and approximately half of her husband's assets (and income therefrom).

The husband appeals from this order on the ground that the Probate Court lacks authority under G.L. c. 208, § 34, to order the transfer of his separate property acquired before marriage and as gifts during marriage. In addition, he maintains that the award, be it "alimony" or "assignment of property," was excessive and plainly wrong. We disagree.

1. General Laws c. 208, § 34, as appearing in St.1975, c. 400, § 33, provides that "[i]n addition to or in lieu of a judgment to pay alimony, the court may assign to either the husband or wife all or any part of the estate of the other." [1] A party's "estate" by definition includes all property to which he holds title, however acquired. Therefore, this provision gives the trial judge discretion to assign to one spouse property of the other spouse whenever and however acquired. See Bianco v. Bianco, 371 Mass. 420, 422, 358 N.E.2d 243 (1976).

---

1. This section, in its entirety, states: "Upon a divorce or upon motion in an action brought at any time after a divorce, the court may make a judgment for either of the parties to pay alimony to the other. In addition to or in lieu of a judgment to pay alimony, the court may assign to either the husband or wife all or any part of the estate of the other. In determining the amount of alimony, if any, to be paid, or in fixing the nature and value of the property, if any, to be so assigned, the court, after hearing the witnesses, if any, of each party, shall consider the length of the marriage, the conduct of the parties during the marriage, the age, health, station, occupation, amount and sources of income, vocational skills, employability, estate, liabilities and needs of each of the parties and the opportunity of each for future acquisition of capital assets and income. The court may also consider the contribution of each of the parties in the acquisition, preservation or appreciation in value of their respective estates."

The husband asserts that the legislative history of St.1974, c. 565 (which amended c. 208, § 34), demonstrates a legislative intent to exclude nonmarital property (property not derived from the marital partnership) from the trial judge's assignment authority. However, we do not resort to legislative history and other sources which clarify legislative intent unless the statute at issue is ambiguous. *Chouinard, petitioner,* 358 Mass. 780, 782, 267 N.E.2d 497 (1971). The language of c. 208, § 34, second sentence, is unambiguous and consistent with the general thrust of § 34, which gives the trial courts a large measure of discretion in settling the financial disputes of parties to a divorce. See *Bianco,* supra at 422–423, 358 N.E.2d 243. Moreover, it is not clear that the legislative history of this statute does in fact show a legislative intent to exclude nonmarital property from the court's discretionary authority to handle divorce settlements. Therefore, we conclude that under G.L. c. 208, § 34, the court may assign to one party in a divorce proceeding all or part of the separate nonmarital property of the other in addition to or in lieu of alimony.

2. General Laws c. 208, § 34, empowers the courts to deal broadly with property and its equitable division incident to a divorce proceeding. *Bianco,* supra at 422, 358 N.E.2d 243. Such broad discretion is necessary in order that the courts can handle the myriad of different fact situations which surround divorces and arrive at a fair financial settlement in each case. See Putnam v. Putnam, 5 Mass.App. __, __, 358 N.E.2d 837 (1977). The statute also requires that before the judge exercises his discretion to award alimony or to assign estate assets he consider all of the criteria enumerated in § 34, third sentence. See note 1, supra. Since § 34, third and fourth sentences (see note 1, supra) define the scope of a trial judge's discretion, *Bianco,* supra at 423, 358 N.E.2d 243, his consideration of factors not enumerated in § 34 would constitute an error of law. Cf. *Putnam,* supra at __–__, 358 N.E.2d 837 (dictum: judge may not award alimony or property purely on the basis of one spouse's blameworthy conduct). Moreover, because § 34 gives the courts such broad discretion, it is important that the record indicate clearly that the judge considered all the mandatory statutory factors. *Bianco,* supra at 423, 358 N.E.2d 243.

The husband made no motion, as required by Rule 52(a) of the Massachusetts Rules of Domestic Relations Procedure (1975), for findings of fact and conclusions of law by the judge. His right to challenge the result read by the judge is thus doubtful, to say the least. Nevertheless, we have examined the record in this case and we observe that it includes evidence concerning each of the mandatory statutory considerations. Furthermore, it includes no evidence that the judge below considered any impermissible factors in deciding to award the wife approximately half of her husband's estate in addition to $30,000 a year alimony (support payments). Thus the record is supportive of the judge's conclusions. The parties were married for almost twenty-seven years, during which time the wife became accustomed to sharing liberally in an income of about $90,000 a year (her "station"). She has little or no ability to support herself or to acquire assets which would support her, whereas her husband has not only a substantial earning capacity but also a likelihood of substantial family inheritance. The wife's income requirements appear to be at least as great as her husband's, and her age and health indicate that she may need an income for a longer period than her husband. No evidence supports the husband's allegation that the judge assigned the husband's assets to his wife because of the husband's marital infidelity.

Therefore, on the record before us, we cannot conclude that the judge's order was plainly wrong and excessive. The judge had discretionary authority both to award any or all of the husband's assets to his wife and to award her alimony. G.L. c. 208, § 34. We add that in future cases under this statute we wish to have findings, whether or not requested by a party (see *Bianco,* supra at 423, 358 N.E.2d 243), showing that the judge below weighed all the statutory factors in reaching his decision and considered no extraneous factors.

Judgment affirmed.

2. How should a legislature select the basic rules that are to govern matrimonial property relations in a country? Historically, the basic marital property regime in a given society tended to reflect the needs and desires of propertied groups in that society. Should law makers in modern republics attempt to ascertain the needs and desires of the majority of couples and to conform the law so far as possible to them? Or should this body of law be constructed with other aims in view, such as protecting the public purse or instilling an ideal of sex equality? Keep in mind that legal issues concerning the property relations between spouses arise not only in connection with dissolution of marriage by divorce, separation or annulment, but also upon the death of a spouse, and in the spouses' dealings with purchasers and creditors. For a comparative general survey of the world's marital property systems, see Rheinstein and Glendon, Interspousal Relations, Ch. 4 in IV International Encyclopedia of Comparative Law 31–191 (1980).

3. No matter how a country's basic matrimonial property regime is selected or what form it takes, it will not be suitable for every couple in the society. Thus, there must be some mechanisms to enable couples to tailor the basic regime to their own particular needs or to displace it altogether. For example, traditionally in separate property jurisdictions, purely voluntary forms of co-ownership such as joint tenancies, tenancies by the entirety and tenancies in common have been available to, and widely used by, married persons. In the civil law countries, most, but not all, of which have had forms of community property, married couples have been free, in varying degrees, to contract for variations in the community regime or to separate their assets. Should there be any limits on a couple's freedom to establish their own matrimonial regime by contract and to contract out of the basic legal rules regarding property distribution upon death and the economic aspects of divorce? To what extent do you think a couple in your state can opt out of its system of marital property rules by contract at the present time? The answer may surprise you. Look up this question in your own state's law, and see generally, Clark, Antenuptial Contracts, 50 University of Colorado Law Review 141 (1978–79), and Glendon, Family Law Reform in the 1980s, 44 Louisiana Law Review 1553 (1984).

For a comparative general survey of contractual regulation of marital property relations, see Rheinstein and Glendon, Interspousal Relations, Chapter 4 in IV International Encyclopedia of Comparative Law 148–165 (1980).

4.   This section has considered the economic aspects of divorce only as they affect the spouses.   Now that you have information about marital property and spousal support law in various countries before you, what do you make of these bodies of law in view of the fact that in all of these countries the majority of divorces (in the United States about three-fifths) involve couples with minor children?   And in view of the further fact that there are in practice relatively few cases where there is extensive property to divide?   How well does existing divorce law in England, France, Germany and the United States respond to the needs of the individuals involved in the statistically most frequent types of divorces?   How can American marriage dissolution law be improved?

5.   In England, the Matrimonial and Family Proceedings Bill of 1984 amended the Matrimonial Causes Act of 1973 to provide that the court, in dealing with financial provision, must give first consideration to the welfare of any children of the family.   Would it be desirable to introduce this factor into the guidelines under American discretionary distribution statutes?

Problem Area 2

THE ROLE OF THE COURTS IN POLICING CONTRACTS FOR UNFAIRNESS

---

1. STANDARD FORM CONTRACTS[1]

In the developed countries, modern contract law is largely the creation of the draftsmen of contracts in standardized forms. Standard terms are usually not negotiated and are frequently accepted by parties who are either unaware of their significance or who accept them because they believe they have no other choice. As it became apparent that the widespread use of such contracts could produce one-sidedness to the undue advantage of the person or organization who formulated their terms, courts and/or legislatures in a number of countries have devoted considerable attention in recent years to the problem of the extent to which unfair or oppressive terms in these contracts should be enforced. In the United States, the main approaches to the problem have been through consumer protection laws and through judicial interpretation of Article 2–302 of the Uniform Commercial Code which denies enforcement to "unconscionable" contracts or clauses.[2] In Germany, it was the courts who took the initiative in dealing with standard form contracts. In the article excerpted below, John P. Dawson describes how the German courts developed "an entirely new and original approach to standardized form contracts, which have been placed in a separate category and subjected to distinct and more rigorous standards of fairness."[3]

---

1. This problem is based on excerpts from Dawson, Unconscionable Coercion: The German Version, 89 Harv.L.Rev. 1041 (1976).

2. See generally, E.A. Farnsworth, Contracts 2d ed. (1990) 310–19.

3. Dawson, supra note 1 at 1042.

A. THE GERMAN RESPONSE TO THE PROBLEM

JOHN P. DAWSON, "UNCONSCIONABLE COERCION: THE GERMAN VERSION"

89 Harvard Law Review 1041 (1976).[4]

[(1) Background: The General Clauses
in the German Civil Code of 1900]

Among the countries whose basic private law has been codified Germany has probably had the most intensive experience with judge-made law produced under the auspices of general clauses. In the German Civil Code, the *Bürgerliches Gesetzbuch,* there are three general clauses that have achieved this kind of prominence and that will be mentioned here. Of these the one whose career has been the most spectacular of all will receive the least attention. This is article 242, whose message is very brief:

> Obligations shall be performed in the manner required by good faith, with regard to commercial usage.

This seemingly innocent provision, which even has a twin sister in our own U.C.C., had at first a modest career. The occasion for its sudden takeoff was the disastrous inflation after World War I. During the years of mounting despair before stabilization was achieved in 1924, the question was more and more insistently asked whether payment of a debt with money whose purchasing power was one hundredth, one millionth, in the end one trillionth of that contracted for, was perfor-mance in "good faith." The German Supreme Court, the Reichsgericht, finally concluded that it was not. The legislature also intervened to "revalorize" broad classes of simple money debts, translating them retroactively into stable money values. But the revision of other trans-actions, in enormous variety, was left to the courts, which sought by individualized methods to redress the manifold and random injustices that the inflation had produced. For this adventurous enterprise, new techniques and new standards of fairness were needed and were pro-duced by the courts through the methods of case law. Generalized and applied in other situations, the requirements of "good faith" have transformed the law of contracts and have penetrated deeply throughout the whole of German private law.

Another general clause, article 826, had become prominent even earlier. It is located in the chapter on wrongful acts, creates what we would call liability in tort, and uses as its standard "good morals":

> One who intentionally injures another by conduct offending good morals must make reparation.

* * *

The general clause that will appear most prominently in the discus-sion that is to follow is article 138, consisting of two paragraphs of which only the first can be described as "general" and will be quoted at this point. It is truly laconic:

4. Reprinted by permission of John P. Dawson and the Harvard Law Review Asso-ciation.

A transaction that offends good morals (*guten Sitten*) is void. Unlike section 2–302 of the U.C.C., article 138 is not locked away in legislation dealing only with one class of transaction, sales of goods, but appears prominently in the introductory "General Part" of the German Civil Code and applies to every legal transaction (*Rechtsgeschäft*)—that is, to all contracts or dispositive acts that are intended by the participants to have legal consequences. The transactions to which it applies are made wholly void as illegal. But article 138, paragraph 1, clearly extends well beyond violations of prohibitions expressed in existing law, for another article in the Code, located nearby (article 134), declares void all transactions that offend on the latter ground. Furthermore, there is at least a linguistic tie between article 138, paragraph 1, and article 826 for both depend on a finding that "good morals" have been offended. Under article 826, of course, the harm must have been *intentionally* done or threatened. Logic does not imperatively require this, but one would expect a consensual transaction to be void under article 138 if it was the product or a constituent part of some wrongful act producing liability under article 826.

* * *

[(2) THE APPROACH OF THE GERMAN COURTS]

The German phrase to describe standardized form contracts has acquired the status of a separate, well-recognized rubric in German law but it is not translatable into meaningful English. *Allgemeine Geschäftsbedingungen* (usually rendered in shorthand, A.G.B.) means literally "general transaction conditions" (or "terms"). The phrase describes an enormous variety of transactions which, merely because of the form in which they appear (documents prepared in advance and duplicated in multiple copies), have been marked off for separate treatment: their validity is determined by different tests and they are subjected to a scrutiny much more intense than that applied to transactions clad in some other form.

It all began without rumbling or portents. The highest court in the German hierarchy (the Reichsgericht, now the Bundesgericht) ordinarily has, through revision proceedings, an extremely limited power to review findings of fact; for this purpose, what the parties to a contract intended by the words they used will be considered a fact. So in 1912 a question arose as to the meaning of language in a policy of accident insurance— were the particular injuries incurred by the plaintiff, the insured, within the categories contained in the policy? It was a standard policy used by the insurer, a large company, in various parts of Germany; the Reichsgericht faced the question of whether it would be powerless if different intermediate courts of appeal, in litigation brought in different districts, read the very same language differently. The court concluded that this would not do. It made the point that the law of insurance required delivery of a copy of the policy to the insured so that he could read it, if he wished, before signing. This requirement, the court said, meant that the insured must know that he is "subjected to provisions that are fixed as a general norm and by which numerous others in existing and future contracts are and will be ruled." This would be especially true if the same form was used by several insurance companies but it would be enough if the provisions were used by only this insurer as "governing rules" for all its own insureds. In any event the language must be read "in its general application" without regard to the particular facts of the case before it, so the Reichsgericht was competent to decide its meaning.[155] The same conclusion was then reached as to a document (articles of incorporation of a mining company) that was much harder to visualize as a "general norm" but that could at least be described as "typical" and intended "to create a firm base for the inner and outer relationships of the enterprise in present and future."[156]

This manner of speaking must have suggested the formula for handling an entirely different problem—how to explain and justify imposing widely broadcast terms on outsiders who were ignorant not only of the particular terms but often of their very existence? When this problem appeared the Reichsgericht offered the explanation that this occurred through a "submission" to provisions that were in widespread use. Conscious adoption or even acquiescence was not needed; it was enough if the provision in question had been broadcast (one is tempted to say promulgated) in some open medium so as to come to general knowledge. Then, in the 1940's, this relatively harmless suggestion was blown up into the thought that the submission was to "a legal order already prepared" by the groups who regularly used the forms, so that their meaning should be taken to be the meaning attributed to them by these groups. If settled and ascertainable readings could not be found there, then the contract forms should be read as statutes are read, searching for meanings consistent with their purposes and with all their provisions viewed as a whole. Still less than before would it matter that the party who "submitted" had the opposite intention or even that he had expressed it clearly at the outset of the transaction. In subjecting himself to "a legal order already prepared," it was for him to learn its governing rules.[160]

---

155. Judgment of Dec. 13, 1912, RG, 81 RGZ 117.

156. Judgment of Feb. 27, 1915, RG, 86 RGZ 283. Similarly, in Judgment of Oct. 18, 1935, RG, 149 RGZ 96, the Reichsgericht found a conditional sale to be a "typical" document whose meaning it could determine, though there was no evidence that it was used by any other sellers, since it "evidently aims to regulate in a unified way the totality of sales contracts of this plaintiff over a wide area, not only the district of the Dresden Oberlandesgericht."

160. The notion of "a legal order already prepared" is most strongly stated in Judgment of Oct. 3, 1942, RG, 170 RGZ

233, but in a context that made it seem almost plausible. The problem did not arise from divergent understandings of the parties. The question was whether a shipment of brown coal (which had spontaneously caught fire) was dangerous cargo within the meaning of the General Affreightment Terms of the Area of the Elbe and Hafel. This set of rules was described by the court as A.G.B., but they had been drawn up by two corporations with public law standing and promulgated by a government minister, so that it was reasonable to lay heavy stress, as the court did, on the broad economic and political purposes that the rules were intended to serve.

This explanation of the Reichsgericht's active role in interpretation of private documents was also used in its handling of debtors' security arrangements, already discussed, in which standardized forms included assignments of rights against others that were to be acquired in the future. Wherever it appeared that such forms were used in an area extending beyond one appellate court district the Reichsgericht claimed full power to determine both meaning and legal effect. The weapon used by the Reichsgericht was not any provision of the Civil Code (e.g., article 138 or 242) but its own invention, a severely strict requirement of definiteness. Two mental operations, not wholly consistent, were used: First, attention was fixed on the document itself with everything outside it rigorously excluded, and second, imagination was then set free to conjure up any "conceivable" (*denkbare*) event in which the rights assigned, especially those to be acquired, were defined unclearly as to incidence or amount. This meant that all "accidental" (*zufällige*) circumstances of the individual transaction must be completely ignored, even though they would, if taken into account, make the meaning perfectly clear. For a "typical" document, it was said, must be read "generically" (*gattungsmässig*), as a creator of norms that would regulate a diversity of transactions and numerous persons in both present and future. The requirement of definiteness, a devastating weapon when used in this way, has since been much relaxed.... But its use in this way confirmed a way of thinking by which the standardized forms as they proliferated were not conceived to be expressions of choice and purpose by the individuals who employed them. They were seen rather as detached and depersonalized sources of widely applicable rules.

There must have been some uneasy questions not far below the surface as to whether some special controls should not be imposed on this private law-making by makers of forms to which others "submitted." But so long as the Reichsgericht functioned—until 1945—the theories it had invented continued to serve their original purpose of justifying the court's active role in interpreting (often nullifying) mass-produced forms, though the court's real objectives went well beyond that of ensuring that they were read consistently nationwide. The injustices that were mass-produced by one-sided drafting of mass-produced forms had long been evident enough. But in one case only did the Reichsgericht assert, and then quite ambiguously, that its power to prevent harsh application of an otherwise valid clause was enlarged because the clause appeared in a standardized contract form that was widely used.[164]

---

164. Judgment of March 31, 1941, RG, [1941–2] Deutsches Recht 1726 (Ed.A). This was a sale of goods with a clause excluding seller's liability for defects. Identifying the form as one in general use (fitting the tests for A.G.B.), the court said that disclaimers of warranty of this kind were valid but that arts. 138 and 242 would justify restrictive interpretation and also action by courts to prevent A.G.B. from having "unbearable consequences." The par-

ties had dealt with each other for years, the practice of the buyer being to send in orders from his own customers which the seller filled by direct shipment to them. As a result the buyer would have no opportunity to examine the shipments himself. The court also stressed that the principal buyer-consignees were the German army, national socialist party organs, and other groups in the public sector. The court may have had some concern for the quality of the ship-

It was not until 1955 that the breakthrough began, with an ingenious twist that gave it a new direction. The Bundesgericht repeated the formulas of the pre-war court: yes, standardized forms in "general" use (A.G.B.) do not depend on the will or purpose of any individual party, for they are prepared in order to provide the base for "an indefinite, large number of transactions in the past, present and future" and constitute "a generally regulated contractual order." Yes, "submission" to this order must be shown. *But* since the one who submits will ordinarily not know the terms of the standardized document he can be considered as submitting only to those terms with which he should "fairly and justly reckon." The converse is equally true. If the draftsmen of the document show concern only for the interests on one side of a two-sided transaction, this disregard of the interests of others contradicts fairness and justice. The provisions of a document prepared and duplicated for widespread use must therefore be interpreted so that justice and fairness will be served, and if its language does not permit this the unjust and unfair provisions will be unforeseeable by the disadvantaged party, offensive to good morals (article 138), and also perhaps provide ground for damage liability for harm intentionally caused (article 826).[165]

This reformulation was quickly recognized as preferable, particularly for its emphasis on the responsibility of the draftsmen who undertake to guide the destinies of persons unknown to them, persons whose resources and opportunities may differ widely, but most of whom will be alike in having only a dim comprehension of the documents tendered to them. If this responsibility is recognized, then those whose interests are to be regulated but who have played no part in choosing the means can expect that those interests will not be callously overridden in search of one-sided advantage. These were to be the central themes repeated in various formulations in the extensive case law that was soon to develop. They met the approval of many authors. One result was a reduced tendency to conceive of the commercial and industrial groups that used, and for the most part originated, the standard forms as themselves makers of rules, almost as though they became small subordinate legislatures, or as though the *consensus utentium,* as in olden times, could generate binding rules of customary law: such notions occasionally reappear but only in residual forms. For even the settled practices of

---

ments they received, but I detect no overtones of Nazi ideology. The solution of the court was simply to direct the lower court to "interpret" the contract "according to good faith."

The case is stated fully because some authors have later described it as a major breakthrough. I would call it a door opened and left slightly ajar.

165. Judgment of March 8, 1955, BGH, 17 BGHZ 1. The action was by a shipper to recover possession of the goods he had shipped against a carrier which claimed,

under its standard contract form, a lien for freight due to it from the consignee, not from the shipper-owner itself. The court conceded that a lien could be created in assets owned by another if the lienor in good faith believed them to be owned by his debtor but concluded that, in a contract form prepared for "general" use by a carrier, neither consignor nor consignee had reason to foresee such an extension of their own risks and of the carrier's self-protection.

organized groups might themselves need to be re-examined as the prefabricated contracts they designed were tested against still more elevated standards of morality and justice, standards that the courts raised steadily higher as the impact of the prefabricated designs grew wider.

It soon appeared better to shift from good morals (article 138) to good faith (article 242) as the Code provision to be invoked, mainly to permit judicial correctives to be made in detail and avoid altogether any suggestion that complex transactions with numerous clauses on printed forms must be held to be void as a whole, as they normally would be under 138, because one or a few clauses had gone astray. The "good faith" standard of article 242 had been used for all kinds of surgery, major and minor, in all kinds of contracts for thirty years; this had become a habit. It is of course possible to discern some bad morals and shift back to 138 if the standardized contract had oppressive clauses so numerous and so interlocked that there was nowhere for a court to begin. But this was rare. In the decisions that will be described shortly (i.e., both soon and briefly) any corrective applied has left the transaction otherwise intact and, unless otherwise noted, the correctives were ascribed to article 242. . . .

In the attempt that will now be made to classify roughly the results so far there are two main purposes—(1) to search for other motives for imposing control, more specific than the broadly stated responsibility of draftsmen to show good faith when by preparing forms for "general" use they transform themselves into quasi-legislators, and (2) to highlight the points at which special controls are imposed that would not be applied to nonstandardized "dickered" transactions.

Frequent statements that a signer is bound only to the terms with which he should "fairly and justly reckon" would suggest that one major motive for intervening would be to prevent "unfair surprise," as the draftsmen of our U.C.C. have phrased it. Thus the German high court gave as a reason—an additional reason—for invalidity, the location of a clause in a place where it would not be expected, even if the document were read with some attention. Still more, where the document bore outward marks of a deliberate effort to jumble clauses and confuse their meaning, this was a separate reason for condemning those clauses, perhaps the entire document.

Under the mantle of preventing surprise, a 1964 case introduced another idea whose implications were broader. It can be phrased as follows: There are some rules of the Code that state the legal consequences of standard and familiar transactions but that are "dispositive" and not mandatory, i.e., departure from them by freely bargained agreement is entirely permissible. These rules nevertheless represent a legislative judgment as to the normal and expected functioning of all the transactions involved. The draftsmen of forms that are intended for and are put to widespread use assume thereby the role of makers of law for a large, undifferentiated mass of users. They therefore have special responsibility to ensure that any abnormal consequences they produce are both (1) fully understood and (2) not unfairly one-sided in favor of those who would project the results on others. The 1964 decision that put forth these ideas involved a contract for services by a broker in finding a willing lender of money. A Code provision on brokers' contracts stated that if a broker is employed to arrange the making of a contract, his commission is earned when that event occurs. By the standardized form used in the particular case (supplied by the broker), he became entitled to the agreed commission by merely finding a lender willing to lend on the principal's terms, whether or not a loan was actually made. The court was clear, as was the text of the Code, that this provision was not mandatory and could be superseded by express agreement—but not so, the court held, where the clause was in a "general" form (A.G.B.), prepared on behalf of one party and taking no account of the interests of the other. This "one-sided departure" from the Code model of a brokerage contract would be unexpected for his client, would therefore violate good faith, and was void.[173] A line of cases followed, involving other service contracts with claims for payments not earned. In these cases also, departures from Code models, permissible when actively bargained for, were denied effect when inserted in standardized forms—in part, at least, because in that setting they would bring surprise. This will be still more true if the Civil Code rules that have been displaced rest on "broad conceptions of justice." The paradox is that in that event it may actually be easier to salvage the contract, for the more compelling and persuasive the conceptions displaced, the more likely it is that the court will read them back in, subsumed under "good faith," which according to the Code (article 157) is to govern the interpretation of all contracts.[175]

One motive that had at least a remote connection with preventing "surprise" could be called the denaturing of the transaction, making illusory the protection it pretended to give—for example, removing all content from a duty to indemnify by casting on those injured a burden of

---

173. Judgment of Nov. 4, 1964, BGH, [1965–1] NJW 246. Cf. Ellsworth Dobbs, Inc. v. Johnson, 50 N.J. 528, 236 A.2d 843, 857 (1967), where a similar provision, giving a real estate broker a fee though the sale fell through by default of the buyer he had found, was declared "unconscionable" and "contrary to the common understanding of men."

175. Judgment of April 16, 1973, BGH, 60 BGHZ 353. Here the defendant had been employed as an engineer to supervise construction of a hotel under a "generally" used form, "Contract Terms for Engineers' Fees." The form entitled the engineer to his full honorarium if he terminated the contract for default by the employer. In disputes with the employer the latter charged defendant with fraud, defendant repudiated the entire contract, and the court assumed that the making of this unproved accusation was a breach by the employer. The principle of justice which, the court held, could not be superseded by a "generally" used form, was essentially the principle of mitigation, that earnings elsewhere that were made possible by the breach, especially if actually earned, must be deducted from defendant's salary claim. The action was brought by the employer for restitution of the full salary that he had already paid defendant. The court directed that any earnings elsewhere that the defendant had made or could have made were recoverable, since good faith in interpretation (art. 157) required this, though the contract form excluded it.

proof that some, at least, could not carry.[176] These cases have some connection with the recurring problems raised by exculpatory clauses. Most frequently litigated of all have been disclaimers of liability by sellers of defective goods, giving buyers at most a "right of withdrawal" if defective goods are not replaced or repaired. Very wide latitude for this form of seller's exculpation is conceded by German courts, even by means of "generally" used forms. Judicial controls are not altogether abandoned, however, for if the buyer's only sanction, his "right of withdrawal," is in any way restricted the disclaimers of liability are brushed aside so that the usual damage liabilities provided by the Code will govern.

The most notable feature of the whole approach to standardized form contracts is that it dispenses with inquiries into the degree to which the particular signer's assent had been impaired. Whether the individual was coerced, had read the form or not, lacked bargaining power, or was "unaware" must be disregarded. As to exculpatory clauses, for example, the test of validity, in the decisions of the pre-war Reichsgericht, was the presence or absence of monopoly, impairing bargaining power in the weaker party; the post-war court seemed for a time to follow the same course but soon shifted ground. Where one possessing a monopoly of an essential service used a standardized form to impose a low ceiling on its liability the ceiling was enforced as entirely fair for the kind of service rendered. In an insurance contract where a term burdensome to the insured was used by all suppliers of that type of insurance, this fact would be worth noting, but the court's role was conceived in broader terms, that of dispensing of "elementary contractual justice" for the large, undefined group who would "submit" to the form. So it was necessary to balance carefully the interests of the insurer against those of numerous unknown but potential insureds, some of whom (one could not predict how many) might be severely deprived; if there could be some, the clause was void as to all.[180] On the

---

176. Judgment of Feb. 17, 1964, BGH, 41 BGHZ 151, involved an owner's action for damage done to household goods while stored in defendant's warehouse. The Civil Code (art. 417) placed the burden on the warehouseman to prove in such a case that the injury was not caused by his fault. The defendant's form contract, on the contrary, required the owner to prove how the injury occurred. The court conceded that the Code provision was not mandatory, so that the burden of proof could have been shifted in this way in a negotiated contract, but concluded that since owners would seldom have the evidence they would need to carry the burden, it was unfair to do this through a "general" form.

Judgment of Feb. 24, 1971, BGH, [1971–1] NJW 1936, held that a supplier of heating oil for a home could not, through a "general" form, throw back on the owner the duty to prevent the oil from overflowing while being poured in, since the owner would seldom have the means to observe, whereas the supplier's delivery man quite surely would.

180. Judgment of April 30, 1969, BGH, 52 BGHZ 86. Here a policy insuring against automobile accident liability had a clause exempting the insurer where the insured had left the scene of the accident without reporting it. The court noted that all liability insurers used such a clause in similar policies so that the court should examine it closely to prevent the imposition of "an undemandable risk on the weaker party." The court concluded that the clause did not require a showing either that loss to the insurer resulted or that the insured had been aware of any injury caused by the accident he had left, so the clause *could* operate on some insureds as a penalty and in a "generally" used form was void.

other hand, if a substantial number of sellers of secondhand trucks do not use the standard form that is used by most, the fact that buyers have some choice is worth mentioning, though it will be necessary still to examine the clauses separately and then appraise their composite effect before the form can, in effect, be certified for "general" use.[181]   In reaching such decisions the features that will be least important will be the pressures at work on the particular signer, what he knew or thought or failed to think.   All these will be "accidents" that cannot affect a generally applicable norm, in whose application it is of the essence that all signers be treated alike so that individualized inquiries can, so far as possible, be dispensed with.

Even two separate transactions that involve different parties and that the parties themselves have tried to disconnect can be brought under a unified control if they have a common documentation in a "generally" used form.   An example is a credit purchase of goods with financing supplied by a third party who desires insulation from disputes between buyer and seller; typically, by excluding all defenses of the buyer based on defects in or nondelivery of the goods sold.   The New Jersey court in such a case resorted to the unconscionability clause of the U.C.C. and struck down as "one-sided" a clause excluding any such defense by buyer against lender.[182]   The German high court had already reached this conclusion in cases where the same documentation had been used for the two transactions, on standardized forms.[183]   The court declared that the draftsmen of the forms and the sellers and lenders who used them must see that a clause excluding buyer's defenses reduced safeguards and increased risks for the buyer, to whom the form used made the series appear as a single, unitary transaction.   Indeed, when the lender turned over to the seller loan application forms, which the seller then induced the buyer to sign with the lender participating in no other way, the lender owed the buyer an independent duty to explain the

181. Judgment of Oct. 8, 1969, BGH, [1969–II] Warneyer, no. 263.   In Judgment of Dec. 13, 1963, LG Tübingen, [1964–2] NJW 1798, a contract for the sale of trucks with terms not significantly different from those in the 1969 case had been condemned indignantly.   The court was explicit that predominant economic power in the sellers did not have to be shown, but pointed out that all dealers in used trucks were members of a central union and all insisted on using the union's form, which when viewed as a whole was so unfair as to show "naked self-seeking" by the members "on the basis of their combination in a union and their resulting position of economic power."

182. Unico v. Owen, 50 N.J. 101, 232 A.2d 405 (1967).

183. Judgment of Oct. 29, 1956, BGH, 22 BGHZ 90 (sale of household goods, with retailer and buyer both signing the lender's form and applying for a loan to the buyer).

Thereafter came Judgment of April 5, 1962, BGH, 37 BGHZ 94 (sale of furnishings for a hotel, with buyer signing on a single form both an order for the goods and a request for a loan); Judgment of Feb. 20, 1967, BGH, 47 BGHZ 217 (sale of three Persian rugs, same form used for sale and loan); Judgment of Nov. 10, 1972, LG Augsburg, [1973–1] NJW 709 (sale of deep freeze equipment with buyer's obligation to pay transferred to a "lease" by a lender, which the seller arranged for the buyer to sign). In all these cases, the recurrent theme was that the protection of buyers should not be impaired by separate references to sale and loan in the same prefabricated documents (A.G.B.).   The second of the three cases emphatically stated that the result would be different if the buyer on his own initiative and on a form that the seller did not sign applied for a loan even though his disclosed purpose was to finance the purchase of specific goods.

risks to the buyer in signing, so that the lender became liable to the buyer for any loss to him caused by his unawareness of these risks.[184]

Thus in the last twenty years an enclave—better described as an extensive territory—has been marked off in German contract law. It is subject to high and exacting standards of fairness, and exceptional powers assumed by courts to strike down or correct terms that fail to meet these high standards. How are the boundaries defined? So far the transactions within it have been selected by a purely external test—the physical garment in which they are clad, a written document previously produced in multiple copies for numerous users. Must they be printed or will xeroxing do? How many copies, how many users? The last question, it seems, contains two parts. A document can have the needed generality of use though it emanated from only a single source if those who "submit" to it are numerous and not predetermined.[185] Signature to a document is not required, for notices posted by operators of parking lots are A.G.B.[186] So are particular clauses (e.g., providing for arbitration) that are widely copied into different forms that are used for differing purposes; for the original point, now deeply submerged, has not been forgotten, that interpretation by the Bundesgericht is needed if such clauses are to mean the same throughout the nation.[187] Must they be printed? Some authors say yes, for the sake of a simple, clear-cut test. But the courts have not as yet been willing to confine themselves so strictly, though some evidence that the document has been or will be duplicated seems to be required.[189] These issues will no doubt be

184. Judgment of Nov. 17, 1960, BGH, 33 BGHZ 293 is the only case in the group that involved really needy customers (married persons living in poverty who bought household furniture that was never delivered). The court laid great stress on the need to protect "typically inexperienced classes of buyers" by imposing high standards of good faith on those who deal with them. The liability of the lender for failure to "explain" did not end up as a liability to pay damages, as one might ordinarily expect. For the "duty to explain" was to be enforced, like other duties, by bringing about the situation that would have resulted if the duty had been performed. With quite a leap the court then concluded that the defendants would not have bought if they had understood and therefore were not liable on the loan, so the lender's action to collect the loan failed.

185. Judgment of Sept. 29, 1960, BGH, 33 BGHZ 216, where the operator of a ship-monitoring service in Hamburg harbor (with a monopoly of the service) successfully used its own special form to limit its liability for negligence to 300 marks but the court was most explicit that the forms used were A.G.B. and must be judged by the tests applied to them.

186. Judgment of May 22, 1968, BGH, [1968–I] Warneyer, no. 129.

187. Judgment of March 5, 1971, BGH, [1971–I] Warneyer, no. 53; Judgment of March 29, 1974, BGH, 62 BGHZ 251.

189. Judgment of March 29, 1974, BGH, 62 BGHZ 251, was a form contract, seemingly typewritten and in fact notarized, for the sale of land on which buildings had been recently constructed. The most objectionable clause was an exemption of the seller from liability for defects in construction, with an assignment, instead, of the seller's rights against the builder and his workmen for any defects in their work. The court concluded that he could not escape in this way liability for defects that were due to his own default, because the terms had been "one-sidedly" imposed by the seller without negotiation and such terms were found in a "not small" number of similar land contracts.

A long, complex and confusing document, prepared (but not printed) in advance by a general contractor and handed over to a sub-contractor to sign without explanation or discussion was held to be correctable by the court under its powers to reinterpret "unreasonable and surprising" A.B.G. that

resolved in legislation now being actively considered by the legislature, for it seems that all now agree on the need for comprehensive legislation. It is likely that many of the solutions reached through court decisions will be thereby confirmed and extended, though it seems unlikely that the powers of courts in maintaining a general oversight over form contracts, outside the limits thus explicitly defined, will be seriously curtailed. For as one distinguished observer has put it, the high court's contributions in this area are considered by many to be a notable achievement, making "worthy of confidence" the regime of free contract to which Germany is committed.[191]

B.   AMERICAN APPROACHES TO STANDARDIZED CONTRACTS

When one reviews American discussions of these themes with the German solutions in mind it becomes plain how misdirected most of them have been. This is all the more strange because there was one writer, Karl Llewellyn, who is still regularly and dutifully cited and who saw the main issues clearly almost forty years ago. He then pointed out how far we have been carried from the open give-and-take in pre-contract bargaining that our contract theories presuppose, by modern mass production of printed-form contracts.[192] Some twenty years later he urged again, this time with rising impatience, that courts and scholars set to work on "agreements" that are mainly composed of multi-copied boilerplate—to devise new techniques for dealing with them, to identify major transaction-types, and "to locate, describe and test proper specifications for an iron core for each." For clauses that were beyond salvaging and that must therefore be struck down, he counted on section 2–302 to provide the needed authority. What he sought to drive home most of all was that as to specific terms in the boilerplate there was usually no assent at all and that it was utterly useless to search for it. Apart from agreement on a few "dickered" terms, there is between proposer and signer not quite a fiduciary relationship but "a plain expression of confidence, asked and accepted,

---

offended good faith. Judgment of April 8, 1975, OLG Frankfurt, [1975–2] NJW 1662. In another recent case another lower court scaled down an "unreasonable, over-reaching" provision for a 50% penalty on buyer's default, contained in a form contract (not printed) for the purchase of office equipment. The provision was declared to offend good faith, BGB, art. 242, though both parties were merchants and the scaling down of penalties is excluded as between merchants by the Handelsgesetz-buch, arts. 348 and 351. Judgment of April 16, 1975, LG Frankfurt, [1975–2] NJW 1519.

191. Ansprachen on the 25th Anniversary of the Bundesgerichtshof by Professor Ernst von Caemmerer, at 21, 25–26, Oct. 3, 1975 (privately printed).

192. Llewellyn, Book Review, 52 Harv. L.Rev. 700, 704 (1939). This appears particularly where he urged judges to see that "free contract means free bargain, and that free bargain presupposes free bargaining; and that where bargaining is absent in fact, the conditions and clauses to be read into a bargain are not those which happen to be printed on the unread paper; but are those which a sane man might reasonably expect to find on that paper." It is worth noting that his comments were made in a review of a book whose main object was to describe the German case law on standardized form contracts as it had developed by that time.

with a corresponding limit on the powers granted," so that there would be no power to impair the "fair meaning" of the dickered terms or insert other terms that were "manifestly unreasonable and unfair." [193]   So brief a summary of his well-known argument cannot do justice to it, but even a brief summary should suggest how closely it parallels the basic elements in the thinking of German courts and scholars.

Standardized form contracts weave in and out of American discussions of unconscionability. They are mentioned quite often. Some authors if pressed might even concede that a very high percentage of the transactions engaged in by most of the present-day population appear in that form. But it is difficult to find an author other than Karl Llewellyn who has plainly said that excessive and unnecessary harshness that has been built into boilerplate is by far the most common source nowadays of problems of unconscionability and that problems coming from this source must be marked off for separate treatment; the territory in which they are located merely adjoins that governed by standard contract law.[194]   Instead we find unconscionability treated as essentially a problem of general contract law which must be solved by finding some failure of assent by the individual signer. One suggestion has been, for example, that we should in each case define the "circle of assent" that surrounds the transaction and then ascertain whether for the particular signer the term in question was near to or far from its center, the object being to ascertain whether the assent manifested was "real" or merely "apparent." [195]   An even more popular explanation is that unconscionable terms are to be explained by inequality in bargaining power, impairing assent. One writer has in fact contended that unconscionability within the meaning of section 2–302 could not exist without this.[196]   So standardized form contracts come to be called "contracts of adhesion," a phrase that is attractively French and that suggests all sorts of things— monopolies and oligopolies that dictate prices, extract immunity for their own misdeeds from victims who helplessly "adhere," and dictate oppressive terms through printed forms that they impose on their victims through superior market power.[197]   Fortunately where section 2–302 has

193. K. Llewellyn, The Common Law Tradition 362–71 (1960).

194. One author does assert, indeed in his opening sentence, that "[s]tandard form contracts probably account for more than ninety-nine per cent of all the contracts now made." But his discussion is so preoccupied with whether they are "democratic" or not and whether they are contracts at all (conflicting answers are given) that I am unable to discover what the author proposed to do about it. Slawson, Standard Form Contracts and Democratic Control of Lawmaking Power, 84 Harv.L.Rev. 529 (1971).

195. Murray, Unconscionability: Unconscionability, 31 U.Pitt.L.Rev. 1 (1969). Severely critical of these tests: Speidel, Un-

consciability, Assent and Consumer Protection, 31 U.Pitt.L.Rev. 359, 371–74 (1970).

196. Comment, Bargaining Power and Unconscionability: A Suggested Approach to UCC Section 2–302, 114 U.Pa.L.Rev. 998, 1001 (1966); in the passages that follow, the tests are further confused by adding "inability to understand" as an alternative source of unequal bargaining power.

197. My own conclusion is that the phrase "contracts of adhesion" has by now accumulated so much debris that it should be discarded altogether. At an earlier stage it was useful in serving as a leading theme for the thoughtful article of Kessler, Contracts of Adhesion—Some Thoughts About Freedom of Contract, 43 Colum.L.Rev. 629

actually been used to invalidate particular clauses—usually exculpatory clauses—there have been no inquiries into the structure and rigidities of the markets in which the particular transactions occurred. As a highly persuasive article has recently suggested, if findings of fact on such issues were essential to determine whether a particular clause was unconscionable, trial of these issues would require the same kind of evidence and last about as long as antitrust suits.[198]

Something useful may come, however, from a section added to the second Restatement of Contracts, a separate provision for "standardized agreements." They are defined as writings that are "regularly used to embody terms of agreements of the same type." The key provisions appear in modest and familiar garb, phrases that we all constantly use in testing the presence or absence of mutual assent. The signer must have "reason to believe" that the writing is thus "regularly used."[199] Then the proposer of the form must have "reason to believe" that the signer would not have signed if he had known that a particular term was included; in that event the challenged clause is "not part of the agreement." This solution needs to be closely studied before its extreme ingenuity becomes apparent. The test seems strict—whether the particular signer would have rejected the entire transaction, not just one clause—and the probe seems to go deep into the signer's psyche: what would he have done if he had known of the term? But not so, and for a very good reason. As the Reporter explained at the Institute meeting, the virtue of the formula proposed was that "it doesn't require the impossible showing of what the party would have done if. . . . I think it's an impossible burden of proof to put on somebody that he would have refused to sign if he had known about this."[200] So the burden is shifted to the opposite party, who can hardly know the signer's psyche as well as the signer himself, and the test is whether the opposite party had "reason" to believe, not what he did believe. It would be especially in standardized transactions that the proposer of the form would have no basis whatever for any belief as to the signer's reaction in the imagined

---

(1943). One author, finding the phrase "wonderfully descriptive," used it to resolve an important semantic problem: the Restatement says that contract law does not require "bargaining," only "bargains," but standardized form transactions in which there is no bargaining can nevertheless be called "bargains" (therefore contracts) since the signer "adheres." Meyer, Contracts of Adhesion and the Doctrine of Fundamental Breach, 50 Va.L.Rev. 1178, 1179–80 (1964). The phrase is no doubt helpful if it brings peace of mind on such questions. How unhelpful it can be made to be is convincingly shown by Slawson, supra note 194, at 549–56.

198. Schwartz, Seller Unequal Bargaining Power and the Judicial Process, 49 Ind. L.J. 367, 384–86 (1974). The argument that appears before the passage cited is mainly concerned with sellers' disclaimers of warranty, and shows how immensely difficult it would be to establish a connection between such clauses when used and superior market power, even where oligopoly can be shown to exist.

199. Restatement (Second) of Contracts § 237(1) (Tent. Draft 1973). Why the signer is thus chosen is not at all clear. It would seem more important that the proponent have "reason to believe" this. Perhaps the object was equal treatment, giving both of them something that they would have "reason to believe."

200. Quoted in Murray, The Parol Evidence Process and Standardized Agreements Under the Restatement (Second) of Contracts, 123 U.Pa.L.Rev. 1342, 1378 (1975).

case. The basis for finding "reason to believe" will, almost always be the terms of the transaction itself. Then the whole process was depersonalized still further by requiring, "wherever reasonable," that the writing be interpreted "as treating alike all those similarly situated," without regard to the actual knowledge or understanding that the signers had in fact.[201]

These expert adaptations of the familiar, much used phrases no doubt carried the Institute as far as it could go in detaching standardized forms from the law of contract. The purpose must have been clear to all concerned. A term that is declared "not part" of the standardized form is presumably denied all legal effect and simply disappears. What the draftsmen of section 237 themselves had in mind is indicated by their own comment on how the proposer's "reason to believe" is to be ascertained: It "may be shown by the prior negotiations or inferred from the circumstances. Reason to believe may be inferred from the fact that the term is bizarre or oppressive, from the fact that it eviscerates the non-standard terms explicitly agreed to, or from the fact that it eliminates the dominant purpose of the transaction."[202] The draftsmen also point out that the second Restatement has its own "good faith" clause[203] and they also point to its "unconscionability" clause, which is U.C.C. 2–302 almost verbatim.[204] But in the Restatement it appears as a principle and a grant of judicial power applying to all contracts, not merely sales of goods. The American Law Institute, it seems, has done its best to equip our courts with general clauses.

Notes and Questions

1. In 1976, as Dawson had predicted, the German legislature adopted a statute to deal with standard form contracts. The Law on Standard Contract Terms, which went into effect in 1977, was essentially a codification of the existing case law on the subject. In two respects, however, the statute went beyond the principles developed in the case law. First, it listed a number of types of clauses which are prohibited entirely and classified others as prohibited unless reasonable. Second, it gave certain types of associations the right to sue to compel the withdrawal from use of such prohibited terms in standard contracts. The statute is described in detail in von Marschall, The New German Law on Standard Contract Terms, 3 Lloyd's Maritime and Commercial Law Quarterly 278 (1979).

---

201. Restatement (Second) of Contracts § 237(2) (Tent. Draft 1973). In justifying this provision, Reporter Braucher almost invoked the equal protection clause of the fourteenth amendment: "when you have a standardized agreement, one of the things about it is that it's supposed to be standard, and treat everybody the same way." Murray, supra note 200, at 1387.

Professor Murray condemns § 237 totally for its departure from tests of signer's assent. He concedes that assent can be impaired by "lack of awareness," and also "lack of choice." If the signer is aware of the questioned term, then the only other ground for attack must be the other party's power to dictate terms, a power he considers to be usually present since standardized form contracts are "contracts of adhesion." Murray, supra note 200, at 1372–89.

202. Restatement (Second) of Contracts § 237, comment (f) (Tent. Draft 1973).

203. Id. § 231: "Every contract imposes upon each party a duty of good faith and fair dealing in its performance and its enforcement."

204. Id. § 234. The cross references are in id. § 237, comment (c).

2. Prior to the 1976 statute, the German courts developed their approach to the problem of standard terms with very little guidance from the legislature. The manner in which they did this illuminates the function of the general clauses within the legal system. It also illustrates how the courts were able to innovate boldly in the area of contract law without undermining either the regime of free contract or confidence in their own authority. Dawson's analysis of why they were able to successfully achieve this is as follows: [5]

> To provide warrant for judges to innovate is precisely the function of general clauses and it is hard to imagine how a codified system could work unless loopholes of this kind were provided. This should occasion no surprise, especially for us who not only expect but actively encourage our judges to be "creative," and we are entirely content when the new law they make is ascribed to an independent authority of their own. It is only when the authority is conferred by a statute (like U.C.C., section 2–302) that the hackles of some persons rise high. In Germany, however, debate could not arise over the propriety of using general clauses in this way but only as to the rate and the scale of judge-made change. If the new inventions, ascribed to good morals and good faith, were to pile up and spread out too rapidly and at random, disruption and disorder were quite sure to result. This, very clearly, has not occurred. The key question, which a trained and responsible group of judges must have had in mind, was whether the German legal order as a whole had means to assimilate the new ideas, some radically new, the many complications and refinements that the judges through their own exposures found to be both rational and needed.

> The means for restoring order could obviously not be supplied by the judges alone but must be drawn as well from the environment that surrounded them. This environment should be briefly sketched, mainly to contrast it with the working conditions of American law. Germany (since 1945, West Germany) has been since 1900 a unitary state most of whose legislation applies nationwide and whose judiciary, unlike our own, is organized in a career service with promotion from within. The judiciary is controlled by a single supreme court, whose jurisdiction is also nationwide, so that judges in the end can be made to speak with one voice, not the fifty, often discordant voices in fifty independent state hierarchies plus the overarching hierarchy of federal courts. So in Germany a highly expert critical literature can concentrate on one coherent body of legislation and decisional law. The quality of this literature contrasts sharply with that of our own legal writing, whose volume alone is enough to ensure that it will remain diffuse and uneven in quality. The vigor and clarity of German legal writing are due of course to many factors but overwhelmingly the most important is the one I have stressed—the continuing commitment of German courts and lawyers to the grand design for a legal order that was constructed by German nineteenth century legal science, that was then expressed in shorthand in the Civil Code of 1900, and has been adjusted, refined and perfected ever since. It may even be that this grand design has retained

5. Dawson, supra note 1 at 1122–24.

its appeal precisely because courts have discovered, through the general clauses, so many avenues of escape. But the systematics on which the Code originally rested have been well learned; they are the common property of all German lawyers. It was surely the discipline implanted by these modes of thought that has induced the strenuous efforts of courts and legal scholars in more recent times to connect up and assimilate the multi-farious new elements, to identify "types" (of fact situation or remedial solution), above all to define the directions taken. In all these efforts legal scholarship has played a most essential role....

So my own conclusion, which falls short of an explanation, will seem on first view to be a paradox—that the boldness and wealth of judicial innovation were an expression of continued confidence in the institutions, methods and disciplines of German law and that without this confidence innovation on such a scale could not have occurred. The thought could be expressed in a metaphor, that judges felt free to wander far afield because within the inherited system they were thoroughly at home and they were determined to maintain a permanent residence there. It was mainly through the general clauses that they were made free to wander and because of the way the Code's general clauses were phrased the wanderings were ostensibly in pursuit of moral ideals. I may have left the impression that they often wandered out over the horizon. If so, I should pause to correct it.

It is true that the moral standards used by the German general clauses—good morals and good faith—made a difference, just as reinstating "conscience" and "good faith" as standards for our courts may make a difference for us. The power conferred on German courts to compel conformity to good morals must have helped, for example, to remove any hesitation that might otherwise have been felt about resting a restrictive rule ... directly and exclusively on a moral judgment, with little concern for its economic repercussions. And German courts have surely found most congenial, and their influence must have been enhanced by, their role as guardians of the nation's conscience; one cannot easily imagine an American state court thundering forth quite so often: "This transaction offends the conscience and sense of decency of all fair and right-thinking persons in the state of [Maine]." But what needs particular emphasis now is that most of the innovations, though ascribed to high-level moral sources, rose at most to an intermediate level. On a scale of moral values where, for example, would estoppel be placed? German courts found estoppel secluded in the good faith clause (242). They have made good use of it for many different purposes as we have made good use of it, especially lately as a ground for enforcing otherwise unenforceable promises. It has an immediate appeal to even a rudimentary sense of fairness, but no one wants to write it on a wall in bronze. Many useful and definable legal ideas like estoppel, qualifications and refinements by the thousands of other rules and doctrines, provide an abundance that has had to be carefully sifted through and fitted back carefully into the basic scheme. In the process the courts themselves have become highly sophisticated in using caselaw techniques. But the continuity, predictability and coherence of German law could not have been maintained to such a high degree if a close working partnership had not been established long before between a career judiciary and legal scholars, both highly trained in and firmly committed to the same comprehensive and highly ordered system of legal ideas.

* * *

The same effort has been made over the whole enormous range of what I have called Germany's caselaw revolution and, I believe, with remarkable success. The courts could never have accomplished this alone. They have been powerfully reinforced by a highly trained and sophisticated legal profession with which they are engaged in a constant and active interchange. But the central reason for the success achieved has been the training, discipline and conscience of the judiciary itself, which have ensured the durability of the legal system through periods of profound political and social change and protected it against more than surface penetration between 1933 and 1945 when the forces of evil assailed it.

3. Dawson states that standard form contracts pose, for the American legal system, "the most persistent and troublesome problems in our law of exchange transactions, problems that we have made almost no progress toward solving." While praising the German advances in the area of legal regulation of standard form contracts, and observing that Americans may have much to learn from them, Dawson nevertheless expresses doubt about whether American courts could or should try to emulate their German counterparts. Dawson, Unconscionable Coercion: The German Version, 89 Harvard Law Review 1041, 1125–26 (1976). Is such doubt justified? Why or why not?

2. EFFECT OF UNFORESEEN CHANGE OF CONDITIONS ON CONTRACTS [6]

As every American law student knows, the avenues of escape from contractual liability in cases where performance is disrupted by unexpected events were narrow indeed in the classical common law of contracts. When circumstances were such as to justify excuse from further performance, the traditional remedy was discharge of the parties to the contract, sometimes accompanied by restitution.[7] The contract law of the German Civil Code of 1900 was similar. It strictly limited the cases where relief for unforeseen change of conditions was permitted, and restricted relief in those cases to discharge from the contract, combined where necessary with restitution of performance that had already taken place.[8]

---

6. This problem is based on two articles by John P. Dawson: Judicial Revision of Frustrated Contracts: Germany, 63 B.U.L.Rev. 1039 (1983) and Judicial Revision of Frustrated Contracts: The United States, 64 B.U.L.Rev. 1 (1984). Excerpts therefrom are reprinted herein with permission of John P. Dawson.

7. Dawson, Judicial Revision of Frustrated Contracts: Germany, 63 B.U.L.Rev. 1039 (1983).

8. German Civil Code, art. 275: "The obligor becomes free of the duty to perform to the extent that the performance becomes impossible after the obligation arose as a

The modern American law of contracts now permits discharge in a variety of situations where performance has become extremely onerous but not literally impossible.[9] Liberalization has occurred in Germany, too, but in recent years has taken a strikingly different course there. In response to the dislocations caused by the disastrous inflation following World War I, German courts first began to relax the strict rules on impossibility of performance. They purported to derive these decisions from the general good faith clause in Article 242 of the Civil Code: "The obligor is bound to carry out his performance in the manner required by good faith with due regard to prevailing usage." They found in this general language adequate authority for holding that rescission was appropriate when supervening events, such as the great inflation, disrupted the "foundations of the transaction" (*Geschäftsgrundlage*).[10] They also found the good faith clause broad enough to authorize occasional experiments with revising frustrated contracts rather than simply cancelling them.

In dealing with the effects of the depression of the early 1930s on contracts, the German courts continued from time to time to exercise the power to adjust rather than dismantle contracts. Then, in the period after World War II, court-ordered reconstruction ceased to be an occasional remedy and became the "standard and preferred solution" for contracts whose "foundations" had been destroyed or undermined by the occurrence of unexpected events.[11] Dawson has written of this development:

> There was no particular reason why the salvaging-by-revising of disrupted contracts should have become standard procedure at the time it did. Courts in the 1950s were not responding to pressing needs of a society in deep and progressive disorder like that of the early 1920s.[12]

The *Volkswagen* case, discussed by Dawson in the excerpt below, demonstrates the degree to which German courts were prepared to extend and multiply the grounds for revising contracts.

A. THE VOLKSWAGEN CASE

The German Basic Law of 1949 established a new high court of ordinary jurisdiction, the *Bundesgerichtshof,* which began to function in 1950. Several of the early decisions of the new court involved transac-

---

result of a circumstance for which he is not responsible.

"An inability of the obligor to perform, intervening after the obligation arose, is equivalent to impossibility." [The remainder of this article consists mainly of clauses enumerating situations of impossibility in which the obligor remains responsible.]

The Civil Code also contains a special section (art. 537) on leases, excusing a lessee from payment of rent when the asset leased becomes unfit for the purpose of the lease.

9. E.g., Uniform Commercial Code § 2–615; Restatement (Second) of Contracts § 261 (1981).

10. Dawson, Judicial Revision of Frustrated Contracts: Germany, 63 B.U.L.Rev. 1039, 1045–51 (1983).

11. Id. at 1075.

12. Id.

tions which had been disrupted by the war. One of these was the *Volkswagen* case: [13]

The plaintiffs in the case were two buyers who had made payments on Volkswagen cars that they had ordered very shortly before the war, in 1938 or 1939. There were 336,000 other buyers who had also made prepayments to the defendant, a corporation organized in 1937 to manufacture "the people's car." This project had the active support of the German Labor Front, a Nazi organization, and Hitler's own personal endorsement. The money prepaid by prospective buyers, totaling 268 million marks, was deposited by the defendant in a Berlin bank in the name of the German Labor Front. The defendant proceeded to build a factory that with the advent of the war was promptly taken over by the government for war production and was then heavily bombed, with destruction estimated at 65 percent. The money prepaid by the buyers was confiscated by the Russians when they reached Berlin. When the defendant after the war commenced producing automobiles the plaintiffs sued to enforce delivery of the cars they had ordered with the price to be fixed by the court if it was willing. When the case reached an intermediate court of appeal in 1951 that court ordered the action dismissed, declaring that the foundations of the contracts had been destroyed. For the dismissal it gave several reasons:

(1) It would be wrong to order the defendant to deliver a car at the original agreed price of 990 marks, the sale price charged by the defendant having risen in the meantime to 4400 marks;

(2) A court did not have the power to bind both parties to new terms that the court, not the parties, had fixed;

(3) A court did not have the means to organize such an enormous number of separate claims, arrange for the payments that were still required and fix delivery schedules for so many buyers.

The Bundesgerichtshof disagreed. It was willing to assume, as were both of the parties, that the foundations of these contracts had indeed been destroyed. But, the high court said, this did not necessarily lead to their termination. "In law one must start from the premise that contracts are to be performed." It was necessary to inquire whether the contracts could be adjusted to the changed situation. "The courts by virtue of article 242 are authorized when the foundations of a transaction have been destroyed to intervene in a contract relation and extensively reshape it. The duties expressed in the contract can in such a case be very considerably changed to the extent this is needed in order to ensure that performance will serve those interests of both parties that deserve to be considered." The lower court had apparently had the misconception that it must be able by its decree to alter the obligations of other buyers who had made their own separate contracts and were not parties to this action. This, as it said, the lower court could not do but clearly it was not necessary. The contracts of the other 336,000 buyers

13. The following is an excerpt from Dawson, Id. at 1083–87.

were relevant in this case only in deciding what performance could fairly be demanded by these two plaintiffs from the defendant. It was for this reason that it was important to know how many other buyers since the war ended had asserted claims under their contracts, how many were able to make the payments that were still due from them, how many in view of the time that had elapsed did not want cars after all and wanted only their money back. With such claims for restitution there would be the question whether they should be awarded for the full amount paid or like other debts that had been incurred before 1948 must be cut down to one-tenth of the original amount and converted at the rate of 1 mark for 10. The lower court must also ascertain whether the defendant had used the money paid in by the buyers to acquire other assets or profits. In order to determine what price the plaintiffs would be required to pay the trial court would need to discover the actual cost of production for a Volkswagen car (on this issue the parties to this case had made contradictory assertions), the present rate of production at the defendant's plant, whether or not this rate could be increased and what percentage of its annual production could be assigned to filling the pre-war contracts without endangering the defendant's economic survival. It was important that the defendant's plant be ordered to produce the maximum number of cars since the trial court must set a deadline for performance of the pre-war contracts in order to ensure that their performance would not be too far prolonged into the distant future.[108]

The trial judge to whom the case was returned must have had the sensation that he was wandering lonely as a cloud among the daffodils as he set about performing these multifarious tasks. He had been told to find out what had happened to 336,000 persons who had bought Volkswagen cars twelve to thirteen years before, six of those years having brought death and migration of Germans on an enormous scale. After the living survivors or the heirs of the dead had been located he would have to send out questionnaires to learn whether they could pay for the new, much more expensive post-war models or preferred to have their money repaid. While the 336,000 buyers were being located and polled the judge could keep busy enough assembling data on the defendant's current production costs, which varied with each model of car, what rate of profit he should allow, whether to give the defendant credit for any of the highly variable overhead costs it had incurred before, during and after the war and whether to take account of the sacrifices of the buyers who had had to wait so long for their cars, how much credit to give the buyers for the payments made before the war that had long since been appropriated by the Russians. Unless the judge was fully experienced in industrial management he would need much help in deciding how great an increase in defendant's production he could safely order, how much added cost (say, through overtime payments) the defendant could afford, whether it would be wise merely to order defendant to postpone delivery on some of its post-war orders while the prewar contracts were being performed and what this would do to defendant's place in the competi-

---

108. 1952 JZ 145 (BGH Oct. 23, 1951).

tive economy of Germany whose rapid and diversified growth was just beginning. Whatever controls over the defendant's deliveries were found to be needed would probably have to be maintained for years to come, for the defendant's incentives to perform the pre-war contracts were not likely to rise any higher at some future time. And it did seem reasonable that a deadline be set, so that buyers to whom cars were to be delivered under mandatory court order would acquire them sometime, at least, before the next war started.

Criticism in Germany of this astonishing case has seemed to me extremely mild. Probably the strongest came from one noted author who merely asked a question—whether the unearthing of so enormous a volume of inaccessible facts and the complexity of the judgment called for in controlling the defendant's production did not require resources far beyond those available to any court.[109] But a more basic question would be—why should such a monumental, unmanageable task be undertaken at all? The high court gave only one reason which it evidently thought sufficient to allay all doubts: "In law it is a basic premise that contracts should be performed." And indeed this short statement might be read as expressing much more than elementary morality. In societies that so greatly depend on private self-regulation through contract it could be thought essential to ensure that the choices made in this way become effective. Wholly laudable though this proposition might therefore be, there would remain one other question— whether it had anything whatever to do with the case. The proposition appeared in the court's opinion not long after its statement that in the court's view (also that of the parties) the foundations of these contracts had been destroyed. This was a figure of speech rendered colorless by constant use, but it did suggest how completely these contracts to make and deliver Volkswagen cars had been wiped out by a series of catastrophes. So the transactions that the high court instructed the trial judge to concoct could be called "contracts" only by way of euphemism and should be contained by quotation marks—the terms for model, price, production year, dates for payment and delivery that a tormented trial judge was ordered to formulate after prolonged and painful effort. This was more clear, no doubt, in the Volkswagen case than in most others because the effort might have to be made on so great a scale. Whether the scale is large or small the "adjustment" of frustrated contracts by courts, as it now operates in German law, does not reinforce or vindicate freedom of contract; the effect is to restrict it. Reinforced is only the power of courts to dictate terms that they themselves invent; no assent by anyone is needed and all dissent is ignored.

In the Volkswagen case itself the two buyers, plaintiffs, had acquiesced in advance in the new and higher price that they had expected

---

109. K. Larenz, Geschäftsgrundlage und Vertragserfüllung 1120–21 (3d ed. 1963). The comment on the decision by G. Kegel, following the text of the opinion as reported in 1952 JZ 147 (1952), offered only the objection that the court should have given some attention to his view that when the foundation of a transaction had been destroyed all gains and losses to either party should be evenly split.

the court to fix.[110]   "Contracts" that were entirely involuntary were to be imposed on the seller only; as to the seller it was clear that it was bound to deliver when the buyers had complied with the terms made up by a court.   And other high court decisions were soon to remove any lingering doubt as to whether a court order could create or increase an obligation to pay without assent newly expressed by the one obligated. . . .

These powers were taken so fully for granted that after 1950 one does not find examples of the evasive tactic that was used in the 1920s during the early stages of court-ordered revision—a short interlude during which the parties were given the opportunity and were encouraged to adjust the transaction by their own agreement.   If in this they did not succeed, one could resort to the pretext that their decision not to agree was the expression of a preference for an "adjustment" devised by a court.   Such transparent pretexts were no longer needed.   Almost everyone by now had become persuaded that it was enough if the parties had failed to provide for the contingency that had thrown their transactions awry.   This of itself produced a gap that it was the duty of courts to fill.

That contracts whose foundations have been destroyed by unexpected events or discoveries will be revised by court order, not rescinded, has become standard doctrine, repeated in many dozens of cases.   In West German decisions reported in the last 30 years I have found no dissent.   One qualifying phrase is often added—when revision is feasible.   By this phrase it is intended, I believe, to exclude situations in which completion of the performances intended in at least rough correspondence with the original design had been altogether prevented, no matter what remedial measures were used.   Such situations are not infrequent.   Illustrations would be a sale in which the subject of the sale has become permanently unusable for the intended purpose [112] or a human agent essential in the performance planned has died and can not be replaced.[113]   There was another sense in which it might be thought that revision was not feasible—if the difficulties and costs in administering judicial remedies would make them sure to fail, would greatly impair their effectiveness or would be out of proportion to the ends that might be gained.   It is on such grounds that in Anglo–American law, courts empowered to give

110.   As described by the court the request of the plaintiff was for delivery "after payment of a sum in an amount and at rates to be fixed by a court." 1952 JZ 145 (1952).

112.   1976 NJW 565 (BGH 1975), sale between club owners of the right to the services of a professional football player who had already accepted a bribe to "throw" a game to an opposing club.   For this he was, after the sale, permanently excluded from playing football by the regulating authorities, so that the "adjustment" usually awarded had to be denied.

113.   1974 MDR 401 (OLG Frankfurt 1973).   This was a sale of chinchillas to be bred for the sale of their fur in what was apparently a profit-sharing enterprise calling for considerable expertise.   After the chinchillas had been delivered the manager of the chinchilla farm, the buyer, died leaving eight minor children, none of whom, strangely enough, was interested in propagating more chinchillas, and no one else was willing.   No "adjustment" was attempted.

equitable relief can deny it, especially specific performance of contract; it would be on such grounds that most of the specific relief that the high court approved in the Volkswagen case surely would have been denied by an American court.   But one would have to look far to find a German case (I have found none) in which the difficulties, uncertainties or costs of manufacturing new terms for frustrated contracts are mentioned as reasons for refusing to undertake the task.

B.   FURTHER DEVELOPMENT OF COURT–ORDERED AD-JUSTMENT OF CONTRACTS IN GERMANY [c]

The revision of contracts that German courts undertook in the 1920s was in the form of changes, almost always upward, in the amounts to be paid in obligations to pay money where money had been promised in exchange for performance of other kinds.   Since 1950 this is still the most common form.   Contract revision can be accomplished, however, in such varied forms as the correction of a document or the transfer or division of particular physical assets.   In reviewing the means that courts have used since 1950 a different question will also arise: where the "adjustments" needed are relatively minor can they be made for minor disruptions that would be entirely insufficient if cancellation of the transaction were the remedy sought?   I believe the reader will be persuaded that this is often the case, that the foundations of a transaction do not need by any means to be reduced to rubble in order for a court to order a correction to offset the effect of an unforeseen event.

Before moving on to the means ordinarily used we should pause for a moment to consider the question whether contract revision can take the form of substituting an entirely different physical subject matter for one that was promised but that could no longer be delivered.   The answer, I believe, is that German courts can do this but rarely do.   The reason for thinking they can is that in one case this is what the Bundesgerichtshof did.   A tract of farm land had been leased to a city-dweller who evidently wished to escape into the open spaces.   He contracted with a builder, defendant in the case, for the erection of a prefabricated house on this land.   To everyone's surprise the local housing officer of the district then refused a permit to erect a housing structure on it.   On first sight this case seemed clear; old-fashioned impossibility of performance would entitle the plaintiff to recover his down payment by way of restitution and this was the remedy the plaintiff sought.   But the defendant builder introduced evidence to show that there was other land some distance away owned by another owner who was willing to lease it to the plaintiff at a rent no higher.   The evidence showed that a building permit could without doubt be secured for this land and that it had air as fresh and a view as good as the land the plaintiff had selected as the building site.   Testimony also showed

c.   Dawson, Judicial Revision of Frus-   1039, 1088–94 (1983).
trated Contracts: Germany, 63 B.U.L.Rev.

that the plaintiff, while the parties were negotiating, had said that his object was to live on land with a good view whose air was clear. The high court concluded that if the defendant proved these contentions when the case was remanded to the trial court the plaintiff would be required to accept his offer and the contract as thus revised would be enforced.[111]

A series of cases in which the revision took one of the usual forms—such as increasing the money price a buyer must pay—may as well begin with a case in which this common form of revision was on a most uncommon ground that the court did not try to explain. Its centerpiece was a large family farm that had remained in the same peasant family for more than three hundred years (since the Thirty Years' War). The plaintiff had married its owner who died in 1946, leaving a life interest in the farm to the plaintiff and the succession thereafter to the defendant, his son by a former marriage.[115] Defendant took possession and control of the farm. Then in 1952 plaintiff, the widow, decided to remarry. She conveyed her interest in the farm to defendant in return for a life-time annuity of 2160 marks a year. The defendant continued to live on and operate the farm until 1962 when he sold it to a corporation for a considerable sum—1,465,000 marks. The report of the case does not indicate that this sale violated any restrictions in the contract itself (or indeed existing anywhere else) on the defendant's power to sell to an outsider. But the high court described the sale as wholly unexpected and said that it produced an "unbearable" disparity between the payments that the plaintiff was to receive for her interest (2160 marks a year for life) and the price that defendant was to be paid, so as to destroy the foundation of the contract. The remedy, however, was not rescission. The defendant must pay a higher price for the interest that the plaintiff had transferred to him ten years before. The trial court was directed to determine what price persons "thinking honorably" would have agreed to accept and pay for her interest if a later sale of the farm to a stranger had been anticipated. From the trial judge this called for a flight of fancy but it was no doubt the only way for the widow to share in her stepson's new wealth, since it is still harder to imagine any ground on which the sale of her interest could itself have been rescinded.[116] One attraction, then, of court-ordered "adjustment"

---

114. 1966 JZ 409 (BGH 1966). A different view was taken, however, in 1972 JZ 120 (OLG Karlsruhe 1971), which involved a contract to deliver over a period of ten years a large quantity of coal (936,000 tons) to be produced in three designated mines in the Ruhr. When the three mines were permanently closed because of their high production costs, the seller offered but was not allowed to deliver coal of the same quality produced at other mines. In dicta the court added that similarly the buyer if he had desired it, could not have demanded coal from other mines.

115. 1972 NJW 152 (BGH 1971). In fact the husband's will had named two sons by the former marriage but one son had died before the transactions that caused all the trouble.

116. 1972 NJW 152 (BGH 1971). Hardest to imagine would be the reason why the widow, who sold her interest when she decided to remarry, would have the slightest concern over whether the family farm remained in the family of a husband who had died years before. Even if a transaction is merely to be "adjusted" its foundation is supposed to have suffered one small tremor, at least.

seems to be that it enables courts to protect interests that in any other kind of proceeding would have to be disregarded.[117]

* * *

So far our concern has been mostly with court-ordered revision that leads to new or additional obligation. Scaling down—or refusing to enforce—an obligation that is enforceable by the usual tests might seem to be for a court less venturesome. The Bundesgerichtshof showed very soon—two years after it had begun to function—that it was equally ready for radical experiments in this other direction. In 1952 it confronted a dispute between two owners of large landed estates in East Germany in an area then held by German armies though it was later conquered by the Russians. On his estate the plaintiff had grown sugar beets that he sold in 1944 to the defendant, who on his land operated a factory for extracting sugar from sugar beets. The factory duly processed the plaintiff's beets and the defendant sold the sugar. The plaintiff (seller) brought an action to recover the proceeds of the sale but before the action could come to trial the Russians confiscated almost all the assets that the defendant owned, leaving him with a tract of 45 acres on which he was trying to scratch out a living. The lower court invoked the "good faith" clause and dismissed the action, giving as its reason that the defendant should not have to pay for the beets after he had lost almost everything else. The high court decided that this went too far, agreeing that article 242, the "good faith" clause, applied to the case but not that it dictated a total discharge. The trial court was instructed to inquire whether it could not scale down and postpone payment so as to enable the defendant to pay some part of his debt if his economic position were later to improve. The high court ended with the usual peroration—the trial court must first assemble more facts.[124]

"Good faith" could also lead to a reduction of debt in strictly mundane transactions in settled times, such as a sale of a second-hand car whose odometer had been altered so as to record incorrectly the

---

117. An example of a quite different kind was 1953 JZ 735 (BGH 1953), where leniency generated by the "good faith" clause was extended to the third parties who might otherwise have suffered some adverse effects. The case mainly concerned a conveyance made in 1942 by one brother to another of a family homestead, in return for the assumption by the grantee of some obligations owed by the grantor to other relatives. The nearest thing to a foundation of the transaction was an expectation on the part of the grantee (but so far as the case showed, not mentioned in their discussions) that the grantor, who was about to join the army, would make his fortune in the army or "in the east." By April, 1945, the adventurous brother found, like millions of other Germans, that his prospects for making his fortune in the army, "the

east," or indeed any place within his reach were indeed grim. So he returned home and sued to recover the estate conveyed in 1942 from the son and heir of his brother (the brother having in the interval died). The court concluded that the plaintiff was entitled to this, though he would be required to make payments to the son and to the dead brother's widow, to whom the brother's will had ordered money payments. Or perhaps, the court said, the farm could be divided up and a part assigned to each. It was not that the son and widow had rights they could independently assert but a decree rendered under the "good faith" clause would and should protect the interests of third parties that the decree might otherwise jeopardize in some way.

124. 1953 MDR 26 (BGH 1952).

mileage it had travelled. The evidence indicated that seller and buyer had both been unaware of the alteration, made presumably by a former owner, so a starting point for remedial measures could be mutual mistake as to an existing attribute of the object sold. But to rescind for mistake it would be necessary for the attribute to be essential and without more in the case this would be hard to show. An inquisitive person might also ask whether any seller's warranties applied. In the case in which these issues arose all seller's warranties, express or implied, had been expressly disclaimed, so there was nothing left but the ultimate recourse, the good faith clause. The court was quite ready to accept the conclusion that a foundation of the sale had been undermined though it made no effort to find out how seriously the usefulness of the car to the buyer was impaired by its added mileage. In any case, the court was clear that it preferred to reduce the price (by the amount its sale value was thereby reduced) rather than cancel the sale and return to the seller a car that in the interval had been driven for three more years. So 1800 marks, the reduction in value through the added mileage, had been overpaid by the buyer on the 6000 mark price and could be recovered by him in this action.[125]

One other sale in which the seller was ordered to reduce the price had the unusual—so far as I know, the unique—feature that the one to whom the court order was addressed did not show the usual docile submission but filed a protest. It was a sale of scrap iron in which the buyer was throughout represented by an exceptionally incompetent agent, described only as *G*. *G*. went to the yard manager of the plaintiff, a dealer in metals, and stated the quantity of scrap iron the buyer wanted without disclosing the purpose (ship ballast) for which the scrap iron would be used. The yard manager quoted *G*. a price of 250 marks for the first delivery, then 290 marks a ton for each later delivery. *G.*, knowing his own total ignorance of metal prices, did not inquire of any other supplier and agreed to buy at those figures. The scrap iron was delivered. It then turned out that the seller's yard-manager understood that the buyer desired a superior grade of scrap—"usable" scrap—and this was the grade that the seller delivered. *G*. had never heard of any distinctions in grades of scrap and in negotiations the question of grade was never raised, though inferior grades costing 98 to 150 marks a ton were entirely suitable for use as ship's ballast. After the buyer had made a small payment on the price the seller sued for the balance, calculated with the figures its yard-manager had quoted. The case almost raised the question whether misunderstanding had prevented formation of a contract but the court passed by this issue without even a nod.[126] It was impressed, however, by the trial court's finding that scrap

125. 1971 JZ 295 (OLG Karlsruhe 1970). The buyer had actually paid the full agreed price, so the remedy had to be recovery of the excess paid—that is, the 1800 marks that the court found to be the reduction in value (from the 6000 mark price) due to the falsified mileage.

126. An advocate of lost causes might have argued that each party had in mind scrap iron of a different grade, the buyer's agent in particular seeking scrap suitable for the buyer's purpose. But the agent had

iron of the higher quality that the seller had delivered was regularly sold by other suppliers for not 290 but 225 marks a ton. So the court concluded that the contract as made was based on a mistake that impaired the foundations of the contract. This, the court said, did not necessarily lead to discharge of the contract but whenever possible to an "adjustment" of its terms. So the most the seller could recover for the scrap iron delivered was the market price, 225 marks a ton.

The seller's protest, briefly summarized by the court, was an appeal to "a free market economy," from which "it derived a right of the parties to fix their prices as they will." The court gave much more space to its own reply: "The truth is that now in conformity with the Constitution the principle that governs is not that of a free but of a social market economy and the plaintiff, as a member of the community that makes it possible for it to conduct its economic affairs unmolested, in security and with success, owes to this community and therefore to its members a corresponding concern and in particular also in fixing prices.... If one wished to concede to every merchant the right to demand what price he pleases, however arbitrary, then good faith would demand that he disclose this to the customer who is unaware that this is occurring, so that the customer can reckon with it." [127]

This was enough, it seems, to quell the spirit of rebellion against court "adjustment" of frustrated contracts. So far as I know, no similar protest has since reappeared.

C. JUDICIAL REVISION OF FRUSTRATED CONTRACTS IN THE UNITED STATES: THE ALCOA CASE

Dawson, in a companion piece to his article on judicial adjustment of contractual relations in Germany,[14] reviewed the development of the traditional American approach to cases of impossibility, frustration of purpose and certain kinds of mistake. He showed how the classical approach was gradually liberalized to permit discharge in cases that fell short of literal impossibility and how courts sometimes revised frustrated contracts by extending standards upon which the contracting parties had already agreed to situations they had not foreseen. He then turned his attention to a group of recent cases in which American courts had been asked to create new substantive provisions without any basis in the parties' own agreement for doing so. This group of cases, discussed in the following excerpt,[15] had in common the fact that performance in each case was alleged to have been seriously disrupted by a widespread increase in the price of some resource that one party needed to have in order to perform.

not disclosed this purpose and the seller had no reason to suspect it.

127. 1963 NJW 1455 (OLG Bremen 1963). The seller still claimed apparently to be an "honorable merchant." He explained the higher price quoted to G. on the ground that the quantity being sold was small enough so that a surcharge of 10 to 20 percent was commonly added to cover higher costs of handling.

14. Dawson, Judicial Revision of Frustrated Contracts: The United States, 64 B.U.L.Rev. 1 (1984).

15. Id. at 23–28.

[These cases] all concerned sales of goods or a service on which the buyer claimed to be so dependent and with performance stretched over a long enough time to make damages for breach hard to calculate. So the buyers in several cases sued for specific performance. This meant that the sellers acquired the seeming advantage of being able to appeal to the discretion of a court exercising "equity" powers, urging it to refuse a remedy within the old equity tradition unless the judge's own standards of good conscience and fairness were fully met by the case before him. From this discretion older decisions had derived a power to impose terms which would not be directly binding on the successful party but with which he must comply in order to secure from the court any aid in enforcing a decree.

This was the dilemma with which the Atlas Corporation sought to confront an Iowa power company to which it had agreed to supply for four years uranium concentrate, to be used for producing nuclear power. The sale price was to rise by small increments from $7.10 a pound in 1975 to $8.45 in 1978. But by 1978 the market price had risen to more than $43.00 a pound and the costs for Atlas of producing it were somewhere in that range. In the year 1976, for example, Atlas claimed that it had incurred a net loss on this contract alone of $1.8 million; larger losses were expected later. To this disaster various factors had contributed, a large increase in wages and other production costs, some of them due to governmental controls aimed at greater safety and environmental protection, but central was a shortage of uranium, leading to higher prices and a decision by Atlas to employ a lower grade. The court was left with questions it could not answer: some, but how much, of Atlas' losses were due to its own decisions, some, but how much, should have been foreseen? It was impossible to track losses to their causes, and a court "cannot pick a price out of the air." So the court granted the specific performance that the buyer had sued for without the "reformation" (price increase) that the seller sought.[57]

There have been other cases in which specific performance sought by buyers has been granted while price revision, even as a mere condition to the remedy granted, was being denied. All the contracts involved commodities whose market price was very likely to rise in response to the sharp rise in the 1970's in petroleum prices. The most emphasized reason for refusing to undertake any price revision was that experienced traders had good reason to foresee a rise in the prices of petroleum and its products. The inclusion in a contract of sale of a clause tied to an index that provided for price escalation was taken to reinforce this conclusion and in the court's view to set limits to the allowance for rises

---

57. Iowa Electric Light & Power Co. v. Atlas Corp., 467 F.Supp. 129 (N.D.Iowa 1978), reversed on other grounds 603 F.2d 1301 (8th Cir.1979), cert. denied 445 U.S. 911, 100 S.Ct. 1090, 63 L.Ed.2d 327 (1980).

in price that the contracting parties had been willing to make.[58] So far as court opinions gave any clues, the fact that these issues arose by way of defense to actions for specific performance did not introduce any different tests than if the supplier were affirmatively suing to secure a discharge. These cases, in other words, in no way suggest the phenomenon so prevalent in West German courts—a readiness to undertake revision of terms in order to "adjust" contracts to unexpected changes— changes that would be entirely insufficient to produce full-scale discharge. If our courts had any such purpose in mind the most plausible way to disguise it would be as a purely defensive maneuver when courts were asked to exercise "equity" powers.

Miscalculation by a supplier reached a new scale of magnitude in the contracts of Westinghouse Electric to supply 49 nuclear power plants with their requirements of uranium. The 27 utilities that owned the sites where these plants were projected wanted assurances before making the necessary huge investment in nuclear plant and equipment, of which Westinghouse was a major supplier. The assurances they received took the form of contracts, mostly made in the early 1970's, for Westinghouse to supply the requirements of uranium for these plants when in operation, at fixed prices—$8.00 or $10.00 (up to $12.00) a pound. They were mostly made in the early 1970's and the market price of uranium began to rise sharply in 1974. In September, 1975, when Westinghouse announced that it could not and would not perform further, the market price approached $40.00 a pound and later went higher. The guesses as to how much Westinghouse would lose if it performed all its contracts for their full terms (on the doubtful assumption they could procure the supplies) started from a base of two billion dollars and went considerably higher. In actions for damages by thirteen power companies, consolidated in a trial that lasted six months, the conclusion reached by the trial judge was that Westinghouse had no sufficient excuse and was liable full scale for expectancy damages.[60] Unfortunately for posterity a reasoned opinion was not filed but this

58. Eastern Air Lines v. Gulf Oil Co., 415 F.Supp. 429, 432–34 (S.D.Fla.1975) (agreement of Gulf to supply Eastern's requirements of jet fuel for 4½ years followed by more than a doubling of the domestic price for oil from newly tapped sources but with Gulf still possessing enough domestic sources to meet these commitments); Publicker Industries v. Union Carbide Co., 17 U.C.C.Rep.Serv. (Callaghan) 989, 990–92 (E.D.Pa.1975) (agreement to supply ethanol for three years with the price of one ingredient almost doubled so as to produce a net loss of $5.8 million); Missouri Public Service Co. v. Peabody Coal Co., 583 S.W.2d 721, 722–23 (Mo.App.1979) (agreement to supply power company its requirements of coal for ten years with price escalation clause using a price index that failed to take account of the increased cost of mine safety so that up to the trial the supplier had lost

$3.4 million), cert. denied 444 U.S. 865, 100 S.Ct. 135, 62 L.Ed.2d 88 (1979).

60. Since this decision has not been reported, the main events have been described only in newspaper reports. The 13 actions for damages brought in different parts of the country were consolidated for trial in Virginia in In re Westinghouse Electric Corp. Uranium Contracts Litigation, 405 F.Supp. 316 (J.P.M.D.L.1975). A useful comment on this aspect appears in Note, In Re Westinghouse: Commercial Impracticibility As A Contractual Defense, 47 UMKC L.Rev. 650 (1979). An excellent account of the economic and legal background and of the astonishing lack of foresight shown by the Westinghouse management is given by Joskow, Commercial Impossibility, The Uranium Market and the Westinghouse Case, 6 J.Legal Stud. 119, 143–50 (1977).

may have been just as well for Westinghouse, since its damage-claim creditors, motivated presumably by their own self-interest in preserving it as a fully functioning enterprise, agreed to settlements that were vastly more lenient than any that a court would have been bold enough to propose.

So the question becomes whether, as the interests at stake rise higher on a scale of magnitude and the complexities of the performances multiply, these are reasons for judges to intervene and impose new terms that to them will seem more workable and fair. This strange inversion of ideas occurred in ... *Aluminum Co. of America v. Essex Group, Inc. (Alcoa),* [where the remedy given] was not damages for losses through performance already completed, but the manufacture of a new price term that was to govern future performance for a potential eight years. The contract thus revised had been made in 1967 by a colossus, the Aluminum Company of American (Alcoa), with another large conglomerate, the Essex Group (Essex), that among other things manufactures metal products. Alcoa undertook for 16 years (extensible by Essex for 5 years more) to smelt specified quantities that Essex supplied of the primary component of aluminum (alumina) and redeliver it to Essex as aluminum.[62] This service was to be performed at a plant owned by Alcoa in Warwick, Indiana.

The price was set at a base figure of 15 cents a pound but included in this total were three components whose prices were variable. One was tied to an index of construction costs nation-wide, another to the costs of labor at the Warwick plant itself, and a third—applied to 3 of the original 15 cents—to an index of wholesale prices for industrial commodities maintained by the United States Department of Labor. The use of this index had been proposed by Alcoa after close study of its past performance had shown that prior to 1967, when the contract was signed, fluctuations in this index had coincided closely with variations in production costs at Alcoa's Warwick plant. For the first seven years after the contract was signed all went well and Alcoa turned a handsome profit on the smelting service it supplied. Then the rise in "non-labor" costs at the Warwick plant, especially the cost of electric energy (a leading element of cost in smelting), exceeded the rise in the Labor Department index, so that in the two years 1977 and 1978 Alcoa lost $12 million, not quite half its profit in the first nine years.[63] For the remaining years Alcoa conjectured that its loss on the contract would exceed $60 million and the judge accepted this estimate though it had no basis in ascertainable facts and was sharply challenged by Essex.

For the evident purpose of opening the way to the "reformation" that Alcoa sought the court strenuously tried to demonstrate that the rise in the cost of energy, occurring years after the contract was formed,

62. Aluminum Co. of America v. Essex Group, Inc., 499 F.Supp. 53 (W.D.Pa.1980).

63. 499 F.Supp. at 59. For the first nine years Alcoa's total profit had slightly exceeded $25 million. In 1977 its loss was $3,415,689.00 and in 1978 $8,620,504.00 for a total of $12,036,193.00. It could hardly be contended that until that point Alcoa had suffered severely.

was a mistake of fact. It was as much a mistake of present fact, I would say, as though at the time two parties agreed on the rental for one day of rooms from which a royal procession could be observed, both parties had believed the king to be a vigorous outdoor type with a strong resistance to colds though later, on the crucial day, a bad cold forced him to stay home in his palace in bed. Describing the parties' miscalculation as a mistake of present fact would change nothing in the case and most certainly would not confer on a court a power to reduce the rent to the sum it found the rented space to be worth for looking out on empty streets. In the *Alcoa* case, I believe, the court was misled by a leading treatise in drawing the inference that for reformation there is no need for an enforceable contract to which the writing was intended and can be made to conform. The court did concede that in the case before it any such purpose could not be accomplished for the contract had said precisely what the parties had intended it to say. But the court flatly rejected "the hoary maxim" that the courts will not make a contract for the parties. So it ordered that the complex scheme for price determination approved by the parties, tied to three price indices, was to be entirely replaced by one invented by the court and shifting completely to a cost-plus basis. Under its scheme the costs of production incurred during each quarter at the Warwick plant were all to be added up after each quarter had ended and Essex was then to pay prices that would ensure to Alcoa for all the aluminum it delivered a profit of one cent a pound.

The judge claimed that in reaching out for this bizarre solution he was inspired by becoming modesty: "the court willingly concedes that the managements of Alcoa and Essex are better able to conduct their business than is the court." But he claimed also that his information, being derived from hindsight, was "far superior" to that of the parties when they had made their contract and that a rule precluding adjustments by courts would have had "the perverse effect" of discouraging the parties from resolving this dispute or future disputes on their own. Only slightly paraphrased, this suggestion seems to mean that when basic provisions are revised by a judge, who knows only what he can learn from presiding at a trial, the result will probably be so unacceptable to both parties that by their own agreement they will reject the dictated terms and reassert the right that they fortunately still retain, to recover control over their own affairs. If that was his object it was soon realized in the *Alcoa* case. The judge's decree was appealed and after argument had been heard in the Court of Appeals for the Third Circuit but before that court could decide, a settlement was reached, Alcoa's action to "reform" was voluntarily dismissed and Alcoa surrendered any rights it had acquired under the trial court decree.

This is, I believe, the only instance in which an American court has claimed power to recast by its own direct order, without some transparent disguise like "reformation," an essential term in an exchange that was still in progress when some unforeseen external event produced major imbalance.

Notes and Questions

1. Dawson, analyzing the development of modern German and American law in cases where unforeseen change precludes further enforcement of a contract, concludes that the readiness with which German courts will undertake to impose changes in the contract upon the parties in order to permit performance to continue constitutes "one of the ways in which the German legal system diverges sharply now from our own." Judicial Revision of Frustrated Contracts: Germany, 63 Boston University Law Review 1039, 1039–40 (1983).

2. Should American courts follow along the road their German counterparts and the district judge in the *Alcoa* case have taken? Professor Speidel apparently would give a qualified affirmative answer for cases involving "long-term supply contracts." Applying a relational approach to contract law, he postulates that in such contracts the parties have a duty to preserve and even to adjust the contractual relationship, a duty which includes an obligation to "bargain in good faith" for revisions when unforeseen change produces "unfair" advantage to one party and corresponding detriment to the other. The sanction for a failure to bargain in good faith, according to Speidel, should be that the court could impose "equitable" terms proposed by the disadvantaged party but rejected by the advantaged party. The problem with the *Alcoa* case, from Speidel's point of view, was only that the court there did not provide the parties with an interval during which they were encouraged to renegotiate the terms of their own agreement. Speidel, *Court–Imposed Price Adjustments Under Long–Term Supply Contracts*, 76 Northwestern Law Review 369, 404–19 (1981).

3. How would you answer the following questions raised by Dawson concerning the *Alcoa* case, the German approach to frustration of performance, and Speidel's position: (1) What would be the likely effect of a broad judicial power to rewrite contract terms upon the reliability and utility of contracts in our society? (2) What in the background, training and experience of a judge enables him to reconcile the divergent interests of the parties and devise terms to govern their future relationship better than the parties themselves? (3) From what source does a judge derive the power to impose a new contract on the parties? For Dawson's full critique of the judicial assumption of power to revise contracts, see Judicial Revision of Frustrated Contracts: The United States, 64 Boston University Law Review 1, 30–39 (1984).

4. How do you explain Dawson's enthusiasm for the bold innovations made by German courts in dealing with standard form contracts and his harsh criticism of the direction they took with frustrated contracts? What, if anything, is different about the two forms of innovation? Consider, in this connection, the view of the role of courts expressed in Dawson, The General Clauses, Viewed from a Distance, which appears at the end of Chapter 5 supra.

5. Stating that the common law approach to frustration of contracts is too rigid, while the rule developed in Germany is "dangerously open to subjective manipulation," Professor Baade writes:

> The obvious way out is a well-drafted *force majeure* clause, spelling out not only the nature of subsequent events entitling the disadvantaged

party to a readjustment, but also the consequences of such disturbances in the equivalence of the contractual relationship. (No sane business-man wants the wooden remedy for frustration, which is simply the excuse of performance.)

Baade, Comparative Law and the Practitioner, 31 Am.J.Comp.Law 499, 510 (1983).

How easy is this solution? How should such a clause be drafted? See Hawkland, The Energy Crisis and Section 2–615 of the Uniform Commercial Code, 79 Commercial L.J. 75 (1974) and Hurst, Drafting Contracts in an Inflationary Era, 28 U.Fla.L.Rev. 879 (1976) for discussion of some of the problems.

Chapter 7

EUROPEAN LAW AND
INSTITUTIONS

In the last few decades, transnational organizations have increasingly affected the legal systems of each of the individual states of Europe. Participation in these political and legal structures has added significant new dimensions to Continental legal traditions. The relevant institutional actors and their respective political roles, the tools and methods of legal culture, and even the normative foundations of national and international law are all affected. The two most far reaching regimes in this respect have been those founded by the Treaties establishing the European Communities, and by the Convention for the Protection of Human Rights and Fundamental Freedoms.

SECTION 1. THE EUROPEAN COMMUNITY

The European Community was born in the wake of European collapse and instability after World War II. Implementing a plan proposed by the French Foreign Minister, Robert Schuman, six European states (Belgium, the Federal Republic of Germany, France, Italy, Luxembourg, and the Netherlands) joined in 1951 to pool their coal and steel industries under the jurisdiction of a supranational High Authority. The Treaty of the European Coal and Steel Community (ECSC), which took effect the following year, was followed in 1957 by the Treaties of Rome, which established the European Atomic Energy Community (Euratom) and the European Economic Community (EEC).[1] Together, the Treaties establishing the European Community sought to create a single, common market in Europe and, more broadly, to bring the European states into ever closer union.

The original six states of the European Community were joined by Denmark, Ireland and the United Kingdom in 1973. Greece acceded to

---

1. Although no formal merger of these three Communities, each with its own foundational treaty, has ever taken place, they have the same membership, common institutions, and the common goal of closer European integration. Accordingly, even though legally still the "European Communities," in political reality as well as common usage they are the "European Community," and that designation will be used here also. Since the 1993 Maastricht Trea-

the Community in 1981, and Spain and Portugal in 1986, bringing the total membership in the Community to 12 States. In recent years, another eight states have applied for membership in the European Community (Turkey, Austria, Cyprus, Malta, Sweden, Finland and Switzerland and Norway [2]), but no new membership is expected to be completed before 1996. Just as significant as the geographic expansion of the Community has been its broadening functional scope. The ECSC and Euratom were essentially restricted to specific economic sectors. The EEC was broader in its aims, but still limited principally to economic liberalization. Gradually, however, the Member States have yielded their sovereignty to give the Community extensive authority over other related matters, such as social, environmental and regional matters. Most recently, the Community has taken large steps toward monetary and political union with the entry into force of the Maastricht Treaty on European Union in November, 1993. Even prior to the Treaty on European Union, however, the European Community had already become an extremely important part of the political and legal landscape of its Member States in a broad range of areas.

A. INSTITUTIONS OF THE EUROPEAN COMMUNITY

The Council of Ministers

The Council is responsible for making the major policy decisions of the Community. Consisting of one representative of each of the Member States (usually the minister of the central government responsible for the particular matters under consideration, such as Agriculture or Labor), the Council meets regularly in Brussels. Although legally a single institution, in practice the Council meets in a variety of specialized groups which are responsible for certain types of issues. For instance, the General Affairs Council is concerned with external relations and broad institutional and policy matters; the Economic and Financial Affairs Council deals with coordination of Member States' economic policies; other Council groups focus on matters such as agriculture, the environment, transportation or the budget of the Community. As a whole, the Council is assisted in its work by a Committee of Permanent Representatives (COREPER), which coordinates the Council's multiple decision-making meetings, and a general secretariat with a staff of about 2000 people. The Presidency of the Council rotates among its members, each of the States holding it for a period of six months.

In general, the Council is the Community's principal lawmaking body.[3] With regard to all but a few areas of high political sensitivity which require unanimity, such as taxation or the rights and interests of workers, the Council reaches decisions by a majority vote. Where there is no express provision to the contrary, a simple majority, with each

ty on European Union, another common designation is "European Union (EU)."

2. The accession of Norway had been attempted in 1973, but was rejected by voters in a national referendum.

3. With regard to the ECSC, however, the Council only deals with a few particularly important decisions.

State having one vote, suffices. More often, however, including in such important areas as the establishment and functioning of the internal market, research and technological development or the environment, a "qualified majority" is required. This procedure, laid down by the Treaties, accords more voting power to larger states than small ones: France, Germany, Italy and the United Kingdom each have ten votes; Spain has eight; Belgium, Greece, the Netherlands and Portugal have five votes apiece; and Luxembourg has two. Of these 76 total votes, 54 are required for a decision.

The European Commission

Although the Council is responsible for adopting Community legislation, it has had to depend on the Commission to draft and present legislative proposals. This "right of initiative" has been inferred from the numerous Treaty provisions that authorize the Council to act "on a proposal of the Commission." However, under the Treaty of European Union, the Commission's right to initiative is no longer exclusive; with regard to common foreign and security policies, and cooperation in judicial and home affairs, the Member States now have concurrent and, in some cases, exclusive, powers to initiate action to be taken by the Council.

The Commission has other important functions as well, foremost among them being the responsibility to enforce Community norms. Considered the guardian of the Treaties, the Commission ensures that their provisions, as well as the measures adopted by the Community institutions, are properly implemented. It has the power to refer cases to the Court of Justice when this is not done, and in some circumstances can grant Member States temporary waivers or derogations from Community rules. In certain areas such as competition law, the Commission has broad investigative powers and the authority to impose fines on individuals or companies in breach of Community regulations.

Finally, the Commission has a quasi-executive responsibility to implement Community policies. The Commission's primary executive powers apply to certain specific economic sectors or activities, including coal and steel, nuclear energy and competition policy. In other areas, the Commission's executive functions are derived from the Council, including the creation of administrative rules for the implementation of Council decisions, the negotiation of treaties and trade agreements and representation of the Community in international organizations, or the management of agricultural markets. In addition, the Commission manages most of the Community budget, through funds and common policies supporting, for instance, the modernization of agriculture, regional development and employment programs, scientific research and international aid to less developed countries.

In exercising their responsibilities, the members of the Commission, unlike members of the Council, are required to be independent of any government or other body, and to act solely in the interests of the Community as a whole. They are appointed by the "common accord" (i.e., unanimity, with no abstentions) of the governments of the Member States, subject to the consent of the European Parliament, for a period of five years. Although the Council has the power to change the number of members of the Commission, it is currently fixed at 17, which in practice has meant that there has been at least one Commissioner from each Member State, with a second from each of the five larger Member States. In its work, the Commission is supported by over 14,000 civil servants in Brussels and Luxembourg, divided into 23 departments, or Directorates–General, responsible for specific policy areas.

The European Parliament

Designated the "Assembly" in the founding treaties, the European Parliament adopted its current name for itself in 1958, and the change was officially recognized by amendment of the Treaties in 1986. It has also changed in the manner of its composition: originally a nominated body whose members were drawn from the parliaments of the Member States, since 1979 the European Parliament has been directly elected by universal suffrage in each of the Member States. It currently has 518 deputies, roughly apportioned according to population: 81 each from France, Germany, Italy and the United Kingdom; 60 from Spain; 25 from the Netherlands; 24 each from Belgium, Greece and Portugal; 16 from Denmark; 15 from Ireland; and 6 from Luxembourg. The three direct elections held so far have been organized under national electoral laws in the Member States, but once elected to their five-year terms, the deputies are organized on the basis of ideologically similar political groups rather than nationality. The Parliament holds its sessions in Strasbourg, but its 19 committees and its political groups generally meet in Brussels, while its general secretariat is based in Luxembourg.

Initially exclusively an advisory and supervisory body within the Community, Parliament has gradually received expanded powers, particularly in budgetary matters and in the general legislative process. The Commission is accountable to Parliament through its annual reports and must defend its actions in open sessions of Parliament. Parliament monitors, comments on and votes on the Commission's program and, although it has never yet done so, it can compel the members of the Commission to resign *en bloc* following a vote of censure supported by a two-thirds majority. Legislatively, Parliament participates in the formulation of directives, regulations and other Community legal decisions in a number of important areas, most notably the completion of the common internal market. It exercises its role primarily by commenting on Commission proposals through the "cooperation procedure" between the Council and Parliament, described in more detail below. In addition, Parliament's assent is required for any further enlargements of the Community and for all international agreements. Under the Treaty of European Union, Parliament's legislative powers have been expanded significantly, to give it powers of co-decision with the Council in a variety of specific areas including the free movement of workers, education, health, culture, consumer protection, research and the environment.

Parliament's most significant role until now, however, has been in the budgetary process. Parliament and the Council review the Commission's draft budget through a back-and-forth process which gives the Council final word over "compulsory" expenditures, which regard primarily agricultural policy, and Parliament the definitive voice on other, "non-compulsory" expenditures. Ultimately, Parliament can either approve or reject the entire budget; in the latter case, as has happened several times so far, the process must begin anew with another draft budget from the Commission.

The European Court of Justice

Based in Luxembourg, the Court of Justice has 13 Judges, assisted by six Advocates General, collectively referred to as Members of the Court. All are appointed for renewable terms of six years by the common accord of the Member States, and according to the EEC Treaty must be "persons whose independence is beyond doubt and who possess the qualifications required for appointment to the highest judicial offices in their respective countries or who are jurisconsults of recognized competence." In practice, the Members of the Court have come from varied professional backgrounds, such as civil service, national judiciaries, academics or legal practice. Also, although not specified by the Treaties, in practice one Judge is appointed from each Member State, with the thirteenth Judge coming from one of the five largest Member States; four Advocates General come from the four largest Member States, while the remaining two positions rotate among the eight smaller Member States. The Court thus unites jurists from several different legal traditions, and conducts its proceedings in any of ten languages.

The role of the Advocates General assisting the Judges has become a unique feature of Community judicial procedure. Though not a Judge, the Advocate General will consider the parties' cases after all submissions have been completed and before the Judges begin their deliberations, and will present a written, reasoned, independent opinion in the case. It will include relevant facts and issues, and recommend a decision to the Judges; it is published alongside the Court's judgment in the European Court reports. As could be expected, the Advocate General's opinion can be quite influential on the Court, whose judgment can often be observed to follow the recommendation closely. At the same time, since the Court of Justice in many cases is both the first and the final recourse of the parties, the Advocate General's recommendation assures that the case will be fully considered twice.

The main function of the Court is to guarantee the proper interpretation and application of the Treaties and other legal instruments adopted by the institutions of the Community. Among other types of proceedings, it reviews Community legislation for compatibility with the Treaties, considers enforcement actions against the Member States for noncompliance with Community law, and provides preliminary rulings clarifying the scope and interpretation of Community law at the request of national courts.

In addition to the Court of Justice, the Community judiciary has since 1989 included a Court of First Instance, created by the Council for the purpose of relieving the burgeoning case load of the Court of Justice, especially in cases requiring more detailed and thorough fact-finding or expertise in complex economic issues. For instance, the Court of First Instance has jurisdiction over cases under the Community competition laws, under the European Coal and Steel Community Treaty, and under the anti-dumping laws.

B. SCOPE AND SUBJECT MATTER OF COMMUNITY LAW

Although frequently described as a "constitutional" order, the European Community does not have a comprehensive constitutional document as such, nor does it have many of the attributes of a fully developed constitutional state, most notably status as an independent sovereign. But it has been given broad, general competence over wide areas of economic and social life, and also draws on a number of key underlying principles and values; together these define the scope of the Community legal order.

The overriding philosophy of the founding Treaties of the Community was a neoliberal faith that the social and economic benefits of market unification will promote peace and prosperity among the peoples of Europe. Accordingly, while peace, unity and security are leitmotifs of Community law and politics, they are to be achieved through the progressive affirmation of the "four fundamental freedoms" of the Community order: free movement of goods, workers, services and capital. In addition, these freedoms are to be exercised on the basis of equality, without discrimination based on nationality.

More concretely, Article 3 of the EEC Treaty specifies the tasks of the Community as follows:

[T]he activities of the Community shall include, as provided in this Treaty and in accordance with the timetable set out therein:

(a) the elimination, as between Member States, of customs duties and of quantitative restrictions on the import and export of goods, and of all other measures having equivalent effect;

(b) the establishment of a common customs tariff and a common commercial policy toward third countries;

(c) the abolition, as between Member States, of obstacles to freedom of movement for persons, services and capital;

(d) the adoption of a common policy in the sphere of agriculture;

(e) the adoption of a common policy in the sphere of transport;

(f) the institution of a system ensuring that competition in the common market is not distorted;

(g) the application of procedures by which the economic policies of Member States can be coordinated and disequilibria in their balances of payments remedied;

(h) the approximation of the laws of Member States to the extent required for the proper functioning of the common market;

(i) the creation of a European Social Fund in order to improve employment opportunities for workers and to contribute to the raising of their standard of living;

(j) the establishment of a European Investment Bank to facilitate the economic expansion of the Community by opening up fresh resources;

(k) the association of the overseas countries and territories in order to increase trade and to promote jointly economic and social development.

In order to achieve these objectives, Article 189 of the EEC Treaty authorizes the Council and Commission to "make regulations, issue directives, take decisions, make recommendations or deliver opinions." Generally speaking, however, the Treaties do not confer on the Community general powers to promote economic integration and liberalization, or even for the accomplishment of the goals specified in Article 3. Rather, in accordance with the principle of the specific attribution of powers, each chapter of the Treaties lays down the extent of Community powers to act, according to the nature of the tasks in question. Thus, for instance, the scope of Community power is much more narrowly defined with regard to competition law (EEC Article 85 et seq.) than in the common agricultural policy (EEC Articles 40(3) and 43(2)).

Nevertheless, these limited, "enumerated" powers of the Community have been extensively supplemented in two different ways. First, in the 1970s the Commission and Council began to use Article 235 of the EEC Treaty to reinforce and extend Community powers in a variety of areas. Article 235 reads:

> If action by the Community should prove necessary to attain, in the course of the operation of the common market, one of the objectives of the Community and this Treaty has not provided the necessary powers, the Council shall, acting unanimously on a proposal from the Commission and after consulting the European Parliament, take the appropriate measures.

In addition to amplifying Community action in areas such as social policy and economic and monetary matters, Article 235 justified the Community's assumption of powers with respect to environmental policy, university research programs, consumer protection and broad energy policy. Subsequently, with the amendment of the founding Treaties by the Single European Act in 1986, these powers were recognized and given Treaty status.

Secondly, the Court of Justice has allowed the fuller exercise of Community functions through its development of a doctrine of implied powers. In order to give effective and meaningful implementation to the powers expressly conferred on Community institutions, the Treaties have been understood to allow implicitly whatever means are necessary to attain the ends legitimately within the Community's domain under the Treaties. For instance, the Court has upheld the Community's capacity to enter into international agreements for the fixing of fishing quotas and to assume other international obligations as an implied power arising from the Community's authority over common agricultural policy.[4]

As might be expected, this expansion in the scope of Community activity has entailed a corresponding erosion of Member State powers. At first, Community powers were all concurrent with the power of Member States. As the Community has regulated certain areas of activity more and more comprehensively, the residual powers of the Member States have been converted increasingly into exclusive Community powers (the legal doctrines which allow this conversion will be discussed further below).

To a significant extent, the incursion of Community norms on Member States is encouraged by the Member States' Treaty obligation to actively and in good faith contribute to European integration. Article 5 of the EEC Treaty establishes this principle of cooperation:

> Member States shall take all appropriate measures, whether general or particular, to ensure fulfillment of the obligations arising out of this Treaty or resulting from action taken by the institutions of the Community. They shall facilitate the achievement of the Community's tasks.

The Article also provides that Member States "shall abstain from any measure which could jeopardize the attainment of the objectives of this Treaty." The Court of Justice has held that the principle of cooperation is one of the fundamental principles of the Community legal structure, and therefore that it plays a preeminent role in the interpretation and application of Community law. In this way it has contributed to the direction of national resources, institutions and law toward Community ends, and to the corresponding strengthening of Community over Member State powers.

As the Maastricht Treaty on European Union is implemented, the relationship between Community and Member State powers will enter a new phase of Community growth and Member State retreat. The Treaty provides for the establishment of a common European currency (although the severe crises of the European monetary union in 1992 and 1993 may cast doubt on the feasibility of this project); common rights of European citizenship; broad new powers for the Community in an array of areas from public health to crime to industrial policy; and a common foreign and security policy.

On the basis of these various powers, Community institutions enact legislation independent of, and binding in, the Member States.

---

4. Kramer, Cases 3, 4 and 6/76, [1976] E.C.R. 1279.

C. SOURCES OF LAW IN THE EUROPEAN COMMUNITY

Community law has a variety of formal foundations and takes a variety of forms. Foremost among the sources of law are the founding Treaties of the Community, with their various protocols and amendments, additions and annexes. Collectively, these are referred to as primary legislation, because they were created directly by the Member States themselves. Subordinate to the primary legislation in authority, but much more common as a source of community norms, is the body of law made by Community institutions acting within the scope of the Treaties, known as secondary legislation.

The forms of secondary legislation vary,[5] in part according to whether there is a need for uniform rules, down to the details, in all of the Member States, or whether instead the Community legislation seeks more simply to allow Member State legal systems to implement a broader policy goal. The Community legal instruments that encroach furthest on national law are regulations. As specified in Article 189 of the EEC Treaty, "a regulation shall have general application. It shall be binding in its entirety and directly applicable in all Member States." That is, regulations do not need to be transformed into domestic law, but directly confer rights and create obligations within the Member States, with which national political institutions are bound to comply and which courts are obliged to safeguard. Regulations have the power to preempt national legislation in a particular area.

On the other hand, directives, according to the EEC Treaty, are "binding, as to the result to be achieved, upon each Member State to which it is addressed, but shall leave to the national authorities the choice of form and methods." Thus, rather than creating new uniform law binding throughout the Community, directives require the Member States to take such measures as may be necessary in order to achieve an aim desired by the community. Directives are "addressed" to Member States, and typically state an objective to be achieved within a given period of time; the means by which to achieve the goal, however, is at the discretion of the addressee. This form of legislation is designed to allow Member States to fashion rules which best suit their particular domestic circumstances while still implementing Community law and policy in a relatively uniform way. The Member States usually do this through new domestic legislation; the overall result on a Community-wide basis is to help harmonize the laws and policies of the various Member States by removing gradually the differences between them.

Since the Community has no single institution that constitutes its "legislature," directives and regulations are enacted by the interaction and cooperation of different Community institutions. The precise procedures of the legislative process depend on the Treaty article on which the legislative initiative rests, and thus vary according to the substantive area being addressed by the legislation. In most cases, as mentioned

---

5. They are also slightly different under the ECSC Treaty than under the EEC and Euratom Treaties; the discussion here will focus on secondary acts under the latter two only.

above, the Commission initiates legislative proposals. A particular department within the Commission will prepare a detailed draft proposal in its field of expertise, and present it to the entire Commission. If adopted by a simple majority, the Commission proposal then goes to the Council, which ultimately will dispose of it. The stages in between can vary, however.

The most straightforward process, and originally the only one giving a role to the European Parliament, is that of consultation: Parliament is consulted on the Commission's proposal before the Council reaches a final decision. Although Parliament's opinion has no binding effect on the Council's decision, it is an indispensable part of the process, as the European Court of Justice has noted:

> The consultation ... is the means which allows the Parliament to play an actual part in the legislative process of the Community. Such power represents an essential factor in the institutional balance intended by the Treaty. Although limited, it reflects at Community level the fundamental democratic principle that the peoples should take part in the exercise of power through the intermediary of a representative assembly. Due consultation of the Parliament in the cases provided for by the Treaty therefore constitutes an essential formality disregard of which means that the measure concerned is void.[6]

In practice, even in cases where the Council is not required to consult with Parliament, it will commonly do so as an optional measure. If during the legislative process the Council or the Commission amends the substance of the original proposal, they are required to reconsult Parliament.[7] In certain cases, when the Council intends to depart from Parliament's opinion, the two institutions have the possibility to seek an agreement through meetings within a Conciliation Committee.

A more complex process, but one giving a more significant role to Parliament, is known as the cooperation procedure. Like the consultation procedure, this involves Parliament's reading of the proposal and its opinion. Instead of taking definitive action, however, the Council then formulates a "common position" which is communicated, with explanations, to Parliament. Parliament is then given an opportunity for a second reading, after which it can either approve the common position, reject it, or propose amendments to it. In the first instance, the Council may proceed to adoption of the measure; in the second case, the Council may only adopt the act by a unanimous vote. The third course, that of Parliamentary amendment, is the most common, and requires the Commission to reexamine the proposal and either leave it intact or adopt the proposed amendments. The Council may then accept the reexamined

---

6. Case 138/79, Roquette Frères v. Council, [1980] E.C.R. 3333, 3360.

7. The Commission may alter its proposal at any time during the procedures, so long as the Council has not yet acted; the Council has a general power of amendment if it acts unanimously.

proposal by a qualified majority, or amend it by unanimous vote. (See Figure 1.)

Figure 1.

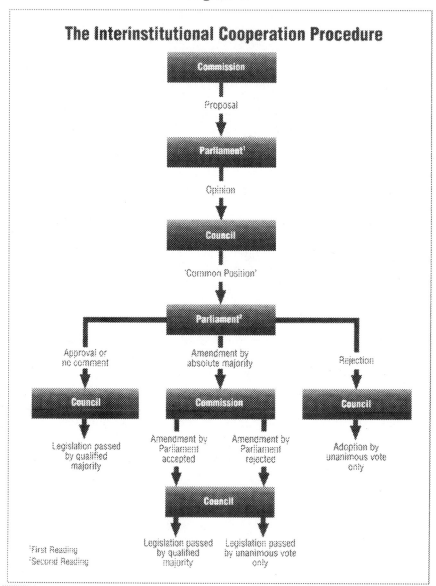

(Source: A Guide to the European Community (E.C. Delegation to the United States, 1991)).

The Treaty on European Union has added a third major legislative procedure to Community law, one which again gives Parliament a more significant voice in the process. Known as the co-decision procedure, it resembles the cooperation procedure in the early stages, with Parliament's first reading of a Commission proposal, the formulation of the

Council's common position, and Parliament's decision to accept, reject or amend the proposal on a second reading. If Parliament expresses its intention to reject the common position, the Council may convene the Conciliation Committee in order to further explain its position. If Parliament subsequently confirms its rejection, the proposal will not go forward. At this stage, or immediately upon the second reading, Parliament may propose amendments, which the Commission will examine before delivering an opinion. The Council may then approve the amendments and adopt the instrument; it must do so by qualified majority if the Commission has delivered a favorable opinion, and unanimously if the Commission's opinion was negative. If the Council does not approve Parliament's amendments, the Conciliation Committee is convened, with the participation of the Commission as well. If the Committee succeeds in producing a joint text, Parliament and the Council may then each adopt the act; rejection by either precludes adoption of the text. In the absence of agreement within the Committee, the Council may confirm its common position, with or without Parliament's amendments, but Parliament may still reject the proposal. In the end, then, under the co-decision procedure Parliament always has the power to veto a proposal.

In addition to regulations and directives, which are clearly of a "legislative" nature, a third legal instrument used by Community institutions, the decision, is more akin to an administrative measure. Unlike the directive, which is only addressed to a state, decisions may also be addressed to individuals or corporations. They require a particular Member State or person to perform or to refrain from a particular action; they could include a fine against persons violating the competition laws, for instance, or a requirement that a State cease to provide a particular form of subsidy to a domestic industry.

Closely related to the secondary legislation of the Community, but not legally binding as such and thus not actually a source of law, are recommendations. These may suggest certain interpretations of Community law, or even recommend detailed rules to be adopted by Member States. Though not creating any legal obligations, recommendations can exert a powerful political influence which may lead to more formal legal results.

Other sources of Community law, beyond secondary legislation, include a variety of Treaties and international agreements, decisions of the Court of Justice, and general principles of law. Each has played an important role in the legal integration of the Community. As mentioned earlier, disagreement over the capacity of the Community to enter into international agreements became the catalyst for the development of the doctrine of implied powers in the Community constitutional structure. Thus, although the founding Treaties themselves only grant very narrow treaty-making powers to the Community institutions, the implied power to negotiate and conclude international treaties with third parties has substantially increased the number of such agreements in recent years.

Court decisions have also grown in scope and importance within the Community legal structure. In addition to being applicable to parties before it, Court decisions are binding on the referring national courts and in some situations are valid *erga omnes,* such as a ruling on the invalidity of a Community act. A prior ruling of the Court on a particular point of Community law can also extinguish national courts' obligations to refer questions of Community law on that matter. In some cases, national courts have explicitly recognized the binding precedential force of prior European Court decisions, even to the point that decisions interpreting Community provisions having direct effect can themselves have an equally direct effect.[8] In these ways, the Court's jurisprudence has acquired some of the attributes of precedent in the common law tradition.

In some areas, judicial interpretation does not simply illuminate Community law, but positively dominates it. Most notably, it is the Court which has judicially developed the concept of "general principles of law" within the Community legal order as an additional source of law. Under Article 164 of the EEC Treaty and parallel provisions of the other founding Treaties, "the Court of Justice shall ensure that in the interpretation and application of this Treaty the law is observed." The language suggests that there is a body of legal principles outside of, and higher than, the text of the Treaty but applicable to it. Other Treaty provisions provide additional support for this concept, notably EEC Article 215, which provides that the non-contractual liability of the Community shall be determined "in accordance with the general principles common to the laws of the Member States." The Court has accordingly looked primarily to the constitutional traditions of the Member States to formulate and apply these unwritten general principles of law within the Community. Some of the more important examples include the principle of proportionality, the principle of legal certainty and the related idea of the protection of legitimate expectations, and the principle of equality.

One of the "general principles" developed by the Court deserves special mention: the Community's obligation to respect fundamental human rights. The founding Treaties make no provision for the application of human rights norms in any way within the Community. Nevertheless, beginning in 1969, the Court began to assert the existence of fundamental rights guarantees as inherent in Community law.[9] These principles were to be drawn from the constitutional traditions common to the member states [10] as well as from "international treaties for the protection of human rights on which the Member States have collaborated or of which they are signatories." [11] The Court's subsequent jurispru-

---

8. See, e.g., Italian Constitutional Court Judgment No. 113 of April 23, 1985, 68 Racc.Uff. 775, 792 (1985).

9. Stauder v. City of Ulm, Case 29/69 [1969] E.C.R. 419, 425.

10. Internationale Handelsgesellschaft v. EVSt, Case 11/70 [1970] E.C.R. 1125, 1134.

11. Nold v. Commission, Case 4/73 [1974] E.C.R. 491, 507.

dence has grown increasingly complex as it has come to recognize a number of specific rights, including but not limited to the right of ownership, the general right of privacy and the privacy of correspondence and of the home, freedom of association, freedom of religion, the freedom to choose and practice a profession, the right to form trade unions and the principle of democracy. The other Community institutions firmly endorsed the Court's case law in a formal Joint Declaration in 1977, and the Community has since incorporated formal references to the European Convention on Human Rights into the Preamble of the Single European Act and Article F of the Treaty on European Union.

One recent example of the Court's use of general principles of law, and especially of human rights norms drawn not just from national constitutions but also international instruments, is the case of Georges Heylens. Heylens, a Belgian football trainer, was offered a position with a professional football team in France. The French Ministry of Youth and Sport refused to recognize Heylens' Belgian education and training and prohibited him from practicing his trade in France, but did not provide any reasons for doing so, and did not provide Heylens with any opportunity for an appeal. When he ignored the order and assumed his position as trainer, criminal charges were brought against him for the unauthorized practice of a profession. The French *Tribunal de Grande Instance*, having doubts about the French law's compatibility with Community law's protection of workers' freedom of movement and right to practice a trade, referred the issue to the European Court of Justice. The European Court explained:

> Since free access to employment is a fundamental right which the Treaty confers individually on each worker in the Community, the existence of a remedy of a judicial nature against any decision of a national authority refusing the benefit of that right is essential in order to secure for the individual effective protection for his right.... [T]hat requirement reflects a general principle of Community law which underlies the constitutional traditions common to the Member States and has been enshrined in Articles 6 and 13 of the European Convention for the Protection of Human Rights and Fundamental Freedoms.[a]

> Effective judicial review, which must be able to cover the legality of the reasons for the contested decision, presupposes in general that the court to which the matter is referred may require the competent authority to notify its reasons. But where, as in this case, it is more particularly a question of a fundamental right secured by the Treaty on Community workers, the latter must also be able to defend that right under the best possible conditions and have the possibility of deciding, with a full knowledge of the relevant facts, whether there is any point in applying to the courts. Consequently, in such circumstances the competent national authority is

---

a. Article 6 protects the right to a fair hearing or trial; Article 13 protects the right to an effective remedy. See infra at pages 374 and 376 for the text of these Articles.

under a duty to inform them of the reasons on which its refusal is based, either in the decision itself or in a subsequent communication made at their request.[12]

The Court's methods in cases such as *Heylens* help broaden the scope of Community law and deepen its legal foundations by drawing on the legal traditions of Member States and international regimes. In doing so, the Court also undoubtedly has contributed to the development of the constitutional structure of the Community and helped to establish the primacy of Community law in the Member States.

D. SUPREMACY OF COMMUNITY LAW IN THE NATIONAL LEGAL SYSTEMS OF MEMBER STATES

The effectiveness of the European Community's constitutional system is contingent on the cooperation of national political and legal institutions in the implementation of Community law. Thus, the effect of the Community on the legal traditions of the individual states of Europe depends profoundly not just on the scope and forms of Community law, but also on the manner in which that law is given effect in domestic law. Of decisive importance in this respect have been the community system of judicial review, and the doctrines of supremacy and of direct effect. These factors, along with the development of the doctrines of implied powers and of human rights mentioned above, were the basis of the transformation of the European Community from a public international legal body to a constitutional order, according to Joseph Weiler.

JOSEPH H.H. WEILER, THE TRANSFORMATION OF EUROPE *

100 Yale Law Journal 2403, 2413–22 (1991).

THE DOCTRINE OF DIRECT EFFECT

The judicial doctrine of direct effect, introduced in 1963[a] and developed subsequently, provides the following presumption: Community legal norms that are clear, precise and self-sufficient (not requiring further legislative measures by the authorities of the Community or the Member States) must be regarded as the law of the land in the sphere of application of Community Law. Direct effect (a rule of construction in result) applies to all actions producing legal effects in the Community: the Treaty itself and secondary legislation. Moreover, with the exception of one type of Community legislation,[24] direct effect operates not

---

12. Unectef v. Heylens, Case 222/86 [1987] E.C.R. 4097, 4117.

* Reprinted with permission of Joseph Weiler and the Yale Law Journal.

a. Van Gend & Loos v. Nederlandse administratie der belastingen, Case 26/62 [1963] E.C.R. 1.

24. Community directives may produce direct effects in the vertical relationship between public authority and individuals but not in the horizontal relationship of individuals *inter se*. *See* Case 148/78, Pubblico Ministerio v. Tullio Ratti, 1979 E.C.R. 1629; Case 152/84, M.H. Marshall v. South-

only in creating enforceable legal obligations between the Member States and individuals, but also among individuals *inter se*. Critically, being part of the law of the land means that Community norms may be invoked by individuals before their state courts, which must provide adequate legal remedies for the E.C. norms just as if they were enacted by the state legislature.

The implications of this doctrine were and are far reaching. The European Court reversed the normal presumption of public international law whereby international legal obligations are result-oriented and addressed to states. Public international law typically allows the internal constitutional order of a state to determine the method and extent to which obligations may, if at all, produce effects for individuals within the legal order of the state. Under the normal canons of international law, even when the international obligation itself, such as a trade agreement or a human rights convention, is intended to bestow rights (or duties) on individuals within a state, if the state fails to bestow the rights, the individual cannot invoke the international obligation before national courts, unless internal constitutional or statutory law, to which public international law is indifferent, provides for such a remedy. The typical remedy under public international law in such a case would be an interstate claim. The main import of the Community doctrine of direct effect was not simply the conceptual change it ushered forth. In practice direct effect meant that Member States violating their Community obligations could not shift the locus of dispute to the interstate or Community plane. They would be faced with legal actions before their own courts at the suit of individuals within their own legal order.

Individuals (and their lawyers) noticed this practical implication, and the number of cases brought on the basis of this doctrine grew exponentially. Effectively, individuals in real cases and controversies (usually against state public authorities) became the principal "guardians" of the legal integrity of Community law within Europe similar to the way that individuals in the United States have been the principal actors in ensuring the vindication of the Bill of Rights and other federal law.

THE DOCTRINE OF SUPREMACY

The doctrine of direct effect might not strike all observers as that revolutionary, especially those observers coming from a monist constitutional order in which the international treaties upon ratification are transposed automatically into the municipal legal order and in which some provisions of international treaties may be recognized as "self-executing." The full impact of direct effect is realized in combination with the second "constitutionalizing" doctrine, supremacy. Unlike some federal constitutions, the Treaty does not include a specific "supremacy clause." However, in a series of cases starting in 1964 [b] the Court has pronounced an uncompromising version of supremacy: in the sphere of

ampton and South–West Hampshire Area Health Authority, 1986 E.C.R. 723.

b. Costa v. ENEL, Case 6/64 [1964] E.C.R. 585.

application of Community law, any Community norm, be it an article of the Treaty (the Constitutional Charter) or a minuscule administrative regulation enacted by the Commission, "trumps" conflicting national law whether enacted before or after the Community norm. Additionally, although this has never been stated explicitly, the Court has the "Kompetenz–Kompetenz" in the Community legal order, i.e., it is the body that determines which norms come within the sphere of application of Community law.[26]

In light of supremacy the full significance of direct effect becomes transparent. Typically, in monist or quasi-monist states like the United States, although treaty provisions, including self-executing ones, may be received automatically into the municipal legal order, their normative status is *equivalent* to national legislation. Thus the normal rule of "later in time" (*lex posteriori derogat lex anteriori*) governs the relationship between the treaty provision and conflicting national legislation. A national legislature unhappy with an internalized treaty norm simply enacts a conflicting national measure and the transposition will have vanished for all internal practical effects. By contrast, in the Community, because of the doctrine of supremacy, the E.C. norm, which by virtue of the doctrine of direct effect must be regarded as the Law of the Land, will prevail even in these circumstances. The combination of the two doctrines means that Community norms that produce direct effects are not merely the Law of the Land but the "Higher Law" of the Land. Parallels to this kind of constitutional architecture may, with very few exceptions, be found only in the internal constitutional order of federal states.

* * *

The Community System of Judicial Review

As mentioned above, the hierarchy of norms within the European Community is typical of a nonunitary system. The Higher Law of the Community is, of course, the Treaty itself. Neither Community organs nor the Member States may violate the Treaty in their legislative and administrative actions. In addition, Member States may not violate Community regulations, directives, and decisions. Not surprisingly, then, the Community features a double-limbed system of judicial review, operating on two levels. Two sets of legislative acts and administrative measures are subject to judicial review: (1) the measures of the Community itself (principally acts of the Council of Ministers, Commission and European Parliament), which are reviewable for conformity with the Treaties; and (2) the acts of the Member States, which are reviewable

---

26. The principle of supremacy can be expressed, not as an absolute rule whereby Community (or federal) law trumps Member State law, but instead as a principle whereby each law is supreme *within its sphere of competence.* This more accurate characterization of supremacy renders crucial the question of defining the spheres of competence and in particular the concomitant institutional question which court will have the final decision as to the definition of spheres, i.e. the question of Kompetenz–Kompetenz....

for their conformity with Community law and policy, including the above-mentioned secondary legislation.

Needless to say, in the context of my discussion of ... Member States' attempts to disregard those obligations they dislike, the effectiveness of review of the second set of measures assumes critical importance. I, therefore, focus only on that aspect of judicial review here.

a.   *Judicial Review at the Community Level*

Either the Commission or an individual Member State may, in accordance with Articles 169–72 of the EEC Treaty, bring an action against a Member State for failure to fulfill its obligations under the Treaty. Generally, this failure takes the form either of inaction in implementing a Community obligation or enactment of a national measure contrary to Community obligations. The existence of a mandatory and *exclusive* forum for adjudication of these types of disputes sets the Community apart from many international organizations.

The role of the Commission is even more special. As one commentator noted, "[u]nder traditional international law the enforcement of treaty obligations is a matter to be settled among the Contracting Parties themselves. Article 169, in contrast, enables an independent Community body, the Commission, to invoke the compulsory jurisdiction of the European Court against a defaulting Member State." [38]

At the same time, the "intergovernmental" character of this procedure and the consequent limitations on its efficacy are clear. Four weaknesses are particularly glaring:

(1) the procedure is political in nature; the Commission (appropriately) may have nonlegal reasons not to initiate a prosecution;

(2) a centralized agency with limited human resources is unable adequately to identify, process and monitor all possible Member State violations and infringements;

(3) Article 169 may be inappropriate to apply to small violations; even if small violations are properly identified, dedicating Commission resources to infringements that do not raise an important principle or create a major economic impact may be wasteful; and finally, and most importantly,

(4) no real enforcement exists; proceedings conclude with a "declaratory" judgment of the European Court without enforcement sanctions.

b.   *Judicial Review at the Member State Level*

The weaknesses of Articles 169–172 are remedied to an extent by judicial review within the judicial systems of the Member States in collaboration with the European Court of Justice. Article 177 provides, inter alia, that when a question concerning the interpretation of the

---

38. Evans, *The Enforcement Procedure*   4 Eur.L.Rev. 442, 443 (1979).
of Article 169 EEC: Commission Discretion,

Treaty is raised before a national court, the court may suspend the national proceedings and request a preliminary ruling from the European Court of Justice in Luxembourg on the correct interpretation of the Treaty. If the national court is the court of last resort, then it must request a European Court ruling. Once this ruling is made, it is remitted back to the national court which gives, on the basis of the ruling, the opinion in the case before it. The national courts and the European Court of Justice are thus integrated into a unitary system of judicial review.

* * *

The fact that the national court renders the final judgment is crucial to the procedure. The binding effect and enforcement value of such a decision, coming from a Member State's own court, may be contrasted with a similar decision handed down in a declaratory fashion by the European Court under the previously discussed Article 169 procedure. A national court opinion takes care of the most dramatic weakness of the Article 169 procedure: the ability of a Member State, *in extremis*, to disregard the strictures of the European Court. Under the 177 procedure this disregard is impossible. A state, in our Western democracies, cannot disobey its own courts.

The other weaknesses of the 169 procedure are also remedied to some extent: individual litigants are usually not politically motivated in bringing their actions; small as well as big violations are adjudicated; and, in terms of monitoring, the Community citizen becomes, willy-nilly, a decentralized agent for monitoring compliance by Member States with their Treaty obligations.

The Article 177 system is not complete, however. Not all violations come before national courts; the success of the system depends on the collaboration between national courts and the European Court of Justice; and Member States may, and often have, utilized the delays of the system to defer ruling.

On the other hand, the overall effect of the judicial remedies cannot be denied. The combination of the "constitutionalization" and the system of judicial remedies to a large extent *nationalized* Community obligations and introduced at the Community level the *habit of obedience* and the respect for the rule of law which traditionally is less associated with international obligations than with national ones.

The collaboration between national courts and the European Court which Weiler considers essential to the Community system of judicial review has not been full and forthcoming. In fact, in some cases, establishing the supremacy of Community law has entailed various degrees of legal struggle.

The constitutional systems of Greece, Luxembourg, the Netherlands, Portugal and Spain provide for basically monist approaches to international law. That is, international law, including treaties such as those founding the European Community, are automatically part of the domestic legal system, without the need for independent national legislation to incorporate them into domestic law. Thus the application of Community law by the judiciaries of these countries generally has been unproblematic. Greece, the Netherlands and Luxembourg not only recognize the higher status of international obligations over national law, but also have constitutional provisions specifically authorizing the delegation of sovereign powers to the Community.[13] In Greece, it should be noted, that provision also prohibits application of treaties violating "the rights of man and the foundations of democratic government," but so far this reservation has apparently not led to Greek resistance to the supremacy of Community law.

Belgium and France also adopt generally monist understandings of international law, but their judiciaries have had slightly more difficulty completely accepting Community supremacy. In particular, the question remained open regarding the continued applicability of Community law when it conflicts with a subsequent national statute. In Belgium, the issue was finally settled in favor of Community law by the *Cour de Cassation* in 1971, when it declared:

> In the event of a conflict between a norm of domestic law and a norm of international law which produces direct effects in the internal legal system, the rule established by the treaty shall prevail. The primacy of the treaty results from the very nature of international treaty law.

> This is *a fortiori* the case when a conflict exists, as in the present case, between a norm of internal law and a norm of Community law.

> The reason is that the treaties which have created Community law have instituted a new legal system in whose favour the Member States have restricted the exercise of their sovereign powers in the areas determined by those treaties.[14]

In France, instead, the Council of State long resisted the supremacy of Community law. The French Constitution establishes the superiority of treaty law over ordinary domestic law,[15] but because the Council of State does not have the power to review acts of Parliament on Constitutional grounds, the Court refused to apply treaty-based Community law over subsequent national statutes. Only in 1989 did it finally accept the primacy of Community acts even over subsequent statutes.[16] The Council of State has also resisted the European Court of Justice's case law

---

13. Article 28, Constitution of Greece; Article 92, Constitution of the Netherlands; Article 49a, Constitution of Luxembourg.

14. Minister for Economic Affairs v. S.A. Fromagerie Franco–Suisse "Le Ski," Judgment of May 21, 1971, [1972] Common Market Law Reports 330, 373.

15. Article 55, Constitution of France.

16. Nicolo, Judgment of October 20, 1989, [1990] 1 Common Market Law Reports 173. See Philippe Manin, The Nicolo Case of the Conseil d'État, 28 Common Market Law Review 499 (1991).

holding that Community directives could have direct effect, but in practice accepted the doctrine in another 1989 case.[17]

In general, Denmark, Ireland and the United Kingdom require national legislation to transform international agreements into national law. Despite the potential difficulties this approach presents in principle (for instance, the possibility that a subsequent national statute will abrogate prior treaty obligations), courts in these three countries have thus far had no difficulty in applying Community law over conflicting provisions of national law. In part, this is due to constitutional (in the case of Ireland) or statutory (in the case of Britain) provisions enacted at the time of accession.[18]

In contrast, the most intractable resistance to the primacy of Community law occurred in the constitutional courts of Italy and Germany. The constitutional systems of both countries require parliamentary approval of international treaties; once parliament has done so, a treaty becomes part of the domestic legal order. This leaves open the possibility that subsequent acts of parliament conflicting with the treaty will supersede it, and also puts into doubt the possibility of the direct applicability of Community legislation. After initial resistance, both countries' constitutional courts came to accept the priority of Community legislation even over subsequent domestic law.

In Italy, the first step toward the acceptance of Community law's supremacy rested on Article 11 of the Constitution, which provides: "Italy consents, on conditions of parity with other States, to limitations of sovereignty necessary to a legal system which assures peace and justice among nations, and promotes and favors organizations dedicated to such purpose." In a series of rulings beginning in 1973, the Italian Constitutional Court arrived at the view that any ordinary state law which is incompatible with a Community norm, even if subsequent in time, is unconstitutional because it would cause Italy to violate its obligations under the Community Treaties, thus indirectly contradicting Article 11. In addition, the Court held that directly applicable Community norms need not, and in fact may not, be received and implemented into domestic law by national statutes.

Although technically making Community law directly applicable and giving it higher status than even subsequent national legislation, the Italian Constitutional Court nevertheless failed to bring its national legal system entirely within the framework of supremacy and judicial review developed by the European Court. The particular nature of constitutional judicial review in Italy gives the Constitutional Court the exclusive authority to annul laws in violation of the Constitution; questions of constitutionality must be referred to it by lower courts. Because the Italian decisions based the supremacy of Community law on its foundation in a national constitutional provision, in theory every ordinary law

---

17. Compagnie Alitalia, Judgment of February 3, 1989, [1990] 1 Common Market Law Reports 248.

18. Article 29, Constitution of Ireland; Section 2(1), European Communities Act of 1972 (United Kingdom).

in conflict with Community law must be ruled unconstitutional. Thus, instead of immediately applying Community law in place of national law, ordinary judges had to first seek a ruling from the Constitutional Court.

In particular, as the 1973 case first recognizing the supremacy of Community law emphasized, the Italian Constitutional Court would review Community legislation for compatibility with basic principles of human rights and constitutional order:

> It is hardly necessary to add that by Article 11 of the Constitution limitations on sovereignty are allowed solely for the purpose of the ends indicated therein, and it should therefore be excluded that such limitations of sovereignty, concretely set out in the Rome Treaty, signed by countries whose systems are based on the principle of the rule of law and guarantee the essential liberties of citizens, can nevertheless give the organs of the EEC an unacceptable power to violate the fundamental principles of our constitutional order or the inalienable rights of man. And it is obvious that if ever Article 189 [a] had to be given such an aberrant interpretation, in such a case the guarantee would always be assured that this Court would control the continuing compatibility of the Treaty with the above-mentioned fundamental principles.[19]

Only in 1984 did the Constitutional Court revise its position and decide that even when a Community norm conflicts with a national law, ordinary judges should apply Community law, without waiting for the Constitutional Court to declare the national law unconstitutional.[20] The complex position of the Italian Court essentially rests on the acknowledgement that the autonomous nature of Community law obviates the need for its integration and transformation into domestic law. Instead, national law is understood to withdraw, allowing a substitution of Community norms for national ones, thus assuring the recognition and guarantee of Community law in Italy.[21]

But despite the Italian Court's substantial acceptance of Community law's supremacy, there remains a residual difference between its approach and that of the European Court. Ultimately, the respect and guarantee of Community law as a higher norm within the domestic legal system still rests on the values and laws of the Italian legal system, in particular on the constitutional requirement of state compliance with international obligations. Thus, as one commentator of the Italian law has remarked:

> [A]lthough the phenomenon [of Community law supremacy] is permanent and unequivocal, it is not completely definitive. Because it

a. Article 189 of the EEC Treaty sets out the legislative competence of the organs of the Community.

19. Frontini v. Ministero delle Finanze, Judgment No. 183 of December 27, 1973, [1974] 2 Common Market Law Reports 372, 389.

20. Granital v. Amministrazione delle Finanze, Judgment No. 170 of June 8, 1984, 21 Common Market Law Review 756 (1984).

21. Paolo Mengozzi, European Community Law 65–69 (1992).

is maintained by the Italian Constitution, the phenomenon remains in effect only so long as the application of Community law over time remains compatible with the fundamental constitutional principles and with the fundamental human rights which the national constitutional system protects.[22]

In fact, as recently as 1989, the Italian Constitutional Court forcefully affirmed that although it will not on an ordinary basis review Community legislation for compatibility with the Constitution, in principle if a rule of Community law violates a fundamental norm of the Constitution concerning human rights, it cannot be applied.[23]

The German Constitutional Court has followed a very similar path in its cautious acceptance of the supremacy of Community law. Basing its decision on the integrity of Community law as an autonomous system of law distinct from the domestic legal order, in 1974 it first acknowledged the primacy of Community law even over subsequent national law:

> [I]n principle, the two legal spheres stand independent of and side by side one another in their validity, and ... in particular, the competent Community organs, including the European Court of Justice, have to rule on the binding force, construction and observance of Community law, and the competent national organs on the binding force, construction and observance of the constitutional law of the Federal Republic of Germany.[24]

Such a transfer of sovereign powers to the institutions of the European Community, made possible in Germany by Article 24(1) of the Constitution, also assures the direct applicability of Community law, without a need for transformation into national law.

At the same time, however, the Court stressed the limitations of the surrender of sovereignty under Article 24 in a manner very similar to the Italian Constitutional Court the previous year:

> Article 24 of the Constitution deals with the transfer of sovereign rights to inter-State institutions. This cannot be taken literally. Like every constitutional provision of a similar fundamental nature, Article 24 of the Constitution must be understood and construed in the overall context of the whole Constitution. That is, it does not open the way to amending the basic structure of the Constitution, which forms the basis of its identity, without a formal amendment to the Constitution.[25]

The Court considered the protection of human rights to be just such a fundamental aspect of the German Basic Law. Yet, it found Community law not to guarantee those rights sufficiently. Therefore, the Court would continue to accept and consider references concerning the applicability of Community laws which could conflict with fundamental rights

22. Id. at 69.

23. Judgment No. 232 of April 21, 1989, 34 Giurisprudenza Costituzionale 1001 (1989).

24. Internationale Handelsgesellschaft v. EVGF, Judgment of May 29, 1974, [1974] Common Market Law Reports 540, 549.

25. Id. at 550.

protected by the German Basic Law, "[a]s long as the integration process has not progressed so far that Community law also receives a catalogue of fundamental rights ... which is adequate in comparison with the catalogue of fundamental rights contained in the Constitution." [26]

By 1986, the German Constitutional Court reconsidered its earlier decision, in light of the European Court's expanded jurisprudence of human rights as well as various formal declarations by the several Community institutions concerning their commitment to protecting those rights. The Court concluded that the Community's legal order had developed an adequate guarantee of the human rights safeguarded by the German Basic Law to reverse the presumption of its earlier decision. Thus, instead of reviewing Community law "so long as" human rights protection was inadequate, the Court would suspend the exercise of its jurisdiction in this area "so long as" the Community continued to protect human rights at least at its then-current level.[27]

E. COMMUNITY LAW AND THE LEGAL TRADITIONS OF MEMBER STATES

The broad and expanding scope of Community law and the forcefulness with which it has penetrated into the domestic legal orders naturally raise the question of Community law's influence on the basic legal traditions of the Member States. In the specific context of our interests here, we might ask whether, to what extent and in what manner have Community law and institutions affected the character of the Continental civil law tradition. National judges are called upon to serve also as actors within the Community legal system; national legislatures are compelled to refashion their laws in accordance with the common policies of the Community. At the most general level, the structure, methods and content of Community law cannot help but infuse the legal consciousness of domestic actors.

At the same time, however, a moment's reflection will show us that such an inquiry is closely related to its inverse, that is, to the influence of the traditions of civil law countries on the European system. For all their differences, the judges and lawmakers in the European Community share the heritage of a common legal tradition, which forms the political, historical, cultural and philosophical substratum of Community law. Indeed, it would be difficult to imagine fashioning such an intricate legal order without fundamentally similar ideas about law. Within the Community institutions, a majority of actors come from within the civil law tradition, and invariably bring with them a common education and practice in the concepts and grammar of civil law discourse. More concretely, the legislation of the Communities relies on national experts, and the Court draws its interpretive and gap-filling principles from

---

26. Id. at 554.

27. Re Wünsche Handelsgesellschaft, Judgment of October 22, 1986, [1987] 3 Common Market Law Reports 225. See also E.R. Lanier, *Solange,* Farewell, 11 B.C. Int'l & Comp.L.Rev. 1 (1988).

common concepts in the law of Member States. When Community law is implemented by national courts, it is done in the context of national procedures, local legal language, and substantively national disputes. In short, the question is one of the reciprocal influence of intermingled legal systems on the development of the civil law tradition within the larger European legal tradition.

One fruitful area of inquiry addresses the role of courts and case law in the legal order. At least one scholar of community law, Paolo Mengozzi, considers this to be a preeminent innovation of Community law which has had profound effects on the national legal systems, particularly with respect to private law.[28] Referring to the general effect of the European Court's interpretive decisions, including the Court's use of general principles, Mengozzi notes that the sources of law to which national judges must look have expanded far beyond the written sources of the Treaties and other legislative acts. Previously, even limited acknowledgment of the binding precedential nature of another court's case law was, in continental countries, reserved almost exclusively for the special case of constitutional courts. In addition, based on Community law ordinary national judges have been called upon not to give effect to the acts of their national legislatures, and to exercise much broader powers than would be normally available under national law in order to ensure implementation of Community law by Member States. In all these respects, Community law entails a reconceptualization of the institutional balance within the constitutional systems of the Member States, including a revision of deeply rooted principles regarding Parliamentary sovereignty and its relation to the exercise of judicial functions.

At the same time, Mengozzi points out, various elements within the Community legal structure mitigate the dominating force of courts and case law.[29] The European Court of Justice has stressed that the application of Community law by national judges is only a minimum, not a sufficient, guarantee of the full application of the Treaties by Member States. The cooperation of other institutions is also required in order to promote greater respect for Community law, in particular through adequately publicized legislation helping to establish the legal certainty of Community norms in the domestic system.

Similarly, Community institutions other than the Court have used various administrative acts to clarify Community law and render it more certain and secure. For instance, the Commission has at various times used "general communications" to address the legal situation within a particular sector of Community law and to serve as a guide for both public authorities regarding their obligations and Community citizens regarding their rights. Although not an authoritative legal text, a general communication helps coordinate case law and written law and sets out the basis on which the Commission will exercise its regulatory

28. Paolo Mengozzi, Diritto Privato e Diritto Comunitario, 21 Trattato di Diritto Privato 185, 187 (Pietro Rescigno, ed. 1987).

29. Id. See also Paolo Mengozzi, European Community Law 78–85 (1992).

and enforcement powers in a given area. Another example is the "negative clearance" in Community competition law, a procedure by which the Commission certifies that a particular business agreement or practice is outside the scope of the competition law without having to refer the matter to judicial decision. The procedure, form and content of a negative clearance essentially provide a form of quasi-judicial legal assistance to businesses.

These and other "nonstandard" administrative acts, according to Mengozzi, do not diminish the importance of case law and adjudication in the Community system. Nevertheless:

> [T]heir existence unequivocally shows that the legal tradition of the continental European countries, the primary protagonists of the Community integration process and the only members of the Community when that process began, has not completely or passively withdrawn. On the contrary, albeit within certain limits, the legal tradition of the continental European countries works against the tendency of the Court of Justice's jurisprudence to become a true source of law. The strongly felt need for legal certainty, the experience of codes and of a single text, as well as the limited analytical study of jurisprudence [i.e., case law] even in university law faculties, so typical and characteristic of the civil law culture of continental Europe, have led the Community institutions not to emphasize the law-creating role of Community jurisprudence by making it the central and privileged element of reference for legal actors. Rather than encourage exclusive reliance on its study, and instead of trying to make legal advisors directly aware of it and thereby leading them to adapt to its novelties, the Community institutions have thought carefully about how to promote alternative instruments (negative clearances and other nonstandard acts created in the context of competition policy) or made recourse to the adoption of instruments (communications) which they considered suitable for conforming, as much as possible, the novelty to tradition. All of this effort is understandable, and even praiseworthy. It should, however, be appreciated in the context of the practical purpose which gave rise to it. To overvalue it and thereby obscure the new importance to be given to the study of case law would be a serious error.[30]

In this way, the innovations of Community law are in dialectical tension with the legal traditions of the civil law countries of continental Europe.

Beyond the processes and methods of the different legal systems, a similar dialectic can be seen between the substantive law of the Community and that of the Member States, whether in traditionally public areas like administrative law, or those areas traditionally governed by the great 19th century civil codes. With regard to the latter, Community law both reflects and helps to further private law's progressive recognition of the contemporary economic and political organization of society.

---

30. Mengozzi, European Community Law 84–85 (1992).

Most directly, Community law has formally established certain legal regimes at variance with traditional civil law constructs, especially in areas such as labor, banking, insurance and consumer law. Various examples can be found of Community legislation or Court decisions departing from the contracts or torts principles of the civil codes. With regard to consumer contracts, for instance, a 1985 Community directive both requires a written contract, and at the same time makes it easier for the consumer to repudiate the contract and be refunded any payment that has already been made. Such developments constitute exceptions to the strict principle of consent traditional to the civil law. Similarly, in an attempt to minimize the competitive distortions of different liability insurance rates for companies operating in different Member States, the Community has regulated the legal regime of liability for defective products. At the national level, such Community constructs have resulted in decisions such as that of a German court refusing to hold a German company in breach of its contract with an Italian company, even though clearly not complying with the express terms of the contract, because those terms violated a Community directive. The court essentially affirmed the primacy of Community private law over the express intent of the parties and the national law which would have enforced it. Examples such as these, which reach to the heart of the principles upon which the civil law has been built, have led at least one commentator to conclude that Community law, far from affecting only peripheral areas of private law, "has produced genuine innovations from the point of view of the theory of the civil law." [31]

In a more indirect and subtle way, Community law can have an even greater impact on the civil law, as a recent European Court case illustrates. In *Marleasing v. La Commercial Internacional de Alimentacion*,[32] one Spanish company sought to rely on a Community directive in its defense against another Spanish company, even though the Spanish government had failed to enact implementing legislation within the period fixed by the directive. Specifically, the plaintiff sought to have the defendant company declared legally null for "lack of legal purpose" under the Spanish Civil Code. The defendant pleaded that the Community directive on company law did not include "lack of legal purpose" among its enumerated grounds for a declaration of nullity. On a reference from the Spanish court, the European Court confirmed that the directive, satisfying the conditions for direct effect, could be relied upon by private parties against the Member State, but not against other private parties. Nevertheless, the Court held that in order to comply with the EEC Treaty, "in applying national law . . . national courts are required to interpret their national law in the light of the wording and the purpose of the Directive." Thus, although Community law could not be relied upon directly in this matter, the Spanish Civil Code should be

31. Tito Ballarino, L'influence du droit communautaire sur la théorie du droit civil, in Perméabilité des ordres juridiques 335, at 336 (Swiss Institute of Comparative Law, 1992). The examples above are drawn from this article.

32. Case 106/89, November 13, 1990, [1990] E.C.R. 4135.

construed in conformity with Community law not to include "lack of legal purpose" as a grounds for a declaration of nullity. Even when Community law does not formally establish variations from domestic private law, therefore, it is bound to weigh heavily on the interpretation of all national law.

Even more broadly, Community law and the civil codes may have their most complex interactions at the level of the fundamental structure and conceptual framework of private law. In an insightful article, Claude Berr has outlined some of the contours of this relationship, with specific reference to the French Civil Code.[33] As French private law continues to adapt to contemporary socio-economic relationships created by Community constructs, Berr argues, their futures are linked. The civil codes have traditionally viewed social and economic relationships in very individualist terms, Berr notes. For example, they have focused on individual employment contracts instead of the collective aspects of labor, such as strikes. French private law has gradually evolved to accommodate such collective phenomena, and Community law reflects and reinforces that progression, particularly in areas of commercial law. Its development of competition law is perhaps the most striking example. A difference between "good" and "bad" competitive practices, based on consideration of a broader market, was a concept largely foreign to traditional private law, but is now finding a place in domestic law as well as at the Community level.

Competition law also illustrates the increasing applications of functional approaches, especially involving the use of economics, to juridical constructs. This marks a significant divergence from the formal foundations of the civil codes. It is indicative of a broader movement in private law from dogmatic toward functional understandings of law, a trend which has found a clear expression in Community law. Community law, in turn, exposes and encourages this movement in domestic law. For instance, Berr notes, national judges addressing disputes involving Community law as well as national law in France seem to be more free to compare and balance the policy interests involved, and to weigh the practical effects of their judgments, instead of (at least outwardly) limiting themselves to formal interpretive concerns.

At the same time, the dogmatic categories of law are themselves breaking down. The traditional French distinction between civil law and commercial law is increasingly irrelevant, for instance. And although Berr acknowledges that the categories of "public" and "private" have long been blurred, the Community legal order "has definitively highlighted the obsolescence of the distinction." The very subjects of Community law—insurance, competition, freedom to establish a business or provide services, the status of workers, including their rights, social security and freedom of movement, and other areas—all constitute

33. Claude J. Berr, L'influence de la Construction Européenne sur l'Evolution Contemporaine du droit Privé Francais, in   Etudes de Droit des Communautés Européennes 1–21 (1984).

intersections of "public" and "private" law, and therefore underscore the disutility of the distinction.

Instead, Berr notes an evolution toward new "poles of coherence" which cut across traditional divisions of private law and develop the law loosely around certain forms of economic activity, like consumption, competition, employment, or professional activity. Again, the Community order is in this respect only a more stark model of a system which has been evolving for some time at the national level. For instance, at least since 1968 there has been an increasing tendency to teach law in French universities according to functional categories rather than dogmatic ones.

Berr does not believe these poles of coherence can yet be properly called "branches" of law, however; they lack the necessary internal coherence and autonomy. Thus, he believes, part of the common future of Community law and national law includes the need for European jurists (including but not limited to private law specialists) to unite the diverse sectors of contemporary law and establish the essential foundations of a true "economic law." This involves "submitting certain current principles of our private law to the crucible of criticism, due in particular to confrontation with public law specialists and to the clarification of European law, and thus setting down the bases of the law for the 21st century."

Berr is certainly correct in emphasizing the role of public law in establishing the new law of Europe, for it has been the area in which the Community legal order has interacted most dynamically and innovatively with the national law of the Member States. On the one hand, public law fields such as administrative law have historically been the most closely tied to the particular social, political and historical circumstances of the states of Europe, and therefore the least susceptible to either comparative study or to *rapprochement* or unification of any kind. Yet, on the other hand, precisely in these areas the European Court has made the most use of its elaboration of the "general principles of law" discussed above. It has thus drawn most explicitly from the principles "common" to the Member States in this area and forged links between them. For this reason, a number of scholars have looked to public law, especially administrative law, for the roots of a new *ius commune* of Europe.[34]

In fashioning the general principles of law of the Community, the European Court has not drawn on the laws of the Member States in any mechanical way, such as a search for the highest or lowest common standard of legal protection, or the need to find a particular rule of law within a set number of Member States' law to then be applied at the Community level. Instead, the Court has sought to extract broad principles from comparative analysis, which may find concrete expres-

---

34. E.g., Jürgen Schwartze, Tendencies Toward a Common Administrative Law in Europe, 16 European Law Review 3 (1991); Ricardo Alonso Garcia, Derecho Comunitario, Derechos Nacionales y Derecho Comun Europeo 227–301 (1989).

sion in very different ways, or perhaps not at all, within any given Member State. The Court then applies the principle to the Community context as it deems most appropriate, not with a view to establishing how any other jurisdiction might decide the same matter. In a sense, it is drawing less on the legal systems of any of the Member States, and more on the more general legal tradition which they share.

A particularly clear example of this process can be seen in the European Court's recognition, in the context of an antitrust investigation, of a limited privilege for attorney-client communications. Following the Advocate General's detailed review of confidentiality privileges in different legal systems, the Court concluded:

> Community law, which derives not only from the economic but also the legal interpenetration of the Member States, must take into account the principles and concepts common to the laws of those States concerning the observance of confidentiality, in particular, as regards certain communications between lawyer and client. That confidentiality serves the requirements, the importance of which is recognized in all of the Member States, that any person must be able, without constraint, to consult a lawyer whose profession entails the giving of independent legal advice to all those in need of it.

> As far as the protection of written communications between lawyer and client is concerned, it is apparent from the legal systems of the Member States that, although the principle of such protection is generally recognized, its scope and the criteria for applying it vary, as has, indeed, been conceded both by the applicant and by the parties who have intervened in support of its conclusions.

> Whilst in some of the Member States the protection against disclosure afforded to written communications between lawyer and client is based principally on a recognition of the very nature of the legal profession, inasmuch as it contributes towards the maintenance of the rule of law, in other Member States the same protection is justified by the more specific requirements (which, moreover, is also recognized in the first-mentioned States) that the rights of the defence must be respected.

> Apart from these differences, however, there are to be found in the national laws of the Member States common criteria inasmuch as those laws protect, in similar circumstances, the confidentiality of written communications between lawyer and client provided that, on the one hand, such communications are made for the purposes and in the interests of the client's rights of defence and, on the other hand, they emanate from independent lawyers, that is to say, lawyers who are not bound to the client by a relationship of employment.

> Viewed in that context Regulation No. 17 must be interpreted as protecting, in its turn, the confidentiality of written communications between lawyer and client subject to those two conditions, and

thus incorporating such elements of that protection as are common to the Member States.[35]

In this way, the Court does not simply replicate particular rules of national law, but interacts with them dynamically, developing the principles in question while drawing from the foundation of national law.

Crucially, these principles and their application, now in altered form, seep back into national legal systems from which they came through the operation of Community law domestically, particularly through national judiciaries. As one judge of the Supreme Court of the Netherlands, who was also a judge of the European Court of Justice, has pointed out:

> [T]he Court of Justice has become one of the major sources of legal innovation in Europe not only because of its position as the Community's judicial institution, but also because of the strength of its comparative methods. National courts take heed to the Court's way of reasoning. As a result, we sometimes see that legal principles which have made their way from the national systems to the Court's case law, in order to be transformed into principles of Community law, make their way back to the national courts. This happens, of course, not only because of their willingness to adopt a certain method of law finding; besides, national courts are often under an obligation to apply rules of Community law.

* * *

> The upshot of these developments is that the application of principles of Community law tends to be generalized. English courts will thus be checking whether a certain government measure was really "proportionate" to its aims, a concept unknown to the common law. And French courts are starting to get worried about the right to a hearing of a private company in administrative matters, just like a common law court might be. This evolution is, probably, not only due to the influence of Community law and the force of the comparative method, but also to the implementation of the European Convention of Human Rights, which has led to the creation of a certain number of uniform standards public authorities are to observe.[36]

The European Court's opening to fundamental human rights is indeed one of the key ingredients in the reciprocal relationship between Community law and national law. It may well be that the new principles which Berr hopes to set out for the law of the 21st century, or the basis for some scholars' hope in a common law of Europe, consist precisely in a common affirmation of certain universal human rights. These form a common substratum to both international regimes and the

---

35. AM & S Europe Ltd. v. Commission of the European Communities, Case 155/79 [1982] E.C.R. 1575, 1610–11.

36. Thijmen Koopmans, The Birth of European Law at the Crossroads of Legal Traditions, 39 Am.J.Comp.L. 493, 505–506 (1991).

several constitutional orders, as well as (incipiently) the European Community. In fact, as we have seen, in defining and protecting fundamental rights the European Court has looked to both Member States' constitutional principles and the European Convention on Human Rights. As a unified statement of fundamental legal norms by all of the European countries, the European Convention on Human Rights is perhaps the single clearest (even if only partial) expression of the political and philosophical principles which animate modern European law. It is appropriate, then, that we also turn to the European regional human rights system, considering it a possible focal point for a "common law of Europe."

SECTION 2. THE EUROPEAN HUMAN RIGHTS SYSTEM

In the aftermath of the second World War, the countries of western Europe agreed to establish a regional Council of Europe for the development of European unity. Impetus for the creation of the Council came in large part from two related goals: the desire to ensure that the horrors of the Nazi dictatorship would never be repeated, and the desire to fortify the West in the face of the expanding power of the Soviet Union. The Statute of the Council of Europe, signed in London in May 1949, accordingly places particular emphasis on human rights and democratic governance. The Preamble declares that the parties are "Reaffirming their devotion to the spiritual and moral values which are the common heritage of their peoples and the true source of individual freedom, political liberty and the rule of law, principles which form the basis of all genuine democracy." Article 3 of the Statute goes on to make these principles a condition of membership in the Council: "Every Member of the Council of Europe must accept the principles of the rule of law and of the enjoyment by all persons within its jurisdiction of human rights and fundamental freedoms."

To this end, one of the first tasks of the Council, including both its Consultative Assembly and the Committee of Ministers,[37] was to create a normative and institutional system for the guarantee of human rights in Europe. The process of drafting and negotiating the provisions of the new European Convention on Human Rights culminated in the signature of the Treaty on November 4, 1950.[38]

When it entered into force on September 3, 1953 (after having been ratified by ten states), the Convention established the first supranational institutional system for the protection and promotion of human rights. Its particular innovative strengths lay not only in making the relations

---

37. Established by the Statute of the Council of Europe, the Committee is a political body consisting of the Minister of Foreign Affairs of each Member State of the Council, serving as representatives of their respective governments.

38. For a description of the drafting and negotiation process, see Mark W. Janis & Richard S. Kay, European Human Rights Law 22–32 (1990).

between a state and its own citizens the object of international obligations (for which there had been modest precedent earlier in the century), but also in the Convention's enforcement mechanisms. The Convention gives individuals as well as states the right to petition the European Commission of Human Rights (Article 25), and confers on the European Court of Human Rights jurisdiction over "all cases concerning the interpretation and application of the present Convention which the High Contracting Parties or the Commission shall refer to it" (Articles 45–46).[39] Given the limited European experience of judicial review until then, the Convention thus marked a significant step toward acceptance of the judicial enforcement of fundamental rights. Substantively, the Convention has also helped to develop a common stratum of foundational principles for the legal and political systems of Europe. As of September, 1993, 28 Member States of the Council of Europe had ratified the Convention.[40]

A. THE RIGHTS PROTECTED

CONVENTION FOR THE PROTECTION OF HUMAN RIGHTS AND FUNDAMENTAL FREEDOMS (1950)

(Selected provisions).

The Governments signatory hereto, being Members of the Council of Europe,

Considering the Universal Declaration of Human Rights proclaimed by the General Assembly of the United Nations on 10th December 1948;

Considering that this declaration aims at securing the universal and effective recognition and observance of the Rights therein declared;

Considering that the aim of the Council of Europe is the achievement of greater unity between its Members and that one of the methods by which that aim is to be pursued is the maintenance and further realization of Human Rights and Fundamental Freedoms;

Reaffirming their profound belief in those Fundamental Freedoms which are the foundation of justice and peace in the world and are best maintained on the one hand by an effective political democracy and on the other by a common understanding and observance of the Human Rights upon which they depend;

Being resolved, as the Governments of European Countries which are likeminded and have a common heritage of political traditions, ideals,

39. Although both Article 25 and Article 46 are optional, all of the contracting States have made special declarations accepting these provisions.

40. These include: Austria, Belgium, Bulgaria, Cyprus, The Czech Republic, Denmark, Finland, France, Germany, Greece, Hungary, Iceland, Ireland, Italy, Liechten- stein, Luxembourg, Malta, Netherlands, Norway, Poland, Portugal, San Marino, The Slovak Republic, Spain, Sweden, Switzerland, Turkey and the United Kingdom. The remaining three Member States, Estonia, Lithuania and Slovenia, had signed but not yet ratified the Convention.

freedom and the rule of law to take the first steps for the collective enforcement of certain of the Rights stated in the Universal Declaration,

Have agreed as follows:

Article 1

The High Contracting Parties shall secure to everyone within their jurisdiction the rights and freedoms defined in Section I of this Convention.

Section I

Article 2

1. Everyone's right to life shall be protected by law. No one shall be deprived of his life intentionally save in the execution of a sentence of a court following his conviction of a crime for which this penalty is provided by law.

2. Deprivation of life shall not be regarded as inflicted in contravention of this Article when it results from the use of force which is no more than absolutely necessary:

(a) in defence of any person from unlawful violence;

(b) in order to effect a lawful arrest or to prevent the escape of a person lawfully detained;

(c) in action lawfully taken for the purpose of quelling a riot or insurrection.

Article 3

No one shall be subjected to torture or to inhuman or degrading treatment or punishment

Article 4

1. No one shall be held in slavery or servitude.

2. No one shall be required to perform forced or compulsory labour.

3. For the purpose of this Article the term "forced or compulsory labour" shall not include:

(a) any work required to be done in the ordinary course of detention imposed according to the provisions of Article 5 of this Convention or during conditional release from such detention;

(b) any service of a military character or, in the case of conscientious objectors in countries where they are recognised, service exacted instead of compulsory military service;

(c) any service exacted in case of an emergency or calamity threatening the life or well-being of the community;

(d) any work or service which forms part of normal civic obligations.

Article 5

1.   Everyone has the right to liberty and security of person. No one shall be deprived of his liberty save in the following cases and in accordance with a procedure prescribed by law:

> (a) the lawful detention of a person after conviction by a competent court;

> (b) the lawful arrest or detention of a person for non-compliance with the lawful order of a court or in order to secure the fulfillment of any obligation prescribed by law;

> (c) the lawful arrest or detention of a person effected for the purpose of bringing him before the competent legal authority on reasonable suspicion of having committed an offence or when it is reasonably considered necessary to prevent his committing an offence or fleeing after having done so;

> (d) the detention of a minor by lawful order for the purpose of educational supervision or his lawful detention for the purpose of bringing him before the competent legal authority;

> (e) the lawful detention of persons for the prevention of the spreading of infectious diseases, of persons of unsound mind, alcoholics or drug addicts or vagrants;

> (f) the lawful arrest or detention of a person to prevent his effecting an unauthorised entry into the country or of a person against whom action is being taken with a view to deportation or extradition.

2.   Everyone who is arrested shall be informed promptly, in a language which he understands, of the reasons for his arrest and of any charge against him.

3.   Everyone arrested or detained in accordance with the provisions of paragraph 1(c) of this Article shall be brought promptly before a judge or other officer authorised by law to exercise judicial power and shall be entitled to trial within a reasonable time or to release pending trial. Release may be conditioned by guarantees to appear for trial.

4.   Everyone who is deprived of his liberty by arrest or detention shall be entitled to take proceedings by which the lawfulness of his detention shall be decided speedily by a court and his release ordered if the detention is not lawful.

5.   Everyone who has been the victim of an arrest or detention in contravention of the provisions of this Article shall have an enforceable right to compensation.

Article 6

1.   In the determination of his civil rights and obligations or of any criminal charge against him, everyone is entitled to a fair and public hearing within a reasonable time by an independent and impartial tribunal established by law. Judgment shall be pronounced publicly but

the press and public may be excluded from all or part of the trial in the interest of morals, public order or national security in a democratic society, where the interests of juveniles or the protection of the private life of the parties so require, or to the extent strictly necessary in the opinion of the court in special circumstances where publicity would prejudice the interests of justice.

2. Everyone charged with a criminal offence shall be presumed innocent until proved guilty according to law.

3. Everyone charged with a criminal offence has the following minimum rights;

(a) to be informed promptly, in a language which he understands and in detail, of the nature and cause of the accusation against him;

(b) to have adequate time and facilities for the preparation of his defence;

(c) to defend himself in person or through legal assistance of his own choosing or, if he has not sufficient means to pay for legal assistance, to be given it free when the interests of justice so require;

(d) to examine or have examined witnesses against him and to obtain the attendance and examination of witnesses on his behalf under the same conditions as witness against him;

(e) to have the assistance of an interpreter if he cannot understand or speak the language used in court.

Article 7

1. No one shall be held guilty of any criminal offence on account of any act or omission which did not constitute a criminal offence under national or international law at the time when it was committed. Nor shall a heavier penalty be imposed than the one that was applicable at the time the criminal offence was committed.

2. This Article shall not prejudice the trial and punishment of any person for any act or omission which, at the time when it was committed, was criminal according to the general principles of law recognized by civilized nations.

Article 8

1. Everyone has the right to respect for his private and family life, his home and correspondence.

2. There shall be no interference by a public authority with the exercise of this right except such as is in accordance with the law and is necessary in a democratic society in the interests of national security, public safety or the economic well-being of the country, for the prevention of disorder of crime, for the protection of health or morals, or for the protection of the rights and freedoms of others.

Article 9

1. Everyone has the right to freedom of thought, conscience and religion; this right includes freedom to change his religion or belief and freedom, either alone or in community with others and in public or private, to manifest his religion or belief, in worship, teaching, practice and observance.

2. Freedom to manifest one's religion or beliefs shall be subject only to such limitations as are prescribed by law and are necessary in a democratic society in the interests of public safety, for the protection of public order, health or morals, or for the protection of the rights and freedoms of others.

Article 10

1. Everyone has the right to freedom of expression. This right shall include freedom to hold opinions and to receive and impart information and ideas without interference by public authority and regardless of frontiers. This Article shall not prevent States from requiring the licensing of broadcasting, television or cinema enterprises.

2. The exercise of these freedoms, since it carries with it duties and responsibilities, may be subject to such formalities, conditions, restrictions or penalties as are prescribed by law and are necessary in a democratic society, in the interests of national security, territorial integrity or public safety, for the prevention of disorder or crime, for the protection of health or morals, for the protection of the reputation of the rights of others, for preventing the disclosure of information received in confidence, or for maintaining the authority or impartiality of the judiciary.

Article 11

1. Everyone has the right to freedom of peaceful assembly and to freedom of association with others, including the right to form and to join trade unions for the protection of his interests.

2. No restrictions shall be placed on the exercise of these rights other than such as are prescribed by law and are necessary in a democratic society in the interests of national security or public safety, for the prevention of disorder or crime, for the protection of health or morals or for the protection of the rights and freedoms of others. This Article shall not prevent the imposition of lawful restrictions on the exercise of these rights by members of the armed forces, of the police or of the administration of the State.

Article 12

Men and women of marriageable age have the right to marry and to found a family, according to the national laws governing the exercise of this right.

Article 13

Everyone whose rights and freedoms are set forth in this Convention are violated shall have an effective remedy before a national authority notwithstanding that the violation has been committed by persons acting in an official capacity.

Article 14

The enjoyment of the rights and freedoms set forth in this Convention shall be secured without discrimination on any ground such as sex, race, colour, language, religion, political or other opinion, national or social origin, association with a national minority, property, birth or other status.

Article 16

Nothing in Articles 10, 11 and 14 shall be regarded as preventing the High Contracting Parties from imposing restrictions on the political activity of aliens.

Article 17

Nothing in this Convention may be interpreted as implying for any State, group or person any right to engage in any activity or perform any act aimed at the destruction of any of the rights and freedoms set forth herein or at their limitation to greater extent than is provided for in the Convention.

———

Three additional rights were considered and subject to negotiations throughout the drafting of the Convention: the right to property, the right to free elections, and the right of parents to choose the kind of education given to their children. However, at first the Committee of Ministers was unable to reach agreement on them. In particular, there was concern over the sensitive issues of state nationalization of industries, accommodation of religious education and its implications for church-state relations, and recognition of the varying forms of representative democratic government. Rather than wait for agreement on these questions, the Committee of Ministers decided to approve the Convention without statements of those rights and to consider them further, leaving them to a separate protocol if necessary. Although this decision provoked strong criticism at the time, consensus on the rights in question followed presently. In March of 1952 the First Protocol to the Convention was opened for signature.

FIRST PROTOCOL (1952)

Article 1

Every natural or legal person is entitled to the peaceful enjoyment of his possessions. No one shall be deprived of his possessions except in the public interest and subject to the conditions provided for by law and by the general principles of international law.

The preceding provisions shall not, however, in any way impair the right of a State to enforce such laws as it deems necessary to control the use of property in accordance with the general interest or to secure the payment of taxes or other contributions or penalties.

Article 2

No person shall be denied the right to education. In the exercise of any functions which it assumes in relation to education and to teaching, the State shall respect the right of parents to ensure such education and teaching in conformity of their own religious and philosophical positions.

Article 3

The High Contracting parties undertake to hold free elections at reasonable intervals by secret ballot, under conditions which will ensure the free expression of the opinion of the people in the choice of the legislature.

In addition to debate about the rights guaranteed in the First Protocol, the drafting and negotiating process included discussion about how to address various economic and social rights, in addition to the political and civil rights that were agreed upon in the Convention. Many of the post-war constitutions of the European states recognized such principles. In the decade following adoption of the Convention, the Council of Europe sought to elaborate a set of common social and economic goals for the Member States. Because of the wide discrepancies in conditions between the social and economic conditions and resources of the different European states, as well as the difficulties in defining standards and devising enforcement procedures, it was thought that a separate instrument would be more appropriate than an expansion of the Convention. Drafted by the Social Committee of the Council of Europe, the European Social Charter was signed in October of 1961 and entered into force in 1965. At present, most of the Contracting Parties to the Convention are also parties to the Social Charter.[41]

The Charter's 19 rights and principles include, among others, the rights of workers, the right to education, health, social security and social welfare services, and protection of the family, especially mothers and children. In recognition of the difficulties in protecting economic and social rights, mentioned above, the Charter sets forth widely varying legal obligations for different rights, and emphasizes their progressive implementation over time. Supervision of the Parties' compliance with the Charter is entrusted to a Committee of Experts, who receive and examine biannual reports from the Contracting Parties. The Committee forwards its conclusions to the Assembly and the Committee of Ministers; the latter can then make recommendations to the Parties concerning their implementation of the rights guaranteed by the Charter.

41. As of September, 1993, the Czech Republic, Hungary, Lichtenstein, Poland, the Slovak Republic and Switzerland had signed but not ratified the Charter; Bulgaria, Estonia, Lithuania, San Marino and Slovenia had not signed it.

In addition to adopting the Social Charter, the Council of Europe has also added to the civil and political rights of the Convention in the years since its adoption. The Fourth Protocol, concluded in 1963, recognized four additional, important rights: freedom from imprisonment for debt; freedom of movement, including the right to leave any country; the right to enter one's own country and freedom from expulsion therefrom; and a prohibition on the collective expulsion of aliens. The next expansion of the substantive guarantees of the Convention did not occur until 1983, with the Sixth Protocol's abolition of capital punishment in times of peace (superseding Article 2 of the Convention). A year later, the Seventh Protocol established five more guarantees: protection of the due process rights of aliens being expelled; the right to appeal in criminal cases; the right to compensation for miscarriages of justice; freedom from being tried twice for the same offence; and the equality of the rights and responsibilities of spouses.

B. THE CONVENTION ORGANS

The principal organs of the European human rights system include the European Commission on Human Rights and the European Court of Human Rights, both of which sit in Strasbourg.

The European Commission of Human Rights

The Commission is composed of a number of members equal to that of the Contracting Parties, no two of whom can be nationals of the same state (although they need not necessarily be from one of the Contracting States at all). They are elected by the Committee of Ministers of the Council of Europe from lists of names submitted by each Member State's delegation to the Consultative Assembly. The candidates must be of "high moral character and must either possess the qualifications required for appointment to high judicial office or be persons of recognised competence in national or international law." During their six-year renewable terms, they cannot be removed from office against their will. They sit on the Commission in their individual capacities, not as representatives of the Member States, and may not hold during their term of office "any position which is incompatible with their independence and impartiality as members of the Commission" (Articles 20–23).

The role of the Commission is to receive applications from states and individuals alleging violations of the Convention. The Commission may only accept an application within six months after all domestic remedies have been exhausted; the petition may not be anonymous, nor may it present substantially the same matter which the Commission or another international body has already examined. The Commission must dismiss any individual petition "which it considers incompatible with the provisions of the present Convention, manifestly ill-founded, or an abuse of the right of petition." In cases which the Commission deems admissible according to those standards, Articles 24–26 provide:

(a) it shall, with a view to ascertaining the facts, undertake together with the representatives of the parties an examination of the petition and, if need be, an investigation, for the effective conduct of which the States concerned shall furnish all necessary facilities, after an exchange of views with the Commission;

(b) it shall at the same time place itself at the disposal of the parties concerned with a view to securing a friendly settlement of the matter on the basis of respect for Human Rights as defined in this Convention.

If a friendly settlement is not reached, the Commission prepares a report of the facts together with its opinion as to whether those facts reveal a breach of the Convention, and submits the report to the Committee of Ministers. In addition, within three months it may refer the case to the Court for a decision. In practice the Commission ordinarily relies on the Court, not the Committee of Ministers, when it seeks to enforce a ruling or to obtain a legally binding result in closely contested cases.

The European Court of Human Rights

Like the members of the Commission, the judges of the Court are nominated by Member States, elected by the Consultative Assembly, must each be nationals of different states, and must meet the same moral and professional standards. They also sit in their individual capacities, not as representatives of their governments, and are not permitted to hold any position incompatible with their independence and impartiality as members of the Court. However, the Court is composed of a number of judges equal to the total number of members of the Council of Europe (not only the number of Contracting Parties of the Convention), and they serve nine-year renewable terms. The Court does not sit permanently, but meets in periodic sessions.[42]

Until now, only the High Contracting Parties and the Commission have had the right to bring cases before the Court.[43] However, the great majority of the Court's cases are brought by the Commission, and most of the suits before the Commission are initiated by private parties. Thus, the Court came to recognize early on that the real "parties in interest" before the Court in such cases are the individuals involved.[44] The access of private parties to the Court has been essential to the development of the system, accounting for an overwhelming proportion

---

42. In October, 1993, the Council of Europe voted to establish a full-time Court, but the change had not been implemented as of the time of this writing.

43. The Ninth Protocol to the Convention, opened for signature in November, 1990 will provide a qualified right to individuals to bring a case before the Court. It will enter into force after it has been rati-

fied by ten Member States of the Council of Europe.

44. In its very first case, for instance, the Court agreed over the objections of Ireland to let lawyers for the individual petitioner argue before it. Lawless Case, Preliminary Objections and Questions of Procedure, Judgment of November 14, 1960 (Series A: Vol. 1, 1961).

of the Court's rapidly growing caseload and output.[45]   In the first ten years of the Court, through 1969, only ten judgments were issued; in the 1970's the number of judgments increased somewhat, but the Court had still only issued a total of 36 judgments by the end of 1979.   The next decade, however, witnessed an extraordinary expansion in the Court's activity.   It gave 58 judgments in the first half of the 1980's, and 111 between 1985 and 1989.   Its current output of decisions is now over 25 annually and still growing.[46]   The case law of the Court has addressed nearly all the provisions of the Convention and is developing into a substantial body of jurisprudence.   Rolv Ryssdal, President of the European Court of Human Rights, has referred to this growth as the development of a "Constitutional Court of Europe":

> The Convention has become the embryo of a European Constitution . . .   Thanks to the firm anchoring of effective political democracy on our continent, the Convention institutions do not nowadays have to deal with gross violations of human rights as occurred in Europe in the 30's and 40's and still occur in too many parts of the world. The typical issue brought before the Commission and the Court is more of a constitutional nature: it embraces the age-long and sensitive problem of the balance to be struck between the general interest of the community and the protection of the individual's fundamental rights.   This is how the Convention and its institutions contribute today to the process of creating [a] United Europe . . .[47]

Clearly, such questions can reach deeply into the legal orders of the separate states of Europe, requiring them to conform to the common "constitutional" principles of the Convention.   A particularly clear and important example of this process can be seen in the following landmark decision of the Court.

MARCKX v. BELGIUM

2 European Human Rights Reporter 330 (1979).

* * *

THE FACTS

A.   *Particular Circumstances of the Case*

8.   Alexandra Marckx was born on 16 October 1973 at Wilrijk, near Antwerp; she is the daughter of Paula Marckx, a Belgian national, who is unmarried and a journalist by profession.   Paula Marckx duly reported Alexandra's birth to the Wilrijk registration officer who informed the District Judge (*juge de paix*) as is required by article 57 *bis* of the Belgian Civil Code in the case of "illegitimate" children.

9.   On 26 October 1973, the District Judge of the first district of Antwerp summoned Paula Marckx to appear before him so as to obtain

45. Mark W. Janis & Richard S. Kay, European Human Rights Law 93–94 (1990).

46. A.H. Robertson & J.G. Merrills, Human Rights in Europe 310–311 (1993).

47. Rolv Ryssdal, On the Road to a European Constitutional Court, in 2 Collected Courses of the Academy of European Law, 1991, Book 2, 9 (1993).

from her the information required to make arrangements for Alexandra's guardianship; at the same time, he informed her of the methods available for recognising her daughter and of the consequences in law of any such recognition (see para. 14 below). He also drew her attention to certain provisions of the Civil Code, including Article 756 which concerns "exceptional" forms of inheritance (*successions "irrégulières"*).

10. On 29 October 1974, Paula Marckx recognised her child in accordance with Article 334 of the Code. She thereby automatically became Alexandra's guardian (Art. 395 *bis*); the family council, on which the sister and certain other relatives of Paula Marckx sat under the chairmanship of the District Judge, was empowered to take in Alexandra's interest various measures provided for by law.

11. On 30 October 1974, Paula Marckx adopted her daughter pursuant to Article 349 of the Civil Code. The procedure, which was that laid down by articles 350 to 356, entailed certain enquiries and involved some expenses. It concluded on 18 April 1975 with a judgment confirming the adoption, the effect whereof was retroactive to the date of the instrument of adoption, namely, 30 October 1974.

12. At the time of her application to the Commission, Ms. Paula Marckx's family included, besides Alexandra, her own mother, Mrs. Victorine Libot, who died in August 1974, and a sister, Mrs. Blanche Marckx.

13. The applicants complain of the Civil Code provisions on the manner of establishing the maternal affiliation of an "illegitimate" child and on the effects of establishing such affiliation as regards both the extent of the child's family relationships and the patrimonial rights of the child and of its mother. The applicants also put in issue the necessity for the mother to adopt the child if she wishes to increase its rights.

B. *Current Law*

(1) Establishment of the Maternal Affiliation of an "Illegitimate" Child

14. Under Belgian law, no legal bond between an unmarried mother and her child results from the mere fact of birth; whilst the birth certificate recorded at the register office suffices to prove the maternal affiliation of the married woman's children (Art. 319 of the Civil Code), the maternal affiliation of an "illegitimate" child is established by means either of a voluntary recognition by the mother or of legal proceedings taken for the purpose (*action en recherche de maternité*). Nevertheless, an unrecognised "illegitimate" child bears its mother's name which must appear on the birth certificate (Art. 57). The appointment of its guardian is a matter for the family council which is presided over by the District Judge.

Under Article 334, recognition, "if not inserted in the birth certificate, shall be effected by a formal deed." Recognition is declaratory and not attributive: it does not create but records the child's status and is retroactive to the date of birth. However, it does not necessarily follow that the person effecting recognition is actually the child's mother; on the contrary, any interested party may claim that the recognition does not correspond to the truth (Art. 339). Many unmarried mothers—about 25 per cent. according to the Government, although the applicants consider this an exaggerated figure—do not recognise their child.

Proceedings to establish maternal affiliation (*action en recherche de maternité*) may be instituted by the child within five years from its attainment of majority or, whilst it is still a minor, by its legal representative with the consent of the family council (Arts. 341a–341c).

(2) Effects of the Establishment of Maternal Affiliation

15. The establishment of maternal affiliation of an "illegitimate" child has limited effects as regards both the extent of its family relationships and the rights of the child and its mother in the matter of inheritance on intestacy and voluntary dispositions.

(a) The Extent of Family Relationships

16. In the context of the maternal affiliation of an "illegitimate" child, Belgian legislation does not employ the concepts of "family" and "relative". Even once such affiliation has been established, it in principle creates a legal bond with the mother alone. The child does not become a member of its mother's family. The law excludes it from that family as regards inheritance rights on intestacy (see para. 17 below). Furthermore, if the child's parents are dead or under an incapacity, it cannot marry, before attaining the age of 21, without consent, which has to be given by its guardian (Art. 159) and not, as is the case for a "legitimate" child, by his grandparents (Art. 150); the law does not expressly create any maintenance obligations, etc., between the child and its grandparents. However, certain texts make provision for exceptions, for example as regards the impediments to marriage (Arts. 161 and 162)....

(b) Rights of a Child Born Out of Wedlock and of His Mother in the Matter of Inheritance on Intestacy and Voluntary Dispositions

17. A recognised "illegitimate" child's rights of inheritance on intestacy are less than those of a "legitimate" child. As appears from Articles 338, 724, 756, 760, 761, 769 to 773 and 913 of the Civil Code, a recognised "illegitimate" child does not have, in the estate of a parent who dies intestate, the status of an heir, but solely that of "exceptional heir" (*successeur irrégulier*): it has to seek a court order putting it in possession of the estate (*envoi en possession*). It is the sole beneficiary of its deceased mother's estate only if she leaves no relatives entitled to inherit (Art. 758); otherwise, its maximum entitlement—which arises when its mother leaves no descendants, ascendants, brothers or sisters—is three-quarters of the share which it would have taken if "legitimate" (Art. 757). Furthermore, the mother may, during her lifetime, reduce that entitlement by one-half. Finally, Article 756 denies to the "illegiti-

mate" child any rights on intestacy in the estates of its mother's relatives.

18.   Recognised "illegitimate" children are also at a disadvantage as regards voluntary dispositions, since Article 908 provides that they "may receive by disposition *inter vivos* or by will no more than their entitlement under the title 'Inheritance on Intestacy' ".

Conversely, the mother of such a child, unless she has no relatives entitled to inherit, may give in her lifetime or bequeath to it only part of her property.   On the other hand, if the child's affiliation has not been established, the mother may so give or bequeath to it the whole of her property, provided that there are no heirs entitled to a reserved portion of her estate (*héritiers réservataires*).   The mother is thus faced with the following alternative: either she recognises the child and loses the possibility of leaving all her estate to it;   or she renounces establishing with it a family relationship in the eyes of the law, in order to retain the possibility of leaving all her estate to it just as she might to a stranger.

(3) Adoption of "Illegitimate" Children by Their Mother

19.   If the mother of a recognised "illegitimate" child remains unmarried, she has but one means of improving its status, namely, "simple" adoption.   In such cases, the age requirements for this form of adoption are eased by Article 345(2)(2) of the Civil Code.   The adopted child acquires over the adopter's estate the rights of a "legitimate" child but, unlike the latter, has no rights on intestacy in the estates of its mother's relatives (Art. 365).

Only legitimation (Art. 331–333) and legitimation by adoption (Arts. 368–370) place an "illegitimate" child on exactly the same footing as a "legitimate" child;   both of these measures presuppose the mother's marriage.

* * *

PROCEEDINGS BEFORE THE COMMISSION

22.   The essence of the applicants' allegations before the Commission was as follows:

— as an "illegitimate" child, Alexandra Marckx is the victim, as a result of certain provisions of the Belgian Civil Code, of a *capitis deminutio* incompatible with Articles 3 and 8 of the Convention;

— this *capitis deminutio* also violates the said articles with respect to Paula Marckx;

— there are instances of discrimination, contrary to Article 14 taken in conjunction with Article 8, between "legitimate" and "illegitimate" children and between unmarried and married mothers;

— the fact that an illegitimate child may be recognised by any man, even if he is not the father, violates Articles 3, 8 and 14;

— Article 1 of Protocol No. 1 is violated by reason of the fact that an unmarried mother is not free to dispose of her property in favour of her child.

[By a majority, the Commission found violations of Article 8, Article 8 in conjunction with Article 14, Article 1 of Protocol No. 1 in conjunction with Article 14, and referred the case to the Court.]

JUDGMENT *

* * *

II. *The merits*

28. The applicants rely basically on Articles 8 and 14 of the Convention. Without overlooking the other provisions which they invoke, The Court has accordingly turned primarily to these two articles in its consideration of the three aspects of the problem referred to it by the Commission: the manner of establishing affiliation, the extent of the child's family relationships, the patrimonial rights of the child and of her mother.

* * *

30. The Court is led in the present case to clarify the meaning and purport of the words "respect for . . . private and family life" [in Article 8 of the Convention], which it has scarcely had the occasion to do until now.

31. The first question for decision is whether the natural tie between Paula and Alexandra Marckx gave rise to a family life protected by Article 8.

By guaranteeing the right to respect for family life, Article 8 presupposes the existence of a family. The Court concurs entirely with the Commission's established case law on a crucial point, namely, that Article 8 makes no distinction between the "legitimate" and the "illegitimate" family. Such a distinction would not be consonant with the word "everyone", and this is confirmed by Article 14 with its prohibition, in the enjoyment of the rights and freedoms enshrined in the Convention, of discrimination grounded on "birth". In addition, the Court notes that the Committee of Ministers of the Council of Europe regards the single woman and her child as one form of family no less than others.

Article 8 thus applies to the "family life" of the "illegitimate" family as it does to that of the "legitimate" family. Besides, it is not disputed that Paula Marckx assumed responsibility for her daughter Alexandra from the moment of her birth and has continuously cared for her, with the result that a real family life existed and still exists between them.

It remains to be ascertained what the "respect" for this family life required of the Belgian legislature in each of the areas covered by the application.

_____

* Drawn up in French and English, the French text being authentic.

By proclaiming in paragraph 1 the right to respect for family life, Article 8 signifies first that the State cannot interfere with the exercise of that right otherwise than in accordance with the strict conditions set out in paragraph 2. As the Court stated in the *Belgian Linguistic Case,* the object of the Article is "essentially" that of protecting the individual against arbitrary interference by the public authorities. Nevertheless, it does not merely compel the State to abstain from such interference: in addition to this primarily negative undertaking, there may be positive obligations inherent in an effective "respect" for family life.

This means, amongst other things, that when the State determines in its domestic legal system the regime applicable to certain family ties such as those between an unmarried mother and her child, it must act in a manner calculated to allow those concerned to lead a normal family life. As envisaged by Article 8, respect for family life implies in particular, in the Court's view, the existence in domestic law of legal safeguards that render possible, as from the moment of birth, the child's integration in its family. In this connection, the State has a choice of various means, but a law that fails to satisfy this requirement violates paragraph 1 of Article 8 without there being any call to examine it under paragraph 2.

Article 8 being therefore relevant to the present case, the Court has to review in detail each of the applicants' complaints in the light of this provision.

32.   ...

The Court's case law shows that, although Article 14 has no independent existence, it may play an important autonomous role by complementing the other normative provisions of the Convention and the Protocols: Article 14 safeguards individuals, placed in similar situations, from any discrimination in the enjoyment of those rights and freedoms set forth in those other provisions. A measure which, although in itself in conformity with the requirements of the Article of the Convention or the Protocols enshrining a given right or freedom, is of a discriminatory nature incompatible with Article 14, therefore violates those two articles taken in conjunction. It is as though Article 14 formed an integral part of each of the provisions laying down rights and freedoms.

Accordingly, and since Article 8 is relevant to the present case (see para. 31 above), it is necessary also to take into account Article 14 in conjunction with Article 8.

33. According to the Court's established case law, a distinction is discriminatory if it "has no objective and reasonable justification", that is, if it does not pursue a "legitimate aim" or if there is not a "reasonable relationship of proportionality between the means employed and the aim sought to be realised".

34. In acting in a manner calculated to allow the family life of an unmarried mother and her child to develop normally (see para. 31

above), the State must avoid any discrimination grounded on birth: this is dictated by Article 14 taken in conjunction with Article 8.

A.   *The Manner of Establishing Alexandra Marckx's Maternal Affiliation*

* * *

1.   *The Alleged Violation of Article 8 of the Convention, Taken Alone*

36.   Paul Marckx was able to establish Alexandra's affiliation only by the means afforded by Article 334 of the Civil Code, namely, recognition. The effect of recognition is declaratory and not attributive: it does not create but records the child's status. It is irrevocable and retroactive to the date of birth. Furthermore, the procedure to be followed hardly presents difficulties: the declaration may take the form of a notarial deed, but it may also be added, at any time and without expense to the record of the birth at the register office (see para. 14 above).

Nevertheless, the necessity to have recourse to such an expedient derived from a refusal fully to acknowledge Paula Marckx's maternity from the moment of the birth. Moreover, in Belgium an unmarried mother is faced with an alternative: if she recognises her child (assuming she wishes to do so), she will at the same time prejudice it since her capacity to give or bequeath her property to it will be restricted; if she desires to retain the possibility of making such dispositions as she chooses in her child's favour, she will be obliged to renounce establishing a family tie with it in law (see para. 18 above). Admittedly, that possibility, which is now open to her in the absence of recognition, would disappear entirely under the current civil code if, as the applicants wish, the mere mention of the mother's name on the birth certificate were to constitute proof of any "illegitimate" child's maternal affiliation. However, the dilemma which exists at present is not consonant with "respect" for family life; it thwarts and impedes the normal development of such life (see para. 31 above)....

The Court thus concludes that there has been a violation of Article 8, taken alone, with respect to the first applicant.

37.   As regards Alexandra Marckx, only one method of establishing her maternal affiliation was available to her under Belgian law, namely, to take legal proceedings for the purpose (*recherche de maternité*). Although a judgment declaring the affiliation of an "illegitimate" child has the same effects as a voluntary recognition, the procedure applicable is, in the nature of things, far more complex. Quite apart from the conditions of proof that have to be satisfied, the legal representative of an infant needs the consent of the family council before he can bring, assuming he wishes to do so, an action for a declaration as to status; it is only after attaining majority that the child can bring such an action itself (see para. 14 above). There is thus a risk that the establishment of affiliation will be time-consuming and that, in the interim, the child will remain separated in law from its mother. This system resulted in a lack of respect for the family life of Alexandra Marckx who, in the eyes of the

law, was motherless from 16 to 29 October 1973. Despite the brevity of this period, there was thus also a violation of Article 8 with respect to the second applicant.

2. *The Alleged Violation of Article 14 of the Convention, Taken in Conjunction With Article 8*

* * *

39. . . .

In the Court's judgment, the fact that some unmarried mothers, unlike Paula Marckx, do not wish to take care of their child cannot justify the rule of Belgian law whereby the establishment of their maternity is conditional on voluntary recognition or a court declaration. In fact, such an attitude is not a general feature of the relationship between unmarried mothers and their children; besides, this is neither claimed by the Government nor proved by the figures they advance. As the Commission points out, it may happen that also a married mother might not wish to bring up her child, and yet, as far as she is concerned, the birth alone will have created the legal bond of affiliation.

Again, the interest of an "illegitimate" child in having such a bond established is no less than that of a "legitimate" child. However, the "illegitimate" child is likely to remain motherless in the eyes of Belgian law. If an "illegitimate" child is not recognised voluntarily, it has only one expedient, namely, an action to establish maternal affiliation (see para. 14 above). A married woman's child also is entitled to institute such an action, but in the vast majority of cases the entries on the birth certificate or, failing that, the constant and factual enjoyment of the status of a legitimate child (*une possession d'état constante*) render this unnecessary.

40. The Government do not deny that the present law favours the traditional family, but they maintain that the law aims at ensuring that family's full development and is therefore founded on objective and reasonable grounds relating to morals and public order (*ordre public*).

The Court recognises that support and encouragement of the traditional family is in itself legitimate or even praiseworthy. However, in the achievement of this end recourse must not be had to measures whose object or result is, as in the present case, to prejudice the "illegitimate" family; the members of the "illegitimate" family enjoy the guarantees of Article 8 on an equal footing with the members of the traditional family.

41. The Government concede that the law at issue may appear open to criticism, but they maintain that the problem of reforming it arose only several years after the entry into force of the European Convention on Human Rights in respect of Belgium (14 June 1955), that is, with the adoption of the Brussels Convention of 12 September 1962 on the Establishment of Maternal Affiliation of Natural Children. . . .

It is true that, at the time when the Convention of 4 November 1950 was drafted, it was regarded as permissible and normal in many European countries to draw a distinction in this area between the "illegitimate" and the "legitimate" family. However, the Court recalls that this Convention must be interpreted in light of present-day conditions. In the instant case, the Court cannot but be struck by the fact that the domestic law of the great majority of the member States of the Council of Europe has evolved and is continuing to evolve, in company with the relevant international instruments, towards full juridical recognition of the maxim *mater semper certa est*.

* * *

43. The distinction complained of therefore lacks objective and reasonable justification. Accordingly, the manner of establishing Alexandra Marckx's maternal affiliation violated, with respect to both applicants, Article 14 taken in conjunction with Article 8.

B. *The Extent in Law of Alexandra Marckx's Family Relationships*

44. Under Belgian law, a "legitimate" child is fully integrated from the moment of its birth into the family of each of its parents, whereas a recognised "illegitimate" child, and even an "adopted" illegitimate child, remains in principle a stranger to its parents' families (see para. 16 above). In fact, the legislation makes provision for some exceptions—and recent case law is tending to add more—but it denies a child born out of wedlock any rights over the estates of its father's or mother's relatives, it does not expressly create any maintenance obligations between it and those relatives, and it empowers its guardian rather than those relatives to give consent, where appropriate, to its marriage, etc.

It thus appears that in certain respects Alexandra never had a legal relationship with her mother's family. . . .

* * *

1. *The Alleged Violation of Article 8 of the Convention, Taken Alone*

45. In the Court's opinion, "family life", within the meaning of Article 8, includes at least the ties between near relatives, for instance, those between grandparents and grandchildren, since such relatives may play a considerable part in family life.

"Respect" for a family life so understood implies an obligation for the State to act in a manner calculated to allow these ties to develop normally (see, *mutatis mutandis,* para. 31 above). Yet the development of the family life of an unmarried mother and her child whom she has recognised may be hindered if the child does not become a member of the mother's family and if the establishment of affiliation has effects only as between the two of them.

* * *

47. There is thus in this connection violation of Article 8, taken alone, with respect to both applicants.

[The Court also found a violation of Article 14 taken in conjunction with Article 8, with regard to the extent in law of Alexandra Marckx's family relationships.]

C.   *On the Patrimonial Rights Relied on by the Applicants*

49. The Civil Code limits, in varying degrees, the rights of an "illegitimate" child and its unmarried mother as regards both inheritance on intestacy and dispositions *inter vivos* or by will (see paras. 17 and 18 above).

Until her recognition on 14 October 1973, the fourteenth day of her life, Alexandra had, by virtue of Article 756, no inheritance rights on intestacy over her mother's estate. On that date she did not acquire the status of presumed heir (*héritière présomptive*) of her mother, but merely that of "exceptional heir" (*successeur irrégulier*). It was only Alexandra's adoption, on 30 October 1974, that conferred on her the rights of a "legitimate" child over Paula Marckx's estate. Moreover, Alexandra has never had any inheritance rights on intestacy as regards the estate of any member of her mother's family.

In the interval between her recognition and her adoption, Alexandra could receive from her mother by disposition *inter vivos* or by will no more than her entitlement under the Code under the title "Inheritance on Intestacy". This restriction on her capacity, like that on Paula Marckx's capacity to dispose of her property, did not exist before 29 October 1973 and disappeared on 30 October 1974.

On the other hand, the Belgian Civil Code confers on "legitimate" children, from the moment of their birth and even of their conception, all those patrimonial rights which it denied and denies Alexandra; the capacity of married women to dispose of their property is not restricted by the Code in the same way as that of Paula Marckx.

* * *

51. The applicants regard the patrimonial rights they claim as forming part of family rights and, hence, being a matter for Article 8. This reasoning is disputed by the Government. Neither does the majority of the Commission agree with the applicants, but, as the Principal Delegate indicated at the hearings, a minority of six members considers the right of succession between children and parents, and between grandchildren and grandparents, to be so closely related to family life that it comes within the sphere of Article 8.

52. The Court shares the view of the minority. Matters of intestate succession—and of disposition—between near relatives prove to be intimately connected with family life. Family life does not include only social, moral or cultural relations, for example in the sphere of children's education; it also comprises interests of a material kind, as is shown by, amongst other things, the obligations in respect of maintenance and the position occupied in the domestic legal systems of the majority of the Contracting States by the institution of the reserved portion of an estate (*réserve héréditaire*). Whilst inheritance rights are not normally exer-

cised until the estate-owner's death, that is, when family life undergoes a change or even comes to an end, this does not mean that no issue concerning such rights may arise before the death: the distribution of the estate may be settled, and in practice fairly often is settled, by the making of a will or of a gift on account of a future inheritance (*avance d'hoirie*); it therefore represents a feature of family life that cannot be disregarded.

53. Nevertheless, it is not a requirement of Article 8 that a child should be entitled to some share in the estates of his parents or even of other near relatives: in the matter of patrimonial rights also, Article 8 leaves in principle to the Contracting States the choice of the means calculated to allow everyone to lead a normal family life (see para. 31 above) and such an entitlement is not indispensable in the pursuit of a normal family life. In consequence, the restrictions which the Belgian Civil Code places on Alexandra Marckx's inheritance rights on intestacy are not of themselves in conflict with the Convention, that is, if they are considered independently of the reasons underlying them. Similar reasoning is to be applied to the question of voluntary dispositions.

54. On the other hand, the distinction made in these two respects between "illegitimate" and "legitimate" children does raise an issue under Articles 14 and 8 when they are taken in conjunction.

55. Until she was adopted on 30 October 1974, Alexandra had only a capacity to receive property from Paula Marckx (see para. 49 above) that was markedly less than which a child born in wedlock would have enjoyed. The Court considers that this difference of treatment, in support of which the Government put forth no special argument, lacks objective and reasonable justification: reference is made, *mutatis mutandis,* to paragraphs 40 and 41 above.

... [I]n common with the Commission, the Court finds that the need to have recourse to adoption in order to eliminate the said difference of treatment involves of itself discrimination. As the applicants emphasised, the procedure employed for this purpose in the present case is one that usually serves to establish legal ties between one individual and another's child; to oblige in practice an unmarried mother to utilise such a procedure if she wishes to improve her own daughter's situation as regards patrimonial rights amounts to disregarding the tie of blood and to using the institution of adoption for an extraneous purpose. Besides, the procedure to be followed is somewhat lengthy and complicated. Above all, the child is left entirely at the mercy of his parent's initiative, for he is unable to apply to the courts for his adoption.

56. Unlike a "legitimate" child, Alexandra had at no time before or after 30 October 1974 had any entitlement on intestacy in the estates of members of Paula Marckx's family (see para. 49 above). Here, again, the Court fails to find any objective and reasonable justification.

* * *

58. The Government also state that they appreciate that an increase in the "illegitimate" child's inheritance rights is considered indispensable; however, in their view, reform should be effected by legislation and without retrospective effect. Their argument runs as follows: if the Court were to find certain rules of Belgian law to be incompatible with the Convention, this would mean that these rules had been contrary to the Convention since its entry into force in respect of Belgium (14 June 1955); the only way to escape such a conclusion would be to accept that the Convention's requirements had increased in the intervening period and to indicate the exact date of the change; failing this, the result of the judgment would be to render many subsequent distributions of estates irregular and open to challenge before the courts, since the limitation period on the two actions available under Belgian law in this connection is 30 years.

The Court is not required to undertake an examination *in abstracto* of the legislative provisions complained of: it is enquiring whether or not their application to Paula and Alexandra Marckx complies with the convention.... Admittedly, it is inevitable that the Court's decision will have effects extending beyond the confines of this particular case, especially since the violations found stem directly from the contested provisions and not from individual measures of implementation, but the decision cannot of itself annul or repeal these provisions: the Court's judgment is essentially declaratory and leaves to the state the choice of the means to be utilised in its domestic legal system for performance of its obligation under Article 53.

Nonetheless, it remains true that the Government have an evident interest in knowing the temporal effect of the present Judgment. On this question, reliance has to be placed on two general principles of law which were recently recalled by the Court of Justice of the European Communities: "the practical consequences of any judicial decision must be carefully taken into account," but "it would be impossible to go so far as to diminish the objectivity of the law and compromise its future application on the ground of the possible repercussions which might result, as regards the past, from such a judicial decision." The European Court of Human Rights interprets the Convention in the light of present-day conditions but it is not unaware that differences of treatment between "illegitimate" and "legitimate" children, for example in the matter of patrimonial rights, were for many years regarded as permissible and normal in a large number of Contracting States (see, *mutatis mutandis,* para. 41 above). Evolution towards equality has been slow and reliance on the Convention to accelerate this evolution was apparently contemplated at a rather late stage.... Having regard to all these circumstances, the principle of legal certainty, which is necessarily inherent in the law of the Convention as in Community Law, dispenses the Belgian State from re-opening legal acts or situations that antedate the delivery of the present Judgment. Moreover, a similar solution is found in certain Contracting States having a constitutional court: their public law limits the retroactive effects of those decisions of that court that annul legislation.

59.   To sum up, Alexandra Marckx was the victim of a breach of Article 14, taken in conjunction with Article 8, by reason both of the restrictions on her capacity to receive property from her mother and of her total lack of inheritance rights on intestacy over the estates of her near relatives on her mother's side.

[The Court went on to find that the distinction in Belgian law between unmarried and married mothers with regard to patrimonial rights violates Article 14 taken in conjunction with Article 8, and also violates Article 14 taken in conjunction with Article 1 of Protocol No. 1, with respect to Paula Marckx. Finally, the Court concluded that the legal rules at issue do not constitute "degrading treatment" under Article 3 of the Convention, and that they fall outside the scope of "the right to marry and to found a family" guaranteed in Article 12. Seven dissenting or partly dissenting opinions were filed.]

Note

Following the *Marckx* decision, lower courts in Belgium immediately began to give effect to the European Court of Human Rights ruling, particularly with regard to the rules of inheritance and the recognition or legitimation of children born of adulterous relationships. However, in 1983 the Court of Cassation held that those articles of the Belgian Civil Code which prohibit recognition of an "illegitimate" child without authorisation of the courts do not violate Articles 8 and 14 of the Convention. In a subsequent decision, the Court of Cassation ruled that Article 8 of the Convention does not have direct effect in Belgium; that is, it does not create subjective, enforceable individual rights in the absence of implementing legislation. The Court of Cassation confirmed this decision in 1986 in a case involving the very inheritance rules which the European Court of Human Rights considered contrary to the Convention in *Marckx*. The Belgian legislature finally brought the country's legislation into compliance with the European Court's decision by the Act of March 31, 1987, which abolished the discriminatory treatment of "adulterine" children. However, the legislature did not give retroactive effect to the new provisions. Belgian courts therefore have continued to apply the discriminatory rules of inheritance with respect to disputes arising after the *Marckx* decision but before the legislative change. In its report of 5 April 1990, the European Commission on Human Rights held unanimously that the Belgian judiciary's refusal to give direct effect to Article 8 and to apply the principles of the *Marckx* decision constituted a new violation of the Convention. The case has been referred to the European Court of Human Rights, where it was pending as of this writing.[48]

As the subsequent struggle over the *Marckx* decision illustrates, the Convention's effect on the legal orders of the individual European states depends crucially on the domestic legal institutions' willingness to acknowl-

---

48. Jörg Polakiewicz & Valérie Jacob–Fultzer, The European Human Rights Con-

vention in Domestic Law (Part I), 12 Hum. Rts.L.J. 65, 72–73 (1991).

edge, incorporate and respect its provisions. But the President of the Commission, Carl Norgaard, asserts that the Convention and the decisions of its institutions undoubtedly have had and continue to have a tangible effect on the law and practice of the member states:

> Firstly, all states have before ratifying the Convention and accepting the right of individual petition under Article 25 and the Court's jurisdiction under Article 46 carefully scrutinized the conformity of their national legislation with the Convention, and in nearly all countries legislation has been changed in order to comply with the requirements of the Convention at this stage. Similarly, in most Convention states any proposed new legislation is carefully examined before it is submitted to parliament in order to secure conformity with the rules of the Convention.

> Secondly, it is possible that the mere existence of a legal right for the individual to complain to an international control organ has a preventive effect in the member states so that possible violations are avoided. Although such an effect is often mentioned and clearly cannot be excluded, it is evident that it can hardly be proven by objective criteria.

> Thirdly, and more concretely, it is a fact that national courts in an increasing number of cases apply the rules of the Convention and the practise from the Convention organs. Naturally, this is especially so in the countries which have incorporated the Convention into national law, i.e., all the member states apart from Great Britain, Ireland, Norway, Sweden, Iceland, and until 1 July 1992, Denmark. But even in those countries, where the courts are not directly bound to apply the Convention, the courts have in an increasing number of cases nevertheless applied the rules of the Convention in the interpretation of national law....

> Fourthly, the most obvious general effect of the decisions taken by the organs in Strasbourg is the number of changes in the legislation of the member states. The number of changes in the individual member states amounts to about 100. In addition, there has been an impressive number of changes in national jurisprudence and administrative practise. Changes of legislation and changes of the practise have occurred in some cases as an element of a friendly settlement concluded before the Commission or the Court, in other cases as a result of decisions by the Commission which [have] been confirmed by the Committee of Ministers, and last but not least as a result of decisions by the Court.[49]

49. Carl Aage Norgaard, The Protection of Human Rights in Europe, in 2 Collected Courses of the Academy of European Law, Book 2, 21, 80–81 (1993).

Chapter 8

THE RISE AND FALL OF THE SOCIALIST LEGAL TRADITION

SECTION 1. INTRODUCTION: A CONCEPTUAL FRAMEWORK

Socialist law was built on the promise of re-invention. Govern your peoples by this law, it urged its client states, and your society will be different from all past societies that were organized under the old legal systems. Its message was as powerful as it was appealing. Very quickly it gained converts from one corner of the globe to another. Pilgrims flocked to Moscow from places as far away as Beijing, Prague and Warsaw to listen to the voiceless motors of Russia's newly invented social machine; to view what they believed was the future of mankind. Little did they realize that socialist law would turn into a revolution that never was. Within fifty years of its checkered history the meteoric rise of socialist law was surpassed only by its apocalyptic fall. As a result of recent defections from its ranks, the socialist legal family today is a caricature of its old self. But, it is far from dead.

Socialist law was originally conceived as a limited Russian experiment in social engineering, but quickly transformed into a universal phenomenon. Like the civil law in France, socialist law in Russia was the product of a bloody revolution that claimed the lives of millions of people. From its humble beginnings in Stalinist Russia of the mid–1930's, socialist law spread like a wild fire to all corners of the globe. Within a span of a little more than one-half century it became the law by which sixty percent of the earth's population governed their lives. As is the case with the civil law, the diverse peoples that adopted socialist law had neither a lingua franca nor a shared cultural history nor a unifying colonial history. Its postulates were attractive to the young revolutionary leaders that wanted to dispense with the old ways of doing things— old legal systems, old political structures and old economic arrangements.

The one thing that was common to all adherents of socialist law was their contemptuous attitude towards law and legal systems in general. They rebelled against all existing systems of law, but saw socialist law as a temporary phenomenon that would wither away, just like the autumn leaves, once it had accomplished its social, economic and political goals. In other words, they believed that the historical mission of socialist law was to engineer the creation of a stateless and lawless society called communism, a society of compulsory happiness and a state of monocytic tranquility in which the "new man" would have no need for laws, lawyers or legal institutions. It was this common political aspiration to reach this graveyard of all legal systems that provided the glue that held this legal sorority together. However, as the European members of this rainbow coalition discovered quite belatedly in the early 1990's, there is an intervening economic stage between socialism and communism and it is called capitalism. These Central and Eastern European countries concluded, therefore, that communism could wait while they experimented with capitalism. As such, they have disembarked from the socialist ship as the latter sails into the twilight.

Like many great civilizations of the past, socialist law soon began to crumble under the sheer wright of its own success. The disintegration of socialist law began with the cataclysmic events that took place in Central and Eastern Europe between 1985–1990: the unfolding of Gorbachev's perestroika in Russia, the ascendancy of the solidarity movement to political power in Poland, the unification of East and West Germany, the dismantling of the Council of Mutual Economic Assistance (COMECON), the collapse of the Warsaw Defense Pact, the dethronement of the communist party in the respective countries, the unleashing of a massive program of privatization of the national economies of all of these countries and the break up of the USSR. The impact of these changes on the life of the socialist legal family was almost fatal.

Following the overthrow of the political yoke of socialism in Central and Eastern Europe in 1989, each one of the countries that once made up the European branch of socialist law embarked upon a comprehensive law reform program that spanned a period of four years (1990–1993). The cumulative results of all of these changes is that the socialist legal family has ceased to be a wholesome family. Of the three legal subgroups that coalesced to form the socialist legal tradition, one—the Central and Eastern European—has abandoned socialist law and returned to its civil law roots. The other two—the Chinese and Southeast Asian as well as the emerging third world cultures—remain faithful to the core tenets of socialist law.

Thus, as we chronicle the reunification of the European branch of socialist law with continental European civil law, we are not proclaiming the death of socialist law per se. This chapter is not a requiem to socialist law. Socialist law lives on in other parts of the world and any report of the death of this legal culture at this time is grossly exaggerated. However, because it has lost what was in essence its heart, socialist law, in our opinion, no longer qualifies to be placed on the same pedestal with the civil law and the common law as one of the major legal traditions in the world today. It is hard to pinpoint the precise time when Central and Eastern Europe conclusively separated from socialist law and rejoined the civil law. We believe, however, that the transition was gradual and took place sometime during 1990–1993.

In the following five sections of this chapter we will examine the genesis of socialist law, the distribution of socialist law before and after 1993, the common core of socialist law, the apocalypse of socialist law and the post–1991 metamorphosis of the European branch of socialist law, with special emphasis on the changes in the legal systems of Russia, Poland and Hungary. The chapter will conclude with an assessment of the lessons of the reunification of the European branch of socialist law with the civil law.

SECTION 2.   THE GENESIS
OF SOCIALIST LAW

As a phenomenon, socialist law traces its roots to Russia of the mid–1930's. The historical chain of events that eventually culminated in the establishment of the socialist family of law began with the 1917 Bolshevik Revolution in Soviet Russia. Ironically, the principal architect of this new "legal order" was Joseph Stalin who saw law as an instrument of political oppression. What began as a Russian experiment in social engineering, soon found its way into other parts of the world. From Russia the revolutionary torch passed on to Mongolia which in 1920 had been transformed into the Mongolian People's Republic and thus became the second oldest socialist country in the world. As a result of the fermentation that took place during World War II, the countries of Central and Eastern Europe joined the growing family of socialist law soon after the conclusion of that war. The most populous country in the world—China—responded to the call to join the marxian socialist countries in 1949. The revolutionary wind of change soon blew through other Southeast Asian countries as Vietnam and Korea lined up behind China. In the late 1950's the small Caribbean island of Cuba joined the fraternity. In the 1960's and early 1970's the family of socialist law continued to add new members in disparate corners of Africa and Asia.

The original intention of the architects of the Soviet legal system was to establish a legal order that had no historical links with the decadent past. They had set out on a clean slate to create a legal system *sui generis*—a legal system that would cure all of the social inequities of law under the tsarist regimes. It would be a legal system that would have no precedent anywhere else in world history, a limited future and that would constitute a revolutionary break with anything that existed prior to 1917. But, instead of producing a radically new legal system they ended up with a system that is both traditional and historically anchored in the past. The history of the Soviet legal system is largely a history of borrowings of legal materials from other legal systems and of assimilation of materials from outside of the law. Between 1917 and

1936 Soviet Russia experimented with different types of law—customary, imperial, Western and Marxist. It was only in the mid–1930's that the Russian government, under the direction of a former seminarian who had now become a professional revolutionary, finally decided to adopt elements of the Western legal system for the Soviet Union. It was the promulgation of the Stalin Constitution of 1936 that finally established Western law in the Soviet Union. Stalin's training in the theology of the Roman Catholic Church and his early years as a seminarian proved critically important in his selection of Western law for Russia. He adopted Western law because he saw in it an element of stability and regimentation. The Soviet state, in Stalin's view, at this time more than at any time in the past needed stability and centralized discipline.

There are haunting parallels between the origins of socialist law in Russia and of civil law in France. The Soviet political leaders adopted Western codes of law for the same reason that Napoleon codified French law. In both situations, a national code helped to consolidate power at the center. With hierarchial codes and regularized procedures, the pattern of human action can be better calculated and directed. As Napoleon needed to reduce the power of the provinces, so the Soviet political leaders sought uniformity throughout the country. Regularity and uniformity provide a basis for efficient manipulation.

Even though Lenin was a lawyer by training he was ambivalent about the form that law should take in a revolutionary state. The true father of modern Soviet law is Iosif Vissarionovich Dzhugashvili (a.k.a. Joseph Stalin). He froze Soviet law in its suppressive state and reversed Marx's and Lenin's earlier views, of its progressive simplification, informality, and evaporation. To Stalin's mind law was not only suppressive but also coercive. To him the victory of socialism in the USSR did not necessarily mean the "winding up" or "withering away" of law in the Soviet Union. On the contrary, the role of law in the USSR would continue to grow until a full communist society was actually put in place. Whereas Lenin believed in a government of men and not of laws, Stalin believed that the rule of man could better be achieved through the rule of law. To Stalin's mind, law had a legitimizing function.

As one would later find out, the imperfections of socialist law are attributable to its faulty design and makeshift construction. The whole system resembles a house that has been slapped together from defective materials in an almost hilarious spirit of improvisation. The mishmash of faulty parts, sloppy workmanship and bad engineering that went into the creation of socialist law nonetheless inspired unwavering confidence in its chief architect, Joseph Stalin, a dictatorial leader who acquired his knowledge of law and legal systems not from any tutored study but from the revolutionary laboratory of Bolshevik Russia.

Predictably, modern Soviet commentators treat with benign neglect the fact that the architects of the Soviet legal system derived inspiration not only from foreign legal systems but also from pre-revolutionary Russian law. They present Soviet law as if it were a monument to the ingenuity and originality of the Soviet legal mind. Soviet law was founded, if one were to rely exclusively on Soviet writings, upon a clean slate by men who were equipped with nothing other than the teachings of Karl Marx, Frederick Engels, and Vladimir Lenin, and a burning determination to sever the umbilical cord linking the new Soviet system with the inequitable past. The founding fathers of Soviet law may well have regarded other systems' notions of law as "almost ridiculous," just as the ancient Romans attributed no importance to outside influences in designing Roman law. The fact remains, however, that the path to Soviet law is paved with stones which were consciously or unconsciously borrowed from other legal systems. Soviet law as it was known prior to its demise in 1991 represented a workable harmonization of the principles of natural justice, the concepts of natural law, structural forms and legal notions that were borrowed both from Roman law and from the civil law tradition, and pre-revolutionary Russian tradition with the general tenets of Marxism–Leninism. This is not to suggest, however, that the Soviet legal system did not make any original contributions to the theory of law. It certainly did.

After the death of Joseph Stalin in 1953 Soviet law underwent a process of fine-tuning. The essential Western features of the system had been put in place in the mid–1930's. The process of de-Stalinization and democratization of Soviet law which took place in the late 1950's was masterminded by Nikita Khrushchev. The spirit of those Khrushchevian reforms was inherited by Leonid Brezhnev, Yurii Andropov, Konstantin Chernenko and Mikhail Gorbachev. The latter Soviet leader presided over the disintegration of socialist law in the USSR. The history of Soviet law was relatively short. It lasted only from 1917–1991. But its impact on legal systems throughout the world will preoccupy legal historians for many centuries to come. It lived a checkered life and left its monumental imprints on legal theory.

SECTION 3. THE DISTRIBUTION OF SOCIALIST LAW BEFORE AND AFTER 1993

Right up to the time of its collapse in 1993 socialist law was a powerful phenomenon in the modern world. Its sphere of influence was neatly packaged into three baskets—the Central and Eastern European, the Chinese and Southeast Asian and the emerging Third World nations. At the height of its glory it was estimated that of every ten persons in the world, six lived under socialist law. The reception of socialist law in the different corners of the globe cuts across cultural, linguistic and racial boundaries. It had been received by such culturally diverse countries as the former Soviet Union, Vietnam and Cuba, and by such racially different societies as Poland, China and Mongolia. The members of the socialist legal family were at different levels of economic development, as is evidenced by the inclusion within the family of such economically advanced countries as Hungary, the former Czechoslovakia and the former East Germany and of such economically underdeveloped societies as Mongolia, China and Albania. Whereas the English language is virtually the lingua franca of the common law system, the socialist legal system, like the civil law system did not evolve a lingua franca. The Russian language, however, was the most influential of the many languages that were used within the family of socialist law. Despite these differences, however, one feature, among others, that was commonly shared by all the members of the socialist family is their legal system.

The Soviet socialist legal system was the oldest national legal system within this legal family. The second oldest socialist legal system was that of Mongolia. The groups of countries that have received socialist law may be divided into two major categories: the older socialist countries and the new or emerging socialist states. Within the first category were the former USSR, Poland, Bulgaria, Hungary, the former Czechoslovakia, Romania, the former Yugoslavia, the former German Democratic Republic, Albania, the People's Republic of China, the People's Republic of Vietnam, the People's Democratic Republic of Korea, Mongolia, and Cuba. The youngest socialist system within this group is Cuba.

Even though socialist law was the product of the Western heritage it had been, like the civil and common law systems, exported to countries that were traditionally not an integral part of the Western culture and civilization. As a result of this historical fact not all the countries in this first group of socialist systems had attained the consummate degree of Westernization of their law. Whereas the legal systems of the former Soviet Union, the countries of Central and Eastern Europe and Cuba had attained the highest degree of integration into the Western legal tradition, those of China and of the countries in Southeast Asia were at varying degrees of Westernization.

From this analysis one would draw the inevitable conclusion that within the socialist legal family there were essentially two sub-groups. Just as one can speak of the English and American sub-groups within the common law or of the Romanist and Germanic sub-groups within the civil law, one could identify two sub-groups within the socialist legal family, Central and East European on the one hand, and the Chinese and Southeast Asian sub-group on the other. The first sub-group included Cuba. Three criteria were used to establish this sub-division within the socialist legal system—the country's attitude towards the rule of law, the leadership style employed by the ruling communist parties in the respective countries, and the historical traditions of the individual societies.

In addition to the foregoing two sub-groups there was also a third grouping of new or emerging socialist legal systems of the modern world. This third basket includes the Democratic Republic of Kampuchea (Cambodia), Laos, Mozambique, Angola, South Yemen, Somalia, Libya, Mali, Senegal, Ethiopia, Guinea, Tanzania and Guyana. It is worth noting that of all the countries in this third group of socialist legal systems, only Guyana and Tanzania had a non-civil law pre-revolutionary legal system.

As a result of the apocalypse of socialist law, which will be examined in greater detail in Section V below, the geographical sphere of influence of socialist laws has been substantially reduced. In 1993 the Central and Eastern European sub-group within socialist law has left the socialist law orbit and reunited with the continental European civil law system. Thus, the distribution of socialist law after 1993 is confined to those countries in baskets 2 and 3 of our foregoing tripartite division of the socialist law world.

SECTION 4. THE COMMON CORE OF SOCIALIST LAW

Even though socialist law has its roots deeply embedded in the civil law tradition, over the years it developed features that are unique to it. There is considerable debate, however, among scholars as to what makes socialist law socialist. On the key question of what elements constitute the idiosyncratic features of socialist law we proffer an approach which proposes to examine socialist law from four integral perspectives: its infrastructure, methodology, ideology and theology. When viewed from the standpoint of the first two dimensions, socialist law may properly be compared with the common law system. When viewed from the standpoint of the third dimension it may be compared with the common and civil law systems. But when looked at from the fourth perspective it is comparable only to such other religious legal systems as Islamic law, Canon law, Jewish law and Hindu law.

A. THE INFRASTRUCTURE AND METHODOLOGY OF SOCIALIST LAW

When viewed from the vantage point of its infrastructure and methodology, no qualitative differences can be identified between socialist law and the civil law. In this regard, socialist law, while introducing some major modifications, still preserves its civil law roots and therefore can be properly contrasted with common law as the valid opposite.

B. THE IDEOLOGY OF SOCIALIST LAW

Socialist law has a mission to accomplish which is radically different from those of the civil and common law systems. To attain its goal socialist law deems it necessary to rearrange the entire political, economic and social orientation of society. Put quite simply, the historical mission of socialist law is to advance the given society toward developed socialism and ultimately toward communism. To achieve this goal, socialist law seeks to liquidate all capitalist and feudal forms of property ownership, to consolidate socialist economic relations, to lift relations within the family from their present level of capitalist or feudal decadence and to realign political power within the society. More than anything else, socialist law is seen as an instrument of social engineering. It is a weapon in the hands of the political governors aimed at achieving the ultimate political goal of establishing a society in which law will no longer be necessary.

From this perspective, the socialist legal system, with some notable exceptions, is characterized by the following elements: an uncompromising recognition of the supreme leadership of the communist party; state ownership of land and the collectivization of the use of land; state ownership of the dominant means of production and distribution; national economic planning as the only acceptable approach to economic development; total mobilization of the entire population for social involvement; and only a grudging tolerance of even the most modest forms of private ownership. Socialist law does not see the construction of socialism as a self-limiting goal, but rather as a stepping stone toward the ideal society called communism. Individual socialist states may vary in their application of the above elements, but these nevertheless represent the common core of socialist law. Socialist law in its purest form may be encountered today in Cuba, North Vietnam and North Korea. During the past few years China has relaxed its application of the non-core elements of socialist legal ideology.

Crucial to a full appreciation of the ideology of the socialist legal system as an autonomous family of law is an understanding of the marxian socialist constitutional arrangements. Among the critically important features of any socialist constitutional system are the following: The typical socialist state regards its constitution not as a legal dogma but as a legal platform for political action. The provisions of the constitution are thus easily amended if political expediency so demands. Also, the process used in the interpretation of any provision of the state constitution is essentially a political rather than a legal process. Because a socialist state constitution serves both as the supreme law of the land and as the supreme codification of the social, economic and political program of the state, it expressly states the general principles of the social, economic and political development of the state.

The Marxian socialist constitution gives the fullest endorsement to state and other forms of socialist property ownership, especially of industrial property, while placing heavy restrictions on all forms of private ownership. To make sure that private ownership does not obstruct the construction of socialism, the socialist state constitution, as a rule, paves the way for easy nationalization of private property if and when public policy so demands. Unfailingly, there is some reference in a socialist state constitution to the class composition of the given society.

In a socialist constitutional system, the general practice is to concentrate political power in the hands of the ruling communist party at the expense of the state organs. This may not necessarily find specific expression in the state constitution. But the reality of all Marxian socialist constitutional systems is that the communist party is both supra-constitutional as well as extra-constitutional. In socialist state constitutions, one typically finds a provision which proclaims the independence of the judiciary. This *de jure* independence, however, is vitiated by other institutional devices within the system. For example, the judges of the highest courts in a prototypical socialist country are elected by, accountable to, and recallable by the corresponding legislative body. This, coupled with the fact that socialist judges are not supposed to "make" law, and that their decisions in specific cases may be overruled by the legislature acting as a supreme appellate instance, renders the independence of the courts problematic. The fact of the matter, therefore, is that in a socialist constitutional system the judiciary is not co-equal with the political branches of government. Rather, it is hierarchically inferior both to the legislature and to the executive branch of government. This makes the socialist judiciary truly the least dangerous branch of the socialist state.

Another prominent feature of a socialist constitutional system is the routine delegation of major government functions to non-governmental organizations. This enables the government to create the semblance that the administration of the affairs of the state is handled through a partnership between the state organs and citizens' organizations. It is customary, for example, for the state to delegate the administration of labor law and other related social legislation to the official trade union organizations and, in exchange for such delegation, to impose direct governmental control over the activities of the trade unions. Furthermore, in order to facilitate the mobilization of the entire population for involvement in various social duties, the socialist constitutional system establishes a network of other non-governmental organizations which are in turn placed under the general supervision of the communist party.

As a general rule, to which there are notable local exceptions, socialist constitutional systems formally recognize only one political party. This party is superimposed over the governmental apparatus as well as over all other state social organizations. In those socialist states with more than one political party, a condition for the existence of a non-communist political party is that it must recognize the leading role of the communist party within that arrangement.

C. THE THEOLOGY OF SOCIALIST LAW

Socialist law as a pseudo-religious category stands in contrast to Hindu, Canon, Jewish and Islamic law. From this vantage point, socialist law is a philosophy whose basic task is the fundamental remaking of the conscience of the people. The purpose of this law is, through an intricate network of legal rules, to inculcate in the people such ideals as high moral soundness, unwavering belief in the ideal nature of life under communism, and self sacrifice for the common good.

As a pseudo-religion, socialist law is a creative reappearance of religion, albeit in a secular and ideological form. Unlike the other religious faiths that look towards Rome and Tubingen, Jerusalem and Damascus, Mecca and Teheran, socialist secular religion looks towards contemporary temples and shrines in Beijing or Ulan Bator. Socialist law is a spiritual ideology. As such it refers to a global system of ideas or symbols which give shape to the whole of history and social reality. It places the community holding the theology, its life, its prospects and its unique character, on the wider range of universal destiny. It gives that community its "vocation" or sense of a special task or significance, an ultimate significance, its history. It is a *Weltanschauung* with a social base and a communal function.

As a symbolic structure uniting and directing a society's life socialist law demands that it must be inwardly and unconditionally participated in by the members of the group in order to be effective, and for the group to be effective. The inward participation has two aspects: intellectual assent to the validity of the symbolic structure of theology and commitment to the obligations of that structure as binding on the self. Thus, societies governed by socialist law are much like older "religious" communities, worried about dissidents and revisionists, and so intent on control of thought, of education, of publications and of art. Because socialist law appeared in an age of science, is founded on pseudo-scientific theories, and is apparently intended to hold together modern technological societies, it may very well be regarded as the first scientific religion in human history. Because it is designed for a scientific society it tends to base its claim to allegiance on its status as "objective science", rather than as divinely revealed or traditionally sacrosanct.

The anatomy of socialist law from its inception to the present reveal its religious character. Even though it is not a religion in the true sense of the word, it clearly has religious dimensions: the claim to ultimacy, the deep relatedness to the normative, the requirement of faith or commitment, the fear of heterodoxy and apostasy, ritual rites and mythologies, the fleet of theologians and missionaries, and its role as providing an interpretation of life as a whole that gives life meaning, significance and purpose. In short, it is an implicit rather than an explicit religion.

SECTION 5. THE APOCALYPSE OF SOCIALIST LAW

The sudden collapse of the Soviet federal state on December 25, 1991 sent shock waves through the entire socialist legal family. This single event triggered the apocalypse of the socialist legal tradition which resulted not in the total extinction of socialist law, but in its fundamental realignment. Henceforth, socialist law had lost its European adherents and ceased to be a European phenomenon. The center of gravity of the shrinking universe of socialist law shifted from Moscow to Beijing. The Central and East European branch of the socialist family broke away from that family tree and rejoined the civil law family from which it had been previously separated. There is a respectable school of thought that would argue that Poland never really left the civil law orbit and that the post–1993 realignment of Polish law should not be categorized as a return of the Polish legal system to the civil law family. Such a viewpoint, just like the one that also contends that pre–1993 European socialist legal systems were actually a subspecies of the civil law tradition, is now moot.

It is ironic that the disintegration of socialist law started in the same country that had given birth to it, i.e., Russia. At the same time that the European branch of socialist law broke away from the socialist legal family, the three federal states within this European group also disintegrated: the former USSR was transformed into 15 independent states; the former Czechoslovakia was divided into the Czech and Slovak republics and the former Yugoslavia is still in the process of defining the national boundaries of the several new states to which it gave birth. One thing that is quite clear is that every member of the former European branch of socialist law had to make a few fundamental changes in its legal system in order to purge itself of the relics of the socialist past and prepare itself for full membership in the civil law family. The nature and scope of these adjustments will be examined in the next section of this essay.

Before we discuss those changes a final observation is in order. As a result of their long existence under the socialist law regime and notwithstanding the readjustments that each one of these countries will have to undergo in order to make the transition from socialist law to civil law, the former European socialist systems will continue for quite a long time to share a few common traits that will set them apart from all the other members of the civil law family. Whereas they are now full-fledged members of the civil law family, they together constitute what could perhaps be described as the fourth sub-group within the civil law family. Thus, henceforth the civil law tradition should be seen as consisting of four legal sub-cultures, i.e., French, Germanic, Latin American and Central–Eastern European.

SECTION 6. THE METAMORPHOSIS OF THE EUROPEAN BRANCH OF THE SOCIALIST LEGAL FAMILY

Between 1936 and 1991 the civil law was totally eclipsed in Russia. A similar submergence of the civil law culture occurred in the Ukraine, Belarus, Armenia, Georgia and Moldova. In the three Baltic republics of Latvia, Lithuania and Estonia, the displacement of the civil law tradition occurred at about the same time that it happened in the remaining countries of Central and Eastern Europe. Now that the blanket of socialist law has been lifted from these countries they find that they must re-tune their respective civil law machines in order to rejoin the civil law fold.

Between January 1991 and September 1993 each one of the former European members of the socialist legal family has subjected all facets of its legal system to cataclysmic reforms in preparation for their re-entry into the civil law orbit. The common core of these reforms are democracy, legality and privatization. The democracy theme permeates the reform of the legislative, electoral and administrative processes. The legality theme guides the reform of the legal institutions, legal professions, legal education and the respective legal procedures. By contrast, the privatization theme runs through every facet of the reform of substantive law. Because of the self-imposed restrictions on the coverage of this casebook, the reform that will be examined here will devote only fleeting attention to changes in substantive law. Rather, the emphasis will be on the metamorphosis of the infrastructure of the respective legal systems, i.e., legal structures, legal actors, procedure, sources of law, the judicial process, and the divisions of law.

Altogether, the reforms of the legal systems of the former European branch of socialist law, not in any particular order of importance, manifest themselves in the following 15 specific forms: privatization of the profession of the notary, revamping of the system of legal education, legalization of the system of private legal education, constitutionalization of judicial review of legislation, democratization of the legislative process, elevation of due process of law to the level of a constitutional principle, introduction of a system of "Government in the Sunshine", retrenchment from a system of secret laws, simplification of access to justice, implementation of a genuine system of separation of powers, bolstering of the status of the law judge, institutionalization of commercial arbitration, overhaul of the judicial system, repudiation of the ideology of socialist law, and a solemn proclamation of the rights and freedoms of man and the citizen—a new bill of rights. Each one of these reforms will be discussed separately.

A. PRIVATIZATION OF THE PROFESSION OF THE NOTARY

Prior to the reforms of 1991–1993 the profession of the notary public in the Central and East European legal systems was a pale imitation of its continental European civil law counterpart. A Russian notary, like his Polish or Czechoslovakian counterpart, lacked the prestige, sophistication and financial wealth of his French or Italian colleague. Prior to 1991 the Russian notary was a faceless civil servant who was paid a fixed salary by the government which employed him without regard to the amount of revenue that he generated for the government. His tasks lacked the depth or the breadth of his French counterpart. He was virtually excluded from real estate transactions which were the mainstay of his continental European civil law counterpart. This pathetic status of the pre–1991 Soviet notary was mirrored in all the other Central and Eastern European legal systems. The socialist notary was nothing more than a dignified law clerk whose sole reason for existence was to place his stamp of approval on legal acts that were presented to him and collect the requisite state fees from the interested parties. He did not draft the legal instruments that were tendered to him for authentication and, in many instances, he was not even knowledgeable in the law governing the instrument that he was called upon to authenticate.

During the reforms of 1990–1993 the profession of the notary public in the Central and East European legal systems was privatized. This meant that notaries were no longer regarded as civil servants and were no longer on state payroll. A good example of this change in the regulation of notarial practice in Central and Eastern European countries took place in Russia. Henceforth, the notary in Russia became a private legal practitioner just like the advocate and the jurisconsult (in-house corporate counsel). A new law of February 11, 1993 (No. 4462–1) "On the Notary" sets forth the procedure for the certification, licensing and regulation of private notaries in Russia. This law recognizes two types of notaries—state and private. This private Russian notary still lacks the key ingredient that defines the prestige of his continental European civil law counterpart, i.e., monopoly over the drafting and registration of real estate transfer documents.

Among the key provisions of this law one may point to the following: to qualify for a notarial commission an applicant must be a Russian citizen, hold a law degree, undergo a minimum of one-year, post-law school apprenticeship, pass the notarial examination and be licensed to engage in notarial practice in Russia; documents that are notarized by state or private notaries shall have the same force of law; a private notary must practice as a member of a notarial chamber, not individually; a licensed notary may not engage in any other income-producing activities during the term of his commission and he may not serve as a broker in any transaction in which he is rendering his notarial services; the clear implication of the foregoing rule is that the same individual may not both a notary and an advocate (attorney) at the same time.

The law further provides that: state notaries shall operate out of state notarial offices; a notary shall confine his practice to his notarial district in which he must maintain an office; within each territorially defined notarial district individuals who need notarial services may go to any one of the notaries licensed to practice within that district; when a notary notarizes a document outside his notarial district such a document is not void by virtue of the ultra vires action of the notary; all private notaries must carry a professional liability insurance; the list in Article 35 of the services that a private notary may provide to a client does not include the drafting of legal instruments—a service which is reserved for advocates; Article 37 lists those notarial services that may be provided by officials of the executive committees of local councils in those remote parts of the country where notaries are not available; similarly, Article 38 enumerates those notarial acts that may be performed by the consular sections of Russian embassies abroad.

Following the example of Russia, many of the other Central and Eastern European legal systems have introduced a bifurcated system of state and private notaries. Even though the Russian private notary is a far cry from his French or Italian counterpart, the mere fact that Russia and the other Central–Eastern European countries have introduced a private notary is a major development in the laws of these countries. The clear separation of the profession of a notary from that of an attorney follows the entrenched tradition in other civilian countries.

B. REVAMPING THE SYSTEM OF LEGAL EDUCATION

Major changes were introduced into the system of legal education in the Central and Eastern European countries during the reforms of 1991–1993. Perhaps the most notable change in this regard is the clear separation between the academic and professional phases of legal education. The professional phase typically follows the academic phase. Whereas the academic phase is provided by law faculties at universities and law institutes, the professional phase consists of a system of apprenticeship in law offices, notarial offices, law courts or other legal institutions. The duration of the apprenticeship varies from one branch of the profession to another. The prospective admittee into the legal profession is allowed to take the professional admission examination after he has completed the mandatory post-law school apprenticeship training. During the academic phase of one's legal education, emphasis is placed on theory rather than on practice. During the practical training a student is placed under the tutelage of an experienced master from whom he learns the nuts and bolts of the law.

Unlike the situation in some civil law countries, e.g., Germany, where the same practical training program is provided for all prospective admittees into the legal profession (i.e., without regard as to the branch of the profession to which the trainee aspires), in Russia the post-law school apprenticeship training is customized for each branch of the profession. Thus, for example, the prospective Russian advocate must undergo all of his practical apprenticeship at a law office and nowhere else. Similarly, the prospective Russian private notary will undergo his post-law school practical training at a notarial office. In other words, the prospective Russian admittee into the legal profession selects the branch of the profession that he wants to get into right after the completion of the academic phase of his legal education but before he commences his practical training.

The practical implication of this Russian system is that an aspiring lawyer does not take just one omnibus "bar examination" that would entitle him to practice law in any of its branches, as does his American counterpart. The aspiring Russian lawyer must take the professional examination that grants admission into the branch of the legal profession to which he aspires. This Russian model follows the French pattern. In Germany, the prospective admittee into the legal profession makes his selection as to the branch of the profession to which he seeks admission after the completion of the common practical training. Some Central and Eastern European countries follow the German model; others, following the Russian example, have adopted the French system.

Another change that took place in the system of legal education in the Central and Eastern European countries is the renaming of the first law degree that is granted by law faculties. Russia also took the lead in instituting this reform. Up until 1991 the first degree that was granted by Russian law faculties was simply called the "diplom", i.e., diploma of law. For those foreign law students who requested a foreign language translation of their Russian law degrees the Russian "diplom" was official translated as "master of laws". Determined to put an end to the confusion as to the precise meaning of its law degrees abroad and as an expression of its desire to become a part of the international system of legal education, Russia changed the appellation of its first law degree from "diplom" to "magistr iuridicheskiikh nauk" (master of laws). The Russian "master of laws" degree is based on the example of the French "maîtrise en droit". Both the French "maîtrise en droit" and the Russian "master of laws" are functionally equivalent to the American "juris doctor" degree. Poland also designates its first law degree as a "master of laws".

C. LEGALIZATION OF THE SYSTEM OF PRIVATE LEGAL EDUCATION

Up until 1991 all Central and Eastern European countries provided legal education to all students (citizens as well as foreigners) free of charge: the students did not pay any tuition fees; in some countries the students were even paid a stipend and provided with free living accommodations as well as a free supply of textbooks. In effect, the law students, like all the other university students, were paid to study. Until 1991 Poland was the least generous of the Central and East European countries in the range of free benefits that it granted to its law students; Russia was the most generous. However, during the reforms of 1990–1993 Russia and Poland have taken steps to institute a limited system of private legal education. Because the constitutions of Poland and Russia continue to recognize the right of the citizens of these countries to free education, including legal education, that right was not taken away during the reforms of 1991–1993. However, both Poland and Russia here interpreted their respective constitutions as not granting the right of free education to foreigners. Poland legitimized this constitutional interpretation by instituting a new policy requiring all foreign students at its law facilities to pay a tuition fee. This was a radical departure from Poland's post-World War II tradition of providing tuition-free legal education to all students regardless of their citizenship status. Poland justified this move on the grounds that it needed to recover some of the costs of operating the universities. Russia quickly followed the example of Poland when it instituted a policy in 1992 requiring all foreign students to pay a tuition fee. But, unlike Poland,

Russia has also given its approval to the establishment of private universities and law institutes where any students, Russian as well as foreign, who so wish may receive legal education. The state regulates the curriculum at such private institutions as well as recognizes the law degrees that the graduates receive. At the present time the private law institutes in Russia tend to offer specialized post-graduate degree courses in subjects such as commercial (business) law, international law and comparative-foreign law. However, the law which authorizes the creation of such private law schools does not limit their curricular authority to just post-graduate training. In the not-too-distant future it is anticipated that these private law schools will expand their offerings to include the entire basic law school curriculum.

D. CONSTITUTIONALIZATION OF JUDICIAL REVIEW OF LEGISLATION

(1) The Grudging Acceptance of the Notion of Judicial Review in Central and Eastern Europe

For quite a long period of time the very thought that a court of law could review and actually invalidate an act of the legislature was deemed utterly unacceptable to the Central and Eastern European countries. Because the legislature was viewed as the supreme embodiment of the state's sovereignty, it was believed that any arrangement that would subject an act of the legislative organ to either pre-enactment or post-enactment judicial scrutiny was tantamount to a derogation from the supremacy of parliament. Another rationale for the rejection of the concept of judicial review of an act of parliament was the belief that, in enacting any law, the legislature acted under the guidance and tutelage of the omnipotent and omniscient communist party. As such, it was believed that any law passed by parliament had already received the blessings of the infallible communist party and that any judicial review of such a legislative act was an indirect challenge to the authority of the communist party. Thus, the total rejection of judicial review in all its forms and manifestation became an integral part of the socialist legal tradition.

Very gradually some of the countries inside this legal tradition began to chip away at the doctrine of no judicial review. Poland was the first to break the ice. She was quickly followed by other Central and Eastern European countries such as Hungary, former Czechoslovakia and former Yugoslavia. These countries experimented with different variations of judicial review of legislative acts: some allowed only pre-enactment review; others combined pre-enactment with post-enactment review; some permitted post-enactment review but not pre-enactment review; whereas some authorized the court to issue only a non-binding opinion whenever it found an act of parliament to be unconstitutional, others empowered the court to invalidate any act of parliament that was found to be unconstitutional. For quite some time the Polish constitutional court was the most active of all the constitutional courts in

Central and Eastern Europe. It boldly took on the Polish Sejm and asserted its authority as the ultimate interpreter of the Polish Constitution.

As Poland, Bulgaria, Hungary, former Czechoslovakia and former Yugoslavia experimented with judicial review, the USSR remained adamant in its opposition to the institution of judicial review. Right up to its demise as a federal state on December 25, 1991 the USSR did not permit even the most timid form of judicial review of legislative acts. A change of mind took place in late 1990 in some of the individual USSR republics and in 1991 Russia became the first of the former republics of the USSR to establish a constitutional court. Russia did not only repudiate USSR old policy of no judicial review, it established a constitutional review mechanism that is even more daring and far more innovative than any of the constitutional courts that had hitherto existed in Central and Eastern Europe. Even Poland's pioneering constitutional court pales by comparison with the new Russian constitutional court. Because of the trailblazing depth and breadth of the jurisdiction of the Russian constitutional court the remaining portion of this analysis will be devoted to a closer look at this Russian novelty.

(2) The Russian Constitutional Court: A Trailblazer in Central and Eastern Europe

The creation of the Russian constitutional court in the fall of 1991 was a cataclysmic departure from Russia's legal tradition and the first credible evidence that Russia was poised to become a genuine *pravovoe gosudarstvo*. As part of the perestroika package, Gorbachev's perestroichniki promised to transform Russia into a "government of laws". But, the historical credit for translating Gorbachev's blueprints into reality went to Boris Nikolaevich Yeltsin, the first democratically elected President of Russia. The court is so alien to the tradition of Soviet law and so unlike anything that bears the mark of "made in Russia", that its creation immediately set off speculation in the West as to which invisible foreign hands guided the structural designing of this novel Russian institution. A more basic question was raised by close observers of Russian legal developments, i.e., will this new court live up to its promise as the new power broker in Russia? On both of these questions the jury's verdict is in and its findings are unequivocal.

A clinical examination of the Russian constitutional court reveals that it is modeled after the German federal constitutional court rather than the U.S. Supreme Court. Any comparison of the political activism of Russia's first Chief Justice Valery D. Zorkin to that of the Chief Justice of the U.S. Supreme Court is fundamentally flawed.

Notwithstanding the celebrated attempts by U.S. consultants to influence the architecture of Russia's constitutional court, the founding fathers of Russia's first experiment in constitutional rule of law elected to emulate the European constitutional tradition as exemplified by post-World War II Germany. But, in designing its own constitutional court,

Russia took a close look at three disparate prototypes, i.e., the French constitutional council, the German federal constitutional court, and the U.S. Supreme Court. After very careful consideration a principled decision was made to emulate the German model. In doing so, however, Russia made a few adjustments to the German import so that it would blend in with the architectural landscape of Russian law.

The establishment of the Russian constitutional court was authorized by legislation of May 6, 1991, but the current court was actually installed in office by the Supreme Soviet on October 30, 1991.

The constitutional foundation for the new court was provided by the Russian Constitution of 1978, as amended. Even though its enabling statute called for a court with 15 justices, the present court has 13 members only one of whom is a woman. At the time of their elevation to the high court, six of the current justices were federal or regional legislators, six were academics and one was a state prosecutor. All 13 of them are lawyers by training and hold lifetime appointment, but must step down at age 65 years.

The court's first Chief Justice was Valery Zorkin whose background was profiled in an article that was published in Rossiskaya Gazeta on June 5, 1993. The article gave the following details about the Chief Justice's background: He was born in 1943 in the Primorskoi Region of Russia. At age 21 he graduated from Moscow State University Law School and went straight to do his post-graduate studies also at Moscow State University Law School. Three years thereafter, i.e., at age 24, he successfully defended his Ph.D. dissertation in 1967. The next 12 years following his Ph.D. degree he was a professor of constitutional law at Moscow State University Law School. In 1978 he successfully defended his LL.D. dissertation on a topic dealing with the positive theory of law. His general areas of expertise are constitutional law and jurisprudence. In 1979 he went to work at the Academy of the Ministry of Internal Affairs of the USSR as a professor of constitutional law and jurisprudence. Between 1986–1991 he was a professor of constitutional law at the law school of the Ministry of Internal Affairs of the USSR. He was elected Chief Justice of the constitutional court in November 1991.

Among the hitherto existing constitutional courts in the world, the U.S. Supreme Court was readily regarded as the most activist. The title of the most activist court in the world today now belongs to the Russian constitutional court. During its short existence it has invalidated decrees of the President of the Russian Republic, voided laws passed by the Supreme Soviet of the Russian Federation, ruled on the constitutionality of federal elections, brokered a political compromise between the executive and legislative branches of the Russian federal government, refereed a jurisdictional dispute between the regional governments of Russia and the central authorities in Moscow and opined on the constitutional parameters of a 1993 national referendum that resulted in a moral but hollow victory for President Yeltsin. When President Yeltsin threatened to convert his April 1993 referendum victory into a national mandate to bypass the conservative Congress of People's Deputies in his efforts to unveil a new Russian constitution, Chief Justice Zorkin quickly cautioned the President against what he called an unconstitutional interpretation of the results of the referendum. When President Yeltsin issued a decree dissolving the Russian parliament in September 1993, the constitutional court opined that the decree was unconstitutional and Chief Justice Zorkin sided with the court's majority in this decision.

Many of Chief Justice Zorkin's constitutional pronouncements are made outside the context of an actual dispute before the court. Thus, for example, the court struck down Yeltsin's order merging the secret police with the interior ministry; voided Yeltsin's decree confiscating the property of the communist party; overturned the President's ban of a right wing party; and modified the President's directive which totally outlawed the communist party. In the later case, the constitutional court held that the part of the President's decree which barred the existence of local units of the communist party was unconstitutional. In all of these case, the President, after some hesitation, willingly agreed to abide by the decision of the court.

The court's flamboyant first Chief Justice did things that might seem totally out of place for a U.S. Supreme Court justice, such as participate in debates before the supreme soviet, make public pronouncements on national radio and television regarding matters that were pending before the court and publicly take positions in political disputes that were destined to wind up in his court.

In an article which was published in Rossiiskaya Gazeta on May 18, 1993, Chief Justice V. Zorkin gave a summary of his May 17, 1993 national television speech in which he made the following points about the controversy surrounding the adoption of a new Russian Constitution: no matter how good the constitution may be, if it was adopted in a manner that is unconstitutional, it will not lead to a national consensus; under the present Russian Constitution there are only two methods that may be used to adopt a new constitution for Russia—adoption by the Supreme Soviet and ratification by the Congress of People's Deputies or adoption in a national referendum; President Yeltsin's fear that the Congress of People's Deputies is not disposed to adopting a new constitution that favors the executive branch is not justified; "I suggest that a Draft Constitution which embodies a sane will of the entire society and prepared on the basis of a wide consensus of the people will be adopted by the Congress of People's Deputies".

At about the same time as his May 17, 1993 article, Chief Justice Zorkin gave an extensive interview to another popular Russian newspaper, "Argnmenty i Fakty" in which he discussed his strained relationship with President Yeltsin. Asked by the interviewer why he had turned from being a friend of Yeltsin into his enemy, he replied "I do not have permanent friends, but I do have a permanent interest in defending the Constitution of Russia. I will not deem myself to be a friend of the President when he begins to act outside the realms of the Constitution.

His real enemies are the advisors who urge him to go outside the permissible boundaries of the Constitution of Russia".

A survey that was conducted by Rossiiskaya Gazeta in July 1993 indicated that the Russian constitutional court's first Chief Justice, Valery Zorkin was becoming a folk hero. The survey asked the readers to indicate the individual that they would like to become the President of Russia if an election were held in 1994. Twenty-nine percent preferred the current Vice President (Rutskoi), 24 percent voted for Zorkin and only 12 percent voted for Yeltsin. In the same poll the readers were asked to indicate their choice for speaker of the Russian parliament if an election were held in 1994. For that position, Zorkin once again came in second. The results were as follows: Khazbulatov (the then speaker of the Russian parliament) received 24 percent of the votes; Zorkin tied with the former President of the USSR (Gorbachev) at 10 percent. Following the "Second October Revolution" of 1993 Khazbulatov was ousted from office and Zorkin, under pressure from President Yeltsin, resigned as the Chief Justice of the Russian Constitutional Court.

To a common law mind all of the aforementioned extra-judicial activities by Chief Justice Zorkin are incompatible with the status of a judge, especially a justice of the highest court in the land. Accordingly, American commentators have uniformly condemned Zorkin's actions as inappropriate behavior for a sitting judge. One explanation for this un-American political interventionism by Chief Justice Zorkin may be found in the nature of the court itself.

Whereas many American constitutional historians contend that U.S. Chief Justices from Marshall to Warren had fostered an activism taking the Court beyond the Supreme Court's mandate under Article 3 of the U.S. Constitution, Chief Justice Zorkin's political activism is clearly permitted under his court's enabling statute. In other words, where activist rulings may be debated as standing outside the permissible parameters of the U.S. Constitution, the interventionist rulings of Chief Justice Zorkin are perfectly proper under Russia's constitutional law.

It is true, however, that right up to the time of the "Second October Revolution" of 1993 the Russian constitutional court tended to side with the legislature against the President. That was not because Chief Justice Zorkin was a political ally of Ruslan I. Khazbulatov, the then chairman of the supreme soviet. After all, Zorkin, like Yeltsin, was until recently a card-carrying member of the communist party. The fact that Zorkin's court sided more often with parliament and less with the President was accidental rather than deliberate. There was nothing in Zorkin's background to suggest that he was an ideological bedfellow of Khazbulatov.

The one conclusion that may be drawn from the foregoing observation is that the similarities between the U.S. Supreme Court and the Russian constitutional court are more apparent than real. By contrast, the differences between these two institutions are quite profound. Consider the following contrasting features of these two courts:

Unlike the U.S. Supreme Court, the Russian constitutional court has an advisory jurisdiction which enables it to give a post-enactment advisory opinion on the constitutionality of an act of parliament or an executive decree outside the context of an actual case and controversy. Such binding advisory opinion may be rendered by the court even without any request for it by either the parliament or the President of the Republic.

Unlike U.S. Supreme Court justices who are appointed by the President with the advice and consent of the Senate, justices of the Russian constitutional court are elected by the supreme soviet upon the nomination of the chairman of the supreme soviet. Also unlike U.S. court, whose Chief Justice is appointed by the President, the Chief Justice of the Russian constitutional court is elected by the general membership of the court itself.

Whereas the U.S. Supreme Court has jurisdiction over constitutional as well as non-constitutional federal law questions, the Russian constitutional court has jurisdiction only over federal constitutional questions. As such, the Russian constitutional court is the supreme court on questions of federal constitutional law and the regular Supreme Court of the Russian Federation is the supreme court on questions of non-constitutional federal law. This idea is borrowed from Germany which, in addition to the federal constitutional court, has five other federal supreme courts. Under this Russian arrangement, appeals on non-constitutional federal law may not be taken from the regular federal courts to the Russian constitutional court. Also, individual citizens whose constitutional rights are violated by any government official or agency may file a constitutional complaint directly with the constitutional court without first exhausting legal remedies in the regular federal courts.

Unlike the U.S. Supreme Court which may use the Chief Justice's annual "State of the Judiciary" message to draw attention to defects in federal law but cannot actually introduce a legislative bill in Congress, the Russian constitutional court has the right of legislative initiative which enables it to introduce a legislative bill in the supreme soviet on its own motion.

Supreme Court justices in the U.S., by both law and tradition must refrain from any direct involvement in the affairs of the legislative and executive branches of their federal government. In contrast, the enabling statute of the Russian constitutional court specifically authorizes the justices to participate in the sessions of the legislature, in meetings of the legislative committees and in meetings of the federal cabinet.

Also unlike the U.S. Supreme Court, which must limit its action in a case to its decision therein, the Russian constitutional court is authorized to issue, in addition to its decision in a case, a "private ruling" in which it addresses the root causes of any established violations of the constitution and urges the offending party to take immediate corrective measures. These private rulings are issued in the form of a separate document.

There are many other intrinsic differences between the U.S. Supreme Court and the Russian constitutional court. But, the foregoing seven features of the Russian constitutional court are an express invitation to that court to be an active participant in the country's political processes. The Chief Justice of the Russian constitutional court is much more than a judicial officer. He is the head of a co-equal department of the Russian federal government. Russia, like the United States subscribes to the principle of separation of powers. But, the practical applications of this constitutional doctrine are different in both systems.

Russian people view the constitutional court as the new power broker in the continuing political battle between parliament and the President. The people's trust in this court is so deep that sometimes the people expect the court to intervene in matters that lie outside its jurisdiction. Thus, for example, on July 29, 1993 the Public Relations Department of the Russian constitutional court issued a public official statement which was published in the July 29, 1993 edition of Rossiiskaya Gazeta. The gist of the statement is as follows: Recent reports in some publications have accused the constitutional court of standing idly by as constitutional rights are being violated and/or threatened by speeches made by certain government officials as well as by certain officials of non-governmental organizations. More specifically, the court is accused of not taking any actions in connection with the events of March 20, 1993. All such criticisms are viewed by the Public Relations Department of the constitutional court as attempts to get the court involved in political battles or, worse still, as an invitation for the court to violate its own charter.

The statement went on to say that "[t]he constitutional court is not authorized to officially react to public statements by private citizens, be they participants in the meeting of the Front of National Salvation [reference here is to recent reports in Russian newspapers that at the Second Congress of the Front of National Salvation many of the speakers called for the "forcible overthrow of the anti-popular regime of President Yeltsin and to establish military-type fighting units of the FNS"] or of Democratic Russia. Such actions would fall within the jurisdiction of the executive department and the relevant law enforcement agencies. Prognosis and the publicly stated intent of certain high-level officials, even if they were expressed in an impermissible form, cannot be the object of judicial proceedings before the constitutional court. Let me remind you that the constitutional court, acting on its own initiative, is authorized to render an opinion, on the constitutionality only of acts or decisions of high-level officials of Russia or of its constituent republics ... The constitutional court ought not and will not react to all sorts of political declarations, no matter how loud such statements are, and the court is not prepared to satisfy the political ambitions of warring factions".

The unrestricted ability of justices of the Russian constitutional court to make pronouncements on constitutional controversies outside the context of an actual case is perhaps best exemplified by what happened in the Izvestiia decision. On May 19, 1993 the constitutional court announced its decision in this famous case.

Briefly stated the facts of the case are as follows: The Izvestiia newspaper was established in 1925 as a self-supporting, self-accounting state enterprise placed under the administrative control of the Presidium of the Supreme Soviet of the USSR. The USSR dissolved on December 25, 1991. By Law of the Russian Federation the Supreme Soviet of the Russian Federation became the successor to the Supreme Soviet of the USSR. Thus, by virtue of this Law, the Izvestiia newspaper, after December 25, 1991, became the property of the Presidium of the Supreme Soviet of the Russian Federation. In February 1992 the editors of the Izvestiia newspaper formed a limited liability partnership to run the newspaper. President Yeltsin threw his support behind the newly reconstituted Izvestiia newspaper, but the Speaker of the Russian parliament, Mr. Ruslan Khazbulatov condemned the newly formed limited liability partnership as an illegal attempt by editors of Izvestiia to operate a newspaper that properly belongs to the Presidium of the Supreme Soviet of the Russian Federation. On July 17, 1992 the Supreme Soviet of the Russian Federation adopted a decree "On the Izvestiia Newspaper" declaring the Izvestiia newspaper as a property of the Supreme Soviet of the Russian Federation. On October 28, 1992, 3,000 employees of Izvestiia met and decided to throw their support behind Khazbulatov.

The issue before the court was whether the Decree of the Supreme Soviet of the Russian Federation of July 17, 1992 "On the Izvestiia Newspaper" (which declared that the newspaper is a property of the Russian legislature) was constitutional. In a very brief and unreasoned opinion the divided court held that the decree was unconstitutional. The majority opinion was written by Justice Gadis Gadzhiev. However, in an article which appeared in Rossiiskaya Gazeta on May 21, 1993 Justice Gadzhiev "clarified" the opinion of the court by supplying the missing reason for the decision. In this newspaper article he made the following points: the decision of the constitutional court did not deal with the issue of property claims involved in this dispute; there are rival claims to ownership of the newspaper by both the Supreme Soviet of the Russian Federation and the executive branch of the Russian federal government; these property claims must go before the Supreme Court of Arbitration which has jurisdiction over them; the Izvestiia Publishing Company is a creature of the Supreme Soviet of the Russian Federation; a contract that would formalize the relationship between the Izvestiia Publishing Company and the Izvestiia newspaper (a newly formed newspaper of which the editors are the sole owners) is being drawn up at this time; the new Izvestiia newspaper is an independent newspaper, separate and distinct from the Izvestiia Publishing Company; at this time the new Izvestiia newspaper is using the printing facilities and premises of the Izvestiia Publishing Company without paying for such use; it is now left to the Supreme Court of Arbitration to decide the amount that must be paid by the Izvestiia newspaper for the use of the property of the Izvestiia Publishing Company.

The remarkable aspect of this controversy is that a justice of the constitutional court and the author of the court's majority opinion in a recently decided case did not hesitate to write an article for a national newspaper to explain the decision of the court in the case and to clarify the issues that were not reached by the court's opinion in the case. He even wrote such an article for a newspaper that is owned and controlled by one of the parties (Rossiiskaya Gazeta is owned by the Supreme Soviet of the Russian Federation) in the recently decided case—and the losing party for that matter.

Along with the President of the Russian Federation and the Chairman of the Supreme Soviet of the Russian Federation, the Chief Justice of the Russian constitutional court is an equal partner in the concerted search for constitutional stability in the country. Former Chief Justice Zorkin explained his activist stance as follows: "... Politics and law cannot be separated by a wall ... Given [our] different political climate, ... the court could [not] sit quietly ... and wait until this or that law arouses controversy. Sometimes emergencies arise and we cannot keep silent."

Supporters as well as opponents of former Chief Justice Zorkin agreed on one thing, i.e., in all of its rulings the constitutional court interpreted the Russian constitution competently and correctly. In an article that appeared in the Rossiskaya Gazeta on May 8, 1993, a leading Russian constitutional scholar, Professor Mikhail Piskotin, noted that the Zorkin court "has acquired a reputation as a competent, responsible and solid institution." He further opined that the court's recent decisions "have once again confirmed its reputation as a genuinely independent and competent instrument of constitutional control".

Under the present conditions in Russia, an activist constitutional court is an insurance against anarchy. Foreign investors look to an activist Russian constitutional court to resolve any political controversy that might disturb the tranquility of the marketplace. As such, Chief Justice Zorkin's political activism was not only desirable but most welcome, and, from the perspective of the "rule of law", the Zorkin court's active intervention in the disputes between the political branches of the Russian federal government was fully supported by the court's enabling statute. Clearly, the court, as it functioned under Zorkin, was not an unconstitutional exercise of the court's police powers. It remains to be seen whether Zorkin's successor as Chief Justice of Russia's Constitutional Court will retrench from the activism of his predecessor. In any case, history will judge the Zorkin court's activism in the context of the political situation in Russia between 1991 and October 1993.

E. DEMOCRATIZATION OF THE LEGISLATIVE PROCESS

Three core elements of the political philosophy of socialist law were a recognition of the leading role of the communist party, rubber stamp parliament and political elections without choices. To the Marxian socialist the communist party represented "the mind, the conscience and the honor of society", it was the self-appointed guardian of society and the guarantor of society's welfare. The notion of the "leading role of the communist party" manifested itself in one of two ways, i.e., a one-party state (as was the case in the former Soviet Union) or a multi-party state in which all the other political parties forcibly agreed to acknowledge the communist party a the primus inter pares (as was the case in pre-Solidarity Poland).

The concept of a rubber stamp parliament meant that parliament was the *pro forma* legislative organ in the society, but it enacted laws under the guidance and watchful eyes of the communist party. Because legislative bills that were presented in parliament had already been debated and approved by the communist party at its closed meetings, the only role left to parliament was to legitimize the will of the communist party. Under this arrangement, law making was similar to the submission of a legal instrument that had been drafted by an attorney to a notary for the latter's notarial stamp. Without this notarial stamp the legal instrument would be invalid, just in the same way that a policy adopted by the communist party would not be regarded as law without the legitimizing but perfunctory function of the parliament.

The notion of political elections without a choice was perfected in the former USSR. Issues were placed on the ballots but the ballots listed only one candidate which the voters were called upon to approve or reject. The only candidate whose name appeared on the ballot was either a member of the communist party or a non-party member who had received the endorsement of the local party organization. Even the choice of issues to be placed on the ballots was controlled by the invisible hands of the communist party. Under this arrangement a political election was an exercise in self-deceit.

With the ascendancy of the Solidarity movement to political power, Poland became the first Central and Eastern European country to attempt serious reform of its political system. In quick succession Poland abandoned the notion of the leading role of the communist party, installed a truly deliberative parliament and revamped its election laws. The Poles have not only abandoned the concept of the leading role of the communist party, but also abrogated the communist party. The building that used to be the national headquarters of the communist party in Warsaw has been converted into a stock exchange. Poland has gone from a situation in which one party (the communist party) controlled parliament to a situation in which there are so many parties in parliament that not one of them controls the legislature all by itself. The architect of these Polish reforms was the Solidarity movement whose leader, Lech Walesa was rewarded with an election to the nation's highest political office—the post of President of the Republic of Poland. Poland's example in parliamentary reforms had been copied throughout Central and Eastern Europe. Even Russia now has a multi-party system, a genuinely deliberative parliament and a democratic electoral system.

But, whereas the forces for the democratization of the legislative process in Poland were led by anti-communists, in Russia the reforms were engineered from within the ranks of the communist party and led by ex-communists such as Boris Yeltsin, Anatoly Sobchak, Gavril Popov and others. These men were all products of the communist party machine and former card-carrying members of the communist party. In Russia, Poland, Hungary, the Slovak and Czech Republics and the three Baltic republics of Latvia, Lithuania and Estonia, the democratization of the legislative process has attained such levels that one could truly proclaim the dawn of Western-style democracy in these countries. However, the results of these reforms are less spectacular in some of the other Central and Eastern European countries, such as Albania, Romania, Belarus, Georgia, Moldova, Armenia and the Ukraine.

F. ELEVATION OF DUE PROCESS OF LAW TO THE LEVEL OF A CONSTITUTIONAL PRINCIPLE

Some of the most profound reforms of the laws of the Central and Eastern European countries have taken place in the sphere of criminal procedure, notably in the areas of substantive and procedural due process. As a result of these changes parties in criminal proceedings have gained more rights and the entire process has become more fair. In the realm of criminal procedure the reforms have dealt specifically with right of counsel, presumption of innocence, the right to an open trial, jury trials and the use of wiretap evidence. In the realm of substantive criminal law the reforms have focused on three issues—a narrowing of the scope of conduct that is deemed criminal, a streamlining of the range of capital offenses and a tightening of the definition of a crime in the criminal code.

It is remarkable that the leader in these reforms is the country that had been most prominently associated with violations of due process of law in the past, i.e., Russia. For this reason our analysis will dwell upon the Russian experience. Prior to the reforms of 1991–1993 a criminal suspect under the Russian system was entitled to retain counsel only at the conclusion of the preliminary investigation. The rationale for this rule was that until the preliminary investigation is completed and the suspect is charged with a crime, the process had not taken on an accusatory character and, therefore, the suspect had neither a need nor a reason to retain counsel. The fallacy of such an argument lies in the fact that irreparable damage could be done and was invariably done to the cause of a criminal defendant in the course of the so-called non-accusatory preliminary investigation. In 1992 the Russian legislature agreed with the latter argument when it amended the Russian code of criminal procedure to allow a criminal suspect to retain counsel during the phase of preliminary investigation. Under this new law all criminal suspects are allowed to retain counsel at the point of first contact with the criminal justice system, i.e., at the point at which he is informed that he is a suspect in the commission of a crime.

The second major reform dealt with the noble principle of the presumption of a criminal defendant's innocence until he is proven guilty. Prior to the recent reforms Russian law embodied a watered down version of the presumption of innocence. Because neither the Russian criminal code nor the Russian code of criminal procedure nor the Russian Constitution explicitly used the term "presumption of innocence", there was some serious doubt in the minds of certain commentators whether Russian law subscribed fully to this concept. To eliminate any doubt about its position in this matter, the Russian Supreme Soviet adopted a law on October 24, 1991 which specifically and for the first time in Russian history employed the term "presumption of innocence" to describe one of the cornerstones of Russian judicial reforms. Subsequently, an amendment to the Russian criminal code specifically and unequivocally stipulated that any defendant in any criminal action shall be presumed innocent of the charge against him and the burden of proving his guilt shall rest entirely with the prosecution who must do so to the inner conviction of the judge. By introducing this change Russia joined the ranks of other Central and Eastern European (notably Poland, Hungary, the Czech and Slovak Republics) countries that had already incorporated the principle of presumption of innocence into their laws.

The third major reform of post–1991 Russian law of criminal procedure dealt with the right to an open trial. In the past Russia had practiced what was then referred to as a "rent-a-crowd" tactic for closing the doors of criminal trials to members of the general public. Under this well-rehearsed maneuver the prosecution would request that a truckload of Russian workers should be given some time off from work and trucked in to the courthouse to serve as "observers" at criminal trials. Typically, these "court observers" would be allowed into the courtroom long before the doors are supposed to be opened to members of the general public. These observers would occupy all the seats in the courtroom. When the doors to the courtroom were supposed to be opened to the general public, persons waiting in line to gain access to the courtroom would be politely but firmly told that all the seats in the courtroom had been taken by what was in effect a rented crowd of sympathetic observers.

The Russian "rent-a-crowd" practice took place even though the laws on the books specifically called for an open trial unless in those few and isolated instances in which the law required a trial to be closed for national security reasons. The change that was introduced in 1992 in Russia did not require a change in the code of criminal procedure. The reform entailed a total ban on the rent-a-crowd practice that had the effect of vitiating the laws on the books.

Perhaps the most dramatic change in Russian law of criminal procedure is the introduction of a limited use of the jury in criminal trials. The new law provides that in ordinary criminal trials the court of first instance shall consist of one law judge and two lay assessors. But, in cases in which the defendant is charged with a crime that carries a death penalty or imprisonment in excess of five years, the trial panel shall be a "jury" which the law defines in parenthesis as "an expanded panel of lay assessors". It should be noted, however, that the new Russian criminal jury operate along the lines of the French court of assizes, rather than the common law jury.

Lastly, the reforms of 1990–1993 have placed severe restrictions on the use of wiretap evidence in criminal trials, through a redefinition of conditions under which a warrant for a wiretap may be granted. The new rule is that evidence obtained through a warrantless wiretap may not be introduced at any criminal trial. More importantly, the new rule provides that such evidence may not be used to convict a defendant in any criminal proceedings.

In the area of substantive criminal law the Russian legislature decriminalized many of the conducts that were hitherto deemed criminally punishable. This meant that the dragnet of the Russian criminal code was systematically reduced in size. Many of the crimes that were taken off the criminal code were rendered criminally harmless as a direct result of the country's switchover to a free market economy. In this sense, privatization of the economy was the single most important factor that compelled a reform of the Russian criminal code.

In addition to deleting many crimes from the criminal code, the Russian parliament also reduced the number of capital offenses. The last of the criminal code reforms dealt with the definition of crimes. As a result of the 1990–1993 revisions of the criminal code, the statutory definition of a crime is more precise and very specific. A juxtaposition of the Russian and Polish criminal codes indicates that there are still more crimes listed in the Russian criminal code than there are in the Polish code. But a careful comparison of the statutory language, severity of criminal punishment and internal organization of both codes no longer reveals any substantial difference between both codes. Both codes have matured to the point of being quite favorably comparable to their continental European counterparts.

G. INTRODUCTION OF A SYSTEM OF "GOVERNMENT IN THE SUNSHINE"

Operating on the assumption that electric light is the best policeman and sunshine—the best disinfectant, the governments of Central and Eastern Europe have instituted some form of "government in the sunshine" to guard against the administrative malpractices that pervaded their systems under the rule of socialist law. A good system of "government in the sunshine" must include three elements, i.e., open meetings of all legislative sessions at which laws are adopted, open meetings of all administrative agencies' rule-making sessions at which rules are promulgated and prompt publication of all new laws. As a result of the reforms of 1990–1993 all Central and Eastern European governments have incorporated the first and third of these "government in the sunshine" elements into their laws. The idea of opening sessions of administrative agency rule-making bodies to the public has not quite yet caught on in Central and Eastern Europe.

Poland was among the first Central and Eastern European countries to grant public access to legislative sessions of parliament. Article 12, para. 1 of the Polish Constitutional Act of October 17, 1992 solemnly proclaims that "the debates of the Sejm shall be open to the public". The public gallery at the Polish Sejm in Warsaw has long been a part of the Polish legislative tradition. Russia, on the other hand, caught on with the idea of a public gallery of its legislature only recently. Up until 1991 Russian law called for open sessions of the Supreme Soviet. In reality, however, there were hardly any non-official members of the public at the Supreme Soviet public gallery. That was so for a combination of reasons: the legislative calendar of the chambers of the Supreme Soviet was not published and thus was unknown to the general public; the security screening system that was in place on the grounds of the parliament building discouraged many people from coming close to that building; and many people thought that because the Supreme Soviet was only a rubber stamp body, there was no sense in going there to observe its meaningless proceedings.

As a result of the reforms of 1990–1993 sessions of the Russian Supreme Soviet are of considerable interest to the general public and many ordinary citizens do in fact take the time to attend these sessions. Additionally, sessions of the Russian Supreme Soviet are broadcast on national radio and reported live on national television. Unlike the situation in the U.S. Congress where the television cameras that are transmitting live broadcasts of sessions of Congress are controlled by the respective houses of Congress, in Russia the television cameras that broadcast live transmissions of sessions of the Supreme Soviet are not controlled by the respective chambers of parliament, but by the independent operators of the television programs.

The one area where Russia has made the most dramatic change in its "government in the sunshine" laws is in the publication of new laws. As a result of the reforms of 1990–1993 Russia now has three parallel systems of law reports—one publishes all laws adopted by parliament, another carries all decrees issued by the President of the Russian Federation and the Council of Ministers of the Russian Federation, a third chronologically publishes all rules and regulations handed down by all federal administrative agencies, including the Central Bank of Russia. Furthermore, a Presidential decree of December 5, 1991 requires all newly issued interdepartmental rules and regulations to be registered with the Ministry of Justice of the Russian Federation which must in turn review them for "conformance with the existing laws of Russia" and ensure their prompt publication in a Russian analogue to the U.S. Code of Federal Regulations (CFR). The skeletal provisions of the Presidential decree of December 5, 1991 were beefed up in two subsequent decrees of the Council of Ministers of the Russian Federation—Decree No. 305 of May 8, 1992 and Decree No. 307 of April 13, 1993. Pursuant to these laws, all interdepartmental normative acts must be published in "Rossiiskie Vesti" within ten days of their submission to the Ministry of Justice for registration.

In addition to the official law reports there is a proliferation of "private" law reports in Russia. The leading national newspapers (such as Rossiiskaya Gazeta, Finansovaya Gazeta and Kommersant) contain regular columns in which the texts of new laws are published. As a result of these public and private publications of new laws, gone are the days when a practitioner of Russian law could argue that new laws were not readily available or that newly promulgated interdepartmental instructions and rulings were not published. The Russian lawyer faces a different kind of problem today, i.e., hyperinflation of legal rules. All three levels of the Russian government—federal, regional and local—put out so many new laws that just trying to keep up with them is like trying to take a sip of water from a fire hydrant. To a more or less degree a system of law reports has been instituted in all of the other Central and Eastern European countries.

H. RETRENCHMENT FROM A SYSTEM OF SECRET LAWS

In any modern state there are compelling national security reasons why certain laws must be kept secret from the general public and circulated only to those government officials who have a need to know the contents of such laws. Typically, these secret laws regulate only the conduct of government officials, not of members of the general public. Prior to 1991 many socialist countries saw secret laws as an ordinary instrument of governmental regulation of public behavior. The former Soviet Union was reputedly the worst abuser of secret laws. At the height of the Stalin administration it was estimated that about one-third of all laws promulgated by the Soviet federal authorities were unpublished.

As part of the reforms of 1991–1992 the government of Russia resolved to do away with the old Soviet practice of abuse of secret laws. The new Russian policy requires that: all laws that affect the legal rights and legitimate interests of the general population must be published; all new laws that fall within this category must be promptly published; all old laws that meet these criteria and are still in effect but had hitherto not been published, must be published as soon as the Ministry of Justice of the Russian Federation makes the requisite determination; an unpublished law may not adversely affect the legal rights and legitimate interests of the ordinary citizen; whenever an unpublished law is being enforced by governmental authorities, the aggrieved party is entitled to assert the secrecy of such law as a defense against its enforcement. This principled retrenchment from a system of secret laws perfectly supplements the earlier introduction of a system of "government in the sunshine" by the Central and Eastern European countries. Both of these policies have now been enacted into laws in all of these former socialist systems as further evidence of their determination to rejoin the continental European civil law tradition.

I. SIMPLIFICATION OF ACCESS TO JUSTICE

A good system of justice is one in which all aggrieved citizens have prompt, affordable and effective access to the courts. Two key ingredients of the affordability of civil justice are the affordability of legal services and the reasonableness of court filing costs. One of the laudatory aspects of the socialist legal tradition was the ease with which ordinary citizens could gain access to justice. In implementing the reforms of 1990–1993 the countries of Central and Eastern Europe preserved as well as sought to improve upon this element of the socialist legal tradition. They introduced new measures aimed at the simplification of access to justice, including the following: substantial reduction in court filing fees; streamlining of the rules relating to pleadings in civil actions; liberalization of the rules governing *pro se* representation in judicial proceedings; imposition of a high level of *pro bono* work requirement on all licensed attorneys; and the institution of changes to ensure efficiency in the operations of small claims courts.

As a backup for the courts, the Central and Eastern European systems here also put in place mechanisms for alternative dispute resolution (ADR) such as conciliation and arbitration. Vehicles for ADR were a prominent feature of socialist law and have maintained such status in the post-socialist legal systems of all Central and Eastern European countries. ADR institutions of former Soviet law such as the comrades' courts, the ad hoc arbitration tribunals, the labor courts, the state arlitrazh courts and the institutional commercial arbitration courts have been totally revamped. Privatization generates litigation and there is no doubt that with the transition of the Russian economy from a centrally planned market to one of free enterprise, the Russian society will become more litigious. It is anticipated that the post–1991 simplification of access to justice will cope with the expected new wave of civil litigation in Russia.

J. IMPLEMENTATION OF A GENUINE SYSTEM OF SEPARATION OF POWERS

Under socialist law the rationale for rejecting the doctrine of separation of power went something like this: in a socialist system the communist party is the leading force in society, the moral conscience of society and the guardian of the state constitution; all governmental institutions, including the legislative and executive divisions of state power, operate under the guidance and tutelage of the communist party; any imminent or actual power struggle between the executive and legislative divisions of state power will be refereed by the communist party; as the custodian of the state constitution, it is the responsibility of the communist party to ensure that the rights of the citizens are not trampled by the government agencies; and, as the referee in the power struggle between the legislative and executive divisions of state power, it was the responsibility of the communist party to ensure that the executive branch does not usurp the powers of the legislature.

This reasoning further contends that since the sole reason for the traditional doctrine of separation of powers is to prevent the tyranny of government and regulate the power struggle between the two political branches of government, such a doctrine is functionally unnecessary in a socialist legal system in view of the oversight role of the communist party within this society. Based on the foregoing argument all socialist countries, following an example of Stalin's Russia, repudiated the doctrine of separation of powers which was condemned as a bourgeois concept.

The simultaneous demise of the communist parties in the respective Central and Eastern European countries led to a rethinking of their attitude towards the doctrine of separation of powers. One by one, beginning with Poland, all of these countries rewrote their constitutions to provide for a separation of powers among the three branches of government—legislative, executive and judicial. Article 1 of Poland's Constitutional Act of October 17, 1992 stated the doctrine of separation of powers quite eloquently as follows: "The State organs of legislative power shall be the Sejm and the Senate of the Republic of Poland; executive power shall be the President of the Republic of Poland and the Council of Ministers; and judicial power shall be the independent courts.". Articles 3–27 spell out the scope of the legislative power that is vested in the Sejm and the Senate, just in the same way that the scope of the executive powers of the President and the Council of Ministers are clearly articulated in Articles 28–69 of this Act.

By contrast, the powers of the Polish courts are enshrined in Articles 56–64 of the Constitutional Provisions of the Constitutional Act of October 17, 1992 on the Mutual Relations Between the Legislative and Executive Institutions of the Republic of Poland and on Local Self–Government. The example of Poland has been emulated throughout Central and Eastern Europe. Thus, for example, as a result of these monumental changes the post-Soviet Russian Constitution, for the first time in Russian constitutional history, uses the term "power" to refer to the judiciary. Hitherto, all Soviet constitutions had referred to the courts as "authority", a term which clearly denoted the inferiority of the courts to the two political branches of the Soviet government. By redesignating the courts as a "power", rather than as an "authority", the post-Soviet Russian constitution has finally recognized the courts as a separate and equal branch of government—at par with the legislative and executive branches. Admittedly, not all civil or common law countries have adopted the doctrine of separation of powers. In order to become full-fledged members of the civil law family the respective countries of Central and Eastern Europe did not have to subscribe to this doctrine. But, by doing so, Russia and Poland have taken a bold step forward—one that neither France nor England has felt compelled to take.

K. BOLSTERING OF THE STATUS OF THE LAW JUDGE

It was an entrenched element of the socialist legal culture to regard the courts as the "least dangerous branch" of government. Consistent with this thinking, courts were treated as hierarchically inferior to parliament and to the executive department of government. As part of this constitutional arrangement the courts were subordinated to the political directors of parliament and even the highest court in the land—the Supreme Court—was required to give an account of its stewardship in an annual report to the parliament. An incident of this cultural treatment of courts under this socialist system was the self-evident fact that socialist judges did not and were not expected to "make" law. In practice the socialist judge was looked down upon even by other members of the legal profession, especially the procurators and the advocates. The ultimate symbol of the lowly status of the socialist judge was the fact that he lacked the power of criminal contempt—any person could defy the orders of a judge in a civil action knowing fully well that the judge could not order his imprisonment. A socialist judge was an object of ridicule not only among his fellow members of the legal fraternity, but also among the general population. The joke among Russian law students used to be that those who managed to graduate with grades in the range of D – average would go on to become judges.

The change in the status of the socialist law judge was slow in coming. It began with the recognition of the courts as an independent branch of government that is co-equal with the two political branches of government. The next change was to grant some law-making authority to the judge. The law-making power of the Central and Eastern European judge is most evident in the area of tort law where the judge has the authority to fill in gaps in the law. The third reform that really elevated the status of the Central and Eastern European judge is the one which grants him the power of criminal contempt. Any person who is held to be in contempt of court in a civil action may now expect not only to pay a fine but also to be sentenced to a term of imprisonment.

The last symbolic gesture in the gradual elevation of the status of the Central and Eastern European law judge is the decision to have him wear a judicial robe during court sessions. In the eyes of the general public, the robe dignifies the judge and enhances his authority, albeit symbolically. The Central and Eastern European judge is still very poorly paid, in comparison with other members of the legal profession. His chambers are still very inadequately furnished, in comparison with the offices of the procurator or the advocate. It is anticipated that with time these status symbols of the Central and Eastern European judge will be upgraded to the prevailing level within the respective country's legal profession.

L. INSTITUTIONALIZATION OF COMMERCIAL ARBITRATION

Commercial arbitration has become a permanent fixture in the legal landscape of all Central and Eastern European countries. It is the most prominent of all the alternative dispute resolution (ADR) mechanisms in these countries. The reform of the law of commercial arbitration in the former socialist countries of Central and Eastern Europe is perhaps most pronounced in Russia where a barrage of new laws were unveiled between 1990–1993. The first of these reformist laws was the Law of the Russian Federation of July 4, 1991 "On the Court of Arbitration". This law established a brand new court of commercial arbitration in Russia and was followed in less than one year by another law—the Code of Arbitration Procedure of the Russian Federation which was promulgated on March 5, 1992 and went into effect on April 15, 1992. This was in turn followed by the adoption on June 26, 1992 of the Temporary Statute "On the Ad Hoc Arbitration Tribunal for the Settlement of Economic Disputes". This latter law expanded the jurisdiction of the ad hoc arbitration tribunals to include the settlement of economic disputes, but specifically precluded these tribunals from hearing cases involving joint ventures unless the parties to such disputes stipulate otherwise. On the same day (June 24, 1992), the Supreme Soviet of the Russian Federation enacted the Statute "On the Procedure for the Amicable Settlement of Disputes". This latter law established a procedure for pre-arbitration settlement of disputes by requiring all parties to any commercial dispute to attempt an amicable settlement of the dispute (conciliation) before any resort to the court of arbitration. Turning from domestic commercial arbitration the Law of the Russian Federation "On International Commercial Arbitration" gave its full endorsement to international commercial arbitration as a method for the settlement of international commercial disputes. The rules of this latter law shall apply if the parties elect to arbitrate their commercial disputes in Russia. However, the rules in Articles 8, 9, 35 and 36 of this law are applicable if the arbitration venue is located outside Russia. It will take quite some time before Moscow, Warsaw or Budapest rivals Paris, London or Stockholm as the preferred European venues for international commercial arbitration.

M. OVERHAUL OF THE JUDICIAL SYSTEM

The court systems that are in place in the respective Central and East European countries prior to 1990 were obviously geared towards the needs of a socialist economy. It was uniformly felt that these socialist-era courts would be ill equipped to regulate the new relationships in a free market system. And so, with the demise of socialist law, each one of these countries embarked upon a comprehensive reform that could methodically give the existing courts a thorough face lift. The clearly articulated purpose of these reforms was to establish a definite line of demarcation between the jurisdictions of the respective judicial hierarchies. Within each national system there would be regular courts (to handle civil and criminal matters), specialized courts (to handle matters such as patent, tax, customs, maritime, labor and administrative law disputes) and constitutional courts (to adjudicate constitutional controversies). These various courts would operate in addition to and against the backdrop of the parallel systems of commercial arbitration or other forms of alternative dispute resolution.

There was no country that was more desperately in need of judicial reform than was Russia. The Supreme Soviet of the Russian Federation recognized this urgent need when it adopted a decree of October 24, 1991 "On the Concept of a Judicial Reform in the Russian Federation". This decree spelled out the philosophy of judicial reform in Russia. Among its key provisions are the following affirmative statements: judicial reform is an indispensable element in Russia's efforts to become a democratic state based on a rule of law; judicial reform must be given top priority in the forthcoming legislative activities of the Russian Supreme Soviet; the goals of judicial reform shall be sixfold—secure the sovereign rights of Russia to enforce justice under law throughout its territory, affirm the judicial power of the courts as an independent branch of government, protect the fundamental rights and freedoms of all citizens under the Constitution of Russia, incorporate into the codes of civil and criminal procedure all of the democratic checks on the activities of the law enforcement agencies, provide the courts and the respective law enforcement agencies with the material and technical support needed to accomplish their tasks, and enhance the accuracy of as well as citizen access to information relating to the operations of the courts and the respective law enforcement agencies.

This Law of October 24, 1991 went on to enumerate the following principles as constituting the foundations of the new Russian judicial reform: the creation of a federal court system in Russia; a recognition of the right to jury trial in those instances that are stipulated by law; expression of the right of aggrieved citizens to challenge any unlawful governmental actions in a court of law; imposition of a strict judicial control over the activities of law enforcement agencies acting within the context of a civil or criminal action; introduction into all judicial proceedings of the triple principles of adversarial contest, equal protection of the law and presumption of the innocence of the criminal defendant; institution of any necessary and proper differentiation between the respective judicial proceedings; and a reaffirmation of the twin principles of independence of the courts and the subordination of the judges only to the law.

In order to comply with this 1991 legislative mandate Russia will have to adopt a new code of civil procedure, code of criminal procedure, law on the courts, law on the status of judges and a law on the correctional institutions (a penitentiary code). If the legislative calendar that was unveiled by the Russian Supreme Soviet in 1991 is followed, all of these new laws will be in place by the end of 1994. By the end of the third quarter of 1993 the schedule was being quite closely adhered to by the Russian parliament. As a direct result of the reforms of 1990–1993 Russia now has three supreme courts—a regular supreme court, a supreme court of arbitration and a constitutional court. This reform is consistent with the practice of France and Germany where there are also several supreme courts.

N. REPUDIATION OF THE IDEOLOGY OF SOCIALIST LAW

The elements of the ideology of socialist law that we described in Section IV–B of this chapter are totally incompatible with membership in the continental European civil law family. To qualify for such membership every Central and Eastern European country had to disavow its socialist ideological past. They did so by dethroning the communist party from its former elevated pedestal as the *primus inter pares* among all recognized political parties in the country, privatization of the national economy, abolition of central planning as a method of regulating the marketplace, and a recommitment to the rule of law. Of all the countries of Central and Eastern Europe Poland was the first to embark upon this path of reform. But, because socialist ideology did not really establish firm roots even in socialist Poland, it was relatively easy for Poland to get rid of its socialist ideological baggage. The degree to which the respective Central and Eastern European countries have purged elements of the ideology of socialism from their system is quite uneven. The highest degree of purge may be noticed in Poland, Hungary, the Czech and Slovak Republics, and in the three Baltic republics of Latvia, Lithuania and Estonia. At the lower end of the purge spectrum will be Albania, Romania, Bulgaria and all of the European republics of the former USSR, including Russia.

O. PROCLAMATION OF THE RIGHTS AND FREEDOMS OF MAN AND THE CITIZEN: THE NEW BILL OF RIGHTS

The quintessence of the legal reforms that were undertaken by all of the Central and Eastern European countries after the demise of socialist law in this region of the world is encapsulated in the new bill of rights that each one of them unveiled in the period between 1990–1993. A juxtaposition of the respective national bills of rights reveals that they tend to follow two patterns as represented by the Polish and Russian approaches. The Polish bill of rights is incorporated into the state constitution by a special constitutional act; the Russian bill of rights is handed down in the form of a solemn declaration by the Supreme Soviet of the Russian Federation. Let us examine these two legislative approaches, beginning with the Polish model.

Subject to a few provisions that were re-enacted and thus continued in force, the Constitution of the Republic of Poland of July 22, 1952 was repealed by the Constitutional Act of October 17, 1992 on the Mutual Relations Between the Legislative and Executive Institutions of the Republic of Poland and on Local Self–Government (hereinafter the Constitutional Act of 1992). The Constitutional Act of 1992 which today constitutes the Constitution of Poland, is divided into two parts—Part I contains 78 articles and is arranged into six chapters; Part II which is known as Constitutional Provisions (hereinafter Constitutional Provisions) contains 106 articles and is arranged into 11 chapters. Chapter 8 (Articles 67–92) of the Constitutional Provisions is entitled "The Fundamental Rights and Duties of Citizens". In addition to articulating the fundamental rights of the Polish citizens in Articles 67–89, the Constitutional Provisions stipulate the constitutional duties that must be borne by all Polish citizens in Articles 90–92.

Prominent among the rights that Polish citizens enjoy under these Constitutional Provisions is equal protection of law irrespective of sex, birth in or out of wedlock, educational attainment, profession, nationality, race, religion, social status and origin. Missing from this list of protected classes of citizens is one that is based on sexual orientation. Thus, the Polish Constitution of 1992 continues to deny equal protection of the law to homosexuals and lesbians. Following Poland's past socialist tradition Article 68 recognizes the right to work as a constitutional right of all Polish citizens, without stating how such a right can be secured by the state in a system of free enterprise economy. Other socialist-era rights that one finds in these Constitutional Provisions include: right to rest and leisure, right to health protection and assistance in the event of sickness or inability to work, the right to benefit from the natural environment, right to free education, right to benefit from cultural achievement and to creatively participate in the development of national culture, and the right to benefit from the achievements of national literature and arts.

Traditional rights such as freedom of speech, of the press and of assembly are enshrined in Article 83. Inviolability of the person is guaranteed to all Polish citizens under Article 87, as are the inviolability of one's home and the privacy of one's correspondence. To conclude the list of rights under this law, Article 89 states that Polish citizens staying abroad, temporarily or permanently, shall enjoy the protection of the Republic of Poland. To dispel any notion that the freedom of speech under this Constitution is absolute, Article 81, para. 2 states that "the spreading of hatred or contempt, the provocation of discord, or humiliation of man on account of national, racial or religious differences, shall be prohibited".

The duties of the Polish citizen includes the duty to: respect the Constitution and the laws of Poland, respect the principles of community life, safeguard public ownership, defend the homeland, perform military service, exercise vigilance against enemies of the nation, carefully guard state secrets and protect the environment. A close analysis of this 1992

Polish Constitution leaves one with the impression that its authors did not quite succeed in expunging from this document the socialist ideals of the Polish Constitution of 1952. Except for a few Western-type clauses that are scattered over the entire document, the Polish Constitution of 1992 still reads like a socialist manifesto. In addition to being less eloquent than its Russian counterpart, the new Polish bill of rights exudes the strong influence of the socialist legal tradition. This is especially noticeable in the array of socialist-era rights that it continues to advocate for Polish citizens.

The Russian bill of rights was handed down in a Decree of November 22, 1991 of the Supreme Soviet of the Russian Federation which is appropriately entitled "The Declaration of the Rights and Freedoms of Man and the Citizen". Its unexpressed motto could very well have been "Liberty, Equality and Fraternity". Not only is its title reminiscent of the French "Declaration of the Rights of Man and Citizen" of August 26, 1789, it is also readily apparent that this law was strongly influenced by the French Constitution of 1958. The French influence on this law is even more apparent as one reads through its eloquent provisions. The Preamble "affirms the rights and freedoms of man, his honor and dignity as deserving of the supreme respect of the society and the state" and goes on to "recognize the necessity to align the laws of the Russian Federation with the generally accepted principles of the rights and freedoms of man in the international community of nations". Like the French Declaration before it, the Russian Declaration of 1991 is based on the premise that "liberty consists in being able to do anything that does not injure another; thus, the only limits to the exercise of natural rights of each man are those that assure to other members of society the enjoyment of the same rights. These limits can only be set by law." If there is any doubt as to the preeminent influence of French scholars in the rebuilding of Russia's new legal system, this document will put an end to it. Post–Soviet Russia is fast emerging as a part of the intellectual empire of France.

Among the rights and freedoms of man and the citizen that this declaration proclaims are the following: the rights and freedoms of man shall belong to him from the time and by virtue of his birth; generally recognized norms of international treaties relating to human rights shall be a direct source of the rights and freedoms of Russian citizens; the enumeration of the rights and freedoms of man and the citizen in this declaration is not exhaustive of the rights and freedoms to which man and the citizen are entitled; rights and freedoms of man and the citizen may be abridged by law only in the interest of protecting the constitutional system, public morality, health, lawful rights and interests of other persons in a democratic society; all persons shall be entitled to equal protection of the law regardless of race, nationality, language, social origin, property status or official position, place of residence, religious preference, belief system, membership in social groups or organizations "and other situations"; right to life; citizens of Russia shall be entitled to an inalienable right to such citizenship.

This law also recognizes traditional rights such as freedom of speech and freedom of thought. What is remarkable about these twin rights is not that they are listed in Article 13 of the Russian Declaration, but that their precise formulation mimics the language used in Article 11 of the French Declaration of 1789. The French document reads "The free communication of thoughts and of opinions is one of the most precious rights of man; accordingly every citizen may speak, write, and publish freely, except that he must answer for the abuse of this liberty in the cases determined by the law". The Russian document echoes as follow "Any person shall have the right to freely communicate his thoughts, his speech as well as express without any restrictions his opinions and convictions. No person may be forced to express his thoughts or convictions."

Other rights that are embodied in the Russian bill of rights include: freedom of movement; freedom from unlawful arrest and of the inviolability of the person; freedom to search for, receive and freely disseminate information; freedom of conscientious objectors to substitute other forms of national service for military service; freedom of assembly and of association; right to private ownership of property; freedom from forced labor; privilege against self incrimination; no person may be compelled to testify against his/her spouse or against a close relative within the degree of relationship defined by law; and the right not to be charged under a retroactive criminal statute.

By virtue of this single legislation Russia has reversed its 75–year human rights tradition. Russian law now subscribes to the notion that: individuals are endowed with certain inalienable rights which accrue to them by virtue of their birth; the rights of a Russian citizen are not limited to those which are enumerated in the positive laws of the state, but may in fact include certain natural law rights; that the exercise of a human right is not conditioned upon the performance of any concomitant duty that may be imposed by the state; a conscientious objector is entitled to refuse military service on the grounds of his religious beliefs; a Russian citizen by birth may not be stripped of such citizenship by the state and may not be thrown out of his native land by the government.

The one principle that rings through this new Russian bill of rights is that rights and freedoms are not absolute; they may be abridged or temporarily suspended by the state under compelling and clearly articulated conditions. Thus, for example, the right to life may be abridged if one is convicted of a capital offense; the right to own private property may be limited by a law which restricts the type of property that individual citizens may own; the right to seek, acquire and freely disseminate information may be abridged by laws intended to protect state secrets; .and the right of free speech may be subject to prior restraint in specific instances stipulated by law. Even in those instances in which there are no prior restraint on free speech, any person who abuses this freedom "must answer for such abuse in the cases determined by law.

The adoption of the Russian bill of rights in 1991 and of the Polish counterpart in 1992 was one credible evidence that the countries of Central and Eastern Europe were ready to be transformed into a "government of laws, not of men". Poland's commitment to the rule of law is enshrined in Article 1 of the Constitutional Provisions of 1992 in the following words: "The Republic of Poland is a democratic state ruled by law and implementing the principles of social justice." As these "lost members" of the civil law family return to their ancestral home after fifty years of experimentation with socialist law, their ability to live up to this solemn promise of the Polish Constitution of 1992 will be put to a serious test.

SECTION 7. CONCLUSION: THE REUNIFICATION OF THE EUROPEAN BRANCH OF SOCIALIST LAW WITH THE CIVIL LAW

In addition to recognizing the reunification of the European branch of socialist law with the civil law, legal historians will also notice an instructive historical parallel between the recent developments in Central and Eastern European law and the early developments of the Roman law phase of the civil law tradition. For the first 400 years of this century much of what is today's Western Europe, including much of England, was Romanized and formed a unified Roman Empire. In 476 A.D. the Germanic tribes invaded, conquered and occupied the Western half of the Roman Empire. As a result of this conquest the Western half of the Roman Empire with its headquarters in Rome was completely cut off from the eastern half of the Roman Empire with its headquarters in Constantinople. While Roman law flourished and prospered in the eastern half of the Roman Empire, Roman law was being vulgarized and bastardized by the Germanic tribes in the western half of the Roman Empire. While the grandeur of Roman law in the eastern half of the Empire was captured in the Justinian Codes (the Corpus Juris Civilis) of 533–534 A.D., the now fragmented and vulgarized Roman law in the western half of the Empire was compiled into what became known as Lex Romana Visigothorum in 506 A.D. Roman law regained its purity and grandeur in the western half of the Roman Empire after both halves of the empire were reunified in 544 A.D. In the meantime the period between 476 A.D. and 544 A.D. became known as the Incubation Period of Roman Law in the western half of the Roman Empire. As the analysis which follows will show, a similar fate befell the civil law in Central and Eastern Europe.

Prior to the forcible imposition of socialism on the countries of Central and Eastern Europe much of what constituted the European branch of the socialist legal family was a part of the European civil law. The imposition of socialism on Russia in 1917 and on Central and Eastern Europe in 1946 parallels the Germanic invasion and occupation of the western half of the Roman Empire in 476 A.D. With the imposition of socialism on those countries, the civil law that was once their legal culture of choice was systematically bastardized, vulgarized and eventually codified as socialist law. In this respect the status of socialist law in Central and Eastern Europe paralleled that of Lex Romana Visigothorum in the western half of the Roman Empire. During the forced incubation of civil law in Central and Eastern Europe, civil law prospered and flourished in continental Western Europe. The reunification of Central and Eastern Europe with continental Western Europe in 1993 is historically analogous to the reunification of the Roman law tradition in both halves of the Roman Empire in 544 A.D.

The lessons that may be learned from this analogy are as follows: first, the process of reacquainting Central and Eastern Europe with the civil law methods and techniques will be painful and protracted; second, until Central and Eastern Europe is fully and completely integrated into the civil law fold, these countries will manifest some common idiosyncracies that will isolate them into a separate chamber within the common home of the civil law. In many respects, the process of reintegrating Central and Eastern Europe into the civil law tradition will be a mirror reflection of the painful process of reintegrating the former Eastern Germany into the common German family.

The third and perhaps the most revealing lesson to be learned from this analogy is that while it was in operation in Central and Eastern Europe socialist law, unlike Lex Romana Visigothorum, was a separate and autonomous legal system that was distinctly different from the civil law system. Under the system of personal law that was followed in the Germanic kingdoms, Roman citizens within these kingdoms were subjected to Roman law, not to Germanic law. Thus, Lex Romana Visigothorum was the special local version of Roman law that was applied to the local Roman population in the Germanic kingdoms. Within these kingdoms Lex Romana Visigothorum existed side by side with the Germanic law which applied to the local German population. By contrast, in Central and Eastern Europe there was only one system of law that was applicable to all citizens and it was socialist law. What happened here was that socialist law borrowed heavily from the civil law. But, in doing so, it evolved into a new and different legal system. Now that the forced incubation of the civil law has ended in Central and Eastern Europe and socialist law has been displaced in these countries, socialism continues its unchallenged existence in other parts of the socialist legal family. Thus, whereas socialist law has lost the notions of Central and Eastern Europe to the civil law, socialist law has not lost its own existence. It exists elsewhere.

Lastly, after their reunification with the civil law, each country in Central and Eastern Europe will continue to show a special affinity with either the French or the German version of the civil law tradition depending on which influence it had prior to the imposition of socialist law on the country. For example, prior to 1946 Polish law was clearly identified with French law. So was Romanian law. After 1993 it is anticipated that the civil law in Poland and Romania will continue to manifest the strong influences of French law, rather than German law. While borrowing a few institutions from German law, it is becoming increasingly clear that post-socialist Russian civil law falls within the sphere of influence of French law. By contrast, it is anticipated that after 1993 civil law in Hungary as well as in the Czech and Slovak republics will resume their pre–1946 strong affinity with German law. What all this means is that after 1993 each Central and Eastern European national law will be operating under two strong conflicting tendencies—a centripetal force that will tend to draw them inward and closer to their subgroup of former socialist laws *and* a centrifugal force that will draw them outward and away from the sub-group of former socialist laws towards the orbit of French or German law.

Part III

THE COMMON LAW TRADITION

Chapter 9

HISTORY, CULTURE AND DISTRIBUTION OF THE COMMON LAW TRADITION

SECTION 1. INTRODUCTION

English common law evolved from necessity; the law was rooted in centralized administration of William, conqueror at Hastings. A single event, the 1066 Norman Conquest, was the progenitor of this tradition, its foundation a unique, "unwritten" constitution and the recorded, but orally rendered decisions of an extraordinarily gifted and respected judiciary. The harmony of a homogeneous society, tested by internal stresses but free of foreign invasion for nearly a millennium, aided an orderly development of legal institutions. Focusing on the resolution of specific, current issues, English law developed insulated from the continental reception of Roman law, and the later emphasis on codification. As Pollock has said, English laws "grew in rugged exclusiveness, disdaining fellowship with the more polished learning of the civilians."[1]

Comprehension of the rule of law in England today, and its litmus role in other common law systems, calls for an understanding of the cardinal incidents in English history which were generative of the slow but persistent development of institutions which comprise the common law tradition.

SECTION 2. ROMAN OCCUPATION

English legal scholars trace the origins of English common law principally to the Norman Conquest. Legal institutions before that time made few lasting contributions. The early law was unwritten, handed down through generations by oral tradition. We know that over centu-

---

1. The principal works on English legal history are the sixteen volumes of W.S. Holdsworth, History of English Law (1922–66) and F. Pollock and F.W. Maitland, History of English Law before the time of Edward I (2d ed. 1898, reissued 1968). A recent useful history is J.H. Baker, An Introduction to English Legal History (3d ed. 1990).

ries tribal laws changed to accord with the times, but we know little with exactitude of when the changes occurred or the precise forces impelling those changes.

Julius Caesar led exploratory expeditions in 55 and 54 B.C. to Southeast England. Disparate Celtic tribes, about whose legal structures Maitland has commented, "The law of one rude folk will always be somewhat like the law of another," [2] supported periodic revolts in Britain against the Roman dominion. A century later Claudius, timidly seeking status as a conquering caesar, chose weak Britain to subdue. Romans ruled much of the island for nearly four centuries. Britain was marked indelibly with Roman culture—the rose, its road system, the Latin language and central heating—but the Romans did not bestow upon the inhabitants the Roman legal system. Britain had not been developed, it had been occupied. Roman law was an incident of occupation. It governed relations between Romans, but it began a decline in 410 A.D. when it appeared that the departing legions would not return. What Rome contributed to the English legal system was indirect, occurring through the survival of remnants of institutional structures of a civilized society.

SECTION 3. ROMAN–NORMAN HIATUS: THE ANGLO–SAXON PERIOD

With the Romans departed, the Britons were left with little but a few Christian missionaries to face Angles, Danes, Jutes and Saxons— again society became dominated by diverse tribal communities, with law predominantly unwritten local custom. There was sufficient cohesion for Pope Gregory's missionary, St. Augustine, to establish Christianity in the late sixth century, giving English kings the imprimatur of the supreme source of justice, but less than the divine right of kings, the latter an important reservation in later centuries. But the efforts of Justinian and the Byzantine jurists in the sixth century in creating the Corpus Juris Civilis were of no greater impact in England as they were occurring than they were five centuries later during their revival.

Anglo–Saxon law possessed elements of Teutonic tribal traditions and customs, but personal wealth began to replace "blood and kin" as the measure of political power. England developed feudal attitudes, but not in the continental sense. Landowners rather than the community or state provided protection to and drew loyalty from the dependent classes. Lords administered justice for their tenants and villani, and their lands provided the source of taxes to defend the nation.

SECTION 4. THE NORMAN CONQUEST

The victory at Hastings by William was more a succession than a conquest. William's claim to the English throne was no less tenuous

---

2. Selected Historical Essays of F.W. Maitland 99 (Cambridge ed. 1957).

than Harold's. The law of England, an aggregate of disparate local customs, was left largely intact by the conqueror. But he confiscated all of the land and then apportioned possession among his most trustworthy followers, extracting pledges of loyalty and service. William allocated the land in a manner to prevent his barons from concentrating their power and challenging William's central authority. This limited holding of the land, with ownership remaining in the sovereign, is today largely theoretical.

William achieved his goal of kingly investiture at Westminster, but duties in Normandy demanded his attention. Establishing centralized rule at Westminster permitted the governance of a large number of Saxons by comparatively few Normans. William's administrative efficiency produced the Domesday survey in 1086, an inventory of all property throughout England, which facilitated a much larger revenue collection.

William resolved matters of royal concern at Westminster; local issues remained in the courts of the shires and hundreds. Only judicial disputes of an extraordinary nature were brought before the king as chief justiciar. Administrative necessity rather than legislative design played the central role in fashioning the early structures of the common law. William's legacy was the creation of a highly centralized legal system.

The transformation of society, including the revival of the study of Roman law, beginning on the continent a few years before the Norman Conquest would have only nominal effect on the development of the English legal system. By the time the clerical scholars from Bologna reached England a largely secular legal institutional structure was sufficiently developed to relegate the influence of Roman law to academic study in the universities. Professional legal communities, the Inns of Court, had secured a hold on legal training.

SECTION 5. ROYAL COURTS

No separation of government functions existed in early Norman England. The king, acting with close advisors in council, the Curia Regis, exercised judicial as well as executive and legislative powers. The council was as mobile as the king. But some functions of the Curia Regis later were delegated to newly created institutions. Judicial powers were assumed by the royal courts, beginning an important unification, the development of a law common throughout England. The three courts which were to develop over the ensuing two and a half centuries affirmed centralized judicial authority.[3] They sat at Westminster even in the absence of the king.

The Court of Exchequer, a judicial offspring of the financial side of the Curia Regis, was the first common law court. It reflected the king's

3. See A. Harding, Law Courts in Medieval England (1973).

paramount interest in efficiently settling tax disputes. Exchequer's initial jurisdiction was more extensive, limited to resolving tax disputes only after the development of the Court of Common Pleas.

The Court of Common Pleas resolved issues between subjects which did not involve a direct interest of the king, thus the name common pleas. The disputes usually dealt with title to land, or personal actions of debt, convenant or detinue. It later developed an exceptional formality of procedure and became an expensive court for litigants.

The third central court was King's Bench, established to hear issues with a direct royal interest, pleas of the Crown. It issued writs of mandamus, prohibition, certiorari and habeas corpus, to control questioned actions of public officials. King's Bench later became an important check on the abuse of prerogative powers of the king. Its civil jurisdiction expanded, encroaching upon the Court of Common Pleas, encompassing most torts through the broadly interpreted writ of trespass and elaborate fictions, and later extending to contracts by the writ of assumpsit.

The English barons were on the verge of rebellion due to the evolution of these common law courts. Although the king's courts did not replace directly the old local shire and hundred courts, if overlapping jurisdiction existed, litigants usually preferred the common law courts. Procedure was more progressive and fairer in the latter, and participants avoided the harsh proof of ordeal or oath of the local courts. This preference eroded the role of local courts and reduced revenue generated from court fees, revenue intensely coveted by both the king and the barons.

SECTION 6.　WRIT SYSTEM

Jurisdiction of the common law courts was limited severely by a writ system. A civil action lay before one of the courts only where a specific writ was available from a high official ("where there is no writ, there is no right"). Issued in the name of and constituting a command from the king, writs were addressed to an official authorizing commencement of specific suits, later known as "forms of action." [4] The system was rigid; selection of the wrong writ resulted in dismissal. The variety of writs, first including the writs of debt, detinue, covenant, replevin and account, later increased. The writ of trespass was added and expanded to encompass ejectment, trover and assumpsit, important to the development of contract and tort. But these nevertheless were limited in scope, and neither the judges nor the chancellor could freely create new writs. The Statute of Westminster 1285, limited the invention of new writs to circumstances similar to those then affording protection.

To increase further the jurisdiction of the common law courts, fictions were invented to extend the circumscribed writs. An example is

---

4. See F.W. Maitland, The Forms of Action at Common Law (1909).

ejectment. It originated as an action available only to a wrongfully ejected leasehold tenant, and was unavailable to a freeholder. But a fiction was created. The freeholder alleged a fictitious lease to a fictitious person, usually John Doe. Doe then alleged that he had been wrongfully ejected by Richard Roe, an equally fictitious character. Doe, the nominal lessee, next sued the ejector. The court had to determine the origin of the alleged lease, raising the issue of who owned the freehold. Thus, the common law court would rule on the title, an issue otherwise reserved to the local courts. This early common law emphasis on procedure was not unlike the early Roman law concentration on forms of actions, on the facts of a case rather than the origination of substantive, abstract legal rules.

SECTION 7. MAGNA CARTA

The progressive loss of jurisdiction of the local shire and hundred courts induced revolt among the English barons. Joined by a similarly aggrieved clergy, the barons in 1215 extracted a charter from King John, later to become venerated as the Magna Carta. It was a self-serving document for the barons, who viewed the charter as a contract to halt their losses of various feudal privileges. But the charter also included a very few stipulations protecting ordinary citizens—provisions which much later endowed it with stature as a constitutional document of exceptional magnitude.

The Magna Carta contributed to the evolutionary demise of the rural courts, a process which continued for three centuries after the Conquest. The common law courts and the writ system were central to this demise, supported by the Crown assuming ownership of all land, and the diminished power of local sheriffs. The Magna Carta denied sheriffs the right to hear pleas of the Crown, and the Statute of Gloucester 1278, was interpreted to severely restrain civil jurisdiction of rural courts.

SECTION 8. ECCLESIASTICAL COURTS

Ecclesiastical courts persisted as rivals to the Royal Courts longer than the rural courts. The ecclesiastical courts applied canon law, the roots of which were firmly in the Roman law. The church vigorously defended its right to try "religious" offenses, including adultery, incest and less distinct offenses against morality. It also assumed civil jurisdiction over family issues, principally marriage and succession, as well as criminal jurisdiction over clergy. "Benefit of Clergy" allowed a convicted cleric to transfer the case from a temporal to an ecclesiastical court for sentencing. This unique doctrine persisted for several centuries, protecting persons with the most transient connection with the church, and ultimately even anyone who could prove literacy. The jurisdictional clash of church and state reached violent dimensions during the Plantagenet period, provoking the murder of Thomas à Becket in 1170 in Canterbury Cathedral. Henry II's reforms dismantled much of the diversity of local law and moved England forward significantly in the development of a law common to the nation, and applicable to all within that nation. Although the church largely forfeited its judicial role, ecclesiastical jurisdiction over family and succession issues persisted until the mid–19th century, when it merged with other civil matters before the Royal Courts. But the imprint of canon law remains to this day on English family and inheritance law.

SECTION 9. EQUITY

The forms of action developed a rigid inflexibility by the early 15th century. A plaintiff unable to obtain a proper writ was left with no remedy. John Austin said that English equity "arose from the sulkiness and obstinacy of the common law courts, which refused to suit themselves to the changes which took place in opinion, and in the circumstances of society." However obstinate it may have been, the common law was not rigid; it accepted new institutions. To counter the severity of the writ system and provide relief other than money damages, the king and later his chancellor, the "keeper of the king's conscience," accepted petitions for equitable relief. Heard in an inquisitorial fashion modeled on canon and Roman law, these equitable proceedings focused on avoiding the strictures of the common law. It was successful, and a formal Court of Chancery soon assumed jurisdiction of pleas in equity.

If the addition of such equitable concepts as injunctive relief and specific performance to supplement the common law was equity's paramount general contribution, the origin of the trust was its most important conceptual addition. The common law did not recognize an interest in a party who was not the titleholder to land. The transfer of property to a party to hold either for the benefit of the grantor, who may have been trying to avoid feudal obligations, or a third party, did not create legal rights enforceable by beneficiaries. The Court of Chancery, acting to fill this acknowledged void in the common law by using its powers to demand good conscience, would rule that the holder of the property must administer it for the benefit of the donor or third party, as specified in the initial grant. From this concept arose an equitable interest held by the beneficiary, the person in possession assuming the status of a trustee obligated to deal with the property considering the nature of the equitable interest of the third party.

The discretion exercised by early Chancellors—John Seldon remarked that equity varied "according to the length of the Chancellor's foot"—by the 18th century had evolved its own procedural rules, paradoxically as rigid as those which equity had been created to avoid.

J. DAWSON, "THE ORACLES OF THE LAW"
2 (1968).*

* * *

One striking thing ... was that these royal judges at all times were so few. A contrast with France will make this more clear. By 1297 the highest royal court in France—the Parlement of Paris—had 51 judges. The total rose to 80 in the following century and to 240 in the eighteenth century. By the eighteenth century, however, twelve other Parlements had been created and the total membership of all thirteen of these high appellate courts was over 1,200. In addition, there were at least 5,000 judges in the inferior royal courts in France and to them could be added some tens of thousands of judges (many of them part-time) in the seignorial courts of the feudal lordships. But in thirteenth century England the Court of Common Pleas ordinarily numbered four or five judges and the King's Bench when it emerged as a separate court, usually had only three. In later times the total membership of the two courts remained about the same—seven or eight—though with variations from year to year. Then in the sixteenth century, when the court of Exchequer acquired a general common law jurisdiction, its complement of judges (four or five) should be added to the total of common law judges. If we ignore the specialized jurisdictions like the Admiralty and the church courts but if the two judges of the Chancery are added, one can make the point shortly by saying that from 1200 to 1800 the permanent judges of the central courts of common law and Chancery, all taken together, rarely exceeded fifteen.

Our present concern is not with the surfeit of judges in France but with the strict economy in judicial manpower that was practiced in England. This strict economy was maintained not only during the rapid growth of the thirteenth century but, as I have said, for centuries thereafter. On first view it would seem a miracle that seven or eight (or later, twelve or thirteen) common law judges could handle all the trials and appellate review of an entire country.

The explanation is partly found in the fact that the coverage of the common law system of remedies was for long severely limited. In the ordering of English society it was a matter of the utmost importance that the crown acquired early a monopoly over prosecutions for major crime, but there remained an enormous range of minor offenses that were punished in the hundred courts, the courts of the manors and towns, and later by the justices of the peace, over whom the central courts exercised a control that was at most sporadic. Civil litigation dealt with the affairs of the relatively prosperous. ... Altogether one can say that at the time of its creation the common law system was remarkable for its range, for its impact on English society and for the power that it mobilized, but that it captured only the key controls, over matters of paramount interest to the crown. ...

A second major explanation can be found in the measures adopted to economize on judges' time. It will be remembered that in the thirteenth

* Reprinted with permission of John P. Dawson and the University of Michigan Law School.

century witnesses did not testify before jury and judges in open court. It was for the jurors themselves to find answers to the questions asked them, using their own private knowledge, gossip in the community, or such other sources as they could tap. By the use of a collective verdict, the sources of their knowledge and the ignorance or dissent of individual members were all effectively buried. This meant that trials could mainly consist of asking the jury the appropriate questions and compelling them to give their answers. It also meant that for many trials no royal justice was needed at all. And so the practice developed in the thirteenth century of appointing judicial commissions of local gentry, "knights of the shire." ...

SECTION 10. JUSTICES OF THE PEACE

The Crusades of the 12th century disrupted rural English life. Returning soldiers had tasted the fruits of conquest. Concern over the maintenance of order in England moved Richard I to name Keepers of the Peace, Dawson's "knights of the shire," commissioned to maintain rural order. Their authority was expanded by the Justices of the Peace Act 1361, granting to "knights, esquires or gentlemen" of the area authority to "pursue, arrest, take and chastise" those breaching the peace.[5] Lesser offenses were tried directly by these lay Justices of the Peace; more serious crimes were referred to the king's judges who conducted County Quarter Sessions four times annually. For 600 years the judicial process for keeping the peace has been lodged principally in the hands of ordinary citizens, rather than a professional judiciary.

SECTION 11. WARS OF THE ROSES

The Wars of the Roses (1455–1471) tested English constitutionalism with civil disturbance, inept domestic rule and factionalism. Englishmen tended to prefer public order over freedom, accepting a firm rule which would have been unacceptable in the absence of the domestic disturbances. Common law institutions were strained, and later subordinated to sovereign decree during the Tudor and Stuart reigns, but they survived this single serious challenge to the common law in English history.

SECTION 12. THE TUDORS

Henry VII (1485–1509), the first of the Tudor kings, created the Court of Star Chamber. Evolving from the judicial remnants of the King's Council, the Star Chamber was vested with extensive criminal jurisdiction, including conspiracies, forgeries and perjury. Its history of coercion to extract confessions and the names of accomplices has identi-

---

5. F. Milton, The English Magistracy 4 (1967). See generally J. Dawson, A History   of Lay Judges (1960).

fied it with unreasoned judicial harshness, but it was not at the time considered particularly repressive. Its fines and punishments were not unduly severe, nor did it impose the death penalty.

The inquisitorial procedure of the Star Chamber had roots in canon and Roman law. It was staffed by lawyers with a civil law education at Oxford and Cambridge, who showed disdain for what they viewed as an overly formal common law system, preferring anything touched by the Renaissance, including the allegedly more understandable civil law. But there was to be no reception of civil law in England. Its influences were limited mainly to aspects of commerce affected by international trade, particularly mercantile and maritime law.

The establishment of Parliament as a legislative chamber separate from the king and his council, although still closely controlled by the king, was a more positive contribution of the Tudor period than the new judicial institutions. The strengthening of Parliament was backed by the proponents of the common law, who feared the gathering power being exercised by the king. A populace benefiting from an improving quality of life and concerned with the unsettling consequences of the abuse of royal power, began to limit the use of the royal prerogative; feudalism was on its deathbed. By the end of the Tudor period Parliament achieved status as the supreme law-making body; only its laws, not sovereign decrees, were binding on the courts.

SECTION 13. THE STUARTS

The sovereign-parliamentary conflict again surfaced under James I (1603–1625), first of the Stuarts. The Star Chamber became an oppressive institution of royal power, giving credibility to its reputation of unjustness which was undeserved at its formation. James would not admit to the philosophy of common law lawyers that ancient royal prerogative powers were divisible, vesting foreign policy and the declaration of war with the king, but assigning other issues to Parliament.

English judges, unlike the common law lawyers, were divided on the issue of sovereign power. Judicial loyalty to the Stuart conception of royal power was attributable to the historical control by the king over the appointment and removal of judges. Edward Coke led the opposition from his position as Chief Justice, ruling persistently to preserve the autonomy of the common law courts.[6]

This divisiveness swelled under Charles I (1625–1649). He convened and then dismissed Parliament with a frequency measured by its loyalty to the Crown. Parliament enacted the Petition of Right 1628, an impermanent attempt to reestablish due process concepts of the Magna Carta, and thus restrict sovereign power. Charles' response was eleven years of rule without a Parliament (1629–1640). When Parliament reconvened, it was hardly repentant. It purged the nation of the Star Chamber and made government ministers accountable to Parliament as

---

6. See E. Coke, Institutes of the Laws of England (1628–1644).

well as to the king. The ensuing civil war was the final test of the separation of powers, a conflict which brought to Charles defeat and execution (1649), followed by several years of ineffectual rule and then Oliver Cromwell's self-appointment as Lord Protector of the Commonwealth. In 1660, eleven years after its demise, the monarchy was restored as the lesser evil.

The House of Lords, abolished after Charles' defeat, was reestablished, with the House of Commons reinforced as being vested with greater initiation and authority. The king conceded to the grievances of Parliament, and confirmed its power over the process of legislation and control of taxation. A bloodless revolution in 1688 established an enduring Protestant royal succession and constitutional government. The Bill of Rights 1689 joined the Magna Carta as a foundation of English constitutionalism. The Bill mandated parliamentary consent for a peacetime standing army, free election of Parliament, parliamentary approval of the suspension of law or levying of taxes, regular parliamentary sessions and limitations on bail, fines and cruel and unusual punishment. The Act of Settlement 1700, created an independent judiciary, members removable only by Parliament. The Act confirmed what Coke had said decades earlier, the sovereign may not dismiss judges.

The common law had survived the tumultuous Stuart era. English political and legal institutions had been altered, but the challenge to the Stuarts did not spring forth from opposition of the same nature as that in France in 1789, where a radical overhaul of the legal system was a consequence of the political revolution. The common law lawyers in England had successfully protected their turf, Coke even once suggesting that common law precepts could not be amended by statute. The threat of civil law notions imposed on English soil, of codification of the very heart of the common law, was for the time dormant.

Nearly as influential within England as Coke, William Blackstone, the Vinerian Professor of English Law at Oxford, wrote his Commentaries on the Laws of England in a readable style and concise form, which allowed them to be easily carried to outlying areas of the colonies. Had Blackstone's work not been available, American lawyers would have been left to Coke's confusing Institutes or the inaccessible and complex case reports, or they even might have turned to civil law codes. Blackstone's impact in America is immeasurable; no other legal book has so affected American legal practice as these published lectures of this once obscure lawyer.

SECTION 14. 19TH CENTURY REFORMS

English law in the 19th century was altered by structural and social legislative reform. Jeremy Bentham and others who had little respect for tradition and the sanctity of precedent, viewed the common law as inordinately slow in responding to social needs. They urged codification to provide certainty and comprehension to the law, and to avoid a social revolution. The conservative judiciary and bar neither desired reform nor believed that legislation should be its source. Parliament became the progenitor of social change, however, enacting laws extending education, creating a competitive civil service exam, broadening House of Commons representation, reforming child labor laws and the Poor Law system, centralizing such government activities as road construction and adopting a freer trade policy by reducing protective tariffs. It did not codify rules, but adopted laws directed to more narrow issues which supplemented rather than replaced English precedent. Although Bentham's influence was apparent in the vast amount of new legislation, he found little support for codification of English law in the tradition of the civil law.

Parliament next turned to make some order out of the fragmented judicial structures. Overlapping jurisdiction and prolonged delays, ridiculed in prose, were reduced by the Judicature Acts 1873. It created a Supreme Court of Judicature consisting of the High Court of Justice and Court of Appeal. The High Court brought together as its new divisions the former courts of Chancery, Queen's Bench, Common Pleas, Exchequer and Exchequer Chamber and Probate, Divorce and Admiralty (the last including some subjects with influences of Roman law). Less than a decade later Common Pleas and Exchequer were merged into the Queen's Bench Division.

At first abolished as an appellate court, the House of Lords soon was restored to its judicial role by the Appellate Jurisdiction Act 1876, restricting its appellate jurisdiction and professionalizing the chamber by limiting members sitting on appeal to the Lord Chancellor, peers who had held high judicial office and newly created judicial peers, named Lords of Appeal in Ordinary. No longer would lay members of the House of Lords sit on legal appeals.

The Judicature Acts hastened the fusion of law and equity. Each division of the High Court was required to apply rules both of law and equity. But equity, that historically infant sibling of law, was to prevail in the event of a conflict. Despite the fusion, the Chancery Division nevertheless has retained to this day much of its original character as the equity court, and matters involving complex equity questions generally are directed to that division.

The rigid forms of action were abolished by the reforms; civil trials henceforth commenced with a general writ of summons. With the addition of a more unified procedure, the contemporary English trial presents far fewer technical obstacles to reaching the substantive issues than earlier existed.

SECTION 15.   THE MODERN PERIOD

Labor and Liberal election victories in the early years of the 20th century markedly altered the structure of English society. The Victorian era was in its finale. Working class dominance in the House of Commons aroused new conflicts with the House of Lords. When the Lords persisted in questioning proposed legislation which its members considered radical, the Commons responded by reducing the legislative power of the Lords, effectively limiting it to a right of delay, permitting neither amendment nor rejection.

The Supreme Court of Judicature was further refined in the Courts Act 1971. Courts of Assize and Quarter Sessions were abolished. The Crown Court assumed criminal jurisdiction and joined the High Court and Court of Appeal as part of the Supreme Court.

English legal institutions have survived centuries of stresses and constitutional crises. The system has shown a remarkable resiliency in adversity. Current issues involving the adoption of a bill of rights, the role of the House of Lords, the progressive fusion of barristers and solicitors and the consultative role of labor unions regarding general policies and proposed legislation will continue to generate stresses on the common law. Its adaptability is illustrated by the distribution of the common law throughout the world. Although some of the strength of English law must be attributable to the homogeneous population in which the law developed, it is a system of justice which has been received in heterogeneous societies with as much ease as the civil law.

SECTION 16. "ENGLISH" LAW

There is some definitional confusion with the term English law, additionally blurred by reference to Great Britain, the United Kingdom, or the Commonwealth. From its origins in Southern England, the common law became the principal basis of the procedure and/or substance of the legal systems for nearly a third of the world's population. It is inappropriate, nonetheless, to suggest that it is English law which exists in the United States or Australia or India or South Africa, or that there is a Commonwealth law applied in the Commonwealth, or a British law of Great Britain. English law applies in England and Wales. Great Britain, the political geographic term for England, Wales and Scotland, has no common legal system. Many English statutes are applicable in Scotland, but the Scottish private law is based primarily on the civil law and principally on Roman law, the result of an alliance with the Continent in the 14th and 15th centuries intended to inhibit recurrent English expansion.[7] After union with England in the Treaty of 1707, the development of Scottish law was influenced largely by the English common law. Parliamentary enactments in many areas of private law were applicable in both England and Scotland. Scottish law remains a curious mix of civil and common law, an appropriate focus for the study of the potential for interrelation between these two legal traditions.

Northern Ireland and Great Britain comprise the United Kingdom, the principal geographic area to which parliamentary expressions apply.

---

7. See G. Paton (ed.), An Introduction to Scottish Legal History (1958).

But, as in the case of Great Britain, the United Kingdom is a larger area than one associates with English law.

English substantive law is not directly applicable outside of England and Wales, and, to a lesser extent, Scotland; however, it retains some authority in many independent nations which were formerly part of the British Empire. The remnant of authority of the House of Lords Judicial Committee of the Privy Council continues a slender connection between England and some former colonies, a role diminished by the independence of former Commonwealth nations and by the Statute of Westminster 1931, the latter granting to Commonwealth legislatures the right to abolish appeals to the Privy Council.

SECTION 17.   DEVOLUTION

Nationalism in Scotland and Wales engendered a demand in the 1970s for a transfer of some government power from London to national assemblies. Included was additional law-making power. Devolution was promoted more strongly in Scotland than in Wales, the former possessing more distinct government institutions and its unique civil law based legal system. A 1978 devolution bill requiring a referendum vote was rejected by Welsh electors. The Scottish voters narrowly approved it, but not by the required forty percent of all registered electors. Devolution in a large measure ended with the referendum, but there will continue to be occasional transfers of government power to local authorities in Scotland and Wales.

SECTION 18.   DISTRIBUTION

Legal systems are often thrust upon nations. They are the consequence of territorial expansion and not of a deliberate and carefully thought out decision regarding which principal legal tradition would best serve the interests of the community. But as they grow they may borrow extensively from other legal systems and traditions. It is rare indeed to find an independent nation with roots in one of the principal western legal traditions, which has not molded that tradition to fit the domestic requirements. As the British Empire grew, English common law fit into the particularly unique institutional framework of each colony. How receptive the colonial inhabitants were towards the reception of the English common law depended upon numerous characteristics of the mode of territorial expansion. The distribution of the English common law has been termed by Dicey as three-fold, those nations "seeded," (i.e., India, Hong Kong), those "settled" (i.e., United States) and those "conquered" (i.e., South Africa). "Seeded" nations are those where elements of the colonial legal system were introduced into a colony which had a relatively advanced society and developed legal system, but where the seeding by the power gaining control was more by negotiation and its apparent "capacity" to conquer, than actually by using force. The common law thus was seeded into such nations as

India and Hong Kong. "Settled" nations are those in which territorial expansion occurred in an area not possessing a strong and developed society and in which the colonial acquisition went to the first settling power. This would include the United States. Finally, "conquered" nations are those in which an element of force was used to wrest power from another authority, which might have been either a strong indigenous authority, or a previous colonizer. South Africa exemplifies this group. In Calvin's Case in 1608 it was ruled that English law was effective when England colonized an area where there was no civilized local law. What legal system will be imposed upon or developed within a colonial power depends both on the inclination of the expanding power to impose its legal system upon the colonial territory, and on the capacity of the colonial territory inhabitants to make changes in the developing theoretical or institutional characteristics of the present legal system.

The distribution of the common law differs from that of the civil law. England was directly linked through its territorial expansion with each of the principal nations in which the common law developed. The direct linkage with Romano–Germanic origins of the civil law system existed in the reception of the civil law within Europe. But expansion external to the European continent and the areas of the Eastern Roman Empire lacked any direct contact with Roman law. Thus, Roman law origins for these nations must be traced through a two-stage linkage, first the Roman law directly linked to European systems and, secondly, that same Roman law traceable through these European systems to a second tier of civil law nations located in many parts of the world.

The common law is a more difficult system to receive. The uniqueness of its origins, embedded in the centralization of the institutional framework subsequent to the Norman Conquest, often generated institutions lacking characteristics facilitating reception. The convenience of codes of civil law nations affords a practical form of reception as well as a theoretical satisfaction of having written down what the law is in a new and often relatively unstable society. But the English matrix of case law and statutes, and the complex language and focus on procedure, formed a tradition which obviously was not created with any thought of facilitating its imposition on foreign lands. Furthermore, the Roman based civil law which was largely private law posed little threat to a new political system tending to favor a voluntary adoption of a codified system.

The world is not easily divided into an orderly pattern of countries which received a single legal tradition. Changes in territorial dominion by colonial powers created some systems possessing elements of more than one of the principal legal traditions. The most notable example is South Africa, where a civil law system (in the Transvaal) based on Roman–Dutch law partially acquiesced to the common law upon England's succession to power.

The distribution of English common law in the three largest areas where there was no well-established system of justice beyond tribal law, occurred in Australia, Canada and the United States. England confronted only a small, indigenous population in Australia, and colonized the continent without expansionist competition from other European nations. Parliament decreed in 1828 that the Australian colony's system was the common law, including English statutes.

Australia developed as a six member federation, each with a constitution and state government, including a parliament. Federal power is limited by the Australian Constitution more severely than in the United States. The Constitution does not protect fundamental, individual rights; the High Court thus may not nullify a federal or state statute as in violation of the rights of individual citizens. United States federalism has evolved over two centuries, its broadly stated Constitution the foundation of a continued and significant growth of central government over previously state controlled activities. Australia has been a federal system for only eighty years; an additional century may witness an increase in federal power not unlike that in the United States.

Both procedure and substantive private law in the several states of Australia are relatively uniform. English appellate decisions, although not binding authority, have remained the foundation for the development of Australian law, an emphasis which will diminish as the quantity of Australian precedent increases. The small population of Australia means a longer period for the development of a substantial body of Australian precedent, however, and the attention to English decisions may endure. Respect for English decisions further is understandable by the peaceful growth of Australia as an independent nation; separation occurred from England without the adversity of a revolution. Australian law remains the most closely identified to English law of all the major nations which trace their legal systems to England. There was no advanced cultural development within the indigenous Australian population, such as was confronted in India, nor was any Australian territory acquired from other European nations, as in the case of South Africa, part of Canada and the United States.

Acquisition by Britain in 1763 of the French settled area of Canada did not lead to a fusion of the legal systems. The English Parliament divided Canada into English and French speaking sections, each with a parliament. It was an unsuccessful experiment terminated in 1840 by the establishment of a common parliament with equal representation. The British North American Act 1867, created the Dominion of Canada, composed of Nova Scotia, Ontario, Quebec and New Brunswick. The relative equality in number of French and English speaking persons was altered by the incorporation of the Northwest Territories acquired from the Hudson Bay Company in 1869, and the joining in the Union in 1871 by British Columbia. Canada thereafter was influenced largely by English government, economic and social structures, although Quebec preserved its civil law system. Unlike later federal constitutions granted by the English Parliament to Commonwealth countries, the 1867 Act gave Parliament authority to approve any constitutional amendments in Canada. But in 1982 Canada adopted a new Constitution and the

British Parliament passed the Canada Act,[8] which relinquished any future right to amend the Canadian Constitution.

The Supreme Court of Canada, functioning as an appellate court for the provincial tribunals, must occasionally apply the Civil Code of Quebec. Its interpretations are influenced by common law methodology. Quebec has a disproportionate participation on the Court, three of the nine members, but it is a minority and there is no weighted voting for cases from Quebec provincial courts.

Important changes in the development of Canadian law have occurred since the 1949 termination of allowing appeals to the Judicial Committee of the Privy Council in England. Additionally, decisions of English appellate courts are no longer binding, although they are treated with respect. A Canadian jurisprudence has developed which includes influences external to the historical affiliation to English law; particular notice is given to legal developments in neighboring United States.

The contiguity of common and civil law systems in Canada and its Province of Quebec, and to a lesser degree in the United States and Louisiana, contrast with the more complex common-civil law relationships in the legal system in South Africa. South African law initially possessed a strong Roman law base, resulting from Dutch governance. Shortly before Napoleon abolished Roman–Dutch law in The Netherlands and replaced it with his famous Code in 1809, England took possession of the Cape and incorporated it into the Empire. English procedure was first imposed on the Roman–Dutch law of the Cape, followed by the adoption of numerous English statutes, principally affecting commerce. Where this mixture of English and Roman–Dutch law was unclear, South African jurists, nearly all of them English trained lawyers, tended to look for guidance to English case law. Political independence for the Union of South Africa in 1910 generated a restoration of Dutch culture, including a resurgence of legal scholarship which concentrated notably on Dutch law. South African law thus is a hybrid system; it possesses Roman–Dutch law substantive elements and aspects of English law procedural methodology and structure.

English settlers in North America, Australia, New Zealand and South Africa did not encounter the highly developed indigenous culture which existed in India. Expansion to India was not by unchallenged settlement, but by permission of the Grand Mogul of India and local leaders. The penetration first consisted of establishing coastal, commercial centers. Internal disorder beset India in the 19th century. The English took advantage of this weakness, extending their influence through transactions with Indian princes, and finally dominating all of India.

Initial attempts to apply the common law in the early 18th century in Madras, Bombay and Calcutta, to both English and Indian parties, were unsuccessful. Hindu and Islamic law were substituted for common

---

8. Canada Act, 1982 (U.K.), 1982, c. 11.

law in land, family and succession matters, a practice which continued in the interior as English governance coalesced. But, except in matters of family and succession law, and religious issues, English trained judges considered the best justice to require the application of English law.

Reform concepts promoted by Bentham found greater reception in India in the early 19th century than in England. Uncertainty existed in Indian law; little truly Indian precedent had developed, and there was substantial inconsistency among Indian courts in determining sources of law. A Law Commission began to codify Indian law, influenced by European codes and by the British acceptance of reforms after the Great Mutiny in 1857. A civil procedure code was adopted in 1859, a criminal code in 1861, and the Indian Succession Act in 1865. The private law of India thus was codified at an early date.

The common law distribution in India, a nation with a strong cultural and religious tradition, illustrates that the expansion of English common law did not require a weak, indigenous population; it could contribute to the administration of justice in a diverse social system.

English law influence extends far beyond the major nations noted above. It has had substantial impact in former English territories in Africa, in some smaller colonies in Asia and in the Caribbean basin. In many of these locations, nevertheless, particularly in Africa, the English law affected a comparatively small percentage of the population. This is not an incident attributable to the nature of English law, but to the structure of the host societies. Such an impact is witnessed also in many areas where the civil law tradition has been received, particularly in nations of Latin America with widely dispersed native communities. Reception of a legal system depends upon the fusion of the local culture with that of the settling nation. Where a cultural assimilation has occurred, the English common law has shown remarkable capacity for adaptation.

Chapter 10

LEGAL STRUCTURES
IN ENGLAND

SECTION 1. THE BRITISH GOVERNMENT

Contemporary parliamentary authority includes direct enactment of legislation and delegation of power to ministers to adopt provisional orders and regulations. There is little separation of legislative and executive institutions. The two are so closely identified that the Prime Minister survives only while retaining the favor of Parliament. Convention dictates that a vote of censure by Parliament of a Prime Minister's actions, or the failure of the government to promote successfully a major bill, will precipitate a call for the dissolution of Parliament and new elections. The system does not support an executive and House of Commons majority from opposing parties.

The mutual dependency of the Prime Minister and the Commons should not suggest a fusion of the two. A philosophical policy schism often evolves after the Prime Minister is appointed. Additionally, the Prime Minister possesses considerable power in directing the executive branch free from direct parliamentary control.

However interrelated may be the executive and the House of Commons, there is a clear separation between the judiciary and the executive-Parliament linkage. Judicial appointments, other than the unique role of the Lord Chancellor, illustrate an absence of political patronage. The immutable requirement for judicial appointment, a long and successful career in advocacy before the courts has resulted in a judiciary nearly devoid of politicians. The English judiciary has evolved from its own highly sectarian source, preserving a clear detachment from the executive and Parliament, however parochial are the internal constraints within the institution of the bar itself.

How does the United States separation of powers differ from the English system? Yardley suggests the United States system is an extreme example.

D.C.M. YARDLEY, "INTRODUCTION TO BRITISH CONSTITUTIONAL LAW" *

75 (6th ed. 1984).

The Constitution of the United States of America, which came into effect on 4 March 1789, probably provides us with the most extreme example of a practical separation of the three fundamental powers. It is based upon a mistaken interpretation by the French writer Montesquieu of the position in England in the eighteenth century, though it should be added that the founding fathers were interested in Montesquieu's views as applied to America, and they were in no way concerned about whether or not he had interpreted the English Constitution of his time accurately. . . . The system in the United States has justly been described as a separation of powers and modified by checks and balances.

Turning to the United Kingdom, it is clear that the three fundamental powers exist, just as they exist in other countries, ... [I]t has become apparent that there is much overlapping between them and between the authorities in which the powers are vested. This is therefore the place at which to summarize the principal factors which in the United Kingdom render it impossible to insist that any strict separation of powers exists. . . .

(1) Members of the government are usually members of one or other of the Houses of Parliament, because it is desirable that all ministers of the Crown should be held responsible to Parliament for their actions. . . . Probably a member of the government may retain his office providing he does not cease to be a member of one of the Houses of Parliament for more than a few months. It is, however, more usual for any minister who takes office without possessing a seat in either House to be created a peer so that he may sit in the Lords. It may be noted that one of the most useful methods of checking up on the activities of ministers or of the government as a whole is the parliamentary question: there is no such parallel possibility in the United States, where members of the government do not sit in Congress, and there is no 'question time'.[a] The concept of ministerial responsibility to Parliament has been copied in the constitutions of most independent Commonwealth countries.

(2) The monarch, who heads the government, also in effect forms the 'third House of Parliament'. Both this point and the last one lead to the common usage of 'Parliament' and 'government' as interchangeable terms, although such a practice is of course incorrect. . . .

---

* Reprinted here and below with permission of Butterworth & Co. (Publishers) Ltd.

a. Members of the government in their role as members of Parliament may be asked questions by other members regarding any subject related to the government member's responsibilities, provided that they do not involve topics which are pending in Parliament.

(3) The monarch is the 'fountain of justice', being technically present in all his courts of law, responsible for many judicial appointments, and exercising the prerogative of mercy in respect of persons convicted in the courts. Thus he plays a part in all three of the fundamental powers.

(4) Parliament is strictly called the 'High Courts of Parliament', and although the House of Commons carries out no judicial functions today, the House of Lords is still the ultimate court of appeal. The Lords of Appeal in Ordinary sit in the House of Lords both as a legislative body and as a court, and they are also Privy Councillors, as is indeed the Speaker of the House of Commons. The Lord Chancellor also plays a part in all three of the powers, being a member of the House of Lords as a legislative body and as a court, responsible for a number of judicial appointments, and also a member of the government.

(5) Although the independence of the judiciary is in practice jealously preserved, superior judges are appointed by the Crown or by the Lord Chancellor, and are removable by the Crown on an address by both Houses of Parliament to the Crown, while inferior judges are appointed and removable by the Lord Chancellor.

* * *

Enough has been said to show the interrelation between the three fundamental powers. It is very probable that the overlapping of powers and authorities insures against arbitrariness. It may be added, finally, that the all-powerful position of Parliament makes it possible for the legislature to make any alteration in the present system which it may wish by simple Act of Parliament. This is not only the method of passing ordinary legislation in the United Kingdom, but it is the procedure for effecting any constitutional amendment whatever.

A. THE HOUSE OF COMMONS

Legislation is adopted by the House of Commons, considered by the House of Lords, and given royal assent by the sovereign. Thus it is important to include the sovereign within the definition of Parliament as a whole. But royal assent *must* be given—the sovereign really has no choice. Legislative power is firmly lodged in the House of Commons, or lower House. But even the Commons is subject to control—by the cabinet, where the most effective base of power exists. Lack of a true bicameral legislature has generated recent discussion of parliamentary reform—directed largely to increasing the power of the House of Lords.

The principal function of the House of Commons—and indeed that of Parliament as a whole—is to enact laws for the overall benefit of the nation. But there is another function that we may tend to overlook, partly because it is related to the different notion of separation of powers in England. It is the role of the Commons to elect the government.[6]

6. W. Bagehot, The English Constitution 150 (1963). The English Constitution
 was first published in 1867. It became a classic and remains today the best introduc-

The House of Commons chooses the Prime Minister. We in the United States follow a different route. We created the electoral college with the idea that it would be composed of some of the most intelligent people in the nation who would deliberate after the national election and choose the most able leader. But it is an anachronism as an American electoral institution and will likely be abolished at some time in the future, although perhaps only when it has functioned so as to cause national surprise or shock. The House of Commons functions quite differently. Bound to some degree by public opinion, the elected House of Commons nevertheless chooses the nation's leader, and perhaps more importantly, may later choose to reject that leader. It is the rejection power that makes the House stand considerably apart from the American system, and causes relations between the chosen Prime Minister and the House of Commons to be, if not cordial, at least frequent. The system tends to result in firm Prime Ministers. Prime Ministers do lead the nation, but the House of Commons follows closely behind, guiding them when it feels the leaders stray too widely.

House of Commons members are elected by a plurality rather than a majority vote. It is commonly referred to as the "first-past-the-post" process. It allows relatively minor changes in voting patterns of the principal parties in the electoral districts to result in meaningful changes in the power balance in Commons. The system does provide for the development of rather close ties between members of the House and their constituents.

Party loyalty and organization are essential to the survival of the parliamentary or government party (that is the party in power, whether Conservative or Labor—the other major party not currently in power is called the opposition party). Serious breaches in loyalty may result in a House of Commons vote contrary to the interests of the government it elected. But such vote would be welcome by the opposition party, ever prepared to confront the parliamentary party in a new election at a time of the latter's weakness.

The Prime Minister appoints a Leader of the House, and the opposition appoints a Leader of the Opposition. Other members are then selected to be "Whips" who maintain discipline and urge attendance and, it goes without saying, loyalty in debate and vote, of the party members. There is far less independent voting by members than in the United States. Were it to be otherwise, the government's very existence might be threatened. Dissolution of Parliament might follow the government's failure to obtain an affirmative vote on a major proposal. It might also come to an end if there is a vote of censure or particularly poor opinion polls. If it does not die an unnatural death, it will do so by lapsing after five years. An extension is permitted only with the concurrence of the House of Lords when there is an emergency. But if the House of Commons decided to enact a statute giving itself extended

tion to the English Constitution. Even though it was published the same year as Disraeli's Reform Act, and thus was immediately outdated, the care with which Bagehot viewed British politics has given his book enduring relevance.

life, could it not do so if it is truly sovereign? It did extend its life during the 1939–45 period. But this was considered an emergency. By convention—a source of law to be discussed in Chapter 11—Parliament would not abuse this rule and when an extension has been decreed, it has been limited, also by convention, to one year at a time. The Prime Minister may choose to dissolve Parliament not only when the situation is bad, but also when it is especially good, with the hope that the people will vote the party in again and give it a new five year lease.

A. SAMPSON, "THE CHANGING ANATOMY OF BRITAIN"
15 (1982).*

... The small chamber, with a floor only sixty-eight feet long, still has the atmosphere of a drawing-room: it is a quarter of the size of the House of Representatives in Washington, which has fewer members. The members crowded on their green leather benches—baying, giggling or sleeping—seem unaware of the public galleries above them. They are not supposed to read their speeches, and their impromptu debates are much more intimate than the speechifying in Washington or Paris. They dawdle in and out of the chamber, bowing to the Speaker and whispering to their colleagues, while in the lobbies, bars and restaurants they pick up their information and gossip. They can all feel the 'mood of the House', which no prime minister can altogether ignore: even Churchill at the height of his wartime power remained (as Attlee described him) 'a good House of Commons man'. And during a crisis such as Suez or the Falklands it is the mood of the House which is ruling the nation.

Even the architecture is now called in question. The wide rectangle, with the rows of members facing each other and the Speaker in the middle, provides the natural stage for two parties competing on the adversary system, seeing every argument as a contest between prosecution and defence. The heroic encounters between Disraeli and Gladstone, Attlee and Churchill, Thatcher and Foot, have become part of Britain's political psychology, accepting that the opposition may suddenly find itself changing sides and becoming the government; and the same two-sided pattern is common to many other British institutions, from football and the law courts to negotiations between 'two sides of industry'....

Most Continental parliaments are very different, laid out like an amphitheatre or semicircle, with deputies facing the President of the Assembly, while each speaker orates from the platform below the President. A British spectator is instantly aware of the difference of atmosphere: it is not so much like a club or a law-court as like a spacious theatre. This was the setting for the French assembly just before the revolution in 1789, when the nobles took up their position of honour on the President's right while the 'third estate' of commoners sat on his left. This ceremonial seating-plan came to symbolise the political differences between conservatives and radicals, with moderates occupying the centre; and by the 1920s British politicians were beginning to call each other 'left' and 'right', even though the words bore no relation to their own seating, and were little understood by ordinary voters.

The French pattern could be said to reflect a more respectful attitude to the state, represented by the President's podium; and Continental deputies did not face the same ordeal of addressing their enemies at close quarters. But the amphitheatres can represent a more flexible system, allowing changing coalitions to show themselves in the seating, or the centre to remain unaligned, while the arguments are not necessarily between opposites and adversaries. Many British critics of the two-party system, including Liberals and Social Democrats, complained that the design of the House of Commons was encouraging out-of-date divisions and arguments: 'The first thing I'd do about parliamentary reform,' said one Social Democrat leader, 'is to call in the carpenters.'

* * *

The House has gradually provided some kind of office for each member—in the towers or courtyards of the Gothic palace itself, in draughty corridors or up winding staircases, or in the cavernous Norman Shaw building across the road. But members never know whether they should be amateurs or professionals, and probably never will. The compactness and the club atmosphere depend on the presence of fairly leisurely individuals with interests outside, while the complexity of government demands specialized committees, time and resources. Without professional resources a member is ill-equipped to question the workings of departments; and he is an easy prey for pressure groups, foreign governments and corporate lobbyists, luring him with retainers, meals and free trips. ...

Members still face great difficulties in grappling with the government departments and nationalised industries. In theory they have sovereignty over them, but in practice they know little about how to control them, and they are up against bureaucrats and ministers who often do not want them to know. The chief ambition of most members (unlike congressmen's) is to become part of the government, so that they never want to appear too rebellious; and it is the traditional debating between the parties which still stimulates many members, ... much more than uncovering the details of bureaucracy and policy-making. But the select committees have undoubtedly brought a new vigour and purpose to the House of Commons, providing a much more serious enquiry into how the country is run, while members with their own offices and secretaries can take their job more professionally than was possible twenty years ago.

* * *

Public participation by approval or disapproval of actions of the House of Commons in the past decade has to a degree limited the power of Commons. The Industrial Relations Act 1971, was never implemented effectively, and consequently was repealed in 1974. A public referendum has been used for two important issues to obtain public support of parliamentary acts. The first confirmed membership in the European Communities by a significant majority in 1975, and the second resulted in the rejection of the 1978 devolution bills for Scotland and Wales. Further use of a referendum following important parliamentary acts may well develop into a form of restraint on the House of Commons.

Question and Note

There is sometimes talk of abolishing the electoral college in the United States. Bagehot has suggested it might have been profitably used in a more expansive manner, such as the role he attributes to the House of Commons in choosing the nation's leader. How does the English structure affect the enactment of laws?

B. THE HOUSE OF LORDS

"The most ancient element of parliament, the House of Lords, has remained the most baffling obstacle to reform over the last two decades, confusing almost everyone with its blend of fact and fantasy, romance and exploitation, comedy and dignity. The whole style of the high Victorian building was calculated to play on past glories. Stained-glass windows shed a red light, while the barons of the Magna Carta look down like saints from the walls, conveying the atmosphere of a grand private chapel which sanctifies the most banal interventions. On the red sofas a few old men fiddle with their deaf-aids, whisper and sometimes sleep, and sitting on a big red pouf stuffed with wool, called "the Woolsack", is a muttering old man in a wig who turns out to be the Lord Chancellor of England, Lord Hailsham, the holder of the most ancient lay office in the kingdom, older than the Norman Conquest." [7]

The House of Lords is less understandable to us in America than the Commons. The House of Lords is not an elected body. The successor of the old *Curia Regis,* it has evolved from an aggregate of noblemen in the 13th century. Membership changed little for centuries. It now includes (of some 1,200 members) Lords Spiritual (certain bishops—about 23 members), Lords Temporal (peers and peeresses, about 1,100 of which about 340 are life, as opposed to hereditary, peers) and the Lords of Appeal in Ordinary (the Law Lords—11 members). It is largely conser-

7. A. Sampson, The Changing Anatomy of Britain 24 (1982).

vative, but often quite adventuresome. A major change was the addition of Life Peers, allowed under the Life Peerages Act in 1948. Since that time there have been relatively few grants of hereditary peerages. Another important change was effected by the Peerage Act 1963, which allowed peers to disclaim their peerage for their lifetime. But they could not disclaim it forever, it would pass to the appropriate heir at the usual time for succession.

A. SAMPSON, "THE CHANGING ANATOMY OF BRITAIN"

24–29 (1982).

. . . Every prime minister since Macmillan has found life peerages an invaluable means to reward their political friends, party benefactors or personal cronies. . . .

The life peers, who include academics, trade unionists, scientists and actors . . . undoubtedly brought some new blood to the Lords; but they have not made it much more relevant to modern Britain. The debates, it is true, are often more thoughtful and better-informed than those in the Commons, with fewer rules and formalities: most of the hereditary 'backwoodsmen' never bother to turn up, and only about three hundred peers attend regularly, . . . But few active tycoons spare the time to speak in debates, and most life peers are already in their sixties, becoming more aloof from practical problems. The House of Lords now looks even more like an old folk's home, as the average age creeps relentlessly up . . . and the younger Lords . . . are inevitably hereditary. Nor can life peerages ever give the House of Lords a political balance like that of the Commons: not just because the hereditary peers are overwhelmingly Tory, but because many Labour life peers have defected to the Conservative benches as they got older. Thus overwhelmingly conservative and elderly, the Lords are an easy prey for any radical critic; but they still defy any practical scheme for reform.

––––––––

The most serious loss of power of the House of Lords resulted from two parliamentary acts, in 1911 and 1949. They limited the role of the House of Lords to little more than a delaying power, and an ability to revise to some minor degree. But is that a more effective role than to have the second house a co-equal? Should a nation have an independent second house which can say "Wait a minute," with regard to a bill endorsed by the other chamber? There have been suggestions for additional reforms, even the abolition of the second house.

T.C. HARTLEY & J.A.G. GRIFFITH, GOVERNMENT AND LAW

(2d ed. 1981).*

Discussions about House of Lords reform are always complicated by the fact that the connection of the House with the aristocracy brings an ideological element into the debate. For this reason attitudes at the two extremes of the political spectrum are often more emotional than rational: the Left favouring the abolition of the House because it dislikes social privilege and the Right coming to the support of the House because of its traditional associations. If, however, one looks at the matter objectively, it seems that in the British context there are two main functions that might be fulfilled by a second chamber. The first is to act as a revising and scrutinizing body—to deal with technical matters not involving party political controversy—and the second is to act as a check on the lower House when it wishes to take action strongly opposed by public opinion. The justification for the first function is that the Commons is often too busy—partly because of its preoccupation with party politics—to give sufficient consideration to the technical aspects of legislation; the justification for the second is that, due to the 'first past the post' electoral system, the composition of the Commons does not always reflect opinion in the country at large.

From some points of view these two possible functions pull in opposite directions: if the first is regarded as predominant, it would be desirable for the House to be composed largely of technocrats and experts; if the second is primary, it would have to be chosen in such a way that it could claim to represent public opinion to a greater degree than the Commons. In the first case, appointment would probably be the most appropriate method of selection; in the second, election by some system of proportional representation would be desirable.

* * *

Questions and Notes

1. A bicameral legislature, such as exists both in the United States and England, does not have to have equal powers. The United States House and Senate are far more equal in power than the House of Commons and House of Lords. Some suggest the English effectively have a unicameral legislature, but it should be apparent that there is an important role of the House of Lords. Do you think an imbalance in the two houses affects achieving the nation's perceived goals of a legislature? Are the houses in England more similar to those in France and Germany? Is imbalance in power a characteristic of a parliamentary system?

2. Is a viable second house of greater use in a parliamentary system such as England or France, in contrast to the separately elected president and more distinct executive branch such as exists in the United States?

Considering the power of Parliament due to the absence of judicial review, what impact would the abolition of the House of Lords have on lawmaking?

3. One may view the concept of the House of Lords as useful in the lawmaking process—that is the appointment for life rather than election for a term—but object to the manner in which that concept operates in the current House of Lords structure. Accepting the use of an elite body, how might it best be used as part of the lawmaking process?

C. THE PRIME MINISTER AND THE SOVEREIGN

The Prime Minister is in an uncertain position. The importance of the position is acknowledged, but the duration is most impermanent. The office expires at the next general election. The power of a serving Prime Minister is considerable, however. The Prime Minister is the head of the party which is in power in Parliament. The system of the Leader of the House and the Whips, combined with the much less powerful role of the House of Lords, gives the Prime Minister power beyond that of the United States president and most other Western leaders.

The most important distinction between the British Prime Minister and the United States President is that the Prime Minister is not elected directly by the people. The aspiring candidate must be chosen from among the leaders of the successful party in the national election for House of Commons seats, not from a public constituency. But the way in which Prime Ministers are selected differs in the two principal parties.

T.C. HARTLEY AND J.A.G. GRIFFITH, "GOVERNMENT AND LAW"

54 (2d ed. 1981).

How in these days does he come to this position? First, he must have been a member of the Conservative or of the Labour party since his youth. And he must have been a member of the House of Commons for many years. He must, in keen competition with many of his contemporaries within his party, have shown ability in the House of Commons and surefootedness in those slippery places where his seniors fought with one another. He should, at certain points in his career, either have thrown in his lot with one of those seniors who then went from success to success; or, at the very least, he should have avoided close identification with others who failed. He must have been picked out for junior office at an early age and have incurred the minimum possible displeasure from those of his contemporaries who were passed over at the same time. And when he came to the top and into contest for the leadership of the party it must have been at a time when his particular qualities were thought to be preferable for reasons which might have had nothing whatever to do with himself. Obviously, then, he must also have luck.

* * *

Until 1965, the Conservative party had no formal procedure for deciding who should be its leader. But in that year a set of rules was adopted and Mr. Heath was the first leader elected under those rules. They provide that the leader shall be elected by a ballot, conducted amongst all the Conservative Members of the House of Commons, under the control of the chairman of the 1922 Committee. ...

In the Labour party, the procedure until 1981 was simpler and less formal. If the election was contested, the Parliamentary Committee devised the timetable for approval by the parliamentary party. ... As in the Conservative party, only Labour M.P.s in the Commons might vote.

... But at a special conference held in January 1981 the system was changed, with the result that the power to choose the leader was to be divided between the trade unions, the constituency parties and the Labour M.P.s in the proportions of 40:30:30 respectively, the votes being cast at the annual conference of the party. It may be that these proportions will be changed so as to give a greater share to M.P.s. But the principle of sharing the power to appoint seems certain to remain.

It is now accepted that each party will always nominate its Leader. If the Leader dies or resigns, the party will select another. If at a general election the governing party is defeated, then the Queen will ask the leader of the successful party to be Prime Minister and to form a Government. Does any power or discretion remain in the Queen? If a Government were re-elected at a general election with the largest number of seats but with less than an overall majority—always a possibility so long as the Liberal or any other third party remains capable of winning seats—and if that Government failed to persuade the third party to support it in the lobbies, then the Government might resign. If so, the Queen would ask the Leader of the second party if he could form a Government and the third party might decide to support the second party and give it a majority in the House. But suppose the Government, re-elected without an overall majority, immediately asked the Queen for a dissolution and for another general election before it had been discovered whether the second party could obtain the support of the third party, could the Queen refuse to grant the dissolution? It seems to us that she could and that, in those circumstances, she should not grant a dissolution until she was sure that no combination of parties or of members could result in a Government with a majority of seats in the House. If the Government party obtained fewer seats than the principal Opposition party, it might still be able to command a majority in the House of Commons and to continue as the Government if a sufficient number of members of other parties or groups were willing to support it.

* * *

Though part of the executive, the sovereign plays a limited role. The sovereign is a ceremonial figure who undertakes state visits, signs documents, receives foreign ambassadors, bestows recommended honors and performs other similar acts. England functions in the name of the sovereign, but the latter acts only upon the advice of ministers. A strong sovereign nevertheless may be influential. The survival of the English monarchy is due principally to its nature as a constitutional monarchy in which the sovereign assumes essentially a symbolic role. By convention the Prime Minister visits frequently with the sovereign to comment on actions taken at Cabinet meetings, offering an interested and astute King or Queen an opportunity for discussion of developing policy and legislation, sometimes referred to as the power to advise, encourage and warn.

The structure of the monarchy and activities of the sovereign are governed by legislation and conventions. The sovereign does exercise the royal prerogative as the historical fountain of justice, but there is no effective remaining independent sovereign power. There are rare rumblings from Labor to abolish the monarchy, but they are not as threatening as the challenges to the other remnant of vested privilege, the House of Lords. Criticism of the monarchy usually is directed to its financial burden to the nation, or to the minor transgressions of subordinate members of the royal family. But on the whole the monarchy seems quite secure, providing it does not allow use of the royal prerogative to stray beyond the symbolic. As Bagehot and Sampson note, the role of the sovereign should not be confused.

W. BAGEHOT, "THE ENGLISH CONSTITUTION"

98 (1963).

The popular theory of the English Constitution involves two errors as to the sovereign. First, in its oldest form at least, it considers him as an "Estate of the Realm", a separate coordinate authority with the House of Lords and the House of Commons. This and much else the sovereign once was, but this he is no longer. That authority could only be exercised by a monarch with a legislative veto. He should be able to reject bills, if not as the House of Commons rejects them, at least as the House of Peers rejects them. But the Queen has no such veto. She must sign her own death-warrant if the two Houses unanimously send it up to her. It is a fiction of the past to ascribe to her legislative power. She has long ceased to have any. Secondly, the ancient theory holds that the Queen is the executive. The American Constitution was made upon a most careful argument, and most of that argument assumes the king to be the administrator of the English Constitution, and an unhereditary substitute for him—*vis.,* a president—to be peremptorily necessary. Living across the Atlantic, and misled by accepted doctrines, the acute framers of the Federal Constitution, even after the keenest attention, did not perceive the Prime Minister to be the principal executive of the British Constitution, and the sovereign a cog in the mechanism. There is, indeed, much excuse for the American legislators in the history of that time. They took their idea of our Constitution from the time when they encountered it. But in the so-called Government of Lord North, George III was the Government. Lord North was not only his appointee, but his agent. The Minister carried on a war which he disapproved and hated, because it was a war which his sovereign approved and liked. Inevitably, therefore, the American Convention believed the King, from whom they had suffered, to be the real executive, and not the Minister, from whom they had not suffered.

A. SAMPSON, "THE CHANGING ANATOMY OF BRITAIN"

14 (1982).

Once a year the monarchy makes contact with democracy in the extraordinary ritual of the state opening of parliament, where officials parade in fancy dress, leaders of the opposition process two-by-two with government ministers, and the Queen reads out the speech which the government has written for her. It can still amaze foreign visitors and infuriate radical members of parliament: 'It's like the *Prisoner of Zenda,*' complained Richard Crossman in 1967, 'but not nearly as smart or well done as it would be at Hollywood. It's more what a real Ruitania would look like—far more comic, more untidy, more homely, less grand'.

But the ritual still illustrates the basis of the British constitution: that the sovereignty of monarchs has passed to the sovereignty of parliament, leaving the monarchy with the trappings of power, while prime ministers are still denied the kind of pomp that is accorded to American and French presidents. The 'dignified' role of the crown in the constitution (as Walter Bagehot described it a century ago) mingles with the 'efficient' role of parliament and the executive. Parliament is the obvious starting point for pursuing what Aneurin Bevan called 'the will o' the wisp of power'. But does parliament still belong to the efficient part, or has it (as Crossman suggested in 1959) joined the monarchy as 'merely one piece of the dignified part'[2] leaving the real power to be wielded in Whitehall or elsewhere?

The above comments on the separation of powers may suggest that separation in England is less extensive—or excessive—than in the United States, but there is one area in which the powers of one branch may not be trespassed upon by another. That is the sovereignty of Parliament. English courts are unable to rule invalid a Parliamentary enactment which has received the assent of the Crown. Parliament may do

2. The Backbench Diaries of Richard   p. 737.
Crossman, Johnathan Cape, London, 1981,

what it wishes, except perhaps in one case. It may not bind itself regarding its future actions. Just as one might challenge some early decisions of the United States Supreme Court which established principles of judicial review, as being inconsistent with views of the founders of the nation, there is similar evidence that the English position might have developed differently.

SECTION 2. JUDICIAL REVIEW

LORD DENNING, "WHAT NEXT IN THE LAW"
319 (1982).*

... Nearly 400 years ago Lord Coke said that:

> "When an Act of Parliament is against right and reason, or repugnant, or impossible to be performed, the common law will control it and adjudge that Act to be void." [2]

This sapling planted by Lord Coke failed to grow in England. It withered and died. But it grew into a strong tree in the United States of America. Under the guidance of the great Chief Justice Marshall, the judges there constantly review legislation: and as constantly set it aside if it is against right and reason or repugnant to the Constitution.

The longer I am in the law—and the more statutes I have to interpret—the more I think the judges here ought to have a power of judicial review of legislation similar to that in the United States: whereby the judges can set aside statutes which are contrary to our unwritten Constitution—in that they are repugnant to reason or to fundamentals. Professor Wade has given a good illustration in his lecture on *Constitutional Fundamentals*. He says:

> "There can be abuse of legislative power, not indeed in the legal sense, but in a distinct constitutional sense, for example if Parliament were to legislate to establish one-party government, or a dictatorship, or in some other way to attack the fundamentals of democracy."

To which I might add—as a matter for debate—if Parliament were to legislate so as to abolish the two-chamber system and have one chamber only. In short, if it were to legislate to abolish the House of Lords, as distinct from reforming it. Would that be an abuse of legislative power? If it were done without a referendum on the very point? I do not doubt that Parliament would have power to reform the House of Lords. The Parliament Act of 1911 contained a recital that

> "... it is intended to substitute for the House of Lords as it at present exists a Second Chamber constituted on a popular instead of a hereditary basis, but such substitution cannot be immediately brought into operation".

---

* Reprinted here and below with permission of Butterworth & Co. (Publishers) Ltd.   **2.** Dr. Bonham's case (1608) 8 Co.Rep. 113b, 118a.

No doubt such a reform would be legitimate; but I doubt whether Parliament could lawfully abolish the Second Chamber altogether. I would expect any such legislation to be challenged in the courts of law; and for the judges to give a ruling on it.

———

What the court must do is to apply the Parliamentary act. That is a view that was stated in the courts of England over a century past. As Lord Denning stated, the idea of Lord Coke in *Dr. Bonham's case* did not grow. Coke's view did not survive the 17th century. The view of *Lee v. Bude and Torrington Railway* has prevailed. There the court stated:

> I would observe, as to these Acts of Parliament, that they are the law of this land; and we do not sit here as a court of appeal from parliament. It was once said,—I think in Hobart,—that if an Act of Parliament were to create a man judge in his own case, the Court might disregard it. That dictum, however, stands as a warning, rather than an authority to be followed. We sit here as servants of the Queen and the legislature. Are we to act as regents over what is done by parliament with the consent of the Queen, lords, and commons? I deny that any such authority exists. If an Act of Parliament has been obtained improperly, it is for the legislature to correct it by repealing it: but, so long as it exists as law, the Courts are bound to obey it. The proceedings here are judicial, not autocratic, which they would be if we could make laws instead of administering them.[1]

When the rule is that an Act of Parliament is sovereign, it might be expected that statutory interpretation becomes especially important. If the court may not invalidate an act directly, it may by interpretive method reduce it to a shadow of its apparent status when it received the assent of the Crown. Statutory interpretation will be discussed in Chapter 11. Here our interest is in the *capacity* of the courts to overrule the action of Parliament. That capacity is more likely to be challenged not when it involves an Act of Parliament which affects solely domestic life in England, but when it deals with some derogation of rules of international law, or might affect the status of an independent nation formerly under the umbrella of the British Empire, or even the relationships of current parts of the United Kingdom. The entry of England into the European Community and the participation in the European Convention on Human Rights has raised difficult and controversial questions.

The role of what might be viewed as external law has become a concern in recent years, with the entry of England into the European Community. It is not really external law that we deal with, however, but the incorporation into the law of England of Community law. Our concern focuses on the question whether Parliament is sufficiently

---

1. (1871) L.R. 6 C.P. 576, 582.

sovereign (if we may measure degrees of sovereignty) to subject England, by the European Communities Act, to an external source of law and, of considerable importance, what impact on England's participation a subsequent act in conflict with Community law would have? The following comments address the issue, showing there is concern and not a little nationalism lurking within the legal profession in England. Lord Denning's view in *Bulmer* stirred much debate.

> ... The treaty does not touch any of the matters which concern solely the mainland of England and the people in it. These are still governed by English law. They are not affected by the treaty. But when we come to matters with a European element, the treaty is like an incoming tide. It flows into the estuaries and up the rivers. It cannot be held back. Parliament has decreed that the treaty is hence-forward to be part of our law. It is equal in force to any statute.[3]

D.C.M. YARDLEY, "INTRODUCTION TO BRITISH CONSTITUTIONAL LAW"

39 (6th Ed.1984).

Does this mean that our Parliament has surrendered some portion of its sovereignty in favour of the Community institutions? Of course Parliament will undoubtedly usually want to do its best to conform with Community legislation, but successive Lord Chancellors have stated that it would remain within the power of Parliament to repeal by a subsequent Act any former Act applying a treaty which had been made. Under the powers enacted by the Referendum Act 1975, the first national consultative referendum was held throughout the United Kingdom, in which the electorate were asked to vote 'Yes' or 'No' to a question whether the United Kingdom should stay in the European Community. In the event there was a convincing majority for the answer 'Yes'. But the very asking of the question suggests that a contrary vote might have led to a later Bill to repeal the European Communities Act 1972. It may be that a specific Act passed later by the United Kingdom Parliament which is directly in conflict with Community legislation would have to be followed by British courts. Sorting out the result of such a clash would seem to be a political, rather than legal, matter for the government, and it may well result in later amending United Kingdom legislation. However it has now been made clear in recent court decisions that the provision in section 2(4) of the European Communities Act 1972 directing the courts to apply Community laws has the effect of precluding them from applying any earlier municipal law which is inconsistent with Community law. Thus in *Macarthys Ltd. v. Smith* [17] the rules of Community law entitling women to equal pay with

---

3. Bulmer Limited v. Bollinger, S.A., [1974] 2 All E.R. 1226, 1231. The *Bulmer* decision is also discussed in chapter 11, section 8, which considers the law of the European Community as a source of law in England.

17. [1981] Q.B. 180, [1981] 1 All E.R. 111.

men were held by the Court of Appeal to be applicable in preference to inconsistent provisions in the Equal Pay Act 1970. Yet this very primacy of Community law is the result of the provisions of the European Communities Act 1972, which could always be repealed or amended by a later Act of Parliament. So far as basic constitutional law is concerned, therefore, entry to the European Community, though envisaged as the first stage in a process of possible European political integration, is in itself not so fundamental a change as it may seem at first sight.

It is in the context of the relationship of an Act of Parliament passed some time ago to a later act which is inconsistent with the former how most questions of Parliamentary sovereignty arise. But another question further adds to this complex sphere a unique framework for consideration of the supremacy of Parliament. It is the question whether Parliament may bind itself in the future. If Parliament can do anything, does that include passing an Act which restricts its power in the future? The answer consistently is no. Blackstone first so stated the reason.

Acts of parliament derogatory from the power of subsequent parliaments bind not. So the statute 11 Hen. VII. c. 1. which directs that no person for assisting a king *de facto* shall be attainted of treason by act of parliament or otherwise, is held to be good only as to common prosecutions for high treason; but will not restrain or clog any parliamentary attainder. Because the legislature, being in trust the sovereign power, is always of equal, always of absolute authority: it acknowledges no superior upon earth, which the prior legislature must have been, if its ordinances could bind a subsequent parliament. And upon the same principle Cicero, in his letters to Atticus, treats with a proper contempt these restraining clauses, which endeavour to tie up the hands of succeeding legislatures. "When you repeal the law itself, says he, you at the same time repeal the prohibitory clause, which guards against such repeal." [4]

D.C.M. YARDLEY, "INTRODUCTION TO BRITISH CONSTITUTIONAL LAW"

34 (6th ed. 1984).

. . . Although Parliament may pass a statute in, say, 1985, by which it can enact some completely new law, yet it is still within the power of Parliament ten years later, or even only six months later, to abolish or alter that law in any way it thinks fit by a later statute, and such alteration, amendment or abolition may even take place by implication from the later enactments, if it is inconsistent with the former. Perhaps the most striking example of Parliament's power to repeal former

4. 1 W. Blackstone, Commentaries 90.

enactments is provided by the Irish Free State Constitution Act 1922, which severed that part of Ireland which is now the Republic of Ireland from the rest of the United Kingdom in flagrant violation of the Act of Union with Ireland 1800, which had declared the union of the two Kingdoms of Great Britain and Ireland to be 'forever'. The 1800 Act also provided for the permanent establishment of the United Church of England and Ireland, yet the Church of Ireland was disestablished by the Irish Church Act 1869. It may be that the provision in the Northern Ireland Constitution Act 1973, s 1, that no part of Northern Ireland may cease to be part of Her Majesty's dominions and of the United Kingdom 'without the consent of the majority of the people of Northern Ireland voting in a poll held for the purposes of this section' would be equally ineffective to prevent such severance if ever the Westminster Parliament were determined to carry it through.

In 1971 Salmon LJ put the position graphically in a case in which a Mr. Blackburn failed to persuade the Court of Appeal to grant a declaration that the United Kingdom application to join the European Community was illegal because it would be an 'irreversible partial surrender of the Sovereignty of the Crown in Parliament'. Salmon LJ said: 'As to Parliament, in the present state of the law, it can enact, amend and repeal any legislation it pleases'.[10] On the other hand, Lord Denning MR in the same case put the practical realities of the issue into perspective. He said: 'We have all been brought up to believe that, in legal theory, one Parliament cannot bind another and that no Act is irreversible. But legal theory does not always march alongside political reality. Take the Statute of Westminster 1931, which takes away the power of Parliament to legislate for the Dominions. Can anyone imagine that Parliament could or would reverse that Statute? Take the Acts which have granted independence to the Dominions and territories overseas. Can anyone imagine that Parliament could or would reverse these laws and take away their independence? Most clearly not. Freedom once given cannot be taken away. Legal theory must give way to practical politics'.

* * *

———

What about the case where *future* acts of Parliament do not clearly evidence an intention to override the Community law. If a clear intention of repeal is not present, there may be a serious problem regarding England's continuation as a member of the Community. The English European Communities Act thus suggests a rule of interpretation that Parliament is presumed not to act inconsistently with Community law. But if there is a clear and express statement of such intent to act inconsistently, then the rule of Parliamentary sovereignty would be fundamentally altered if the later act were held unlawful. Even the

10. Blackburn v. A.G. [1971] 1 W.L.R. 1037, 1041.

suggested rule of interpretation causes unsettled moments for the Parliamentary purist—who believes that nothing Parliament may say, however express or deemed intended by the words of the act, can be subordinated to *any* earlier act.

An additional entry of England into the community of the continent raises even more perplexing issues of judicial review and the possibility of declaring an Act of Parliament unlawful. That is the 1966 acceptance of competence of the European Commission of Human Rights, set forth in the European Convention on Human Rights. England signed the Convention in 1950, but has not enacted any law incorporating the Convention into English law. But the participation of England allows the legality of any Act of Parliament to be challenged by any private individual before the Court in Strasbourg. The *Thalidomide* and *Spycatcher* decisions illustrate how the European Court of Human Rights in Strasbourg has become a form of judicial review, not binding on the English courts but of influence on the Parliament (and executive) in London in inducing amendments to existing laws or the enactment of new laws consistent with the Strasbourg Court's rulings, however contrary to earlier English court rulings.

After several hundred children were born with deformities to mothers who had taken the drug thalidomide between 1959 and 1961, numerous cases were initiated against the drug company. Some were settled and in 1968 the company offered a settlement conditional on all remaining plaintiffs agreements. Five refused. Little further progress in either settlement or commencing trial ensued and in late 1972 the Sunday Times published the first of a series of articles on the tragedy of the young children. The Attorney–General, after complaint by the company, sought and obtained an injunction in the Queen's Bench Division of the High Court against the publication of any further articles. On appeal the House of Lords held that the publication was a contempt of court which prejudiced the pending litigation or was likely to cause public prejudgment on the issue.[1] The Lords were not interpreting an act of Parliament but ruling on a common law principle not addressed by the courts in this century. The Attorney–General was acting in "a constitutional role as guardian of the public interest."[2] Nowhere in the decision was reference made to the European Convention.

The Times took the matter to the European Court of Human Rights at Strasbourg, charging principally that the injunction based on such a broad definition of contempt violated Article 10 of the European Convention on Human Rights, which is the freedom of expression provision of the Convention.[3]

---

1. Attorney–General v. Times Newspapers, [1974] A.C. 273.

2. Id. at 279.

3. Article 10(1) states that "Everyone has the right of freedom of expression. The right shall include freedom to hold opinions and to receive and impart information and ideas without interference by public authority and regardless of frontiers." Article 10(2) adds, "The exercise of these freedoms, since it carries with it duties and responsi-

THE SUNDAY TIMES v. UNITED KINGDOM

2 EHRR 245 (1979–80).

* * *

45.   It is clear that there was an 'interference by public authority' in the exercise of the applicants' freedom of expression, which is guaranteed by paragraph 1 of Article 10.   Such an interference entails a 'violation' of Article 10 if it does not fall within one of the exceptions provided for in paragraph 2 (HANDYSIDE v UK (1976)). . . .   The Court therefore has to examine in turn whether the interference in the present case was 'prescribed by law', whether it had an aim or aims that is or are legitimate under Article 10(2) and whether it was 'necessary in a democratic society' for the aforesaid aim or aims.

A.   WAS THE INTERFERENCE 'PRESCRIBED BY LAW'?

46.   The applicants argue, inter alia, that the law of contempt of court, both before and after the decision of the House of Lords, was so vague and uncertain and the principles enunciated by that decision so novel that the restraint imposed cannot be regarded as 'prescribed by law'.   The Government maintain that it suffices, in this context, that the restraint was in accordance with the law; they plead, in the alternative, that on the facts of the case the restraint was at least 'roughly foreseeable'.   This latter test had been referred to by the Commission in its report, although there it merely proceeded on the assumption that the principles applied by the House of Lords were 'prescribed by law'. However, at the hearing on 25 April 1978, the Commission's Principal Delegate added that, in view of the uncertainties of the law, the restraint was not 'prescribed by law', at least when the injunction was first granted in 1972.

47.   The Court observes that the word 'law' in the expression 'prescribed by law' covers not only statute but also unwritten law. Accordingly, the Court does not attach importance here to the fact that contempt of court is a creature of the common law and not of legislation. It would clearly be contrary to the intention of the drafters of the Convention to hold that a restriction imposed by virtue of the common law is not 'prescribed by law' on the sole ground that it is not enunciated in legislation: this would deprive a common law State which is Party to the Convention of the protection of Article 10(2) and strike at the very roots of the State's legal system.

In fact, the applicants do not argue that the expression 'prescribed by law' necessitates legislation in every case; their submission is that legislation is required only if—as in the present case—the common law rules are so uncertain that they do not satisfy what the applicants

bilities, may be subject to such formalities, conditions, restrictions or penalties as are prescribed by law and are necessary in a democratic society, . . . public safety, . . . for the protection of the reputation or rights of others, . . . or for maintaining the authority and impartiality of the judiciary.''

maintain is the concept enshrined in that expression, namely, the principle of legal certainty.

48. The expression 'prescribed by law' appears in paragraph 2 of Articles 9, 10 and 11 of the Convention, the equivalent in the French text being in each case 'prevues par la loi'. However, when the same French expression appears in Article 8(2) of the Convention, in Article 1 of Protocol No 1 and in Article 2 of Protocol No 4, it is rendered in the English text as 'in accordance with the law', 'provided for by law' and 'in accordance with law', respectively. Thus confronted with versions of a law-making treaty which are equally authentic but not exactly the same, the Court must interpret them in a way that reconciles them as far as possible and is most appropriate in order to realise the aim and achieve the object of the treaty See WEMHOFF v GERMANY (1968) ... and the Vienna Convention on the Law of Treaties of 23 May 1969, art. 33 (4).

49. In the Court's opinion, the following are two of the requirements that flow from the expression 'prescribed by law'. First, the law must be adequately accessible: the citizen must be able to have an indication that is adequate in the circumstances of the legal rules applicable to a given case. Secondly, a norm cannot be regarded as a 'law' unless it is formulated with sufficient precision to enable the citizen to regulate his conduct: he must be able—if need be with appropriate advice—to foresee, to a degree that is reasonable in the circumstances, the consequences which a given action may entail. Those consequences need not be foreseeable with absolute certainty: experience shows, this to be unattainable. Again, whilst certainty is highly desirable, it may bring in its train excessive rigidity and the law must be able to keep pace with changing circumstances. Accordingly, many laws are inevitably couched in terms which, to a greater or lesser extent, are vague and whose interpretation and application are questions of practice.

50. In the present case, the question whether these requirements of accessibility and foreseeability were satisfied is complicated by the fact that different principles were relied on by the various Law Lords concerned. The Divisional Court had applied the principle that a deliberate attempt to influence the settlement of pending proceedings by bringing public pressure to bear on a party constitutes contempt of court. Certain members of the House of Lords also alluded to this principle, whereas others preferred the principle that it is contempt of court to publish material which prejudges, or is likely to cause public prejudgment of, the issues raised in pending litigation.

51. The applicants do not claim to have been without an indication that was adequate in the circumstances of the 'pressure principle'....

The Court also considers that there can be no doubt that the 'pressure principle' was formulated with sufficient precision to enable the applicants to foresee to the appropriate degree the consequences which publication of the draft article might entail....

* * *

52.   The applicants contend, on the other hand, that the prejudgment principle was novel and that they therefore could not have had an
adequate indication of its existence....

* * *

To sum up, the Court does not consider that the applicants were
without an indication that was adequate in the circumstances of the
existence of the 'prejudgment principle'. Even if the Court does have
certain doubts concerning the precision with which that principle was
formulated at the relevant time, it considers that the applicants were
able to foresee, to a degree that was reasonable in the circumstances, a
risk that publication of the draft article might fall foul of the principle.

53.   The interference with the applicants' freedom of expression
was thus 'prescribed by law' within the meaning of Article 10(2).

B.   DID THE INTERFERENCE HAVE AIMS THAT
ARE LEGITIMATE UNDER ARTICLE 10(2)?

54.   In the view of the applicants, the Government and the minority
of the Commission, the law of contempt of court serves the purpose of
safeguarding not only the impartiality and authority of the judiciary but
also the rights and interests of litigants.

The majority of the Commission, on the other hand, whilst accepting
that the law of contempt had the general aim of securing the fair
administration of justice and that it thereby seeks to achieve purposes
similar to those envisaged in Article 10(2) where it speaks of maintaining
the authority and impartiality of the judiciary, considered that it was not
called upon to examine separately whether the law has the further
purpose of protecting the rights of others.

55.   The court first emphasises that the expression 'authority and
impartiality of the judiciary' has to be understood 'within the meaning of
the Convention'....

The term 'judiciary' ('pouvoir judiciaire') comprises the machinery
of justice or the judicial branch of government as well as the judges in
their official capacity. The phrase 'authority of the judiciary' includes,
in particular, the notion that the courts are, and are accepted by the
public at large as being, the proper forum for the ascertainment of legal
rights and obligations and the settlement of disputes relative thereto;
further, that the public at large have respect for and confidence in the
courts' capacity to fulfil that function.

* * *

56.   In the present case, the Court shares the view of the majority
of the Commission that, in so far as the law of contempt may serve to
protect the rights of litigants, this purpose is already included in the
phrase 'maintaining the authority and impartiality of the judiciary': the
rights so protected are the rights of individuals in their capacity as
litigants, that is, as persons involved in the machinery of justice, and the
authority of that machinery will not be maintained unless protection is

afforded to all those involved in or having recourse to it. It is therefore not necessary to consider as a separate issue whether the law of contempt has the further purpose of safeguarding 'the rights of others'.

57. It remains to be examined whether the aim of the interference with the applicants' freedom of expression was the maintenance of the authority and impartiality of the judiciary.

None of the Law Lords concerned based his decision on the ground that the proposed article might have an influence on the 'impartiality' of the judiciary. This ground was also not pleaded before the Court and can be left out of account.

The reasons why the draft article was regarded as objectionable by the House of Lords ... may be briefly summarised as follows:

—by 'prejudging' the issue of negligence, it would have led to disrespect for the processes of the law or interfered with the administration of justice; it was of a kind that would expose Distillers to Public and prejudicial discussion of the merits of their case, such exposure being objectionable as it inhibits suitors generally from having recourse to the courts;

—it would subject Distillers to pressure and to the prejudices of prejudgment of the issues in the litigation, and the law of contempt was designed to prevent interference with recourse to the courts;

—prejudgment by the press would have led inevitably in this case to replies by the parties, thereby creating the danger of a 'trial by newspaper' incompatible with the proper administration of justice;

—the courts owe it to the parties to protect them from the prejudices of prejudgment which involves their having to participate in the flurries of pre-trial publicity.

The Court regards all these various reasons as falling within the aim of maintaining the 'authority ... of the judiciary' as interpreted by the Court in the second sub-paragraph of paragraph 55 above.

Accordingly, the interference with the applicants' freedom of expression had an aim that is legitimate under Article 10(2).

C. WAS THE INTERFERENCE 'NECESSARY IN A DEMOCRATIC SOCIETY' FOR MAINTAINING THE AUTHORITY OF THE JUDICIARY?

58. The applicants submit and the majority of the Commission are of the opinion that the said interference was not 'necessary' within the meaning of Article 10(2). The Government contend that the minority of the Commission was correct in reaching a contrary conclusion and rely, in particular, on the margin of appreciation enjoyed by the House of Lords in the matter.

59. The Court has already had the occasion in its above-mentioned HANDYSIDE judgment to state its understanding of the phrase 'necessary in a democratic society', the nature of its functions in the examination of issues turning on that phrase and the manner in which it will perform those functions.

The Court has noted that, whilst the adjective 'necessary', within the meaning of Article 10(2), is not synonymous with 'indispensable', neither has it the flexibility of such expressions as 'admissible', 'ordinary', 'useful', 'reasonable' or 'desirable' and that it implies the existence of a 'pressing social need'. . . .

In the second place, the Court has underlined that the initial responsibility for securing the rights and freedoms enshrined in the Convention lies with the individual Contracting States. Accordingly, 'Article 10(2) leaves to the Contracting States a margin of appreciation. This margin is given both to the domestic legislator . . . and to the bodies, judicial amongst others, that are called upon to interpret and apply the laws in force'. . . .

'Nevertheless, Article 10(2) does not give the Contracting States an unlimited power of appreciation'. 'The Court . . . is empowered to give the final ruling on whether a "restriction" . . . is reconcilable with freedom of expression as protected by Article 10. The domestic margin of appreciation thus goes hand in hand with a European supervision', which 'covers not only basic legislation but also the decision applying it, even one given by an independent court'. . . .

* * *

60. Both the minority of the Commission and the Government attach importance to the fact that the institution of contempt of court is peculiar to common law countries and suggest that the concluding words of Article 10(2) were designed to cover this institution which has no equivalent in many other member States of the Council of Europe.

However, even if this were so, the Court considers that the reason for the insertion of those words would have been to ensure that the general aims of the law of contempt of court should be considered legitimate aims under Article 10(2) but not to make that law the standard by which to assess whether a given measure was 'necessary'. If and to the extent that Article 10(2) was prompted by the notion underlying either English law of contempt of court or any other similar domestic institution, it cannot have adopted them as they stood: it transposed them into an autonomous context. It is 'necessity' in terms of the Convention which the Court has to assess, its role being to review the conformity of national acts with the standards of that instrument.

* * *

61. Again, the Court cannot hold that the injunction was not 'necessary' simply because it could or would not have been granted under a different legal system. As noted in the BELGIAN LINGUISTIC CASE, the main purpose of the Convention is 'to lay down certain international standards to be observed by the Contracting States in their relations with persons under their jurisdiction'. . . . This does not mean that absolute uniformity is required and, indeed, since the Contracting States remain free to choose the measures which they consider appropri-

ate, the Court cannot be oblivious of the substantive or procedural features of their respective domestic laws. . . .

62. It must now be decided whether the 'interference' complained of corresponded to a 'pressing social need', whether it was 'proportionate to the legitimate aim pursued', whether the reasons given by the national authorities to justify it are 'relevant and sufficient under Article 10(2)'. . . .

* * *

65. The Government's reply is that it is a matter of balancing the public interest in freedom of expression and the public interest in the fair administration of justice; they stress that the injunction was a temporary measure and say that the balance, on being struck again in 1976 when the situation had changed, fell on the other side.

This brings the Court to the circumstances surrounding the thalidomide case and the grant of the injunction.

As the Court remarked in its HANDYSIDE judgment, freedom of expression constitutes one of the essential foundations of a democratic society; subject to paragraph 2 of Article 10, it is applicable not only to information or ideas that are favourably received or regarded as inoffensive or as a matter of indifference, but also to those that offend, shock or disturb the State or any sector of the population. . . .

These principles are of particular importance as far as the press is concerned. They are equally applicable to the field of the administration of justice, which serves the interests of the community at large and requires the co-operation of an enlightened public. There is general recognition of the fact that the court cannot operate in a vacuum. Whilst they are the forum for the settlement of disputes, this does not mean that there can be no prior discussion of disputes elsewhere, but it in specialised journals, in the general press or amongst the public at large. Furthermore, whilst the mass media must not overstep the bounds imposed in the interests of the proper administration of justice, it is incumbent on them to impart information and ideas concerning matters that come before the courts just as in other areas of public interest. Not only do the media have the task of imparting such information and ideas: the public also has a right to receive them (See mutatis mutandis, KJELDSEN, BUSK AND PEDERSEN v DENMARK (1976)). . . .

To assess whether the interference complained of was based on 'sufficient' reasons which rendered it 'necessary in a democratic society', account must thus be taken of any public interest aspect of the case. The Court observes in this connection that, following a balancing of the conflicting interests involved, an absolute rule was formulated by certain of the Law Lords to the effect that it was not permissible to prejudge issues in pending cases: it was considered that the law would be too uncertain if the balance were to be struck anew in each case. . . . Whilst emphasising it is not its function to pronounce itself on an interpretation of English law adopted in the House of Lords (See, mutatis mutandis, RINGEISEN v AUSTRIA (1971)), ... the Court points out that it has to take a different approach. The Court is faced not with a choice between two conflicting principles, but with a principle of freedom of expression that is subject to a number of exceptions which must be narrowly interpreted (See, mutatis mutandis, KLASS v GERMANY, 2 EHRR at p 214, para 42). In the second place, the Court's supervision under Article 10 covers not only the basic legislation but also the decision applying it (See HANDYSIDE v UK).... It is not sufficient that the interference involved belongs to that class of the exceptions listed in Article 10(2) which has been invoked; neither is it sufficient that the interference was imposed because its subject-matter fell within a particular category or was caught by a legal rule formulated in general or absolute terms: the Court has to be satisfied that the interference was necessary having regard to the facts and circumstances prevailing in the specific case before it.

66. The thalidomide disaster was a matter of undisputed public concern. It posed the question whether the powerful company which had marketed the drug bore legal or moral responsibility towards hundreds of individuals experiencing an appalling personal tragedy or whether the victims could demand or hope for indemnification only from the community as a whole; fundamental issues concerning protection against and compensation for injuries resulting from scientific developments were raised and may facets of the existing law on these subjects were called in question.

As the Court has already observed, Article 10 guarantees not only the freedom of the press to inform the public but also the right of the public to be properly informed....

In the present case, the families of numerous victims of the tragedy, who were unaware of the legal difficulties involved, had a vital interest in knowing all the underlying facts and the various possible solutions. They could be deprived of this information, which was crucially important for them, only if it appeared absolutely certain that its diffusion would have presented a threat to the 'authority of the judiciary'.

* * *

67. Having regard to all the circumstances of the case and on the basis of the approach described in paragraph 65 above, the Court concludes that the interference complained of did not correspond to a social need sufficiently pressing to outweigh the public interest in freedom of expression within the meaning of the Convention. The Court therefore finds the reasons for the restraint imposed on the applicants not to be sufficient under Article 10(2). That restraint proves not to be proportionate to the legitimate aim pursued; it was not necessary in a democratic society for maintaining the authority of the judiciary.

68. There has accordingly been a violation of Article 10.

* * *

Joint Dissenting Opinion....

1. With respect, we are unable to share the opinion of the majority of our colleagues that the contested interference with freedom of expression was contrary to the Convention because it could not be deemed necessary in a democratic society for maintaining the authority and impartiality of the judiciary, within the meaning of Article 10(2) of the Convention.

* * *

4. The difference of opinion separating us from our colleagues concerns above all the necessity of the interference and the margin of appreciation which, in this connection, is to be allowed to the national authorities.

* * *

7. The Court has already had the occasion, notably in HANDY-SIDE v UK (1976), ... to state the correct approach to the interpretation and application of the phrase 'necessary in a democratic society', within the meaning of Article 10(2), and to indicate both what its obligations are when faced with issues relating to the interpretation or application of this provision and the manner in which it means to perform those obligations.

* * *

10. In the United Kingdom, the law of contempt constitutes one of the means designed to safeguard the proper functioning of the courts. As has been said above, the authors of the Convention had this law in mind when they introduced the notion of maintaining 'the authority and impartiality of the judiciary'....

The task of ensuring that the law of contempt is observed falls to the domestic courts. In this respect, it would appear undeniable to us that the House of Lords is in principle better qualified than our Court to decide whether, in factual circumstances which are for the House to assess, a given form of restriction on freedom of expression is necessary for maintaining, in a democratic society, the judiciary's authority within the United Kingdom itself.

This cannot be taken to the point of allowing that every restriction on freedom of expression adjudged by the domestic courts to be necessary for observance of the law of contempt must also be considered necessary under the Convention.

While the domestic courts' assessment of the prejudicial consequences that a given publication might have on the due administration of justice in the United Kingdom should in principle be respected, it is nevertheless possible that the measures deemed necessary to avert such consequences overstep the bounds of what is 'necessary in a democratic society' within the meaning of Article 10(2).... The Court, in its consideration of the matter, must pay particular heed to this fundamental factor in the Convention system.

* * *

12.   The applicants submitted before the Court that the actions brought by the parents against Distillers were 'dormant' at the relevant time.   In its report on the present case, the European Commission of Human Rights considered firstly that it was somewhat improbable that the great majority of the actions, then subject to negotiation, would eventuate in a court judgment and secondly that, as regards the actions brought by the parents who as a matter of principle were not willing to opt for settlement, no court decision could be anticipated in the foreseeable future.

Assessment of the state of the actions in question depended on what could be expected at the relevant time in relation to the development of the negotiations, on the probability of a settlement, on the eventuality that certain of the parents would accept a settlement and discontinue their actions whilst others would pursue them, and in general on what were the more or less immediate prospects either of a settlement or of judgment in court.

For the purposes of such an assessment, which covered a wealth of contemporary facts and points of procedure, the national judge must, in this respect also, be taken as being in principle in a better position than the Court. . . .   In our view, the House of Lords was 'entitled to think' that in the circumstances then obtaining the actions concerned could not be regarded as 'dormant'.

13.   The considerations set out above led us to conclude that the domestic courts' evaluation of the risk of seeing the article concerned interfere with the due administration of justice, as well as their assessment of the necessity of the measure to be taken within the context of the domestic law, must be regarded as reasonable.

As has already been pointed out . . ., it is nevertheless for the Court to determine whether, on the strength of this evaluation, the restraint on the publication was proportionate to the legitimate aim pursued and can be deemed necessary in a democratic society for the maintenance of the authority and impartiality of the judiciary, within the meaning of Article 10(2).

This determination involves that the Court should take into account not only the interests of justice, which according to the domestic courts made it necessary to impose the restraint at the relevant time, but also the consequences of this measure for the freedom of the press, a freedom which figures amongst those guaranteed by the Convention as one of the essential foundations of a 'democratic society' and as one of the basic conditions for that society's progress and development (See, mutatis mutandis, HANDYSIDE v UK). . . .

* * *

15. As regards the duration of the restraint, it should be noted that the sole aim of the injunction granted was to ensure that for a certain time premature publications should not be able to prejudice the due administration of justice in relation to specific litigation. According to the House of Lords, the necessity to restrain publication of the article stemmed from the state, at the time of its decision, of the actions pending. Their Lordships foresaw the possibility that the situation might change, that, even before the proceedings had been finally terminated, the balance between the interests of justice and those of the freedom of the press might shift, and that the injunction might be discharged.

* * *

16. In the light of the considerations set out below, we conclude that the interference with freedom of expression, adjudged by the national courts in the instant case to be necessary according to the law of contempt in the interests of the due administration of justice, did not overstep the limits of what might be deemed necessary in a democratic society for the maintenance of 'the authority and impartiality of the judiciary' within the meaning of Article 10(2).

On the basis of the material before the Court, we consider that no infringement of the requirements of Article 10 has been established.

* * *

The European Court ruling, approximately 50 pages long, was 11 to nine. In addition to the dissents, three of the majority filed separate concurring opinions. The Times asked for costs. The United Kingdom opposed on the grounds that the 11–9 decision suggested that only a small majority believed there was fault. By 13 to 3 the Court awarded the Times its costs.

The United Kingdom Parliament enacted the Contempt of Court Act 1981, certainly influenced by the European Court decision.[4] Thus the Parliament, rather than the English courts, effectively overruled the decision of the House of Lords. The Contempt of Court Act eliminated the "prejudging the issue" test, leaving as the sole test interference with the course of justice.

The *Thalidomide* case did not involve judicial review of an act of Parliament. The European Court was reviewing a common law principle under Article 10. It would soon have an opportunity to revisit that review, although the new Contempt of Court Act is not at issue.[5]

4. The matter had been under study for several years and was the subject of a report of a committee known as the Phillimore Report. The final report, rendered after the House of Lords decision, was critical of the Lords' definition of contempt.

5. The Act preserves common law contempt. It adds a strict liability rule which was determined not to be an issue.

Peter Wright, former officer of the British Secret Service, MI5, wrote memoirs about his service. They included some rather damaging allegations about the British intelligence service and the loyalty of several members. Several newspapers, principally those involved in the *Thalidomide* case, published some outlines or excerpts of the book. The Attorney General obtained an injunction (3–2 vote to essentially preserve an injunction until trial) against further publication. The book was not published in England but was published elsewhere and copies were distributed privately in England. Although the initial English House of Lords *Thalidomide* decision contains no reference to the European Convention or Court, the first House of Lords *Spycatcher* decision illustrates the increasing importance and role of the Convention in English judicial decisions. The following are some extracts from the first House of Lords *Spycatcher* ruling:

ATTORNEY–GENERAL v. GUARDIAN NEWSPAPERS

[1987] 3 ALL ER 316, 343.

Lord Bridge of Harwich.

* * *

... Having no written constitution, we have no equivalent in our law to the First Amendment to the Constitution of the United States of America. Some think that puts freedom of speech on too lofty a pedestal. Perhaps they are right. We have not adopted as part of our law the European Convention on Human Rights ... to which this country is a signatory. Many think that we should. I have hitherto not been of that persuasion, in large part because I have had confidence in the capacity of the common law to safeguard the fundamental freedoms essential to a free society including the right to freedom of speech which is specifically safeguarded by art 10 of the convention. ... If the government are determined to fight to maintain the ban to the end, they will face inevitable condemnation and humiliation by the European Court of Human Rights in Strasbourg. Long before that they will have been condemned at the bar of public opinion in the free world.

Lord Brandon of Oakbrook.

* * *

... The public right to freedom cannot, even in a democratic country such as the United Kingdom, be absolute. It is necessarily subject to certain exceptions, of which the protection of national security is one. This is expressly recognised in art 10(2) of the Convention for the Protection of Human Rights and Fundamental Freedoms ..., to which the United Kingdom has adhered although its provisions have not been incorporated into our domestic law.

* * *

LORD TEMPLEMAN.

* * *

My Lords, this appeal involves a conflict between the right of the public to be protected by the security service and the right of the public to be supplied with full information by the press. This appeal therefore involves consideration of the European Convention on Human Rights (Convention for the Protection of Human Rights and Fundamental Freedoms (Rome, 4 November 1950; TS 71 (1953); Cmd 8969)) to which the British government adheres....

* * *

In *Sunday Times v UK* (1979) 2 EHRR 245 the European Court of Human Rights decided by a majority of 11 to 9 that there had been a violation of the convention by reason of the judgment of this House which restrained the Sunday Times from publishing—

> 'Any article which prejudices the issues of negligence, breach of contract or breach of duty or deals with the evidence relating to any of the said issues arising in any actions pending or imminent against Distillers ... in respect of the development, distribution or use of the drug Thalidomide.'

The European Court pointed out that this House applying domestic law had balanced the public interest in freedom of expression and the public interest in the due of administration of justice. But the European Court—

> 'is faced not with the choice between two conflicting principles but with a principle of freedom of expression which is subject to a number of exceptions which must be narrowly interpreted ... It is not sufficient that the interference involved belongs to that class of exceptions listed in Article 10 which has been invoked; neither is it sufficient that the interference was imposed because its subject-matter fell within a particular category or was caught by a legal rule formulated in general or absolute terms; the Court has to be satisfied that the interference was necessary having regard to the facts and circumstances prevailing in the specific case before it.'

* * *

The question is therefore whether the interference with freedom of expression constituted by the Millett injunctions was, on 30 July 1987 when they were continued by this House, necessary in a democratic society in the interests of national security, for protecting the reputation or rights of others, for preventing the disclosure of information received in confidence or for maintaining the authority and impartiality of the judiciary having regard to the facts and circumstances prevailing on 30 July 1987 and in the light of the events which had happened....

* * *

In my opinion, therefore, the injunctions are necessary in terms of the convention because harm will be caused to the security service if the press insist on disclosing to their readers not the general nature of Mr Wright's uncorroborated allegations but the mass circumstantial hearsay contained in *Spycatcher* relating to the security service and its activities.

* * *

LORD ACKNER.

* * *

(1) THE EUROPEAN CONVENTION ON HUMAN RIGHTS

Counsel for the Sunday Times laid great emphasis on the provisions of art 10 of the European Convention on Human Rights ..., dealing with the freedom of expression. Article 10(2) provides qualifications and exceptions to which the exercise of free expression may be made subject. They include such conditions—

> 'as are prescribed by Law and are necessary in a democratic society in the interests of National Security ... for the protection of the ... rights of others, for preventing the disclosure of information received in confidence ...'

Given that it is accepted that the Crown has an arguable case for a permanent injunction, that damages are a useless remedy, that there exists a significant public interest factor and that your Lordships are concerned only with a pre-trial restraint on publication. I see no prospect of the convention availing the appellants. Indeed, I adopt all my learned and noble friend Lord Templeman has said in his closely reasoned judgment as to the relevance and applicability of art 10, and I fully support the conclusion at which he, unlike my noble and learned friend Lord Bridge, arrives.

* * *

LORD OLIVER OF AYLMERTON.*

* * *

———

The newspapers took the matter to the European Court at Strasbourg, challenging the injunctions under Article 10, among others.[6] The Court, by a 14 to 10 vote, found no violation of Article 10 until July 30, 1987, the time the House of Lords ruled, but unanimously found a violation after that date.[7]

---

* Lord Oliver made no reference to the Convention.

6. The process takes the matter first to the Commission and then to the Court. The Commission voted 6–5 that Article 10 was violated before July 30th, and unanimously that it was violated thereafter.

7. The Observer and the Guardian v. United Kingdom, (1992) 14 EHRR 153; The Sunday Times v. United Kingdom, (1992) 14 EHRR 229.

Notes and Questions

1. The first English court *Spycatcher* decision included comments about the European Convention by all but one Lord. What was the purpose of the comments of the Lords in the first English court *Spycatcher?* Were the Lords concerned with the prestige of the House of Lords? The impact of any adverse European Court decision on the English law? Fairness to the parties involved? Merely responding to arguments of counsel? Possible disclosure about practices of the intelligence service pursuing political rather than national security goals? Breach of duty of confidentiality? What does Lord Brandon mean when he refers to the Convention as a document "to which the United Kingdom has adhered although its provisions have not been incorporated into our domestic law"? Isn't Lord Templeton actually applying the Convention when he says "the injunctions are necessary in terms of the convention because ..."? What is Lord Ackner's view? Perhaps the Lords comments regarding the Convention were made only to respond to counsel for the newspapers, who argued the applicability of the Convention.

2. In the European Court's *Spycatcher* decision, the majority decision referred almost exclusively to previous European Court decisions, while the partial dissents referred largely to United States Supreme Court decisions to object to the majority's view that there was no violation of Article 10 until July 30, 1987.

3. The European Court based its decision at least partly on the "insufficient foreseeability" of English domestic law. The House of Lords decisions are certainly difficult to interpret. Each Lord renders a separate opinion. Each searches for common law principles applicable to the case. The civil law tradition dominated judiciary of the European Court seem to feel that the "unwritten" common law may itself be unfair to those it purports to govern.

4. The *Spycatcher* episode added much to the debate regarding adoption of a Bill of Rights. The proponents of such adoption pointed to *Spycatcher* as evidence of the inability of the English judiciary to protect citizen's rights. But opponents suggested that the Lords had considered the Convention in rendering their decision, especially Lord Templeton. Thus, if a Bill of Rights (either the European Convention or a separate UK Bill of Rights) were adopted, would the House of Lords be likely to rule any differently?

5. Is the Convention "creeping" into English law? Although the House of Lords majority may not believe so, perhaps the Court of Appeal (from which the next members of the House of Lords usually come) believes differently. Consider the comments of the Court of Appeal below, in a case brought by journalists seeking to have quashed Home Secretary imposed restrictions regarding broadcasting direct statements by representatives of proscribed organizations in Northern Ireland because they breached Article 10 of the European Convention:

R. v. SECRETARY OF STATE FOR THE HOME DEPARTMENT, EX PARTE BRIND

[1991] 1 AC 696, [1990] 1 ALL ER 469, [1990] 2 WLR 787.

LORD DONALDSON OF LYMINGTON MR.

* * *

It will undoubtedly strike some people as strange that, the directives having been approved by Parliament, the courts should be prepared to entertain applications to judicially review them, since Parliament is supreme under our constitution. I can well understand such a reaction and it is very important that it should be answered and dispelled.

Parliament is indeed supreme, subject to immaterial exceptions stemming from European Community law, which does not include the European Convention on Human Rights.... If Parliament had passed an Act containing the restrictions imposed by the Home Secretary's directives, the courts could and would have had nothing to consider or say. However, where Parliament authorizes ministers to take executive action, it is the duty of the courts in appropriate cases to consider whether ministers have exceeded that authority....

* * *

THE EUROPEAN CONVENTION ON HUMAN RIGHTS

There have been a number of cases in which the European Convention on Human Rights has been introduced into the argument and has, accordingly, featured in the judgments. In most of them the reference has been fleeting and usually consisted of an assertion, in which I would concur, that you have to look long and hard before you can detect any difference between the English common law and the principles set out in the convention, at least if the convention is viewed through English judicial eyes. However, in this case we are invited to grapple with the fundamental question of the effect of the convention as distinct from any common law to the like effect....

The convention is contained in an international treaty to which the United Kingdom is a party and, by art 1, binds its signatories to 'secure to everyone within their jurisdiction the rights and freedoms defined in Section 1 of this Convention'. The United Kingdom government can give effect to this treaty obligation in more than one way. It could, for example, 'domesticate' or 'patriate' the convention itself, as has been done in the case of the treaties mentioned in the European Communities Act 1972, and there are many well-informed supporters of this course. Their view has not, as yet, prevailed. If it had done so, the convention would have been part of English domestic law. Alternatively, it can review English common and statute law with a view to amending it, if and in so far as it is inconsistent with the convention, at the same time seeking to ensure that all new statute law is consistent with it. This is the course which has in fact been adopted. Whether it has been wholly successful is a matter for the European Court of Human Rights in Strasbourg and not for the English courts. By contrast, the duty of the English courts is to decide disputes in accordance with English domestic law as it is, and not as it would be if full effect were given to this country's obligations under the treaty, assuming that there is any difference between the two.

It follows from this that in most cases the English courts will be wholly unconcerned with the terms of the convention. The sole exception is when the terms of primary legislation are fairly capable of bearing two or more meanings and the court, in pursuance of its duty to apply domestic law, is concerned to divine and define its true and only meaning. In that situation various prima facie rules of construction have to be applied, such as that, in the absence of very clear words indicating the contrary, legislation is not retrospective or penal in effect. To these can be added, in appropriate cases, a presumption that Parliament has legislated in a manner consistent, rather than inconsistent, with the United Kingdom's treaty obligations.

* * *

RALPH GIBSON LJ. . . .

The first ground of appeal was based on the European Convention on Human Rights. . . .

* * *

Counsel for the applicants acknowledged that the obligation of the United Kingdom to secure the right to freedom of expression, as guaranteed by art 10, and to secure that right under the domestic legal order, cannot be effected in the courts of this country where the alleged violation is required by Act of Parliament, because the convention does not require the availability of a domestic remedy to challenge the compatibility of the statute with the convention. In such a case, counsel for the applicant also acknowledged, the convention provides a remedy for a violation only on the international plane, i.e., before the European Commission and Court of Human Rights.

It was next submitted that the rights and freedoms of the convention have not been expressly incorporated by statute into the domestic law of this country because successive governments have considered that it was unnecessary to take that step so as to comply with the obligations imposed by the convention. Successive governments must be taken, it was said, to have assumed that the existing arrangements within our domestic legal order comply with those obligations so that the convention rights and remedies are directly secured and so that there are effective national remedies.

* * *

Thus the courts of this country now refer, and must now refer, to the relevant provisions of the convention, and to the judgments of the

European Court of Human Rights, interpreting those provisions for the purpose of ensuring, where possible, that our domestic law is in conformity with the convention. That must be done when construing legislation, as when reviewing the exercise of administrative discretion or declaring and applying the common law. Only if an Act of Parliament cannot be construed so as to be consistent with the convention must the courts of this country apply the statute and leave the complainant to seek redress in Strasbourg.

* * *

Before giving consideration to the cases relied on by counsel for the applicants it is necessary, I think, to define the point of constitutional principle which counsel for the Secretary of State has raised against the applicants' main argument on this point. It is uncomplicated. An international treaty such as the European Convention on Human Rights is made by the executive government. It does not directly affect the domestic law of this country, which can be changed only by Parliament. It is not within the powers of the court, by application of a rule of statutory construction, to import into the laws of this country provisions of a treaty for direct application by the court. Only Parliament can do that. It would be usurpation of the legislative power of Parliament for the court to do more than to construe the legislation which Parliament has passed in order to establish its meaning. To do that it may, and must, apply the rules of construction of statutes established in our law and by reference to which Parliament legislates. The court will, therefore, construe the primary legislation in that way. The court may have regard to a relevant treaty obligation in that process of construction. Thereafter, the court must apply the law of this country in deciding whether the act of the minister under the legislation is lawful or not. The court cannot, said counsel for the Secretary of State, decide whether an act of the minister, which is lawfully within the power given by Parliament, is a breach of the obligation of the United Kingdom under the convention.

* * *

McCOWAN LJ. Counsel for the applicants argued before this court that recourse to art 10 of the European Convention on Human Rights ... can be had because there is an ambiguity in the language of the relevant statutory provision, s 29(3) of the Broadcasting Act 1981....

* * *

... I am unpersuaded by counsel for the applicants that there is any ambiguity in the language of s 29(3). It follows, in my judgment, that art 10 of the European Convention on Human Rights has no part to play in the determination of this case. It is to be noted that the Divisional Court, which thought otherwise, having looked at art 10, did not find that it assisted the applicants' case.

* * *

Now to a final and rather curious situation which also raised questions of the sovereignty of Parliament. The English Parliament is sovereign in England, Wales, Northern Ireland and, one would think, also in Scotland. But this last was challenged in the well known Royal Numerals case, *MacCormick v. Lord Advocate.*[8] Queen Elizabeth I was the first queen in England to use that name. But she was not Queen of Scotland—she reigned before the Treaty of Union between England and Scotland was signed in 1707. When Queen Elizabeth in 1952 ascended to the throne and assumed the title Queen Elizabeth II, use of the II was disputed because there had never been a Queen Elizabeth I for Scotland. The use of II was authorized by the Royal Titles Act of 1953. Was it in conflict with the Treaty of Union which declared that any law which was inconsistent with the terms of the Treaty was void? That included any subsequent acts of the Parliaments of England and Scotland. Did the Treaty possess some special status as an act so important that it was not subject to later alteration by Parliament? The case was before the Court of Session in Edinburgh. But it did not have to answer the question. The petitioner was found to have no standing to sue. The court did suggest, however, that the Treaty did not forbid the use of the numeral, and that had the 1953 Act been inconsistent with the Treaty, then the later Act would not have been effective unless approved in Scotland. Some questions were left unanswered. Who would speak for the people of Scotland? All of the people through a vote? There was no experience for that form of inquiry. No other challenges have ever been forthcoming. It may be that the European Commission on Human Rights would be the body to give advice on the issue. However uncertain the issue remains, it seems that Parliament is sovereign in the United Kingdom, with an asterisk needed next to the name of Scotland.

Questions and Notes

1. Would it violate your notions of separation of powers to have the President and the cabinet appear one day each month in a joint session of Congress to answer questions from members of Congress—a parallel to the practice in England and many other nations? What effect on the passage of laws might such a practice have?

2. When Lord Denning suggests English courts should have the right to overrule statutes, is he correctly interpreting the United States Constitution when he notes the Supreme Court will overrule a statute if it "is against right and reason or repugnant to the Constitution"?

3. Were the United States to join the European Community, how different from that in England would the entry process be with regard to the role of the executive, legislative and judicial institutions? Assuming United States membership in the EC, what would be the effect of an act passed by

8. 1953 S.C. 396.

Congress which did not specifically withdraw the United States from the EC, but which was clearly in conflict with provisions of the Rome Treaty?

4.   Has the European Court at Strasbourg become a quasi-constitutional court for England?   Where would you place it in the judicial hierarchy?

5.   Fine minds have long debated the extent of the authority of the English Parliament.   Do you agree that the *only* thing Parliament cannot do is act so as to bind itself in the future?   Isn't the sovereignty of Parliament limited by the affirmative actions it has taken subsequent to decisions of the European Court at Strasbourg?   Could the United States Congress bind itself in the future?   Why does the issue appear more important in the English legal system?

SECTION 3.   THE JUDICIAL STRUCTURE

When courts of a system are studied, the tendency is to focus upon the traditional or regular courts of law where criminal or civil proceedings occur.   Special courts and tribunals or administrative hearing bodies receive comparatively scant attention.   In common law systems, where the judicial process leads to the event of a trial, this emphasis is even stronger because people attend the more spectacular of these events much as they might attend a play or the cinema.   The tradition of the English courts—with robed and wigged participants—exaggerates this focus.   But were one to make inquiry into where the largest number of decisions are made regarding peoples' everyday lives, then the administrative tribunals assume their proper importance.   They are less incidents of the development of the common law, than the development of advanced societies with complex governmental structures.   The civil law nations in Europe reflect a parallel development in the use of administrative tribunals.   We nevertheless are drawn to the ordinary courts to outline the way in which disputes are resolved.   They may be undergoing a process of chipping away at their jurisdiction.   But they are where most major civil and criminal events continue to be resolved.

Our interest in the courts of England will focus on several issues. Some outline of the ordinary courts is necessary to illustrate how England has structured these courts over the years.   As the chapter on history has suggested, they are very much a product of sequential events since the Norman Conquest.   They have changed very slowly; we might expect, therefore, that many of their characteristics reflect historic moments in developments which have flowed from the currents of the times.

The English court system evolved from just such currents—the desire of the king to hear matters of importance to the crown, and the concern of the barons that they consequently would lose both power and revenue by such a transfer to the developing central courts.   The English courts evolved through the centuries to serve perceived needs, at least those perceived by persons in authority.   In the late 19th century, the system was refined by the Supreme Court of Judicature Acts 1873.

Nearly a century later some modest restructuring occurred with the passage of the Courts Act 1971.

The courts nevertheless have continued to retain characteristics associated with the structures formed during the three centuries following the Norman Conquest. The system, despite its erosion by the creation of hundreds of tribunals, remains essentially unitary. All courts, both civil and criminal, lead to the Court of Appeal and the House of Lords. That actually applies to most administrative tribunals as well. The English system, more than other common law systems, preserves rather extensive appeal rights for those whose initial trials or hearings were before administrative tribunals. It should be noted, and continually reemphasized, that although there has been an erosion in the use of the regular or ordinary courts, considering the nature of hearings before administrative tribunals, there is a reasonably clear distinction between subject matter. The ordinary courts remain the dominant dispute resolving fora for conflicts between private citizens. The extensive number of administrative tribunals largely hear what we would call public law with more comfort were we civil law trained. They are matters between the private citizen and some governmental body.

It is less than a century ago that Dicey made his controversial and much criticized claim that there was no difference between public and private law in England.[9] Nor did England possess an equivalent to the French *droit administratif*. Certainly there has never been an attempt to systematically allocate matters between public and private law. Lacking a constitutional document which either reaffirms the Dicey view, or defines public and private law, the door has been open for the development of the public-private dichotomy. There now exists in England what one might well label a *droit administratif*. But it is not separate to the extent it is in France. France has long had special courts for public law matters. And not only the courts of first instance, but a full hierarchy ascending to the *conseil d'état*. The unitary nature of the English system causes public law matters to be fed into the High Court. Concerned with the proliferation of special tribunals and their separation from the traditional judicial process, the government has appointed special commissions to review this conflict. The Franks Committee report in 1957, the most extensive recent review, led to the Tribunal and Inquiries Act 1958, which permitted judicial review by the law courts of decisions of a number of tribunals. But many decisions remain outside the regular court system. The permitted review is not without some cost, often involving an extensive and expensive delay in the establishment of government promoted services. But the involvement of the ordinary legal process through judicial review remains to many the only adequate way to protect the rights of individuals affected by the actions of the government. It also assures the barristers of retaining some participation in the resolution of public issues. As public law has increased its reach into the lives of citizens, the solicitors have furthered

9. A.V. Dicey, Law of the Constitution 183 (4th ed 1893).

their role as advocates. It is one thing to be kept out of the regular courts—it is another to shift subject matter jurisdiction away from the regular courts to ones which admit solicitors as advocates.

In viewing the High Court, one may ask if law and equity have really been fused. A similar question arises if inquiry is made into the role of Lincoln's Inn as a chancery inn, in contrast to the type of practice barristers pursue who have chambers in Gray's, Middle Temple or Inner Temple. But law and equity have been brought together, if not institutionally and perceptually fused. The fusion is better viewed as one stage of many movements, together and apart, of characteristics of the system and occurring over the centuries. The above mentioned development of an English public law is an example of some judicial separation. The same is true of the impact of the entry of England to the European Communities. The European Court of Justice is the court of last resort on issues of Community law.

Ordinary courts in England most generally are classified as superior or inferior. Inferior courts, the jurisdiction of which is limited both geographically and according to the nature of subject matter, include those civil and criminal courts which decide the vast majority of disputes, the county and magistrates' courts, respectively. Superior court jurisdiction is limited neither geographically nor by value, and exists in the Crown Court, High Court, Court of Appeal and House of Lords. The most important special courts include the Judicial Committee of the Privy Council and Restrictive Practices Court.

The structures and jurisdiction of the English court system are less surprising to an American observer than several particular characteristics, such as the extensive use of lay judges for minor criminal matters in magistrates' courts, the more active participation of judges in court proceedings, the comparative minor use of juries in civil trials, the less adversary nature of proceedings, and the colorful ceremonial trappings of court dress.

The following two charts show the system of English courts which, in figure one, depict civil jurisdiction, and in figure two, criminal jurisdiction. The unitary nature of the courts should be evident. There may be divisions to deal with criminal matters, but they are divisions of an integrated court system. Apart from the separate magistrates' courts and crown courts for criminal matters, and the county courts for civil matters, the depictions are exclusively of the High Court, the Court of Appeal and the House of Lords. If we were to outline the entire English system of courts and tribunals, these charts would be vastly extended. But the Court of Appeal and House of Lords would continue to appear at the top as the harbors of jurisdiction for appeals from a good many of the special courts and tribunals.

R.M. JACKSON, "JACKSON'S MACHINERY OF JUSTICE"

39 (8th ed. 1989).*

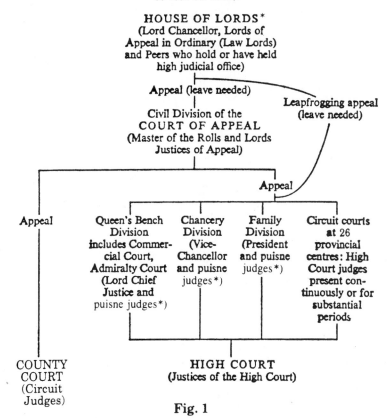

Fig. 1

* Judges other than the heads of divisions are referred to as puisne judges.

* Reprinted here and below with permission of Cambridge University Press and   R.M. Jackson.

R.M. JACKSON, "JACKSON'S MACHINERY OF JUSTICE"

211 (8th ed. 1989).

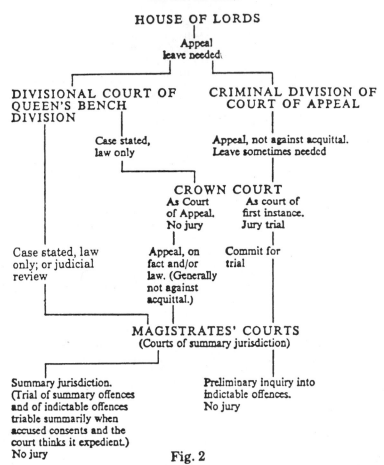

Fig. 2

A. COUNTY COURTS

County courts resolve comparatively minor civil matters. A county court is the forum in which the English citizen is most likely to appear in civil litigation. Arranged in districts, they convene as courts of first instance with appeals directly to the Court of Appeal for most issues, but to a divisional court of the Chancery Division of the High Court for matters of bankruptcy.

The shire and hundreds courts, which developed before the Conquest and which largely had declined or perished for lack of use by the Middle Ages, were the historical predecessors of the county courts. The modern county court traces its origins to the County Court Act 1846, and notably differs from the superior courts by dispersions into every corner of England and Wales, thus providing a local forum for civil disputes. The County Court Act 1959, broadened the jurisdiction of these courts, extending it beyond simple matters of contract and tort to probate of small estates, equity jurisdiction and, in some courts, limited admiralty matters and undefended divorces. The county courts are also assigned jurisdiction of some social legislation, but a large amount is confined to special tribunals.

Procedure in the county courts is simplified in contrast to the High Court, and costs are lower. The county court judges are professional judges; they are experienced barristers appointed in the same manner as to the superior courts, by the sovereign at the recommendation of the Lord Chancellor. Assisting these courts is a Registrar, a solicitor who serves as administrative chief of the court, who has authority to hear and decide both pre-trial motions and small claims. The Registrar actually is a second judge for minor cases. Solicitors as well as barristers may appear as advocates before the county courts, an intrusion by the former into the usually well preserved barristers' domain.

The county court is a familiar court to an American observer. With its comparative informality, its single professional judge, and its broad jurisdiction over less complex civil disputes involving modest sums, the county court serves as the most important adjudicatory body for private, civil matters throughout England and Wales.

B. MAGISTRATES' COURTS

If the structure and function of the county courts appear to differ little from methods of resolving comparatively minor civil matters in many common law systems, the structure of the magistrates' courts may seem most unique. Established throughout England and Wales, magistrates' courts primarily are staffed by ordinary but carefully chosen citizens. Part-time lay members sit in collegiate form without a jury to resolve in summary form the great bulk of minor criminal charges. Three magistrates usually sit, choosing their own chairman.

The use of lay as opposed to professional judges for less serious criminal matters has strong historical roots. The return of English soldiers nourished with plundering from the continental wars and the Crusades, and the loss of as much as one-half of the population from the Black Death, encouraged government control of both wages and the free movement of persons. A few of the most influential persons in each community were appointed to keep the peace under the Justices of the Peace Act 1361. Now nearly twenty thousand justices, or magistrates, serve throughout England and Wales. Appointed by the Lord Chancellor from nominations of local commissions, the magistrates accept office as a public duty, for the prestige of being a part of the judicial system and being permitted to append to their names the initials J.P. They were compensated in earlier years, but the remuneration has been abolished. The lay magistrates are assisted by a law trained clerk, in larger cities a full-time position, but in smaller towns a part-time local solicitor. The clerk advises on procedural and substantive issues, but at the magistrates' request may participate in the discussion leading to judgment.

Magistrates are often referred to as "the great unpaid," or by critics as "the great unlearned," an opprobrium which applies only to the lay magistrates. In the larger cities, full-time, salaried, law trained stipendiary magistrates sit in the magistrates' courts. The stipendiary magistrates, who are usually solicitors, sit not in collegiate form, but alone.

Criminal jurisdiction is the paramount role of the magistrates' courts in the system of English justice. Summary offenses, those generally of a minor character, are tried without a jury. The benefit is speed and the low cost of appearance, in contrast to a proceeding before the Crown Court. The disadvantage is a highly probable conviction. A large percentage of magistrates' cases are violations of the road traffic acts and regulations, although most persons so charged plead guilty and submit by mail specified fines without a personal court appearance. Certain indictable offenses may be tried before a magistrates' court, but the more serious are tried in the Crown Court.

The magistrates' court plays an important role involving young persons. When the court convenes to hear juvenile offenses, it assumes a status separate from the criminal environment of magistrates' court proceedings. The juvenile proceeding is closed to the public, press coverage is limited and at least one of the required three lay justices must be female. This special status carries through to any issue requiring detention, which usually will be in a community home rather than confinement with adult offenders.

Jurisdiction of the magistrates' courts extends beyond its principal criminal law responsibility to include minor civil issues involving the collection of specific debts, such as national insurance contributions and utility charges, licensing matters, and some juvenile and domestic issues.

The magistrate system involves an extraordinary use of lay persons to adjudicate the vast majority of minor offenses committed within a community. It has no significant parallel in the United States, but rather is more closely identified with various comrades' courts in socialist law systems, although it lacks the political function of such tribunals.

The magistrates' courts render their justice in an informal setting. That setting is described below.

MICHAEL W. GORDON, AN AMERICAN IN BOW STREET

140 New Law Journal 437 (1990) *

Brian Hilliard suggested in "Brooklyn Justice" (*New Law Journal*, September 22, 1989, p 1272), that one must "look long and hard to be satisfied" that justice had been done in the Brooklyn court he visited. In the magistrates' court at Bow Street in London, to view justice one must watch carefully and not blink.

Courtroom # 2 at Bow Street is not unlike the maze at Hampton Court Palace. It is challenging to pass through unscathed, and when one does exit, it is difficult to relate exactly what occurred. The Bow

* Reprinted with permission of Butterworth & Co. (Publishers) Ltd.

Street courtroom is a grouping of numerous oak compartments with little doors. Each compartment has a very specific purpose—the judicial contribution to keeping England tidy. One is labelled "counsel", another "solicitors." Counsel's is raised slightly, closer to the judge, and further from the accused, than that for solicitors. England's split profession is partly sustained by some good English oak. But there are termites in that oak, bringing down the barriers between barristers and solicitors. That is another story, however, told episodically in living colour, by way of green papers and white papers and responses from red faced barristers.

Other compartments in the courtroom are for the inspector, the probation officer, and the usher.

10:30. The session begins. The clerk sits below the elevated bench. An ominous green, iron-frame, waist-high cage faces the bench. It is the dock, placing the accused on centre stage. I sit on a bench which holds about a dozen people. Another two dozen stand behind us. The usher commands all to rise as Judge Jeremy Connor enters and sits. By the time the public realises they may sit the first case is over. The accused had entered the dock, pleaded guilty and become £25 poorer.

10:32. Michael Kubie is in the dock. He is asked whether he wants to see the evidence against him. Kubie stammers "yes", uncertain what it means. He is given a file and steps down to read it.

10:33. Mario Mitkova, a Yugoslav, grasps the green rail and expresses his lack of understanding of the proceedings. He is charged with stealing three cassettes. Mitkova speaks halting English. He pleads guilty. Mr. Connor asks him why he had taken them. Mitkova stammers that he intended to buy them but realised he had not paid after leaving the store (the realisation was probably strongest after he was apprehended).

"Were you dishonest?" asks the judge.

"No," responds Mitkova. Connor sets the trial for five weeks later and Mitkova leaves the courtroom. Three minutes have passed. It would have been four had the clerk suggested to him that he had a choice of being tried before the Crown Court. In most cases the clerk raced through her monologue about the accused's right to decide whether to be tried before the magistrates' court or the Crown Court; if the former and the person is found guilty, believing the sanctions of the magistrates' court to be too lenient, the magistrate could refer the matter to the Crown Court for sentencing. "I sentence you to be sentenced by the Crown Court." It sounds like double jeopardy. If the crime tried in the magistrates' court merits punishment beyond what that court may impose, it would seem appropriate to extend that court's sanctions, at least for stipendiary magistrates.

10:36. George Watson has spent the weekend in jail after being found drunk. In two minutes time he pleads not guilty and trial is set.

10:38. Another drunkenness charge, against Peter Wilesworth. He pleads guilty and the clerk notes a previous conviction barely a week earlier on the same charge, plus assaulting a police constable. That had been worth £81 and the new charge brings 40. He saved 41 by not swinging this time.

10:39. Robert Law. Obstructing the police. He quickly pleads guilty. His file is momentarily misplaced. £50 and out.

10:50. George Smith is in the dock for less than a minute and leaves £40 poorer, with permission to pay in three weeks.

10:51. David Benn is charged with playing a musical instrument in the underground at Piccadilly.

"Have you done this before?" asks Mr. Connor.

"Yes, about £12 worth on an earlier charge," replies Benn.

"Forty-five pounds." He pays four, the rest by Saturday.

Benn leaves to return to the underground to resume earning his living. Part of the four pounds he pays may have come from me. I always give some change to subway musicians. Benn's case consumes just one minute.

10:52. Two dishevelled men are led in, adding to the courtroom a new odour. They had been holding up traffic and insulting people in Covent Garden. £50.

10:54. A young man had ridden the underground without paying.

"Why did you do this?" queries the judge.

"I must have dropped my ticket," replies the accused.

"Guilty or not guilty?" asks the clerk.

"Not guilty," responds Mr. Connor, who sets the trial for Saturday, five days later.

He is led out of the dock asking the usher "What happened—what did they do to me?" Exactly one minute has passed, a truly blank period in his life. He leaves the court in a daze, told to return Saturday.

10:55. The next accused has been fined £20 by the time I look up again. He had failed to pay £70 of a previous £90 fine. Requesting payment at £5 a week, the magistrate gives him 14 days to pay the total.

10:57. Oliver Sharkey and Dennis Turner. "Obstructing the highway", a charge that I would hear frequently. Were these pedestrians who did not cross the street quickly enough? Or drunks stopping cars? Neither. They were minor merchants, selling trinkets on the sidewalk. With the underground musicians, these cases comprise a kind of "commercial division" of the magistrates' court. The trend is more encouraging than the cases I had heard in the same court 16 years earlier, when drunkenness, importuning and prostitution dominated.

One trader pleads guilty and parts with £40, 20 on the spot and 20 by Saturday, after he has had time to sell some more trinkets. The other pleads not guilty.

11:01. Lisa Ann Bonner is called. The woman next to me rises and steps to the dock. The usher escorts another from the holding room. She is Anne Conner. There is confusion but it is Anne Conner's turn. Time passes. Jeremy Connor asks, "What's this case about in a handful of words?" It is misuse of a credit card by a young visiting Nigerian.

"Is she a woman of good character?" asks the magistrate. Sureties are ordered to assure her return.

11:05. Lisa Ann Bonner returns; highway obstruction again. She had pleaded not guilty but never returned for the trial on a similar charge four months earlier.

"Why didn't you return," asks the clerk.

"I don't remember not returning."

Jeremy Connor notes, "You must have known you had to come back. What was your excuse?" Before she can reply he adds, "Not guilty to the failure to appear." The clerk orders, "Stand down."

Bonner leaves the dock with a confused look on her face, stands for a moment as though waiting to see if anyone is going to give her some instructions, shrugs her shoulders and walks out. Would she forget to return again?

11:08. A non-appearance is set over to 2:00 at the request of a solicitor.

11:08. Charges of assaulting a police constable and abusive and threatening conduct. Not guilty to both. Three previous offences are noted and trial is set for early January.

11:10. William McCall in the dock. Needs advice. Postponed.

11:12. The magistrate orders the arrest of two who have not appeared.

11:20. Sheridan Lee. How much can he pay? When? He is out of the dock before I can tell what he is charged with.

11:24. Ed Wade, case No 41, wants to know why he didn't go before case No 43. Judge Connor replies, "We jump all around." Wade was on the railway without paying. He pleads guilty. The clerk inquires, "Why didn't you have a ticket?" "I had a round trip ticket. I lost the return part but I was going to pay."

The judge asks, "You are saying you were not guilty. Were you intending to be dishonest?" "No." "Then you are pleading not guilty." "No, guilty." responds Wade. "Seventy-five pounds. 14 days to pay." concludes Jeremy Connor.

11:26. Michael Kubie by now has seen the evidence against him. He asks for a delay. Granted.

11:27. Peter Wilkenson and Richard McCarthy plead guilty. Fined.

11:27. David Johnson arrives late, apologises and faces his charge of trading without a license, another method to discourage street traders.

Clerk, "You were here before?" "Yes." A frequent response to this question. "Forty-five pounds," says Jeremy Connor.

11:28. Anspar Ahmed pleads guilty to obstructing the highway and sacrifices a modest £10.

An hour in Courtroom No 2 has passed. Nothing of a serious nature has been before the court. Few questions are asked as to why the acts were done. No educational role of the court. An enormous waste of national funds. Each of the charges could have been more efficiently dealt with by paying by post, as in the case of many traffic offences.

Few of the defendants were aware of the procedure they were facing. There was no time for learning. Henry Ford would have been proud of the assembly line process adopted by the magistrates' court. Not one drunk charged left with an admonition not to drink again, nor a reference to alcohol abuse treatment. Not one person riding public transportation without paying was told that his actions increased the costs for others. Not one merchant charged with highway obstruction or selling without a licence was informed of the licensing process or advised of the safety problems of blocking pedestrians.

Jeremy Connor was invariably polite, never showing frustration. British decorum was maintained. The process apparently satisfied the judge, the clerk, the Crown prosecutors, the usher, and the probation officer. It undoubtedly had very little effect on any one or more of those accused. The drunks were probably back drinking, the merchants spreading their wares on the sidewalks of Covent Garden, and the others returning home on free rides on the underground.

If justice was seen to have been done, it was seen only by those who had administered it, not by those who had stood nervously in the dock for their allotted minute or two. Little different than the Brooklyn court observed by Brian Hilliard, this Bow Street court had not altered the lives of those charged in any real way. Both courts offered illustrations of cultural attributes of their respective systems of justice. Neither offered much more.

SYBILLE BEDFORD, "THE FACES OF JUSTICE"
33–57, 86–92 (1961).*

The magistrates, professional and lay, dispense instantaneous justice every working morning of the year. Summary, in half the cases, means dispatch from charge to sentence in one breath. People are brought into the dock still steaming with their deeds. Not here, the well-rounded lawyers' contest, the fine-culled point, the slanted pleadings—these courts are in the market place.

* Reprinted here and below with permission of Sybille Bedford, author of The Faces   of Justice, A Traveller's Report, Simon & Schuster, N.Y.

Put your hand in a pocket, strike a blow, snatch the orange, smile at the stranger, curse the cabby, cry your odds, and the law has swooped and has you by the scruff and in you go before the bench with your shopping bag, your load of beer, your evening clothes. . . .

"This is number one sir, Patrick O'Connor."

"Patrick O'Connor, you are charged with being drunk in the street. Do you plead guilty or not guilty?"

"Guilty."

"This was at ten forty-five P.M. yesterday your Worship, in the North Elms Road."

"Any trouble?"

"No trouble."

"Pay ten shillings."

"This way. *This* way."

"This is number two sir, Joseph Andrew White."

Quick as small-arms fire. Burst cracks on burst from floor to bench to box, from box to bench to dock.

* * *

All of this has reeled by as fast as print. The dovetailed entrances and exits, the sustained antiphonal flow, the quick probe from the chair, the hint of cadenza, the conclusive click—ten cases, a dozen cases, twenty cases put up, put through their paces, judged and gone, and it is hardly more than a quarter of an hour since court has opened. Each man at his post on his toes, and each man with what he must contribute on his file, his ledger, his notebook, on his clipboard, on the tip of his tongue, and all the time the man in the chair must have his hand on the reins and his mind on every word, on every move, on every point. He is also usually engaged in writing.

* * *

There are eleven of these courts in London alone. Doing this kind of work, sitting—without a break—every day of the year except Sundays and the four Bank Holidays, trying to catch up, trying to get through their lists. The lists are always full. At Lambeth, at Clerkenwell, at Shoreditch and Soho and Fulham and Marylebone, at Tower Bridge, the same daily teamwork, the same processions rounded through the docks, the wheels grinding small and quick.

* * *

Each metropolitan magistrate's court, police court it used to be called, has two full-time (stipendiary) magistrates who sit alternately. Except Bow Street, which has four. Bow Street and Great Marlborough Street, the most metropolitan of the courts, London definitely, not London area, are to the magistrature what Paris and Washington are to the diplomatic service. Stipendiaries, unlike the lay justices who sit on most of the country benches and who sit perhaps once a fortnight each, are professionals. ... Also, unlike the lay J.P.s who must be at least a pair, one single stipendiary forms a court, that is, he may try cases without additional members on the bench; in fact he is the bench. The appointment is for life, or rather until retirement age. ...

Men come to the magisterial bench when they are between forty and fifty, and they stay there. To turn back, to go back to the bar, is not practicable; no magistrate so far has been made a High Court judge. A dead-end job then, and one must feel that this should not be so. There is a point when experience becomes self-defeating. That particular compound of pace and pressure and importance and triviality must be fraying or blunting as the years go by. Think of dealing every morning of your life with all those men and women in what to them is an hour of great fear—the responsibility: five seconds' inattention may work an injustice. The helplessness: you don't make the laws, you can't change the people. The repetition!

Each court has a different tone. Some magistrates run theirs like a High Court, some like a regiment. Some pride themselves on their good manners; some maintain an exceptionally cordial relationship with the police. Two or three think and speak like lawyers; the rest are also lawyers, but turned schoolmasters, civil servants or committeemen. At one London court the senior magistrate is a woman. The repertoire, on the other hand, is determined by the neighbourhood. In certain districts the breaches of the peace mainly take place at home—assault, blows between men and wives, mothers and sons, lodger trouble; in others, the emphasis is on the street—betting, soliciting, obstruction, that new bugbear, whether by costermonger's barrow or by motor car. The traipse of morning-after drunks is ubiquitous, but in the West End used to be outnumbered by prostitutes six to one.

* * *

Magistrates' courts have another side which in London comes into its own in the early afternoon. People appear to answer charges brought against them by their neighbours, to discuss their means or to be reconciled to their wives. Although the magistrates cannot grant a divorce, their matrimonial jurisdiction covers a good deal of the remaining ground. They have power to make out separation and noncohabitation orders, maintenance orders and affiliation orders, that is power to compel a man to support his wife, his children and his bastards. They can override a parent's refusal to allow a minor child to marry, and they preside at proceedings known as matrimonials.

Matrimonials are held in closed court with the gallery seats cleared and the press forbidden to report; most people would still call them public. There are present, besides the magistrate, the contending couple and the clerk, half a dozen policemen in their various functions, possibly some social worker or law student, a probation officer and an usher. No disclosures are barred.

"He's been sleeping in the garage for the last fortnight," the wife says from the witness box.

"Only because *she's* been so nervous—"

The magistrate is not trying so much to apportion who was right or wrong but to sort the general situation and find out what the parties really want and whether what they want may still be feasible. He will say, and not for the first time, "Will you be silent, Mr Jones. You will be able to tell your story presently. First we hear one side, then we hear the other, as it has gone on for fifteen hundred years."

* * *

"*Arrears* of eight pounds, fifteen shillings, sir, from an order of ten shillings a week for the wife and fifteen shillings for a child made in 1948."

This order is a maintenance order, and this is how it comes into being. A man goes off; the wife applies to the court, the court summons the husband, tries to find out about his earnings and general circumstances, then makes out an order to pay so and so much a week to the wife, so much for each child. (If the man chose not to turn up, it would amount to contempt of court and a warrant of arrest might be made out eventually. He could try to disappear. It is no longer easy.) The money must be paid weekly into court; the women come and call for it at the pay office. No order is immutable. The man may come to earn less, a child grow to need more, grow up; the wife may marry again. Either party can apply for a change of order. On the other hand a day may come when the man hasn't paid because he won't or can't, and he is summoned for what is called arrears.

In a lounge suit, folded overcoat on his arm, he stands before the bar—*outside* the dock—and says he is a man's hairdresser's assistant and business has been bad.

"??"

"Well, sir, for us it was. People want less haircuts in the cold weather." Now things are looking up again. How long does he think it will take him to catch up? He could, he says, he's sure, manage another pound a week above the usual.

"Adjourned for four weeks: pay or appear." The magistrate marks his register. "You understand, Mr Roberts, if you pay regularly every week, you need not come. [Touch of bonhommie: Mr Roberts is one of the rarer birds] We don't want to see *you*, we want to see your money." Brief smile; dismissal.

Next a workingman in working clothes. "Arrears for twenty-three pounds, seven shillings and sixpence, sir, from an order of seven shillings, sixpence for the wife and ten shillings for a child in 1958."

"Is that correct, Mr Thompson?"

"I don't think that it is."

The magistrate is not having any. "Very well. Then please go outside to the accounts office and see for yourself."

Time is filled by calling a Mr Hilbert....

* * *

Thompson is back and concedes the £23.7.6.

"Well, why haven't you paid?"

He's been out of a job.

"Come and tell us about it from the witness box."

Thompson is marched over and swears to tell the whole truth.

"You haven't paid for—twenty-three weeks I make it, is that right? Everybody seems to be better at figures than I am...."

"Twenty-three weeks, sir," says the clerk.

"Let me see, this order was made in 1958.... *You haven't paid anything at all?*"

No reaction.

"Out of a job all that time?"

"You know how it is, your Honour, the building trade—"

"May I see your yellow card?"

"What yellow card?"

"The card from the Labour Exchange, aren't you getting unemployment relief?"

[Tone of self-congratulation] "I've never been near the Labour Exchange in my life."

"What have you been living on?"

[Wooden-faced, yet smug] "My married daughter."

"How do you expect your wife and child to live?"

"There's plenty of ways."

"On National Assistance? At public expense?"

"There's others what do it."

"Thompson, I'm not going to waste any more time over you. Adjourned for two weeks: pay or serve warrant."

And if Thompson *will not* pay, the last answer is prison from where he *cannot* pay. It's our old friend, the deterrent: a gamble.

R. BLYTHE, "AKENFIELD"

Ch. 15 The Law 268 (1969).*

MRS. CHRISTIAN ANNERSLEY, aged fifty-five, MAGISTRATE and CHAIRMAN OF THE BENCH

I think that what I actually enjoy about the Bench is that it is simply endlessly interesting.... I often ask myself if I have a sense of power at this moment—does it give me this? I think it probably does. I think I am probably better than other people—then I know I'm not! ... And there is no doubt that today's magistrate is a far better person than his predecessor. He goes to conferences, he goes to prisons, reads the law and does try to find out. Whereas before it was simply Colonel Bloggs who prided himself on being just an ordinary decent chap, and all this implies. Rigidity. Ignorance. If I am going to send a country boy to an approved school I want to know what the school is like....

There are seven magistrates but we never sit more than five at a time.... We elect our own Chairman every three years, also our Deputy and the Chairman of the Juvenile Bench. Then there is the Licensing Committee; no magistrate who is in the brewery trade can sit on this. As I have said, we have always been upper class, which I think is a bad mistake. We did have a working-class magistrate years ago and he was always right. It was fascinating. We'd have this great strapping fellow come up, a horsecoper or something, and we'd all agree to fine him so much, when our working-class friend would add another £10. Then out would come a huge wadge of notes, fingers would be licked and ten of them would be peeled off. He always understood who could pay, who should be made to pay and how much.

In the village there was always the Bad Family. Every village had one and we knew them all. They came up over and over again, and we watched them going slowly, inevitably downhill. I remember one young man and his predestination as a Bad Family person seemed to shine out of him, so that he simply hadn't a chance. He deteriorated. He deteriorated and we watched. It was terrible really. I have remembered him all this time, one of the small percentage of people who go wrong and who will keep on going wrong whatever you do. It is a dreadful thing to say, but nothing can make any difference for some people. Since then, I have visited schools and borstals, prisons and hospitals, and there they are. One can pick them out. They are cursed in some way. Nobody knows what with really.... I don't think that these poor men feel cursed themselves; they just think that although they haven't managed to beat the law this time, they might the next. Hard to help—hard to reach. I think that they feel shame but I'm not really sure. Our village Bad Family—father and three grown-up sons—doesn't feel any shame I am sure. Their lives are a little war, winning and losing, mostly losing. When they lose it is simply, 'That bloody old policeman has got me again!' Our Bad Family isn't bad at all—just stupid. But they'd sooner be called bad than stupid.

* * *

I think that the relationship between the police and the Bench is very good, although they get a bit fed-up with us because we are so lenient. The police are, on the whole, straightforward and trying to do their best. Now and then you get a bad 'un, a type who must go too far. But when you consider how they are provoked, they are marvellous people. I think that the provocation of the police is too cruel for words. And the village policeman has a wretched time really. His loneliness is rarely understood.... I really don't know why any young countryman should choose the police force as a profession. It is a tedious, trying, unnaturally isolated job—and poorly paid.

* * *

An average day at our court isn't very spectacular. Four licensing extensions, three motor-car slight accidents with written-in pleas of Guilty—£5—£10—£20—£30 each and license endorsed. Then, the police having had their radar stationed at various points, you will have about ten cars doing between thirty and forty miles an hour. There is an automatic scale of fines for these offences. Then five bicycles with insufficient brakes or something. Then the young man who got drunk on Saturday and shouted you-know-what, or perhaps he hit somebody with a brick. Then you might have a defended case of dangerous driving, which will take time, or a bit of breaking-and-entering. We never have any of these dear young modern protestors—they don't come our way. We have to pass plans for all the pub alterations. No murders—I have never had a murder case in twenty-five years—and no poachers now. No lead-stealing from the church roof—that was the most popular crime in Suffolk just after the war. But there has been a great increase in stealing valuable things from inside the churches, and the thieves are rarely ever caught.

* * *

When we need a new magistrate on our Bench we ask for a specific person by name. A special committee chaired by the Lord Lieutenant considers our choice. This committee is made up of magistrates from all the Benches in the area but the actual membership is kept very secret. It meets twice a year, when various names are brought forward and approved. It is getting more and more political, but in Suffolk it is probably less political than anywhere else. We all feel very strongly about these political considerations and pressures and do our utmost to get a true cross-section of the social element in the local villages. We aren't succeeding but it remains our aim and object. It is still difficult to have a really working-class person because they can't get off work and also because one really does need to be fairly well educated to do the work. Of course, you get a lot of so-called educated middle-class folk who are frightfully stupid, so one can't generalize. One of the best magistrates in Suffolk is a railway porter....

It is getting harder and harder to get lay magistrates, especially now that they are wanting younger and younger people. Few young men can afford the time and young women have no one they can leave their children with for two or more whole days a month. And although travelling expenses are allowed, there are still a great number of people who simply couldn't afford to be a J.P. So the trend is towards more stipendiaries. All the same, people still like being magistrates—love it!

All of us worry about sentencing. It is our chief worry. We attend all kinds of courses and conferences to discuss it and how to achieve uniformity or something approaching it. When I first started, the basic rule was to find out a person's means and fine him accordingly. Was he married? What was his rent? How many children? We even did this with the bicycle-lamp cases! But now, with affluence, the whole picture has changed. When you can afford a car you can afford a uniform fine, this is what it amounts to. But disparity occurs all over Suffolk still, so justice certainly doesn't appear to have been done. I think that one can say that the problem is almost entirely confined to motoring offences. People remain puzzled by the seeming haphazards of sentencing, one Bench in the west obviously fierce, our Bench notoriously soft.... And now we've all got to get used to a new thing altogether—the suspended sentence.

We sit every fortnight but it is soon going to have to be every week. We used to get everything finished by lunch-time but now it takes all day, and yet we are a little backwater so far as Benches go. We know everybody and it can be a bit embarrassing when a personal friend comes up! Then you can either pretend it's all a great joke or you can sit back. Any magistrate can push his chair back if he doesn't want to sit on a case. We're rather a dull Bench really but people come to watch us and everything we say is lavishly reported in the local press. I must say that these reports are not very good. In fact, not at all good. They often get it all wrong and the cases, to my mind, are still too much part of amusement and entertainment....

* * *

After all these years I'm beginning to feel that I shan't be sorry to give it up, because there are so many things for which there is no answer. There are so many ways in which you know you're doing the wrong thing—because there is no right thing to do. You know at heart where prison is no answer, yet the man will be sent to prison. The prisons—I visit so many of them—are still way behind everything. And then there is this conflict of reform versus punishment. And I'm really honestly and truly, having been liberal and 'psychological' for all my life, coming to the conclusion that punishment is a good thing. That punishment really gets it off the chest of a great many people. They think, 'Well, I've paid!' If people can accept the fact that they have paid they can either go on being a happy criminal or they can stop being a criminal. So I don't think that punishment is a bad thing. I used to think it was, but I don't now. There now, after all my years as a reformer! It is rather a cleansing thing. Certain people are destroyed—

killed—by the present method. Justice is not done to these people. A very wrong result comes out....

And then there are the risks you take with human beings. There's a boy and you think, yes, he's exactly the right sort to send to a detention centre. Well, he may *not* be. It may do him good, it may leave him quite untouched, but—and this is more likely—it may do him great harm. You, sitting there on the country Bench, may in a word send this boy whom you have never seen before to complete destruction. This is what weighs on one's mind. I always come home frightfully worried and wretched if I've sent somebody to prison or to a detention centre. I am so moved by the plight of many of the people who come up, but I'm harder than I used to be. The truth of the matter is that most of the people who come up at a court like ours don't come from 'bad backgrounds'. Most of the boys in borstals are from bad backgrounds— town and city backgrounds usually. Only two per cent of the borstal inmates are village boys. This fact tells one something.

————

With the lay magistrates in a place of importance—both as to location and authority—a conflict arose between the magistrates with their significant power, but limited legal knowledge, and the clerks with their lesser authority, but greater legal knowledge. When there is an issue of law the magistrates ordinarily will ask the clerk for an opinion. But the *decision* has for decades been thought to be within the province of the magistrates alone. The clerk may only retire with the magistrates if invited. Two decades later the view had altered considerably. Magistrates never made their decisions alone and the law was changing to reflect the necessary role of the clerk. The view the decision should not be that of the justices and their clerk, but that of the justices alone, was overturned. First the notion of the role of the clerk as severely limited was eroded by suggesting that legislation had become more complex and the magistrates should not be discouraged from seeking the help of the clerk on law and practice issues.[10] Later, when a magistrates' bench overruled their clerk's opinion as to the endorsement of a defendant's driving license, the court stated that the justices *must* accept the advice of the clerk in such instances.[11] The Magistrates' Association now recommends to its members that in all but the most routine cases, the clerk should be consulted before the verdict and sentencing.

Questions and Notes

1. Could the magistrates' system function in the United States? Should they be paid? Would the appellation J.P. or some alternative mean as much to persons in the United States as it does in England?

2. Why should the system use paid (stipendiary) magistrates in the cities? They are former barristers or solicitors. Does that provide a dual

10. R. v. Southhampton Justices ex parte Atherton [1974] Crim.L.R. 108.

11. Jones v. Nicks [1977] R.T.R. 72.

system with different procedures and results? The role of the law clerk would seem much less important where there is a stipendiary magistrate. From the viewpoint of the clerk, would not a position with a lay magistrates' court offer greater prestige, power and challenges? Does that not suggest a very different system of justice in cities and rural areas?

3. Are there offsetting benefits to the lack of professional judges on the magistrates' court? Consider that the court is perhaps not so much changed as rearranged. The clerk sits below the bench, but is asked for advice on issues of law. The magistrates sit elevated in the rear center and make factual determinations and rulings on the law, but usually make the latter with the advice of the clerk. What if we moved the clerk onto the bench and placed the magistrates in a box off to the right? Are we not then really in the same form as many courts in the United States? Perhaps we should give more consideration to how courtrooms are arranged than we do. Where do the people making legal and factual determinations sit? How do they appear to the accused? Who should wear the robes and wigs?

4. Is it fair to suggest that a benefit of the lay magistrates' court is that most judges who would serve for very long periods of time on that level bench would not be very good judges? Should we be using highly trained persons for more complex (not necessarily important) judicial work? Or is it appropriate to keep the existing system in the United States since we have so many law graduates? Perhaps we should even have three professional judges on the bench—would you agree?

5. Is it possible for consistent justice throughout the nation to be achieved with lay magistrates? If not would there be any more or less consistency than with single professional judges?

6. There has been some movement in England towards closing magistrates' courts (which usually meet only once every two weeks) and having the matters heard in similar courts in the nearest larger community. Does this diminish any of the benefits of the system?

7. Dawson suggests that "the English respect for law is still partly due to the important share that laymen still have in administering it." J. Dawson, A History of Lay Judges 145 (1960). Does this seem plausible? Another related question is: are we adequately using in our legal system the vast human resources which the lay public constitutes?

8. Being judged by one's peers seems to be part of the historical constitutional fabric of the common law. Is it not therefore more appropriate to use lay judges in common law systems than in civil law systems?

9. How do you react to Mrs. Annersley's feeling that there are "bad families" about which nothing can be done?

10. Does the legal process before a stipendiary magistrate in Bedford's *Faces of Justice* appear similar to what you have viewed in United States courts, or how you think the process should function if you have not viewed such proceedings? If it differs, which system would you prefer to face on a charge of drunken behavior, or petty theft, or any other summary (misdemeanor) offense?

11. How extensive a jurisdiction would you entrust to lay magistrates? Juvenile matters? Family issues such as post-divorce matters (non-payment

of alimony or child support, etc.)? Could they also deal as effectively with civil issues of relatively minor amount, thus relieving some of the burden on the county courts?

12. How much additional role should the magistrates' clerk have? Should he have the sole authority to rule on the admissibility of evidence? Should he be able to sum up the defendant's points of law? At what point would we then have him exchange places with the magistrates, and place them to the side in a jury box?

C. THE HIGH COURT

When we speak of the Royal Courts of Justice, usually we mean the High Court and the Court of Appeal, housed in an imposing building on the Strand in London. The Supreme Court of Judicature Acts 1873, created the High Court by bringing together the courts of civil jurisdiction which had been formed shortly after the Conquest. The High Court was constituted in five divisions—Chancery; Probate, Divorce and Admiralty ("wills, wives and wrecks"); Queen's Bench; Common Pleas and Exchequer. Common Pleas and Exchequer were merged into the Queen's Bench Division in 1880. The Courts Act 1971, abolished the Probate, Divorce and Admiralty Division, dividing its responsibilities among Queen's Bench, Chancery and a newly created Family Division.

This divisional structure is partially illusory. Each of the three divisions theoretically has equal jurisdictional competency, although the Rules of the Supreme Court express an allocation of matters to separate divisions. Matrimonial cases in the High Court are heard in the Family Division, and Chancery is assigned numerous matters which have a traditional equity nature. A High Court judge assigned to any division, nevertheless, may exercise jurisdiction over an issue which under the Rules of the Supreme Court technically is allocated to another division.

The Chancery Division, presided over by the Lord Chancellor, almost always sits in London. Chancery judges are not noted for travelling on circuit, although the Courts Act permits sessions of any division to be held anywhere in England or Wales. Chancery tends to concentrate on issues of an equitable nature earlier assigned to its predecessor, the Court of Chancery, including estate administration, trusts, mortgages, certain interests in land, partnership dissolution and bankruptcy of companies and some revenue matters. It has a limited appellate jurisdiction, allowing a single judge to hear appeals from the Commissioner of Inland Revenue, or two judges to sit for appeals of bankruptcy decisions from county courts. By far the most are revenue appeals.

The Family Division—a President is its chief judge—has original jurisdiction of matrimony, legitimacy, adoption, guardianship and various disputes between spouses. Its limited appellate jurisdiction involves guardianship, adoption, matrimonial and affiliation appeals from magistrates' and county courts.

The broadest civil jurisdiction, original and appellate, is assigned to the Queen's Bench Division. It also is given limited criminal appeals. The Queen's Bench broader jurisdiction, encompassing many contract and tort actions, is attributable to its being the successor to three of the original divisions of the early High Court—Queen's Bench, Common Pleas and Exchequer. Additionally, it is charged with admiralty jurisdiction, a unique function evolving from the transfer of admiralty issues from the former Probate, Divorce and Admiralty Division to Queen's Bench in the 1971 reform.

By far the largest number of cases before the High Court are heard in London. Although the widely dispersed county courts dispose of most minor civil matters, the more complex cases of higher value tend to be tried in London, much due to the concentration of barristers in London. But the High Court judges in the Queen's Bench Division do sit throughout the country, often hearing High Court cases on a circuit which has scheduled additionally the same judge to sit for criminal matters in local Crown Courts.

Civil appellate jurisdiction of the Queen's Bench is limited, involving a single judge deciding certain appeals from tribunals and from interlocutory orders of Queen's Bench Division masters. Two or more Queen's Bench Division judges may hear some civil appeals from magistrates' courts, or from the limited civil jurisdiction of the Crown Courts.

The Queen's Bench Division is the only division of the High Court with any criminal jurisdiction. Two or three judges may sit as an appellate court in limited appeals from the magistrates' courts or Crown Courts.

Complaints about the High Court are not dissimilar to complaints about the regular courts in many systems, not limited either to England or even common law systems as a group. They relate to costs, delay and procedures which are complex and perceived more as obstacles than as assistance in achieving a just result. But some of the concerns regarding the High Court relate to its structure and the residue of jurisdictional rivalries which began with the formation of the central courts not long after the conquest. There have been the two major court reforms noted above, but there has never been a reform based on the proposal that the whole court system should be arranged with one primary goal—to provide the best system of justice. There are too many obstacles for such a proposal to succeed. Too many vested interests, too much judicial infrastructure to alter, too much in cultural acceptance of the system as at least adequate. The legal institutions of a nation bear the scars of history. And also some gold stars and medals of achievement. Such characteristics should be even more apparent in England, where the courts have existed with tracings of the past for nearly a millenium. The following comments on the High Court are thus addressed to problems common to many systems, but the resolutions of which are burdened with incidents of history.

B. ABEL–SMITH AND R. STEVENS, "IN SEARCH OF JUSTICE"

64, 87, 21 (1968).*

Traditionally, the core of English justice is said to be a 'united' High Court based in London but serving the provinces with regular visits from itinerant judges. Quantitatively, however, this court is a very small part of the judicial system. Moreover, from the point of view of the litigant, the High Court appears united more in theory than in practice, organized as it is in separate divisions performing separate functions. Not knowing in what respects the High Court is the superior court, the citizen may well see it as just one of a confusing number of judicial bodies to which particular types of dispute must be taken. Each area has its magistrates' court, its county court and an array of separate specialized tribunals, such as the Rent Assessment committee. There is no one court which deals with all legal matters. As a result, the citizen often needs legal advice simply to discover which is the correct judicial body to which he should take his particular problem.

Lawyers regard the High Court as the core of the system because it handles the more serious criminal offences and civil cases involving the larger sums of money, and until recently it had exclusive control over such solemn matters as divorce. The desire to keep the superior courts for such limited matters, buttressed by the underlying assumption that the number of High Court judges should be kept small, has been one important reason for the steady proliferation of other judicial bodies and other methods for solving disputes which, in other countries, might be thought appropriate for the ordinary courts. . . .

* * *

There is such a danger that High Court hearings will be slow, inconvenient and expensive that potential litigants try to find ways of avoiding them. The unpleasantness of litigation encourages persons to settle their disputes if this is at all possible. (In some respects this may be good; but equally it may be harmful.) Businessmen also make extensive use of private arbitration to resolve their disagreements. Some arbitration procedures cover particular commodities or trades; others are established for general purposes by chambers of commerce in each locality. Thus arbitration tribunals provide provincial businessmen with 'courts' which can be convened whenever required and act as a substitute for provincial courts. While such arbitrations are sometimes as slow and expensive as the courts, businessmen normally find them psychologically preferable to court proceedings. The publicity and adversary mentality of the courtroom are absent; even the judge is generally 'one of us' and generally will sit at dates and times convenient to parties. In some cases a lawyer will act as sole arbitrator, in other cases a lawyer chairs a tribunal of local businessmen. Much more common, however, is a panel of laymen with expertise in the relevant field, an attribute which even High Court judges often lack.

* * *

The basis of the division of jurisdiction between the High Court and the County Court can be seriously questioned. At present the distinction rests primarily on how much money is in dispute. Historically, ... the whole development of the court structure has been strongly influenced by the desire to meet the needs of the poorer litigant for whom the High Court was intolerably expensive. If High Court litigation had been less expensive, all litigation might have been kept in a united High Court, which in turn might have developed branches sitting continuously in different parts of the country much earlier. The problem of the poorer litigant might then have been met by providing free or subsidized legal help on a large scale. Rather than contemplate this cost, the first response of Parliament over a century ago, not unnaturally in view of the social state of England, was to develop cheaper courts for those who could not afford to use the High Courts and for matters where the costs of the High Court would have made it uneconomic to take the matter to court—the county courts. Thus the principle was introduced that there should be two standards of justice—a higher and more costly standard when a relatively large sum of money was at stake and a lower and cheaper standard when a smaller sum of money was at stake.

Presumably the costly apparatus of the High Court is expected to increase the statistical chance of arriving at the truth. (At least this was the main argument which, for 110 years, prevented divorce jurisdiction being given to the county courts.) At first sight it may seem only sensible that the costs of litigation, whoever pays them, should be in some reasonable proportion to the financial gain in winning it. But this overlooks the fact that a sum of £100 can be of very much greater importance to a small tradesman than the sum of £1,000 to a large and prosperous company. What appears to be a petty matter can be of immense importance directly or indirectly to those who seek the decision.

But assuming that it is advantageous to have legally-trained judges, the poorer section of society has an even more legitimate grievance than the tradesman who is forced to resort to the county courts. Recognizing that the county court was too slow and expensive to meet the needs of the working classes and that county court judges did not enjoy the confidence of trade-union leaders (a lesson finally learnt with the experience of workmen's compensation), Parliament allowed magistrates increasing civil jurisdiction and created a series of administrative tribunals. The vast bulk of the cases heard by these bodies are not such as would be of major concern to those who are comfortably off. But such matters are often of major importance to those who are not. The tribunals are, nevertheless, staffed largely by laymen often without the benefit of any legal advice. Such courts and tribunals may in fact be more sympathetic to a wider sector of society. But less than the best form of justice is all that is provided to settle those types of dispute which may be of critical concern to the vast majority of the population.

Thus rather than have one court with one procedure to deal with matters of importance to both rich and poor, or finding a way of giving full legal help to those who could not afford to purchase it, Parliament— in keeping with the social spirit of the period—developed three classes of courts. Just as children were divided into three types of school— 'grammar,' 'technical' and 'modern'—to fit the structure of occupations, so litigation has been divided into High Court, county court, magistrates' court/tribunal according to the assumed importance of the matter.

* * *

[O]ne solution which has frequently been canvassed is that of giving unlimited jurisdiction to the county court, without abolishing the High Court. All cases would then begin in the county court and would be transferred to the High Court only if both parties (and the county court judge) agreed. In 1954 Professor L.C.B. Gower justified such a far-reaching plan on the ground that 'we do not force anyone who wants a square meal to go to the Ritz, but recognize that some will prefer Lyons or the A.B.C., notwithstanding that the cuisine and the service may be less superb. Why, then, should we force litigants to pay for the luxury of the High Court, if they prefer the humbler diet of the county court?' Where both parties want a High Court hearing and both are paying for it themselves, we see no objection to their obtaining it. Where only one party wants a High Court hearing we suggest that the county court judge should decide. In exercising this discretion the judge would, it is hoped, take into account the importance of the matter to each party and submissions made by one or other party about the legal complexities which are likely to arise.

It would, moreover, seem that, if the extension of the county court jurisdiction were coupled with a willingness to provide sufficient judges, there would be no reason why the advantages of the county court should be lost to the small claimant. Even today a well-run county court takes cases which are easy to dispose of on one day and cases that are likely to last several hours on another. Turning the county court into the basic court would not only help the courts become far more open to the ordinary man in the street, but hopefully the less formal atmosphere of the county court would survive the broadening of the jurisdiction.

* * *

———

Because the English trial is a single event, delay may be used by solicitors as a tactical maneuver in the hope that new evidence will appear, a settlement will be more likely, some key parties may pass away, etc. Would the elimination of the trial as an event alter this? The alternative would seem to be not unlike the case process in a civil nation. If one is concerned with trespassing on vested interests, this suggestion seems certain to succeed in raising the ire of some legal actors. Abel–Smith and Stevens have also noted:

> It has been suggested that, instead of being scheduled as single events, trials could be broken down into component parts with the result that trial judges would have a number of different cases under consideration at any one time. During one day, for example, a judge might hear a witness in one case because he could conveniently appear at that time, then a submission on a legal point by counsel in a second case, and then some point in a third case. This system, it is suggested, would not only avoid the psychological trauma of the one-shot battle, but the courts would be offering a much more convenient service to their customers. An extension of this is argued by those who would encourage the informality of the court procedure to such an extent that the judge, even in a civil case, would follow the continental 'inquisitorial' system. Such a system might be no better than the present adversary system in providing a service to the public and helping to establish the facts. But, if the opposition of the Bar could be overcome (the system would make a separate breed of advocates less necessary), experiments along these lines ought at least to be tried.[12]

Notes and Questions

1. The court system as described in the articles appears to provide different levels of justice to different categories of litigants. The measure to determine which level or forum one must use is not what one can afford to or may wish to pay. Should *any* litigant be able to choose a less costly forum rather than be sent to one only when the amount in controversy is less? If such were to be the rule, what would be the impact on the legal institutions? If there is only one ordinary court for all civil matters, such as exists in many civil law nations, is there any other restructuring of the courts that is necessary, such as referring more matters to tribunals? In other words can one court deal with all issues—or must there be a division on some basis, such as the amount in controversy or the nature of the actions? See Gower, The Cost of Litigation, 17 Modern Law Review 1 (1954).

2. The suggestion that the same judges hear both civil and criminal matters partly is based on the view that it gives them some diversity of work and reduces boredom. Is that offset by the possible reduced capacity to deal with this diversity as effectively as when the judges are specialists? Are the differences in the structures in Germany and France attributable to any of the problems seen in the English system? How close to the English structure are the courts in your state?

3. If we give the lowest courts unlimited jurisdiction, thus allowing parties to choose between the High Court and the county court—would this be a way to achieve fusion? Would it result in the demise of the High

---

12. B. Abel–Smith and R. Stevens, In Search of Justice 209 (1968).

Court? Or would it simply shift a few matters to the county court where both parties believe that level of justice is sufficient? To what extent should we allow, and do different systems allow, the parties rather than the system to determine where the matter will be heard?

4. Are the High Courts limited in what they hear and where they hear it because of a view that that is how it should be, or because there are pressures to keep the elite judiciary small and the consequences include a limited jurisdiction court? Do any other nations do this?

5. The High Court's limited jurisdiction may be a factor in the creation of the many special tribunals. Had the High Court been able to deal with all those issues and do so rapidly and cheaply, would the tribunals have developed? Is the development of the use of tribunals in the United States, France and Germany attributable to the same reason?

D. CROWN COURTS

The Crown Court is a superior court of criminal jurisdiction on a level comparable to the civil jurisdiction of the High Court. The divisions of the High Court have evolved over centuries, however, while the Crown Court was created by the Courts Acts 1971. It is, nevertheless, part of an evolutionary process of criminal courts. Hearing indictable offenses, the more serious crimes, the Crown Court has replaced Quarter Sessions and Assizes. The latter were local courts, their organization and administration varying throughout the country. Special criminal courts convened in several of the larger cities. The Central Criminal Court Act 1834, created the famous Assize Court for Greater London, popularly known as the "Old Bailey."

The geographic distribution of the English population was altered when urbanization accelerated in the late 18th century, and the very different characteristics of local criminal courts became apparent. Uniformity was thought desirable and best achieved through a national system of criminal courts with some consistency in structure and administration. The Courts Act 1971 established a single superior criminal court, made part of the Supreme Court of Judicature and designated the Crown Court. The Crown Court is convened throughout the year in contrast to the abolished Quarter Sessions.

There was no unification of judicial qualification when the court structure was changed; the Crown Court cannot be said to have its own judges. The judges rather consist of all the judges of the High Court, plus Circuit judges, Recorders and Justices of the Peace. They sit alone. It is possible for a collegiate form to convene, but it does not tend to happen. A Justice of the Peace may serve if there is also a judge of the High Court present, but the former sit principally when there is a hearing on an appeal or an issue of committal for sentence.

Supplementary to the jurisdiction of the Crown Court over the principal indictable offenses, are its roles for appeals from the magistrates' courts and as a sentencing tribunal after conviction in a magistrates' court. A magistrates' court may transfer sentencing to the

Crown Court if the magistrates believe that their own sentencing powers are inadequate considering the severity of the crime.

The question of who sits in the Crown Court is indeed somewhat confusing. The English experience is unique. Tracing criminal and civil jurisdiction from the most minor to the most major of issues surely must be puzzling for a French or West German lawyer. The issues are divided in France and West Germany. There is less confusion between the latter nations and England with regard to who sits, what they are called, why there is more use of lay judges for criminal but professional judges for civil (county court) matters, and where the courts sit (out, on the fringe, or in) in the High Court structure. Jackson discusses some of the changes occurring in the past two decades and the remaining complexities.

R.M. JACKSON, "JACKSON'S MACHINERY OF JUSTICE"

176 (8th ed. 1989).

The essence of the system which we now have for trying cases on indictment is that there is notionally only one higher court, namely the Crown Court, which is separate from the High Court, but is organised and run together with the High Court as part of an integrated system. Just as the High Court consists of a number of judges sitting for the most part singly in court-rooms in London or twenty-six places in the provinces, so the Crown Court consists of judges (with juries in cases that are defended) sitting singly or in some cases with justices of the peace in court-rooms at some 90 centres in London and elsewhere in England and Wales. The Crown Court thus sits at more centres than the High Court, and necessarily also uses a bigger pool of judges. High Court Judges sit in the Crown Court, and have jurisdiction to try any kind of case there, but are used only for the most serious cases. The bulk of the work is done by Circuit Judges, Recorders and Assistant Recorders....

For the purpose of administering the higher courts, civil as well as criminal, England and Wales is divided into six circuits, each based on a major city: Midland and Oxford (Birmingham), North Eastern (Leeds), Northern (Manchester), South–Eastern (London), Wales and Chester (Cardiff) and Western (Bristol). Each has its own staff of administrators, and its own presiding judge. Within each circuit there are a number of court centres which are ranked in three levels of importance, and at all of them the Crown Court sits. The first-tier and second-tier centres are regularly visited by High Court Judges,[1] and there the full range of indictable offences can be tried. The third-tier centres are usually visited only by Circuit Judges and Recorders, and are for the trial of less weighty matters. The various centres are listed in an

---

1. The difference between a first- and a second-tier centre is that High Court Judges sit at first-tier centres for the conduct of civil business.

Appendix to this book, together with a map. The system is less rigid than the map suggests, however, and can be adjusted, temporarily or otherwise, to meet demand. Section 78 of the Supreme Court Act 1981 provides that any Crown Court business may be conducted at any time or place in England and Wales which the Lord Chancellor may direct. Thus High Court Judges are sometimes sent to third-tier centres, and the Crown Court occasionally sits at remote places—Penzance, for example—which are not regular centres at all.

Because High Court Judges are considered more suitable than Circuit Judges and Recorders for handling difficult and sensitive cases, rules are made to distribute cases to the type of judge who is best fitted to deal with it. By section 75 of the Supreme Court Act 1981 the Lord Chief Justice, with the concurrence of the Lord Chancellor, issues Practice Directions which grade indictable offences in various categories of seriousness and allocate them between the different types of Crown Court judge. Directions given in 1987 set up a four-fold classification. Class 1 consists of a small number of offences of the greatest difficulty and seriousness which must always be tried by a High Court Judge; it includes treason, murder, and offences under the Official Secrets Act 1911 s.1. A particular murder may, however, be released for trial by a Circuit Judge approved by the Lord Chief Justice. Class 2 comprises a small number of slightly less serious offences, which must be tried by a High Court Judge unless the presiding judge of the Circuit orders otherwise in a particular case: manslaughter, abortion and related offences, rape, sexual intercourse with girls under 13, sedition, mutiny and certain other offences. Rapes and serious sexual offences against children may only be released for trial before a Circuit Judge who has been approved by the Lord Chief Justice. Class 4, which is very large, consists of offences which, although triable by a High Court Judge, are normally to be tried by a Circuit Judge or a Recorder. It includes wounding, theft, fraud, robbery, burglary, and reckless driving. Class 3 is a residual category consisting of all offences not in any of the other classes. These may be tried by any judge competent to sit in the Crown Court and no legislative preference is expressed. Causing death by reckless driving, for example, comes into this category. Class 3 offences are normally listed for trial by a High Court Judge.

As a matter of law any Crown Court has jurisdiction to try any indictable offence from any part of the country. Where a case is sent for trial is in the first instance a matter for the magistrates at the committal proceedings. The magistrates are not completely free to send the case where they please, however, because defined catchment areas are fixed by the presiding judges of the circuits and the magistrates are expected to adhere to these. For offences in class 1, 2 or 3 they will commit to the most convenient first- or second-tier court. For a class 4 offence they commit to the Crown Court which has been administratively designated as the normal court to receive their committals; if this is a third-tier court they may nevertheless commit to a first- or second-tier court if they think there are circumstances which make trial before a High Court

Judge desirable. The court officials who prepare the lists have power to overrule the decision of the magistrates and to send the case to a different court, a power which enables them to divert cases around legal traffic-jams in particular locations. The place where a case is to be tried may be hotly disputed, not only on grounds of convenience but also because of allegations of local racial or other influences, any of which may be thought to affect jurors. For this reason both the prosecutor and the defendant are given a right to object to a proposed venue, and such objections must be heard in open court before a High Court Judge.

The Crown Court system is almost entirely based on rational analysis and planning and there is only one marked survival of ancient privilege: nothing must appear to be altered that affects the dignity of the City of London. The Crown Court sitting in the City of London accordingly continues to be known as the Central Criminal Court (Old Bailey) and the Lord Mayor of the City and the Aldermen of the City are entitled, as they were in the past, to sit as judges in the Old Bailey (which they have in fact done only in a ceremonial way). The working judges in the Old Bailey are the visiting Queen's Bench Division judges, the Recorder, the Common Serjeant, and a number of Circuit Judges. The Recorder continues to be appointed by the City (and then is appointed by the Crown to exercise judicial functions) and the Common Serjeant continues to be appointed by the Crown, but by statute both are now Circuit Judges. The City continues to own the court-house but must make it available for courts and must not alter it without consent of the Lord Chancellor.

Justices of the Peace were members of the court in the days of County Quarter Sessions, and when these were abolished in 1971 there was much discussion as to whether they should play any part in the Crown Court. The Beeching Commission recommended that justices should sit (but only as assessors) but by the Courts Act 1971 they were given a definite place as full members of the court for certain purposes. When the Crown Court is sitting as an appeal court from decisions in the magistrates' court, or dealing with cases committed by a magistrates' court to the Crown Court for sentence, it is required by statute to sit with a number of justices of the peace in addition to a judge (and there is no jury). For most purposes there must be not less than two and not more than four, but the number varies according to the type of business, and for licensing appeals and appeals from a juvenile court there are further requirements about their sex and experience. The details are to be found in the Crown Court Rules which are made by a statutory Committee.

For trials on indictment the presence of justices is possible but not mandatory. The Practice Direction which classifies offences for trial before the various types of judge originally decreed that all Class 4 offences were suitable for Circuit Judges or Recorders sitting with justices, but in 1986 the Direction was revised so that magistrates are only to be used in proceedings for Class 4 offences where the defendant pleads guilty. This means that they may take part in sentencing offenders but no longer in trials where the defendant's guilt is contested. In all the instances when justices sit they are theoretically full members of the court, and it is provided by statute that in the event of disagreement the decision may be by a majority, subject to the judge's casting vote if the panel is evenly divided; but a Court of Appeal decision limits this to decisions on point of fact, and lays down that on any question of law the justices must accept the judge's ruling.

* * *

Notes and Questions

1. Is the Crown Court a High Court when a High Court judge sits, but a different court when a circuit judge sits? Does the nature of the court determine who will sit, or does the sitting judge give the title to the court? What are the obstacles to simply having judges called Crown Court judges?

2. Is the division of summary and indictable (what we would essentially call misdemeanor and felony) offenses between the magistrates' and Crown Courts unique to the English system? Are the Crown Courts better equipped to deal with issues that normally come before the magistrates' courts (but where the accused accepts the offer to have the matter transferred to the Crown Court), than the magistrates' courts are able to deal with indictable offenses?

3. The Courts Act 1971 was for the most part not controversial. But the provisions regarding the qualifications to be appointed a circuit judge or Recorder and to have a right of advocacy in the Crown Court raised the expected concern of the barristers. Another foot of turf was being pulled away from their yard. The bill as initially introduced was intended to preserve the Bar's rights in these areas. But the Bar lost. Much fuel for the fear of fusion, about which there will be more in the next chapter.

E. THE COURT OF APPEAL

The Court of Appeal is part of the Supreme Court of Judicature, and is exclusively a court of appellate jurisdiction. Its jurisdiction extends to both civil and criminal matters. Civil jurisdiction involves appeals from the High Court, county courts and certain administrative courts and tribunals. The criminal side primarily hears appeals from the Crown Courts. The court is thus the point at which nearly all disputes merge if further proceedings are intended, a feature characteristic of most common law systems, in contrast to having parallel levels of appeal for several judicial hierarchies.

The Lords Justices of Appeal are the principal judges of the Court of Appeals, the Master of the Rolls and the Lord Chief Justice are the administrative heads of civil and criminal matters, respectively. The Lord Chancellor, the Lord Chief Justice, the Master of the Rolls, the President of the Family Division of the High Court, the former Lord Chancellor, and the Lords of Appeal in Ordinary are all ex-officio judges. During times of substantial caseload, the Lord Chancellor may temporarily add a judge of the High Court, illustrative of the absence of absolutes in the identification of certain judicial positions with a single, specific court.

Appellate decisions are rendered in collegiate form, by three judges, although in some limited circumstances one or two judges may appear, usually to determine application for leave to appeal. If a particularly important issue of law is before the court, five or more judges may sit, although the resulting decision possesses no greater authority than one emanating from the more common three judge court.

Both the Court of Appeal and the House of Lords acting as an appellate court sit in London. But the nature of the appeal differs from the trial. It becomes more like the civil law process. It is largely documentary in the United States—there is a concentration on arguments of law supported by prepared briefs. But as will be discussed in the section on appellate procedure, chapter 12, section 4, the English appeal differs from its counterpart in the United States because the appeal in England is more oral. It nevertheless is not a trial in the common law sense of an event. There is thus less of a burden on the parties—usually only the lawyers attend the proceedings. There has been little demand in England to decentralize the appellate stage. Nor has there been such demand in states in the United States where appeals may be centralized in the capital city. But in many states there is an appeal stage which is decentralized.

But there is another concern—the duplication of appeals with two stages.

R.M. JACKSON, "JACKSON'S MACHINERY OF JUSTICE"
95 (8th ed. 1989).

... It is difficult to justify two appeal courts. It may be argued that at any given time either the Court of Appeal or the House of Lords is the better tribunal, or they are both equally good, so that on either hypothesis there is no need for both of them. The result upon litigants is that an appeal to the Court of Appeal is not necessarily final, so that if the case is taken on to the House of Lords the whole of the costs in the Court of Appeal appear wasted. It is sometimes disquieting to find that a litigant may lose a case, although the majority of judges find for him. If the trial judge finds in favour of A and against B, and then B appeals to the Court of Appeal where all three judges uphold the decision in A's favour, B may yet win in the House of Lords because out of the five judges sitting there three may be in his favour and two may be against him; the result is that altogether six judges favour A's case and three judges favour B's case, yet B wins. Since costs normally follow the event, A must pay B's costs in the trial court (where A won) and in the Court of Appeal (where A also won) and in the House of Lords where he lost; and of course he must also pay his own costs in all three courts.

There is some weighty evidence in favour of having a single appeal court.... Higher law courts and especially final appeal courts raise questions about their social utility....

... To many lawyers, an important part of their function is developing and adapting the law in the light of changing conditions, and if this is accepted as one of the reasons for their existence then it makes sense to keep the House of Lords as a less busy, more fully-staffed appeal court which is able to give particular attention to difficult and developing areas of the law. But a problem arises with the House of Lords as presently constituted if what one is looking for is the ideal expert court. With only nine Law Lords and a few extra helpers, it is not always possible—as it usually is possible in the Court of Appeal—to ensure that a case in the House of Lords is always heard by a panel at least one member of which has expert knowledge of the area of law in question. This, more than anything, probably explains the poor record of the House of Lords in criminal cases over the years.

* * *

The strongest argument for retaining a second appeal court is the rigidity of the Court of Appeal. So long as the Court of Appeal holds that it is bound by its own decisions, there must from time to time be poor results through attempts to follow previous decisions that have come to be regarded as wrong or seriously inconvenient or conflicting. This deficiency in the Court of Appeal can be tolerated so long as 'there is always the House of Lords to put things right', though adherents of that view omit to say who it is that pays the bills of costs. But this line of argument really amounts to saying that we must retain the House of Lords in order to avoid altering the habits of the Court of Appeal.

Establishment of a single appeal court would not be free of any difficulty. Abolition of the Court of Appeal, so that all appeals would go direct to the House of Lords, would require so much reorganisation to deal with the volume of work that the character of the House of Lords would be lost in the process. Abolition of the appellate jurisdiction of the House of Lords, so that the Court of Appeal would be the final court, would offer less difficulty and to the English lawyer it might seem the simplest step. It must, however, be remembered that the House of Lords is a United Kingdom court. There are always some members appointed from Scotland and from time to time someone from Northern Ireland. Some important parts of law, including much of commercial law and law relating to road traffic, is the same all over the United Kingdom, and it is most desirable that there should be a single appellate court whose decisions are authoritative in every part of the kingdom. We have gained greatly from having Scots lawyers in the House of Lords, for there is perhaps no better stimulus to legal thought than contact with other systems of law....

F. THE HOUSE OF LORDS

The judicial role of the House of Lords antedates its legislative role. But few of its early judicial functions as part of the Curia Regis survive. Its current role is chiefly as the senior appellate court.

Decisions of the House of Lords prior to the 19th century did not command considerable respect. They often were rendered by House of Lords members who were not lawyers. It remains possible in theory for the entire House of Lords to hear an appeal, including both its legislative and judicial members. But in practice decisions are now rendered by the Appellate Committee of the House of Lords, which includes only professional members. The judges include the presiding Lord Chancellor, and the Lords of Appeal in Ordinary, called Law Lords. The Law Lords are chosen either by direct appointment from among the most eminent barristers or by elevating a judge from a lower court. Almost always the appointments are made from the Court of Appeal. A benefit of such appointment is a life peerage, to a degree offsetting the rather modest salary. One or two of the Law Lords are from Scotland, and are assigned to appeals from the highest Scottish court of appeal, the Court of Session.

But the elevation to the House of Lords from the Court of Appeal is not considered by all to be a promotion in anything but prestige and title. Lord Denning, who moved from the Court of Appeal to the House of Lords and then back to head the Court of Appeal as Master of the Rolls, said this about the elevation:

> To go from the Court of Appeal to the House of Lords is like going into retirement. It is rather like the senior partner retiring and becoming a consultant. In the Court of Appeal you are under continuous pressure. In the House of Lords you are relaxed and at ease. You sit four days a week. Sometimes less. Sometimes short days. You reserve every judgment, with ample time to think it over and to write it.[13]

We are interested in the House of Lords in its judicial capacity—we have noted above its role as a legislative body. There is some overlap of the functions of its members. The person designated a Law Lord, or Lord of Appeal in Ordinary, is a member of the House of Lords and secondly a judge in that chamber. But he is appointed to be a judge rather than a legislator. If he does participate in the legislative sessions, and many do actively, he is not to speak on matters which involve party politics. He is supposed to limit his activities to legal issues and to voting on social questions. This role contrasts with the participation of members of the House of Lords who are not Law Lords, but who might wish to sit when the Law Lords hear appeals. They may not. In the middle of the 18th century it was established by convention that lay peers do not vote on judicial appeals.

At the head of the Law Lords is the Lord Chancellor, appointed by the Prime Minister to serve for the duration of the government. He has multiple roles. He is an administrator; he rarely hears cases with the Law Lords. He presides both in the House of Lords in its judicial capacity and over the Judicial Committee of the Privy Council, heads the Chancery Division of the High Court, is an ex-officio member of the

13. Lord Denning, The Family Story 184 (1981).

Court of Appeal, and is responsible for the county court system, all in addition to other judicial duties. But he is also a member of the executive, usually in service in the Prime Minister's cabinet. And finally, the Lord Chancellor is a legislator; he sits as Speaker (chairman) of the House of Lords.

The setting for appeals before the House of Lords is far less formal than in the Royal Courts on the Strand. The judges appear in business suits, sitting on the same level as counsel in what appears more a conference room than a court room. But some of the trappings of the colorful dress of the English system are present. Barristers wear their robes and wigs. If the case is one of those few heard in the Chamber of the House of Lords, then there is greater formality, but those cases amount to less than ten percent of the appeals to the House of Lords.

The Law Lords are given by their clerk a single page summary outlining the case and the issue presented on appeal. It additionally states the names of the appearing barristers. Oral argument is presented much in the same manner as in the Court of Appeal, and a hearing may go on for two weeks or more, although most do not extend beyond several days. The time for oral appeal at this highest court is thus significantly longer than the limited oral argument allowed by the United States Supreme Court. But much of the time of the appeal involves reading from the record and from cases supporting the barristers' arguments. At the close of the oral argument, unlike the Court of Appeal where judgments are rendered immediately, the judges tend to reserve their decision. In rare cases, they may decide the case but provide an opinion with their reasoning at some future date.

The Law Lords have some limited time for work in chambers. They generally sit four days a week and, if a case ends before the end of the day, they may decide not to go on to the next case but rather spend time working on opinions in chambers. Each of the Law Lords writes a separate opinion and sends it to the other judges who sat on the case. If their views are quite different, they may meet and attempt to reconcile those differences, but they do so informally. Decisions of the House of Lords illustrate that there is little attempt to render a harmonious decision or one which might be said to be a decision of the court rather than of the judges. The tradition is for the judges to state individual views in their separate opinions. Some half dozen weeks after the hearing, the Law Lords sit to announce opinions in an atmosphere far more formal than during the oral argument. The meeting takes place in the regular chamber where the Lords meet in legislative session, and the Lord Chancellor speaks from the Woolsack after the session is opened by prayers. But the only persons likely to be in attendance are the judges who sat on the appeal and barristers and solicitors involved in the cases. The judges read their separate opinions in each case, except for the rare occasion when they have agreed on an opinion for the entire court. It can be a time consuming practice, often taking two or more hours. But some of the Law Lords may omit portions of their opinion, moving rapidly to their reasons for their position. At the end of the reading, the Lord Chancellor tallies the vote and the appeal is concluded.

The jurisdiction of the House of Lords is predominantly appellate, and is almost exclusively related to matters from the Court of Appeal in England, although it is also the final court of appeal for Scotland and Northern Ireland. Either the Court of Appeal or the Appeals Committee of the House of Lords must grant leave for an appeal. Since the Administration of Justice Act 1969, some limited leap-frogging appeals are permitted directly from the High Court to the House of Lords.

Question

We will return to the courts in the chapter on procedure. The material above should illustrate the nature of the courts as institutions of the legal system, and how the structures differ from those in the United States and in civil and socialist law systems. One cannot conclude that the House of Lords is the same as the Supreme Court of the United States. In both what it does and the esteem it possesses, the United States Supreme Court is a full step above the lower federal appellate courts in the United States. Justices on the Supreme Court do not go back to become chief judges of the federal courts of appeals, as Lord Denning moved from the House of Lords to head the Court of Appeal. Is the House of Lords just another step in the appeal process? Does it serve a higher role in the appeal process in contrast to how we view United States Supreme Court decisions, with regard to the prestige of its decisions with legal actors and the public?

G. JUDICIAL COMMITTEE OF THE PRIVY COUNCIL

The Privy Council is also a judicial evolution of the Curia Regis. It was created initially to hear appeals from the Channel Islands and the Isle of Man. Later known as the Privy Council, it assumed the role as the final court of appeals for courts from throughout the Empire. The royal prerogative was its source of power. The Privy Council's minor local jurisdiction diminished when the scope of the royal prerogative was limited following the constitutional conflicts in the Stuart period. The Privy Council later refined its unique role as a judicial body limited to hearing appeals from the Commonwealth, aided by the creation of the Judicial Committee, whose members were limited to professional judges, which assumed responsibility for all judicial matters of the Privy Council. The Judicial Committee survives as part of the English court system. Its judges are those Privy Councillors who have held high judicial office in the United Kingdom or other parts of the Commonwealth. But only a few appointments were made from the Commonwealth prior to 1962, by which time political changes in the Commonwealth had reduced the jurisdiction of the Judicial Committee. Commonwealth nations acquiring independence generally established national appellate courts, terminating or reducing appeals to the Judicial Committee. Canada, India, South Africa and most other former Commonwealth members have abolished appeals to the Judicial Committee. . . . A few former Commonwealth nations continue to use the Judicial Committee as the final court of appeal.

Had Commonwealth representation been increased significantly prior to 1962, the Judicial Committee might have survived as a far more consequential institution. But it never altered its status as a central court sitting in London, requiring Commonwealth Judicial Committee members to travel considerable distances to participate in deliberations. The relative inactivity of the Committee did not demand the full time presence of its members, and Commonwealth participants usually did not terminate service on their national courts. Once prestigious, this judicial vestige is now of minor stature; its future is bound securely to the fortunes of the Commonwealth.

The process used in the Privy Council differs from that of the House of Lords. Unlike the hearing in the House of Lords, the judges on the Privy Council reach a single opinion. No concurring opinions are written, nor are dissents permitted. The nature of the decision differs from an appeal from the lower courts in England. The decision of the Judicial Committee of the Privy Council goes to the sovereign, who then conveys that decision to the particular court in whatever nation or Commonwealth member from which it has been submitted. In the same manner as hearings before the House of Lords, Privy Council hearings are informal and judgment is reserved. Because there is an opinion rendered by the court, the judge who has been assigned the task of drafting the opinion will meet with the other judges to achieve final agreement. Even if there is a strong dissent, it will not find expression in the final decision.

When the decision has been completed, the final part is read by one of the judges during a regular sitting of the House of Lords as a judicial body. The sovereign does not give assent to the decision in the same form as rendered to legislative acts of Parliament. Decisions of the Judicial Committee are accepted by the sovereign at a formal meeting of the full Privy Council. The difference in the process of sovereign consent illustrates the judicial independence of the Judicial Committee, an independence which parallels that of the House of Lords in its regular appellate capacity.

As noted above, the frequency of reference of appeals to the Privy Council is decreasing. The more developed nations of the Commonwealth tend to feel comfortable with their own appellate structures. But for some of the less developed nations, having the Privy Council as a court of last resort gives additional credibility to the judicial system as a whole. This does not mean that the Privy Council will accept any appeal which it receives. Being across the sea and increasingly isolated from the culture of newly independent former colonies, the Privy Council may not feel able to deal effectively with some issues. The following case illustrates this concern.

RAGHO PRASAD v. THE QUEEN (P.C.)

[1981] 1 W.L.R. 469.*

The judgment of their Lordships was delivered by LORD DIPLOCK.

At a trial in the Supreme Court of Fiji, held before Stuart J. and five assessors, Ragho Prasad (the defendant) was convicted of murdering his father, and sentenced to life imprisonment. He appealed to the Fiji Court of Appeal against his conviction, on the ground of various alleged errors and other defects in the judge's summing up to the assessors, whose unanimous opinion, with which the judge concurred, was that the defendant was guilty of murder. . . .

* * *

The practice of the Judicial Committee in the exercise of its appellate jurisdiction in criminal matters was authoritatively stated by Lord Sumner in *Ibrahaim v. The King* [1914] A.C. 599, 614–615. The practice remains unchanged, and the whole passage bears repetition:

> "Leave to appeal is not granted 'except where some clear departure from the requirements of justice' exists: . . . nor unless 'by a disregard of the forms of legal process, or by some violation of the principles of natural justice or otherwise, substantial and grave injustice has been done': . . . . It is true that these are cases of applications for special leave to appeal, but the Board has repeatedly treated applications for leave to appeal and the hearing of criminal appeals as being upon the same footing: . . . . The Board cannot give leave to appeal where the grounds suggested could not sustain the appeal itself; and, conversely, it cannot allow an appeal on grounds that would not have sufficed for the grant of permission to bring it. Misdirection, as such, even irregularity as such, will not suffice: . . . . There must be something which, in the particular case, deprives the accused of the substance of fair trial and the protection of the law, or which, in general, tends to divert the due and orderly administration of the law into a new course, which may be drawn into an evil precedent in future. . . ."

To this their Lordships would only add that courts of appeal composed of judges more familiar than members of this Board can hope to be with local conditions and social attitudes, are in a better position than their Lordships to assess the likely effect of any misdirection or irregularity upon a jury or other deciders of fact in a criminal case. This is all the more so where, as in Fiji, the mode of trial is not the same as in England or Scotland. There is no jury; the trial is before a judge and assessors to the number of not less than four in capital cases. The judge sums up to them; each then states his individual opinion as to the guilt of the accused; although permitted to consult with one another they are not obliged to do so; and the ultimate decider of fact (as well as law) is the

* Reprinted with permission of The Incorporated Council of Law Reporting.

judge himself who need not conform to the opinions of the assessors, even though they be unanimous, if he thinks that their opinions are wrong. The field of comment upon evidence that is proper to a judge in summing up to a jury in a trial in which they are collectively the exclusive deciders of fact is not necessarily the same as in summing up to assessors whose function it is to help the judge in making up his own mind as the sole ultimate determiner of fact.

H. SPECIAL COURTS AND TRIBUNALS

In nearly every advanced society, whatever its legal tradition, the price of its degree of advancement seems to be extensive government regulation of the lives of the citizens. The ordinary courts cannot bear the burden of this additional load of dispute resolution. And, as noted above, they are often viewed as inadequate to deal with these issues because of the cost, delay and procedural complexities they have accrued along the path of development. The national response has been to create new structures to deal with these issues. Many questions surround these structures. Are they to be given the stature of courts or considered lower level tribunals? Will there be an appeal allowed into the regular court system? Who will have the right of advocacy in these courts? Will their jurisdiction infringe upon the regular courts or are they truly limited to new issues?

One often sees writing and hears lectures on how the materials in a text or casebook, the curriculum of a law school as a whole, or the general focus of attention is on the very limited area of the regular courts, and even more specifically, the appellate courts. People's everyday lives may be affected more by the myriad of tribunals than the regular courts. They may be denied social security benefits. A person's small store is fined for sanitary violations. Price controls hurt their profit. The son is denied a deferment and must forego college. The daughter is denied a real estate license. But the structures which deal with these issues are given comparatively scant attention. It is a practice this chapter follows as well. Perhaps not so blindly.

Though the special courts and tribunals do come into people's lives so frequently, we nevertheless tend not to perceive them as the institutions to which we turn for many major issues, nor do we consider them part of the essential structures which make up the central fabric of our system of justice. Those roles are reserved for the regular courts. With regard to the civil courts, that is where we go if we are seriously injured by another in an automobile accident. Or where difficult property disputes are resolved, such as rights of ingress to our homes. They loom large in our lives as being the courts where the really serious issues can be heard. And they may be where we take our appeals from either lower regular courts or special courts and tribunals. This touches upon a sensitive issue which is resolved in different ways in different systems. That is to what degree should the regular appellate courts reserve jurisdiction over appeals from all forms of hearing bodies?

The ordinary courts also are essential to our perception of the use of the legal system for dealing with crimes. Almost any charge we are likely to face, from running a red light to the most serious felonies, goes to the regular courts. There are tribunals which have the ability to levy fines for violations of the law. But again our perception of the kinds of activity over which the regular courts have jurisdiction tends to elevate the regular courts above the tribunals.

What we would consider subordinate tribunals in our system may be given far greater status in another. Consider, for example, the German hierarchy of courts as discussed in Chapter 2, section 5. Alongside the hierarchy which possesses civil and criminal jurisdiction are other hierarchies. Not just lower courts but full hierarchies which ascend to their own final court of appeal. One such hierarchy is social security. It is co-equal in the institutional structure with the civil law. It does not have such status in the English system, nor in the United States. And even in Germany, if one asks if they are really perceptually co-equals, the response is likely to be no. The civil hierarchy is given greater stature. It is at least partly so because of the greater reverence for the civil code than the social security laws. In the same way, we have greater reverence for the sources of law which govern civil matters in the common law systems—precedent of the courts and legislation, than we have for the laws which govern social security issues—administrative rulings and legislation.

Whether one agrees or disagrees with the above, we must consider the tribunals. The comments above do not suggest the lack of importance of these special courts and tribunals in the common law systems, but offer some reasons why we tend to discuss them after we discuss the regular courts. Perhaps the most visible is the Restrictive Practices Court, hearing a broad range of issues related to monopolies and restrictive practices. It is the most important court in England to use an aldermanry composition of judges. Professional judges from the High Court, Court of Session in Scotland and Supreme Court of Northern Ireland, one of whom serves as president, share the bench with ten lay persons who possess special knowledge of industry, commerce or public affairs. But the special courts do not share the respect the bar accords the ordinary courts. Of even less stature are the numerous tribunals.... Their procedures are less formal, more rapid and less expensive than proceedings in the regular courts, but they are criticized for denying individuals their right to appear before the ordinary courts. Lay participation on tribunals is far more extensive than in the regular courts. Solicitors may appear as advocates, but even they are not required in many tribunals.

The development of special tribunals with lay judges is viewed by some as a way of preventing social legislation from being excessively strictly construed by the conservative English judiciary. But the judiciary has reacted. The Tribunals and Inquiries Act 1958, increased professional judicial control over the tribunals, foremost through the participation of the Lord Chancellor in appointing members. Further control is exercised by channeling appeals from tribunals to various parts of the Supreme Court, usually to the Queen's Bench Division of the High Court.

Dispute resolution in England by the ordinary courts as a right continues to be eroded. Any encroachment on the role of the ordinary courts by administrative tribunals is generally weighed very carefully. No formal, recognized separate court hierarchy has developed for private and public law issues, as exists in many civil law nations. But there is nearly one for some public matters, such as social security. Administrative justice in England, viewed by many, particularly the organized bar, with less than reverence, nevertheless continues to increase in scope and has a notable effect on the lives of all English citizens.

B. ABEL–SMITH AND R. STEVENS, "IN SEARCH OF JUSTICE"

68, 77, 218 (1968).

The simple generalization that disputes with the State (other than those involving criminal law) are heard by administrative tribunals and disputes with other citizens are heard by civil courts has too many exceptions to be useful. The citizen can sue the State for breaches of contract, nuisances or torts in the ordinary courts in the same way as he can sue a private citizen. Some disputes with the State are decided by the Minister (or in practice normally his officials), and there is no appeal on fact or law to any court or tribunal nor any way of bringing such disputes before the ordinary courts. Some disputes between citizens go before administrative tribunals (for example, those concerning rents); others go before arbitral tribunals.

* * *

The composition of tribunals varies greatly both in the number of persons acting in a judicial capacity and in their background and training. Nearly all tribunals have legally qualified chairmen; ... The members of the various tribunals tend to be chosen because of their knowledge or experience of the subject matter under adjudication....

* * *

In an earlier chapter we showed that the responsibilities for deciding disputes and articulating the law were divided among a spectrum of adjudicating bodies in a way which conformed to no rational pattern. We found no coherent theory which explained why some responsibilities were exercised by courts and others by tribunals or which accounted for the way in which the various responsibilities were distributed among the different courts. Courts and tribunals do not, however, encompass all procedures of adjudication. There remain many matters which are still decided by Ministers and local authorities....

* * *

Similarly, just as we saw that the distribution of responsibilities between tribunals and courts is largely arbitrary, so, it turns out, is the distribution of responsibilities for decisions between Ministers (and their civil servants) on the one hand and courts and tribunals on the other. The decisions which have to be made in government do not fall neatly into specific pigeonholes. . . .

* * *

The assumption that certain things are inherently justiciable and others are non-justiciable has been largely abandoned by modern scholars, if not by all lawyers. As the Franks Committee noted: 'What is judicial has been worked out and given expression by generations of judges. Its distinction from what is administrative recalls great constitutional victories and marks the essential difference in the nature of the decisions of the judiciary and the executive.' But no immutable lines exist. Public dissatisfaction with the working of the courts could lead Parliament to transfer further work from the courts to the tribunals.

Thus changes in the law could take away from the courts a number of matters they presently handle. . . . the bulk of the work of the courts consists in debt cases, matrimonial cases, and negligence claims. Tribunals could be established to handle each of these. The county courts are primarily debt-collecting agencies. If tradesmen or companies are able to get judgement entered in that court, then the debtor is liable to be thrown into prison if he fails to pay under the order, on the ground that he is in contempt of court. Such a haphazard method of allowing the courts to be used to enforce debts has caused doubt for some time. It does not exist in Scotland, nor in most common-law jurisdictions, and the system is unlikely to survive much longer in England. . . .

* * *

A foreign non-lawyer who was unaware of the prestige of the British judiciary and of traditional concepts such as the separation of powers, which have come to be associated with courts rather than tribunals, might well ask what the difference really is between a court and a tribunal. What does it matter if some particular adversary procedures have come to be called courts while others are described as tribunals? Both are normally established under statutes. Both interpret laws made by or under statute as well as their own case law, although the latter may be more flexible under administrative tribunals. Both are normally chaired by persons appointed by the Lord Chancellor, although in the case of most courts there are no other members of the bench.

We would argue that such differences as there are between them are not in any sense fundamental but at most differences in degree. Tribunals tend to include a much wider range of skills on the bench; and the most significant hallmark of policy-oriented tribunals is specialization. The most cursory examination of the courts shows that the decision-makers consist of lawyers or laymen or both. Trusted laymen (J.P.s) staff the majority of magistrates' courts. They also sit with legally qualified chairmen at county quarter sessions. Unselected laymen, although to a much more limited extent than formerly, take decisions as jurors—on guilt in criminal cases or on 'penalties' in civil cases (for example not only about whether there is liability but also about how much compensation should be paid in a libel case).

Tribunals, on the other hand, normally use as decision-takers, and not just as witnesses, persons with specialized experience (employers or trade unionists) and persons with professional skills other than legal skills. . . .

With respect to the court-substitute type of tribunals we would argue that the chief features which distinguish them from the regular courts are their cheapness, their speed and efficiency, their privacy and their informality. . . .

* * *

Some lawyers would argue that there was a further fundamental difference between the two streams. Courts are said to be administering rules of law while tribunals are thought to be administering both law and policy. We would maintain that no such clear line can or should be drawn. Indeed it was the evolution of this myth which helped establish the tribunal system by convincing the judges of the ordinary courts that they were concerned with legal but not with policy questions. But continued insistence on this unsatisfactory distinction makes it increasingly difficult to entrust new matters to the courts or to merge courts and tribunals. Properly understood, tribunals are a more modern form of court. In some cases they may have more discretion than the courts, and this is particularly true of the policy-oriented tribunals. But certainly they have no more discretion than the Chancery Division has in handling trusts, wards or companies. Conversely the court-substitute tribunals are often as precedent-conscious as, and may even exercise a much narrower discretion than, the ordinary courts.

But we would reaffirm our position that there is no fundamental difference between courts and tribunals. We would argue, therefore, that every effort should be made to merge the two. A well-structured court system, with reformed and flexible procedures based on the county court or Civil Tribunal, with specialized 'lists,' might then offer a general adjudicatory system, with a spectrum of judges specialized in the many fields in which a potential litigant might be interested.

The actual work currently done by the courts is largely accidental. At the same time, very few matters could not be done by courts. All the work done by tribunals could be done by courts; and much more besides. Principles could be devised which would enable courts to determine even such politically contentious matters as the rate of income tax or the boundaries of constituencies. Moreover, the principles might not need to be much more 'discretionary' than many of the 'rules' applied by the courts. It is, however, unlikely that a responsible democracy would allow matters of this kind to be settled by courts—as they involve such a strong element of political choice that it is thought they should be taken by either an elected body or a body responsible to an elected body.

It is in the light of this background that the present function of the courts should be re-examined. Our thesis is not a destructive one: we are anxious to make the courts more useful to society. But to do this it is necessary to show that just as many of the matters now handled by tribunals could be handled by courts, so many of the substantive problems currently handled by the courts could be handled by other decision-making agencies. Once this is realized, the potential role for courts and lawyers may well be vastly extended; and the arid dispute between lawyers (who feel that only decisions taken in courts are really pure) and non-lawyers (who feel that any dispute which ends up in the hands of lawyers is evidence of a basically unhealthy society) may then be ended.

While politicians and political scientists, psychologists, sociologists and public administrators now regard decision-making as some form of spectrum, ranging from the highly principled to the discretionary, lawyers still tend to see issues as legal and non-legal. They are still haunted by the idea popularized by Dicey that lawyers are the sole guardians of principled doctrines, and that to the courts alone has been granted an understanding of the mysteries of objectivity and impartiality. They ignore the fact that few decisions anywhere in government are totally unprincipled, and choose to ignore the developments in the psychology of decision-making which show that an element of discretion exists even in decisions which on their surface may seem entirely principled.

Out of these myths lawyers have built certain other myths. They illogically insist on the crucial importance of the independence of the judges, as protectors of civil liberties—yet they have never spelt out clearly what these civil liberties are (except in the constitutions of dependent territories), nor made clear how they reconcile such alleged protection with their denial of any clear law-making role for the judges. They claim an impartiality for the judiciary, ignoring the inevitable 'inarticulate premises,' which other disciplines would now accept. Yet they use these various doctrines to claim a privileged status for the judges and the common law. Perhaps it is desirable in an age of increasing centralization that centres of power should grow up outside the executive and legislature. But too often the claims made for the independence of the judges and the courts are emotional and spiritual rather than intellectual.

It is true that progress has been made since some of the hysterical outbursts of the 1930s. But, alas, much of the legal and judicial mystique has lapped over into the 1960s and may well plague the 1970s. As a distinguished civil servant recently wrote:

> The Lawyer of England, unlike his colleagues in the Roman law countries, has behind him a professional history which tends to separate him from the administrator. He is not accustomed to think of justice, as they do in France, as a 'government service like

the provision of education or roads'. He is conscious of belonging to a kind of independent corporation, knowing that 'Parliament only passes statutes affecting the organization of the courts on the advice or suggestion of the legal profession'. He is haunted by the ghost of Sir Edward Coke, and is inclined to believe in the common law as in a power independent of the state, forgetting that in so far as Parliamentary supremacy was established in 1688 the standing of the common law fell with that of the royal prerogative.*

When a new issue is raised, or someone suggests a new departure in government, there is a danger that lawyers respond with generalized observations about the 'separation of powers' or 'responsible government'. Such claims are not without foundation, but they are sometimes used to mask unjustifiable positions. When an attempt is made to take some new jurisdiction from a non-judicial body and give it to the ordinary courts—as in the case of the establishment of the Restrictive Practices Court—the judges recoil in horror, announcing that they could not possibly handle such a matter, since they would then be involved in determining questions of policy rather than legal questions. At the same time, when some traditional area of competence like workmen's compensation or rent restriction is removed from the courts and given to tribunals (or someone suggests the removal of divorce or negligence actions), some elements in the legal profession are prepared to make unthinking remarks about attempts 'to weaken the independence of the judges' or 'to destroy the Rule of Law'. There are even occasional references to Magna Carta and the Bill of Rights.

Question

Any merger of tribunals with the courts would raise the issues of the increase in the number of judges, the possible addition of lay judges and how to maintain the prestige of the judiciary. Is the prestige attributable to the exclusivity of the judiciary? If all administrative tribunal issues were to be transferred to a merged system, would it be necessary to hear them all before judges with the background currently possessed by English judges? But many disputes are complex. How would you organize the judiciary in a merged system?

I. ENGLAND AND THE EUROPEAN COURT OF JUSTICE

The entry of England into the European Communities by enactment of the European Communities Act 1972, added a new judicial institution of then uncertain scope. But it was obvious to the observer that the European Court of Justice would be an important part of the system. Not a new lowly tribunal with appeals fed into the regular court system, but a court which would for certain issues nudge aside the House of Lords from its lofty setting above the pack. Would the Law Lords quietly accept this nudge? English judges have had long years of protecting their territory, first as barristers fending off the persistent

---

* C.H. Sisson, The Spirit of British Administration 73 (2d ed 1965).

solicitors who wish additional rights of advocacy, then as judges keeping jurisdiction over as much subject matter as possible, and at least retaining substantial rights over appeals.

With the entry of England, the 1957 Treaty of Rome became part of the law of the United Kingdom. Some comment has been made earlier in this chapter regarding the sovereignty of Parliament and the Community. We will discuss this also in the section devoted to sources of law in Chapter 13. At this point we are interested principally in the Community as a new institutional structure, and especially in the added court, the European Court of Justice.

Because the final authority for the interpretation of Community law is the European Court of Justice in Luxembourg, an important part of English law is being developed by a judicial institution not only with a composition which differs from the ordinary English superior courts, but with a strong balance in favor of judges from civil law systems. One should not identify the court as a civil law court, however, but it does possess a structure likely to create a Community law with predominant influences from civil law jurisprudence.

Of interest is the extent to which decisions of the European Court will bear a resemblance to decisions of civil law courts, disclosing a more abstract nature which may render them less usable as precedent than decisions from common law systems. This nevertheless presupposes that decisions of the Court have some precedential value. Nothing in the organizational structure of the Court suggests such an intention, and the pattern of decisions supports this view. One may well expect, however, that judges of the Court trained in the common law may place greater emphasis on past decisions of the Court, particularly where they contain substantive analysis rather than abstract statements.

The addition of the European Court of Justice to English judicial institutions is one of the most important changes in English common law in several centuries. The lack of an enforcement procedure for the European Court of Justice, however, may mean that its decisions will have less impact in England than decisions of domestic courts. There is evidence of this to-date in some EC nations. Several decisions of the European Court have been ignored by nations against whose interests they have been rendered.

Chapter 11

LEGAL ACTORS IN ENGLAND

SECTION 1. INTRODUCTION

There is always a curiosity about how other people live and what they do. It fills books and popular magazines. It has captured a special name—biography, and become of such interest that we even peer directly into private lives by authors' discussions of their own lives—autobiography. As actors in a very special profession—whether having only recently crossed the law school threshold, or nearing the end of a lifetime career—knowing how our counterparts function in other legal systems takes on an added meaning. We may become better at our own tasks, and we should have more compassion and tolerance for our foreign colleagues. As we have seen in Chapter 3, legal actors in France and Germany may carry some labels with which we are familiar, but they may serve fundamentally different roles in society. The civil law notary is only one example.

The cast of characters in the common law includes some who do not differ markedly from those in civil law systems. There are practitioners who represent parties. There are persons who decide disputes. And there are those who train these persons to undertake their roles. But who these people are, and how they carry out those basic roles of the profession, differ not only from their counterparts in civil law systems, but differ within the common law tradition from system to system. What we call them and what they are assigned to do in the system, i.e., barristers assigned to represent clients at certain stages of a proceeding, magistrates assigned to settle criminal matters of lesser importance, are less significant to the comparatist than how they undertake their roles, how they are perceived by the public (and by themselves and others within the profession) and what tensions exist between them as they exercise their roles and others who review their acts from the sole measure of their effectiveness in the administration of justice. The English legal profession is philosophically a closed shop. Anthony Sampson noted that:

> All the conservatism, and exclusiveness of old institutions is to
> be found in the legal profession, which has grown up alongside the

old universities, as part of the classic route to parliament and political power, with its roots deep in history and religion: 'that great Gothic structure of authority,' as John Mortimer calls it, 'with its stone buttresses of power and its ancient ecclesiastical ornaments'. The law is the most extreme British example of a closed and self-regulating community, with all its strengths and weaknesses. Its proud traditions can enable judges to stand apart from the state apparatus, as the ultimate guarantors of human liberties; but they have also enabled lawyers to resist reforms more stubbornly than anyone, and to fortify their own privileges. Right-wing lawyers love to complain about the monopolies and restrictive practices of trade unions while they enjoy the most restrictive monopoly of all, protected by one of the oldest trade unions.[1]

We should know, through our years of education in the United States, of a few of the romanticized characteristics of some of the English actors. We recall Dicken's descriptions of Chancery in *Bleak House*. We have read of, or seen photographs or paintings depicting, the robed and wigged judges and barristers. Only our judges in the United States wear robes—and wigs are found nowhere among the tools of the trade. These superficial distinctions cannot be overlooked. The garments of office play a function in the rituals and machinery of justice. But we will go much deeper. From the form and substance of legal education, to the division of tasks between specialists (barristers and solicitors), to the existence of actors scarcely found in the United States (masters and lay magistrates), the English system is startlingly at contrast to our way of allocating roles to legal actors. That should be apparent as we begin where we must begin—in the education to practice law.

SECTION 2.   LEGAL EDUCATION

As professions evolve over long periods of time, the preparation stage for the profession tends to shift from on-site or apprentice training conducted by those actively functioning as practitioners, to institutions created for or adapted to the purpose of training. Those institutions may be under the close scrutiny of the profession. Indeed they may exist as organizations *of* the profession. Or they may be completely disassociated and often multi-disciplinary institutions. The university serves the latter role, the Bar and Law Society operated schools and Inns of Court the former. If the roles co-exist in both types of institutions, tensions are certain to evolve over role allocation.

The evolutionary shift of the educational role (academic *and* vocational) may be from apprenticeship directly to the university, without the establishment of a bar operated training site. This has been the experience in the United States. Law was for many decades learned in a law office under the supervision of practitioners. The development of

---

1. A. Sampson, The Changing Anatomy of Britain 149 (1982).

law faculties in universities provided an alternative. They became attractive to students who could afford the cost of a university education. They were likely to receive a more predictable offering of training. It was further attractive to the practitioner who may have lost a poorly paid (if at all) assistant, but who no longer had to spend so much valuable time in conducting the prospective lawyer's professional education.

The shift from learning in a lawyer's office to the university has evolved much more slowly in England. And it involved a unique institution—the Inns of Court. For those who seek to become courtroom advocates, the Inns have been and continue to be the single most important focus of one's attention. The law student in the United States concentrates on passing through the concentrated confines of university and law school training, culminated by passing a bar examination. He is then thrust into a wide expanse of geographic choice, and a life of contact with a considerable variety of people. There may be a similar pattern for the English law student who chooses to become a solicitor, but with a smaller territory in which to settle. But for the prospective barrister, the culmination of his education and the call to the Bar thrusts him not outward but into the cloistered atmosphere of the Inns of Court. His contact thenceforth is limited largely to his clerk, solicitors and judges who some years before pursued the same confined existence. Change is evolving slowly. Barristers now more frequently than before appear before non-professional courts and before lower level professional courts, and solicitors are slowly gaining increased rights of audience.

The study of civil law in the English universities developed as an academic discipline, much as one would study Greek history or English literature. Lawyers learned the common law in the courts. Qualification to practice law in England either as a barrister or a solicitor has never required a university legal education, although a law baccalaureate increasingly is the path selected by those intending a legal career. The decision to become a barrister or a solicitor—one may not be both in England—frequently is postponed until university graduation. Personal economics may be the deciding factor; becoming a barrister remains more costly. But the large amount of criminal work paid for by the government offers barristers hope of modest early remuneration.

The separation of solicitors and barristers evolved during the first two centuries after the Conquest. Persons appearing before the new common law courts were often assisted by one of a number of attorneys or advocates who spent their days milling about the courts. The attorneys or advocates initially were associated with the church, which had a dominant role in many areas of law. But as the church power waned, the advisors primarily were laymen. Sergeants and barristers carved out their niche as courtroom advocates, assisted in preparing the litigation by attorneys or, in the Court of Chancery, solicitors. The distinction between attorneys and solicitors, and the position of sergeant, were later abolished. The separation of the barristers and solicitors, however, has been preserved.

University teaching of law was for a long period unrelated to legal practice. Courses in the civil law, principally Roman law, were part of the general, university educational offerings; they were academic and theoretical rather than professional courses. The common law as an academic study was introduced to universities quite late. Blackstone lectured on common law at Oxford in the mid–18th century, as the first Vinerian Professor. A common law chair was established at Cambridge, and English law courses were introduced in University College and King's College in London. There was no rush to enroll. The number of students studying law in universities increased slowly. Training for legal practice, contrary to the continental custom, continued to be governed by the profession, not the universities. Law as an academic discipline in England evolved long after it had been firmly established on the continent. Irnerius gave his first lectures on Justinian's Digest at Bologna in the 11th century, when legal studies were becoming both systematic and scientific.

Few legal actors now believe that one should enter the practice of law either as a barrister or solicitor without first studying law at a university or polytechnic. A significant majority of recently qualifying barristers and solicitors possess law degrees. But unlike the practice in the United States and many other countries, the professions have not adopted this requirement as a mandatory qualification. The training of barristers in the Inns of Court and of solicitors through articles has such strong historical roots that the shift of training of members of the legal profession from close control of the profession to the universities has come very slowly. Suggestions that the vocational stage of training be provided by the universities and polytechnics rather than by the profession was approved by a majority of the Ormrod Committee, but opposed by a minority of the Committee which represent the profession. They prevailed. As discussed below, vocational training for both barristers and solicitors remains outside of the scope of the universities and under the control of the professions. But there is some encroachment on the training of the vocational stage for solicitors, since several universities (former polytechnics) offer the course leading to the Final Exam for prospective solicitors.

The quality of the instruction in the Inns of Court has long been criticized. A select committee in 1846 concluded that there was no adequate legal education available in England and that what was available was considerably inferior to that in the "more civilised states of Europe and America." [2] It was this report that stirred Oxford and Cambridge to establish law degrees, and later led to the creation of additional law faculties first at the University of London and later in

2. Report of the Select Committee on Legal Education, 1846, Vol. X, British Parli- amentary Papers, p. lvi, para. 2.

several of the provincial universities. But English law was taught much as was Roman law, as a liberal arts course with an emphasis on jurisprudence. Those prospective barristers and solicitors who did attend the university, tended to favor reading the classics or some other subject than law. Schools were not financially well endowed, and most young men interested in legal careers went directly into the Inns of Court or solicitors' offices as articled clerks. There was thus both a lack of interest on the part of prospective members of the profession in attending law programs in the universities, and an inability of the universities themselves to agree that law was an appropriate part of the university curriculum.

However slowly change has come to legal education in England, it has in fact come.

B. ROSHIER AND H. TEFF, "LAW AND SOCIETY IN ENGLAND"

179–181 (1980).*

The process of becoming a lawyer is relevant to the provision of legal services, because it helps to perpetuate certain distinctive features of the profession which reduce its capacity to meet the reasonable expectations of the public. Academic legal education is markedly influenced by the profession's views on what it is appropriate for a budding lawyer to study. Vocational training and professional entry requirements tend in practice to restrict admission to people from a comparatively narrow social range, conspicuously so in the case of the Bar, with its profoundly traditional and conservative ethos.

The legal profession is overwhelmingly a graduate one, increasingly composed of law graduates. By granting partial exemption from professional examinations to graduates who have passed specified "core" subjects (Constitutional and Administrative Law, Contract, Torts, Criminal Law, Land Law and Trusts), the Law Society and the Bar Council retain a measure of indirect control over academic law courses. We have referred earlier to criticisms of these courses for putting disproportionate emphasis on common law subjects, traditionally conceived, and on a narrowly analytical approach to legal study. We have also noted the recent attempts to broaden legal education. Clearly, teaching the law in context and the development of clinical legal education could help to create a broader conception of the lawyer's social role, especially in so far as such courses focus on the problems of the poor.

Just as tribunals have in practice assumed more importance for most people than the courts, so legal education is beginning to come to grips with previously neglected areas of law with which tribunals are concerned, such as housing, social security, and immigration. But it is

* Reprinted here and below with permission of B. Roshier and H. Teff, and Tavi-   stock Publications.

very much a beginning. The bulk of academic law teaching reveals an uneasy compromise between a liberal educational ideal and vocational demands....

* * *

If there has been reluctance to innovate at the academic stage, vocational training has in the past been notoriously unimaginative and uninspired, demanding little more of the student than a very retentive memory and being largely devoid of exercises to impart practical skills. Several of the worst features of these courses have recently been eliminated, but despite new proposals (as suggested, for example, in the Ormrod Report, 1971) no radical restructuring has taken place.[a]

The cost of becoming a lawyer obviously plays some part in determining the social class composition of the profession. This is notoriously the case at the Bar. The prospective barrister faces considerable expense in qualifying, maintaining himself during the twelve-month period of apprenticeship known as pupillage and often in his early years at the Bar.[1] This of course assumes that he is one of the approximately 50 per cent to be offered a place in a set of barristers' chambers. Practising from chambers is a prerequisite of a career at the Bar, which has the effect of limiting competition. The hazards are such that few will take the risk without access to private means. Solicitors during their apprenticeship as articled clerks face a much less daunting prospect, though their initial remuneration is also relatively modest.

Without impugning the high standards of the bulk of legal practitioners, it is difficult to imagine that someone asked to devise a blueprint for the organization of the legal profession would construct a system which closely resembled the one we now have. A whole network of restrictive practices persists, allegedly to preserve standards but often of seemingly questionable value when measured against the criterion of public interest in more competition and reduced cost. Yet precisely because it is the system we have, advocates of fusion or at least of less rigid separation, and of other reforms, are expected to provide elaborate justifications, while traditionalists need offer little more than dubious rationalizations of the *status quo,* coupled with blunt denials that criticism is well founded: 'The assertion that the two branches are of unequal status is quite simply false: the difference is of function'.[b]

In the United States, there is little opportunity to stray from the path of training requiring both an undergraduate degree (in no particular subject, a Bachelor of Education with a major in recreation will suffice, though it will hardly be persuasive to admissions committees in

a. Report of the (Ormrod) Committee on Legal Education, 1971, Cmnd. 4595.

1. Since 1991 law chambers have made available awards for pupils.

b. A. Leggatt, "Why Fusion is a Consummation not to be Wished," Law Society's Gazette 978, 24 Nov. (1976).

law schools) and a law degree. But England has always held open the door to practice to university graduates with non-law degrees, and also to those without any university education, through the characterization as "mature" students of those with some non-legal experience or qualification.

M. ZANDER, "LEGAL SERVICES FOR THE COMMUNITY"
144 (1978).*

[L]egal education of those who are not law graduates is considerably worse. There are four categories. For both branches there is the graduate who has read some subject other than law, and the mature entrant (over 25) who has some non-legal experience or qualifications. For the solicitors' branch there are also former Fellows of the Institute of Legal Executives and school-leavers. The non-law graduate or mature entrant can complete the academic stage of training by taking the new Common Professional Examination (CPE) in six 'core' subjects. . . . The Law Society announced in 1975 that from 1980 school-leavers would not be eligible for admission entry into articles. But, under pressure from City firms and other elements in the profession that resented the cost of putting a son or daughter through university, it withdrew and in 1977 announced that school-leavers would, after all, be able to come into the profession direct. The proposed scheme of training for school-leavers was announced in December 1977. They were to have the same 'A' level qualifications as would be necessary to get into university. They would then be required to take the first year law degree course at a polytechnic and pass four 'core' subjects. This would be followed by study (at a polytechnic, or privately or through a correspondence course) for an examination consisting of another four law subjects—the remaining two 'core' subjects plus two others. They would then be ready to take the Final and two years of articles like graduates.

It is inevitable that the courses for those not studying for law degrees will be considerably inferior in quality to those for degree courses. They will, for one thing, be significantly shorter in time. (The one-year CPE course clearly cannot be the equivalent of a three-year degree course. Even the six core subjects to be taught in the CPE course will receive less time than in the degree course.) The teachers will be less able—the quality of teachers in polytechnics is generally lower than in universities and that in technical schools is generally lower than in polytechnics. At institutions teaching for both the law degree and the CPE, the latters' students are likely to be treated and regarded as second-class citizens. Whatever arrangements are made for the academic training of school-leavers, they are likely to be no better than for those who take the CPE—and may be worse.

* * *

* Reprinted here and below with permission of Maurice Temple Smith Ltd.

[T]he quality of legal education in the law faculties has improved. Until recently the liberality of legal education was thought to depend chiefly on the subject-matter taught. Thus, Roman law, jurisprudence, international law, legal history or common law subjects were fit topics for a liberal education; company law, labour law, tax law and statute-dominated subjects were not. This view has now been largely rejected.... If a subject is one in which principles can be discovered and reasons for facts and decisions can be related to the principles, such a subject can be made the basis for liberal education. The most 'practical' of legal subjects can be taught so as to illuminate the workings of society and the clashes of social, economic, political and philosophical values implicit in legal rules. Equally, the most 'academic' of subjects can be taught in a dry, pedantic, narrow manner which is the antithesis of the spirit of liberal education.

Practical subjects are now normal ingredients in the law school menu. Moreover, the range of optional subjects has in recent years been broadening very considerably.... The quality of legal textbooks has risen noticeably in the past generation. Some teachers are trying to involve their students in real-life problems—mostly through legal advice services run by students under the supervision of staff and to a lesser extent through studies of the legal system. The profession unquestionably feels that legal education at the university is more relevant than in the past.

Its main defect, however, is that, in spite of the undoubted improvements, legal education in most universities and polytechnics is somewhat pedestrian. Worthy, but dull, is probably a not unfair description of the average course. In most law faculties students are never required to write anything longer than the weekly three or four page essay. They therefore never learn the skill of using the library for a piece of research.... Law journals edited by law students, normal in North America, are virtually non-existent. Even the new moves towards involvement in the provision of actual legal services and tentative steps towards some form of clinical legal education affect only a tiny number of students. The style or method of teaching in many instances still leans too heavily on requiring mastery of 'black letter law'—rules as rules rather than as illustrations of principles. The great American law schools have the advantage that they do not have to teach the law of their own states since the students come from all over the country. Teachers can focus on the fundamentals of their subject by reference to practice and results of that practice in different jurisdictions. The English law teacher is much more likely simply to teach the law of England without reference even to comparison with Scotland. Even at the best institutions, therefore, the general level of the education offered does not deserve more than moderate praise. It is distinctly better than even twenty years ago, but there is still a long way to go before the general standards of our best courses match the intellectual quality of the courses offered by the twenty or so leading American law schools.

———

Persons interested in a career in law today generally attend one of the approximately fifty universities or polytechnics which offer a first degree in law. Acquiring a law degree with completion of stipulated core subjects fulfills a substantial part of the mandatory barrister or solicitor training. The teaching is more concentrated on legal rules and sources than their practical application. In contrast, law school in the United States has become increasingly vocational. Clinical programs abound. They serve an educational function to a degree disputed and discussed at length by academics and practitioners. They may have a high educational content, or they may do little other than serve some perceived community need. But also considered vocational to the English system are courses in procedure and evidence, which are less so thought of in United States legal education. They are viewed as substantive law courses, usually no less so than contracts, torts or company law. Those who are hired to teach them usually are those who also teach other substantive courses. But they are also taught by those hired primarily to teach in legal clinic programs, being the substantive courses most closely related to the clinical work. The English law school curriculum has little focus on vocational subjects, but a course in evidence is offered at most schools and, although procedure is not offered as a separate course, it is hardly possible to learn English substantive law without learning procedure. One reason is that common law developed through procedure—with writs and fictions, with law and equity. Procedure had a tenacity that caused it to dominate the machinery of justice until a little over a century ago.

What is allocated to the university as its role in legal education is reflected by the course offerings. They may appear quite limited from the experience of a law student in the United States. But in England, because one studies law in what we call the undergraduate years, the student is more a generalist than is the case in the United States. The United States law student enters law school with a background of four years of essentially (and to most legal actors preferably) non-law courses, and then concentrates with few exceptions exclusively on law subjects. It is in this context that one should consider the curricular offerings not of law schools, but of universities and polytechnics offering law study. The following is that of the London School of Economics in the University of London.

First Year (the Intermediate Examination)

Public Law	Law of Contract and Torts
Law of Property I	English Legal System

Second Year (the Part I Examination)

Law of Obligations	Criminal Law

Optional Courses to the value of two courses

Third Year (the Part II Examination)
Jurisprudence
Optional Courses to the value of three courses

Optional Courses
Not all of the optional courses are taught every year.

Property II	Law and the Environment
Public International Law	Law of Corporate Insolvency
Labour Law	Political, Legal and Economic
Law of Business Associations	Anthropology
Intoduction to European Law	Law of Evidence
International Protection of	Conflict of Laws
Human Rights	Domestic Relations
Legal and Social Change	Administrative Law
since 1750	Women and the Law
Civil Liberties	Taxation
Computers, Information and	Law of Restitution
the Law	

Also available are (1) "outside" courses, meaning one course in another major field, (2) a law course from another college within the University of London, and (3) some six "half subjects," two of which constitute a full course. The graduate law (LL.M.) curriculum is extensive, but attended mainly by foreign students.

The LL.B. is awarded on the basis of written examinations. If one passes the first two years and is allowed to enter the third year, failure is very unlikely, although the person may receive the lowest passing grade. Very few graduates receive first class honors, more receive an "upper second", with the majority receiving a "lower second". At least an "upper second" is normally needed to pursue the barrister track after law school.

The training which follows a university education, and which also follows the decision to pursue the career of either a barrister or solicitor, is principally vocational. But it is also academic for those who have not taken the required law courses at the university, and for those who have entered by the route of the mature student.

An expectant barrister next joins one of the four Inns of Court, maintains the required "dining terms" and registers for the vocational training. The vocational or professional stage requires a year in attendance at the Inns of Court School of Law for those intending to practice in the United Kingdom. The bar candidate participates in substantive courses, practical exercises, and ultimately sits for the vocational examinations. This procedure is not inexpensive; it is undertaken in London and for many constitutes a financial obstacle. Government financial support has helped somewhat.

The professional stage concentrates on practical courses including Procedure and Evidence, both considered elementary courses in United States university legal education. A participant also must select two substantive courses. The quality of the courses has been strongly criticized.

Even the vocational courses conducted by the Law Society's College of Law and the Inns of Court Council of Legal Education have been poorly evaluated. Before 1968 reforms, teaching was almost entirely part-time, and since the lectures tended to lack any depth and attendance was not compulsory, most prospective practitioners enrolled in a commercial cram course. But in 1969 full-time teachers were appointed and the focus of the course altered from academic to practical. The Inns of Court Council of Legal Education training for prospective barristers has moved away from a primary focus on lectures to exercises in drafting, simulation, required viewing of actual court sessions and classes in advocacy. There is a greater linkage between this training and what the fledgling barrister will face during pupillage and the first years of practice at the Bar. The Law Society's College of Law conducts the vocational stage for prospective solicitors. Earlier experience with this stage of training was not unlike that at the Bar with respect to being the focal point of considerable criticism and leading students to take cram courses. Reforms were less forthcoming than for the vocational education of barristers. A Law Society proposal in 1974, that a one year mandatory course should be required, which would go beyond the traditional lectures to a focus on practical experience, was rejected by the profession. It would have been costly and it would have eliminated former training as articled clerks, although after the proposed new examination a three year service in a solicitor's office would have been required prior to being permitted to practice individually. Articles have been continued, the vocational stage now conducted either by the College of Law or several polytechnics, concluded by the Final Examination. Solicitors taking on articled clerks are required to provide experience in several areas, and it is important for graduates seeking articles to be aware of what those areas may be, since one may otherwise be assigned to areas beyond the articled clerk's interest.

An historical vestige which remains a requirement for becoming a barrister is "taking dinner" at the chosen Inn of Court. Those reading the law in earlier decades lived in their Inns, but pressures of space ultimately forced them out. Taking meals at one's Inn of Court has been substituted for residence. It does offer some collegiality. But the concept of mingling with senior barristers over an evening meal unfortunately has become more of an entry and departure without risking indigestion, or dining if a seat is available, and little more than being witness to the presence of one's seniors.

Completion of the vocational stage examinations leads next to a call to the Bar and a search for a one year pupillage with a junior barrister, intended to entail additional, supervised, practical instruction. The fortunate pupil may divide time between two chambers, gaining experience in different areas of concentration. The workload and cramped space of barristers often limits the pupillage to mostly self study in a law library, but the time must be endured before the new barrister may accept individual briefs. During the first six months of the pupillage the new barrister may not accept briefs, but even during the last six months the pupil is not likely to have many briefs. Berlins and Dyer have noted that a pupillage is insecure,

> because there is no guarantee that the pupil will be able to stay in the same chambers after his year is over. The barrister can only practice if he is offered a 'seat' or 'tenancy' in a set of chambers.... A young barrister may be allowed to 'squat' in chambers at the end of his pupillage, ... hoping for a chance of tenancy. Eventually, many abandon the Bar, ...[3]

Becoming a solicitor is, if not less academic, certainly less expensive. Completing the academic stage, a would-be solicitor registers at the Law Society's College of Law to undertake the vocational or professional stage. There is some parallel to the professional training of a prospective barrister in the Inns of Court School of Law, but the Law Society's teaching is directed to the special function of the solicitor. The candidate then becomes an articled clerk to one or more solicitors or to a governmental unit. The clerk is poorly compensated, but usually is better off than the fledgling barrister. The more conscientious firms provide their articled clerks with a variety of experiences, including moving them from one department to another where the size of the firm allows specialization. The less fortunate articled clerks, perhaps as many as one-third of them, receive no instruction at all, but pass their days much on their own doing minor, routine tasks (even their own typing), and biding their time until the "training" is over and they qualify as solicitors. When the period of articles is over, the new solicitor's name is added to a list maintained by the Master of the Rolls.

There has not been a total fusion of the education of the barrister and the solicitor, but earning a satisfactory law degree, or passing the Common Professional Examination by those with a non-law degree, fulfills the academic stage for both prospective barristers and solicitors. Law has become a graduate profession, the school leaver who once could become apprenticed to a barrister or solicitor and separately study for the exams must now do formal study. The unfading distinction in the legal education of barrister and solicitor candidates is at the professional stage. It appears remote that this stage will be merged unless there is an outright fusion of the two functions. That fusion was rejected by a Royal Commission study in 1979,[4] but the changes wrought in the two professions during the past few decades show an inexorable movement towards, rather than away from, fusion.

How well prepared is the fledgling barrister or solicitor upon being called to the Bar or enrolled in the list of the Law Society? The following comments show some of the problems with the apprenticeship in England.

3. M. Berlins and C. Dyer, "The Law Machine" 37 (3d ed. 1989).

4. Report of the Royal Commission on Legal Services, 1979, Cmnd. 7648.

K. EVANS, "ADVOCACY AT THE BAR"

3 (1983).*

If they find it, they will spend an aggregate of twelve months in somebody's chambers, watching how law is actually practised. Depending on their luck, the teaching that they receive during pupillage will be good, mediocre or virtually non-existent. Again, depending on their luck, they might or might not, during their second six months, get into court and hear the sound of their own voices. The lucky pupil will find himself or herself in a company with a pupil master who enjoys teaching and whose example is a good one, and in chambers where at the end of his 'first six' months he will regularly get sent to the magistrates' court to adjourn cases, to make simple bail applications, to deal with pleas of guilty and perhaps even to handle simple fights. If the chambers where he is have a mixed practice he may find himself before the Master in Chambers doing simple applications and before the county court judge on any number of small matters.

The odd thing is, however, that he will have received a very curious training for all of this. He will be standing there in court, passing himself off to the world as a real-life barrister. Yet his pupil master will hear none of this. The pupil master will never have heard his pupil speak in court, will never have had the opportunity of saying, 'No, no. That's *not* the way to do it!', will never have the chance of correcting the pupil's glaring errors and blundering early steps.

And why not? Because the system makes no provision for it. The pupil master is busy and when he is in court his client expects *him* to ask the questions, to address the judge and do the talking. Rarely, very rarely does the chance arise when one can safely say to one's pupil: 'I want you to take the next witness: just ask him so and so'. I have been able to do this just three times in fourteen years. And even if the master does get the chance of standing the pupil on his feet to break his duck with a few terrified sentences, the chance that he will be able to watch him do it again is almost non-existent. What happens in busy chambers is that the 'second six' pupil will be sent off to court to learn for himself by trial and error, and if the public realised just how little we do as a profession to train our newcomers, there would be a justifiable outcry.

* * *

England is not alone in this. America is even worse. There the new arrival can set up on the day he qualifies without any pupillage at all. And indeed it is generally accepted throughout the English-speaking world that the standards of the English Bar are by and large among the best. But as many a juryman and magistrate will tell you, that isn't

* Reprinted here and below with permis-   Publications Limited.
sion of K. Evans and Financial Training

saying much. Great advocacy is still very much to be found at the English Bar but our general standards, especially among the younger members, are low. Perhaps they always have been. It is high time that something were done about it.

R. HAZELL (ed.), "THE BAR ON TRIAL"
88, 94 (1978).*

Not only is the training provided within chambers sometimes excessively narrow, but at the moment training for the Bar is confined exclusively to practical experience acquired within the Bar. No attempt is made to introduce the young barrister to skills or disciplines other than his own, or to give him practical experience of related professions, or indeed of related aspects of the legal system. The most obvious blind spot is in relation to the other branch of the legal profession itself. Barristers will spend the whole of their professional lives advising solicitors, but the vast majority embark on their careers without any practical experience of how a firm of solicitors operates.

In most other jurisdictions where there is a split profession this is not the case. In Australia and South Africa it is standard practice (though not a professional requirement) for would-be barristers to spend a couple of years training first in a solicitor's office; in Scotland an intrant is *required* to spend 21 months with a solicitor before he can start 'devilling' (pupillage) for a practising advocate. The Scottish Faculty of Advocates says that it regards the period in a solicitor's office as 'invaluable', and it is not difficult to see why. Solicitors are the consumers of the Bar's services, and any barrister who has worked in a solicitor's office must have a much clearer idea of what solicitors expect and require of barristers, and will be far better equipped to provide his solicitor-clients with sensible and useful advice.

* * *

Lack of payment for his work is not the only indignity a pupil has to suffer. In many other little ways he is made to feel unwanted, transient, a second-class citizen. In a number of chambers pupils are not allowed to use the telephone, nor can they be telephoned: the clerks are told (or themselves decide) not to take calls for pupils. In one set of chambers where I was a pupil we were not even allowed to share in the chambers' supply of tea and coffee!

* * *

It is true that some barristers, for the noblest of reasons, feel very strongly that all students who hope to practise (however forlornly) should have the chance to do pupillage; but the numbers of those currently embarking on pupillage so far exceed the numbers of those who can hope to enter practice that some chambers are already deliberately trying to cut down on the number of pupils they take in. They

* Reprinted here and below with permission of Quartet Books.

have no room for them afterwards, and feel that it is dishonest to offer pupillage to people who have no prospect of practising. This policy may appear harsh; but I think myself that it is right. Not only is a great deal of individual misery avoided, but a considerable body of highly skilled people is put to better use: it is pointless wasting the time of pupils (and of their masters) training them for a profession in which they will not be able to remain. However, whether a given individual will be able to find a tenancy depends so much at the moment on his being in the right place at the right time that one can sympathize with those who feel that everyone should at least have the chance to draw a ticket in the lottery.

Notes and Questions

1. As is true in civil law systems, legal education in England and most common law nations is undergraduate training. The degrees differ. Some institutions offer a B.A. in Law. Others an LL.B. Do you believe you would receive an adequate training to practice law were it to be an undergraduate offering, perhaps followed by a year of vocational study, a bar exam and a brief apprenticeship or pupillage? If you believe the undergraduate program would be inadequate to carry such an educational role, do you also believe that the even shorter three year period for the baccalaureate in England therefore produces persons not adequately and/or not as well prepared to practice?

2. Does the English system do a better job of allocating the academic and vocational stages of a legal education? Should they be segregated at all?

3. Casebooks such as those we use in the United States are not in common use in English legal education, though in recent years a few have been written. Why did the case method develop in the United States rather than in England? It may seem ironic that there is an increasing use of casebook collections in England at the time criticism of the case method seems quite extensive in the United States. Does the goal of a legal education in England differ to the extent that casebooks would seem more or less useful as a teaching tool there?

4. If you can make an assessment of the legal education system in England with the above materials, what might your main concerns be were you to be studying in England now instead of the United States? Would you in any way appear to be better off under the English system?

5. Does the English system better prepare the English lawyer to think conceptually, to place law in the context of society, and, as mentioned in note 3 to Chapter 3, section 1, above, acquire the "grammar of the law"?

6. Are the arguments against fusion persuasive to you—forgetting if you can your notions of its discriminatory aspects?

7. The obstacles to becoming a lawyer that women encounter are not the patrimony of American women. Might there be more, and more subtle, obstacles in the English system? Many women choose the solicitor route because the barrister obstacles appear greater. Does this create an over-looked argument for fusion—that the divided profession functions in an unacceptably discriminatory manner by allowing women into the profession,

but by shunting them off to the solicitor side to preserve the maleness of the Inns and bench?

8. Zander suggests that the apprenticeship system allows some control over numbers entering the profession. But it also may be used to control who enters the profession. If one is to criticize the vocational training stage in England, and the lack of such a stage in the United States, it is the bar of practicing lawyers who must bear the criticism. In Germany, control of the vocational stage, and even the first *Refendar* examinations at the end of one's academic training, is firmly lodged in the courts. Would the system function better in England or the United States if there were more governance by the courts? Or should the training be regulated by legislation on the basis that it is in the public's interest to have better preparation of lawyers before they are admitted to practice?

SECTION 3. LEGAL PROFESSIONS

The civil law system offers, or rather demands from the law graduate, a choice from a wider list of legal professions than we think of in the common law systems. The reason principally is because we add the judiciary to the choices at the time of qualification in civil and socialist systems. And we may also add the notary as a special profession. The choice in the common law systems is not whether to represent clients or to be a judge, or perhaps to be a notary. It is a single choice. Whom to represent. Will one be a private practitioner with a variety of clients, or house counsel representing a single, usually corporate, client, or even choosing to represent the government by becoming a government lawyer, which one should distinguish from being a lawyer (law graduate) in government.

In contrast to the United States, England and several other common law nations have split the profession into those who deal directly with clients, the solicitors, and those who are called upon by solicitors to answer special legal questions, prepare papers, and most importantly, do the work of advocacy in the higher courts, the barristers. We have seen that the split comes not at the time of entry into practice, but during the educational process. The choice, once made, is rarely reversed.

It is difficult for the United States law student to realize how difficult and emotional this decision can be for an English student. The United States student graduating from law school and passing a bar is a lawyer. There is no further choice to be made which in any way is as significant as the barrister-solicitor decision. A United States graduate may choose to be a Wall Street lawyer or a small town sole practitioner, a trial lawyer or an office work lawyer. But he is still called *Lawyer*. The English division raises one overriding question for the comparatist. Does the split profession lead to a better delivery of legal services? That is a question to which we should return after reading about what solicitors and barristers do.

A. SOLICITORS

The origin of the solicitor is less elitist than that of the barrister, and the solicitor's work has been less romanticized than the trial advocacy of the wigged and robed barrister. Attorneys who worked directly with clients preparing litigation for disputes before the King's Bench and Common Pleas courts usually did not possess the educational level of barristers. Nor did they present the actual cases in court. The role of advocate was carefully protected by the barristers. The term solicitor initially applied to an attorney appearing in the Chancery Court; that same role was called a proctor before the admiralty and ecclesiastical courts. These attorneys, solicitors and proctors—all later called solicitors—were first jointly housed with barristers in the Inns of Court, but the solicitors were ejected in the late 16th century and organized their own association.

Solicitors outnumber barristers seven to one. The more than 55,-000 practicing and employed solicitors in the United Kingdom are not as concentrated in London as are the barristers. Solicitors practicing in London do not have their offices within monastic chambers like the barristers' Inns of Court.

The life of the solicitor is on the whole more relaxed than the barrister's, though the solicitor is less apt to achieve the fame accessible to a successful barrister, which may culminate in judicial appointment to the High Court. The solicitor may reach the heights of compensation of the most successful barrister, however, and an average solicitor is more likely to achieve a comfortable financial position than his counterpart at the bar. Some new solicitors choose to accept a salaried position with a government authority or in industry, but the majority seek employment with a firm of solicitors.

The work of the solicitor is concentrated in the areas of conveyancing and estate law, in advising on business matters, and for some, litigation preparation and, in the lower courts, some advocacy. In the major cities large firms of solicitors often concentrate on advice to industry. They are quite similar to large firms in the United States, with the exception of refraining from the advocacy jurisdiction of the barrister.

Solicitors, like United States lawyers, may have their offices in large cities, or in tiny hamlets. It is a choice not facing the barrister, whose decision is whether to practice from chambers in London, or to have chambers in one of the other principal cities in England or Wales.

Expectation of partnership after some years as a salaried associate parallels the participation in a law firm in the United States, although the solicitor is expected to buy in to the partnership and, unless he has sufficient resources, he may have to remain a salaried employee. A solicitor who is a partner in a large and well known firm may expect sizable financial rewards, and also will benefit from the work of his articled clerks, assistant solicitors and junior partners. Large firms nevertheless are the exception; most solicitors practice alone or in a small group.

The solicitor traditionally has been a law office practitioner, advising clients on legal, and often personal and business, matters. The solicitor does accompany the associated barrister to court to assist in a trial, but the role of courtroom adversary is preserved and protected by the barristers. More recently, solicitors have gained authority to act as advocates in the lower courts. They appear in magistrates' courts, in county courts, in some tribunals, and, in limited circumstances approved by the Lord Chancellor, in criminal matters before the Crown Courts. They have nearly the same rights of audience as barristers in the European Court. They are chipping away at the boundaries of the barristers' preserve, and there is a tension between the two professions of which the public largely is unaware.

Several developments in the 1980s affected the role of the solicitor. Solicitors lost their monopoly on property conveyancing, having to share that work with estate agents. It was the largest contributor to the income of many solicitors. This loss spurred the solicitors' interest in acquiring new territory, especially increased rights of audience in the courts. Two developments were thought to perhaps provide additional rights of audience. The first was the creation of the Crown Prosecution Service (CPS) in 1985, a new, independent prosecution service which would employ some 1,500 barristers and solicitors as full time prosecutors. Solicitors hoped that they would have a right to appear in all criminal cases, including matters before the Crown Courts. The plan was condemned by Bar members, who viewed it as an encroachment on the barristers' exclusive domain. The issue of such increased rights was deferred to the second area, the then ongoing consideration of reforming legal services, ultimately leading to the Courts and Legal Services Act of 1990. The results, explored below, were disappointing to the solicitors. They gained more rights in theory than rights in actuality.

Although solicitors may not have gained rights to the higher courts, the Courts and Legal Services Act transferred considerable business from the High Court to the county courts. This essentially means much more advocacy work for solicitors. The same results from the transfer of business from the Crown Court to the magistrates' courts.

B. BARRISTERS

> Their work "leaves very little time for friendship, travel or art.... That explains why most successful barristers are hardly worth sitting next at dinner—they yawn so."

Virginia Woolf, Three Guineas (1938).

There are few institutions in England more tradition-bound than that of the some 6,600 practicing barristers (4,600 practicing in London). Isolated in their Inns of Court, barristers view with a mixture of alarm and disdain any encroachment on their domain by the larger group of solicitors. The 1979 Royal Commission report brought a breath of relief to the barristers; it recommended perpetuation of the division of the profession. The Courts and Legal Services Act of 1990 may result in rights of audience for solicitors but its implementation is in the hands of the judges, who may not open the door very wide to solicitors.

Four Inns of Court survive: Gray's Inn, Lincoln's Inn, Inner Temple and Middle Temple. Sergeants' Inn, composed of the more senior barristers, and the Chancery Inn, earlier were merged with other Inns.

M. BERLINS AND C. DYER, "THE LAW MACHINE"

43 (3d ed. 1989).

... Stepping from the bustle of Fleet Street into the courtyards and lawns of the Temple is like taking a trip backwards in time.... Lord Gifford, whose chambers are an exception, located not in the Inns but in an ordinary office building in Covent Garden, finds the atmosphere of the Inns attractive but 'very corrupting':

> Barristers who operate from London spend their whole working life either in that little precinct, that little enclave of the Inns of Court, or they go into courts which themselves are very artificial theatres, cut off from the real world. And when you think that a number of the people we're talking about have spent their early life anyway in some way set apart—they may have been to public schools or they may have been to an old university—it enhances this feeling that we are something special, something above the rest, some special breed of being.

A. SAMPSON, "THE CHANGING ANATOMY OF BRITAIN"

152 (1982).

... The Inns have retained more completely than Oxbridge colleges their ancient autonomy and privileges. Their constitution was described by Sir Frederick Pollock in 1922 as 'a survival of medieval republican oligarchy, the purest, I should think, to be found in Europe'; and it has not changed much since for the Inns have refused to delegate real power to the barristers' professional body, the Bar Council. During the heyday of Victorian reformers in the 1860s and 1870s they resisted pressures much more successfully than parliament, universities, the civil service or the army: they refused to change their constitutions and provide a system of legal education, and they remain today uncontrolled by any statute. They are ruled by their 'benchers,' the self-perpetuating senior lawyers who sit at high table, and their wealth remains secret, since they are (almost uniquely) exempted from publishing accounts.

R. HAZELL, (ed.), "THE BAR ON TRIAL"

48 (1978).

* * *

The Ormrod Committee [on Legal Education 1971] appeared to disagree about the value of dining and its associated traditions:

'It is difficult to evaluate it reliably. It may play some part in the process of identification and in laying the foundations of that corporate spirit which is a real and important characteristic of the Bar. This object would be fostered if the practice of barristers and students dining at *separate* tables in hall was done away with altogether. On the other hand, the necessity to make frequent journeys to London can be a hardship.... We do not wish to destroy the positive advantage of this tradition, but we think that it is essential that it should be adapted to present day conditions....'

Sir Robert Megarry, in an otherwise approving account of life at the Bar, also expressed doubts about the value of dining: 'Conversation at the students' table tends toward the personal, the trivial and the political.... Today it is difficult to find any students who can see any value or utility in the ritual of dining in Hall. The food, it is said, is poor or scanty or both, and the conversation does no more than pass the time, but the Inn requires it, so one must go through the pointless ceremony.'

In response to these criticisms the Inns have in recent years made some effort to improve the value of dinners. Moots are occasionally held, and on one or two evenings a term there may be an after-dinner speaker; but only a small proportion of students ever take part in the moots, and since the after-dinner lectures are optional a number of students leave hall before the lecture begins. It is clear that the original rationale of dining, according to which the students learned from the wisdom and experience of older barristers, can never be recaptured, for the simple reason that on most nights there are few if any practising barristers to be seen; they have all gone home to their wives and families, and apart from a token number of Benchers dining separately at High Table the Hall is almost entirely occupied by students. In these circumstances any attempt to restore to dinners their educational purpose can meet with only very limited success; and if the Inns really wish to pursue in earnest their (eminently laudable) aim of increasing the contact between students and practitioners some other means must be found. There can be little doubt that attendance at a residential course, which included moots, debates, lectures and discussions, in the company of Benchers and barristers would fulfil the aim of the Inns much more effectively than attendance at a series of dinners where, as often as not, the student only meets other students and his sole purpose is to eat dinner and leave as quickly as possible.

* * *

Within the Inns themselves one simple change would effect a revolution almost overnight: if one could only turn the clock back a hundred years to the days of Serjeants' Inn, when the judges on appointment automatically left their old Inns, the Inns would be governed by barristers again. It is traditional at the Bar to ignore the difference between barristers and judges, and to say with Sir John Donaldson that 'the reality is that "the profession" consists of "Bench and Bar" and not the Bar alone'. The Pearce Committee certainly went along with this, adding for its part that it did 'not want to lose the benefit of the wisdom and experience of those who have become Judges'.

It is high time that this particular fiction was laid to rest. The profession is the Bar and not the Bench and Bar. A judge is a barrister no longer, but a salaried official of the state; and his interests and concerns are very different from those of a busy self-employed professional man or woman. Certainly judges have wisdom and experience; so do all those in other walks of life who have arrived at the end of their professional careers. But in no other profession is it suggested that the wisdom and experience of retired practitioners entitle them to continue to play an active part in the government of the profession—let alone to dominate it, as the judges do in the Inns. The Bar can benefit from their wisdom and experience without abandoning its right to govern its own institutions. Although Serjeants' Inn can never be revived, it would not be difficult to provide that while judges could remain members of their Inns, and even Benchers, they should do so in a non-executive, purely honorific capacity.

This change coupled with direct election of the executive benchers would serve to end almost all the inefficiencies and absurdities of which barristers at the moment complain. If they were dissatisfied with the management of their Inn the remedy would lie in their own hands. But it would not exempt the Inns from continuing to be the proper objects of public concern. It would be naive to suppose that the moment the Bar takes over the Inns all the abuses would cease; one cannot ignore the danger that the Inns will be regarded simply as clubs, and that the profession will not take seriously its responsibilities for the education and training of students and the career development of young barristers.

———

Once a barrister is settled into chambers after completing the year of pupillage, he begins his practice of advocacy, of drafting documents and of rendering opinions. The barrister does not have direct contact with the client. Where there is a need to confer with the client the barrister will meet only in the presence of the solicitor, and usually in the chambers of the barrister. Barristers may not form partnerships, as may solicitors, although they do work together in chambers, sharing a clerk and secretarial assistance. The clerk is more of an office manager; he negotiates his barristers' fees with solicitors and usually receives a commission as compensation. The fees are not fixed, but are set according to the complexity of the case and the reputation of the barrister. The fees are paid to the barrister by the solicitor, who may require an advance from his client to avoid having to pay the barrister without receiving the expected source of that payment, the fee owing from the client, as well as an admonishment from the Law Society.

Barristers do considerable office work, preparing wills, contracts, and drafts and written opinions. But their protected monopoly and the role which makes them so distinctive is as advocates in the Royal Courts and House of Lords. The successful barrister must be able to assimilate rapidly a great number of facts, possess a sound awareness of procedure and the rules of evidence, and use that knowledge in court where his capacity to think and respond immediately will determine his future.

Particular barristers often are sought by solicitors because of the former's specialization, and a firm of solicitors will generally direct work to a select list of barristers. If the work is of only a nominal level of skill, a junior barrister may be associated. For a complex matter, a Queen's Counsel may be preferred. That role is discussed below.

It is advocacy for which the barrister is known. It may well begin in the magistrates' courts.

R. HAZELL (ed.), "THE BAR ON TRIAL"
87 (1978).

When I first appeared in a magistrates' court to represent a client of my own I had only been in such a court twice before, during 15 months of pupillage. This was because all three of my pupilmasters had practices confined almost exclusively to the High Court. Such an experience is quite common among pupils, and something about which the Ormrod Committee expressed specific concern:

> 'The danger that the pupil will not receive a sufficiently wide experience is a real one. Most pupilmasters are aware of this, and try to ensure that their pupils have the opportunity of spending part of the time with other members of chambers, particularly the younger ones who are doing the sort of work which the pupil will be doing when he has completed his pupillage, for example, in county courts and magistrates' courts.'

The experience of most of those who have contributed to this book is that this latter statement is untrue. The Ormrod Report continued:

> 'We think that this attitude should be encouraged, and that it should be generally accepted ... that part of the obligation of the master to the pupil is to ensure that he gets as much, and as varied, an experience as the chambers can provide.'

One way in which the committee suggested this might be achieved would be 'by altering the basis of pupillage, so that the pupil becomes a pupil of a set of chambers (rather than of one member), or by the head of chambers assuming responsibility for seeing that the pupils in his chambers get as wide an experience as possible.... While there are definite advantages in a pupil having a specific master, the emphasis should be upon "reading in chambers" rather than solely with an individual barrister.' In order to prevent an inexperienced young barrister like myself from being let loose on an unsuspecting public this proposal should be incorporated in the code of ethics as a professional obligation. A very firm lead needs to be given from above directing that each head of chambers should either assume responsibility himself for the training received by the pupils in his chambers, or should appoint some other member of chambers to do so.

* * *

His advocacy will take him to other courts, indeed he has little choice in the matter. He must accept offered briefs. It is the "cab-rank rule". As K. Evans notes:

> Because the Bar as a whole has seen, over the centuries, how mistaken an individual and initial impression can be, and because as a profession we abhor the thought that an accused person might find himself standing in the dock with no one to defend him,.... [P]roviding a barrister is available to take the case and providing it is within his field of expertise and the fee is reasonable, then he *must* take the brief. If he refuses, he can be hauled up before the Professional Conduct Committee and disciplined for his refusal. If he privately thinks that his client is guilty, that is of no consequence. He is an advocate, not a judge.[5]

M. BERLINS AND C. DYER, "THE LAW MACHINE"
40 (3d ed. 1989).

The brief to appear for the defence in a criminal trial is also the cause of one of the main criticisms about the system, the late return of briefs. Barristers operate by a cab-rank rule. Like taxi-drivers they can't pick and choose their clients, nor even which side they are on. But because one trial will end earlier than expected and another will go on much longer, a clerk will often double-book a barrister, rather as travel agencies or airlines overbook, to make sure that he isn't left with an empty, and hence unpaid-for, day. The briefs that the barristers can't handle then have to be returned to be reallocated, usually to another member of the chambers who happens to be free—sometimes to someone more junior. Perhaps as many as one-third of briefs are returned in this way, and sometimes the return is made very late—the evening before the trial. All this may seem sensible and efficient from the Bar's point of view, but it can be a disaster for the client. He has been told by his solicitor that a particular barrister is appearing on his behalf, and comes

---

5. K. Evans, Advocacy at the Bar 29 (1983). Professor Michael Zander suggests that the cab rank rule is a myth, and that it is now used as an indirect means for barristers to limit rights of audience to higher courts. See M. Zander, The Myth of the Cab Rank, 140 New Law Journal 558 (1990).

to court to find another. Often he believes—sometimes justifiably—that the new counsel foisted on him is inferior, and doesn't properly know the case. It leads to bitterness and loss of confidence in the system of justice. . . .

* * *

———

A lawyer in the United States usually is aware of his schedule for the ensuing few weeks, although it is never certain how long a trial will be delayed, nor how long it will last once started. Because the English barrister receives his briefs from his clerk, which may occur the afternoon before the trial, there is considerable uncertainty for a barrister as to just where he might be tomorrow or in the next few days. The comments of two young barristers illustrate the daily life of an advocate, and the external forces which guide one's schedule.

E. USHER, "CAREERS IN THE LAW IN ENGLAND AND WALES"

52, 49 (1982).*

The best way I can describe my job is to outline a fairly typical week:

Sunday: After dinner at about 8 pm I did some preparation on the brief I had for the next morning and worked until midnight. It is quite normal for me to have to work at weekends, especially between October and July. The courts take a summer break, and when term starts in the autumn I manage to keep abreast of things during the week, but as Christmas approaches and I spend more time in court and become progressively more tired, I have to start working at weekends to keep up.

Monday: At 7 am I got up and drove to Maidstone Crown Court and was in court from 10 am to 12.30 pm, opposing an appeal against conviction by a man convicted of dangerous driving. His application was unsuccessful. The case finished early so I decided to take a long lunch break, and was back in chambers around 4 pm. I then drafted a pleading in a civil case I had been instructed in, and at 5 pm three briefs for the following day were delivered to me. I worked on these until 6.30 pm and then went home. After dinner I did a further hour-and-a-half's work on the briefs.

Tuesday: I was up again at 7 am and caught the 8.35 train from Liverpool Street to Cambridge, arriving at court by 10 am. The three briefs were to appear as prosecuting counsel to oppose appeals against sentence that were being brought by three people, two convicted of causing actual bodily harm, and the other of a motoring offence. I had read the papers on the train and discussed the cases with my instructing

* Reprinted with permission of Kogan Page, Ltd.

solicitors for half-an-hour, and I was then in court from 10.30 am to 12.30 pm, and from 1.30 pm to 4.30 pm. My clerk told me I was to be back in Cambridge again next day and that the briefs were in chambers, so I went back to London and picked up the papers at about 7 pm and went home. I should have read the briefs that night but as I didn't get home until 8 pm, I confess that after dinner I fell asleep in an armchair at about 9 pm!

Wednesday: I took the same train to Cambridge, reading the papers on the way. This time I was to prosecute a shoplifter, and oppose the appeal against conviction of a man found guilty of stealing from his employer. I was in court the whole day, and returned to chambers to collect Thursday's papers. I worked on these for an hour and then went home where I did a further three hours' work, finishing around midnight.

Thursday: I caught the 8.10 am train from Victoria to Canterbury, arriving before 10 am, having gone over the papers on the train. I had been briefed in a civil case in which I was defending a man whose landlord was trying to evict him. The case proved to be too long to be heard in the time the court had set aside for it, so it was adjourned, part-heard, at lunch-time. I went back to chambers and worked on a set of civil papers. I had been instructed to advise in a contractual matter and to settle pleadings if I felt it was an appropriate case to fight. I was home by 8 pm.

Friday: I was in chambers all day working on papers. I try to return paperwork to solicitors in about a fortnight, and it certainly helps if I can have an uninterrupted day once in a while. Without that I have to work on papers after court and at weekends. That day I worked until 7 pm.

Whilst it is true that barristers earn above the average income, it must be clear from the outline of my week that no one joins the profession just for the money, and if you took the hourly rate for the job it is obvious that you could earn a lot more doing something else requiring a similar level of responsibility and skill. What I enjoy is the control I have over what I do—on Monday I took a long lunch break and as a result I had to work late, but that was my choice and I didn't have to explain it to anyone.

* * *

You get used to having to wear black, in time, and you learn what clothes look neat and feel comfortable with the formal color and gown— you also get used to your career being incompatible with an ordered social life! In the second six months as a pupil you 'get on your feet' and can represent clients in court. Again, I remember my first brief, not so much for the case itself as for the surrounding circumstances. It was in the summer and I had been hanging around chambers for a couple of days hoping that the clerk might give me a brief. Finally, on a particularly lovely afternoon, I decided to give up my vigil and go and play tennis, and I had just made all the arrangements when the clerk told me I could go to court instead if I wanted to! Faced with the prospect of my first case, the game went by the board. I soon realised why barristers never make firm social commitments midweek. You can never be sure that you won't have to work in an evening, and, if you take on criminal cases, you have the added problem that the Crown Courts, except in particularly complex or lengthy cases, do not publish the lists of the cases they will hear the next day until about 4 pm on the afternoon before. So it is not until that time that you know whether you will be in court, or where. If you are in court you will probably need to spend the evening reading the papers. Of course, no matter how inconvenient this may be, no barrister, particularly one starting at the Bar, will ever want to turn work away. It has not been unknown for me to go to the theatre and leave at the first interval to go and work on papers for the next day. To have a career at the Bar you have to be prepared to arrange the rest of your life around it and you have to enjoy what you are doing enough not to resent that.

. . . When you start, you'll be in the magistrates courts dealing with people accused of shoplifting; driving offences; minor robberies, burglaries and juvenile crime. It is unlikely that you will start by defending hard-fought cases. You will probably be making applications for bail for your clients or representing them at committal or remand hearings, or simply making pleas in mitigation on their behalf in cases where they have pleaded guilty to the charge. At about the time you start dealing with 'fights' in the magistrates courts you will probably start receiving briefs to undertake the smaller matters in the Crown Courts.

Equally, if you start with civil cases you won't be dealing with contested divorces or High Court disputes over defectively-built public buildings, but you may appear in magistrates courts representing wives in undefended claims for maintenance from their husbands, and you will often be asked to advise on smaller consumer problems. As your experience grows, so will the level of responsibility and you will soon have the opportunity to take on a variety of county court cases such as disputes between landlords and tenants; parents over children; buyers and sellers over products or payments.

* * *

The way your practice builds up, and the success you achieve, is largely dependent on your clerk. It is the clerk who persuades a solicitor to try you out and who assesses when you are ready to take on more difficult cases. A good clerk will build up not only your practice, but also your confidence to match it. Slowly you will start to specialise to some extent, since it is extremely difficult to keep abreast of developments in the law right across the board, and also your clients will look to you not only to advise them on their legal position but to give a prediction of what is likely to happen to them. . . .

* * *

———

Barristers with at least ten years experience may decide to "take silk," substituting silk for stuff robes and assuming the title Queen's Counsel.   Those who do not choose to be Queen's Counsels (the Lord Chancellor must give his consent) remain junior barristers throughout their careers.   About ten percent of English barristers take silk. Queen's Counsel (or leader) status, once limited to barristers working for the Crown, is now sought by barristers in general practice who hope they possess a sufficiently strong reputation to encourage solicitors to retain them for more complex and, consequently, more highly compensated matters, and to limit their work to advocacy and giving oral and written opinions.   Until recently a Queen's Counsel had to appear in court with a junior barrister as an assistant, a requirement abolished in an attempt to reduce legal fees.   But it is perpetuated now as a custom.   A Queen's Counsel will not often go to court without a junior, and a clerk may not be willing to brief a Queen's Counsel who does not follow the rule.   The attempt to change the rule was thought to assist some who had taken silk unwisely, who did not have a sufficient reputation to draw the higher fees necessary to pay both the Queen's Counsel and a junior barrister.

A Queen's Counsel who does not succeed financially must not return to junior status.   A way of alleviating an unwise choice is to seek and accept some minor judicial appointment.   Seeking Queen's Counsel status thus is one more risk in a profession already filled with obstacles. But if success is achieved as a leader, the financial rewards are quite substantial.

The barrister has carefully defended his courtroom turf, and his feeling of superiority over the solicitors.   He remains reluctant to accept change that will alter his status, a reluctance which often results in an unfavorable public attitude.

R. HAZELL (ed.), "THE BAR ON TRIAL"
30 (1978).

Officially the Bar is no longer the senior branch of the legal profession, but unofficially there is a widespread feeling that barristers are still the superiors of solicitors, both intellectually and socially.... Today the Bar continues to maintain its unofficial seniority in a host of different ways.   Some have already been mentioned: the monopoly over virtually all judicial appointments, the wearing of wigs, the different rows occupied in court.   And in other little ways the status differences are preserved: other counsel are referred to in court as 'my learned friend,' solicitors simply as 'my friend'.   When a solicitor wants to write a letter to a barrister on a professional matter he cannot do so direct, but has to write to him through his clerk.   When barristers were consulted in 1973 over the design of new court buildings, they asked that whenever reasonably possible counsel should not be asked to share a room with solicitors for luncheon. And when a conference is held, however busy the solicitor and however junior the barrister, it is always the solicitor who comes to see the barrister, and never *vice versa;* indeed it is a breach of professional etiquette for counsel (save in the most exceptional circumstances) to go to the solicitor.

There are few barristers nowadays who would defend these differences simply for reasons of snobbery; although a senior barrister (now a Q.C.) once told me that he was opposed to fusion because solicitors were not really gentlemen, and we were. But a large number of barristers simply enjoy being different. It may be asked whether there is any harm in this; the answer I think is provided by Lord Goodman in his comment on the wearing of robes. Most barristers like the importance conferred on them by their wigs and gowns, and will zealously defend the tradition as lending dignity to court proceedings and authority to counsel. This is Lord Goodman's reaction:

> 'I do feel that it is no longer appropriate, and indeed faintly ridiculous, that grown members of a learned profession should wear period costumes. This is particularly so since they adopt the convention of our undergraduate days, that the honourable nature of a garment is reflected by its age and tatters. But I also believe that there is a more important aspect of the wig and gown than the question of maintaining a tradition or discarding it. I think it reflects an attitude on the part of the people who wear it which is no longer a relevant or contemporary one. It serves to maintain differences and distinctions which I believe should be minimized and not stressed.'

* * *

There is one other way in which the conventions and traditions of the Bar affect the development of the law and its institutions, and that is by ensuring that barristers who challenge the conventions do not reach positions of importance in which they can influence these matters. Outwardly the Bar has a reputation for tolerance and respect for differing views and eccentricities, but this tolerance only exists within clearly defined limits. Almost any senior barrister will privately give examples of colleagues who were passed over or made to wait for silk or the Bench, simply because they did not conform; and anyone whose nonconformism extends to challenging the practices and traditions of the Bar itself puts his career in serious jeopardy. But of course such cases are extremely rare: most barristers are conformist by training, if not by temperament, and for those few who are not the ceremonies, rules and patterns of behaviour in the Inns soon ensure that they pay proper respect to the ethos and traditions of the Bar which are inculcated into them by their elders.

The organization of barristers' chambers reflects the prohibition of any formal partnership association by barristers, although there is much sharing among barristers of the expenses of operating a practice. They are in many ways *de facto* partnerships, as Hazell notes.

> The first thing which is worth remarking is that in many respects chambers are already partnerships in fact, though not in law. The most important respect is that chambers share a common fund of goodwill. If one member of chambers damages this, all will suffer; if one member prospers, the others will benefit also. In matters of organization chambers are also run as partnerships. Most chambers have a collective insurance policy to indemnify their members against liability for negligence; and chambers expenses on rent, secretarial facilities, law reports, postage etc., are apportioned not by keeping individual accounts, but *pro rata*. The only respect in which chambers are not already partnerships is that the rules of etiquette strictly forbid barristers from sharing work or fees as partners.[6]

The barrister's life to a surprising degree is governed by the clerk of chambers, who may be better paid than most if not all of the barristers in the chambers, and whose favor is crucial for the new barrister to succeed. No institution like that of the barristers' clerk exists in the United States, nor in other common law systems, even where the profession similarly has not been fused.

R. HAZELL (ed.), "THE BAR ON TRIAL"
109, 106, 122 (1978).

In fact the fees for almost all paperwork are fairly standard, which is why there is normally no previous agreement as to fees when counsel is asked to advise or to draft a pleading; the clerk sends out a fee-note after the papers have been returned to the solicitor, and provided the fee is reasonably close to the market rate for the work done there is not usually any difficulty.

Brief fees are a different story. These are wide open to negotiation and vary enormously—from £15 (the norm for a small case in the magistrates' court) to £25,000 (the figure paid to a leader in a recent commercial action which involved months of preparation). The brief fee is the fee for preparing the case and for the first five hours of the hearing: if the case lasts for longer than one day the barrister is paid a further fee known as a 'refresher,' which may range from £25 to £200 per day. The brief fee must be marked on the brief before counsel goes into court; oddly, the refreshers are often not agreed until after the case is over.

Brief fees give clerks the most scope for negotiation—negotiation in which the barrister can play no direct part, except in cases of 'special

---

6. R. Hazell (ed.), The Bar on Trial 124 (1978).

difficulty'. The Bar Council's justification for excluding the barrister is that he is not himself competent to judge what is a proper fee: 'The basis of the rule is not that it would be "ungentlemanly" for counsel to deal directly with fees. The basis of the rule is that this is a matter better left to someone able objectively to assess what is a proper fee.' This is an extraordinary argument, since only the barrister who has done or is about to do the work knows how much work was or is involved. This is particularly the case with advisory work. Sometimes the barrister feels the clerk has charged far too little; sometimes that he has charged far too much. The question is, whose opinion is right—the barrister who has done the work, or the clerk who knows what the market will bear? Most barristers would agree that the market rates for various categories of work are quite out of proportion to the skill and effort involved: advisory work, except at the specialist Bars, is on the whole grossly underpaid, while certain classes of court appearance (e.g. Crown Court criminal work) have in the past been overremunerated. One reason why fees have become such an indefensible lottery is that they are negotiated by clerks who do not themselves do the work.

* * *

What barristers lose at the interlocutory stages they hope to make up on the brief fee when an action comes to trial. Inevitably because so few actions come to trial (the proportion is only between one and two per cent) brief fees are disproportionately large. . . .

* * *

This swings-and-roundabouts system of remuneration severely penalizes litigants whose cases come to trial and subsidizes those whose cases are settled beforehand. It also engenders in barristers a cynicism about the whole Alice-in-Wonderland system of fees which leads to passive acquiescence in one of the most anomalous rules of all, which is that once a brief has been delivered the brief fee has to be paid, even if the case subsequently does not go to trial. Although the brief fee is meant to be payment for the preparation of the case and the first five hours of the trial, a barrister is entitled to his full fee even if the case is settled on the day after delivery of his brief and he has not had time to undo the ribbon.

The only justification for this rule is that when a case is settled at the last moment a barrister will not normally find alternative court work for that particular day. But he can get on with his paperwork; in such circumstances a barrister may deserve to be paid for preparing the case for trial, but he certainly does not deserve to be paid for the first five hours of a trial which does not take place. Nor does he deserve to receive any brief fee in those cases which settle well before the last moment and before the barrister has started to prepare the case for trial.

The rule is one reason why briefs tend to be delivered at the very last moment to counsel, leaving them with insufficient time to prepare the case properly. If there is any hope of a settlement the solicitors will hang on to the brief, thus saving their client the expense of paying counsel for a trial which never takes place.

* * *

Clerks are such an entrenched feature of the chambers' organization in this country that it is difficult for most English barristers to imagine how they could possibly operate without them. Indeed they would probably be amazed to learn that in other countries where there is a separate Bar, divided from the solicitors' branch of the profession on exactly the same lines as our own, the barristers manage to get along without clerks at all. In Ireland, for example, barristers arrange their appointments and negotiate their fees directly with solicitors, and no one has suggested that this has corrupted their professional or ethical standards.

South Africa provides an even better comparison, because there the Bar has an identical chambers structure to that in England (in Dublin and Belfast the barristers all practise from a common Library). Their chambers (called 'Groups') are about the same size or slightly larger; they employ the usual telephonists and typists, and there is an office manager called the Group Secretary, who may also do the accounts and send out fee-notes. When a solicitor wishes to brief counsel he talks to the barrister direct—each barrister keeps his own diary, and it is contrary to professional etiquette for him to arrange to be in two different courts on the same day. Fees are a matter of direct negotiation between barrister and solicitor; and to protect young barristers there are scales of minimum fees for most of the standard types of work. Young barristers, in South Africa and in Ireland, receive most of their early work either through contacts (in South Africa almost every barrister works in a solicitor's office before going to the Bar) or on the recommendation of their pupilmasters or other more senior barristers— people who are in a better position to judge the true worth of a beginner than the clerk, who has never seen him in action in court, nor read his work on paper.

The same system operates in Australia (in those states which have a separate Bar). There they do have clerks, but they are simply administrators; the barristers negotiate their own fees and arrange their own timetables. Beginners are passed down returns by their seniors—not necessarily even from the same chambers: with no clerk eager for his percentage there is not the same anxiety to keep a brief in chambers that exists in England. The barrister giving away the brief is merely anxious to find the best possible substitute available, in order not to let down 'his' solicitors. And, as in South Africa, the vast majority of young barristers do not go straight to the Bar but work first for a firm of solicitors for a couple of years, in order to gain practical experience and to ensure a steady supply of work when they do start at the Bar. Again, it has never been suggested that the South African and Australian Bars have any but the highest ethical standards.

In all these countries barristers do the same work as in England and they operate under essentially the same code of conduct. In none of them do they obtain their work or negotiate their fees through the medium of a clerk. The conclusion is inescapable; that in these two crucial respects the English clerk is dispensable. How they acquired their present position of power it is hard to say; but the sooner barristers have the courage to manage their own affairs without being ruled by their clerks the better life will be for themselves, and the better the service will be for their clients.

———

Barristers' clerks traditionally have been compensated by a percentage of the fee they negotiate for their barristers. It is a major source of criticism, both by outsiders and by barristers. A ten percent clerk's fee has been a source of pride, and a source of considerable income. Some say it causes clerks to extract excessive fees from solicitors, and suggest that the barrister effectively is paid ninety percent of the clerk's fee.

Attempts to alter the fee system illustrate the conflict. Barristers in one chambers suggested that the clerk reduce his share from ten to eight percent. He agreed only if he would no longer have to pay the two junior clerks from his share. The barristers rejected his demand and dismissed the clerk, who was unsuccessful before the industrial tribunal because he was an independent self-employed contractor, and could not have been unfairly dismissed. The stage seems set for change: either lower percentages or salaries.

It is not only his commissions which a clerk may lose—he may lose some of his barristers.

J. FLOOD, "BARRISTERS' CLERKS"

25 (1983).*

Apart from losing part of his commission, the other main contingency a senior clerk faces is the loss of some of his barristers. If a set of chambers fragments owing to, say, personality differences among the members a senior effectively has two choices. Either he can revert to junior status in a different set, something not often done, or he can join one of the segments. One clerk had two such schisms occur. On the first occasion he aligned himself with the break-away faction, which involved him in a search for new chambers. The second time he lost five out of thirty barristers, and his junior went too.

These splits usually occur when a middle-range barrister (of, say, ten years' call) rebels against the authority of the head of chambers and wants to establish his own, taking like-minded colleagues with him. An astute clerk must be constantly aware of the shifts in mood of his barristers, and any possible emotional confrontations. His job is to

* Reprinted with permission of Manchester University Press.

monitor drifts towards disequilibrium and draw them back into equilibrium if necessary and if possible.

Other losses occur as a result of official and judicial appointments. And they can have a dramatic effect on the clerk's profit margin. Most of these appointments are from among Queen's Counsel, who are not only profitable but also, in many instances, are the mainstay of the chambers' reputation. The following example is extreme, but it shows in a magnified way the effects of such losses. A clerk in his late twenties was promoted to senior in a very successful specialist chambers which was, however, quite small, with only nine members. In the space of a few years he lost his three most senior counsel—all silks—to the Bench. They were appointed prematurely over the heads of several other eminent QCs in that specialist bar. At the age of thirty-three the clerk was left with no silks, too much tail and a smaller income than when he started. The danger is exacerbated when there is only one QC in the chambers. A replacement should always be ready to fill the vacant slot.

The entry of women into the legal profession in the United States has moved with considerable speed. So has their admission to the role of solicitor in England. But they have not been so successful in surmounting the numerous obstacles to becoming successful barristers. They have not only their male barrister colleagues to convince, but the clerk of chambers and the solicitors who come to the chambers seeking a barrister. It has been a slow process.

R. HAZELL (ed.), "THE BAR ON TRIAL"
148 (1978).

It was not until May 1922 that Ivy Williams became the first woman barrister and was called to the Bar by the Inner Temple.

It has been a long struggle punctuated by the unsuccessful applications of many women, including Christabel Pankhurst, and the successful application of Bertha Cave in 1902—an oversight by Gray's Inn which was rapidly corrected when the Benchers realized what had happened. She appealed to a tribunal of eight judges presided over by the Lord Chancellor himself; they confirmed the Benchers' decision. Their conclusion was based on a fine old principle of English law: there was no precedent for women being called to the English Bar—and the judges were not going to create one. It was not until the passage of the Sex Disqualification (Removal) Act 1919 that the admission of women was forced upon the Inns by Parliament; and since that date the acceptance of women has continued to be slow and grudging.

* * *

The stage at which women suffer because of their sex is not in arranging pupillage but in looking for a tenancy. . . .

Women also suffer more than men from the expense of starting at the Bar. Banks are frequently less willing to give them the generous overdraft facilities which are essential in one's first two years; and although Inn scholarships are available, some are specifically closed to women. Of the remainder, few are awarded to women and even when they are the amount received is sometimes smaller than that received by men of similar means and ability. The Awards Committee of one Inn told a working-class graduate that she was "irresponsible" for coming to the Bar with no resources whatsoever. They asked her patiently and sympathetically: 'Wouldn't you be better off considering becoming a solicitor ... a civil servant ... a law teacher?' In fact, anything rather than a barrister. She did not receive an award.

However the main stumbling block is simply prejudice, and this reveals itself most strongly at the crucial stage in a woman's career, when she is looking for a tenancy. Most chambers openly admit a 'no women' policy, and continue to do so despite the Sex Discrimination Act 1975 (which does not apply to the Bar, since sets of chambers are not partnerships and tenants are not employed). One particular set of chambers which has always been known to have a no woman policy (amended to a 'no other woman' policy after the daughter of the Head of Chambers was admitted) has blatantly refused a woman applicant on the grounds of her sex. Others do not have the same confidence that they are beyond the law and hide their discrimination behind all sorts of excuses. Either the woman was not up to the standard of the men who applied or for sound economic reasons she did not suit the vacancy.

* * *

It is also frequently pointed out that at the Bar women receive equal pay with men for equal work, and always have done. The problem is that women frequently fail to get equal work.

There are still great difficulties facing a woman who wishes to practise outside the traditional fields of crime and divorce. At the Chancery Bar there are only seven or eight women barristers in active practice, while virtually none break into the specialized fields of tax or commercial law, patents or planning. These are the more lucrative areas of practice, as well as being intellectually more demanding; but it has never been suggested that academically women lack the ability to succeed in these fields—if only given the chance.

* * *

Even at the common law Bar where all the women are concentrated they tend to remain clustered on the lower rungs of the ladder without the encouragement and variety of work given to their male contemporaries. To find the reasons for this it is necessary to look at the three people who decide which barrister is the right one for the job: in ascending order of importance these are the client, the solicitor and the clerk.

The Bar Council does not recognize that prejudice might come from the clerk, but lays the blame squarely with the client:

> 'The prejudice against women emanates from the lay client who wishes to have a male barrister to conduct his case. The same prejudice exists between the patient and the surgeon, hence, no doubt, the small number of women surgeons. Accordingly a solicitor is as a general rule reluctant to recommend women barristers.'

It is true that some clients are prejudiced against women barristers, and may be prompted to complain, especially where a last-minute change of counsel leaves them being represented by a woman where previously their barrister was a man. However it is relatively rare that a client actually declines the services of a woman barrister.

More frequently, as the Bar Council says, solicitors will screen the pool of barristers available for the case, and if they feel the client might be a little awkward they will play safe and brief a man. Sexism can however operate from a different angle, with solicitors taking a fancy to a pretty woman and briefing her in preference and to the envy of her male colleagues. One such squatter was told that her chambers had decided not to give her a tenancy because she had been getting 'too friendly with solicitors'.

* * *

... Clerks generally regard their 10% as better invested in a man than in a woman in the long term. The clerk will be reluctant to help a woman build up her practice when any day she may marry, produce children and leave a gap in chambers. 'It's like backing horses, women often fall at the first fence,' was how one of them put it. Childbearing hampers every woman's struggle for equality and the break in her working life which this involves tells against her even in a profession where she is self-employed and the profits are her profits. The power of the clerk in the system is immense and few Heads of Chambers would have the courage to demand the entry of women where a clerk was against it. Even fewer Heads of Chambers will insist that a woman gets her share of the interesting work and is not left simply to pick up the crumbs.

And that is how most of the male bar would have us leave it, with the blame resting principally on the villainous clerks. Yet most of them at heart agree with the clerks' attitude. As one Head of Chambers put it: 'It's nice to have a pretty face around; the trouble is some young chap is bound to notice her charms and then what will chambers do?' Another Q.C., the Head of a large set, denied any taint of prejudice: 'I've got two women in my chambers, one older and past marrying, the other younger but so plain that the chance is remote'—words spoken in jest, perhaps, but with a grain of truth behind them. Younger men can also be found who protest that it is their clerks alone who quash any attempt to introduce women; but their inaction speaks louder than their words.

Notes and Questions

1. The United States does not have a divided profession, but lawyers tend to specialize after entry into practice. Some lawyers with primarily an office practice occasionally go to court. But it is usually a minor court. The English solicitor has won admission to practice before the lower courts, and thus his work overlaps with that of the barrister in those courts. Former Chief Justice Burger of the United States Supreme Court showed a rather strong affection for the skills of the English barrister as an advocate. It is a view shared by many who have witnessed barristers in court in England. Should we expand the concept of certification to severely limit those allowed to practice in major courts to lawyers with a certain number of years experience? But where would the experience be gained? In inferior courts? As a form of juniors assisting a certified advocate in major courts? Would it be better to adopt a split profession to achieve such a goal? Would the English view work in the broad expanses of the American landscape, or is its success at least partly due to the small size of England and the highly centralized legal system?

2. Were barristers to be stripped of their robes and wigs and forced out of the Inns to work in regular office locations around London and the rest of the country, would they be any less effective? Would it open the profession to a degree which might suggest some loss in effectiveness is balanced by the greater access to being a barrister, as well as the greater access to their services? This makes an assumption that barristers might be consulted directly by clients. Why should they not be so retained?

3. If the United States were to adopt a more severe certification process for courtroom advocates, would this tend to place other lawyers in a second class status? At what point in separating the profession would you think some of the detriments might appear?

4. Are the Inns part of the cause of the complaints about the professional split, or are they places where barristers may do their highly specialized work in quiet, free from distractions of others? Everyone certainly knows where they are. If everyone had more direct access to them, would there be as many complaints?

C. FUSION OR INCREASED RIGHTS OF ADVOCACY FOR SOLICITORS

In England, many advocate removal of the distinction between the barrister and the solicitor. As expected, the barristers reject such a move, while the solicitors tend to favor greater access to the courts as advocates, although not total fusion. They wish to gain access to *all* of the courts. The discussion of fusion is useful in considering whether a split or fused profession offers better legal services. The first serious study of the possibility of fusion was the 1979 Royal Commission report.

THE ROYAL COMMISSION ON LEGAL SERVICES

Final Report, ch. 17, Comnd. 7648 (1979).*

Some might argue that our entire system of justice should be changed so that it resembled the other systems we have mentioned.... Our task, in any event, was to examine the organisation of the profession on the basis of our present legal system and the present rules of court procedure. In this system the quality of advocacy remains an essential component of the quality of justice.

Even if our system were modified so that less was done by means of the spoken word, it would not follow that the quality of advocacy would cease to have importance. In the United States judges of the superior courts have, in their law clerks, professional assistants of high quality. A great deal of legal argument is committed to paper, in the form of briefs. In those circumstances it might be thought that the standard of advocacy would be a matter of less concern. The contrary is the case. The Honourable Warren Burger, Chief Justice of the United States of America, told us in oral evidence of his concern for the standards of advocacy in his jurisdiction, and of the difficulties which arose from advocacy of poor quality. He said:—

> My observation from sitting in trial of cases in the *nisi prius* court was that something less than half of the lawyers who appeared there were minimally qualified to perform their function ... over a long period of time I undertook to take soundings in state courts and in federal courts throughout the country, and the most pessimistic view was that only 25 per cent of the lawyers appearing in our courts were really qualified to represent their clients properly and to move the case along adequately. Some judges placed it as high as 75 per cent. Somewhere near the mid-way mark is probably correct, and it will vary to some extent from place to place.

The chief Justice remarked that cases were dealt with in British courts more quickly than in American, and went on:—

> From time to time I have been asked how I account for this. It is not easy to account for it but an over-simplification perhaps is that in your courts generally you have three experts who have all been trained in the same tradition and in the same pattern. The judge almost by definition has been one of the leading members of the Bar, and the two advocates appearing before him are trained in the same way the judge was trained. This is not so on our side ... the trial of a case resembles in a way a three-legged stool. If any one of the legs is very much shorter than the other you have not got a very good stool. If any one of them is weaker than the other the stool might collapse if weight is put on it. In our system, unfortunately, too often all three of the legs of the stool are not as competent as they should be.... Even if you have a very experi-

* Reprinted with permission by Her Majesty's Stationery Office.

enced judge and he has two mediocre, badly-trained or untrained advocates before him he has difficulty.

The Attitude of the Profession

Members of both branches would find some advantages in a fused profession. Firms of solicitors, particularly the larger, could expect to gain, materially and in prestige, by having as partners barristers who were the acknowledged leaders in various fields. Barristers, particularly those in the lower and middle ranges of income, might earn in a solicitors' firm as much as or more than they could at the Bar, with the additional advantages of greater security and provision for retirement. The start of professional practice would be easier in a fused profession than it now is at the Bar. In spite of these advantages, the weight of evidence from both branches of the profession is opposed to fusion....

The Main Criticisms

Of the many witnesses who submitted evidence on the structure of the profession, a small minority advocated fusion. These witnesses put forward three main criticisms of the two-branch profession, that it was inefficient, harmed the confidence of clients and was more expensive. It was argued that these defects could be cured by the creation of a fused profession.

Efficiency

The efficiency of the two-branch profession was criticised on the grounds that the structure caused failures in communication and was a source of delay. Failures in communication were said to arise because the professional relationship between barrister and solicitor was distant and formal, because the written instructions sent to counsel were in some cases inadequate and late in arriving and because barristers were reluctant to complain about inadequate instructions for fear of offending a solicitor client. There was also said to be poor service when a brief was returned by a barrister at a late stage, because the barrister to whom it was reallocated had insufficient time to make himself familiar with the case and with the client....

Problems of communication would not arise if the advocate in a case personally undertook the necessary preparatory work. We doubt whether, even in a fused profession, this could be done as a matter of regular practice, except in minor cases. If a partner in a firm of solicitors did all the work now sent to a barrister, he would face practical difficulties in dealing with both preparatory work and advocacy, even if he thought it desirable to do so. A solicitor who specialises in advocacy told us that he did not himself interview witnesses or prepare a case for trial. He found it best to deal with his cases at the same stage, and in the same way, as a barrister. If a small firm had no partner to do the work, it would have to retain another firm as agents to undertake advocacy on behalf of its clients. In any circumstances where an advocate did not undertake the preparatory work, communication would not necessarily be any better than at present. The main reason why essential material is omitted from a brief is that the case has been inefficiently prepared, and this is as likely to occur in one system as in another.

DELAY

* * *

We think it an exaggeration to say that periods of delay are necessarily doubled under the present system, but it is clearly correct that, if cases must wait first for a solictor's and then for a barrister's attention, there will be an increase in the total time taken to complete the work. It is, however, possible only to speculate on the improvement to be expected in a fused profession. . . .

* * *

It was suggested that clients received more efficient and quicker service in foreign countries in which unified professions operate. The majority of the witnesses who submitted evidence on this point however held the opposite view. This is illustrated by the evidence of ... a former barrister and manager of a shipowners' insurance association, undertaking worldwide legal business, who said:—

* * *

Lawyers are always blamed for being too slow. The English system perhaps accentuates this, in that unlike, for example, the United States, there is only one real bite at the cherry. The trial is the focal point. In the United States, the evidence of fact comes out separately from the trial, often almost at once, through depositions. In France, the court will appoint surveyors who will report on the facts. In Germany, the judge will pick off the issues one by one. In England, law and facts are all decided at one time and, not unnaturally, particularly in a big case, there is a long delay between incident and final judgment. However it is not my experience that English claims remain open longer than those for other countries. On the contrary, the experience of the solicitors and the detached advice of counsel tends to lead to early settlements ... I do not believe that fusion would tend to speed up our legal services. On the contrary, it would tend to reduce the number of experienced advocates available and, hence, in my view, increase the delays.

RETURN OF BRIEFS

Many of the present criticisms of the quality of service provided by the profession relate to the return of briefs. It was argued that, in a fused profession, the function of representation would be spread among a larger number of practitioners, reducing the risk of clashes of engagements. Against this, it was pointed out that the working lives of most barristers were organised for the conduct of advocacy and that there had been built up a system of communication solely concerned with the listing of cases and appearance in court. ... Our conclusion is that, in a fused profession, the number of additional advocates is unlikely to be so great as to lead to an appreciable reduction in the problem of clashes of engagements, and that these would be less easy to cope with than at present, because of the loss of some of the advantage of quick and informal communication between barristers and their clerks which is possible under present centralised arrangements.

CONFIDENCE OF THE CLIENT

Some of those who advocated fusion argued that the present divided profession reduced the client's confidence in the quality of the service received. The barristers working in the Wellington Street Chambers said:—

> A considerable degree of mutual confidence is required, if the client is to communicate and the lawyer is to understand. The sooner and more fully the trial advocate is brought into the case, the better will be the advocacy. The divided profession is an obstacle, often fatal, to this relationship. The client must first express his or her problem to a solicitor, and may in doing so come to trust and have confidence in the solicitor, only to learn that the advocate in court will be someone else. Thereafter at best, the client will be taken to see counsel, and start a second time to establish a relationship of understanding and confidence.

The Legal Action Group said:—

> We think that the "detachment" which the Bar claim as an advantage of separateness is rarely so. What the barrister calls detachment the client may well view as ignorance of his case and circumstances. It matters not that the client may be wrong, and that the barrister in fact knows quite as much as the court needs to know: if clients are left with the feeling that the legal profession does not bother on their behalf, then public confidence in the legal system suffers.

These witnesses stated that it is common practice, particularly in criminal cases, for the client not to meet his counsel until the day of the hearing.

There was also criticism of the situation arising when a brief is returned, so that a client, who may have established a good relationship with the barrister intended to represent him, encounters a total stranger on the day of the hearing. In these circumstances, as the organisation Justice remarked:—

> Nothing is more calculated to shake the lay client's confidence in the legal system than to be told at the last minute that X cannot take the case and it will have to be done by Y, who has not previously been involved and indeed may belong to a different set of chambers.

We agree with this view and make recommendations ... on this point. As we said ... however, we doubt whether fusion would solve this particular problem since there is no reason to suppose that advocates in a fused profession would be more successful than barristers under present arrangements in avoiding clashes of engagements and consequent withdrawals.

It was argued against the view that barristers are too remote from their clients that it is a benefit to clients to have a detached second opinion, and that if they are properly informed about the arrangements by which they are to be advised and represented, and if those arrangements are properly carried out, the divided profession offers a superior service.... [A] director of a firm of marine insurers, who are frequently involved in litigation in many parts of the world, expressed this view.

> The detachment from both the pressures of the potential litigant and the documentary spadework which barristers enjoy quite definitely produces advice of a judicial quality markedly absent from most opinions given by lawyers in Europe or the USA. This does not mean that an English barrister will not advise a client with full enthusiasm on the various alternative courses open to him if he wants to pursue them, but certainly for our insurance purposes we find invaluable the element of warning (which English barristers would never fail to give) whether or not any particular course of action is likely to prevail at law.

In its evidence the Council of HM Circuit Judges quoted one of its number as saying:—

> ... for some eight years ... I was a solicitor-advocate appearing almost daily in the magistrates' courts and taking many criminal cases. I often took my own statements, always interviewed the client and generally the witnesses, if any. In these circumstances it was very difficult to preserve the correct balance between one's duty to one's client and one's duty to the Court. The relationship with the client was too close and when I subsequently practised in the criminal courts as a member of the Bar the situation was quite different and the presence of the solicitor or his clerk acted as a buffer so that I could take a more detached view of the case possibly to the benefit of the client and certainly to the benefit of the Court.

The contrasting arguments set out in the previous paragraphs may both have some justification, but in relation to different classes of cases. In the larger civil actions, in particular in commercial proceedings and in serious criminal cases, there are clear advantages in bringing in a specialist advocate and in most such cases we believe that the client benefits from such representation. In the smaller cases, and in particular in minor criminal cases, in which solicitors already have rights of audience, a client with no previous knowledge of the law may find it disconcerting that it is necessary to instruct counsel and that his own solicitor, in whom he has confided, does not handle the case alone from start to finish. For the reasons already given, we are not persuaded that fusion of the two branches of the legal profession would, in itself, overcome this problem.

Cost of Legal Services

Those who submitted evidence in favour of fusion argued that, by reducing the number of lawyers involved in a case, legal work would, in general, be done more cheaply in a fused profession. As Professor Zander put it, "there would be only one taximeter instead of two or three". Against this, the Senate argued that it was a fallacy to suppose that a two-branch profession led to two people doing the work of one and said that any double-manning could and should be eliminated under the present system. It concluded, "there may be a few residual instances of unavoidable duplication of effort which would be offset many times over by the cost-effectiveness of separation". This point was also made in the evidence of the London Criminal Courts Solicitors' Association.

We have no doubt that in a fused profession the costs of legal services would escalate enormously, the range of choice available would decline and the degree of specialisation possible in the present system would also decline.... The result of fusion would be a general decline in the service offered to the clients at a considerably increased cost.

* * *

It has been argued that, even if the fees actually incurred are somewhat higher than they would be under a fused system, the present system is more cost effective. For example, it has been suggested that the effect of the intervention of a barrister is often to promote negotiations for a settlement, on which he can advise more objectively than a solicitor who has identified himself with the client and the client's wish to pursue the proceedings. It is impossible to quantify any saving which arises in this way. We are satisfied however that the independent view which is brought to bear by counsel can have the effect of limiting the issues or bringing about a settlement. Other things being equal, this may represent an important saving in time and cost to the client.

Purpose of the Present Restrictions

The two-branch profession is maintained by the rules which restrict the rights of audience of solicitors and access to barristers by lay clients. These rules have, in each case, a direct and an indirect object. The direct object of the rule governing rights of audience is to ensure, so far as possible, that advocacy in matters of substance is performed only by practitioners who specialise in it, and who have the time and the facilities to do so. The direct object of the rule which prevents access save through a solicitor by the client to the barrister is to ensure that barristers are free from hour-to-hour distractions and that specialist matters with which they deal are presented to them by a lawyer who has already identified the issues and sifted out the relevant facts, rather than by the lay client himself who can only present his problem as a whole. The object is not to put the barrister at a distance from his client, but to ensure, so far as possible, that his specialist skills are efficiently used, that he is ensured, so far as possible, the time necessary to concentrate

on them and—this is put forward very much as a secondary objective—
that he remains sufficiently detached from his client to be able to give
him advice which is wholly objective. The indirect object of both these
rules is to prevent the fusion and blurring of the two categories of
practitioner, by ensuring that the solicitor does not undertake work for
which a barrister is required and by ensuring that the barrister is not
diverted to functions outside his specialty functions which can be better
performed by the solicitor.

* * *

QUALITY OF SERVICE

The reason given by nearly all the witnesses, including the judges,
for their opposition to fusion was that it would lead to a serious fall in
the quality of advocacy and hence also, because of the nature of court
proceedings, in the quality of judicial decisions. They argued that this
would damage not merely the interests of individual litigants, but the
administration of justice itself. In the following paragraphs we set out
these arguments in more detail.

ACCESS TO ADVOCATES

* * *

If the two branches of the profession were fused, it is likely that the
larger firms of solicitors would seek to consolidate their position by
inviting the leading barristers to join them as partners. This would
enable these firms to provide most services likely to be required by their
clients. Medium-sized firms of solicitors might wish to take one or more
barristers into partnership to provide some, at least, of the services
which they could not provide for their clients without them. To take
one barrister only into a partnership would in practice be unlikely to be
effective for this purpose. For example, if a firm absorbed a barrister
who was skilled in criminal law and advocacy it would need another
barrister if it wished to provide a comprehensive service in, for example,
chancery work. It is unlikely that many such firms could provide
enough work to keep one or more barristers employed solely as advocates
unless they were able to obtain instructions on a regular basis from
smaller firms of solicitors. In the event, many firms would not be able
to recruit barristers because there would be too few to go round. This
difficulty would be exacerbated if a large number of barristers decided to
set up their own firms which they are not at present permitted to do.

The likely consequences of the situation that we have described are
set out in the evidence of a barrister with knowledge of practice both in
this country and in California who said:—

> Once the ability to instruct counsel is removed, by fusion, the
> tendency will be for lawyers to set themselves up as law firms
> providing a comprehensive service with 'trial lawyers' salaried by
> the firm. This will lead to bigger firms with bigger premises and
> the one man firm practising in the poorer areas will have to join the

big firm in the richer area. My experience of law firms in California is that none have their offices in the poorer areas; in these parts the only lawyers available are young enthusiasts who set up legal 'co-operatives' and are more concerned with righting political and economic injustices than doing day to day case work. I believe that the 'local' solicitor makes an important contribution to the present system in the United Kingdom and that his existence would be imperilled by fusion.

* * *

As the law becomes more complex and as the need for specialisation increases, solicitors' firms are likely to continue to increase in size by mergers and amalgamations and by natural growth. Up to a certain point, size has advantages both for the firm and for the clients. It is possible to specialise to a greater extent and thereby to offer the client a higher degree of technical expertise in certain classes of work. For these and other reasons the level of earnings in large firms is higher than in small ones and the provision for pensions is better. If, however, the pattern of the profession were to move too far towards a small number of large firms, as we believe would tend to happen in a fused profession, the effect would be to diminish the number of firms available to the public and thus to limit competition and freedom of choice, especially in smaller towns and rural areas. Such a development would clearly be against the public interest.

* * *

In a fused profession, a partner in a small firm or a sole practitioner, one of whose clients required the services of an advocate, would either have to refer the client to another firm or undertake the advocacy himself, whether or not he was able satisfactorily to do so. If the case were referred to another firm to act as agents for advocacy alone, the criticisms of the present system, such as the cost of employing two lawyers and the need for one to brief the other, would apply. The cost could be expected to be higher, because, as we pointed out in paragraph 17.7, a solicitor's overhead expenses are appreciably higher than a barrister's. Moreover, it would be more difficult to obtain the services of a suitable advocate from amongst those employed in firms of solicitors, because their dispersal would complicate the process of selection and because the chosen advocate might prefer, quite properly, to give priority to the existing clients of his own firm. This could lead to the undesirable situation that, because only those litigants who retained the services of a large firm with advocacy partners would be assured of an advocacy service of the highest standard, there would be greater disparity than at present in the standards of advocacy on either side in cases coming before the courts.

* * *

Selection of Judges

Nearly all the judges are recruited from among the senior members of the Bar, although it has recently become possible for a solicitor, who has served as a recorder for three years, to be appointed a circuit judge and nine solicitors have been so appointed. The Lord Chancellor's Department stressed to us that it is necessary for the Lord Chancellor to have the fullest possible information about candidates for appointment to judicial office. This is available under the present system because the number of practising barristers is not great, because their talents are well known in the profession and are often on public display and because the Lord Chancellor and his senior advisers are likely to have personal knowledge of the most senior members of the Bar. Fusion would increase the numbers available for consideration but might increase the possibility of making an unsuitable choice.

The Effect of Present Trends

Because of the growing trend towards specialisation and the need at all levels for effective advocacy, we think it likely that, if the profession were fused, there would be a demand for the kind of service which is now provided by the Bar. This is visualised by those who support fusion, one of whom, Mr. A. Huxley, said in evidence:—

> ... in my submission there must be, even if one has fusion, a rump of the Bar. Call it what you will, there will be some kind of lump advocacy labour, in other words, a pool on which one can draw for a particular case. That has to exist even under a fused system.

This view is supported by experience in other jurisdictions, in particular New Zealand and Australia. When the legal profession began to operate in these countries the distances which practitioners had to travel were often considerable, communications were bad and slow and the countries were sparsely inhabited. In these conditions no separate Bars were established. In more recent times specialist Bars have developed in order to meet an increasing demand for specialisation in the practice of the law. The results are said to have been beneficial....

* * *

In New Zealand a number of lawyers practise as barristers, although the profession is not formally divided. The former Chief Justice, ..., expressed the view in oral evidence that formal division, on the British pattern, was unlikely. Whilst agreeing that the system worked well in New Zealand, his colleague ... said:—

> I am one of those who does subscribe to this concept of a separate Bar and I make no secret of the fact that I think it is one of the great British achievements to have evolved such a system or institution. One would be somewhat dismayed to find that in the country of its birth it was either abolished or radically altered. I think that the idea of an independent body of men and women, specialists and skilled in their type of legal service, and not mere paid agents for the clients but recognising that they owe some

responsibility to the courts and having the confidence of the courts, and the standard of ethics and professional skill that tends to go with that, is an extremely valuable concept, and long may that continue.

SUMMARY

In the light of all the considerations set out above we have reached the following conclusions. We consider it likely that in a fused profession there would be an unacceptable reduction in the number and spread of the smaller firms of solicitors and an increase in the proportion of large city firms. This would accentuate the present uneven distribution of solicitors and reduce the choice and availability of legal services. We are satisfied that in the future there will be a greater need for specialisation. Fusion would disperse the specialist service which is now provided by the Bar and we consider that this would operate against the public interest. In a large firm with an advocate partner there would be readier communication than is usual between solicitor and barrister; but this advantage would not be realised in a fused profession to the extent that it proved necessary for the smaller firm to refer its clients to larger firms for an advocacy service.

In terms of cost, it is difficult to make accurate estimates, because they depend heavily on assumptions. On balance, we believe that in small cases there might be some saving, but that in the larger cases this would not be so and the expense might be greater. With regard to the administration of justice, the weight of evidence is strongly to the effect that a two-branch profession is more likely than a fused one to ensure the high quality of advocacy which is indispensable, so long as our system remains in its present form, to secure the proper quality of justice. These considerations lead us to the unanimous conclusion that it is in the public interest for the legal profession to be organised, as at present, in two branches.

———

The Royal Commission report laid to rest the issue of fusion for several years. In 1986 the Marre Committee (five barristers, five solicitors and five independent members) was established to consider solicitors' rights of advocacy in the higher courts, a possible step considerably short of a fully fused profession. The Marre Committee report in 1988 failed to reach agreement on the main issue. The Lord Chancellor soon thereafter announced that government "Green Papers" would be forthcoming on several issues involving the future of the legal profession. Three Green Papers were issued in early 1989. They suggested basing rights of audience to the courts not on the status of barrister or solicitor, but on qualification, and suggested the use of "advocacy certificates." Any full advocacy certificate holder would therefore be eligible for judicial appointment to the higher courts. Solicitors would lose their monopoly on conveyancing, the title Queen's Counsel would be open to solicitors, clients would have direct access to barristers, barristers could practice outside chambers, barristers' clerks would not be required, barristers could form partnerships and could even join in partnerships with solicitors, and some form of contingency fee could be adopted. The solicitors welcomed the proposals, they benefitted from essentially every decision except the loss of their conveyancing monopoly. But the barristers attacked the proposals and commenced a bitter campaign against nearly every recommendation. Many senior judges, normally unresponsive to such reports, spoke out as though the independent legal profession and judiciary was on the brink of extermination. The vast majority of the criticism appeared more based on protecting privileges than delivering the best possible legal services. Debate in the House of Lords was for the most part critical, no debate occurred in Commons. After hearing numerous points of view, the Lord Chancellor issued a White Paper in July, 1989. The sweeping changes had been drastically modified. The central issue of rights of audience for solicitors was decided in favor of the barristers. Solicitors no longer would be prohibited from advocacy in the highest courts, but the barristers would control their access. Several months later the Courts and Legal Services Bill was introduced, and became law in 1990. Professor Zander comments on the Courts and Legal Services Bill.

ZANDER, "THE THATCHER GOVERNMENT'S ONSLAUGHT ON THE LAWYERS: WHO WON?"

24 International Lawyer 753 (1990).

* * *

Apart from the unexpected length and complexity of the Bill, there were few surprises. The greatest perhaps was how narrowly the government intended to confine the discretion of the four senior "designated judges" who will have to approve any proposed changes in regard to rights of audience.

The Bill ... defines "the statutory objective" and "the general principle." ... The statutory objective is "the development of legal services in England and Wales (and in particular the development of advocacy, litigation, conveyancing and probate services) by making provision for new ways of providing such services and a wider choice of providing them." New, it appeared, was by definition to be deemed good. There was at first no public interest test. But after protests during the debates in the House of Lords, the government introduced an amendment adding at the end of the definition the words "while maintaining the proper and efficient administration of justice."

The general principle ... is that the question of rights of audience for different categories of persons should be determined *only* by reference to: (a) whether the person concerned is qualified "in accordance with the educational and training requirements appropriate to the court or proceedings"; (b) whether he is a member of a professional or other body which (i) has rules of conduct governing the conduct of its members, (ii) has an effective mechanism for enforcing those rules of conduct, and (iii) is likely to enforce them. Again, when the Bill was first published there was no requirement that consideration be given also to any test of the public interest. It was obvious that the government hoped to give as little scope as possible to the designated judges' veto.

But as a result of criticism in the House of Lords, the government introduced an amendment that somewhat expanded the definition of the general principle by adding (c) consideration whether the professional (or other) body's rules of conduct were appropriate to the interests of the proper and efficient administration of justice. This still did not, however, seem to permit an inquiry into whether it would be in the public interest for members of the body (say, solicitors) to have the rights of audience proposed.

The government was defeated in the House of Lords on one potentially very significant further part of the definition of the general principle. An amendment moved by Lord Alexander (a past chairman of the Bar), added to the definition of the general principle that in regard to rights of audience in the higher courts the body had to have a rule equivalent to the Bar's "cab rank rule." This rule requires a barrister to take any case offered in a field of work in which the barrister practices provided that the barrister is free to take the case and is offered a proper fee. The rule prohibits a barrister from discriminating between clients on the ground that the barrister does not like or does not want to represent the client.

* * *

[T]he ... government ... accept[ed] the principle, though it would introduce its own revised version of the Alexander amendment applying the nondiscrimination principle to all cases, not just those in the higher courts. Much turns on the precise definition of the cab rank rule adopted by the government—which was unfortunately not available in time to be included here. The Bar hopes that the effect of the rule would be to reduce the attractions of advocacy in the higher courts for solicitors and thus minimize the threat of competition from the solicitors' branch. The Law Society hopes that the new rule will not affect the way solicitors operate their practices too seriously [153] and that some solicitor-advocates will be encouraged to exercise any new rights of audience granted.

If the new rule were only to apply to the higher courts, the Bar's hopes might be realistic. But since it will apply to advocacy in all the

---

153. A great debate was generated, *a propos*, by the revelation that two highly respected firms of solicitors did not act for defendants in rape cases. It would seem that such policies would have to be abandoned in the face of the new rule.

courts it seems likely that it will be drafted in such a way as to leave the status quo broadly unaffected.

* * *

The White Paper and the Bill, in marked contrast to the Green Papers, were well received in most quarters. The profession is relieved in particular that the crucial issue of partnerships between barristers and solicitors and between lawyers and nonlawyers is still to be determined in essence by professional self-regulation. Whether or not solicitors eventually opt for multidisciplinary partnerships, this arrangement virtually guarantees the continuation of the divided profession more or less in its present form.

The judges have won a right of veto over proposed changes in regard to rights of audience. The solicitors' branch immediately expressed concern that the judges might simply block extended rights of audience for solicitors in the name of the "public interest." It remains to be seen whether these fears prove realistic. That they are far from being a fantasy was shown in the first public comment by a judge when the Master of the Rolls, Lord Donaldson, ..., signalled his view that the judges might wish to insist that in regard to much work in the higher courts (including criminal cases and judicial review work) only full-time advocates taking instructions from other lawyers should be eligible. If the judges persist in this approach, in spite of a clear contrary view from the new broadly based Advisory Committee, they would indeed be thwarting the balance of the new scheme proposed by the White Paper.[156] But the precise balance of power between the Advisory Committee and the four designated judges and which of them is to be "top dog" is one of the imponderables of the government's legislation. In the writer's view the Advisory Committee is intended to be the chief policy maker, but the judges may take a different view.

The White Paper gave the Bar a victory in control over issues such as the right of barristers to practice in partnership and the right of lay clients to go directly to barristers. The threat of competition from lawyers employed by the Crown Prosecution Service has also probably receded.[158] The solicitors' branch too has won important victories, in regard to extended rights of audience in the higher courts, in the right of appointment as Queen's Counsel and to the higher levels of the judicia-

---

156. The importance of the battle over rights of audience, it must be said in passing though, will be less important than before, as more work is transferred from the higher to the lower courts where solicitors can already appear as advocates. The government's plan to implement the main proposals of the Civil Justice Review, for instance, will mean the transfer of virtually all personal injury cases to the county court.

158. There was an ominous note for the Bar, however, in the statement by the Attorney General on the Bill's Second Reading in the House of Commons that the proposed new cab rank rule would have to be adjusted so as to allow employed advocates "to act only for their employers in whatever court of proceedings in which they may have a right of audience." The Bar is understandably terrified of the possibility that the Crown Prosecution Service would be given rights of audience in the crown courts.

ry, and, above all, in the restrictions imposed on competition from financial institutions (which are so severe as greatly to diminish, if not wholly to eliminate, the threat of such competition). The judges, the Bar, and the solicitors' branch all feel that the White Paper and the Bill represented a significant retreat by the Government on the vital question of independence of the profession and self-regulation.

On the other hand, the Lord Chancellor by no means gave up the whole of his original package, and many of the alterations he accepted still represent valuable advances from the previous status quo. I personally believe that the most important development in the long run will prove to be the establishment of an Advisory Committee with a majority of lay members. If the right persons are appointed to serve on this body (reform minded but not too radical), it could play an invaluable, constructive role as a catalyst for change.

* * *

... I share the widely held view that the White Paper and the Bill represent a great improvement on the Green Papers. But, as an exemplar of how to conduct an exercise in reform, the whole exercise seems to me to fall a good way short of the ideal.

First, it was exceedingly unfortunate that it generated so much heat and indeed produced so much bad feeling. Not all the blame for this can fairly be laid at the door of the government. The Bar, in particular, handled its response to the Green Papers, especially in the early weeks of the campaign, in a manner that verged on hysteria and that seemed unworthy of a great profession. Nor did all the judges who took part in the debate conduct themselves with the discretion that one might reasonably expect from seasoned members of the English judiciary. Several of them made public statements that, even at the time, seemed "over the top." [163]

But it is right to say that even though the judges and the Bar were arguably wrong to be so intemperate in their response, one cannot be sure that the Lord Chancellor would otherwise have paid as much attention to what they had to say. Possibly, the unreasonable way in which they presented their views made an impact that could not have been achieved by a more moderate stance.

Moreover, there is no denying that they were sorely provoked. The government put forward highly controversial plans that were completely at variance with what the Royal Commission on Legal Services had recommended and the government itself had previously accepted. It gave no explanation of its dramatic change of policy. It launched its proposals with a great fanfare under a banner of radical reform. Those directly affected saw the proposals as posing a serious or even a mortal threat. The government then allowed an inadequate period for consul-

---

163. A signal instance was the suggestion by Lord Lane, Lord Chief Justice, that the Green Paper was "one of the most sinister documents ever to emerge from Government."

tation. In spite of protestations from the Lord Chancellor to the contrary, most commentators gained the clear impression that there would be little scope for modification of the proposals, and that they would be forced through regardless of the opposition.... This impression was strengthened by the way that the Lord Chancellor stumped the country making speeches in support of his so-called consultation papers. One might have expected him to have sat apart waiting to see what response his proposals might bring.

If a government plans to introduce major changes with significant potential impact on important institutions it should make every effort to ensure that it has done its homework. The critics were right, I believe, to say that many of the proposals in the Green Papers were poorly thought out. The fact that they were ultimately dropped was a mercy. But many of them should never have been put forward at all.

The Green Papers represented an attempt at reform by what might be called the Big Bang. Predictably, they aroused intense opposition. The only unpredictable factor was the precise intensity of the reaction. Some believe that it was all a Machiavellian plot by the Lord Chancellor to put forward outrageous proposals which would attract so much flak that he would then retreat to carefully prepared positions considerably more daring than he could otherwise have attained. I do not share this view. I do not think that Lord Mackay anticipated quite how furious everyone would be—the more striking considering how personally liked and respected he is. But that the proposals would be deeply unpopular with the profession and the judges was obvious. The fact that, in the end, the government had to beat a fairly massive retreat shows, at the least, that its original judgment of what was desirable was seriously at fault. The first test of politically sound solutions to problems is whether they can be implemented. These failed the first test and had to be discarded. Through a combination of luck and skill, the Lord Chancellor managed to convey an impression of having pulled off a successful coup by achieving a compromise more or less acceptable to all. Certainly, he deserves credit for having the integrity to admit that the original proposals required drastic modification. But one would not expect less from Lord Mackay.

The pity was that the Green Papers provoked a huge and, I believe, completely unnecessary row, which will, I fear, have had the consequence not only of creating much regrettable ill-feeling all around, but of damaging confidence in the good sense of government in general and of the Lord Chancellor's Department in particular.

The effect of the legislation on legal services remains to be seen. There are four key uncertainties: (1) what new rights of audience will be given to solicitors in private practice and to what extent will solicitors exercise them; (2) whether salaried Crown Prosecution Service lawyers will be permitted to appear as advocates in the crown courts; (3) whether financial institutions will engage seriously in competition with solicitors for conveyancing work; and (4) whether solicitors will eventually be allowed by the Law Society to join in partnership with nonlawyers. The eventual judgment on the value of the Government's legislation will turn on the answers to those questions—and their consequences.

R. HAZELL (ed.), "THE BAR ON TRIAL"
187, 176 (1978).

* * *

The best testing ground for observing the effects of fusion is Australia, which provides a rich variety of different systems among its different States. Victoria is the system most commonly examined, but the other States are no less instructive. In Victoria the profession was fused by the Amalgamation Act 1891. Since then all lawyers have qualified and been entitled to practise as barristers or solicitors or both; the interesting thing is that those who wished to specialize as advocates continued to practise as 'barristers', and to refuse instructions except through a 'solicitor', and so it has remained ever since. The divided profession has continued but it is a *de facto* rather than a *de jure* division; those who choose to practise as solicitors have exactly the same rights of audience in all courts as barristers, and those solicitors who regularly appear in the courts are in effect practising as both (and are known as 'amalgams'). These amalgams nevertheless brief members of the Bar in cases where they think this is desirable.

It is often argued that because the profession has remained divided fusion in Victoria has been a failure. But on the contrary, what it has achieved is to sweep away the whole mesh of monopolies and restrictive practices and to allow the Bar to survive and be seen to survive on its own merits. In our system a client involved in proceedings in the higher courts is forced to take in and pay for a barrister whether one is needed or not. In Victoria when a specialist advocate is needed and the client can afford one he is briefed; in other cases the solicitor will argue the case himself.

Specialists exist in every legal system, whether fused or divided. It is because of the need for specialist advocates (and subject-specialists) that a separate Bar has continued in Victoria; and there is no reason to suppose that exactly the same would not happen in this country. The Bar can also take courage from the experience of other States in Australia. In New South Wales there is a *de jure* division of the profession but the Bar has no monopoly of rights of audience; it continues to survive. In South Australia and West Australia the profession is unified, but in the 1960s a separate Bar on the same lines as in Victoria has emerged and exists side by side with what is in substance the North American system. Individual partners in firms of 'amalgams' still do most of the court work (briefed by one of their partners, or by another firm), but some practitioners have decided to practise as barristers taking instructions only from 'solicitors'. In both States the Bar is still very small; but it has come into existence to meet a need, and as in Victoria it survives on its merits—there is never any obligation to brief counsel. The client instructs a second lawyer because he thinks his advice or advocacy is worthwhile.

The evidence from Australia and from the fused systems in the United States and Canada should allay the fears of those who believe that fusion would bring to an end the possibility of seeking expert help, whether with advocacy or a legal problem. Even if the English profession were fully fused the Bar would continue to exist. . . .

SECTION 4.   THE JUDICIARY

Very young judges are not encountered in England. The route to the scarlet and ermine robes and cumbrous wigs of the judiciary is neither by career choice, as in most civil law nations, nor by political appointment or election, as in the United States. Advancing to the English bench is a long and orderly process with appointment rarely granted before the age of 40.[7] That appointment is invariably made from the ranks of barristers. Although the 1990 reforms allow appointment of a solicitor who has been granted access to and has practiced before the higher courts. The judiciary thus created has an esteem unparalleled in other systems. The English legal system owes its reputation, and its reception by others, as much to its personalities as to its principles.

Even were entry procedures to advocacy measurably altered, the change would not affect the judiciary for many years. As a barrister (or solicitor advocate) progresses through the stages of the profession, from a junior member to Queen's Counsel to the bench, a measure of conservatism tends to evolve. Judges rightly appreciate that they have passed stern tests in achieving judicial appointment, and they are not given to very much self-criticism. A few have criticized this process as discouraging any judicial reform suggested from within the judiciary, and as constituting a body which often acts counter to parliamentary enactments by a severely restrictive approach to statutory interpretation.

The English judiciary certainly is not an aggregation of judicial activists, but that is one of its noteworthy strengths. The nature of legal reform in England rarely has involved drastic alteration (note the strong, adverse response to the Green Papers discussed above), rather the evolution and modification of current institutions to accommodate changing social needs. There is no reason why the legal profession cannot adjust where necessary, and avoid the dislocations of any extreme and abrupt fundamental changes. The current structure has matured over centuries and is viewed from many areas of the world as a crucial structure to an orderly society, as an irreplaceable backbone to a system

---

7. A more recent increase in appointments in the early 40's is at least partly attributable to the 72 and 75 years mandatory retirement age.

which has provided strength to the nation in numerous times of national crises.

Entry into the judiciary only after long years as an advocate, generally at least ten years for the High Court, illustrates that becoming a judge signifies the culmination of a career rather than the pursuit of a new one. Few judges ever leave the bench to commence a new endeavor. A judge who does step down often elicits a negative response from the bar, partially because the prestige and a life peerage, if granted, do not terminate with the judicial resignation.

Barristers are drawn to the judiciary at the height of their careers, for the most part from the position of Queen's Counsel, because of the prestige, the challenge and a knighthood or peerage if appointed to the High Court or above.

M. BERLINS AND C. DYER, "THE LAW MACHINE"

65, 60 (3d ed. 1989).

* * *

Most barristers who become judges—certainly those in London— have already spent twenty-five or even more years working, and often eating and drinking, in the rarified and somewhat artificial atmosphere of the Inns of Court with their obscure and ancient customs and traditions.[a] When they become judges the cocoon is tightened around them. The dignity of their office and the importance of being seen to be impartial and uncontroversial often demands that they distance themselves from their former habits and haunts, and even friends. The result can be an increasing remoteness from the mainstream of society. The longer they serve as judges, the more they may appear to be out of touch with the problems of the ordinary person. The charge is made against them that they live in an ivory tower, remote from the vicissitudes of most people's daily lives, unable from their lofty heights to appreciate the difficulties that lesser humans face. How true is that?

* * *

At the High Court level, becoming a judge is by invitation only and it is the Lord Chancellor who does the inviting. He chooses from a small and limited pool—senior barristers, almost always experienced QCs. The only formal qualification is that the candidate should have been in practice for at least ten years. In former days, when the Bar was small, the Lord Chancellor knew all the able QCs personally and could assess which of them were good judge material. It is much more difficult now. He cannot know everyone; he has to base his appointments on advice

a. Professors in England are correctly viewed as lacking the necessary court experience to be appointed to the trial bench, and there is a greater general hostility towards law professors in England than in the United States. But they are hardly venerated in the United States, as they are in many civil law nations. A not insignificant number of American law professors do become judges. For a discussion of the civil law professor, see section 3 of Chapter 3.

from other judges, senior lawyers, and reports from his departmental officials. It is largely an informal process. A judge who has been particularly impressed (or the opposite) with the performance of a barrister who has appeared before him might tell the Lord Chancellor so. Reputations spread. Little by little a dossier is built up. There will also be information about barristers from occasions when they have applied for lesser appointments; to become QCs or recorders, for instance. All is stored on pink cards in the Lord Chancellor's department. So by the time a senior barrister comes to be considered for the High Court bench, the Lord Chancellor has quite a lot of information on him or her which he can supplement by further enquiries from anyone who knows the candidate. And almost all candidates for the High Court bench have been recorders, so their judicial ability is not entirely unknown. Lord Elwyn–Jones, the Lord Chancellor in the 1974–79 Labour administration:

> You have his whole background, experience and what people have found him to be good at and not so good at—sometimes referees are inclined to turn every goose into a swan; sometimes they are alarmingly in the other direction.

There is finally a meeting between the Lord Chancellor and his senior judges. An informal short list is discussed. Usually one name emerges as the strongest, but the final decision is the Lord Chancellor's alone.

———

The acceptance of a judgeship distinctly is not motivated by monetary gain. Judicial salaries are notably less than the earnings of a successful barrister. Nor will the salary increase to a meaningful degree if a judge later moves to a higher court. Where salary differentials exist between superior court judicial positions they are nominal, and thus promotion is not sought for financial gain. Furthermore, there is no overwhelming expectation of periodic promotion, although the selection of judges for the superior courts usually involves elevation from a lower judicial level. The view of the English barrister toward his role and future as a judge thus contrasts with that of the civil law judge, where promotion through the full hierarchy is a major expectation and, in fact, a necessity of the system since few judicial appointments are made from outside the ranks of professional judges.

Where do the judges come from? They are often criticized for their homogeneity, and their conservativeness. But they are much less often challenged for their effectiveness as impartial triers of disputes.

J. GRIFFITH, "THE POLITICS OF THE JUDICIARY"
27 (1981).*

From time to time in recent years, analyses have been made, based on information in reference books, of the social background of the more senior judiciary.

The most comprehensive in terms of social class origins covers the period from 1820 to 1968.

* * *

Over the whole period the dominance of the upper and upper middle classes is overwhelming. . . .

* * *

School education is a good indicator of social and economic class background, particularly as the relative cost of attendance at one of the independent 'public' schools has changed little, until very recently. It must also be remembered that university education at Oxford and Cambridge before 1945 (when those who are now judges attended) was also very largely a middle-class activity. . . .

* * *

The age of the full-time judiciary has remained constant over many years: the average on appointment has been about fifty-two or -three and the average of all those in office has been about sixty. Inevitably, given the system of promotion, the average age is highest in the Court of Appeal and the House of Lords, at about sixty-five and sixty-eight years respectively.

* * *

. . . [I]n broad terms, four out of five full-time professional judges are products of public schools, and of Oxford or Cambridge. Occasionally the brilliant lower-middle-class or working-class boy has won his place in this distinguished gathering. . . . To become a successful barrister, . . ., it is necessary to have financial support and so the background has to be that of the reasonably well-to-do family which, as a matter of course, sends its sons to public schools and then either straight to the bar or first to Oxford or Cambridge.

Nevertheless, some men and women have, since the middle 1960s, benefited from the expansion of university education, from the growth of law faculties in universities, and from the wider availability of this education and, with little private income, have been able (largely because of the increase in publicly financed legal aid) to make a living at the bar. By the mid–1980s some of these will move into the ranks of successful barristers from whom judicial appointments are made. Only then shall we be able to assess how far the dominance of the public schools and (what is of much less significance) of Oxford and Cambridge has begun to lessen. And not until the 1990s shall we know whether (as seems most unlikely) judicial attitudes have changed as a result.

* * *

* Reprinted with permission of Manchester University Press.

K. EVANS, "ADVOCACY AT THE BAR"

86 (1983).

Make no mistake about it. Some of the English judiciary are indeed the finest judges in the world. And appearing before one of those excellent judges is a delightful experience. It is like playing in, or watching, a match that is faultlessly refereed. But it is far more than that. To appear in court before a wise and impartial judge who regards impartiality as his duty and who understands what the English system was really intended to be about—to appear before such a judge is a true privilege, an exhilarating experience. There is an atmosphere in the court of such a judge which is conducive to getting the right result. One feels that one is doing a good job with proper tools and with proper materials. Everything is in tune. And at the end *everybody* comes away feeling that there could have been no fairer trial, whatever the result.

Unfortunately such judges are not noticeably in the majority. Many barristers feel that the really good judges are outnumbered. Whatever be the right proportion you are as likely as not to find yourself before a judge who does *not* match up to the expected standards of impartiality. You have to be prepared, therefore, for what you are likely to encounter and you have to know what to do about it—in so far as anything can be done. This is what the 'anti-boot' device is all about, and in order to use it properly you need to know a little more about how some judges fall short of the standards that our propaganda has led us to expect of them.

Let us consider, then, what we were taught to expect of the English judge. We were taught, were we not, that there are two major kinds of criminal trial—the 'inquisitorial' system that operates throughout Europe and in many other parts of the world, and the 'accusatorial' system that operates wherever the Common Law has been adopted, that is to say, in broad terms, wherever the English language is spoken? The first of these, the inquisitorial system, involves the judge taking an active part in establishing the facts, asking questions on his own initiative and frequently conducting virtually the whole of the examination of a witness before asking the *avocat* if *he* has any questions. In the accusatorial system, on the other hand, the judge acts as an impartial umpire watching over a kind of forensic tennis match played by advocates. If those advocates know their job then ideally the judge ought to be able to sit there throughout the trial saying virtually nothing.

Back in the mists of time the advice given to a new judge in England was that he should take a sip of holy water at the beginning of the day and hold it in his mouth until the end. One new appointee to the bench is said to have propped up in front of him so that he could see it at all times, a card with the clearly printed message 'Shut up'. After more than a generation on the bench one distinguished American judge still has a card where only he can see it, reading 'Be quiet'. Another story is told about a brand new judge who took his place on the bench determined to achieve such standards of self-restraint. At the end of his first day he thought he had done remarkably well and went round to his old chambers to see a friend who had been appearing in front of him all day.

'How did I do?' asked the new judge, confidently.

'Not bad at all, dear boy,' said the other. 'But you really must stop talking so much.'

It is obviously very difficult. We appoint our judges almost entirely from the ranks of barristers who have been earning their living for at least the previous twenty-odd years by talking. It is no wonder that it comes so hard for them to make the change and overnight to control their inclination to intervene and to question: in a word, to talk far too much. But as the great Bacon wrote in his essay *Of Judicature,* 'An over-speaking judge is no well-tuned cymball', and the aim of our judiciary is always in theory at least to sit there in as much silence as possible, interfering only when necessary to ensure that the rules are properly complied with.

* * *

Returning to what we were taught to expect of our judges, and noting that comparative silence was one thing, the next and overwhelmingly important expectation was that they should be scrupulously impartial. And this is where many of them fall short. Perhaps it has always been like this: one cannot know. But without any doubt, there is throughout the length and breadth of this land a distinct bias on the part of a lot of our judges. What seems to be a vast majority of them favour the prosecution and lean against the defence. If you find this hard to believe go and talk to a barrister who divides his time between prosecuting and defending. Ask him about the differences. Making the change from defending to prosecuting has been described as being similar to the difference between riding a bicycle uphill with the wind against you and downhill with the wind behind. It is a strange and in some ways an embarrassing feeling, when turning to prosecute after a long time defending, suddenly to find that the judge is with you, that there is this helping hand coming from the bench, that the umpire is playing on your side.

There is no doubt that this is all too often so. Nor is there any doubt that it has been getting worse. It is now an open topic of conversation at the Bar. It is not written about in the press nor discussed on the television. No Parliamentary inquiry or debate looks into the question of whether our judges are doing their job properly. There is no generally known system of inspection, no generally known system of checking on or reporting on how our judges are doing. We have no generally known committee that aims to advise anyone on whether the appointment to the bench was a good one or not. Short of a complex system that was last used in the 1700s, there is no known way of getting rid of the tyrant in the judge's seat or of making him do what he is paid to do. Once appointed, our judges are to all intents and purposes there for the rest of their working days, right up to retirement. And in the case of some of them, their retirement is awaited with impatience by all those who feel that British justice ought to be something of which we can be proud.

———

The English judiciary staffing the superior courts is a relatively small group, about 100, but increasing as more persons turn to the courts to resolve disputes. The increased number of judges in England has only modestly diminished judicial prestige. The enhanced role of legislation in contrast to judge made law has had a more severe impact. The judges of England with a lasting place in history—Mansfield, Coke, Bacon—thrived in an era where there were few judges and little challenge to the preeminence of precedent as the source of the common law. The judiciary in the United States may be associated with judicial activism, but the English judiciary tends not to issue rulings which grant to individuals rights that demand substantial national expenditure, believing that area to be the responsibility of Parliament.

The appointment of English judges to the superior court from among the barristers is a convention dating to the 13th century. The absence of elected judges lends a consistency to the English judiciary which does not exist in the United States, where the selection practice varies from one state to another, and even within a particular state with respect to different levels of the judiciary. A benefit of a judiciary homogeneous in experience and reputation, both within a given level of the court system and from one level to another, is the lack of a sense of need for an appeal to reach a more experienced or competent judge. The English system tends to assure one of meeting competency at even the lowest level, thereby reducing the indispensability of an appeal for a fair hearing.

Judges hold office for life, they may be removed by the sovereign only if in breach of good behavior and only at the request of both the House of Lords and House of Commons. Removal has never occurred. Lifetime service is permitted of judicial appointees to age 72 or 75, virtually a decade longer than allowed other government officials. Before the age limit of 75 was placed on superior court judges, many served to a very advanced age; Lord Halsbury sat nearly until his death at 93, exceeding Oliver Wendell Holmes' service until 90. Permitting lengthy service does reduce the possibility of a judge retiring and returning to other full time work, although it may result in ineffective service by judges who become incapacitated in later years.

Life peerages are invariably granted to the Lord Chancellor, the Lords of Appeal, the Master of the Rolls, the Lord Chief Justice, the President of the Family Division of the High Court, and occasionally to other judges of the Royal Courts. Every judge of the High Court or Court of Appeals is knighted, if they are not peers. As peers, they may sit as legislators in the House of Lords, but convention dictates that they avoid political issues and not stray far afield from law reform.

The Court of Appeal is not only the most influential court, but its civil side is undoubtedly the most burdened court in England. The judges sit every day and all day for a full five days each week. A few judgments are reserved and, since there is no time for preparing those judgments during the week, judges often must work on weekends. But their work load does not make them difficult to deal with, as Evans notes:

> Oddly enough, they are not a terrifying court if you are absolutely prepared. They are, with the House of Lords, the most conversational court of the lot. Be prepared to abandon your script almost at once. You are in there to answer questions. More than any other court they are lawyers who enjoy talking to economical lawyers. Infinite respect, perfect preparation, a point worth taking their time over and a clear demonstration that you understand the value of time are all you need. If you have these they will listen, help, question and, indeed, tolerate your inexperience. They are the most unforgiving court in the land to the inadequately prepared and to the time-waster. To the well prepared and the meter watcher they are the nicest tribunal of all—with the possible exception of the Lords.[8]

Lord Denning, after several years on the House of Lords, returned to the Court of Appeal, but in the capacity of the Master of the Rolls, the head of its civil side. Few persons have been appointed to the Court of Appeal without time as a trial judge, almost always in one of the divisions of the High Court. Lord Denning has suggested that persons appointed to the Court of Appeal without trial experience would have been better appeal judges had they served on the trial bench. He notes:

> Sir Wilfred Greene, my predecessor as Master of the Rolls, lacked it. He was preeminent as an advocate in points of law. He was appointed straight from the Bar to the Court of Appeal. He had been brought up in Chancery where every word of a witness is believed unless the judge says otherwise. In the Court of Appeal Wilfrid Greene would try cases on the transcript. He would take the shorthand notes, read out an answer of a witness and say to us at the Bar: 'How can you say that in view of the evidence?' We would answer: 'The judge may not have accepted it'. He would reply: 'Then he ought to have said so'. Not having said so, his decision was reversed. Irrefutable logic. Unanswerable from the Bar. But leading to a wrong determination of the appeal. Moral for an Appeal Judge: Beware of logic. It has misled better men than you.[9]

When Lord Denning moved from the Court of Appeal to the House of Lords he suggested that it was like "going into retirement." The

---

8. K. Evans, Advocacy at the Bar 187 (1983).

9. Lord Denning, The Family Story 170 (1981).

House of Lords places considerably less pressure on its judges. A Law Lord might sit four or fewer days per week, and the work days are often considerably shorter than the lengthy hours judges spend on the Court of Appeals. With judgment reserved in the House of Lords and time to spend in chambers, the pace is considerably less. Denning did not wish to retire when he was appointed to the House of Lords. He was young (58) and active. He not only sat as a judge, but as a Lord in the legislative chamber, limiting his activity to speaking and voting on social questions and legal questions, but refraining, as tradition requires, from speaking or voting on matters involving party politics.

Lord Denning was the most important and controversial judge of the past several decades, at least the most independent who made his views public. He stood out as an anachronism among the English judiciary, but he is acknowledged to have been the most significant force in the judiciary since Lord Mansfield in the 18th century. Anthony Sampson wrote:

> He made the most of his own independence, as an old judge whom no one can shut up. He enjoyed appearing on television, against the Lord Chancellor's wishes, and distancing himself from the administrators and legislators. His preoccupation has been with the problem of freedom under the law: 'What matters in England,' he said in his Hamlyn Lecture in 1949, 'is that each man should be free to develop his own personality to the full; and the only duties which should restrict this freedom are those which are necessary to enable everyone else to do the same.' His concern for the individual has brought him repeatedly up against the powers of the administration and trade unions: 'Properly exercised the new powers of the executive lead to the welfare state; but abused they lead to the totalitarian state.' [10]

Although the English judge is usually viewed as possessing skills allowing him to perform his job well, there is some question as to whether they always come to the bench prepared to do certain specialized tasks to which they may be assigned, such as those relating to family matters. Doubt is also cast on whether a career as an advocate prepares one to assume the neutral role of a judge. Berlins and Dyer have noted that:

> It is one of the quirks of the system that a judge, once appointed, may be allocated to an area of the law about which he knows very little. It is quite common, for instance, for a barrister who has spent his entire professional career doing civil work to be called on to try serious criminal cases, or for someone whose practice was mainly in the criminal courts to have to decide divorce disputes. There is an unspoken, perhaps arrogant, assumption that anyone good enough to be appointed to the bench has the ability to turn his hand to any branch of the law. Sir Neville Faulks, a former High Court judge, admits in his autobiography that when he was appoint-

10. A. Sampson, The Changing Anatomy of Britain 160 (1982).

ed as a judge to try divorce cases—a subject about which he knew little since his practice at the Bar had been in libel—he spent the Christmas vacation 'reading very carefully *Rayden on Divorce.*' That, it seems, was his only training for the job to which he had been appointed. In practice the results of our rather haphazard system are mixed. Many a judge becomes known for his mastery of a field that he hardly touched as a barrister, but there are others who only feel at ease in the speciality they developed at the Bar.[11]

Besides the appointments to ordinary and special courts staffed by professional judges, lesser judicial appointments are available as a master, or registrar, or as a stipendiary magistrate. Masters and registrars undertake the duties of processing cases before trial, a task left to ordinary judges in many nations. The English master has developed a reputation for a remarkable expertise in passing judgment on pre-trial motions, and especially in reducing the issues to be heard by the judge by overseeing the collection of facts and seeking the agreement of the litigants on minor issues. Not infrequently is the work of the master so effective that the dispute is resolved without the need of a trial. If trial is nevertheless required, the master may assign it to a County Court or determine that it should be heard in the High Court in London or on circuit.

A second minor judicial position is an appointment to a magistrates' court, to sit individually in a large city, in contrast to the lay magistrates who convene in collegiate form in the rural areas. The professional magistrate, called a stipendiary magistrate, assumes repetitious and intense work, handling a vast number of minor criminal cases. He generally sits daily, which may produce a boredom that is not a burden to the lay magistrate in the rural areas, who serves only weekly or every second week.

Among the non-professional judges, the lay magistrate is unique to the viewer from abroad. It is the lay magistrates who decide the vast majority of criminal matters, grantedly those lumped at the minor end of the scale of gravity. They are an example of the use of unpaid lay persons to a degree unknown in most common law systems, certainly in the United States.

A. SAMPSON, "THE CHANGING ANATOMY OF BRITAIN"

154 (1982).

The average citizen is much more likely to appear before a magistrate than before a judge; and the great bulk of British justice is carried out not by professional lawyers but by unpaid magistrates who sit on the bench only one day a week or a fortnight. A magistrates' court provides a complete contrast to the pomp of a law court, with no wigs, no gowns and often no lawyers. The three justices sit below a modest lion-and-

---

11. M. Berlins and C. Dyer, The Law Machine 68 (3d ed. 1989).

unicorn, only slightly removed from the courtroom, with a magistrates' clerk below who can advise them on points of law. The courtroom is often full of mothers, friends or relations and the atmosphere is far less male than the higher courts. The exchanges are brisk and matter-of-fact and only when lawyers appear are they caught up in legal rigmarole.

* * *

After the Second World War the magistrates were still very unrepresentative and often eccentric: a quarter were aged over seventy and fourteen were over ninety. Nearly all were Tories. In the country many were large landowners, as they had been six hundred years earlier. In the towns mayors, ex-mayors and London aldermen automatically became magistrates, often autocratic ones. The Lord Chancellor selected the others through a secretive and elaborate oldboy network, and since magistrates dispensed licences for pubs and gaming (which they still do) they could sometimes have corrupt motives.

Many socialists expected the post-war Labour government to abolish amateur justices altogether in favour of a professional bench. But successive Lord Chancellors found it so convenient and flexible, compared to the legal bureaucracy, that they reformed it instead. They gradually changed the political balance: by 1977 34 per cent of magistrates were Conservative, 31 per cent Labour and 14 per cent Liberal. They brought in many more women, who now make up about a third of all magistrates. They insisted on compulsory retirement, first at seventy-two, then at seventy (or sixty-five in juvenile courts). And they tried, with much less success, to broaden the class basis. Lord Gardiner even tried to find some farm labourers to be JPs, but their trade union could only come up with two candidates. By 1962 the first black magistrate was appointed in Nottingham, but by 1977 there were still only seventy-nine immigrant JPs. Black magistrates were much needed as urban crime increased, but they were still hard to recruit.

K. EVANS, "ADVOCACY AT THE BAR"
192, 196 (1983).

You will find that some lay benches are utterly charming and intelligent. Others you will encounter that are rough, rude and apparently dense. Most come somewhere in between the two extremes. But you simply must remember that in their neighbourhood they are quite powerful people and some of them are, understandably, a bit conscious of it....

... As responsible people of their neighbourhood they have an instinctive admiration for the fact that you distinguished yourself in your studies and had the pertinacity to carry them through to the point of qualifying as a lawyer. You in your turn ought to have in mind that by being chosen to be the justices of the peace of their neighbourhood they too have distinguished themselves.

Be aware of this potential 'balance of respect', because it is both justified and useful. There is not uncommonly a tendency among some young advocates to think of the lay justices as being a crowd of woodentops, as people who think illogically, who cannot be relied upon to come up with a sensible decision and who, being unqualified, are somehow inferior. That is such a silly mistake.

Of course, the justices can be perverse, and of course their absence of training in legal thought sometimes creates a communication gap between bench and lawyer. But if you start to think of them as inferiors you will inevitably talk down to them. That is the flavour that will inform your advocacy. You will never get the sympathy of your court and it will serve you right. Quite apart from anything else, they might, despite their appearance, be better qualified, better educated and cleverer than you. Hidden behind their usually unexceptionable facades you might find all manner of interesting backgrounds.

* * *

[Evans also comments on the non-professional judges on statutory tribunals].

Here you have a legally qualified chairman and, usually, two laymen who are representatives of political or factional interests. The rules are *very* much eased up here. *If what you say sounds like advocacy, then you are doing it wrong.* The atmosphere is much more one of quietly trying to find out the right thing to do.

These tribunals often feel more like a well run committee meeting than a court of law. Fastidious politeness is required, as always, and a great deal of quiet kindness. Non-lawyers often appear as advocates and it will do you a power of good to play down your 'lawyerliness'. The helpful, 'well groomed civil servant' approach is called for. Never a purple passage, please. Never the expansive phrase or gesture. Quiet, totally well organised, efficient and gentle: those words pretty well describe the kind of young advocate who goes down well in the tribunals.

It is a knack that you will develop, the ability to be very slightly self-effacing in these quasi-courts. They hold no terrors at all to the well-prepared. Their members are patient and respectful of competent lawyers. There are no tetchy clerks. Formality is at an absolute minimum. Go along to them determined just to be a well-prepared, nice individual. When you have to discuss law, do so with a measure of reluctance, despite the fact that labour law can be as complex as anything that the Vice–Chancellor might have to deal with. To sum it up in a sentence, avoid appearing to be a lawyer before the statutory tribunals. Go along there as someone whose presence is just going to be of assistance in the important work they have to do.

M. BERLINS AND C. DYER, "THE LAW MACHINE"
(3d ed. 1989).

... The process of choosing magistrates is subtle and secretive. There are no competitive examinations, and the only public trawl is through the occasional newspaper advertisement. Constitutionally, the appointment of magistrates lies with the Lord Chancellor, but in practice the task of choosing suitable candidates has been given to advisory committees all around the country. ... The Lord Chancellor relies heavily on the advisory committees, who have the local knowledge and the opportunity to assess and interview those they think might have the qualities to sit on the bench.

There are 95 advisory committees in England and Wales, each with responsibility for a specified area. The curious and controversial fact about these committees is that, they do not at present publicly reveal the identity of their members, except for the secretaries (so that those putting a name forward know to whom to write). The traditional reason given for this secrecy is to prevent committee members being lobbied.

That anonymity is soon to be abolished. From the end of 1992 advisory committees will be obliged to make public the names of their members....

* * *

... The Lord Chancellor's department admits that one of the reasons there are not more working-class magistrates is because they don't come to the attention of the advisory committees in the same way as middle-class candidates do—they don't move in the same circles or belong to the same clubs. Those that become active in politics or trade union affairs might be recommended by their party or union officials, but others may just never have their ability noticed and brought to the attention of the advisory committee.

There are other reasons too. Working-class people are often loath to allow their names to be put forward, either through lack of interest or because they fear that their job or promotion prospects might be endangered by their absences from work; or even on the ground that becoming a JP would cause tensions with their workmates and colleagues. ... If a working JP loses his job, he might find it difficult to get another once a prospective employer finds out he has to have a day off every fortnight. ... Magistrates may also have to sacrifice part of their pay: the loss of earnings allowance (£27.50 a full day; £13.75 if they just sit for a morning) is less than most skilled workers earn. There should be no difficulty, in theory, about absences from work. Under the law, employers cannot object to their workers' taking time off to sit on the bench. In practice, however, there are many subtle ways in which an employer can make his displeasure known.

Whatever the reasons for the disproportionate social balance, it has led to comments that there is too much of a gap between the mainly middle-class, white, comfortably-off magistrates and the typical defendants who appear before them. Magistrates, it is suggested, cannot really understand the problems of the kind of people they try. If true, this would seem to contradict one of the aims of the system of lay justices.

More recently, concern has been expressed about the low proportion of magistrates from the ethnic communities, especially West Indian, Indian and Pakistani. The latest figures show that fewer than 2 per cent of magistrates are black or Asian. ...

The attempt to get more women on the bench has been more successful—partly because many more women than men are not in full-time work—and the ratio of men to women is now about 4 to 3 (16,000 men and 12,000 women approximately).

* * *

Training for new JPs is divided into two parts. After they are appointed but before sitting for the first time, they are given lectures, amounting to around eight hours, on their duties and their jurisdiction, the practice and procedure of the court and methods of punishment and treatment. They also have to sit as observers in a few different courts to see them in action from the public's point of view. After the first part of training magistrates are entitled to sit on the bench, though only in the company of far more experienced colleagues.

The second stage of training is held within six to nine months. It is a more intensive course also lasting around eight hours in which magistrates discuss with their clerk the laws they have to apply in more detail, and participate in practical exercises on bail and sentencing, two of the most important decisions they have to make. In the sentencing exercise, conducted by the justices' clerk, the magistrates are given the backgrounds of convicted offenders and details of their crimes, and have to decide how to deal with them. They discuss the options, which include an absolute or conditional discharge, a fine, probation, community service, imprisonment. They also attend lectures by probation officers and other officials involved with the courts. In addition, they visit a prison, a youth custody centre, and see various forms of non-custodial schemes in action.

All this still does not add up to anything remotely close to a professional education. How can we allow such thinly trained people to take on such awesome responsibilities? The answer is three-fold. First, the people chosen are supposed to have exhibited already in their careers, or in work for their community, or in some other way, the kind of qualities that will make them capable of judging and sentencing others with commonsense and understanding. Second, they can acquire experience gradually, from sitting on the bench under the guidance of more senior JPs. They also have to attend annual brush-up courses. Third, they lean heavily on their justices' clerk to fill the gaps in their legal knowledge or experience.

K. EVANS, "ADVOCACY AT THE BAR"
193 (1983).

Come now to that remarkable English official, the clerk to the justices. Out in the provinces he's often a retired solicitor in late middle age. In the big cities he or she might be a fully qualified barrister or solicitor or an unqualified but trained civil servant. The function of the clerk is to advise the lay justices on the law, to run the court and to take depositions.

In the old days everywhere, and nowadays in many places still, you would be forgiven for thinking that the proprietor of the court was the clerk himself. Some of them still dominate their courts to a quite astonishing degree. Comyn J, as a very young junior, doodled a verse on his way back from the West Country once:

> I'm the power beneath the throne:
> I'm the way the wind has blown:
> I'm the man who knows his 'Stone'.
> I'm the Clerk!

Now the right relationship with the clerk is probably more of a hit or miss affair than anything else in advocacy. It is a strange office that he occupies—the lawyer who acts as some kind of major-domo to the unqualified justices, a sort of butler or master of ceremonies to the laymen, a learned adviser but not, in theory at least, a decision taker. He decides so much, yet the ultimate decisions aren't his.

In all of this he may be thoroughly happy. He may never have seen himself in wig and gown enthralling an Old Bailey jury. He may hug himself in warm self-congratulation whenever he thinks of his regulated pensionable life. He may on the other hand be as desperate as Jude the Obscure, hating every last moment of his safe existence and resenting bitterly the carefree young advocates who have snapped up chances that he either failed to grasp himself or never had. He may be neither of these. He may just be a grumpy old solicitor who has got tired to death of the job. He may be a tough, stiff-necked, bossy individual who adores the power he exercises. He may be a kind, contented chap who enjoys every minute of his interesting and useful profession.

. . . [T]he clerk is the part of the lay bench court that is in the habit of talking back. Very often he interrupts.

'What is the relevance of that?'

'How can that be right?'

If you are not ready for this and don't know how to cope, the clerk can throw you off balance with ease.

M. BERLINS AND C. DYER, "THE LAW MACHINE"
83 (3d ed. 1989).

The lay magistrates' system in England and Wales is undoubtedly very quick, very cheap and pretty rough and ready. It is also reasonably efficient. Four main criticisms are made against it.

First, it is said that magistrates are too hasty and crude in the justice they dispense, that a magistrates' court can sometimes be confusing for the people who pass through it, and that injustice can result.

* * *

The second criticism is that magistrates tend to be prosecution-minded and too inclined to believe police witnesses automatically. A London solicitor summarises what many who specialize in the criminal field feel—he points out that, especially in country areas:

> ... the same magistrates see the same police giving evidence all the time and it follows therefore that they establish some sort of rapport, some sort of relationship with those individual police officers. That, coupled with the fact that the magistrates tend to come from an area of the community which does not have adverse contact with the police generally, tends to result in the lay magistrates accepting without question the evidence of police.

Another solicitor puts it this way:

> Clearly the way in which they look upon the police is governed and conditioned by their own social background and how they perceive the police to be. They are naive in many ways when they consider whether or not a police officer is telling the truth, as the view that they tend to hold is that a police officer has no reason not to tell the truth. They do not give the impression of looking on evidence presented by a police officer and a defendant in a completely even-handed manner.

* * *

The third main criticism is that there is too much of a social barrier between the magistrates and the defendants. If that is so and if indeed injustice does result, it is a difficult matter to put right. The Lord Chancellor's department tries hard to get a wider social and ethnic spread of justices. That it has not sufficiently succeeded is largely due to complex factors outside its control.

The fourth criticism is that magistrates are conviction-minded. It is widely believed that an accused has a better chance of being acquitted by a jury than by magistrates. Statistics are difficult to come by, partly because it was recently discovered that the magistrates' court figures which formed the basis of comparisons had been wrongly collated. Research using correct data is limited to relatively small samples, but the results suggest that magistrates convict up to 75 per cent of defendants who plead not guilty before them, whereas the acquittal rate for defendants choosing trial by jury is about 50 per cent. Magistrates argue that this merely shows that they are less often taken in than juries, not that they are convicting many innocent defendants. But some critics believe that wrongful, as well as justified, convictions are more likely in magistrates' trials, mainly because magistrates' courts do not have the time to be as thorough.

Whatever its faults, most lawyers and others who have come into contact with the system believe that on the whole it works. Magistrates deliver justice enormously cheaply (proportionately, England has easily the lowest bill for judicial services of any developed country), and relatively speedily and efficiently. The lay magistracy does the job asked of it and it offers good value for money. No serious contenders have been proposed to replace it and it is likely to remain the cornerstone of our justice system for the foreseeable future.

* * *

... Originally appointed when the reputation of the lay magistracy was at a low ebb, the few stipendiaries have remained part of the system. For the most part, stipendiary and lay justices co-exist reasonably happily together, even when they inhabit the same court. There has never been any serious call either to replace lay with paid justices altogether or to do away with the stipendiaries. Nevertheless, it is widely accepted that stipendiaries dispense a different kind of justice from that meted out by part-time justices, though there is no agreement as to which is preferable: some say that the full-time 'stipe' quickly becomes case-hardened and strict, others say that he is much more professional and fair.

Who makes a good magistrate?

SYBILLE BEDFORD, "THE FACES OF JUSTICE"
71 (1961).

I once asked a professional magistrate what he considered to be his first duty. "The keeping of the peace," he said, "and the rehabilitation of the individual. They go together. Although sometimes there is conflict...."

The good magistrate, one might say, must be a good man. And possibly a contented one. He ought not to be too high-strung; a man with a Dostoevsky view of life would wear himself to a frazzle in six months. (Dickens of course would have done splendidly, in his youth at least.) As a barrister put it, "Oh, a happily married chap, you know; garden, kind heart, good health and not too much out for himself." Another magistrate named the qualities, in that order: "Humanity; common sense; humility; a little law, a very clever chap would be wasted; a sense of humour." To which one might add, imagination, some experience of life and an ability to absorb the unexpected.

The not-so-good magistrate is a man who talks with his head down, who seldom takes his nose out of the ledger. He does not look at the people who speak to him. He hurries them along with *hnhn's* and *well's*. He interrupts witnesses, and when there is counsel he takes the examination out of his mouth. He browbeats young barristers. He gives everybody a sense of the scarcity of his time. He does not appear to listen. He pretends to be unable to understand what people say to him. He is sarcastic when it is too easy. He makes up his mind, or appears to have made up his mind, at the beginning of a case. He loses his temper not because it might be necessary, but because he loses it. He loses it, not because he has been tried beyond endurance, but because it is a cherished exercise. He shows contempt for his customers and his place of work, and he betrays his sense that he is made of different clay.

Questions and Notes

1. Is the judicial appointment power of the Lord Chancellor a contribution to or a detraction from the generally held high opinion of the English judiciary?

2. Why is the English judiciary considered to be apolitical? It does not seem to be attributable to appointment at middle-age in light of the experience in the United States of appointing many judges in middle-age *because* of established political beliefs. But is the English appointment process really devoid of politics or is it in fact *overwhelmingly* political?

3. The extensive use of lay magistrates is more comparable to comrades courts in the USSR than to any part of the American legal system. When you read the materials in the socialist legal tradition, consider how lay persons are used in each system. Is their role really the same?

Chapter 12

PROCEDURE IN ENGLAND

SECTION 1. INTRODUCTION

Procedure in the development of common law stood at the forefront. Substance followed some distance behind. Procedure was molded and developed and has attained a status with recognizable characteristics deserving of our attention. While we shall discuss the process of a civil suit and a criminal charge, including the appeal, our attention will focus on several elements of the process which serve to illustrate some fundamental differences between the root common law system and what we have learned as procedure in the United States. Perhaps the most significant and important is the jury system. Not only is the use of the jury system different—its near absence in England for civil cases is often surprising to an American observer—but the way in which it is selected and reaches its conclusion has profound implications for the manner in which legal services function in the two nations. Of further note is the different attitude expressed in the two nations towards the public's right to know regarding the unfolding of events during the prosecution of a crime. Constitutionalists in the United States tend to shudder at the restrictions on the press in England, enforced under contempt rules. Finally, the appeal process in England is a more oral process than in the United States. Less supported by briefs and limited oral argument, the English process may be viewed by American observers as consuming too much time in court. Some attempts have been made to speed the process, essentially by use of an abbreviated, written note of the argument to be presented at the oral hearing. Few of these observers are left unimpressed with the exercise of judicial skills as the English judges render a decision orally immediately upon conclusion of the appeal—the famous American judicial phrase "I reserve judgment" seems to have little home in England. These materials should suggest that procedure reflects much of how a nation wishes its legal system to function. Let us now begin to consider some different ways in which the legal actors function within their principal legal institutions—the courts.

SECTION 2. CIVIL PROCEDURE

A. GENERAL

English civil procedure developed internally, that is, within the court system itself, to meet immediate needs. Rules which resolved questions of how the course of an action would proceed were established on-the-spot by the King's Courts. The development of English civil procedure, particularly since the 16th century, has constituted a process of refinement, of periodic alterations to correct immediate deficiencies which distracted the court from reaching a just result. This development contrasts significantly with the more methodical, external development of civil procedure in most civil law nations, where it is guided by legislative enactments and by the writings of law faculty, detached from any particular, current dispute. The civil law lawyer consequently views his system of procedure as more logical and rational in development.

An extraordinary transformation has occurred in English civil procedure from its dominant role in the early stages of the formation of English law. That dominance was demonstrated by the inflexible forms of action in the writ process, reflected in the statement "where there is no writ there is no right." Comparatively little substantive law existed in the initial decades of the development of English law, it evolved over a long period of time through judicial pronouncements, each issued within the strict procedural framework. The legal relationships of ordinary persons, such as in contracts and torts, grew slowly from the aggregation of specific decisions. As substantive legal rules accumulated in the reported decisions, the dominant role of the strict procedural elements declined. English civil procedure is considerably more flexible than during the early centuries of its development. There is no longer any general attitude that procedure overshadows the substantive law. Once governed by an almost mystical unwritten scheme, for a century now English civil procedure substantially has been codified. Rules of the Supreme Court, originally authorized by the Judicature Acts 1873, now regulate most civil proceedings in the Supreme Court, and there are corresponding rules for the county courts and for criminal proceedings in the magistrates' courts.[1]

The complexity of the pretrial stage of an action initially depends on the rules regulating service of process. In a federal system, such as the United States, the serving of process to obtain jurisdiction over a person located in a different governmental unit meets with numerous conflicts. Such complexity does not exist within England, although similar issues mandates an adaptation of English procedural law to the jurisdictional conflicts arising from England's participation in the European Community and the EC Convention on Jurisdiction and the Enforcement of Judgments 1968 (Brussells Convention).

---

1. Procedure in the county courts and magistrates' courts, as well as the Supreme Court, is discussed in T. Ingman, The English Legal Process, ch. 1 (1983).

Civil proceedings begin by the appropriate court office issuing a writ of a summons to commence the action. The writ includes only enough information to apprise the defendant of the nature of the action. It is unlike the earlier, strict forms of action, which required a plaintiff to choose his form correctly or face dismissal. The writ is a command in the name of the sovereign to enter an appearance before the court. The "appearance" is accomplished by sending an acknowledgment of service to the court office which issued the writ.

The pleadings follow the appearance, and are quite similar to the process in other common law systems. But they tend to be briefer and more specific than American pleadings. The parties may be made to produce certain documents or, quite rarely, answer specific written interrogatories, but the English discovery system does not allow a pretrial oral deposition. The pretrial stage thus appears to be almost exclusively a written, documentary process. But this is not so. The applications, such as those for injunctions or discovery or to strike certain pleadings, are argued orally. And, as is true of most appeals, the oral arguments are made without briefs. Some of the pretrial work is accomplished by solicitors, but the barristers who will argue at the trial consult and draft required documents.

The English legal system contributes to the pretrial stage the expertise of a "master" (District "registrar" in the provinces). A master is a former barrister or solicitor who accepts this position of less prestige, but less pressure, than a judge, and who is as skillful in procedure as the judge who will try the final issues is in interpreting substantive law. Masters perform numerous functions intended to refine the case for trial, or bring it to an early conclusion by way of settlement or withdrawal. They rule on interlocutory requests for interrogatories or the discovery of documents, proposed amendments to the pleadings and requirements for security. If the master has performed his task well, the issues will have been narrowed to those truly in conflict. Documenting evidence will have been collected, and the judge at trial will have been relieved of confronting many procedural conflicts which may burden the proceeding and confuse the participants. Acting in the quiet of his office or a hearing room, away from the publicity, openness and formality of the courtroom, the master plays an important role in preparing cases so that the oral, trial stage may proceed without delay, and in contributing to litigation a degree of uniformity which allows the trial stage to focus on the substantive issues. His is not an unhurried role, however, and he often pressures parties to resolve the case themselves.

B. KAPLAN, "AN AMERICAN LAWYER IN THE QUEEN'S COURTS: IMPRESSIONS OF ENGLISH CIVIL PROCEDURE"

69 Michigan Law Review 821 (1971).*

* * *

The masters deal with a variety of matters, but one of their better known performances occurs at "summons for directions." The plaintiff must bring on this summons within a month after the close of the pleadings. It is a theater for applications by both sides and also for settling the arrangements for trial. The master will handle the parties' demands concerning the pleadings—largely applications for particulars and amendments—and questions of interrogatories and perhaps documentary discovery. So, also, with the cooperation of the parties, the master runs over the possibilities of expediting and shortening the proof at trial; he fixes the mode and place of trial. With exceptions here and there, the masters' work is routinized. A summons for directions will usually be disposed of in one to three minutes. Barristers are not often in attendance; in fact, the parties are commonly represented not by the solicitors proper but by their unadmitted clerks. Masters' calendars are heavy and their decisions are made on the spot. . . .

One begins by thinking of the summons for directions as being analogous to the American "pretrial conference," allowing always for the fact that with us it is the judges who do the work. Indeed, the summons for directions was referred to for comparison in the original Advisory Committee's note to Federal Rule 16, which established the pretrial conference. Our conference, however, has turned out to be so variable as to complicate assessment, comparative or otherwise. It appears in the Federal Rules as a device to be used in the court's discretion. In some courts it is used hardly at all; in others it is regularly used but in a perfunctory way; in still others it is cultivated intensively. The pretrial conference figures importantly in the conduct of large, complex cases where it has been used under strong judicial initiative and impulsion to organize the conduct of discovery by the parties, to concentrate the parties' interlocutory motions, to frame issues of fact and law superseding the pleadings *pro tanto,* and to make other arrangements anticipating ultimate trial. Discussion of settlement comes in quite naturally, and is encouraged and even initiated by some judges. But it should be added that the once-current idea that the American pretrial conference in fact hastened and multiplied settlements was left in doubt by field investigation of an ordinary run of cases in the state courts of New Jersey.

There has been some sentiment in the United States for employing practice masters, and we hear of two federal district courts that have utilized so-called pretrial examiners or pretrial masters to help with pretrial conferences. The English masters are indeed attractive figures, working hard and efficiently to mop up the interlocutory applications with little levy upon the time of the judges. One connects the masters' work with the fact that procedure in England has been put in the adjective or subordinate place where it seems to belong; one connects it

* Reprinted with permission of Benjamin Kaplan and the Michigan Law Review.

with a boast that the English can make with more claim to truth than ourselves, that cases are not decided on points of practice which are, in Pounds' words, "the mere etiquette of justice." However, the qualities of the milieu in which English masters operate must be appreciated. There can be relatively few important, potentially dispositive questions that arise upon the face of an English action. For England is a legal unit without the complications of competency, jurisdiction, and venue that can bedevil an action in a federal system—Walt Whitman might have been thinking of legal federalism when he wrote: "Here is not merely a nation but a teeming Nation of nations." ... So also the masters are spared the kinds of questions that can arise from the ramifications of the American discovery process....

In their turn, enthusiasts of the American pretrial conference have been pressing it on the English, to become there an adjunct, perhaps, to the summons for directions. The conference, however, is most plausible as a means of ordering and arranging massive cases with the usual imprecise pleadings and sprawling discovery. The wisdom of using it in the bulk of English actions—that is, relatively small actions—is thus dubious, as, indeed, is also the wisdom of applying it routinely to American cases. Adoption of the conference in personal-injury cases would seem at odds with the recommendation to routinize further the summons for directions. Again, there are peculiarly English objections to adopting our conference. Barristers would have to be briefed to attend a conference, which of course would mean a fee. Moreover, it might be thought awkward—destructive of the image of the office—to have masters edging up to settlements. Of course the idea of using the judges themselves to manage such conferences would go down even harder. In all events, the Winn Committee rejected the idea of a pretrial conference in the same breath with its disapproval of American discovery.

———

The English trial is an oral process. This was necessarily so in earlier times when jury members were usually illiterate; presenting written evidence would have been futile. But the oral process also is mandated by the nature of the trial today. Continuation of the deliberate and often time consuming written procedures which dominate the pretrial stage is no longer appropriate when all the parties have gathered for the trial. The parties expect its conduct to proceed without undue postponement. The English trial, as in most common law nations, is "an event." It begins with all parties present and proceeds to its conclusion while they remain. This oral proceeding exhibits the skills of the English advocate.... The English view their trial stage as necessitating rapid comprehension and response, skills which are often not possessed by trial lawyers in nations which do not limit trial advocacy to specialists, including the United States....

The oral process of an English civil trial is familiar to any common law system observer.... But the English civil trial judge often plays an active role in directly questioning the parties, to clarify for his own sake conflicting or unclear matters, or even to commence a new line of questioning which he may perceive as important, but which had been ignored by counsel. Judicial participation is important in a civil trial where either party may decide not to introduce evidence. The judge may be able to extract what one counsel prefers not to mention, and the other ignores.

Although England's civil procedure once followed extremely strict procedures, an English trial today appears less disrupted by the application of strict rules of evidence. Evidence precluded in the United States often is admitted unchallenged in an English proceeding, and a barrister certainly is more hesitant in objecting to a line of inquiry presented by the judge than by opposing counsel.

English common law almost never affords the parties a trial with judge and jury in civil cases. The use of a civil trial jury varies throughout common law systems. The United States extends the right to trial by jury well beyond practice in England.

Questions

Would the concept of masters be appropriate for the American legal system? How would we have to, as Kaplan notes, modify the voltage of our system? Were they to be used, who should be eligible to be a master? Should they assume a role of trying to encourage (coerce) settlements, or should that be left to the trial judge?

B. THE JURY IN CIVIL CASES

The jury is a product of the evolutionary process that we call the common law. As there are parallels in the common law use of precedent to the way it was used in Roman law, there are parallels to the common law jury in Roman law. The Lex Servilia in 104 B.C. allowed both parties to propose 100 judices, and each to then reject 50 from the list of the other. But the parallels are just that, and not roots. The Roman practice did not find acceptance on the Continent. The jury was introduced to English law in the thirteenth century. It was a welcome replacement for the ecclesiastical ordeals. But the juries were at first not randomly selected persons. They usually were persons who lived in such closeness to the event that they could decide without hearing evidence. They *knew* about the event. Over the centuries they would evolve into that bulwark of the common law, the impartial jury. Sometimes impartial, often impugned. There may be no element of the common law tradition which has been more vilified and more sanctified. To an outside observer, it appears that we select a dozen persons totally ignorant of the facts, and hardly likely to ever comprehend the testimony, much less remember it at the time of deliberation, allow lawyers to attempt to twist the minds of the jurors into a mold favorable to one side or the other, and then send them into a locked room until they tire of debating and the weakest give in to the strongest. Advocates in England have spoken more kindly, Blackstone noting that trial by jury

... ever has been, and I trust ever will be, looked upon as the glory of English law ...   The liberties of England cannot but subsist so long as this palladium remains sacred and inviolate.[2]

And Lord Devlin stated that:

... [N]o tyrant could afford to leave a subject's freedom in the hands of twelve of his countrymen.   So that trial by jury is more than an instrument of justice and more than one wheel of the constitution: it is the lamp that shows that freedom lives.[3]

However altered the jury may be in England and other common law nations, it has played a major role in the development of the legal structure.   Lords Devlin and Denning comment further on the use of the jury in England.

LORD DEVLIN, "TRIAL BY JURY"
4 (1956).*

The English jury is not what it is because some lawgiver so decreed but because that is the way it has grown up.   Indeed, its invention by a lawgiver is inconceivable.   We are used to it and know that it works; if we were not, we should say that it embodies a ridiculous and impracticable idea. . . .   Theoretically it ought not to be possible to successfully enforce the criminal law by such means.

How is it done?   Two answers to that question can be given at once. The first is that the account which I have just given of the jury process, though not inaccurate, is a very superficial one.   There is a great deal going on beneath the surface that tends to shape the jury's verdict. Most lawyers would readily assent to the generalisation that the jury is the sole judge of all questions of fact and the jury itself is invariably told that it is; but it is a generalisation that, when one stops to think more about it, is found to need a good deal of qualifying.   The second answer is that the jury system is not something that was planned on paper and has to be made to work in practice.   It developed that way simply because that was the way in which it was found to work and for no other reason.

It began as something quite different and the nature of its origin is shown by its name.   A juror was a man who was compelled by the King to take an oath.   It was the Normans who brought over this device whereby the spiritual forces could be made to perform a temporal service and the immense efficacy which they possessed in medieval times used for the King's own ends.   The oath then was so strong a guarantor of veracity that, provided that the men who were compelled so to answer were the men who must know the truth about a matter, there could be no better way of getting at the facts. . . .   The King used it for obtaining

---

2. 1 Commentaries III 379.

3. Lord Devlin, Trial by Jury 164 (1956).

* Reprinted here and below with permission of Sweet & Maxwell Ltd.

information which he wanted for administrative purposes, for example, in the compilation of the Domesday Book, and the people who were compelled to answer were those who lived in the place where the inquiry was being held and who must therefore know the facts. Thus the jury originated as a body of men used in an inquisition or, in the English term, an inquest. . . .

But the inquest was not at first associated with the administration of justice. Indeed justice was not thought to need any form of preliminary inquiry. Disputes were settled simply by one of the disputants proving himself by one means or another to be the better man. Trial by battle was one obvious way; it too was introduced by the Normans and was not liked by the English. Or a man might show the superiority of his own oath by bringing as many of his neighbors as he could as compurgators to swear to the value of it and then some process of oath-counting, possibly ending in a fight, went on. It is all very reminiscent of school-boy justice. Trial by ordeal was the most popular of the recognised means; and perhaps deservedly so by comparison with the others, because it was believed to signify the divine acceptance of a claim.

It was King Henry II who was directly responsible for turning the jury into an instrument for doing justice and Pope Innocent III who was indirectly responsible for its development as a peculiarly English institution. Henry II understood well the importance of extending the royal jurisdiction as a means of enlarging the royal power; and also the royal purse, for the conduct of litigation was in those days a profitable business. A jury which gave the King information for administrative purposes could also be used to give him information which would enable him to decide a dispute. . . . They were men drawn from the neighbourhood who were taken to have knowledge of all the relevant facts (anyone who was ignorant was rejected) and were bound to answer upon their oath and according to their knowledge which of the two disputants was entitled to the land. When a party got twelve oaths in his favour, he won. This is the origin of the trial jury, though there was as yet no sort of trial in the modern sense. . . .

* * *

In November 1215 Pope Innocent III prohibited trial by ordeal. . . . On the Continent, where the science of law and legal procedure was much further advanced than in England, the judges were quick to devise new and more rational forms of proving guilt. In England—the Crown was then in the infancy of Henry III—the judges who went out on circuit were left to improvise. . . . Something had to be devised and it was natural that the judges should use the jury. . . .

At first no sharp distinction was drawn between the jurors who presented and those who tried. . . . The process was still, and for many years remained, an inquest—an inquiry of those who were supposed to know. Until 1948, after the jury had been sworn to try treason or felony, a proclamation was made in these terms—

"If any one can inform my Lords the King's Justices, or the King's Attorney–General, on this Inquest to be taken between our Sovereign Lord the King and the Prisoner at the Bar, of any Treasons, Murders, Felonies or Misdemeanours, done or committed by the Prisoner at the Bar, let him come forth and he shall be heard, for the Prisoner now stands at the Bar upon his Deliverance."

* * *

The words illustrate vividly one stage in the metamorphosis of the jury, the stage in which they were changing from a body that acted on its own inherent knowledge into one that received information from outside. At first, the information was supplementary and given haphazardly—perhaps privately to one or two of the jurors by the plaintiff or defendant (much as a party interested in the decision of a committee might nowadays buttonhole one of the members and put his point of view) or perhaps publicly in response to a general invitation. The idea of the reception of evidence matured slowly....

... [W]ill you note two things which especially contribute to an understanding of the way the jury works to-day? The first is that judge and jury were never formally created as separate institutions; there was never any separation of powers, never any conscious decision by anyone that questions of law ought to be decided by lawyers and those of fact by laymen. The jury derived all its powers from the judge and from his willingness to accept its verdict; even now, if he were to refuse to do so, he would offend against no statute and his judgment would be good until reversed by a higher court. In theory the jury is still an instrument used by the judge to help him to arrive at a right decision; ... The verdict has no legal effect until judgment is entered upon it. The jury's function was always, and still is, simply to answer the question so that judgment may be given. Its place in the trial has become important not because it has been granted or usurped additional powers but simply because the coming of rational methods of proof has given to the task of fact-finding an importance unrecognised by thirteenth-century judges; if they had recognised it, they would probably have kept the task for themselves. We talk nowadays of the province of law and the province of fact almost as if they were separate jurisdictions, and sometimes of judges encroaching on the jury's province....

The other point is that the origin of the jury's verdict explains a unique feature of it that is still of the first importance. Judges give their reasons, either so as to satisfy the parties or because they themselves want to justify their judgments.... The jury just says yes or no. Indeed, it is not allowed to expand upon that and its reasons may not be inquired into. It is the oracle deprived of the right of being ambiguous. The jury was in its origin as oracular as the ordeal: neither was conceived in reason: the verdict, no more than the result of the ordeal, was open to rational criticism. This immunity has been largely retained and is still an essential characteristic of the system.

LORD DENNING, "WHAT NEXT IN THE LAW"

33 (1982).

* * *

You must not suppose ... that trial by jury has remained unchanged. It has been altered beyond recognition. It has been whittled away. It no longer subsists in civil cases in England save for libel. It is still retained in criminal cases of any consequence, but it has defects which cause concern....

* * *

As we move into the nineteenth century, we find that juries were treated in a more civilised manner. They were not starved or locked up so as to secure unanimity. They were not carried round the circuit in a waggon. If there was a disagreement—even if one only dissented—there was no verdict. There had to be a new trial. The judge would try to get them to agree but, if it was unsuccessful, the judge used no threats and no pressure. He ordered a new trial. If on a retrial there was still a disagreement, the prosecution used to drop the case.

But still throughout the nineteenth century the jury played the predominant role in the decision of all cases. Not only in criminal cases, but also in civil cases. The jury were in the eye of the law all 'reasonable men'. They were all householders. They were all male, middle-class and middle-aged. Their verdicts did represent the views of right-minded people. The nineteenth century was the golden age of trial by jury.

But the judges sought to exercise more control over juries. They did it sometimes by holding that there was no case to go to the jury. They did it at other times by holding that the verdict was perverse and by ordering a new trial. They gave them directions on points of law— which the jury had to follow. And so forth. The trials of the nineteenth century became not so much 'trial by jury' as 'trial by judge and jury'....

* * *

[T]rial by jury dominated the administration of justice in England right up to the end of the First World War. Everyone had confidence in it. The jurors were not chosen at random from the whole population. They were chosen from a select band of the middle classes. They were responsible heads of households—who came without pay—not so much even as their expenses. Never was any one of them challenged. Each was educated and of good understanding. Each was a worthy representative of the 'reasonable man' so well respected by the law.

There have been so many reforms—good or bad—in my time that I hardly know where to begin.

The first is the virtual disappearance in civil cases of trial by jury. Up till the First World War there was a right of trial by jury—the overwhelming number of civil cases were tried by jury. During the war the judges were given a discretion whether to order a jury or not. This was continued after the war. But the courts still gave priority to trial by jury. The position was well stated by Lord Justice Atkin in the important case of *Ford v. Blurton* [(1922) 38 TLR 801 at 805]:

> 'Trial by jury, except in the very limited classes of cases assigned to the Chancery Court, is an essential principle of our law. It has been the bulwark of liberty, the shield of the poor from the oppression of the rich and powerful. Anyone who knows the history of our law knows that many of the liberties of the subject were originally established and are maintained by the verdicts of juries in *civil cases.* Many will think that at the present time the danger of attack by powerful private organisations or by encroachments of the executive is not diminishing. It is not without importance that the right now taken away is expressly established as part of the American constitution.... Hitherto, notwithstanding the far-reaching changes of the Judicature Acts, the right to trial by *jury has been substantially maintained....*

> I do not myself see any inconvenience in trying before a jury contested facts, even though upon their ascertainment questions of law may emerge.'

That feeling was still prevalent in my early days at the Bar. Most personal injury cases were tried by a judge and jury. Leading counsel used to be paid 10 guineas for him and 2 guineas for his clerk. A '10 and 2 shout' it was called.

Over the years, however, parties have come to ask less and less for juries in civil cases. Eventually it was a decision of the Court of Appeal in 1965 which transformed everything. The case was *Ward v. James.* [(1966) 1 QB 273]. As Master of the Rolls I convened a full court of five judges. Both sides agreed to accept our decision and not to appeal to the House of Lords. It was a case where a warrant officer in the Army was badly injured in a road accident. He was left with both his arms and his legs paralysed. The damages would be very large. He wanted them to be assessed by a jury. We held that he had no right to a jury. The court in their discretion could refuse it. In the course of the judgment the court laid down guide-lines for the exercise of the discretion. These have been so interpreted that no one gets a trial by jury now in any civil case except in a very rare case in which by statute it is explicitly provided that the party has a right to trial by jury. The most important of these exceptions are in libel cases....

In 1967 the rule requiring unanimity was abrogated. Instead a verdict of a majority of ten to two was to be accepted. I confess that I was against the change. I spoke against it in the House of Lords. But the voting was seventy-four to eight in favour of majority verdicts.

The reasoning for the change was impressive. It was based on the new type of crime. This was highly organised by men who robbed banks and stole huge sums. If they were charged, one of their friends or associates would try to bribe or threaten one of the jurors—or his wife or relative—and induce that juror to disagree. This was possible in any long case. Time after time this happened. A case would go on for three or four weeks. The evidence would be clear and convincing. But at the end there would be a disagreement of the jury. It was an affront to justice—and a great waste of time and money. To try and circumvent this, the police had to put a guard on the jurors and their relatives. Lord Stonham for the Home Office told the House of Lords that

> 'there are 82 police officers, plus a detective inspector and a detective sergeant, engaged in aiding the jury in one case'.

* * *

In view of this menace to justice, the House overwhelmingly approved the introduction of majority verdicts. It may be possible to bribe or threaten one or two of the jurors, but it is not very likely to be successful in more.

WARD v. JAMES

Court of Appeal [England].
[1966] 1 Q.B. 273.*

LORD DENNING M.R. read the following judgment. In the spring of 1962 the plaintiff was a warrant officer in the Army. He was serving in West Germany. He was aged 34, a married man with two children. On May 20, 1962, he was off duty. He was a passenger in a car driven by another military man, the defendant. They were going along the road from Lüneberg to Drogeniendorf. There was an accident in which the plaintiff was very severely injured. His back was broken. Both his arms and both his legs were paralysed. He can never recover. In medical terms he is a permanent quadraplegic. He was taken to the hospital at Stoke Mandeville where much skill is devoted to the treatment and training of persons so afflicted. He is able to get into a wheel-chair and to use it, and he has some use of his arms.

On December 14, 1962, an action was brought on his behalf against the driver of the car for negligence. The driver denied negligence and did not admit the damage. It is unlikely that there will be any serious contest on liability. The substantial question is: what damages should be awarded?

On July 23, 1963, on the summons for directions, the plaintiff asked for trial by jury. Master Lawrence so ordered. The defendant appealed. On July 30, 1963, Roskill J. dismissed the appeal. So the case *was* to be tried by jury. It was set down for trial in the jury list and was about to come on for hearing. Then on November 2, 1964 (15 months after trial

---

* Reprinted with permission of The Incorporated Council of Law Reporting.

by jury was ordered) the defendant sought to have the mode of trial altered. He wanted trial by judge alone. He applied for leave to appeal out of time. On November 10, 1964, Sellers and Russell L.JJ. enlarged the time for appealing, gave leave to appeal from the order of Roskill J. and ordered that the appeal be heard by a full court. Both parties have agreed to accept the decision of the full court and not to appeal to the House of Lords. The reason why leave was given was so that the views of the full court might be obtained on the question of trial by jury in personal injury cases.

Up to the year 1854 all civil cases in the courts of common law were tried by juries. There was no other mode of trial available. Since 1854 trial by jury in civil cases has gradually lessened until it is now only some 2 per cent. of the whole. I will not now go through the history of the enactments from 1854 onwards; it can be found in the judgment of the court in *Ford v. Blurton.* I will go straight to the governing enactment today, which is section 6 of the Administration of Justice (Miscellaneous Provisions) Act, 1933. It gives a right to trial by jury to a party in the Queen's Bench Division where fraud is charged against that party, or a claim is made for libel, slander, malicious prosecution, false imprisonment, seduction, or breach of promise of marriage. Then for all the remaining cases (which include personal injury cases) it says: "But, save as aforesaid, any action to be tried in that Division may, in the discretion of the court or a judge, be ordered to be tried either with or without a jury."

* * *

In my opinion *Hope's* case was a decision simply on the construction of the Act and the rules then in force. It decided that the mode of trial was in the discretion of the court or a judge, without his being fettered by any *presumption of law* in favour of or against a jury. It did not decide that the discretion of the judge in chambers was absolute, or incapable of review by the Court of Appeal. That point was never discussed at all.

* * *

In *Sims v. William Howard & Son Ltd.* this court laid down a rule for the guidance of the judges. It said that in personal injury cases a jury should not be ordered except in special circumstances. This rule has been challenged. It is said to be an unwarranted fetter on the discretion of the judges. Yet it is of the first importance that some guidance should be given—else you would find one judge ordering a jury, the next refusing it, and no one would know where he stood. It might make all the difference to the ultimate result of the case. This would give rise to much dissatisfaction. It is an essential attribute of justice in a community that similar decisions should be given in similar cases, and this applies as much to mode of trial as anything else. The only way of achieving this is for the courts to set out the considerations which should guide the judges in the normal exercise of their discretion. And that is what has been done in scores of cases where a discretion has been entrusted to the judges.

* * *

The cases all show that, when a statute gives discretion, the courts must not fetter it by rigid rules from which a judge is never at liberty to depart. Nevertheless the courts can lay down the considerations which should be borne in mind in exercising the discretion, and point out those considerations which should be ignored. This will normally determine the way in which the discretion is exercised, and thus ensure some measure of uniformity of decision. From time to time the considerations may change as public policy changes, and so the pattern of decision may change: this is all part of the evolutionary process. We have seen it in the way that discretion is exercised in divorce cases. So also in the mode of trial. Whereas it was common to order trial by jury, now it is rare.

Let it not be supposed that this court is in any way opposed to trial by jury. It has been the bulwark of our liberties too long for any of us to seek to alter it. Whenever a man is on trial for serious crime, or when in a civil case a man's honour or integrity is at stake, or when one or the other party must be deliberately lying, then trial by jury has no equal. But in personal injury cases trial by jury has given place of late to trial by judge alone, the reason being simply this, that in these cases trial by a judge alone is more acceptable to the great majority of people. Rarely does a party ask in these cases for a jury. When a solicitor gives advice, it runs in this way: "If I were you, I should not ask for a jury. I should have a judge alone. You do know where you stand with a judge, and if he goes wrong, you can always go to the Court of Appeal. But as for a jury, you never know what they will do, and if they do go wrong, there is no putting them right. The Court of Appeal hardly ever interferes with the verdict of a jury." So the client decides on judge alone. That is why jury trials have declined. It is because they are not asked for. Lord Devlin shows this in his book [The Hamlyn Lectures, eighth series, Trial by Jury, ch. 6], p. 133.

This important consequence follows: the judges alone, and not juries, in the great majority of cases, decide whether there is negligence or not. They set the standard of care to be expected of the reasonable man. They also assess the damages. They see, so far as they can, that like sums are given for like injuries. They set the standard for awards. Hence there is uniformity of decision. This has its impact on decisions as to the mode of trial. If a party asks for a jury in an ordinary personal injury case, the court naturally asks: "Why do you want a jury when nearly everyone else is content with judge alone?" I am afraid it is often because he has a weak case, or desires to appeal to sympathy. If no good reason is given, then the court orders trial by judge alone. Hence we find that nowadays the discretion in the ordinary run of personal injury cases is in favour of judge alone. It is no sufficient reason for departing from it simply to provide a "guinea-pig" case....

For many years, however, it has been said that serious injuries afford a good reason for ordering trial by jury. At any rate, it is a consideration which should be given great weight.... Recent experience has led to some doubts being held on this score. It begins to look as if a jury is an unsuitable tribunal to assess damages for grave injuries, at any rate in those cases where a man is greatly reduced in his activities. He is deprived of much that makes life worthwhile. No money can compensate for the loss. Yet compensation has to be given in money. The problem is insoluble. To meet it, the judges have evolved a conventional measure. They go by their experience in comparable cases. But the juries have nothing to go by.

* * *

[R]ecent cases show the desirability of three things: First, *assessability:* In cases of grave injury, where the body is wrecked or the brain destroyed, it is very difficult to assess a fair compensation in money, so difficult that the award must basically be a conventional figure, derived from experience or from awards in comparable cases. Secondly, *uniformity:* There should be some measure of uniformity in awards so that similar decisions are given in similar cases; otherwise there will be great dissatisfaction in the community, and much criticism of the administration of justice. Thirdly, *predictability:* Parties should be able to predict with some measure of accuracy the sum which is likely to be awarded in a particular case, for by this means cases can be settled peaceably and not brought to court, a thing very much to the public good. None of these three is achieved when the damages are left at large to the jury. Under the present practice the judge does not give them any help at all to assess the figure. The result is that awards may vary greatly, from being much too high to much too low. There is no uniformity and no predictability.

I would add this. The assessment of damages is almost as difficult as the sentencing of offenders. In each it is important that similar decisions should be given in similar cases. Some measure of uniformity is achieved in criminal cases by leaving the sentence always to the judge, with an appeal to the Court of Criminal Appeal. We can hardly put damages on a like footing. But cannot we do more than at present to secure some measure of uniformity?

One remedy that has been suggested is that the Court of Appeal should be more ready to correct the verdict of a jury. This court should correct it in much the same way as it corrects the decision of a judge. After all, the test which it applies is very much the same. This court can interfere with the figure awarded by a *jury* if it is "out of all proportion to the circumstances of the case." It can interfere with the figure awarded by a *judge* if it is "a wholly erroneous estimate of the damage suffered." In each case "excess implies some standard which has been exceeded" ..., and the only standard which this court can apply is to take the conventional figure awarded in comparable cases and see how far the award is above or below it.

Although the test is so similar, nevertheless in practice the result is very different. In case after case this court has held that it cannot interfere with a jury as readily as with a judge.... One reason for this difference is the difficulty of showing the basis of the jury's award. They give no reasons. They find no facts. Their verdict is as inscrutable as the sphinx. So you cannot pick holes in it. Another reason is the very great hesitation which this court feels before it interferes with the verdict of a jury. This hesitation is right enough when the jury have all the relevant materials before them, but not when they are ignorant of them. In cases of personal injury the jury are ignorant. The award is basically a conventional figure, but the jury are not told what that figure is. No wonder they go wrong sometimes! When they do, they would be the first to wish it to be put right. Take *Every v. Miles:* If the jury knew that the conventional figure for loss of a leg was between £4,000 and £6,000, they would wish their figure of £2,000 to be corrected.

We cannot change the principle on which those cases were decided, but we can, I think, alter the emphasis. In future this court will not feel the same hesitation as it formerly did in upsetting an award of damages by a jury. If it is "out of all proportion to the circumstances of the case" (that is, if it is far too high or far too low), this court will set it aside. On setting it aside this court has power, I think, to order the fresh assessment to be made by a judge alone. This could not be done in the old days when there was a right to trial by jury. But now that the mode of trial is a matter of discretion, this court can, on granting a new trial, order that it be held by a judge alone....

... The other remedy that has been suggested is that the jury should be given more guidance. Two possible ways are put forward: (i) By referring them to awards in comparable cases; (ii) by telling them the conventional figure. I will take them in order.

(i) *Comparable cases.* Before 1951 it was not the practice for counsel to refer the court or the jury to awards in comparable cases. It is obvious that counsel could not call witnesses to give the figures in other cases. Nor could counsel give figures himself from his own experience or from the books. If counsel sought to refer to any comparable case, it would be rejected out of hand on the ground that it was res inter alios acta. Since *Bird v. Cocking & Sons Ltd.* in 1951 a change has set in. When the case is tried by a judge alone, or heard on appeal by the Court of Appeal, counsel is allowed to refer to awards in comparable cases. This is because we now recognise that the award is basically a conventional figure, and in order to arrive at it, it is relevant to refer to comparable cases. If this be so before a judge alone, or the Court of Appeal, why should it not also be so in trial by jury? Why should the jury not receive the same guidance as a judge?

This sounds well in theory, but in practice it is open to strong objection. During the argument before us both counsel agreed that it would not do. See what would happen! Each counsel would refer the jury to cases which he believed were comparable but which were not really so. Speeches would be taken up with the one counsel citing analogies and the other destroying them. Then the judge would have to review them all again in his summing-up. The inevitable result would be that the minds of the jury would be distracted from the instant case and left in confusion.

If counsel cannot refer the jury to comparable cases, neither can the judge. He cannot, on his own initiative, drag out from the books, or from his own experience, other awards (and tell the jury of them) when counsel have not had any opportunity of commenting on them, or distinguishing them. All in all, I am quite satisfied that the present practice should be maintained where the jury are not told of awards in comparable cases.

(ii) *Conventional figures.* Another suggestion is that the jury should be told of the conventional figures in this way, that the judge should be at liberty in his discretion to indicate to the jury the upper and lower limits of the sum which in his view it would be reasonable to award. Thus in the case of the loss of a leg, he might indicate that the conventional figure is between £4,000 and £6,000. This proposal has many attractions. It would give the jury the guidance which they at present lack. But here again we come up against a serious objection. If the judge can mention figures to the jury, then counsel must also be able to mention figures to them. Once that happened, we get into the same trouble again. Each counsel would, in duty bound, pitch the figures as high or as low as he dared. Then the judge would give his views on the rival figures. The proceedings would be in danger of developing into an auction. The objections are so great that both counsel before us agreed that counsel ought not to be at liberty to mention figures to the jury. If this be so, I think that the judge should not do so either.

Apart from this, it seems to me that if the judge were at liberty to mention the upper and lower limits, then in order to be of any real guidance, they would have to be somewhat narrow limits. It would be no use his telling the jury (as judges have done in the past) for the loss of a leg: "Do be reasonable. Don't give as much as £100,000, or as little as £100." The judge would have to come nearer home and say: "The conventional figure in such a case as this is between £4,000 and £6,000." But if he can give them narrow limits of that kind, there is little point in having a jury at all. You might as well let the judge assess the figure himself.

I come to the conclusion, therefore, that we must follow the existing practice, and we cannot sanction any departure from it.

Conclusion. The result of it all is this: We have come in recent years to realise that the award of damages in personal injury cases is basically a conventional figure derived from experience and from awards in comparable cases. Yet the jury are not allowed to know what that conventional figure is. The judge knows it, but the jury do not. This is a most material consideration which a judge must bear in mind when deciding whether or not to order trial by jury. So important is it that the judge ought not, in a personal injury case, to order trial by jury save in exceptional circumstances. Even when the issue of liability is one fit to be tried by a jury, nevertheless he might think it fit to order that the damages be assessed by a judge alone.

The Present Case. At long last I come to the present case. On July 30, 1963, when it was before Roskill J., he exercised his discretion in the light of the considerations then current. He had not the benefit of the three decisions since then.... Nor, of course, had he the guidance which I hope is to be found in the present judgment. The defendants acquiesced in the order for trial by jury for months and months. It was not until the case was just about to come for trial before a jury that they sought to change the mode of trial to judge alone. It seems to me that they come too late. I am not disposed in these circumstances to interfere with the order made by the judge, and all the more so when I think that, if the jury should go seriously wrong, this court will not feel the same hesitation as it formerly did in upsetting them.

I would therefore dismiss this appeal.

SELLERS L.J. I agree.

PEARSON L.J. I agree.

DAVIES L.J. I agree.

LORD DENNING M.R. DIPLOCK L.J. cannot be here this morning, but he authorises me to say that he agrees.

Appeal dismissed with costs.

———

Ward v. James was the practical end of civil jury trials. Professor Zander suggests that there have been only a dozen or two per year since *Ward*.

HODGES v. HARLAND & WOLFF, LIMITED

Court of Appeal [England].
[1965] All E.R. 1086.*

LORD DENNING, M.R.: We have yet once more to consider the mode of trial of a personal injury case. Mr. Hodges, the plaintiff, in 1962 was a painter at the King George V Dock at Silvertown. In the course of his employment he was operating a diesel driven air compressor. There was a spindle on that machine revolving at a great number of revolutions a minute. Unfortunately it was not guarded, as it should have been under the regulations. While the plaintiff was operating it, it caught his trousers and tore them. It tore off his penis and severely injured him in that part of the body. He brings this action for damages in which he includes a claim for loss of future earnings which he puts at £8 a week.

The defence is that the accident was in part his own fault. Also the damage is not admitted.

When the question of the mode of trial came before Master Clayton, he apparently expressed the view that it would be a proper case for trial by jury, but he felt himself bound by the decisions of this court to order trial by judge alone. When the matter came to the judge, Lyell, J., he considered the cases, and in particular the principle of uniformity. He thought that nevertheless this was a case for trial by jury, and he so ordered. Now the defendants appeal to this court and ask for trial by judge alone. Naturally enough, we have been referred to the recent decision of this court in *Ward v. James*. It is a mistake to suppose that this court in that case took away the right to trial by jury. It was not this court but Parliament itself which years ago took away any absolute right to trial by jury and left it to the discretion of the judges. This court in *Ward v. James* affirmed that discretion and said that, as the statute has given a discretion to the judge, this court would not fetter it by rigid rules from which the judge was never at liberty to depart. What *Ward v. James* did do was this. It laid down the considerations which should be borne in mind by a judge when exercising his discretion: and it is apparent that, on those considerations, the result will ordinarily be trial by judge alone. It will not result in trial by jury save in exceptional circumstances. That is no great change. It has been the position for many years. As it happened, in *Ward v. James* itself, the result was trial by jury.

In this present case the judge, it seems to me, has borne all the relevant considerations in mind. He said, "this is a unique case". So it is. Counsel for the defendants urged that there were one or two cases in the books where a man had retained the sexual urge without the ability to perform the sexual act. That may be so; but they were very different from this. I think that the judge was well entitled to take the view that this was an exceptional case, and in the circumstances to exercise his discretion in favour of trial by jury. Indeed, when a judge exercises his discretion and takes all the relevant considerations into account, it is well settled that the burden is on anyone coming to this court to show that he was wrong. I see nothing wrong in the way that Lyell, J., dealt with this case in ordering trial by jury.

* * *

I think that this case was properly decided by the judge. The appeal fails and must be dismissed.

Davies, L.J.: I agree....

Salmon, L.J.

* * *

I would dismiss the appeal.

The jury died in England in most civil cases for a variety of reasons. These reasons are important to us in the United States, since if they are reasons based on the nature of the jury as an institution of resolving civil disputes, then we might seriously consider jury reform. But if the reasons are based more on cultural characteristics which are not present in the United States, then it should not be abolished unless more sound argument may be made. We consider the jury to be one of the central elements of our system of justice. These materials on the English jury may leave some doubt as to its continuing appropriateness in civil, or even criminal, processes.

Notes and Questions

1. Is the jury any longer useful for civil trials in the United States? Is there any more reason to say yes to a civil jury trial for the fact situation in *Hodges?* What about the statutory right providing for juries in cases of libel, slander or malicious prosecution—do they merit right rather than discretion?

2. Are there other areas than those protected in England by statute where we might wish to preserve the civil jury trial?

3. The use of the jury in criminal trials remains a strongly protected right in common law systems. Is there any more reason to preserve that right than in civil cases?

4. Contrast the standard in the *Ward v. James* case, where the court stated that damages should be "a conventional figure derived from experience and from awards in comparable cases", with the practice in the United States.

SECTION 3. CRIMINAL PROCEDURE

A. GENERAL

The London criminal courts are filled with tourists during the summer months. Seats are often at a premium at the Central Criminal Court (Old Bailey) and the Bow Street Magistrates' Court. Even a lay observer could note contrasts from the American system. The most obvious seem superficial and traditional: the wearing of wigs and robes; the accused alone in the dock; police officers testifying by reading from their notes. But these simple and more obvious observations are part of a larger aggregate of variations from the American system of criminal procedure. And they are more than form. They have evolved over centuries. They have improved and become more civilized.

Until the late 16th century, an accused was detained until trial with no opportunity to prepare a defense. He was not informed of the evidence to be used against him, or of those who would testify for the prosecution. Nor could he call any witnesses on his own behalf. He could not even have counsel were he accused of treason or a felony. He stood isolated against the state. The changes in criminal procedure in the past few centuries, and most importantly since the mid to late 19th century, are almost without exception changes that benefit the accused. But there is less public criticism in England than in the United States that the balance has swung too far in favor of protecting the interests of the accused, to the detriment of society. The process nevertheless retains elements of the earlier trial—the notion that it is a form of combat.

The English and American systems have been subjected to their own separate stresses and reform movements. Significant differences have evolved. The primary focus of Graham in the following article is on reform of the American system, not to present an objective analysis of the English system. But he makes useful observations on some differences in the two systems.

M. GRAHAM, "COMMENTS ON THE ENGLISH CRIMINAL JURY TRIAL," FROM "TIGHTENING THE REINS OF JUSTICE IN AMERICA"

228 (1983).*

The English approach to criminal justice from arrest of the accused on suspicion through rules governing appeal strongly favors the prosecution. The system may fairly be described as a well-oiled, cost-efficient, prosecution-oriented machine. Speaking generally, solicitors are not permitted to interfere with police interrogation. Failure by the police to obey rules and laws governing interrogation and search and seizure will rarely result in evidence being treated as inadmissible. Police interrogation is extremely effective, resulting in the introduction of a written or oral admission or confession in roughly 64 percent of all contested trials in the Crown Court. The effect that evidence elicited by the police during interrogation from an accused has upon the rate of guilty pleas is self-evident. Not surprisingly, 92 percent of all defendants plead guilty in the Magistrates' Court, while 60 percent of those committed for trial in the Crown Court also plead guilty.

The legal machinery prior to trial, from initial appearance to arraignment, is simple, quick, and cost efficient. The police prepare statements of witnesses and provide them to the defense prior to the uncontested Section 1 committal. The police also freely disclose exhibits to the accused. In turn, the accused provides a Notice of Alibi defense. Only the police see witnesses for the prosecution prior to trial. Legal executives employed by defense solicitors interview the accused and take statements from defense witnesses. Rarely does anyone on the defense side attempt to interview a prosecution witness. Neither the prosecuting solicitor's office nor the defense solicitor employs private investigators.

* Reprinted from Tightening the Reins of Justice in America: A Comparative Analysis of the Criminal Jury Trial in England and the United States, by Michael H. Graham, Greenwood Press, Westport, Ct. 1983, with permission of the publisher.

The image of a well-oiled, cost-efficient, prosecution-oriented machine of justice applies with equal force at trial. Summary trials before magistrates tend to be short and to the point. The result is a 75 percent conviction rate. Considering that as many as 40 percent of the 25 percent of trials resulting in an acquittal stem from the inability of the prosecution, for a combination of reasons, to produce evidence constituting a prima facie case, the percentage of convictions at the Magistrates' Court approaches 85 percent. The structure of the Crown Court trial has been examined in depth. The Crown Court has a 53 percent conviction rate, which rises to over 67 percent after accounting for acquittals ordered by the court and directions by the court to the jury to acquit. A high conviction rate in the Crown Court should be expected with respect to serious crime. Not only does the presence of incriminating statements in 64 percent of all contested cases favor the prosecution, but, when compared with American trials, every English variation except one tends to facilitate a conviction. These variations include:

1. Placement of the accused in the dock.

2. Placement of counsel next to each other.

3. Wigs and robes worn by counsel.

4. Counsel's inability to leave his assigned location during trial.

5. Lack of voir dire.

6. Lack of prosecution witness interviewing by the defense.

7. Day-before perusal of the Brief.

8. Lack of meaningful communication between counsel and the defendant.

9. Permitting police officers to read from their notes in open court.

10. Inability of counsel to seriously attack the character of prosecution witnesses without opening the door to use of prior convictions of the accused to impeach.

11. Lack of recross-examination.

12. Placement of defendant's opening speech following the close of the prosecution's case in chief.

13. Summary of evidence and comment upon credibility being included in the court's summation to the jury.

14. Defining reasonable doubt as "satisfied that you are sure."

15. The absence at all stages of the trial of an emphasis upon the presumption of innocence, the burden of proof resting upon the prosecution, and the concept of proof beyond reasonable doubt.

16. The overall detachment exhibited by defense counsel.

The one factor operating in favor of the accused is the prohibition in practice against use of the accused's prior convictions to impeach credibility. As a result, defendants testify in approximately 95 percent of all Crown Court trials. The importance of this factor to the outcome of the trial can be appreciated by considering that the Chicago jury study indicated that, when a defendant's criminal record is known and the prosecution's case has contradictions, the defendant's chances of conviction are 65 percent, as compared to a 38 percent rate when the conviction is not known. Accordingly, assuming cases having contradictions, a fair assumption with respect to most cases actually tried, and a defendant testifying free from impeachment by means of his prior convictions, in England one could expect roughly a 38 percent conviction rate, not the nearly 64 percent conviction rate observed. It is suggested that the sixteen factors listed above account for much of the variation between what would be expected and what is observed.

There are many individual aspects and broad approaches exemplified in the English criminal justice system worthy of in-depth exploration and analysis by those concerned with the continuing breakdown of law and order in the United States. We should commend the emphasis in England on simple, speedy, effective, and cost-efficient procedures and rules capable of being understood and applied by those responsible. ...

* * *

No simple answer explains why the law in England with respect to trial practice lacks the rigorous analysis found in the United States. Probably the most important factor is one of attitude. The English hold themselves out to be fair and capable of fairness. Decisions by reasonable men can accommodate the interests of disputants at the time of the dispute. It thus becomes unnecessary to attempt in advance to account for all contingencies, to identify and precisely articulate concerns, or to require procedures that address the appearance of impropriety rather than its reality. In their place stands the notion that, given basic principles of justice, a fair man can come to a fair result once apprised of the facts. Accordingly, business agreements in England are shorter than in America. Concern is with basic principles, referred to as heads of agreement, not minute details. English solicitors would hardly negotiate with great zeal a clause defining the rights of the parties in case of condemnation to a three-year lease in a new building on Sixth Avenue in New York. New York attorneys would take this seriously, but not the English solicitor, whose attitude would be that fair men could and would resolve the question justly when it arose if it ever arose.

This sense of fairness, based on the interest and capacity of individuals to be fair if given the basic facts, has many implications concerning the jury trial we have been examining. It is directly related to the fourth and last practice of particular concern—the apparent detachment, lack of interest, and lack of aggressiveness displayed by counsel. Because of the nature of the criminal jury trial, this detachment is more significant when displayed by counsel for the accused. Undoubtedly in comparison with American defense attorneys, the jury does not feel the presence of the defense barrister in the trial. How the concept of fairness interacts in the criminal justice system with the structure of the trial, the concept of a divided profession, and the absence of rigorous legal analysis to create this appearance of detachment is extremely difficult to pinpoint. All that can reasonably be attempted is to describe the resultant interplay of these relevant considerations, as exhibited by the barrister in the criminal jury trial.

The English criminal jury trial to a marvelous extent keeps its eye on the ball—the guilt or innocence of the accused. The trial unfolds as a search for truth in the same sense that a parent faced with two screaming children goes about determining who started the fight....

The barrister thus seeks to have the case decided on the contested facts very much as does the parent of the two fighting children. The barrister asks the jury to act like the parent of the fighting children and inflict punishment only if it is sure which version of the story is true. The barrister seeks a fair determination, not an unjust victory. It is thus to be expected that, in comparison to the American defense attorney, the barrister appears detached and uncommitted to the cause of his client.

Incidents associated with the divided profession serve to reinforce both the appearance and actuality of counsel's detachment. Barristers usually prepare the case solely during the evening before trial. Each reads his Brief, consisting mostly of witness statements submitted at the Section 1 committal. Neither speaks to any witness other than experts prior to trial, except that the defense barrister normally confirms the accused's position with respect to disputed facts during a conference with him immediately before trial. Counsel often resolve matters concerning admissibility of evidence prior to trial. The Briefs tell counsel little about the background of the witnesses or the witnesses' ability to acquire the personal knowledge stated and even less about other possible avenues of impeachment. Almost never will the barrister have himself visited the scene of the crime. Combined with the rules relating to challenge and imputations of character, cross-examination of prosecution witnesses often amounts to little more than defense counsel putting the accused's story to the witness to be denied. Cross-examination of defense witnesses often amounts to little more than prosecution counsel putting the Crown's contentions to the witness to be denied.

The structure of the trial itself adds greatly to the impression of detachment. The opposing barristers are located next to each other wearing identical wigs and robes. Because the accused sits in the dock at the rear of the courtroom, the jury never sees him communicate directly with his counsel. There is no voir dire, and thus no opportunity for defense counsel to ingratiate himself and his client with the jury. Defense counsel's opening speech, if permitted, takes place after the close of the prosecution's case in chief and after defense counsel has already been obliged to put the accused's case to prosecution witnesses. Immediately following defense counsel's closing speech, the court in its summation summarizes the evidence and may comment on the credibility of witnesses. Any attempt by counsel in his closing speech to distract the jury from the matter truly at hand or to improperly characterize the evidence will be dealt with harshly by the judge in his summing up.

Contrast the image of the barrister with that often exhibited by defense attorneys in the United States—the defense attorney who puts the state to its proof on all issues, never stipulating to anything or agreeing that witness statements dealing with uncontested matters may be read; the defense attorney who stresses the presumption of innocence and the burden of persuasion on the prosecution to establish each and every element of the offense beyond a reasonable doubt during voir dire, opening, and closing and who insists on such concepts being fully explored once again in the court's instructions on the law; the defense attorney who objects to anything objectionable, and to many questions and exhibits that are not: the defense attorney who frequently attempts to interject extraneous matters in the hope of creating a reasonable doubt in the minds of the jury; the defense attorney who, at all stages of the trial, sells himself and his apparent but often unreal belief in the innocence of his client to the jury; the defense attorney who seeks an acquittal, not a fair determination of guilt or innocence.

An interesting question arises as to why, in England, barristers representing the accused do not become more aggressive in their examination and speeches and more demanding of change in the structure of the trial itself. If securing a high acquittal rate were paramount to the defense barrister, more aggressive advocacy would be observed, and demands for changes in trial practice such as permitting voir dire examination, permitting the accused to sit near counsel, and permitting the defense to make an earlier opening speech would have been heard. It is clear, however, that securing acquittals is not the principal objective of the defense barrister. Nor is the objective to any great extent one of putting on a good show in defeat, as it is for many privately retained defense counsel in the United States.

In representing his client, the barrister rarely acquires the role of the aggressive advocate assumed most frequently by defense counsel in the United States. Generally speaking, the barrister representing the accused in England, unlike the defense attorney representing the defendant in America, does not proceed upon the notion that his function is to obtain an acquittal by enforcing each and every rule applicable to the trial in the hope that the prosecution will falter. Nor does the defense barrister consider it proper to interject irrelevant matters into the case to confuse the jury, to require witnesses testifying as to uncontested matters to appear in court, to object to break the flow of damaging testimony, to turn the trial into an accusation against the complainant or the police where not called for clearly by the evidence, or to ask the jury to try the prosecutor, the judge, or society rather than the accused. Moreover, the defense barrister does not consider it his function to attempt to convince the trier of fact that the accused must be innocent by selling himself and his relationship with the accused to the jury, to consciously build into the trial error to be argued on appeal, or to seek with great intensity a hung jury on the theory that a hung jury is, in most instances, the functional equivalent of an acquittal.

In its place, the defense barrister adopts the overall stance that, notwithstanding the prosecutor's burden of proof, the accused should normally put forth his contentions as to the relevant matters of the case, leaving it for the jury to determine whether they are "satisfied that they are sure" of his guilt after hearing both versions of the relevant events. Accordingly, the accused testifies in roughly 95 percent of the jury trials in the Crown Court.... The absence of voir dire and the timing of the opening speech by defense counsel reduces the opportunity to stress reasonable doubt before the jury....

What is the objective of defense counsel if it is not simply winning or putting on a good show? Is it merely a search for the truth for the sake of truth? It is suggested that it is too idealistic and unreal to ascribe the restraint and detachment exhibited by defense barristers solely to a search for justice. If not solely truth, what else? It has been said that barristers try their cases to obtain the approval of the presiding judge. This claim is difficult to evaluate. On the one hand, the barristers observed and consulted in Birmingham expressed no greater respect for members of the judiciary or ambition to join their ranks than attorneys of similar age and experience in the United States. On the other hand, the power of the English trial judge to influence the outcome of the trial through various means, including the questioning of witnesses as well as the tone and content of his summing up, clearly makes it disadvantageous to have the judge take a personal dislike to a barrister. The difficulty in securing reversals on appeal on the basis of errors committed by the court further inhibits counsel taking any action likely to irritate the trial judge. The fact that the same trial judge sits in civil cases in bench-only trials adds to the chilling effect. Finally, social pressure is placed upon counsel to conform by virtue of the judiciary being senior members of the Inns of Court. Thus, on balance, it is probably fair to say that the desire of the court to have the trial proceed in the customary civilized manner results in counsel exercising more restraint than otherwise might prevail.

Other factors are also at work. The division of the bar leading to barristers preparing cases for trial in civil or criminal cases, motions, and pleas in mitigation each night for the next day requires that all court proceedings be conducted in a steady, low-key manner. Barristers for the most part work alone; the hordes of young associates available to the litigating partner in large American law firms are not available to the barrister. Any preparation in criminal cases must be done either by the barrister, by the Crown Court assistant, or by the legal executive. Moreover, lawyers, like everyone else, cannot maintain a fever pitch day after day, year after year. For the barrister to appear in court as often as he does necessitates accommodations between counsel. Evidence must be capable of being offered with a minimum of foundation, and cross-examination must be simple and straightforward. Counsel for the prosecution frequently has little time for anything but to become sufficiently familiar with the facts to make an opening statement and lead the witnesses through their statements. Counsel for the defense has little time to do anything but prepare to put the accused's version of the facts to prosecution witnesses on cross-examination and to prepare a well-reasoned closing speech. Neither counsel has time to develop a profile of ideal jurors, to explore the factual basis of potential areas of cross-examination not obvious from the witness's statement, or to research the law in support of an objection to the admissibility of evidence. Each counsel is assisted by the conciliatory attitude toward resolving questions of admissibility and the almost casual handling of exhibits. Each counsel is assisted by conditional witness orders, which permit the reading of uncontested evidence in the form of a witness statement to the jury.

Moreover, there is job satisfaction in being a barrister for the accused. Many defendants are acquitted. Not as many receive acquittals as might be anticipated with more aggressive representation, but there are many acquittals nonetheless. In addition, unlike many defense attorneys in the United States, the English barrister understands the importance of his plea in mitigation in connection with sentencing. Barristers and solicitors alike consider it a personal triumph when they are able to secure a fair, if not favorable, sentence for their client considering all of the surrounding circumstances.

In searching for reasons underlying the restraint and detachment exhibited by defense barristers, it is extremely important to realize that tomorrow is a new day, and that today's defense barrister will be tomorrow's prosecutor. With the exception of a few barristers, principally in London, who represent only the prosecution, and even fewer who only appear for the defense, barristers appear for both the prosecution and the defense. These same barristers also appear in civil matters for both the plaintiff and the defendant. Unlike the criminal defense attorney in America, who either wins representing the accused or not at all, the barrister in England knows that tomorrow he will be presenting the prosecution's case opposed by another barrister acting in the same way as he did today. Each barrister knows that only if each barrister acts in accordance with expected tradition, taking into consideration the plight of a brother at the bar, will each be able to carry on in the manner to which each is accustomed. Finally, the fact that the relatively few barristers in England are grouped together in chambers, where an officer's club attitude prevails, certainly serves to restrain counsel from taking any action in court that will embarrass a fellow barrister and thereby raise the level of hostility among barristers.

––––––––

The comments of Graham are almost exclusively devoted to the role of the defense counsel, a barrister in the Crown Court or either a barrister or solicitor in the magistrates' court. It is counsel for the prosecution which has undergone the most significant change by the adoption of the Crown Prosecution Service (CPS) in the Prosecution of Offenses Act 1985. Before this act police undertook the prosecution of most cases in magistrates' courts, although barristers were retained to represent the charging authority in more complex magistrates' court cases, and in the Crown Court. Under the CPS, some 2,000 professional prosecutors serve as prosecutors. Police undertake the investigation phase, while the CPS lawyers do the advocacy in court. The CPS has had a very difficult gestation period, criticized by police, judges, magistrates and their clerks, and the probation service. But there has been an increasing acceptance for this very significant change to the criminal justice system. Perhaps the most contentious issue is the right of solicitor-CPS prosecutors to appear in the Crown Court, currently denied. A barrister-CPS prosecutor has that right by virtue of being a barrister (not by virtue of being competent). Solicitors have urged the admission of solicitors-CPS members to appear in the more complex Crown Court cases, but this has not been granted based upon being members of the CPS, they must gain rights of audience as discussed in the chapter above on Legal Actors.

Civil procedure tends to be not greatly dissimilar between different courts. The amount in controversy usually determines the level of court with jurisdiction. There is a greater variation of procedural characteristics in criminal proceedings in different courts, directly related to the seriousness of the offense. Seriousness is usually the basis in any legal tradition for determining which criminal procedure will apply. While the goal in civil litigation is to determine liability and damages, a criminal proceeding may involve, in addition to determination of guilt, an educational element, loss of freedom or physical retribution, or a mandated work requirement. Offenses are classified. The least serious (summary offenses in England, misdemeanors in the United States) may require nothing more than the payment of a fine by mail, with a notation in the court records of the financial satisfaction of the wrong. As the summary offense becomes more serious in England, persons must appear in person before the magistrates' court, to be tried by lay peers (or in the large cities a single professional stipendiary magistrate) without a jury. The procedure is less formal than more serious crimes demand (indictable offenses, not unlike the felony in the United States), where a jury will be convened and rules of evidence become stricter and more carefully followed. The complexity of the procedure in a criminal prosecution is directly related to the gravity of what society may demand for one's guilt. No such indictable-summary classification existed during the early years of the development of common law. Other than trial by ordeal, all trials were by judge and jury. To use the current labels, all were indictable.

It is the police who recently prosecuted in the magistrates' courts. This function was the most distinguishing characteristic in contrast to the role of police in the United States. But many towns appointed local solicitors as prosecutors. This alleviated some of the criticism of "police advocacy." A police prosecutor usually lacks the indifferent attitude as to the outcome of the case, which is quite necessary if the prosecutor, as an advocate, is to assist the court in reaching a just conclusion. The state is not in a win or lose position, it wins as much if an innocent person is acquitted as when a guilty person is convicted. The creation of the CPS essentially relegated the police to investigation, with CPS lawyers doing the in court prosecution.

The early American criminal law system was more liberal in allowing legal representation to the defendant, but in terms of both allowance and funding of defense counsel, the two systems are not now greatly divergent. English legal aid does tend to exist more within the traditional professional structure than in the United States, where separate public defender offices have prevailed. That English professional structure, where barristers and judges have common roots and comprise a homogeneous fraternity, tends to give an American observer the impression that there is a closer bond between counsel and the judge than counsel and his client, a bond that may lead the barristers to present a less rigorous defense than his American counterpart.

The English law of arrest may seem vague to an American observer. It has evolved from suits for false imprisonment and resisting arrest. Warrants are used less frequently in England, both because of the pattern of success in issuing summons (mostly limited in the United States to traffic violations) even for some serious crimes, and because the issuance of a warrant may require a concurrent decision as to bail, which is not part of the warrant process in the United States.

The English policeman is more limited in arresting for offenses committed in his presence; if a misdemeanor either it must constitute a breach of the peace, which is not clearly defined in English law, or the officer must rely on an increasing number of specific statutes. The limitations on the English policeman's powers reflect the relatively homogeneous nature of the population, and the absence of fear on the part of a citizen stopped by a policeman. But that is changing rapidly in the larger cities; the negative caution an American feels if stopped by police increasingly is shared by many persons in England. It affects the relationship at the time a policeman has little more than a suspicion, and it brings to the relationship the adversary element of the later stages of the criminal process.

Although he does not prepare the case, it is the judge who determines the relevancy of evidence, his decision guided by limiting statutes and a considerable bulk of precedent. The English judge must not only rule on what evidence may be admitted, but, unlike an American judge, he may himself participate in molding the finished product, the final aggregate of facts upon which either he or the jury will decide guilt or innocence. The judge may recall witnesses or introduce new witnesses (rarely and with the consent of both counsel), and he may question witnesses either to remove doubt based on earlier testimony, or to inquire more deeply into matters which he believes were only superficially treated. But when he intervenes to do more than clarify an ambiguity, he raises the question of the point at which his questioning alters the nature of the process from adversarial to inquisitorial. Where a trial judge had allegedly intervened too much, the Court of Appeal discussed the judge's role as an inquisitor.[a]

Notes and Questions

1. Do you agree with Graham's reasons for his preference for the English system? Is the English burden of proof in fact different? Are the differences he describes based on considerations of achieving a more just system—reaching a higher percentage of acquittals of the innocent and convictions of the guilty at a not unreasonable cost to society? Or is the system intent on achieving adequacy while preserving style?

2. Since in Crown Court both counsel for the Crown and the accused are regular barristers, who may represent opposite sides the next day, is the English system more likely to achieve a just result? Is there likely to be less motivation on the part of the barrister for the Crown to obtain a conviction for reasons extrinsic to fairness and justice than in the American system?

3. Were professional prosecuting counsel established, would the balance exist which currently results from a barrister being a defense counsel one day, and a prosecuting counsel the next? Would it cause the development of a more rigid defense bar among those barristers who chose not to leave their independent status and accept government positions as prosecuting counsel, but to remain and represent the only available criminal law clients, the accused persons?

4. Is the English system of police advocacy inconsistent with notions of an accusatorial system?

5. What would be the effect on the role of an American trial lawyer if the judge asked as many questions as in an English trial?

B. THE JURY—USE IN CRIMINAL TRIALS

The near absence of juries in civil law trials has been discussed in the previous section. We noted the contrasts in jury use in general regarding the selection process and the lack of a *voir dire* in England as we know it in the United States. But the jury vetting process does function as a means of eliminating prospective jurors, however different it may be from the American *voir dire*. The English process has elements of secrecy and obviously is not viewed as an effective means for defense counsel to challenge prospective jurors. It is a process tilted sharply toward the interests of the prosecution. If those interests are to achieve a just result, rather than to "win", then perhaps it is not in fact tilted against the defendant, but in favor of fairness.

The use of the jury in England in criminal trials remains important, but not in terms of numbers. Most crimes are disposed of in the magistrates' courts. But the more serious crimes continue to be tried before a jury in a Crown Court. This is a right which exists in most

a. Jones v. National Coal Board [1957] 2 Q.B. (C.A.).

common law nations. The procedural elements in selecting the jury and in the nature of its verdict, however, vary markedly among the systems. In some systems, the alterations to the judge and jury have been so extensive that the result appears closer to a civil law mixed form of decision making. Within each system, and across the boundaries of legal traditions, the goal appears to be how best may a mix of lay and professional persons be used to seek a fair and just result. The United States clings to the use of the jury more tenaciously than does England.

The English jury is one of the institutions of trial procedure which was implanted in the extensive and culturally diverse Empire. The development of the jury in several common law nations assumed attributes not dissimilar to the collegiate courts of first instance in some civil law nations. The professional judge was joined by lay assessors. A few members of the jury moved from the jury box to the bench—the remainder went home. But in some nations there was a reluctance to move the lay assessors to the bench—they sat instead apart from him, appearing more like a small jury than a collegiate bench. Mawer outlines some of this commonwealth development. Is it at all significant how the system places its professional and lay participants in the courtroom? Should we not be more concerned with what role they each serve? Who decides issues of fact? Issues of law? Do lay members have the power to overrule the professional judge where the former participate in legal issue decisions? What might be the best separation of responsibilities from the perspective of a just legal machinery? And what might be the most appropriate courtroom layout (1) to fulfill that goal, and (2) considering cultural and social elements such as the impact on the litigants or accused of a separation of judge and jury/assessors. Or should we use a single bench where all sit in a uniform level of apparent importance?

R.K. MAWER, "JURIES AND ASSESSORS IN CRIMINAL TRIALS IN SOME COMMONWEALTH COUNTRIES: A PRELIMINARY SURVEY"

10 Int'l & Comp.L.Q. 892 (1961).*

[I]t is interesting to observe that whereas at the beginning of the present century jury trial was favoured not only in India but in many of the colonies, the position today is very different. The problems of working the jury system have been so great that trial by a judge sitting with assessors is now more generally preferred. Already, trial by jury has been abolished in eleven Indian States. Other States are expected to do the same. Recently, the Law Commission in India recommended the abolition of the jury system on an all-India basis, saying that the jury system was time-consuming and expensive, and had been a failure. The State Law Ministers who met in Srinagar in 1960 left it to the State

* Reprinted with permission of the British Institute of International and Comparative Law.

Governments to introduce or abolish the jury system in the light of the circumstances prevailing in each area. There is no provision for trial by jury in the East and Central African territories such as Uganda, Tanganyika, Northern Rhodesia and Nyasaland. In Ghana and Sierra Leone there is no jury trial in those parts which are (or were) protectorates, as opposed to colonies; moreover, jury trial in Ghana is limited to crimes punishable by death or life imprisonment. In Kenya, as in Fiji, jury trial is confined to Europeans. In Fiji, a proposal to abolish jury trial entirely, in favour of trial by a judge and assessors in all cases, is now under consideration. In Sierra Leone, jury trial in non-capital offences may be excluded by order of the court, which is made as of course upon the application of the Attorney–General. In the Eastern Region of Nigeria there is, currently, neither jury trial nor trial with assessors; the judge sits alone in all criminal cases. It is interesting to speculate whether, in time, England will be the last country in which the jury system is preserved.

* * *

The development of the alternative method of trial by a judge sitting with assessors has been most interesting. There was some early use of assessors in India, where it was felt that a European judge could better administer justice if he had the benefit of the opinion of respectable local inhabitants acquainted with local custom and habits. However, the question as to whether a judge can take into consideration his assessors' opinions upon a custom which has not been proved in evidence, has given rise to somewhat conflicting decisions in the Court of Appeal for Eastern Africa. . . .

Although the literal meaning of assessors is those who sit by the side of another, the assessors do not, in many colonial territories, sit by the side of the trial judge, but are set apart from him, like a jury. Indeed it may be possible to detect a growing tendency to assimilate the functions of assessors with those of a jury. It is of course true that the opinions of the assessors are not, in general, binding upon the trial judge, although at one time in Malaya the judge was unable to overrule the assessors if they agreed; he could only order a retrial. Furthermore, judges normally sum up to the assessors, and such summings-up are tending more and more to conform with the requirements of a summing-up to a jury. There is generally no statutory obligation upon the judge to sum up, and the omission to do so has been held not to be fatal to a conviction but it is clearly desirable except in the very simplest cases.

After the summing up, it is now usual in many territories to allow the assessors to retire, like a jury, if they wish. When the assessors return, each assessor gives his opinion as to the guilt or otherwise of the accused. The opinions need not of course be unanimous. Like a jury, the assessors are discharged when the admissibility of an alleged confession is tried. However an inquiry as to the fitness of an accused to plead is held by the trial judge without the assistance of the assessors. While the trial judge, who has absolute power to give effect to his own views, may well differ from the assessors, even if they are unanimous, he is nevertheless bound to give great weight to their opinions when preparing the judgment of the court. Certainly the opinions of the assessors must not be used by a trial judge merely to fortify, in his judgment, the views he may have indicated in his summing up—but otherwise disregarded. The judge will not lightly disregard the assessors' opinions, particularly where knowledge of village life and custom is relevant.

Although therefore it seems that the original purpose of the assessor system was merely to provide the judge with assistance upon local custom and habits, assessors have, over the years, tended to assume a status approaching that of jurors. . . .

Notes and Questions

1. When a nation moves from using a jury to trial solely before a judge, the judge will be around to criticize after the trial. But a jury goes home and is no longer available for responding to criticism. Also a single juror may escape from his individual responsibility by being part of a group—but the judge stands alone to face his shortcomings. Are these effective reasons for moving away from use of the jury?

2. The report of the Royal Commission on Criminal Justice in 1993 recommended that the defendant ought to lose the right to choose trial by jury. Many defendants, in an estimated 35,000 cases per year, reject trial before a magistrate's court for a jury trial in the Crown Court. The recommended procedure is that when the prosecution and defense cannot agree, the magistrates would decide whether the case remains in the magistrate's court or goes to the Crown Court. It is a much debated issue. Some view it as a cost cutting measure, others to reduce the more frequent acquittals in the Crown Court, others to avoid having to appoint more judges to the Crown Court (which might include having to appoint solicitors). The Bar was not pleased with the recommendation—it would keep many matters before the magistrate's courts where solicitors may appear, rather than having them transferred to the Crown Court where solicitors' rights are very limited.

C. THE JURY IN CRIMINAL CASES—SELECTION

The variation in the United States and English decisions to use the jury in civil trials evolves from whether it is an effective institution in achieving a just resolution of civil disputes. Two quite distinct conclusions have been reached. Similarly, the two systems have reached different conclusions on how best to select a jury (both the jury panel and those members of the panel who will hear a particular case).

Empanelling a jury requires the preparation of a list of persons qualified to serve, excusing some on that list for particular reasons, and the selection of persons remaining on the list to serve at a specific trial. There are thus several stages for variation to arise in jury selection determination in different legal systems. How is eligibility determined? If the list of potential jurors achieves the desired selection goals, are they markedly altered by either granting jury panel member requests for dismissal, or through challenges to willing members made for cause or peremptorily, or by jury vetting by the state—the practice of removing potential jurors by the prosecution by having police check the records of potential jurors for evidence of serious offenses which would evidence susceptibility to pressure or bias. In considering the variations between practice in the United States and England in jury procedures, apart from the *use* of the jury, questions arise regarding the balance of rights of the prosecution and defense with respect to challenges and vetting, and the role and numerical limitation on the form of challenges—cause and peremptory.

The changes prompted by the Morris Committee in 1965 enlarged the pool and the composition. No longer were juries, as Lord Devlin had commented, "predominantly male, middle-aged, middle-minded and middle-class."

The jury had been male because few women satisfied the property qualifications. It had been middle-aged because the age limits were twenty-one to sixty, now changed to eighteen to sixty-five, and it had been middle-minded and middle-class because exempted were principally peers, members of Parliament, country and town councillors, lawyers, clergymen, a variety of medical persons, soldiers and sailors, policemen and post office workers.

Lord Devlin had noted the apparent inconsistency between the limited qualification and much earlier granted universal suffrage.

> It may seem surprising that in a country which has had universal suffrage for longer than a generation the jury should still rest upon a comparatively narrow base. Looked at from that angle, the argument for a change seems very strong. But it might be dangerous, so long as the unanimity rule is retained, to equate the jury franchise with the right to vote. No one expects the country to be unanimous in favour of the Conservative Party, but the jury must be unanimously for a plaintiff or a defendant. The approach to unanimity must be helped to some extent by the fact that the jury is drawn from the central bloc of the population and it is difficult to estimate what the effect might be of the inclusion of more diversified elements. If unanimity is insisted upon and the narrow franchise is preferred, it is no doubt right that juries should be taken out of the middle of the community where safe judgment is most likely to repose.[4]

The new exempt list was basically limited to judges, persons involved with the administration of justice and the clergy—a decided decrease in the scope of those excused by law, rather than by the court.

It is the dismissal of a prospective juror by the court which in English law is at considerable variance with the United States practice. Challenges to the entire panel are infrequent in both systems, but in

4. Lord Devlin, Trial by Jury 22 (1956).

English law challenges for cause are almost never made and peremptory challenges have been abolished. Turning again to Lord Devlin, he describes the situation in the mid–1950s.

L. DEVLIN, "TRIAL BY JURY"

20 (1956).

Although the challenging of jurors is now so little used, I have dealt with it in some detail for two reasons. The first is that it is important that the right should exist and be recognised. Trial by jury will be useless as a safeguard for the subject, as it has proved useless in the past, if it means trial by a packed jury. Therefore the precautions which the law takes to secure that a jury is unbiased and independent must be preserved and understood; the fact that they have not been necessary in the last hundred years or so does not mean that they will never be necessary again.

The second reason is that the disappearance of the challenge in England can usefully be contrasted with the practice in the United States. It is always interesting to see the same institution developing differently in different climates. The jury system in the United States has in the years of its independent existence diverged acutely from the English in this matter of the challenge.... The *voir dire* has become in the United States a pre-trial procedure of great importance, in which the advocates on each side vie with one another to secure a jury of individuals whom they think look favourably on their client's case. To some extent the position under the common law has been altered. In all states peremptory challenges have been allowed in civil causes as they never were at common law; in most states the number varies from two to six; in the Federal Court each party is entitled to three peremptory challenges. There is no rule, as there is in England, that counsel must show a prima facie ground for challenge before he can interrogate the proposed juror. Moreover, counsel is allowed to interrogate within reasonable limits for the purpose of deciding whether to exercise a peremptory challenge. The possibility of bias is very widely explored and a prospective juror seems to be asked an infinity of questions about his views. If a plaintiff's case rests on an oral contract, has he a prejudice in favour of contracts being in writing? If the defendant is wealthy, would that influence him in assessing damages? If a party is a foreigner, would he dislike that? If the defendant is a bank, has the juror ever had his overdraft harshly treated? If the juror discloses that he has a predisposition on any of these matters, nevertheless if he declares that his opinion will yield to the evidence and that he will give his verdict according to the evidence and to the law that is laid down by the court, he cannot usually be successfully challenged for cause unless there is some reason for discrediting his declaration.

Naturally it is not very often that a juror will either admit to a rooted prejudice or assert that he would maintain it in the teeth of the evidence. But that does not greatly diminish the importance of the *voir dire.* By a careful exercise of peremptories, but still more by a skilful use of his power of questioning and of the opportunities which it gives for making a personal contact with the jury, the advocate will seek to secure a jury of individuals favourably disposed towards himself and his case. The textbooks (for in the United States textbooks are not confined as they are here mainly to theoretical matters, but deal in detail with the practical conduct of the case) make this quite clear. The selection of the jury is considered a "fine art" which the advocate must carefully study. The *voir dire* offers the advocate "an opportunity of educating the jury on the issues in the case"; a chance to "create a favourable atmosphere" or "condition the jury to the desired viewpoint." It is the right time at which to make a frank disclosure of any difficulties there may be—such as a client's criminal record or past history of motor accidents—and "extract a promise" from the jurors that they will not allow these things to prejudice their verdict. It is part of the art that an advocate should be alert to detect jurors who seem unsympathetic and get rid of them if he can by the use of his peremptories.

The *voir dire* can occupy quite an appreciable time.... I do not think that this procedure would now be acceptable to English ideas, not so much because it may add substantially to the length of the trial as because in its American form it conflicts with our traditional methods of advocacy. By the end of it the advocate has found out a good deal about the jurors and it is inevitable that his conduct of the case and his style of oratory will be influenced by the desire to appeal to them as individuals. The English tradition is that advocacy should be quite impersonal: counsel should not say what they think or feel; they should simply submit their case. Likewise, they should address the jury as an impersonal body of twelve and the less they know about them as men and women the better.

In fact they know nothing at all about them; and it is very doubtful whether they would be allowed to find out anything very much. In a case over a century ago, where the charge was obtaining goods by fraud, counsel for the defence wanted to ask each juror whether he was a member of an association for the prosecution of persons committing frauds upon tradesmen. The judge refused to allow it, saying:—"It is quite a new course to catechise a jury in this way." I can guess that an American advocate would be astounded by this. There may be, he would say, a juryman who is so predisposed to one side or the other as to make him by common consent an unfit judge; what is done to detect and eradicate such a man? The answer is that nothing is done and that unless his predisposition happens by chance to be known to the parties or their solicitors, he will undoubtedly serve on the jury. We can defend the obsolescence of the challenge only by claiming that such people are rare and that individual prejudices become so diluted in the jury-room that they count for little in the end.

Nevertheless, there can be a degree of laxity that is almost indefensible. Often counsel and solicitors do not bother even to observe a juror while he is taking the oath. How otherwise can one account for the fact that after a trial in Wales conducted in English two jurors were able to make an affidavit saying that they understood no English? ...

* * *

———

There appears to be some tension in English practice between the need to allow challenges to remove potential jurors who threaten a just result, and the concern that the challenge not be used to create a stacked jury, which, as Lord Devlin notes, may make trial by jury useless to the subject. It may well be useless to the accused if the prosecution stacks the jury, or useless to the state if that stacking is accomplished by the counsel for the accused. If both are equally adept at stacking, is the result a fair panel or a skewed assemblage of positive and negative biases far distant from what the English system continues to hold as the best available practice—taking pot luck with few exceptions? ... Lord Denning's view is of a much more narrow group from which to select the jury, or a more restrictive selection of the panel to choose those "sensible and responsible members of the community." He talks about the practice of "vetting" the jury.

LORD DENNING, "WHAT NEXT IN THE LAW"
62 (1982).

* * *

By making everyone qualified to sit on a jury, it led inevitably to the practice of 'jury vetting'. The prosecuting authorities naturally wanted to exclude criminals—who would presumably be biased in favour of their companions in crime. It would lead to the guilty being acquitted. So the practice grew up in some places of the prosecuting authorities searching through the criminal records—and checking them against the jury panel—and objecting to them. Was this 'jury vetting' lawful or not?

There are two rival philosophies. One philosophy says that the parties to a dispute ought to know whether the jurors are suitable to try the case. They ought to have access to the antecedents of the persons on the panel: so that they may be able to object to those who are unsuitable to sit in judgment. That philosophy prevails in the United States of America. So much so that the parties in that country can cross-examine the potential jurors before they are sworn: not only about their previous convictions, but also upon their occupations, their views on this matter or that which may arise in the course of the hearing—so as to see if they are prejudiced in any way.

That philosophy has never prevailed in England. Our philosophy is that the jury should be selected at random—from a panel of persons who are nominated at random. We believe that twelve persons selected at random are likely to be a cross-section of the people as a whole—and thus represent the views of the common man. Some may be moral.

Others not. Some may be honest. Others not. Some may be bad drivers with many convictions for motoring offenses. Others may not have a single thing against them. The parties must take them as they come. There are a few exceptions. Someone may be disqualified. Another may be banned because the prosecution has asked that he 'stand by for the Crown', that is, because the prosecution can ask that he does not serve as a juror. ... But subject to these exceptions, the principle of English law is that the jurors should be selected at random.

In recent times, however, there has been a change. Some prosecuting authorities seem sometimes to have searched through the criminal records—and the records of Special Branch—checking to see if any of those on the jury panel have anything entered against their names; and then, if they think any one of them is unsuitable, to require them to 'stand by for the Crown'. This is called a 'jury check' or 'jury vetting'. In the House of Commons in 1980 the Attorney–General disclosed that

> 'The Northamptonshire police were checking all jury panels against Criminal Records Office records. This information was passed on to prosecuting counsel.'

This sort of thing can be done without anyone outside the police force knowing anything about it.

In *R v. Sheffield Crown Court, ex parte Brownlow* [[1980] 1 WLR 892], I thought that it was unconstitutional. I said:

> 'To my mind it is unconstitutional for the police authorities to engage in "jury vetting". So long as a person is eligible for jury service, and is not disqualified, I cannot think it right that, behind his back, the police should go through his record so as to enable him to be asked to "stand by for the Crown", or to be challenged by the defense. If this sort of thing is to be allowed, what comes of a man's right of privacy? He is bound to serve on a jury when summoned. Is he thereby liable to have his past record raked up against him— and presented on a plate to prosecuting and defending lawyers—who may use it to keep him out of the jury—and, who knows, it may become known to his neighbours and those about him?'

My view was rebutted by Lord Justice Lawton in the more recent case of R v. Mason.[1] On a trial for burglary, the Crown objected to four jurors: and asked them to 'stand by for the Crown' because they had previous convictions. The accused was found guilty and then complained of 'jury vetting'. The Court of Appeal held that it was perfectly lawful. Lord Justice Lawton said:

> 'The facts which have been revealed show that some scrutiny of jury panels is necessary if disqualified persons are to be excluded from juries. The police are the only authority able to do this. Since it is a criminal offence for a person to serve on a jury knowing that he is disqualified, for the police to scrutinise the list of potential jurors to see if any are disqualified is to do no more than to perform their

---

1. [1980] 3 WLR 617.

usual function of preventing the commission of offences. In the course of looking at criminal records convictions are likely to be revealed which do not amount to disqualifications. We can see no reason why information about such convictions should not be passed on to prosecuting counsel. He may consider that a juror with a conviction for burglary would be unsuitable to sit on a jury trying a burglary; and if he does so he can exercise the Crown's rights. Many persons, but not burglars, would probably think that he should.

'The practice of supplying prosecuting counsel with information about potential jurors' convictions has been followed during the whole of our professional lives, and almost certainly for generations before us. It is not unlawful, and has not until recently been thought to be unsatisfactory.'

I stand corrected.

* * *

To my mind this is what should happen: There should be a qualification for service as a juror so that a jury is composed of sensible and responsible members of the community. It should be representative of the best of them of whatever sex or colour, and of whatever age or occupation. Service as a juror should be regarded as a service to the community—as indeed it is. It should command the respect of the people generally—much as service as a magistrate does now. Those on the jury list should be selected in much the same way as magistrates are now. Sometimes people apply. Sometimes they are recommended by others. Always references are required. Interviews are held to assess suitability. In the make-up of the jurors' list, the magistrate could be of the greatest help. It should be part of their function to make up the jury list for their neighborhood.

In this way I suggest that trial by jury can be retained as the great institution it always has been. Otherwise, I suggest it should be replaced by trial by judge and assessors.

―――――

We are accustomed in America to think of removing potential jurors only by means of either a challenge for cause or a limited number of peremptory challenges. This occurs after the jury list is prepared. It is conducted in open court. But potential jurors may be removed at an earlier stage. The qualifications for serving constitute a determination of who should be removed, by not permitting them to qualify in the first instance. Thus, minors are removed from the list of those qualified. So might be persons on active duty in military service. But even after these classifications are followed to prepare the list, should the state be able to remove any other persons for any reason? If so should they be removed before the selection of the jury begins, or should the state give the information to the prosecuting office so that he might challenge for cause?

Challenges for cause are rarely used in England. In 1978 information was disclosed that in terrorism criminal trials, the police and military were searching their files for information regarding potential jurors' loyalty, record of any criminal activity and even what seemed attitudinal traits, reflected by participation in demonstrations. Some prospective jurors were removed. Is this practicing of jury vetting really a secret and unlimited peremptory challenge available exclusively to the prosecution? Does it illustrate a deficiency which could be corrected by use of the challenge for cause? Is it inconsistent with the 1973 Practice Direction which stated that

> [A] jury consists of 12 individuals chosen at random from the appropriate panel.... A juror should be excused if closely concerned in the facts of the particular case.... It is contrary to established practice for jurors to be excused on more general grounds such as race, religion or political beliefs or occupation.[5]

Does this preclude the lengthy examination of jurors as it exists in America?

Questions

1. Do you agree with the age limits for jury qualification in England (18–65)?

2. The English view towards challenges to the jury panel is remarkably different from the American practice. How would you explain the differences in terms of a just system to someone from a nation which does not use the jury? If you were that third party nation observer, how would you be likely to respond to the question: Which is the more just system—the English or the American?

3. Would the concept of "stand by for the Crown" be acceptable in the United States?

D. THE JURY—VERDICT

Another striking difference in the jury procedure involves the verdict. The majority verdict in criminal cases appears to be a practice whose time has come. It is being adopted in various states in the United States, and the pattern has been to allow a smaller majority than the English view. The accused is believed to have enough in his favor under modern procedural rules, and the impact of a single (or small minority) obstinate juror is thought to justify this important change from the early common law adherence to the unanimous verdict. Thus the difference is not between or among common law national systems, but between contemporary practice and the historical mandate of a unanimous verdict. The difference which does exist is diminishing. The verdict in

---

5. [1973] 1 All E.R. 240.

English criminal law long mandated unanimity. The Criminal Justice Act 1967 (later reinforced in the Juries Act 1974), introduced a major change, the majority verdict.

CRIMINAL JUSTICE ACT 1967
C. 80.

13.—(1) Subject to the following provisions of this section, the verdict of a jury in criminal proceedings need not be unanimous if—

(a) in a case where there are not less than eleven jurors, ten of them agree on the verdict; and

(b) in a case where there are ten jurors, nine of them agree on the verdict;

and a verdict authorised by this subsection is hereafter in this section referred to as "a majority verdict".

(2) A court shall not accept a majority verdict of guilty unless the foreman of the jury has stated in open court the number of jurors who respectively agreed to and dissented from the verdict.

(3) A court shall not accept a majority verdict unless it appears to the court that the jury have had not less than two hours for deliberation or such longer period as the court thinks reasonable having regard to the nature and complexity of the case.

———

An attempt is first made to achieve a unanimous verdict. It is only when that fails that a majority verdict is allowed. Lord Devlin offers some observations on the requirement of unanimity, written before the adoption of a majority verdict.

LORD DEVLIN, "TRIAL BY JURY"
48 (1956).

. . . Why is the verdict of a jury thought to require a degree of assent which for most purposes would be rejected as impracticable? The answer is that no one ever planned that it should be that way; the rule is simply an antique. Twelve witnesses were required to support the winning party and naturally for that purpose their testimony had to be unanimous; when the twelve witnesses were translated into judges, the unanimity rule, notwithstanding that its original significance had then departed, remained with them. . . . It is of course not unique, in the law or elsewhere, to find something retained long after the reason for creating it has vanished. Judges wear ermine in winter because they once needed to keep themselves warm; but it does not seriously impede their movements and anyway they now keep most of it for ceremonial occasions. The singular thing about the unanimity rule is that it is retained as the active principle of the verdict.

* * *

The requirement survives notwithstanding that the older and harsher methods of obtaining unanimity have now been abandoned. The imprisonment of nonconformists was soon given up as being too drastic; but for centuries after that it was habitual to keep the jury confined until it reached agreement, however long it took. Blackstone notes, though with the implication that the practice was obsolete, that a judge need not wait for the verdict beyond the end of the assize, but could take the jury with him to the next town in a cart. Both before and after Blackstone's time the rule was that the jury was to be kept without meat, drink, fire or candle; this continued until 1870 and was strictly enforced. Here is an example from Elizabethan days which reads like a cautionary tale from the Garden of Eden:—

> "The Jury being withdrawn after Evidence, and remaining a long Time without concluding on their Verdict, the Officers, who attended them, seeing their Delay, searched them, and found that some had Figs and others had Pippins; which being moved to the Court, they were examined on Oath, and two of them confessed that they had eaten Figs before they were agreed on their Verdict, and three confessed that they had Pippins, but had not eat any of them; and that this was unknown to the Parties. Those who had eaten were each of them fined five Pounds, and those who had not eaten the Pippins, were each of them fined forty Shillins; but the Verdict was, upon great consideration, and Conference with the other Judges, held to be good."

About the same time John Mucklow was fined twenty shillings for being found with "sugar-candy and liquorish." It is very difficult for a minority to hold out indefinitely in such conditions and without pippins or liquorish, and it is obvious that many verdicts so obtained must in fact have been majority verdicts, however they were made to appear— perhaps even minority verdicts if the minority was determined enough. All this is very reminiscent of the verdict's origin. What was sought was not a rational conclusion but a sign, something akin to the result of the ordeal or to triumph in battle; the process could not be determined until it was obtained and, once obtained, the methods of obtaining it were thought less important than the fact that it was there. The defects of the rule were seriously studied during the nineteenth century by the Commissioners for the Reform of the Criminal Law and others and recommendations made for its modification which, like so many other recommendations on legal subjects, have passed into oblivion.

The practice of keeping a jury into the night or without refreshments and other amenities is now obsolete. But as recently as 1908 a jury who said they were unable to agree were told by the judge that they would be locked up for two hours; they found the prisoner guilty and the Court of Criminal Appeal considered the procedure to be regular. Today it is very unusual for a jury to be out for more than four or five hours. If after three or four hours they come back into court to say that they cannot agree, it is customary to ask them to make a further effort to sink their differences; and if that fails, they are discharged. There must then be a new trial. In a criminal case it is almost conventional now to accept a second disagreement as tantamount to an acquittal and to drop the prosecution....

The extent to which a jury can be exhorted into unanimity is a delicate question. The fundamental principle is that while it is right that every member of the jury should take into account the opinions of the others, he must not assent to a verdict that goes against his conscience. A direction given by Mr. Justice Finlay is now very generally used:—

> "In the first place, I desire to point out to you how vitally important it is that you should agree. I am not prepared yet to release you, because the consequences—the enormous expenditure of public money in this case, the consequences to the public and to every member of the public—are so grave that it is a matter of most vital importance that you should agree, and I must ask you to make another effort to agree. The other matter which I should like to say a word on is simply this, that with a view to agreeing there must inevitably be some give and take. I would exhort any member or members of the Jury who may be disposed to differ from their comrades, to consider the matter carefully, to weigh what is said to them, to remember, if they are a small minority—I do not know—to remember that they may be wrong, and while I would not for one moment suggest to a single member of the Jury to be false to his oath, I would most strongly urge upon all of you and upon each individual among you the extreme importance from the point of view of the Prisoner and from the point of view of the public and from every point of view, of agreeing."

In 1919 a direction was approved by the Court of Criminal Appeal that I think might now be treated as questionable: "If a substantial number take one view, as a rule it is expedient that the others should subordinate their views to the majority." In 1936 in the Court of Appeal Lord Wright said: "If a judge does tell the jury that the minority must give in to the majority simply to avoid a difference of opinion, that is a misdirection in law." A judge may emphasise the misfortune of disagreement, but must not create the impression in the minds of the jurors that there is a legal duty to agree at any cost.

It might be supposed that, when all physical pressure on the jury was removed, disagreements would increase. Another factor which one would suppose might tend towards an increase is the spread of education and loss of class-consciousness; the leadership of one or two socially superior men is now less likely to be accepted. ...

Since no one knows what goes on in the jury room, one can only speculate about the nature of disagreements. I think it probable that they fall into two quite distinct classes. The first is the genuine disagreement between two more or less evenly balanced views and the second is the minority of one eccentric. The advisability of modifying the unanimity rule has, I think, to be considered differently in relation to the two classes.

I do not think that there would be any support for the view that verdicts should go by a bare majority. Reformers generally have suggested a majority of eight to four or nine to three. Moreover, they have recognised that it would be very undesirable if a poll were to be taken at the outset and a majority verdict reached before there had been a strenuous attempt to secure unanimity. To meet this point one suggestion has been that a majority verdict should not be accepted until, say, six hours after the jury has first retired. This still leaves the danger that a majority will settle down from the beginning to play out time; and most people would be unhappy at the thought of a minority of three or four being overridden unless the majority verdict was, as it were, accompanied by some convincing assurance that it was the only way out of the deadlock. Another suggestion, which would erase this last criticism, is that the taking of a majority verdict should be at the discretion of the judge. The difficulty about that is that there is no way in which the judge could satisfy himself that the possibilities of unanimity had really been exhausted and no principle upon which the discretion could be exercised. It would be as appropriate in all cases as in none. If it was to be exercised in every or in the great bulk of cases, it would have the same effect on the jury as if it were a written rule. If in few or none (which is much more likely, for the strength of the law is precedent and, where there is none, it is the habit of judges to proceed with great caution), it would give no substantial relief. An important point that has been made by Dr. Evatt is that the taking of a majority verdict may endanger the practice of secrecy; there may be speculation about the reasons for the dissension, and a minority that has been overruled may be tempted to give tongue.

Notwithstanding these objections I should myself be happy to see a majority verdict taken in civil cases subject to safeguards of the type I have been discussing. Modifications of this sort have now been introduced into many of the states of America and Australia. In some the reform has been extended to the criminal verdict, and of course in Scotland the verdict has always gone by a majority. In crime I should prefer to stick to the English habit. Whatever its origin, unanimity is now so ingrained in our procedure that its eradication would seem to take from the verdict a virtue that in the criminal law it needs. The criminal verdict is based on the absence of reasonable doubt. If there were a dissenting minority of a third or a quarter, that would of itself suggest to the popular mind the existence of a reasonable doubt and might impair public confidence in the criminal verdict.

There is, I believe, much well-informed support for the view that the other type of disagreement—that caused by the odd eccentric—should be tackled. The man whose spiritual home is the minority of one and who, often in compensation for his social ineffectiveness, delights in the power of veto, is a nuisance; and there can be no doubt that every now and again he turns up on a jury. A majority of eleven would probably be taken by the public as proving that the outsider was a crank rather than as showing that there was any real possibility of the defence being right.

But the fact is, I believe, that the eccentrics do not turn up often enough and so the demand for reform is not strong enough to defeat the faith reposed in traditional and well-tried methods. The evil caused by disagreements is not great. When they occur, they can sometimes be grievous to the parties concerned and they are always expensive, but they are not numerous enough to create a general problem. The sense of satisfaction obtainable from complete unanimity is itself a valuable thing and it would be sacrificed if even one dissentient were overruled. Since no one really knows how the jury works or indeed can satisfactorily explain to a theorist why it works at all, it is wise not to tamper with it until the need for alteration is shown to be overwhelming. If an institution has been constructed to plan, we may have some confidence in improvements suggested by planners. But the jury, like so many English institutions, has been constructed biologically rather than mechanically. In the fields of legal and political science the English have found the green fingers of gardeners more useful than precision instruments.

————

Lord Hailsham makes the interesting comment that the jury is venerated, but not trusted. If you accept his view, is it reason for moving towards eliminating the jury? Is there any reason to think that if lay assessors are used, that they would be any more trusted than a jury? They would be more carefully chosen than juries. Isn't the magistrates' court a rejection of the jury but a recognition that lay persons may have a role in the determination of guilt or innocence in criminal proceedings?

But Lord Hailsham nevertheless believes the jury will survive in England. One may question whether the English jury is truly a random selection. But it is more so than in America, and his comment that the American system is not the direction English law would be apt to go in seems well taken. He emphasizes the popularity of the jury. Is it a popularity based on romanticized notions of the "Twelfth Man" saving an innocent person after gruelling hours of convincing his brethren in a hot jury room? Or is it, as Lord Hailsham mentions, a system strengthened by the "sense of responsibility of the average individual citizen?" How do you believe the jury is viewed in the United States? By lay persons who have never served? By those who have served? By nontrial lawyers who presumably have considerable knowledge of the law and what it intends to achieve, but have no vested interests in the preservation of the jury? Lord Hailsham comments:

LORD HAILSHAM, "HAMLYN REVISITED: THE BRITISH LEGAL SYSTEM TODAY"

39 (1983).

Will the jury survive indefinitely as the only method of trial in criminal cases on indictment? So far as I know it still commands the respect of the profession and the public, from Lord Devlin at the summit to the individual in the street. All the same some doubts begin to be expressed, and some abuses plain. ... There have been repeated attempts, discovered usually only in the cases in which they have failed, to intimidate or bribe jurors, so easily followed home or made the subject of threatening telephone calls. There is the immense problem of trying long cases of commercial frauds which may run into months' duration. Not only is the evidence often immensely technical, and extremely complex, but the mere fact that members of a jury selected to try a case of this nature must make themselves available for months of continuous sitting during consecutive weeks precludes a random choice, besides imposing great hardship on those unable to excuse themselves. The American method of selection, involving careful examination of personal backgrounds, is certainly unattractive to an English practitioner, accustomed as he is to random selection. But is the comparison altogether to our advantage? Recent examples have been disclosed of persons sitting on juries with known criminal records, some with long strings of serious offences to their discredit. In one case which came to my knowledge, a defendant, ultimately convicted after, I think, more than one trial, had boasted before arraignment that no English jury would convict him. He had some reason for this boast. He had five previous acquittals on serious charges. He was either extremely unlucky in being falsely accused five times, or extremely lucky in his juries or perhaps it was not luck at all.

The strength of the jury system lies in the sense of responsibility of the average individual citizen where his own personal interests are not involved; the perfectly proper distrust of the public, and therefore of jurors, of persons in authority, including police, judges, counsel, public officials and experts; and the fact that each particular jury, once its period of service is over, never reassembles, and therefore can acquire no reputation for lenience or severity, or indeed bias of any kind. It remains, I am sure, in the field of criminal law at least, a popular institution, to interfere with which would cause widespread consternation. Nevertheless, false convictions as well as perverse acquittals do take place perhaps more often than is supposed (especially when the question is one of identity) and, unless there has been a misdirection on the part of the judge, or some other irregularity in the trial, they are almost impossible to upset, except in the unlikely event of the convicted person, ... actually being able to prove his innocence after all attempts at appeal have failed. Have we in the field of this venerated institution really evolved the most perfect system? Would a reasoned judgment by a mixed court composed of laymen with a lawyer in the chair, combined, as it would have to be, with a wider right of appeal on fact, achieve less haphazard results? The difficulty with criminal law is that you cannot without good reason experiment with the liberties of human beings. Personally I would welcome an experiment on these lines limited to cases where the defendant consented and to the longer type of contested commercial fraud.

———

The criminal procedure systems of different common law nations may reflect very contrasting treatment, but there is a more common element to the sentencing process, namely, judicial discretion. Although there is some limited movement toward mandatory, fixed sentences, the generally wide judicial discretion contrasts with the more strict trial procedures. There is one feature in English sentencing which is unknown in the United States. Where a defendant, having been found guilty by a magistrates' court, is believed by the magistrates to have committed a crime for which the magistrates lack authority to grant sufficient sentencing, the magistrates may refer the matter to the Crown Court for the imposition of sentence. A defendant appearing before a magistrates' court thus must be aware that the sentencing limitations of the magistrates' courts are supplemented by those of the Crown Court. If a defendant before a magistrates' court believes there is a likelihood of a reference to the Crown Court for sentencing, he may well prefer to have the entire matter referred to the Crown Court for trial. The reason accused persons tend to avoid requesting a trial in the Crown Court, however, is an expectation of a modest sentence by magistrates in return for an almost certain conviction.

Notes and Questions

1. The 1967 Criminal Justice Act applied only to criminal trials. The Courts Act 1971, § 39, extended the majority verdict to civil trials, although it applies to the much reduced use of a jury in civil litigation. The same rule applies as expressed in the Criminal Justice Act for juries of ten or more. For the county court, a majority verdict is seven of the eight jurors. The two hour deliberation rule for criminal trials is altered to a reasonable time considering the nature and complexity of the case.

2. A majority verdict may avoid one problem of unanimity—keeping a jury panel together for so long that decisions are based more on a desire to escape jury confinement than to reach a just result. Mischief may occur in attempting to force a conclusion upon a jury. But that could occur when there is a ten person jury and a persistent 8–2 split, with a 9–1 vote needed to convict. Would it not be preferable to alter the conditions in which juries discuss the facts and determine whether or not to adopt a majority verdict for the reasons that such practice is not unjust? In other words, should the unanimous verdict be altered because it deteriorates when it is cold and jurors are hungry, or should we give them food and some heat and say "Get about your business?" Is a better approach to consider, as Lord Devlin did shortly before the majority verdict was adopted, the impracticability of the unanimity rule?

SECTION 4. APPELLATE PROCEDURE

A. GENERAL

In the early development of the common law, an appeal lay only to challenge an error on the record. One sought a writ of error, and then pursued a process which to us seems unwieldy. A review of the judgment, alleging that the court reached the wrong conclusion, later was recognized in the Chancery Court. Thus appeals developed as part of the common law, recognized not by statute, but in the same manner as other rights, as the "way things ought to be", by the judiciary. When the rural courts were abolished, the right of appeal was incorporated into the statutory framework, the primary source being the Judicature Acts.

An appellant now seeks to reverse the judgment as incorrect in law, which in a narrow sense constitutes a rehearing since the judgment may be reversed or some other judgment substituted. But it is not a rehearing in the manner of the rehearing of a civil law appellate court, where new evidence will be heard and there is a de novo proceeding. New evidence may be presented in the English appeal, but it very rarely is, and is accepted only where it (1) could not have been obtained for use at the trial, (2) suggests an important influence on the result and (3) seems reasonably creditable. The most frequent acceptance of new evidence is in an interlocutory appeal, not an appeal from the trial judgment.

Although the appellate court does rehear the case, English judges are far more hesitant to interfere with the discretionary power of trial judges than in the United States. But they do often overrule procedural determinations.

The statutory scheme designates the Court of Appeal as the appellate body of the Supreme Court to which appeals are directed from divisions of the High Court, from the county courts or from interlocutory orders of judges in chambers or masters on pretrial issues.

The Court of Appeal uniquely is an appellate court, a characteristic also of the judicial role of the House of Lords. Both have very limited, special original jurisdiction. The trial courts, contrastingly, possess an extremely qualified role in the appellate process.

The Court of Appeal has both civil and criminal divisions. In the civil division a judge in chambers hears appeals from High Court masters or registrars in the form of a full rehearing, but country court registrar decisions are heard in the form of a true appeal, without rehearing. Orders from High Court or county court judges are generally by right, with leave required only in certain exceptions. Only certain High Court orders may "leapfrog" the Court of Appeal and be heard directly by the House of Lords. While the High Court is essentially not a court of appeal for the lower county court in civil matters, on the criminal side in summary trials in the magistrate's courts the Crown Court (criminal parallel to but not part of the High Court) does hear appeals on conviction and sentencing issues. Additionally some appeals (essentially issues of law) are allowed from the magistrate's courts to the Queen's Bench Division of the High Court. The Queen's Bench Division of the High Court is principally a court of first instance for *civil* matters, possessing no *civil* appeal jurisdiction from the lower civil courts (county courts). But it does sit as an appellate court in *criminal* matters for appeals by way of case stated alleging the decision of the magistrate's court to have been wrong in law or in excess of jurisdiction. A decision of the Queen's Bench in such case could be appealed to the House of Lords, bypassing the Court of Appeal. In contrast to *summary* trial appeals, appeals following trial on *indictment* in the Crown Court go to the Court of Appeal (Criminal Division). Further appeal is to the House of Lords. If this framework seems convoluted (as it does even more when one overlays the framework with who sits for appeals, especially criminal appeals), it is the process of judicial evolution, not of planning a civil and criminal appellate system.

A new level of judicial review has been added with the participation in the European Community. The European Court of Justice hears *references* from English courts. It is perhaps incorrect to call the European Court of Justice an appellate court, since a reference to the court is less an appeal than a request for a ruling on European law which will be binding on the referring English court. The Treaty of Rome, the creator of the European Community, is unlike English legislation. The latter is more exact and English judges tend to limit the application of legislation only to those circumstances which precisely fit the wording of the statute. But the Treaty of Rome often states general principles, and where the English courts interpret its provisions, the judges must consider the intent and spirit of the Treaty—they ought not act as "traditional" English judges.

If it is appropriate to describe the European Court of Justice as part of the English judicial structure but not an appellate court, it may be appropriate to describe the European Court of Human Rights in Strasbourg as not part of the English judicial structure but an appellate court. Britain has signed the European Convention on Human Rights, but has not made the Convention English law. Thus parties do not technically "appeal" to the European Court of Human Rights from English court decisions, but it is often decisions of the English courts (such as those discussed in Chapter 10) which cause aggrieved parties to take their cases to the European Court—in a very real sense constituting an appeal of the English court ruling.

The Treaty is unlike English legislation. The latter is more exact and judges tend to limit its application only to those circumstances which precisely fit the wording of the statute. But the Treaty often states general principles, and where English courts interpret its provisions, the judges must consider the intent and spirit of the Treaty. They must not act as "traditional" English judges.

As in the United States, some appeals in England are a matter of right, others require judicial permission. In England, immediately after a decision is rendered by the Court of Appeal, a party may ask the court for leave to appeal. The judges usually respond immediately, rather than reserving judgment. If the request is denied, then the party may ask the House of Lords to permit the appeal, thus giving two chances for the review. The Appeal Committee of the House of Lords hears oral arguments on the petition, and, much like the judges of the Court of Appeal, responds immediately without reserving judgment.

An appeal may require an accurate transcript of the trial process. Modern machines are replacing the fountain pen. Will better transcripts increase the rate of appeal, or simply make those brought more effectively heard? The dialogue below illustrates the tedious process of trying to keep up with the witness.

SYBILLE BEDFORD, "THE FACES OF JUSTICE"
61 (1961).

... The witness reads the oath, gives and spells her name, her address and occupation: she runs a sweetshop in Belgravia....

"He came into the shop, I thought he was a child, I thought he was going to buy a bar of chocolate or something, suddenly he puts up a revolver—"

The clerk says, "Just a moment, madam, not quite so fast if you please."

The witness stops in her tracks. The magistrate leans over and explains to her that she has to be followed by pen.

"Oh, I see."

"Yes, madam?" says the clerk.

[A bit off her stride]: "Well, then he said to me—"

The clerk [firmly]: " 'He came into the shop—'?"

"... and suddenly he put a revolver on the counter, it was covered with a handkerchief, a silk handkerchief, but I could see the muzzle, I hardly believed my eyes, and he said—"

"One moment—"

" 'Give me your money!' I was stunned, I didn't answer. Then he said—"

"Yes—?"

" 'Oh, come on.' So I whipped up the flap, very quickly, like this, and it flung off the revolver—"

"—?"

"... and he made for the door—I ran after him—I called out to people—in the street and a man—a man got hold of a policeman. ... They caught him."

"Do you see him here?"

"Yes," she says; without looking.

"Where?"

"There."

In due course the evidence is read back. Human speech is not easily caught up with, even with a fast fountain pen. It comes out something like this:

> He came into the shop. I thought he was going to purchase something. He suddenly put a revolver on the counter, a handkerchief was placed over it. He said, "Give me your money." I was so stunned that I made no answer. He said, "Oh, come on." I brought up the flap of the counter, the revolver fell and he made for the door. I followed him into the street where I attracted the attention of a passer-by who called the police. I identified the accused in court today.

The witness signed this record (the deposition), left the box and was asked to sit down in the back of the court.

A major contrast with the United States system in allowing appeals is the limitation in England of criminal appeals to the Court of Appeal from the Crown Court. The Criminal Division of the Court of Appeal is permitted to allow an appeal and quash the decision. Or it may order a retrial but only if there is fresh evidence. Finally, it may "apply the proviso." That permits the court to agree that there is reason for the appeal, but to halt further proceedings because "no substantial miscarriage of justice occurred." Studies have suggested that in many of these cases, serious error had occurred.

Both civil and criminal appeal courts have power to receive fresh evidence. This includes the production of documents and the appearance of witnesses. It is a power which should be, according to the rules, and is, according to practice, exercised very sparingly. It gives rise to witnesses attempting to change their testimony, which may lead the court to believe that if the witness lied the first time, there is no reason to believe the truth will come out on a repeat appearance.

LADD v. MARSHALL

Court of Appeals.
(1954) 1 W.L.R. 1489.*

DENNING, L.J.

It is very rare that application is made to this court for a new trial on the ground that a witness has told a lie. The principles to be applied

* Reprinted with permission of The Incorporated Court of Law Reporting.

are the same as those always applied when fresh evidence is sought to be introduced. To justify the reception of fresh evidence on a new trial, three conditions must be fulfilled: first, it must be shown that the evidence could not have been obtained with reasonable diligence for use at the trial; secondly, the evidence must be such that, if given, it would probably have an important influence on the result of the case, though it need not be decisive; thirdly, the evidence must be such as is presumably to be believed, or in other words, it must be apparently credible, though it need not be incontrovertible.

We have to apply those principles to the case where a witness comes and says: 'I told a lie but nevertheless I now want to tell the truth.' It seems to me that the fresh evidence of such a witness will not as a rule satisfy the third condition. A confessed liar cannot usually be accepted as being credible. To justify the reception of the fresh evidence, some good reason must be shown why a lie was told in the first instance, and good ground given for thinking the witness will tell the truth on the second occasion. If it was proved that the witness had been bribed or coerced into telling a lie at the trial, and is now anxious to tell the truth, that would, I think, be a ground for a new trial and it would not be necessary to resort to an action to set aside the judgment on the ground of fraud. Again, if it was proved that the witness made a mistake on a most important matter and wished to put it right, and the circumstances were so well explained that his fresh evidence was presumably to be believed, then again there would be ground for a new trial.... But this is not a case of bribery or coercion, nor of a mistake. It seems to me that Mrs. Marshall is not a person who in the new situation is presumably to be believed. She endeavoured to show that she was coerced by her husband, but on reading through the affidavits on both sides, it seems to me that the suggestion of coercion comes to nothing. She does not seem to have been in fear of her husband at all. I am afraid it is simply a case where a witness who has told a lie at the first hearing now wants to say something different. It would be contrary to all principle for that to be the ground for a new trial. In my judgment this appeal and the motion should be dismissed.

PARKER and HUDSON LJJ concurred.

———

Ordering a retrial in criminal cases in circumstances other than where there is fresh evidence has been debated and studied extensively in England. Views have been divided. A report by a JUSTICE committee in 1964 discussed the issue.

JUSTICE, POWER TO ORDER A RETRIAL, 1964.*

SHOULD THE COURT HAVE UNLIMITED POWER TO ORDER NEW TRIALS ON APPEALS FROM CONVICTION?

12. This Committee is no better able than its predecessors to reach agreement. Four of its members ... consider that the court should not have such power, nine ... consider that it should. The arguments put forward by the opposing sides change little and are expounded ... in the Tucker Report.** In the end the decision is made in the light of the individual's own experience, his conception of the requirements of justice, and his knowledge of the workings of other legal systems.

* * *

16. Those of us who say that the court should not have such power base their views on the following grounds:

(*a*) The absence of a general power to order a new trial is a humane feature of English criminal procedure. It ensures that once the jury has given its verdict the accused person cannot be subjected for a second time to the ordeal of a criminal trial. To maintain this practice is a mark of strength rather than weakness in our judicial system.

(*b*) This power should not be granted unless the need for it has been clearly and conclusively established. The statistics supplied to the committee indicate that no more than forty-five to fifty new trials would be likely to be ordered in a year, and possibly considerably less. These figures do not suggest that considerations of public safety require the removal of this safeguard to the freedom of the individual. On the other hand we are satisfied that there is a danger that, once granted, this power would be used increasingly....

(*c*) The majority of reported cases in which the Court of Criminal Appeal has complained of the lack of this power are ones where the court, although allowing the appeal, clearly suspected the guilt of the appellant but were unable to apply the proviso to s. 4 of the Criminal Appeal Act, 1907, and say that no substantial miscarriage of justice had actually occurred. Every accused person is entitled to be tried properly, and if he has been convicted in an irregular manner, it is not unreasonable that he should be released. It is not the fault of the accused if his first trial was not conducted properly. By the principle of autrefois acquit the prosecution are denied a second attempt to prove the guilt of an accused. There is no reason why the judicial system should be granted a second attempt to give him a fair and proper trial.

* Reprinted with permission of the Law Society.

** The Tucker Report was the conclusion of the Departmental Committee on New Trials in Criminal Cases, See Cmnd. Papers 9150 (1954).

(*d*) There is no evidence to support the suggestion that the Court of Criminal Appeal might be more ready to grant a new trial in cases where appeals are at present dismissed. To suggest that they would do so in cases where the proviso is at present applied, is to suggest that it is being applied improperly. The committee have received no representations to this effect. There is force in the suggestion that it would be desirable if the Court of Criminal Appeal were more ready to set aside the jury's verdict in cases where the conviction appears to be against the weight of the evidence, but there is no reason to think that a general power to order a new trial would produce this result. If the court is of the opinion that there may well have been a miscarriage of justice, it should quash the conviction as it now has express power to do.

(*e*) There must be real doubt as to the fairness of a second trial. The fact that the accused has already been convicted, his antecedents, adverse comments by the judge at the first trial or by the Court of Criminal Appeal itself, are all matters that may have received publicity and come to the notice of the second jury. Moreover, some jurors might conclude that the Court of Criminal Appeal considered the accused probably guilty in granting a new trial. Even if the second jury were able to disregard all such matters, it is doubtful whether justice would appear to be done. This objection can no longer be lightly dismissed following the unanimous recommendations of the Departmental (Tucker) Committee on Preliminary Proceedings in Magistrates' Courts (Cmnd. 479, July 1958) against publication of reports of committal proceedings until the trial has been concluded, or the accused discharged by the magistrates.

(*f*) Experience of new trials (where a jury at the first hearing has been discharged owing to disagreement or for some other reason) does not argue in favour of new trials. Nearly all practitioners, whether appearing for prosecution or defence, dislike new trials intensely. The evidence is stale, successful cross-examination can seldom be repeated, and in many subtle ways the prosecution are at a considerable advantage at the new trial.

(*g*) The Tucker Committee considered a substantial volume of evidence from Commonwealth countries, and the majority did not find the experience of these countries to have great persuasive force. The further evidence before this committee has not caused us to take any different view.

(*h*) Those who argue in favour of new trials consider that the power should only be exercised once. There can be no logical reason for this. The concession impliedly admits the oppressive nature of new trials. . . .

17. Those members of the committee who say that the court should have such power base their view on the following grounds:

(*a*) The principle object of any system of criminal justice is to convict the guilty and acquit the innocent. We believe that a general power in a criminal appeal court to order a new trial would, if wisely applied, contribute to both ends.

(*b*) We believe that a large majority of the relatively few cases on which a wholly innocent man is convicted are cases of mistaken identity: the evidence of identity is 'thin' and the judge appears to take that view, but the jury convict. The Court of Criminal Appeal, we think inevitably in such a case, while not feeling that the case is satisfactory, are unable to supplant the jury who have seen and heard the witnesses, whom the court has not seen or heard. We do not believe that under the existing law in such cases the Court of Criminal Appeal either could, or ever would, quash the conviction. But they could and should, if they have the power, order a new trial.

(*c*) There are cases in which an obviously guilty man is convicted on overwhelming evidence but appeals on the ground of misdirection or misrepresentation of evidence. It is difficult, and in practice rare, for the court to apply the proviso in such a case because they cannot be sure what a jury, properly directed, would have done. So far as can be discovered, the proviso has never been applied, for example, where cross-examination as to character has been wrongly admitted however clear the appellant's guilt is. In the result an obviously guilty man goes free, with the effect which that has (*a*) on the public, (*b*) on honest witnesses who gave truthful evidence, (*c*) on the jury who have given the true verdict, (*d*) on the victim whose neighbours, knowing that the man has 'got off,' sometimes conclude that the victim must have been lying after all, and (*e*) sometimes on the man's next victim in a crime which he could not have committed if his conviction had not been quashed.

(*d*) The Court of Criminal Appeal has always found the application of the proviso a question of great difficulty. As Lord Goddard said in the 1948 debates:

> 'The difficulty which the court so often feels in applying the proviso is one of the principal reasons why we often think that there should be a new trial. It is almost beyond the wit of man to say in every case, and certainly from the point of view of doing justice to the prisoner, whether if so and so had not happened in the course of the case, and if such a direction had not been given, a jury would assuredly have come to the same conclusion.'

In the Commonwealth countries where there is power to order a new trial it has been used where the Court of Criminal Appeal here would apply the proviso. A new trial is fairer to the accused than having his appeal dismissed by an application of the proviso....

(*e*) The courts hearing criminal appeals in Australia, Canada and New Zealand all have the power to order a new trial. Lawyers in these Commonwealth countries have been consulted and the substance of what they say is that the Bar accepts that the power to order a new trial is desirable and beneficial, that it works well, and that their experience gives no ground for thinking that the fears which have been expressed about it in England are valid. These views have been formed after nine years more experience than those countries had at the time of the Tucker Committee. New trials also exist in India and Eire.

————

For the most part the English appeal follows an orderly process through each step in the judicial hierarchy. Direct appeals which omit one level, the "leap frogging" process, are presented to the House of Lords from the High Court, but only in a very limited number of cases where there is agreement of the parties and a question of law of some public importance.

The emphasis of the English appeal is on an oral process. Karlen has studied the English system of appeals and notes some very important distinctions. In the three decades since his observations, some changes have been made to speed the process, but it remains largely an oral process.

DELMAR KARLEN, "APPEALS IN ENGLAND AND THE UNITED STATES"

78 Law Quarterly Rev. 371 (1962).*

The American method of handling appeals, though historically derived from England, is today fundamentally different from the English method. In the United States, oral arguments are limited in duration and secondary in importance to written briefs; in England, they are unlimited in duration and of primary importance, written briefs being virtually unknown.[a] In the United States, the judges do most of their work in chambers; in England, they do most of it in open court. In the United States, decisions are ordinarily reserved and handed down in written form; in England, they are ordinarily pronounced orally immediately on close of argument.[b] Such are some of the major differences between the two patterns.

To assert that there are distinct national patterns is not to gainsay the fact that in both countries great diversity exists from one appellate court to another. This seems inevitable in the United States, with its separate judicial systems for each of the fifty quasi-sovereign states and another for the federal government. But the situation is not very different in England despite its unitary, compact government. Substan-

* Reprinted with permission of Sweet & Maxwell Ltd.

a. Unlimited oral argument remains, but written presentations are now more common.

b. This is changing. Many decisions of the Court of Appeal are reserved.

tial differences exist from one court to another. For example, in the Court of Criminal Appeal the judges customarily read the record of proceedings below in advance of oral argument, whereas in the Court of Appeal they do not.[c] In the House of Lords, each judge ordinarily renders his own opinion, whereas in the Privy Council a single opinion for the entire court is prepared. ... The number of judges who sit, the way in which they go about their work, the manner in which their decisions are announced—such characteristics vary widely from one court to another, not only within the United States, but also in England. Nevertheless, in each country a distinctive national pattern can be discerned.

* * *

PAPERS ON APPEAL

An outstanding difference between the two nations is the fact that "briefs" are required in the United States, whereas in England they are not. The brief is a full-dress argument in writing, often running fifty or more printed or mimeographed pages in length. It states the facts, outlines the claimed errors in the proceedings below, and cites and discusses the authorities claimed to justify reversal or affirmance. The appellant serves his brief on the other side well in advance of the time for oral argument, and the respondent then serves his answering brief on the appellant, again well in advance of oral argument. Sometimes the appellant serves a reply brief.

In England such a document is virtually unknown. The closest approach to it is the "case" normally required from both sides in the House of Lords and Privy Council. This, however, is a very abbreviated paper, seldom running more than six or seven pages in length, and is intended only as a preliminary outline of the extended oral argument to be made later. It does not discuss authorities in detail, or argue the propositions of law to be relied upon. Relatively few cases are cited (although this may be attributable more to the English theory of precedent than to the form which papers on appeal take). In the other appellate courts of England, no written arguments of any kind are used.

In both England and the United States, the judges are furnished with a record on appeal. It consists of the notice of appeal, pleadings and other formal documents, the judgment below, and so much of the evidence as may be relevant as to the questions raised on appeal. There is this difference, however. In England, there is almost always a reasoned (though often extemporaneous) opinion by the judge below, outlining the evidence, the authorities relied upon, the decision and the reasons therefor. In the United States, such a document is frequently lacking. If the case has been tried by jury, as many cases are, in place of a reasoned opinion, there will be simply the judge's instructions to the jury, without any citation of the authorities upon which his propositions of law are based. If the case has been tried without a jury, there

c. They now do.

ordinarily will be only formalised findings of fact and conclusions of law, again without the citation of authorities. Sometimes there is a reasoned opinion below, as where the case has gone through an intermediate stage of appeal, but this is the exception rather than the rule.

* * *

ORAL ARGUMENT

In the United States, oral arguments are secondary in importance to the briefs, and are rigidly limited in duration. In the United States Supreme Court, one hour is allowed to each side, but in many appellate courts, less time than that is permitted, frequently no more than fifteen minutes or a half-hour for each side. Reading by counsel is frowned upon. The judges do not wish to hear what they can read for themselves. They expect to get all the information they need about the judgment below, the evidence, and the authorities relied upon from studying the briefs and record on appeal. They do not even encourage counsel to discuss in detail the precedents claimed to govern the decision, preferring to do that job by themselves in the relative privacy of their chambers, with or without the assistance of law clerks.

In England, where there are no written briefs, oral arguments are all-important. They are never arbitrarily limited in duration. While some last for only a few minutes, others go on for many days, even weeks. The only controls ordinarily exercised over the time of oral argument are informal, *ad hoc* suggestions from the judges. Thus when counsel wishes to cite a case as authority, the presiding judge may ask him: for what proposition? If the judges indicate that they accept the proposition as stated, there is no need to read the case. Similarly if counsel has persuaded the judges on a certain point, they may indicate that it is unnecessary for him to pursue it further. If counsel for the appellant, by the time he finishes his argument, has failed to persuade the court that the decision below should be reversed or modified, the court informs counsel for the respondent that it does not wish to hear from him at all, and proceeds forthwith to deliver judgment. Despite such controls as these, the time spent in England in oral argument tends to be very much greater than that spent in the United States.[11]

* * *

THE DECISION

In England, few decisions are either reserved or written. In the Court of Appeal, the practice is for each judge to express his individual views orally and extemporaneously immediately upon the close of argument. In the Court of Criminal Appeal a single opinion for the court is customarily announced, but almost always orally and extemporaneously.

---

11. In 1982 the Master of the Rolls made some attempt to speed up the appeal process in the Court of Appeal. He adopted the procedure used in the House of Lords which requires appeal judges to read written submissions before the oral hearing. Additionally, judgments are to be handed out, not read in court.

Only in the House of Lords and the Privy Council are decisions customarily reserved and written.

The American approach entails different internal operating procedures than are usual in England. Conferences, both formal and informal, are a prominent feature of American practice. So are exchanges of memoranda and draft opinions. On the other hand, since reading and writing are by their nature solitary operations, American judges—who are compelled to do much of both—spend many, if not most, of their working hours alone. They are frequently required to shift their attention from one case to another and then back again, because, with cases being heard in batches, several are awaiting decision at any given time.

To the limited extent that the English practice conforms to the American pattern, the same internal procedures doubtless apply. In the great majority of English appeals, however, the judges follow a vastly different routine. Most of their working time is spent together sitting on the bench, listening and talking rather than reading and writing. The discussions they hold are brief and seemingly casual—although highly economical, by reason of the fact that cases are heard and decided one at a time. The judges' minds are already focused on the problems at hand and not distracted by other cases which have been heard and are awaiting decision. They whisper between themselves on the bench; they converse as they walk to and from the courtroom; and they indirectly make comments to each other as they carry on Socratic dialogues with counsel. But they do not ordinarily exchange memoranda or draft opinions or engage in full scale conferences.

In short, the appellate judge in England spends most of his working time in open court, relatively little in chambers, whereas his counterpart in America spends most of his working time in chambers, and relatively little in open court. This is neatly illustrated by the times of sitting for comparable courts in the two nations. In the United States Court of Appeals for the Second Circuit, each judge hears arguments one week out of four, and uses the other three for studying briefs and records on appeal, conferring with his brother judges, and writing opinions. By way of contrast, each judge on the English Court of Appeal hears arguments from 10:30 a.m. to 1 p.m. and from 2 p.m. to 4:15 p.m. day after day, five days a week, throughout each term.

* * *

CONCEPTION OF ROLE

In England, appellate judges tend to regard their job as complete when they reach a correct conclusion on the case presented to them. They are inclined to worry relatively little about the effect of their decision as a precedent. They cannot even be sure that it will ever be published in the law reports. Even if they know that it will, they may be content to leave its ultimate published form primarily to the law reporters. Furthermore, they are so imbued with the idea of the supremacy of Parliament that they do not think much about their own law-making functions. For these reasons, an appeal is regarded as little more than an extension of the original trial. Symptomatic of this attitude are these facts: (1) in both the Court of Appeal and the Court of Criminal Appeal it is possible for the court to take new evidence; (2) litigants are very often present at the argument of an appeal, especially in the Court of Criminal Appeal, where the accused ordinarily has a right to be present.

In the United States, the appellate process is given greater prominence than in England. It is treated as something quite distinct from the trial process, and, in a sense, more important. Appellate judges ordinarily are assured of publication of every opinion they write. They need not usually concern themselves directly with litigants or even with questions of fact, but may concentrate on questions of law and policy. In so far as they deal with constitutional problems, they are dealing with matters beyond even the reach of ordinary legislative processes. In so far as they deal with the common law, they conceive it to be their duty to reform rules which they consider unjust or obsolete. They place greater stress on their law-making function than do their English cousins, being at least as interested in laying down guide-lines for the future as in deciding the cases before them correctly.

FINALITY

In England, appeals terminate litigation, subject only to the possibility of further review in a higher court or a retrial in the court below. Rehearings are not permitted in any type of case. Even new trials are prohibited in criminal cases: if an error is found which the reviewing court cannot classify as harmless, it has no alternative but to quash the conviction and set the accused free. There is no federal system to create conflicts between different jurisdictions and thus permit successive applications for the same relief to different tribunals. There is no expansion of the writ of habeas corpus or any similar remedy in such a way as to allow the re-examination of judgments rendered by legally constituted tribunals acting within their jurisdiction. Finally, the doctrine of precedent is sufficiently rigid to render pointless any re-litigation of a question once unequivocally decided. If a citizen is unhappy about the law, he had better seek corrective action in Parliament rather than squander his wealth on hopeless litigation.

In the United States, appellate decisions possess less finality. New trials can be granted in all types of cases, criminal as well as civil. Rehearings are frequently asked and occasionally allowed. Existing side by side with appeals are a variety of methods of collateral attack, including habeas corpus, sometimes entailing successive re-examination of a single case by courts of co-ordinate jurisdiction.

* * *

The oral argument has been a part of English procedure for centuries. Oral arguments are considerably more extensive than in courts of appeal in the United States. Considerable time is spent by American lawyers in the preparation of written briefs which contain arguments and requests. They are read by the judges (in theory and usually in practice) before the oral hearing. The oral hearing in America usually is strictly limited to a designated number of minutes, often 20 to 30. No such limitation is placed on the English barrister appearing in the Court of Appeal. Lord Denning has suggested that considerable pressure was placed on him while he was Master of Rolls to adopt the United States system, but that he continuously resisted such change.

His belief, and that held by many English jurists, is that an open dialogue is the best way of reaching correct decisions. But that creates an issue of how extensively the appellate judge should participate in the oral process. When should the judge begin asking questions and how many should be asked? The generally accepted procedure in England is to allow the barrister to present the case until legitimate questions are raised from the oral presentation. Since many of the judges have not read any of the papers beforehand, they do not enter the court room with predetermined questions which they are lying in wait to ask. If a judge begins to raise questions early in the oral argument, then counsel may feel that the judge had predetermined the result from reading papers before the oral hearing.

One problem that obviously arises with the relatively unlimited appellate oral hearing in England is stopping counsel who speaks far too long. Lord Denning suggests that "The best method is to sit quiet and say nothing. Let him run down. Show no interest in what he is saying. Once you show any interest, he will start off again."[6] Denning offers other methods as well:

> ... Other methods have their uses. Take a few hints from Touchstone. There is the *Retort courteous:* 'I think we have that point, Mr. Smith'. There is the *Quip modest:* When counsel complained that he had been stopped by the Judge below, the Master of the Rolls said, 'How did he do that, Mr. Smith?' 'By falsely pretending to be "with me"', was the answer. There is the *Reply churlish:* 'You must give us credit for a little intelligence, Mr. Smith'. To which you may get the answer, 'That was the mistake I made in the Court below'. Next there is the *Reproof valiant:* When the advocate said, 'I am sorry to be taking up so much of Your Lordship's time'—'Time, Mr. Smith', said the Master of the Rolls, 'You've exhausted time and trespassed upon eternity'. Next there is the *Countercheck quarrelsome:* 'You've said that three times already'. Finally the *Lie circumstantial* and the *Lie direct:* 'We cannot listen to you any longer. We will give judgment now'. Against him.[7]

6. Lord Denning, The Family Story 205   **7.** Id.
(1981).

The unreserved or "off-the-cuff" judgments have been the mark of the Court of Appeal, but increasingly judgments are reserved, as is the practice in the House of Lords.

The need for law clerks largely is absent in England. Since extensive briefs are not used and judges render their opinions extemporaneously upon completion of oral argument, clerks serve little purpose prior to the appeal. Nor are they later needed, as it is the law reporters who check the facts and citations and make the cases more readable, not law clerks. But the law reporter has a far more important role in the English system. He determines which decisions will be published in Law Reports, and thus join the accessible fabric of the common law of England.

There are few appellate judges in England—some two to three dozen on the Court of Appeal and House of Lords. They all sit in London. The appellate process is highly centralized. But the process does not require the presence of the clients, it is a written and oral documentary process. The centralization and limited number of judges does offer a consistency in decision making generally absent in the United States, further enhanced by the process of appointing appellate judges, discussed earlier, which creates a judiciary more consistently competent than in common law systems where judicial selection more closely approximates that in the United States.

The relatively small number of judges in England is made possible by the limited frequency of appeal. Although the incidence of appeal has been increasing troublesomely in the last decade, nevertheless it is correct to note that there remains a greater public belief in England than in the United States that issues are dealt with competently at lower levels and that there is little likelihood of a reversal on appeal. The recent increase in appeals has placed a substantial burden on the appellate court structure, and it has altered the nature of lower court proceedings. The preservation of the right to appeal and its documentation has assumed an important role in the course of the trial stage.

Notes and Questions

1. The appeal to the House of Lords is really a second appeal. There is one Court of Appeal and one House of Lords, meaning the House of Lords in perhaps five percent of the cases before the Court of Appeal revisits the exact same issues the Court of Appeal considered. A second opinion may be appropriate in advance of a prostectomy or mastectomy, but is it appropriate after a panel of Court of Appeal judges have rendered their opinion? For a system which places a premium on the costs of legal services delivered, is the House of Lords simply redundant?

2. An oral process may be appropriate for itinerant justices sitting in rural provinces where it is impossible to adequately provide the justices with written submissions before they arrive. Perhaps the most important question is less the orality of presenting the lower court record, which is increasingly accomplished by written process, than the limitations on oral presentation of the reasons for the appeal. Where briefs are used, is it

appropriate to save the best for oral argument? If all the arguments are presented in the brief, why give even 20 minutes to present the case? If the briefs have been read, would not the time be best used for questioning and debate? The English system seems to preserve time for debate. Is that debate in the form of the drunk using the lamppost, more for support than illumination?

Chapter 13

LEGAL RULES IN ENGLAND

SECTION 1. SOURCES OF LAW

Sources of law pertain not to how an ordinary citizen believes his conduct is governed, but to where courts look in determining what legal rules are applicable to resolve a specific dispute. Tradition often separates sources into written and unwritten. It is a confusing distinction, intended to contrast laws which have been formally enacted from those which have not been enacted, the latter including judicial decisions and customs, and, important in English law, conventions and the royal prerogative. The variety of sources of English law attest to its nature as a *method* of administering justice.

Classification of sources is less important than their assigned values, particularly when the sources represent conflicting rules. How judges perceive the value of different sources additionally affects the manner in which they will apply a governing source of law. Value allocation to sources within a system is a slow, evolutionary process. English judges traditionally have been less inclined to defer unquestioningly to legislation, particularly social reform legislation, than United States judges.[1] Disdain for social legislation has diminished slowly. The legal profession in England has bred an independent and pervasive sense of what is right. Paramount is a sensitivity for preserving an individual right to contract freely and to alienate property. Social change is thought to be introduced appropriately through the adaptation of precedent to new circumstances, not by means of legislation. The judiciary believes that due accord to social changes is illustrated by the development of common law decisions. Although there is no dispute that legislation is the source of law which has authority over all other sources, and that legislation increasingly is assuming the major role as a source of law, the fabric of the common law is its precedent, and the vast number of volumes of "unwritten" law is the foremost distinguishing feature of the common law tradition.

---

1. The Law Commission in England, charged with the development and reform of law, has not always been favorably viewed. Its suggestion in 1966 that it might extensively codify the law brought sharp criticism. See H. Hahlo, Here Lies the Common Law: Rest in Peace, 30 Modern L.Rev. 241 (1967).

SECTION 2. PRECEDENT

A. REPORTING OF CASES

In any legal system, what judges have said in addressing issues in earlier disputes is likely to be of interest in subsequent cases with similar facts. If a judge assumes that earlier decisions in his court and in higher courts were dealt with competently, there is no reason to suppose, in the absence of changed circumstances, that a similar result would be inappropriate. Continuity and predictability of the law are positive attributes. The theoretical *usefulness* of prior case law should not be any less in a legal system where judges do not have to follow earlier decisions, than where they are compelled to follow them, presupposing access to the substantive law in the earlier cases through an effective reporting system.

Precedents are only as functional as their reporting. If reports were not available, precedent would have little value. Courts might refer to previous decisions judges recalled, but there would be little value in the system to decisions which could not be used by advocates as well as judges. Who reports cases and what they contain thus are questions which should be considered before discussing the binding nature of case law and judicial interpretation of prior decisions.

English law reports developed very slowly, without government participation. They continue to be the product of a private enterprise system which chooses which cases shall be reported, often on the basis of the economics of including a particular judgment. Yearbooks developed in the late 13th century, consisting essentially of notes compiled by advocates, but under no pretext that they were to be used by judges as precedent. Still, they were used for that purpose occasionally, increasingly so by the 15th century. When publication of the yearbooks ceased, private reports were produced, initially under the name of the particular law reporter. They proliferated for three centuries until, in the mid–19th century, a semiofficial council was formed for the purpose of reporting cases in England and Wales. Their Law Reports, which have now replaced most of the private series, are not the exclusive location for the publication of cases, but convention suggests that they are the reports which should be referred to when citing decisions.

The system of reporting is less formal than in the United States. In both nations, the publishing of decisions is left to private enterprise, but there is considerable difference in the official status of reports, in how decisions are selected for reporting, in the form of the decision rendered by the judges and in the volume of case reporting. Dawson outlines some of the unique attributes of the English system, and how it differs from the United States method.

J. DAWSON, "THE ORACLES OF THE LAW"

83 (1968).*

Thus the responsibility of English judges in reporting the results of their work is for the most part indirect and disguised. Where written opinions are drafted by the judges themselves, as is now usual practice in decisions by the House of Lords, reporters presumably take fewer liberties. But most opinions in other courts, even at the intermediate appellate level, are still delivered extemporaneously at the conclusion of oral argument. It then becomes the reporter's task to ensure that these oral comments are reduced to readable English. Through usage, not rule, drafts of opinions that have been selected for inclusion in the Law Reports are submitted to the judges for criticism and comment. The opportunity thus given to edit the drafts before publication makes it possible to describe them as "approved" by the judges. But the extent to which revisions will be suggested depends on the choice of each individual judge, since this aid is bestowed "purely as a matter of grace." On the other hand, many cases are reported, not in this approved series (one cannot call it an "official" series), but by various private enterprisers with no other safeguard than a certificate by a barrister that he has reported what he heard. Here the only protection is a disclaimer entered later by the judge, asserting that he has been misquoted.

The cases to be included in the Law Reports are selected by the reporters, not by the judges, and the tests for inclusion are rigorous. About 70 per cent of the decisions by the House of Lords and the Privy Council are ordinarily reported, but in the Court of Appeal only about 25 per cent appear in the "approved" series. More surprising is the freedom of the reporters to omit passages that they consider dicta or of no lasting interest to the profession; such surgery can be used even on written opinions in the House of Lords. It does seem true that "Having a considerable measure of control over what cases are to be published and in what form, [the reporter] determines to a very large extent the content of English case law for the future."

As conceptions of precedent have petrified, the rigorous tests of the authorized reporters have raised problems of another kind. Many cases that they decide to exclude are reported in other series with no review by the judges, the only requirement being that they be vouched for by a barrister. Proposals to restrict or eliminate these competing series were rejected by the Chancellor's Commission on Law Reporting in 1940, as striking at the base of "one of the pillars of freedom, that the administration of justice must be public." But cases reported outside the authorized series are considered binding in the same degree as those appearing in the authorized series. So are decisions that have never been published anywhere but are filed in the form of stenographer's

* Reprinted with permission of John P.   Law School.
Dawson and the University of Michigan

transcripts in the library of the high court, where they are available to all barristers and to others by special permission. They are "unexploded land mines, ready to do damage." To defuse them somewhat Arthur Goodhart in 1940 offered a compromise—that official shorthand reporters transcribe all opinions delivered in courts of record and that their transcripts be promptly reviewed by the judges. This proposal was rejected by the Chancellor's Committee on Law Reporting on the grounds that it would be too costly, would impose on the judges an additional burden, and as unnecessary anyway, since the competition of reporters in the market preserves all that is worth preserving, and the residue is "a rubbish heap in which a jewel will rarely, if ever, be discovered."

The study of history has one disadvantage, that it revives old ghosts. Modern English discussions of the law reports seem at times to recall the image of a small group of men all wearing the coif, engaged in intimate colloquy in a fenced enclave of Westminster Hall. In the scene envisaged it would not matter if judges spoke hastily or were grossly misquoted. It surely would then be "purely as a matter of grace" that a judge would correct a summary of his remarks that had been noted down by some ready learner. Such corrections would serve no great purpose in any event, for what was said or done in a particular case counted little in the sum of transmitted doctrine. The scheme for law reporting that has now been in use in England for 100 years was adopted when a radical change in attitudes was already well under way. Its adoption was entirely due to the initiative taken by the bar, motivated primarily by its own self-interest. The bar retains important control through the editing by its nominal agents, the authorized reporters, and still more through the freedom of individual barristers to select and report, without any editing by the judges, whatever they find to be worth reporting. These haphazard methods and diffused responsibilities seem a strange survival when matched against the vastly increased power that the pronouncements of English judges have now acquired.

In methods of law reporting, as in other ways that our case law is administered, a different course has been followed in the United States. Many reasons explain the great and widening gulf between England and the United States that became apparent late in the nineteenth century. Without attempting to assign all the reasons, one can note the lack of legal training of many early American judges, the distrust of the judiciary that was often expressed, the great dearth of books, an open, undifferentiated and undisciplined bar, the involvement of courts in public law issues, the novelty of many of the problems they faced. In an environment so different, conceptions of precedent and of the responsibility of judges were certain to differ. Without the protective screen of a small, expert, and closely allied bar, American courts stood out in greater isolation, while their creative role was more evident.

In law reporting the American states for a time followed the English example and relied on private enterprise. The first published book of law reports appeared in Connecticut in 1789, giving cases decided in the previous four years. In Massachusetts, New York, Pennsylvania, North and South Carolina, and Virginia series appeared in the near neighborhood of 1800. These were produced by private individuals, though some were "authorized" in the sense that the judges gave them close cooperation or reviewed the product. Very soon, however, statutes in several states provided for the appointment of official reporters who were usually paid a modest stipend with a share in the profits of public sale. By 1810 four states had adopted this expedient; by 1835, sixteen. In several states where official reporters had not been appointed, judges of appellate courts published reports on their own initiative. By 1850 substantially all states then members of the Union had assigned to their highest appellate courts official reporters whose purely ministerial duty it was to publish opinions that the judges had written.

The struggle that ensued was not over the desirability of written, as against oral, opinions but over the demands made on appellate courts that they file written opinions in *every* case. By 1830 statutes had been passed in at least six states imposing this requirement. A few courts retaliated by declaring such statutes to be unconstitutional as interferences with the judicial function. In other states legislatures were persuaded to concede some discretion to appellate courts in selecting the cases that were sufficiently novel or important to require written opinions. But the main tendency has been to preserve and extend the requirement, even to reinforce it by constitutional provisions. The net result now is that 29 states, 15 by constitution and 14 by statute, require their highest courts to write opinions in *all* cases in which they render final decisions. In the other states practice varies widely as to the percentage of cases decided by appellate courts without explanatory opinions. In New York this percentage is exceptionally high, in the neighborhood of 70 per cent. We have shown no disposition to follow France, Germany, and Italy in imposing the requirement of written opinions on trial courts as well. But it is clear everywhere that if opinions of any of our high courts are published the responsibility for writing them and the choice whether or not to publish them (where there is any choice) resides in the deciding court. We conceive this responsibility to be attached to the office, one that cannot be discharged through intermediaries.

One thesis of this study will be that on the continent of Europe officially published judicial decisions—an invention essentially of the nineteenth century—have transformed the relationship of courts to other agencies for legal development, both by compelling judges to participate in reasoned exposition of legal rules and by fixing on them direct responsibility for the reasons they are required to publish. This form of accountability for the public authority they exercise has been imposed on courts by deliberate political decision after extended public debate, as it has been in many American states. The burden imposed on continental judges, trial as well as appellate, is a heavy one. It can be justified in part by the value of published reasons as a guarantee of consistency and conformity to law but still more by the incentive to thoughtfulness and care that is supplied where the decision-maker must dredge up the reasons that were persuasive to him and place them in writing on his own responsibility, whether they are published or not. In England it was no novelty for judges to be expositors of legal rules or to state their reasons in public. It seemed a minor change, though it implied some recognition of their own duty to a wider public, when English judges on their own initiative undertook in the early nineteenth century to appoint "authorized" reporters. When this device failed and the bar took over the reporting function, the cooperation of judges with reporters named by the bar was still conceived as wholly voluntary. But a judge who had had an opportunity to review a draft prepared by one of these reporters would no doubt find it difficult to enter a subsequent disclaimer. The net result is that English judges, by a transition that was almost imperceptible, came to assume full responsibility for the reports they had "authorized." Without contest and indeed with almost no discussion they became directly accountable for what they do, and—still more important—for what they say.

———

The format of reporting largely determines its usefulness as precedent. Effective employment as precedent is possible only where a decision is reported in a form which makes it usable by judges in future cases. The form of reporting has thus tended to develop in a style which assures the utility of these private ventures. Reported cases in England, as in the United States, briefly outline the facts and the legal issue which has been presented, and give reasons, often quite lengthy, for reaching a particular decision. But in English cases, facts are perceived differently than in the United States. Factual differentiation often is carried to an extreme in the United States, certainly more than in England. English precedent consequently is more likely to serve as a forceful value in future cases.

The number of reported decisions in the United States far exceeds that in England. That is to be expected. The United States is not only much larger, and more litigious, but the federal system adds an overlay of federal cases to the myriad of state decisions. The largest states add more than a dozen volumes a year to the already immense aggregate of reports, and the federal courts produce an additional 50–60 annually.[2] Many of the reported cases in the United States merely add additional cites to long held legal principles. The English system tends to add only cases which make some contribution to the development of the law, whether it is to further a principle or a retrenchment. The duplication of precedent on the same principle adds to the cost of litigation. Lawyers must research the repetitive cases and may be compelled to distinguish each one from the fact situation at hand. Considerable reliance is

2. Additional cases not published in bound fashion exist due to such services as   WESTLAW.

placed on services which digest case principles, and the product of most research of practicing lawyers is only as effective as the preparation of the digests. How much valuable precedent is overlooked in the bloated reporter system remains unknown.

That a system has reported decisions, which is increasingly an attribute of civil law as well as common law systems, does not therefore mean they are valued by the system *pari passu* with another legal system. They may not have value within the system in deciding future cases. Or they may have some value but not as we perceive that value in the United States. Decisions in civil law nations often refer to earlier cases as "teaching" something. But this does not mean the judge is compelled to learn the principle, or if he does learn it to apply it in his own case. Even within one system, precedential value may vary depending on the court which has rendered the decision, and the relationship of the court which rendered the decision to the court which is asked to consider it.

Where precedent has value assigned by the system, a characteristic most associated with the common law tradition, some general rules tend to exist. The decisions of lower courts are not binding on higher courts. The decisions of higher courts are binding on lower courts—at least the decisions of the *highest* are binding on lower courts. The more difficult question is whether the decisions of one court are binding on that same court in the future, and if that is a divisional court at a particular level, whether the decisions, if binding on the same division, are also binding on other divisions. The rules in the English system will illustrate both that they differ from those in the United States, and expectedly from civil law systems, and that they are rules in motion—changing to meet the demands of the times.

B. THE BINDING NATURE OF CASES

The binding nature of past cases, what we call *stare rationibus decidendis,* or more commonly but less accurately, *stare decisis,* functions more easily in a unified court hierarchy. If all matters come before a single court of appeal, there is less likelihood that the judges of that court will not follow a previous decision in their court, or a higher appellate court, than where the decision was rendered in a court of appeal on a similar level, or even higher level, in a separate hierarchy. Certainly, a case is more likely to be offered as binding when it is a case of similar substantive issues—the opportunity for a case in one hierarchy, for example the labor court hierarchy, to present rules which are relevant to resolve a case in another, for example the civil hierarchy, occurs with limited frequency. But it does occur, and the single hierarchy affords an easier aggregate forum for the development of rules of *stare decisis.* In considering the binding nature of decisions in the English system, one should consider, therefore, how such rules might be applied in a civil law or socialist law system, as well as how they have developed in the United States.

To start at the top one might refer to the decisions of the European Court of Justice and their binding nature on English courts. But this discussion is deferred to Section 8 of this Chapter, where several unique aspects of that court as a source of law to a common law system will be considered. We start rather with the House of Lords. Its decisions are binding on lower courts. No one seriously questions this rule. It is a respect for higher judicial authority and is followed not only throughout the common law systems, but has close parallels in many civil law systems. For decades it was assumed that the House of Lords would follow its own decisions. In 1898 it held that it was bound by its own decisions.[3] However subject to criticism over the years, this remained a firm rule. But in 1966 the Lord Chancellor announced a reversal of this policy.

> Their Lordships regard the use of precedent as an indispensable foundation upon which to decide what is the law and its application to individual cases. It provides at least some degree of certainty upon which individuals can rely in the conduct of their affairs, as well as a basis for orderly development of legal rules.

> Their Lordships nevertheless recognise that too rigid adherence to precedent may lead to injustice in a particular case and also unduly restrict the proper development of the law. They propose therefore to modify their present practice and, while treating former decisions of this House as normally binding, to depart from a previous decision when it appears right to do so.

> In this connection they will bear in mind the danger of disturbing retrospectively the basis on which contracts, settlements of property and fiscal arrangements have been entered into and also the especial need for certainty as to the criminal law.

> This announcement is not intended to affect the use of precedent elsewhere than in this House.[4]

The foregoing announcement was generally supported by the press and the Bar. Made to allow the House of Lords to consider more favorably well-reasoned decisions of the superior courts than earlier decisions of its own judges, and to allow the judges to consider changed conditions, it was not expected to have an early and momentous effect on the substance of English law. There have been few instances of reliance on the new rule. The Lord Chancellor and the Law Lords retained no list of decisions which they were waiting to overrule. Nor have the Law Lords been ready to overrule past decisions solely because they thought they had been decided incorrectly. They have rather expressed the idea

---

3. London Tramways v. London County Council [1898] A.C. 375. The decision affirmed what was the view generally believed to have existed since the decision in Beamish v. Beamish (1861) 9 H.L.C. 274.

4. Practice Statement [1966] 1 W.L.R. 1234.

that there should exist some broad issue of justice or public policy, not the construction of complicated provisions of a statute.[5]

That the House of Lords might consider following a Court of Appeal or even lower High Court opinion, rather than an earlier opinion of its own, may be partly attributable to the greater homogeneity of the English courts than is characteristic of many other common law systems. Homogeneity should be understood here in the sense that the judges are all cut from the same cloth. They have been eminent barristers, usually Queen's Counsels. We may think someone qualified to be on a federal district court, or even the court of appeals, but not the Supreme Court. That is much less said about English judges, though it is the more able who work their way up to the Court of Appeal and to the House of Lords. But, as noted above in discussing the House of Lords as a judicial institution, some believe the Court of Appeal to be the more important court in the sense of handing down more decisions which retain lasting influence. That is not so in the United States, due largely to geography. In England there is one Court of Appeal for the whole nation. It is located in London. It is thus much like the House of Lords. But in the United States there are many courts of appeal. The important decisions are widely spread among them. Were we to have a single court of appeal in Washington, might it not have the elevated prestige possessed by the Court of Appeal in England?

We are not suggesting that the House of Lords is in any way bound by decisions of the Court of Appeal. The position of the Lords is that it recognizes that the binding nature of decisions of any court has a potential for creating mischief in the rational development of the law. The Lords prefer to be free to follow good decisions, not any decisions tied less to the value of the substance of the decision, than to the level of the court which rendered the decision. We should note, however, that the direction of the Law Lords is not to say: we do not wish to follow previous decisions of our court so that we may say anything we wish, but so that we may consider decisions of other tribunals which have put forth valuable and appropriate interpretations of the law. Of course the court will go beyond its own decisions and those of lower courts. The Practice Statement was meant to allow the Law Lords to consider the needs of society over time. But the reference to wanting to also consider decisions of other, lower English courts illustrates the pull of precedent in shaping new policy. It emphasizes the value we place on precedent, even though we may wish to reject it as mandating compliance.

Only brief note need be made regarding the obligation of lower courts to follow the dictates of the highest court, and generally any court higher than the one rendering the decision. But if the court of appeal next closest to the court whose decisions are at issue is very close to the

---

5. Jones v. Secretary of State for Social Services [1972] 1 A.C. 944, interpreting a statute previously interpreted in In Re Dowling [1967] 1 A.C. 725. See also Herrington v. British Railways Board [1972] A.C. 877; Miliangos [1976] A.C. 443; Fitzleet Estates v. Cherry [1977] 1 W.L.R. 1345; Johanna Oldendorff [1974] A.C. 479; Vestey v. I.R.C. [1980] A.C. 1148.

higher court in the respect given to the former's decisions and the homogeneity of its judges, and if the lower court is a single national court in the same location as the highest court, perhaps there is a greater likelihood that the lower court will be inclined at times to ignore, if not actually and untactfully reject, the highest court's decisions. This has occurred in England, in the rulings of a self-admitted "turbulent judge"—Lord Denning. In *Broome v. Cassell,* the Court of Appeal held unanimously that the House of Lords had been wrong in an earlier decision.[6] Lord Denning comments on his experience; he was one of the justices on the Court of Appeal.

LORD DENNING, "THE DISCIPLINE OF LAW"
310 (1979).*

In my judgment I had ventured to criticise some of the reasoning in the House in *Rookes v. Barnard* about exemplary damages. I put it much too strongly. After detailing my reasons, I said:

'All this leads me to the conclusion that, if ever there was a decision of the House of Lords given per incuriam, this was it. The explanation is that the House, as a matter of legal theory, thought that exemplary damages had no place in the civil code, and ought to be eliminated from it; but as they could not be eliminated altogether, they ought to be confined within the strictest possible limits, no matter how illogical those limits were'.

I am sorry that I ever said it. It earned for me a severe rebuke by the House of Lords. They specially convened seven Law Lords to hear the appeal.[2] But, in mitigation, I may say that they appreciated the difficulties which had been presented by *Rookes v. Barnard.* Viscount Dilhorne went so far as to dissent from it. He thought it was in conflict with a previous decision of the House of Lords and that the *Rookes v. Barnard* approach was wrong. In addition Lord Wilberforce gave convincing reasons for thinking that the legal theory underlying *Rookes v. Barnard* was wrong. He said:

'... It cannot lightly be taken for granted, even as a matter of theory, that the purpose of the law of tort is compensation, still less that it ought to be ... or that there is something inappropriate or illogical or anomalous (a question-begging word) in including a punitive element in civil damages, ...'.

and he said:

'My Lords, I think there was much merit in what I understand was the older system, before *Rookes v. Barnard* [1964] AC 1129. I agree with the Court of Appeal that in substance, though not perhaps philosophically or linguistically, this was clear and as ex-

6. [1971] 2 Q.B. 354.   **2.** [1972] A.C. 1027.

* Reprinted here and below with permission of Butterworth & Co. (Publishers) Ltd.

plained above I doubt if there was any confusion as to what the jury should do'.

Added to those wise words, there is the fact that Canada, Australia and the United States have retained the doctrine of exemplary damages as previously understood and have not been led away along the path of *Rookes v. Barnard*.

* * *

. . . If you read the speeches of the seven in *Cassell & Co Ltd (No. 2) v. Broome* you will see that they saw the difficulties presented by *Rookes v. Barnard*. Yet all but one of them felt they were bound by it. Was it not right for the Court of Appeal to point out those difficulties? So that the House might, if it thought fit, escape from them. I am afraid that my fault lay in my insubordination to the authority of the House. This is what Lord Hailsham of St. Marylebone, the Lord Chancellor, had to say about it: [1]

'. . . I am driven to the conclusion that when the Court of Appeal described the decision in *Rookes v. Barnard* as decided "per incuriam" or "unworkable" they really only meant that they did not agree with it. But, in my view, even if this were not so, it is not open to the Court of Appeal to give gratuitous advice to judges of first instance to ignore decisions of the House of Lords in this way and, if it were open to the Court of Appeal to do so, it would be highly undesirable. The course taken would have put judges of first instance in an embarrassing position, as driving them to take sides in an unedifying dispute between the Court of Appeal or three members of it (for there is no guarantee that other Lords Justices would have followed them and no particular reason why they should) and the House of Lords. But, much worse than this, litigants would not have known where they stood. None could have reached finality short of the House of Lords, and, in the meantime, the task of their professional advisers of advising them either as to their rights, or as to the probable cost of obtaining or defending them, would have been, quite literally, impossible. Whatever the merits, chaos would have reigned until the dispute was settled, and, in legal matters, some degree of certainty is at least as valuable a part of justice as perfection.

'The fact is, and I hope it will never be necessary to say so again, that, in the hierarchical system of courts which exists in this country, it is necessary for each lower tier, including the Court of Appeal, to accept loyally the decisions of the higher tiers. Where decisions manifestly conflict, the decision in *Young v. Bristol Aeroplane Co Ltd* [1944] KB 718 offers guidance to each tier in matters affecting its own decisions. It does not entitle it to question considered decisions in the upper tiers with the same freedom . . .'.

---

1. [1972] A.C. 1072.

Yes—I had been guilty—of lese majesty. I had impugned the authority of the House. That must never be done by anyone save the House itself. Least of all by the turbulent Master of the Rolls.[1]

When we shift the issue of precedent as binding to the next level, that is whether the courts below the highest court are bound by their own decisions, we begin to discover even less established rules. The Court of Appeal in England must follow decisions of the House of Lords. The federal courts of appeal in the United States must follow the decisions of the Supreme Court. But must they follow their own decisions? No absolute rule is present in the United States. Would it be appropriate for one circuit court of appeal to be bound by its own decisions but not by the decisions of other circuits? Does not the system of multiple circuits tend to cause the rule to be less forceful, less binding in mandate? Is the English experience of the Court of Appeal any different from that of United States circuit courts? State courts? The Court of Appeals and House of Lords decisions in *Davis v. Johnson* are addressed to the question of whether the lower appellate court can deviate from its earlier decisions.

DAVIS v. JOHNSON

[1979] A.C. 264.*

[The case involved the interpretation of the Domestic Violence and Matrimonial Proceedings Act 1976. One issue was whether the court was bound by two previous (and quite recent) interpretations of the Act by the same Court of Appeal.]

LORD DENNING M.R.

I turn to the second important point: Can we depart from those two cases? Although convinced that they are wrong, are we at liberty to depart from them? What is the correct practice for this court to follow?

On principle, it seems to me that, while this court should regard itself as normally bound by a previous decision of the court, nevertheless it should be at liberty to depart from it if it is convinced that the previous decision was wrong. What is the argument to the contrary? It is said that if an error has been made, this court has no option but to continue the error and leave it to be corrected by the House of Lords. The answer is this: the House of Lords may never have an opportunity to correct the error: and thus it may be perpetuated indefinitely, perhaps for ever.... It took 60 years before the erroneous decision in *Carlisle and Cumberland Banking Co. v. Bragg* [1911] 1 K.B. 489 was overruled by the House of Lords in *Gallie v. Lee* [1971] A.C. 1004....

1. "Who will free me from this turbulent priest?" (Henry II of Thomas à Becket).

* Reprinted here and below with permission of The Incorporated Council of Law Reporting.

Apart from monetary considerations, there have been many instances where cases have been settled pending an appeal to the House of Lords: or, for one reason or another, not taken there, especially with claims against insurance companies or big employers. When such a body has obtained a decision of this court in its favour, it will buy off an appeal to the House of Lords by paying ample compensation to the appellant. By so doing, it will have a legal precedent on its side which it can use with effect in later cases.... By such means an erroneous decision on a point of law can again be perpetuated for ever. Even if all those objections are put on one side and there is an appeal to the House of Lords, it usually takes 12 months or more for the House of Lords to reach its decision. What then is the position of the lower courts meanwhile? They are in a dilemma. Either they have to apply the erroneous decision of the Court of Appeal, or they have to adjourn all fresh cases to await the decision of the House of Lords. That has often happened. So justice is delayed—and often denied—by the lapse of time before the error is corrected. The present case is a crying instance. If it took the ordinary course of appeals to the House, it would take some months before it was decided. Meanwhile many women would be denied the protection which Parliament intended they should have. They would be subjected to violence without redress: because the judges in the county court would have to say to them: "We are sorry but the Court of Appeal says we have no jurisdiction to help you." We were told that, in this very case, because of the urgency, the House might take special measures to hear it before Christmas. But, even so, I doubt whether they would be able to give their decision until well on in the New Year. In order to avoid all the delay—and the injustice consequent upon it—it seems to me that this court, being convinced that the two previous decisions were wrong, should have the power to correct them and give these women the protection which Parliament intended they should have. It was suggested that, if we did this, the judges in the county court would be in a dilemma. They would not know whether to follow the two previous decisions or the later decision of this court. There would be no such dilemma. They should follow this later decision. Such a position always arises whenever the House of Lords correct an error made by a previous decision. The lower courts, of course, follow the latest decision. The general rule is that, where there are conflicting decisions of courts of co-ordinate jurisdiction, the later decision is to be preferred, if it is reached after full consideration of the earlier decision ....

So much for principle. But what about our precedents? What about *Young v. Bristol Aeroplane Co. Ltd.* [1944] K.B. 718?

I will first state the position as it was before the year 1944. The Court of Appeal in its present form was established in 1873. It was then the final court of appeal. Appeals to the House of Lords were abolished by that Act and only restored a year or two later. The Court of Appeal inherited the jurisdiction of the previous courts of appeal such as the Exchequer Chamber and the Court of Appeal in Chancery. Those earlier courts had always had power to reconsider and review the law as laid down in previous decisions: and, if that law was found to be wrong, to correct it: but without disturbing the actual decision....

* * *

The change came about in 1944. In *Young v. Bristol Aeroplane Co. Ltd.* [1944] K.B. 718 the court overruled the practice of a century. Lord Greene M.R., sitting with a court of five, laid down that this court is bound to follow its previous decision as well as those of courts of coordinate jurisdiction: subject to only three exceptions: (i) where there are two conflicting decisions, (ii) where a previous decision cannot stand with a decision of the House of Lords, (iii) if a previous decision was given per incuriam.

It is to be noticed that the court laid down that proposition as a rule of law. That was quite the contrary of what Lord Esher had declared in *The Vera Cruz* in 1884. He said it arose only as a matter of judicial comity.

Events have proved that in this respect Lord Esher was right and Lord Greene was wrong. I say this because the House of Lords in 1898 had held itself bound by its own previous decisions as a rule of law: see *London Street Tramways Co. Ltd. v. London County Council* .... But yet in 1966 it discarded that rule....

* * *

That shows conclusively that a rule as to precedent (which any court lays down for itself) is not a rule of law at all. It is simply a practice of usage laid down by the court itself for its own guidance: and, as such, the successors of that court can alter that practice or amend it or set up other guide lines, just as the House of Lords did in 1966. Even as the judges in *Young v. Bristol Aeroplane Co. Ltd.* ... thought fit to discard the practice of a century and declare a new practice or usage, so we in 1977 can discard the guide lines of 1944 and set up new guide lines of our own or revert to the old practice laid down by Lord Esher. Nothing said in the House of Lords, before or since, can stop us from doing so. Anything said about it there must needs be obiter dicta....

* * *

So I suggest that we are entitled to lay down new guide lines. To my mind, this court should apply similar guide lines to those adopted by the House of Lords in 1966. Whenever it appears to this court that a previous decision was wrong, we should be at liberty to depart from it if we think it right to do so. Normally—in nearly every case of course—we would adhere to it. But in an exceptional case we are at liberty to depart from it.

* * *

The truth is that the list of exceptions from *Young v. Bristol Aeroplane Co. Ltd.* ... is now getting so large that they are in process of eating up the rule itself: and we would do well simply to follow the same practice as the House of Lords.

* * *

CUMMING-BRUCE L.J. . . .

* * *

. . . It seems to me that in any system of law the undoubted public advantages of certainty in civil proceedings must be purchased at the price of the risk of injustice in difficult individual situations. I would think that the present practice holds the balance just about right. . . . I consider that we are bound to act in accordance with the practice as stated in *Young's* case and *Morelle's* case [1955] 2 Q.B. 379. This is because I consider that the constitutional functions of their Lordships sitting in their judicial capacity includes the function of declaring with authority the extent to which the Court of Appeal is bound by its previous decisions, and the function of defining with authority the exceptional situations in which it is open to this court to depart from a previous decision. . . .

[On appeal, the 3–2 decision favoring Lord Denning's view did not fare well. The five Law Lords rejected the idea that the Court of Appeal did not have to follow its own rulings.]

DAVIS v. JOHNSON

[1979] A.C. 317.*

LORD DIPLOCK . . .

* * *

So far as civil matters are concerned the law upon this question is now clear and unassailable. It has been so for more than 30 years. I do not find it necessary to trace the origin and development of the doctrine of stare decisis before the present structure of the courts was created in 1875. In that structure the Court of Appeal in civil actions has always played, save in a few exceptional matters, an intermediate and not a final appellate role. . . .

* * *

. . . In an appellate court of last resort a balance must be struck between the need on the one side for the legal certainty resulting from the binding effect of previous decisions, and, on the other side the avoidance of undue restriction on the proper development of the law. In the case of an intermediate appellate court, however, the second desideratum can be taken care of by appeal to a superior appellate court, if reasonable means of access to it are available; while the risk to the first desideratum, legal certainty, if the court is not bound by its own previous decisions grows even greater with increasing membership and

* Reprinted with permission of The Incorporated Council of Law Reporting.

the number of three-judge divisions in which it sits .... So the balance does not lie in the same place as in the case of a court of last resort. That is why the Lord Chancellor's announcement about the future attitude towards precedent of the House of Lords in its judicial capacity concluded with the words: "This announcement is not intended to affect the use of precedent elsewhere than in this House."

Much has been said in the instant case about the delay and expense which would have been involved if the Court of Appeal had treated itself as bound by its previous decision ..., so as to make it necessary for the respondent to come to this House to argue that those decisions should be overruled. But a similar reasoning could also be used to justify any High Court or county court judge in refusing to follow a decision of the Court of Appeal which he thought was wrong....

* * *

In my opinion, this House should take this occasion to re-affirm expressly, unequivocally and unanimously that the rule laid down in the *Bristol Aeroplane* case ... as to stare decisis is still binding on the Court of Appeal.

* * *

Viscount Dilhorne. ...

* * *

In 1966 consideration was given to whether as a matter of law this House was bound to follow its earlier decision. After considerable discussion it was agreed that it was not, and so the announcement to which my noble and learned friend refers was made. "If the House of Lords is not bound by its previous decision, why should we be?" so the argument runs, an argument that could be advanced in every court of record in the land, but an argument which ignores the unique character of the House of Lords sitting judicially. It is a character not possessed by any other court and herein lies the fallacy in the argument. This House is not bound by any previous decision to which it may have come. It can, if it wishes, reach a contrary conclusion. This is so whether or not the House is sitting to discharge its judicial functions. This is the ground on which those who were parties to the announcement made in 1966 felt, I think, that it could be made without impropriety. It is not a ground available to any other court and the fact that this House made that announcement is consequently no argument which can properly be advanced to support the view that the Court of Appeal or any other court has similar liberty of action.

* * *

Lord Kilbrandon. ...

* * *

My Lords, I do not find it necessary to add anything to what has been said by my noble and learned friends on the subjects of the handling of precedents by the Court of Appeal, and of judicial reference to the Parliamentary debates. I entirely agree with their opinions.

* * *

LORD SALMON. . . .

* * *

I am afraid that I disagree with Lord Denning M.R. when he says that the Court of Appeal is not absolutely bound by its own decisions and may depart from them just as your Lordships may depart from yours. As my noble and learned friend Lord Diplock has pointed out, the announcement made in 1966 by Lord Gardiner L.C. about the future attitudes of this House towards precedent ended with the words: "This announcement is not intended to affect the use of precedent elsewhere than in this House." I would also point out that that announcement was made with the unanimous approval of all the Law Lords: and that, by contrast, the overwhelming majority of the present Lords Justices have expressed the view that the principle of stare decisis still prevails and should continue to prevail in the Court of Appeal. I do not understand how, in these circumstances, it is even arguable that it does not.

I sympathise with the views expressed on this topic by Lord Denning M.R., but until such time, if ever, as all his colleagues in the Court of Appeal agree with those views, stare decisis must still hold the field. I think that this may be no bad thing. There are now as many as 17 Lords Justices in the Court of Appeal, and I fear that if stare decisis disappears from that court there is a real risk that there might be a plethora of conflicting decisions which would create a state of irremediable confusion and uncertainty in the law. This would do far more harm than the occasional unjust result which stare decisis sometimes produces but which can be remedied by an appeal to your Lordships' House. I recognise, as Cumming–Bruce L.J. points out, that only those who qualify for legal aid or the very rich can afford to bring such an appeal. This difficulty could however be surmounted if when the Court of Appeal gave leave to appeal from a decision it has felt bound to make by an authority with which it disagreed, it had a power conferred on it by Parliament to order the appellants' and/or the respondents' costs of the appeal to be paid out of public funds. This would be a very rare occurrence and the consequent expenditure of public funds would be minimal.

* * *

LORD SCARMAN. . . .

* * *

. . . I have had the advantage of reading in draft the speeches of my noble and learned friends, Lord Diplock and Viscount Dilhorne. I agree with what my Lord, Lord Diplock, has said on the principle of stare decisis in the Court of Appeal.

———

The above decisions of the Court of Appeal and House of Lords illustrate another point of comparison in *stare decisis* in England and the United States. The English decisions contain several opinions. That is the common practice. From which does one draw the principle of the case, the *ratio decidendi?* There is no common opinion, a fact which also is true of the Divisional Court decisions.

R. CROSS, "THE RATIO DECIDENDI AND A PLURALITY OF SPEECHES IN THE HOUSE OF LORDS"

93 Law Quarterly Rev. 378, 379 (1977).*

There is of course no trouble when each of several speeches, or a majority of several speeches, contain the same *ratio decidendi* and this is what usually happens, but difficulties begin to arise when, although several speeches concur in a particular conclusion, they each treat different facts as material. "How," asks Professor Goodhart, "do we determine the principle of a case in which there are several opinions which agree as to the result, but differ on the material facts on which they are based?" His answer is that "The principle of the case is limited to the sum of all the facts held to be material by the various judges." Literally construed, this answer cannot always be right for it would mean that if a majority was in favour of a broad ratio based on facts A, B and C, while the minority favoured a narrower ratio which included fact D, the broad ratio would not be authoritative. When more than one judgment is delivered it is simpler, and more in accordance with the practice of the courts in determining the *ratio decidendi* of a case, to do one's sums in terms of the *rationes decidendi* of the different judges.

Where there is no majority in favour of a particular ratio, it is difficult to escape the conclusion that a case is only authority for what it actually decides. What else can be said of a case decided by a House of Lords with five members unanimously in favour of judgment for the plaintiff, when ratio A is propounded in two of the speeches, ratio B in two others which declare ratio A to be unacceptable, while the fifth speech not only propounds ratio C but also dissents from ratios A and B? There are three *rationes decidendi,* but none with any claim to be described as that of the House of Lords. What of a case heard by a House of Lords with five members in which five points are raised by the appellant and each law lord is for the appellant on a different point though against him on the other four? According to the English practice

* Reprinted with permission of Sweet & Maxwell Ltd.

the appellant will win though he lost four to one on each of the points. Lord Simonds is said to have described this as a "familiar proposition." I am inclined to think that this was one of the few occasions on which his Lordship was guilty of hyperbole, but the mere reference to such a possibility is thought-provoking. It is open to question whether the result can be said to be just *inter partes,* and it is doubtful whether the performance as a whole could be of much assistance in the development of the law. There would be five *rationes decidendi,* each of them condemned by four out of five law lords. A lower court could presumably choose between them, or, if it could conjure up a sixth rule, apply that one, provided always that the facts of the case before it were reasonably distinguishable from those which gave rise to the litigation before the House of Lords.

* * *

A Law Lord should always have his consumers in mind, and his principal consumers are practitioners and less exalted judges who are certainly more busy and probably less learned than he is. This is especially true of the Law Lord called upon to give judgment on the criminal law and he should bear in mind the following remarks in the report of the Donovan Committee on the Court of Criminal Appeal:

> "It is of considerable advantage, we think, that those who have to administer the criminal law and who are bound by the decisions of the Court of Criminal Appeal should have one judgment only expounding the relevant law rather than have to consider several judgments in one case and possibly have to distill out of these a ground of decision which is common to all."

The Committee was recommending the continuance of the provision in the Criminal Appeal Act 1907 that there should only be more than one judgment in the Court of Criminal Appeal when the presiding judge stated that it would be convenient for separate judgments to be pronounced. Separate judgments were seldom pronounced in the Court of Criminal Appeal and I am not sure that any have been given in the Criminal Division of the Court of Appeal. If there were ever to be a similar provision with regard to the criminal jurisdiction of the House of Lords, I would hope that there would be more separate speeches than there have been separate judgments under the Criminal Appeal Acts of 1907 and 1966. Even when there is no question of fundamental disagreement, separate speeches can serve a useful purpose by stressing or adding to, points in previous speeches.

Provided it was liberally construed by the presiding judge, I would welcome a provision under which criminal appeals to the House of Lords were normally disposed of in a single speech. I think there is all the difference in the world between the functions of the House of Lords in civil and criminal cases. The assistance of the development of the law by the formulation of principles is so much more appropriate in the former. In criminal cases one particular certified point has to be clarified. The common law is a dynamic force in tort and contract in a way that it is not in the case of the criminal law.

Even if we cannot have the norm of single speeches in criminal appeals to the House of Lords, might we not have, in civil and criminal cases alike, a greater co-ordination of the speeches? It does seem that this is a matter which is dealt with more happily in the United States Supreme Court than in the House of Lords. If the regular practice were to have a leading speech, followed by assentient speeches with a clear indication of why they were being made, and, where necessary, dissentient speeches, the ordinary mortal would experience less difficulty in determining the *ratio decidendi* and it is even possible that the number of cases which are only authority for what they actually decide would diminish.

———

The rule of *stare decisis* in England reflects characteristics of the judicial institutional structure. It also reflects the attitudes of those judges sitting in the highest court as to the role of the various levels of courts, and the degree of eminence given their own decisions. Other nations have different views of *stare decisis*. Do they relate to their institutional structures or to notions of how a machinery of justice should best function? Are decisions binding because of the eminence of the issuing court, or because the legal system needs to have decisions of certain levels binding for reasons of stability, predictability, fairness and cost?

R. CROSS, "PRECEDENT IN ENGLISH LAW"

12 (3d ed 1977).*

* * *

Contrast With Parts of the Commonwealth

The Judicial Committee of the Privy Council used to be the final court of appeal for all Commonwealth countries outside the United Kingdom. The Judicial Committee has never considered itself to be absolutely bound by its own previous decisions on any appeal. The form in which the decisions are expressed is often said to militate against the adoption of a rigid rule of precedent, for the judgment of the Committee consists of advice tendered to the Sovereign together with the reasons upon which such advice is based. Another factor which makes for a less strict rule of *stare decisis* is the comparative frequency upon which the Privy Council is called upon to deal with appeals on questions of constitutional law, but there are several cases which were not concerned with constitutional law in which the Committee has dissented from the

* Rupert Cross, Precedent in English Law   Oxford University Press.
(3d ed 1977). Reprinted by permission of

advice which it gave on a former occasion. The Judicial Committee is, however, strongly disposed to adhere to its previous decisions. The decisions of the Privy Council are only of strong persuasive authority in the English courts.

The right of appeal to the Privy Council has been abolished in some Commonwealth countries, including Canada.... In the days when there was still an appeal to the Privy Council, the Supreme Court of Canada regarded itself as bound by its own past decisions although there was a saving clause relating to "exceptional circumstances". Since the abolition of the right of appeal to the Privy Council, the Supreme Court of Canada has claimed the power of declining to follow its own past decisions as it is the successor to the final appellate jurisdiction of the Privy Council which is not bound by its own past decisions.

The High Court of Australia does not regard itself as absolutely bound by its own past decisions. As long ago as 1879 it was said to be of the utmost importance that in all parts of the Empire where English law prevails, the interpretation of that law by the courts should be as nearly as possible the same. It is for this reason that, in the absence of some special local consideration to justify a deviation, the Australian and Canadian courts would be loath to differ from decisions of the House of Lords, but there does not appear to be any question of the decisions of the House being binding in either country. The High Court of Australia in fact stated that a leading decision on the English criminal law (since largely overruled by an English statute) was to be treated as no authority in Australia,[1] and the Judicial Committee of the Privy Council has held in a civil case that the Australian High Court was right not to follow a decision of the House of Lords on exemplary damages.[2]

The desirability of having the same common law throughout the Commonwealth is not as self-evident as it is sometimes made to appear. Much depends on the branch of the law concerned. In commercial matters, for example, where members of the different Commonwealth countries are liable to be affected by the same rule, there is much to be said for uniformity; but the demand for uniformity in other spheres may militate against useful developments. For historical reasons, Australian and Canadian judges may, *faute de mieux,* have to start their thinking with English law, but there is no obvious merit in their binding themselves to adopt the English solution. The first answer to a legal problem is not necessarily the right one, and each of two answers may be equally meritorious.

COMPARISON WITH FRANCE [a]

* * *

1. Parker v. R., [1963] A.L.R. 524.
2. Australian Consolidated Press, Ltd. v. Uren [1967] 2 All E.R. 523. [Editor's note: Australia no longer uses the Judicial Committee for appeals. English cases, however, are often referred to in researching a point of law.]

a. Precedent in civil law traditions is discussed in Section 3 of Chapter 5.

. . . To quote a distinguished French legal writer: 'The practice of the courts does not become a source of law until it is definitely fixed by the repetition of precedents which are in agreement on a single point.'[3]

* * *

Three of the principal reasons for the difference between the French and English approaches to the doctrine of precedent are that the need for certainty in the law was formerly felt more keenly by the English judge than most of the judges on the Continent, the highly centralized nature of the hierarchy of the English courts, and the difference in the position of the judges in the two countries.

The Need for Certainty

. . . The continental judge has no doubt always wanted the law to be certain as much as the English judge, but he has felt the need less keenly because of the background of rules provided first by Roman law and codified custom, and later by the codes of the Napoleonic era. These resulted in a large measure of certainty in European law. Roman law was never 'received' in England, and we have never had a code in the sense of a written statement of the entirety of the law. 'English justice, if it were not to remain fluid and unstable, required a strong cement. This was found in the common-law doctrine of precedent with its essential and peculiar emphasis on rigidity and certainty.'[2]

The Hierarchy of the Courts

The French judicial system is based on the division of the country into districts. So far as civil cases are concerned, each district has a court of first instance and a court of appeal. The district courts of first instance are not bound by their own previous decisions or those of any other district court of first instance, nor are such courts of first instance bound by the previous decisions of their own appellate court or that of any other district. The district appellate courts are not bound by their own past decisions or those of any other district court of appeal. There is a right of appeal on points of law from the district appellate court to the *Cour de Cassation* in Paris. In theory, this body is not bound by any previous decision of its own, and the district courts are not bound to follow an individual decision of the *Cour de Cassation* in a previous case. . . .

* * *

3. Lambert, 'Case-method in Canada', 39 Yale L.J. 1 at p. 14. A helpful account of the operation of precedent in France together with examples of the judgments of French courts is given by Lawson, 'Negligence in Civil Law', pp. 231–5. See also Esmein, Revue trimestrielle de droit civil, v. i, p. 5 (1902); Encyclopédie Dalloz, v. iii, p. 17; 'Le Droit privé français', by Ripert, v. i, p. 9; O. Kahn–Freund, C. Lévy and B. Rudden, A Sourcebook of French Law, pp. 98–140. In Spain it seems that two decisions of the Supreme Court constitute a 'doctrina' binding on inferior courts, though the Supreme Court may later alter the 'doctrina' (Neville Brown, 'The Sources of Spanish Law', 5 Int.Comp.L.Q. 367 (1956)).

2. Precedent in English and Continental Law, 50 L.Q.R. 40, 62 (1934).

With a system of courts as decentralized as that which has just been sketched, it would have been difficult for France to have evolved a doctrine of precedent as rigid in every respect as our own. Even if the *Cour de Cassation* had come to treat itself and the district courts as absolutely bound by each of its past decisions, there would almost inevitably have been considerable flexibility at the level of the district courts of appeal. It would have been too much to expect anything approximating to the uniformity of decision demanded of the English judges. French law owes its uniformity to the various codes in which it is declared and to *la doctrine*—the opinions of jurists—rather than to *la jurisprudence*.

The Different Position of the Judges

. . . In the first place, there are fewer judges of our superior courts than there are members of the French judiciary. Secondly, the French judiciary is not, like ours, recruited from the Bar but from the civil service, and thirdly, many French judges are relatively young and inexperienced men. . . . The result is that the judiciary tends to be considered as less important in France than in England, and, although it is difficult to assess the significance of these matters, it is generally, and probably rightly, assumed that they help to explain the greater regard which is paid to case-law in this country than that which is paid to it on the Continent. Still more important is the fact that the judges have been the architects of English law.

> The common law is a monument to the judicial activity of the common law judge. He, not the legislator or the scholar, created the common law. He still enjoys the prestige of that accomplishment.[1]

Further Reasons for the Difference

Allowance must also be made for the difference in the structure of the judgments of English and French courts . . . and for the vast number of cases decided by the *Cour de Cassation*. A rule that a single precedent should be binding would be unlikely to develop when it was difficult to discover a precise *ratio decidendi* and it is not always easy to extract a precise *ratio* from a French judgment. A rule that one single decision of an appellate court should suffice to constitute a binding precedent is hardly likely to develop in a jurisdiction in which there are numerous appeals. The House of Lords only hears some 30 appeals from the English courts each year, but some 10,000 cases are dealt with annually by the different chambers of the *Cour de Cassation*.

Notwithstanding the great theoretical difference between the English and French approaches to case-law, and the total absence of rules of precedent in France, the two systems have more in common than might be supposed. In the first place, French judges and writers pay the greatest respect to the past decisions of the *Cour de Cassation*.

---

1. A. Von Mehren, The Civil Law System 839.

Secondly, the manner in which the English judges interpret the *ratio decidendi* of a case tends to assimilate their attitude towards a legal problem to that of their French counterparts. . . .

* * *

. . . It would be wrong to say that, in deciding case D, an English High Court judge of first instance considers cases A and B, decided by the Court of Appeal, together with case C, decided by another High Court judge of first instance, in order to see whether the law has become 'definitely fixed by the repetition of precedents which are in agreement on a single point'. However, his attitude towards the *ratio decidendi* of case A might be profoundly affected by the observations of the judges in cases B and C. English case-law is not the same as *la jurisprudence*, but it is a mistake to suppose that our judges permanently inhabit a wilderness of single instances. If, for the time being, we ignore the difference in the form in which the English and French judges express their conclusions, it seems that the divergence between the two systems is most noticeable when there is only one important decision on the point before the court, as was the case in *Beamish v. Beamish*. It is quite possible that a French judge of first instance would have felt himself as much bound to follow *Simonin v. Mallac* as did Sir Jocelyn Simon in *Padolecchia v. Padolecchia,* although this would be on account of the fact that *Simonin v. Mallac* had been followed on numerous occasions rather than on account of the fact that the decision had received the blessing of appellate courts on relatively few occasions. A further respect in which the two systems of case-law differ profoundly is due to Art. 5 of the Civil Code which prohibits a judge from laying down general rules. It is not uncommon for the judgments of English appellate courts to lay down rules, concerning the quantum of damages for example, to be followed by lower courts in the future. This could hardly happen in France.

————

We have seen some comparative commentary on the use of *stare decisis* in common law systems and a civil law system, France. Scotland has a civil law base with an imposed English law overlay penetrating many layers. One of the more interesting systems is that in South Africa. No primary code exists. Roman–Dutch law was subjected to additions of English law. Some characteristics have remained. One is that higher court judgments are binding on lower courts. There is less of a feeling in South Africa than in Scotland (or perhaps Quebec) that the common law will smother the civil law base. South African courts readily look abroad for guidance. While it might be expected that they would look to the civil law systems, it is often to the common law of England that they turn for the interpretation of statutes. Hahlo and Kahn discuss the reasons:

H. HAHLO AND E. KAHN, "THE SOUTH AFRICAN LEGAL SYSTEM"
592 (1968).*

... [I]t has been suggested that if we have to look for guidance to other legal systems, attention should be paid to 'those systems of the West European continent which, though codified, have their roots in the same historical soil as our law', rather than to English law. It is only necessary to read modern Dutch, French or German law reports to discover that this admonition, sound as it may be in theory, does not work out in practice, the reason being that modern Continental systems are codified, whereas the Roman–Dutch law is not. Continental judgments inevitably argue on specific code provisions, whereas courts in countries with non-codified systems argue on abstract non-verbalized principles. This explains why our judges in the past derived greater assistance from the judgments of English, Scottish and American courts than from the judgments of Continental tribunals, and will continue to do so in the future. More help can probably be obtained from modern Continental treatises, but even they are 'code-directed'. The reason why the courts of Quebec have been able to find so much aid in modern French *jurisprudence* and *doctrine* is that the *Code civil* of Quebec is substantially identical with the *Code Napoléon*. It would seem that a non-codified civilian system can derive better guidance from the non-codified law of England than from the codified civilian systems of the Continent.

In their approach to the interpretation of statutes, too, the courts of South Africa have always found more assistance in the law of England than in the *jurisprudence* of Continental countries, and again, the explanation is that South African and English law are non-codified systems, whereas Continental systems are in the form of codes. In countries with codified systems of law statutes take the form of amendments to the Code and have to be fitted into the general legislative scheme. In countries with non-codified systems, on the other hand, statutes create islands in the sea of the common law and have to be interpreted accordingly. Should English law be codified, as appears not unlikely at the moment, it may well have the effect of cutting the tie between South African and English law.

Notes and Questions

1. Two years after the *Broome v. Cassell* decision, the Court of Appeal again departed from a ruling of the House of Lords. The House of Lords had earlier ruled that English judgments should be given in sterling. *Havana Railways* [1961] A.C. 1007, 1052. The Court of Appeals ruled that the reasons for that rule had ceased to exist. *Schorsch Meier G.m.b.h. v. Henning* [1975] 1 Q.B. 416. The case was not appealed to the House of Lords. But later the issue was before the Law Lords in *Miliangos v. George*

Frank (Textiles) Ltd. [1976] A.C. 443. The Law Lords exhumed their earlier *Havana Railways* decision that the Court of Appeal had attempted to bury forever. It did not bother the Lords that the Court of Appeal said it had to follow its own earlier decision in *Schorsch Meier.* The Lords said the Court of Appeal was incorrect in departing from the earlier House of Lords *Havana Railways* decision. But it then decided that the rule on currency should be changed, the same conclusion reached by the Court of Appeal in *Schorsch Meier.* If the Court of Appeal in *Schorsch Meier* had followed the earlier Lords *Havana Railways* decision and ruled the judgment had to be in sterling, then in the later *Miliangos* case they would have been compelled to rule the same way. The plaintiff probably would not have appealed, but have accepted the judgment in sterling. Then the House of Lords would not have had an opportunity to itself overrule its earlier *Havana Railways* decision, all to the harm of England's overseas trade. See Lord Denning, The Discipline of Law 308 (1979). How would you respond, were you sitting on appeal, to Lord Denning's logic? Is this a case where the rule of strict observance of the highest court's decisions should not be followed? If so should the same allowance be made for courts on even a lower level? Since the appeal rate in England is considerably lower than in the United States, does Lord Denning's view make more sense—that the plaintiff would not have appealed?

2. Could the Court of Appeal adopt by rule a view similar to the House of Lords that it is no longer bound by its own decisions? Should it be left to the courts to decide this issue?

3. If the previous opinions of a court are binding, will the court be likely to find a way around the previous interpretation? Lawyers are trained to distinguish previous decisions from their present case. Would it be better to accept the opinion of the Court of Appeal that it should be able to forthrightly reject earlier opinions? At least that will cause the court to say the earlier decision was wrong and we are going to change the rule, rather than the earlier decision was wrong but we must follow it so we will find a way to distinguish it from the case at hand. A second alternative would be for the court to hold the previous case to have been given *per incuriam.* It is a doctrine to be used with tact and caution, allowing a previous decision to be rejected because it was "given in ignorance or forgetfulness of some inconsistent statutory provision or of some authority binding on the court concerned; so that in such cases some part of the decision or some step in the reasoning on which it was based is found, on that account, to be demonstrably wrong." Morelle v. Wakeling [1955] 2 Q.B. 379, 406 (Court of Appeal).

4. Greater flexibility is allowed the Court of Appeal in following decisions involving criminal law. Why should this be so? Would this flexibility be appropriate to public law? To certain judicial hierarchies, for example in the German system, but not in others?

5. Do opinions identified with individual judges affect *stare decisis* differently than opinions of a collegial court, such as those rendered in civil law nations?

6. How do you view the rule of *stare decisis* in the United States in contrast to England? Did the English Practice Statement of the House of Lords bring the English view more into line with that in the United States?

7. Mr. Justice Frankfurter said that "The ultimate touchstone of constitutionality is the Constitution itself, and not what we do about it." Graves v. New York, 306 U.S. 466, 491, 59 S.Ct. 595, 603 (1939). Decisions interpreting the Constitution are secondary to the Constitution itself. Thus decisions may be less likely to follow earlier decisions than what a given court believes the Constitution itself to say. See A. Goodhart, Case Law in England and America, Essays in Jurisprudence and the Common Law (1931). It is difficult to amend the United States Constitution. It is far easier to alter a previous interpretation of its provisions by avoiding the earlier decision and turning directly to the provisions of the Constitution.

One might ask whether there is too much focus on the process in the United States on separating the *ratio decidendi* from the chaff (and possibly important dictum), or whether other systems do not place sufficient emphasis on the process, to the detriment of these persons when later acting as advocates. But our interest is not in comparative education at this point, but on how systems approach the maze of decisional verbiage with the goal of seeking the often elusive rule of law on which the court reached its conclusion.

The process of determining the *ratio decidendi* does not affect the judicial process in civil law nations to the same extent as in common law systems. This is understandable. Decisions of such civil law courts as the French Cour de Cassation do not when read show much in common with common law cases. The French civil courts' decisions do not read in general discourse fashion—they attempt to succinctly state the reasons for the decision.

Determining the *ratio decidendi* has been given almost as much attention in the writings of English observers of the system as the most loquacious decisions they would dissect. John Austin may be the progenitor of this discourse, he made reference to the term, *ratio decidendi* in his lectures on jurisprudence.[7] Arthur Goodhart set forth a framework for finding the *ratio decidendi,* which became very influential in England,[8] but which has been criticized by later observers, including Julius Stone. Stone rejected the Goodhart view as being prescriptive,[9] suggesting it was rather descriptive and offering his own view that "the process is basically one of choosing an appropriate level of generality. There is thus implicit in a decided case a number of *rationes decidendi.*"[10] The American realists would respond that searching for the *ratio*

---

7. Vol. II at 627 (ed. Campbell 5th ed. 1885).

8. Essays in Jurisprudence and the Common Law 25 (1931).

9. The Ratio of the Ratio Decidendi, 22 Modern L.R. 597 (1959).

10. J. Farrar and A. Dugdale, Introduction to Legal Method 87 (2d ed 1984). The development of English theory regarding

decidendi and *obiter dictum* is a fruitless search. The analysis of a case and the determination of what the judge has said as *ratio decidendi* and what he has said as *obiter dictum* becomes important only in the context of what a later judge says about a previous case. The rule in case A is what the judge in case B says it is. As Cross suggests, they (realists) consider rather seriously a joke made to a Lord of Appeal in Ordinary that "The rule is quite simple, if you agree with the other bloke you say it is part of the *ratio;* if you don't you say it is *obiter dictum,* with the implication that he is a congenital idiot." [11] But one must not ascribe this view only to the American realists, it is a view shared by persons in England and all systems with decisions regarded as of precedential value. Nor is the American Realists' view accepted throughout the United States. These views are less specific systems-based views than they are differing views which are present in every system. If it is difficult for a civil law observer to separate law from dictum in reading a common law decision, some comfort should be found in the fact that often persons trained in the common law cannot agree on the distinction in a given case.

Case law binding upon courts may have assumed a diminished role in the English legal system, but legislation faces a gauntlet of interpretation by the courts. Decisions which interpret legislation become a source of law as much as the laws which they interpret. The existence of interpretive decisions of a parliamentary act tends to give a sense of comfort to English lawyers and judges. Until judicially interpreted, laws are frequently believed to lack the authority which arises with judicial sanctification. While this should in no way diminish the fact of the supremacy of Parliament, it does illustrate that where the interpretations of statutes possess independent status and authority, the statute alone may be viewed as incomplete until it has been interpreted.

Certainty, precision and flexibility are thought to be characteristics of precedent as a binding source of law. Once a decision has been rendered involving particular facts, there is some assurance that in a subsequent identical fact situation a similar conclusion will be reached. Common law lawyers nevertheless have become exceptionally skillful at distinguishing fact situations, and making it difficult to accept that identical situations ever recur. The aggregate of judicial decisions in England constitutes an extensive framework, illustrating how varying disputed facts have been resolved. To the English lawyer it is inconceivable that these variations could be foreseen, or included, in statutes. The most exhaustive code cannot offer solutions to all possible situations. It must of necessity have some measure of abstractness. A civil law judge has the task of resolving a case from broad statutory principles and underlying theories of the "essence."

the ratio decidendi is outlined in R. Cross, Precedent in English Law 38 (3d ed 1977).

11. R. Cross, Precedent in English Law 51 (3d ed 1977), citing Journal of the Soci-ety of Public Teachers of Law (N.S.) 359 (1950).

English common law has attributes both of flexibility and rigidity. Decisions are less binding than might at first be assumed. They are also distinguishable, to a degree that sometimes suggests inappropriateness rather than difference. The English judge, nevertheless, often is more reluctant than American judges to ignore a decision which appears to dictate what may seem at the time to be an inappropriate or unjust resolution. The resulting opinion may state that however regrettable a particular decision might appear, the law on the subject is settled by earlier precedent, and any change must be mandated by an act of Parliament. The degree of rigidity of a common law system thus depends on judicial attitude. The greater homogeneity of judges in England, in contrast to the diversity that exists in the United States with an extensive state court system, tends to identify the English system as one of stronger judicial compulsion to follow precedent, and of fewer variances in attitudes throughout the judicial system.

No system possesses a written law governing all conceivable disputes. Judges must therefore create new law. It may not be very obvious to an observer of a common law system that a judge has "made" law. What effectively is new law may appear to have at least some identity with elements of one or more previous decisions, in contrast to a similar situation in a civil law system, where the judge-made law may have at best a tenuous identification with abstract statutes.

C. JUDICIAL STYLE

Judicial opinions reflect characteristics of a legal system. They may tell us how and why judges reach particular conclusions. Goutal has studied decisions involving third party beneficiary contracts from France, England and the United States to attempt to learn how judges justify their conclusions. He considered the length of opinions, the schemes of reasoning employed and the tone of the opinions. His piece brought a response from Lawson.

J.L. GOUTAL, "CHARACTERISTICS OF JUDICIAL STYLE IN FRANCE, ENGLAND AND THE U.S.A."

24 American Journal of Comparative Law 43 (1976).*

A. PATTERNS OF LEGAL REASONING

In order to establish a relationship between the normative sources and their decisions, judges will follow—or will appear to follow—a logical route. In this process the whole range of patterns of reasoning is open to them, and a study of cases shows that judges actually resort to a great variety of them: deduction ("from general rules to other general rules or to particular cases"), induction ("the building up of a general rule from many particular cases"), analogy (from a case showing some resemblance

* Reprinted with permission of the American Society of Comparative Law.

with the case at bar), reasoning by specific example (temporarily leaving the case in order to abstract a rule from a case thought similar, the solution to which is clear or easy to reach), statistical syllogism (inferring from knowledge that a high percentage of elements in a group have characteristic Z, the conclusion that any element of this group has characteristic Z), *reductio ad absurdum* (arriving at a conclusion through elimination of alternatives by showing that some proposition ... implies a self *contradiction*). However, case reading also shows that some judges tend to use certain reasoning patterns more often than others, and that other judges are dedicated exclusively to other schemes of reasoning. Clearly, in none of our legal systems is there a black-letter rule directing judges to use certain forms of reasoning rather than others. Do judges then feel compelled by some unstated command? Or is it that the system in which they act requires the use of certain patterns?

France

French courts, with amazing regularity, ever since the Revolution, have practiced deduction and nothing but deduction. At the opening of the opinion, a perfectly abstract and general principle will be stated, from which the court will reach its decision through a strictly deductive process: "Under [*Vue*] Art. 1121 of the Civil Code—Whereas the law allows valid contracts to be made for the benefit of third persons as soon as the promisee has an interest in the performance of such contract...." The principle will possibly be commented upon or reworded in order to fit into the hypothesis of the case: "Whereas such an interest need not be a financial one but may simply be of a moral or affective nature...." Thereupon follows the hypothesis of facts, albeit in a highly refined form: "Whereas it appears from the 'sovereign' findings of the trial judges that Jules Dupont, being the father of Alfred Dupont, had a clear interest in performance of Durant's promise to take Alfred to the Elk City rodeo"; followed the conclusion: "Whereas the trial judges thereby rested their judgment for Alfred Dupont on valid grounds; on these grounds: affirms...." A plain syllogism, the pattern all decisions of the Cour de Cassation follow. Decisions of courts of appeal will elaborate more on the facts, and the conclusion will differ slightly from that in this model (because courts of appeal do not review decisions in the same manner as the Cour de Cassation; but this is irrelevant for our purposes), but the logical structure will be the same: a simple, clean-cut deduction from premises stated in the form of an abstract principle, normally drawn from statute....

England

In contrast, English decisions by no means adhere exclusively to a particular pattern of reasoning, but use a broad range of logical (and illogical) schemes. The opinion will not normally start with a principle: there is no emphasis on deduction. Instead it will begin with a careful, smooth, often lengthy exposé of facts, which judges do not mind putting as a story: "Old Peter Beswick was a coal merchant.... All he had was a lorry, scales and weights." It is almost like telling a tale: "There is in

Lancashire a river called Eller Brook.…" The judge then proceeds to explain the situation, taking care to be understandable rather than strictly relevant; this is in sharp contrast with his French colleague who sacrifices more often than not, comprehension to relevance. The exposé of facts in an English judgment is not the minor premise of a syllogism as it is in a French judgment where the judges are condemned to strict relevance if they wish to preserve the justificatory value of their opinion (as we shall see below). This distinction is crucial: the French opinion, in which reasoning starts at the first line, is nothing but a pure form of reasoning, whereas the English opinion, in which reasoning appears only after a lengthy introduction, is a discursive process, incidentally integrating various forms of reasoning.

Variety is the key word here—another crucial difference which makes it difficult to build a model as we did for the French case and as we shall do for the American. The reasoning will at times be formal deduction from an acceptably clear statute, the rule of which is applied through a plain syllogism. However, this ideal description fits very few English cases. For one thing, who has ever seen a clear statute? Think of the Road Traffic Act, 1972 s. 68 which requires that an automobile "carry two lamps, each showing to the front a white light *visible from a reasonable distance.* " Even if we do not pick such extreme examples, it seems that a statute with plain wording is to English minds devoid of legal significance until it has been reworded, explained into something particular, concrete, and reasonable (as opposed to formally rational): unlike their French colleagues, English judges regard principles as repugnant.… No matter what the official doctrine, the rule laid down by statute is not really treated differently from "the rule in *X v. Y* " laid down by precedent: it does not make sense until analysis and explanation has revealed "what the statute amounts to." And this gives the deductive process a peculiar touch, if indeed deduction is still conceivable in such a context.

More typical and frequent is the use by English judges of inductive reasoning. Most common is reasoning by example. Writers will use that expression in its plain sense to mean the extension process of the technique of precedent. However, here we think it helpful to use it in a more particular sense to describe the very original process of the judge who seeks to reason on something like a laboratory model, and we shall call it "reasoning by specific example." Assume the question is whether a stevedore can rely on a clause in the bill of lading limiting the liability of the carrier and of his servants or agents. The judge will pick a different situation about which he is confident that a) he can easily find a solution, and b) he will be able to draw a parallel with the case at bar. "For instance, if the shipowner owned another ship which negligently ran into this one, that would be an independent tort for which the shipowner would be liable." …

Instances of such reasoning by way of a specific example are quite frequent among English judges, both in the 19th century and now. Moreover, the use of such reasoning is virtually unique to them: we have not found a single instance among French decisions and, if we may anticipate, very few among American decisions. A little later we shall try to explain what this imports.

In the third type of reasoning we have found in English opinions, the judge reaches a conclusion by ruling out the various possible solutions through testing them against a certain position. The scheme is as follows: "Either we decide A or we decide B; if we decide A, C follows; but C is inconsistent with the well settled proposition D. Therefore, we cannot decide A. If we decide B, etc. . . .". We shall call this *reductio ad absurdum*. This type of reasoning was found abundantly in both 19th and 20th century cases. For example Brett L.J. in *Rayner v. Preston:* ". . . it seems wrong to say that the one is a trustee for the other . . . if the vendor were a trustee of the property for the vendee, if it would seem to follow that all the product, all the value of the property . . . ought . . . to belong to the vendee." (This is not the case; therefore he is not a trustee. Let us try something else.) . . . Again, this type of reasoning is typical of English courts; we have not found one *reductio ad absurdum* in French decisions, and very few in American ones.

We now come to the fourth and fifth forms of reasoning: analogy and precedent. "Reasoning by analogy" is sometimes used by writers to refer to the technique of precedent. We would like to take the expression in a strict sense because, like reasoning by specific example, its use shows interesting characteristics of English judges.

Reasoning by analogy involves two situations which have one or more crucial features in common, and thus make it tempting to apply the rule known to govern one situation to the second. "Such being the case in respect of goods, the question is whether a similar rule applies to the carriage of passengers." The judge does not say "Despite some discrepancies, case A is essentially similar to case B; therefore we shall apply to Case B the rule in case A." This would be, as one shall soon see, the application of precedent, i.e., a *normative* process yielding a *binding* conclusion. In analogy, the judge only refers to a rule in case A as giving him an idea how to solve the question in case B: the process is only *indicative*. Accordingly, this type of reasoning is used in support of central arguments themselves weak. But it is also typical of English opinions inasmuch as it fits the English pattern of piling up arguments. It will usually follow the citation of more formal and convincing authorities and sources, and give a final touch to the point the judge is trying to make: "In further support of the rule in respect to passengers, I would refer to the Carriage by Air Act, 1932."

The fifth and last characteristic type of reasoning is the application of precedent. As already noted, writers generally call it either reasoning by example or by analogy, or are content to classify it broadly in the category of induction. However, it appears to me (an outsider's view) that application of precedent involves a very special type of reasoning which the words "example," "analogy," or "induction" do not adequately describe. Indeed, it seems that application of precedent involves several different reasoning patterns which make it a hybrid type. It can be analyzed in a two-tier process; in the first stage the judge will abstract a rule from one or more cases: this is induction. But in the second stage (usually clearly detached from the first one) he will apply this rule, formally expressed in general terms but resting on a highly differentiated factual background, to the facts of the case at bar: this is deduction, and it usually shows that feature of inevitability ("I am bound to decide that . . .") so typical of deductive reasoning. But the process of precedent application accumulates the traits and stigmas of each of its two tiers: substantively, it is as creative, as loose, and as weak as induction; formally, it is as safe and as limiting as deduction: a very original scheme of reasoning, which is found nowhere in French cases.

Precedent, then, is not analogy. As E.R. Emmet points out, "The whole point of . . . analogy is that the things compared are basically dissimilar." Whereas the central point in the application of precedent is that the cases, despite some differences, are *basically similar.* Hence, the cogent inference. If the application of precedent were an argument by analogy, there would be no concept of the binding force of precedent: "In fact, then, analogies may be useful in illustrating points . . . but they can never be used to establish a conclusion."

* * *

United States

In American opinions most of the reasoning patterns we have already considered will be found again. However, some of them wear a somewhat different aspect, and one new form should be added to our typology.

This new form is statistical syllogism. The judge notes that a number of cases have received a certain solution, and induces therefrom that the case at bar could very well deserve the same solution. "By the great majority of courts in this country, it is regarded as unjust for the promisor not to perform as he promised in return for a consideration." (Conclusion: why not hold the same in this case?) Unlike precedent, there is nothing normative in this process, no appeal to hierarchy or formal authority; it only suggests a way to solve the question without any hint of anything binding—very much like analogy. However, unlike analogy, the stress is not on that crucial trait common to two situations otherwise different; on the contrary, it assumes that the cases are roughly similar (the test is that they can be broadly grouped in the same class, e.g., third party beneficiary contracts) and puts the stress on the sheer frequency of the decisions. Thus, it combines two antagonistic features: although its substantial justificatory value is next to nothing (the fact that everyone does something does not show why it is good), its persuasive value is extremely high, much higher generally than that of analogy. The latter, as we have seen, is normally used as a collateral, supplemental argument. In contrast, statistical reasoning yields a central argument.

The other kinds of reasoning—specific example, *reductio,* analogy, precedent, deduction—undergo dramatic changes in America. For one thing, the first three become extremely rare; "example," in particular, virtually disappears. Secondly, precedent and deduction have merged and yielded to a dual form of deduction. We shall explain this by constructing a model.

The short opening paragraph of the opinion will usually place the case in its procedural context: "This is an appeal from a decision of the District Court of Yoyo County in favor of appellee, The Grand National Casualty Co., on a contract between appellant, John Smith III, and the Hard Labor Construction Company." The judge in a dry but lengthy manner will recite the facts: "Material allegations of the amended petition read: the Hard Labor Company entered into a contract with the Board of Regents of a New Mexico state college for the construction of an astrological science laboratory for a total amount of $30,000.00; the Grand National Casualty issued a performance bond. . . ." No storytelling style, no fantasy; whether out of inability to write a mellow account of the facts or simply a quest for rigor, the judge in any event will put a stress on relevance unknown to his English colleague, but in a sense akin to the preoccupation of French appellate judges. After the exposé of facts, he will go through each point, either defined in his own terms or, more frequently, as set out in the brief. So far, no reasoning has appeared. The reasoning scheme, as in English cases, will not start until after the end of that lengthy factual information: unlike the French judgment, the American one is a discursive process in which formal reasoning is a collateral element. This is one of the (few) traits it has retained from its English ancestry.

The process assumes highly original characteristics. The judge will cite the rule he finds governing, and state his conclusion in the same telegram-style sentence, followed by citation of some encyclopedia, the Restatement, Corbin on Contracts and an avalanche of cases. Generally, one will look in vain for explanations: "Plaintiff can recover. It is now well established in this jurisdiction that a third party may avail himself of a contract made by others for his benefit, whether designated therein as beneficiary or not. New Mexico Digest, Sect. 12; Am.Jur.Contracts p. 825; 4 Corbin on Contracts; Lawrence Coal Co. v. Shanklin, 25 N.M. 404, 183 P. 435; Southwestern Portland Cement Co. v. Williams, 32 N.M. 68."

This is a deduction of a very particular style. The rule is drawn from statute, precedent, the Restatement, encyclopedias, or textbooks. All these sources are cited together, at the same level: they all seem to have the same authority and the same justificatory value. As a result, the inductive part of precedential reasoning has vanished and only the deductive stage is left. We shall comment in a moment on this striking departure from the English tradition.

Further, the structure of the syllogism is peculiar: the conclusion is usually given in the first sentence, which also contains the major premise, while the minor premise (which would be the proposition of fact) is omitted: the facts have already been set out in the lengthy opening of the opinion, and the judge is not going to repeat them in his hurried syllogisms. The premise and the conclusion are concentrated in one sentence, and the middle proposition omitted: a process we feel like calling a collapsible syllogism, to be found only in American decisions. Sometimes, the deduction is so perfectly collapsible that it simply disappears. Here is a striking example, the full text of a dissenting opinion.

"TAFT, JUSTICE (dissenting).

See *Brotherton v. Merritt–Chapman & Scott Corp.*, 2 Cir., 1954, 213 F.2d 477; *Clark v. P.M. Hennessey Construction Co.*, 1913, 122 Minn. 476, 142 N.W. 873; *Reed v. Adams Steel & Wire Works,* 1914, 57 1914, Ind.App. 259, 106 N.E. 882; Restatement of the Law of Contracts illustration under Section 147, 12 American Jurisprudence, 834, Section 281."

At other times, however, the syllogism unfolds. The rule is drawn from some source and stated for its own sake and without any rush: "According to Restatement of the Law of Contracts, Section 133, a person is a creditor beneficiary if the performance of the promise will satisfy an actual, supposed or asserted duty of the promisee to the beneficiary and is not intended as a gift" (understood: and such a beneficiary can recover). Then the judge will comment upon the rule and construe it in order to arrive at a form that fits the hypothesis of the case at bar: "The most frequent examples of the creditor-beneficiary situation outlined in the texts are those where one person contracts to pay the debts of another, but this need not always be the case. It is pointed out, as follows, in 4 Corbin on Contracts, 97, Sec. 787: "The promises on which a creditor beneficiary has been given judgment are nearly all cases where...." So much for the rule, i.e., the major premise of the syllogism. Then comes a full scale minor premise in which the judge will verify that the hypothesis of fact fits the norm: "The State of Ohio owed certain duties to plaintiff.... Among those duties was that of providing plaintiff with a site ... and of doing those things which it promised to do.... The performance of those duties was undertaken by the defendants under their contracts with the State of Ohio. Since the contracts between the defendants and the state ... provided ... for the performance of certain obligations owed by the state to the plaintiff, it would seem that plaintiff falls squarely within the definition of 'creditor-beneficiary'." The conclusion is not stated (that the beneficiary, being a creditor-beneficiary, can therefore recover), but one should not be too demanding.

So, the judge will consider each point in turn, normally through a deductive reasoning, either unfolded or, in most cases, "collapsible." When he has gone through all the points, a short sentence will state the conclusion, often accompanied by procedural directions: "The decision of the court below is affirmed. The cause will be remanded to the court below for further proceedings in accordance with this opinion."

Such a model fits only a majority of cases (whereas the French one seems to fit 99%). Some courts will utilize different patterns, like the Supreme Court of Delaware which renders opinions in a fashion strikingly close to the English tradition or, to a lesser extent, the Court of Appeals of New York. And even in jurisdictions where the current pattern conforms with the model, the court will at times depart from its habitual dryness: the judge will pause to explain a point, he will occasionally take time to discuss a case or he will make a personal remark. Of course, it should finally be noted that our model does not escape the limitations inherent in its very nature. Like any schematization, it may at times appear as an over-simplification and will not account fully for a complex reality. Inasmuch as it remains a Common Law decision, the American decision escapes an ideal description. The extent to which it is amenable to such a description probably reflects a good measure of its integration of Civil Law techniques. The point is that it appeared possible to establish such a model, whereas this proved impossible with England; that this model was centered on deductive reasoning; that the standard deduction appeared to be "collapsible" syllogism. Taken together, these three traits characterize American opinions and show the departure from Common Law fashions.

* * *

Conclusion

Such are the findings which can be drawn from examination of those two crucial elements of the "path of justification." As anticipated, they revealed, explained and confirmed some important ideas or notions characteristic of the three legal systems: their historical experiences, the position of their judiciaries, the techniques of their law, its sources, the roles of judges, academics, counsels, in the construction and operation of the system.

But other ideas were somewhat unexpected and, in a sense, new. We refer to the closeness of many features, tendencies and symptoms in the American and the French legal systems: the systematization and, to a point, the abstraction of the legal sources, a common taste for deductive reasoning, a certain problem of legitimacy, a certain mass treatment of justification processes. In these many aspects, the legal system of America is surprisingly close to that of France, surprisingly remote from that of England.

And there was something more impressive yet. The path of justification showed in both France and America a complex of three features which puts them in sharp opposition to England. In both systems the length of opinions hardly grew (though it did in England), opinions are on the short side, and courts are addicted to deductive reasoning. ...

Essentially, justification consists in deduction from an abstract, systematized source—Code, statute book, encyclopedia, Restatement, normalized precedent. In America the process was brought forth by the trend toward standardization and a certain crisis of legitimacy; in

France it resulted from a major crisis of legitimacy and a certain deal of standardization.

By contrast, England, where the "path of justification" witnessed no standardization and no legitimacy crisis, was spared that decadence of justification. The great length of judicial opinions and variety of reasoning patterns, on the contrary, witnessed the high level of individualization and attention typical of scrupulous craftsmanship.

F. LAWSON, "COMPARATIVE JUDICIAL STYLE"

25 American Journal of Comparative Law 364 (1977). *

... I would not venture to comment on his article were it not that I think that his very perceptive and appreciative description of English judicial style needs to have something added to it by way of supplement. ...

Of course in a study of this kind one can only start from a survey of published material. The reports are indeed unlikely to lead one astray in American law, where virtually all appellate decisions are reported, or in France, where they are at any rate handed down in writing, but one misses a great deal if one confines oneself to the published English decisions. For although most House of Lords decisions are normally published, the decisions of the Court of Appeal are in principle published only where they are thought to contain a material contribution to the law. Since unpublished decisions are almost certainly shorter than published decisions, the cogency of Mr. Goutal's statistical examination of the length of English decisions may be called in question, or rather, it should perhaps be emphasized that it is confined to decisions which have been arrived at with greater than usual difficulty. I shall have more to say about this later.

The selective English practice of publishing decisions might have little significance for such a study were it not that unpublished appellate decisions have almost certainly not been handed down in writing, but delivered orally from the Bench immediately after the close of oral argument or after a very short interval. ...

Accordingly we must start from the position that the oral judgment is the rule. Moreover, it is based entirely on oral argument. Although "cases" are submitted in advance to the House of Lords, they can, in Professor Karlen's words, "best perhaps be described as advance written outlines of oral arguments to be presented later," and although the Court of Appeal has access to the reasoning on which the judgment in the court below was based, there is nothing in English practice like the American brief.

Finally, there is no place in the English system for the judicial conference; indeed there is seldom any time for it. The judges may be able to exchange a few words during an adjournment or *sotto voce* on the

* Reprinted with permission of the American Society of Comparative Law.

Bench at the close of the argument. Then the presiding judge will usually start speaking and the others may add a few words or merely concur.

All of this is highly personal. The arguments are not confined within specific limits of time, though Counsel do not waste the Court's time and the judges have means of letting them know when they have heard enough. The judges consider it their business to deal with all the serious arguments that are put forward, though naturally they concentrate their attention on those that are most important. Speaking generally, they confine themselves to the arguments of Counsel, though they may open new lines of thought by putting questions. They do not find for themselves the material for decision. They do not go home to do extensive research and they have no one to help them like the American law clerks.

Moreover, English judges are taken from the ranks of successful advocates, not office lawyers, as is common in America, and they have not spent most of their life following a judicial career, as in France. Thus not only do they look to advocates for informative and persuasive arguments, but they carry their own advocacy with them to the Bench. After Counsel on both sides have sought to persuade the judges in opposite directions, the judges try to deal with their arguments and persuade them that their decisions are correct. They are, as it were, the third side of an argumentative triangle. Moreover, the judges in the Court of Appeal have to contemplate the possibility of an appeal to the House of Lords and they are, so to speak, using their judgments as advocating the point of view which they support. Hence I should prefer not to use the word justification, like Mr. Goutal, but to say that the judges are trying to persuade the profession and the public and, it may be, the House of Lords; and a judge does not change his persuasive habit when he becomes a Law Lord, that is to say, a judicial member of the House of Lords.

It would be idle to expect English judges to write in a less discursive manner than the way they speak. Judgment will be reserved in order to give the judges time for consideration, and no doubt the written judgment will usually be a more finished product. But it will be on the same general lines as an oral judgment. It will be designed to show, above all, the way a judge's mind has worked and how he arrived at his decision.

The contrast to French style and practice is admirably brought out by Mr. Goutal and I need add nothing. I am very hesitant in commenting on his treatment of American opinions, but I think he misses some points. He very properly draws attention to what he calls the "statistical syllogism," that is to say, the practice of looking at the way in which a question has been decided in several jurisdictions and identifying majority and minority opinions. He very properly says that although its "substantial justificatory value is next to nothing . . . its persuasive value is extremely high." An allusion to the notion of *communis opinio,* the search for which is not unknown in France until the Cour de

Cassation has spoken, and the formation of something in the nature of a judicial custom, would be very much in point. Moreover, the practice is almost inevitable in a country where, except for federal questions, there is no one court of final appeal. The single ultimate jurisdiction of the House of Lords leaves no room for it in England and indeed the Judicial Committee of the Privy Council has been able to ensure substantial uniformity of common law and equity throughout the Commonwealth. This is an important reason for the greater part that precedent plays in British judicial practice than in that of France or the United States.

Secondly, the drastic curtailment of the time available for oral advocacy before American appellate courts has helped to make the preparation of argument not only a written but also a corporate enterprise, especially in the large metropolitan firms, and concurrently with the development of the judicial conference, the appellate opinion has become corporate also. I think this corporate, one might almost say bureaucratic, element in American practice has combined with the search of a *communis opinio* to cause the convergence between American and French judicial styles and their divergence from the English.

Although in all three countries the judges work upon materials, including arguments, presented to them by the practising lawyers in the case, in England the discussion takes place between the Bench and the Bar, whereas in America and France a large part of it, perhaps the most important part, is among the judges and their auxiliaries, law clerks in the former and *avocats-généraux* in the latter.

SECTION 3. CUSTOM

Custom as a source of law is present in every legal tradition. The English common law has drawn extensively upon local custom; the Normans did not import a legal system from the continent. Indeed, according to Blackstone, the common law was nothing other than "the custom of the realm from time immemorial", which the judges as "living oracles" were to discover. Local custom in England assumed an important function in aiding English judges in resolving specific disputes. Custom was a basis for much of the early criminal law, as well as for such family prescriptions as the rights of parents.

Some local custom also existed separate from the common law, usually involving rules which were applicable to a very small group of people within a local community. These rules constituted exceptions to the common law. Local custom separate from the common law included rules regulating local fishermen, such as where they could dry their nets, or stipulating the characteristics of a right of way. Custom in this form differs from custom which is part of the common law only in its narrow and limited application, and its variance from the common law. With the passage of time, local customs often come to be modified to evolve into general customs which are integrated as part of the common law.

The initial establishment of custom requires proof that it existed uninterrupted for a long period of time, and that it existed by common consent rather than by the use of force. Also, it must be consistent with other customs, contain certainty and be accepted as obligatory and of significant importance. And it must be reasonable.

Can a custom be law before receiving any judicial affirmation? Or does it only become law when a court draws it from use into print? If a court adopts a custom as the basis for a decision is it not doing so because the custom already possesses status as law? If a court refused to accept an alleged custom, it either was not a custom or at least was not sufficiently a custom to constitute law. The adoption of a custom by a court allows the court to make a ruling without limiting its sources to precedent or legislation. If precedent does not exist as a primary source, then custom would seem to be of even greater potential use to a court seeking to expand its jurisdiction, or seeking to avoid an appearance of law-making by identifying an acceptable source. If the permissible source is a statute, but that statute is susceptible of varying interpretations, the use of custom as a source may avoid the charge of judicial law-making. If the custom supports the legislation little objection is likely to come forth, others may even suggest that there was no custom nor any need for mention of the custom, because the statute could be interpreted expansively to cover the case. If the custom is not supportive but is not inconsistent with the statute, then there is greater potential challenge, but as long as the statutory scheme does not seem violated, the custom should receive at least equivocal acceptance. Where the custom is inconsistent with the statute, however, a charge of judicial law-making is difficult to avoid. The use of such a custom in a civil law system would appear less acceptable than in a common law system. This is so, not because a custom inconsistent with a statute has any priority in common law, but because multiple sources are more recognized. It is also easier to use such custom where the court is not compelled to give reasons supporting its conclusion.

SECTION 4.   CONVENTIONS

Conventions are an influential source of English law, and, along with custom, constitute the unwritten legal sources. Convention dictates expected conduct in the functioning of the judicial system as well as other institutions. No act of Parliament specifies that there must be a Prime Minister, nor outlines the method by which the Prime Minister is chosen. It is according to convention that a Prime Minister is selected from the parliamentary or majority party, and that if the Prime Minister fails on a vote of confidence or a major government proposal, a resignation should follow. Convention additionally limits the conduct of the sovereign. It is convention which caused King Edward to abdicate; a monarch should not marry a divorced person. It is also by convention that the sovereign carefully limits any exercise of the royal prerogative, and follows the advice of the Prime Minister in making cabinet and ministerial appointments and in granting royal assent to acts of Parliament.

Within the judicial structure, convention has long played a role in determining the respect to be given to the decisions of other courts, the right to issue dissents and the commencement of certain disputes before a specific court, even though other courts possess concurrent jurisdiction. The several courts acts have codified and altered convention, but it remains an integral element of the structure of these institutions.

Convention exists in every society; it is a part of every legal system. It prevails more successfully in a system where there is little emphasis on the codification of rules. Convention thus is less important in civil law systems. A homogeneous society probably is more conducive to admitting convention where tradition plays an important role, where the expectations of one individual with regard to the conduct of others tend to be common throughout the population. Convention is a flexible source of law, but nevertheless a source of exceptional importance in the machinery of justice in England.

SECTION 5. ROYAL PREROGATIVE

Powers of the English monarch are severely limited. Sovereignty of the crown, as contrasted with sovereignty of Parliament, is essentially a sovereignty symbolizing loyalty to the monarch. The power of the monarch, called the royal prerogative, includes various rights exercised directly by the sovereign, with a subordinate sense of the prerogative constituting powers exercised by the government on behalf of the sovereign.

The judicial system was highly centralized in the beginning years of Norman rule in England. The king was the supreme source of justice. Various devices such as the writ system allowed the royal courts to increase their jurisdiction at the expense of local, rural courts. The power of the king went unchallenged until the Magna Carta 1215, the first formal check on royal power acceded to by the king. The will of the king was no longer the law, though several centuries later civil strife occurred over the issue of the scope of royal power. The use of the royal prerogative surged in the 16th century with the establishment of the Star Chamber. The Stuart kings extensively enlarged the royal prerogative, based on their conceptions of the king's divine right. This challenge was met by common law advocates, and by the end of the 17th century the prerogative was returned to a state of diminished exercise. The royal prerogative was never again the source of authority for the creation of new courts, such as the Star Chamber.

The royal prerogative diminished even further with the Petition of Right Act 1860, which increased a citizen's ability to seek recourse against the sovereign for alleged wrongs. The sovereign's immunity from civil proceedings again was altered by the Crown Proceedings Act 1947, all but eliminating ancient rules restricting procedures against the sovereign.

Comparatively little remains of the royal prerogative, although the monarch still plays an important role in the functioning of the government. A few formal powers remain, essentially summoning and dissolving Parliament, rendering royal assent to bills, presiding over the Privy Council, conferring honors, granting pardons, appointing some state officers, approving cabinet and ministerial appointments, appointing leading clerics, and concluding treaties. Many of these are illusory powers. Nevertheless, the monarch does not personally select the Prime Minister, but acts according to the will of the leaders of the parliamentary party. It is unlikely that the royal prerogative will increase in scope in the future. The monarchy is more a symbol than a source of authority. The royal prerogative is at the command of Parliament.

R. LACEY, "MAJESTY, THE ROYAL PREROGATIVE"
209, 225 (1977). *

Elizabeth II's preference has consistently been not to get involved in politics. Sir Henry Marten raised her on Bagehot's historic definition of the monarch's role vis-à-vis the Prime Minister—to be consulted, to encourage, and (occasionally) to warn—and she has never had the inclination to go beyond these three rights. . . .

But in the decade following the resignation of Winston Churchill in 1955 Elizabeth II found herself drawn into politics in a fashion neither she nor anyone else had anticipated, creating what seemed to some a sinister intrusion of the royal prerogative, but which reflected rather the shyness of a woman whose upbringing had prepared her better for her representative than for any executive functions. Her parents had not trained her to choose prime ministers, rather the reverse, and this coincided with her own instincts. . . .

But the basic problem stemmed not from her but from the Conservative party's lack of a mechanism for electing its leader. 'Emergence,' a semi-mystical fixing upon the right man for the job, was the process which had served it well enough until the reign of Elizabeth II and even into her early years, for Anthony Eden had been the clearly acknowledged successor to Churchill in 1955. . . .

. . . 'Emergence,' an undefined process whereby undefined elders took undefined soundings of undefined groups within the party, prevailed, and it was because this process was twice required, in 1957 and 1963, to interpret party opinion when no clearly overwhelming consensus prevailed, that Elizabeth II became directly involved in political controversy—and did not prove herself any more capable than the other participants of emerging from that sort of scrum unmuddied.

The 1957 controversy followed directly from Suez. . . .

* * *

On 8 January 1957 Eden arrived at Sandringham to tell the Queen his doctor's verdict [that he must resign due to poor health], and next day she travelled to London to receive his resignation. It has been stated that he gave her no advice as to his successor, but she did in fact request it and acted on his suggestion that Lord Salisbury should be asked to take soundings informally among members of the Cabinet....

... Lord Salisbury at once assumed the rôle allotted him and proposed, with Lord Kilmuir, the Lord Chancellor, to interview the ministers one by one. Selwyn Lloyd, the Foreign Secretary, objected to this procedure being carried out by two peers. But no one else shared his misgivings. Salisbury and Kilmuir held the Queen's commission. They held the two senior traditional posts in the Cabinet—Lord President and Lord Chancellor, respectively—they were generally regarded, next to Churchill, as the elder statesmen of the Conservative party, and they were accepted in this rôle for the very reason that they were not themselves candidates for the party leadership.

The two peers went to Lord Salisbury's room in the Privy Council offices, and one by one the Cabinet ministers appeared before them....

The Harolds [Macmillan, as opposed to R.A. Butler] had it, by 'an overwhelming majority'....

Lord Butler himself today agrees with this assessment. 'I was in a state of being suspect at that very moment when the choice of government was made,' he said in an interview with the author in May 1976. 'And there is no doubt that the Cabinet, by a majority, voted for Macmillan. It wasn't such a difficult choice.' As the political correspondent of the *Times* wrote at the time, 'the impression has grown that those opposed to him [Butler] were more likely to make trouble in the event of his becoming Prime Minister than were the smaller number of the Conservatives who may have been opposed to the selection of Mr. Macmillan.'

But this understanding of the Conservative psychology in January 1957 was rare. As soon as the news of Eden's resignation was known, it was generally assumed outside the Parliamentary party that Butler would take over. And the press shared and fostered this impression. His indecisiveness, a grave disadvantage in the eyes of several Cabinet colleagues, was not widely appreciated and it was, by contrast, Harold Macmillan who appeared dated and moth-eaten. The agility behind his calculated Edwardian somnolence was not appreciated. On the morning of Thursday, 10 January 1957, the newspapers—with the exception of the *Times,* which was noncommittal—were unanimous in predicting that R.A. Butler would be summoned to Buckingham Palace and invited to form a government.

At eleven o'clock that morning Lord Salisbury was driven to the Palace, and he told the Queen the results of his soundings of the Cabinet, the Party Chairman, the Chief Whip and the Chairman of the 1922 Committee. Her Private Secretary, Lascelles' former assistant, Sir Michael Adeane, contacted two influential conservative peers, Lords

Chandos and Waverley, and Winston Churchill also arrived, at Elizabeth II's invitation.

* * *

Meanwhile Macmillan ..., was awaiting the verdict in the official residence of the Chancellor of the Exchequer at No. 11 Downing Street.... 'At noon Sir Michael Adeane rang up and asked me to be at the Palace at 2 o'clock. So it was settled.'

There was an immediate cry of injured surprise, and sinister explanations were advanced for the Queen's making such a totally unexpected choice. She had allowed herself to be manipulated....

But this was unfair. Lord Salisbury had revelled in the rôle accorded him and was delighted with the result of his polls.... Yet he was no more than a head counter, and if blame was to be assigned for the ammunition supplied to conspiracy theorists it belonged more properly with the Queen herself. The evidence suggests that justice was done. Harold Macmillan had a better chance of commanding a solid majority in the House of Commons in January 1957 than R.A. Butler, and outsiders who thought otherwise were several months out of date. But justice was not, at the time, clearly seen to have been done. It was a miscalculation for Elizabeth II to let it appear she had selected a prime minister to run her country solely on the say-so of two elderly men with no clearly defined constitutional function. The fact that she knew them both personally and had consulted others (Chandos and Waverley) privately was enough for her. But it was a naïve view of how public opinion worked, and could only be excused in terms of her secluded upbringing.

* * *

As it was, Elizabeth II laid herself open to the charge of favouritism. The prerogative became involved willy-nilly in the political controversies surrounding the rejection of R.A. Butler, and the fact that Macmillan accomplished a feat of political wizardry once he became Prime Minister in pulling his party together to achieve a sweeping victory in the 1959 election did not improve the temper of his political opponents. The Crown suffered in the backlash, coming to be seen as part of a phenomenon newly identified in the late 1950s, the Establishment, a grouse-shooting, Conservative-voting oligarchy nominated as the root of the nation's malaise by the satire industry which sprang up in the disillusionment that followed Suez.

* * *

... If open leadership elections had been held, Macmillan would almost certainly have won convincingly on the first occasion.... But the royal prerogative did not bring out the pragmatic wisdom of this choice. Rather it masked it. It injected mystery, melodrama even, into the straightforward process in which the participants themselves were supposed to be expert—the counting of heads. And in her eagerness to avoid political involvement Elizabeth II got the worst of both worlds. It was not her fault that the emergency right of royal intervention was dragged into politics. But once involved she was half-hearted.... She was not seen to act independently. There was safety in numbers, but instead she appeared to relinquish her responsibilities to individuals as vulnerable as Lord Salisbury was to the charge of personal bias.

＊ ＊ ＊

It was the mechanism that was at fault.... On 25 February 1965 was published the first-ever open 'Procedure for the Selection of the Leader of the Conservative and Unionist Party.' Conservative leaders would in future be elected by ballots of the members representing the party in the House of Commons, and these ballots would be organised not by the leadership but by backbenchers, through the 1922 Committee. The backbenchers were the source of any Consérvative prime minister's support in Parliament, and it was only logical that their democratic significance should be recognised democratically. This left the royal prerogative strictly for the occasions when the mechanisms of democracy got into a genuine deadlock they could not resolve without the help of a presiding agency seen to be fair, strong-willed, and independent.

———

The idea that the ruler of a nation possesses power by virtue of the office is one which may conflict with notions or formalized arrangements of separation of powers. Where the powers are divided by a constitution, as in the United States, the thought that the president has also assumed some prerogative powers either by virtue of his office, because the constitutional drafters did not allocate all power, or by some osmotic transfer from the former sovereign to the new head-of-state, may lead to tensions between the various elements of the state which have been allocated power. One only has to read such United States cases as *United States v. Curtiss–Wright Export Corp.,*[12] *Youngstown Sheet & Tube Co. v. Sawyer,*[13] or *Dames & Moore v. Regan,*[14] to realize that constitutional powers in the United States include something more than constitutional powers, and among the extra-constitutional powers may be an element of prerogative power.

One modern day instance of the use of prerogative powers by a leader of a former part of the British Empire occurred when the Governor–General of Australia in 1975 dissolved the Australian Parliament and dismissed the Prime Minister and his government. It was not an action taken at the request of the government, but solely by the Governor–General after the government was unable to convince the Parliament to enact government proposed laws, and had neither re-

---

12. 299 U.S. 304, 57 S.Ct. 216, 81 L.Ed. 255 (1936).

13. 343 U.S. 579, 72 S.Ct. 863, 96 L.Ed. 1153 (1952).

14. 453 U.S. 654, 101 S.Ct. 2972, 69 L.Ed.2d 918 (1981).

signed nor called on the Governor–General to dissolve Parliament so that a general election might be held. It is a rare example of a rare use of the prerogative power, not meant to suggest that such power also rests in the hands of the President of the United States, but illustrative of the prerogative power in certain common law nations as an element of the constitutional sources of law.

SECTION 6. LEGISLATION

The authority of legislation in England or the United States, or in any other common law nation, may appear quite fundamental to observers in each nation. Enactments of the principal legislative bodies become law which must be followed. In the United States, complex questions about the effectiveness of the legislation may arise because of the existence of both federal and state legislatures. Is the matter enumerated in the Constitution for the federal congress? Is the matter one of specific residual delegation to the states, and thus not for federal action? These questions do not arise in England; parliamentary enactments are not questioned by challenging legislative competence. With few exceptions, Parliament is sovereign in legislating domestic law. It may enact unwise laws which the courts nevertheless in theory are bound to apply. The English constitution does not contain fundamental rights which may lead to parliamentary decrees being invalidated by the courts as unconstitutional. This should not suggest, however, that there exists an unchallenged acceptance of all acts of Parliament. The vast amount of statutory law is thought by many judges to be inconsistent with and a threat to the stability of the common law. Legislation gains authority when judicially interpreted and methods of judicial interpretation by the English courts are more highly refined than in the United States. Absent the ability to rule legislation unconstitutional, the English courts have finely tuned a system by which legislation is interpreted. Courts thus have significant influence on the post-enactment development of statutory law, since enacted law is only effective when the courts permit it to be applied.

Where there is no judicial review of statutes, as in England, a court may effectively nullify a statute by the method of construction. Is the court in the following excerpt merely strictly construing the act, or is it using the common law to effectively diminish the value of the act?

NATIONAL ASSISTANCE BOARD v. WILKINSON
[1952] 2 Q.B. 648, 661.*

* * *

DEVLIN J. . . . It is a well-established principle of construction that a statute is not to be taken as effecting a fundamental alteration in the general law unless it uses words that point unmistakably to that conclu-

---

* Reprinted with permission of The Incorporated Council of Law Reporting.

sion. Accordingly, if the words "a man shall be liable to maintain his wife" in section 42 of the National Assistance Act, 1948, stood by themselves, I should read them subject to the common law, and should not conclude that they were intended to disturb the principle that a wife forfeited her right to maintenance by the commission of a matrimonial offence. Against this it is argued that the initial phrase "for the purposes of this Act" makes it possible to give the wide words that follow their full meaning without altering the general law. The same sort of wide words was, however, used in the Poor Law Act, 1927, s. 41(1), which provides that it shall be the duty of a husband of a poor person to maintain her. These words are not subject to any limitation of the purposes of the Act, and they are moreover contained in a consolidating Act. I could not, therefore, hold that the Act of 1927 altered the common law; and it is noteworthy that no one has in 20 years ever suggested that it did. But if words of this sort are not to be widely and literally construed in 1927, why should they in 1948? The qualifying phrase "for the purposes of this Act" is not, in my judgment, sufficient to effect the alteration. The use of the phrase is sufficiently explained by the inclusion in the section of a novel liability in the case of women, and by a wish to avoid the consequences, as demonstrated in *Middlesex C.C. v. Nathan,* of the unrestricted words in the Act of 1927.

It is another principle of statutory construction that the court leans against an interpretation which produces unjust and arbitrary consequences. I think it would be unjust if a husband were compelled to support a wife in open and admitted adultery; and it would be arbitrary if the amount of money he had to spend on her depended on the speed with which he was able to obtain his decree absolute.

Any statute is capable of being viewed from several different perspectives. The English have developed several rules of interpretation. What rule is adopted may depend on what is the responsibility of the judiciary in interpreting statutes. We saw above the conflict in interpreting previous cases. Some judges are reluctant to follow previous decisions and rather openly express their reluctance, others share the same disdain for an earlier decision but find a way to distinguish it, and still others may apply, however reluctantly, the earlier decision because that is how they view their responsibility toward the precedent as a source of law. With regard to statutes, there may be a strong personal antipathy to a particular statute, but no judge would simply rule that it is not binding. He might, however, emasculate the statute by his method of interpretation, just as he might a previous case with which he disagrees.

One may approach statutory interpretation through a strict rule, a literal interpretation of the statute without regard to what such ruling does to reason or justice. The literal approach has much support in the

English cases. The following excerpts illustrate how literal the literal approach may be.

REG. v. JUDGE OF THE CITY OF LONDON COURT
(1892) 1 Q.B. 273, 290.**

LORD ESHER ...

Jessel, M.R., says that the words of s. 2 are quite clear, and that, if the words of an Act of Parliament are clear, you must take them in their ordinary and natural meaning, unless that meaning produces a manifest absurdity. Now, I say that no such rule of construction was ever laid down before. If the words of an Act are clear, you must follow them, even though they lead to a manifest absurdity. The Court has nothing to do with the question whether the legislature has committed an absurdity. In my opinion, the rule has always been this—if the words of an Act admit of two interpretations, then they are not clear; and if one interpretation leads to an absurdity, and the other does not, the Court will conclude that the legislature did not intend to lead to an absurdity, and will adopt the other interpretation. If the learned judge meant to say that, when the meaning of general words is (if you look at them by themselves) clear, that determines their construction at once, even though from the context—from other parts of the same Act—you can see that they were intended to have a different meaning; if he meant to say that you cannot look at the context—at another part of the Act—to see what is the real meaning, then again I say he has laid down a new rule of interpretation, which, unless we are obliged to follow it in the particular case, I would not follow. ....

DUPONT STEELS LTD. v. SIRS
[1980] 1 All E.R. 529, 541.**

LORD DIPLOCK.... My Lords, at a time when more and more cases involve the application of legislation which gives effect to policies that are the subject of bitter public and parliamentary controversy, it cannot be too strongly emphasised that the British Constitution, though largely unwritten, is firmly based on the separation of powers: Parliament makes the laws, the judiciary interpret them. When Parliament legislates to remedy what the majority of its members at the time perceive to be a defect or a lacuna in the existing law (whether it be the written law enacted by existing statutes or the unwritten common law as it has been expounded by the judges in decided cases), the role of the judiciary is confined to ascertaining from the words that Parliament has approved as expressing its intention what that intention was, and to giving effect to it. Where the meaning of the statutory words is plain and unambiguous it is not for the judges to invent fancied ambiguities as an excuse for

** Reprinted with permission of The In-
corporated Council of Law Reporting.

** Reprinted with permission of Butter-
worth & Co. (Publishers) Ltd.

failing to give effect to its plain meaning because they themselves consider that the consequences of doing so would be inexpedient, or even unjust or immoral. In controversial matters such as are involved in industrial relations there is room for differences of opinion as to what is expedient, what is just and what is morally justifiable. Under our Constitution it is Parliament's opinion on these matters that is paramount.

A statute passed to remedy what is perceived by Parliament to be a defect in the existing law may in actual operation turn out to have injurious consequences that Parliament did not anticipate at the time the statute was passed; if it had, it would have made some provision in the Act in order to prevent them. It is at least possible that Parliament, when the 1974 and 1976 Acts were passed, did not anticipate that so widespread and crippling use as has in fact occurred would be made of sympathetic withdrawals of labour and of secondary blacking and picketing in support of sectional interests able to exercise 'industrial muscle'. But if this be the case it is for Parliament, not for the judiciary, to decide whether any changes should be made to the law as stated in the Acts, and if so, what are the precise limits that ought to be imposed on the immunity from liability for torts committed in the course of taking industrial action. These are matters on which there is a wide legislative choice, the exercise of which is likely to be influenced by the political complexion of the government and the state of public opinion at the time amending legislation is under consideration.

It endangers continued public confidence in the political impartiality of the judiciary, which is essential to the continuance of the rule of law, if judges, under the guise of interpretation, provide their own preferred amendments to statutes which experience of their operation has shown to have had consequences that members of the court before whom the matter comes consider to be injurious to the public interest.... So in relation to s 13(1) of the 1974 Act, for a judge (who is always dealing with an individual case) to pose himself the question, 'Can Parliament really have intended that the acts that were done in this particular case should have the benefit of the immunity?' is to risk straying beyond his constitutional role as interpreter of the enacted law and assume a power to decide at his own discretion whether or not to apply the general law to a particular case. The legitimate questions for a judge in his role as interpreter of the enacted law are, 'How has Parliament, by the words that it has used in the statute to express its intentions, defined the category of acts that are entitled to the immunity? Do the acts done in this particular case fall within that description?'

G. WILLIAMS, "THE MEANING OF LITERAL INTERPRETATION"
131 New Law Journal 1128, 1129 (1981).*

Lord Diplock says that in interpreting a statute the court must decide whether it is plain and unambiguous—two words that presumably mean the same thing. If it is plain the words must be applied, and the judges must not invent "fancied ambiguities". If however the statute is really ambiguous the court may, presumably, adopt the meaning that best fits with the apparent intention of the legislation.

However, the question for the court is not whether the statute is ambiguous in the abstract—ambiguous to the ordinary reader who has not in mind the particular problem that has arisen. The question is whether it is ambiguous in relation to the facts presented to the court. And there will be two sides, each arguing for a different interpretation of the Act in relation to those facts. A court that decides that the statute is unambiguous decides that the alternative interpretation is impossible on the wording. . . .

It is convenient to distinguish between the primary meaning of words (their most obvious or central meaning) and a secondary meaning (a meaning that can be coaxed out of the words by argument). Secondary meanings are sometimes thought of in terms of implication. The court finds from the general purpose of the statute that it must be using words in either a less or a more extended sense or otherwise in a different sense from the one they would normally bear.

The recognition of secondary meaning is compelled by the rule that words are to be interpreted in their context. We understand the meaning of words from their context, and in ordinary life the context includes not only other words used at the same time but the whole human or social situation in which the words are used. Professor Zander, in his excellent book *The Law–Making Process,* gives the example of parents asking a child-minder to keep the children amused by teaching them a card game. In the parents' absence the child-minder teaches the children to play strip poker. There is no doubt that strip poker is a card game, but also no doubt that it was not the sort of card game intended by the instructions given. One knows this not from anything the parents have said but from customary ideas as to the proper upbringing and behaviour of children. It would be nonsense in these circumstances for the child-minder to assert that all he did was to ascertain from the words the parents used as expressing their intention what that intention was, and that the expression "card game" in its natural and ordinary meaning refers to a game played with cards. Certainly it is true that one ascertains a person's intention from his words, but one considers the words in the circumstances and for the purpose for which they were uttered. Lord Edmund–Davies put the point in relation to the interpretation of statutes as follows (*Morris v. Beardmore* [1981] AC at 459):

"A statute does not exist in limbo. It has a background, it rests on an assumption that it will operate only in a certain climate and

* Reprinted with permission of Butter-worth & Co. (Publishers) Ltd.

that circumstances of a certain sort will prevail."

If the court accepts a secondary meaning, it may be natural to express this by rephrasing the statute to explain how it is now to be understood. In one case Lord Edmund–Davies objected to a secondary meaning attached to statutory words by the majority of his fellow-peers, saying: "This is redrafting with a vengeance" (*Royal College of Nursing v. DHSS* [1981] 2 WLR at 303). But he said this because he rejected the proposed secondary meaning. Stigmatising it as redrafting was only a way of saying that it was inconsistent with the "true" meaning of the Act. If the recognition of a secondary meaning arises from what Lord Edmund–Davies himself called the background of the Act, it cannot logically be rejected on the ground that it amounts to redrafting.

Statements of the literal rule sometimes misleadingly imply that if the primary meaning of the words is clear no recourse can be had to a secondary meaning. This does not represent the practice of the courts, and it misunderstands the way in which we use language (since we do not always use words in their primary meaning). Whether or not the court can be persuaded to attach a secondary meaning to the words of the legislature depends upon many considerations varying with the individual case; it does not depend on the question whether the primary meaning is plain and unambiguous—whatever that may mean.

Some statements of the literal rule, again, are open to objection because they overlook the distinction between primary and secondary meaning and the opportunity this gives to the courts to choose between different possible meanings. Lord Diplock said that the role of the judiciary is confined to ascertaining Parliament's intention from the words it has approved. But when the primary and secondary meaning of the words differ, the choice between these meanings cannot always be made by examining "the words that Parliament has approved". Similar objection may be made to a remark of Lord Wilberforce (*Royal College of Nursing v. DHSS* [1981] 2 WLR at 294):

> "There is one course which the courts cannot take; they cannot fill gaps; they cannot by asking the question 'What would Parliament have done in this current case—not being one in contemplation—if the facts had been before it?' attempt themselves to supply the answer, if the answer is not to be found in the terms of the Act itself".

As has already been said, this kind of remark is in one sense a truism, but it is a misleading truism because it mistakenly suggests that the court has *only* to read the Act.

Judges certainly differ in their readiness to reorganise secondary meanings, and they may mask their real motivations by speaking of literal interpretation and of words being plain and unambiguous; but such language is not controlling. Some judges tend to be of a formalistic, legalistic turn of mind while other are more socially conscious. Then again a judge may have strong social or moral views in relation to one type of activity but not in relation to another. If the judge is sufficiently convinced that it was the intention of Parliament to cover the situation (or would have been its intention if it had thought of it), or else that this situation ought socially or morally to be covered, he will strive to find a secondary meaning (or to imply words into the statute) in order to cover it; if he either believes that it ought not to be covered or is not satisfied that Parliament intended it to be covered he will be disposed to say that it cannot be brought within the statutory words.

I have stated in the previous paragraphs what I believe to be the practice of the judges, but would add that a judge ought always to subordinate his preferences to the apparent intention of the statute. He should give effect to his own ethical opinions only to the extent that it seems reasonable to assume that they were shared by Parliament, or would have been shared if Parliament had addressed itself to the matter.

————

The admission of an absurdity as the result of a literal application of a law led to the creation of a second approach, the "golden rule." Where the literal approach leads to an absurdity, a repugnance, an inconvenience or an inconsistency, then another meaning may be sought. But what degree of absurdity, or inconvenience, will allow the search for a better meaning? The rule opens the door, as far as the judges wish it to open, to a decision based on social policy or political preference. Is it preferable to trust the judiciary to use considerable discretion in opening the door, or to reject the golden rule and leave the door shut, with an absurd result standing naked before the door, unable to come in and gain the flimsiest garment of reasonableness or justice? Discretion wisely used may avoid public hostility to a system which applies rules so as to achieve results which are admitted on the bench to be deviants from the aggregate body of fair and just opinions. What must be stressed is that the rule does not permit one to open the door quickly and widely and to enter the domain of unfettered justification. It is a rule applied only after the literal rule is first attempted—and because one of the above undesirable conclusions arises. Then, the golden rule permits a search for a more reasonable meaning. The Adler decision tends to support the use of the rule, but it should be remembered that as a rule, the golden rule achieves legitimacy only because the first applied literal rule is also deemed a legitimate rule of construction.

ADLER v. GEORGE

[1964] 2 Q.B. 7, 9. *

Lord Parker C.J. This is an appeal by way of case stated from a decision of justices for the county of Norfolk sitting at Downham Market who convicted the defendant of an offence contrary to section 3 of the Official Secrets Act, 1920, in that, in the vicinity of a prohibited place, namely, Marham Royal Air Force station, he obstructed a member of

* Reprinted with permission of The Incorporated Council of Law Reporting.

Her Majesty's Forces engaged in security duty in relation to the said prohibited place.

Section 3 provides that:

"No person in the vicinity of any prohibited place shall obstruct, knowingly mislead or otherwise interfere with or impede, the chief officer or a superintendent or other officer of police, or any member of His Majesty's forces engaged on guard, sentry, patrol, or other similar duty in relation to the prohibited place, and, if any person acts in contravention of, or fails to comply with, this provision, he shall be guilty of a misdemeanour."

In the present case the defendant had obtained access to—it matters not how—and was on the Air Force station on May 11, 1963, and there and then, it was found, he obstructed a member of Her Majesty's Royal Air Force.

The sole point here, and a point ably argued by the defendant, is that if he was on the station he could not be in the vicinity of the station, and it is only an offence under this section to obstruct a member of Her Majesty's Forces while he is in the vicinity of the station. The defendant has referred to the natural meaning of "vicinity," which I take to be, quite generally, the state of being near in space, and he says that it is inapt to and does not cover being in fact on the station as in the present case.

I am quite satisfied that this is a case where no violence is done to the language by reading the words "in the vicinity of" as meaning "in or in the vicinity of." Here is a section in an Act of Parliament designed to prevent interference with members of Her Majesty's forces, among others, who are engaged on guard, sentry, patrol or other similar duty in relation to a prohibited place such as this station. It would be extraordinary, I venture to think it would be absurd, if an indictable offence was thereby created when the obstruction took place outside the precincts of the station, albeit in the vicinity, and no offence at all was created if the obstruction occurred on the station itself.... There may be, of course, many contexts in which "vicinity" must be confined to its literal meaning of "being near in space" but under this section, I am quite clear that the context demands that the words should be construed in the way I have said. I would dismiss this appeal.

Neither the literal approach nor the golden rule seeks to consider the aim toward which the legislature was directing its efforts. Even the golden rule concentrates on the words of the statute, extracting a meaning from those words more reasonable than the words which the literal approach extracts. To consider what the legislature was trying to correct or achieve is called the mischief rule. Why was the statute passed? What mischief was it meant to remedy? The statute should be read consistently with the goal of the legislature. While this might suggest seeking the legislative history of the act, it does not in England admit the depth of search permitted in the United States. The English mischief rule seems to the American lawyer quite limited. Lord Diplock has given the meaning of the rule.

BLACK–CLAWSON LTD. v. PAPIERWERKE A.G.
(1975) A.C. 591, 638. *

LORD DIPLOCK . . .

* * *

[W]hen it was laid down, the "mischief" rule did not require the court to travel beyond the actual words of the statute itself to identify "the mischief and defect for which the common law did not provide," for this would have been stated in the preamble. It was a rule of construction of the actual words appearing in the statute and nothing else. In construing modern statutes which contain no preambles to serve as aids to the construction of enacting words the "mischief" rule must be used with caution to justify any reference to extraneous documents for this purpose. If the enacting words are plain and unambiguous in themselves there is no need to have recourse to any "mischief" rule. To speak of mischief and of remedy is to describe the obverse and the reverse of a single coin. The former is that part of the existing law that is changed by the plain words of the Act; the latter is the change that these words made in it.

———

In the mischief rule we are moving away from the words of the statute to attempt to discover what those words mean. Judges are not content with being limited to reading the words. The words may be ambiguous. They may lead to an absurd result. The judges do not wish such result to cause discredit to the system and they seek a better meaning. Thus they look to external sources. But what are the permitted limits of their search? Before we consider those limits, and how they differ from an external search for statutory meaning in the United States, we should note that there may be another reason for such an inquiry. There may have been a gap in the statute. Something may appear to have been left out. The words of the statute may be clear, but they may not cover the case at hand. They may be close. Should the judges fill in the gap? One may wish first to know how broad the gap is. Let us assume it is not so broad that most persons would agree that it should not be filled, but rather sufficiently narrow to create a question of (1) whether it should be filled, or (2) whether the conclusion should be (a) that the statute does not at all address the issue, or (b) that the statute should be applied as best as it can without recognition of a gap.

* Reprinted with permission of The Incorporated Council of Law Reporting.

Lord Denning was a champion of filling the gap. He wrote of statutory interpretation while Master of the Rolls and advocated a change. The view he expressed, a purposive approach, began to gain favor. But he wrote four years later, soon after his retirement, that the flood tide of change was ebbing and that the grammatical approach was returning. It is a question of constitutional importance. Do judges have the power to fill gaps, a power which is one of law-making and thought by most to be reserved to Parliament?

LORD DENNING, "THE DISCIPLINE OF LAW"
9 (1979).

Beyond doubt the task of the lawyer—and of the judge—is to find out the intention of Parliament. In doing this, you must, of course, start with the words used in the statute: but not end with them—as some people seem to think. You must discover the meaning of the words. I have known statutes where there is no discernible meaning. Then we can say with the King in *Alice in Wonderland:* 'If there's no meaning in it, that saves a world of trouble, you know, as we needn't try to find any'. But in most cases there is some meaning: so we have to go on as the King did: 'And yet I don't know', he went on, 'I seem to see some meaning in it after all'.

... The meaning for which we should seek is the meaning of the Statute as it appears to those who have to obey it—and to those who have to advise them what to do about it; in short, to lawyers like yourselves. Now the Statute does not come to such folk as if they were eccentrics cut off from all that is happening around them. The Statute comes to them as men of affairs—who have their own feeling for the meaning of the words and know the reason why the Act was passed— just as if it had been fully set out in a preamble. So it has been held very rightly that you can inquire into the mischief which gave rise to the Statute—to see what was the evil which it was sought to remedy. You can for this purpose look at the Reports of Royal Commissions, of Departmental Committees and Inquiries, Law Reform Committees—and the like. So can the Judges. But oddly enough the Judges cannot look at what the responsible Minister said to Parliament—at the object of the Statute as he explained it to the House—or to the meaning of the words as he understood them. Hansard is for the Judges a closed book. But not for you. You can read what was said in the House and adopt it as part of your argument—so long as you do not acknowledge the source. The writers of law books can go further. They can give the very words from Hansard with chapter and verse. You can then read the whole to the Judges.... The first case in which there was an opportunity to advocate a new approach to the interpretation of statutes was *Seaford Court Estates Ltd v. Asher*.[1] I was a very junior Lord Justice of Appeal of only six months' standing. Lord Greene MR was presiding with

1. [1949] 2 K.B. 481.

Asquith LJ and me.   It was a case where the rent of a flat had been
increased from £175 a year to £250 a year.   The increase was because
the landlord agreed to provide the hot water for the flat.   The tenant
freely agreed to pay the £250 but then tried to get it reduced to £175.
He had no merits at all.   His argument depended on giving a literal
meaning to the word 'burden' in the Rent Act 1920.   It was a situation
which Parliament never foresaw and for which it had made no provision.
We reserved judgment for four weeks.   I prepared my judgment and
showed it to Lord Greene.   He agreed with it and said so in his own
judgment.   Lord Justice Asquith also agreed with it.   So it had backing
of the first order.   This is what I said:

> 'The question for decision in this case is whether we are at
> liberty to extend the ordinary meaning of 'burden' so as to include a
> contingent burden of the kind I have described.   Now this court has
> already held that this sub-section is to be liberally construed so as to
> give effect to the governing principles embodied in the legislation
> ... and I think we should do the same.

> 'Whenever a statute comes up for consideration it must be
> remembered that it is not within human powers to foresee the
> manifold sets of facts which may arise, and, even if it were, it is not
> possible to provide for them in terms free from all ambiguity.   The
> English language is not an instrument of mathematical precision.
> Our literature would be much the poorer if it were.   This is where
> the draftsmen of Acts of Parliament have often been unfairly criti-
> cized.   A judge, believing himself to be fettered by the supposed rule
> that he must look to the language and nothing else, laments that the
> draftsmen have not provided for this or that, or have been guilty of
> some or other ambiguity.   It would certainly save the judges trouble
> if Acts of Parliament were drafted with divine prescience and perfect
> clarity.   In the absence of it, when a defect appears a judge cannot
> simply fold his hands and blame the draftsman.   He must set to
> work on the constructive task of finding the intention of Parliament,
> and he must do this not only from the language of the statute, but
> also from a consideration of the social conditions which gave rise to
> it, and of the mischief which it was passed to remedy, and then he
> must supplement the written word so as to give 'force and life' to
> the intention of the legislature.   That was clearly laid down by the
> resolution of the judges in *Heydon's* case, and it is the safest guide
> today.   Good practical advice on the subject was given about the
> same time by Plowden.... Put into homely metaphor it is this: A
> judge should ask himself the question: If the makers of the Act had
> themselves come across this ruck in the texture of it, how would
> they have straightened it out?   He must then do as they would have
> done.   A judge must not alter the material of which it is woven, but
> he can and should iron out the creases.

> 'Approaching this case in that way, I cannot help feeling that
> the legislature had not specifically in mind a contingent burden such
> as we have here.   If it had would it not have put it on the same

footing as an actual burden? I think it would. It would have permitted an increase of rent when the terms were so changed as to put a positive legal burden on the landlord'.

The case went to the House of Lords and our decision was upheld but it was there put by the majority of the House on traditional grounds. Lord MacDermott (who dissented) took the literal meaning. He thought I had stated the principles 'rather widely' [1].

The new approach did not last long. Only a year later it was roundly condemned by the House of Lords. It was in *Magor and St Mellons Rural District Council v. Newport Corporation* [2]. The Newport Corporation had expanded its boundaries by taking in goodly parts of the two Magor and St. Mellons Rural Districts—taking in the richest parts paying a large amount of rates. The Act provided for reasonable compensation to the two District Councils. Then the Minister made an Order amalgamating the two District Councils into one. On that account the Newport Corporation sought to reduce the compensation to nothing. This seemed to me most unjust. The Newport Corporation sought to rely on the literal meaning of the Order. They succeeded in all Courts. I protested in the Court of Appeal, saying:

> 'This was so obviously the intention of the Minister's Order that I have no patience with an ultra-legalistic interpretation which would deprive (the appellants) of their rights altogether. I would repeat what I said in *Seaford Court Estates Ltd v. Asher*. We do not sit here to pull the language of Parliament and of Ministers to pieces and make nonsense of it. That is an easy thing to do, and it is a thing to which lawyers are too often prone. We sit here to find out the intention of Parliament and of Ministers and carry it out, and we do this better by filling in the gaps and making sense of the enactment than by opening it up to destructive analysis'.

My protest carried some weight with Lord Radcliffe. He had the best mind of anyone of his time. He rejected the strict literal view saying: 'I regard this as an injustice' [1], but all the others insisted upon it. Lord Simonds was a dominating intellect but cast in a most conservative mould. He rejected my proposition that it was 'the duty of the Court to find out the intention of Parliament—and not only of Parliament but of Ministers also'. He said that it 'cannot by any means be supported. The duty of the Court is to interpret the words which the legislature has used'. That is the traditional view expressed, as usual, by Lord Simonds in his most dogmatic fashion. He went on to pour scorn in these words:

> '... The court, having discovered the intention of Parliament and of Ministers too, must proceed to fill in the gaps. What the legislature has not written, the court must write. This proposition, which restates in a new form the view expressed by the Lord Justice

---

1. [1950] 1 All E.R. 1018, 1029.

2. [1951] 2 All E.R. 839.

1. [1951] 2 All E.R. 839, 849.

in the earlier case of *Seaford Court Estates Ltd v. Asher* (to which the Lord Justice himself refers), cannot be supported. It appears to me to be a naked usurpation of the legislative function under the thin disguise of interpretation. And it is the less justifiable when it is guesswork with what material the legislature would, if it had discovered the gap, have filled it in. If a gap is disclosed, the remedy lies in an amending Act'.

So injustice was done. The new approach was scotched. It took a long time to bring it to life again. Yet gradually it came. Even in the House of Lords, some Law Lords began to say—quite contrary to Lord Simonds—that it was their task to find out the intention of Parliament: and that they would adapt the words of the statute—put a strained construction on them if need be, to carry out that intention. Thus in *Nimmo v. Alexander* [2] Lord Wilberforce said:

> 'If I thought that Parliament's intention could not be carried out, or even would be less effectively implemented, unless one particular (even though unnatural) construction were placed on the words it has used, I would endeavour to adopt that construction'.

And in *Kammins v. Zenith Investments Ltd,* [1] Lord Diplock drew a clear distinction between the 'literal approach' and the 'purposive approach', and used the purposive approach to solve the question.

There remained only one further push needed. It was provided by Sir David Renton in the Report of his Committee [2].

> 'We see no reason why the Courts should not respond in the way indicated by Lord Denning. The Courts should, in our view, approach legislation determined, above all, to give effect to the intention of Parliament. We see promising signs that this consideration is uppermost in the minds of the members of the highest tribunal in this country'.

Thus encouraged, I soon found occasion to restate the principle I had stated nearly thirty years before. . . .

* * *

LORD DENNING, "THE CLOSING CHAPTER"
99 (1983).

Two years ago that attitude [the view of Lord Simonds in the previous piece and a later decision which refuses to fill any gap] was severely criticised by Lord Diplock. It was in *Fothergill v. Monarch Airlines.* [3] He quoted Lord Simonds and called it a 'narrowly semantic approach'. He said that it had left an 'unhappy legacy'. It had influenced the parliamentary draftsmen for the worse. It had led them to adopt the 'current English style of legislative draftsmanship'.

2.   [1968] A.C. 107, 130.   **2.**   Cmnd. 6053, para. 19.2.

1.   [1971] A.C. 850, 881.   **3.**   [1981] A.C. 251, 280.

They tried to 'provide in express detail what is to be done in each of all the foreseeable varieties of circumstances'. In short, they tried to think of every contingency and to fill the gap. An impossible task. No one can think of everything.

In view of that criticism, I would ask the question: Nowadays, if the courts come across a gap in a statute, can they fill it? Can they remedy the omission by doing what good sense and justice require? This question lies at the heart of statutory interpretation today. In order to answer it, I now come to some recent cases. In one of them the House of Lords filled a gap and did justice. In the others the gap was not filled and injustice resulted.

Mr. Fothergill went for a holiday on a package tour. He insured his luggage with an insurance company. He came home by air to Luton airport. He got his suitcase and found that it was badly damaged. He went to the reception desk and reported it. The lady filled in a form:

> Nature of Damage: Side seam completely parted from case. Damage occurred on inbound flight.

Mr. Fothergill did not at that time complain that any of the contents were missing. He went home to Colchester with his damaged suitcase. When he opened it, he found that his shirt was missing. He claimed on his insurance company, £12 for the damage to the suitcase and £16.50 for the loss of the shirt. His insurance company paid him for both.

But nobody told the airline about the loss of the shirt. No complaint was made to them for over three months. Then the insurance company, by virtue of their right of subrogation, made a claim. The airline admitted liability for the damage to the suitcase (because they had been notified of it within seven days) but they denied liability for the loss of the shirt (because they had received no complaint about it for three months). They said that, in case of pilferage, it was important that they should be notified of it promptly so that they could check it at once.

Mr. Fothergill's insurance company took it up as a test case. They brought an action in Mr. Fothergill's name against the airline. They relied on an Article in the Warsaw Convention. It laid down seven days as the time limit for a complaint:

> In the case of *damage*, the person entitled to delivery must complain to the carrier forthwith after the discovery of the *damage*, and, at the latest, within seven days from the date of receipt of the baggage.

The great contest was as to the meaning of the word 'damage' in that Article. Mr. Fothergill's insurance company said that it only applied to the damage to the suitcase, and not to the loss of the shirt. There was, they said, no time-bar for the loss of the shirt. So complaint could be made to the airline about it for the first time even after several months had passed.

Both the trial judge and the majority of the Court of Appeal (with me dissenting) accepted that view. They held that 'damage' meant physical damage and did not include partial loss of contents. So, despite the lateness of the claim, the airline were held liable for the missing shirt.

But the House of Lords reversed them. They accepted—or at any rate Lord Scarman did—that 'damage' in its ordinary sense meant damage and did not include loss. But the whole House went on to hold that in this Article 'damage' included 'partial loss of contents'. They filled in a gap in the Article by reading it as if it said 'in the case of damage or partial loss of contents'. They justified their attitude by reliance on a purposive interpretation. Lord Wilberforce took the considerations relevant to the word 'damage' in its literal sense, and said: [1]

> If one then inquires whether these considerations are relevant to a case of partial loss of objects contained in baggage, the answer cannot be doubtful: they clearly are.... There seems to be no sense in making a distinction between damage to baggage ... and loss of contents.

Lord Scarman said

> If, therefore, the literal construction be legitimate, I would dismiss the appeal. But, in my judgment, it is not. It makes commercial sense to apply, if it be possible, the same time limits for giving notice of a complaint of partial loss of contents as for one of physical damage: and I am equally in no doubt that it is the duty of the English courts to apply, if possible, an interpretation which meets the commercial purpose of the Convention. In my judgment, such an interpretation is possible.

So the Lords did what good sense required. It would be unjust to allow a complaint of pilferage to be made months or even years afterward.

In later cases, however, the House of Lords have refused to fill in a gap. The first is one where students from overseas were claiming they were entitled as of right to have their university fees paid by the local authorities. It is *R v. Barnet London Borough Council, ex parte Nilish Shah*.[2] I will take one of the students as an example. Hamid Akbarali lived with his parents in Pakistan. He went to school there. But in 1975, when he was 18, he wanted to become an engineer. The best place for training was England. His parents could pay for it. In order to get an entry to England he had to satisfy the authorities that he could meet the cost of the course and his own maintenance, and that he would leave at the end of the course. He did satisfy them. He was granted a student's visa. This gave him leave to enter for 12 months, and it was continued on the same basis each year. He went daily to a technical college here from January 1975 to September 1978. He lived at Kings' Road, Chelsea, in a rented flat. His parents paid for it. He returned

---

1. [1981] A.C. 251, 273.   2. [1983] 2 W.L.R. 16.

twice to Pakistan—in 1977 and 1978—on holiday visiting his parents. In October 1978 he started a course at Chelsea College in London, studying for a BSc degree. His parents paid his fees at the College and the cost of his maintenance. That was in accordance with the conditions of his student's visa.

Then he heard that he might be entitled to a mandatory grant from the local education authority, and thus save his parents the expense. That was because under the Education Act 1962 and the Regulations made in 1979, an authority was under a duty to pay an award to a person who is 'ordinarily resident' in the area throughout the three years before starting the course. The crucial question was whether he was 'ordinarily resident' in Chelsea during the three years 1975 to 1978. In their literal meaning the words 'ordinarily resident' mean that the person must be habitually and normally resident here, apart from temporary or occasional absences of long or short duration. That was true of Akbarali. He was habitually and normally resident in Chelsea, even though his home was in Pakistan and he went back there occasionally for holidays.

On the literal approach, therefore, Akbarali was entitled to a mandatory grant. He had brought himself within the literal meaning of the words.

The Court of Appeal refused to accept the literal meaning. They rejected Akbarali's claim. I said: [1]

> In these circumstances I think we must abandon our traditional method of interpretation. The rebuffs in *Magor and St Mellons Rural District Council v. Newport Corpn* [1952] AC 189 no longer hurt. We must ourselves fill in the gaps which Parliament has left. We must do our best to legislate for a state of affairs for which Parliament has not legislated. We must say what is the meaning of the words 'ordinarily resident' in the context of the situation brought about by the Immigration Act 1971.
>
> On this approach, it is my opinion that, whenever a boy comes from overseas on a student's visa, which is renewed every year, he is not to be regarded as 'ordinarily resident' here. He is allowed to enter on the terms that he or his parents or friends will pay all his fees and expenses whilst he is here, and that he will leave this country when his leave comes to an end. Such a boy is not 'ordinarily resident' here. No matter whether he goes home for holidays or not. No matter whether his parents are dead and he has no home to go to overseas. Suffice it that he has to leave at the end of his time, unless renewed.

In coming to this conclusion I was much influenced by the observations of Lord Justice Ormrod when this case had come before the Divisional Court: [1]

1.   [1982] Q.B. 688, 720.   1.   [1982] Q.B. 688, 704.

We are fortified in our construction of this regulation by the reflection that it is almost inconceivable that Parliament could have intended to bestow major awards for higher education, out of public funds, on persons permitted to enter this country on a temporary basis, solely for the purpose of engaging in courses of study at their own expense. Such an improbable result is not to be accepted if it can properly be avoided.

This meant filling in a gap. The Education Act 1962 and the 1979 Regulations had not dealt with the position of students coming from overseas on students' visas. It must have been overlooked. If they had dealt with it, they would have excluded them from any right to a mandatory grant. They would have inserted words for the purpose. It was inconceivable that they would have omitted to deal with it if they had thought of it.

Could this oversight be corrected by the judges? The Court of Appeal thought it could. But the House of Lords took a different view. There was only one speech. It was by Lord Scarman. The others agreed with it. They held that overseas students were 'ordinarily resident' for the three years in England: and that, on the wording of the statute, they were entitled to a grant. Lord Scarman said that the Court of Appeal

> were influenced by their own views of policy and by the immigration status of the students.[1]

He then said:

> The way in which they used policy was, in my judgment, an impermissible approach to the interpretation of statutory language. Judges may not interpret statutes in the light of their own views as to policy. They may, of course, adopt a purposive interpretation if they can find in the statute read as a whole, or in material to which they are permitted by law to refer, as aids to interpretation, an expression of Parliament's purpose or policy. But that is not this case. The Education Act's only guidance is the requirement contained in the Regulations that, to be eligible for a mandatory award, a student must have been ordinarily resident in the United Kingdom for three years. There is no hint of any other restriction, provided, of course, he has the educational qualifications and his conduct is satisfactory.

In other words, the Court of Appeal ought not to have filled in the gap as they did.

The House of Lords' decision was viewed with dismay by the Council for Local Education Authorities. For them it was said in *The Times:*

> It is quite a bombshell. The financial implications are quite serious. Unless legislation is introduced as a matter of urgency it looks as though many who have been classified as overseas students

---

1. [1983] 2 W.L.R. 16, 30.

will now be classed as home students, paying lower fees and entitled to mandatory grants.

The Times had a headline: 'Councils alarmed by grant ruling. It is also embarrassing for the Government.' Professor Zander wrote an article in *The Guardian* of 22 December 1982 describing it as:

> A blinkered way to lay down the law ... This is to go back to the bad old traditional literal-minded approach—with the judge looking for the solution to problems in the dictionary.

* * *

The next case in the House of Lords was equally startling. It is *Griffiths v. Secretary of State for the Environment.*[1] Mr. Griffiths wanted to develop his land. The Secretary of State refused to grant planning permission. Mr. Griffiths wished to appeal to the High Court. The statute gave him six weeks from the date on which 'action is taken' by the Secretary of State. The House of Lords, by a majority, held that 'the action' was taken at the moment when some officer in the department put the date-stamp on the decision-letter. That date was final, even though the letter was never posted, or was lost in the post, so that it never reached Mr. Griffiths: and he had no notice of the decision.

Lord Scarman dissented. He said that it was unjust that Mr. Griffiths should have lost his right of appeal before he had any notice of 'the action'. Lord Scarman said:

> I would not hold that Parliament intended anything so arbitrary.

Lord Elwyn–Jones said that the result was 'regrettable', but he did not formally dissent.

There was a simple way of doing justice. It was to fill in the gap by saying that the six weeks ran from the date on which Mr. Griffiths received notice. But the majority refused to fill in the gap.

* * *

In a debate in the House of Lords on 15 December 1982 the Lord Chancellor suggested that statutory interpretation raised a constitutional question. He asked:

> Are we not really in the presence of a political and constitutional problem which is endemic in our parliamentary institution to a greater extent than has wholly been realised?
>
> ... We should remember that much of what we are complaining of is actually due to the balances and checks which we have come to accept as part of our constitutional liberty.

As I see it, that balance is this: Parliament enacts statute law and the judges interpret it. Statute law is necessarily expressed in words.

---

1. [1983] 2 W.L.R. 172.

Parliament decides upon the words. The judges say what those words mean.

In one pan of the scales you put the proposition that every citizen is bound by the words which Parliament has used, and by the words only. That is the check upon Parliament. In the other pan you put the proposition that the judges are not to add to or subtract from the words. They are not to legislate. That is the check upon the judges.

The Lord Chancellor spoke of his experience of legislators:

> How often when a minister has said, 'The courts will take a sensible view of this' have I heard the words from the back benches, 'Well, let us have it written into the statute'?

According to this point of view, our constitution requires legislation in such detail as to preclude any misunderstanding. In going into detail, the draftsmen are only fulfilling a constitutional requirement.

To my mind there is this answer:

Legislation in detail has been found by experience to be self-defeating. It leads to statutory provisions which are so complicated as to be obscure and unintelligible. When this happens, it offends the fundamental principle that a statute should be so expressed as to be readily understood by those who are affected by it.

It is this principle—the principle of clarity—which should prevail. Accordingly, legislation in detail should be abandoned and replaced by legislation in principle. By this I mean that our statutes should expound principles in clear language and should leave the details, where necessary, to be worked out by some other means or in some other way. That was one of the recommendations of Lord Renton's Committee. It was in paragraph 10.13 of their Report, Cmnd 6053. Even so, there are bound to be gaps—due to oversight or lack of foresight or to draftsmanship. These gaps should be filled in by the judges according to their own good sense. They can and should be trusted thus far. They developed the common law in that way. They should be trusted, likewise, with the statute law.

I find very apposite the eloquent plea for clarity which Lord Renton made at the end of his opening speech in the debate in the House of Lords:

> If our Acts of Parliament cannot be understood even by clever experts it not only brings the law into contempt, it brings Parliament into contempt. It is a disservice to our democracy; it weakens the rights of the individual; it eases the way for wrongdoers and it places honest, humble people at the mercy of the state. In the name of reason and justice, *Let's get it straight!*

To my mind, the one way to get it straight is for Parliament to use plain, simple language expressing principles, and for the judges to fill in the gaps in a statute so as to do what good sense requires.

In his Hamlyn Lecture just delivered, Lord Hailsham of Saint Marylebone has said that statute law has assumed a vastly increased importance and that this

> has greatly accentuated the need for fresh thinking about the draftsmanship and interpretation of statutes.

The Times in a leader on 21 May 1983 says that 'his timing could hardly have been better'. It suggests a solution in these words:

> What seems to be needed is some movement on both fronts: (a) a broader style of legislative drafting on the one hand, and (b) a somewhat more purposive approach to statutory interpretation by the courts.... It is probably inevitable that greater simplicity in legislative drafting will confer a greater discretion on the courts in interpreting statutes, but there is no alternative if the law is to remain accessible to the people.

––––––––

The view of Lord Denning may be welcomed by many outside the aggregate of legal actors, and a not inconsiderable number within, but his view does not represent the majority of the legal profession. The comments of Lord Devlin may be more indicative of the norm.

P. DEVLIN, "THE JUDGE"

14 (1981).*

* * *

I turn now to statute law. Judges, I have accepted, have a responsibility for the common law, but in my opinion they have none for statute law; their duty is simply to interpret and apply it and not to obstruct. I remain unconvinced that there is anything basically wrong with the rule of construction that words in a statute should be given their natural and ordinary meaning. The rule does not insist on a literal interpretation or require the construction of a statute without regard to its manifest purpose. There should be, as Lord Diplock has said, 'a purposive approach to the Act as a whole to ascertain the social ends it was intended to achieve and the practical means by which it was expected to achieve them'. But in the end the words must be taken to mean what they say and not what their interpreter would like them to say; the statute is the master and not the servant of the judgment.

In the past judges have been obstructive. But the source of the obstruction, it is very important to note, has been the refusal of judges to act on the ordinary meaning of words. They looked for the philosophy behind the Act and what they found was a Victorian Bill of Rights, favouring (subject to the observance of the accepted standards of morali-

* The Judge by Patrick Devlin (1979).   sity Press.
Reprinted by permission of Oxford Univer-

ty) the liberty of the individual, the freedom of contract, and the sacredness of property, and which was highly suspicious of taxation. If the Act interfered with these notions, the judges tended either to assume that it could not mean what it said or to minimize the interference by giving the intrusive words the narrowest possible construction, even to the point of pedantry.

No doubt judges, like any other body of elderly men who have lived on the whole unadventurous lives, tend to be old-fashioned in their ideas. This is a fact of nature which reformers must accept. It is silly to invite the older generation to make free with Acts of Parliament and then to abuse them if the results are unpleasing to advanced thinkers. Not that everything can always be blamed on the conservatism of judges. Statutes are not philosophical treatises and the philosophy behind them, if there is one, is often half-baked. Those who want judges to search for meanings beyond words should first examine some case histories. Let me give you one which recently came to my notice and which, I can assure you, is quite typical.

The Harbours, Docks and Piers Clauses Act 1847 is not a statute infused with a high social purpose, but it is a good example of the sort of statute with which judges habitually deal. Section 74 provides that any damage done by a vessel to a harbour, dock, or pier shall be paid for by the owner of the vessel; in order to make sure that there should be no judicial quibbling about what is a vessel, the statute says 'every vessel or float of timber', but otherwise it is written in normal English. Yet when a case of damage arose at Durham Assizes in 1875, only two out of the seven judges who ultimately had to consider the case could bring themselves to believe that the statute meant what it said and actually imposed absolute liability. Note that the majority judges were taking the liberal view. The common law at that time was seeking to free itself from primitive notions of absolute liability and was at the commencement of a great development in the law of negligence; surely the Act must be made to fit in with the rational idea that liability followed upon fault.

This decision of the House of Lords in *River Wear Commissioners v. Adamson* [1] is one of quite a number of its sort which trouble the law of England. The point I want to take from it is that the departure from the natural and ordinary meaning of words usually leads to confusion. Five judges are no more likely to agree than five philosophers upon the philosophy behind an Act of Parliament and five different judges are likely to have five different ideas about the right escape route from the prison of the text. The House of Lords in the *River Wear* case certainly decided that section 74 should not be given its literal meaning. But beyond that, and in spite of several judicial inquests at the highest level, the courts have not yet arrived at any general agreement about what section 74 does mean. After a century it is still fermenting in judicial

---

1. [1877] 2 A.C. 743.

thought. One of its legacies recently split the High Court of Australia three to two.

Today we should have no difficulty with section 74. Its language fits in nicely with the new philosophy that negligence does not matter and that the statutory object in such a case is simply to make clear who is to take out the insurance policy. Perhaps Parliament in 1847 had a prophetic glimpse of the twentieth-century philosophy, but it is far more likely that it had no philosophical thoughts at all.

So while in theory there is room for judicial activism in the development of a statute when the consensus is clear, I doubt whether in practice it would be productive. The judicial expansion of statutes from the Statute of Frauds onwards has not usually been successful. It would be surprising if it had been. You cannot hope for effective co-operation between bodies which are not expected to converse with each other. 'The organs of government are partners in the enterprise of lawmaking,' Professor Jaffe writes, 'courts and legislatures are in the law business together.' He refers to the 'potentiality' of a fruitful partnership and interaction between them. If this is meant as more than metaphorical, ways and means as yet unmentioned will have to be devised for effectuating the joint enterprise; one partner cannot be left guessing about what the other is doing and why. In a country such as the United States in which the legislature and the executive are independent of each other, it would perhaps be possible, granted some considerable relaxation in the doctrine of the separation of powers, to have legislators and judges working together in a communion which did not imperil essential freedoms. In a country like Britain it would be impossible. For the British Parliament, while it acts as an independent check on legislation brought forward by the executive, is not an independent legislature. Legislation in Britain is introduced by the executive and, when it has been enacted at the behest of the executive, is frequently implemented by ministerial regulation. Thus the executive commands both the principle and the detail of the statute. Is the judge in the case to go into partnership with the government of the day? On such a statute as, for example, the Industrial Relations Act 1971? Is he to ring up the appropriate Minister and get his views about the next step? Without this sort of conversation the judge, bent on developing the law, is at worst heading for a collision and at best groping in the dark; with it the judge abandons his role of arbiter between the government and the governed.

I appreciate that radical reformers may take a fundamentally different view from mine about the function of the judiciary. They may see it not as arbitrating between citizens and as holding the balance between the state and the individual but as one of the three branches of the government. They may see the need for social reform as demanding that all three arms of the government should smite in unison for its achievement. Judges should give social leadership, they say. What if they are harnessed to an Act of Parliament? They are still free to gallop with it towards the social millennium, treating the sections that rumble along behind as but the wagons that are packed with fodder for progressive judgments.

If judges were men endowed for such a task they would not truly be judges. In every society there is a division between rulers and ruled. The first mark of a free and orderly society is that the boundaries between the two should be guarded and trespasses from one side or the other independently and impartially determined. The keepers of these boundaries cannot also be among the outriders. The judges are the keepers of the law and the qualities they need for that task are not those of the creative lawmaker. The creative lawmaker is the squire of the social reformer and the quality they both need is enthusiasm. But enthusiasm is rarely consistent with impartiality and never with the appearance of it.

Why is it, I ask in conclusion, that the denunciators of judicial inactivity so rarely pause to throw even a passing curse at the legislators who ought really to be doing the job. They seem so often to swallow without noticing it the quite preposterous excuse that Parliament has no time and to take only a perfunctory interest in an institution such as the Law Commission. Progressives of course are in a hurry to get things done and judges with their plenitude of power could apparently get them done so quickly; there seems to be no limit to what they could do if only they would unshackle themselves from their precedents. It is a great temptation to cast the judiciary as an elite which will bypass the traffic-laden ways of the democratic process. But it would only apparently be a bypass. In truth it would be a road that would never rejoin the highway but would lead inevitably, however long and winding the path, to the totalitarian state.

SECTION 7. THE CONSTITUTION

Defining the constitutional law of the United Kingdom is made complex by the absence of a single constitutional document. Most common law nations have a constitutional document, although this does not mean it includes a bill of rights or that the constitution grants the judiciary the power of judicial review of legislation for constitutional inconsistencies. But the absence of a single document of British constitutional law has led to the creation of a myth. British constitutional law is frequently noted as being based on an "unwritten constitution." It is true only in the sense that constitutional law is not contained in a single document; the complex and abstract nature of the British Constitution results from it being an aggregation of numerous sources, mostly written but all identifiable. Changes in any of the sources which comprise the British Constitution will alter its total structure, making it more flexible than many constitutions.

The Constitution is affected by most traditional sources of English law, including the royal prerogative, conventions, common law, a few of the more important acts of Parliament, and, more recently, the addition of acts of the European Communities. Clarity of identifying the British Constitution is dependent upon recognizing its sources. The existence of custom, conventions and the royal prerogative do not render this an easy task.

The most important elements of the British Constitution are the Magna Carta, the Petition of Right 1628, and several statutes enacted by Parliament. The Act of Union with Scotland 1707, while classified as a parliamentary act, has a special status over most other acts, a status given also to the Bill of Rights 1689. The Act of Settlement 1700, and the Habeas Corpus Act 1679, are additionally constituent elements of British constitutionalism. Whether a law has the aura of constitutionalism is unknown until the courts have discussed that issue, which they only infrequently do. Thus it is difficult to classify a legal rule. Uniquely important is the European Communities Act 1972, which joined England to the European Communities. This added a new source of law, the law-making bodies of the Communities. Community law takes precedence over domestic United Kingdom law. If not applied by the United Kingdom courts, it will be by the European Court of Justice.

External to the direct and indirect effects of acts of Parliament on the British Constitution are custom and the English common law. The most significant constitutional aspect of the common law is the role of judicial decisions in protecting civil liberties. The 17th century Bill of Rights does not guarantee individual liberties. Where such rights are protected, the sources of law are various conventions, judicial decisions and statutes. A contemporary, written bill of rights in England has been sought by many for years. But many argue against a modern bill of rights. Lord Denning, who often sides with those suggesting change, in this case has written against such a bill.

LORD DENNING, "WHAT NEXT IN THE LAW"

271 (1982).

There has been much discussion on whether we should have a Bill of Rights....

The demand for a Bill of Rights arises from like causes as those in the past. There is a feeling among ordinary people that rights and freedoms of the individual have been eroded beyond measure: and that the law, as at present administered, is no longer able to protect the citizen against the pressures of the government, the trade unions, and other all-powerful bodies. So they cry: 'Let us have a Bill of Rights'.

* * *

Macaulay describes the importance of the Bill of Rights [1689] in these words:

'The Declaration of Rights, though it made nothing law which had not been law before, contained the germ of the law which gave religious freedom to the Dissenter, of the law which secured the independence of the Judges, of the law which limited the duration of Parliaments, of the law which placed the liberty of the press under the protection of juries, of the law which prohibited the slave trade, of the law which abolished the sacramental test, of the law which relieved the Roman Catholics from civil disabilities, of the law which reformed the representative system, of every good law which has been passed during more than a century and a half, of every good law which may hereafter, in the course of ages, be found necessary to promote the public weal, and to satisfy the demands of public opinion.' [a]

If we are to have a new Bill of Rights, will it too be the germ of the law which, in the complexities of modern society, maintains the rights and freedoms of the individual against the all-powerful bodies that stride about the place?

I would digress here to remind you that our forefathers who went to America took with them the 'rights of Englishmen'. They took with them, too, our Bill of Rights of 1689 and Blackstone's Commentaries. After they obtained their independence in 1776 they established on 17 September 1787 the Constitution of the United States. This set out the structure with a President, a Senate and a House of Representatives, and so forth. But one James Madison took the lead in pressing for a Bill of Rights after the English pattern. He said:

'I believe that the great mass of the people who opposed it (the Constitution), disliked it because it did not contain effectual provisions against the encroachments on particular rights, and those safeguards which they have been long accustomed to have interposed between them and the magistrate who exercises the sovereign power.'

James Madison got his amendments accepted by the Senate and approved by the House of Representatives. They were ratified by the states. . . .

* * *

Every word of those amendments has been the subject of close consideration by the Supreme Court of the United States. You could fill a whole library with decisions on the meaning of 'due process of law'. The cost in time and money has been enormous. Our own Bill of Rights has not. I do not suppose it has been invoked more than a dozen times in the last 300 years. If we are to have a new Bill of Rights, will there be thousands of cases upon it? Will our courts be cluttered up with frivolous or vexatious actions and complaints?

* * *

. . . On 24 October 1945 the United Nations Organisation was formed. On 10 December 1948 the General Assembly approved the Universal Declaration of Human Rights. This set out in thirty articles a

---

a. III History of England 1311.

'Bill of Rights' for the inhabitants of all the nations of the world. They sound very impressive.   * * *

* * *

That Universal Declaration was absolutely useless for one decisive reason. There was no means of enforcing it. There was no court to give orders. There were no litigants to appear before it. There were no police to arrest offenders. Any one of the nations who signed it could cock a snook at it. And many did so. It can be expunged from any list of Bills of Rights. It was a declaration of pious aspirations—not of enforceable rights.

Nevertheless, the Universal Declaration did have an important effect for the continent of Europe. It led to the Council of Europe founded in 1949. The Council produced the Convention for the Protection of Human Rights and Fundamental Freedoms which in 1950 was signed on behalf of the United Kingdom and ratified by the Government. But it has never been made part of our law. It remains an international treaty conferring obligations between the signatory countries on an international level, but without any legal force within the United Kingdom.

Whenever anyone speaks of a Bill of Rights nowadays, most people think that the practical way of doing it would be for Parliament to pass a statute making the European Convention part of our law. The latest Bill (which, as I have said, passed all its stages in the House of Lords) says simply:

> 'The Convention ... shall without any reservation immediately upon the passing of this Act have the force of law, and shall be enforceable by action in the courts of the United Kingdom.'

Is this desirable or not? I will first consider the way in which the courts approach the Convention nowadays. Next, I will consider what the effect would be if the Convention were made expressly part of our law.

If one or other party wishes to rely on an article of the Convention, we do not shut him up. We do not say: 'It is not part of our law. We will not look at it.' We do look at it—as if we were doing an exercise in comparative law—to see how other countries have tackled the problem. We do not go into the details of it or into masses of cases upon it. We take the article that is relied upon. We look to see if the line of approach is one which appeals to us as being correct. If so, we use it as a support for our decision. If it does not appeal to us—or if the article is too hedged about with exceptions—we put it on one side. We go about our business—of finding out the English law on the topic—without regard to the Convention....

* * *

Even at present, although the European Convention is not part of our law, nevertheless there is a means by which pressure can be brought upon us to change our law—so as to conform to it. It is because of the European Court of Human Rights which sits at Strasbourg.

Although the decisions of that Court are not binding on us, the United Kingdom has recognised its jurisdiction to the extent that cases from the United Kingdom can be referred to it. This recognition has recently been extended for another five years. So we get cases in which the Court at Strasbourg has held that the United Kingdom has violated the Convention. That ruling cannot change our law. But it means that pressure can be brought on Parliament to change it.

* * *

The proposal is that the European Convention should be made part of our law and be enforceable in our courts—with ultimately an appeal to the European Court of Human Rights sitting at Strasbourg.

I would emphasise here that the European Convention would become completely part of our law—just as much as Community law is now. This follows from two important articles in the Convention:

> '1. The high Contracting Parties shall secure to everyone within their jurisdiction the rights and freedoms defined in Section 1 of this Convention.'

Mark that article. It would mean that our courts would have to take the very words of the European Convention—and apply them in our courts as part of our law.

> '13. Everyone whose rights and freedoms as set forth in this Convention are violated shall have an effective remedy before a national authority....'

Mark that article too. It would mean that whenever a person alleged a violation of the Convention, he could bring a claim before our courts. It might be far-fetched. It might be unreasonable. But the courts would have to examine it and give effect to it.

Article 45 deals with the jurisdiction of the European Court of Human Rights at Strasbourg:

> 'The jurisdiction of the Court shall extend to all cases concerning the interpretation and application of the present Convention which the High Contracting Parties or the Commission shall refer to it.'

Mark that article too. It would mean that the Court at Strasbourg would have not only jurisdiction over the *interpretation* of the Convention—but also the *application* of it. That is, it would actually decide cases which were referred to it.

Thus you see that if the European Convention should become part of our law, it would go much further than we do in regard to the Treaty of Rome.... It would make the Court at Strasbourg the supreme judicial tribunal over us—superior to the House of Lords—in the actual decision of cases.

* * *

To my mind it would be very unfortunate for our English judges—who will have interpreted the Convention in one way—to be overruled by the European Court of Human Rights at Strasbourg. The English judges would have the 'feel' of the case. They will see how it should be decided in the light of the circumstances prevailing in England. They should not be overruled by judges who have no knowledge of the circumstances in England.

Rather than incorporate the Convention, it seems to me that the present approach is just about right. Let the English courts have regard to the principles and exceptions set out in the Convention, but not so as to be bound by them. . . . Let it be for our Parliament to decide whether or not to apply its decisions and make them part of our law. Do not let us be bound by decisions of judges who do not know our way of life—nor anything of our common law.

———

A final element of the British Constitution is that part of custom referred to as conventions, an important part of the framework of both the Constitution and ordinary English law. The source of conventions and their enforcement is less identifiable than other constitutional elements. Convention evolves principally from a non-judicial precedent established over decades if not centuries, of consistent conduct. Pressures for continuance are the expectations of the public and the convenience of the existence of the conventions. Illustrative of the role of conventions and the impact on constitutionalism is the convention that the sovereign will only exercise the royal prerogative when ministerial advice to do so is rendered. Also attributable to a convention is the requirement that ministers are responsible to Parliament, and that the government must not ignore the wishes of Parliament as expressed in legislation. Conventions tend to become sanctified as the years of their recognition and observance accumulate. They are thus less frequently found, or followed, in the newly independent nations.

In addition to the absence of a single written constitutional document, there is no court with authority to rule on the issue of constitutionality of acts of Parliament. A parliamentary act is supreme. If it conflicts with an earlier act of Parliament, or with precedent, the earlier law is modified, not violated. This might suggest that it is absolutely clear that no act of Parliament can be challenged. For Parliament to pass an act inconsistent with the Act of Union with Scotland, or with the European Communities Act, but which was not intentionally directed to altering those important acts, a court would face the difficult problem of construing them as abolishing or amending those earlier acts, or being unintentionally in violation of those acts and thus invalid. What measure of parliamentary activity is necessary to amend or abrogate an important earlier parliamentary act is unclear, particularly where that earlier act is part of the aggregate which collectively is known as the British Constitution. But it does not appear that legislation in England is assigned different values, not by Parliament, but by those through whose test it must survive, the English judiciary. Though they may not declare an act unconstitutional, they are most adept at nullifying the impact of parliamentary acts viewed as particularly objectionable to the administration of justice.

Nations which have adopted the common law have invariably chosen to have a written constitution. That should not be surprising. The unwritten constitution of Britain is the product of centuries of accretion of a variety of rules from diverse sources. A nation granted or grasping independence tends to reject the idea of an unwritten constitution not because that form has not worked in England, but because the newly independent nation usually has ideas of what the fundamental law should state—and a writing is a natural consequence of the circumstances of modern nationhood.

The study of constitutional law as a source in common law systems is one of the more interesting subjects of comparative study. Constitutions reflect values, and the most fundamental values at that. The choice of parliamentary government versus the presidential system, the separation of powers, judicial review and individual rights are often addressed by the drafters. How these choices are made will reflect characteristics of the local culture not necessarily consistent with the former colonial rule.

Question

Lord Denning does not discuss the benefit of a separate English Bill of Rights, with the House of Lords as the final arbiter. Are his arguments re making the European Convention part of English law helpful in answering the question "Should England have its own Bill of Rights?".

SECTION 8. THE LAW OF THE EUROPEAN ECONOMIC COMMUNITY IN ENGLAND

Ratification of the Treaty of Accession and the European Communities Act 1972, initiated England's entry into the European Communities (European Economic Community, European Coal and Steel Community, and European Atomic Energy Community). England follows the dualist theory of international law; a treaty does not by accession become the law of the United Kingdom. The Treaty of Accession was thus not self-executing; Parliament had to act to give England's participation legal standing. Parliament not only accepted Community law existing at the time of the Act, but it agreed to adopt directly applicable Community legislation of the Council or Commission enacted subsequent to entry. Parliament thus delegated law making power to Community institutions, although limited to rights and obligations created by the text of the treaties.

Community legislation which is not directly applicable requires parliamentary action to become effective in the United Kingdom. Such legislation may be implemented by statute or, the more likely course under the 1972 Act, by subordinate legislation adopted by the English executive under delegated authority.

Community law includes sources beyond the treaties and secondary legislation. Decisions of the European Court of Justice may become an important source of law, both as precedent in that Court and in courts in the United Kingdom. A decision of the Court of Justice does not nullify a member state law, but the decision must be followed in member state courts if it pertains to the meaning or effect of the treaties, or the meaning or validity of a Community instrument. United Kingdom courts are bound by European Court of Justice decisions. Were Community law to become unacceptable in the United Kingdom, the only method to renounce that law would be political, not judicial, mandating a withdrawal from the Community by repealing the European Communities Act. The effect of any action less than withdrawal, such as an act of Parliament in conflict with the European Communities Act, remains a matter of some debate. The traditional view that one Parliament cannot bind another tends to prevail. Parliament has been sensitive in avoiding passing laws in conflict with the acts of union and of emancipation of the colonies and dominions. It would seem similarly aware of problems associated with passing laws in conflict with participation in the Communities.

The impact of Community law is thus relatively unchallenged. But how large an impact it will make is uncertain. It may be, as Lord Denning has stated, like a tide.

BULMER LTD. v. BOLLINGER S.A.

[1974] 2 All E.R. 1226, 1231.*

LORD DENNING, M.R. . . .

* * *

The first and fundamental point is that the treaty concerns only those matters which have a European element, that is to say, matters which affect people or property in the nine countries of the Common Market besides ourselves. The treaty does not touch any of the matters which concern solely the mainland of England and the people in it. These are still governed by English law. They are not affected by the treaty. But when we come to matters with a European element, the treaty is like an incoming tide. . . . Parliament has decreed that the treaty is henceforward to be part of our law. It is equal in force to any statute. . . . The statute is expressed in forthright terms which are

* Reprinted here and below with permission of Butterworth & Co. (Publishers) Ltd.

absolute and all-embracing. Any rights or obligations created by the treaty are to be given legal effect in England without more ado. Any remedies or procedures provided by the treaty are to be made available here without being open to question. In future, in transactions which cross the frontiers, we must no longer speak or think of English law as something on its own. We must speak and think of Community law, of Community rights and obligations, and we must give effect to them. This means a great effort for the lawyers. We have to learn a new system. The treaty, with the regulations and directives, covers many volumes. The case law is contained in hundreds of reported cases both in the European Court of Justice and in the national courts of the nine. Many must be studied before the right result can be reached. We must get down to it.

The Treaty of Rome, as is customary with law-making in European nations, was drafted with broad general principles. They are subject to many different interpretations. The English courts thus confront legislation quite different from English legislation. It requires them to do what they are usually disinclined to do—to fill the gaps. The European Court of Justice may help by giving an interpretation of Community law—indeed, that is what the Court exists for. It does not decide individual cases.

BULMER LTD. v. BOLLINGER S.A.

[1974] 2 All E.R. 1226, 1232.

Lord Denning, M.R. ...

* * *

It is important to distinguish between the task of interpreting the treaty—to see what it means—and the task of *applying* it—to apply its provisions to the case in hand. Let me put on one side the task of *applying* the treaty. On this matter in our courts the English judges have the final word. They are the only judges who are empowered to decide the case itself. They have to find the facts, to state the issues, to give judgment for one side or the other, and to see that the judgment is enforced.

Before the English judges can apply the treaty, they have to see what it means and what is its effect. In the task of *interpreting* the treaty, the English judges are no longer the final authority. They no longer carry the law in their breasts. They are no longer in a position to give rulings which are of binding force. The supreme tribunal for *interpreting* the treaty is the European Court of Justice at Luxembourg. Our Parliament has so decreed....

But even though Community law does not contain the precision of words and sentences more typical of English law, English judges have been willing to speculate as to what was intended by the drafters. The noteworthy English decisions to date, guided considerably by the rulings of former Master of the Rolls Lord Denning, illustrate a distinct preference to reach conclusions without the participation of the European Court. But even though interpretive rulings have not been the norm, the rulings of the English courts have tended to comply with the spirit of the European treaties. If the English courts consistently avoid requesting interpretive rulings, a body of United Kingdom domestic precedent interpreting Community law might develop which is quite different from the aggregate of Community law emanating from the European Court and other member nations.

The presence of Community law as a source of English law has caused English judges to rethink some of their reluctance towards the purposive approach to statutory interpretation. Denning's views have found more acceptance with Community law interpretation than with the statutes of Parliament.

BULMER LTD. v. BOLLINGER S.A.

[1974] 2 All.E.R. 1226, 1236.

LORD DENNING, M.R. . . .

* * *

In view of these considerations, it is apparent that in very many cases the English courts will interpret the treaty themselves. They will not refer the question to the European Court at Luxembourg. What then are the principles of interpretation to be applied? Beyond doubt the English courts must follow the same principles as the European Court. Otherwise there would be differences between the countries of the nine. That would never do. All the courts of all nine countries should interpret the treaty in the same way. They should all apply the same principles. It is enjoined on the English courts by s 3 of the European Communities Act 1972, which I have read.

What a task is thus set before us! The treaty is quite unlike any of the enactments to which we have become accustomed. The draftsmen of our statutes have striven to express themselves with the utmost exactness. They have tried to foresee all possible circumstances that may arise and to provide for them. They have sacrificed style and simplicity. They have foregone brevity. They have become long and involved. In consequence, the judges have followed suit. They interpret a statute as applying only to the circumstances covered by the very words. They give them a literal interpretation. If the words of the statute do not cover a new situation—which was not foreseen—the judges hold that they have no power to fill the gap. To do so would be a 'naked usurpation of the legislative function'.... The gap must remain open until Parliament finds time to fill it.

How different is this treaty. It lays down general principles. It expresses its aims and purposes. All in sentences of moderate length and commendable style. But it lacks precision. It uses words and phrases without defining what they mean. An English lawyer would look for an interpretation clause, but he would look in vain. There is none. All the way through the treaty there are gaps and lacunae. These have to be filled in by the judges, or by regulations or directives. It is the European way....

Likewise the regulations and directives. They are enacted by the Council of Ministers sitting in Brussels for everyone to obey. They are quite unlike our statutory instruments. They have to give the reasons on which they are based: see art 190 of the EEC Treaty. So they start off with pages of preambles, 'whereas' and 'whereas' and 'whereas'. These show the purpose and intent of the regulations and directives. Then follow the provisions which are to be obeyed. Here again words and phrases are used without defining their import.... In case of difficulty, recourse is had to the preambles. These are useful to show the purpose and intent behind it all. But much is left to the judges. The enactments give only an outline plan. The details are to be filled in by the judges.

Seeing these differences, what are the English courts to do when they are faced with a problem of interpretation? They must follow the European pattern. No longer must they examine the words in meticulous detail. No longer must they argue about the precise grammatical sense. They must look to the purpose or intent. To quote the words of the European Court in the *Da Costa* case; they must limit themselves to deducing from 'the wording and the spirit of the treaty the meaning of the Community rules ...'. They must not confine themselves to the English text. They must consider, if need be, all the authentic texts, of which there are now eight. They must divine the spirit of the treaty and gain inspiration from it. If they find a gap, they must fill it as best they can. They must do what the framers of the instrument would have done if they had thought about it. So we must do the same. Those are the principles, as I understand it, on which the European Court acts.

————

Filling the gaps is consistent with the nature of the Community law, and has support in European Court decisions. The Court has stated that:

> In the absence of such legislation [by the Commission], it is for the competent courts to fill the resulting lacuna in a manner which is consistent with the aim of protecting fishing stocks and which also takes into account the fact that protection of fishing nets should be

permitted.[15]

The role of the European Court remains quite different when it fills gaps. An English court may, in the absence of legislative clarity, retreat to the common law. It may suggest that it is applying a principle of the common law, though it may challenge the best of minds to find that principle anywhere in the foggy parameters of the common law. The European Court has no such latitude. They talk rather in terms of general principles of law as they create new rules. Both are involved in judge made law, but with different justifications to assuage the fears that the judges are stepping beyond the line which limits their authority.

Notes and Questions

1. Because the decisions of the European Court are not absolutely binding on the Court in future cases, what if the English House of Lords does not wish to follow a previous opinion of the Court? Does it have the same latitude to reject the earlier European Court opinion? The answer appears to be no—the House of Lords should refer the point, not the case, to the European Court for reconsideration of its earlier decision. But that is the only mandatory reference to the Court, no other English court is so required to refer a question to the Court.

2. If judges are permitted to fill in the gap, it may mean reserving judgment, as Lord Denning mentioned in his discussion of the *Seaford Court Estates* case. Thus, is the objection to his concepts of statutory interpretation based on the possible effect on the judicial process rather than on the substance of his theory?

3. Is the process of enacting a bill in England suggestive of a different approach to statutory interpretation?

15. Christine Marie (1983) 147 J.P.N. 520, 522.

Chapter 14

DIVISIONS OF ENGLISH LAW

SECTION 1. LAW AND EQUITY

Where alternative systems of justice exist, conflict is bound to occur. Equity supplemented the common law by offering compatible remedies in some cases, but in others it produced a direct clash with the common law. The Court of Chancery often issued an equitable injunction ordering an individual to cease an action which had been commanded by a common law court. The success of the equitable remedies depended on the ability of the sovereign to exercise prerogative powers. Objections to the injunctive power of Chancery ultimately waned in the early 18th century, when the rules of equity had become nearly as rigid as those of the common law. The Judicature Acts 1873, finally transferred the powers of the common law courts and courts of equity to the newly established Supreme Court of Judicature. No division of the High Court may issue an injunction to restrain a proceeding in another division, ending the most controversial dispute between the two systems. The fusion nevertheless was not absolute. Traditionally legal remedies remained a matter of right, those of equity continued to be discretionary, but the administrative conflicts were abolished.

The courts of equity served a function of allowing a just remedy where the common law had grown too rigid. Could not equity be used today to serve the function of filling gaps in the law, as discussed in the previous chapter on legislation as a source and legislative interpretation? That champion of gap filling, Lord Denning makes such a plea for a "new equity."

L. DENNING, "THE FAMILY STORY"
175–177 (1981).*

This philosophy of mine is very akin to the philosophy upon which the doctrine of equity is founded. During my time as a Lord Justice, I gave a lecture which I like to think had some impact. It was in 1952 in University College, London, under the title *The need for a new equity.*

* Reprinted with permission of Butterworths & Co. (Publishing) Ltd.

Every student knows what equity is. It arises out of the tendency of all law to become rigid. The rules of law, when enunciated by legislators or judges, are usually founded on reasons which appear satisfactory at the time. Once these rules are given the force of law, however, they must be obeyed for their own sake, and not for the goodness of the reasons which prompted them. No society can permit its members to disobey its laws simply because they disapprove of the reasons for them. The rule therefore becomes the important thing, not the reasons for it. In the course of time the reasons may cease to be valid: but the rules remain binding. New days may bring the people into new ways of life and give them new outlooks: and with these changes there may come a need for new rules of law, to control the new order and to reflect the new outlook. The old rules must then be modified or else the society itself will stagnate. This truth was observed and well stated by Sir Henry Maine nearly a hundred years ago:

> 'Social necessities and social opinion are always more or less in advance of law. We may come indefinitely near to the closing of the gap between them, but it has a perpetual tendency to reopen. Law is stable; these societies we are speaking of are progressive. The greater or less happiness of a people depends on the degree of promptitude with which the gulf is narrowed'.

In those days in 1952 the gap might be closed (a) by equity or (b) by legislation. But these had been unavailing. As to equity I said:

> We are much too modern and sophisticated to believe in a law of nature; and that is all that equity was. Whether you take Roman equity as administered by the praetors, or English equity as administered by the Lord Chancellor, in each case equity invoked the principles of natural justice. Equity claimed that these principles had priority over all the laws then existing: and therefore that these principles could be prayed in aid to mitigate their harshness or to soften their rigidity. Thus although a man might be entitled at law to use his land as he pleased, nevertheless equity would not let him do so if it would be contrary to good faith. So it invented the trust. Although a man might be entitled at law to insist on the binding force of a contract, nevertheless equity would not allow him to do so if it had been induced by a misrepresentation, even though it was an innocent misrepresentation. In the days of Lord Nottingham and Lord Hardwicke equity was very fluid and adaptable but in the hands of Lord Eldon it became rigid and technical: and it has remained so ever since.

When counsel sought to rely on the equity in a case, Lord Justice Bowen in 1890 said with judicial gravity:

> When I hear of an 'equity' in a case like this, I am reminded of a blind man—in a dark room—looking for a black hat—which isn't there!

Harman J said in 1950 that 'Equity is presumed not to be past the age of child-bearing'. But in 1952 it had no child living which was not at least 100 years old.

As to legislation I said:

Parliament is much too busy to do all it should for law reform. Crisis follows upon crisis; and one major debate on another major debate. Foreign policy, economic affairs, defence and social services claim the attention of the legislature to such an extent that there is no time for them to consider the injustices caused by decisions of the courts of law. Even if they do find time, they can never remedy the injustice in the case itself. They cannot, or at any rate should not, legislate retrospectively. The aggrieved party must suffer under the injustice, and content himself with the reflection that his case has brought it to light. Then Parliament can remedy it for others in the future, if it can find time to do so, but it cannot remedy it for the original sufferer.

In 1952 I concluded the address with these words:

I repeat again: Where is the new equity to be found? Not in the Judges, for they are forbidden to legislate. Not in the House of Lords, for they are bound by their own mistakes or, to put it more accurately, bound by their past decisions even though they have become out of date. It is, I think, to be found in the new spirit which is alive in our universities. There must rise up another Bentham to expose the fallacies and failings of the past and to point the way to a new age and a new equity. We stand at the threshold of a new Elizabethan era. Let us play a worthy part in it.

Since I gave the address in 1952 a good deal has been done. The universities have played the worthy part I besought of them. The teachers and the students—especially the students—have supported the cause of reform. Work of the first importance has been done by the Law Reform Commission established in 1965 by Lord Gardiner. We have also the Resolution of the Lords in 1966 that they would no longer be absolutely bound by their own decisions. But there remains a great deal that can yet be done by the judges. That is why I put my first priority— Let justice be done. The judges should so handle precedent—and should so interpret statutes—as to do justice—in a way fitted for the needs of the times in which we live.

SECTION 2. PUBLIC AND PRIVATE LAW

Division of common law systems into private and public law is referred to infrequently. A division is more often noted in terms of what is known as substantive, as opposed to procedural, law. Were the system to be classified under the headings of public and private law, private law would include laws of contract, torts and property. Additionally so categorized would be family law, succession and trusts. Criminal law would constitute a major part of the public law, as would constitutional and administrative law, and procedure. Civil law nations often employ entirely separate hierarchies of courts for public and private law. While there are specific common law courts in England for criminal law, the principal criminal law courts, the Crown Courts, are part of the Supreme Court of Judicature. Appeals may lie to different divisions, but both civil and criminal matters are heard in the same appellate court. The other major section of public law, the law of the constitution, is allocated in the main to administrative tribunals, but the common law appellate court system retains jurisdiction over most administrative appeals.

Lord Denning has argued that there is a public law division developing in England that is different from private law.

LORD DENNING, "THE CLOSING CHAPTER"

117 (1983).

In recent years there has been a revolution in our constitution. It is in the relations between the public authorities and the citizen: and the emergence of a difference between public law and private law.

In my young days we regarded Dicey's *Law of the Constitution* with almost as much reverence as the Bible. He wrote it in 1885 and declared that there is in England no difference between public and private law; and that we have no system of *droit administratif* as they have in France. He said:

> We mean, . . . when we speak of the 'rule of law' as a characteristic of our country, not only that with us no man is above the law, but (what is a different thing) that here every man, whatever be his rank or condition, is subject to the ordinary law of the realm and amenable to the jurisdiction of the ordinary tribunals.

His views were repeated in Halsbury's *Laws of England*. Under the title 'Constitutional Law'—in all four editions—it is said and still said:

> Nevertheless the boundaries of constitutional law have never been satisfactorily defined, partly because there is no constitutional document possessing an extraordinary sanctity, partly because the constitutional rules are susceptible of change, and partly because there is no fundamental difference between public law and private law and it is not possible to assign exclusive provinces to each. Thus, generally speaking, the same courts of law have jurisdiction whether the case raises questions of public or private law.

* * *

This was in complete contrast to the law laid down by Justinian for the Roman empire and still prevailing in Europe today. In the very forefront of the *Institutes* of Justinian it is said that there is a fundamental difference between public law and private law:

The precepts of the law are these: to live honestly, not to injure your neighbour, to render each man his due. This study is divided into two parts, public and private. The public part is that which relates to the nature of public authority in Rome: the private part is that which appertains to the affairs of individual persons.

In the last few years we have thrown over Dicey and gone back to Justinian. In *O'Reilly v. Mackman* I was able to say.[1]

In modern times we have come to recognize two separate fields of law: one of private law, the other of public law. Private law regulates the affairs of subjects as between themselves. Public law regulates the affairs of subjects vis-á-vis public authorities.

The reason for the change-over into two fields is because, during the last 30 years, we have established a comprehensive system of administrative law. It bears some little resemblance to the *droit administratif* of France in that it fulfils a dual purpose. On the one hand it gives the subject an efficient remedy against a public authority. On the other hand it protects a public authority from being harassed by busybodies and cranks.

But it differs from the *droit administratif* in that it is all within the jurisdiction of the High Court: whereas in France the distinction is so complete that there is a different hierarchy of courts. Private law culminates in the *cour de cassation:* public law in the *conseil d'état.*

It is in the realm of remedies that public law has made the most spectacular advance. The Court of Appeal made a preliminary skirmish on 30 June 1982, a little before I retired, in *O'Reilly v. Mackman.* But the main assault was made by the House of Lords in two cases decided on 25 November 1982 after I retired. They are *O'Reilly v. Mackman* [2] and *Cocks v. Thanet District Council.* [3]

In order to understand the significance of these two decisions, you should know that for 100 years before 1950 the only remedies in public law known to the English courts were the old prerogative writs of certiorari, mandamus and prohibition. These were of very limited scope and suffered from many procedural disadvantages.

After 1950 there were advances on two fronts. One advance was to extend the remedy by prerogative writs so as to cover many more misdoings by public authorities: such as errors of law on the face of the record, and going outside their jurisdiction, and so forth. The other advance was to develop the remedy by ordinary actions so as to make the equitable remedies of declaration and injunction available against public authorities for breach of public law.

Each of these advances had its advantages and disadvantages. The complainant chose whichever suited him best. If he wanted to quash a decision of a public authority, he would go by certiorari. If he wanted to

---

1. [1982] 3 W.L.R. 604, 619.   **3.** [1982] 3 W.L.R. 1121.

2. [1982] 3 W.L.R. 1096.

compel it to do its duty, he would ask for mandamus. If a declaration would suit his book—to declare what was its duty—he would issue a writ in an ordinary action. Likewise if he wanted an injunction to stop it breaking this duty, he would also issue a writ. Some of the most important cases in public law were decided in actions for declarations, such as *Barnard v. National Dock Labour Board,*[4] *Pyx Granite Co. Ltd. v. Ministry of Housing and Local Government,*[1] *Ridge v. Baldwin*[2] and *Anisminic Ltd. v. Foreign Compensation Commission.*[3]

The procedures became so diverse that on 8 December 1969 the Law Commission

> were formally requested by Lord Gardiner (the Lord Chancellor), in pursuance of section 3(1)(e) of the Law Commissions Act 1965, 'to review the existing remedies for the judicial control of administrative acts and omissions with a view to evolving a simpler and more effective procedure.'

Many regretted that these terms of reference were limited to procedure: but they need not have worried. By reforming procedure the way was laid open for the judges to reform the substantive law. In amending the law of procedure, the judges have reformed the substantive law as well. This has always been the case. Sir Henry Maine put it in this way:

> So great is the ascendancy of the Law of Actions in the infancy of Courts of Justice, that substantive law has at first the look of being gradually secreted in the interstices of procedure.

The Law Commission made their report in March 1976 (Law Com no 73). It was implemented by Rules of Court (Order 53) in 1977 and given statutory force in 1981 by section 31 of the Supreme Court Act 1981. It combined all the former remedies into one proceeding called Judicial Review. At one stroke the courts could grant whatever relief was appropriate. Not only certiorari and mandamus, but also declaration and injunction. Even damages. The procedure was much more simple and expeditious. Just a summons instead of a writ. No formal pleadings. The evidence was given by affidavit. As a rule no cross-examination, no discovery, and so forth. But there were important safeguards. In particular, in order to qualify, the applicant had to get the leave of a judge.

The statute is phrased in flexible terms. It gives scope for development. It uses the words 'having regard to'. Those words are very indefinite. The result is that the courts are not bound hand and foot by the previous law. They are to 'have regard to' it. So the previous law as to who are—and who are not—public authorities, is not absolutely binding. Nor is the previous law as to the matters in respect of which

4. [1953] 2 Q.B. 18. **2.** [1964] A.C. 40.

1. [1960] A.C. 260. **3.** [1969] 2 A.C. 147.

relief may be granted. This means that the judges can develop the public law as they think best. That they have done and are doing.

The first thing to notice is that public law is confined to 'public authorities'. What are 'public authorities'? There is only one avenue of approach. It is by asking, in the words of section 31(2)(b) of the Supreme Court Act 1981: What is the 'nature of the persons and bodies against whom relief may be granted by such orders', that is, by mandamus, prohibition or certiorari?

These are divided into two main categories:

First, the persons or bodies who have legal authority to determine questions affecting the common law or statutory rights or obligations of other persons as individuals. That is the formula stated by Lord Justice Atkin in *R v. Electricity Comrs, ex parte London Electricity Joint Committee Co. (1920) Ltd* [1] as broadened by Lord Diplock in *O'Reilly v. Mackman.* [2]

Second, the persons or bodies who are entrusted by Parliament with functions, powers and duties which involve the making of decisions of a public nature. That goes back to the time of Chief Justice Holt who said in 1691:

> This Court will examine the proceedings of all jurisdictions erected by Act of Parliament. And if they, under pretence of such Act, proceed to incroach jurisdiction to themselves greater than the Act warrants, this Court will send a certiorari to them, to have their proceedings returned here; to the end that this Court may see, that they keep themselves within their jurisdiction: and if they exceed it, to restrain them. And the examination of such matters is more proper for this Court. [1]

To which I would add the words of Lord Goddard CJ in *R v. National Joint Council for Dental Technicians, ex parte Neate:* [2]

> The bodies to which in modern times the remedies of these prerogative writs have been applied have all been statutory bodies on whom Parliament has conferred statutory powers and duties which, when exercised, may lead to the detriment of subjects who may have to submit to their jurisdiction.

But those categories are not exhaustive. The courts can extend them to any other person or body of a public nature exercising public duties which it is desirable to control by the remedy of judicial review.

There are many cases which give guidance, but I will just give some illustrations.

Every body which is created by statute—and whose powers and duties are defined by statute—is a 'public authority'. So Government departments, local authorities, police authorities, and statutory under-

---

1. [1924] 1 K.B. 171, 205.
2. [1982] 3 W.L.R. 1096, 1104.

1. R. v. Inhabitants—in Glamorganshire (1691) 1 Ld Raym 580.
2. [1953] 1 Q.B. 704, 707.

takings and corporations, are all 'public authorities'. So are members of a statutory tribunal or inquiry, and the board of visitors of a prison. The Criminal Injuries Compensation Board is a public authority. So also, I suggest, is a university incorporated by royal charter: and the managers of a state school. So is the Boundary Commission: and the Committee of Lloyd's.

But a limited liability company incorporated under the Companies Acts is not a 'public authority', nor is an unincorporated association like the Jockey Club. You may ask: What about trade unions? No case has arisen on the point, but in view of the many statutes regulating their powers and duties, they may be a 'public authority'.

ADMINISTRATIVE JUSTICE: SOME NECESSARY REFORMS

Report of the Committee of the JUSTICE.
All Souls Review of Administrative Law in the United Kingdom 168 (1988).*

* * *

7.1. In this chapter we address ourselves to two questions. The first question is whether there is a need to create a new court or to restructure the existing courts system so as to deal more efficiently with administrative law cases. We add some comments about the powers of the court. Second, we ask whether the substantive law as applied by the courts in such cases is in need of reform.

An Administrative Court?

7.2. Until recently there was a body of opinion which advocated fundamental change in the courts system to deal with the growing volume of disputes between citizens and public authorities. One possibility which was much discussed was the creation of an Administrative Court, on the lines of the French Conseil d'Etat. This court would have been separate from the High Court and might have had investigatory powers. It could have been composed of both judges and laymen. Its jurisdiction would have extended not only to legal disputes of the kind which courts are used to handling in the administrative field but also to allegations about the malfunctioning of the public service....

7.3. Since the time when these proposals were first actively considered the position has changed. There has been the procedural reform ... namely, the new Order 53 providing for the application for judicial review. We have made clear our view that this has proved a significant advance enabling cases against public authorities to be brought on for hearing before a single judge with great expedition. While we have also made it clear ... that there are various aspects of the rules which stand in need of amendment, we do not support any proposal for the creation of a completely new Administrative Division of the High Court along the lines earlier proposed. There is nothing that such a division could

* Reprinted with permission of the Oxford University Press and JUSTICE.

achieve that cannot be achieved through existing machinery. In practice, though not in name, there is already a functional segregation of administrative law cases and they are generally tried by specialist judges. There seems to us to be no need to amend the Judicature Acts so as to replace the flexibility of the present system with the rigidity of a separate division.

7.4. For much the same reasons we find ourselves opposed to the introduction of anything on the lines of a Conseil d'Etat. There are, however, some additional objections. It has to be appreciated that in the wake of a revolution the Conseil d'Etat was created to discharge specific tasks. In the course of its life it has undergone considerable change and development. It is not possible, as it were, to pick up such an institution, set it down in alien soil, and expect it to flourish. The membership of the Conseil is composed in large part of administrators who were trained as lawyers. It would be difficult to recruit such a category from the departments here. If a Conseil d'Etat were to be introduced, questions would arise as to whether it was to be given an exclusive area of jurisdiction as in France. If so, it might be necessary to follow the French precedent and to have a separate court or tribunal to decide whether borderline cases should be dealt with by the ordinary courts or by the Conseil. Our view is that the courts are now acting so vigorously and effectively that there is no case for undertaking a novel experiment for which the nation's constitutional history has not prepared it. If there are particular doctrines of law applied by the Conseil d'Etat which would be an improvement on English law, then these should certainly be considered with a view to their adoption, but further than that it seems both unnecessary and undesirable to go.

POWERS OF THE COURT

7.5. The powers of the court on judicial review are more circumscribed than they are on an appeal. The court cannot substitute its own opinion for the opinion formed by the decision-maker—so long, that is, as he has applied the law correctly and followed the correct procedure. In *Chief Constable of the North Wales Police v. Evans* [1982] 1 WLR 1155, 1161 the Lord Chancellor, Lord Hailsham of St Marylebone, said: 'The purpose of judicial review is to ensure that the individual receives fair treatment, and not to ensure that the authority, after according fair treatment, reaches on a matter which it is authorised by law to decide for itself a conclusion which is correct in the eyes of the court.' This means that there remains a wide area within which the decision-maker is not open to challenge. This covers such matters as finding the primary facts on evidence fairly admitted and making the critical appreciation, for example, as to whether, in the light of all relevant planning considerations, the applicant should be granted planning permission.

JUDICIAL REVIEW AND FACT-FINDING

7.6. While the overall position is as we have stated it above, we must draw attention to two decisions which may indicate that the courts in certain (possibly very rare) cases will be willing to go behind the facts found or the inferences drawn by the decision-maker. We refer to the House of Lords decision in *R. v. Secretary of State for the Home Department*, ex parte *Khera* and *Khawaja* [1984] AC 74 and the Privy Council decision in the Mount Erebus disaster case (*Mahon v. Air New Zealand Limited* [1984] AC 808).

Khawaja

7.7. All the Law Lords who took part in the decisions in *Khera* and *Khawaja* held that the court could re-examine the factual question whether in each case the applicant for judicial review was an 'illegal entrant' within the meaning of the Immigration Act, 1971. On this re-examination further evidence could be looked at and the court was not confined to the material which was before the immigration officer. Four of their Lordships proceeded on the basis that proof that the applicant was an illegal entrant was a 'precedent fact' which had to be established before the immigration officer had any power to exclude or deport. Other terminology used in the case is 'collateral question' or 'jurisdictional fact'. The theory underlying this approach is that the decision-maker has no power to act unless a certain state of facts exists. Thus, a rent tribunal only has jurisdiction if the premises are, in the view of the court, a dwelling house (*R. v. Hackney Rent Tribunal* [1951] 2 KB 15). So in *Eleko v. Government of Nigeria* [1931] AC 662, the Governor only had power to order deportation if the applicant was a 'native chief'. The rent tribunal in the first of these cases and the Governor in the second could not confer jurisdiction upon themselves by erroneously believing certain facts to exist which did not exist.

7.8. In the *Khawaja* case great emphasis is laid (and properly laid) on the fact that the case concerned the liberty of the subject and this made it especially important for the court to be vigilant to see that no deportation order was made if the facts did not justify the order. But, although four of their Lordships justified their re-examination of the facts and receipt of further evidence on the basis of 'precedent fact', it seems that Lord Wilberforce expressly rejected this theory. He, nevertheless, thought that it was open to the court to go into the question whether on the facts it had been established that the applicants were illegal entrants. He said (p. 105):

> The court's investigation of the facts is of a supervisory character and not by way of appeal ... It should appraise the quality of the evidence and decide whether that justifies the conclusion reached, e.g., whether it justifies a conclusion that the applicant obtained permission to enter by fraud or deceit. An allegation that he has done so being of a serious character and involving issues of personal liberty, requires a corresponding degree of satisfaction as to the evidence. If the court is not satisfied with any part of the evidence, it may remit the matter for reconsideration or itself receive further evidence. It should quash the detention order where the evidence was not such as the authorities should have relied on or where the

evidence received does not justify the decision reached or, of course, for any serious procedural irregularity.

7.9. Taking Lord Wilberforce's language, the power of a reviewing court to 'appraise the quality of the evidence' and to 'receive further evidence' seems to be moving very close to a power to reexamine the primary facts. We do not at all dissent from the proposition that a case involving personal liberty should make the court vigilant to ensure that deportation orders and the like are only made when the facts justify them, but, if the underlying principle is sound, we think that there are other classes of case where the reviewing court should be equally vigilant in its scrutiny of the facts. By way of illustration we would cite cases involving a man's livelihood or his reputation.

THE EREBUS CASE

7.10. The Privy Council case *Mahon v. Air New Zealand Limited and others* was just such a case involving reputation. The Royal Commissioner who had been appointed to investigate an air disaster in Antarctica included in his report highly critical passages which were seriously damaging to the reputations of the airline and of named individuals. The Privy Council said that a Commissioner conducting such an inquiry must base his decision upon evidence that has some probative value. They defined this as meaning that 'the finding must be based upon some material that tends logically to show the existence of facts consistent with the finding and that the reasoning supportive of the finding, if it be disclosed, is not logically self-contradictory'.... After a lengthy consideration of the evidence their Lordships concluded that certain critical findings of fact were arrived at by a process of reasoning that was self-contradictory. (The judgment also proceeded on the ground that the Royal Commissioner had failed to observe the rules of natural justice.)

7.11. The double use of the adverb 'logically' in this quotation ('... material that tends logically to show the existence of facts consistent with the finding ...' and '... reasoning supportive of the finding ... not logically self-contradictory') appears to open the door to the judges of the reviewing court substituting their own conclusions on fact and inferences for those of the decision-maker if they are unconvinced by the route which he has followed.

FURTHER DEVELOPMENTS IN JUDICIAL REVIEW OF FACT-FINDING

7.12. It is impossible to forecast how the courts will utilize these new tools for getting behind the facts found by the decision-maker. Perhaps both cases should be treated as special and as not laying down any general rule. The only comment that we can safely make is that if these cases were to be generally applied the gap between judicial review and appeal would be narrowed notwithstanding repeated judicial pronouncements (to be found in the *Erebus* case as elsewhere) to the effect that review is a very different process from appeal. There is, we believe, a risk that if reopening the facts became a common practice, judicial review itself might come under attack.

THE SUBSTANTIVE LAW

7.13. In our Discussion Paper ... we drew attention to the change of attitude of the courts towards judicial scrutiny of the activities of the administrator. This has manifested itself over the last thirty years and has ended an era styled by Professor Sir William Wade *Constitutional Fundamentals* (Hamlyn Lectures), 1980, p. 63) as the courts' 'period of amnesia'. There are many decisions which demonstrate the positive attitude which the courts currently adopt....

7.14. We have asked ourselves in what respects the existing substantive law is inadequate. By way of answer we single out specific instances in the following paragraphs....

REASONS

7.15. [W]e think that there should be a statutory obligation to give reasons on request for administrative decisions. Although the Donoughmore Committee in 1932 called the giving of reasons the third principle of natural justice, the courts have not taken that view and (with fairly rare exceptions) have allowed administrators to decide without giving any indication of their thought processes.

COMPENSATION

7.16. We think that there should be compensation for the citizen who suffers loss as a direct result of unlawful administrative action. The law already covers cases of negligence and other recognized torts but there is a wide area ... where no compensation is available even though financial loss can be shown to have followed directly from wrongful action of an administrative character.

BAD ADVICE BY OFFICIALS

7.17. There should be some protection for the citizen where erroneous advice or a misleading assurance has been given by a public official. The law already covers cases where negligent advice can be shown to have caused financial loss. Sometimes liability can be established in contract where a public official was able to, and did, bind his employer. Cases do, however, arise which are not so covered. For instance, an official may, without personal negligence, give an assurance that planning permission for a certain use of land is not needed. The individual relies upon that assurance and later discovers that the assurance is incorrect. He then seeks planning permission and it is refused. Apparently the individual is without a legal remedy in this situation. He cannot even assert that the local authority is estopped from enforcing the planning law against him, since the Court of Appeal's decision in *Western Fish Products Ltd. v. Penwith DC* [1981] 2 All ER 204 comes close to excluding for all practical purposes the law of estoppel from the realm of the exercise of statutory powers. The subsequent House of Lords decision in *R. v. Inland Revenue Commissioners,* ex parte *Preston* [1985] AC 835 is to the same effect. In *A.-G. of Hong Kong v. Ng Yuen Shiu* [1983] 2 AC 629, the Judicial Committee of the Privy Council held that the Hong Kong government was bound by an undertaking given that an illegal immigrant's case would be considered on its merits. In that case, the court was able to give due protection to the individual against unfair treatment, but there was no overriding statutory duty to be surmounted. In cases where the court is unable to provide an adequate remedy, it will be within the purview of the ombudsmen (both parliamentary and local) to investigate and report on the circumstances, and if justified to recommend the payment of compensation. We accept that, if public authorities are to be held liable for incorrect or misleading statements, a possible reaction to this would be that officials will be instructed not to offer any advice, or will in any event be reluctant to give advice. But we cannot accept that the administration should be able inadvertently to cause loss or injustice and not be required to alleviate the consequences for the individual.

LATE CHALLENGE TO COMPULSORY PURCHASE ORDERS ON THE GROUND OF FRAUD.

7.18. We think that the rule in *Smith v. East Elloe RDC* [1956] AC 736 and *R. v. Secretary of State for the Environment,* ex parte *Ostler* [1977] QB 122 (that a compulsory purchase order (CPO) cannot be questioned on the grounds of fraud or bad faith once the statutory time-limit for challenge—normally six weeks—has expired) should be reversed by legislation. While we recognize the very strong arguments of certainty and convenience in support of not disturbing an act that has such consequences as a CPO, it seems to us quite fundamental to our law that fraud or bad faith vitiates any transaction, and it is dangerous to protect the administration from investigation by the courts in such cases. The remedy in damages against the individual guilty of fraud or bad faith (recognized in *East Elloe*) is not enough. In principle a CPO and any similar order or scheme procured by fraud should be capable of being set aside by the court notwithstanding the expiry of the statutory time-limit. The circumstances may, of course, be such that the powers of the court are invoked at so late a stage that any attempt to set the CPO aside would be a *brutum fulmen* or work injustice to innocent third parties. In such a case, the successful plaintiff who has established fraud should be allowed to recover damages from the local authority or other public body for provable loss inflicted on him in excess of the compensation (if any) already awarded to him for the taking of his land. It may well be that in many cases damages would suffice, and it would only be in rare cases that the CPO itself would need to be set aside.[1]

ERROR OF LAW WHICH DOES NOT APPEAR ON THE FACE OF THE RECORD

7.19. We think that the old rule that a decision can only be quashed by certiorari for error of law where the error appears on the face of the record can no longer be justified. Where it can be demonstrated that the decision was actually vitiated by an error of law the court should not be prevented by any technical rule from striking down

---

1. One of the Committee, Sir John Boynton, dissents from the view expressed in paragraph 7.18. He believes that in the interests of finality and certainty the CPO should not be open to any attack after the statutory period has elapsed.

the decision. We believe that if our recommendation about the obligation to supply full reasons on request were to be implemented the occasions when the 'record' would fail to reveal the error would be much rarer, especially if our further recommendation is adopted that the statement of reasons and findings should be deemed to form part of the record. But even without this reform we consider the old technical rule to be indefensible. That this now seems to be the opinion of the House of Lords appears from Lord Diplock's speech in *O'Reilly v. Mackman* [1983] 2 AC 237 (the other Law Lords concurred and did not deliver separate judgments). The view is there expressed that as a result of the *Anisminic* case ([1969] 2 AC 147) the distinction between errors of law within and without the jurisdiction has virtually to be disregarded.[2] In the section of the Australian statute referred to in paragraph 6.33 above (which gives a statutory list of the grounds for judicial review) the relevant head is expressed as follows: 'that the decision involved an error of law, whether or not the error appears on the record of the decision'. It is to be hoped that the English courts will now act on the same basis by following Lord Diplock's guidance.

SECTION 3. COMMERCIAL AND COMMON (CIVIL) LAW

Commercial law is often separately administered in civil law nations. It evolved within the fairs and markets of the Middle Ages, creating what became known as the law merchant. Commercial law might have developed within England as a largely separate system existing parallel to the common law. But it substantially had assimilated into the common law by the 17th century, although it retained a separate significance, because judges recognized that commercial rules chiefly were based on the practices of merchants and traders. Commercial usage constituted custom. The common law rule requiring proof of the existence of a custom from a very early time was not required in commercial litigation. Current custom was acceptable as long as it did not conflict with common law decisions. In the late 19th century, most of the law merchant was incorporated into statutes, including the Bills of Exchange Act of 1882, the Partnership Act 1890, and the Sale of Goods Act 1893. While the law merchant had its own separate and important origin, little of that isolation remains today in English law.

From these English commercial acts the United States evolved a set of its own commercial laws, the 1896 Uniform Negotiable Instruments Law, the 1909 Bills of Lading Act, the 1906 Uniform Warehouse Receipts Act and the most important commercial law, the Uniform Commercial

---

2. It is difficult to reconcile this *obiter dictum* with authorities to the contrary, in particular the Privy Council decision in the *South East Asia Fire Brick* case [1981] AC 363. The cases are collected in Wade, *Administrative Law*, 5th edn., pp. 264–7 and to them we would add *Stevenson v. Barham* [1977] 163 CLR 190, 201 (per Mason and Jacobs, JJ. in the High Court of Australia) and *Glenville Homes Pty. Ltd. v. Builders Licensing Board* (1981) 2 NSWLR 608; 4 ALD 358, 359 (per Hope and Samuels JJA in the Court of Appeal of New South Wales).

Code, adopted first in Pennsylvania in 1953. Because commercial law was assimilated into the common law and did not develop as a parallel subject of law, the term "commercial law" has quite a different meaning than that on the continent. There are no separate courts in most common law countries for commercial law problems, although there are special courts for certain commercial matters, such as the bankruptcy courts in the United States and the Restrictive Practices Court in England. But there is in England a Commercial Court, which is part of the Queen's Bench Division of the High Court. It now has statutory status and may develop into a specialized court with a status similar to the Admiralty Court, also a part of the Queen's Bench Division. The judges are High Court judges assigned to the Commercial Court because of their expertise in commercial law. The Court has gained popularity and respect. But the Commercial Court is not a separate, specialized court outside the civil court structure, as in some civil law nations.

Note

When the Uniform Commercial Code was passed, the question was raised whether it was a code in the civil sense. The same had been asked of the earlier laws of commerce mentioned above, but even more so about the UCC, partly because it was called a code. Thus we have two questions raised by the commercial law enactments. Do common law systems have a separate commercial law apart from the common law? And are they codifying laws in the tradition of the civil law? The same answer responds to both inquiries. The commercial law remains part of the common law, although we have seen fit to produce collections of all the provisions in a consolidated law. But it is not separate from the common law—we should not so suggest because to do so implies that the common law is a parallel to the civil law of the continental nations. The civil law is the substantive heart of the law of those nations, surrounded by many additions of unquestioned importance in the aggregate of substantive law. The common law is rather an identification term, not one which refers to a particular area of substance.

Rather than ask whether there is a division between commercial and common law, the better question is whether the enactment of such laws as the UCC are indicative of a movement toward codification in the civil law sense. The answer is no. The purpose and function of the UCC is distinguishable from the civil codes of civil law systems. But the UCC may be identified with the movement toward greater use of statutes to govern particular areas, which has its parallels in civil law nations but should not be confused with codifying laws.

The UCC was not the result of a general movement for unification of laws within the United States, which motivated the enactment of many of the European codes in the 19th century. Many of the Western European nations possessed extremely diverse commercial laws, laws which impeded commerce and thus motivated the adoption of uniform laws intended to assist international commerce, and therefore national development on the Continent. Codification became the method of unification. There was quite clearly no strong popular support of a Uniform Commercial Code in the United States. Absolute uniformity was not intended to be achieved by the

UCC, the provisions of which leave both gaps in the Code itself, and are subject to varying interpretations in the different state jurisdictions.

The French Civil Code, and several other civil law codes have represented a conscious and profound break with the past. Although the principal codes evolving from the major European reforms were the civil codes, revision of the commercial law was often undertaken simultaneously. The Uniform Commercial Code did not evolve from any social reform movement. There was comparatively little reform of commercial practices in the UCC; it is for the most part a restatement of existing law with an adoption of the "better rule." The most significant changes sought to adjust commercial transactions to the realities of 20th century commercial transactions, not to deal with new theories of jurisprudence.

An additional distinguishing feature between the Uniform Commercial Code and civil law codes of Europe is the process of revision. In the short existence of the UCC there have been several official texts, the most recent in 1972. It thus appears that the Uniform Commercial Code will continue to be reviewed and altered as the necessities of commercial transactions dictate that change.

The comparatively frequent restatement of the Uniform Commercial Code also occurs because of the recognition that UCC provisions will be interpreted differently in the more than 50 different jurisdictions. The obvious way to avoid having the law become increasing dissimilar in various jurisdictions is to periodically analyze the various interpretations, seek agreement as to the best resolution to meet commercial necessities and then suggest revisions to regain a measure of uniformity.

The great codes of Europe have tended not to be changed in this fashion. One only has to mention for illustration the French Code Civil, more than 170 years old, and the German code, over 80 years old, neither of which has been superseded. Revision is an immense undertaking, and there exists no current movement for the form of social reform which motivated their initial evolution. The tendency has been to alter codes by statutes which speak to certain parts of the code. This static aspect of the European code has not evoked a paralleled experience in the Uniform Commercial Code. Alterations to the Uniform Commercial Code in the future will continue as frequently as commercial requirements dictate.

The concept of codification of law in the United States remains in a state of some controversy. In preparing the Uniform Commercial Code, as well as in other uniform laws, the question invariably arises as to whether there should be *any* codification. This question has long since been resolved in civil law nations, which assume codification as a fundamental basis of jurisprudence. Attention in those nations now focuses on the relationship of civil and commercial laws, i.e., the fusion or the separation of the areas.

An additional dichotomy exists with the concept of unification. Laws may be codified but not fully unified. There is an obvious partial unification when a draft law serves as a basis for new codes throughout the United States, as in the case of the Uniform Commercial Code. But the issue of uniformity is not fully resolved in the United States in the sense that commercial laws continue to be left to state determination. Were unification truly an important issue, commercial law would be federalized to guarantee total unification.

*

Index

References are to Pages

†